Introduction to African American Studies

Transdisciplinary Approaches and Implications

Introduction to African American Studies
TRANSDISCIPLINARY APPROACHES AND IMPLICATIONS

James Stewart

Talmadge Anderson

INPRINT EDITIONS

Introduction to African American Studies
Transdisciplinary Approaches and Implications

Published 2007, 2015, 2018, 2021 INPRINT EDITIONS. All Rights Reserved.

Library of Congress Number: 2007934669

ISBN-13: 978-1-58073-039-6

Printed by BCP Digital Printing, Inc.
An affiliate company of Black Classic Press

To review or purchase Black Classic Press and INPRINT EDITIONS books, visit *www.blackclassicbooks.com.*

ı may also obtain a list of titles by writing to:
Classic Press

'14
)1203

Dedication

This edition of *Introduction to African American Studies, Transdisciplinary Approaches and Implications* is dedicated to my former co-author Talmadge Anderson. Talmadge transitioned to the realm of the ancestors on June 3, 2011, in Savannah, Georgia, at the age of 78. His life was one that manifested an enduring commitment to the uplift of people of African descent. Talmadge's activism and scholarship were exemplars of the type of social responsibility and engaged academic excellence that are the hallmarks of African American Studies.

Talmadge earned a B.A. degree in business from Savannah State College in 1953. After graduating, he served three years in the U.S. Army. Subsequently, he earned an MBA from Atlanta University in 1958. During the late 1950s and 1960s, Talmadge held various academic positions. He served as Chair of the Department of Business at Lane College during the 1958-59 academic year, taught at Allen University from 1959-1962, held the position of department chair at St. Augustine's College from 1963-1965, and taught at Bethune-Cookman from 1966-67 and West Virginia Institute of Technology from 1968-1970.

In 1970, Talmadge moved to the institution where he would devote the next 25 years of his professional life, Washington State University (WSU). In this year, he assumed the role of Director of Black Studies and was also appointed as a faculty member in the College of Business Administration and Economics. Talmadge's skillful and pragmatic leadership produced a broad interdisciplinary program that was the first in the region to offer classes like Swahili, Introduction to Black America, Black Psychology, Black Politics, and Black Sociology. Students were exposed to Talmadge's expertise in business and economics through his Black Economics course.

Talmadge exemplified the active embrace of a transdiscplinary approach to African American Studies in 1975 when he founded the Heritage House, the university's first African American cultural center. His innovations included a research library, art exhibit space, and meeting space for African American students and organizations, faculty, and the entire WSU community. The facility provided an accessible forum for the campus community to discuss issues relevant to Africans throughout the Diaspora. One year after his retirement in 1995, the Heritage House was renamed the Talmadge Anderson Heritage House (TAHH) in his honor, and it continues the legacy established by its founder. The TAHH houses a collection of art and artifacts, books, and music, as well as films and video that celebrate African and African American heritage. The Martin Luther King, Jr. Freedom School is housed in the facility, along with the University's Diversity Education Program office.

The strong commitment to academic excellence Talmadge exhibited was manifested both collectively and individually. In 1977, he founded and served as the first editor of *The Western Journal of Black Studies* which has become one of the discipline's premier scholarly publications. The names of scholar activists whose work has been published in the journal are too numerous to list here. In his own research, Talmadge displayed the same type of commitment to careful inquiry that he expected of contributors to the journal. Talmadge's 1992 text, *Introduction to African American Studies: Cultural Concepts and Theory* (*Kendall Hunt Publishing Co.*, 1994) is the foundation of this edition and its predecessor. His 1990 monograph, *Black Studies: Theory, Method, and Cultural Perspectives* (*Washington State University Press*, 1990), is another important contribution to establishing the intellectual contours of African American Studies.

Talmadge's scholarly production was not limited to monographs. His significant journal articles include: "Black Economic Liberation Under Capitalism" (*The Black Scholar*, 1970); "An Ideological Treatise on Black Publications and Black Writers, The Evolvement of *The Western Journal of Black Studies*" (*The Serials Librarian*, 1984); "Black Entrepreneurship and Concepts Toward Economic Coexistence" (*The Western Journal of Black Studies*, 1982); "Black Encounter of Racism and Elitism in White Academe" (*Journal of Black Studies*, 1988); (*The Western Journal of Black Studies*, 1990); and (*Journal of Black Studies*, 1992).

The leadership and engagement provided by Talmadge Anderson will be sorely missed – not only by his African American Studies extended family, but even more so by his biological family that includes five children and several grandchildren. May Talmadge rest in peace in the company of the host of freedom fighters that have preceded him.

James B. Stewart

Table of Contents

Chapter 3
THE HISTORY OF AFRICANS IN AMERICA

Chapter 4
AFRICAN AMERICAN SOCIETY AND CULTURE

Chapter 5
BLACK PSYCHOLOGY AND PSYCHOLOGICAL WELL-BEING..**181**

Chapter 6
POLITICS AND PUBLIC POLICY 213

Chapter 7
INDIVIDUAL AND COLLECTIVE ECONOMIC EMPOWERMENT 279

Chapter 8
AFRICAN AMERICAN ARTS AND HUMANITIES 325

"I Can't Breathe." July 17, 2014, *Eric Garner.*
"I Can't Breathe." May 25, 2020, *George Floyd.*

Author's Note 2021
Facing Old and New Challenges

The lengthy note provided in the 2018 edition of this text presented many indicators documenting the escalating public and private threats to Black well-being that manifested during the first two years of the Trump administration. That discussion informed my call to Black/Africana Studies (B/AS) scholar/activists to focus on designing strategies "that not only protect hard-fought gains, but also help to rebuild liberatory momentum." Developments since 2018 have forcefully underscored the need for such a robust response, as ongoing efforts to further entrench white supremacist ideology and enact derivative public policies intensify.

As described in the 2018 note, contemporary efforts to reinforce the subordinate status of people of African descent, viewed in historical perspective, bear easily identifiable similarities to tactics deployed to dismantle post-Civil War Reconstruction policies and usher in the infamous Jim Crow era. Since 2018, the rightward shift in the collective US psyche has been accelerating and is congealing into a formation characterized by noted scholar Henry Giroux as "American Fascism."[1] During the Trump presidency, this ominous societal mindset gained significant traction due to his actions, public pronouncements and especially his Twitter messages. The most notable example of Trump's early promotion of white supremacist ideology was his characterization of the right-wing extremists who perpetrated violence at a 2017 "Unite the Right" demonstration in Charlottesville, Virginia, as "very fine people."[2]

Parroting the narrative advanced by Trump, several of his acolytes later attempted to defend the January 6, 2021, armed insurrection at the US Capitol by advancing a deeply flawed comparison between those violent insurrectionists and the protestors who responded, mostly peacefully, to the murder of George Floyd by police officers in Minneapolis on May 25, 2020.[3] Trump actively incited the Capitol insurrection, and it clearly is not alarmist to envision a future in which Trumpism morphs into future physical attacks by right-wing zealots targeting Black Americans, harkening back to the heyday of the Ku Klux Klan.

The contemporary resurgence of anti-Black racism can be thought of as the product of a societal affliction that I call "Post-Obama Racial Trauma" or PORT. PORT manifests as cognitive and emotional anguish precipitated by the Obama presidency, which produced a high degree of cognitive dissonance among those who never could have imagined such a development.

For many Trump supporters, this dissonance invokes several types of responses that evidence a retreat from rationality. A significant cadre of Trump acolytes interpret his "Make America Great Again" slogan as a promise to erase all evidence of the Obama presidency. It thereby provides a collective antidote for PORT, symptoms of which include a propensity to subscribe to outlandish conspiracy theories such as QAnon and Nazi-era tropes such as the so-called white-replacement conspiracy theory, which posits the existence of a deliberate plot to enact social policies designed to achieve the extinction of whites.

Trump has been especially successful in spreading PORT through his blustering personality and use of techniques that bear strong similarities to those deployed by cult leader Jim Jones and the fictional Pied Piper. The mass delirium exhibited by Trump's most fervent loyalists can be appropriately compared to the collective hysteria associated with the 17th century Salem, Massachusetts, witch trials. Trump accurately described the state of the American psyche when he boastfully declared in 2016: "I could stand in the middle of 5th Avenue and shoot somebody, and I wouldn't lose voters."[4]

Trump's defeat in 2020 did not stop the spread of PORT. In many ways, it accelerated its contagion. For example, since 2017, Black activists have experienced a growing backlash in response to the aggressive campaign against police killings of Blacks initiated by the Black Lives Matter (BLM) Movement. The ensuing wave of protests challenging police killings of African Americans prompted white legislators in almost 20 states to introduce bills intended to restrict citizens' right to protest.[5] Fortunately, most of those bills were never enacted into law; however, a very repressive "anti-riot" bill was enacted in Florida in 2021. The provisions in that law include specifications of new criminal offenses and increased penalties for targeting law enforcement and participating in violent or disorderly assemblies. More ominously, the Florida law gives automobile drivers the right to plow right through demonstrators if they feel threatened, without fear of prosecution and provides immunity from civil charges.[6] Such a scenario actually caused the death of a protestor during the 2017 Charlottesville protest, and since then over 100 persons around the country have been hit by automobiles during protests catalyzed by the murder of George Floyd.[7]

Efforts to restrict the right to protest are expanding even as the racial disparity in police killings persists. At least 135 Black men and women have been killed by police since 2015. Analyzing data for the period from 2013 to 2018, Edwards, Lee, and Esposito found that 1 in every 1,000 Black men are at risk of being killed by police over the course of their lives. Furthermore, Black men are about 2.5 times more likely to be victims of summary executions by police over their life courses than are white men;[8] and Black women are about 1.4 times more likely to be killed by police than are white women.[9] To this last point, it should be remembered that the murder of Breonna Taylor on March 13, 2020, occurred some two months before that of George Floyd.

The tendency of some police officers to resort to the use of lethal force against Black Americans has its origins, to a large extent, in those officers' prior military service. Approximately 20 percent of US police officers are military veterans who frequently bring militaristic mindsets to their work in the law enforcement profession.[10] From this perspective, recent exposés of the prevalence of white racial-extremist adherents in the armed forces is particularly troubling. A 2021 Pentagon report warns that domestic extremists pose a serious threat to the military through their efforts to recruit service members into their movement. According to that report, "Military members are highly prized by these groups as they bring legitimacy to their causes and enhance their ability to carry out attacks."[11] Military veterans influenced by radical racist ideologies who transition into law enforcement thereby pose a significant potential threat to the life and liberty of Black citizens. Their involvement further compounds the threats emanating from non-veterans who absorb racist ideologies from other social entanglements.

The influx of ex-military service people into law enforcement has proceeded concurrently with the militarization of local police departments. As Wayne McElrath and his colleagues (2020) report, this militarization results in local police taking on "the appearance, armament, and behavior of soldiers at war" in ways that make "the public both less safe and less free." This posture, these authors contend, means that "those who encounter militarized police, whether in their daily lives or at a demonstration, are far more likely to end up dead or injured as a consequence of an officer's militarized mindset."[12]

Overt efforts to restrict the electoral power of Black Americans have been intensifying since the Supreme Court gutted key sections of the 1965 Voting Rights Act in their 2013 *Shelby County v. Holder* decision. Almost immediately following that decision, legislators in Texas and North Carolina introduced new voting restrictions intended to curtail the voting rights of their respective states' Black citizens. The North Carolina provisions were so blatantly racially discriminatory that the Supreme Court later ruled in 2017 that the districts had violated Constitutional guarantees.[13] Despite this minor setback, efforts to enact Black-targeted voter suppression laws are expanding. Such efforts are a direct response to the critical role played by Black voters in defeating Donald Trump in the 2020 presidential election and producing Democratic Party victories in the 2021 Georgia Senate election. As reported by the Brennan Center for Social Justice, as of February 2021, "thirty-three states have introduced, prefiled, or enacted over 165 restrictive voting bills…in a backlash to historic voter turnout in the 2020 general election and grounded in a rash of baseless and racist allegations of voter fraud and election irregularities."[14]

The Election Integrity Act of 2021 passed in Georgia was the first major post-2020 election voter-suppression law. The racially discriminatory provisions identified in a detailed *New York Times* analysis of the Georgia statute include enhanced restrictions on absentee balloting, elimination of mobile voting centers, and reduction in the number of ballot drop boxes. The law further empowers the Republican-controlled Georgia legislature to exercise more control over the state's board of elections and to suspend county election officials.[15] This latter provision allows state legislators to overturn future election results in predominantly Black urban counties. Foreseeably, forcing Black voters to vote in person and restricting the number of available voting sites will not only generate long lines that discourage voter participation but will also expose Black voters to direct intimidation by racist poll watchers.

The resort to voter suppression legislation to blunt Black electoral power is motivated in part by the failure of direct voter intimidation and misinformation dissemination efforts. Belle (2020) reports that conservatives invested $20 million during the 2020 election season to place 50,000 people to "guard the vote" during early voting and on Election Day. According to Belle, then-President Trump called these poll watchers his "Army for Trump."[16]

Efforts to suppress the Black vote via dissemination of misinformation online date back to the 2016 election. For example, in 2016, an article entitled "How to be a Ni**** on Twitter" was posted on the white-supremacist website, *The Daily Stormer*. That article informed the site's constituents about how to create fake accounts that would appear to be owned and operated by Black people. Such accounts, the article explained, were intended to "create a state of chaos on Twitter, among the Black Twitter population, by sowing distrust and suspicion, causing blacks to panic."[17] Domestic racists also aggressively trolled Black activists in 2020. As the Associated Press reported in July 2020 after the murder of George Floyd, a network of Facebook groups, launched primarily by conservative and pro-gun activists, shifted their conversations to attacks on Black Lives Matter and the nationwide protests over the killing of Black men and women.[18]

Black voters were specifically targeted by foreign interests intending to foment racial division and support the white-supremacist agenda of Donald Trump. For example, prior to the 2016 election, a Russian troll farm created the "Blacktivist" channel on YouTube, whose content highlighted violent acts directed at Black men and received over 11 million visits.[19] Foreign trolls continued their nefarious activities targeting Black online users in the run up to the 2020 election. In August 2020, Facebook removed hundreds of accounts from a foreign troll farm whose posters were posing as African American supporters of Trump and QAnon. That troll farm was based in Romania and pushed content on Instagram under names like "BlackPeopleVoteForTrump" and on Facebook under "We Love Our President."[20]

B/AS scholar/activists should be especially concerned going forward about a particularly insidious manifestation of resurgent anti-Black racism—namely, efforts to rewrite both the historical record and the current narrative describing the existence and impact of institutional racism. The historical precedent for this effort is the "Lost Cause" movement propagated by ex-Confederates following the Civil War. As described on the "Inclusive Historian" website (2020), the Lost Cause ideology "perpetuated the narrative of racial difference that had begun in slavery, describing competent white people well-practiced in self-control and incompetent African Americans simultaneously unserious and dangerous, preferring loyal deference to actual participation in public and political life."[21] It additionally posited that "black men and women who acted the parts of loyal and submissive servants" are to be "celebrated and promoted."[22] Moreover, "the Lost Cause was not just about the past. Among the white ruling class in the former Confederate States, it set expectations for the present and the future. It supported the white southern worldview that revered the past, deferred to elite rule, enforced conservative social values, exalted rural life, and marginalized black people."[23]

Clear echoes of the Lost Cause ideology can be found in the contemporary era's anti-Black discourse.[24] The role of historical amnesia in intensifying the resurgence of anti-Black racism was illustrated in 2017 when Trump cited the long-deceased Frederick Douglass as someone who was currently making important contributions to Black well-being! [25] Trump later issued an Executive Order in September 2020 prohibiting DEI (Diversity, Equity, and Inclusion) training in federal agencies. That order, which subsequently was rescinded by President Biden, prohibited government contractors from providing "any workplace training that inculcates in its employees" training on race or sex diversity, equity, or inclusion involving 11 "divisive concepts." The forbidden concepts characterized as "anti-American" and "divisive" included anything that might make someone "feel discomfort, guilt, anguish, or any other form of psychological distress on account of his or her race or sex." One example used to illustrate such prohibited discourse was workplace diversity trainings that suggest "men and members of certain races, as well as our most venerable institutions, are inherently sexist and racist."[26] Trump's action was precipitated by concurrent right-wing attacks on Critical Race Theory and the *New York Times'* publication of "The 1619 Project," a journalistic series that seeks to "reframe US history by putting the legacy of slavery and the contributions of Black Americans at its center."[27]

As described by *Encyclopedia Britannica*, Critical Race Theory (CRT) is an "intellectual movement and loosely organized framework of legal analysis based on the premise that race is not a natural, biologically grounded feature of physically distinct subgroups of human beings but a socially constructed (culturally invented) category that is used to oppress and exploit people of colour." Critical Race theorists hold that "the law and legal institutions in the United States are inherently racist insofar as they function to create and maintain social, economic, and political inequalities between whites and nonwhites, especially African Americans."[28] Although the origins of CRT date back to 1989, it has recently become a favorite target of neo-Lost Cause advocates. As Char Adams (2021) observes, "A cluster of bills that aim to prohibit teaching critical race theory in K-12 schools have popped up in the last year." States where legislators have introduced bills prohibiting CRT instruction include Idaho, Tennessee, and Rhode Island.[29]

The 1619 Project, conceived and spearheaded by Pulitzer Prize-winning reporter Nikole Hannah-Jones, produced a long-form reframing of US history that locates slavery and the contributions of African Americans as the cornerstone of the national narrative.[30] Trump's opposition to such a narrative was foreshadowed by his failure to coordinate his White House's Black History Month commemorations with the Association for the Study of African American Life and History (ASALH), as had been the precedent established by previous administrations. State lawmakers in several states have since attempted to follow Trump's lead in attacking the 1619 Project's narrative.[31] In April 2021, for instance, Senator Mitch McConnell (R-KY) sent a letter to the Secretary of Education demanding the removal of any proposals incorporating the 1619 Project into their curricula from federal grant programs.[32] Censorship of antiracist narratives has also begun to infect higher education, as demonstrated in March 2021, when officials at Boise State University canceled 52 sections of a diversity course after complaints from a state legislator.[33]

These widespread censorship efforts are critical elements of the neo-Lost Cause movement. Indeed, several prominent Republicans have contributed to the spread of this ideology, which denies the existence of institutionalized racism. Among these were former Attorney General William Barr, who openly disputed assertions that the US justice system treats Blacks differently than whites.[34] Republican South Carolina Senator, Lindsey Graham, went even further, issuing a public denial that systemic racism exists in the US.[35]

All of the foregoing has contributed to muted responses from politicians and policymakers to the declarations issued by the American Medical Association (AMA) and the Centers for Disease Control (CDC) characterizing racism as a public health crisis. As a June 2020 AMA statement asserts: "The AMA recognizes that racism in its systemic, structural, institutional, and interpersonal forms is an urgent threat to public health, the advancement of health equity, and a barrier to excellence in the delivery of medical care."[36] In a similar vein, the CDC declared the following in April 2021:

> What we know is this: racism is a serious public health threat that directly affects the well-being of millions of Americans. As a result, it affects the health of our entire nation. Racism is not just the discrimination against one group based on the color of their skin or their race or ethnicity, but the structural barriers that impact racial and ethnic groups differently to influence where a person lives, where they work, where their children play, and where they worship and gather in community. These social determinants of health have life-long negative effects on the mental and physical health of individuals in communities of color.[37]

Notably, both the AMA and CDC statements appropriately recognize that Black Americans were experiencing a variety of inequities long before the COVID-19 pandemic erupted in 2020.

Various economic metrics including unemployment rates, income levels, poverty rates, and wealth holdings document the disproportionate vulnerabilities that confronted Blacks as the pandemic approached. Since the formal collection of unemployment data by race began, the unemployment rate for Blacks has consistently been approximately twice that of whites. In February 2020, immediately preceding the pandemic onset, the unemployment rate for Black men was 5.8 percent compared to 2.9 percent for white men. The comparable rates for Black and white women, respectively, were 4.8 percent and 2.8 percent. It is also important to recognize that Black workers make up a disproportionate share of so-called "essential workers" who have been forced to work in settings that pose significant risk of contracting and spreading COVID-19. Although Black workers account for about 12 percent of all workers, they make up about one in six, or slightly over 16 percent, of all frontline-industry workers.[38] The employment challenges facing African Americans have created persisting income gaps relative to whites. As Valerie Wilson (2020) reports, the median household income for white households in 2018 was 70 percent higher than that of Black households: $70,642 versus $41,692.[39]

As would be expected, employment and earnings disparities are mirrored when poverty rates are examined, and the historically large gap between the poverty rates of Blacks and Hispanics compared to those of whites persists. In 2018, the poverty rates for Black and Hispanic families were 18.8 and 16.1 percent, respectively, compared to 5.7 percent for non-Hispanic white families. Although the poverty rates for Black and Hispanic families reached all-time lows in 2019 (16.9 and 14.4 percent, respectively), the gap between these rates and those of non-Hispanic white families (4.9 percent) declined only slightly. [40]

The persistence of these economic disparities over many generations has been a major contributing factor to the enormous gap in wealth holdings between Blacks and whites. Wealth holdings constitute a critical resource for overcoming the type of disruptions created by the pandemic. Neil Bhutta et al. (2020), for example, found that the white-Black gap in median wealth was little changed—from $163,700 in 2016 to $164,100 in 2019—and the white-Hispanic gap fell modestly, from $160,000 in 2016 to $152,100 in 2019.[41]

The debilitating effects of racism on Black Americans has been exacerbated further by the COVID-19 pandemic. Black Americans have experienced disproportionate COVID-19 mortality, partly due to underlying health conditions fueled by limited access to primary care and insurance coverage. African Americans are also overrepresented among the throngs of "essential" workers forced to endure high risks of exposure to the coronavirus. CDC data released in April 2021 indicate that, since the onset of the pandemic, African Americans were about 10 percent more likely to have contracted COVID-19 than were non-Hispanic white Americans; however, African Americans were 2.8 times more likely to have been hospitalized after contracting COVID-19 and 1.9 times more likely to die after contracting the disease. For Hispanics, the infection rate was twice as great, the hospitalization rate three times as great, and the mortality rate 2.3 times larger than that of non-Hispanic white Americans.[42]

Disparities in healthcare coverage have contributed significantly to disparities in hospitalization and death rates. For example, Black workers are 60 percent more likely to be uninsured than white workers, are less likely to have paid sick days, and have less ability to work from home than do white workers.[43] Racial segregation and housing discrimination have also played important roles in generating differences in the likelihood of contracting COVID-19. Several studies have documented that members of racial/ethnic "minority" groups who contracted COVID-19 were more likely to live in areas with higher population density and more housing units or inadequate housing such as that lacking indoor plumbing.[44] The greater likelihood of having underlying health conditions, many of which result from historically conditioned disparities in the social determinants of health, also fuel disparities in negative

COVID-19 outcomes. The higher obesity rates of Blacks and Hispanics, as well as higher blood pressure and a greater prevalence of diabetes, have all contributed to disproportionate hospitalization and mortality rates.[45]

Without a substantial injection of federal assistance, the COVID-19 pandemic would have dramatically increased the poverty rates for all groups. According to the Urban Institute (2020), the 2020 poverty rates for Black individuals (not families), for example, would have been 20.5 percent. As a result of the federal stimulus payments distributed that year, expanded unemployment assistance, and other transfers, the 2020 poverty rate for Black individuals was projected to be 15.2 percent.[46] These projections, however, do not consider the inequitable access to stimulus checks and unemployment benefits experienced by many African Americans. Many unemployed Blacks, as well as Black citizens generally, faced unanticipated difficulties in accessing support via the Coronavirus Aid, Relief, and Economic Security Act (CARES Act) because they were "unbanked"—that is, they did not have a savings or checking account, into which most of these government aid funds were disbursed electronically. According to a 2018 report, 16.9 percent of Black households were unbanked in 2017 compared with just 3.0 percent of white households.[47]

Difficulty in accessing support has also contributed to disproportionate food insecurity and housing challenges. In March 2021, sixteen percent of Black households reported that they sometimes or often did not have enough to eat,[48] while 22 percent of Black renters claimed they were not caught up with their rent.[49] Nonetheless, of the top 10 states receiving the most rental assistance per renter household in 2021, more than half had a white population of more than 80 percent.[50] Black homeowners confronted similar issues. Over the period from 1984 to 2017, the rate at which Black homeowners were forced to become renters was 80 percent greater than the rate for whites.[51]

The COVID-19 pandemic also wreaked havoc on the fortunes of Black-owned businesses. The number of African American business owners plummeted from 1.1 million in February 2020 to 640,000 in April 2020. This loss of 440,000 Black business owners represented a 41 percent decline from the previous level.[52] Employees of Black-owned businesses were disproportionately affected by the pandemic, with the largest percentage of losses in the arts, entertainment, and recreation fields; accommodation and food services; and other service industries. These three sectors accounted for almost a third (32.3 percent) of Black-owned businesses but just 18.8 percent of white-owned businesses.[53]

The decline in Black-owned businesses was further exacerbated by the disproportionate barriers Black entrepreneurs encountered in obtaining assistance from the federal government. A survey based on May 2020 data found that a majority (51 percent) of Black and Latinx small business owners who sought federal assistance requested less than $20,000 in temporary funding while only about 12 percent received the assistance they requested. Almost two-thirds (41 percent) reported that they had either received no assistance or were still waiting for a decision (21 percent).[54]

Overall, the experiences of African Americans since 2018 fully support the finding noted in *US News & World Report*'s *Best Countries 2021* that the US is among the 10 worst countries for racial equality.[55] This finding was based on analyses of how 78 countries have elevated the importance of addressing racial inequities. The metric used was part of the report's social-purpose sub-ranking, which assesses a country's racial equity and commitment to social justice. Development of the metric was a response to the social dislocations generated by the COVID-19 pandemic, the ensuing sharp economic downturn, and worldwide calls for social justice and an end to inequality.[56]

Fighting the Powers and Keeping the Faith

Confronting Police Violence

As emphasized throughout this volume, a distinguishing feature of Black/Africana Studies is its emphasis on Black agency—that is, on active efforts to overcome racism, including PORT, and elevate the status of people of African descent. Focusing first on the battle to curtail police and civilian violence, Buchanan et al. (2020) estimated that between 15 and 26 million people participated in Black Lives Matter (BLM) protests in the United States during 2020, making that movement one of the largest in US history.[57] The efforts of the BLM Movement have been buttressed by unprecedented support from professional athletes in a wide range of sports. For example, the protest initiated by African American pro football quarterback Colin Kaepernick in 2016 set the stage for subsequent advocacy by Black professional athletes in several sports. Although Kaepernick has apparently been shunned for life by the National Football League (NFL) for kneeling during the national anthem, NFL Commissioner Roger Goodell recently publicly apologized to the League's Black players for his organization's failure to respond appropriately to their concerns; he also encouraged players of all races to engage in peaceful protest.[58] Goodell's apology was occasioned by the release of a video in which several prominent NFL players, including Deshaun Watson, Odell Beckham Jr., DeAndre Hopkins, Saquon Barkley, Sterling Shepard, and Jamal Adams, challenged the NFL to confront racism directly.[59]

In July 2020, fully 300 of the National Basketball Association's (NBA) 350 players decided to have one of eleven slogans printed on the back of their jerseys in lieu of their last names. The available slogans included "Black Lives Matter," "Say Their Names," and "I Can't Breathe."[60] This collective statement came on the heels of active support for the BLM Movement by major NBA star players including Carmello Anthony, Stephen Curry, Paul George, Lebron James, Chris Paul, and Dwayne Wade. The power of the NBA's African American players was in full view when Black members of the Milwaukee Bucks refused to play in Game 5 of the NBA playoffs on August 26, 2020, following the police shooting of Jacob Blake, effectively postponing that game.

African American players in the Women's National Basketball Association (WNBA) have been equally assertive in their support for the BLM Movement. Following the Milwaukee

Bucks' lead, three WNBA games were postponed in the wake of Jacob Blake's murder. As noted by Erica Ayala (2020), however, the WNBA's African American players have a long record of social advocacy. They were, Ayala observed, "among the first athletes to wear warm-up shirts with social justice messaging affirming Black Lives Matter, hold media blackouts and even kneel during the national anthem." Maya Moore, an MVP (Most Valuable Player)-ranked member of the Minnesota Lynx postponed her career in 2016 to help reverse the conviction of Jonathan Irons, a Black man wrongfully sentenced as a teenager to a 50-year prison term. Additionally, WNBA players Renee Montgomery of the Atlanta Dream and Natasha Cloud of the Washington Mystics sat out during the 2020 season to work on social justice projects.[61] Black female tennis stars Coco Gauff, Naomi Osaka, and Sloan Stephens were also highly visible in their support of BLM. Perhaps the most unexpected support from Black athletes came from professional race car driver Bubba Wallace, who drove a car with a Black Lives Matter paint scheme at a Martinsville Speedway race in 2020; and from Lewis Hamilton, a Black British driver on the Formula One racing circuit.

Musical artists have a long tradition of producing liberatory fare.[62] Thus, it is not surprising that anti-police violence initiatives and the BLM Movement have garnered strong support in recent years. Representative songs released in 2020 include "I Can't Breathe" by H.E.R., "The Bigger Picture" by Lil Baby, "Get Up" by T Pain, "2020 Riots: How Many Times" by Trey Songz, and "FTP" by YG. On June 2, 2020, the entire music industry observed "Black Out Tuesday" spurred by the murders of African Americans George Floyd, Breonna Taylor, and Ahmaud Arbery. As noted by the HB (Hollywood Branded) Team, "Major labels, publishing and public relations companies and artists took a day to provide a space for the voices who need it most, sharing the message of solidarity in the fight against racism. Everything from music and video releases to publicity updates were put on hold."[63] Reportedly, artists associated with various genres—among them Kanye West, The Weeknd, and Drake—have donated close to $3 million to organizations whose agendas are compatible with the BLM Movement such as the National Bail-Out Collective and Colin Kaepernick's Know Your Rights Camp, as well as providing direct support to the Floyd, Taylor, and Arbery families.[64]

BLM has expanded into a global operation: the Black Lives Matter Global Network Foundation, Inc. As described on its website, the mission of that organization, which is based in the US, UK, and Canada, is "to eradicate white supremacy and build local power to intervene in violence inflicted on Black communities by the state and vigilantes."[65] We The Protestors (WTP) is another organization actively engaged in combating police violence. Its website states that it has "built the most comprehensive database of police violence in the nation" and has "used the data to identify effective policy solutions and supported movement organizers to enact these policies at every level of government."[66] One WTP initiative, Campaign Zero, encourages policymakers to focus on solutions with the strongest evidence of effectiveness at reducing police violence.[67] Another organization, The Not Fucking Around Coalition (NFAC), headed by Grand Master Jay, is taking a more aggressive stance against racial violence. Its goals include "empowering Black citizens through training them on proper use of firearms and establishing a framework [for an]...inter-city security force that can patrol or self-police Black neighborhoods."[68] The broader self-defense agenda of the NFAC reflects concerns about possible violence perpetrated by right-wing zealots. For these and similar organizations, the 2015 massacre of Black worshippers at Emanuel A.M.E. Church in Charleston, South Carolina, is a potent reminder of the potentially dire consequences of inadequate community vigilance.

Attorney Benjamin Crump has achieved national recognition for his success in obtaining financial settlements for the families of Black victims of police killings. Sometimes referred to as "Black America's Attorney General," Crump's victories include a $12-million settlement in the Breonna Taylor case and a $27-million settlement in the George Floyd case. More multi-million-dollar settlements are likely to be forthcoming.[69]

Empowering Black Voters and Fighting Voter Suppression

Without a doubt, Black voters played a critical role in forging the 2020 election victory of President Joe Biden and Vice President Kamala Harris. It is also significant that 57 African Americans currently are serving in the US House of Representatives compared to 50 in the 115th Congress (2017–18). Overall, Black voter turnout in 2020 increased by 14 percent compared to 2016, with 90 percent of Black voters supporting the Democratic Party ticket. The difference between the number of Blacks voting Democratic versus Republican was greater than the Biden-Harris ticket's margin of victory in the key states of Arizona, Georgia, Michigan, Nevada, Pennsylvania, and Wisconsin.

Despite these successes, several cautionary observations are in order. The percentage of Blacks supporting the Democratic ticket in 2020 was less than that evidenced in 2012 and 2016. While 93 percent of Black women voted Democratic, only 86 percent of Black men did, and Black women accounted for 59 percent of all votes cast by Black voters. Notably, 37 percent of voting-age Blacks did not vote in the 2020 election.[70] This low voter participation rate was surprising given the extensive efforts undertaken to mobilize Black voter turnout. In its focus on voter engagement, for example, the National Association for the Advancement of Colored People (NAACP) spent $15 million to encourage voters to get to the polls using a mix of social media, text messages, and radio ads. The NAACP's target states included Michigan, Pennsylvania, Wisconsin, Georgia, Texas, and Alabama.[71]

A Black Georgia politician, Stacey Abrams, was unquestionably the most visible opponent of voter suppression and advocate for fair elections leading up to the 2020 elections. Abrams founded an organization named Fair Fight in 2018 after losing her bid for the Georgia gubernatorial election. She subsequently established another organization, Fair Fight 2020, in anticipation of the need to fund and train voter-protection teams in 20 battleground states during the 2020 election cycle.[72] She has been credited with engineering Georgia Democratic victories in both the 2020 presidential campaign and the 2021 Senatorial runoff election.

Abrams' efforts were complemented by the efforts of the Atlanta Hip Hop community. As recounted by Elliott McLaughlin (2020), "Atlanta's hip-hop community hit the streets and beauty and barber shops, took to Instagram and YouTube, and helped voter drives turn Georgia from red to blue." Moreover, Hip Hop activists continued their efforts in the runup to the 2021 Georgia Senatorial runoff election.[73] On the national scene, a group of Black athletes and entertainers launched the More Than A Vote initiative in June 2020 with the goal of energizing, educating, and protecting Black voters as well as fighting systemic racism and protecting Black communities generally.[74]

In response to Georgia's voter-suppression laws, an impressive group of 72 high-level Black business executives issued a public statement denouncing those efforts. That statement, published in the *New York Times* on March 31, 2021 was titled "Memo to Corporate America: The Fierce Urgency is Now." It called for corporations to "publicly oppose any discriminatory legislation and all measures designed to limit Americans' ability to vote." As it further stated: "Corporate America must support our nation's fundamental democratic principles and marshal its collective influence to ensure fairness and equity for all.... We call upon our colleagues in Corporate America to join us in taking a non-partisan stand for equality and democracy."[75] The Georgia law was also challenged by the Georgia NAACP and other voting rights organizations.[76] Similar legal challenges can be anticipated as efforts expand around the country to enact voter-suppression legislation masquerading as voting-reform initiatives.

Confronting White Supremacist Symbols and Narratives

Efforts to remove Confederate statues and monuments from public spaces have been some of the most visible strategies used to combat the neo-Lost Cause ideology. According to the Southern Poverty Law Center, social protests catalyzed the removal of 168 Confederate monuments from public spaces in 2020. It is important to remember, however, that approximately 700 such monuments currently remain in public spaces around the country.[77] Consequently, continuing advocacy will be necessary to maintain the momentum of the monument-removal movement.

In addition to the previously discussed 1619 Project, an antiracist educational initiative is challenging the neo-Lost Cause narrative. Ibram X. Kendi is the most visible spokesperson for this initiative, which has been spurred by the popularity of his bestselling book, *How to be An Antiracist.*[78] The neo-Lost Cause narrative is also being neutralized by a wave of liberatory creative production including several recent biopics and documentary films. Notable recent films focusing on visible activists include *Harriet* (2019), *Just Mercy* (2019), *Self Made* (2020), *John Lewis: Good Trouble* (2020), and *One Night in Miami* (2020). Poignant portrayals of Black struggle include *The Hate You Give* (2018), *Queen and Slim* (2019), and *The United States vs. Billie Holiday* (2021). Novelist/essayist James Baldwin has provided a wealth of material fueling the development of cinematic counter-narratives as illustrated by two recent films drawing from his life and works: *I am Not Your Negro* (2016) and *If Beale Street Could Talk* (2018).

The HBO mini-series *Watchmen* (2019) deserves special mention for its rebuttal to the neo-Lost Cause narrative. The series reimagines the original DC Comic superhero saga, focusing on issues of racial trauma. The initial episode, for example, revisits the 1921 Tulsa, Oklahoma, massacre, and much of the series' action centers around a character named Angela Abar (played by Regina King), a Tulsa police detective who also goes by the name Sister Night. In the Tulsa of 2019, Abar continually confronts the legacy of the 1921 pogrom. Analogous to the historically corrective role adopted by the 1977 mini-series *Roots*, *Watchmen* foregrounds the historical record of violence and destruction experienced by Black Americans in a creative format.[79] The abiding significance of the Tulsa Massacre is further underscored by the plans of basketball star LeBron James and his Springhill production company to partner with CNN Films to produce a documentary examining that violent event. That program, "Dreamland: The Rise and Fall of Black Wall Street, aired to national audiences on CNN on May 31, 2021."[80]

African Americans have stepped up their use of social media to confront neo-Lost Cause narratives since 2018. As noted by researcher Brooke Auxier, from 2015 to 2020, Black social media users have been "more likely than their counterparts from some other racial and ethnic backgrounds to engage in different types of political activities on social media and to believe these activities are more effective."[81]

Pandemic Recovery and Community Revitalization

Achieving a sustainable recovery trajectory from the COVID-19 pandemic will require a concerted collective commitment. Vaccination inequity is the latest in a continuing pattern of disparate treatment. After March 1, 2021, the share of the population that had received at least one dose of a COVID-19 vaccine increased among all racial/ethnic groups, but disparities for Black and Hispanic people have persisted and widened. As of April 2021, the percentage of whites who had received at least one COVID-19 vaccine dose (38 percent) was 1.6 times higher than that for Black (24 percent.)[82] Several factors are contributing to this inequity, including limited access to vaccination sites, lack of access to online vaccination-registration portals, and hesitancy regarding public health interventions associated with historical abuses such as the infamous Tuskegee Syphilis Experiment. Another limiting factor is the closure of several urban hospitals that historically have served disproportionate percentages of Black and Latinx patients. Many of the patients who use these facilities have been forced to seek out emergency-room treatment as an alternative to their limited access to primary health care providers.[83]

Abdul-Mutakabbir et al. (2021) have proposed a three-tier model to address barriers to vaccine delivery in African American communities. The three components of their model are (1) engagement of Black faith leaders; (2) promotion of vaccine education by Black health-care professionals; and (3) increasing accessibility of vaccination clinics by situating them in Black communities, thereby eliminating the need for online registration and scheduling. To this end, Black churches around the country have organized COVID-19 vaccination clinics for their members and local neighborhood residents.[84] Several Black celebrities have made public service announcements to address the problem of vaccine hesitancy including Vice President Kamala Harris, former First Lady Michele Obama, sports notables like Hank Aaron and Kareem Abdul-Jabbar, and film stars Samuel L. Jackson and Tyler Perry.[85]

The disproportionate misery heaped on Black Americans by the current pandemic underscores the need for a comprehensive approach to addressing the historically conditioned sources of health disparities. Such an approach must also address well-known environmental dangers that disproportionately affect African Americans such as air pollution and proximity to brownfields as well as lesser-examined problems like exposure to household pests and the role of urban heat islands that exacerbate health problems. Urban heat islands are locations within metropolises that are significantly warmer than surrounding rural areas, primarily as a result of extensive paving that captures heat and the associated absence of trees that can aid in heat absorption.[86] Edward Wallace (2021) has introduced the concept of the "Damaging Constitution" to emphasize the fact that the country's founding document "does not require local and state governments to provide any goods or services to the public, whatsoever, unless they want to." The absence of mandated national norms has catalyzed gross racial and geographical disparities in the availability and quality of medical services.[87]

Concurrent with the pursuit of systematic pandemic-recovery efforts is the urgent need to coordinate the impressive array of self-help initiatives underway to foster long-term uplift in Black communities. Black entertainers and athletes are playing an important role in this effort. For example, NBA stars Carmelo Anthony, Dwyane Wade, and Chris Paul have established the Social Change Fund, an organization whose aim is "to provide more opportunities in Black and Brown communities, nationwide—expanding education, economic equity, efforts to end police brutality, advocating for voting rights and supporting civic engagement."[88]

Operating at the grass-roots level are organizations like Community Movement Builders (CMB), which is committed to fostering community development. CMB is a member-based "collective of black people creating sustainable, self-determining communities through cooperative economic advancement and collective community organizing."[89] The Pittsburgh Community Stabilization Fund is a CMB affiliate that is fighting gentrification by helping "long-term neighborhood residents pay bills or make critical home improvements to avoid eviction, foreclosure, or a forced sale of their property.[90]

Another movement underway aims to revitalize Tulsa's Black Wall Street, a once-prosperous business district that was destroyed by white rioters in 1921. In April 2020, the National Park Service announced a $500,000 grant for building renovation in the Tulsa Black Wall Street area.[91] This effort was expanded in June 2020 with the initiation of a $10 million major rebuilding campaign. Riffing on this initiative, a plan was announced soon afterward to undertake a similar project to revitalize Detroit, Michigan's Black Bottom neighborhood, which was decimated in the 1950s to make way for Interstate 375.[92]

Impressive revitalization efforts are emerging in rural African American communities as well. One example is the Hope Enterprise Corporation (HOPE), a partnership of development organizations dedicated to strengthening communities, building assets, and improving lives in the Delta and other economically distressed parts of Alabama, Arkansas, Louisiana, Mississippi, and Tennessee predominated by African Americans. HOPE has provided financial services, leveraged private and public resources, and shaped policies that have benefited more than a million residents in one of the nation's most persistently poor rural regions.[93] Evoking memories of the Soul City project spearheaded by attorney Floyd McKissick Jr. in the early 1970s, another organization, The Freedom Georgia Initiative, spearheaded the August 2020 purchase by a group of 19 Black families of over 96 acres of land in Toomsboro, Georgia, to create a "safe haven" and self-sustaining community for Black people.[94]

The future prospects for Black farmers seem to be brightening. Black farmers have been fighting for decades to obtain relief for the systemic discrimination they have experienced at the hands of the US Department of Agriculture—inequities that have contributed to a 90-percent decline in the amount of Black-owned farmland since 1910. The 2021 Emergency Relief for Farmers of Color Act, introduced by Georgia's first and newly elected Black Senator, Raphael Warnock (D-GA), forgives up to 120 percent of the value of all loans granted to Black farmers from the Department of Agriculture or from private lending sources guaranteed by the USDA.[95]

The Reparations Movement has also gained significant momentum since 2018, as evidenced by the mounting attention given to the 2020 book, *From Here to Equality: Reparations for Black Americans in the Twenty-First Century*, by William Darity and Kristen Mullen.[96] More importantly, that movement is gaining traction via legislative initiatives, community-specific undertakings, and systematic research. At the national level, H.R. 40, the Commission to Study and Develop Reparation Proposals for African Americans Act, was re-introduced in Congress on January 4, 2021, by Representative Sheila Jackson Lee (D-TX). As proposed, this commission would be charged with examining slavery and discrimination in the colonies and the United States from 1619 to the present and recommending appropriate remedies. The bill, which was reported out of committee at the House of Representatives level in April 2021, mandates that the commission identify (1) the role of the federal and state governments in supporting the institution of slavery, (2) forms of discrimination in the public and private sectors against freed slaves and their descendants, and (3) lingering negative effects of slavery on living African Americans and society.[97]

At the state and local levels, California recently announced its own H.R. 40-style commission via a law that creates a nine-member task force charged with informing Californians about slavery and exploring ways that state might provide reparations to its African American citizens.[98] Additionally, the mayor of Providence, Rhode Island, signed an executive order in July 2020 creating a "truth-telling, reconciliation and municipal reparations process" intended to determine the feasibility of providing reparations payments to that city's Black residents.[99]

Some municipalities have gone even further and have established concrete reparations implementation programs. In March 2021, for example, the Evanston, Illinois, city council voted to make the first $400,000 round of payments that are part of a $10 million decade-long reparations commitment. Evanston's initial distribution will provide $25,000 to a small number of eligible Black residents for home repairs, down payments, or mortgage payments as a response to the community's historically racist housing policies.[100] In a similar vein in July 2020, Asheville, North Carolina, approved reparations for Black residents to promote home ownership and business opportunities.[101]

Universities are also coming to grips with their involvement in, and benefits derived from, the institution of slavery. Jesuit-affiliated Georgetown has received the most attention as a result of it announcing a plan in 2019 to pay $400,000 a year to create a fund for reparations to the descendants of 272 enslaved Blacks sold by the institution. In March 2021, the Jesuit order pledged $100 million to atone for its use of enslaved labor and its sales of enslaved Blacks. The renaming of buildings on the campus of Rutgers University after prominent African Americans including Sojourner Truth, who was once enslaved by the family of a Rutgers president, is another significant development. In the wake of a 2018 report documenting its role in perpetuating enslavement, the University of Virginia founded the Universities Studying Slavery Consortium, which includes about 40 schools that are sharing resources to research their historical connections to the slavery regime.[102]

Addressing the pandemic-induced educational difficulties experienced by Black children must be a top priority for the nation's pandemic-recovery efforts. According to a December 2020 report, Black and Hispanic students are twice as likely as white students to have had no live contact with their teachers over the previous week; they are also three to six percentage points less likely to be receiving consistent live instruction. Although racial/ethnic gaps in access to a computer or comparable device and similar disparities in internet access have narrowed since spring 2021, Black and Hispanic households are still three to four percentage points less likely than white households to have reliable access to devices and three to six percentage points less likely to have reliable access to the internet. As the report concluded, if current pedagogical practices are maintained without adjustment, students of color stood to lose 11 to 12 months of learning by June 2021; targeted action, however, could help reduce this loss to 6 to 8 months.[103] Concurrent with this necessary focus on basic skills is the need to ensure that post-pandemic instruction reflects best practices in culturally responsive pedagogy. As Matthew Lynch (2016) maintains: "Culturally responsive pedagogy is a student-centered approach to teaching in which the students' unique cultural strengths are identified and nurtured to promote student achievement and a sense of well-being about the student's cultural place in the world."[104]

In the longer term, the type of educational interventions necessary to help African Americans break out of the cycle of disempowerment could be funded by reparations proceeds. V. P. Franklin (2012, 2013) has proposed the creation of a "Reparations Superfund" that could be used "to fund projects in public schools to promote the arts and music and in private institutions offering supplemental education in the form of music and arts programs." Additionally, this Superfund could "target and support alternatives to the current emphasis on 'high stakes testing' and test preparation that contributes mightily to the high dropout rates." It could also "help to support maternal and early childhood health care program and interventions that target young children and place them in a 'health-care network' administered by health care professionals who have experience implementing these programs successfully in African American communities or neighborhoods."[105]

The need to ensure that African American students are encouraged to consider careers in high-tech fields is also critical so Blacks are not relegated to the digital backwaters. Black Tech Nation (BTN), a Pittsburgh-based, multi-faceted tech group, is one organization addressing this issue. BTN, according to its website, is about "building a #DigitalWakanda"—a reference to the advanced technology portrayed in the fictional Afro-futuristic nation where much of the action in the 2018 blockbuster movie, *Black Panther*, takes place. "Through education, digital media, recruitment, and funding for Black technologists and entrepreneurs," its website continues, BTN focuses on "uplifting Black technologists, educating and supporting our members, creating employment and funding opportunities, providing access to the 'right people' in the industry, producing digital events and workshops, and advocating for tech equity across our industry."[106]

Other positive developments in higher education signal the potential for a robust pandemic-recovery trajectory for African Americans. In his 2019 commencement address at Morehouse College, Black billionaire Robert Smith announced he was donating an estimated $41 million to pay for the educational debts of that institution's 400 graduating seniors. His philanthropy affords those recipients the luxury of pursuing graduate study, entrepreneurial ventures, and other potentially community-elevating activities absent the conventional financial barriers that typically face new US undergrads.[107] More recently, philanthropists McKenzie Scott, Scott Hastings, and Hastings' spouse Patty Quillin made donations to selected HBCUs totaling some $250 million. The primary beneficiaries were Howard University, Xavier University of Louisiana, Hampton University, Morehouse College, Spelman College, and Tuskegee University.[108] These gifts should position those schools to play an extremely active and visible role in advancing post-pandemic recovery and community revitalization nationwide. In a similar vein, the recent upgrading of several Black/Africana Studies units to departments at several American institutions of higher education—St. Louis University, Louisiana State University, Stanford University, Bowdoin College, Michigan State University, and Washington University, among them—should allow B/AS scholar/activists affiliated with these and other institutions to expand their roles in promoting the intellectual, material, and spiritual liberation of people of African descent.

James B. Stewart
Summer 2021

xxxi

Endnotes

1. Henry Giroux, *American Nightmare: Facing the Challenge of Fascism* (City Lights Open Media) City Lights Publishers; City Lights Open Media edition (July 10, 2018)

2. Jordyn Phelps, "Trump Defends 2017 'Very Fine People' Comments, Calls Robert E. Lee 'A Great General,'" *abcnews.com*. URL: https://abcnews.go.com/Politics/trump-defends-2017-fine-people-comments-calls-robert/story?id=62653478. (April 26, 2019).

3. Kiara Brantley-Jones, "False Equivalency Between Black Lives Matter and Capitol Siege: Experts, Advocates," *abcnews.com*. URL: https://abcnews.go.com/US/false-equivalency-black-lives-matter-capitol-siege-experts/story?id=75251279. (January 16, 2021).

4. Jeremy Diamond, "Trump: I Could 'Shoot Somebody and I Wouldn't Lose Voters,'" *cnn.com*. URL: https://www.cnn.com/2016/01/23/politics/donald-trump-shoot-somebody-support/index.html. (January 24, 2016).

5. ACLU, "Anti-Protest Bills Around the Country," *aclu.org*. URL: https://www.aclu.org/issues/free-speech/rights-protesters/anti-protest-bills-around-country.

6. Michael Putney, "Florida Gov. Ron DeSantis' Anti-riot-bill Expect to Pass, Will Make Penalties Harsher." *Local10.com*. URL: https://www.local10.com/news/politics/2021/04/03/florida-gov-ron-desantis-controversial-anti-riot-bill-will-make-penalties-stiffer/. (April 3, 2021).

7. Grace Hauck, "Cars have Hit Demonstrators 104 Times Since George Floyd Protests Began, *usatoday.com*. URL: https://www.usatoday.com/story/news/nation/2020/07/08/vehicle-ramming-attacks-66-us-since-may-27/5397700002/. (Updated September 27, 2020).

8. Frank Edwards, Hedwig Lee, and Michael Esposito, "Risk of Being Killed by Police Use of Force in the United States by Age, Race–Ethnicity, and Sex, *PNAS* 116 (34). URL: www.pnas.org/cgi/doi/10.1073/pnas.1821204116. (August 20, 2019).

9. Ibid.

10. Steve Early and Suzanne Gordon, "Trading One Uniform for Another: Can Police be "Demilitarized" When So Many Cops are Military Veterans?" *CounterPunch.org*. URL: https://www.counterpunch.org/2020/06/22/trading-one-uniform-for-another-can-police-be-de-militarized-when-so-many-cops-are-military-veterans/. (June 22, 2020).

11. John M. Donnelly, Pentagon Report Reveals Inroads White Supremacists Have Made in Military, *rollcall.com*. URL: https://www.rollcall.com/2021/02/16/pentagon-report-reveals-inroads-white-supremacists-have-made-in-military/. (February 16, 2021).

12. Wayne McElrath and Sarah Turberville, "Poisoning Our Police: How the Militarization Mindset Threatens Constitutional Rights and Public Safety," *pogo.org*. URL: https://www.pogo.org/analysis/2020/06/poisoning-our-police-how-the-militarization-mindset-threatens-constitutional-rights-and-public-safety/. (June 9, 2020).

13. Vann Newkirk II, "The Supreme Court Finds North Carolina's Racial Gerrymandering Unconstitutional," *theatlantic.com*. URL: https://www.theatlantic.com/politics/archive/2017/05/north-carolina-gerrymandering/527592/. (May 22, 2017).

14. "Voting Laws Roundup: February 2021." URL: https://www.brennancenter.org/our-work/research-reports/voting-laws-roundup-february-2021.

15. Nick Corasaniti and Reid Epstein, "What Georgia's Voting Law Really Does," *nytimes.com*. URL: https://www.nytimes.com/2021/04/02/us/politics/georgia-voting-law-annotated.html. (April 2, 2021).

16. Elly Belle, "Black Voter Intimidation is More Present Than Ever—Here's How Activists are Fighting Back," *yahoo.com*. URL: https://www.yahoo.com/now/black-voter-intimidation-more-presen175430679.html?guccounter=1&guce_referrer=aHR0cHM6Ly93d3cuZ29vZ2xlLmNvbS8&guce_referrer_sig=AQAAAFv4MI0i9Ljw-QmT7ny6-OeAXDkBascQgR0Tdaz-ZauJUJM7UpwIAW97iPnEjNkjY4bzYJqW8eU518eU3tlfTBQCLCZ2wN6XM9Zl888PqHYRY5dd4MvdloxrZKuDyPIWYuj4XTMuy-UASej5Dn5MmfMvxScqo3UNCHI3w2ujWl9OJ

17. N. Rashid, "The Emergence of the White Troll Behind a Black Face," *npr.org*. URL: https://www.npr.org/sections/codeswitch/2017/03/21/520522240/the-emergence-of-the-white-troll-behind-a-black-face. (March 21, 2017).

18. Associated Press, "Network of Facebook Groups Shifts Attacks from Stay-at-home Orders to Black Lives Matter," *marketwatch.com*. URL: https://www.marketwatch.com/story/network-of-facebook-groups-shifts-attacks-from-stay-at-home-orders-to-black-lives-matter-2020-07-05. (July 5, 2020).

19. The Select Committee on Intelligence, United States Senate. "Senate (U)Report of The Select Committee on Intelligence, United States Senate, on Russian Active Measures Campaigns and Interference in the 2016 U.S. Election, Volume 2: Russia's Use of Social Media with Additional Views. Report 116-xx. URL: https://www.intelligence.senate.gov/sites/default/files/documents/Report_Volume2.pdf. (2019).

20. D. Freelon, et al., "Black Trolls Matter: Racial and Ideological Asymmetries in Social Media Disinformation," *Social Science Computer Review*, 1-19 (2020).

21. "Lost Cause Myth,"*inclusivehistorian.com*. URL: https://inclusivehistorian.com/lost-cause-myth/. (May 13, 2020).

22. Ibid.

23. "Lost Cause Myth," op. cit.

24. Clint Smith, "Why Confederate Lies Live On," *theatlantic.com*. URL: https://www.theatlantic.com/magazine/archive/2021/06/confederate-lost-cause-myth/618711/. (June 2021).

25. Cleve Wotson, "Trump Implied Frederick Douglass was Alive. The Abolitionist's Family Offered a 'History Lesson,'" *washingpost.com*. URL: https://www.washingtonpost.com/news/post-nation/wp/2017/02/02/trump-implied-frederick-douglass-was-alive-the-abolitionists-family-offered-a-history-lesson/. (February 2, 2017).

26. "Executive Order on Combating Race and Sex Stereotyping," *Law & Justice.* Issued on September 22, 2020.

27. Schwartz, Sarah, "Lawmakers Push to Ban '1619 Project' From Schools," *edweek.org*. URL: https://www.edweek.org/teaching-learning/lawmakers-push-to-ban-1619-project-from-schools/2021/02. (February 3, 2021).

28. "Critical Race Theory, *Britannica.com.* URL: https://www.britannica.com/topic/critical-race-theory.

29. Char Adams, "How Trump Ignited the Fight over Critical Race Theory in Schools," *nbc.com*. URL: https://www.nbcnews.com/news/nbcblk/how-trump-ignited-fight-over-critical-race-theory-schools-n1266701. (May 10, 2021).

30. *"The 1619 Project," The New York Times (August 14, 2019).*

31. Barbara Rodriguez, "Republican State Lawmakers Want to Punish Schools That Teach the 1619 Project," *usatoday.com*. URL: https://www.usatoday.com/story/news/education/2021/02/10/slavery-and-history-states-threaten-funding-schools-teach-1619-project/4454195001/. (February 10, 2021).

32. Ryan Nobles, "McConnell Sends Letter to Education Secretary Demanding Removal of the 1619 Project from Federal Grant Programs, *cnn.com*. URL: https://www.cnn.com/2021/04/30/politics/mcconnell-1619-project-education-secretary/index.html. (April 30, 2021).

33. Nell Gluckman, Why Did a University Suspend its Mandatory Diversity Course? *Chronicle.com.* URL: https://www.chronicle.com/article/why-did-a-university-suspend-its-mandatory-diversity-course?cid=gen_sign_in&cid2=gen_login_refresh. (March 18, 2021).

34. Caitlin Oprysko, "Barr: 'I Don't Think There are 2 Justice Systems' for Black and White Americans," *politico.com*. URL: https://www.politico.com/news/2020/09/02/barr-race-justice-system-407929. (September 2, 2020).

35. Devan Cole, "Graham Denies Systemic Racism Exists in US and Says 'America's not a racist country,'" *cnn.com.* URL: https://www.cnn.com/2021/04/25/politics/lindsey-graham-systemic-racism-america/index.html. (April 25, 2021).

36. "AMA Board of Trustees pledges action against racism, police brutality," *ama-assn.org*. URL: https://www.ama-assn.org/press-center/ama-statements/ama-board-trustees-pledges-action-against-racism-police-brutality. (June 7, 2020).

37. "Media Statement from CDC Director Rochelle P. Walensky, MD, MPH, on Racism and Health," *cdc. gov*. URL:https://www.cdc.gov/media/releases/2021/s0408-racism-health.html.

38. Hye Jin Rho, Haley Brown, and Shawn Fremstad, *A Basic Demographic Profile of Workers in Frontline Industries*. Center for Economic and Policy Research, April 2020.

39. Valerie Wilson, "Inequities Exposed: How COVID-19 Widened Racial Inequities in Education, Health, and the Workforce." Testimony before the U.S. House of Representatives Committee on Education and Labor. *epi.org*. URL: https://www.epi.org/publication/covid-19-inequities-wilson-testimony/. (June 22, 2020).

40. US Census Bureau, "Table 2. Poverty Status of People by Family Relationship, Race, and Hispanic Origin: 1959 to 2019." *census.gov*. URL: https://www.census.gov/data/tables/time-series/demo/income-poverty/historical-poverty-people.html. (Visited April 30, 2021).

41. Neil Bhutta, et al., "The Fed—Disparities in Wealth by Race and Ethnicity in the 2019 Survey of Consumer Finances." *federalreserve.gov*. URL: https://www.federalreserve.gov/econres/notes/feds-notes/disparities-in-wealth-by-race-and-ethnicity-in-the-2019-survey-of-consumer-finances-20200928.htm. (September 28, 2020).

42. Centers for Disease Control, "Risk for COVID-19 Infection, Hospitalization, and Death by Race/Ethnicity." *cdc.gov*. URL: https://www.cdc.gov/coronavirus/2019-ncov/covid-data/investigations-discovery/hospitalization-death-by-race-ethnicity.html#print. (Updated April 23, 2021).

43. Valerie Wilson, "Inequities Exposed: How COVID-19 Widened Racial Inequities in Education, Health, and the Workforce." Testimony before the U.S. House of Representatives Committee on Education and Labor. *epi.org*. URL: https://www.epi.org/publication/covid-19-inequities-wilson-testimony/. (June 22, 2020).

44. See A. K. Okoh, et al. "Coronavirus Disease 19 in Minority Populations of Newark, New Jersey," *International Journal for Equity in Health*. 19 (93), 2020; and D. Rodriguez-Lonear, et al., "American Indian Reservations and COVID-19: Correlates of Early Infection Rates in the Pandemic," *Journal of Public Health Management and Practice*. 24 (4), 2020; 371-377.

45. See M, El Chaar, K. King, and A. Galvez Lima, "Are Black and Hispanic Persons Disproportionately Affected by COVID-19 Because of Higher Obesity Rates?" *Surgery for Obesity & Related Diseases*, 2020; J. A. W. Gold, et al., "Characteristics and Clinical Outcomes of Adult Patients Hospitalized with COVID-19—Georgia, March 2020. *Morbidity & Mortality Weekly Report*. 69 (18), 2020; 545-50; and V. Gayam, et al., "Clinical Characteristics and Predictors of Mortality in African-Americans with COVID-19 from an Inner-city Community Teaching Hospital in New York," *Journal of Medical Virology*, 2020.

46. Linda Giannarelli, Laura Wheaton, and Gregory Acs, "2020 Poverty Projections." *urban.org*. Table 2: Projected 2020 Annual Poverty Rates with and without COVID-19 Pandemic Response Policies. URL: https://www.urban.org/sites/default/files/publication/102521/2020-poverty-projections.pdf. (July 2020).

47. Gerald Apaam, et al., *2017 FDIC National Survey of Unbanked and Underbanked Households*. Federal Deposit Insurance Corporation. (October 2018).

48. "Tracking the COVID-19 Recession's Effects on Food, Housing, and Employment Hardships," *cbpp.org*. URL: https://www.cbpp.org/sites/default/files/atoms/files/8-13-20pov.pdf.

49. Ibid.

50. Romina Ruiz-Goiriena and Aleszu Bajak, "How Much Rent Relief Will I Get? You're More Likely to Get Help if You're White and Live in Rural America," *usatoday.com*. URL: https://www.usatoday.com/story/news/nation/2021/02/10/covid-rent-relief-emergency-rental-assistance-not-enough-big-states/4413471001/. (February 11, 2021).

51. Gregory Sharp, Ellen Whitehead, and Matthew Hall, "Tapped Out? Racial Disparities in Extrahousehold Kin Resources and the Loss of Homeownership," *Demography* 57 (September, 2020).

52. Robert W. Fairlie, "The Impact of Covid-19 on Small Business Owners: Evidence of Early-Stage Losses from the April 2020 Current Population Survey." *Working Paper 27309*. URL: http://www.nber.org/papers/w27309.

53. Elise Gould and Valerie Wilson, "Black Workers Face Two of the Most Lethal Preexisting Conditions for Coronavirus—Racism and Economic Inequality,"*epi.org.* URL: https://www.epi.org/publication/black-workers-covid/. (June 1, 2020).

54. Global Strategy Group for Color of Change and Unidos, "Federal Stimulus Survey Findings," *unidosus.org.* URL: https://www.unidosus.org/about-us/media/press/releases/051820-UnidosUS-Press-Release-COVID-19-Survey-Black-and-Latino-Small-BusinessNIDOSUS.

55. Kevin Drew, "Survey: U.S. Among 10 Worst Countries for Racial Equality," *usnews.com.* URL: https://www.usnews.com/news/best-countries/articles/2021-04-13/us-is-one-of-the-10-worst-countries-for-racial-equality. (April 13, 2021)

56. U.S. News Staff, "Methodology: How the 2021 Best Countries Were Ranked," *usnews.com.* URL: https://www.usnews.com/news/best-countries/articles/methodology Among 10 Worst Countries for Racial Equality. (April 13, 2021).

57. Larry Buchanan, Quoctrung Bui, and Jugal Patel, "Black Lives Matter May Be the Largest Movement in U.S. History," *The New York Times.* (July 3, 2020).

58. Rob Maaddi, "Colin Kaepernick has More Support Now, Still Long Way to Go," *denverpost.com.* URL: https://www.denverpost.com/2020/06/06/colin-kaepernick-more-support/. (June 6, 2020).

59. Joseph Staszewski, "NFL Stars Deliver Challenge to League in Black Lives Matter Video," *nypost.com.* URL: https://nypost.com/2020/06/05/nfl-players-deliver-challenge-to-league-in-black-lives-matter-video/. (June 5, 2020).

60. The Undefeated, "Social Justice Messages Each NBA Player is Wearing on his Jersey," *theundefeated.com.* URL: https://theundefeated.com/features/social-justice-messages-each-nba-player-is-wearing-on-his-jersey/. (July 31, 2020).

61. Erica L. Ayala, "The NBA's Walkout is Historic. But the WNBA Paved the Way. *Washingtonpost.com.* URL: https://www.washingtonpost.com/outlook/2020/08/29/nba-wnba-racial-injustice/. (August 29, 2020).

62. James B. Stewart, "Message in the Music: Political Commentary in Black Popular Music from Rhythm and Blues to Early Hip Hop," in "The History of Hip Hop," Special Issue of *The Journal of African American History*, 90 (3) (Summer 2005), 196-225.

63. HB Team, "The Music Industry Responds to Ongoing Black Lives Matter Protests in America," *hypebeast.com.* URL: https://hypebeast.com/2020/6/artists-statements-black-lives-matter-protests-america-roundup. (June 4, 2020).

64. "Second Take: Hip-hop Artists Take on Activist Roles in BLM Movement Through Musical Commentary, Protest," *dailybruin.com.* URL: https://dailybruin.com/2020/06/29/second-take-hip-hop-artists-take-on-activist-roles-in-blm-movement-through-musical-commentary-protest. (May 12, 2021).

65. "Black Lives Matter," *blacklivesmatter.com.* URL: https://blacklivesmatter.com.

66. "We the Protestors," *wetheprotestors.org. URL:* http://www.wetheprotesters.org.

67. "Campaign Zero," *joincampaignzero.org.* URL: https://www.joincampaignzero.org/#vision.

68. Tess Owen, "'If You Attack Us, We Will Kill You': The Not Fucking Around Coalition Wants to Protect Black Americans," *vice.com.* URL: https://www.vice.com/en/article/3anz38/the-not-fucking-around-coalition-wants-to-protect-black-americans. (October 28, 2020).

69. "'Black America's Attorney General' Represents Families of People Killed by Police." *npr.org.* URL: https://www.npr.org/2021/03/09/975382854/black-americas-attorney-general-represents-families-of-people-killed-by-police. (March 9, 2021).

70. Yair Ghitza and Jonathan Robinson, "What Happened in 2020," *catalyst.us.* URL: https://catalist.us/wh-national/.

71. Jenese Harris, "Historic Black Voter Turnout in 2020 Presidential Election," *news4jax.com.* URL: https://www.news4jax.com/vote-2020/2020/11/10/historic-black-voter-turnout-in-2020-presidential-election/. (November 10, 2020).

72. "Stacey Abrams," *Fairfight.com.* URL: https://fairfight.com/about-fair-fight/.

73. Eliott C. McLaughlin, "How Atlanta Rappers Helped Flip the White House (and They're Hustling to Flip the US Senate), *cnn.com.* URL: https://www.cnn.com/2020/12/29/politics/atlanta-hip-hop-flip-election-senate-white-house/index.html. (December 29, 2020).

74. "We are Black Athletes and Artists Working Together to Fight Systemic Racism and Educate, Energize, and Protect Our Community," *morethanavote.org*. URL: https://www.morethanavote.org/who-we-are/.

75. Palash Ghosh, "Dozens of Black Executives Urge Corporate America to Battle Restrictive Voting Laws, Report Says," *forbes.com*. URL: https://www.forbes.com/sites/palashghosh/2021/03/31/dozens-of-black-executives-urge-corporate-america-to-battle-restrictive-voting-laws-report-says/?sh=56fa21bd5d7c. (March 31, 2021).

76. Melissa Quinn and Adam Brewster, "Georgia NAACP and Voting Rights Groups Challenge Sweeping Georgia Voting Law," *cbsnews.com*. URL: https://www.cbsnews.com/news/georgia-voting-law-naacp-lawsuit/. (March 29, 2021).

77. Rachel Treisman, "Nearly 100 Confederate Monuments Removed in 2020, Report Says; More Than 700 Remain," *npr.org*. URL: https://www.npr.org/2021/02/23/970610428/nearly-100-confederate-monuments-removed-in-2020-report-says-more-than-700-remai. (February 23, 2021).

78. Rebecca Koenig, "How to Be an Antiracist Educator: An Interview with Ibram X. Kendi," *edsurge.com*, URL: https://www.edsurge.com/news/2020-12-01-how-to-be-an-antiracist-educator-an-interview-with-ibram-x-kendi. (December 1, 2020).

79. Emily Nussbaum, "The Incendiary Aims of HBO's 'Watchmen,'" *newyorker.com*. URL: https://www.newyorker.com/magazine/2019/12/09/the-incendiary-aims-of-hbos-watchmen.

80. Zoe Christen Jones, "Lebron James to Produce Documentary on 1921 Tulsa Race Massacre," *cbsnews.com*. URL: https://www.cbsnews.com/news/lebron-james-production-company-announces-tulsa-massacre-documentary-black-wall-street/. (October 26, 2020).

81. Brooke Auxier, "Social Media Continue to be Important Political Outlets for Black Americans," *pewresearch.org*. URL: https://www.pewresearch.org/fact-tank/2020/12/11/social-media-continue-to-be-important-political-outlets-for-black-americans/. (December 11, 2020).

82. Nambi Ndugga, et al., "Latest Data on COVID-19 Vaccinations Race/Ethnicity," *kff.org*. URL:https://www.kff.org/coronavirus-covid-19/issue-brief/latest-data-on-covid-19-vaccinations-race-ethnicity/. (April 28, 2021).

83. Joseph P. Williams, "Code Red: The Grim State of Urban Hospitals," *usnews.com*. URL: https://www.usnews.com/news/healthiest-communities/articles/2019-07-10/poor-minorities-bear-the-brunt-as-urban-hospitals-close. (July 10, 2019).

84. Jacinda C. Abdul-Mutakabbir, et al., 'A Three-tiered Approach to Address Barriers to COVID-19 Vaccine Delivery in the Black Community, *thelancet.com*. URL: https://www.thelancet.com/action/showPdf?pii=S2214-109X%2821%2900099-1. (March 10, 2021).

85. Essence, "These Black Public Figures Said Yes to the COVID-19 Vaccine," *essence.com*. URL: https://www.essence.com/news/these-black-celebs-said-yes-to-the-covid-19-vaccine/. (February 3, 2021).

86. United States Environmental Protection Agency, "Heat Island Impacts," *epa.gov*. URL: https://www.epa.gov/heatislands/heat-island-impacts#health. (Visited April 30, 2021).

87. Edward Wallace, *Disparities in Urban Health: The Wounds of Policies and Legal Doctrines*. (Baltimore, John Hopkins Press, 2021).

88. Jade Lawson, "Black Entertainers, Athletes Converge to Deliver Messages of Social Activism," *abcnews.com*. URL: https://abcnews.go.com/US?black-entertainers-athletes-converge-deliver-social-activism/story?id=72117198. (August 1, 2020).

89. "Community Movement Builders." URL: http://www.communitymovementbuilders.org/our-mission-and-values.html.

90. "The Pittsburgh Community Stabilization Fund (PCSF)." URL http://www.communitymovementbuilders.org/community-stabilization-fund.html.

91. Dana Givens, "Tulsa's Black Wall Street Has Received a Grant to be Modernized," *blackenterprise.com*. URL: https://www.blackenterprise.com/tulsas-black-wall-street-has-received-a-grant-to-be-modernized/. (April 15, 2020).

92. Jasmin Barmore, "Campaign to Rebuild Black Wall Street Could Extend to Detroit," *detroitnews.com*. URL: https://www.detroitnews.com/story/news/local/detroit-city/2020/06/18/campaign-rebuild-black-wall-street-could-extend-detroit/3214278001/. (June 18, 2020).

93.   "Hope Enterprise Corporation." URL: https://hopecu.org/about/hope-enterprise-corporation/.

94.   19 BOTWC Staff, "Families Purchased Over 90 acres of Land in GA to Create a City Safe for Black People," *becauseofthemwecan.com*. URL: https://www.becauseofthemwecan.com/blogs/culture/19-families-purchased-96-71-acres-of-land-in-georgia-to-create-a-city-safe-for-black-people. (August 26, 2020).

95.   Chuck Abbott, "After 20 Years of Advocacy, Black Farmers Finally Get Debt Relief," *agriculture.com*. URL: https://www.agriculture.com/news/business/after-20-years-of-advocacy-black-farmers-finally-get-debt-relief. (March 9, 2021).

96.   William Darity and Kristen Mullen, *From Here to Equality, Reparations for Black Americans in the Twenty-First Century*. (Chapel Hill, NC, 2020).

97.   "H.R. 40—Commission to Study and Develop Reparations Proposals for African Americans Act. *congress.gov.* URL: https://www.congress.gov/bill/117th-congress/house-bill/40.

98.   Madeline Holcombe, "California Passes a First-of-its-kind Law to Consider Reparations for Slavery," *cnn.com*. URL: https://www.cnn.com/2020/10/01/us/california-bill-slavery-reparations-trnd/index.html. (October 1, 2020).

99.   Philip Marcelo, "Providence Mayor Launches Reparations Process," *usnews.com*. URL: https://www.usnews.com/news/best-states/rhode-island/articles/2020-07-15/providence-mayor-launches-reparations-process. (July 16, 2020).

100.   Brendan O'Brien and Joseph Ax, "Chicago Suburb's Plan to Pay Black Residents Reparations Could be a National Model, *reuters.com*. URL: https://www.reuters.com/article/us-usa-race-reparations/chicago-suburbs-plan-to-pay-black-residents-reparations-could-be-a-national-model-idUSKBN2BD0B8. (March 21, 2021).

101.   Neil Vigdor, "North Carolina City Approves Reparations for Black Residents," *nytimes.com*. URL: https://www.nytimes.com/2020/07/16/us/reparations-asheville-nc.html. (July 16, 2020).

102.   Tracy Scott Forson, "Enslaved Labor Built These Universities. Now They are Starting to Repay the Debt," *usatoday.com*. URL: https://www.usatoday.com/story/news/education/2020/02/12/colleges-slavery-offering-atonement-reparations/2612821001/. (October 14, 2020).

103.   Emma Dorn, et al., "COVID-19 and Learning Loss—Disparities Grow and Students Need Help, *mckinsey.com*. URL: https://www.mckinsey.com/industries/public-and-social-sector/our-insights/covid-19-and-learning-loss-disparities-grow-and-students-need-help. (December 8, 2020).

104.   Matthew Lynch, "What is Culturally Responsive Pedagogy? *theadvocate.org*. URL: https://www.mckinsey.com/industries/public-and-social-sector/our-insights/covid-19-and-learning-loss-disparities-grow-and-students-need-help. (April 21, 2016).

105.   V. P. Franklin's commentaries focusing on reparations include: "Introduction – African Americans and Movements for Reparations: Past, Present, and Future," *The Journal of African American History*, 97 [Winter-Spring 2012], 1-12; "Reparations Superfund: Needed Now More Than Ever, *The Journal of African American History* 97:4 [Fall 2012], 371-375; "Commentary - Reparations as a Development Strategy: The CARICOM Reparations Commission," *The Journal of African American History* 98:3 [Summer 2013], 363-366.

106.   "Black Tech Nation," *blacktechnation.com*. URL: https://blacktechnation.com.

107.   P. R. Lockhart, "The Morehouse Debt Cancellation and the Growing Black Student Debt Crisis," *vox.com*. URL: https://www.vox.com/identities/2019/5/20/18632801/morehouse-commencement-robert-f-smith-student-debt-hbcu. (May 20, 2019).

108.   Kiara Brantley-Jones, "6 Historically Black Colleges Receive Millions in Record Donations from Mackenzie Scott, Amazon Boss Jeff Bezos' Ex-Wife," *abcnews.com*. URL: https://abcnews.go.com/US/black-colleges-receive-millions-record-donations-mackenzie-scott/story?id=72068091. (July 31, 2020).

Note to the Second Edition

The significantly altered social, economic, political, and cultural landscapes in the wake of the 2016 election necessitated the inclusion of this brief overview statement. A more detailed treatment of relevant developments will be included in the third edition of the text.

James B. Stewart
November 2018

The night of November 7, 2016, my daughter told her seven-year-old son that Hillary Clinton would be declared President-elect of the United States the next day. She happily informed him that this announcement would mark a seminal historical moment, ultimately culminating in the inauguration of the first female Chief Executive of this country. Understandably, he was confused the next morning when he found out about the presumably unforeseen election result. Donald Trump, widely criticized for racist, sexist and xenophobic rants and actions, had scored a decisive Electoral College victory and was indeed declared President-elect.

My African American grandson attends a Spanish-immersion elementary school. His first effort to interpret this disconcerting news was to ask, in earnest, if the election result meant that his classmates would be deported! In all likelihood this query reflected his exposure to xenophobic campaign rhetoric promising deportation of undocumented aliens and a Mexico-financed wall on the southern border. Even more troubling, my grandson's second attempt to process the election result was to ask if the outcome meant that he and his family would be sent back to Africa!

At one level one can only marvel at how the mind of an academically talented second grader could intuit a relationship between a twenty-first century political contest and the Atlantic slave trade that initiated massive population dislocations that disrupted and distorted African societies and families. However, at another level his innocent inquiry challenges us to examine in more detail the extent to which historical linkages between economic forces and racial tensions have contemporary parallels.

The 2016 election clearly marks a truly pivotal and distressing moment in the ongoing efforts to overcome the ongoing battle against white supremacy. Unquestionably, the election of Donald Trump as successor to Barack Obama as President of the United States will have far ranging and long lasting negative consequences for African Americans. How could what seemed to be a seemingly progressive social and political trajectory during the Obama presidency so rapidly deteriorate into an overtly racist counter-revolution?

Many years ago W.E.B. Du Bois reminded us:

> "We can only understand the present by continually referring to and studying the past; when any one of the intricate phenomena of our daily life puzzles us; when there arises religious problems, political problems, race problems, we must always remember that while their solution lies in the present, their cause and their explanation lie in the past."[1]

From this perspective, the election of Donald Trump and its attendant consequences constitute a convergence of various developments with identifiable historical antecedents. And these historical antecedents and their contemporary manifestations are infected with a socially ingrained commitment to the preservation of white supremacy at all costs.

Celebrated author, Ta-Nehisi Coates, maintains in *We Were Eight Years in Power, An American Tragedy*, that the election of Donald Trump is a direct outcome of the presidency of Barack Obama. He argues convincingly, "The symbolic power of Barack Obama's presidency—that whiteness was no longer strong enough to prevent peons from taking up residence in the castle—assaulted the most deeply rooted notions of white supremacy and instilled fear in its adherents and beneficiaries. And it was that fear that gave the symbols Donald Trump deployed—the symbols of racism—enough potency to make him president and, thus, put him in position to injure the world."[2]

The title of Coates' book is drawn from an 1895 commentary by Black South Carolina Reconstruction-era Congressman, Thomas Miller, regarding the backlash that reinstated white supremacy in the former Confederate states. Coates quotes Miller as declaring:

> "We were eight years in power. We had built schoolhouses, established charitable institutions, built and maintained the penitentiary system, provided for the education of the deaf and dumb, rebuilt the ferries. In short, we had reconstructed the State and placed it upon the road to posterity."[3]

Unlike the scenario described by Miller, the Obama presidency, in the face of unyielding Republican legislative intransigence, was only successful in advancing a few broad-based progressive policy initiatives. Nevertheless, a widespread racist backlash to the presence of a Black person in the nation's highest elected office, coupled with organized resistance from entrenched elites to efforts to provide universal health care, preserve the environment, and protect consumers against exploitation by financial institutions were sufficient to lay the groundwork for a major reactionary offensive that culminated in Trump's electoral victory. In the same vein that Miller woefully observed the wholesale dismantling of progressive Reconstruction institutions, Trump has undertaken an almost pathological effort to erase all vestiges of the Obama presidency.

Nevertheless, it would be a gross misunderstanding to focus solely on Trump as the source of contemporary threats to black well-being. Of course, there is no question that he personally encouraged and catalyzed the current racist backlash, beginning even before his infamous support for claims that Barack Obama was not a U.S. citizen. However, Trump is simply the face of a broader reactionary cabal that utilizes white supremacist ideology to advance the interests of well-entrenched elites. To illustrate, noted historian, Nancy MacLean, has produced an in-depth examination of the machinations of the infamous Koch brothers, principal figures in promoting right-wing libertarian policies. She concludes,

> "what this cause really seeks is a return to oligarchy, to a world in which both economic and effective political power are to be concentrated in the hands of a few. It would like to reinstate the kind of political economy that prevailed in America at the opening of the twentieth century, when mass disenfranchisement of voters and the legal treatment of labor unions as illegitimate enabled large corporations and wealthy individuals to dominate Congress and most state governments alike, and to feel secure that the nation's courts would not interfere with their reign."[4]

Consistent with Du Bois's observation regarding the relationships among the study of the past and the understanding of current developments, Africana Studies researchers recognize the need to scrutinize closely similarities between the post-Reconstruction era and contemporary interplay of social, political and economic forces. This type of inquiry can provide important guidance for interpreting contemporary developments and, equally important, for developing effective resistance strategies.

A comparison of developments during the post-Reconstruction era and the current moment reveals several important parallels. During both periods there was a dramatic shift in the sector(s) producing economic growth. The earlier shift involved a transition from an agricultural to an industrial economy. The current transition involves a shift from an industrial to an information and service-dominated economy. Both shifts induced major dislocations for workers and resistance efforts were frustrated by policies limiting union organization. In both periods the implementation of pro-business policies exacerbated income and wealth inequality and, along with employment dislocations, catalyzed the emergence of populist movements with strong anti-immigrant and racist overtones. In the post-Reconstruction period entrenched interests were successful in scapegoating Blacks for the worsening plight of non-elite Whites, and cultivating support for reduced enforcement of civil rights laws, increased voter suppression, reducing the influence of Black elected officials, and violent and non-violent racist intimidation.

Early in Trump's tenure there are a number of developments that are disturbingly similar to their historical antecedents. Several early actions by the Trump administration provide strong indications that the efforts to reverse the limited progress made by Blacks will intensify rather than abate. Examples include initial efforts to reduce funding for Historically Black Colleges and Universities (subsequently reversed after public outcry), a directive from Attorney General Sessions mandating review agreements intended to curtail hyper-policing of Black communities and excessive use of force, and a directive reinstating harsh sentencing guidelines for drug offenders.

In August 2017, the FBI produced an Intelligence Assessment focusing on so-called "Black Identity Extremists," perhaps signaling a revival of the surveillance and disruption tactics used during the Civil Rights era.[5] And the racist national mindset emerging from the White House is apparently trickling down to the state level. In 2017, the NAACP issued a travel advisory warning African Americans about the possibility of experiencing discrimination during trips to Missouri.

Alongside government-based retrenchment of Black civil liberties and attacks targeting Black institutions, there is an increasing threat of discrimination in the private sector. The NAACP issued a travel warning in 2017 directed at American Airlines in the wake of alleged discrimination experienced by several Black customers. The potential for increased discrimination in housing markets has increased as a result of the institutionalization of the short-term rental market through Airbnb. It is not clear that existing anti-discrimination laws cover such rentals and a study by Benjamin Edelman, Michael Luca and Dan Svirsky found strong evidence that many owners discriminate against potential Black renters.[6]

These developments, along with others, are deeply troubling and increase the urgency of designing strategies that not only protect hard-fought gains, but also help to rebuild liberatory momentum. For some it may be tempting to pursue protective efforts through a broad-based populist resistance movement to counter the worst manifestations of Trumpism but, unfortunately, there is no discrete set of issues that unify the various constituencies. In addition, historical inter-racial efforts, such as the nineteenth century Populist Movement, have failed, in part, because of culturally-based divergence between Black and White resistance tactics. This record suggests the need for Blacks to focus on adapting historically successful community-based self-help strategies as a primary strategy, rather than relying on nebulous inter-racial alliances.

In early 2017, threats and protests erupted in New Orleans, Louisiana, and Charlottesville, Virginia, over the actual and/or planned removal of statues commemorating the Confederacy.[7] Subsequently, white nationalist rallies have been held in several cities. According to the Southern Poverty Law Center (SPLC), the number of chapters of the Ku Klux Klan increased from 72 in 2014 to 190 in 2015. Anger about the removal of the Confederate flag from the South Carolina capital grounds in 2015, in response to the June 2015 reparations massacre of nine Black churchgoers in Charleston, was one reason for this growth. The SPLC noted that "rallies in favor of the battle flag were held in 26 states—concentrated, but by no means limited to the South—and reflected widespread white anger that the tide in the country was turning against them."[8]

Obviously, there is a need for active self-defense against extra-legal and quasi-legal physical assaults in response to increased anti-Black racial intimidation by right-wing hate groups.

Community organizations committed to confronting this form of racial intimidation may develop useful insights by examining the historical example of the African Blood Brotherhood (ABB) founded by Cyril Briggs in 1917 to confront the Ku Klux Klan.

In the case of police killings, the Black Lives Matter (BLM) movement has emerged as the primary resistance formation. In many respects this movement reprises one of the thrusts of the Black Panther Party for Self-Defense.[9] Aside from direct confrontation precipitated by specific incidents, there is also a role for organized community surveillance patrols to shadow police patrolling Black communities and post videos of confrontations between citizens and police on the Internet. Incursions into Black communities by racist hate groups would also be documented. This strategy would channel the historical efforts of the NAACP, Ida Wells-Barnett, and other individual and media activists to broadcast widely information about the horrific epidemic of lynching and physical intimidation of Black citizens.

Broad-based political mobilization at both the grassroots and national levels has been another effective strategy for combating intensifying racial oppression. Notable historical examples include the Niagara Movement, the NAACP, and the Women's Club Movement. The organization of both the NAACP and the Women's Clubs featured local affiliates supported by a national infrastructure. Although the NAACP and organizations supporting complementary agendas persist, in the digital age, organizations that require continued, face-to-face personal interaction are difficult to sustain. Consequently, building new counterparts to these organizations and replicating the type of mobilization and constant engagement that allowed historical protest organizations to serve as effective weapons against oppression will prove to be extremely difficult, if not impossible.

However, the digital age is creating new opportunities for younger African Americans to mobilize quickly to confront assaults and cultural affronts. As an example, in Spring 2017, graduates of several historically Black colleges and universities waged almost contemporaneous protests challenging decisions by college administrators to invite officials of the Trump administration as keynote speakers.[10] Notably, there has been a dramatic increase in the activities of right-wing groups on college campuses.[11] Reactions to these incursions could evolve potentially into a new national Black student resistance movement.

Historically, both political mobilization and community uplift were catalyzed by a dramatic increase in literacy. During the period 1895-1915, more than 1200 Black newspapers had provided critical information to Black readers. By 1910, there were still 275 Black newspapers in operation with a circulation of one half million. Cultural pride and cultural memory preservation were promoted by Carter G. Woodson, with the formation of the Association for the Study of Negro Life and History in 1915, the activities of W.E.B. Du Bois as editor of the *Crisis*, and the Garvey Movement. These organizations and initiatives created the momentum culminating in the Harlem Renaissance. The associated mantra of the "New Negro" not only asserted the strength and beauty of Black culture, but also signaled an intention to confront oppression aggressively, as epitomized by Claude McKay's classic poem, "If We Must Die."[12]

Unfortunately, many of the organizations and organs that provided vital, liberatory sustenance in the past have either ceased to exist or have lost their vitality. However, new formations are emerging that have the potential to channel the historical dynamism while also leveraging contemporary technological capabilities. Although the Black Press is but a shadow of its former self, positive developments in other arenas, including television and social media, have enhanced the capacity to reach large audiences. For younger African Americans the rapidly expanding number of Black bloggers, especially Black women, provides a powerful means of information sharing.[13]

Hip Hop also has the potential to expand its role as a vehicle for community revitalization and political mobilization. In response to the protests initiated by Black Lives Matter, a number of "conscious" Hip Hop artists wrote and performed songs that both reinforced the message of BLM and, also, trumpeted Black pride and active resistance to oppression.[14] Some professional football players, spurred by Colin Kaepernick, continue to stage protests in support of the issues foregrounded by BLM.[15] Collectively, these various developments could signal the beginning of a modern counterpart to the Harlem Renaissance.

Perhaps the most daunting challenge facing freedom fighters in the era of Donald Trump is advancing the battle to obtain Reparations for the almost incalculable damage incurred by Blacks during (and subsequent to) the era of enslavement (and subsequently). Historically, a proposal developed by Walter Vaughn, published in 1891, was one of the first formal efforts to seek reparations for Blacks in the U.S. Vaughn's "Freedom Pension Bill" was described as "a rational proposition to grant pensions to persons of color emancipated from slavery." The efforts of Callie House provide the most direct historical counterpart to the contemporary Reparations Movement. House championed the cause for reparations for the previously enslaved through the National Ex-Slave Mutual Relief, Bounty and Pension Association, chartered in 1898. By 1900, the organization's membership had ballooned to 300,000.[16]

The contemporary movement has been spearheaded by a number of organizations including the Republic of New Africa, the National Coalition of Blacks for Reparations in America, and the African Reparations Movement. A number of states and municipalities have passed legislation requiring corporations to divulge links with slavery, including in California, Chicago, and Los Angeles. Several recent developments have provided new momentum for the movement. Caribbean nations released the "CARICOM Ten Point Program" in March 2014 demanding reparations, as well as proposals to generate a parallel "Ten Point Program" for reparations payments to African Americans in the United States.

The CARICOM Ten Point Program focuses on "reparations as a development strategy." Their goal is to use reparations payments to deal collectively with pressing economic and educational problems facing the citizens in the Caribbean that trace their origins to the underdevelopment imposed by slavery, slave trading, native genocide and economic exploitation by the European nations. The fourteen CARICOM nations voted unanimously to seek reparations and demand: 1) an official apology from slave trading nations; 2) support for repatriation programs for those desiring resettlement in Africa; 3) the creation of an indigenous peoples development program; 4) support for Caribbean cultural institutions, such as museums and research centers; 5) the launching of public health programs to address the high rates of hypertension and type II diabetes; 6) the mounting of illiteracy elimination programs; 7) the expansion of knowledge of Africa through school and cultural exchange programs; 8) the development of rehabilitation programs to overcome the psychological trauma produced by enslavement and under-development; 9) the transfer of knowledge of the latest technology and science into the training of Caribbean youth; and 10) the reduction of domestic debt and cancellation of international debt.[17]

My reading of the historical record and contemporary social, political and economic dynamics engenders confidence that variants of the various different resistance strategies described previously will blossom and consolidate. Consequently, I intend to tell my grandson that, although conditions may worsen before they improve, people of African descent will survive the current and coming assaults and continue the march along the slow and winding road toward true liberation and full realization of our human potential. I also plan to express my expectation that someday he will become a member of the conscious cadre of freedom workers who will guide us through the next stage of the ongoing freedom struggle.

Endnotes

1   W.E.B. Du Bois, "The Beginnings of Slavery," *Voice of the Negro 2* (February, 1905), 104.

2   Ta-Nehisi Coates, *We Were Eight Years in Power, An American Tragedy*. New York: One World Publishing, 2017, xvi.

3   Ibid., xiii.

4   Nancy MacClean, *Democracy in Chains, The Deep History of the Radical Right's Stealth Plan for America*. New York: Viking Press, 2017, xxxii.

5   Federal Bureau of Investigation, *Black Identity Extremists Likely Motivated to Target Law Enforcement Officers*. Intelligence Assessment. (3 August 2017). URL: https://assets.documentcloud.org/documents/4067711/BIE-Redacted.pdf

6   Benjamin Edelman, Michael Luca, and Dan Svirsky, "Racial Discrimination in the Sharing Economy: Evidence from a Field Experiment," *American Economic Journal: Applied Economics, 9* (April 2017), 1- 22. URL: http://www.benedelman.org/publications/airbnb-guest-discrimination-2016-09-16.pdf

7   See "Behind the Fight to Remove Confederate Statues in the South," CBS News, April 13, 2017. URL: http://www.cbsnews.com/news/confederate-statues-removal-south-charlottesville-virginia/

8   Mark Potok, "The Year in Hate and Extremism," *Intelligence Report*. Southern Policy Law Center. (February 15, 2017). URL: https://www.splcenter.org/fighting-hate/intelligence-report/2017/year-hate-and-extremism

9   See Minkah Makalani, *For the Liberation of Black People Everywhere: The African Blood Brotherhood, Black Radicalism, and Pan-African Liberation in the New Negro Movement, 1917-1936*. Urbana, IL: University of Illinois at Urbana-Champaign, 2004. PhD dissertation

10 See, for example, "Students at a Historically Black School Protest Betsy Devos' Commencement Address," Thinkprogress.org. URL: https://thinkprogress.org/hbcu-students-protest-betsy-devos-8e2512ab9c6f

11 See, for example, Marilyn Mayo, "Alt Right Groups Target Campuses with Fliers, " adl.org. (December 7, 2016). URL: https://www.adl.org/blog/alt-right-groups-target-campuses-with-fliers

12   For more information about these developments see James Stewart and Talmadge Anderson, *Introduction to African American Studies, Transdisciplinary Approaches and Implications*. Revised and Expanded. Baltimore: Black College Press, 2007. Claude McKay's poem can be found at https://www.poetryfoundation.org/poems-and-poets/poems/detail/44694

13 *Black Enterprise* magazine has designated July 2017 as "Black Blogger Month."

14   See, for example, Alexander Billet, "The New Anthems of Resistance: Hip-Hop and Black Lives Matter," *inthesetimes.com*. URL: http://inthesetimes.com/article/18333/hip-hop-black-lives-matter-kendrick-lamar-janelle-monae

15 See Jay Kang, "How Colin Kaepernick's Protest is Connecting Playing Fields to the Streets," The *New York Times Magazine* (October 11, 2016). URL: https://www.nytimes.com/2016/10/16/magazine/how-colin-kaepernicks-protest-is-connecting-playing-fields-to-the-streets.html

16 For more information about the efforts of Callie House see Mary Frances Berry, *My Face Is Black Is True: Callie House and the Struggle for Ex-Slave Reparations*. (New York: Knopf, 2005) and James Turner, J. (2006). "Callie House: The Pursuit of Reparations as a Means for Social Justice," *The Journal of African American History 91* (3) (Summer 2006), 305-310.

17 See "CARICOM Ten Point Plan for Reparatory Justice." *Caricom.com*. URL: http://www.caricom.org/caricom-ten-point-plan-for-reparatory-justice/

Introduction to
the Second Edition

In this single-author, second edition of *Introduction to African American Studies: Transdisciplinary Approaches and Implications*, every effort has been made to remain true to the original intent of my deceased former co-author, Talmadge Anderson. While the book's dedication attempts to summarize Talmadge's many contributions to shaping the contours of African American Studies, it alone cannot do justice to the importance of his role in this enterprise.

As his health declined, Talmadge urged me to foreground the Obama phenomenon in the revised edition. I have attempted to follow his dictate. Throughout the book, the reader will find discussions that focus on the implications of the 2008 election and the 2012 re-election of Barack Obama for issues of concern to African American scholar-activists. Given the increasing impact of globalization on the lives of people of African descent, an extensive discussion of the engagement of African Americans with international affairs, especially with respect to Africa and the African Diaspora, has also been added.

There are also other important changes reflected in this second iteration of the text. First and foremost, the mantra of "social responsibility" is emphasized throughout. Discussions of initiatives that illustrate how African American Studies scholarship is being used, and/or can be used, to guide practical interventions to improve the quality of life for the discipline's constituents are embedded in several chapters. More importantly, a list of possible "Social Responsibility Projects" is provided at the end of each chapter to assist readers in designing their own African-American Studies-inspired programs and interventions. This emphasis attempts to resurrect the original thrust of African American Studies, i.e., to generate knowledge that can contribute directly to positive social change. In recent years, in this author's estimation, too much scholarship has tended toward the esoteric, unfortunately mimicking the ivory tower-orientation of much of what is gener-ated in the academy.

There is also an expanded discussion of the various approaces to the study of the experiences of people of African descent that all claim kinship to either African American or Africana Studies. It is increasingly difficult to make definitive statements about what qualifies as bona fide African American/Africana Studies scholarship. In some cases this is a positive development that reflects creativity and the crossing of traditional boundaries. However, in some other cases, critical examination of the premises underlying some approaches raises the question of whether they are even minimally compatible with the original mission and central values of the discipline.

The empirical/statistical material has been updated in all chapters. It is critically important that African American Studies specialists remain familiar with the magnitude of both historical and current indicators and their trends in designing strategies to address the negative conditions confronting our constituents. In a similar vein, the discussion of science and technology has been significantly expanded to reflect the growing impact of both on the lives of every global citizen.

I am especially excited about the inclusion of a substantial amount of visual material to complement the narrative. The visuals not only add an important aesthetic sensibility, they also help to highlight the emphasis on the transdisciplinary, encouraging readers to use multiple senses simultaneously while considering how different genres are interwoven.

Hopefully, this revised version of *Introduction to African American Studies: Transdisciplinary Approaches and Implications* will experience the same, if not an even greater, positive reception as the first edition. Thanks to all who have communicated their appreciation of this effort. Indeed, it is your inspiration that has sustained me during the many, many months that producing this revised edition has consumed!

James B. Stewart
2015

Transdisciplinary Approaches and Implications: A Note to Readers

There is an ongoing debate as to whether African American Studies is a discipline, or a multidisciplinary or interdisciplinary field. Some scholars assert that African American Studies is a discipline because scholars in African American Studies use a well-defined common approach in examining history, politics, and the family in the same way as scholars in the disciplines of economics, sociology, and political science. Other scholars consider African American Studies multidisciplinary, a field somewhat comparable to the field of education in which scholars employ a variety of disciplinary lenses—be they anthropological, psychological, historical, etc.,—to study the African world experience. In this model the boundaries between traditional disciplines are accepted, and researchers in African American Studies simply conduct discipline-based analyses of particular topics. Finally, another group of scholars insists that African American Studies is interdisciplinary, an enterprise that generates distinctive analyses by combining perspectives from different traditional disciplines and synthesizing them into a unique framework of analysis.

The concept of African American Studies that provides the foundation for this text is *transdisciplinary*. This term conveys the idea that adequate examination of the experiences of people of African descent requires tools of analysis that go beyond those used within traditional academic disciplines. Whereas Transdisciplinary African American Studies makes use of established disciplinary perspectives, it focuses equal attention on using other ways of knowing to generate broader and richer interpretations of the experiences of people of African descent. Similar to the interdisciplinary model, the goal of Transdisciplinary African American Studies is to generate distinctive analyses that yield richer insights than those emerging from narrowly structured disciplinary studies.

There is widespread agreement that many areas of cultural knowledge are necessary to understand the complexity of the Africana experience. Transdisciplinary African American Studies recognizes the need to embrace indigenous cultural knowledge attained through visual and oral accounts that are outside the traditional boundaries of humanistic and scientific discourse. In the sense that thought precedes speech, and orature precedes literature, indigenous knowledge sometimes precedes "scientific" acceptance. In sum, Transdisciplinary African American Studies is an evolving intellectual/activist enterprise that synthesizes traditionally ignored traditional, contemporary, and future ways of knowing to conduct analyses capable of leading to improvements in the well-being of people of African descent.

—The Authors

The Great Temple of Ramses II in Abu Simbel, Egypt

Anthony Browder

Acknowledgments

I am deeply indebted for the tremendous support received from many sources in the course of producing this text. First and foremost, I want to thank my spouse and best friend, Caryl Sheffield, for enduring many hours of isolation as I wrestled with the revisions. My motivation to proceed was consistently re-energized by suggestions from users, and inquiries regarding my progress in completing the update.

I have been, and continue to be, rejuvenated by the unswerving commitment of Black Classic Press to publish work of the highest quality. Paul Coates and Natalie Stokes-Peters are true visionaries who understand the compelling need to amplify the voices of Africa and the African Diaspora in the ongoing ideological and conceptual debates surrounding history, culture, and society. Natalie again proved to be a true genius at coordinating the various processes necessary to bring this publication to fruition. Of course, she had the assistance of dedicated staff, including D. Kamili Anderson, Jean Church, Marcia Cross-Briscoe, Apryl Motley, Lynn Suruma and Kamau Sennaar. I would also like to express my gratitude to Dr. Alfred Young for reading the text in its entirety prior to publication. I am forever grateful to all who worked so hard to make the second edition of *Intro* a reality!

There a people, now forgotten, discovered, while others were yet barbarians, the elements of the arts and sciences. A race of men, now rejected from society for their sable skin and frizzled hair, founded on the study of the laws of nature, those civil and religious systems which still govern the universe.

C.F. Volney
The Ruins of Empires
1793

Chapter 1

Foundations of African American Studies

Introduction

African Americans

The issue of whether racial classifications such as African American continue to be relevant in the twenty-first century has emerged as critics argue that young people are increasingly embracing multiple heritages and multiracialism as a defining category. Champions of multiracialism gained additional traction with the election of President Barack Obama. Obama's victory was heralded by many as solid evidence of the United States' transition to a "post-racial" society. Their narrative highlighted the Kenyan origins of Obama's father and the fact that Obama's mother was a White woman reared in the Midwest. Multiracialism advocates also noted that Obama spent many of his formative years in Hawaii and Indonesia, and that he subsequently was raised in his White grandparents' household in Kansas.

Even given these facts, President Obama declared himself to be Black when he completed his 2010 Census form.[1] In fact, ninety-three percent of the 41.3 million persons identifying themselves as Black or African American in the 2010 Census chose only this designation, despite having the opportunity to select multiple heritages. Among those who claimed multiple heritages, approximately 1.9 million indicated Black/White ancestries; 280,000 described their ancestries as Black/American Indian; 143,000 indicated Black/Asian ancestry; and 24,000 chose the Black/Native Hawaiian and/or Pacific Islander category.

The growing number of immigrants from African and Caribbean countries also complicates how the term *African American* is understood. In 2009, nearly three-fourths (74.4 percent) of the African-born population reported their race as Black or African American, either alone or in combination with another race. This group accounted for a third of all foreign-born Blacks and about three percent of the total Black population in the United States.

It is important to note, however, that racial self-identification varied widely by African country of origin. Nearly all immigrants from West African countries and Ethiopia reported their race as Black or African American. In contrast, very few immigrants from Algeria, Egypt, and Morocco selected this classification.[2] In a similar vein, the diverse demographics of the various Caribbean countries lead to large variation in the salience of the African American classification. In 2009, the countries of origin for the vast majority of Caribbean immigrants were Cuba (28.6 percent), the Dominican Republic (22.9 percent), Jamaica (18.8 percent), Haiti (15.5 percent), and Trinidad and Tobago (6.4 percent).[3] Though it is important to recognize the variations in contemporary constructions of Black and African American racial identities, African American Studies addresses these issues from the vantage point of the historical experiences of the modal descendants of Africans who were forcibly kidnapped, enslaved, transported to the Western hemisphere, and ultimately relocated to the geographical space that later became designated as the United States of America. Although history reveals that Africans accompanied the early European explorers of the Americas a hundred years preceding the landing of the first captive Africans at Jamestown in 1619, Blacks were the first numerically significant involuntary immigrants to the New World.[4] Whereas the overwhelming majority of other immigrant groups came to America voluntarily in pursuit of political freedom and economic opportunity, the African presence in America, by contrast, was based on economic exploitation and the denial of freedom.

Africans in America were robbed of their human dignity and commoditized into capital goods (the enslaved) to promote the development and economic growth of America and Europe. The nature of their subjugation and treatment at the hands of White European-American enslavers constituted a form of racism based on color that had never before been practiced anywhere in the world. African immigrants were forcibly denied their language, history, culture, ancestral ties, and homeland affiliations. African American women were raped and otherwise forced into miscegenation with enslavers. Such violations often resulted in the sale of mixed-race offspring as chattel property. Although such extremely oppressive conditions and inhuman acts may no longer prevail, the legacy of enslavement and its effects still linger in the psyche and social orientation of many African Americans. Emancipation, Reconstruction, the Civil Rights Movement, and resulting laws and enactments have failed to accord African Americans complete equality of opportunity or a full measure of social justice. Institutional racism, prejudice, and discrimination continue to impede the advancement of African Americans in education, employment, and political empowerment.

Nevertheless, despite the legacy of enslavement, segregation, and continuing disheartening discrimination, African Americans, in the face of daunting odds, have exhibited resilience and a robust capacity for perseverance against oppression. History provides no record of any other people who were captured, shipped thousands of miles, and sold like cattle or who endured four hundred years of enslavement and racial degradation, yet survived, achieved, and progressed in the same land and in the presence of their former enslavers. This phenomenon should be considered in any comparison of the African American experience with the experiences of other immigrant groups.

Racial Identification

Africans in the New World were denied recognition of their humanity and national origins. Consequently, their identities, designations, and names were arbitrarily decided by their captors and enslavers. In Europe and America, Africans were called by or given negative and colloquial titles or names such as "nigger," "darkie," "colored," and "negro." The debate concerning a racial/national identity or name for Americans of African descent has not yet been fully resolved.

Sterling Stuckey offered a comprehensive historical account of the dilemma and controversy of Black identity in his book, *Slave Culture: Nationalist Theory and the Foundations of Black America*. Another commentator, Beverly H. Wright, suggests that Black Americans' choice of a name for their racial identification has been influenced by social and political environments, by the locus of control, and by changes in ideology during each era of progress or social movement.[5] During the height of the Civil Rights Movement of the 1960s, for example, millions of Black Americans embraced the ideology of Black Power and self-determination, thus emphatically rejecting any name or identity imposed on them by White Americans.

The 1960s have been characterized as an era of social and political reformation of the American polity. During that decade, both older and younger Black Americans insisted that the gulf be closed between the theoretical precepts set forth by the US Constitution with regard to equality and justice for all citizens and America's practice and conformity to the law. For Americans of African descent, it was a period of active rebellion against all forms of White racism and the prevailing ideology of White supremacy. They demanded and agitated for reform.

The Civil Rights Movement of the 1960s signaled a rebirth of African American pride in their race, history, and culture that was reflective of the Harlem Renaissance. A faction of African American participants in the drama of the 1960s revived that earlier era's ideology of self-empowerment, self-sufficiency, self-determination, self-help, and self-respect. More importantly, they felt that it was time the descendants of Africa reasserted their own identity. It was time for self-naming.

In European and Western historical thought and folklore, both the color and the word *black* have negative and ominous connotations. Black connotes that which is soiled, dirty, foul, horrible, wicked, evil, or bad. The European concept of the devil is black.[6] Thus, it has been easy for White Americans and Europeans to associate negative connotations of blackness with the dark-skinned peoples of Africa. Furthermore, as a religious rationale for the unjust and oppressive treatment of African people, Whites introduced the biblical myth of Noah's son Ham, in which God willed that Ham's son and all his descendants be Black and banished into the depths of Africa (Egypt). Subsequently, older generations of African Americans had been socialized to believe that Blackness was bad and that the pigmentation of their skin was disadvantageous. Many revered White or light-skinned persons and engaged in futile attempts at skin lightening. However, in the 1960s, in defiance of the White/European American conceptualization of Blackness, Americans of African descent rejected—permanently—the term *Negro* and replaced it with *Black*.

As Stokely Carmichael and Charles V. Hamilton state in *Black Power: The Politics of Liberation in America*: "Black people must redefine themselves, and only they can do that... There is a growing resentment of the word 'Negro,' for example, because this term is the invention of our oppressor."[7] The underlying motive for adoption of *Black* as their new racial identification was psychological. After centuries of being socialized to believe that both the color and word have pejorative implications, Black Americans needed a form of reverse psychology to correct such negative imagery. Therefore, during and after the 1960s, exclamations, slogans, and clichés such as "Black Power," "Black Pride," and "Black is Beautiful" served to reverse and supplant the negative Eurocentric connotations of blackness.

This new identification of Blacks in America was almost immediately accepted, nationally and internationally. Blacks refused to respond to or create any form or document that used the terms *Negro* or *Colored*. Consequently, all federal, state, and local government offices; schools and colleges; private organizations; and enterprises were compelled to revise various forms and documents to comply with the new self-definition and identity of Black Americans.

The adoption of Black identity was not intended to preclude or diminish use of the term *African* when referring to Black people. The terms *African, Afro-American, and African American* have always been used by Black Americans. Many Black institutions and organizations including, for example, the African Methodist Episcopal Church, were chartered using African as part of their names. By contrast, few Whites used the term African to reference Black citizens in any form or circumstance prior to the Civil Rights Movement of the 1960s.

In 1988, a group of Black leaders met in Chicago to discuss national goals and objectives for Americans of African descent. The Reverend Jesse Jackson, a prominent Black political figure, suggested at that meeting that all Blacks be identified officially as African Americans. In Jackson's words, "To be called African Americans has cultural integrity. It puts us in our proper historical context."[8]

In the present-day context, the discussion concerning the use or designation of the terms Black or African American poses no real dilemma. Depending on their application or intent, both terms currently are proper and correct. African American is appropriate if used to apply to Black citizens of the United States or North America. The term may also be applicable to Blacks living in South America; however, African American is not correct with reference to Black people in Africa or in the Diaspora. The term Black, which is universal and inclusive in concept, can be used to describe all Black people of African ancestry. This book is titled *Introduction to African American Studies* because it focuses on the history, culture, and experience of Blacks in the United States of America. The global significance of the word Black is additionally reflected in this book by its capitalization when used as either a proper noun or adjective in reference to people of African descent.

It is important that students of the African American or Black experience not become confused and automatically associate the term *minority* as an interchangeable designation for Black people in the United States or for Africans throughout the world. Minority has been coined, bureaucratically and conveniently, by federal agencies to refer to all non-White citizens. In recent years, however, Blacks have become increasingly apprehensive when they are referred to or perceived as minorities for the following reasons. First, minority is a derivative of the word *minor*, which means "less than, under, or subordinate to." Minor is also commonly used to refer to one who is under full legal age and thus not fully grown. Second, use of the term minority can be psychologically detrimental to a people if they have been socialized into believing that they are perpetually perceived as and relegated to a minor rank or role in the society. Psychologically and politically, however, the term may have been initiated and designated precisely for this purpose.

A third reason for the inappropriateness of minority as a racial identification for African Americans is that it falsely assumes that a group or population of people is in the minority at all times and in all situations. African people are not a world minority. White or European people, on the other hand, are minorities in comparison to African and Asian world populations. Finally, current self-identification choices of Black Americans may be transitional. If racism is eradicated from American society and if total freedom, justice, and equality are accorded to Blacks, the term *American* may then be sufficient for all citizens.

Definition, Scope, Purpose, and Objectives

Definition

The scope and meaning of African American Studies and of the more generic terms *Black Studies* and *Africana Studies* have evolved continually since the field was established in schools, colleges, and universities in the late 1960s. (A discussion of the origin of African American Studies follows later in this chapter.) The political and social confrontations preceding the establishment of African American Studies do not diminish its significance as a field of study in any way. In fact, the controversy surrounding this latter field creates an opportunity for the exploration of critical social issues.

The absence of a single, definitive term to characterize the field reflects its wide geographical coverage. Africana Studies has become the most popular global nomenclature for departments and programs in this discipline. The variety of labels used in addition to Africana Studies generally reflects different geographic areas of concentration: African, African American, and African Caribbean Studies. Diaspora Studies is sometimes used for studies of populations of acknowledged African descent not located on the African continent. For the sake of ease of exposition, the various terms (i.e., Africana Studies, Black Studies, and African American Studies) are used interchangeably throughout this text, although the typical reference will be to the experiences of African Americans in the United States.

Within this broader context, African American Studies may be defined as a field of study that systematically treats the past and present experiences, characteristics, achievements, issues, and problems of Black

citizens of the United States who are of African origin and background. It does not begin with the African enslavement in America but rather with their heritage and ancestral roots in Africa. Further, African American Studies concentrates on the distinctiveness of Black people and their interrelationship with White American society as well as with other American racial and ethnic groups.

In accordance with our earlier discussion of the centrality of self-determination, defining and conceptualizing African American Studies is a task that belongs to Black Americans and other Black people of African origin. Others may contribute perspectives, but the initiative and final definition must derive from an African ethos or worldview. Over time and through a process of academic maturation, functional definitions and a consensus of the African American Studies concept have been achieved. The eventual unified approach in defining and developing this discipline contributed to its phenomenal development and institutionalization.

Vivian Gordon defines and explains the broad scope and nature of African American Studies thusly:

> [African American] Black Studies may be defined as an analysis of the factors and conditions which have affected the economic, psychological, legal and moral status of the African in America as well as the African in Diaspora. Not only is Black Studies concerned with the culture of the Afro-American ethnic, as historically and sociologically defined by the traditional literature, it is also concerned with the development of new approaches to the study of the Black experience and with the development of social policies which will impact positively upon the lives of Black people.[9]

Gordon admits, however, that her definition may be imprecise and that it may remain so into the foreseeable future because the boundaries of the field are subject to debate.

Scope

The root or origin of the identity, culture, history, and philosophy of Blacks in the United States is Africa. Therefore, any academically legitimate or valid study of Black people in America must include, to some extent, a study of the customs, characteristics, traditions, languages, and mannerisms of the peoples native to the continent of Africa, for even after four hundred years of White American and European cultural hegemony, African traits remain identifiable among Black Americans. Likewise, the complexity of Black American social and psychological identity is reflected in the various titles used to demarcate and identify the academic area treating the study of African people in America and in the Diaspora. The most common descriptive titles used to identify over two hundred programs that offer structured opportunities to study the experiences of Black Americans include African American Studies, Afro-American Studies, African American and African Studies, African and African American Studies, Africana Studies, Black Studies, and Pan-African Studies. Some of the variations in titles relate to differences in geographical focus of the programs or curricula. In other cases, a broad umbrella conception is suggested by a completely different title. For example, the program at the University of Wisconsin-Milwaukee parenthetically augments Afro-American Studies with the term "Africology." Thus, the description of the program reads as follows:

> Afro-American Studies (Africology) is the normative and empirical inquiry into the life histories and life prospects of peoples of primarily African origin, especially those who live in the United States and Canada, Africa, the Caribbean, as well as Central and South America. Its purpose is to educate students to describe, explain, evaluate and predict actions, events and phenomena that structure the life experiences and possibilities of [B]lacks in the several societies in which they live.[10]

Afro-American Studies: A People's College Primer, a volume published by Abdul Alkalimat and Associates, uses the more standard terminology, interpreting Afro-American Studies as encompassing the study of Black people on the "entire American hemisphere, including North, Central, and South America, the Caribbean, and northern countries like Newfoundland and Greenland."[11]

Although it has always been conceptualized as an interdisciplinary field of study, African American Studies has developed within the existing structures and boundaries of the human experience reflected in traditional academic disciplines. This means that African American Studies curricula generally are organized according to preexisting disciplinary demarcations; however, a comprehensive approach to African American Studies deals with the history, sociology, psychology, politics, and creative arts of the Black experience because its goal is to examine the African American experience holistically.

Classical and traditional African societies serve as the initial focus of historical inquiry in African American Studies. Familiarity with African societies provides a context for assessing the ethical and material implications of these societies' early encounters with Islamic and European societies. This background is necessary to appreciate the long-term significance of the slave trade and enslavement, the resistance waged by enslaved Blacks, the Civil War, Emancipation and Reconstruction, Jim Crow segregation and discrimination, and the protests and other political action that fueled the success of the modern Civil Rights Movement in the United States. Sociological topics that receive significant attention in African American Studies include the dynamics of the Black family; Black male/female relationships, sex roles, and patterns of behavior; racism and discrimination; growth and development in Black communities; education; health and welfare; church and religion; sports; and crime and delinquency. A variety of individual and collective psychological topics are relevant, including the psychology of oppression, socialization patterns, personality development and alienation, self-concept and identity, and collective identification. Insights from the disciplines of political science and economics are useful for understanding theories and ideologies of Black empowerment, electoral participation and influences, social movements, employment discrimination, collective economic development strategies, and entrepreneurship.

The cultural dimensions of African Americans are reflected in their literature, poetry, music, dance, and other performing and visual arts. These cultural attributes of American Blacks might be categorized as Afrocentric creative arts or as the humanities of African Americans. Additionally, in the modern world, it is essential to focus attention on how rapid changes in science and technology are creating new challenges and opening up new opportunities to address persisting inequities among the races. Because African American Studies seeks to develop and impart knowledge that contributes to positive social change, it is important to examine how current and prospective public policies are likely to alter the social, cultural, political, and economic milieu.

A common misperception of African American Studies is that it is limited in scope to the study of only the Black experience and culture. Clearly, however, the range of relevant topics enumerated previously cannot be explored systematically without taking into account how African Americans are connected to American and world human experiences. The trans-Atlantic slave trade affected the political and economic destinies of millions of people and of many countries other than the United States. The liberation and civil rights struggles of African Americans have received international attention and have served as models for parallel struggles by other oppressed populations such as South Africans. Black Americans have influenced American foreign policy decisions in many areas of the so-called Third World and especially in South Africa. The music, dance, and entertainment talents of African Americans have permeated world cultures and are widely admired and imitated. Indeed, the impact of the African American experience is global.

Purpose

African American Studies warrants particular academic interest because it is a branch of knowledge that was deliberately slighted or expunged from the American scheme of education. Critical issues pertaining to its development and social problems between Black and White Americans will continue as long as the field of study is treated as being outside the main sphere of the educational process. Indeed, the ignoble and deplorable history and contemporary state of race relations in the United States might be attributed to the failure of the educational system to reveal and to treat the African experience in America with respect. This statement can be made with certitude and without qualification because of the nature and role that education plays in developing the minds, attitudes, and values of a society.

Education is a process of learning and development that influences the character of human interpersonal relationships. Education is the social vehicle by which values and culture are transmitted, but it can be much more. It can be used as a political tool for rallying, uplifting, and glorifying one group while simultaneously alienating, oppressing, and denigrating another. Further, negative educational outcomes for some groups can be institutionalized by the omission of the study of truth and facts as well as by inequitable educational policies. African American Studies was born to confront such unethical educational approaches.

In the classic text, *Introduction to the Foundations of American Education*, James A. Johnson and his colleagues very clearly and cogently discuss the role, commitment, and purpose of American education through an examination of its schools. They perceive the role of education not only as a preserver of traditions and heritage but also as a vehicle for adapting historically based understandings to address contemporary problems. More importantly, they assert that education should function as a positive agent for change in society. They further claim that American education has a commitment to the universality of education, social and economic liberation, and equality of opportunity consistent with the democratic principles of the Republic. One of its most important purposes is that it seeks to satisfy the normative and psychological needs of students.[12]

An alternate view is that the American education system has substantially failed to fulfill its role, commitment, and purposes for most citizens of African descent. America has never been fully committed to proportional or equal educational resources, facilities, and opportunities for Black Americans. Upon examining the textbooks and curricula of American public schools, colleges, and universities, one discovers that the country's European heritage is examined extensively, but the monumental role Africa and Africans have played historically and presently in the development of America into a superpower is given inadequate attention. American education has been slow and largely ineffectual in readjusting to modern perceptions and realities of race and culture, especially with regard to African Americans, Africans, and the people of the Third World. Educational interventions have not succeeded in changing racist attitudes, values, and ideologies that have crystallized over centuries characterized by racial oppression, exploitation, injustice, violence, hatred, and discrimination. African American Studies confronts this challenge directly by offering an educational corrective to historical omissions, distortions, oversights, and cultural myths pertaining to Black Americans and other peoples of African descent.

American education has had a lonely, limited impact in providing societal enlightenment and moral guidance relevant to efforts by Black Americans to achieve political, social, and economic liberation.

1

Educators, administrators, and textbook authors have been reluctant to give more than cursory attention to discrimination and institutional racism. Consequently, individual and collective strategies that emerge from traditional discourses are inadequate to address the underlying sources of persistent inequities that Black Americans experience.

African American Studies has a very different social and political orientation. It emphasizes the study of the effects and implications of racism, inequality, and injustice on the historical and contemporary life chances of Black people. It directly attacks the casual, slight, and often stereotypical treatment of Blacks that negatively affects the social psychology of African American students in educational curricula and textbooks. African American Studies also enhances the education of White students by neutralizing the omission, distortion, and depreciation of the role and contributions of Black Americans that instill and sustain false notions of White supremacy and European preeminence.

The education that American students receive in the traditional disciplines of the social and behavioral sciences and in the humanities cannot be considered wholly adequate in the modern world without systematic exposure to material examining the contributions of African Americans and other non-White groups to the growth and development of world culture. For example, the enslavement of Africans, the abolition of slavery, the emancipation of the enslaved, and the many subsequent civil rights struggles that have ensued have all had—and continue to have–a direct and profound effect on American religion, politics, and economics. Who would deny that African American/African ethos and culture have influenced the arts of White America? Notwithstanding, the dominant American society's proclivity toward ethnocentrism and institutional racism marginalizes the discussion of this shared legacy, thus leading to uniform approaches in dealing with the larger world and the replication of oppressive encounters instead of the generation of mutual respect between Blacks and Whites.

The purpose, function, and rationale for African American Studies are to expand and impart knowledge through scholarly research, theoretical inquiry, and policy analysis. For the sake of authenticity and to realize its full potential, African American Studies must extend beyond traditional approaches developed by other disciplines. It must approach history with a critical eye and with the goal of educational and social improvement. The most challenging purpose and rationale for the field are to effect social reform of the racist tradition of American society.

Objectives

When considering any of the various academic disciplines or fields of study active today, a student or other interested person logically would be concerned about each field's social objectives and practical applications. Opponents and skeptics of African American Studies question the academic validity and professional application of knowledge oriented to the study of people of African descent. Such criticisms ignore the fact that African American Studies is today an established branch of knowledge in the broad and infinite realm of education. African American Studies was initiated on the campuses of educational institutions nationwide because it is the function of schools and colleges to provide the broadest feasible range of subjects to students.

In addition to the role, commitment, and purposes of education discussed above, education is a process of developing one's knowledge, mind, skills, and character. A liberal education is, in some ways, more socially valuable than specialized training because it prepares one to think creatively, theoretically, and intellectually about a broad range of subjects and human phenomena. Thus, when one receives a degree or certificate in African American Studies, that education is not usually limited to courses related only to Black or African people. Like any other curriculum or program, students of that discipline are required to take courses in mathematics and science as well as a core of subjects in the traditional disciplines of the social and behavioral sciences and the humanities. Should they choose to concentrate more on a subject area such as African American Studies, the objectives of a liberal education are still being served and theoretical or philosophical thought is not diminished.

Society seeks and requires foremost an educated person. The primary objective of an African American Studies curriculum, regardless of race or color, is education for positive and productive citizenship. Questions regarding the practical or occupational use of African American Studies can also be asked of Shakespearean Studies, Medieval Literature, or American Studies. Yet, most of the hundreds of annual graduates in these fields find gainful employment not only in academe but also in government, industry, and many other occupational settings.

For African Americans, African American Studies is as essential to their normative and psychological well being as White Studies are to White Americans or Europeans. It is socially and psychologically dysfunctional to be unfamiliar with one's own culture and heritage. White students have been socialized to believe that the material studied in their classes reflects universal rather than European-based scholarship. Consequently, many do not understand why other groups clamor for distinctive programs with group-identified titles. However, as more White students are exposed to courses in these specialized areas, many begin to understand how the group-specific character of traditional disciplines is disguised. They are then in a better position to take a more critical and informed approach to questioning conventional interpretations and cultural myths. A truly universal education requires that one be acquainted with the culture of various racial/ethnic groups.

In addition to endowing students with marketable intellectual skills, African American Studies was initiated and developed with several other objectives in mind. During the early 1970s, a task force funded by the US Department of Health, Education, and Welfare was charged with the responsibility of making a limited but systematic inquiry into the status of African American Studies programs at a selected number of American institutions of higher education. The task force was concerned with the definition, purpose, and objectives of these programs. The group found a variety of statements defining program objectives, including the following:[13]

- to provide an understanding of the life, history, and culture of Afro-Americans—an awareness of the Black experience;
- to develop the tools of inquiry necessary for research and publication;
- to provide an opportunity to acquire skills and knowledge for building the Black community;
- to provide an understanding of the current social, economic, and psychological condition of Black people;
- to provide an understanding of racism as an element in American life;
- to liberate Black people;

- to provide specialized training and to develop professionals;
- to humanize American education and American society;
- to explode myths about Blacks;
- to help fashion a Black identity;
- to provide an opportunity to experiment with art forms expressing the Black experience;
- to academically scrutinize the entire ethical and economic structure of the United States, exposing the gulf between the ideals of the Constitution and the actual practice of human equality and social justice;
- to reveal the personal and social consequences of racism and to prepare students for the work which will help destroy that aspect of American society;
- to provide interdisciplinary study in the arts, sciences, and humanities from Black perspectives;
- to provide meaningful human study experience which in itself might serve as a career or complement the professions in the fields of sociology, psychology, social work, politics, economics, education, law, and the humanities.

To reiterate, the goal and utility of African American Studies are to serve as an educationally beneficial and intellectually broadening field of study for all students regardless of race or ethnic origin. As an interdisciplinary field, African American Studies may enhance the self-concept and self-esteem of Black Americans, but it also serves conversely to eliminate the negative and stereotypic attitudes that White people may have relative to Black life and history and, especially, to the Black community.

The wholistic approach to African American Studies in this text is deeply influenced by the life and work of renowned scholar-activist W. E. B. Du Bois. James Stewart has described several of Du Bois' legacies to contemporary African American Studies, two of which are his use of various methodologies to examine the experiences of people of African descent and his emphasis on the dissemination of information through multiple communication outlets. Du Bois's professional career also reflects a bridging of academic research and community outreach.[14] His idea of the historically Black college and university serves as a model for the continual development of African American Studies. According to Du Bois:

> The university must become not simply a center of knowledge but a center of applied knowledge and guide of action... .Starting with present conditions and using the facts and the knowledge of the present situation of American Negroes, the Negro university expands toward the possession and the conquest of all knowledge. It seeks from a beginning of the history of the Negro in America and in Africa to interpret all history; from a beginning of social development among slaves and freedmen in America and Negro tribes and kingdoms in Africa, to interpret and understand the social development of all mankind in all ages. It seeks to reach modern science of matter and life from the surroundings and habits and attitudes of American Negroes and thus lead up to understanding of life and matter in the universe.[15]

The centrality of Du Bois's vision to the interpretation of African American Studies in this text will be evident to the reader. The works of many authors are referenced, but Du Bois's writings are cited throughout the volume. As the most eminent scholar-activist of his generation and as a visionary who anticipated the challenges and opportunities that confront contemporary African American Studies, Du Bois merits the heavy reliance on his work that you will see throughout this work.

Foundation and Philosophy

Basis and Development of Thought

African American Studies does not attribute the basis of its foundation and philosophy to any of the classical European Greek and Roman philosophers, nor to medieval philosophers who were persons of a leisure class sustained by a rank-and-order system of feudalism. Aristotle, Plato, and others wrestled philosophically with the ontological and theological facets of human existence. Somehow, in their profound musing, they theorized and developed a rationale for human servitude and subjugation based on superiority and inferiority of biology, heritage, values, and culture. The reasoning of these early White European philosophers provided the intellectual basis and academic framework for a succession of eighteenth-, nineteenth-, and early twentieth-century White European and American scholars who depreciated Africa in their writings. Hegelian and Darwinist philosophies and theories imply that there exists a so-called natural hierarchy among human races, with Europeans or Caucasians at the apex. European intellectuals such as David Hume, Thomas Arnold, Count de Gobineau, and Houston Stewart Chamberlain, as well as Americans such as John Burgess of Columbia University, developed derogatory theories about the Black race or African people that were consistent with Hegelian and Darwinist thought.[16]

African American Studies is significantly antithetical to the racist social theory of European philosophers and intellectuals. By contrast, African American Studies is founded on and grounded in an African or Afrocentric worldview. The philosophy of the discipline grew out of the collective philosophical thought, writings, rhetoric, and political strategies put forth by Black intellectuals and freedom fighters during centuries of struggle that encompass the pre-enslavement, enslavement, abolition, emancipation, and Reconstruction eras. The field's philosophical foundations received additional impetus during the Harlem Renaissance and subsequently as Blacks intensified their liberation struggles during the eras of the Civil Rights and Black Power movements. Therefore, much of the content and social theory of African American Studies reflects, to some extent, the oppressive social, political, and economic experiences of Black Americans during these periods. Although protest, petition, and racial vindication are primary themes in African American Studies, its philosophical foundation is much broader.

Philosophy in this discussion refers to how a people perceive and interpret the nature of human existence, world phenomena, human conduct, and creativity. The history, culture, and status of a people within the world community affect their worldview and perception of reality. The perceptions and interpretations of those at the top of the social, political, or economic order may be different from those at the bottom. For generations, many Black Americans have had to interpret the world from an oppressed state and within a hostile environment; however, the thought and perceptions of Black intellectuals are not any less profound or invalid simply because they may express social protest and racial vindication. Furthermore, the orientation and foundation of African American Studies provides the intellectual framework for the interpretation of Black art and literature.

African American Studies is based on the philosophy, culture, aesthetic, and historical experiences of Black people in America. The diversity of these experiences has evoked a myriad of different philosophical responses from Black Americans. African American Studies attempts to treat and place into perspective the philosophies and ideological leanings of eminent Black intellectuals, writers, artists, and social and political activists from 1619 to the present time. African American Studies is also inclusive of the works of all writers and scholars, regardless of race or national origin, who have contributed without stereotypical prejudice and racist intent to the revelation and development of the Black experience.

For the purposes of African American Studies, the terms *philosophy* or *philosopher* must not be defined or perceived totally from the scientific ideal or value-neutrality standard of Eurocentric academic ideology. White American and European scholars or intellectuals traditionally have viewed African American and African philosophic perspectives with disdain and regarded them as insignificant relative to so-called universal learning and knowledge. Black writers and intellectuals generally have not been concerned with Eurocentric futuristic and abstract social and political theory; instead, they have concentrated more or less on philosophical subjects relating to protest, race survival, and liberation. Their perspectives and concepts mirror the true sociopolitical and economic status of Blacks in American society.

Because of the protestant, race vindicating, and controversial nature of Black philosophical perspectives, White social scientists often dismiss such studies as polemical, propagandistic, or unscholarly. Thus, Black or African philosophical perspective generally is excluded from the accepted textbooks of American social theory. As Leonard Harris writes in book, *Philosophy Born of Struggle*: "…[the world] to see Afro-Americans as humans and as peers. World unduly reluctant to embrace, and unwilling to know, messages of truth, insight, sound argument, cogent methods because of their source. Yet fraudulently prides itself on color-blindness quality."[17]

context of African American Studies, philosopher may be one with acuity of perception, clarity of diction, and integrity of purpose who has contributed profound perspectives and concepts to the understanding of world phenomena and human conduct, especially those affecting the existence and survival of people of African descent. Such a person may be without formal education, as was Malcolm X, or he or she may have earned a Harvard PhD, as did Alain Locke. African American Studies does not depend solely on those who historically and traditionally have denied the human equality and views of Black people to validate their foundation and philosophy or to sanction the purveyors of their perspectives and concepts. Philosophical concepts, writings, and studies by Africans in America existed centuries before the first formal academic program in African American Studies was initiated in the United States in 1968.

Black Philosophers and Philosophy of the Eighteenth and Nineteenth Centuries

It may be useful for students of African American Studies to become familiar with some of the most eminent Black scholars, writers, intellectuals, and ideologists before discussing the controversial origin of African American Studies programs at colleges and universities throughout America. Consistent with the definition of an African American philosopher or Black philosophy used in this text, numerous eighteenth- and nineteenth-century figures have contributed to the philosophical orientation and foundation of this discipline. Again, it is not important whether such persons are recognized as philosophers or intellectuals in the classical Eurocentric tradition; what is essential is that they are sufficiently liberated intellectually to define terms and concepts within an independent, Afrocentric framework.

The eighteenth and nineteenth centuries were the most oppressive eras for Africans in America, yet persons of great insight and intelligence arose from the masses of subjugated Africans even then. They were insightful because they sought learning and knowledge. They were intelligent because it is unintelligent *not* to resist oppression. Many of these Africans in America resisted oppression and espoused ideological theories and concepts of liberation. To this extent and in the context of African American Studies, they were both philosophic and prophetic.

Because of the deliberate and intensive efforts of early American historians to create and sustain the image of African inferiority, history may never reveal all of the philosophical attributes and literary contributions of Blacks who lived in America during the eighteenth and nineteenth centuries. It is impossible, however, to suppress the liberationist thought and writings of some of these early African Americans because of their impressive logic, eloquence, and dynamism.

Historically, much of African American philosophy has been concerned with the deliverance of Blacks from bondage and oppression, and much is related to social theory and political protest. Most African American leaders and intellectuals of the eighteenth and nineteenth centuries were noted for their stirring rhetoric, prophetic speeches, and writings on abolition. Among the most notable of male exponents were David Walker, Henry Highland Garnet, and Frederick Douglass. African American female philosopher/activists also played a critical role in framing the liberation discourse. The pioneering work of several African American women historians has been critical in uncovering the unique contributions of African American women to the Black freedom struggle.[18] The activities of Sojourner Truth, Mary Ann Shadd, and Maria Stewart are particularly noteworthy. There are also, of course, many other men and women whose philosophies and ideologies are of interest, many of whom will be mentioned or alluded to throughout this text.

David Walker (1785–1830)

As an author and abolitionist, David Walker could aptly be considered the father of militant Black liberation ideology. He was one of the most eminent, if not the first, African American to foster pride in Blackness, Black unity, and Black consciousness through literary means. His belief that Africans were being exploited and oppressed throughout the world led him to pen a plea for the universal emancipation of Black people. This concept may have planted the seed of the Pan-African Movement that emerged in the twentieth century.

Walker was born in Wilmington, North Carolina, of a free mother and an enslaved father. After traveling and living many years in the South, he moved to Boston in 1827. A self-educated man, he became famous and revered among many Africans in America for his book *David Walker's Appeal: To the Coloured Citizens of the World*, which was addressed in particular and very expressly to those Blacks in the United States of America. Walker's *Appeal* was candid and inflammatory in its condemnation of White Christianity for its role in aiding and abetting slavery, and his text exhorted Blacks to resist bondage and overthrow their enslavers.

The book was circulated clandestinely to Blacks and Whites in the North and South, but particularly in the southern states, where it sparked a tide of panic among White government officials and citizens. *David Walker's Appeal* marked an end to moral suasion to end slavery. Instead, more violence and oppression followed. A price was placed on Walker's head, and although he was urged to flee to Canada for safety, he remained in Boston. After completing a third edition of his book, David Walker was found dead under mysterious circumstances in 1830.

Sojourner Truth (1797?–1883)

Abolitionist, women's rights activist, and preacher Sojourner Truth (whose birth name was Isabella) was born in upstate New York. She labored for a succession of five enslavers until July 4, 1827, when slavery was finally abolished in the state of New York. A powerful speaker and singer, Truth began walking through Long Island and Connecticut, speaking to people about her life and her relationship with God. She was encouraged by friends to go to the Northampton Association, a cooperative community dedicated to abolitionism, pacifism, equality, and the betterment of human life. After moving there in 1843, she met progressive thinkers like William Lloyd Garrison, Frederick Douglass, and David Ruggles as well as several local abolitionists.

Although Truth never learned to read or write, she dictated her memoirs to Olive Gilbert, and they were published in 1850 as *The Narrative of Sojourner Truth: A Northern Slave*. Her book and presence as a speaker made her a sought-after figure on the anti-slavery and woman's rights lecture circuit. Over the next decade, she traveled and spoke widely. She is best known for the famous "Ain't I a Woman?" speech she gave at the woman's rights convention in Akron, Ohio, in 1851.

After the Emancipation Proclamation was issued, Truth relocated to Washington, DC, where, in her late sixties, she began working with emancipated Blacks in the newly created Freedman's Village. Refusing to face the indignities of Jim Crow segregation on streetcars, she fought for the desegregation of public transportation in the nation's capital during the Civil War. She was successful in having the Jim Crow car removed from the city's streetcar system. After the Civil War, she set out on a final crusade to gain support for a land distribution program for freedmen and freedwomen that Congress refused to enact.[19]

Maria Stewart (1803–1879)

Born Maria Miller in Hartford, Connecticut, Maria Stewart entered the public realm following the untimely death of her husband in 1829. She began speaking out against tyranny, victimization, and injustice and wrote several essays challenging slavery and political and economic exploitation. Like David Walker, her target audience was the Black community rather than White abolitionists. She urged Blacks to exercise virtue and character so that Whites would recognize the equality of the races.

Stewart's first essay, "Religion And The Pure Principles Of Morality, The Sure Foundation On Which We Must Build," was published in 1831 in the abolitionist newspaper, *The Liberator.* Her essay was noteworthy not only for its content but also because it was the first political manifesto written by an African American woman. In it, Stewart entreated Blacks to develop their talents fully and argued that both the Bible and the Constitution provided all people with the universal birthright of justice and freedom.

Stewart spoke out against the Colonization Movement, which sought to repatriate African Americans back to Africa, emphasizing the irony of Blacks being encouraged to leave behind the land that they had played such a major role in enriching. As she declared in one speech, "…before I [would] go, the bayonet shall pierce me through." Following the Civil War, Stewart worked as a teacher. In the early 1870s, she was appointed matron of the Freedmen's Hospital in Washington, DC. In the late 1870s, she published a new edition of her collected work that included letters from friends and colleagues.[20]

Henry Highland Garnet (1815–1882)

Being African and yet an American resulted in conflicted personalities and contradictory ideologies for many Black intellectuals and abolitionists of the nineteenth century. In the twentieth century, W. E. B. Du Bois described such conflicted psychological and behavioral phenomena as "double consciousness," or "two-ness of thought." Henry Highland Garnet represents a case in point of that duality. He was born

in Maryland, escaped enslavement with his parents, and moved to Pennsylvania in 1824. He had a thirst for knowledge and education and eventually graduated from Oneida Institute in 1840. At Oneida, he was no doubt exposed to the classical studies of Greek and Latin. Garnet was a refined man and became an outstanding scholar, minister, writer, and educator. Seemingly, he had faith in American institutions and believed that ultimately the principles of the Declaration of Independence and the American Constitution would be realized. He recruited Black troops for the Union Army and ended his career as an American emissary to the Republic of Liberia.

Yet Garnet vehemently opposed White supremacy, advocated revolution to overthrow the system of slavery, and rejected the spirit of democratic capitalism and materialism. He is recognized as a forerunner of the political militancy of the Black Church. He also is regarded by many as the father of Black Nationalism because he promoted and supported Black self-determination, self-reliance, self-esteem, self-defense, and a back-to-Africa emigration scheme. Garnet's nationalist ideology was a forerunner to those of Marcus Garvey, Malcolm X, and many others of the twentieth century. He is renowned for his inflammatory antislavery speech "Address to the Slaves of the United States of America," which he delivered at the Convention of Free Colored People in Buffalo, New York, in 1843. Garnet admired David Walker and, that same year, he reissued the second edition of *David Walker's Appeal* and included his own "Address to the Slaves of the United States of America" in the book.

Frederick A. Douglass (1817–1895)

The social philosophies and political objectives of African Americans today are as varied and diverse as those of their Black eighteenth- and nineteenth-century predecessors. Whereas a significant percentage of African Americans subscribe to the Africanist/Black Nationalist, separatist, and militant philosophies of David Walker and Henry Highland Garnet, many others embrace the integrationist, assimilationist, and Afro-Saxonist ideologies of Frederick Douglass. Douglass's integrationist/assimilationist ideals greatly influenced the social philosophy and political objectives of African Americans throughout much of the twentieth century, at least until the late 1960s.

Born into slavery in Tuckahoe, Talbot County, Maryland, Douglass witnessed and endured during his tenure as a bondservant some of the most brutal and inhuman treatment ever recorded in history. He escaped enslavement in 1838, arriving safely in New York City, and eventually joined the Abolitionist Movement. Largely self-educated, Douglass became one of the most articulate and impressive orators of the period. He captured the attention of the leading and formidable White abolitionist of his day, William Lloyd Garrison, who was editor of the abolitionist newspaper, *The Liberator*. Douglass fell under the influence of Garrison, and they worked together as abolitionists until differences in ideological approaches to end slavery caused a rift in their relationship.

Garrison's philosophy of using moral suasion, of appealing to the notions of the common humanity shared by all peoples and of nonviolence greatly shaped Frederick Douglass's thinking and political ideology with respect to slavery. Like contemporary White liberals, Garrison did not encourage or support the idea of Blacks using political processes and militancy to achieve abolitionist objectives. Douglass, however, felt that moral suasion alone was insufficient.

Having spent over twenty years of his life in abject enslavement, perhaps the influence of Garrison on Douglass can explain why he formed and advocated an integrationist and assimilationist philosophy. Douglass did not approve of any organization that was distinctively racial. He believed that the slave system deprived both the enslaver and the enslaved of human dignity. He always fostered the notion of Black/White equality and challenged the ideology of White supremacy and the myth of Black and African inferiority. Yet, Douglass also harbored a rather Eurocentric perception of Africa. He opposed most colonization or back-to-Africa movements. Many of his speeches and campaigns were devoted to the support of women's suffrage and equal rights crusades, which were dominated totally by White women. After the death of his first wife, he married a White woman. Douglass's philosophical ambivalence relative to race consciousness reflects the duality of the psychological and cultural realities of the African American's existence and experience in America.[21]

Mary Ann Shadd Cary (1823–1893)

Mary Ann Shadd was born a free Black in Wilmington, Delaware. She moved to Windsor, Ontario, Canada, when the 1850 Fugitive Slave Act threatened to enslave free northern Blacks and return to slavery those Blacks who had escaped bondage. She established a school in Windsor in 1851 to serve the needs of Black refugees from the United States.

Shadd became the first Black woman in North America to edit a weekly paper, the *Provincial Freeman*, in 1853. Designed to cover the lives of Canadian Blacks and promote the cause of Black refugees to Canada, the paper included antislavery editorials and articles on women and their contributions. Shadd lectured frequently in the United States and, in 1855, she became the first woman to speak at the National Negro Convention. Frederick Douglass said that she gave one of the most convincing and telling speeches in favor of Canadian emigration. Shadd eventually abandoned her belief in emigration but maintained a strong desire for Black autonomy and Black self-help.

Shadd left Canada following her husband Thomas Cary's death in 1860 and became a recruiter for the Union army. While living in Washington, DC, she established a school for Black children and attended Howard University Law School. She became the first Black female lawyer in the United States when she graduated in 1870 at the age of 60. As a lawyer, she worked for Blacks to gain the right to vote and was one of a few women to receive the right to vote in federal elections. She organized the Colored Women's Progressive Franchise, which was dedicated to women's rights, in 1880.[22]

Collective Legacy

Black abolitionists of the eighteenth and nineteenth centuries developed the philosophical foundation for the social philosophy and political ideology of African Americans of the twentieth century. Their philosophical legacy—and those of twentieth-century scholars, intellectuals, and commentators—provided the historical and cultural basis for the demand for and eventual institution of African American Studies. The following discussion focuses on six Black intellectuals and one charismatic leader of the late nineteenth and early twentieth centuries. They contributed significantly to the philosophical and literary foundations that guided the systematic study of Black Americans long before the formal advent of African American Studies programs at colleges and universities.

Late Nineteenth- and Early Twentieth-Centuries' Black Philosophers and Intellectuals

Late nineteenth-century African American male and female philosophers, along with the philosopher-intellectuals of the early twentieth century, provided the basic social theory and ideological bases on which African American Studies was founded. This period produced a cadre of Blacks who were educated at America's prestigious universities under the tutelage of eminent White professors and trained in the academic regimen of scientific idealism or abstract, objective, and empirical methodological research. W. E. B. Du Bois, Booker T. Washington, Charles S. Johnson, E. Franklin Frazier, Carter G. Woodson, Alain Locke, and Marcus Garvey are the prominent male figures featured in this section. Anna Julia Cooper, Ida B. Wells-Barnett, Mary Church Terrell, and Zora Neale Hurston are the important female contributors highlighted in this overview.

Black sociologists and historians have played an especially important role in providing the intellectual thought that undergirds African American Studies. Sociology, simply defined, is the study of group life and human interaction. Because much of African American philosophy is related to social theory, social analysis, and social protest, sociology has been a suitable discipline for research of Black social organization and culture. Sociologist Nathan Hare, who will be discussed in the next chapter, is recognized as the father of formal African American Studies programs in the United States. Three of the other scholars to be discussed in this text were sociologists as well—namely, W. E. B. Du Bois, Charles S. Johnson, and E. Franklin Frazier. Although Du Bois earned his PhD in history, his pioneering, community-based sociological research set the early standards for the African American Studies field.

Historian Carter G. Woodson is acclaimed as the father of modern Black historiography. Woodson is extolled not only for his contributions to Black history but also for his philosophy of African American education and independent Black thought. Although many historians, both Black and White, have challenged conventional racist historical interpretations of the Black experience and have produced progressive works in the twentieth century, Woodson occupies a special status because of his unique effort to promote the study of African American history in local communities. He accomplished this through the establishment of chapters of the Association for the Study of Negro Life and History, and the creation of Negro History Week (since renamed and expanded to the current Black History Month).

Booker T. Washington might appropriately be considered a nineteenth-century figure, however, his controversial accommodationist philosophy carried over well into the twentieth century. Marcus Garvey was an important African-centered intellectual and philosopher. His Black cultural nationalist ideology was the mantra of the Black Power and Black Studies advocates and activists of the 1960s. Alain Locke was formally trained in traditional European and American philosophy at Harvard University. As one of the principal architects of the New Negro Movement and the Harlem Renaissance, Locke believed that each cultural group has its own identity and is entitled to protect and promote it. He also asserted that the claim to a distinctive cultural identity need not conflict with the claim to American citizenship.

Anna Julia Cooper was a staunch proponent of gender equality who rejected Booker T. Washington's educational philosophy in her efforts to prepare African American women to attend college. As a lecturer and organizer, she spoke at the 1893 World's Congress of Representative Women and the Pan-African Congress of 1900. Ida B. Wells-Barnett was a fearless antilynching crusader who used her talents as a journalist to promote social justice. She was one of two African American women who signed "the Call" to establish the National Association for the Advancement of Colored People (NAACP) in 1909. Mary Church Terrell, who was also instrumental in forming the NAACP, is best known as cofounder of the Federation of Afro-American Women and first president of the National Association of Colored Women. Zora Neale Hurston was a trained anthropologist who established important precedents for conducting research on Black communities through her meticulous efforts to document and record Black folk culture. She is best known for her seminal novel, *Their Eyes Were Watching God*.

Booker T. Washington (1856–1915)

The so-called "accommodationist" philosophy of Booker T. Washington had an immeasurable effect on the lives and condition of millions of African Americans. Accommodationist is the term historians use to describe Washington's philosophy of capitulating to White racism, oppression, and segregation in the South. He formally expressed his ideas in a speech he made at the Cotton States Exposition in Atlanta in 1895. Whites praised Washington's address and hailed him as a prudent leader of the Negro people. The speech propelled Washington to national fame.

1

W. E. B. Du Bois later described the speech as the "Atlanta Compromise." In essence, Washington stated that Blacks: 1) would accept second-class citizenship and segregation; 2) should not agitate for desegregation and political equality; and 3) must limit their education to agriculture, the industrial arts and crafts, and the professions. His statement that "in all things that are purely social, [the races] can be as separate as the fingers, yet one as the hand in all things essential to mutual progress" drew the loudest applause from the hundreds of Whites in the audience.[23]

Many Blacks, including W. E. B. Du Bois, considered the ideas and implications of Washington's speech as socially retrogressive and predicated on "Uncle Tomism." Others surmised that Washington's opinions were highly practical, considering the reality of the circumstances at that time. Ironically, aspects of his philosophy appealed to some Black entrepreneurs and professionals because their success or the profitability of their businesses depended partly and unfortunately on the oppressive and exploitative system of segregation.

In a sense, the notion of Black independence or domestic nationalism was implicit in Washington's philosophy. His speech alluded to nationalist tenets of self-help and self-determination. He stressed the importance of economics and Black entrepreneurship, in his founding of the Negro Business League, whose members included African American business proprietors. One could say that Booker T. Washington propagated the concept of Black capitalism, yet his philosophy of accommodation is considered by many to be a betrayal of the ideals of human equality and civil rights. Washington's social and economic philosophies continue to spark much debate and controversy in African American Studies, but the overall effects of his ideas and influence cannot be assessed definitively.

Washington was also an educator. His educational accomplishments as the founder and principal of the Tuskegee Institute in Alabama afforded him significant influence among southern Blacks. A substantial number of Black professionals supported both him and his ideology. Washington and his supporters represented a formidable political force known as the "Tuskegee Machine."[24] After his Atlanta speech, Whites crowned him the national leader of the Black race.

Booker T. Washington may not be considered an intellectual *per se*, but he was certainly a cunning practical philosopher who used his ideas to win influence among White Americans. This, in turn, endowed him with power among Blacks. He used that power overtly and covertly to force his will or political ideology on a large segment of the Black population. Like Frederick Douglass, he experienced enslavement from birth, and, also like Douglass, his particular philosophy had a profound impact on the social and political conditions of African Americans for almost a century.

Anna Julia Cooper (1858–1964)

The philosophical and political perspectives and activities of prominent Black men have received more attention than those of their female counterparts. However, during the late nineteenth and early twentieth centuries, African American women made seminal contributions to the understanding of Black culture and to mobilizing support to confront injustices. In fact, one of the major contributions of contemporary African American Studies has been the recovery and articulation of the important roles played by Black women in the ongoing liberation struggle.

Like that of W. E. B. Du Bois, Anna Julia Cooper's life spanned the final years of slavery and the Civil Rights Movement of the 1960s. Cooper received her bachelor's and master's degrees from Ohio's Oberlin College. She taught at M Street High School in Washington, DC, for many years, acceding to the role of principal in 1902. Cooper was the subject of public controversy because her educational philosophy emphasized preparing African American students for college. Her students attended prestigious colleges and universities, including Harvard, Brown, Oberlin, Yale, Amherst, Dartmouth, and Radcliffe. Washington, DC's elites, many of whom subscribed to Booker T. Washington's educational philosophy, conspired to thwart Cooper's efforts and succeeded in getting her removed from her teaching and administrative positions.

Cooper received her doctorate from the University of Paris in 1925, becoming the fourth African American woman to achieve that level of academic distinction. The title of her dissertation was "Slavery and the French Revolutionists." Prior to writing her dissertation, however, Cooper had established herself as a major philosophical thinker in her first and only full-length book, *A Voice from the South by a Black Woman from the South*, published in 1892. Her activism included formal presentations at the 1900 Pan-African Congress. In 1905, she helped found the Colored Women's YWCA (a division of the Young

Women's Christian Association); and in 1912, she was the major force behind the establishment of the colored women's branch of the YWCA in Washington, DC. Cooper continued her philosophical explorations throughout her life and wrote through much of the 1940s, even as she approached the age of ninety.[25]

Ida B. Wells-Barnett (1862–1931)

Ida B. Wells-Barnett is widely regarded as one of the most uncompromising leaders and most ardent defenders of democracy in the United States. Her professional career began as a schoolteacher, but her crusade for racial justice began in Memphis in 1884, when a conductor for the Chesapeake & Ohio Railroad Company asked her to give up her seat to a White man. Wells-Barnett had to be forcefully removed from the train. She later sued the railroad. Although she won in the local courts, the Supreme Court of Tennessee reversed the lower court's ruling.

Many newspapers approached Wells-Barnett to obtain accounts of her challenge to White supremacy. That exposure enabled her to establish a career as a professional journalist. She became a partner at the *Free Speech and Headlight* newspaper in 1889. Following the lynching of three of her friends in 1892, Wells-Barnett launched a fierce anti-lynching crusade. She used her newspaper to articulate and propagate a self-defense philosophy that advocated the use of economic clout and relocation to combat structural violence. Wells-Barnett was forced to flee Memphis after White reactionaries burned down the newspaper's offices and threatened to lynch her.

After relocating to Chicago, Wells-Barnett helped develop numerous African American women's and reform organizations, but she remained diligent in her anti-lynching crusade. She wrote a book on the topic, *Southern Horrors: Lynch Law in All Its Phases*. In alliance with reformer Jane Addams, Wells-Barnett successfully blocked the establishment of segregated schools in Chicago, Illinois. In 1906, she joined with W. E. B. Du Bois and others to further the Niagara Movement, becoming one of the founding members of the NAACP. She was also among the few Black leaders to explicitly oppose Booker T. Washington and his strategies. As a result, she was labeled a radical and prevented from assuming any leadership position within the NAACP. Wells-Barnett continued her activism until the end of her life, which included an unsuccessful campaign for the Illinois State legislature in 1930 that gave her the distinction of being one of the first Black women to run for public office in the United States.[26]

Mary Church Terrell (1863–1954)

Like her contemporary Ida B. Wells-Barnett, Mary Church Terrell had roots in Memphis, Tennessee. Following graduation from Oberlin College in 1884, she taught at a Black secondary school in Washington and at Wilberforce College in Ohio. Terrell was acquainted with both Frederick Douglass and Booker T. Washington, and she worked with Douglass on several civil rights campaigns.

Terrell became an active member of the National American Woman Suffrage Association, and she was particularly concerned about ensuring that the organization continued to fight for suffrage for Black women. Concurrently, she was actively involved in developing organizations within the Black community. She too was a founding member of the NAACP. In collaboration with Josephine Ruffin, Terrell formed the Federation of Afro-American Women. She was selected as the first president of the National Association of Colored Women in 1896.

Terrell articulated her philosophical and experiential perspectives in several books, including her autobiography, titled *A Colored Woman in a White World*, published in 1940. A staunch freedom fighter throughout her life and although well advanced in age, she was actively involved in the struggle against segregation in public eating places in Washington in the early 1950s.[27]

William Edward Burghardt Du Bois (1868–1963)

W. E. B. Du Bois is acknowledged as an outstanding scholar, author, social critic, and egalitarian social activist. Having received his PhD from Harvard University, he was firmly established in the tradition of the scientific method of research and empiricism. He authored numerous books, many of which reflected his empiricist orientation toward studying and researching the life and history of African Americans.

Du Bois possessed a kind of philosophical ambivalence relative to the integration and eventual assimilation of Blacks into the mainstream of White society. He advocated and worked toward the realization of integration, yet; on the other hand, he rationalized the necessity for Blacks to maintain separate institutions operating within Black communities. He was one of the founders of the NAACP, an organization that was and continues to be dedicated to the achievement of the wholesale integration of Blacks and Whites into

American society. However, Du Bois's exaltation of Black culture, color, and consciousness, and his insistence on the retention of separate Black organizations and institutions, led to his eventual dismissal from the NAACP. Prophetically, he feared the negative psychological effects on African Americans of being inundated with White and European history, culture, and social values. Du Bois was not the absolute integrationist and assimilationist that Frederick Douglass was. He was, however, a philosophical and psychological example of his own theory of Black "double-consciousness ... two-ness ... and warring ideals."[28]

Contrary to what some may contend, Du Bois was not the originator or first advocate of Black cultural consciousness or awareness and Pan-Africanist ideology. Much of what we now call Du Boisian philosophy had already been expressed by David Walker, Henry Highland Garnet, and Frederick Douglass. Indeed, recognition and lionization of Du Bois as a major proponent of African American Studies ideology developed and waxed strongly after the establishment of formal academic programs in the discipline. Nonetheless, Du Bois was the forerunner among Black scholars in performing specific studies of African Americans in the United States in the early twentieth century. Although his work did not lead to or constitute a formalization of academic programs in African American Studies during his academic tenure or lifetime, he did urge and propose a plan for Black-oriented curricula at predominantly Black colleges. His efforts were not realized because of his retirement and a reduction in funds allocated for the project.[29]

Ideologically, Du Bois believed that African Americans should produce a cadre of intellectuals dedicated to uplifting the social, economic, and political condition of the Black masses. He referred to this cadre as the "Talented Tenth." He warned, however, that this group should not perceive itself as elitist and detached from those masses but as servants to the oppressed and uneducated.[30] His philosophy of racial uplift conflicted sharply with the leading Black public figure of that era, accommodationist Booker T. Washington.

Carter G. Woodson (1875–1950)

African Americans acclaim Woodson as the "father of Black history." There is no question that Woodson was pioneering and assertive in reestablishing the long neglected heritage and history of Black people in the United States and elsewhere, yet it is equally significant to note that Woodson provided the philosophical basis and rationale for Black intellectual and educational independence. In Woodson's day, with White and Jewish scholars virtually in complete control and authority over the study of African Americans and Africans, it was difficult for African American researchers to achieve any measure of scholarly independence and recognition of their works. More importantly, few Blacks before Woodson had the insight and courage to challenge White control of Black scholarship.[31]

Woodson rightfully may be acclaimed a philosopher, historian, scholar-educator, and intellectual activist. He earned his PhD from Harvard University in 1912 and subsequently studied at the Sorbonne in Paris. In 1915, he founded the Association for the Study of Negro Life and History (the name was later changed to the Association for the Study of Afro-American Life and History). This organization was chartered not only for the study of Black history but also for the study of all aspects of African American life and experience. In 1916, he founded and published the *Journal of Negro History* and, in 1920, he established Associated Publishers as an independent publishing affiliate of the Association for the Study of Negro Life and History. In 1926, Woodson initiated the observance and celebration of Negro History Week, which has since been extended and is now observed as Black History Month. He also founded the *Negro History Bulletin* in 1937.

Woodson decried the irrelevancy of traditional American education to Black life long before Black students demanded the establishment of African American Studies in 1968. With simplicity and candor, he explained how American education and Black educators had failed African American youth in his 1933 classic work, *The Mis-education of the Negro*. The thesis of his book is that although Blacks have been physically emancipated from enslavement, their socialization in the Americas has kept them in intellectual bondage. As Woodson observed:

> When you control a man's thinking you do not have to worry about his actions. You do not have to tell him not to stand here or go yonder. He will find his "proper place" and will stay in it. You do not need to send him to the back door. He will go without being told. In fact, if there is no back door, he will cut one for his special benefit. His education makes it necessary.[32]

Like Du Bois, Woodson believed that the role of Black intellectuals was to serve the Black masses, not to be a detached elite. Woodson was astutely philosophic and prophetic in his criticism and theories addressing the social, political, and economic conditions and challenges facing Black people in America. *The Mis-education of the Negro* was a synthesis of the wisdom, ideologies, and prophesies of David Walker, Henry Highland Garnet, Frederick Douglass, W. E. B. Du Bois, and Booker T. Washington.

Alain Leroy Locke (1886–1954)

Alain Locke was formally educated and trained in the field of philosophy. Having received his PhD from Harvard in 1918, Locke became the quintessential philosopher of an intellectual stature generally associated with elite universities such as Harvard, Oxford, and the University of Berlin. His philosophical interest and contributions were in the area of value theory. Locke's theories of values and of value conflict and resolution contribute much toward an analysis of American racism. They also offer important insights into the contemporary concept of cultural pluralism. Locke wrote several books and numerous articles relating to the social and behavioral sciences, humanities, education, and religion.

It is important to recognize Alain Locke as a major contributor to the theoretical foundation of African American Studies. He made important contributions to both the New Negro Movement and the Harlem Renaissance. Although he may not be widely known or acclaimed, he was a contemporary of W. E. B. Du Bois, Booker T. Washington, Carter G. Woodson, E. Franklin Frazier, Charles S. Johnson, and Marcus Garvey. Locke maintained a quiet presence among these men, and his works influenced or complemented their ideologies in a reasoned yet elitist way. He spent his entire professional career at the predominantly Black Howard University as a professor of philosophy. While at Howard, he helped to shape the philosophical orientation of thousands of Black students and intellectuals who would, after his demise in 1954, become participants and professionals in the field of African American Studies.

Locke was a strong advocate of Black education, adult education, and particularly Black culture in education. Indeed, he was philosophically prophetic in what he wrote and described in his most profound work, "Enter the New Negro," published in 1925. In that essay, he apparently foresaw the restlessness and growing intolerance of Blacks to White racism and the eventual Black revolt and American reform movements of the 1960s. He was also insightful with regard to the race-value arguments brought on by the affirmative action initiatives and programs of the 1960s and the continuing controversy surrounding such initiatives in the twenty-first century. Many knowledgeable analysts regard Locke as a major interpreter of African American culture.[33]

Marcus Garvey (1887–1940)

Any discussion of the philosophies that have shaped African Americans' understanding of self and society would be incomplete without an account of the charismatic and dynamic influence of Marcus Garvey. Although Garvey may not have been considered as intellectually astute as his contemporaries or peers, he equaled them or even surpassed them in ideological keenness and persuasiveness. In a technical sense, Garvey was not an American, but he was Black and his ethos was indisputably African. Moreover, the economic and social courses of action he advocated have made an indelible impression on the philosophy and ideological opinions of millions of African Americans and Blacks worldwide during the early twentieth century and even today.

Garvey was born in Jamaica, West Indies, and received his early education there. He became a printer by trade, making several attempts at and achieving some success in newspaper publishing. Reared under the exploitative rule of British colonialism, Garvey began early to protest and organize against poverty and bad working conditions. He left Jamaica in 1909 and traveled abroad to Costa Rica, Panama, and several other Latin American countries. There, he witnessed much of the same demeaning and oppressive treatment accorded people of African descent by the European colonial powers. Subsequently, he moved to England, living there for a few years and attending London University.

Upon his return home, Garvey organized the Jamaica Improvement Association, which would serve later as a model for an American branch of the organization, to be called the Universal Negro Improvement Association (UNIA). The UNIA became the ideological base for the launching and development of Garvey and Garveyism as major political forces. The provocative and idiomatic slogans—"Back to Africa," "Africa for the Africans" and "Black is Beautiful"— were the rallying themes of the UNIA, and Black self-sufficiency and self-determination were its motivating economic objectives.

Black leaders, foes, friends, integrationists, separatists, Pan-Africanists, and nationalists have acclaimed Garvey as the greatest booster of the African American's spirit of self-pride. He propagated a notion and movement of defiance against White racism and White supremacy in the United States. W. E. B. Du Bois and E. Franklin Frazier, although critical of Garvey's personality, ego, and administrative incompetency, hailed him as a leader of the Black masses across all socioeconomic strata or income groups. As Frazier observed, "the Garvey Movement is a crowd movement essentially different from any other social phenomenon among [Blacks]."[34]

Garvey instilled within the hearts and minds of Black people not only a philosophy and ideology of freedom but also a psychology of liberation. Garvey and Garveyism emerged during the cultural revival and revelation period of the Harlem Renaissance. The splendor and the enchantment of the "Black Pride" ideology of the Garveyites accentuated and complemented the cultural creativity of African American writers and artists of the Harlem Renaissance.

The Garvey movement and the UNIA coexisted with other Black freedom-seeking organizations. While the other leaders and organizations focused on and fought for social and political enfranchisement, Garvey's emphasis and priority were economic. He understood clearly that, for the masses of Blacks, social integration and politics were secondary to their impoverished economic status. He introduced to the Black masses the idea that capitalism practiced and mastered by Blacks can operate to uplift and dignify African people. Conversely, he taught them that monopoly capitalism controlled by Whites was being used to exploit and oppress Blacks. In many ways, the philosophies of Marcus Garvey and Booker T. Washington are similar, especially in terms of their emphases on separatism and economic independence. Harold Cruse alludes to these similarities when he writes, "[I]t was not so much that Washington was against civil rights as he was instinctively opposed to the ideals of noneconomic liberalism that dominated the civil rights traditions."[35] It may seem paradoxical that Booker T. Washington was condemned by many Blacks for his acceptance of White separatist ideology, yet Marcus Garvey was lauded by the Black masses for his advocacy of race separation. The difference, of course, is that Washington endorsed unequal or inequitable segregation or separation of the races. Garvey's separatism demanded race equality. Moreover, there is a fundamental difference between forced segregation and voluntary separation.

Garvey's mismanagement of his Black Star Shipping Line and a myriad of other economic ventures, covert and overt persecution of him by both the American and British governments, and a growing resentment by Black leaders for his endorsement of White racist segregation policies led to the decline and demise of Garveyism and Garvey. However, Garvey predicted that his cause would rise again. This prophecy was realized during the 1960s when African American students and Black Nationalists such as Kwame Ture (Stokely Carmichael), Elijah Muhammad, Malcolm X, and many others espoused many of Garvey's philosophies and ideologies. The concept of Black nationhood and the symbolic red, black, and green colors of the Garvey movement were flaunted and flourished during the civil rights revolt of the 1960s and 1970s. The philosophy and idealism of Marcus Garvey are embraced today by millions of Black Americans and represent a significant political factor and social paradigm in the foundation of African American Studies.

Zora Neale Hurston (1891?–1960)

Zora Neale Hurston was an enigmatic figure whose views regarding race and strategies to combat inequality shifted over time. Born in Notasulga, Alabama, Hurston grew up in Eatonville, Florida, and later attended Howard University. Drawn by the visibility of the major Harlem Renaissance figures, she moved to New York City in 1925 and began writing fiction. Subsequently she began studying anthropology and ethnology at Barnard College under Franz Boaz and received a six-month grant enabling her to collect African American folklore in the South. Thus, unlike the early Frazier, she was committed to the idea that African Americans had a distinctive culture that warranted study and appreciation.

When Hurston began working as an ethnologist, she combined fiction with her knowledge of culture to produce unique types of treatises. Her best-known work is *Their Eyes Were Watching God*, published in 1937. The novel sparked controversy because it did not conform to existing stereotypes. During the 1930s and early 1940s, Hurston completed graduate work at Columbia University and published four novels and an autobiography. After a trip to the Caribbean, Hurston became so intrigued by the practice of voodoo that she began incorporating ritualistic elements into her novels and stories.

Although the White literati praised her work, some Black literati challenged Hurston, noting that none of her works addressed the issue of White racism toward Blacks. Hurston called her detractors "niggerati" for what she perceived as their narrow-minded criticism of her views on race. Her racial politics became increasingly problematic over time. In fact, her credibility evaporated completely when she attacked the civil rights struggle and began supporting ultraconservative politicians. She died in poverty and obscurity.

Hurston's trajectory is difficult to explain, but it may reflect, in part, perspectives assimilated during her advanced studies. She was trained as a social-constructionist anthropologist, a school of thought which asserts that race is a vacuous concept. Her case is additionally interesting because she is widely viewed as a forerunner to contemporary Black conservative thinkers who question the validity of African American Studies. It is important to note, however, that Hurston has achieved almost iconic status for her literary works, and especially for her novel *Their Eyes Were Watching God*.

Charles S. Johnson (1893–1956)

African American scholars have traditionally acquired expertise in research methods through study at major American and European universities. The standards by which research is evaluated have been set forth in Eurocentric paradigms. These paradigms emphasize objectivity and empiricism as critical ingredients of good scholarship. Charles S. Johnson acquired solid research skills while studying at the University of Chicago through his association with renowned urban sociologist Robert E. Park and other eminent professors.

Johnson resisted incorporating protest ideology into his scholarship for the sake of having his work "accepted" as professional despite the climate of intense racism and segregation under which most of his studies were conducted. Nevertheless, his work on Black rural and urban life is important to the sociological field and, particularly, to African American Studies. He is credited with creating broader interest in social research and analysis of the Black community. Though he was not ideological or particularly

philosophical in an explicit sense, he used the statistical and empirical data and analyses contained in his studies to document and provide the rationale for rallying public opinion against the injustice of segregation and the evils of racism. The lack or even a hint of protest or ideological militancy in his works may be attributed to the fact that financial support for many of his studies came from government sources or White philanthropy.[36] Johnson never earned a degree above the Bachelor of Arts, yet his studies were as perceptive, as interpretative of the ethos of Blacks, and as eloquently written as those authored by W. E. B. Du Bois.

Du Bois's 1899 study, *The Philadelphia Negro*, provided the model for researching Black communities that Johnson and Frazier subsequently followed. Johnson, Frazier, and Du Bois were all useful to their mentors and White researchers interested in studying African Americans because they were indigenous to the Black community.

E. Franklin Frazier (1894–1962)

Early Black philosophers and intellectuals functioned outside the realm of the university establishment and without the influence and authority that academe conferred. Their writings and oratory were related almost entirely to abolition social protest, and social reform issues. Beginning in the early twentieth century, more Blacks were admitted to northern White universities, and some earned advanced or doctoral degrees. Equipped with academic rank and authority, they applied university training and research methodology to examine the social organization and culture of African Americans.

E. Franklin Frazier was especially productive and prolific in the sociological study of African American life, conditions, and experiences. He earned his PhD in sociology from the University of Chicago, where he was chiefly influenced by Robert E. Park and other eminent White sociologists identified with the University of Chicago sociological school of thought. Frazier's research and publications focused principally on the Black family, Black intra-class structure, and institutions in the Black community, specifically Black-owned businesses and the Black Church. Ideologically, Frazier was an integrationist, and this integrationist orientation and philosophy permeated and influenced his works. His studies and conclusions on the Black family, the Black middle-class, and Black businesses sparked much debate, at least among African American scholars and intellectuals.

Some of Frazier's studies might easily be perceived as highly critical and even satirical. In his book, *The Negro Family in the United States*, he submitted that social factors such as the high incidence of female-headed households, children born out of wedlock, divorce, poverty, crime, and delinquency have contributed to disorganization of the Black family. Daniel Moynihan, author of a United States Department of Labor report on the Negro family (*The Negro Family: A Case for National Action*), used Frazier's analysis as a basis to claim that the Black family was a "tangle of pathology"—one that exhibited substantial dysfunctionality because of its matriarchal structure. Black civil rights proponents perceived the Moynihan report as an attack on the Black family and a distraction from the real issue of racism in American society.

Frazier also contended that enslavement had destroyed all vestiges of African heritage and culture relative to Black behavioral and social patterns. Many African American scholars criticized his theory at the time, and African American Studies scholars in the late twentieth century firmly rejected it. Many Black intellectuals welcomed the meticulous and comprehensive research by Melville J. Herskovits, a White anthropologist, in his study *The Myth of the Negro Past*, which was a refutation of Frazier's thesis of the destruction of African culture.[37]

Frazier's 1957 work, *Black Bourgeoisie*, provoked the wrath and resentment of the African American middle-class social stratum at which it was directed. Some analysts regarded the work as a sardonic and satirical literary ridicule of the Black middle-class's unsuccessful efforts to emulate White culture and White social and economic institutions. The book additionally generated class antagonism between low-income and middle-class African Americans. Many low-income Blacks who felt that well-to-do Blacks were indifferent to their plight praised the book, especially during the Civil Rights Movement.

Black Bourgeoisie is applicable to, or descriptive of, any oppressed or colonized group that aspires to emulate the coveted position of their oppressor. One must realize, however, that E. Franklin Frazier was an ardent integrationist. As such, he believed that Blacks must fully and successfully adopt and practice White middle-class values and culture if the ultimate goal of assimilation was ever to be achieved. Frazier asserted in *Black Bourgeoisie* that African Americans have not been successful or sufficiently expeditious in the mastery of White middle-class values and culture. He

substantially moderated his philosophy and advocacy of integration as the panacea for the race problem in the United States prior to his death in 1962.

Regardless of the debate and controversy provoked by some of Frazier's works, his books and articles are valuable resources that have contributed to the academic development of African American Studies. They provide students with an opportunity to study and analyze social theory and intraracial social science studies authored by a prominent African American scholar.

African American/Black Philosophy and Social Change

A people's philosophy derives from exposure to physical, social, cultural, political, and economic phenomena or experiences unique to their survival or existence. Their experiences forge a collective perception of the universe that engenders a distinctive worldview or philosophy of life. Differences in the historical circumstances shaping the development efforts of different groups are likely to produce significant variance in worldviews. Different types of wisdom and understanding are likely to emerge among disparate groups depending upon their particular status or condition in world society. The manner in which groups interact with each other exacerbate such worldview variations. A sustained pattern of systematic racial oppression has created few opportunities to bridge or reconcile the divergent worldviews of Blacks and Whites.

At the same time, philosophy is both transmittable and transient. White American philosophy and worldview did not begin with the landing of the Mayflower and the arrival of the Pilgrims on what later became America. Correspondingly, the genesis of African American thought and intellect emerged long before the first slave ship arrived on those shores. Despite the Europeans' denial of the equality of African peoples and the destruction of much of African civilization, there was and still exists an African philosophy distinct from that of Europeans. The written and unwritten thought, knowledge, and wisdom of Africans have been passed down from generation to generation. Great African thinkers have always existed in the societies of the Egyptians, Bantus, Zulus, Tauregs, Kikiyus, Sudanese, and countless others. The ancient African empires of Ghana, Mali, and Songhay were once the centers of African thought and intellect. The Songhay Empire and the University of Sankore at Timbuctoo were in existence over a hundred years after the slave trade started.[38]

There is no reason for African Americans or Black people to relate solely to European or American classical and neoclassical philosophers for enlightenment on their own plight and destiny. The philosophies of Socrates, Plato, Aristotle, Hegel, and Marx on virtue and morality were derived from a social milieu of tensions between leisure-class and feudalistic lifestyles and between bourgeois and proletarian life circumstances. Axioms and prescriptive assessments of human conduct based on traditional European models are largely incomparable and certainly not completely applicable to the experience of chattel slavery, racism, segregation, and discrimination endured by Africans in America. As stated above, however, philosophy is not only transmittable but also transient. After successive civil and human rights struggles and triumphs, culminating with the Civil Rights Movement of the 1960s, African American thought and philosophy began to shift away from purely social protest to a new stage of liberation ideology. This new philosophy is not focused on the social but rather is predicated on the achievement of complete political and intellectual liberation.

The 1960s also addressed the long-neglected subject of women's liberation and especially Black women's liberation. African American women's protest thought and activities during the eighteenth and early nineteenth centuries were unheralded and sometimes unpublicized. Black women such as Harriet Tubman, Sojourner Truth, Anna Julia Cooper, Mary Church Terrell, Ida B. Wells-Barnett, Maria W. Stewart, and many others played major roles in the formulation of an African American philosophy and in laying the foundation for African American Studies. These women projected their philosophy through their activities, if not always through oratory or "learned" literature.

The discovery or rediscovery, revelation, analysis, and interpretation of the works and activities of historical and contemporary African American philosophers, writers, and artists are a major mission and research task of African American Studies. Every academic discipline necessarily builds on the legacy left by its predecessors as later generations of scholars expand on the founders' original vision. In addition, the idea of making this knowledge a part of world history and of making American education relevant to Blacks was the intellectually "liberated" basis for the institution of African American Studies.

Questions & Exercises

1. What factors differentiate the history and experience of African Americans from those of Asian, Latino, and Native Americans?

2. Define African American Studies and enumerate its major educational and social objectives.

3. If the term *Black* is used to name or identify a race of people, should it be capitalized or lowercased?

4. If the history and experience of Black citizens of the United States were integrated fully and equitably into American textbooks, would that obviate the need for a separate discipline of African American Studies?

5. Prepare a brief paper comparing the social, political, and economic philosophies of Booker T. Washington, W. E. B. Du Bois, and Marcus Garvey.

6. Study the histories or biographies of early Black women human-rights activists such as Harriet Tubman, Sojourner Truth, Anna Julia Cooper, Mary Church Terrell, Ida B. Wells-Barnett, and Maria W. Stewart. What were their social, political, or economic philosophies beyond the abolition of slavery?

7. Obtain a copy of *David Walker's Appeal* and Henry Highland Garnet's "Address to the Slaves of the United States of America." Compare their philosophies and rhetoric to those of Black Civil Rights activists of the 1960s such as Malcolm X, Stokely Carmichael, Angela Davis, or Martin Luther King, Jr.

Social Responsibility Projects

1. Discuss the issue of racial classifications with family members and acquaint them with the current controversies regarding single- versus multiple-identity choices.

2. Organize a Facebook group to explore the pros and cons of single- versus multiple-racial classifications.

3. Determine what racial classifications your institution uses to classify students from various African and Caribbean countries by requesting a demographic breakdown of its Black students. Write a report presenting your findings and disseminate the results through your student newspaper.

4. Organize a panel discussion on racial identity with panelists representing African Americans who identify solely as Black, those claiming multiple identities, and Blacks of African and Caribbean origins.

5. Contact student groups on campus that represent various subsets of the Black population and encourage them to develop programs that encourage collaboration and an understanding of shared interests.

NOTES AND REFERENCES

1. Sam Roberts and Peter Baker, "Asked to Declare His Race, Obama Checks 'Black,'" *New York Times*, April 2, 2010. http://www.nytimes.com/2010/04/03/us/politics/03census.html

2. Kristen McCabe, "African Immigrants in the United States," *US in Focus*. Migration Policy Institute (July 2011). http://www.migrationinformation.org/USfocus/display.cfm?id=847.

3. Kristen McCabe, "Caribbean Immigrants in the United States," *US in Focus*. Migration Policy Institute (April 2011). http://www.migrationinformation.org/USfocus/display.cfm?id=834

4. See Ivan Van Sertima, *They Came Before Columbus: The African Presence in Ancient America* (New York: Random House, 1976).

5. B. H. Wright, "Ideological Change and Black Identity during Civil Rights Movements," *Western Journal of Black Studies* 5 (Fall 1981): 186-95.

6. See Joel Kovel, *White Racism: A Psychohistory* (New York: Vintage Books, 1971), 62-63. In fact, the *Oxford English Dictionary* and *Webster's Dictionary* define the term *Black* as "evil," "wicked," and "bad," in addition to other meanings.

7. Stokely Carmichael and Charles V. Hamilton, *Black Power: The Politics of Liberation in Americas Politics* (New York: Vintage Books, 1967), 37.

8. L. Ludlow, "Assorted Reactions to Calling Blacks African Americans," *San Francisco Examiner*, December 22, 1988, A-4.

9. Vivian V. Gordon, "The Coming of Age of Black Studies," *Western Journal of Black Studies* 5 (Fall 1981): 233.

10. Cited from program announcement, "Opt for Undergraduate Studies in Afro-American Studies," College of Letters & Science, The University of Wisconsin-Milwaukee, 1991.

11. See A. Alkalimat and Associates, *Introduction to Afro-American Studies: A Peoples College Primer* (Chicago: 21st Century Publications, 1986).

12. James A. Johnson, et al., *Introduction to the Foundations of Education* (Boston: Allyn & Bacon, 1969), 12-13.

13. The objectives listed here and other findings of the task force can be found in the published report, *Black Studies: Issues in Their Institutional Survival* (Washington, DC: US Department of Health, Education, and Welfare, 1976).

14. James Stewart, "The Legacy of W.E.B. Du Bois for Contemporary Black Studies," *The Journal of Negro Education* 53 (3): 296-311.

15. W. E. B. Du Bois, "The Field and Function of the Negro College." Alumni Reunion Address, Fisk University, 1933. Reprinted in Herbert Aptheker, ed., *The Education of Black People: Ten Critiques 1906-1960* (Amherst: University of Massachusetts Press, 1973), 95-96.

16. For a comprehensive study of how European and American philosophers and intellectuals introduced racism and degraded Africa, see St. Clair Drake, *Black Folk Here and There* (Los Angeles: University of California, Center for Afro-American Studies, 1987), 13-42. See also, Chukwuemeka Onwubu, "The Intellectual Foundation of Racism," in Talmadge Anderson, ed., *Black Studies: Theory, Methods and Cultural Perspectives* (Pullman: Washington State University Press, 1990), 77-88.

17. Leonard Harris, *Philosophy Born of Struggle* (Dubuque, IA: Kendall/Hunt, 1983), ix.

18. See, for example, Darlene Clark Hine, ed., *Black Women's History: Theory and Practice* (Brooklyn, NY: Carlson Publishers, 1990) and Darlene Clark Hine, Elsa Barkley Brown, and Rosalyn Terborg-Penn, eds., *Black Women in America: An Historical Encyclopedia* (Brooklyn, NY: Carlson Publishers, 1993).

19. A large body of writing on the life and work of Sojourner Truth is available. For one of the most insightful explorations, see Nell Painter, *Sojourner Truth: A Life, A Symbol* (New York: W. W. Norton, 1996).

20. For a comprehensive examination of Maria Stewart that includes her writings, see Marilyn Richardson, ed., *Maria W. Stewart, America's First Black Woman Political Writer: Essays and Speeches* (Bloomington: Indiana University Press, 1987).

21. Biographical data on Walker, Garnet, and Douglass are common and numerous. See Association of Afro-American Life and History (ASALH), *The International Library of Afro-American Life and History* (Washington, DC: ASALH, 1976); Sterling Stuckey, *Slave Culture* (New York: Oxford University Press, 1987); and Philip Foner, ed., *The Life and Writings of Frederick Douglass*, 4 vols. (New York: International Publishers, 1975).

22. For an extensive analysis of Mary Ann Shadd's life and activities, see J. Rhodes, *Mary Ann Shadd Cary: The Black Press and Protest in the Nineteenth Century* (Bloomington: Indiana University Press, 1998).

23. Bernard A. Weisberger, *Booker T. Washington* (New York: Mentor Books, New American Library, 1972), 83-87.

24. Manning Marable, *W. E. B. Du Bois: Black Radical Democrat* (Boston: Twayne Publishers, 1986), 42-43.

25. For a recent examination of Anna Julia Cooper, see Karen Johnson, *Uplifting the Women and the Race: The Lives, Educational Philosophies, and Social Activism of Anna Julia Cooper and Nannie Helen Burroughs* (New York: Garland, 2000).

26. The activism of Ida B. Wells-Barnett is the subject of a recent monograph: Patricia A. Schechter, *Ida B. Wells-Barnett and American Reform, 1880-1930* (Chapel Hill: University of North Carolina Press, 2001).

27. For a detailed exploration of the life and writings of Mary Church Terrell, see Beverly W. Jones, *Quest for Equality: The Life and Writings of Mary Eliza Church Terrell, 1863-1954* (Brooklyn: Carlson, 1990).

28. These quotes are from W. E. B. Du Bois, *The Souls of Black Folk* (New York: New American Library, 1969), 45.

29. See W. E. B. Du Bois, *The Autobiography of W. E. B. Du Bois* (New York: International Publishers, 1968), 313-30.

30. Marable, *W. E. B. Du Bois*, 147.

31. For a profound study on the plight of the Black intellectual, see Harold Cruse, *The Crisis of the Negro Intellectual* (New York: William Morrow, 1967. Reprint, New York: Quill, 1984), 96-111, 451-75.

32. Carter G. Woodson, *The Mis-education of the Negro* (Washington, DC: Associated Publishers, 1933. Reprint, 1969), xxxiii.

33. See John Washington, *Alain Locke and Philosophy: A Quest for Cultural Pluralism* (New York: Greenwood Press, 1986), 78-98, 120-31.

34. See John Henrik Clarke, ed., *Marcus Garvey and the Vision of Africa* (New York: Vintage Books, 1974), 3-9, 237.

35. Ibid.

36. Richard Robbins, "Charles S. Johnson: Scholarship, Advocacy, and Role Balance," in James E. Blackwell and Morris Janowitz, eds., *Black Sociologists: Historical and Contemporary Perspectives* (Chicago: University of Chicago Press, 1974), 72-73.

37. See G. F. Edwards, "E. Franklin Frazier," in James E. Blackwell and Morris Janowitz, eds., *Black Sociologists: Historical and Contemporary Perspectives* (Chicago: University of Chicago Press, 1974), 92-97. See also Melvin Herskovits, *The Myth of the Negro Past* (Boston: Harper & Brothers, 1941. Reprint, Boston: Beacon Press, 1958).

38. John Henrik Clarke, "The University of Sankore at Timbuctoo: A Neglected Achievement in Black Intellectual History," *Western Journal of Black Studies* 1 (June 1977): 142-46.

Chapter 2

Introduction and Development of African American Studies

Demand, Controversy, and Institutionalization

Evolution of the Student Movement in America

The first formal academic program in African American Studies was established in 1968 under the moniker of Black Studies. The initiation of African American Studies programs and departments at institutions of higher learning followed a nontraditional or inverse process in comparison with traditional disciplines or fields of study. The ideas and efforts leading to the establishment of African American Studies did not originate with academic administrators and faculty in accordance with custom. Demands for the formalization of programs and curricula in the study of African Americans began with Black students who were aided and abetted not only by professional, ordinary, and "street" people of the Black community but also by enlightened White students. The emergence of student power and the powerful effect Black students had on the moral consciousness of White America compelled schools, colleges, and universities to reassess their academic mission and social objectives.

Historically, students steeped in the classical philosophies of their academic mentors and guided by the traditional purpose and role of institutions of higher learning have influenced human progress and social change. However, in many countries throughout the world, students have rebelled against tradition and forced change in social customs and political policies through organized protest, rioting, and strikes. Until

the 1960s, American students seemingly accepted the college or university as a bastion of the privileged elite in pursuit of liberal education and professionalism.

The 1960s was marked by the emergence of student power. Students began to challenge the meaning and purpose of education and forced colleges and universities to reexamine their role and function in American society. Students questioned the societal tradition and purpose of institutionalized education and sought to reform the structure and curriculum of colleges and universities. African American students at historically Black institutions initiated the student revolt by challenging the racist and segregationist traditions of the American South. The students demonstrated that education should and did serve to enlighten a people relative to their civil rights and social justice. Education empowered them with the courage of free expression and the determination to seek truth.

White students were concerned with free speech, shared student-university governance, ideological diversity, social idealism, and humanitarian goals and objectives. They also questioned the morality of the university's complicity with corporations, the military, and the Central Intelligence Agency (CIA), especially in relation to the Vietnam War. Whereas White students sought to legitimize radical politics and to revolutionize the system, Black student protests and demands clearly were focused on American racism, segregation, civil rights, discrimination, and the establishment of African American Studies programs. White students often joined and supported Black students' civil rights and African American Studies initiatives. Student demands, protests, and rebellions did not always occur within a peaceful milieu, however. The Student Power Movement of the 1960s provoked unprecedented incidents of violence and disruption on campus and in their surrounding communities.[1]

The struggle for civil rights and social equality led to student rebellions and subsequently to the demand and formal establishment of African American Studies. These events were influenced by the rising expectations among African Americans resulting from a series of historical events. The socioeconomic and political status of Blacks in the United States has tended to improve after each American war or international conflict. Blacks, particularly Black men, have served loyally and valiantly in the US armed forces and have fought abroad in many wars to protect the liberty and rights of others that were denied to them at home. Each time, upon their return to the United States or their discharge from the armed services, they have been less inclined to accept the degradation of racism and the status of second-class citizens. This was particularly evident in the aftermath of World War II and even more so during and after the Korean conflict. Moreover, African Americans' inevitable participation in the workforces of wartime industries improved their economic condition and resources.

Despite the vast economic disparity that existed between Whites and Blacks in the US, the minor gains that accrued to Black people as a result of World War II sparked new hopes and fueled their determination to resist segregation and to fight the dehumanizing institution of racism. Civil rights organizations such as the National Association for the Advancement of Colored People (NAACP) renewed their legal initiatives and appeals in the courts to end racial discrimination and segregation. It was the sons and daughters of Black parents who had gained courage and the means to fight racism and segregation during World War II, the Korean conflict, and the post-war periods who precipitated the student movements and rebellions of the 1960s.[2]

The United States Supreme Court's decision in *Brown v. Board of Education of Topeka, Kansas* on May 17, 1954, was a groundbreaking event that seeded the Black student rebellion of the 1960s. In that case, the Supreme Court ruled that racial segregation in public schools was unconstitutional. The ruling provoked a wave of White protests and a series of lynchings, bombings, and other violent and repressive activities by White supremacist groups directed at African

Americans in the southern United States. White southern lawyers hastened to prepare briefs and suits to appeal, forestall, or resist the school desegregation ruling. Black civil rights organizations and their attorneys attempted to implement the law by initiating test actions or cases in elementary and secondary public schools in the eleven hard-core segregationist states of the South.

Avid segregationists obstructed with terror and violence the efforts of school boards to comply with the law. One of the most notable resistance cases occurred at Central High School in Little Rock, Arkansas, where President Eisenhower had to federalize that state's National Guard in order to enforce the law and allow Black students to enter the school. Similar scenarios of resistance, confrontation, and enforcement were repeated in the arena of higher education when African Americans attempted to enroll as students at the universities of Alabama, Georgia, and Mississippi. The gauntlet for integration and equality was cast down, with Black students serving as both pawns and protagonists.

Less than two years after the *Brown v. Board of Education* Supreme Court ruling, Rosa Parks, a Black woman, challenged the segregationist policies of Montgomery, Alabama, by refusing to relinquish her seat on a bus to a White man and move to the rear of the bus. When she adamantly refused to move after repeated requests by the bus driver, the driver summoned the police, and she was arrested. This incident incited an unprecedented stance of unity among the Blacks of Montgomery and triggered a massive Black boycott of the city's transit system. The Black community there organized the Montgomery Improvement Association and selected a young clergyman, Martin Luther King, Jr., to head the boycott movement. Under King's leadership and the association's rallies and fund raising efforts, the Montgomery bus boycott achieved national and world attention and support. It ignited a spirit of defiance to racism in Black America and eventually led to similar resistance movements throughout the country.

King adopted Mahatma Gandhi's philosophy of nonviolent protest during the boycott. His strategies of nonviolence and civil disobedience became a model for future protest movements in the United States, especially for dissident students of the 1960s. The favorable Supreme Court school desegregation decision and the triumphant success in desegregating the Montgomery buses swelled the liberation aspirations of the younger Black generation, which became increasingly impatient with the slow pace of securing freedom through the courts and with the "gradualistic" approach of traditional civil rights leaders and organizations. African Americans also felt betrayed by the ineffectiveness and lack of enforcement of the *Brown* decision. Four years after the ruling, southern schools and universities remained virtually segregated and unequal.

On February 1, 1960, four students from the historically Black North Carolina Agricultural and Technical College in Greensboro seated themselves at the segregated lunch counter of a Woolworth's store. They were refused service, yet they sat quietly and read their textbooks. They were jeered at and threatened, but they sat passively. The store closed the counter, but they returned the next day. The students exercised the techniques and tactics of nonviolent protest and passive resistance. When the media published news of the sit-in, thousands of students began similar sit-ins in towns and cities throughout the South where Black colleges were located. Within weeks, between fifty- and seventy-thousand persons had participated in sit-ins or demonstrated on behalf of the movement. Thousands were arrested and several were killed. Police brutality was rampant.

The dynamic growth and spread of the sit-ins throughout the South led to the formation of the most formidable African American student organization in the history of America. Martin Luther King, Jr., and Ella Baker of the Southern Christian Leadership Conference (SCLC) called a meeting of student representatives from all Black colleges. Over two hundred people attended that conference, which was held in Raleigh, North Carolina, on April 15, 1960. Out of this meeting, the Student Nonviolent Coordinating Committee (SNCC) was born.[3]

The eventual establishment of African American Studies programs and departments in educational institutions in the United States is broadly but indirectly related to the formation of SNCC. The sit-ins began a revolutionary student movement focused on abolishing racial segregation and discrimination, and they gained momentum as a broader assault on Jim Crow segregation was undertaken. During the spring and summer of 1961, SNCC participated with the Congress of Racial Equality (CORE) in the execution of dangerous and sometimes violent Freedom Rides throughout the South. The Freedom Rides were designed to exercise the rights of Blacks to use interstate public transportation without discrimination. Although the Supreme Court had ruled segregation in carriers and terminal facilities unconstitutional fourteen years earlier, fear and the threat of arrest or violence inhibited Blacks from exercising this right in the deep South. SNCC also diversified its concerns and activities from Freedom Rides to Black voter registration and political reform throughout the South.

In association largely with CORE, SNCC organized grassroots Blacks and coordinated massive voter registration drives. Their efforts were met with terror and violence from southern Whites who were resistant to relinquishing their hold on the White supremacist political structures. SNCC was also instrumental in organizing an independent Black political organization in Lowndes County, Alabama, called the Black Panther Party. By the mid-1960s, under the leadership of Kwame Ture (formerly known as Stokely Carmichael), the ideological bent of SNCC changed from integration to independent Black politics, self-determination, and economic self-sufficiency. Carmichael used the slogan "Black Power" to define this new ideology. The term *Black Power* was controversial and subject to various interpretations; however, it resurrected Marcus Garvey's earlier concepts of race pride, self-respect, self-help, and Black consciousness.

The social revolutionary role that SNCC played, and its achievements in the liberation of African Americans during the 1960s, are too extensive to discuss in detail in this book. It is important, however, to state that the influence and social revolutionary ideology of African American students were not limited to the geographical confines of the American South and East; they also took root in the West. The new nationalist and militant emphasis of SNCC probably influenced the formation and ideology of a more radical Black student/community organization in California. The Black Panthers, founded in Oakland, California, in 1966, adopted the name and symbol of the defunct SNCC Black Panther political party of the Lowndes County (Alabama) Freedom Organization.[4]

By 1967, the idea of Black Power and of African Americans controlling the social, political and economic institutions in their community began to make sense and gain support throughout Black America. However, it was evident that if Black self-determination and self-sufficiency were to become a reality, African Americans would have to raise their educational levels and technological competencies. Consequently, the strategy and base of operations of the Black Student Movement generally shifted from the town to the campus. When students redirected their attention to the campus, they discovered that the educational policies and academic curricula of the colleges and universities reflected and promoted the same racial inequities and social injustices as the broader society.

They concluded that the American higher education, perhaps more than any other institution, denigrated the humanity of Black people and consequently posed a formidable barrier to the realization of Black pride, self-development, and self-determination. For education to benefit African Americans, they concurred that colleges and universities had to become more responsive to the needs of the Black community and more relevant to Black culture. Thus, the students organized to demand and negotiate change. The most widespread name chosen for such organizations was Black Student Union. These various organizations issued the challenge and set the course that would bring about a revolution in American education.[5]

The Genesis of African American Studies: The Black Studies Program at San Francisco State College

It was merely incidental that the first African American Studies academic program was initiated at San Francisco State College (SFSC). The shift of Black students' focus from social and economic integration to educational reform, academic parity, and Black Power was a national phenomenon. The nature and intensity of racism at predominantly White colleges and universities led African American students to revel increasingly in their African heritage and culture. Therefore, it was inevitable that the absence of the culture and experience of Africans in America in the university curriculum would become a burning issue and demand. Indeed, almost concurrent with SFSC's concession to the demand for and creation of a Black Studies Department in 1968, students at other major institutions were using disruptive tactics and making similar and related appeals. Students at Stanford, Columbia, Northwestern, Cornell, and Ohio State universities were concerned with the adoption of African American history courses, increasing the recruitment

of Black students, employment of initial or additional Black faculty, and the provision of special buildings for Black American culture or habitation. Thus, after the historic strike and political controversy over Black Studies and other social issues at San Francisco State, the demand and establishment of similar programs and courses accelerated throughout the nation.

Before summarizing the factors that led to the establishment of the first Black Studies Department, the role and position of students should be examined. The term *student* defines one who occupationally acquires knowledge—that is, one who is a processor and product of studying. When a person enrolls as a student in an educational institution, his or her status as a civilian is considered suspended relative to certain civic responsibilities or forms of accountability. In essence, students are favored with a mythical shield of invulnerability. Therefore, they are effective, quasi-civilian agents for promoting and engendering social change.

Economic paradoxes, along with the racial and class income differentials of the 1960s, exacerbated the deteriorating social conditions of racial and ethnic minorities in the United States. These circumstances gave rise to increased student discontent with the role and performance of higher education institutions. In California and particularly in the Black and other Third World communities near San Francisco State, students began to develop their own ideas about the role and responsibility of the college for reaching out to the educationally deprived and economically disadvantaged.

During periods of economic upturn and prosperity, many affluent White students tend to relax their materialistic pursuits and adherence to the principles of the "establishment" and become more socially oriented and committed. Conversely, the paradox of an inflationary-recession raises the unfulfilled socioeconomic expectations of the underclass and provokes unrest and discontent in Black and Third World communities. A tax cut and accelerated expenditure on the Vietnam War, which took place during the mid- and late-1960s, produced a climate of economic uncertainty among some groups of White students, so they focused their attention on both social and war-and-peace issues.

The student government at SFSC had a significant fund of $300,000 from compulsory student-body fees. White student activists were able to direct much of these funds toward the development of a tutorial program to help children living in distressed neighborhoods and the underprivileged. They also supported other educational and sociopolitical community programs, including the Mississippi Summer Project. The students also created an Experimental College focusing on social and educational indoctrination, which its initiators hoped would lead to social reform.

The idea and success of these White student programs, in conjunction with the initiation and rise of the Black Student Union (BSU) and its Black consciousness and Black Power orientation, set the stage for the unfolding drama surrounding the battle for African American Studies. Black student activists coopted the model of the White student programs and, with the support of the student government fund, launched a number of Black arts and culture courses at SFSC's Experimental College. In the summer of 1966, Jimmy Garrett, a SNCC organizer from Watts (in south Los Angeles) and a San Francisco State College student, founded a BSU on that campus. He was not content, however, with confining the Black Studies courses to the Experimental College. Garrett vigorously campaigned for the incorporation of Black Studies courses into the college's academic departments, but his ultimate goal was the establishment of a Black Studies Department.[6]

Dr. Nathan Hare, an SFSC professor, was tasked by then-SFSC president John Summerskill to develop and coordinate a Black Studies curriculum.[7] Summerskill, who had been an early opponent of the United States' role in the Vietnam War, previously had been criticized for failing to control violent student demonstrations. Less than two years after becoming president of San Francisco State in 1966, he was put on probation by the trustees of the California State College system. When the trustees learned of his intentions to support a Black Studies initiative, they postponed implementation of the program. Summerskill resigned in May 1968 while campus buildings were occupied as part of a student sit-in.[8] His successor, Robert Smith, was subsequently succeeded by Samuel I. Hayakawa, who rose to national prominence by suppressing disorders on the campus. Having exhausted all viable means and appeals, Black students became exasperated and called for a strike on November 6, 1968, effectively closing the college.

The strike called by the SFSC Black Student Union was based on a myriad of issues and grievances affecting various campus groups; however, the most incisive petition among the demands was for the immediate establishment of a Black Studies Department. The strike gained the support and joint participation of various Third World student organizations including the Asian-American Political Alliance (AAPA), the Mexican-American Student Confederation (MASC), the Latin American Student Organization (LASO), the Philippine-American Collegiate Endeavor (PACE), and the Intercollegiate Chinese for Social Action (ICSA). In coalition with the Black Student Union, these groups formed an umbrella organization called the Third World Liberation Front (TWLF). Their combined organizations submitted a list of fifteen non-negotiable demands to the administration. The Students for a Democratic Society (SDS), a radical White student organization, also supported and participated in the strike as well as other unaffiliated White students.[9]

The strike was successful, and the students were victorious. By the end of 1968, San Francisco State College was the first institution of higher education formally to establish a formal department of Black Studies, and Nathan Hare was appointed its first coordinator or head. After the 1968 student rebellion and strike, the number of African American Studies courses, programs, and departments proliferated, not only in institutions of higher education but in many elementary and secondary schools as units and courses. Moreover, African American Studies served as the vanguard and model for the subsequent implementation of Chicano Studies, Asian American Studies, Native American Studies, and even Women's Studies.

Expanding the History of the Development of African American Studies

Though it is important to give appropriate recognition to the path-breaking nature of developments at San Francisco State, it is important to acknowledge earlier student-initiated efforts to establish African American Studies programs, especially at historically Black colleges and universities (HBCUs). In a special issue of the *Journal of African American History (JAAH)*, author Derrick White laments the finding that "research on the history of Black Studies has not paid significant attention to the field's origins at Historically Black Colleges and Universities."[10] In that same issue, Ibram Rogers highlights important events that occurred as early as 1965 at several HBCUs including Tuskegee, Howard, Southern, and Hampton.[11] Major milestones at predominantly White institutions highlighted additionally by *JAAH* contributors Delores Aldridge and Carlene Young include protests by African American students at Northwestern University in 1968 and the establishment of the first African American and African Studies bachelor's degree program in the South at Emory University in 1971.[12] In contrast to the role of student protests in forcing institutions to establish African American Studies units, Yale University students were able to catalyze a major two-day symposium exploring the educational ramifications of African American Studies without initiating a major protest.[13] The movement to institutionalize African American Studies was also spurred by organizations such as the Institute of the Black World.[14]

African American Studies and Educational Democracy

Democratization of American Education

The demand for and establishment of African American Studies signaled the waning influence of the integrationist or assimilationist philosophy espoused by Frederick Douglass. Integration and the remote hope of assimilation had been the primary social and political objectives of Black civil rights movements since Emancipation. Although the accommodationist-segregationist philosophy of Booker T. Washington and the subsequent Black nationalist-separatist ideology of Marcus Garvey had widespread appeal and support among certain socioeconomic classes of African Americans, racial integration had always been perceived by most Blacks as the panacea for race problems in America. However, the integration-oriented campaigns of Black students changed when their attention shifted from town to campus. Their educational demands were quite separatist and Garveyian in nature. To understand the complexity of this paradoxical change of emphasis from integrationist to race-specific educational concerns, it is necessary to discuss the racially exclusive nature of American education.

American education professes to the ideals of democracy, equality of opportunity, and protection of the rights and dignity of all citizens. These ideals are all but ignored in their application to America's more than thirty million citizens of African descent. Black Americans are almost compelled to subscribe to and adopt White Western Anglo-Saxon history and culture, yet they are denied equal opportunity and access to social and political power. "Americanization" for Blacks requires their social and cultural adaptation to White middle-class norms and European values. Thus, the White-ethnocentric character of American education, in cause and effect, gives rise not only to White nationalism but also to institutional racism. The exclusion of the African American experience belies the democratic intent of education and makes the social platitude of integration a myth.

Democracy fosters the principles of equality of rights, opportunity, and treatment. Although democracy is based on the theory of majority rule, its egalitarian orientation provides for the maintenance and protection of minority rights and dignity. The race-specific or separatist implications of African American Studies may well be interpreted as a cry for the fulfillment of the democratic ideal of education. Educational exclusivity and racism were the bases of the demand for African American Studies. Any policy of integration that requires African Americans to relinquish their heritage, culture, and racial identity and become largely invisible within the culture of the dominant society is undemocratic.

The establishment of African American Studies programs was, and still is, perceived by some as signaling a trend toward separatism or even segregation. The democratic implications inherent in the institution of African American Studies have been lost because of confusion over the definitions or differences between the terms *segregation* and *separatism*. Segregation refers to a policy of enforced apartness (as in *apartheid*) under the control of an oppressor or dominant race. Separation is the voluntary act of one race to collectively separate from another in pursuit of its own social, economic, or political freedom and self-actualization. As Nathan Hare observed:

> Segregation exists when somebody sets you apart for characteristics they deem to be inferior. Separation is the act of moving away or seeking independence of mind or space yourself, for your own reasons at your own time. There is a crucial psychological difference between the two which is too often missed.[15]

The unresponsiveness of Whites to Blacks' demands to end educational racism and acknowledge the contributions of African American life and experience to the history and development of the United States led to a series of separatist demands on campuses nationwide. Black students and the Black community took American schools, colleges, and universities to task for teaching the equality of mankind while institutionalizing inequality in the educational curricula. According to Preston Wilcox:

> The rash of Black Studies programs is a direct reflection of the failure of "integrated," White supremacist education. Black students are refusing to attempt to fully integrate themselves into racist institutions which educate Black students to hate themselves as Blacks. White controlled institutions of higher education have systematically overlooked the intellectual and political interests of [thirty] million Black people and persisted in talking about the right of free inquiry and academic freedom.[16]

Race-specific studies related to African Americans and to other American racial-ethnic populations were instituted to coexist, in a relative sense, with studies of White Americans. Although the various ethnic-racial studies programs represent a giant step toward democratizing American education, the nation's educational system remains one of the major institutions perpetuating racialist and racist ideas. It also continues to focus almost solely on the White American-Eurocentric experience while neglecting or ignoring the presence, interests, and contributions of African Americans. The only other democratic and viable alternative to separate African American Studies programs is the equitable integration into the American educational curricula of the life experiences and contributions of Black Americans to the history and development of the United States.

The Educational Relevance of Race

The race of an individual or group is of primary concern and importance in American society. Race has a profound impact on the level of social attainment, the degree of political empowerment, and the opportunity for economic advancement of many groups in the United States, especially African Americans. When a person's or group's life-choice and political and economic status or condition are affected or determined by race, the resulting social phenomenon is racism. Those who have the power to implement and enforce the policies and conditions of racism are oppressors or racists; the human objects or victims of racism become the oppressed. Therefore, if education is to serve as a liberating agent and satisfy a person's or group's normative and psychological needs, it is logical to assume that the education relevant to the oppressor might be much different for or even irrelevant to the oppressed.

Race, particularly in America, is a biological, social, and cultural construct that conditions interpersonal relationships as well as collective perceptions of reality. The biological characteristics identified with race are transmitted hereditarily, whereas those that are sociocultural and attitudinal are acquired or learned. Color or phenotype has been a primary dimension in the historical development of theories about race and racial characteristics. Historically, Euro-Western anthropologists claimed to identify three main races: Negroid or Black, Mongoloid or Yellow-Brown, and Caucasoid or White.[17] The various commentators went beyond simple classification and assigned rankings to each group by characterizing members of the Caucasoid type (Caucasians) as the most advanced and members of the Negroid group (the Blacks of and from Africa) as the least developed.

Scholars of African descent have challenged the unidimensional approach to racial classification. In his 1897 essay, *The Conservation of Races*, W.E.B. Du Bois argued that "the wonderful developments of human history teach that the grosser physical differences of color, hair, and bone go but a short way toward explaining the different roles which groups of men have played in Human Progress." He went on to acknowledge the existence of "differences—subtle, delicate and elusive, though they may be—which have silently but definitely separated men into groups. While these subtle forces have generally followed the natural cleavage of common blood, descent, and physical peculiarities, they have at other times swept across and ignored these. At all times, however, they have divided human beings into races."[18]

Du Bois's enlargement of the concept of race beyond simple phenotype introduces the concept of ethnicity. Ethnicity defines individuals who consider themselves, or who are considered by others, to share common characteristics that differentiate them from other collectives in a society, within which they develop distinct cultural behaviors. The term was first coined to clarify misconceptions about the term *race*. Although members of an ethnic group may be identifiable in terms of racial attributes, they may also share other cultural characteristics such as religion, occupation, language, or politics.

This is clearly the distinction to which Du Bois alluded in his 1897 query: "What, then, is a race? It is a vast family of human beings, generally of common blood and language, always of common history, traditions, and impulses, who are both voluntarily and involuntarily striving together for the accomplishment of certain more or less vividly conceived ideals of life."[19] He reiterated this view some fifty years later by asserting that Africans were "not simply a physical entity: a black people, or a people descended from black folk but, what all races really are, a cultural group."[20] Unfortunately, such a nuanced understanding of race, ethnicity, and culture has not informed educational theory and practice, nor has it informed social policy in the United States.

In the United States, where race and color are of immense social and political significance, the demand for educational relevance according to race has unequivocal validity. The prospect for universal education is diminished when world human phenomena and/or "civilization" is viewed from only the White American-European perspective. During the twentieth century, the world was influenced heavily by White Western art, technology, thought, sociopolitical experiences, and religious or moral values. Although much of the foundations of Western culture had been borrowed from other cultural traditions, including those developed in many African societies, this cultural borrowing was rarely acknowledged; and systematic efforts were undertaken to destroy other social systems. In the words of Alioune Diop, the European or White race "has crushed the language of others, has violated the spirituality of others, devalued the technological or artistic experience of others, humiliated, and paralyzed the creativity of others."[21] Diop's indictment of Europeans as practitioners of cultural genocide is especially relevant to Africans and African Americans.

US textbooks and public education glorify the American and European nexus, but they are virtually mute on the concomitant role of people of African descent in America's development and their influence on its art and culture. Some progressive White scholars have acknowledged this institutionalized marginalization. John H. Bunzel, for example, captures the essence of Black students' concern for educational relevance when he states that "the Black Students' Union, their educational problem at San Francisco State is clear and unambiguous: they read White literature, study White families, analyze White music, survey White civilizations, examine White cultures, probe White psychologies. In a word, the college curriculum is White-culture-bound."[22]

In a multiracial society, education must be made relevant to the cultural, political, and social interests and aspirations of all racial/ethnic groups. An educational system must be designed pedagogically to have a positive influence on the cognitive and affective learning outcomes of all racial/ethnic groups relative to their ethos and cultures. Academic programs and curricula that have the effect of abetting oppression are irrelevant to members of oppressed racial/ethnic groups. Such an educational system only benefits the vested interests of the racial/ethnic collective it is designed to serve.

It is educationally sound and beneficial to teach and to study race and races as long as racial ethnocentrism, domination, and superiority are analyzed critically and emphasis is placed on the equality, interrelatedness, and interdependence of all races. Cultural, technological, and social borrowing or exchange has taken place among racial and ethnic groups ever since the beginning of time. To presume that all customs, arts, science, and technology that are worthwhile and deserving of mention are the product of the culture, ingenuity, and intellect of Europeans is preposterous. Africans were among the early contributors to the culture, science, and technology of world civilization. Yet in American textbooks, there is little, if any, positive inclusion or treatment of any group except Europeans.

This does not mean that Eurocentric culture is bad or negative; however, it does imply that no single group's culture can meet the needs or serve the interests of all humankind. In the absence of a philosophy of cultural/racial relativism, cultural hierarchy determines the character of race relations. Cultural ranking also produces the basis for racism. Racism inevitably results in the inequitable sharing of economic goods and political power; thus, there is a direct relationship between race and educational relevancy. Education has the potential of fostering the cultural supremacy of one racial/ethnic group while making the culture of another irrelevant.

Contemporary Concepts and Approaches

Black Consciousness and Community Orientation

Nathan Hare, a sociologist and the developer of the first Black Studies curriculum, emphasized that Blackness and strong connections to a community base are the measures of an authentic African American Studies program. Blackness or Black consciousness, he wrote, is necessary to counterbalance the longstanding psychological effects of White cultural imperialism. For the same reason, he recommended that the education of African Americans should be primarily concerned with or centered in the African American community.

Hare concluded that education and research, though primary missions, should be applied to promote Black community problem solving and social action. His concept of Black Consciousness and Community Orientation (BCCO) is consistent with the idea of relevance in education.[23] He further concluded that the emphasis he placed on Black culture and the Black community in no way makes African American Studies irrelevant to White society. In addressing the relevance of Black Studies to Whites, Hare states:

> However, a racist society cannot be healed merely by solving the problems of its black victims alone. The black condition does not exist in a vacuum; we cannot solve the problems of the black race without solving the problems of the society which produced and sustains the predicament of blacks. At the same time as we transform the black community, through course-related community activities, white students duplicating this work in their communities—predominantly—may operate to transform the white community and thus a racist American society.[24]

In other words, African American Studies cannot be relevant to the needs of the Black community if it is not dedicated to the task of bringing about political and social change within the entire society.

Universal relevance is achieved through Black consciousness and community engagement by including research and analysis of other groups generally defined as races. African American Studies is virtually of little value if it only engages in the study of the Black condition (victim analysis). Hare's initial curriculum included courses related to the study of oppressed peoples in all parts of the world and of their past and present liberation movements—those that succeeded and those that failed. His BCCO concept of African American Studies is implicitly separatist in theme and tone even though it actually has promoted democracy and equitable integration. This concept and others also whetted the intellectual curiosity and social awareness of millions of Whites. Not only were the early African American Studies classrooms integrated, but the African American Studies movement resulted in the hiring of a few thousand Black faculty and staff at previously all-White colleges and universities. Thus, relatively speaking, the institutionalization of African American Studies accomplished more integration in higher education than centuries of integrationist-assimilationist appeals and ideology.[25]

From its inception, the Hare philosophy or model of Black Studies was socially and politically revolutionary. Ideological and pedagogical Blackness constituted the educational foundation, but the instructional and research focus was not limited merely to the study of Blackness or of Black history and culture. It also encompasses an *expressive* or *affective* phase designed to give African Americans knowledge of their history and instill within them a sense of self-pride and collective destiny. This aspect of the program indirectly benefits Whites by helping to change their false notions of superiority and correcting many of their distorted views of African American life and history.

A second phase could be considered *functional* or *pragmatic*. It serves the purpose of increasing professional, scientific, and technical skills within the Black community through the use of new teaching techniques and methodology that use terms and concepts easily understood by Black people. Courses that produce such socioeconomic skills might be labeled Black Politics, Black Economics, Black Science, Blacks in Mathematics, and so forth. Hare's curriculum design ensures that African American Studies, or education generally, is made more relevant to the Black community and its needs. At the same time, that community is made more relevant to (or involved in) the educational process.[26] His ideas and concepts, which were based on the Student Movement and Black Power philosophy of the 1960s, significantly influenced subsequent curriculum development in African American Studies.

The Kawaida Theory of Maulana Karenga

Maulana Karenga's Kawaida Theory provides a somewhat different conceptual approach to the development of African American Studies. Basically, Kawaida is a synthesis of Black Nationalist, Pan-Africanist, and socialist thought and practice. Karenga's theory and Hare's concept differ partly in their diagnostic, prescriptive, and critical assessment of African American culture and the Black condition in American society.

Karenga posited that African American culture and African consciousness have been affected dysfunctionally by the dominant European American society. To rectify this sociocultural imbalance and counteract the psychological effects of oppression, theories and programs of sociocultural reconstruction must be developed. Kawaida theory asserts that Africans in the Diaspora are estranged from their natural or positive values and thus in need of cultural and social reconstruction. It further describes and critiques the African American experience and condition and then prescribes corrective social and cultural theory.[27]

Karenga's perspective on African American culture is reflective of E. Franklin Frazier's contention (discussed in Chapter 1) that Blacks in America have suffered the loss of their African culture and social heritage. As he contends: "The key crisis in Black life is the cultural crisis, that is, the crisis in views and values. The vision crisis is defined by a deficient and ineffective grasp of self, society, and the world, and the value crisis by incorrect and self-limiting categories of commitment, and priorities which in turn limit our human possibilities."[28] Consequently, his theory of Black culture has attracted some critics. One especially critical aspect of Karenga's work lies in his assertion that views and values are the principal determinants of culture when, in reality, they are only a few among a myriad of other elements. Some critics claim that Kawaida Theory seems to imply that the cultural crisis and the deficient and ineffective self-conception that Blacks suffer should be blamed on Blacks themselves rather than on the racist nature and effects of American society. In subsequent writings, however, Karenga clearly identifies European oppression of various types as the source of African Americans' cultural disconnection, thus distancing himself from Frazier's views.

Technical criticism of Kawaida Theory aside, its principles have served as a guide for the initiation of numerous African American Studies courses and as an important basis for philosophical thought and discussion. As a corrective of real or perceived dysfunctions in Black social organization, Kawaida Theory offers seven fundamental tenets (the *Nguzo Saba*) as core elements of a new value system:

1. *Umoja* (Unity)
2. *Kujichagulia* (Self-Determination)
3. *Ujima* (Collective Work and Responsibility)
4. *Ujamaa* (Cooperative Economics)
5. *Nia* (Purpose)
6. *Kuumba* (Creativity)
7. *Imani* (Faith)

In several African American Studies courses and for a number of Black Nationalist-oriented individuals and households throughout the United States, these principles serve as popular referents in discussions and analyses of African American family life or Black male/female relationships. African American Studies curricula or textbooks organized around Kawaida Theory also incorporate Karenga's seven basic areas of culture: Mythology, History, Social Organization, Economic Organization, Political Organization, Creative Motif, and Ethos.[29]

Although the African American Studies ideologies of Maulana Karenga and Nathan Hare are somewhat different, they are not oppositional or contradictory. They differ primarily in political leanings and social focus. Whereas both Karenga and Hare may appear separatist or anti-integrationist in their social outlook, Hare is not an avid Black Cultural Nationalist. Implicit in Hare's works is the notion that celebrating African American history and African culture is neither the major objective nor the end of the struggle for Black liberation and education.

Afrocentricity: Concept and Approach

Afrocentricity (or Africentricity) as an intellectual foundation of the African American experience has existed since the eighteenth century. The implications of Afrocentricity were evident in the nineteenth-century abolitionist and emigrationist oratory, thought, and philosophy of David Walker, Henry Highland Garnet, Martin Delany, and numerous other Black philosophers of that period. The theme

2

of Afrocentricity is also evident in the political ideologies of prominent twentieth-century figures such as Marcus Garvey, Elijah Muhammad, Malcolm X, and Kwame Ture (Stokely Carmichael). However, from a modern and more clearly defined academic perspective, Molefi K. Asante is regarded as the leading theoretician of the concept of Afrocentricity. The concept also has been utilized by a significant number of Black behavioral and social scientists. Leading Afrocentric psychologists include Joseph Baldwin, Na'im Akbar, Linda James Myers, Wade Nobles, and Daudi Azibo. The works of contemporary Black social scientists Leonard Jeffries, Dona Richards, Ronald Walters, James Turner, Jacob Carruthers, and many others also reflect an Afrocentric perspective.

Asante defines Afrocentricity as a way of viewing and interpreting universal phenomena from African historical and cultural perspectives. He maintains that African American Studies must be viewed as an extension of African history and culture beginning with the primacy of classical African civilizations. Thus, any analysis of Black or African American culture and experience that is not based on Afrocentric theory and philosophy may lead to erroneous results or conclusions.[30]

The fundamental premise of the Afrocentric approach to African American Studies is that each race or racial/ethnic group develops its own perception and interpretation of the environment and the world. Different racial/cultural groups or populations have distinct ways of conceiving their existence and the order of the universe. The term used to describe the various conceptions racial/cultural groups hold concerning nature and the universe is *worldview*. In other words, a worldview includes cosmology, epistemology, and ontology. A people's worldview will cause them to respond to and to place different values on social, spiritual, physical, and material realities in conformity with their history and culture.[31]

The principles of Afrocentricity complement the educational objectives of Maulana Karenga's Kawaida Theory. For example, Afrocentricity provides guidance for the correction of the cultural crisis and deficiency in perception and values that Kawaida theory ascribes to African Americans. By using Afrocentric criteria to identify and critique negative external influences, individuals will be better able to embrace the more wholesome values articulated in Kawaida Theory.

Afrocentricity has had an important influence on the development of African American Studies.

Its emphasis on the use of African thought, philosophy, and values as frames of reference for study and research provides a clear point of demarcation from traditional Eurocentric studies purporting to offer insights into the lives of people of African descent. Proponents of Afrocentricity maintain that prior to the academic formalization of African American Studies, what was passed on about the Black experience in most courses was misinformation. That misinformation reflected biases derived from the use of Eurocentric concepts and perspectives to interpret the lives and behavior of people of African descent. However, the principal argument for Afrocentric courses and programs is not based on opposition to Eurocentricity. Afrocentric-oriented African American Studies promotes the idea that—along with Greek, Roman, or European culture and civilization—African culture, myths, legends, literature, and thought constitute parallel manifestations of human achievement. In short, it contends that the European worldview is not universally applicable to all peoples.

Class Analysis and African American Studies

Abdul Alkalimat and his associates have been in the forefront of promoting Marxian class analysis as a competitor to cultural nationalism as an ideological foundation for African American Studies. Their framework was first articulated in the text, *Introduction to African American Studies*, first published in the 1970s and now available online.[32] The core construct presented in that text is the authors' idea of a "paradigm of unity," which they argue provides a framework within which all points of view can coexist. They further advance the critical claim that class, more than any other social factor, influences the nature of every other aspect of society. While foregrounding class, they maintain that "[r]ace, nationality, and consciousness exist independently, each with its own 'substance and logic of development.'"[33] From this vantage point, they use the paradigm of unity to examine African American history as "a dynamic process of historical periodization."[34]

The Alkalimat team's periodization scheme posits three periods of "social cohesion"—that is, slavery, rural life, and urban life, along with three periods of social disruption: emancipation, migration, and crisis. They additionally claim that "[a]ll aspects of the Afro-American experience fall into this historical paradigm," and that "[w]ith a paradigm of unity, and with this method [historical periodization], all knowledge of the Black experience can be synthesized as part of a cumulative process."[35]

Du Bois provides important guidance in examining the impact of capitalism on African American life through his progressive integration of class analysis into his research. In 1954, for example, he acknowledged that his original interpretations of the trans-Atlantic slave trade failed to give appropriate attention to the economic motivations behind American slavery. Specifically, he proclaimed that "if the influence of economic motives on the action of mankind ever had clearer illustration it was in the modern history of the African race, and particularly in America.[36] He further maintained that his 1935 work, *Black Reconstruction*, was his first major publication reflecting the synthesis of his Marxist-influenced approaches to historical investigation.[37]

Cultural Studies and African American Studies

In recent years cultural studies has become highly visible in many African American Studies units in a manner that hearkens back to the Beatles "British invasion" of the US in the early 1960s. Many scholars uncomfortable with the type of cultural-nationalist formulations introduced by African American Studies scholar-activists, such as Maulana Karenga and Molefi Asante, have gravitated toward what is perceived as a less politically charged framework. One such framework is that of the "Black Atlantic," which foregrounds the construct of *hybridity* to challenge the idea that individuals can be identified with a single cultural reference group. The Black Atlantic paradigm calls for a reduction of emphasis on the experiences of people of African descent who are the progeny of those Africans whose locus of enslavement was the United States.[38] This approach, they maintain, involves "tak[ing] the Atlantic as one single, complex unit of analysis and us[ing] it to produce an explicitly transnational and intercultural perspective."[39]

The extent to which this line of inquiry has generated new insights is debatable. Hybridity has always been an organic aspect of the experiences of people of African descent in the US. It is manifested via skin-color and hair-texture politics and unwritten social mores, all of which were overlaid by the "one-drop rule," which prescribed racial identification

in the larger US landscape. Both historically and in the contemporary world, people of African descent, both those from African countries and from all portions of the African Diaspora, have found space to live and actively participate in the lifespace created by the descendants of the victims of the holocaust of enslavement in the US.

African Americans' solid commitments to transnational liberatory and identity concerns have been manifested in many ways. These include the various Pan-African Congresses and the work of Black expatriates such as those who relocated to France. As Darlene Clark Hine and Stephen Smalls have noted, World War I led to a critical mass of African Americans establishing residence in France. They maintain that "the interwar taste for exoticism and black culture, plus the popularity of jazz, made Paris a center for hundreds of African American performers."[40] A second wave of African American expatriates, including Richard Wright, James Baldwin, and Chester Himes, spent significant time in Paris in the 1950s.

Some critics argue that the Black Atlantic approach to racial identity reinterpretation reflects what Boris Groys describes as the commercialization of African American cultural identity in the international media and tourist markets."[41] These critics contend that the failure to find their non-US, multiracial, reference-group identities represented within the conventional discourse of African American Studies led Black Atlantic theorists to develop, commodify, and market an alternative narrative successfully to some major educational institutions. The resulting discourse provides outsiders with safe opportunities to engage in intellectual voyeurism with an international flavor. According to this line of argument, the demand for the intellectual products of cultural studies commentators by the accommodating institutions is fueled partly by a desire to neuter the traditionally oppositional political tenor of "mainstream" African American Studies.[42]

Post-Structuralism and African American Studies

Some scholars who self-identify with African American Studies (primarily literary critics) have wholeheartedly embraced Jacques Derrida's deconstruction approach to inquiry, despite his own caution regarding the need to pursue that project cautiously.[43] Deconstruction is, in essence, a theory of literary criticism that questions traditional assumptions about certainty, identity, and truth. A principal assertion is that words can only refer to other words and that it is impossible to derive a singular meaning from a text. Subsequently, the only meanings of significance are those supplied by readers themselves, all of which have equal validity. Derrida's claims regarding the equivalent validity of alternative textual interpretations has been used to deny the existence of a master historical narrative that chronicles a shared collective experience. This school of thought foregrounds a scenario in which multiple narratives describing various historical trajectories are intertwined, yet none can claim primacy over any other. This logic further undermines the construct of collective political struggle fueled by shared experiences and racial identification, which is, of course, an anathema to the original mission of African American Studies, which maintained that an organic relationship between inquiry and struggle must be reenergized continuously.

Some post-structuralist commentators who identify themselves with African American Studies argue that many of the traditional linguistic conventions used to characterize the experiences of people of African descent have become anachronisms due to the march of modernity (this assertion is also made by Cultural Studies proponents). Such arguments imply the need for Black people to reduce the amount of their collective energies devoted to confronting racial oppression and redirect those interests toward individualized concerns.

There are, however, those post-structuralist theorists who have come to very different conclusions about the role of so-called "identity politics" in the contemporary world. For example, Boris Groys has issued the following clarion call for the revival of radical politics and radical aesthetics:

> One must be committed to radical aesthetics to accept radical politics—and this sense of commitment produces relatively closed communities united by an identical project, by an identical vision, by an identical historical goal. The way of radical art and politics does not take us from closed premodern societies to open societies and markets. Rather, it takes us from relatively open societies to closed communities based on common commitments.[44]

To paraphrase Groys, the counter-claim to assertions about the anachronistic nature of identity politics is that such movements are absolutely essential to survival in the contemporary era of globalization. This is precisely the stance Du Bois articulated in 1948 in "Race Relations 1917-1947."[45] In that article, Du Bois identified what might be termed the "leveling effect of capitalism on cultural diversity" as one of the major threats associated with the progressive expansion of monopoly capitalism:

> The result of world-wide class strife has been to lead civilization in America and Western Europe toward conformity to certain standards which became predominant in the 19th century. We have refused continually to admit the right of difference. The type of education, the standards and ideals of literature and art, the methods of government must be brought very largely to one single white European standard.[46]

In a more specific warning, Du Bois raises the specter of the disappearance of a distinctive African American culture:

> If this [leveling of culture patterns] is going to continue to be the attitude of the modern world, then we face a serious difficulty in so-called race problems. They will become less and less matters of race, so far as we regard race as biological difference. But what is even more important, they will even become less and less matters of conflicting cultures.[47]

Challengers to traditional African American Studies often interpret post-structuralist philosophy as supporting the view that political motivations should be divorced from humanistic and artistic endeavors. However, regarding the question of the role of identity politics *per se*, some post-structuralist thinkers reject the conventional wisdom. To illustrate, in discussing the relationship between art and politics, Jacques Ranciére argues that art and politics are always intermixed—that is, "politics has its aesthetics, and aesthetics has its politics."[48] Ranciére's core message to political progressives is that "it is up to the various forms of politics to appropriate, for their own proper use, the modes of presentation or the means of establishing explanatory sequences produced by artistic practices rather than the other way around."[49] Thus, he invites activists to impose political meaning on appropriate artistic representations. Ideally, such appropriation must be undertaken in collusion with the artist; but even outside the artist's intention, an art object may still become a powerful weapon in a liberation arsenal.

African Studies and African American Studies

The intellectual hegemony of the African Studies establishment persists with respect to the study of Africa. This hegemony has produced research paradigms that generally represent African peoples as a disparate collection of distinctive ethnic collectives with few common cultural attributes. Ironically, some interests within African Studies are now seeking to expand the definition of that field to include the African Diaspora and to extend external hegemony by redefining both the concept of Africa and of the Diaspora! To put this new hegemonic thrust in perspective, however, one should recall, as Aubrey observes, that traditionally "White Africanists are more likely to define Africa by its continental boundaries, and many still by its sub-Saharan delineation."[50]

Increasingly, a "new" conception of African studies that includes the study of the Diaspora is being adopted by members of the African Studies establishment. Alpers and Roberts, for example, report that "many of them have embraced the concept that Africa and its diasporas are equally the subject of African studies."[51] They further argue that "an important corollary to having a greater inclusion of diasporas in the subject matter of African studies is imagining the Africa we know as many Africas, through a human geography that is not continent bound."[52] Expanding on this emergent paradigm, Alpers and Roberts insist that it is appropriate to write "of African *diasporas* in the plural, instead of a single African diaspora."[53]

These conceptualizations are inconsistent with the views of many Black Africanists. Even though Aubrey notes the greater tendency of "African American Africanists to define Africa as the continent and its diaspora," he contends that they have rejected mainstream efforts to fragment the experience of peoples of African descent into loosely connected micro-organisms.[54] In Aubrey's words, "For African Americans in African studies, the tendency is strong to define Africa as the continent and the diaspora together, inextricably linking Africans by continent of origin, color, and condition."[55]

The intellectual tradition of Black Africanists that Aubrey describes is one that lays the foundation for them to forge partnerships with African American Studies scholar-activists. Aubrey insists that "more African Americans in African studies are shifting more resolutely toward a redefinition of Africa that is in line with the definition of leader Pan-Africanist African Americans and continental Africans such as Du Bois, Nkrumah, and Azikwe...Pan-African frameworks are being used more frequently to look at problems, prospects, and possibilities of global Africa."[56] As a further indication of the potential for partnership, Aubrey notes that "some African Americans and continental Africans are revisiting proposals for merging African studies with African American/Black studies—a difficult endeavor, as African American studies programs generally are plagued with problems."[57]

Reaffirming the Original Mission of African American Studies

The preceding discussion demonstrates that post-structuralist European philosophy need not be at odds with the original mission of African American Studies. Indeed, invoking insights from some variants of this body of thought can strengthen claims advanced by African American Studies scholar-activists. The larger issue, however, is whether this literature adds much to the knowledge base of the discipline. Much of the same ground has been either previously, or was concurrently, plowed by an acknowledged progenitor to the field such as W.E.B. Du Bois. Yet, in addition to Du Bois, serious examination of the life and work of Anna Julia Cooper can provide useful insights regarding the exploration of gender dynamics consistent with the directions suggested by post-structuralists. As Shirley Moody-Turner and James Stewart argue:

> Central to Cooper's theoretical position is a critique of Western ethnocentric epistemologies and a call for both new sites of knowledge and new approaches to interpreting such knowledge. Positivism, as well as claims to "objectivity" and "pure reason," bore the brunt of Cooper critiques; especially when these epistemological approaches were employed to draw conclusions about "the Negro."[58]

In her 1892 article, "The Negro as Presented in American Literature," Cooper critiques the so-called "scientific" approach to the study and representation of African Americans. She was a forerunner in connecting scholarship to direct action in her work with the Hampton Folklore Society (the first predominantly Black folklore society in the US). Cooper put her theories into practice, imploring African American folklorists to "free themselves from the Anglo-Saxon standards by which their own traditions were judged primitive and lacking."[59] She urged Black folklorists to "collect and present folklore based on their own observations, memories, and experiences rather than rely on popular constructions of black folklore."[60] In this way, Cooper challenged Western claims to "certified" knowledge, especially insofar as that certified knowledge pertained to African Americans. She then worked to validate African Americans as both producers and theorizers of alternative forms of knowledge or, as she stated, "when we have been sized up and written down by others, we need not feel that the last word is said and the oracles sealed."[61] As she explained, there are gifts "far better than seeing ourselves as others see us."[62] Cooper's efforts to foreground Black folklore as collected by Black folklorists is clearly within the African American Studies tradition of documenting and preserving cultural knowledge in a way that challenges uncritical, "objective" approaches to representing the cultural traditions of Africana peoples and instead locates agency with the producers of such cultural knowledge.

While recognizing the ongoing search for new knowledge reflected by the efforts to introduce new paradigms in African American Studies discourse, the enduring precedents established by Du Bois and Cooper inform the approach to the analysis of the contours of the experiences of people of African descent presented in this text. At the same time, it is important to consider how these traditions must be adapted to reflect societal changes.

Toward New Paradigms and Methodologies

Developing New Research and Analytical Frameworks

It is evident from the preceding discussion that African American Studies arose from the throes of a social movement. Although the field was established before its theoretical objectives and research methods were clearly defined, the initial proponents and architects of African American Studies were soon convinced that many of the traditional Euro-American research models used to investigate and analyze the Black experience were flawed or inappropriate. Indeed, much of the racist and stereotypical theory relating to the African American experience has resulted from flawed Eurocentric analyses based on the so-called value-free or objective scientific method.

Historically, much of the implicitly racist social and government policies affecting the quality of life of African Americans and Africans have been based on theoretical constructs used by White Americans and Europeans that are inconsistent with the social and cultural realities of Black people or the Black community. Because Blacks are, in general, oppressed in American and European societies a value-free, objective, or detached approach and methodology toward the liberation of Black people from oppression would be, for the African American scholar, insensitive if not masochistic. Surely, a salient purpose of African American Studies is to effect social, political, and economic change. In the absence of counter-cultural values, those who are part of the system and who benefit from institutional racism may employ paradigms and research methodology that tend to sustain the sociopolitical and economic status quo to preserve their self-interests.

Many African American Studies theorists have rejected the comparative, equilibrium, and value-neutrality paradigms and methodologies of White social science. The comparative approach uses White, middle-class norms and values as the standard for analyzing and evaluating Black social and behavioral characteristics. The equilibrium model treats the status quo as a desirable state of affairs and regards change in such circumstances as risky disruption. As a consequence, the model emphasizes conformity and assimilation as strategies to overcome disadvantage. Serious deficiencies also are inherent in the objective or value-neutral methodology in relation to the lives and conditions of African Americans.[63] Recognition of this fact led to the call in the early 1970s for the creation of a "Black social science."[64] Within the proposed Black social science, terminology employed in research would avoid sanitized descriptions and bring oppressive relationships into sharp relief. This transformative linguistic convention would reinforce political commitments to undertake social science-based research to counteract racism and discrimination and improve the life circumstances of people of African descent.

Racism, neocolonialism, prejudice, and discrimination influence the life conditions and affect the worldviews of Black people. Consequently, new study models and research methodologies will have to be constructed or traditional ones significantly modified to take into account the different social realities of African Americans. Nathan Hare, in his initial conception of Black Studies, challenged African American social theorists to undertake the task of formulating new or alternate research models for the study of Blacks. As he wrote: "The Black scholar must develop new and appropriate norms and values, new institutional structures. In order to be effective in this regard, he must also develop and be guided by a new ideology. Out of this new ideology will evolve a new methodology, although in some regards it will subsume and overlap existing norms of scholarly endeavor."[65]

The development of new or modified theoretical and empirical paradigms for authenticating and explicating the African American experience is necessary if the Black Consciousness and Community Orientation (BCCO) concepts of Nathan Hare, the Kawaida (corrective) Theory of Maulana Karenga, or the Afrocentric school of thought of Molefi Asante are to be realized. African Americans are not Europeans, nor are they the "natural" adapters of Western culture. Any comprehensive study of Black Americans must take into consideration the implications of their common African origins and the continuing influence of an Afrocentric ethos or worldview on their ways of living and understanding social relations. As an illustration, Duane Champagne has suggested that further refinement of African American Studies research approaches should involve the study of "group processes of institutional change within their transocietal and historical contexts" so that empirical knowledge can be accumulated "about specific processes of social change."[66] Using such evidence, Champagne argues, will allow theory to be generated "by inductive means, through comparisons of results from accumulated historical and comparative studies."[67]

The Paradoxes of Cultural Pluralism, Diversity, and Americanization

The American population is comprised of many diverse racial and ethnic groups. Yet, the American educational system has not moved progressively toward formulating curriculum models, pedagogical approaches, and methodological designs that serve all American citizens equitably. The "melting pot" theory that postulates a homogeneous or national American culture is a mythical concept insofar as African Americans are concerned. African Americans, perhaps more than any other American racial/ethnic group, have little if any possibility of ever being assimilated, the reason being a matter primarily of color and of the derogatory status White Americans impute to Black people. Therefore, as a result of social alienation and political and economic disfranchisement, many Black Americans have, either voluntarily or necessarily, opted for a separate social, cultural, and even *national* identity.

Assertion of a separate racial or ethnic social/cultural identity has been pursued not only by African Americans. Such a posture has been adopted to some extent by various other "conspicuous" American minority populations as well. However, assertion of a distinctive racial/ethnic cultural identity by specific non-White populations conflicts with the goal of national homogeneity or *Americanization*,[68] which, in essence, means conformity by all citizens to the dominant or majority American culture. The term *American* is implicitly and almost exclusively meant to refer to White Anglo-Saxons. For political and patriotic reasons, America expects Blacks to become Americanized without according them full rights and privileges of citizenship. Whites offer to Blacks the opportunity for Americanization, but the equity of integration is denied and assimilation is virtually impossible.

The socialization objective of American education has produced ambivalence among African Americans. African American Studies was demanded and established as a solution to the cultural and identity dilemma—to coexist as a corrective to American education. Separate racial/ethnic cultural programs have been instituted with the idea and intent of promoting cultural pluralism. Although cultural pluralism is espoused as an educational means of improving race relations and preserving national unity, the practice and implications of cultural pluralism challenge the traditional concept of Americanization.

In referring to racial stratification and education, John Ogbu suggests that Blacks, in particular, have had to forge their own collective social identity and cultural frame of reference. What has resulted is an opposing or oppositional Black cultural identity in relation to White culture and society.[69] Black Americans, collectively, have little hope of ever becoming assimilated into the mainstream of White American society. Consequently, many have subscribed to a form of African American nationalism in response to European American nationalism or Anglo-Saxon Americanism. Increasingly, Africa is being proposed as the historical, social, and psychological frame of cultural reference in the study and research of Black Americans.

Racial and ethnic assertion in the United States has not been limited to African Americans. Native Americans, Asian Americans, Mexican Americans, and Latino Americans have observed the cultural-pluralist (separatist) or cultural-nationalist trend of Blacks and have moved toward a greater degree of racial/ethnic assertion. The goal of Americanization for achieving a national homogeneity is giving way to an oppositional heterogeneity of races and ethnic groups. For the most part, Blacks have been unwilling to submerge or lose their African heritage and culture in exchange for an inequitable measure of Americanization or integration. Furthermore, cultural pluralism and "cultural diversity" will inevitably lead to some functional separateness among racial and ethnic minorities. The social product of promoting cultural diversity is cultural specificity.

Demographers project that if current Latino, Asian, and Black immigration and birth rates continue at the present rate, by the year 2050 Whites (non-Latino) will represent less than half of the total US population. Clearly, there is a need to develop new or alternative theoretical formulations and research paradigms for differentiating, analyzing, and describing the diverse populations of America. The historical and continuing maladies of racism, discrimination, prejudice, and racial conflict in American society encourage and, indeed, compel Blacks and other oppressed minority groups to respond with racial/ethnic assertion or self-determination. Thus, the growth and development of African American Studies and other ethnic studies programs continue.

The socially curative propositions of cultural pluralism, cultural diversity, and integration have not substantially affected the unequal social, political, and economic conditions of African Americans. Until institutional racism and anti-Black and anti-African attitudes and sentiments no longer shape social dynamics in the United States, the trend toward Black cultural assertion and Afrocentricity will probably increase. Contemporarily, for African Americans, there is no viable alternative.

The original vision of the founders of African American Studies must be enlarged to address several emerging challenges that did not appear critical in the 1960s. Many of these challenges are linked, either directly or indirectly, to the phenomenon of increasing globalization. The major demographic transformation mentioned previously will not only erase the traditional numerical majority status of Whites, it will also reduce the representation of the African American population. African American Studies theorists and researchers must be at the forefront of developing political strategies to ensure that these shifts do not result in diminished momentum in the ongoing struggle for freedom and social justice from reduced influence in some venues such as electoral politics. Developing such strategies may require new thinking regarding the development of alliances with other groups who also perceive the need to assert a distinctive identity such as Latinos. Both populations are in jeopardy of being relegated to the backwaters of the political-economic system as massive changes sweep through the global economy. Access to good employment opportunities and high-quality public goods are two shared concerns that could serve as the foundation for a functional alliance. Advancing such a coalition will not be easy. African American Studies scholars must be in the vanguard in efforts to identify opportunities for collaboration and education of both groups about the structural nature of the forces that work against the pursuit of common interests.

Unlike the 1960s and early 1970s when there was an organic relationship between creative production and social protest, in today's world popular culture is shaped increasingly by economic considerations. As popular culture becomes increasingly commercialized, external forces co-opt its liberating potential. At the same time, some creative artists have made the conscious decision to forego fame and fortune in favor of speaking truth to power. It is the responsibility of contemporary African American Studies theorists and researchers to engage popular culture more directly than has been the case to date and to create partnerships with progressive artists to pursue new strategies for disseminating knowledge from African American Studies.

African American Studies theorists and researchers must also extend the scope of the field to pay greater attention to issues of scientific and technological development and their impact on people of African descent. The basic challenge has been stated by Maulana Karenga in the following terms: "The question is ... how to synthesize the need and growth of science and technology with the need for human sensitivity and morality or how to humanize nature without denaturalizing and dehumanizing humans? Europe by its own admission has failed in this project. It now falls on Africans and other Third World peoples to demonstrate its possibility."[70] In a similar vein, Saneh Chamarik has argued that the general problem is to answer the question of how "non-colonial science and creativity can be promoted and developed ... as a liberating tool ... for transforming all the productive forces available to society into a balanced and self-sustaining process of growth and development."[71]

The challenges associated with neutralizing the adverse consequences of unbridled scientific and technological developments are greater than ever. As Tomovic observes, in contrast to older regimes, in the modern era "promoting technology becomes an organized social activity rather than one involving only individuals or companies."[72] Specialists in African American Studies must step forth and meet this challenge in the spirit of the values of self-reliance and self-determination that have shaped the development of the field. As Chamarik suggests, "[F]undamentally, the question of self-reliance in science and technology is concerned with cultural freedom and creativity that have been lost in the process of forced industrialization."[73]

All of the mandates issued as challenges for the ongoing development of African American Studies focus on the need for increased engagement with contemporary public policy crises. As the discipline continues to engage in historical resurrection and in forging a new future for people of African descent, it must be guided by Du Bois's dictum:

> We can only understand the present by continually referring to and studying the past, when any one of the intricate phenomena of our daily life puzzles us, when there arises religious problems, political problems, race problems, we must always remember that while their solution lies in the present, their cause and their explanation lie in the past.[74]

Questions & Exercises

1. What were the fundamental social and educational concerns of Black students that led them to protest the status quo and petition for the development of African American Studies during the 1960s?

2. Why did so many White students advocate and support the move to establish Black Studies programs at predominantly White colleges and universities?

3. Relate the educational rationale for African American Studies to the political and economic objectives of the Civil Rights Movement of the 1950s and 1960s.

4. Who was the "father" of formal African American Studies programs in the US? Name other major proponents of the African American Studies movement.

5. Are *cultural pluralism*, *multiethnicity*, and *cultural diversity* synonymous terms insofar as American education is concerned?

6. Write a position paper discussing how race and culture should be reflected in courses included in the general education curriculum of colleges and universities.

7. Give an analysis and evaluation of Nathan Hare's Black Consciousness and Community Orientation, Maulana Karenga's Kawaida Theory, and Molefi Asante's Afrocentricity paradigms or approaches to African American Studies.

8. Is the American educational system free of political influence, political content, and White-nationalistic orientation? Discuss.

9. Historically and universally, students have effected social and political change through protest and demonstration. What gives students this unique ability, power, and influence?

10. What did you learn from textbooks or were taught about African Americans during your own elementary and public school experiences? Discuss.

Social Responsibility Projects

1. Determine if an annual Kwanzaa celebration takes place at your institution and/or in your home community. If such programs do exist, volunteer to help implement a Kwanzaa program and solicit participation from your classmates and/or neighbors. If not, organize a group to plan and carry out a Kwanzaa celebration.

2. Organize a group to research the history of the African American Studies unit at your institution, if any, and disseminate the findings to your campus's student body.

3. Conduct a student survey to identify ways to strengthen support for the African American Studies program on your campus.

4. Collect information about options for graduate study in African American Studies and share that information with students at your institution who are majoring and minoring in the subject.

5. Contact African American Studies majors and minors at other institutions and develop collaborative projects that reflect the mission of African American Studies.

Notes and References

1. For a dialectical study of student-university and student-societal conflict, see Edward Bander, ed., *Turmoil on the Campus* (New York: H. W. Wilson, 1970).

2. See Benjamin Quarles, *The Negro in the Making of America* (New York: Macmillan, 1969; reprinted by Collier Books, 1970), 215-38. Also compare to Lerone Bennett, Jr., *Before the Mayflower* (Chicago: Johnson Publishing, 1982; reprinted by Penguin Books, 1984), 360-85.

3. Howard Zinn, *SNCC: The New Abolitionists* (Boston: Beacon Press, 1965), 16-39.

4. Sol Stern, "The Call of the Black Panthers," in August Meier and Elliot Rudwick, eds., *Black Protest in the Sixties*, (Chicago: New York Times Company, 1970; reprinted by Quadrangle Books), 230-42.

5. See also Harry Edwards, *Black Students* (London: The Free Press and Collier-Macmillan, 1970).

6. James McEvoy and Abraham Miller, eds., *Black Power and Student Rebellion* (Belmont CA: Wadsworth, 1969; reprinted by Barlow & Shapiro), 286-97, Gitlin, 298-306.

7. Letter from Nathan Hare to Talmadge Anderson, October 26, 2007.

8. Glenn Fowler, "John Summerskill is Dead at 65; Led San Francisco State in 60," *New York Times* (June 15, 1990). http://www.nytimes.com/1990/06/15/obituaries/john-summerskill-is-dead-at-65-led-san-francisco-state-in-60-s.html?pagewanted=1

9. Ibid., 278-79.

10. Derrick White, "An Independent Approach to Black Studies: The Institute of the Black World (IBW) and its Evaluation and Support of Black Studies," in Jonathan Fenderson, James Stewart and Kabria Baumgartner, eds., *Expanding the History of the Black Studies Movement. A Special Issue of the Journal of African American Studies* (2012).

11. Ibram Rogers, "The Black Campus Movement and the Institutionalization of Black Studies, 1965-1970," in Jonathan Fenderson, James Stewart and Kabria Baumgartner, eds., *Expanding the History of the Black Studies Movement. A Special Issue of the Journal of African American Studies* (2012).

12. Delores Aldridge and Carlene Young, "Preface," in Delores Aldridge and Carlene Young, eds., *Out of the Revolution, The Development of Africana Studies* (Lanham, MD: Lexington Books, 2000).

13. Jonathan Fenderson, James Stewart, and Kabria Baumgartner, "Introduction," in Jonathan Fenderson, James Stewart, and Kabria Baumgartner, eds., *Expanding the History of the Black Studies Movement. A Special Issue of the Journal of African American Studies* (2012).

14. White, "An Independent Approach to Black Studies," 70-71.

15. Nathan Hare, *The Hare Plan* (San Francisco: The Black Think Tank, 1991), 56-57.

16. Preston Wilcox, "Integration or Separatism in Education: K-12." *Integrated Education: Race and Schools* 43 (Jan.-Feb. 1970). Reprinted by Integrated Education Associates, Chicago, IL.

17. See Ruth Benedict, *Race: Science and Politics* (New York: Viking Press, 1945), 9-18; see also O. Klineberg, *Race Differences* (New York: Harper & Brothers, 1935), 20-24.

18. W. E. B. Du Bois, *The Conservation of Races*, American Negro Academy Occasional Papers No. 2. (1897). Reprinted in Philip Foner, ed., *W. E. B. Du Bois Speaks: Speeches and Addresses 1890-1919* (New York: Pathfinder Press), 75.

19. Ibid.

20. W. E. B. Du Bois, "The Talented Tenth Memorial Address," *Boule Journal* 15 (October 1948): 3-13.

21. Cheik Anta Diop, "Cultural Well-Being," *First World 2* (1979): 8-9.

22. John Bunzel, "Black Studies at San Francisco State," *The Public Interest* (c. August 1968), 26-27.

23. Much of the information explaining this concept has been obtained by the author in discussion with and from materials furnished by Nathan Hare, a colleague and friend.

24. Nathan Hare, "Questions and Answers About Black Studies," *Massachusetts Review, Directions in Black Studies* (Autumn 1969): 733.

25. See Nathan Hare, "The Meaning of Black Studies," *The Graduate Journal*, University of Texas at Austin, 8 (1971): 453-56.

26. Hare, "Questions and Answers About Black Studies," 727.

27. Maulana Ron Karenga, *Kawaida Theory: An Introductory Outline* (Inglewood CA: Kawaida Publications, 1980).

28. Ibid., 17.

29. Karenga, *Kawaida Theory*, 17-22; 44-46.

30. See Molefi Asante, *Afrocentricity: The Theory of Social Change* (New York: Amulefi, 1980), 5-26.

31. Donna Richards, "Implications of African-American Spirituality," in *African Culture: The Rhythms of Unity*, Molefi Asante and Kariamu Asante (Westport: Greenwood Press, 1985), 207-10.

32. "Introduction to Afro-American Studies." http://eblackstudies.org/intro/

33. "Introduction to Afro-American Studies." http://eblackstudies.org/intro/chapter1.htm

2

34. Ibid.

35. Ibid. Although Alkalimat et al.'s paradigm of unity does not constitute the foundation of the present text, readers should keep in mind the overarching role of capitalist expansion in shaping the historical narrative recounted in Chapter 3. Issues of class divisions among African Americans are addressed later in this text, particularly in Chapters 4 and 7.

36. W.E.B. Du Bois, *The Suppression of the African Slave Trade to the United States of America, 1638-1870* (New York: Schocken Books, 1969), xxxii.

37. Ibid.

38. See, for example, Kwame Appiah, *In My Father's House: Africa in the Philosophy of Culture.* (New York: Oxford University Pres, 1992) and Paul Gilroy, *The Black Atlantic: Modernity and Double-Consciousness* (Cambridge, MA: Harvard University Press, 1993).

39. Gilroy, *The Black Atlantic*, 15.

40. Darlene Clark Hine and Stephen Small, *Black Europe and the African Diaspora.* (Urbana: University of Illinois Press, 2009), 185.

41. Boris Groys, *Art Power* (Cambridge, MA: The MIT Press), 151.

42. Issues of identity are addressed primarily in Chapter 5. Creating closer connections between research and direct efforts to improve the life circumstances of people of African descent are emphasized throughout the text.

43. For a good summary of Derrida's ideas, see the *Stanford Encyclopedia of Philosophy*. http://plato.stanford.edu/entries/derrida/.

44. Groys, *Art Power*, 153.

45. W. E. B Du Bois, "Race Relations: 1917-1947," *Phylon* 9 (3), (1948): 234-247.

46. Ibid, 245.

47. Ibid, 247.

48. Jacques Ranciére, *The Politics of Aesthetics.* Translated by G. Rockhill. (New York: Continuum, 2004), 62.

49. Ranciére, *The Politics of Aesthetics*, 64-5.

50. Lisa Aubrey, "African Americans in the United States and African Studies," *African Issues* 30 (2), 2002: 19.

51. Edward Alpers and Allen Roberts, "What is African Studies? Some Reflections." *African Issues* 30 (2), 2002: 14.

52. Ibid, 14.

53. Ibid.

54. Aubrey, "African Americans in the United States and African Studies," 19.

55. Ibid, 20.

56. Ibid, 21.

57. Ibid, 22.

58. Shirley Moody-Turner and James Stewart, "Gendering Africana Studies: Insights from Anna Julia Cooper," *African American Review 43* (1), Spring 2009: 35-44.

59. Shirley Moody, "Anna Julia Cooper, Charles Chesnutt, and The Hampton Folklore Society—Constructing a Black Folk Aesthetic through Folklore and Memory," in Lovalerie King and Linda Selzer, eds., *New Essays on the African American Novel: From Hurston and Ellison to Morrison and Whitehead.* (New York: Palgrave, 2008), 18.

60. Moody, "Anna Julia Cooper, Charles Chesnutt, and The Hampton Folklore Society," 18.

61. Julia Cooper, "The Negro as Presented in American Literature" (1892) in Charles Lemert and Esme Bhan, eds., *The Voice of Anna Julia Cooper, Including A Voice from the South and Other Important Essays, Papers and Lectures* (Lanham, MD: Rowman & Littlefield, 1998), 159.

62. Cooper, "The Negro as Presented in American Literature," 159.

63. See Ronald Taylor, "The Study of Black People: A Survey of Empirical and Theoretical Models," 10-15; and Terry Kershaw, "The Emerging Paradigm in Black Studies," in Talmadge Anderson, ed., *Black Studies: Theory, Method, and Cultural Perspectives* (Pullman: Washington State University Press, 1990), 16-24.

64. See the various essays in Joyce Ladner, ed., *The Death of White Sociology* (New York: Random House, 1973).

65. Nathan Hare, "The Challenge of a Black Scholar," *Black Scholar* (December 1969): 6.

66. Duane Champagne, "Toward a Multidimensional Historical Comparative Methodology: Context, Process, and Causality," in J. Stanfield and R. Dennis, eds., *Race and Ethnicity in Research Methods* (Newbury Park, CA: Sage Publications, 1993), 253.

67. Ibid.

68. William Peterson, Michael Novak, and Philip Gleason, *Concepts of Ethnicity* (Cambridge: Belknap Press of Harvard University Press, 1982), 84-89.

69. John Ogbu, "Racial Stratification and Education," in G. Thomas, ed., *US Race Relations in the 1980s and 1990s,* (New York: Hemisphere Publishing, 1990): 15-18.

70. Maulana Karenga, *Introduction to Black Studies* (Los Angeles: Kawaida Publications, 1982), 73.

71. Saneh Chamarik, "Technological Self-reliance and Cultural Freedom," in Christopher Weeramantry, ed., *Human Rights and Scientific and Technological Development* (New York: United Nations Press, 1990), 48.

72. R. Tomovic, "Technology and Society," in Anouar Abdel-Malek, Gregory Blue, and Miroslav Pecujlic, eds., *Science and Technology in the Transformation of the World.* Proceedings of the First International Seminar on the Transformation of the World (Belgrade, Yugoslavia, October 1979), 58-59.

73. Chamarik, "Technological Self-reliance and Cultural Freedom," 49.

74. W. E. B. Du Bois, "The Beginning of Slavery," *Voice of the Negro* 2 (February 1905): 104.

2

Chapter 3

The History of Africans in America

The Primacy of History in African American Studies

Historical studies provide the foundation for all other types of inquiries in African American Studies. Maulana Karenga asserts that Black History is "indispensable to the introduction and development of all other subject areas [because it] places them in perspective, establishes their origins and development, and thus aids in critical discussion and understanding of them."[1] According to Robert Harris, the conduct of historical research within African American Studies has benefited significantly from advances in African American historiography:

Afro-American historiography, with its own conceptual and methodological concerns, is now poised to illuminate the Afro-American past in a manner that will broaden and deepen our knowledge of black people in this country. The writing of Afro-American history is no longer undertaken principally to revise the work of wrongheaded White historians, to discern divine providence, to show black participation in the nation's growth and development, to prove the inevitability of black equality, or to demonstrate the inexorable progress made by Afro-Americans. It is conducted as a distinct area of inquiry, within the discipline of history, with black people as its primary focus to reveal their thought and activities over time and place.[2]

The study of history within African American Studies incorporates the field's overarching ideological principles. As Manning Marable contends, African American Studies treats the history of African Americans as "a history of struggle rooted in the concept that human beings collectively made their own history [throughout which they] fought to maintain their unique identity as a people and to secure by whatever means, the economic and political tools for self-determination [and] self-reliance."[3]

African American Studies attempts to balance two approaches to historical research that can be described as *macro-level* and *micro-level* historiography. Most contemporary historical research examining the experiences of people of African descent is best characterized as *social history*. Social history emphasizes the examination of social structures and the interaction of different groups in society as opposed to affairs of state or national developments. Within African American Studies, micro-level social history research is framed necessarily by a macro-level master narrative that foregrounds classical and traditional Africa and that highlights the manner in which African origins and the historical experiences of African people continue to influence the circumstances of African Americans. From this perspective, macro-narrative emphasizes the impact of the trans-Atlantic slave trade on the historical and contemporary generations of Black people. Issues of cultural stability, sustainability, adaptation, and cooptation are important concepts within this framework.

The impetus within African American Studies for a micro-level historiography can be traced to a complaint raised by W. E. B. Du Bois, who claimed that "we have the record of kings and gentlemen ad nauseam and in stupid detail, but the common run of human beings, and particularly of the half or wholly submerged working group, the world has saved all too little of authentic record and tried to forget or ignore even the little saved."[4] This type of historiography utilizes different methodologies than are required for macro-level historical inquiry. Thus, Du Bois utilized participant observation and laypersons to collect case studies and first-person accounts to put flesh on the macro-level narrative that describes the modal experience of African Americans.

Within recent African American Studies historiography, important studies of local leadership and local institutions have facilitated the mobilization of everyday people to become actively engaged in the struggle for freedom and justice during the Civil Rights and Black Power movements. This research fills a critical void, but does not completely address Du Bois's concerns. Such studies of leadership must be complemented by information about the lives and motives of grassroots soldiers in the freedom struggle.

In contemporary times, Black genealogy studies can provide a vehicle for collecting valuable information about the efforts of such individuals and families to live out the version of history Marable described. Advances in genetic research are creating new opportunities for African Americans to gain more concrete information about their geographical origins than had been possible in the past. Large-scale excavation of family histories has the potential for refining the master narratives in macro-level African American Studies historiography. The growing interest in Black family reunions could constitute one venue for collecting this information.

The macro-level approach to the study of African American history requires that ancient Africa serve as the initial focus of inquiry. Importantly, it also recognizes that the study of the experiences of people of African descent within African American Studies is not an isolationist project. As Du Bois so cogently observed, "It seeks from a beginning of the history of the Negro in America and in Africa to interpret all history; from a beginning of social development among enslaved Africans and freed men in America and Negro tribes and kingdoms in Africa, to interpret and understand the social development of all mankind in all ages."[5]

The Heritage of Africa

African Civilizations Before European Domination

If the concept of civilization refers to a people who have reached a high stage of social and cultural development and who function under a high order of social organization, then early African civilizations matched and, in many aspects, surpassed the much-acclaimed civilizations of ancient Europe and Asia. Europeans perpetrated the myth that Africa had no history or civilization of world significance in order to glorify themselves and to establish White cultural hegemony over Africa and its peoples. The denigration of African history and culture also served as moral or religious justification for the trans-Atlantic slave trade and for Europe's colonization of Africa.

Africans were, in fact, among the first builders of dynamic civilizations and of great cities, city-states, kingdoms, and empires. They were also early developers of agriculture in the cultivation of soil and the planting and sowing of domestic crops. Animal domestication, iron smelting, and tool making appeared among various African populations from about 4300 to 250 BC. Africans were the forerunners or concurrent contributors to science, engineering, metallurgy, medicine, architecture, and the fine arts.

The findings of twentieth-century anthropologists and archaeologists support the theory that African peoples were the earliest fabricators of wood, stone, and other natural materials into survival tools and devices. In 1959, Louis S. B. Leakey, a noted British paleontologist, discovered the fossil remains of a prehistoric, humanlike creature in Olduvai Gorge in Tanzania, East Africa, which he named *Homo habilis*, meaning *skillful man*. The skull and teeth construction of *Homo habilis* were adapted for meat eating, which would indicate a reliance on tools or animal-killing devices. The fossil's hands had opposable thumbs and forefingers necessary for tool making.

The earliest Stone Age culture emerged in Africa, where evidence of stone or pebble-like tools has been found throughout the continent. Because *Homo habilis* dates back over two million years, scientists believe that humans or humankind began in Africa and migrated to Asia, Europe, and other regions of the world. Before Leakey's discovery of *Homo habilis*, scientists thought that humankind began in Asia because the fossil remains of Peking Man and Java Man were excavated from that continent. We do not know precisely when Africans became regular users of fire, but objects or devices made of iron have been found in Egypt dating as early as 2000 BC. Rock paintings, etchings, and engravings of animals and other figures discovered in several African countries reveal the expressive cultures of prehistoric African societies. Historical and contemporary research and discoveries attest to the early evolution of African civilization.[6]

Given the undeniably advanced civilization of the Egyptians, White historians have attempted to claim Egypt as an extension of European culture. Obviously, the question or point of concern for Europeans is the race or color of the Egyptians. If the ancient Egyptians were Black—in the context of contemporary conceptions of race—the European myth of African intellectual inferiority would be invalidated. The ancient Egyptians, however, were of mixed racial stock, with physical and genetic characteristics of both Africans and Europeans. Nonetheless, Greek writers and philosophers described the Egyptians as Black. Drawings, etchings, and sculptures discovered by archaeologists and other researchers reveal the Egyptians as exhibiting mostly so-called Negroid features, although it may be argued that some also show European and Asian characteristics. The Sphinx displays the image of a Pharaoh with the head of a Black man.

The massive migration of Black Ethiopians during the time of the Hyksos invasion (c. 1700-1500 BC) made Egypt more African than ever. *Ethiopian* was the name the ancient Greeks used to describe Africans of dark hue. The word *Ethios* means *burnt*; and the word *ops* refers to the face—thus, *burnt faces*. Ethiopians eventually dominated the political life and organizations of Egypt. By the eighth century BC, Ethiopia had gained complete control of Egypt and ruled over it for more than a century until Egypt was conquered by the Assyrians.

Black people therefore contributed significantly to the ingenious achievements of ancient Egypt. The Egyptians invented writing with a form of alphabet. They made paper from plants and developed ink from the juices of various plants. They are most noted for the construction of the Great Pyramids (tombs) and other monuments, the preservation of the dead through embalming, and the invention of the calendar as well as their contributions to mathematics. They

also were advanced in the use of metals and the creation of jewelry and objects from gold and silver.

Egypt may have been populated by racially mixed peoples, but it was, and remains, culturally and geographically an integral part of Africa. The Black or African cultural influence permeated Egyptian civilization. Although the achievements of the Egyptians have received much focus and credit over the centuries, the African nations to the south of Egypt—Kush, Nubia, and Ethiopia, among them–developed advanced civilizations independent of Egyptian influence. Indeed, these nations contributed to and participated in the cultural and technological achievements of Egypt.

Throughout the span of human existence, trade and other forms of commerce have flourished where ready access to waterways or established land routes existed. Such economic activity has been a primary factor in the formation of villages, towns, cities, states, nations, or empires. Ancient Africa followed this natural course in the development of sociopolitical and geographical units that produced various cultures and civilizations. The phenomenal development of Egypt or Northeast Africa may be attributed to the transitory and migratory nature of the peoples who traveled within the fluctuating borders of the nations there and who influenced the area externally. Geographically, Egypt was located at the crossroads leading from Asia and Europe into Africa. The Nile River connected it economically and socially with southeastern African nations and kingdoms. Egypt's productive agricultural economy derived from the fertile land of the overflowing Nile. The gold mines below the First Cataract of the Nile provided the sources of wealth necessary for the development of a great civilization. Commerce flourished and attracted not only Africans from the south but also European traders from the north via the Mediterranean Sea and Asians from the Red Sea. However, it was gold that drew Caucasian peoples to the area from many countries, near and far. As the numbers of White and Asiatic peoples increased in Egypt, the fortune and status of Blacks declined.[7]

The development of African civilizations was not limited to Egypt and northeastern Africa. Social, political, agricultural, and commercial development of northern interior and western Africa occurred contemporaneously with that of Egypt and with territories along the Nile. Carthage, a city-state established by the Phoenicians in the year 814 BC, was a major trading post and entrepôt in the western Mediterranean Sea before and after its conquest by the Romans in 146 BC. Commerce was the foundation of the Carthaginian economy, and traders practiced a unique form of silent bartering with Africans in the interior. Carthaginians sought to establish markets along the Atlantic coast of Africa, but the extent to which they were successful is not known.

The western Sudan abounded in gold, ivory, and various agricultural products from Lake Chad to the Atlantic. Trade routes were established along the Atlantic coast of Africa and, as a result, numerous African groups, villages, towns, and cities emerged from the Western Sahara to Equatorial Guinea. Goods and products originating in the west and western Sudan were sold to North African Berbers, who, in turn, traded them with Europeans and Asians. For the most part, gold was their principal export; and they imported salt, skins, cloth, jewelry, weapons, and metal cooking utensils.

Africa is a vast, topographically varied continent with a complex human population. The history of its peoples and of its development of its thousands of ancient cities, kingdoms, and empires would require hundreds of volumes. The preceding and following discussions reveal that, prior to the European conquest and imposition of the slave trade, progressive and dynamic African civilizations existed that contributed immensely to the development of world society. The ancestral roots of most African Americans, however, likely can be traced to West Africa because this is the region where most enslaved Africans bound for the Americas were captured, purchased, and dispatched. Consequently, this text will highlight three great Western Sudan or West African empires that rose and declined from the beginning of the eighth to the end of the eighteenth century. Some historians refer to this period as the Golden Age of West Africa.

Ghana

The ancient kingdom of Ghana is one of the oldest and most significant West African political states. The date of its origin is not known precisely; however, the recovered records do show that more than forty-four kings had ruled Ghana successively by the year 300 AD. Located in the western Sudan northeast of the Senegal River and northwest of the Niger River, the Ghanaian empire at its height spanned the territory that presently encompasses Mali, Guinea, the Gambia,

Senegal, and a portion of Mauritania. The territorial expansion of the Ghanaian empire resulted mostly from peaceful alliances with neighboring cities and states, but there were some conquests.

The Ghanaians were an agricultural and trading people. The country was located strategically along the trans-Saharan trade routes. Gold was the principal commodity that contributed to Ghana's wealth and power. Although Ghana may not have had complete control of the Wangara gold mines where the gold was produced, it reaped immense profits through the levying of import and export taxes on traders passing through Ghanaian territories. Gold was so abundant that it was decreed that only the king could possess gold bars and that the people could use only the gold dust. This was necessary to circumvent the erosion or depreciation of the value of gold. Gold was the primary medium of exchange, but salt, a product not plentiful in Ghana, was also valuable and used for exchange purposes.

The economy of Ghana was diversified. Gold was not the only metal it produced and from which it benefited. Ghana had engaged in iron mining and manufacturing for over a thousand years before the Europeans came to Africa. The presence of skilled iron workers enabled formation of a powerful, large army equipped with awesome weapons that intimidated neighboring countries and potential enemies. Besides having astute traders and merchants, Ghana also had expert craftsmen, including goldsmiths, blacksmiths, coppersmiths, potters, cloth weavers, stone smiths, carpenters, and furniture makers. Ghana was a trading empire that sold agricultural, consumer, and commercial products as well as slaves. Slavery to the Ghanaians, however, was different in both meaning and practice from that of the institutionalized European and American slavery practiced from the sixteenth to the nineteenth centuries.

During the year 1062 AD, a Muslim religious sect called the *Almoravides*, invaded Ghana to force its people to convert to Islam. The Ghanaian empire resisted for more than ten years, but in 1077, the capital city of Kumbi fell to the invaders. The Almoravides Muslim movement disintegrated when their leader died in 1087, but dissonance among its former member states and the destructive effects of the Almoravides prevented Ghana from restoring its empire. By the year 1240, Ghana entered into a period of economic decline that was compounded by a series of droughts.

Mali

Following the destruction and decline of Ghana, small kingdoms formerly under the Ghanaian empire competed for its wealth and position in the Western Sudan. The Black kingdom of Mali emerged as the strongest organized state in the year 1235, but the origin of Mali dates back to the seventh century AD. Unlike Ghana, Mali's kings (called *mansas*) embraced the Muslim religion, which served to strengthen its ties with the Islamic world. Though the Mali rulers adopted Islam, the masses of the Malian people retained their traditional beliefs. Nevertheless, Sundiata, the king of Mali, formed alliances with neighboring Muslim rulers and soon became the most influential and powerful person in West Africa. He subdued all of the smaller states—Kaniaga, Diara, Soso, and Galam—that formerly constituted Ghana and took control of the gold mining regions of Wangara. Mali was primarily an agricultural economy, yet there was a substantial skilled craft sector that included weaving, dyeing, tanning, blacksmithery, and the smithing of gold, silver, and copper.

Mansa Musa I, a successor to Sundiata, made the Mali empire renowned in Africa, the Middle East, and Europe. In 1324, Mansa Musa made a historic pilgrimage to Mecca. The journey was unusual because it was possibly the first time a Black Sudanese king traveled from western Africa through Egypt to Mecca. The Mansa Musa's entourage to Mecca comprised more than seventy thousand persons, including soldiers, logistical personnel, and servants. They brought with them twelve tons of gold borne by eighty camels. The Mansa Musa gratuitously distributed gold and gifts to his hosts and to prominent citizens along the way. Islamic scholars, including es-Saheli, a poet and architect, accompanied him on his return. Es-Saheli supervised the construction of several magnificent temples and buildings throughout the empire and especially in Timbuktu. These massive edifices helped to demonstrate the power and prestige of the Mali empire.

The geographical expanse of the Mali empire was equivalent to that of western Europe. It encompassed what later became French West Africa, including Senegal, the Gambia, Mali, and parts of Nigeria and Upper Volta. The empire of Mali began to decline by 1550. It was weakened by the incursions of the Songhay, attacks from the Mossi, and the malicious designs of the Portuguese.

Songhay

The rise and fall of the Songhay empire are particularly significant because at its apex Songhay was the most highly advanced society on the African continent. Its destruction set in motion events that would pave the way for the Atlantic slave trade and the myth that African peoples lacked civilization. Contrary to common belief, Africans were among the first people to foster the idea of the university. They were learned in literature, art, and the sciences long before the continent came under the influence of Western European culture. The kingdom of Songhay probably began in the early eighth century, at Gao, a somewhat centrally located city in the Western Sudan. However, its emergence as a kingdom capable of challenging the empire of Mali did not occur until the fifteenth century. Mali and Songhay had been parts of the Ghanaian domain. Following the decline of Ghana, Songhay had developed into a formidable kingdom and became a matter of concern to the Mansa Musa of the established empire of Mali. When the Mansa Musa returned from his pilgrimage to Mecca, he visited the captured city of Gao and took two sons of the king of Songhay as hostages to assure the loyalty of Songhay to Mali. After the death of the Mansa Musa, one son escaped and founded the Sunni dynasty in 1355 that subsequently challenged and brought about the downfall of the Mali empire.

Sunni Ali, a succeeding Songhay monarch, conquered and incorporated most of the cities and kingdoms of the former Malian empire and of the Niger region, which included Timbuktu and Jenne. These two cities, established during the Malian empire, had already become renowned educational centers; Timbuktu was the home to the University of Sankore. After conquering the kingdom of Mali, Songhay became the dominant and most revered empire in West Africa.

When Sunni Ali died in a drowning accident in 1492, his son, who was not a devout Muslim, succeeded him on the throne. The son's failure to convert to Islam led to his dethronement, and Askia Mohammed, a Muslim general, became the ruler of Songhay. Askia Mohammed, an exceptionally competent ruler, continued Sunni Ali's vision of conquest and expansion. He brought the Mossi territory in Upper Volta and most of the seven Hausa States of contemporary Nigeria under his rule.

3

As a devout Muslim, Mohammed made a pilgrimage to Mecca in similar style and fashion as the Mansa Musa of Mali had done in 1324. He returned with a host of Islamic scholars, teachers, scientists, and professionals to aid him in building an efficient centralized administration and in developing cultural and intellectual centers of education in Timbuktu, Jenne, and other major cities throughout the Songhay empire. The establishment of schools, colleges, and universities, and the resurrection of Black learning, was the significant contribution that the Songhay empire made to African peoples. The University of Sankore at Timbuktu offered courses in law, literature, astronomy, medicine, music, mathematics, and other subject areas that constitute modern school and college curricula. The university and other schools in the empire attracted students and scholars from all over Africa, the Middle East, and Europe.

Besides deriving benefits from achievements in education and scholarship, the Songhay empire consolidated the agricultural, trade, and commercial interests of the former empires of Ghana and Mali. It became the economic hub of Western Africa, but a series of destructive events led to the decline and fall of the empire of Songhay. Askia Mohammed's eldest son dethroned him, and civil wars and Moroccan invasions so weakened Songhay that recovery of its former glory was impossible. The Moroccans had a smaller army than Songhay, but they were aided by Spanish mercenaries with firearms. Together, the invaders defeated the Songhay army. They plundered and destroyed the established educational institutions, including the libraries and original works of many scholars, but the ruins of the University of Sankore still stand in the Mali Republic.

The number of early African cities, kingdoms, and empires—and the extent and quality of their civilizations—are not limited to the northeastern, northern, and the western Sudan regions of the African continent. Several states rose and declined in the fifteenth century among the Hausa people in the region east of Songhay that now constitutes the nation of Nigeria in modern Africa. The Kanem-Bornu empire, which existed under King Idris Alooma between 1580 and 1617, encroached on the Hausa states east and west of Lake Chad. Several Black kingdoms also developed south of the Sudan along the Guinea coast in the thirteenth and fourteenth centuries. These kingdoms included the forest states of Dahomey, Ife, Oyo,

and Benin. The kingdom of the Congo, a confederation of several smaller states, comprised the area south from the mouth of the Congo River. It was one of the first African regions to come under the influence and domination of Europeans. African peoples south of the Congo founded kingdoms in the region of South Africa that included the Zulu, Basuto, Khoi, and San peoples. Medieval East African states developed, and civilizations emerged in much the same manner as in northern and western Africa. (Selected major developments in African history, many of which have been discussed in previous sections of this volume, are summarized in Table 3.1.)

African civilizations—like those of European, Asian, and other cultures of the world—developed unique characteristics that reflected the specific influences of climate and environment. Not all pre-European or pre-colonial African peoples were racially or ethnically homogeneous; however, significant similarities existed across groups in terms of their collective psyches and philosophical, ideological, and cultural worldviews. This common worldview reflected Africa's unique climates, rivers, desert, mountains, lakes, flora, and fauna. The imperialistic intrusion of the Europeans and the cultural hegemony imposed upon Black peoples further strengthened the common thread of African unity. All of these factors contributed to what modern Black social theorists describe as an Afrocentric worldview with regard to the unity of origin and the common struggle of African peoples.

Contrary to Western European notions, ancient Africa was rich in its own traditions of religion, philosophy, creative arts, and literature. African religious beliefs and customs prior to and independent of Islam were comparable to those of other peoples of the world. Many African societies embraced common beliefs in deism or mythologies of creation and animistic worship. The most widespread indigenous religious practices of Africans typically included veneration of ancestors.

Africans believed that the spirits of their ancestors exercised surveillance and influence over their daily lives. Despite the heterogeneity of ancient Black states and peoples, there existed a collective African philosophy that was transmitted from generation to generation, written and unwritten. Just as in Europe and Asia, there were great African philosophers in Egypt, the Western Sudan, and in southern and eastern Africa. These great thinkers expounded and prophesied on life, death, love, beauty, good, evil, and other aspects of human reality. Oral literature in the form of proverbs, parables, folktales, short stories, myths, and legends abounded throughout Africa. Literature, art, music, and dance served functional purposes in African societies.

TABLE 3.1
ABBREVIATED TIMELINE OF AFRICAN HISTORY
PRIOR TO THE ATLANTIC SLAVE TRADE

4 million BC	Earliest humans in East Africa
c. 2000 BC	Agriculture is developed in the Niger River Valley
3200–30 BC:	**Ancient Egypt**
3100-2686 BC	The Early Dynastic Period
2686-2181 BC	The Old Kingdom
2181-2040 BC	The First Intermediate Period
2133-1786 BC	The Middle Kingdom
1786-1567 BC	The Second Intermediate Period
1567-1085 BC	The New Kingdom
1085-341 BC	The Late Dynastic Period
332-30 BC	The Ptolemaic Period
200 BC–AD 400:	**Urbanization South of the Sahara**
c. 100 BC	Introduction of ironw-working in the area south of Sudan by the Bantu people
AD 1	Beginnings of the East African city-states
AD 100	Beginnings of Bantu migration
AD 400	Founding of the urban center Jenne-Jeno in Nigeria
400–1500:	**Kingdoms and Empires**
300-700	Kingdom of Axum
c. 900	Beginnings of the Sudanese kingdoms
c. 900-1100	Kingdom of Ghana
c. 1200	Beginning of the Hausa city-states
c. 1200-1450	Kingdom of Mali
900s-1400s	Great Zimbabwe
c. 1450	Oyo empire founded
1460-1591	Songhay empire

Source: This abbreviated version of the African History Timeline was developed by David W. Koeller as part of Northpark University's Web Chronology Project, WebChron, (*http://campus.northpark. edu/history/WebChron/Africa/Africa.html*).

The dynamic, but in some ways stifling, influence of Islam did not significantly affect the lay or common peoples of ancient Africa. Their leaders, kings, and dynastic rulers may have subscribed to or adopted the Muslim religion for economic and political benefits, but they did not use excessive force to convert subjects. In fact, Islamic religious practices generally fostered egalitarianism and, in a reciprocal way, enhanced the educational and economic conditions of Blacks. On the other hand, Christianity, as it was introduced to Africa by Europeans, claimed the doctrine of equality in theory while practicing Black domination and White supremacy in reality.[8]

Pre-colonial Africans functioned under similar traditions of social organization, religion, political structure, judicial practice, and arts creation. Throughout most of Africa, the family, community, village, state, and kingdom were formed and functioned under a hierarchal system of kinship. The kinship and amalgamated kinship systems of pre-colonial Africa were rigid institutions. Kinship lines were often the basis of political rule or dynasty. Agricultural production and guild practice (e.g., in the arts and crafts) also followed the lines of the kinship system through the extended family.

In the pre-colonial kinship system, an individual had little status or security outside the family clan. The family was the beginning, nucleus, and basis of social organization. Various African groups and nations practiced patrilineal or matrilineal family systems of authority and descent in accordance with their ethnic and cultural traditions. Polygamy was a functional family pattern in most societies, but socially imposed economic conditions discouraged its widespread practice. The monogamous nuclear familial structure did not become a social standard until after the European Christian influence came to dominate the African continent.

Before the imperialistic and hegemonic intrusion of Europeans into Africa, Black societies and kingdoms possessed all the elements that Europeans ascribe to civilization. Yet, for centuries, European historians wrote of world civilizations without acknowledging the existence of any civilizations in Africa except that of Egypt. Even today, White scholars and historians deny or reluctantly admit the Black and African ancestry of the Egyptians. The truth of the matter, however, is that in antiquity Africa gave to Europe and the rest of the world as much as it had received in terms of culture and civilization.[9]

Background and Beginning of the Atlantic Slave Trade

Slavery, the subjugation of a group by another to perform work or services without pay or compensation, has existed throughout human history. Slavery existed many millennia before the Middle Ages in Europe, Asia, and Africa; however, ancient practices of slavery were not based specifically on the race or color of individuals or groups. Whites, Blacks, and other peoples not only enslaved individuals from other groups but also members of their own groups. For the most part and prior to 1500 AD, European and African traders and merchants negotiated and traded in gold, agricultural products, and slaves without regard to the color or race of the latter as a fundamental factor or social condition of enslavement. Persons conscripted into slavery generally were captives who had been conquered or subjugated as a result of intergroup and intragroup conflicts or warfare. No particular systematic or automatic subordinate social or political role was assigned to Africans because of their race or color, but discrimination based on myriad factors—including religion, myths, and stereotypes—would eventually lead to the designation of Africans as the primary victims of enslavement.

Slavery in any form is cruel and oppressive, but ancient slave customs and practices generally were more humane than the human bondage practiced during and after the sixteenth century. Prior to that time, slaves were often of the same race and nationality as their slaveholders. In some societies, slave status had a limited term or specified tenure. Slaves could purchase their freedom; and they could, and often did, intermarry with their slave masters. They could own property and possessed certain rights as human beings. However, the basis, nature, and character of early slavery were changed drastically by the European incursion into Africa.

The economic development of Europe and the Americas was spurred from the fourteenth until the early nineteenth century by the exploitation of Africa and Africans. A more succinct statement is that Europe and the Americas were developed at the cost of the underdevelopment of Africa.[10] Several European peoples including the English, Portuguese, French, Spanish, Dutch, and Swedes participated in and profited from the rape of Africa's physical resources and the marketing of Black human bodies. Portugal may have been in the vanguard of this activity, but eventually England and the United States of America would emerge as the principal beneficiaries and leaders of the Atlantic slave trade.

Prince Henry "the Navigator," a member of the Portuguese royal family, was primarily responsible for opening up West Africa for exploitation and for revealing its substantial material resources and economic potential to Europeans. Prince Henry's preoccupation with oceanic navigation or the maritime arts led to the unprecedented exploration of Africa by Europeans that eventually resulted in the Atlantic slave trade. Henry had learned, from participants in the school for sailors that he had established, about the trade routes of the Western Sudan leading to the great city of Timbuktu and about the legendary gold mines of Wangara. Portugal was perhaps the most familiar with northwest Africa bordering the Atlantic because of its historical military encounters with the Muslims and Berbers. Having either defeated or made peace with Islamic forces, the Portuguese were heady with the prospect of foreign exploration in Africa.

The Portuguese developed sturdy, easily navigable ships called *caravels* that facilitated their raiding of the West African coast in their search for gold and adventure. After numerous failed attempts at penetrating beyond the coast of Morocco, one of the Portuguese voyages was successful in sailing beyond the Western Sahara and reporting the discovery of people and cities to Prince Henry. In 1441, a Portuguese caravel brought back a few captives that included Black Africans. As Portuguese expeditions went farther south towards the coast of Guinea, they were encouraged to seize and return with more Black captives.

In 1444, Lancarote, a Portuguese captain, planned and executed a series of kidnapping raids off the coast of Guinea and brought back over two hundred African men, women, and children to Portugal. The Africans were sold at public auction. Oliver Ransford, a scholar of the African slave trade, writes of this event:

> August 1444 remains one of the saddest dates in the history of man—white as well as black—and we are still paying for what followed that auction in the meadow outside Lagos. For the profit made that morning by Lancarote's sailors and the enormous financial potential it disclosed, committed western Europe to the continuance of this trade in human flesh.[11]

England's ascendancy to a world power began near the end of the fifteenth century after the reign of Elizabeth I. Wars and domestic disorganization initially prevented England from participating competitively in the exploration of Africa and the so-called New World. (The term *New World* applies to the European perception of the Americas and the West Indies; obviously, the land was not new to its original inhabitants.) However, after the defeat of the Spanish Armada and Henry VIII's unification of England under Protestantism during the early fifteenth century, the British were prepared to challenge the naval and commercial interests of Portugal, Spain, France, and other European nations.

England moved aggressively during the sixteenth century to establish colonies in the West Indies and in North America. English and French plantation colonies produced tobacco as a major cash crop until the market price fell and thus created the need for a new product for diversification. The Dutch introduced sugar to the French and English colonies and developed a profitable and booming world market for sugar. Sugar cultivation in the West Indies was a major factor and rationale for the development of the Atlantic slave trade.

Sugar production required large capital outlays, extensive land areas, and many laborers. Consequently, the number of European settlers and planters in the West Indies were insufficient to fertilize, grow, weed, harvest, and process the cane into sugar. To sustain the commercial and industrial revitalization of Europe, the colonizers did not hesitate to demand enslaved Africans to help them solve their labor problem. All the European colonizers of the West Indies, North America, and South America resorted to slavery as the solution.

Spain and Portugal played prominent roles in establishing beliefs that endorsed the large-scale enslavement of Africans. Portugal's military conflicts with the dark-skinned Muslim Moors of northwest Africa resulted in the capture of many Africans and their relegation to serfdom or enslavement. Although color or race may not have been the basic reason for their denigrating treatment of Africans, black skin soon became a symbol of subordinate status for the Portuguese. Elsewhere in Europe, domestic servitude and slavery without regard to race or color was common. Indeed, the systems of slavery of medieval Europe, Asia, and Africa prior to the heightening of the Atlantic slave trade were more humane. Slaves were vested with certain rights and often became simply menial residents of an estate or were freed after a predetermined tenure of servitude. However, the existence of these relatively less permanent variations of slavery does not in any way diminish or condone the basic incompatibility of the institution with modern conceptions of human rights and dignity.[12]

The critical role of the Spanish and Portuguese in the initial phases of the trans-Atlantic slave trade was diminished after the discovery of North America and the West Indies. The English, French, and White American settlers then assumed the leading role in the trade, creating a racist system as they sought to exploit rich new agricultural resources. Europeans subsequently employed a number of specious moral arguments of racial inferiority based on color to rationalize the enslavement of African people. The Protestant and Catholic clergy, for example, sanctioned slavery on religious grounds—that is, they maintained that the "heathen" Africans needed to be brought under the influence of Christendom and civilized for their salvation's sake. The real or underlying motive for the enslavement of Africans, however, was the economic and industrial development of Europe, which was substantially based and dependent on the plantation economies of the New World and the West Indies.

England benefited substantially more from African slavery than did other European countries. During the seventeenth century, the British slave colonies produced more than a fourth of all British imports and exports of merchandise and agricultural products. Thus, the British economy was highly dependent on slavery. Slavery spurred the development of Europe and in time the United States. New markets, produce, materials, and lands were required to sustain the new commercial renaissance and expansionist designs of the Europeans. These needs and demands created a market for enslaved Africans and thus the intensification of the Atlantic slave trade.[13]

The actual number of captive Africans transported to the Americas and the West Indies cannot be determined. A consensus of findings, however, even from modest estimates, suggests that at least ten million survived the voyage. Millions more were murdered, died from sickness, or committed suicide during the period of the trans-Atlantic slave trade, which extended for more than four centuries.

Few will deny that some African chiefs or rulers were complicit with Europeans in the initial stages of African slavery. War captives and criminals detained in some African societies were exchanged with Europeans for trinkets and other valuables. The greed that influenced African chiefs to cooperate with European slave traders is humanly inexcusable but few, if any, of

59

the chiefs or co-conspirators could have known of the unprecedented inhuman and cruel system of enslavement that awaited their African kinsmen in the New World. When African societies awakened and became conscious of the magnitude and horrors of slave marketing for their own societies, it was too late.

The naval, military, and weapons superiority of the Europeans rendered Africans helpless to end the trade. The English, French, and Dutch established trading posts or forts along the coast of West Africa to facilitate and defend their sordid business. The British, for example, invented the highly efficient and profitable triangular trade process, a three-way system of profit. It worked this way: Africans were bought on the African Gold Coast with New England rum and then traded in the West Indies for sugar or molasses, which was brought back to New England to be manufactured into rum. If the demand and markets for sugar, tobacco, cotton, and condiments had not existed, slavery on such a vast scale would not have developed. If morality had triumphed over markets, there would have been no slave trade. The slave colonies of the New World existed to supply goods to the mother countries that the colonial powers could not produce or provide for themselves.

It would be difficult to imagine the terror, horror, and suffering that African captives experienced awaiting embarkation to points unknown and to uncertain fates. African captives were herded, chained, branded, and guarded while waiting for slave ships to stop at the European commercial depots or forts located along the West African coast from Senegal to Angola. The captives were of various backgrounds, languages, and cultures. Not all were prisoners of war or incarcerated offenders, however. Many were farmers, merchants, artisans, members of rival royal families, and common people captured especially for the slave trade. Most were acquired along the coastal regions, but many were marched coastward from the deep interior of the African forests. It is generally assumed that the majority of African Americans originated from West Africa, but it remains practically impossible to determine any Black American's precise state, city, or clan of origin.

On the voyage to the New World, Blacks were packed like sardines below the main decks of the slave vessels and chained together by their legs, wrists, or necks. Sickness and epidemics often afflicted both the enslaved African cargo and the ships' crews. Extreme heat compounded the foulness of the air on board the

ships. Naked captive African men and women lay for hours and days in their own defecation, blood, and mucus, which covered the floors. Thousands committed suicide or died from harsh and cruel treatment and punishment while in transit from Africa to the New World. Resistance, revolt, and mutiny were not uncommon, and thousands died in such attempts. The estimate is that only one out of five enslaved Africans survived the voyage.

The trans-Atlantic slave trade was a system founded on human cruelty and exploitation. It was motivated by economic greed, social deviance, and psychological and moral turpitude. European capitalists sought the least costly sources of labor, and they and their supporters concocted religious and social justifications to support the barbaric practices that bolstered that system. Ironically, justifications for slavery involved designating Africans as savage, uncivilized heathens. These stereotypes were increasingly promoted as the volume of trade in Africans increased. Interestingly, the decline of the empire of Songhay and of its University of Sankore at Timbuktu, one of Africa's greatest academic and intellectual civilizations, coincided with the mounting slave trade.

The best available evidence indicates that approximately 11.3 million enslaved Africans arrived in the Western Hemisphere between 1450 and 1867. Only about 3.5 percent of this total were captured and transported between 1450 and 1600. Another twelve percent of the victims of the trade were introduced into the Western hemisphere between 1601 and 1700. The majority of enslaved Africans that survived the voyage found themselves in the Western hemisphere between 1701 and 1800, with another thirty-one percent being forcefully introduced to the Western hemisphere between 1801 and 1867.

The year 1680 is from the original source and was determined by data availability. All African Americans in these colonies even in those where slavery was legal in 1680 were enslaved. Table 3.2 shows the relationship between the year in which slavery was legalized in each of the American colonies and the size of the African American population in those colonies in 1680. The legalization of slavery was clearly associated with increases in the size of the African American population. However, it is important to remember that free persons were also present in all of the colonies even after the legalization of slavery.

TABLE 3.2
A COMPARISON OF THE YEAR IN WHICH
SLAVERY WAS LEGALIZED IN EACH OF THE AMERICAN
COLONIES AND THE SIZE OF THE AFRICAN AMERICAN
POPULATION, BY COLONY

Colony	Year Slavery was Legalized	Number of African Americans in Each Colony by 1680
Connecticut	1650	50
Delaware	1721	55
Georgia	1755	0
Maryland	1663–64	1,611
Massachusetts	1641	170
New Hampshire	1714	75
New Jersey	1702	200
New York	1655	8,996
North Carolina	1715	210
Pennsylvania	1700	200
Rhode Island	1703	175
South Carolina	1682	200
Virginia	1661	3,000

Source: Schomburg Center for Research in Black Culture, *The Atlantic Slave Trade: Migration Resources*, http://www.inmotionaame.org/gallery/detail.cfm?migration=1&topic=1&id=1_005M&type=map

African Bondage and Oppression in America

The Institution of Slavery in America: 1619–1783

Africans began a horrid period of servitude and enslavement in what is now the United States in 1619 in Jamestown, Virginia. Historians note, however, that the first twenty Blacks who disembarked from the Dutch vessel moored at the Jamestown port were actually indentured servants and not slaves. Nevertheless, most writers concur that the Africans were brought to the English colony of Virginia against their will. The available documents further suggest that they had been captured by Dutch privateers, sold to the colonial government, and then distributed among the White settlers. If those Africans were indentured servants, it simply meant that they had a binding and legal obligation to work for another person until their fixed term of indenture expired. Given that probably no records exist of their eventual disposition or fate, they may have become free at some time in their lives.

A fine line of distinction must be drawn between involuntary servitude and enslavement, especially when human beings are captured, transported, and sold against their free will. When the twenty Africans arrived in Jamestown, no formal recognition or authorization of slavery existed. Laws authorizing enslavement, *per se*, would not to be enacted until forty years later.

A few years prior to 1619, the settlers of the colony of Virginia had discovered the profitability of raising and exporting tobacco to England. Tobacco cultivation required sizable tracts of land and a large labor force. Consequently, hundreds of White voluntary and involuntary workers and servants were shipped to the colonies from England. Plantations in the various regions of the South developed around different base crops: tobacco in Virginia and Maryland, rice or indigo in South Carolina, and sugar in the West Indies. The colonial government allotted fifty acres of land per servant or worker to the planters or settlers. The more servants a settler could acquire, the more land he could acquire.

White indentured servants provided only a temporary source of labor because the term of their indentures was fixed at five or seven years. Efforts to force Native Americans into involuntary labor were unsuccessful. Native Americans who fought unsuccessfully against the English colonists were captured and reduced to involuntary servitude. However, they proved unsuitable for plantation labor because their familiarity with the local environment enabled them to escape from enslavement. Their susceptibility to diseases introduced by Europeans also made them unsuitable for servitude. The involuntary arrival of Africans in 1619 was timely and opportune for the settlers. Millions of Africans would follow those initial twenty to America, and their status as slaves and their treatment as such would become more clearly defined by colonial law.[14]

The influx of millions of Africans into the southern colonies of America occurred partly as the result of the difficult circumstances England faced in the West Indies and the Caribbean. For decades, England had reigned supreme and prospered handsomely from sugar production on its West Indian and Caribbean island plantations. The English brought millions of captive Africans to British colonies in Barbados, Jamaica, Bermuda, the Bahamas, Trinidad, and other islands. They imported millions more to the Spanish islands of Cuba and Puerto Rico and to the islands colonized by the French, including Guadeloupe and Martinique. The eventual result was a surplus of enslaved Africans in these locations, as enslaved populations outnumbered slaveholders on hundreds of plantations. Consequently, uprisings, revolts, and runaways among the enslaved became epidemic.

The most inhumane, brutal, and cruel punishments imaginable were inflicted on Black men, women, and children in an effort to control the soaring African populations. Enslaved Africans were burned, whipped, and hanged. Their tongues and noses were often slit. Owners used clubs to break their arms, legs, and backs in order to demonstrate their might, but such sadistic and inhumane treatment did not stem the tide of insurrection and runaways. Some of the enslaved Africans escaped into the forests and mountains and repelled the European military expeditions sent to reclaim them. These escapees, called *maroons,* often won their independence in this manner. Other slave insurrectionist groups were also successful in achieving independence.[15] The problems of slave control and Anglo-French conflict in the West Indies and Caribbean were compounded by a glut of sugar in the market. This situation led England to direct more attention to its North American colonies. When the prosperity of the West Indies and Caribbean declined, millions of Africans from these British possessions were relocated to the North American colonies.

Africans brought to the southern American colonies were immediately relegated to a status subordinate to the indentured servant. Because they were Black, conspicuously different, and could not blend in with the Native American or White indentured servants, the latter of whom were physically indistinguishable from the White settlers, escape was extremely difficult. The colonists realized very early that it was much more profitable and convenient to conscript Africans into slavery to satisfy the ever-increasing demand for cheap labor. Thus, slavery soon was regarded as a permanent solution to their labor problems. As St. Clair Drake and other scholars have pointed out, racial slavery *per se* may not have originated in the American southern colonies, but the American practice of confining slavery and perpetual servitude exclusively to Blacks, of forbidding their assimilation into New World societies, and of predicating African subjugation on an ideology of White supremacy revolutionized world traditions of human bondage.

If there was any ambivalence on the part of the Virginia colony regarding the status and treatment of the initial Africans on American soil, it was soon resolved. By the year 1750, slavery was recognized and sanctioned by law in all the American colonies. These laws clearly differentiated the status and treatment of enslaved Blacks from other classes of servants. Especially in the southern colonies, enslaved Africans had no rights except those arbitrarily determined by individual slave masters. Blacks, their children, and future descendants were purchased and sold into perpetual enslavement as chattel property with no legal rights as human beings. Table 3.3 shows the African American population of each of the American colonies by 1750.

TABLE 3.3
SIZE OF THE AFRICAN AMERICAN POPULATION IN THE AMERICAN COLONIES BY 1750, BY COLONY

Colony	African American Population in 1750
Connecticut	2,598
Delaware	1,035
Georgia	1,000
Maryland	24,031
Massachusetts	3,035
New Hampshire	500
New Jersey	4,366
New York	8,996
North Carolina	11,000
Pennsylvania	2,063
Rhode Island	2,408
South Carolina	30,000
Virginia	60,000

Source: Schomburg Center for Research in Black Culture, *The Atlantic Slave Trade: Migration Resources,* http://www.inmotionaame.org/gallery/detail.cfm?migration=1&topic=1&id=1_005M&type=map

The condition, treatment, and experience endured by enslaved Blacks in each colony or colonial region depended on myriad domestic and international economic and commercial factors. The cultivation of tobacco, cotton, rice, indigo, timber, pitch, and turpentine in Maryland, Virginia, the Carolinas, and Georgia was labor-intensive and differed substantially from agricultural and more industrialized economic activities in the middle and New England colonies. Furthermore, the intensity and severity of the work imposed on enslaved Africans were related largely to market demands in England for specialized crops and products. The British economy depended heavily on plantation colonies and the increased use of the labor of the enslaved. Not only were tobacco, cotton, and other commodities produced for export to England, but complementary and reciprocal markets also developed among the southern, middle, and New England colonies. The American colonies provided products to each other that each could not produce independently in sufficient quantities to satisfy domestic consumption demands.[16]

Regional differences in the commercial and industrial economies and in the social traditions of the American colonies resulted in some degree of variation in the treatment of slaves after 1750. For example, labor requirements in the non-agriculturally based or more commercial-industrialized economies of the Middle and New England colonies contrasted vastly with the labor-intensive agricultural plantations of the South. The nature of much of the work in the colonies north of Maryland required that the slaves possess limited reading ability and education, which induced a somewhat less oppressive variant of slavery.

The religious influence of the Quakers and Puritans also contributed to the evolution of a comparatively milder form of slavery in the Middle and New England colonies. The English Quakers of the Middle colonies constantly tried to improve the plight of enslaved Blacks by providing them with religious education and by promoting antislavery sentiment among colonists. This was particularly true in Pennsylvania, Delaware, and New Jersey. Consequently, the enslaved populations in these three colonies never reached significant proportions. The New York colony maintained the strictest and harshest slave system of the Middle colonies. During the early seventeenth century, slave codes were enacted in New York forbidding the congregation of more than three slaves, legalizing the whipping of those guilty of the slightest infractions, and setting curfews and nullifying any regard for Blacks as a result of baptism. These laws were enacted to control increasing numbers of Africans who had begun to engage in rebellious acts and insurrections. Perpetrators of rebellious acts and insurrections were subjected to horrifying punishment or death.

By 1771, discontent with the importation of enslaved Africans began to surface in all the colonies. This discontent was based on fear of a Black uprising as the proportion of enslaved Africans in the population increased. Slave management concerns and policies always followed a similar course. Whenever slave populations threatened the security of White colonists,

cruel and restrictive slave codes were enacted and brutal punishment was prescribed to contain or control any potential Black insurrection. Restrictions on importation of enslaved Africans constituted another method of control.

For the American colonists, the Revolutionary War (1775–1783), fought for freedom and independence from Britain, created a moral paradox *vis-à-vis* their own enslavement of Africans. The institution of slavery maintained by the American colonies was inconsistent with the principles motivating the conflict with England. Consequently, in some quarters, the issue of whether to permit the enlistment and arming of Blacks in the war against England created a major dilemma.

Black participation in colonial military ventures was not new. Blacks had served in the Anglo-French conflict, Native American and colonist battles, and in all colonial wars between 1689 and 1763, including the French and Indian War (1755-63). In many campaigns, Blacks fought alongside Whites and received equal pay. If Black soldiers distinguished themselves in the line of duty, they were usually granted their freedom. In the Revolutionary War, however, Blacks fought only a few weeks before being excluded from service.[17]

In the summer of 1775, General George Washington issued an order not to enlist Blacks into the military. Subsequent policies of the Council of War rejected the use of both slave and free Blacks in the army. In an effort to capitalize on the American colonists' rejection of Blacks for military service, Lord Dunmore, the British governor of Virginia, issued a proclamation in November 1775 inviting all able-bodied indentured servants and Blacks, free or enslaved, to serve in the British military. The move by the British to enlist Blacks provoked the concern of the colonial army because it was logical to assume that hundreds of Africans would flock to join his Majesty's troops. General Washington then sought to reverse his previous order rejecting Black enlistment. In January 1776, Congress granted Washington's request to enlist only free Blacks in the continental army. Prior to the American colonists' reversal of policy, hundreds of Black runaways and enslaved Africans from Virginia, Maryland, and the Carolinas had escaped to the British lines. They so bolstered the British position that the colonists further reversed their policy and permitted the recruitment of both free and enslaved Blacks to join their ranks. However, Georgia and South Carolina never formally approved of Black enlistment and service in the military. Approximately five-thousand Blacks served in both the American and British armies during the duration of the war. Blacks were used as pawns, fighting for their British and American oppressors with the hope of being rewarded, eventually, with manumission (freedom) if they survived the war.[18]

Slavery After the American Revolutionary War

The American war for independence gave hope to millions of Africans that their history of suffering and human bondage would end or be ameliorated. Such expectations soon proved to be contrary to the majority will of the now-independent Americans. The feelings of guilt and hypocrisy that fueled antislavery sentiment before and during the war faded with the British surrender at Yorktown. What resulted after the war were regional reinterpretations and modified forms of slavery and human oppression. In the northern colonies, the general pattern was a gradual movement toward the abolishment of slavery. Even before the cessation of the war, Vermont had moved to abolish slavery in 1777, and Pennsylvania followed in 1780 with a gradual emancipation plan. Immediately after the war, the state of Massachusetts declared slavery unconstitutional. Subsequently, New Hampshire, Connecticut, Rhode Island, New York, and New Jersey provided for the gradual manumission of slaves. By 1807, all the northern states had passed emancipation laws. There emerged in the North a category of African that John Hope Franklin describes as "quasi-free Negroes."[19] In 1787, the new national government of the former thirteen colonies enacted statutes stipulating that the Northwest Territory be developed exclusive of slavery. Eventually, this meant that the five states carved out of the Northwest Territory—Indiana, Illinois, Ohio, Michigan, and Wisconsin—became non-slave states upon their admission to the Union.

The South not only did not make any move to abolish slavery, it also became even more recalcitrant to the idea of manumission and even more vengeful toward enslaved Blacks. Evidently, the axiomatic expression, "All men are created equal," authored by Thomas Jefferson and incorporated into the Declaration of Independence, did not wield the same moral force in the South as it may have in the North. The apparent ambivalence between Jefferson's egalitarian philosophy of freedom and his active participation in the practice of slavery served to reinforce the will of the South to resist all antislavery notions and to pursue human bondage and oppression with an even greater passion.

In drafting their new constitution, the founding fathers totally ignored the question of slavery except through an implicit recognition of Africans as chattel property. The resulting document was predicated on compromise and reconciliation of the interests of the North and South in order to preserve the American union. On the matter of representation and taxation based on population, for example, there arose the problem of counting Blacks in the "free" North versus the non-free South. As a compromise measure, the Constitution of the United States of America, without mentioning slavery or race, relegated the status of Black Americans to "three-fifths" of a person. Further compromises were evident in the dispute over the continued importation of enslaved Africans and in the adjudication of rights in the case of escaped indentured servants or laborers. The constitutional problem of dealing with escaped Africans would resurface again with the passage of the Fugitive Slave Law of 1850.

In essence, White America's independence from the tyranny and oppression of Britain resulted in few changes in the plight of Africans, especially in the southern United States. Ironically, the freedom gained by White Americans through the War of Independence made them freer than ever to oppress Africans and deny to Africans the same human dignity and freedom they had so valiantly sought and fought for from England. In the aftermath of the Revolutionary War, slavery grew and intensified in the South, and real freedom was denied to "free" Blacks in the North. Thus, from American independence were sown the seeds of the most unique forms of racial slavery and racism ever practiced in the world.

The Middle and New England colonies had initiated steps to declare slavery unconstitutional during the Revolutionary War period, and by the end of the war, at least on paper, human bondage above the Mason-Dixon Line had come to an end. Out of the quasi-free, post-Revolutionary War milieu of northern states, viable free African communities emerged and Black persons of distinction were able to contribute to the public good. Religious organizations, antislavery groups, and persons of antislavery sentiment increased their efforts to provide opportunity for Blacks to learn to read and write or to obtain an education. Often on their own initiative, Blacks became self-educated. Various White religious denominations and churches permitted Africans to join and allowed them to participate on a subordinate basis. With a modicum of opportunity and freedom, quasi-free Blacks and former enslaved Africans developed a spirit of self-worth, protest, and self-determination that would later serve as the foundation for the abolitionist movement.

The intelligence and the literary and oratory talents of some former enslaved Africans and quasi-free Blacks captured the interest of Whites, who promoted them and enabled the practical application of their abilities. Phillis Wheatley, a former slave of a Boston family, distinguished herself as a Black female poet during the era of the Revolutionary War. Her most notable works were published between 1773 and 1784. Contemporary scholars of Black literature debate whether her poems related, even implicitly, to the plight of Africans, but during her lifetime, any hint of protest in her works would have been detrimental to her welfare. In 1786, Jupiter Hammon, a former slave who became a minister and poet, wrote *An Address to the Negroes of the State of New York*, which was delivered to the African Society of New York City. Hammon's poetry was religious in nature, and his oratory advocated the rewards of a Black afterlife and gradualism in dealing with slavery and oppression.

Sylviane Diouf maintains that African Muslims, who comprised at least ten percent of the enslaved Black population, "arrived in the Americas with a tradition of Arabic literacy that they struggled to preserve."[20] This literacy, argues Diouf, "set them apart from most slaves and many slaveholders but became the basis of their disproportionate influence in slave communities and, in some instances, their key to freedom."[21]

In time, learned and articulate, quasi-free Blacks applied their limited opportunities and abilities to register protest and to submit petitions decrying inequality and slavery throughout the new independent American republic. James Forten of Philadelphia was born free in 1766 and became a highly successful businessman as a sail maker. In 1797, he joined several other Blacks in the city of Philadelphia in petitioning Congress against the slave trade. He was also one of the signers of a petition in 1800 requesting Congress to alter the Fugitive Slave Act of 1793. Forten was opposed to emigration or back-to-Africa schemes. By contrast, Paul Cuffee of Massachusetts, a Black shipbuilder and owner, went to Africa in 1811 to investigate the possibility of resettling free Blacks in Africa. Like Forten, Prince Hall, a preacher, participated in the presentation of a number of petitions to end slavery between 1773 and 1788. Hall, having obtained a charter from the Masons in England to establish the first African Lodge, is recognized as the founding father of Black Freemasonry in America. He also lobbied for the establishment of schools for Black children in Boston. Yet Hall, like Cuffee, supported plans for Black emigration to Africa, and he might be called one of the earliest advocates of Black nationalism.[22]

The scientific and literary achievements of Benjamin Banneker during the period following the Revolutionary War are testimonials to the intellectual equality of African people. Banneker was born in Maryland of a free White woman and a slave father. He was fortunate to have received an education at a school organized for White children, but to which a few Blacks were admitted. He developed into a mathematician, astronomer, and an inventor. He wrote an almanac that was published annually from 1792-1802. Thomas Jefferson learned of his abilities and achievements and recommended him to serve with the surveying commission to lay out the boundary lines and streets for the District of Columbia.

The period following the Revolutionary War to the War of 1812 marked the beginning of the separate and independent Black Church in America. The first northern independent Black church effort took place in Philadelphia. Separate Black churches and independent African religious denominations were established as a result of the hostile and derogatory treatment Blacks experienced when they attempted to worship in the same edifice with Whites. Richard Allen was an active worshipper at the White St. George's Methodist Church of Philadelphia. One Sunday, Allen and two of his companions were pulled from their knees while praying and ordered to move to the balcony. Allen and one of his companions, Absalom Jones, left St. George's and subsequently founded the Free African Society of Philadelphia. Through this organization, Richard Allen founded the Bethel African Methodist Episcopal (AME) Church in Philadelphia in 1794. Branches of the Bethel AME were established in Maryland, Delaware, and New Jersey. The AME Church gradually developed into a national Black religious denomination. Hostility from Whites also prompted the founding of the African Methodist Episcopal Zion Church denomination in New York in 1796. Around 1809, separate Black Baptist churches were organized in Boston, New York, and Philadelphia.

Southern Blacks rarely, if ever, had the opportunity to worship with Whites. Nevertheless, separate Black Baptist churches in the South were organized during and after the Revolutionary War period. The First Southern African Baptist church of record was formed at Silver Bluff on the South Carolina side of the Savannah River about twelve miles from Augusta, Georgia. After the treaty ending the war was signed, this congregation evolved into the First African Baptist Church of Augusta. During the same period, George Liele, a slave, started a Black Baptist church in Savannah. However, after the war, he left for Jamaica. Another slave, Andrew Bryan, continued Liele's efforts and in January 1788, the First Baptist Church of Savannah was founded. Blacks continued to form their own separate churches in the North and South during this period. Whites began to forbid the formation of Black churches in the South, especially after the Denmark Vesey-led slave uprising of 1822.[23] The light of hope for the end of human bondage and oppression that had begun to shine dimly by the end of the Revolutionary War was soon to be extinguished as the Industrial Revolution got underway in America after the War of 1812.

"King Cotton" and the Revival of Slavery in the South

As noted by the eminent Black historian Benjamin Quarles in discussing the impact of cotton on slavery states: "Cotton was a powerful stimulant to slavery; the two seemed to have been made for each other."[24] Eli Whitney's cotton gin, invented in 1793, increased the convenience and profitability of producing cotton in the South. The technological breakthrough in the process of separating the cotton fiber from the seed of the plant effectively accelerated the demand for cotton. Before the cotton gin, the South produced a few thousand bales of cotton, but production rose to more than a half-million bales after the War of 1812. Cotton—like sugar, tobacco, rice, and indigo—created a need for unlimited cheap or free labor. It also promoted the resurgence and intensification of slavery.

Despite the impact of cotton on slavery, historians James Dormon and Robert Jones cast doubt on the idea that slavery would have declined eventually if the cotton gin had not been invented. They contend that slavery had become institutionalized in the hearts and minds of White southerners and that the economy of the South was inextricably tied to slavery. The belief of many Whites in the natural inferiority of Africans, the long history of racial slavery in the Americas, and the prevailing ideology of White supremacy would have made any effort to abolish slavery improbable in the absence of some major unforeseen development.[25]

The War of 1812 was waged essentially to satisfy the westward expansionist designs of the new American republic. The soil and climate of the South and Southwest regions including Louisiana, Alabama, Mississippi, and Georgia were extremely favorable for producing cotton. Consequently, the plantation system was extended progressively into these territories. The acquisition and availability of more land necessitated the demand for an unlimited supply of Black slave labor.

Historically, materialism, ethnocentrism, and greed have been inextricably connected to the practice of slavery, but the European and American proclivity and passion for human slavery exceeded the rationale for goods and markets. More so than their northern kin, southern Whites manifested a mean and xenophobic attitude toward Blacks that defied explanation. Undoubtedly, their anti-African posture was psychopathically motivated. This perhaps is the only way to explain how Whites were so inured and emotionally immune to the inhumane treatment they inflicted upon Blacks under the plantation system of the South. The vilest violation of African humanity was the southern slave masters' practice of slave breeding. After Congress banned the importation of enslaved Africans in 1807, the American slave population began to decline, thus creating a shortage of slave labor. Although some scholars estimate that over two-hundred-fifty-thousand enslaved Africans were smuggled into the country during the fifty years following the restrictive law, the unlimited and profitable demand for enslaved Africans escalated the practice of domestic slave breeding. This practice often involved the slave masters' sexual manipulation of slave women, the use of Black male "studs" to copulate with female slaves, and a reward-and-punishment system to induce slave women to produce offspring. The breeding and marketing of enslaved Africans became nearly as profitable as producing and selling cotton.

The "cotton kingdom" developed in the lower southern states of South Carolina, Mississippi, Georgia, and Alabama. The upper southern states of Virginia, Kentucky, Maryland, Tennessee, and North Carolina, however, supplied the lower states with thousands of enslaved Africans annually. Saunders Redding describes vividly and compassionately how the slave traders gathered their human cargoes and marched them overland to the Deep South:

> The slave gangs of men, women and children slunk along in a double line. The manacles that fastened the left wrist of one to the right wrist of another chafed the flesh. Running through a link in the gyves and binding the whole gang together was the coffle chain with links of iron as thick as a man's finger. The sun was hot, or the wind was raw and piercing; the roads were rutted. At night the gang rested; at dawn the march began.[26]

Most towns in the Deep South had slave markets, auction blocks, and pens. Slave traders made no distinction among men, women, mother, father, husband, wife, or children—they were all sold indiscriminately, jointly or individually, with profit being the only consideration. Some Africans were traded especially as concubines and studs.

The illegal importing, breeding, and kidnapping of enslaved Africans constituted a major economic enterprise in the American South. A substantial number of the relatively small population of "free" Blacks were often kidnapped, sold, and re-enslaved. Slave codes designed for the purpose of denigrating and controlling Blacks during the pre-Revolutionary War period were reinforced, and new codes were enacted in the South. Enslaved Blacks had no rights; their treatment and fate depended solely on the merciless whims and desires of slave masters or the dreaded slave drivers. They could be lashed, maimed, tortured, or killed at the will of their tormentors at any time. A slave's day from dawn to dusk was filled with the strenuous tasks of hoeing, digging, plowing, planting, chopping, picking, fixing, cleaning, lifting, or whatever work might be required to maintain the plantation. Enslaved Africans could be worked eighteen to nineteen hours per day, and as Redding states, "There was no law that said they could not be worked to death."[27]

Enslaved Blacks generally lived in one-room windowless huts or shacks with cracks in the walls and dirt floors. They were not insulated from the rain, wind, or snow, and the smoke from heating and cooking was suffocating. Enslaved Blacks usually slept on pallets of rags. Two or more families shared a cabin or hut. They customarily made their own crude furniture and utensils. Their diets consisted mostly of salt pork, corn meal, molasses, and dried beans. Black autobiographies record that the food was sometimes sufficient in bulk but totally unbalanced and not sufficiently nutritious to sustain a person's physical endurance and health. Sickness and death from epidemics of yellow fever, tuberculosis, cholera, malaria, and other diseases were a constant plight in the slave quarters. Of course, the lot of enslaved Africans invariably depended on the humaneness or cruelty of the slave master.[28]

During the Civil Rights Movement and student revolts of the late twentieth century, many references and analogies were made to Malcolm X's characterization and description of the "house negro" and the "field negro." The house slave or servant worked and often lived in the home of the slave master and slave mistress. House slaves were perceived by many as enjoying a privileged and elite position. The house slave ate the same food or leftovers as the slave master and wore the used and discarded clothes of the slave master's family. The house slave's duties included housekeeping, cooking, gardening, caring for the infants or children of the slave master and mistress, and serving the general and intimate needs of their White owners. The house slave was usually spared the arduous, back-breaking work in the fields and generally was not the object of torture and brutality accorded the field slave. The field slave, on the other hand, was beaten and suffered immensely from morning to night. He or she lived in a hut or shack, wore inadequate clothing, and ate the lowest quality of food. In Malcolm X's words, "The Negro in the field caught hell."

Whereas Malcolm X portrayed a sharp contrast in the treatment of house slave and field slave, John Blassingame's work suggests that the cruelty inflicted on both was similar and differed only in kind. The house slave had to be available at all times, even to the vengeful and sadistic desires of his or her owners, and functioned always under the watchful eyes of the slave master and mistress. Female house slaves were often exploited sexually, for breeding purposes

3

or for pleasure; the millions of mixed-blood Africans or mulattoes attest to their plight. Nevertheless, many conclude that house slaves tended to be more loyal to their owners while field slaves tended to hate their masters and mistresses. Both Malcolm X and Blassingame maintained that the sociological dichotomy of the house slave and field slave is reflected in contemporary Black life and relationships.[29]

In assessing the contributions of Blacks to pre-Civil war economic growth, it is important to recognize that Black labor was exploited outside of plantation agriculture as well. A useful context for discussing this issue is provided by Robert Fogel's claim that although the nonagricultural sector accounted for less than a quarter of southern output in 1840, it was the source of about forty percent of all the increase in the region's per capita income during the last two decades of the antebellum era."[30] As Mark Smith observes, "The South had about one-third of the nation's railroad mileage in 1860 and the network was financed primarily from southern and not northern investment capital."[31] Not only was this rail network self-financed, enslaved Blacks supplied the labor used in its construction. According to Richard Starobin, the South accounted for approximately twenty percent of invested industrial capital in the 1850s. Southern industry was tied intricately to plantation agriculture (e.g., textile manufacturing), which made extensive use of slave labor. In the 1850s, between 160,000 and 260,000 slaves worked in industry, with four-fifths owned directly by industrial entrepreneurs. Starobin reports that industries employing slave labor were more profitable than similar industries employing either integrated, slavefree, or free work forces.[32]

Slavery was also a normal feature of southern cities. In 1860, there were approximately 70,000 urban slaves. The population of both free and enslaved Blacks in southern cities declined between 1850 and 1860, however, as the demand for agricultural labor increased. More succinctly, enslaved Blacks were relocated from the cities to plantations because redeployment into cotton production yielded greater returns to their owners. In discussing slavery in urban areas, Richard Wade has noted that public control replaced private supervision by owners because many enslaved Blacks were allowed to "hire their own time" and to "live out" or find their own residence. These arrangements reduced owners' involvement in negotiating contractual arrangements for the employment and maintenance of enslaved Blacks. The result was lower costs and higher profits for owners.

Blacks involved in such arrangements were able to capture some of the returns from their human capital. Often owners were paid fixed amounts that were less than the amounts earned even after accounting for maintenance expenses.[33] As Joe Trotter notes, artisans were "the most numerous of the self-hires," and they included "carpenters, tailors, seamstresses, and mechanics."[34] Despite these impressive demonstrations of Black ingenuity and managerial ability, it is important to keep in mind, as Roger Ransom and Richard Sutch conclude, that "only about 6 percent of adult male slaves held occupations above those of agricultural worker, unskilled laborer, or house servant."[35]

In the face of the inhumane, oppressive, and generally merciless aspects of slavery, the anomaly of the "free" or "quasi-free" Black created a persistent paradox. Shortly before the Civil War, the population of so-called non-slave Blacks in America numbered slightly less than half a million. Almost half this number lived in the South. The term *free* is qualified because no Black person in either the North or South was actually free. Although the free Blacks of the South were not owned by individual slave masters, they were, in essence, the property of and subject to the will of every White person in their community, town, or state. In most southern states, these quasi-free Africans were required to carry a pass to certify their non-slave status. Generally, they were not allowed to vote, hold public office, nor permitted to testify against a White person in courts of law. They were also subject to curfew, forbidden the right of assembly, and could be virtually re-enslaved upon the slightest infraction of a law or ordinance. Anyone of a dark hue was burdened with proving his or her non-slave status. The degrees of freedom enjoyed by free Blacks varied from state to state, however, and also varied from one region or particular circumstance to another.

Several factors permitted the free Black population of the South to grow and develop from 1790 to 1860. Hundreds of free Blacks earned their freedom as a result of their participation in the American War for Independence. Some slave owners, out of conscience or because of their inability to maintain their enslaved Africans, simply set them free. Blacks often would run away to escape bondage, and some were able to purchase their freedom.

Despite their unequal status and restricted position, some free Blacks acquired property and became relatively wealthy. Some even became slaveholders themselves, but historians seem to agree that many of these better-off free Blacks used their newfound wealth to purchase their loved ones, relatives, or friends from the grips of White slavery.[36] The presence and growth of free Blacks caused uneasiness among southern Whites, as did the problem of distinguishing lighter-skinned free Blacks from Whites. In his definitive study, *Slaves Without Masters*,[37] Ira Berlin implies that more than fifty percent of all free Blacks were mulattoes, typically the illegitimate offspring of White men and Black women. A small percentage resulted from relationships between Black fathers and Native American or White women. Many White-skinned Blacks passed over the color line into White society. Each state government, through legislation and court decisions, established its own specifications of racial identity associated with peoples of African descent. These racial subclassifications differentiated African Americans into categories purported to designate their degree of African ancestry. Categories such as mulatto, quadroon, and octoroon were given official status, not only to distinguish patterns of descent but also to assign differential opportunities; nonetheless, any discernible Black trait or traceable "drop" of African blood barred a person from being viewed as White. Given that the social foundation of American intergroup relations, then and since, is based on race and color, these divisions were deemed necessary to maintain distinct racial lines for the perpetuation of racism and a racist ideology.[38] As such, both the quasi-free and enslaved Africans were perceived as being inferior or less than equal to Whites, whether in the free states of the North or the slave states of the South.

The form of racial slavery based on color, as introduced by Europeans to the Americas, also affected the survival and base instincts of the Africans in the New World. Color and class divisions and conflict of interests developed between free and enslaved Africans and tended to deter their unified resistance to the slave system. Ira Berlin gives a descriptive and plausible account of the tenuous and suspicious relationship that sometimes existed between enslaved and free Blacks. He claims that Whites created the schism between free or mulatto Blacks and bondservants to exploit their division and maintain control over both groups. They encouraged free Blacks to inform on the

slaves in return for privileges or economic rewards and coerced house slaves to inform on field slaves to demonstrate their loyalty to their slave masters.[39] The strategy of divide and conquer contributed, then and now, to the thwarting of the freedom goals and objectives of African peoples.

The deliberate creation of color-class differences among the Africans in the Americas caused some Blacks to falter both in their concept of self-identity and their collective sense of responsibility for the freedom of their race. Three major slave uprisings between 1800 and 1831 failed because house slaves or mulattoes betrayed the confidence of the revolt leaders. Though such betrayals resulted in disastrous consequences, they were not typical of all relationships between free Blacks and enslaved Blacks.

Slave Resistance, Rebellion, and White Fears

Slavery failed to provoke the moral consciousness of Whites in the Americas partly because most Whites conveniently adopted a rationale that Blacks were providentially inferior, unintelligent, docile, and childlike by nature. Therefore, it is not surprising that, as late as the early twentieth century, some White scholars promoted the unfounded theory that Blacks accepted their subjugated plight and endured the resulting brutality, pain, and suffering with geniality and passivity. Black scholars, on the other hand, overwhelmingly rejected the asinine notion that the whole race of African people had a proclivity for masochism. They conversely rejected the equally unintelligent notion that all members of the Caucasian race were afflicted with sadistic tendencies.

In *American Negro Slave Revolts*, a comprehensive and seminal work that refutes the "docile slave" stereotype, Herbert Aptheker provides evidence of some 250 Black slave revolts or insurrections in the Western Hemisphere. He also describes various tactics of resistance employed by individual slaves. He notes, for example, that slaves feigned illness, employed self-mutilation, refused to work, engaged in sabotage and strikes, and attempted and often succeeded in escaping. They also resorted to arson and to poisoning and assassinating slave masters.[40] Historian Stanley M. Elkins' insinuation that the intellect and will to rebel resided only in the non-slave, literate Black is a suspect and unproven stereotype.[41] The fact that freer and more educated Blacks often initiated rebellions and fomented resistance to slavery affirms the concern and

3

compassion that the better-off class of African Americans sustained for their less fortunate brothers and sisters.

Enumerating many of the recorded slave revolts or treating any single incident at great length would be impractical in a survey study. Notably, however, one of the earliest recorded slave rebellions took place at Stono, South Carolina, in 1739, when twenty or so slaves seized some firearms and killed their guards and all other Whites who got in their way. They marched, burned buildings, and chanted freedom songs on their way to Florida where they hoped to escape. They were eventually met and attacked by a detachment of militia. Some were killed; others dispersed, but they were later captured and killed. Several slave revolts occurred between 1739 and 1790 in the Atlantic states, including New York and New Jersey.

Virginia experienced a disproportionately large number of revolts. In 1800, Gabriel Prosser and Jack Bowler conspired to lead a revolt near Richmond. They and their accomplices secretly acquired and stored an arsenal of firearms and bullets, and fashioned crude swords and bayonets. On the day the revolt was to have taken place, over a thousand slaves gathered on the outskirts of Richmond with the intent of attacking. Prosser's rebellion failed, however, not only because he was betrayed by two house slaves but also because fate intervened in the form of a massive thunderstorm with torrential rain. The storm destroyed a key bridge and made passage impossible. The conspirators were forced to disband, the militia was dispatched, and scores of insurgents were rounded up and executed. Prosser escaped immediate capture, but he was betrayed again by two Black informers while trying to escape by boat. He and other rebels were hanged.

Denmark Vesey is reported to have been a literate slave and expert carpenter who purchased his freedom with money won from a lottery. He was a respected member of the free Black community of Charleston, South Carolina, known for his antislavery, human-equality outlook, and oratory. Impressed with the successful Black revolution in Haiti, Vesey took a long period to organize his own revolt. It was one of the most meticulously planned and threatening rebellions of African slaves in the history of Virginia. Vesey's attempt to recruit a house slave to the rebellion's cause proved to be an error in judgment. The house "negro" informed Whites of the conspiracy before it fully

materialized. As a consequence, Vesey and hundreds of his Black conspirators were arrested, tried, and executed. The Vesey conspiracy caused heightened alarm among Whites in Virginia and elsewhere throughout the South, so fearful were they of the inevitability of future rebellions. They subsequently forbade Black church organizations and religious practices from taking place and carefully scrutinized other Black gatherings of any type.

It was Nat Turner who led and executed the most famous slave revolt of the nineteenth century. Indeed, Turner's rebellion involved the greatest number of participants and was perhaps the bloodiest in terms of the large number of both Whites and Blacks killed. Turner undoubtedly inherited his strong will and resolution from his father and mother. His father escaped to the North while Nat was still a boy, and his mother often swore that she would rather have killed her infant son than to see him sold into slavery. Turner learned early to read and write. He was highly religious and became a Baptist preacher, claiming to have had divine visions of slave insurrections and freedom since his youth. He planned his revolt with extreme secrecy, having learned via newspaper accounts how other attempts had been betrayed.

On the day of the uprising, White farmers, slaveholders, and any other White person who got in the way were systematically killed. As the rebellion progressed, it began to meet with increasing armed resistance from Whites, who mobilized the militia. With their overwhelming firepower and numbers, the Whites squelched the revolt. Mass executions, mutilations, and horrid tortures followed the insurrection. Turner, however, eluded his pursuers for over two months but was eventually captured, convicted, and hanged. Before he was executed, he purportedly dictated his confession of the conspiracy, which inspired a spirit of revolution among many African peoples.[42]

The African American slave experience continues to be a fertile field of scholarly research and speculation, but only African Americans—who were and still are affected socially, psychologically, and politically from slavery—have a true grasp and feeling for the extent and scope of its destructive consequences. Despite the systems of White control exercised on the plantations, which required the creation and promotion of class divisions among the slaves, most of the significant slave revolts were precipitated by so-called free Blacks. This proves that free Blacks were not really free. True, some house slaves and near-White Blacks betrayed enslaved Blacks' attempts at freedom and were blindly loyal to their White masters, but there was obviously also much cooperation and complicity on the part of Blacks from all sectors in planning and organizing the revolts that did occur. Additionally, Black preachers, church groups, and various religious advocates against human inequality and oppression were major proponents in many slave uprisings.

The social dynamics that existed among Africans during the era of slavery continue to be manifested and are functional still in the African American societies of the contemporary era. Like the so-called free Blacks of the slave period who fought for the liberation of all Africans, many members of today's Black middle-class or African Americans also carry on the struggle of the enslaved Black masses for freedom and uplift. Courageous and freedom-minded Black ministers and members of the Black Church continue to protest against racism. Indeed, they are often at the forefront of efforts to challenge the structural inequality that persists into the early twenty-first century. It may not be plausible, however, to expect those who have benefited from slavery to lionize Gabriel Prosser, Denmark Vesey, and Nat Turner of the eighteenth and nineteenth centuries; or for them to idolize Marcus Garvey and Malcolm X of the twentieth century as upholding the values upon which the American republic was founded. Notwithstanding, many Blacks today celebrate these individuals as champions in the ongoing struggle for justice and freedom.

Rising Abolitionism: Causes and Effects

The axiomatic saying that "if someone has to let you be free, you may never be free" directly relates to the indispensable role Africans played to free themselves from the bonds of slavery. Because the power of government and law remains overwhelmingly in the hands of Whites, much of the literature treating the abolition of slavery in America addresses only the political machinations of the executive, legislative, and judicial branches in either opposing or abetting antislavery movements. Many traditional and revisionist historians have played down the importance of African Americans' involvement in the abolitionist movement, but Black people in this nation have always been the foremost instigators for their own freedom. Acknowledging Black Americans' role in their own liberation, Herbert Aptheker writes:

Slavery was the unique experience of black people in the United States... They alone endured it, survived it, and combated it. They were the first and most lasting Abolitionists. Their conspiracies and insurrections, individual struggles, systematic flights, maroon communities, efforts to buy freedom, cultural solidity, creation of antislavery organizations and publications—all preceded the black-white united efforts.[43]

Relatedly, it would be inaccurate to say that all Europeans or Whites supported and encouraged slavery. Individuals and groups of various ethnic origins and nationalities who opposed slavery in America were known as abolitionists. Abolition-oriented individuals and organizations first emerged in Britain, the country that virtually originated the "unique" concept and practice of trans-Atlantic slavery and benefited most from its earlier perpetration.

Antislavery sentiment and activity in the former American colonies subsided somewhat after the Revolutionary War because citizens of the northern states had essentially appeased their consciences by making slavery theoretically unconstitutional. However, after the War of 1812, slavery became even more essential for the development of the cotton economy of the South. Southern plantations and businesses sought a revival and extension of slavery, not a reduction or abolition of it. Therefore, the interests and dispositions of the South were diametrically opposed to those of the North. This engendered a contentious and politically divisive relationship between "free" states and "slave" states. The South was adamant about maintaining slavery and rationalized the enslavement of Blacks based on notions of their inferiority. The South also enjoyed a trade and commercial advantage over the North given its reliance on unpaid or slave labor and lower tariffs.

As new territories and states developed in the American West, their designation as free or slave became increasingly important in determining the balance of power between North and South. Ultimately, the issue of slavery or freedom for Blacks determined whether or not the South would secede from the Union. To circumvent the threat of secession, the North and South made compromises to maintain a balance of free and slave states and territories. The Ordinance of 1787 abolished slavery in the territory north of the Ohio and east of the Mississippi rivers. This area included the future states of Ohio, Illinois,

Indiana, Michigan, Wisconsin, and Minnesota. Alabama, Mississippi, Louisiana, Florida, Texas, Arkansas, Tennessee, and Kentucky were admitted as slave states, which equalized the numbers of free and slave states. The threat of disequilibrium occurred when the Missouri territory petitioned for admission to the Union as a slave state. A member of the House of Representatives, James Tallmadge, proposed an amendment that would prohibit slavery in the new state of Missouri. The amendment did not pass, but Congress moved to admit Maine as a free state along with Missouri as a slave state to preserve the balance between North and South. This 1820 action became known as the Missouri Compromise.

Prior to the enactment of the Missouri Compromise, the importation of slaves had been prohibited by law as of January 1, 1808. Unscrupulous slavers regularly ignored this prohibition, resulting in thousands of enslaved Blacks being imported into the United States between 1808 and 1860. According to Sylviane Diouf, the last recorded group of captive Africans was brought to the Atlantic River, north of Mobile, Alabama, in the summer of 1860.[44]

Several compromises were made in 1850 to preserve harmony and balance between the North and South. The one that stirred the most intense antislavery sentiment was the Fugitive Slave Act. The Fugitive Slave Law allowed slave owners to pursue and reclaim alleged slaves or fugitives without due process; the alleged slave was not permitted to testify in his or her own behalf, and heavy penalties were imposed on anyone providing aid to the fugitive or assisting in his or her escape. Northerners questioned the constitutionality of the Act on the grounds that its ultimate effect was to suspend the writ of *habeas corpus*.[45]

The Supreme Court's decision in the *Dred Scott* case of 1857 provoked further constitutional controversy and antislavery protest. Dred Scott was an enslaved Black who originally lived in Missouri, a territory in which slavery was legal, but he was taken by his master to Illinois, where slavery was outlawed and where he lived for a number of years. Scott subsequently returned with his master to the slave state of Missouri, where he eventually saved enough money to purchase his freedom. His master refused this request, and through a benefactor lawyer, Scott sued the man. Scott contended that since he had lived in a free state, he was entitled to his freedom even upon his return to the slave state of Missouri. A lower court ruled in Scott's favor, but the Missouri Supreme Court reversed the decision. The case was appealed all the way to the US Supreme Court. In the Court's ruling, Chief Justice Roger B. Taney, a southerner, declared in essence that Blacks, being members of an inferior race, were not and could not become citizens of the United States. Thus, Blacks were not eligible to bring suit in US courts.[46]

The Missouri Compromise, Fugitive Slave Law, and the *Dred Scott* decision served to arouse and intensify antislavery sentiment and abolitionist activity in the United States. The morally unconscionable and inhumane oppressive actions perpetrated in the South did not quell the spirit of resistance and drive for freedom evidenced by Africans in America. Slave insurrections, mass runaways, and other acts of defiance instilled fear, desperation, and doubt in the minds of many southern Whites concerning their untenable position on human bondage. Not only did southern recalcitrance sow the seeds of Civil War, the controversies surrounding slavery intensified the agitation for abolition and led to the emergence of the most righteous, eloquent, courageous, and daring men and women of both races in the history of humankind.

In the absence of military might, the most potent weapons of the defenseless and powerless are the pen, oratory, and moral suasion. Armed with one or a combination of these methods of protest, abolitionists petitioned and lobbied state and federal legislative bodies seeking the repeal of slave trade and fugitive slave laws. Abolitionists formed antislavery societies to aid slaves in escaping, and they published and disseminated antislavery newspapers and underground publications. Among the renowned Black abolitionists from 1829 until the eve of the Civil War were men such as David Walker, Henry Highland Garnet, and Frederick Douglass. Harriet Tubman and Sojourner Truth were outstanding among Black female abolitionists. (The critical role of abolitionist thought in shaping Black philosophy and political ideology was discussed at length in Chapter 1.)

The genesis of Black cultural nationalism and Pan-Africanism is reflected in *David Walker's Appeal to the Coloured Citizens of the World*. Henry Highland Garnet was one of the first African Americans to embrace the concept of freedom by any means necessary, including violent revolution. The charismatic leader Malcolm X echoed Garnet's theme during the mid-twentieth century. Nevertheless, Frederick Douglass's integrationist and assimilationist philosophy and goals dominated the political ideology of most Blacks until the mid-1960s.

Douglass was perhaps the most famous and eloquent Black orator of the abolitionist period. His assimilationist ideology did not diminish the acidic and invective quality of his speeches. If he was an integrationist, certainly he was a militant one, as the following excerpt from a speech he delivered August 4, 1857, clearly reflects:

If there is no struggle there is no progress. Those who profess to favor freedom and yet deprecate agitation, are men who want crops without plowing up the ground, they want rain without thunder and lightning. They want the ocean without the awful roar of its many waters. This struggle may be a moral one, or it may be a physical one, and it may be both moral and physical, but it must be a struggle. Power concedes nothing without a demand. It never did and it never will. Find out just what any people will quietly submit to and you have found out the exact measure of injustice and wrong which will be imposed upon them, and these will continue till they are resisted with either words or blows, or with both. The limits of tyrants are prescribed by the endurance of those whom they oppress... If we ever get free from the oppressions and wrongs heaped upon us, we must pay for their removal ... by suffering, by sacrifice, and if needs be, by our lives and the lives of others.[47]

One of the most effective abolitionist initiatives that eroded the institution of slavery involved the assistance provided to support the escape of thousands of slaves through the Underground Railroad. The term *Underground Railroad* is a metaphor for the various secretive ways and means abolitionists used to enable fugitive slaves to escape to free states and Canada. Hundreds of persons, White and Black, were involved in this surreptitious activity. The most prominent figure in the Underground Railroad movement was a Black woman, Harriet Tubman. Tubman escaped from slavery as a young woman and subsequently was instrumental in forming a network of secret way stations to aid in the escape of other slaves. She led at least nineteen missions into the South to free hundreds of Blacks from the shackles of slavery. After 1860, she became active in antislavery meetings and also participated in the women's rights movement.

Sojourner Truth was the most prominent Black female orator of the abolitionist period. She was a self-styled preacher who felt that she had a divine mission to travel (sojourn) and spread the (truth) about slavery. She was born a slave around 1797 but was freed by the New York State Emancipation Act of 1827. Truth was very active in the Underground Railroad and in the antislavery movement. Although it was not customary during this period for women to speak at public meetings, she is noted historically for a speech she was reluctantly permitted to deliver at the second National Woman's Suffrage Convention held in Akron, Ohio, in 1852. The speech was titled, "And Ain't I a Woman?"

The press was a major force and tool of the abolitionists. Of the hundreds of White abolitionists, William Lloyd Garrison stands out as one who used publications and the press effectively in the antislavery movement. Garrison founded *The Liberator*, an inflammatory antislavery newspaper that was published from 1831 to 1865. In 1827, two educated Blacks, John Russwurm and Samuel E. Cornish, founded *Freedom's Journal*, the first journal edited by and for Blacks in America. Although *Freedom's Journal* was not totally an abolitionist newspaper, it gave Africans their own independent vehicle to express and disseminate their views. Frederick Douglass also used the press to attack slavery. In December 1847, he launched his own newspaper, *The North Star*, later titled *Frederick Douglass' Paper*. Subsequently, he initiated the *Douglass' Monthly*, which he published from 1859 to 1863.[48]

Although White abolitionists were numerous, few risked death or gave their life for the cause of ending slavery as did John Brown. John Brown demonstrated his passionate opposition to slavery through militant and violent acts of aggression against the White establishment. He designed and executed a scheme to recruit and arm slaves, establish guerilla forces in the mountains, and fire on or defeat any government militia attacking them. He conferred with Black abolitionists such as Frederick Douglass and Harriet Tubman, but they declined to participate based on their assessment that the plan was not likely to succeed. Nevertheless, Brown and a small contingent of followers, including three of his sons and five Blacks, assaulted Harpers Ferry, a Federal armory in West Virginia, in October 1859. The group succeeded in capturing the facility and resisting until they were defeated by Federal troops. Brown and two of the survivors of the coup were tried and hanged. The only survivor who escaped execution was Osborne Anderson, an African American, who avoided capture and returned to Canada, the country from which he had emigrated during the early 1850s. Brown, however, became a widely regarded martyr for the abolitionist cause, and the political and psychological implications of his feat exacerbated tensions between the North and South.

Increasing national and international antislavery sentiment, slave escapes and insurrections, conflicting economic and social interests between North and South, and the rising tide of abolitionist activities made slavery the paramount political issue confronting the US federal government. Maintaining the fragile balance between free and slave states in the face of increasing threats of secession by southern politicians created a trenchant political dilemma for the newly elected sixteenth President of the United States, Abraham Lincoln.

Abraham Lincoln, Civil War, and Emancipation

Abraham Lincoln was a moral and political enigma. Historians can only guess or surmise the extent of his moral consciousness concerning slavery. Most would agree that he was politically astute but that his moral attitude toward Blacks and slavery vacillated in proportion to what was politically expedient. Prior to assuming the presidency, Lincoln was reported to have made several antislavery statements. He also indicated his opposition to the expansion of slavery into the new US territories. Yet, the pattern of his political and social decisions with regard to Blacks during the Civil War was ambiguous to the extent that his true feelings will never be known. Notwithstanding, the political disarray and factionalism of the Democrats over the slavery issue assured his election as a moderate Republican president in 1860.

Lincoln was the political heir of the turmoil and tension created by the North–South conflict over slavery that his predecessor James Buchanan could not resolve. The North had gained the balance of power with the admission of the western territories of Oregon, California, and Minnesota as free states. The South's economy was based on cotton and slave labor, and it was imperative that slavery be maintained despite the North's antislavery sentiment. As a result, the secession of the South became imminent. South

Carolina was the first southern "cotton" state to secede and was followed by Mississippi, Alabama, Georgia, Florida, Louisiana, and eventually Texas. Delegates from the secessionist states convened in Montgomery, Alabama, and formed a new government; thus, the Confederacy was born.

The new Confederacy seized federal forts and properties; laid siege to Fort Sumter in Charleston, South Carolina; and fired on a federal vessel entering the port of Charleston. When Lincoln attempted to supply provisions for Fort Sumter, the Confederacy demanded that federal troops evacuate the facility. The troops refused and were fired on by Confederate forces. The federal defenders returned fire, but the overwhelming firepower and advantage of the Confederacy forced the surrender of Fort Sumter. Thus, on April 14, 1861, the American Civil War commenced.

Lincoln had taken a cautionary stance regarding this turn of events in his inaugural address by indicating he would not intervene with force to prevent secession unless the Confederacy provoked and initiated attack or violence first. However, after the war had begun, he acted with military efficiency in requiring the governments of the northern states to muster militia and recruit volunteers to defeat the southern insurgency. As both sides prepared for battle, North Carolina, Arkansas, Virginia, and Tennessee joined the Confederacy. The border states of Maryland, Kentucky, and Missouri remained quasi-loyal, if not fully loyal, and under the control of the Union.

The war was to be a long, bloody, and costly undertaking for both the Union and the Confederacy, and it was fought principally over the issue of slavery. The argument that the war was fought to preserve the Union thus is irrelevant because the preservation of the Union and slavery were inextricably tied together.

Blacks in America generally regarded the war as a godsend. Thousands, both "free" and enslaved, sought to join the ranks of the Union army with hopes of earning gratitude from the North and freedom from southern slavery and oppression. However, at the beginning of the Civil War, Blacks were forbidden from joining the Union army. This posture of the Union War Department soon changed as military manpower shortages occurred throughout the North. The decision to use Black troops was motivated by a decline in White volunteer enlistment and the absence of authorized general conscription. The Militia Act of 1862 authorized the use of Black troops when states could not meet their voluntary quotas, but the act was ineffective in recruiting and maintaining adequate military personnel levels. In March 1863, a national Conscription Act was passed that lacked a racial clause. This indicated that Lincoln planned to use all sources of manpower available. A loophole in the Militia Act of 1862 enabled the War Department to pay Black soldiers less than Whites even though they had, upon enlistment, been promised equal pay. This injustice prevailed until the protests of Black soldiers, supported by a few White sympathizers and coupled with the need to recruit more Africans to the war effort, led to the enactment of the Army Appropriation Act of 1864 that equalized military pay.[49]

Nearly four hundred thousand Blacks served in the Union army, about half of whom were considered combat troops. The others were assigned various duties in military service units. Africans also performed service in the Union navy. Service in the Union military offered Blacks the opportunity to achieve freedom not only for themselves but also to fight for the abolition of slavery. Nevertheless, service in the Union army for Blacks was not without pain and suffering inflicted by White officers and institutionalized racism. Joseph T. Glatthaar relates in his book, *Forged in Battle*, how Black soldiers were discriminated against in promotion and appointment as officers, slandered as being inferior and incompetent, denied medical care and treatment, issued poorer quality weapons and equipment, subjected to various forms of punishment and brutality, and regularly subjected to all forms of racism. Black soldiers experienced various degrees of racism across units and, in some regions, more than in others.[50]

Despite suffering humiliation and racism, Black troops served the Union armed forces with valor and distinction. The Black military experience in the Confederacy was a different story. Slaves were used to grow, harvest, and serve food for the Confederate army. Some were hired out to the army to work in labor gangs and on military construction projects. Although some accounts suggest that southern "freedmen" served with the Confederate army, the South never fully approved of arming Blacks, whether free or slave, in the Civil War. When battle losses and dire manpower shortages eventually forced the South to sanction the use of slaves to combat Union forces, it was too late. The defeat of the Confederacy was imminent, and the North had won.[51]

Slavery was advantageous to the South in its war effort. Lincoln therefore decided to abolish slavery wherever it benefited the Confederacy. As mentioned above, slavery was connected inextricably to the war and the objective of preserving the Union. Consequently, as early as August 1861, Lincoln began making selective and strategic plans that would have emancipating effects on enslaved Blacks. Congress passed a Confiscation Law that allowed the Union army to confiscate the property of rebels used for insurrection purposes, including slaves. The Fugitive Slave Law that required federal authorities to return runaway slaves to their southern masters was nullified. In July 1862, a second Confiscation Law was passed that provided for the seizure of the property of rebels and the emancipation of slaves only in those states that had seceded from the Union. After the Union victory at the battle of Antietam on September 17, 1862, Lincoln issued a preliminary emancipation proclamation on September 22, 1862, that was scheduled to become final and effective on January 1, 1863. The proclamation affected only those states that were still at War with the Union, however, and allowed slavery to continue in the border states.

Abraham Lincoln's true moral conviction on slavery and Blacks will never be known. He was assassinated on April 14, 1865. Much controversy exists among scholars regarding the interpretation of Lincoln's speeches and actions and his attitude toward freedom and equality for Africans in America. Some believe that the "Great Emancipator" epithet bestowed on Lincoln is misplaced considering his racial attitudes and support of emigration schemes to relocate Blacks to Africa, Haiti, or Panama. Historian LaWanda Cox offers one of the strongest defenses of Lincoln's procedures and policies regarding Black emancipation. She suggests that freedom for Blacks was foremost in Lincoln's mind, but that he was equally concerned about having a constitutional base for emancipation that would withstand judicial scrutiny. Cox asserts that "the [Lincoln] criticism reflects late twentieth-century conscience more accurately than mid-nineteenth-century realities."[52] Lerone Bennett, Jr., on the other hand, offers a very different interpretation of Lincoln's views and actions in his book, *Forced into Glory: Abraham Lincoln's White Dream*.[53] Bennett views Lincoln's ambiguous and ambivalent statements and actions on the issue of Black freedom as indicative of the self-preservation motive of a politician.

3

Most politicians tend to react positively or negatively to an issue based on factors that might enhance their popular image or preserve their political office. That being the case, Lincoln was not unlike his predecessor Thomas Jefferson on the question of slavery. Jefferson's real feelings about slavery were obscured by myriad contradictions. One might compare the inconsistencies of Jefferson and Lincoln regarding Black Americans with the views and actions of twentieth-century President Lyndon Baines Johnson. Johnson built his career as a state politician and US senator opposing freedom and civil rights for Blacks. He was elected to serve as vice president during the presidency of John F. Kennedy. With Kennedy's assassination in 1963, Johnson became president. After assuming the presidency, Johnson reversed his opposition to equality for Blacks and proceeded to use the influence and authority of his office to achieve enactment of the most significant Civil Rights legislation in the history of America.

African Americans and the Rise and Fall of Reconstruction

Reconstruction was a program to rebuild the physical properties of the South; to restore whatever good relations might have existed between White southerners and northerners before the Civil War; and to resolve the two-centuries-old issues of slavery and human inequality. Eventually, it succeeded in rebuilding the political and economic structures of the South and in achieving at least a working relationship between the Union victors and the former Confederacy. Nonetheless, Reconstruction never succeeded in reforming the collective hearts, minds, and attitudes of White southerners toward Africans.

Lincoln had proposed some fundamental plans for reconstruction before his death, and his successor, Andrew Johnson, sought to interpret and follow through with Lincoln's ideas. The South had been devastated both in lives and property. It lost over two billion dollars in slave assets once emancipation was effected. Despite the suffering and devastation the South experienced as a result of the war, White southerners were not repentant of their stance on Africans and slavery. They vengefully opposed all laws and attempts to bring about the equality of Blacks. A wide geopolitical schism developed between northern Republicans and southern Democrats. The Republican

North traditionally ranged from moderate to liberal on the issues of Black freedom and equality. Republicans saw the enfranchising of Blacks as a means to increase their numbers and influence in the South.

Neither the Emancipation Proclamation nor the Civil War completely resolved the issue of African freedom and equality. Congress enacted three Reconstruction Amendments to address the status of Africans. The Thirteenth Amendment of 1865 abolished slavery; the Fourteenth, ratified in 1868, conferred on Blacks the rights of citizenship; and the Fifteenth, passed in 1870, extended voting rights to former slaves. Southern state delegations rejected the Reconstruction Amendments and enacted laws or "Black Codes" that, in effect, reduced the status of Africans to inferior, second-class citizens despite Emancipation. The Black Codes amounted to legally "sanitized" versions of the old slave codes. They were designed to re-subjugate Blacks to virtual slave or indentured servant status. The codes limited Blacks to mostly agricultural forms of employment, restricted their areas of residence, and permitted them only segregated and unequal educational opportunity. However, as noted historian Benjamin Quarles has pointed out, the Black Codes differed slightly from the slave codes in that they generally allowed Blacks the right to own property, to make and to enforce contracts, to sue and be sued in cases involving other Blacks, and to have legal intraracial marriages.[54]

Newly freed Blacks were coerced into providing agricultural labor through formalized labor contracts. Additionally, food, clothing, housing, medical care, and access to garden plots, hunting grounds, and fishing waters that previously had been provided by plantation owners now had to be purchased in cash. Given that most Blacks did not have cash, they were forced into sharecropping and tenancy arrangements that kept them in perpetual debt.

The treatment of the supposedly emancipated Africans by southerners was so unjust and severe that the Republican-dominated Congress was prompted to investigate and propose bills that would grant relief to Africans and assure their civil rights. The Congress proposed an extension of the activities of the Freedmen's Bureau. The Freedmen's Bureau was an agency of the War Department established in March 1865 to assist former slaves and impoverished Whites in employment, health programs, labor or wage contract disputes, and in the development of schools.

Congress also proposed a Civil Rights bill that essentially was to become the Fourteenth Amendment. President Johnson vetoed both of these bills, basically on the grounds that they provided more than the former slaves deserved and were capable of handling. The Republican Congress easily overrode the president's veto and went on to pass the Fourteenth Amendment on June 13, 1866, pending its ratification by the states. To force southerners to comply with the Civil Rights measures, the Reconstruction Act of March 2, 1867, was enacted. The act specified that the defiant former states of the Confederacy were to be divided into five military districts, with each one governed by a major general. The generals were to prepare the states for readmission to the Union by organizing a constitutional convention comprising delegates elected by voters. No state would be admitted until it had ratified the Fourteenth Amendment.

Following the ratification of the Fourteenth and Fifteenth Amendments and during the brief period of Reconstruction, many African Americans were elected or appointed to serve in various political and public offices. Under the auspices and enforcement of their civil rights by the federal government, Blacks served as senators, legislators, and in a number of lesser state and federal public offices. Hiram R. Revels and Blanche K. Bruce, two Blacks from Mississippi, served in the US Senate, and fourteen other Blacks sat in the House of Representatives. Contrary to racist myths and stereotypes, most African American officials competently and diligently executed the duties of their offices. As historians J. G. Randall and David Donald maintain, "It should be added that the few [Blacks] who served in high offices were mostly men of ability and integrity."[55] Despite these accomplishments, the Reconstruction experiment was destined to fail because efforts by African Americans to take advantage of what appeared to be unprecedented opportunities were frustrated by the actions of southern planters, military leaders, and government officials.

Ulysses Grant succeeded Andrew Johnson as president of the United States. During the early phase of the Grant administration, the country was undergoing territorial and diplomatic expansion and rapid development in industry and technology. However, Grant's tenure of office was marred by corruption and scandals that were attributed largely to his ineptitude or unfitness for the presidency. Even before the end of his second term of office, southern Democrats and their northern counterparts had gained basic control of the legislature. Radical or liberal Republicans who had championed and safeguarded Black Reconstruction in the South had begun to lose moderate Republican support. An economic depression plagued the second half of the Grant term, and the attention of the country turned from the problems of the South and from the civil and human rights of Blacks to what were construed as the more urgent matters of the national debt, currency, tariffs, and property rights.

Radical Republicans and carpetbaggers were able to gain widespread political influence in the South. Black voters were instrumental in the election of Republican state governments and Republican members to the US House of Representatives and Senate throughout the South. Although some of the carpetbaggers were corrupt opportunists, many others were sincerely interested in promoting the well-being of formerly enslaved African Americans. White Democrats, fearful of the rise and threat of Black Republicanism in the South, resorted to intimidation and terror to discourage Blacks from participating in the electoral process. Terrorist organizations like the Ku Klux Klan and other White secret societies perpetrated violence, arson, murder, and other acts designed to instill fear in Blacks and suppress their participation in Republican politics. White racist Democrats soon reigned supreme in all the southern states. The Republican tide that had swept in Reconstruction and relief from oppression for Africans waned.

The final death knell for Reconstruction was the election of Rutherford B. Hayes as president in 1876. To win the office, Hayes made a series of compromises and pledges to end southern racial reformism and to reconcile the interests of the North and South. Hayes recalled the remaining federal troops and Reconstruction-enforcement officers from the South. The US Supreme Court also became indifferent and hostile to the equal citizenship rights that the Reconstruction amendments had supposedly bestowed on Africans. Its rulings were unfavorable to Blacks in a number of Reconstruction cases, even those involving the Fifteenth Amendment that guaranteed all citizens the right to vote. The federal government further abandoned the former slaves by neglecting enforcement of civil rights and safeguards of Black freedom. Thus, Reconstruction ended with the fate of African Americans left once again to the merciless and oppressive racist designs of reactionary southern Whites. The

3

scenario of Black–White relations from 1865 to 1877 is reflective of what would occur between 1960 and 2000—namely, social revolution, reconstruction, and retrogression.

From "Neoslavery" to Protest and Social Transformation

Renewal and Intensification of Oppression and Violence

After Reconstruction ended, African Americans experienced a modified form of racial subjugation that could be described as *neoslavery*. This form of oppression differed from traditional American slavery only in that Blacks were no longer the chattel property of Whites. Constitutionally and theoretically, but not in practice, they were supposed to be free and equal. African Americans, especially in the South, were stripped of almost every vestige of citizenship rights. They were denied justice, due process, and protection of the law as prescribed by the Constitution.

Eminent Black scholar W. E. B. Du Bois describes the fate and condition of Africans in the South after the fall of Reconstruction as a step back toward slavery. Du Bois's account of this reversion emphasizes the economic necessity of southern Whites to perpetuate the subjugation of Blacks after Emancipation because former slaves were still the South's major economic asset. The Civil War had destroyed the economic foundations of the South, and the South could not rebuild without exploiting the labor of Africans and denying their humanity.[56] Economics alone, however, can neither explain nor rationalize the virulent hatred Whites had for Blacks or their obsession with holding African people in perpetual servitude. The psychological dimensions of southern Whites' attitudes toward and treatment of Blacks have yet to be investigated.

The former Confederate states defied both the Fourteenth Amendment, which afforded equal citizenship rights to Blacks, and the Fifteenth Amendment, which afforded the right to vote to all citizens. The Civil Rights Act of 1875, which mandated that African Americans be afforded equal and full access to public facilities and conveyances, was also ignored. Instead, the southern states nearly jointly and successively began to pass so-called "Jim Crow" laws designed to

circumvent and to nullify the Constitution and any federal laws enacted to protect the citizenship status of Blacks.

Jim Crow more aptly describes the laws and statutes that were passed to segregate Blacks from Whites in every facet of southern life, including education, transportation, and housing. Through mob violence, terrorist group activities, and lynching, Whites sought to discourage Blacks from asserting their citizenship rights. The most blatant affront to constitutional law was the set of unscrupulous and cruel practices used to discourage and deny Black people the right to vote. Mississippi, with a majority-Black population in 1890, took the lead in eliminating Black voters. Each voter was compelled to pay a poll tax of two dollars, and one could not vote if previously convicted of certain misdemeanors.

Strict and ridiculous literacy competencies were required of Blacks as a condition for voting in southern states. Louisiana, for example, wrote and adopted a grandfather clause in 1898 to restrict Black voter participation. The clause granted the voting franchise "to any person who, although lacking the requisite education and property, had been eligible to vote on January 1, 1866, or who was the son or grandson of a person eligible to vote on that date."[57] All the former Confederate states contrived "legal" and effective strategies for disfranchising Blacks by the first decade of the twentieth century.

White southern Democrats dominated the politics of the South. Conditions in cities, both in the South and the North, were no more hospitable. The presence of Blacks in cities, although not expanding significantly at the time, was perceived as a threat to the new European immigrants who began to pour into major cities in large numbers in the 1870s. Subsequently, race riots targeting Blacks broke out in Philadelphia in 1871; Danville, Virginia, in 1883; Wilmington, North Carolina, in 1898; and New York City in 1900.

Successive US Presidents from 1885 to 1893—Rutherford B. Hayes, James A. Garfield, Chester A. Arthur, Grover Cleveland, and Benjamin Harrison—either ignored or failed to enforce constitutional measures that were intended to ensure the equal citizenship rights of African people. The US Supreme Court, through its distorted interpretations of the Fourteenth Amendment, consistently rendered decisions favorable to the racist and segregationist designs of White southerners. Financial linkages between southern businessmen and property owners and between the industrial and commercial interests of northern Democrats induced many northern Whites to ignore neoslavery developments in the South.

The emergence of the Populist Party of 1891 served briefly to garner the support of poor Whites and Blacks in opposition to both the Democratic and Republican parties. However, this experiment failed when all the political camps began to exploit and intimidate Blacks in competition for their votes. White southerners recognized the threat of Black political participation and moved swiftly toward complete disfranchisement of African Americans. The stranglehold of White supremacist ideology tightened on Blacks in the South as they were subjected increasingly to terror, violence, lynching, and murder. Some of these same practices reared their ugly heads in the North as well. Segregation, race purity enforcement, discrimination, and assertions of African inferiority—based on so-called biblical and scientific rationales—became operating principles of southern politics. Jim Crow practices ranged from the extreme to the ridiculous, from segregated restrooms to separate Bibles in the courtroom.[58] A new form of slavery and a virulent era of racism had begun.

In a very few situations, enterprising and creative African Americans were able to create vibrant and stable communities that were somewhat insulated from the outside racist sociopolitical environment. In each of these communities, the development of a strong Black capitalist sector was tied integrally to a broader-based economic development strategy. In Durham, North Carolina, for example, Black-owned and operated life insurance companies and banks undergirded the development of a strong capitalist sector. Du Bois praised Durham as a model of how successful Black communities could be established in an effort to create what he describes as a "group economy."[59]

Black Migration, Education, Protest, and Accommodation

There was little hope for change of the oppressive plight of African Americans in the North or South at the end of the nineteenth century. Although segregation was not as rampant or extreme in the North, economic discrimination in employment opportunity, housing, and social services for Blacks was equally appalling. If any vestige of hope remained, it was found in the US Constitution

and federal Civil Rights laws that, in words and theory, guaranteed freedom, justice, and equality for all citizens. Much of this hope faded in 1896, however, when the Supreme Court upheld a Louisiana law requiring segregated facilities for Blacks and Whites. In a case brought by Homer A. Plessy, a Black man who had been ejected from a "Whites-only" railway car, the Court ruled that the Louisiana Jim-Crow policy of separate-but-equal was legal. With this one sweeping decision in *Plessy v. Ferguson*, the Court gave constitutional approval to Jim Crowism or *de jure* segregation. The Court's separate-but-equal ruling would negatively affect the social, economic, and political life of African Americans for the next sixty-eight years, well into the twentieth century.

In essence, the Court ruled that separate-but-equal public facilities or accommodations did not violate the Fourteenth Amendment. Superficially, the decision appeared reasonable; the Court mandated equality of separate facilities. Indeed, if Black public schools, housing, and other accommodations or facilities had been made equal and on par with those available to Whites, much of the racial conflict and claims of injustice might have subsided. However, the equitable separation of the races never occurred. Public facilities, accommodations, assets, services, and other provisions for Blacks were always demonstrably inferior or second-class to those of Whites. The inequitable practice of the separate-but-equal doctrine worsened the oppressive educational and economic conditions of Blacks in the South. Whereas schools for Whites were modern, sufficiently staffed, and equipped with the best instructional aids, Blacks attended comparatively run-down schools with poorly prepared teachers and obsolete or inadequate educational supplies and equipment. Education was also rapidly emerging as the key to equitable employment opportunity. Without education, Blacks were relegated to low-paying, menial, labor-intensive, and hazardous jobs with no hope of advancement. Thus, many Blacks were locked into an inextricable cycle of poverty.

Despite the Court's iniquitous ruling and other monumental setbacks of the late nineteenth century, Blacks sought freedom not only of body but also of thought and mind. Concerning this struggle, W. E. B. Du Bois observes:

It is but human experience to find that the complete suppression of a race is impossible. Despite inner discouragement and submission to the oppression of others there persisted the mighty spirit, the emotional rebound that kept a vast number struggling

3

for its rights, for self-expression, and for social uplift.[60]

The separate-but-equal doctrine was a catalyst for discontent among Black people of the South. Thousands resorted to migration to escape segregation, discrimination, and poverty. Small migrations of Blacks from the South to the North and West began during and shortly after the Civil War, but the great exodus to which historians refer, of African Americans from the South, began during the early twentieth century. Blacks unquestionably fled the South in such large numbers because of the extreme oppression, segregation, violence, and intimidation they suffered under White racist southern society and particularly under plantation owners. Moreover, after the severe drought, crop failures, and cotton boll weevil plague of 1915–16, plantation owners and Black sharecroppers and tenants were hard-pressed to subsist. Thus, thousands of Blacks left the South simply to feed their families.

Benjamin Quarles writes that the earlier migration from 1879 to 1890 of Blacks to the West—that is, to the states of Oklahoma, Kansas, Texas, Nebraska, and Iowa—was stymied because of extreme cold and hardship. As he notes: "Some of the migrants were thus able to weather the storm, eventually finding jobs or obtaining public lands. But others returned to the South or struck out in new directions."[61] Organized migrations sometimes occurred, as in the case of the two hundred thousand *exodusters* who migrated to the Midwest, especially to Kansas and Oklahoma, in the late 1870s. Indeed, a movement was launched to make Oklahoma and Texas all-Black states.

By far, however, the largest migration of Blacks from 1890 to 1920 was northward. Although figures from different sources vary, during this period more than a million Black southerners left the South to live in large urban centers of the North. Florette Henri reported that "by 1920, almost 40 percent of the Black population in the North was concentrated in the eight cities of Chicago, Detroit, New York, Cleveland, Cincinnati, Columbus, Philadelphia, and Pittsburgh."[62] In addition to the desire to escape Jim Crow, racial violence, and lynching, Black migrants were also seeking social and economic betterment. The Industrial Revolution created jobs that paid significantly higher wages than could be obtained in the South. Furthermore, the absence of overt and extreme segregation in public conveyances, schools, facilities, and accommodations in the North enabled the African American migrants to regain a sense of human dignity and self-respect. Even in the metropolitan areas of the North, Blacks were discriminated against in union membership, in specific employment opportunities, and in housing.

The exodus of Blacks from the South created economic problems for White southerners. Exploitation, injustice, and brutality suffered at the hands of Whites caused Africans to flee the South. Yet, the economy of the southern states was still heavily dependent on cheap Black labor and the peonage system. Consequently, southern officials attempted to restrict and prevent the tide of Black migration to the North and West. Norman Hodges relates how Blacks were intimidated and forced back to farms, refused railway and bus tickets, arrested as vagrants, and even beaten to stem their exodus.[63] White southerners have always had a paradoxical and ironic relationship with Black people. Many have, historically, mistreated and enslaved Africans and have refused to live equitably and harmoniously with Blacks although their economic and political survival was inextricably tied to the continuing presence of Blacks.

Migration to the North did not end the racism, discrimination, suffering, and violence experienced by many African Americans. What Blacks experienced were differences in the nature, degree, types, and intensity of racist treatment, along with hardship. The large influx of Blacks to northern cities and towns was destined to create conflict and arouse prejudice and resentment among northern Whites. The problem of providing housing, employment, health, and social services for the tides of migrants was an overriding concern and issue for urban officials and politicians. Mostly unskilled and uneducated, Blacks were forced to live in deteriorating sections of cities and live in overcrowded units in hovels and ghetto structures. Conditions of squalor and deprivation caused widespread disease and deaths. Thousands died from tuberculosis, pneumonia, and venereal disease. Health agencies were hard-pressed to provide care for both indigenous residents and migrants. Black infant mortality rates were disproportionately high.

Structural unemployment, dislocation, and impoverished conditions contributed to problems of crime, alcohol, drugs, and other forms of deviance in the ghetto. Exhibiting no understanding of the historical and sociological circumstances leading to the deplorable conditions among Black urban dwellers, many northerners regarded migrant Blacks as criminally prone social misfits. Blacks also had to compete with the flood of European immigrants for various industrial and commercial jobs, both skilled and unskilled. From 1900 to 1920, this competition created interethnic or interracial conflict that resulted in several race riots. These developments made the transition from the South to the North a tenuous proposition for Blacks; even so, few chose to return to the South. Overall, Black people's life chances, educational opportunities, and possibilities for social justice were somewhat better in the North. Furthermore, the lynching of African Americans throughout the United States increased dramatically from 1890 to 1920, with most of the incidents occurring in the South.

The Black Church was a major institution in giving important assistance to and in sustaining the perseverance of Black southern migrants. W. E. B. Du Bois observes, in his classic work, *The Souls of Black Folk*, that "the Negro Church is the social center of Negro life in the United States, and the most characteristic expression of African character."[64] The church served as the social and spiritual link to the southern homeland the Black migrants had left behind. On the other hand, the migrants inspired within the northern churches a deepening sense of solidarity and community. With increased memberships, Black churches sponsored various programs to care for the sick, feed the hungry, and assist new migrants in finding housing and employment.

The Black Women's Club Movement also played an important role in providing supportive services to Black urban residents. Two pre-existing organizations merged in 1895 to form the National Association of Colored Women with the motto, "Lifting as We Climb." The clubs that were part of this federation provided support to the aged and the infirm as well as medical care, child care, and related services to Black families.[65]

The first decade of the twentieth century was marked not only by Black migration but also by mob violence, race riots, and lynchings in the North and South. It was inevitable that Blacks, especially those of the North, would seek to organize, protest, and petition the government for protection and relief. Theodore Roosevelt ascended to the American presidency in 1901 and, like most politicians of his day, turned a deaf ear to the plight of Blacks. The National Association for the Advancement of Colored People (NAACP) was organized in 1909, with W. E. B. Du Bois as one of its charter members. Its purpose was to work toward ending segregation and the lynching of Blacks, to fight for equal education, and generally to demand that the

provisions of the Fourteenth and Fifteenth Amendments be enforced. In 1911, the National Urban League (NUL) was founded as a result of a merger of three older organizations. Its main objective was to facilitate the entry of Black migrant workers into the industrialized job markets of the northern urban centers.

Black protest and self-uplift in the twentieth century involved a number of self-help efforts, including those of the Niagara Movement, the National Association of Colored Women, and various African American lodges and societies. It expanded to encompass organizations with an interracial support base such as the NAACP and the NUL. The establishment of Black churches and educational institutions during the latter part of the nineteenth century served as the foundation for these organizations and for the Civil Rights Movement of the entire twentieth century. After the Civil War and during Reconstruction, African American church denominations were instrumental in establishing schools and colleges for the Black population. White religious and philanthropic organizations of the North assisted the independent Black educational institutions and also established other schools and colleges for African Americans. During the late nineteenth century, major White liberal universities of the North had begun to admit and graduate select African Americans.

Given the increased educational opportunities of the late 1800s and early 1900s and despite the general climate of repression and oppression, learned and talented African Americans made outstanding contributions to business and industry as inventors and entrepreneurs. In the arts and humanities, they began to create and express Black culture in literature, poetry, art, and music. For example, Jan Matzeliger (1852–1889) invented a shoe-lasting machine that revolutionized the shoemaking industry and made shoe lasting by hand obsolete. Elijah McCoy (1845–1929) patented more than fifty inventions related to the mechanical lubrication of rail locomotives. Matzeliger and McCoy were only two among hundreds of African American inventors from the seventeenth to the twentieth century. Some were able to have their inventions patented, but others were denied this right.[66]

Novelists Charles Waddell Chestnutt (1858–1932) and Zora Neale Hurston (1903–1960), poets Paul Laurence Dunbar (1872–1906) and Claude McKay (1890–1948), artists Henry O. Tanner (1859–1937) and William Harper (1873–1910), musician Joseph (King) Oliver (1885–1938), and composer W. C. Handy

3

(1873–1958) were among the many notable exponents of African American culture during this period. Literally an explosion of Black cultural arts and letters took place during the Harlem Renaissance, which began at the height of the exodus of Blacks from the South before and during World War I and lasted for more than two decades. The Harlem Renaissance will be discussed in more detail in the chapter exploring African American cultural arts and creativity.

Education dispels ignorance, bolsters courage, and gives insight into the important social phenomena that shape human relationships. Frederick Douglass, the largely self-educated, eloquent, and fiery Black leader during and throughout the abolitionist, emancipation, and Reconstruction periods, indisputably articulated the major social philosophy of African Americans. Douglass championed and fought for the assimilationist goal of social, political, economic, and educational equality of Blacks and Whites. In an ironic turn of fate, Frederick Douglass died in 1895, the year before the US Supreme Court rendered its infamous *Plessy vs. Ferguson* (separate-but-equal) decision that legitimized racial apartheid in the United States. Douglass's death left a temporary void in the philosophical direction of African Americans; but a new cadre of Black educated elites was already forming who would challenge, modify, or extend his social philosophy.

Douglass's demise cleared the way for the ascendancy of Booker T. Washington to the top realm of African American leadership. Washington, educated at Hampton Institute in Virginia, was the principal of a school established by White southern philanthropists for Blacks in Alabama. That school would later become Tuskegee Institute. Washington espoused a social philosophy that was, in many ways, diametrically opposed to that of Frederick Douglass, but there were certain aspects of his ideology for Black liberation that appeared logical, feasible, and practical in the context of race relations during his era. Washington's views should be interpreted in a contextual frame that focuses on the Supreme Court's codification of separate-but-equal as the law of the land.

Washington seemed to endorse Jim Crowism and segregation by conceding the political disfranchisement of African Americans and discouraging an immediate struggle for equality and civil rights. He proposed that Blacks should strive to master the crafts and vocational trades and forsake aspirations to excel in the professional and liberal arts fields. He exhorted Blacks to emulate or adopt White Victorian principles of manners and cleanliness, and advocated self-help and self-improvement. Washington also encouraged and promoted Black independent entrepreneurship. Given this social philosophy, it is not surprising that he won the hearts, minds, and influence of Whites throughout the United States.

In his address to the Atlanta Exposition of 1895, Washington detailed essential elements of his racial social philosophy. He spoke with much humility and eloquence, maintaining that, "In all things that are purely social we [Blacks and Whites] can be as separate as the fingers, yet one as the hand in all things essential to mutual progress."[67] On the issue of racial and social equality, he claimed the following: "The wisest among my race understand that the agitation of questions of social equality is the extremist folly, and that progress in the enjoyment of all the privileges that will come to us must be the result of severe and constant struggle rather than of artificial forcing."[68] Following his Atlanta Exposition address, Washington was highly recognized and praised by Presidents Theodore Roosevelt and William Howard Taft. Several White industrialists and philanthropists gave him financial aid and support for Tuskegee Institute.

A fair analysis of the full context of Washington's address beyond his obvious submission to White interests and sensitivities might reveal a few practical and logical approaches to Black survival and development under the conditions of that time. Some contemporary Black social theorists detect elements of Black Nationalism in Booker T. Washington's philosophy. Others regard Washington as an "Uncle Tom" who pawned the best interests of African Americans to ensure his White-appointed role as the leader of the Black race.

Booker T. Washington did not escape criticism from his African American peers or fellow educated elites. Foremost among those who opposed his social philosophy and disagreed with the accommodationist theme of his Atlanta speech were W.E.B. Du Bois and William Monroe Trotter. Du Bois and Trotter, graduates of Harvard University, were opposed to Washington's philosophy. They advocated liberal instead of vocational education for Blacks, sought to repeal segregationist laws, petitioned to halt lynching, and demanded that the government enforce the constitutional provisions of equal citizenship and voting rights. Leading educated Black women who fought against lynching and segregation included Ida B. Wells Barnett and Mary Church Terrell. They, along with other detractors of Washington, continued to promote the integrationist ideals of Frederick Douglass.

Booker T. Washington and his social philosophy did have some support among African Americans, but he was lauded and praised largely by Whites, many of whom were avowed racists and haters of African people. The adulation that Whites had for Washington did not affect or diminish the lynchings, mob violence, mutilations, and terror directed toward African Americans during the time of his leadership. Race relations actually worsened. Over three thousand Black men and women had been lynched by 1915, the year that Washington died. By the time Du Bois, Trotter, and twenty or more Black professional men met near Buffalo, New York, to organize the Niagara Movement, the Black masses had begun to turn away from accommodation and submission as viable responses to racism and White oppression.[69]

World War I, Segregation, Riots, and Black Nationalism

African Americans endured extremely abusive, inhumane, and violent treatment from Whites during and after World War I. The war spurred an increase in Black migration from the South to the North and energized a new spirit of resiliency and resolve among Blacks to struggle against oppression. World War I temporarily restricted the inflow of European immigrants and created job opportunities for Blacks in the North. The need for Black industrial workers, coupled with a recession in southern agriculture, catalyzed a mass migration of between seven hundred thousand and one million Blacks from the South to northern and western cities. White workers protested the employment of Black workers in industrial enterprises.

A special Office of Negro Economics was established during the war to increase social acceptance of Black workers and discourage more Blacks from migrating from the South. Blacks, however, increasingly ignored efforts to slow their northern migration, and Black workers responded to the opposition of White workers in several ways. They worked, for example, as strikebreakers, and they formed all-Black unions.

When the United States decided to enter the War in Europe, in March 1917, thousands of Blacks rushed to volunteer. Initially, they were rebuffed. The attitude and disposition of the federal government with regard to Black enlistment in World War I were consistent with the precedents set during the Revolutionary War, War of 1812, and the Civil War. Nevertheless, after passage of the Selective Service Act, which required all able-bodied male citizens between the ages of twenty-one and thirty-one to register, Blacks were accepted into the armed services. Of the more than two million African Americans who registered during the early draft period, approximately three hundred-seventy thousand—a disproportionately large number—served. Most were assigned to segregated labor and support military units.[70]

At the outbreak of the War in Europe in 1914, Blacks were too preoccupied with protesting the spate of murders, lynchings, and incidents of mob violence in the United States to form a collective opinion on the world conflict. In 1917, more than one hundred Blacks were killed and millions of dollars in property damage occurred in the Black community of East Saint Louis, Illinois, as a result of White mob violence and race riots. Racial violence erupted wherever large numbers of Blacks entered the large cities. However, most Blacks supported the war and opted for the opportunity, once again, to win the right of full citizenship and to become equal participants in American democracy. W. E. B. Du Bois even urged Blacks to put aside their grievances with White America and "close ranks" during the war effort. William Monroe Trotter dissented from this point of view, however, and continued to demand equal rights and the integration of the armed services.

The enlistment and service of Blacks in the military did not lessen the hostility of White civilians toward African American soldiers. Racial tensions and violence actually heightened in towns and cities where Black troops were stationed. Black soldiers were greeted with contempt from Whites, strictly segregated, and denied admission to theaters, restaurants, and other public facilities. Clashes between White civilian authorities and Black soldiers occurred frequently.

The most notable of such incidents resulted in a riot in Houston, Texas, in the summer of 1917. The riot started when a Black soldier intervened as a White policeman assaulted a Black woman. The police arrested and jailed both the woman and the soldier. When members of the Black soldier's unit inquired about the incident, they were physically attacked and shots were fired at them. Rumors quickly developed that Black soldiers were being brutalized or murdered by the police. That night, over one hundred Black soldiers broke into their armory, took ammunition and arms, and marched into the city. Several Whites, including five policemen, and two Blacks were killed. White federal troops and Texas militia eventually disarmed the Black soldiers. The Army hastened to make examples of the insurrectionists. One hundred fifty-six men were court-martialed

3

for mutiny. Of the sixty-three who were tried, forty-one received life sentences, four received shorter sentences, five were acquitted, and thirteen were hanged before any appeal could be mounted.

Black soldiers suffered humiliation and insults not only in the United States but also while stationed overseas, where they were discouraged and prohibited from socializing with White European women and were taunted with racial epithets. The National Association for the Advancement of Colored People (NAACP) was at the forefront in protesting and petitioning the government to investigate and relieve the plight of Blacks in the military. NAACP officials were instrumental in the establishment of a school for the development of Black commissioned officers. As a result, at least fourteen hundred Black officers were commissioned and later served during the war, even though the top field grade officers in the segregated units were usually White. Ironically, Black leaders and organizations appealed for more Black soldiers to be assigned to combat or frontline service. Eventually, as in the case of previous wars, manpower demands compelled the formation of various Black combat units and regiments.

Despite the racist and bigoted treatment accorded African American soldiers, treatment that would have dampened the *esprit de corps* of even the most avid patriots, Black companies and regiments served the American military with gallantry and distinction. According to historian Lerone Bennett:

> Three of these regiments—the 369th, the 371st and the 372nd—received the Croix de Guerre for valor, and the fourth covered itself with distinction in battles in Argonne Forest. The 369th...was the first allied unit to reach the Rhine [River, in Germany]. Although the 369th was under fire for 191 days, it never lost a foot of ground, a trench or a soldier through capture. No less courageous was the 370th...which was commanded almost entirely by black officers and which fought the last battle of the war.[71]

If Black soldiers and citizens expected gratitude or redemption from racial bigotry and oppression for their exemplary service and patriotism after the war, their expectations were soon dispelled. The cessation and slowdown of wartime industries resulted in mass layoffs and unemployment. Migration problems and racial tensions combined with African Americans' increasing intolerance of racism, especially after their contributions

and sacrifices during the war, brought on new conflicts, riots, and resistance. After the war and during the summer of 1919, a succession of riots erupted in Chicago, Washington, DC, Omaha, Knoxville, Charleston, and Longview, Texas. Whites as well as Blacks were killed, an indication that passivity to White violence was a thing of the past. A large segment of the Black population adopted an aggressive self-defense ideology.[72]

Following what some historians refer to as the "Red Summer" of 1919, Marcus Garvey, a Black man from Jamaica, took the public stage. Garvey was destined to become the leader of the first mass Black ideological movement in African American history. His emergence as a charismatic leader who promoted Black pride, reveled in the ancient history of Africa, and advocated Black self-help and self-determination was both fortuitous and timely for African Americans. Blacks were disillusioned after witnessing a resurgence of White hate, discrimination, violence, and terrorist organizations in the post-World War I period. The formal appeals, moral suasion, and patient strivings of Black intellectuals during this time were insufficient to placate the Black masses. They needed and found in Marcus Garvey a savior or a "Moses" who could lead them to liberation and instill within them a new feeling of self-esteem.[73] The essence of Garvey's ideology might be described as Black Nationalism. His philosophy influenced Black thought during the 1920s, was revived during the 1960s, and persists to this day among a significant segment of the Black population.

The Decades of Enlightenment, Depression, and the "New Deal"

The period from 1920 to 1940 was pivotal in establishing the foundation for a gradual upswing in the fate and fortune of African Americans. New expectations had been created by the unprecedented opportunities made possible by World War I, and Blacks were not inclined to allow these gains to be revoked without a fight. A major depression in the agricultural sector between 1920 and 1927 spurred renewed Black migration to the North and led to increased tensions between Black and White workers. Although some White labor interests attempted to reduce these conflicts by organizing Black workers, Blacks themselves undertook major self-organizing activities—another manifestation of their renewed racial pride and self-confidence.

African American creativity in the arts, literature, and music blossomed and flourished from the mid-1920s until 1940 as part of the so-called "Harlem Renaissance" movement. Although writers and historians maintain that the nucleus of this era's Black cultural movement was New York's Harlem borough, the contributors, activities, and impact of the period encompassed all of Black America. Few would deny, however, that Marcus Garvey's philosophy and crusade of African pride, self-esteem, and self-determination inspired and nurtured Black cultural, social, and economic industry during this era.

Few Black historians have attempted to connect or relate changes in the Black community with corresponding social and ideological changes occurring among White Americans. In *The National Experience*, however, historian John M. Blum and his coauthors contend that a mood of nonconformity and dissent emerged during the post-World War I period among a significant segment of the White population. They claim that some Whites had begun to reject materialism and the corporate ethos and had embraced progressive ideals of literature, art, and intellectualism. For these Whites, the era was defined by Sigmund Freud's psychological theories focusing on the seminal role of conflict in shaping sexual identity and human nature. White American novelists Ernest Hemingway and William Faulkner and the poet T. S. Eliot reflected this changed outlook in their literary contributions to the broader society. Thus, the weariness of the post-war period, coupled with the social pathology evident in the race relations of the time, engendered some rebellion and radicalism, even in White society. Blum et al. elucidate this phenomenon thusly:

> One symbol of their [Blacks'] protest was jazz, with its sensuality, its spontaneity, its atavistic rhythms, and with the sinuous and intimate dancing it inspired. Jazz was ungenteel, even un-Caucasian, above all uninhibited. It expressed not only protest and art of a kind but also a controversial change in sexual mores.[74]

There is, of course, no way to prove any direct relationship between the liberated spirit of oppressed Blacks during the Harlem Renaissance and the radicalism that developed among some White Americans in the post-World War I period. However, it is more than speculative to say that the burst of artistic talent, literary genius,

and scholarship demonstrated by Blacks caused Whites to view Black people from a different perspective.

Several political gains accrued to Blacks during this period. The rapid growth of the national economy following the recession immediately after the war was a significant factor in African American cultural and intellectual development. The nation came close to achieving full employment during the presidential terms of Warren G. Harding and Calvin Coolidge because of industrial mechanization, the proliferation of factories, and the implementation of mass-production techniques in manufacturing. Although Blacks generally were relegated to the lowest-paying and most menial jobs, their job opportunities and incomes improved with the healthy general economy. White trade and labor unions, however, practiced systematic discrimination against Black workers and job seekers. Blacks therefore engaged in various self-organizing efforts. These initiatives included the formation of the American Negro Labor Congress and the Brotherhood of Sleeping Car Porters (BCSCP) in 1925. At its apex, the latter group, organized by A. Philip Randolph as a direct response to the exclusionary practices of the White railroad brotherhoods, had a membership of 35,000. The BSCP became affiliated with the American Federation of Labor (AFL) in 1929 but was unable to alter the AFL's traditional racist posture. In discussing these efforts, Joe Trotter notes that: "[D]espite little success in changing the material conditions of Black workers during the 1920s, the BCSP and other Black labor organizations established the groundwork for a more vigorous labor movement during the New Deal era of the 1930s."[75]

Economic prosperity from 1920 to 1929 did not stem the tide of injustice, racism, and discrimination toward African Americans. Racial hostilities and conflicts were common throughout the country and lynching invariably continued in the South. Moreover, the large-scale migration by Blacks out of the South in the 1920s set in motion a continuing decline in the amount of farmland owned by Blacks, which had reached a high point of twenty-million acres in 1920.

The Black exodus from the South not only caused a surge in population in the North but also became a major influence in shaping northern urban politics, a reality that persists to this day. Despite the Republican Party's betrayal of Blacks after Reconstruction, most African Americans perceived the party of Abraham Lincoln as more supportive of civil rights than the Democratic Party. Thus, once liberated from the racist Democratic stronghold of the South, Blacks in the North tended to vote Republican. In their efforts to remain politically competitive with the northern Republicans, White northern Democrats attempted to attract African Americans to the Democratic Party. Their efforts included offering small political amenities and appointments to Blacks.

The Republicans and Democrats were not the only political parties interested in Black voters, however. The Socialist and Communist parties of America also sought political alliances with African Americans, but neither was successful in attracting a significant number of African Americans to their ranks. The labor-class ideologies of the socialists and communists have never gained widespread acceptance by Blacks, nor have large numbers of Blacks deemed them directly relevant to many of the race-specific problems facing Black people in America. There were, however, several notable exceptions to this observation. For example, the African Blood Brotherhood (ABB), founded by West Indian journalist Cyril Briggs, was a radical Black liberation organization that eventually developed ties to the Communist Party.

Briggs initially worked for New York City's *Amsterdam News*, but quit because he perceived censorship of his ideas regarding racial separatism. He launched his own monthly magazine, *The Crusader*, in November 1918; and organized the ABB in early 1919. At its peak, *The Crusader's* circulation was about 36,000. The ABB's national headquarters was in New York City, with various "posts" located in other parts of the country. Its membership probably never exceeded three thousand.

The formal linking of the ABB to the Communist Party occurred in 1921 when Briggs joined the organization. The Communist Party hoped to use the ABB to mobilize support among the Black working class. Publication of *The Crusader* ceased in 1922, but Briggs continued to operate the Crusader News Service, partially in an effort to fight the ideology of Marcus Garvey, which Briggs opposed as capitalist in nature. The ABB was dissolved in the early 1920s, and many of its members became affiliated with various other Communist and Communist-leaning organizations.[76]

African Americans began to demonstrate an unprecedented proclivity toward political independence during the latter 1920s. This pattern was evident in the national presidential election of 1928, when Alfred E. Smith ran as a Democrat against the Republican Herbert Hoover. Hoover espoused the capitalist virtues of individualism, *laissez–faire* capitalism, corporation rights,

and business prosperity. He was indisputably conservative and implicitly White-supremacist in his ideologies. Al Smith may not have been classified as a liberal, but as governor of New York he advocated for strong public assistance programs and civil liberty protections. He was also a Catholic. The Democrats did not win the election, but Blacks voted for Smith and the Democratic Party in surprisingly large numbers that year. This demonstrated that the Republicans could no longer depend on the automatic support of African Americans. The end of the 1920s thus would usher in a new era of Black politics and mark a dramatic change in the nation's political orientation.

Herbert Hoover rode the crest of the nation's economic prosperity for several months following his election in 1928, but no one could have predicted the abrupt economic crash that occurred near the end of 1929. The ensuing Great Depression lasted well into the 1930s. Economists attributed the major causes of the Great Depression to speculation fever, dubious and manipulative stock market schemes, technological displacement of workers, sagging farm prices, and unsound monetary policies of the banking system. Regardless of the specific causes of the nation's economic crash, the unemployment rate soared to over thirty percent and did not fall below fifteen percent during the entire decade of the 1930s.

The Great Depression resulted in financial loss and impoverishment for millions. Its impact was particularly acute for Black Americans, who had been relegated to the bottom of the economic ladder. Various policies designed to end the Great Depression failed throughout the Hoover administration. By the end of Hoover's term of office in 1933, the nation was ready for change and for a leader with imaginative ideas for resolving the country's myriad economic woes and problems. It was virtually presupposed that a Democrat would succeed Hoover because the four years of economic adversity were generally attributed to the Republican administration. The Democrats nominated and were successful in electing Franklin Delano Roosevelt, an astute northern politician, to the presidency in 1932. For the first time since Reconstruction, African Americans voted in significant numbers in support of Democratic candidates. There was, however, a certain political irony in the Black support of the Democrats: the stronghold of the Democratic Party was located in the American South, where racial inequality, segregation, and discrimination continued to flourish. Consequently, a vote for the

Democratic Party also meant a vote for Jim Crowism. Nevertheless, Blacks and Whites wanted a change from the status quo of widespread economic depression and poverty.

Franklin Roosevelt assumed office and began vigorous implementation of his campaign proposal of a "New Deal" for the American society. Almost immediately, the Congress passed more than fifteen bills proposed by Roosevelt. These pieces of legislation were designed to rectify the practices and shortcomings of the banking and financial system, grant assistance and relief to farmers and agriculture, decrease the unemployment rate, establish guidelines and policies for labor and wages, and provide a national plan for social security for all Americans. New Deal programs such as the Works Progress Administration (WPA), Civilian Conservation Corps (CCC), and the National Youth Administration, designed to put people to work, were of particular benefit to poor Whites and Blacks. Many of the New Deal programs were based on the Keynesian economic theory of using compensatory government spending to stimulate economic recovery.[77]

Roosevelt's New Deal policies were not enacted specifically to help African Americans, but Blacks benefited to some extent, even though many were victimized by discrimination in several federal programs. Discrimination was especially rampant in the New Deal programs focused on the agricultural sector. Provisions in the Agricultural Adjustment Act of 1933 allowed landowners to expropriate a large portion of transfer payments ostensibly intended for tenants, among whom Blacks were disproportionately overrepresented. Southern interests also attempted to institute differential legal minimum wages for Blacks and Whites through the National Industrial Recovery Act of 1933. This initiative was thwarted, however, largely as a result of the efforts of the NAACP.

Roosevelt was reserved and publicly noncommittal on civil rights for fear of offending some Whites or losing southern support for his New Deal policies. Notwithstanding, Blacks helped to reelect Roosevelt in 1936, 1940, and 1944; and little doubt remains that significant progress occurred in the ongoing struggle of African Americans for full citizenship during Roosevelt's four terms as president. Roosevelt revived the practice instituted by former presidents Theodore Roosevelt and William Howard Taft of using a cadre of highly qualified African Americans as his consultants or advisors on matters of race relations and civil rights. This group was known as President Roosevelt's "Black Cabinet." The President's wife, Eleanor Roosevelt, was a staunch advocate and activist for the rights and equality of African Americans. She befriended and valued the advice of Mary McLeod Bethune, the renowned Black educator and the only African American woman member of the Black Cabinet.

New Deal and Roosevelt administration actions resulted in improvements in federal employment practices and influenced changes in social and economic practices affecting Blacks. World War II would further increase economic expansion and improve the plight of African Americans. In many respects, World War II would set the stage for a major transition in the status of African Americans.

World War II and Strides Toward Racial Progress

American wars have affected the role, status, and progress of African Americans. From the Revolutionary War of 1775 to the Vietnam War of the 1960s, Whites have found it difficult to reconcile fighting for the American creed of "freedom and justice for all" with their unjust and oppressive treatment of Black Americans. World War II brought these contradictions into sharp relief.

The outbreak of World War II obviated the need for large-scale compensatory government spending measures to stimulate the national economy. European demands for munitions to resist the invasions of Nazi Germany had stimulated recovery in the defense industry long before America entered the War in December 1941. Employment in the United States had begun to increase, and the average White American worker was beginning to receive increases in wages and salaries. Initially, however, the new prosperity did not trickle down to African Americans. Blacks were deliberately discriminated against and excluded from employment in defense industry firms. In the nation's industrial centers, where thousands of qualified African Americans lived, the recruitment of workers was restricted to Whites.

The abject injustice of discrimination against African Americans in the defense industry provoked strong protest from Black leaders and some liberal Whites. Blacks picketed racist defense plants and firms throughout the country. A. Philip Randolph, founder of the Brotherhood of Sleeping Car Porters, organized the most successful protest movement. Randolph threatened a march on Washington involving thousands of

3

Blacks if the Roosevelt administration did not investigate and end the discriminatory hiring practices. A few days before the march was scheduled to take place, President Roosevelt conceded to meet with Randolph and other Black leaders. As a result, Roosevelt agreed to establish the Fair Employment Practices Commission. The success of the Randolph organization no doubt inspired the young Black leader James Farmer to organize the Congress of Racial Equality (CORE) and collaborate with the National Urban League (NUL) and the NAACP to fight racism and discrimination. This initiative was the genesis of modern Black nonviolent protest movements that would play a pivotal role in the struggle for freedom and full citizenship for African Americans throughout the twentieth century.

The exclusionary and discriminatory treatment Black civilians experienced in the defense industry was no less deplorable than the racism and Jim Crowism that Black volunteers and draftees confronted at the hands of the War Department and the armed forces. At the beginning of World War II, fewer than twenty thousand African Americans were in the armed services. The War Department's policy was to enlist Blacks in proportion to their numbers in the general population. Blacks were systematically excluded from the Marine Corps, Army Air Corps, and other elite military units. Blacks in the military were relegated to serve in segregated, labor-intensive, and menial support units. Even though the Selective Service Act of 1940 contained a nondiscrimination clause, the official position of the War Department was as follows: "The policy of the War Department is not to intermingle colored and white enlisted personnel in the same regimental organizations. This policy has been proved satisfactory over a long period of years and to make changes would produce situations destructive to morale and [be] detrimental to preparations for national defense."[78]

In response to protests from Black leaders and manpower shortages, the War Department and the Roosevelt administration were forced to modify some of the discriminatory policies. Officer candidate schools were established where Whites and Blacks trained together. Housing, mess, and recreational facilities were subject to local installation control; and posts with large numbers of Black officers tended to have segregated housing and mess facilities. In 1942, the War Department declared that Black officers could, under specified conditions, command White enlisted troops but that they would be prohibited from commanding White officers. Blacks who completed Officer Candidate School were usually college-educated northerners with no previous military experience or familiarity with the Jim Crow South, where many of the new installations were built.

The heroism of a Black messman, Dorie Miller, stationed on the USS Arizona during the Japanese attack on Pearl Harbor on December 7, 1941, influenced the Navy to change its policy of allowing Blacks to serve only as cooks. As a result, before the end of the war, a relatively few African Americans were commissioned naval officers. However, with a few experimental exceptions, the policy of racial segregation in the armed forces remained intact throughout the duration of the war. In 1945, White and Black units were integrated briefly for an assault against the Germans. Before war's end, more than seven hundred thousand African Americans had served in the different branches of the armed forces. About a half-million of them saw service overseas in various combat units and fighting capacities.[79]

Generally, Black military units and individual African American service men and women served with honor and distinction during World War II. They did so despite discriminatory treatment from their White counterparts-in-arms and contempt and hostility from White civilians. Wherever Black troops were based in the United States, racial incidents and clashes with the civilian populace seemed inevitable. Violent race riots erupted during the war years in Detroit, Los Angeles, and New York. Social injustices, beatings, and lynchings continued in the South, and race relations grew increasingly tense in the North. These experiences would serve to energize Black political efforts to seek freedom and full citizenship during and after World War II.

World War II was unequivocally beneficial in improving the status and prospects of Black Americans. Black men and women had proved they were not cowards and were capable of mastering weapons of war, engage in warfare, and kill as well as Whites. African American civilian and armed service personnel obtained vocational, technical, and scientific training and skills in defense firms and in military occupations that enabled millions of them to become more employable and economically self-sufficient. The war years were also an important testing ground for a new generation or cadre of Black intellectuals, professionals, and leaders who later became visible and recognized by the White establishment.

The new vanguard of Black leadership was politically sophisticated and as daring in the freedom struggle as their predecessors were in the struggle against slavery. By employing bloc-voting strategies in the North and in the South where they could vote, Blacks were able to exact concessions on civil rights issues from both the Democratic and Republican parties. The ability to exercise leverage within the Democratic Party was especially pronounced because the shift from traditional political loyalty to the Republicans was regularly producing eighty- to ninety-percent Black support for Democrats in elections. Thus, Franklin D. Roosevelt soon replaced Abraham Lincoln as the symbolical political benefactor of African Americans.

Roosevelt died on April 12, 1945, only a few months before the Japanese surrendered, an event that marked the end of World War II. Harry S. Truman, Roosevelt's vice president, subsequently became the thirty-third President of the United States. Truman, a native of Missouri, had a penchant for fairness, as evidenced in his 1948 election slogan calling for a "Fair Deal" for America, an extrapolation of Roosevelt's New Deal policies and programs. Truman was the first president to promote, publicly and actively, a comprehensive program of civil rights policies and legislation. In 1946, he appointed a special Commission on Civil Rights. That Commission's 1947 report, *To Secure These Rights*, made sweeping proposals for legislation to address the issues of lynching, poll taxes, and segregation. Truman subsequently proposed legislation to Congress that included many of the Commission's recommendations, but that body repeatedly failed to pass any of his initiatives.

Truman's call during the 1948 election for legislation to ban lynching, poll taxes, and segregated public transportation, and to enact fair employment practices legislation caused many southerners to defect from the Democratic Party and form the Dixiecrat Party. Despite the lack of support from southern Democrats, Truman narrowly won re-election. His election was aided significantly by the northern Black vote. Truman was never successful in securing the passage, by both houses of the Congress, of any of his proposed civil rights measures. Nonetheless, he advanced social justice, desegregation, and civil rights for African American through the issuance of Executive Orders.

On July 26, 1948, for example, Truman issued Executive Order 9981, which ended segregation in the armed forces. Desegregation of the armed forces was the first major institutional challenge to the prevailing separate-but-equal doctrine that had defined the course of race relations since 1896. Although Truman's order did not immediately result in equity or solve all of the racial problems within the armed services, in time the military complied and demonstrated the economic efficacy, logic, fairness, and practicality of integration. Truman's Executive Order also served to alter the views of many individual southerners about traditional racial protocols. In the military, Blacks were routinely placed in positions of authority over Whites. It is also important to note that on the same date Truman issued the military desegregation order, he simultaneously issued Executive Order 9980 barring discrimination in federal employment and in work performed under federal government contracts.

Several developments during the 1950s increased the momentum of the drive to obtain full civil rights for African Americans. The NAACP, bolstered by its growing influence and successes during the 1930s and 1940s, was incessant in mounting court challenges to legally sanctioned racial segregation. The Korean War (1950–1953) yielded additional proof of the workability of racial desegregation and thus accelerated the process of integration in the armed services. Desegregation of the Federal Civil Service and nondiscriminatory employment practices instituted by defense contractors led to significantly expanded employment opportunities for Blacks. Given President Truman's efforts to achieve fair and equal treatment for Black Americans and the NAACP's successful legal challenges and moral suasion, the number of White sympathizers for racial justice increased, even in the South. However, the most essential and effective development—indeed, the development that eventually would produce the demise of Jim Crow—was the gradual ideological shift within the US Supreme Court. This shift manifested as a growing tendency to issue decisions that chipped away at the edifice of institutional discrimination that the Court had created previously.

The Court's momentous decision against racial segregation occurred on May 17, 1954, in *Brown v. Board of Education of Topeka, Kansas*. In that case, Thurgood Marshall, the special counsel for the NAACP, argued that segregation was inherently unconstitutional, that it stigmatized an entire race, and that it thereby denied Blacks equal protection under the law as guaranteed by the Fourteenth Amendment. Chief Justice Earl Warren and the other members of the Court agreed. Thus, after fifty-eight years, the separate-but-equal clause upheld in *Plessy v. Ferguson* in 1896 was overturned.

The southern response and opposition to the Supreme Court's ruling was discussed briefly in Chapter

3

2 in relation to the genesis of African American Studies, but the magnitude of White southern resistance and defiance to the desegregation ruling requires further treatment. The traditional, segregationist states varied in their adoption of one or more of the following responses or stances: reluctant conformance, token and symbolic compliance, or outright defiance. Gradual voluntary desegregation occurred primarily in the border states of Delaware, Maryland, West Virginia, Kentucky, Missouri, and Oklahoma, along with the District of Columbia. Desegregation in a few school districts in Texas and Arkansas occurred briefly before state politicians mounted formal opposition. The upper southern states such as Virginia and Tennessee adopted a pattern of gradual token integration, just sufficient to suggest minimal compliance with the law. More than one hundred southern US senators and congressmen signed a document dubbed the "Southern Manifesto," which declared the 1954 Supreme Court decision to be in violation of the Constitution. Their response, in essence, according to a report of the US Commission on Civil Rights, was one of defiance and included "the adoption of resolutions which purportedly nullified the Court's decision and 'interposed' the States' authority between the Federal Government and the people; called for the impeachment of Supreme Court Justices; and provided for the closing of schools if that became the only alternative to desegregation."[80]

Violent and armed confrontations between community residents and state or federal militia occurred at public schools in various southern states where Black students and their parents attempted to test or comply with the Supreme Court's ruling. The Ku Klux Klan and other hate groups were rejuvenated to bolster the desegregation resistance movement. The mob violence and riots that erupted in Clinton, Tennessee, and in several small towns in Kentucky required the National Guard to be called in to assure the safety of African American children attempting to enter the previously all-White schools. One of the most famous incidents occurred in Little Rock, Arkansas, when Governor Orval Faubus defied the local school board's decision to integrate Central High School in September 1957 and used the local National Guard to prevent Black students from entering the school. President Dwight D. Eisenhower asked Faubus to withdraw the National Guard, but when the Black students returned to Central High the next day, they were blocked once again from entering the school by vehement, screaming Whites. Eisenhower then federalized the National Guard and ordered a thousand paratroopers to Little Rock to escort the Black students to class. Prince Edward County, Virginia, closed its public schools to avoid having to integrate them and provided tuition grants for White children to attend private schools. The Court, however, ordered the county to reopen the schools. Overall, gradualism, legal schemes, and procedural delays were used to thwart the Court's order to desegregate "with all deliberate speed."

Not only were African Americans denied admission to formerly all-White public elementary and secondary schools, they were also barred from state colleges and universities. There were several notable legal cases involving turbulence, civilian or state resistance, NAACP litigation, and intervention by federal marshals. They include cases relating to University of Alabama Black student Autherine Lucy (1956), University of Mississippi Black student James Meredith (1962), and University of Georgia Black students Charlayne Hunter and Hamilton Holmes (1960). The NAACP and its Legal Defense and Educational Fund represented African Americans in virtually all of the school desegregation cases. Although public school, college, and university desegregation has been public policy since the 1960s, it is yet to be implemented successfully or fully in the United States, and court decisions in the 1990s and first decade of the twenty-first century suggest that the future of desegregation efforts is a diminishing one.

President Dwight D. Eisenhower, former General and Supreme Commander of Allied Forces in Europe, governed the country during the crucial beginning and crux of the modern Civil Rights Movement. Eisenhower had a penchant for moderation and military orderliness in his approach to political issues, management, and delegation of authority. Though he is alleged to have espoused racist views personally, his administration proposed new civil rights legislation during both his terms as president. On April 29, 1957, for instance, Congress passed the first civil rights bill for Blacks since the Reconstruction bill of 1875. The legislation was enacted primarily to protect the voting rights of African Americans. It created a Federal Civil Rights Commission to make recommendations to government in the areas of voting, employment, and education.

The Civil Rights Movement and the Post-Civil Rights Era, 1955–2012

The Struggles and Politics of Nonviolent Protest

After the historic 1954 desegregation decision by the US Supreme Court, Blacks intensified their struggle for full constitutional rights and citizenship. Some Whites, however, especially those in the Deep South, were equally determined to prevent African Americans from achieving the equal rights and protection of the Constitution. It is nonetheless debatable as to which specific racial event was the catalyst of the mass Civil Rights Movement of the twentieth century. Many believe the Montgomery, Alabama, transit boycott by thousands of Blacks in December 1955 triggered the movement. If the mass action of the Civil Rights Movement began with the Montgomery bus boycott, then the collective national spirit and mood for Black rebellion started with the brutal lynchings of Blacks that had taken place in Mississippi earlier in 1955. The most notorious was the kidnapping and murdering of a Black fourteen-year-old boy, Emmett Till, for having allegedly whistled at a White woman on August 28, 1955, in Money, Mississippi. Till's body—beaten, mutilated, and shot to death—was found in the Tallahatchie River. Despite clear evidence of guilt, an all-White, all-male jury acquitted the two White defendants of the murder. The murder of Emmett Till gained international attention and fired the moral indignation of both Blacks and many Whites. The mood and tone for African American rebellion nationwide had been set.

In December 1955, thousands of Blacks organized the widely heralded Montgomery bus boycott when Rosa Parks, a Black woman and member of the NAACP, refused to yield her seat to a White man as the segregationist law required. Her subsequent arrest precipitated a thirty-eight-day boycott, which was sustained until the federal courts ruled that segregation on public transportation was illegal. The inspiration generated by the Montgomery bus boycott's success encouraged African Americans to launch similar civil rights challenges all over the country. National and international media coverage of the boycott propelled the Reverend Martin Luther King, Jr., elected to head the Montgomery protest movement, into world focus. King, who received a PhD in systematic theology from Boston University, became a major charismatic figure and leader of the Civil Rights Movement. He was the founder and leading exponent of the philosophy of nonviolent social protest in America. King was assassinated on April 4, 1968, but he remains a celebrated figure of the Civil Rights Movement of the twentieth century.

The *Brown v. Board of Education of Topeka, Kansas*, desegregation decision and the Montgomery bus boycott served as important catalysts for the myriad school segregation cases, challenges, and violent incidents of the 1950s. The Eisenhower administration was forced to confront the social turmoil associated with the early stages of the Civil Rights Movement, while President John F. Kennedy had the leadership reins during the equally turbulent early 1960s. As pointed out in the preceding chapter, the southern Black student sit-in movement of 1960 successfully challenged segregation in public accommodations. The student organization SNCC (for Student Nonviolent Coordinating Committee) encountered tremendous resistance and terrorism in response to its Freedom Rides and voter registration efforts. By the time Kennedy was inaugurated president in 1961, the issue of racial oppression and the struggle of African Americans for human equality in America had become significant political issues in the court of world opinion.

The contradiction between the freedom and justice creed of the United States and the second-class citizenship of the country's largest minority was a source of embarrassment to many White politicians and intellectuals. Therefore, it was prudent that Kennedy include civil rights in his "New Frontier" Democratic platform. The Democrats could hardly have won the election without bloc voting by northern Blacks, which was reinforced by the increasing number of Black registered voters in the South. Despite his electoral debt to Blacks, Kennedy did not move immediately to propose new civil rights legislation. However, in 1962 a Constitutional Amendment making the poll tax illegal was passed, and Kennedy took executive action to address discrimination in voting rights, employment, education, and public transportation. Kennedy, more than any previous president, publicly and emphatically denounced racial injustice in America routinely in speeches in the North and South.

The period from 1963 to 1965 was the turning point in the Civil Rights Movement. During spring 1963, Martin Luther King, Jr., and other Black leaders staged a protest rally and march in Birmingham and led a series of mass demonstrations in the South demanding equal rights and access in employment, housing, and public accommodations. Thousands of demonstrators were arrested, including King. On June 12, 1963, Medgar Evers, a field secretary for the NAACP in Mississippi, was assassinated in front of his home by a White segregationist.

The courage and perseverance of the many men and women who put their lives on the line in the battle for racial justice created a groundswell of energy that culminated in the largest ever mass-organized rally demanding freedom and justice for all citizens: the March on Washington for Jobs and Freedom, on August 28, 1963. Nearly a quarter-million Blacks and Whites marched peacefully from the Washington Monument to the Lincoln Memorial. At this event, King delivered his famous "I Have a Dream" speech. Less than a month after the March, on September 15, 1963, four young Black girls were killed in the bombing of a Black church in Birmingham, Alabama. Prior to and during the events of 1963, President Kennedy had submitted to Congress a comprehensive civil rights bill. The bill provided for the federal government to file suit to desegregate public accommodation and to assure African Americans equal educational and employment opportunity. It was debated, modified, negotiated, and delayed by both houses of Congress and was not passed during the Kennedy administration. It took the assassination of President Kennedy on November 22, 1963, to break down the walls of resistance of those firmly committed to a White supremacist regime on Capitol Hill.

Many historians are reluctant to give credit to President Lyndon Baines Johnson for advancing the civil rights agenda. Johnson subordinated his southern roots and made civil rights for Blacks a major concern after Kennedy's assassination. He pushed through the Congress the most far-reaching civil rights legislation in the history of the United States. On June 10, 1964, Congress passed the strong Civil Rights Act initially proposed by President Kennedy. A Voting Rights Act, which eliminated all devious policies and barriers for Black registration and voting, especially in the South, was passed on August 6, 1965. It is doubtful that these laws and other civil rights measures would have passed without the political astuteness and southern influence of Lyndon B. Johnson. Johnson also continued the Kennedy practice of appointing African Americans to high-level judicial, government, and ambassadorial positions. His most notable appointment was that of Thurgood Marshall as the first Black to become a Justice of the US Supreme Court.

Not surprisingly, recalcitrant Whites made few voluntary concessions on civil rights during the 1960s. The advances that were made resulted from the struggles, sufferings, and sacrifices of the blood and lives of Black people and some of their allies. The progress of African Americans occurred in an environment of White racist reprisals and acts of violence. These threats led to the creation of self-defense initiatives in numerous locations. For example, a group of Black men in Jonesboro, Louisiana, established the Deacons for Defense and Justice in February 1965 to protect civil rights activists. According to Lance Hill, "the Deacons guarded marches, patrolled the black community to ward off night riders, engaged in shoot-outs with Klansmen, and even defied local police in armed confrontations."[81] At the end of 1966, members of the Deacons numbered in the hundreds, and they were spread across twenty-one chapters in Louisiana and Mississippi.[82]

White activists and allies in the Civil Rights Movement were not spared from the wrath of those White supremacists who considered them turncoats or traitors. The bodies of three civil rights workers, two White and one Black, were discovered in Philadelphia, Mississippi, in August 1964. Eighteen White segregationists were charged with conspiracy to deprive the three victims of their civil rights. In 1965, James Reeb, a White minister, was killed in Selma, Alabama, and Viola Liuzzo, a White woman, was killed after the Selma-to-Montgomery march. A few other Whites were killed or wounded while participating in civil rights demonstrations. More than fifty race riots, numerous church burnings, and hundreds of other acts of racial violence occurred in cities throughout the United States during the 1960s.[83]

Prominent Black leaders and their respective organizations during the Civil Rights Movement of the 1960s included Martin Luther King, Jr., leader of the Southern Christian Leadership Council (SCLC); Roy Wilkins, head of the NAACP; James Farmer and Floyd B. McKissick of the Congress of Racial Equality, or CORE; Stokely Carmichael and H. "Rap" Brown of SNCC; and Whitney Young of the National Urban League (NUL). Ella Baker was one of the most prominent female leaders during this period. Baker was active in the NAACP, SCLC, and SNCC. As Barbara Ransby observes, though most of Baker's political associations were with Black men, her "most significant and sustaining relationships were with a group of women activists" including Septima Clark, Fannie Lou Hamer, and Dianne Nash.[84] For the most part, these male and female leaders embraced the integrationist objectives and assimilationist ideal of nineteenth-century Black philosopher, Frederick Douglass.

The dynamic and charismatic Muslim minister Malcolm X took a very different ideological position in his efforts to liberate the Black masses. His message to Black people was antithetical to that of King and the other leaders of the Civil Rights Movement. Malcolm X employed satanic images to portray Whites, opposed integration, stressed self-help, promoted Pan-Africanism, and urged Blacks to achieve liberation "by any means necessary,"[85] not excluding violence. Malcolm X's philosophy represented, in part, a revival of Marcus Garvey's ideology. It appealed to the rising number of Black students and to many older African Americans who had grown weary and cynical of the gradual and peaceful approaches of traditional Black leaders. Though Malcolm X was assassinated on February 21, 1965, as a result of his defection from Elijah Muhammad's Nation of Islam, his philosophy and exhortations influenced the politics and civil rights activities of many African Americans throughout the late 1960s and the 1970s and experienced a brief revival in the early 1990s.

The assassinations of Malcolm X and Martin Luther King, Jr., were visible indicators of the vulnerability of national Black leaders. Without such leaders, the potential for sporadic urban violence increased as the frustration of the masses of African Americans simmered, fermenting just below the surface in Black communities. Despite the previously discussed legislative gains in civil rights, the basic living conditions of most Blacks did not improve significantly in the 1960s; however, the defeat of Jim Crow and institutional discrimination had created a tide of rising but unfulfilled expectations. Any small spark could ignite such a combustible mixture, and conflicts between White police forces and Black community residents kindled the explosion in many cities.

A race riot erupted in the Watts section of Los Angeles, California, in August 1965, leaving thirty-four people dead. This was the first of many such conflagrations that occurred across the country over the next four years. Devastating riots also rocked Chicago in 1966 and Detroit and Newark in 1967. The following year, after the assassination of Martin Luther King, Jr., rioting erupted in many cities, including the nation's capital. In July 1967, while rioting was still underway in Detroit, Michigan, President Johnson appointed a National Advisory Commission on Civil Disorders, popularly known as the Kerner Commission after its chairman, former Illinois Governor Otto Kerner. The Kerner Commission was charged to analyze the specific causes for the riots and the factors contributing to a worsening racial climate and to propose potential remedies. It released its report seven months later, concluding that urban violence reflected the profound frustration of inner-city Blacks and that racism was deeply embedded in American society. The report's most famous passage warned that the United States was "moving toward two societies, one black, and one white—separate and unequal." The commission supported its conclusions by describing the discrimination, chronic poverty, high unemployment, poor schools, inadequate housing, lack of access to health care, and systematic police bias and brutality disproportionately experienced by Black Americans. The report offered a large number of recommendations to address all the problem areas, but by 1968 Richard M. Nixon had been elected to the presidency as a result of a conservative White backlash, thus ensuring that the Kerner Commission's recommendations would be largely ignored.[86]

Black Power, Black Nationalist, and Black Pride ideologies, which were revived during the Black student movements of the late sixties and especially after King's assassination, fortified the spirit of resistance and rebellion of millions of African Americans. The young generations and even the newly emergent Black middle class began to revel in their African heritage and many adopted African customs, dress, and names. Several groups, including the Black Panther Party based in Oakland, California, were openly critical of the oppressive nature of the capitalist system and of social injustice and police brutality. A significant number of Blacks serving in the armed forces during the Vietnam War, were influenced politically by Black Nationalism and by the philosophies of Marcus Garvey and Malcolm X; this sparked many racial incidents in combat and garrison units. Protests also erupted at historically Black colleges and universities, as the demands of African American students demonstrating for social justice, academic equality, or Black Studies at Jackson State College, Southern University, and South Carolina State College were met with violence resulting in several deaths and hundreds of arrests.

The new Black ideology and its motivations were bound to provoke clashes with White authorities and African American communities across the nation. Black "radicals" as well as student and community activists were harassed and arrested routinely by the police.

Huey Newton, George Jackson, Joanne Chesimard, Fred Hampton, Bobby Seale, and Eldridge Cleaver of the Black Panthers; the Reverend Ben Chavis of North Carolina's Wilmington Ten; and Angela Davis, a Communist professor at the University of California-Los Angeles, are only some of the most prominent Blacks who were incarcerated on various questionable charges. For the first time, race, racialism, and racism were not the only factors motivating Whites to brutalize and imprison Blacks. African Americans were also being incarcerated and held as political prisoners.

In this cauldron of national disunity, disorder, and White backlash, it was easy for Republican Richard Nixon to defeat the Democratic candidate, Hubert Humphrey, in the 1968 presidential election. Nixon rode to power by appealing to White southern Democrats. He promised to restore law and order, resist "forced-integration" and school bussing, and eliminate or reduce welfare and social programs. In the 1972 election, Nixon captured forty-nine of the fifty states and for the first time, the South voted overwhelmingly for a Republican president.

Liberation Struggles and Electoral Politics

The Civil Rights Movement of the 1960s resulted in a increase of the Black middle class from thirteen percent in 1960 to twenty-seven percent in 1970. Though a relative decrease in the number of middle-class African Americans was noted after 1975, by 1984, the proportion had increased to thirty-nine percent.

Improvement in the economic conditions of African Americans could be attributed to the Civil Rights Act of 1964 and specifically to Title VII, which prohibits discrimination in employment and job advancement policies based on race, sex, or national origin. Title VII and Affirmative Action programs contributed significantly to the increase of the Black middle class and to its occupational diversity.[87] Moreover, the Federal Job Corps as well as federally and privately supported job training programs improved the economic status of Black Americans. Tokenistic hiring of Blacks in non-traditional executive and administrative positions in corporations, state and federal agencies, and at predominantly White colleges and universities increased as well. Black communities experienced artificially low unemployment rates because of high participation rates in the military during the Vietnam War era, which ended in 1973. In general, the first half of the decade of the seventies was a milestone of economic progress for African

Americans, but it was not without racial conflicts, racism, and sociopolitical setbacks. Improvement in the condition of Blacks provoked resentment and reprisals by many Whites.

President Nixon did not disappoint his southern constituency and other White conservative supporters. During his first term in office, Nixon changed the ideological make-up of federal courts by appointing White conservatives to vacant judgeships. The social and legal philosophy of the US Supreme Court was altered drastically with the confirmation of Harry Blackmun, Lewis F. Powell, William Rehnquist, and the conservative federal jurist Warren Burger, the latter of whom succeeded the retiring Earl Warren as Chief Justice of the Supreme Court. The judicial foundation for a reversal of the gains won by Black Americans was firmly in place.

Paradoxically, these retrenchments occurred during a period in which African Americans achieved dramatic increases in electoral representation. By 1970, the diligent and sacrificial efforts of SNCC and other civil rights organizations to promote Black voter education and registration had begun to reap significant political dividends for African Americans nationwide. Increased African American voter participation was made possible through the momentous Voting Rights Act of 1965, which was extended and amended by Congress in 1970, 1975, 1982, and 1991. The increase in the number of African Americans elected to the US House of Representatives, mostly from predominantly Black districts, led to the formation of the Congressional Black Caucus (CBC) during the ninety-second Congress (1971-1973). The number of Black elected officials increased from 280 in 1965 to 1,469 in 1970; still, their ranks constituted less than one-half of one percent of all elected officials nationwide.

Nixon was unable to fully his implement civil rights retrenchment plans because he was forced to resign before the end of his second term as a result of the Watergate "break-in" scandal. When Nixon resigned on August 9, 1973, Vice President Gerald R. Ford completed the remaining term of his office. Ford's brief term was haunted by the suspicion that he had made a prearranged deal to grant a presidential pardon to Nixon for any crimes he may have committed in the Watergate fiasco. President Ford inherited an ailing national economy with a soaring unemployment rate. He was unable to win the 1976 election on his own merit, suffering defeat at the hands of Democrat Jimmy Carter from

Georgia, who became the first President from the deep South since before the Civil War.

President Carter, however, attempted to halt the reversal of civil rights gains initiated during the Nixon administration. He promoted Title VII and Affirmative Action programs, enforced the Voting Rights Act and other civil rights statues, and appointed African Americans to high federal and cabinet posts. He appointed more Blacks, Hispanics, and women to federal judgeships than any of his predecessors, but no vacancies on the US Supreme Court occurred during his four-year term in office.

Carter's positive attention to civil rights was in recognition of the decisive Black bloc vote he garnered during the 1976 election. Indeed, he profited politically from the millions of African Americans who became voters as a result of the work of civil rights organizations and the Voting Right Act, especially in the South. He nonetheless lost his bid for reelection in 1980 to Ronald Reagan, a Republican from California, due to a number of economic and foreign policy failures attributed to him by the American public. Ironically, this loss occurred at the same time that the electoral representation of Blacks was expanding. By 1980, the number of Black elected officials had increased to 4,912. This represented approximately one percent of the 490,200 elective offices in the United States. The largest increases were in the South where Black voter registration previously had been obstructed or denied.[88]

Despite Black electoral gains, Reagan revived and advanced the same type of anti-Black and anti-civil rights policies instituted by former President Nixon. Reagan Republicanism represented the interests of rich conservative Whites, corporations, White ethnic immigrants, and the millions of White southerners who defected from the Democratic Party during Nixon's campaigns. Reagan's constituents were fed up with the array of civil rights statutes and with equal opportunity and affirmative action programs designed to remedy the historical affects of slavery and racism suffered by African Americans. He moved swiftly to discredit or dismantle federally funded poverty, job training, and affirmative action programs.

The Reagan administration treated the goals and timetables of Affirmative Action programs as forms of "reverse discrimination" that disadvantaged deserving White men. Reagan appointed arch-conservatives to head the Equal Employment Opportunity Commission (EEOC) and the United States Civil Rights Commission (USCRC) who, in turn, reduced sharply or invalidated thousands of discrimination suits filed against employers.[89] He continued the Nixon strategy of stacking the lower federal courts with very conservative justices. In 1981, Reagan made his first appointment to the Supreme Court, conservative Sandra Day O'Connor, the first woman confirmed for the highest court. When conservative Chief Justice Warren E. Burger retired, Reagan proposed William H. Rehnquist, a sitting member of the Court, to become the Chief Justice. Two of Reagan's nominees to the Supreme Court whose judicial records demonstrated their disdain for civil rights and antidiscrimination laws were not confirmed, but conservatives Antonin Scalia and Anthony M. Kennedy did win confirmation. Thus, before the end of his second term in office, Reagan had tilted the balance of the Supreme Court and numerous other federal courts of appeal toward conservatism and an anti-civil rights ideology.

White racists and hate groups were emboldened by Reagan's anti-civil rights posture. Racial attacks and harassment against Blacks and other minorities increased dramatically during his second term in office. Racial incidents and bigotry spread on major college campuses, and recruitment of African American faculty and students at these institutions decreased. The Reagan administration also introduced sharp cuts in minority financial aid that limited college access for poor Black and other non-White students. The long-term effect of these policies has been to slow the entry of Blacks into key professions including academe, medicine, and law.

The corporate world was also affected by the neoconservative stance of the Reagan Administration. Many companies relaxed their efforts to promote African Americans into mid-level management positions or above. Although the Black middle class grew significantly between the 1960s and the 1980s, the Black-White salary gap widened. Advances in racial integration in schools and housing were minimal during the Reagan years.[90]

The retrogressive civil rights policies of the Reagan administration galvanized and increased the political participation and activism of many African Americans. Blacks developed political strength to influence at least 220 electoral votes and elect almost twenty percent of Democratic convention delegates in the national election. The number of big-city Black mayors and elected local and state officials continued to increase as well. The 1984 presidential candidacy of the Reverend Jesse Jackson, a former lieutenant of Martin Luther King, Jr.'s, was of historic significance. Jackson, a charismatic and articulate Black Baptist minister, made a strong showing in the Democratic Party primary elections among Black and minority voters nationwide. His second presidential campaign in 1988 was even more impressive. On his second attempt, he attracted a significant number of White votes in various states. In the so-called "Super Tuesday" primary of March 8, 1988, Jackson was victorious in five Deep South states and came in second in eight other southern and border states by garnering twenty-eight percent of the popular vote.[91] Jackson's popularity among Blacks stemmed, in part, from the worsening of their economic position under Reagan's leadership; Whites supported Jackson for many of the same reasons. Globalization had catalyzed loss of large numbers of jobs in manufacturing across the country, and Jackson ran on a populist platform that emphasized the shared misery experienced by working-class Blacks and Whites alike.

The Democrats subsequently failed to field a strong candidate in the 1988 election, and George H. W. Bush, Sr., was elected president. This enabled the continued implementation of conservative racial and social policies. Bush easily beat the lackluster Democratic candidate, Michael Dukakis. The campaign provided an early indication of Bush's approach to racial issues. He exploited White voters' concerns with law and order and stereotypes about Black criminality to mobilize electoral support. Willie Horton, a Black prison inmate who had committed violent crimes while on prison furlough, was featured repeatedly in Bush's television political advertisements.

Once elected president, Bush approached racial issues less clumsily than did his immediate predecessor. In contrast to Reagan, George H. W. Bush appointed several eminently qualified African Americans to relatively important positions within his administration. Among his most significant Black appointments were Louis Sullivan as secretary of Health and Human Services and General Colin Powell as chairman of the Joint Chiefs of Staff in the Department of Defense.

At the same time, however, Bush continued a pattern of stacking the Supreme Court with extremely conservative justices. When moderate Justice William Brennan, Jr., announced his retirement in 1990, Bush nominated conservative Judge David Souter of the US Court of Appeals for the First Circuit in Boston as Brennan's replacement. When Thurgood Marshall, the only African American Supreme Court Justice, announced

his retirement in the summer of 1991, George Bush named Clarence Thomas, also an African American but a staunch conservative, to fill Marshall's slot. Thomas's nomination sparked national controversy because of his unenthusiastic prosecution of discrimination cases filed while he was chairman of the federal Equal Employment Opportunity Commission (EEOC) and his indifference to affirmative action and women's rights issues.

Blacks were divided in their assessment of Thomas, but conservative Republicans vigorously supported his nomination and defended him against charges of serious sexual improprieties brought against him by an African American woman. Despite the controversy, in October 1991, the Senate confirmed Thomas as the 106th Justice of the Supreme Court by one of the narrowest margins in American history.

The Millennium Challenge—The 1990s and Beyond

Burdened by a stagnant economy and the fallout from the first Gulf War, George H. W. Bush was unable to win reelection, and Democrat William Jefferson Clinton was elected president in 1992. The former governor of Arkansas positioned himself as a "New Democrat" by rejecting many of the traditional liberal positions of the Democratic Party. As a consequence, while neutralizing legislative attempts to turn back the clock on civil rights, Clinton proposed no new initiatives to address racial inequalities during his first term. He was still able to maintain Black support because during his two terms he presided over the longest economic expansion in US history. Many Blacks were able to improve their economic status significantly during this period, and Clinton was able to introduce welfare reform policies with little opposition even though those policies had the potential to worsen the circumstances of the most vulnerable as soon as the economic boom eroded.

Meanwhile, the conservative Supreme Court justices appointed by President Clinton's predecessors had begun a retrenchment process on civil rights issues that even Congress was unable to fathom. In 1991, Congress passed a new Civil Rights Act to counteract the effects of six 1989 Supreme Court rulings that had seriously weakened the protections against employment discrimination provided by Title VII of the Civil Rights Act of 1964. However, the Supreme Court continued its assaults on civil rights statutory protections through lawsuits filed by various conservative groups.

Public support among Whites for civil rights retrenchment saw an increase as a result of the pressures placed upon White workers' quality of life from the massive socioeconomic restructuring that was taking place globally. Concerns about the deterioration of their personal circumstances provided fertile ground for misleading propaganda which claimed that the enforcement of Title VII was the source of Whites' declining economic fortunes.

The 1995 Supreme Court decision in *Adarand Constructors v. Pena* further reshaped the landscape of affirmative action enforcement. In *Adarand*, by a five-to-four vote, strict scrutiny was established as the standard of constitutional review for federal affirmative action programs that use racial or ethnic classifications as the basis for decision-making.[92] Blacks attempted to counteract these assaults by using strategies that had proved successful during the Civil Rights Movement. Spurred by the call to arms issued by Nation of Islam leader Minister Louis Farrakhan and the National African American Leadership Summit, several hundred thousand African American men journeyed to Washington on October 16, 1995, to participate in the Million Man March in search of inspiration, fellowship, and empowerment. Although crowd estimates vary, most agree that the event was the largest gathering in the nation's capital since the March on Washington in 1963. The widespread support for the Million Man March reflected growing Black people's frustration with many persisting problems, including the decline of Black males enrolled in higher education and the increasing incarceration of Black males in America. Although many celebrities were actively involved in this event as speakers and performers, the spirit of the march was grassroots. It gathered everyone from businessmen to barbers and people from small towns and urban centers. The participants ended the Million Man March with a pledge to recommit themselves to uplifting their community.

A year later, national newspapers and magazines continued to report positive effects of the march. Black fathers indicated that they were becoming more involved with their young sons, Black community groups were organizing, and Black volunteerism was flourishing in urban areas like Atlanta and Chicago. Many participants also noted that they came away from the march inspired to start their own small businesses and community organizations and indicated their progress toward achieving those goals.[93]

The Million Man March, along with mounting criticism of his failure to address issues of racial inequality directly, pushed President Clinton to announce a new initiative during his second term. In a speech to the graduating class of the University of California-San Diego on July 14, 1997, Clinton announced the creation of his "One America in the 21st Century: The President's Initiative on Race" program, which he established by Executive Order 13050. The order called for the creation of a commission that would be charged with conducting a "great and unprecedented conversation about race" throughout the nation and eventually preparing a final report summarizing its findings. The eminent African American historian John Hope Franklin was selected to chair the commission. Clinton described the initiative as a major new effort to "lift the burden of race and redeem the promise of America" at the dawn of the new millennium. Commission members spent the next fifteen months traveling the country, meeting and listening to Americans who revealed how race and racism have affected their lives. These meetings focused on the role of race in civil rights enforcement, education, poverty, employment, housing, stereotyping, administration of justice, health care, and immigration.[94]

The commission's work was overshadowed to some extent by the racially motivated murder of James Byrd in Jasper, Texas, on June 7, 1998. In that case, three White men tied Byrd, a Black man, to the back of a pickup truck and dragged him two miles down a country road to his death.[95] This modern-day lynching summoned up memories of the spate of lynchings that characterized the Jim Crow era. That same September, President Clinton's commission released its report, *One America in the 21st Century: Forging a New Future*. The report begins by discussing the goals and visions held by most Americans—ranging from a belief in fairness and justice to the desire for adequate and affordable health care. It then confronts the legacy of racism in America and examines current data which show that "although minorities and people of color have made progress in terms of the indicators to measure quality of life, persistent barriers to their full inclusion in American society remain." It also emphasizes the growing diversity of the US population, along with the need to include all Americans in discussions about race. In a chapter titled "Bridging the Gap," the report offers recommendations for various areas.[96]

There was little support for implementing any of the commission's recommendations, and this initiative quickly faded from public view. The election of George

W. Bush, son of former President George H. W. Bush, in 2000, in what proved to be the most controversial election since the 1870s, ensured that previous Republican efforts to retrench civil rights protections would be renewed. Bush's victory over former Vice President Al Gore eventually had to be certified by the Supreme Court amid allegations of disfranchisement of Black and other voters, primarily in Florida but in other states as well. The disfranchisement charges brought back memories of the unconscionable strategies used to deny the vote to Blacks after the Civil War.

Bush moved to squelch this controversy by using the same strategy employed by his father—namely, making highly visible appointments of African Americans to disguise systematic retrenchment efforts. His most notable appointments were Condoleeza Rice as National Security Advisor, former General Colin Powell as Secretary of State, and Rod Paige as Secretary of Education. Battles over affirmative action in higher education would be the arena where his conservative agenda would become transparent. Bush also devised a strategy to neutralize the influence of traditional civil rights organizations on the voting behavior of Blacks by introducing a series of faith-based funding initiatives designed to influence Black ministers to support the conservative Republican social agenda. Bush later became the first President since Herbert Hoover who did not attend an NAACP convention during his term in office.

Although the previously discussed *Adarand* case focused on the administrative component of affirmative action, its standards apply to any classification that makes race or ethnicity a basis for decision making, including higher education. Prior to the *Adarand* decision, the principal guidance regarding diversity in higher education was provided in Justice Powell's opinion in *Regents of the University of California v. Bakke* (1978).[97] The Court revisited these issues in the *Gratz v. Bollinger* and *Grutter v. Bollinger* cases (which were decided by the US Supreme Court in June 2003). These cases involved challenges to the University of Michigan's minority admissions policies. President Bush directed the Justice Department to intervene in support of the plaintiffs, reversing the posture adopted by former president Clinton.

The five-to-four *Grutter* decision authored by Justice Sandra Day O'Connor affirmed former Justice Powell's earlier position in *Bakke* that student body diversity is a compelling interest that can justify the narrowly tailored use of race in university admissions. O'Connor signaled that the Court was only willing to continue such policies for another twenty-five years, however.[98] This time limit placed by the Court on affirmative action interventions to address racial inequality introduced a new sense of urgency to efforts to achieve racial equality. Viewed in historical perspective, contemporary patterns of retrenchment in the enforcement of civil rights legislation and related policies over the last decade and a half bear remarkable similarities to developments in the second half of the nineteenth century, including the demise of Reconstruction, the nullification of the Civil Rights Law of 1875, and the judicial institutionalization of the separate-but-equal doctrine in the Supreme Court's 1896 *Plessy v. Ferguson* decision.

This sense of urgency was heightened by the reelection of George W. Bush as president in November 2004. Bush not only successfully mobilized broad-based support from his core White conservative constituency but also built upon the wedge established in the 2000 election between liberal and conservative Blacks by taking advantage of highly visible controversies surrounding abortion and gay marriage rights. Many conservative Black religious leaders subordinated traditional political and economic concerns and urged constituents to support the Republican ticket solely on the basis of their shared views on these two issues. Black Republicans played an especially critical role in producing a Bush victory in Ohio, the state that succeeded Florida in its role in 2000 as the key state providing an electoral victory and the one most mired in controversy over charges of Black voter suppression.

Buoyed by his electoral victory, Bush quickly claimed a mandate to expand the implementation of a range of conservative public policies that negatively affect the daily lives of Blacks and other historically marginalized groups. (The specific aspects of many of these policies and their adverse effects on the educational, economic, and social advancement of many African Americans will be discussed in subsequent chapters.) The most graphic example of the potential for widespread harm to befall Blacks at the hands of a neglectful or unfriendly federal government is the continuing misery faced by many Black former New Orleans residents in the wake of Hurricane Katrina, which struck in August 2005. For example, Steve Sternberg reports that the death rate in New Orleans in 2006 was forty-seven percent higher than that for the two years prior to the catastrophe, largely as a result of the loss of seven hospitals and 4,500 doctors.[99]

The election of Barack Hussein Obama as President of the United States in November 2008, and his re-election in November 2012, are seen by many as events with unparalleled potential to advance the fight for justice and progress in racial matters. (The implications of the Obama presidency for the future of African Americans are explored in detail in succeeding chapters.) In some respects, Obama's election can be said to have ushered in a new era in African American history. This new historical era entails growing formal public acknowledgment of the historical struggles for freedom and justice waged by African Americans and the relevance of these struggles for all U.S. citizens. These sentiments are embedded, for example, in the discourses surrounding President Obama's election and re-election. Additionally, several important milestones have served and are continuing to serve to formally institutionalize the continuing record of struggle for racial justice. These include the centennial celebrations of various major organizations such as the NAACP, the Urban League, and a number of Black fraternities and sororities.

The new Martin Luther King, Jr., Memorial on the National Mall in Washington, DC, dedicated in fall 2011, is certainly the most visible testimonial to the battles waged during the last half of the twentieth century. Looking back further in history, the new African American Civil War Memorial and Museum, whose grand opening took place in July 2011, is particularly significant. This museum is designed to help visitors understand "the African American's heroic and largely unknown role in maintaining the Union and securing the blessing of liberty for all Americans."[100] The efforts of the museum are certainly timely as the celebration of the sesquicentennial anniversary of the Civil War proceeds. The 2011 Black History Month theme announced by the Association for the Study of African American Life and History (ASALH) was "African Americans and the Civil War."

Construction of the National Museum of African American History and Culture is slated to begin on the National Mall in 2012, and the edifice is scheduled to be completed in 2016. This museum's goals include providing visitors with opportunities to explore the depth and breadth of the African American experience. Its exhibits will use African American culture as a means to understand how a people's lives, stories, histories, and cultures are shaped and informed by both national and international considerations.[101]

Last but not least, the Carter G. Woodson Home National Historic Site is scheduled for public unveiling in 2016. Woodson, known as the "Father of Black History," helped found the Association for the Study of Negro Life and History (which later became the ASALH). His home was designated as a National Historic Site through legislation enacted in 2003.[102]

African American Studies specialists welcome these public testimonials to the ongoing significance of African American history. The visibility of the various events and projects will undoubtedly expand interest in the discipline and guide succeeding generations of students from all racial/ethnic groups to enroll in courses, pursue majors in the discipline, and carry on the centuries-long struggle for racial justice in the United States and around the world.

3

Questions & Exercises

1. All races and cultures have made scientific, technical, and aesthetic contributions to world development and human progress. What are some of the early contributions Africa and African people gave to the world?

2. Study and discuss medieval (476 -1450 AD) contacts between Europeans and Africans. If race and color were not significant prejudicial factors during this period, when and why did they develop?

3. Discuss some common factors that contributed to the rise and decline of the ancient West African empires of Ghana, Mali, and Songhay?

4. What were the social, political, and economic motives of Europeans in initiating slavery and the trans-Atlantic slave trade?

5. Discuss the changing attitudes of White Americans toward slavery before and after the Revolutionary War and leading up to and after the Civil War.

6. Explain the political and economic factors that prevailed in the South and North that led to the failure of Reconstruction.

7. Study Abraham Lincoln's attitudes toward Blacks. Should he truly be remembered as the "Great Emancipator"?

8. After each American war, Blacks have made significant social, political, and economic gains. What were some of the gains made after World War I, World War II, the Korean Conflict, and the Vietnam War?

9. Discuss the progress or lack of progress African Americans have made since the Civil Rights Movement of the 1960s to the present.

Social Responsibility Projects

1. Organize a group of students to conduct an assessment of how African American history is taught in history courses at your institution.

2. Organize a college branch of the Association for the Study of African American Life and History (ASALH).

3. Organize a group of students to raise funds to attend the annual conferences of ASALH and the National Council for Black Studies.

4. Organize a group of students to develop programming for Black History Month activities.

5. Organize fellow students and family members to visit important historical sites relevant to African Americans, including new museums and monuments.

3

NOTES AND REFERENCES

1. Maulana Karenga, *Introduction to Black Studies, 1st. ed.* (Los Angeles: University of Sankore Press, 1982), 3.

2. Robert L. Harris, Jr., "Coming of Age: The Transformation of Afro-American Historiography," in *Paradigms in Black Studies*, A. Alkalimat, ed. (Chicago: Twenty-First Century Books & Publications, 1990), 53-72.

3. Manning Marable, "The Modern Miseducation of the Negro: Critiques of Black History Curricula," in *Black Studies Curriculum Development Course Evaluations, Conference I*, Institute of the Black World, ed. (Atlanta: Institute of the Black World, 1981), C1-C28.

4. W. E. B. Du Bois," Preface," In H. Aptheker, ed., *A Documentary History of the Negro People in the United States.* (New York: Citadel Press, 1951).

5. W. E. B. Du Bois, "The Field and Function of the Negro College," *Alumni Reunion Address*, Fisk University, 1933. Reprinted in *W. E. B. Du Bois: The Education of Black People, Ten Critiques 1900-1960*, Herbert Aptheker, ed. (Amherst: University of Massachusetts Press, 1973), 83-102.

6. Joseph Harris, *Africans and Their History* (New York: New American Library, 1972), 26-33.

7. See Chancellor Williams, *The Destruction of Black Civilization* (Chicago: Third World Press, 1974), 62-100.

8. St. Clair Drake, *Black Folk Here and There, Vol. 2* (Los Angeles: Center for Afro-American Studies, University of California, 1990), 77-100.

9. See John Henrik Clarke, "Introduction," in J. Jackson, *Introduction to African Civilizations*, 3-35.

10. See, for example, Walter Rodney, *How Europe Underdeveloped Africa* (London: Bogle L'Ouverture, 1972).

11. Oliver Ransford, *The Slave Trade: The Story of Transatlantic Slavery* (London: John Murray Publishers, 1971), 40.

12. Drake, *Black Folk Here and There*, Chapter 7.

13. Patrick Richardson, *Empire and Slavery* (London: Longmans, Green & Co., 1968), 3-21.

14. John M. Blum, *The National Experience: A History of the United States, 2d ed.* (New York: Harcourt, Brace & World, 1968), 53-55.

15. Ransford, *The Slave Trade*, 96-120.

16. Richardson gives a detailed account of the market mechanisms of colonial American slavery in *Empire and Slavery*, 14-34. The treatment of the economic factors influencing the status and treatment of slaves has special significance for the present discussion.

17. See Warren L. Young, *Minorities and the Military* (Westport, CT: Greenwood Press, 1982), 192-93.

18. John Hope Franklin, *From Slavery to Freedom* (New York: Knopf, 1967), 130-40.

19. The use of the term *Negro* in reference to Black Americans virtually ceased in popular and academic discourse after 1968 except as a term of derision applied to persons perceived to engage in social and political behavior at variance with general tendencies among Blacks. The first edition of John Hope Franklin's book, *From Slavery to Freedom*, was originally published in 1967.

20. Sylviane Diouf, *Servants of Allah: African Muslims Enslaved in the Americas* (New York: New York University Press, 1998), 3.

21. Ibid.

22. See Gary B. Nash, *Race and Revolution* (Madison, WI: Madison House, 1990), 57-87.

23. Charles Wesley, *In Freedom's Footsteps* (Cornwell's Heights, PA: International Library of Afro-American Life and History, 1976), 113-15.

24. Benjamin Quarles, *The Negro in the Making of America* (New York: Macmillan, 1969; Collier, 1970), 63.

25. James Dormon and Robert Jones, *The Afro-American Experience* (New York: Wiley, 1974), 126-27.

26. Saunders Redding, *They Came in Chains* (Philadelphia: Lippincott, 1950; 1969), 70.

27. Ibid., p. 56.

28. See John Blassingame, *The Slave Community* (New York: Oxford University Press, 1979).

29. See George Breitman, ed., *Malcolm X Speaks: Selected Speeches and Statements* (New York: Grove Press, 1966), 10-17; and Blassingame, *The Slave Community*, 250-57.

30. Robert Fogel, *Without Consent or Contract, The Rise and Fall of American Slavery* (New York: W. W. Norton, 1989), 101.

31. Mark Smith, *Debating Slavery, Economy and Society in the Antebellum American South* (Cambridge, UK: Cambridge University Press, 1998), 4.

32. Richard Starobin, *Industrial Slavery in the Old South* (New York: Oxford University Press, 1970).

33. Richard Wade, *Slavery in the Cities: The South, 1820-1860* (New York: Oxford University Press, 1964).

34. Joe Trotter, *The African American Experience* (Boston: Houghton Mifflin, 2001), 167.

35. Roger Ransom and Richard Sutch, *One Kind of Freedom: The Economic Consequences of Emancipation* (New York: Cambridge University Press, 1977), 15.

36. See, for example, Franklin, *From Slavery to Freedom*, 224.

37. Ira Berlin, *Slaves Without Masters* (New York: Vintage Books, 1976).

38. See, for example, Cheryl I. Harris, "Whiteness as Property" *Harvard Law Review, 106* (June 1993): 1709-91; and A. Leon Higginbotham, *In the Matter of Color, Race and the American Legal Process: The Colonial Period* (New York: Oxford University Press, 1978).

39. See Berlin, *Slaves Without Masters*, 250-82. Berlin not only relates the occasional divisions between free and enslaved Blacks but also gives a balanced account of their mutual support and cooperation.

40. Herbert Aptheker, *American Negro Slave Revolts* (New York: Columbia University Press, 1943).

41. See Stanley Elkins, *Slavery* (Chicago: The University of Chicago Press, 1959), 138-39.

42. For more on slave revolts, see Harvey Wish, "American Slave Insurrections Before 1861," *Journal of Negro History, 22* (July 1937): 229-320, see also Philip Foner, *History of Black Americans* (Westport CT: Greenwood Press, 1983), 131-62.

43. Herbert Aptheker, *Abolitionism* (Boston: Twayne Publishers, 1989), xiii.

44. Sylviane Diouf, *Dreams of Alabama: The Slave Ship Clotilda and the Story of the Last Africans Brought to America* (New York: Oxford University Press, 2007), 1.

45. Inferences regarding the relationship between the Fugitive Slave Act of 1850 and twentieth-century Supreme Court philosophy and debate are discussed in Ena I. Farley, "The Fugitive Slave Law of 1850 Revisited," *Western Journal of Black Studies* (Summer 1979): 110-15.

46. More detailed background and analysis of the *Dred Scott* case are provided by James G. Randall and David H. Donald, *The Civil War and Reconstruction* (Boston: D. C. Heath, 1961), 108-13.

47. From a speech Douglass delivered at the West India Emancipation at Canandaigua, New York, reprinted in Philip Foner, *The Life and Writings of Frederick Douglass* (New York: International Publishers, 1975 and 1950), 437.

48. For a history of Black periodicals and newspapers, see W. Daniel, *Black Journals of the United States* (Westport CT: Greenwood Press, 1982).

49. Young, *Minorities and the Military*, 195-99. See also Joseph T. Glatthaar, *Forged in Battle: The Civil War Alliance of Black Soldiers and White Officers* (New York: Meridian, 1991).

50. Glatthaar, *Forged in Battle*, 169-206.

51. Young, *Minorities and the Military*, 198-99.

52. See Lawanda Cox, *Lincoln and Black Freedom* (Columbia: University of South Carolina Press, 1981), 11-12, 30.

53. Lerone Bennett, Jr., *Forced into Glory: Abraham Lincoln's White Dream* (Chicago: Johnson Publishing, 1999).

54. Quarles, *The Negro in the Making of America*, 130-31.

55. Randall and Donald, *The Civil War and Reconstruction*, 622-23.

56. W. E. B. Du Bois, *Black Reconstruction in America 1860-1880* (New York: Atheneum, 1971), 670-71.

57. US Committee on Civil Rights, *Freedom to be Free: A Report to the President* (Washington, DC: Government Printing Office, 1963), 57.

58. See C. Vann Woodard, *The Strange Career of Jim Crow* (New York: Oxford University Press, 1966) for an interesting account of Jim Crowism in the South.

59. W. E. B. Du Bois, "The Upbuilding of Black Durham," *World's Work, 13* (January 1912): 334-38.

60. Du Bois, *Black Reconstruction in America 1860-1880*, 702.

61. Quarles, *The Negro in the Making of America*, 159.

62. See Florette Henri, *Black Migration: Movement North, 1900-1920* (Garden City, NY: Anchor Books, 1976), 69.

63. Norman Hodges, *Black History* (New York: Monarch Press, 1971), 145-46.

64. For a "poetic" description of the nature of the Black Church, see W.E.B. Du Bois, *The Souls of Black Folk* (New York: Signet Classics, 1969), 210-25.

65. For more information about the Black Women's Club Movement, see Darlene Hine and Kathleen Thompson, *A Shining Thread of Hope, The History of Black Women in America* (New York: Broadway Books, 1998), 177-83.

66. For a detailed and pictorial account of Black inventors and their problems with the patent process, see Portia P. James, *The Real McCoy* (Washington, DC: Smithsonian Institution Press, 1989).

67. Louis R. Harlan, ed., *The Booker T. Washington Papers*, Vol. 3, (Urbana: University of Illinois Press, 1974), 583–587.

68. Louis R. Harlan, ed., *The Booker T. Washington Papers*, Vol. 3, (Urbana: University of Illinois Press, 1974), 583–587.

69. Bennett, *Before the Mayflower*, 336-39.

70. See Lawrence Dunbar Reddick, "The Negro Policy of the U.S. Army," *Journal of Negro History*, 34 (1949).

71. Bennett, *Before the Mayflower*, 347-48.

72. Only a cursory account of the many race riots that occurred from 1916 to 1920 can be reported in this survey work. For more information, see Mary Frances Berry, *Black Resistance/White Law* (New York: Appleton-Century-Crofts, 1971), 139-73.

3

73.   Garvey's philosophy and work, along with the rise and decline of his movement, are discussed in Chapter 1. Further discussion of Garvey and his contributions to Black liberation struggles can be found in succeeding chapters on African American politics and economics.

74.   Blum, *The National Experience*, 651.

75.   Joe W. Trotter, *The African American Experience* (Boston: Houghton Mifflin, 2001), 294.

76.   See Barbara Bair, "The Crusader," in Mary J. Buhle, Paul Buhle, and Dan Georgakis (eds), *Encyclopedia of the American Left, 1st edition*, 170-171; and Mark Solomon, *The Cry Was Unity: Communists and African Americans, 1917-1936*, chapters 1 and 2.

77.   Some familiarity with basic principles of economics might be helpful in understanding the technical aspects of how the New Deal programs affected economic recovery.

78.   US Commission on Civil Rights, *Freedom to Be Free* (Washington, DC: Government Printing Office, 1963), 114-15.

79.   See Franklin, *From Slavery to Freedom*, Chapter 29; also Quarles, *The Negro in the Making of America*, Chapter 9; Reddick, "The Negro Policy of the U.S. Army"; Richard Dalfiume, *Desegregation of the US Armed Forces* (Kansas City: University of Missouri Press, 1969).

80.   US Commission on Civil Rights, *Freedom to Be Free*, 152-53.

81.   Lance Hill, *The Deacons for Defense: Armed Resistance and the Civil Rights Movement* (Chapel Hill: The University of North Carolina Press, 2004), 2.

82.   Ibid.

83.   Two of the most detailed and concise chronologies of notable events and of the Civil Rights Movement are Alton Hornsby, Jr.'s, *The Black Almanac* (Woodbury, NY: Barron's Educational Series, 1973) and Lerone Bennett, Jr.'s, *Before the Mayflower*, 557-607.

84.   Barbara Ransby, *Ella Baker and the Black Freedom Movement* (Chapel Hill: The University of North Carolina Press, 2003), 4.

85.   Malcolm X, *By Any Means Necessary*, George Breitman, ed. (New York: Pathfinder Press, 1970).

86.   National Advisory Commission on Civil Disorders, *Report of the National Advisory Commission on Civil Disorders* (Washington, DC: US Government Printing Office, 1968).

87.   See Bart Landry, "The New Black Middle Class (Part I)," *Focus, Joint Center for Political Studies* (September 1987): 5-7.

88.   *Focus* (Washington, DC: Joint Center for Political Studies, December 1980), 6.

89.   See C. Calvin Smith, "The Civil Rights Legacy of Ronald Reagan," *Western Journal of Black Studies 14* (Summer 1990): 102-14.

90.   See *Business Week* (March 14, 1988), 63-69, also, *Newsweek* (March 7, 1988), 18-45.

91.   Joint Center for Political Studies, *Political Trendletter* (March 1988).

92.   *Adarand Constructors, Inc. v. Pena*, 515 U.S. 200 (1995). The strict scrutiny standard replaced the more lenient intermediate scrutiny standard, which required only that an important governmental interest be served by the racial classification and that it be substantially related to the achievement of the program's objective. In addition to advancing a compelling goal, the Court mandated that the use of race must also be narrowly tailored only after prior consideration of race-neutral alternatives and operationalized via individualized consideration of persons seeking the benefit of a racial classification rather than using groups as a unit of analysis.

93.   The Million Man March Pledge can be found at the following website: http://www.africawithin.com/mmm/mmmpledge.htm. For a comprehensive treatment of the March, see Haki Madhubuti and Maulana Karenga, *Million Man March/Day of Absence: A Commemorative Anthology: Speeches, Commentary, Photography, Poetry, Illustrations, Documents* (Chicago: Third World Press, 1996).

94.   Basic information about former President Clinton's Initiative on Race was accessed at the following website: http://clinton4.nara.gov/Initiatives/OneAmerica/america_onrace.html.

95.   Information about the lynching of James Byrd was found at the Texas NAACP website: http://www.texasnaacp.org/jasper.htm.

96.   President's Initiative on Race Advisory Board, *One America in the 21st Century: Forging a New Future* (Washington, DC US Government Printing Office, November 1998).

97.   Powell had argued that "increasing the racial and ethnic diversity of the student body at a university constitutes a compelling interest, because it enriches the academic experience on campus."

98.   Information about the *Grutter* case can be obtained at the following website: http://caselaw.lp.findlaw.com/cgi-bin/getcase.pl?court=US&navby=case&vol=000&invol=02-241.

99.   Steve Sternberg, "New Orleans Deaths up 47%," *USA Today* (June 22-24, 2007), A-1.

100.   "Grand Opening Celebration: The New African American Civil War Memorial and Museum," http://www.afroamcivilwar.org/splash.php/.

101.   Lonnie Bunch, "A Vision for the National Museum of African American History and Culture," http://nmaahc.si.edu/section/about_us.

102.   "Association for the Study of African American Life and History," http://www.asalh.org/WoodsonHome.html.

Chapter 4

African American Society and Culture

Sociology and African Americans

The field of sociology originated in Europe. A morass of social and political upheavals had transformed eighteenth and nineteenth century European societies. The decline of feudalism and church authority, the institutional foundations that had shaped the Middle Ages, set the stage for power struggles that included revolutions, religious wars, class conflicts, and assertions of racial superiority. French philosopher Auguste Comte (1798–1857) coined the term *sociology* in 1839, with the intention that it would become a science to study human order and relational harmony. Comte, as some contemporary sociologists assert, "was a strong believer in what nowadays would be called law and order."[1] French scholar Emile Durkheim (1858–1917) and German sociologist Max Weber (1864–1920) were early major contributors to sociology. The point of this historical reference is to establish that sociology as social theory was founded upon and derived from a European and not an African worldview.

Sociology, generally defined, is the study of the relationships, values, beliefs, and organizational structures of societal groups. The prefix *socio*, meaning society, when combined with *-ology*, which infers study or science, implies the study of society. Classical European sociologists or philosophers studied social values, beliefs, behaviors, and organizational propensities to learn how to establish and to control order within the society. Both Comte and Durkheim were concerned with discovering and affecting humanistic codes of values and morality outside the realm and

dogma of conventional religion or church. Durkheim saw the school system as an alternative institution for instilling normative values and beliefs. Max Weber related human values and behavior to economics and linked the "Protestant ethic" to the development of capitalism. Weber is noted, too, for his conceptualization of the term *ideal type*, which proposes certain typical ideal patterns of social or nonsocial behavior for purposes of comparison. In the execution of his theories, Weber championed the notion of objective social science.[2]

Western European sociological theory has significantly affected the social, political, and economic plight of African Americans and Africans. Although the study of sociology had its origins in the revolutions, religious feuds, and class conflicts of Europe, it was inevitably influenced by the African or Atlantic slave trade that flourished from the sixteenth until well into the nineteenth century. The subjugation of Africans by Europeans and the racial oppression of Blacks in the Americas were not addressed explicitly by classical sociologists. One wonders how such pathological conduct—relative to values, morals, behavior, and human relationships—could be ignored in the course of undertaking their sociological investigations.

Sociology began to take root in the United States at the height of racial segregation, violence, and oppression, near the end of the nineteenth and the beginning of the twentieth centuries. Early American sociologists, such as, William G. Sumner, George Herbert Mead, Robert Park, and several others, were influenced by the classical social theory of Europe. The order theories of Comte, social Darwinism of Spencer, secular humanism of Durkheim, and the ideal type theory and scientific objectivism of Weber were all taught at various American universities and often applied in discussing African Americans. Thus, early American sociology generated a European-inspired paradigm for interpreting and altering the conditions of Africans.

Although sociology is a popular subject among Whites and Blacks, its appeal to the two races might be different. The apparent interest of White sociologists in human organizations, interactions, and values has been for the purpose of theorizing and establishing social mechanisms for order, control, and equilibrium. Thus, as Butler A. Jones notes, "The early academic and public image of sociology was reformistic and problem oriented."[3] On the other hand, many African Americans perceive sociology, figuratively, as a medium of social introspection relative to racism and racial inequity in the political and economic spheres of American society. It is small wonder that Black sociologists, among others, have taken the lead in critically examining the social system and in fermenting social protest. Indeed, Black sociologists and historians were prominent in the demand for and development of African American or Black Studies programs.

Blacks were particularly affected and influenced by the work and "empiricist tradition" of the sociology faculty at the University of Chicago. Led by Robert Park, the school conducted research and field studies in urban sociology on racial antagonism, not only in relation to African Americans but also in relation to the growing populations of European immigrants in the Midwest. As indicated in Chapter 1, members of the "Chicago school" trained two eminent Black sociologists. Sociology as an academic discipline has a long tradition in the curricula of predominantly Black colleges and among African American academic professionals and students. Although W.E.B. Du Bois was basically an historian by training, his most significant scholarly contributions were sociologically oriented. Generally, the most significant works of African American scholars and writers have been in the areas of sociology and history. Even during the classical era of sociology (1890–1930), White scholars were reluctant to examine the sociology of race except to imply the inherent inferiority of Blacks and to rationalize academically the subordinate societal position of African people. Many White scholars favored applying sociological theory to the resolution of the problems of Blacks in society. The "Chicago school" trained a few Black sociologists, notably E. Franklin Frazier and

Charles S. Johnson, and used them to collect and present data on the social conditions of Blacks in urban and rural environments. W.E.B. Du Bois was asked to research the social and political conditions of Blacks in Philadelphia in 1896. Consequently, he produced his renowned study *The Philadelphia Negro*. For the most part, Blacks were intended to be the subjects of sociology, and not sociologists to the extent that they would formulate theory.[4]

Many Black sociologists view sociology and its theoretical approaches from a different perspective than Whites. African Americans have perceived sociology as a field that can create theories of Black liberation and can propose guidelines for social, political, and economic equality. Because African Americans occupy an oppressed status in the society, many Black sociologists have chosen not to study or practice sociology from a detached or value-free stance. Progress for Black people has occurred not as a result of scholarly objectivity, but from a subjective approach and active involvement of African American scholars.

In addition, many African American scholars are suspicious of an emphasis on quantitative research as the primary means of conducting sociological research at the expense of the discipline's capacity to produce meaningful insights. Rushton Coulburn and W. E. B. Du Bois expressed such concerns in 1942 when they cautioned:

> If sociology describes and classifies more fully, realistically, and accurately than the other social sciences, let it describe only that which is susceptible of full and realistic classification ....Change and movement have to be further explained, but the sociologist, even the sociologist who has conceived a meaningful-causal system, dare not be too clear that it is man who causes movement and change, that would so constrict the validity of sociology.[5]

E. Franklin Frazier expresses similar concerns and reminds researchers:

> The question of methods and techniques in sociological research just as in other fields of scientific inquiry is inseparable from the conceptual organization of the discipline ....In so many so-called sociological studies this simple fact is forgotten and virtuosity in the use of methods and techniques becomes an end in itself... Many statistical

studies lack sociological significance because they fail to show any organic relationship among the elements which they utilize for analysis.[6]

Coulburn and Du Bois perceived a growing tension between understanding the experiences of people of African descent grounded in historical research and the shorter-term quantitative studies preferred by sociologists. They drew critical distinctions between sociological and historical approaches to the study of the human condition in 1943:

> If ... the area of human initiative is as broad and decisive as history has assumed, then the realm of sociology is the comparatively narrow one of the measurable in human action. On the other hand, if physical, chemical, and biological law and but partially known determinants in the fields of psychology so condition human action that little or nothing is left for human initiative—which is from the point of view of orthodox science, chance— then the sociologist becomes everything and the historian simply his recorder.[7]

Du Bois had earlier believed that it was possible to resolve the tensions between historical and sociological studies of African Americans by undertaking a century-long research program in which ten topics would be studied in succession—one each year. Du Bois believed that this approach would produce "a continuous record on the condition and development of a group of 10 to 20 millions of men—a body of sociological material unsurpassed in human annals."[8] Central to Du Bois' approach was insistence that the research design focus on an in-depth analysis of the Black experience, rather than on comparative research. Or, in his words, "the careful exhaustive study of the isolated group, then, is the ideal of the sociologist of the 20th century—from that may come... at last careful, cautious generalization and formulation."[9]

The perceptual conflict in sociological inferences and objectives, grounded in different intent, experience, and worldviews between African and European peoples, led to the concept of *Black Sociology*.[10] This initiative developed concomitantly with the establishment of Black Studies programs in the 1960s. While much of sociological theory is basic and common to all human nature, values, mores, and beliefs can differ significantly across racial/ethnic groups. Cultural

and behavioral patterns based on a people's values are more authentically conveyed and are more apt to be correctly interpreted by members of the same race or ethnic group. Moreover, Europeans and American Whites had characterized Africans as having no civilization, history, or values of significance. Whites used the subjugation and colonization of Africa, and the enslavement, segregation, and oppression of Blacks in America, as evidence to support their belief in Black inferiority. The exponents of a Black sociology reasoned that it was detrimental to the African American self-image and self-concept to be uncritical of traditional sociology and of the terms, concepts, and approaches it employed to study Black people. Advocates of a Black sociology feared that certain sociological theories, and paradigms or frames of reference, would function to serve the interests of White domination rather than Black liberation.

Anthropologist Marimba Ani (Dona Richards) admonishes against the uncritical use of Western European social scientific theory as it relates to Black or African peoples:

> Contrary to the propaganda of academia, white social theory does not represent a universally valid and "objective" body of thought, nor a neutral tool to be used for the purpose of understanding human experience. It might be argued, instead, that it represents a particular view of the world as seen from the perspective of supposed Western European superiority, and that an image of the inferiority of African civilization is inherent in the terms, definitions, and theoretical models on which [much] white social theory is based.[11]

The appropriate starting points for undertaking sociological investigations are the theories of human development and social organization advanced by eminent Black intellectuals. Du Bois, for example, contended that the measurement of human progress— and, in particular, comparison across groups—was extremely difficult and fraught with the potential for biases and misrepresentations. His reason was that "we are so ignorant of the ordinary facts relating to conditions of life, and because, above all, criteria of life and the objects of living are so diverse."[12] He hypothesized that, in the absence of external intervention, all distinctive cultural groups proceed through four stages of development: (1) organization to provide the means of subsistence; (2) creation of accumulation

4

mechanisms to ensure that future subsistence is guaranteed; (3) introduction of formal mechanisms to ensure harmonious social relations and the intergenerational transmission of values, beliefs, and commitments; and (4) establishment of intercultural contacts that facilitate sharing of ideas and trade in goods and services.

The key element in Du Bois's model is the emphasis on group self-definition and an indigenously determined trajectory of societal development. He believed that European domination disrupted this normal developmental pattern among Africans and that self-determined development among African Americans had been thwarted by the holocaust of enslavement. Nevertheless, he lauded African Americans for having succeeded in creating viable social institutions despite the oppressive barriers that had to be overcome. Du Bois's perspective provides the guidance for sociological inquiry in African American Studies. Two of the principal goals of sociological inquiry in African American Studies are

1. to identify historical models of social organization among Africans and African Americans that were functional and have the potential for successful adaptation and contemporary deployment; and
2. to develop new approaches to social organization consistent with historical values that serve current needs.

Race, Racism, Color, Culture, and African Americans

Race, racism, color, and culture are factors that have determined the nature and extent of the social and sociological relationships of Black people in America since their involuntary arrival in 1619. More than a century earlier, European philosophers and explorers had pronounced the native inhabitants of the African continent "inferior" in relation to the race, color, and culture of Europeans. The concept of race, especially, has been and continues to be a controversial and indefinable term. Despite the lack of universal agreement on the meaning of race, most anthropologists suggest that race has a biological dimension. In popular discourse, race refers to certain physical characteristics of people in the world or within a society with diverse

populations. Otto Klineberg writes in support of this perspective:

> A race, then, may be defined as a large group of men possessing in common certain physical characteristics which are determined by heredity. The other, non-physical, qualities which have been ascribed to races are in this sense secondary, in that they do not belong to the concept or definition of race; they are not used, for example, in race classification.[13]

Klineberg's classic work, *Race Differences*, seems to reject the notion that such physiognomical qualities as mental ability, intelligence, character, morality, and cultural proclivities have any relation to race.

For classification purposes, the races of mankind have been traditionally divided into three general physical-type categories: Negroid or black, Mongoloid or yellow, and Caucasian or White. Consistent with the physical-difference theory of race, other racial characteristics are considered, such as, eye color and form, hair color and texture, shape of nose, bodily stature, and cephalic index (the maximum breadth to the maximum length of the head, seen from on top and expressed in percentage). Anthropologists caution against making any absolute racial characterizations based on physical factors because of historical migrations, conquests, and the inevitable intermingling of peoples.[14]

The issue of race was used, historically, as a pretext to conceal the ethnocentric-xenophobic beliefs and attitudes of pre-capitalist European nomadism. The concept of racial superiority, rank, and differentiation gained much acclaim when Count de Gobineau, a French aristocrat, published his *Essay on the Inequality of Human Races* (1853-1857). Initially, Gobineau's essay may have been inspired by the class conflicts of Europe, but his "racial-type" theories and racist doctrines served to give moral support for Europe's colonization of Africa and, certainly, as a rationale for White enslavement and oppression of African Americans. Early rank-type racial theories, such as Gobineau's, evolved into the phenomenon of nineteenth and twentieth century American racism. Racism has been, and continues to be, a primary sociological factor affecting the social organization and the political and economic conditions of African Americans.

Racism, unlike race, is a definitive concept. The problem of racism is not one of definition but of proving that it is operative to skeptics who are not victimized by its effects. Yet, racism is very much perceptible and concrete to an individual or a group subjected to its practice. Racism has been defined both as a belief in the innate superiority of one's own race and as an ideology of racial privilege. However, racism goes beyond individuals' beliefs and attitudes. Racism is not only a racialist dogma but an enforceable practice of racial persecution and domination. For racism to exist, a person or race must possess the power to effect, assert, or enforce disadvantages and discrimination on another individual or population. Since the first twenty captive Africans were brought to Jamestown in 1619, Whites have always maintained the power to enforce social, political, and economic disadvantages on Blacks.

While legislative enactments and cultural refinement have caused a significant reduction in individual acts of racism against African Americans, institutional racism has remained relatively the same—although it has become more sophisticated in practice. Institutional racism is imperceptibly embodied in the policies of the social, political, and economic institutions of the society, and it is designed to restrict the access of Blacks or other subordinate racial-ethnic minority groups to social benefits. In his discussion of economic forces and institutional racism, Robert B. Hill differentiates between prejudice and discrimination. Hill states, "[P]rejudice involves negative attitudes or beliefs about racial or ethnic groups, while discrimination involves negative treatment of them."[15] Racism, in all of its forms and attributes, is an integral dimension of the sociological experiences of African Americans.

Universal antagonism between peoples of the world exists, in part, because of the widespread acceptance of the traditional racial classifications used to ascribe social roles. Yet, most respected social theorists and scholars agree that "skin color, of itself, however, has very limited scientific use as a criterion of these primary races."[16] Not only is skin color an ambiguous indicator of geographical origin and of imprecise usefulness in differentiating among "races," it also has no predictive value in determining intelligence, character, values, morality, or culture. Nonetheless, African Americans have probably suffered more social disadvantage and antagonism because of their color than any other race or group. Within the monolithic perception of race and color, White skin color yields a decisive advantage in American society.

White Europeans generated negative associations with the color black or blackness, partly as a moral or religious rationalization for the capture, transportation, and enslavement of Africans. It was economically convenient and morally consoling to translate biblical myths and cultural superstitions regarding blackness into a justification for Black slavery. Black sociologist/ anthropologist St. Clair Drake has written a definitive work on the origins of prejudice against dark-skinned people in *Black Folk Here and There*. Interestingly, he is not able to identify any consistent symbolism or myth— religious or secular—that would explain Europeans', or, indeed, any people's, prejudice against the color black.[17]

Racial and cultural antagonisms between White and non-White peoples have existed since the Middle Ages. Peoples classified as non-White comprise approximately seventy-five percent of the world's population, whereas Whites represent a clear minority. Yet, at present, those who authentically or opportunistically classify themselves as White generally subject non-Whites to cultural, political, and economic domination. Psychiatrist Frances Cress Welsing proposes a controversial theory to explain White ethnocentric or xenophobic behavior toward non-White or colored peoples. *The Cress Theory of Color-Confrontation* posits:

> ... Whites are also vulnerable to their sense of numerical inadequacy. The behavioral manifestations or expressions of their sense of this inadequacy in their numbers become apparent in the drive or need to divide the massive majority of "non-Whites" into fractional as well as frictional minorities. This is viewed as a key and fundamental behavioral response to their own minority status in the known universe.[18]

Welsing further suggests that Whites' obsession with achieving superiority over peoples of color, fascination with materialistic acquisition and accumulation, and quest for more potent technologies and political power are psychologically motivated to sustain White supremacy. However, the most controversial aspect of Welsing's theory is not so much the numerical inadequacy of Whites, but their genetic inability to produce color. She argues that the inability to produce the skin pigments of melanin, which are responsible for skin

4

coloration, is a genetic deficiency and that Whites do desire to have colored skins.

If the sociological and biological phenomenon of color has psychologically affected European Americans, it has also influenced the social relationships and intraracial social structures of African Americans. The dichotomous White-master and Black-slave relationships of the era of American slavery inevitably led to widespread miscegenation. The sexual liberties taken by White masters victimized African females and resulted in large numbers of human beings with mixed Black and White ancestry. Africans with visible evidence of European color and physical characteristics were termed *mulattoes, quadroons, octoroons,* etc., to indicate the extent of African ancestry. Although light-skinned Africans were not allowed to escape the caste of the Black race, they were often accorded privileges and benefits that were denied dark-complexioned Africans. The superior rank and economic status of Whites caused Blacks to equate wealth and power with white color or whiteness. Thus, a nominal but significant class structure—based on color—developed among African Americans during slavery, and it persisted as a major determinant of social networks until the Black Power and Black Pride movement of the 1960s. In recent years, color has again become a factor in differentiating opportunities and a factor affecting social networks, as the number of children produced by biracial unions has increased.

In spite of the lack of scientific evidence that color is an absolute determinant of race, *skin color* is a major criterion for ranking human groups as superior or inferior in America and in Europe. Antagonistic social relations that developed from the color-hierarchy of early American life still prevail and affect the conscious or sub-conscious behavior of Blacks and Whites in their daily life experiences. The American value system is based significantly on race/skin-color and White supremacy. Historically, Black Americans have adopted a variety of coping strategies in the search for social betterment and economic survival. Thousands of light-skinned African Americans or mulattoes "pass" for White, and some have passed permanently into the White race to benefit from the privileges that whiteness allows. More significant is that thousands of other African Americans could "pass" but have chosen, and still choose, to remain true to their African heritage and fight for a society that will be free of color discrimination. Color and race remain germane to an examination of the sociology of African Americans.[19]

From an Afrocentric perspective, culture is clearly related to race, although some social scientists dispute the notion that an absolute correlation between race and culture exists. Furthermore, there is a tendency among many Euro-American social theorists to deny that African American culture is significantly different from that of the dominant White American society. Sociologist Jerry D. Rose concedes that there is "at least a rough correlation between the distribution of racial types and of cultural forms...." However, he attributes the origin of such distinctions to the geographic isolation of groups. He appears to suggest that when isolation is broken down, cultural differentiation is diminished or dissolved.[20]

The debate relative to the correlation of culture and race exists, essentially, because the concept of culture is used to convey a variety of different ideas. *Culture* has various meanings to different groups or peoples. Culture includes more than an individual's or group's customs, language, artifacts, and physical environment. History, social experience, values, and beliefs are equally important in the understanding of culture because these factors constitute a people's worldview. To understand a people's culture is to understand its worldview.

African American culture is distinctive not only in terms of the contrast between African and European cultures, but also because of different and conflicting worldviews pertaining to racial experiences and race relations. Although Blacks and Whites share the same land space, their social and racial experiences are different. The African American view of America is one of historical slavery and segregation and of contemporary discrimination and socioeconomic inequality. Blacks' beliefs and values are focused on the attainment of racial and social justice. Moreover, Blacks remain generally "isolated" residentially from Whites. America is still, basically, a "segregated" Black and White society. The contrast between the collective social, political, and economic positions or statuses of African Americans and Whites is striking and vast. The relative positions of power and influence of Blacks and Whites have not changed. It is inconceivable that from these phenomena one could deny the existence of a distinct African American culture.

This reality can be overshadowed by excessive attention to recent trends in residential segregation. Sociologists and demographers use a variety of statistical indices to examine trends in residential racial segregation. The dissimilarity index is one of the most widely used metrics. It measures the relative separation or integration of groups across all neighborhoods of a city or metropolitan area. If the White-Black dissimilarity index of a city were 65, for example, that would mean that 65 percent of White people would need to move to another neighborhood to make the distribution of Whites and Blacks even across all neighborhoods. This 65 percent figure is provided only as an example. Clearly, such a value indicates a high degree of residential segregation, and it serves as a useful benchmark for assessing the actual data presented in table 4.1.

TABLE 4.1
BLACK-WHITE DISSIMILARITY INDICES
Selected Cities 1960–2010

Metro Area	1960	1970	1990	2000	2010
New York	.743	.737	.809	.802	.780
Los Angeles	.883	.884	.727	.700	.678
Chicago	.913	.911	.844	.812	.764
Washington	.788	.811	.655	.638	.623
San Francisco	.784	.770	.670	.657	.620
Philadelphia	.796	.780	.752	.710	.684
Boston	.807	.807	.685	.676	.640
Detroit	.873	.889	.876	.857	.753
Dallas	.810	.869	.628	.598	.566
Houston	.800	.781	.655	.657	.614
Atlanta	.766	.821	.663	.643	.590
Miami	.889	.861	.714	.692	.648
Seattle	.889	.803	.565	.524	.491
Phoenix	.793	.776	.501	.451	.436
Cleveland	.904	.905	.828	.782	.741

Source: 1960 and 1970 Cutler/Glaeser/Vigdor Segregation Data
http://trinity.aas.duke.edu/~jvigdor/segregation/
1990, 2000, 2010 University of Michigan, Population Studies Center, Institute for Social Research http://www.psc.isr.umich.edu/dis/census/segregation2010.html

Table 4.1 contains dissimilarity indices for selected U.S. metropolitan areas. The indices cover the period 1960–2010, to allow the examination of long-term trends consistent with the methodological guidance provided by Du Bois and the historiographic emphasis of African American Studies. As can be seen from a cursory examination of the data, all areas experienced a decline in Black-White segregation. However, following the methodological protocols of African American Studies, it is important to look at this

phenomenon over a longer period of time. The data indicate that extremely high levels of segregation still exist in many cities. This segregation reinforces cultural distinctiveness *vis-à-vis* African Americans and White Americans. This pattern obviously has a long history that predates 1960. Thus, it would be unrealistic to expect that such well-established patterns could be wholly transformed even over six decades (1960–2010).

Moreover, declines in residential segregation provide little information about patterns of interracial interaction. However, the available information suggests that residential segregation is not a good indicator of the degree of cross-cultural intercourse. As an example, the proverbial claim that 10:30 A.M. on Sunday morning is the most racially segregated time of the week remains valid. In a recent survey, although 51 percent of pastors claimed that their churches are "multicultural," in more than 80 percent of the congregations in America, at least 90 percent of the congregants are of the same racial group.[21]

In many situations where extensive Black–White interaction cannot be avoided and where potential competition for status and power exists, such as the workplace, high levels of racial tension persist. Avoidance of Blacks in the workplace by Whites is typically no longer feasible in the post-Civil Rights/post-Industrial regime. The charge that many Blacks who now occupy higher status positions are unqualified or under-qualified is one indicator of how Whites are reacting to disruption of the traditional status hierarchy of positions, where Whites occupied higher status occupations and Blacks were relegated to lower level jobs. Cohn argues that "the workplace is the primary stratifying institution in our society," and that even though "blacks and Whites are likely to work in racially mixed occupations, high-status jobs, however, [still] have a lot of Whites and relatively few blacks [and] low-status jobs have fewer Whites and more blacks."[22] In 2010, most African American men were employed in construction, maintenance, production, operative, and transportation occupations (36.5%). Service was the most prevalent occupational category for African American women (28.3 percent).

It is important to exercise great care in describing the complexities of the situation of Blacks in the U.S. Racialism, racism, and the ethnocentric ideology of color in the United States have forced African Americans to develop a culture that is significantly different from that of the dominant White society. African

4

Americans tend to reject the term or concept "subculture," which some sociologists use to describe the culture of a minority population. The prefix "sub" connotes a culture that is "less than" or "inferior to" the larger culture. Cultures should not be systematically ranked but considered relative to each other. When cultures are "ranked" according to race, the inevitable result is racism. Because of racialism, racism, discrimination, and oppression, African Americans have developed a distinctive culture that reflects their unique experiences in this society and that continues to be influenced by aspects of traditional African cultures—cultures that have survived and have adapted to function in the contemporary world. Therefore, race has a direct correlation to the culture of African Americans. As Amuzie Chimezie observes:

> It is true that Blacks participate in Euro-American culture, however, most of the participation is effected through coercion and the use of punishment if one fails to participate. Also, it is doubtful whether a majority of Blacks relate to the White part of the cultural dualism in their community with the same feeling as they do to the Black part.[23]

Of course, the "punishment" that Chimezie refers to is related to the social, economic, and political costs, such as education and employment that African Americans would be deprived of if they failed to embrace White American culture to some extent. Caroline Torrance argues that "Although Blacks support the ideology of American society it is not for the same reasons as Whites, but because of high levels of Black consciousness."[24]

Arab scholar A. Abdel-Daim identifies four levels of culture: local, national, regional [world region], and universal.[25] However, two additional levels of culture must be considered in analyzing the circumstances of African Americans. The major differences between Black and White American cultures are manifested at the neighborhood and family levels. It is at these two levels of cultural separation that even the superficial effects of integration have failed.

In developing a perspective on whether Black total acculturation into American society can ever be realized it is useful to consider the assimilation variables or possibilities that Milton M. Gordon outlines in *Assimilation in American Life*. Gordon lists the subprocesses or conditions that must exist before a minority racial/ethnic group might be culturally or behaviorally assimilated into a dominant society or culture as follows:

1. Change of cultural patterns to those of host society.
2. Large-scale entrance into cliques, clubs, and institutions of host society, on primary group level.
3. Large-scale intermarriage.
4. Development of sense of peoplehood based on host society.
5. Absence of prejudice.
6. Absence of discrimination.
7. Absence of value and power conflict.[26]

Gordon proposed that the preceding conditions should be thought of as steps or stages in the assimilation process. It must be pointed out that his assimilation variables apply to, or have more relevance for, White European ethnic and immigrant populations. After well over a century of emancipation from slavery, Blacks have not made significant collective progress relative to Gordon's assimilation stages. Although the acculturation of White European ethnic groups might have been delayed, race, racism, and color or culture did not prevent them from becoming fully assimilated into American society on a voluntary basis. The panacea for racial problems and antagonism proposed by social psychologists in "contact theory" or through desegregation has failed to change the racial status and power dynamic between Blacks and Whites in the United States to any significant degree.

The Call for a "Black Sociology"

The persisting patterns of racial isolation, exclusion, and oppression African Americans experience impelled efforts to construct a "Black Sociology." This initiative was derived from the premise that peoples of African descent possess a distinct ethos, culture, and worldview. Diaspora Blacks, such as African Americans, have retained sufficient elements of their African psyche and culture to differentiate themselves despite the imposition of slavery and oppression by Europeans and White Americans. As Ronald W. Walters states, "Black life has been distinctive and separate enough to constitute its own uniqueness and it is on the basis of that uniqueness that the ideology and the methodology of Black social science rests."[27] Nathan Hare, the first coordinator and developer of a formal Black/African American Studies academic unit, foresaw the need for Black scholars to develop appropriate new norms and values, new or adaptive research methodologies, and new ideologies to authenticate the academic nature of the Black experience.

In simple terms, sociology is the study of human group life. This definition may be a true assessment of the field, but the theoretical underpinnings and implications of sociological study depend on which human group is studied and which group or people is conducting the study. There are major differences between the social experiences and cultures of African and European peoples, or the Black and White races, that should be addressed and questioned in assessing the efficacy of alternative research paradigms. Given persisting differences in socialization and experiences between Blacks and Whites, how valid is the sociological study of Blacks or Africans when it is based solely on the social experience, philosophy, and ideology of Whites or Europeans? Should Blacks be judged, or judge themselves, according to White or European behavioral norms or standards? Is universal sociological thought limited to the exclusive theoretical constructs and world-views of White classical and neoclassical scholars and philosophers? Is fair or balanced consideration accorded the philosophical social perspectives of scholars of African and Asian descent? Finally, is it logical that Black scholars should define and interpret their own social experience and develop new approaches or adapt traditional methodologies for the study of African peoples? These questions are posed simply as a premise and justification for an Afrocentric orientation to sociology applied to African Americans.

Robert Staples, an eminent Black sociologist, feels that many of the traditional ways of studying sociology are overwhelmingly influenced by and based on White norms, mores, and values. Thus, there is the tendency to glorify Whites and to patronize or demean Blacks and other non-White groups. He points out that the Chicago school of sociologists and White sociologists, in general, focused on and studied the so-called problem of Black populations, such as, low-income families, single parents, and emotionally disturbed or academically non-achieving or delinquent children and youths. Although some of their methodologies were appropriate, the ideologies that influenced the interpretation of the research data were

not. Staples criticizes traditional sociology for often attempting to function as a pure science by seeking "objectively" to study group life without much concern for the practical use of such knowledge. He postulates that Black sociology, of necessity, must function as an applied science with the objective of applying sociological theory to the liberation and development of the Black community. Staples concurs with the contention that Blacks and Whites in American society share little in common in political and economic participation, social experience, and culture. Consequently, the specific need for Black sociology is to study the Black experience and culture as an internal social system and to analyze external constraints on African American life and institutions.[28]

The functionalist, conflict theory, and symbolic interactionism paradigms have been the principal empirical and theoretical sociological models for the study of human or group values, behaviors, and social relationships. Functionalism is a theory derived from Auguste Comte's order and morality concept of sociological objectives. Neoclassical sociologists, such as, Talcott Parsons and Robert Merton, have contributed to the development or modification of the functionalist approach. Functionalism assumes a normative consensus of values within societies and social institutions that constitutes an order or equilibrium state. Any individual, group or phenomenon that disrupts or upsets the societal equilibrium is considered problematic, and the source of the disturbance must be reordered and controlled to restore order and equilibrium. Civil law is considered a constructive means of readjusting society and restoring order.

Conflict theorists maintain the opposite view. They regard conflict as normal and inevitable when competing groups contend for power, advantageous position, and scarce resources. Conflicts are eliminated through institutional suppression of the dissident or rebellious group in favor of the dominant group. The dominant group's values and ideas exercise a cultural hegemony over subordinate societies or groups.

Symbolic interactionism is a social-psychological theory that emphasizes the self as a social object and entity that is changed, weakened, strengthened, or otherwise affected in its interaction with others.

The preceding brief explanations of the prevailing major sociological paradigms—functionalism, value-conflict, and symbolic interactionism—have

4

been presented to highlight their ideological implications in studies on the African American experience. The common scheme of traditional Western sociological models is to gain knowledge of human behavior, values, beliefs, or cultures for the purpose of ranking and controlling specific segments of the society. The biological theories of Charles Darwin and the sociological ideology of Herbert Spencer (social Darwinism) are reflected in the social objectives of European and Euro-American sociology. In essence, much of the theory implicitly fosters the ideology of European dominance and superiority. By labeling Africans or the underclass as intellectually inferior, misfit, morally deficient or deviant, the rationale for colonialism and slavery was promoted and sustained.

What becomes evident is that the definition and interpretation of social phenomena are affected by race, culture, and historical consciousness. It is interesting that the victims of slavery and racism were adjudged socially and psychologically deviant or pathological, whereas the perpetrators of inhumane practices (slave masters and racists) were perceived as socially, morally, and psychologically healthy and superior. Runaway and rebellious slaves, for example, were perceived as disrupters of order and deviants by most Whites, but Africans viewed them and their acts as positive and heroic. In Black inner cities, hustling, pimping, or minor drug trafficking are often perceived as effective coping and survival activities. Conversely, the same behavior is viewed as deviant and threatening to the maintenance of law and order by many traditional sociologists. This example illustrates that African Americans and European Americans do not always share the same perceptions of social behavior and conduct. Without the countervailing force of a Black sociological perspective, this disjunction can easily lead traditional researchers to misinterpret behaviors and advocate ineffective policies to address presumed causes of contra-cultural activities. Without a Black sociological perspective or approach, traditional sociology might well be meaningless or of little benefit to the Black community.

Not all Black social theorists subscribe to the need for new paradigms for the study of African Americans. Many apply traditional approaches and methodological constructs to Black life, especially in the absence of alternatives. Afrocentric scholars, many of whom matured professionally within the African American/ Black Studies field after 1968, are perhaps the most insistent on developing new constructs, or adapting

conventional ones, that challenge traditional positivist approaches to the Black experience. The positivist methodological protocol relies on the findings of previous empirical and theoretical data; the construction of research instruments based on the researcher's common sense knowledge of social processes; and the execution of experiments, observations, surveys, or interviews with value neutrality as the guiding principle. The method of positivism is ahistorical, and the results often reestablish and reinforce the status quo.

Critical methodology offers an improvement over positivism because it requires the investigation of all intragroup strata, studies the historical development of the group, and develops a global understanding of the political and economic experiences of the social group. Furthermore, it compares conditions with understanding, analyzes the prevailing ideology, discovers imminent possibilities for action, identifies fundamental contradictions, and educates in order to effect improvement. Although the two methodologies are different, for the purposes of Black Studies, Terry Kershaw suggests a synthesis of positivist and critical approaches in exploratory efforts to create new or appropriate sociological protocols and methodologies.[29]

The task of developing new or revised models for researching and analyzing the Black experience is challenging in a world where White social theory and definitions dominate. Available research funding to study the positive dimensions of the Black experience is declining. Nevertheless, it is imperative that the Black social scientist be self-determining and free to develop paradigms for the study of African Americans. The true extent of a people's freedom depends on their ability and courage to define, validate, and legitimatize their own experience and achievements. Dennis Forsythe states that "it is the task of Black sociology to stress the uniqueness of the Black experience and to see that knowledge collected on Blacks is used for change rather than for control."[30]

Institutions in Black Communities

Du Bois's model of group development, discussed previously, emphasizes institution building as a measure of success for increasing survival prospects and enabling full realization of human potential. He recognized that establishing stable family arrangements, religious bodies, and educational conventions was essential for wholesome social development. He felt that care had to be taken so that sharp class divisions did not emerge between the more and less privileged. Externally imposed barriers to the normal development of these institutions among African Americans have led to uneven social development, including undue emphasis on some activities and institutions that can retard rather than enhance development.

Advocates of African American Studies focus on understanding the operation of social institutions that either contribute significantly to enhanced community well-being or that have the potential to affect its well-being adversely if appropriate interventions are not undertaken. This is, in essence, the same approach Du Bois took in outlining his model of social progress. Du Bois championed institutions that cultivate positive social values, expand the body of available knowledge and information, and promote harmonious relationships. In modern terms, such institutions can be described as contributing to the creation of "social capital." Social capital builds community strength and well-being by allowing persons and communities to mobilize greater resources and achieve common goals through enhanced social connectedness, social trust, and community identity. The sustained creation of social capital requires: (1) widespread involvement of individuals in community organizations and activities; (2) conditions that foster feelings of safety; (3) dense social networks; (4) a shared understanding of the value of life; and (5) a commitment to activities that bring internally-controlled resources, such as paid employment, into the community. Using this analytical framework, some contemporary researchers see the problems of alienated youth and the poor in inner city communities as the consequences of social capital having been transferred out of Black communities concomitant with a decline in traditional forms of social capital in the urban core.

In the spirit of Du Bois's model of social development, the family, religious, and educational institutions will be examined as major traditional sources of social capital. We will also examine sports and young adult collectives, two other institutions that have had mixed effects on the creation of social capital because of their disproportionate influence on the lives of younger cohorts of African Americans.

The African American Family

The union of males and females for the purpose of procreation, extension of ancestral lineage, and propagation of the human species is a universal phenomenon. The social laws, modes, and practices that determine the genesis of the conjugal union or relationship between males and females to perform the functions of procreation and ancestral propagation have always varied in accordance with group cultures and customs. Each basic human unit that is united and related to perform these functions is described as a "family." Because family initiations and practices vary across different racial or ethnic cultural groups or societies, the African American family should be studied from an African-centered or Afrocentric perspective. It is also important to recognize that conceptions of family are constantly evolving as non-traditional configurations, such as, same-sex households and blended families, become more prevalent.

This discussion will not focus extensively on the classic and ongoing debate of some scholars about whether or not the Black American family has retained sufficient African cultural traits to be truly distinctive from European culture. However, it is essential to emphasize that many scholars of the African and African American experiences affirm that the African American family has retained numerous cultural characteristics and practices that originated among various African cultural groups across the continent.[31] Even in the absence of explicit evidence, it is logical to assume that certain latent cultural traits prevail in spite of Black slavery and oppression. In fact, oppression, racism, and discrimination have caused many Blacks, more or less, to reject White or European values or culture and to rediscover and revel in their African heritage. This orientation is exemplified by the growing popularity of African attire, the increasing choice of African names, the expanding efforts to emulate traditional African value systems, and the celebration of Kwanzaa by Black Americans—a practice that emerged after the 1960s Black Power movement. In other words, if much of African familial culture was lost during slavery, it is now being rediscovered and reconsidered after almost four centuries.

There is no doubt that European influence and domination have diminished the influence of traditional African familial values and practices in the lives of Black Americans. Yet, familiarity with the features of traditional African family structures provides an important context for understanding elements of African American culture. African family structures are based on kinship and descent systems that are significantly different from those of Europeans. Both matrilineal and patrilineal family systems are practiced in Africa. The matrilineal family designates kinship exclusively through the lineage or ancestry of the mother. Conversely, patrilineal societies determine kinship strictly through the father's lineage.

Different cultural groups have had various marital forms, such as monogamy, polygamy, polygyny, and polyandry. *Monogamy* involves a male or female having only one spouse, whereas *polygamy* allows a person to have more than one partner in marriage. When a man has more than one spouse it is called *polygyny*, and when a woman is married to more than one it is known as *polyandry*. The extended family is central to most African societies, in contrast with a focus on the nuclear family in the Western tradition. The extended family includes even distant relatives, ritualistically adopted kin, and multiple related family units, sometimes living within the same residential complex.[32] Matrilineage, patrilineage, and the various other marital forms were functional within the respective societies in which they operated. The community observed and enforced strict rules of behavior and conduct based on the cultural norms of each society.

The differences between African and European familial traditions were a source of frustration to enslaved African Americans. European civilizations regarded patrilineage and monogamous relationships as culturally superior to other practices. Initially, Africans attempted to continue their African familial traditions in the slave quarters of America. However, African traditional family customs were forcibly eroded or modified to conform to the concepts of Christianity. Slave masters determined the extent to which familial relations and activities could be manifested. In spite of the liberties that masters took with slave women, the White church encouraged Blacks to practice Christian monogamous relationships. White ministers of the South preached against adultery and fornication but were faced with a dilemma when married slaves were sold and separated. Scholars Blassingame and Gutman seem to indicate that, ironically, enslaved Blacks did adopt a preference for two parent households or functionally monogamous families. Enduring two-parent relationships and households formed during slavery were recorded

and reported among former enslaved Africans many years after Emancipation.[33] The evidence is conclusive that slavery did not totally destroy Black family culture or diminish the value of the functional benefits of the African concept of the extended family. After Emancipation, many formerly enslaved Blacks vigorously attempted to find kin that had been sold apart from their relatives, had run away, or were residing elsewhere for various other reasons. There was also a more stable family tradition that developed among many free Blacks during the slavery era. Frazier sees free Black families during slavery as an ideal type and insists that "it was among this class that family traditions became firmly established before the Civil War."[34]

The contemporary Black family has been the subject of more sociological inquiries than any other aspect of African American society. There is an ongoing debate regarding the extent to which current difficulties are directly linked to the era of enslavement. Many social theorists have proposed that the African American family has been irreparably weakened and remains unstable because of historic and chronic racism and discrimination. A significant segment of the Black population lives in circumstances in which high crime rates, vice, juvenile delinquency, drug and alcohol abuse, and ineffective schools are prevalent. Daniel P. Moynihan argues in his study, *The Negro Family: The Case for National Action*, that the reason for deviancy and educational underachievement of youths is that the Black family is characterized by a large number of female-headed households, illegitimate births, and absent fathers. Borrowing heavily from arguments first put forth by E. Franklin Frazier, Moynihan proclaims that slavery had destroyed the quality of African American family life and left it in "a tangle of pathology," which, in consequence, impeded the progress of Black Americans.[35]

The Moynihan study provoked national concern and reaction among Black and White scholars, spawning two conflicting theories intended to rebut the Moynihan thesis. Rutledge Dennis describes the two competing schools of thought as the "Weak-Family Theory" and the "Strong-Family Theory." The Weak-Family Theory concurs to some extent with Moynihan's assessment that slavery did affect Black family development but contends that weakness and instability have been caused more by the social, political, economic, and psychological effects of persistent racism since slavery. Although they do not discount the effects of slavery and of contemporary racism, the Strong-Family Theory proponents emphasize the survivability and adaptability of the African American family as indicators of its strength and viability.[36]

The Weak-Family concept was rejected by a host of notable Black scholars that include Andrew Billingsley, Robert B. Hill, and Robert Staples.[37] Billingsley used the case study method to support his counterclaims, and Hill employed empirical-quantitative methods to produce contravening evidence. Staples rejected the Moynihan thesis on Afrocentric ideological grounds. Strong-Family theorists propose that the Black family should be evaluated within the context of its own social reality. Thus, variations from White patterns should be understood, in part, as adaptive coping strategies influenced by African heritage.

Those who argue that oppressive factors have contributed to deviance and the instability of the Black family believe that strength and viability cannot be achieved until racism and discrimination have been eliminated. Weak-Family theorists define the optimum family model and structure in terms of White middle-class norms. Black families that approximate White middle-class standards are perceived to be stronger and more stable than those exhibiting different arrangements and functioning styles. Nathan Hare criticizes the Strong-Family school of thought because it has the effect of absolving White people of blame for their racist and oppressive role in weakening the African American family. Yet, he applauds promotion of an independent spirit and Black pride reflected in the interpretations of Strong-Family proponents.[38]

The difference between the two Black family theories might be analogous to "seeing the glass half full or half empty." Blacks often subscribe to the social definitions of White society although their perceptions of social phenomena might differ. An Afrocentric theorist, for instance, may repudiate the term *illegitimacy* for Black children born out of wedlock or without a formal father. Strong-Family and Afrocentric theorists may regard children born out of conventional wedlock as an inevitable human social occurrence arising from Black male unemployment and imposed racial poverty. There is no such thing as an illegitimate human being with reference to birth; but, here again, the dominant society determines social legitimacy and illegitimacy.

A case in point is the growing number of White women who yearn for children and hasten to take advantage of scientific medical advances in producing human life through "test-tube" babies, surrogate motherhood, genetic engineering, and frozen human embryos. The questions of legitimacy and the absence or identity of the biological father are seldom if ever applied or considered. Furthermore, as an outcome of the White feminist movement, the stigma attached to being an unmarried mother has been reduced, as more women pursue professional careers.

The differing interpretations posed by the two theories suggest the need to examine carefully the available data relevant for resolving the points of disagreement. Consistent with the methodological emphasis in African American Studies on scrutinizing long-term trends, the data in Table 4.2 track change in the relative prevalence of various family arrangements among Blacks between 1950 and 2010. While there is a drastic decline in the representation rate for married couple families since 1950, the sharpest decline occurred between 1970 and 1980, a decade in which the Vietnam War and economic stagnation dominated the social landscape. The decline slowed between 1990 and 2000, a period that overlaps partially with the longest economic expansion in U.S. history. A slight reversal occurred between 2000 and 2010. The pattern experienced for married couple households is mirrored by corresponding changes in the representation rate of female-headed households. However, the changes in the percentages of female-headed households across the decades exhibit less variation than is the case for married couples. It is also important to note the increase in the prevalence of households headed by unmarried males beginning in the 1990s. Taken together, these data could be interpreted as evidence of "residual strength" that can be tapped and utilized if favorable economic and social conditions exist. This is, of course, not to deny the challenges to viable family functioning faced by single heads of households.

Finally, it is also important to recognize that significant growth is occurring in the number of single-sex households among African Americans. In 2008, the American Community Survey reported that African Americans accounted for 4.5 percent of male same-sex households, and 7.7 percent of female same sex-households. These percentages imply that in 2008 there were approximately 16,800 male and 22,700 female single-sex African American households.[39]

4

TABLE 4.2

CHANGES IN THE COMPOSITION OF BLACK FAMILIES*
1950 – 2010

Percentage Representation

Family Type	1950	1960	1970	1980	1990	2000	2010
Married Couple	78	74	68	56	50	45	46
Female Householder No spouse present	18	22	28	40	44	47	44
Male Householder No spouse present	4	4	4	4	6	8	10

Source: "Black Americans: A Profile," Bureau of the Census Statistical Brief SB?93-2 (March 1993); Jesse McKinnon and Lynne M. Casper, "America's Families and Living Arrangements," Current Population Reports (2000); Data for 2010 is from Table F1. Family Households/1, by Type, Age of Own Children, Age of Family Members, and Age, Race and Hispanic Origin/2 of Householder: 2010. http://www.census.gov/population/socdemo/hh-fam/cps2010/tabF1-blkalone.xls

There is no question that there is a legitimate need to focus detailed attention on the situation in which children are conceived and reared. Although African American Studies eschews uncontextualized comparisons of social indicators for different racial/ethnic groups, in discussions of trends in births to unwed women versus married women such comparisons can be illuminating. The data in Table 4.3 confirm the disproportionate prevalence of births to unwed women among African Americans compared to other groups. However, consistent with the pattern observed for family arrangements, the proportion of births to Black unwed mothers declined between 1995 and 2002—a period dominated by the economic expansion. In contrast, Whites and Hispanics experienced a continuous increase in the proportion of births to unwed mothers during this period. By 2010, the proportion of births to unmarried women had increased significantly for all three racial/ethnic groups, with the proportion of African American births to unwed mothers exceeding seventy percent.

TABLE 4.3

PERCENTAGE OF BIRTHS TO UNMARRIED WOMEN
Selected Years, 1980 – 2010

Percentage Representation

Race/Ethnicity	1980	1985	1990	1995	2002	2010
Black	56.1	61.2	66.5	69.9	68.2	72.5
White, non-Hispanic	9.6	12.4	16.9	21.2	23.0	29.0
Hispanic	23.6	29.5	36.7	40.8	43.5	53.4
TOTAL	18.4	22.0	28.0	32.2	34.0	40.8

Source: 1980 – 2002, Child Trends Databank, http://www.childtrendsdatabank.org/figures/75-Figure-1.gif 2010 National Vital Statistics Report, "Births: Final Data for 2010," 61 (1), August 28, 2012 http://www.cdc.gov/nchs/data/nvsr/nvsr61/nvsr61_01.pdf

The hypothesized relationships described by Wilkerson and Gresham are complex and require separate considerations of several issues. First, they raise the issue of the extent to which Black males are able to engage the U.S. economic system in ways that allow them to perform expected roles *vis-à-vis* provision of support to families. Data detailing the labor market experiences of Black men over the last forty years are presented in Table 4.4, with comparative data for white men included as points of reference.

Three separate but related indicators are provided. The first two columns present the labor force participation rates for Black and White men (LFPR). This is the proportion of men 20 years or older who are either employed or unemployed, divided by the total number of males in that age group. The middle two columns contain the employment/population ratios for both groups (Emp/Pop). This is the ratio of the number of men 20 or over who are employed divided by the total size of the 20 and over population for each group. The last two columns provide unemployment rate data, that is, the percentage of men over 20 who are unemployed divided by the total number of men in that age range who are in the labor force (URATE).

TABLE 4.4

LABOR FORCE PARTICIPATION AND UNEMPLOYMENT TRENDS
BLACK AND WHITE MEN
Selected Years, 1972 – 2011

Percentage Representation

Year	White LFPR	Black LFPR	White Emp/Pop	Black Emp/Pop	White Unem Rate	Black Unem Rate
1972	82.0	78.5	79.0	73.0	3.6	7.0
1975	80.7	76.0	75.7	66.5	6.2	12.5
1980	79.8	75.1	75.6	65.8	5.3	12.4
1985	78.5	74.4	74.3	64.6	5.4	13.2
1990	78.5	75.0	75.1	67.1	4.3	10.4
1995	77.1	72.5	73.8	66.1	4.3	8.8
2000	77.1	72.8	74.9	67.7	2.8	6.9
2005	76.2	71.3	73.3	64.7	3.8	9.2
2010	74.6	69.5	67.9	57.5	8.9	17.3
2011	71.3	64.2	65.3	52.8	8.3	17.8

Source: U.S. Census Bureau, Current Population Survey. Labor Force Statistics from the Current Population Survey. http://www.bls.gov/cps/.

The LFPR data indicate a fairly stable structural difference between Black and White men, with White men exhibiting a 4-5 point larger percentage participation rate. The EMP/POP data exhibit a similar pattern. However, for Black males there was a much sharper decline between 1972 and 1985 than for White males, which would be expected to have severe negative implications for the viability of Black families during that period. The unemployment data document the well-known pattern, with the rate for Black males more than twice that of Whites. It is important to note that the rate for Black males does not reach single digit levels after 1972 until the decade of the 1990s, a period when the decline in married couple families started to stabilize. However, by 2005, the Black male unemployment rate was again approaching double digits and has increased dramatically during the most recent recession and anemic recovery.

TABLE 4.5
AFRICAN AMERICANS AS A PERCENTAGE OF ACTIVE DUTY ENLISTED PERSONNEL AND OFFICERS
Selected Years, 1976 – 2007
Percentage Representation

Year	Enlisted Percentage	Officer Percentage
1976	16.6	3.4
1979	21.2	4.7
1989	22.1	6.7
2003	19.1	8.9
2007	18.5	9.1
2010	18.1	9.4

Source: 1976-1989 – Defense Equal Opportunity Management Institute, "Twenty-Seven Year Demographic Trends, Active Duty Forces 1977-2004; 2003-2007 - Defense Equal Opportunity Management Institute, "FY Summary Representation of Race/Ethnicity Groups and Women in the Active Armed Forces, 1997-2007" 2010 - Defense Equal Opportunity Management Institute, "FY Summary Representation of Race/Ethnicity Groups and Women in the Active Armed Forces, 2004-2010"

For many African Americans, persisting labor market discrimination and limited educational opportunities have made the military a viable alternative to civilian employment, especially since the advent of the all-volunteer military in 1974. In the military, each service person is assigned an occupational specialty and receives the requisite training to perform assigned duties. Although Blacks are disproportionately represented in the lowest skill occupations, the fixed pay scales based upon rank limit earnings differentials compared to the civilian sector. The representation of Blacks in the enlisted and officer ranks for selected years is presented in Table 4.5. Representation of Black enlisted personnel continued to increase

into the early 1990s, but has declined subsequently, partly in response to increases in armed conflicts in Iraq and Afghanistan. In contrast, the representation of Black officers has continued to climb. Representation of Black enlisted personnel and officers is greatest in the Army and smallest in the Marines. In 2010, for example Black enlisted representation in the Army and Marines, respectively, was 21.5 percent and 10.9 percent. In 1997, Black enlisted representation in the Army was 29.7 percent.[40]

It is also necessary to recognize how the extensive incarceration of African Americans affects labor force statistics and outcomes. As an example, a large number of Black males are under the control of the criminal justice system and are, therefore, unable to function in familial roles. The continuing calamity of Black male incarceration has been characterized as "The New Jim Crow" by Michelle Alexander.[41]

In 1980, the number of Black and White males admitted to state and federal prisons were, respectively, 58,412 and 82,417. By 1990, these figures had ballooned to 169,500 and 169,300, respectively. The data in Table 4.6 present more recent information about the numbers of incarcerated Black and White males. The numbers appear to have plateaued for both groups, but the number of incarcerated males remains near its historic high.

TABLE 4.6
BLACK AND WHITE MALES IN STATE AND FEDERAL PRISONS AND LOCAL JAILS
Selected Years, 2000 – 2008
Number of Admissions

Year	Black Inmates	White Inmates
2000	791,600	663,700
2002	818,900	630,700
2005	806,200	688,700
2008	846,000	712,500
2009	841,000	693,800

Source: *Prison Inmates at Midyear - Statistical Tables.* Bureau of Justice Statistics, various years

The preceding assessment highlights the need to examine trends in the magnitude of economic resources available to support Black families. Table 4.7 presents median Black family income for several family types from 1970 - 2011. Median family income is the income of the family that would be exactly in the middle if families were ranked from highest to lowest income. The data presented are in what is termed "real dollars"; that is, they are adjusted for inflation over the last forty years, so that income for those years is expressed in what would be the equivalent amounts in 2011. This allows an assessment of the extent of improvement in living standards.

Several key conclusions can be drawn from the table. First, there was no significant improvement in the circumstances of any type of family until the 1990s, with the most significant improvements occurring between 1995 and 2000. Second, the families that experienced the greatest improvement in well-being were married couple families in which both partners were in the labor force. In fact, such families experienced significant improvements in income between 1975 and 1990, while the incomes of other types of families were largely stagnant during the same period. Third, the incomes of all family types were either stagnant or declined between 2000 and 2011, with the exception of married couples in which the wife was not in the labor force. Income fell sharply for households headed by single men.

TABLE 4.7
MEDIAN BLACK FAMILY INCOME BY FAMILY TYPE
Selected Years, 1970 – 2011
(Constant 2011 $)
Median Income

Year	All families	Married couple wife in lf	Married couple wife not in lf	Female head no spouse present	Male head no spouse present
1970	32,456	50,248	30,812	18,484	34,896
1975	33,368	54,562	32,471	18,617	34,037
1980	32,936	59,238	32,274	19,296	32,632
1985	33,461	60,802	30,158	18,548	32,723
1990	35,737	66,791	33,919	20,227	36,446
1995	38,056	71,120	37,378	21,987	36,887
2000	43,983	76,495	39,372	26,912	41,876
2005	40,857	76,616	37,317	25,302	36,070
2010	39,811	75,719	41,066	25,144	33,291
2011	40,495	75,101	42,475	25,309	36,477

Source: U.S. Census Bureau, Historical Income Tables, Table F-7.
http://www.census.gov/hhes/income/histinc/f07b.html

These data suggest that there is a more complex pattern of strengths and weaknesses among Black families than either the strong or weak family theories have considered. This changing pattern is driven by changes in the relative economic position of Black men and women.

Table 4.8 tracks the median income of Black men and women across several age ranges for the same time period. For men ages 25-34, the median income has actually declined since 1970, while women in this age range have increased their median income by over $3,000. Income for men 35-44 years old has been essentially unchanged while income for women has grown by slightly over $11,000. As a result, what was a difference of over $13,000 in 1970 had been reduced to about $2,500 in 2011. The greatest relative improvement for women has occurred for women in the 45-54 age range. In 1970, women earned almost $17,000 less than men did; but, by 2011, this deficit had been cut to slightly over $5,000.

TABLE 4.8
MEDIAN INCOME OF BLACK MEN AND WOMEN AGES 25-34
Selected Years, 1970 – 2011
(Constant 2011 $)
Median Income

Year	Men 25-34	Men 35-44	Men 45-54	Women 25-34	Women 35-44	Women 45-54
1970	28,802	31,500	30,161	17,771	17,239	12,462
1975	31,361	32,946	27,846	19,529	17,746	15,462
1980	28,607	32,853	29,828	18,604	18,807	15,845
1985	27,223	33,803	33,967	16,621	22,228	20,284
1990	25,435	33,527	33,807	16,919	24,747	22,509
1995	26,451	30,602	31,855	18,946	24,147	23,949
2000	30,661	35,551	35,488	26,451	28,801	28,472
2005	27,235	36,254	35,378	23,529	29,803	27,752
2010	24,799	32,577	31,754	22,390	29,506	25,798
2011	25,850	31,987	30,814	21,209	28,252	25,338

Source: U.S. Census Bureau, Historical Income Tables, Table P-8.
http://www.census.gov/hhes/www/income/data/historical/people/P08B_2011.xls

This new policy increased the instability of the incomes of single female heads of household, with potentially catastrophic results, as suggested by the large increases in the unemployment rate of Black women between 2000 and 2005. The impact of these policy changes on black female unemployment have been compounded by the most recent recession and has led to an increase in the unemployment rate to 14.1 percent in 2011, a level not seen previously.

TABLE 4.9
LABOR FORCE PARTICIPATION AND UNEMPLOYMENT TRENDS
BLACK AND WHITE WOMEN
Selected Years, 1972 – 2010
Percentage Representation

Year	WHITE LFPR	BLACK LFPR	WHITE EMP/POP	BLACK EMP/POP	WHITE UNEM RATE	BLACK UNEM RATE
1972	42.7	51.2	40.6	46.5	4.9	9.0
1975	45.3	51.1	41.9	44.9	7.5	12.2
1980	50.6	55.6	47.8	49.1	5.6	11.9
1985	54.0	58.6	51.0	50.9	5.7	13.1
1990	57.6	60.6	55.2	54.7	4.1	9.7
1995	59.2	61.4	56.7	56.1	4.3	8.6
2000	59.9	65.4	58.0	61.3	3.1	6.2
2005	59.7	64.4	57.4	58.9	3.9	8.5
2010	59.9	63.2	55.6	55.1	7.2	12.8
2011	58.0	59.1	53.7	50.8	7.5	14.1

Source: U.S. Census Bureau, Current Population Survey. Labor Force Statistics from the Current Population Survey. http://www.bls.gov/cps/

The previous discussion regarding the military as an alternative to civilian employment applies to both African American men and women. Table 4.10 shows the number and percentage of African American female enlisted personnel and officers for selected years.

TABLE 4.10
NUMBERS AND PERCENTAGE REPRESENTATION OF FEMALE
AFRICAN AMERICAN ENLISTED PERSONNEL AND OFFICERS
Selected Years, 1993 – 2007

Year	Number of Enlisted	Percentage Representation	Number of Officers	Percentage Representation
1993	57,108	33.5	4,308	13.1
1997	57,421	34.3	4,366	13.8
2001	61,714	35.0	5,141	15.8
2003	59,556	32.8	5,695	16.0
2007	50,682	30.5	5,842	16.8
2010	51,907	30.4	6,568	17.2

Source: 1993-2003 – Defense Equal Opportunity Management Institute, "Twenty-Seven Year Demographic Trends, Active Duty Forces 1977-2004; 2007 - Defense Equal Opportunity Management Institute, "FY Summary Representation of Race/Ethnicity Groups and Women in the Active Armed Forces, 1997-2007"

Note that the percentage representation of African American women, *vis-à-vis* all military women,

is significantly larger than for men. As is the case for men, the percentage representation is greatest in the army and smallest in the Marines (excluding the Coast Guard). In 2010, African American women comprised 39.4 percent of Army enlisted personnel (46.7 percent in 1997) and 16.5 percent of Marine enlisted personnel (26.4 percent in 1997). As is the case for men, Black representation in the enlisted ranks has declined subsequently, partly in response to increases in armed conflicts in Iraq and Afghanistan.[42] In contrast to men, there has been a slight increase in enlisted personnel between 2007 and 2010.

The disastrous effects of incarceration on the well-being of African Americans impacts women directly, as it does men. Table 4.11 presents information about the levels of incarceration of Black women with data for White women provided as points of reference. It is notable that the number of incarcerated Black women has remained relatively stable while that for White women has increased dramatically since 2002.

TABLE 4.11
BLACK AND WHITE FEMALES IN STATE AND FEDERAL
PRISONS AND LOCAL JAILS
Selected Years, 2000 - 2009
Number of Admissions

Year	Black Inmates	White Inmates
2000	69,500	63,700
2002	65,600	68,800
2005	65,700	88,600
2008	67,800	94,500
2009	62,800	92,100

Source: *Prison Inmates at Midyear-Statistical Tables*. Bureau of Justice Statistics (various years)

The labor market barriers and incarceration patterns discussed previously have contributed directly to the trends in the proportion of all types of Black families living in poverty, shown in Table 4.12. For all family types, there was a significant decline in the proportion of families living in poverty between 1995 and 2000, followed by a drastic upturn, especially for male-headed households. However, even for this group, the poverty rate is significantly less than that for single women, which has been consistently over 40 per cent except in 2000.

TABLE 4.12
PERCENT OF BLACK FAMILIES WITH CHILDREN UNDER 18
IN POVERTY BY FAMILY TYPE
Selected Years, 1975 – 2009

Year	All Families	Married Couples	Female Head	Male Head No Spouse Present
1975	33.9	16.5	50.1	13.0
1980	35.5	15.5	49.4	17.7
1985	39.9	18.0	50.5	22.9
1990	37.2	14.3	48.1	20.6
1995	34.1	9.9	45.1	19.5
2000	25.3	6.7	34.3	16.3
2005	28.4	9.3	42.0	29.2
2010	33.9	12.2	47.6	40.1
2011	32.8	12.2	47.3	28.8

Source: U.S. Census Bureau, Historical Poverty Tables, Table 4.
http://www.census.gov/hhes/www/poverty/data/historical/hstpov4.xls

Male-Female Conflicts and Family Dynamics

The strengths and weaknesses of African American families can only be fully appreciated by analyzing the historical social relationships and the prevailing politico-psychological issues contributing to problems or conflicts between Black males and females. In general, American society subscribes to gender specific socialization of males and females that reproduce traditional notions of masculinity and femininity. But beyond this social reality, Black males and females have been experiencing, and continue to experience, different modes of socialization because of the effects of slavery, racism, discrimination, and the ever present influence of White cultural hegemony.

Historically, the divergent treatment and roles of Black men and women began with their forced voyage to the New World on slave vessels. The men and boys were shackled and chained in holds below deck, while some of the slave women and girls were allowed to roam on deck. Enslaved Black women were considered too weak to attempt to revolt or escape. Invariably, members of the ships' crews subjected some women to rape and other forms of sexual exploitation. Owners attached special economic value to enslaved females because of their reproductive ability and their potential use as sexual objects. Many young slave girls were used as breeders, concubines, or prostitutes, depending on their owners' assessments and preferences. Differential male and female roles were based solely on

the economic interests of the owner. Owners determined how much care enslaved women received during pregnancy and the treatment or attention given to their children. Enslaved Black women were forced to be at the disposal of owners and allowed only incidentally to function as daughters, wives, or mothers.[43]

During slavery, the Black male was virtually emasculated with respect to domestic relations. He had to seek permission from the enslaver to court or marry an enslaved woman. Although historians do record that some enslavers did respect the sanctity of enslaved families and marital unions,[44] the Black father was often separated from his enslaved mate and their children. In general, Black men could not protect girlfriends, daughters, wives, or mothers from physical or sexual abuse without suffering physical punishment or being killed.

This is the context in which Barbara Omolade argues that "the historical oppression of black women and men should have created social equality between them, but even after the end of slavery when the white patriarch receded, maleness and femaleness continued to be defined by patriarchal structures, with black men declaring wardship over black women. In the black community, the norm of manhood was patriarchal power, while the norm of womanhood was submission to patriarchal power, though both men and women selected which aspects of these norms they would emphasize."[45]

Externally imposed gender role-socialization practices continue to distort Black male–female relationships. Various social theorists suggest that race, racism, and discrimination exacerbate tensions associated with the differential socialization of African American males and females.[46] Moreover, racism results in differences in White/Black gender role expectations that can also affect Black male/female conflict.

Sociologist Clyde W. Franklin, while not denying the reality of the socialization effects of racism on African American life and behavior, initially proposed that White racism is a conditional rather than a causal variable in producing and perpetuating Black male/female conflict. In his opinion, White racism alone was an inadequate and illogical explanation for the causes of Black male/female conflict.[47] However, in a subsequent essay, Franklin suggests those differential perceptions of masculinity and the "acting out" of masculine roles between Black and White males could be a causative factor contributing to Black male/female conflict. The socialization of Black males into "White" definitions of masculinity, including power, dominance, competitiveness, aggressiveness, non-emotionalism, and non-feelingness could have conflictive effects in Black male/female relationships.[48]

According to sociologist K. Sue Jewell, a major dimension of Black male/female conflict may be attributed to the "definitions" assigned to White and Black Americans through the media. Traditionally, positive definitions and images are assigned to White males and females and negative ones to Black males and females. White supremacy is the basis on which both positive and negative definitions were developed.[49] White males, for example, are disproportionately depicted as authoritative, competent, courageous, and fully in charge and protective of their families. Black men are usually portrayed as submissive, subservient, dependent, cowardly, or simple. White women are typically depicted in the media in roles in which they are subordinate to White males and fixated on housekeeping and childrearing. On the other hand, Black women are portrayed as dominant, physically large and threatening, and more competent and self-sufficient than the Black male. These stereotypical images caused many Black males and females to aspire to the White "idea" and to negate each other. Television programs such as *The Jeffersons, Good Times, What's Happening, Gimme a Break*, and, more recently, *Martin, My Wife and Kids*, and *The Bernie Mac Show* embody and reinforce such stereotypes.

Negative characterizations of Black males and females disseminated through media imagery perpetuate dysfunctional aspects of male and female relationships that developed during the slavery era and persisted into the post-bellum period. Different reactions to the negative effects of the imagery of the domineering Black woman and emasculated Black male were a source of friction between Black males and females during the Black Power movement of the 1960s. Black males viewed their protest and rebellious activities as a sign that manhood lost during slavery was finally being regained. Consequently, some expected Black women to assume subordinate roles that would simply be supportive of the males' struggle. Thus, many African Americans had internalized the stereotypical and negative role definitions leading to conflicts in Black male/female relationships during the Black Power movement.[50]

The media continues to be a socializing influence that perpetuates perceptions of White supremacy, racial stereotypes, and mythical sexual roles and imagery. Contemporary Hip-Hop culture has reintroduced the emphasis on misogyny and hypersexuality that complements externally imposed distortions of male/female relationships. This phenomenon has been described previously as the "pimp-whore" complex in Black male/female relationships.[51] David Pilgrim argues that the "Jezebel" has replaced the Mammy as the dominant image of Black women in American popular culture, and the Black woman as prostitute has become a staple in Hollywood movies. Moreover, he asserts that this pattern is complemented by "televised music videos, especially those by gangsta rap performers, [who] portray scantily clad, nubile Black women who thrust their hips to lyrics which often depict them as 'hos, skeezers, and bitches'..."[52] Jewell implies that conflict between the sexes and the races are inevitable if such negative definitions are internalized rather than rejected.[53]

Between 1993 and 1998, Blacks were victimized by intimate partners at significantly higher rates than persons of any other race. Black females experienced intimate partner violence at a rate 35 percent higher than that of White females, and about 22 times the rate of women of other races. Black males experienced intimate partner violence at a rate about 62 percent higher than that of White males, and about 22 times the rate of men of other races.[54] Black women are more likely than other groups to report their victimization to police.[55]

It is equally important to note, however, that lethal incidences of intimate partner violence among Blacks have declined more rapidly than among other groups. Since 1976, the number of Black females killed by intimates dropped 45 percent, and the number of Black males killed fell by 74 percent. In contrast, the decline for White males was 44 percent, but the number of White females killed actually increased. The disproportionate decline in lethal incidences of intimate partner violence among Blacks is largely due to the low marriage rate of Blacks, because most intimate partner killings involve married couples.[56]

There are significant class and structural issues that affect patterns of intimate partner violence. Women on welfare are more likely than others to experience domestic violence. For unmarried Black women, cuts in Aid to Families with Dependent Children (AFDC) levels increase the likelihood of experiencing violence.[57] The preceding overview suggests the need for several policy initiatives. There is a pressing

4

need to strengthen community efforts to develop "early warning" systems to detect persons at risk of experiencing domestic violence as well as community resolution mechanisms. Such mechanisms would not only serve to reduce violence but also to limit external interventions by police and other authorities that often lead to additional violence. Such internal support and resolution systems would also increase rates of reporting.

The imputation of matriarchy as a fundamental characteristic of the Black family and negative perceptions of matriarchy are two of the most divisive issues threatening the harmony of African American male and female relationships. Although Western societies have always regarded matriarchal societies as culturally inferior, from a global historical perspective this viewpoint is totally unjustified. The fact that matrilineal and patrilineal forms of family relationships were normal, accepted practices in African societies has been documented earlier in this chapter. The noted African scholar Cheikh Anta Diop insists that matriarchy "is not the distinctive trait of any particular people but has controlled at a given time the social organization of all the peoples of the earth."[58] Unfortunately, some African Americans have appended a negative connotation of female domination to the basic concept. Many African American men, sensitive to the historically emasculated role of Black males in slavery and during the oppressive Jim Crow era of the South, began to lean ideologically toward Eurocentric "paternalism," which is unrelated to African patriarchy. The Western and White American concept of patriarchy or paternalism translates as masculine imperialism and feminine passivity. African patrilineal and matrilineal family systems did not function to establish male or female superiority or inferiority but to comply with social laws governing ancestral inheritance and descent.

The matriarchy issue sparked interest in reexamining sexual roles in African American marital relationships. Differential historical and economic factors reduce the significance of comparing Black with White sexual roles and attitudes. Nevertheless, African Americans are inevitably influenced to some degree by White social paradigms. Therefore, attempts have been made to fit the analysis of Black marital sexual roles into the conventional sociological classifications of traditional, contemporary or modern, and egalitarian. The traditional arrangement differentiates marital

or mate responsibilities on a sexual basis. In a marriage, the husband has the primary responsibility for financially supporting the family, and the wife has the basic responsibility for maintaining the home and for child rearing. Contemporary or modern sex-role proponents reject the notion of ascribing any responsibilities or activities on a sexual basis. The egalitarian philosophy developed from the socioeconomic necessity of both husband and wife, or man and woman, having to work to support the home or household. Egalitarian relationships operate with the understanding that the professions or occupations of both partners are of equal importance, and the male and the female practice shared responsibility in the management and execution of home or household duties.

As illustrated by the data in the previous section, socioeconomic necessity has consistently generated higher rates of labor force participation for married Black women than their White counterparts. Therefore, it is not surprising that a study by the Institute for Urban Affairs and Research found that more than 80 percent of Blacks who were polled support the egalitarian division of family tasks. The study revealed that most African Americans believe that both spouses should be employed, but, in spite of dual employment, 85 percent agreed that motherhood is the most fulfilling experience a woman can have.[59]

Although egalitarianism has proven to be a functional adaptation in many African American marital and intimate relationships, there is an ongoing need to confront dysfunctional manifestations of hierarchy that hamper collective empowerment. One approach to addressing this issue has involved the exploration of the extent to which tenets associated with feminism can be adapted to address concerns specific to the circumstances facing Black women. It was evident from the beginning that the basis, grievances, and objectives of the Feminist Movement were not totally compatible with the plight of Black women. In the first place, the contemporary Feminist Movement was initially founded by White women and was based on their dissatisfaction with White male-dominated society. Secondly, the White Feminist Movement was primarily concerned with sexism, but Black women were faced with the social reality of being oppressed on the basis of both sex and race. In response to this reality, Black feminist organizations were soon organized to deal with unique problems and issues of Black women, which included sexism and racism. As observed by

Aaronette White, "the contemporary black feminist movement took most of its shape during the late 1960s and early 1970s" fueled, in part, by "dissatisfaction with the sexism of black civil rights organizations and the racism of white feminist organizations." [60]

Black Feminism's linkages to the Feminist Movement sparked suspicions among many in the traditional Civil Rights community because of perceptions that the struggle against racial subordination was being supplanted by an emphasis on combating sexism. Because both Black men and Black women are oppressed by White society on the basis of race, separate efforts to liberate either the Black man or woman were argued to be counterproductive to the crusade to free the entire Black family—men, women, and children. Some Black women questioned other Black women regarding the logic and feasibility of forming alliances with the White Feminists because many White women have historically oppressed Black women and men on the basis of skin color. Conversely, many Black men viewed both Black feminists and White feminists as a threat to their own liberation struggles, manhood, or masculinity. Particularly in the area of employment opportunity, Black feminists were accused of working unwittingly with White feminists against the interests of Black men. As an example, Hare writes that "almost to the exact extent that the white female has entered the labor force the black male has been pushed out of it, with obvious consequences for black sexual and family relationships... plus the white female's proximity and intimate relationship to the white male foreordained her privileged access to the necessarily limited new jobs."[61]

Although many Black women may not accept all of the tenets espoused by Black feminists, they still share many of the concerns of the Feminist Movement. Some of the common concerns usually expressed are sexual discrimination in employment, government and private support for day-care centers, improved health-care facilities for women, legal and inexpensive abortion, and violence in domestic relationships. African Americans generally support many of the objectives of Black feminists. In fact, there are concrete examples of how Black feminists have successfully organized coalitions that have enhanced the quality of life for both Back women and Black men. A large-scale anti-rape campaign organized in connection with the highly publicized rape trial of former heavyweight boxing champion Mike Tyson is one

example. Based on her study of this campaign, White concludes that the campaign demonstrates that "Black women as well as Black men are willing to participate in antirape collective action" and that a Black feminist framework can "transcend the master frames of the Black nationalist-civil rights and feminist social movements and serve as the nexus between the movements" [62] In another study, White found that men who subscribe to Black feminist ideals have developed distinctive parenting styles, using Black feminist principles as a guide, that emphasize nurturing and active engagement with children. She asserts that "African American feminist fathers seek radical solutions to fatherhood issues without excusing African American men from financial responsibility for their children or reinstating any patriarchal, heterosexist, or economic principles that feed the system."[63]

These examples demonstrate the potential for collective development when Black males and females organize with, rather than against, each other. Expanding the type of examples described previously could play an important role in resolving conflicts between African American males and females. Within African American Studies, a group of women has developed an alternative to Black feminist approaches that provides a means of addressing gender oppression concurrent with a united front against racist oppression. Africana womanist scholars, which include Delores Aldridge, Vivian Gordon, and Clenora Hudson-Weems, have all published important works outlining what can be described as an Africana women's studies paradigm. Although these scholars recognize the need to confront gender-based oppression, they focus on its intersection and overlap with racial oppression in diminishing the well-being of Africana women. Thus, Africana womanists work collectively both to address Africana women's issues, and in cooperation with Africana men and Africana Studies organizations, to combat racial oppression. Their approach to initiating change is obviously much more closely aligned with the original vision of African American Studies than that of Black feminists.[64]

Another avenue for examining Black male/female relationships is identifying the structural factors that condition these relationships. The sex ratio, the number of males per 100 females, is an extremely valuable analytical tool that allows the type of examination of long-term trends characteristic of African American Studies methodology. W. E. B. Du Bois was one of the first analysts to recognize the importance of the sex ratio in shaping male/female relationships and community well being. Studying Black migration patterns in the early twentieth century, he observed an excessive number of females to males in some cities. Du Bois argued that "present economic demand draws the [N]egro women to the city and keeps the men in the country, causing a dangerous disproportion of the sexes." He also expressed concern that low wages and a rising cost of living were forcing Black men and women to delay marriage "to an age dangerously late."[65] His recognition of the complex interaction among the sex ratio, economic opportunities, male/female interactions, and family formation is useful in examining the data presented below in Table 4.13, which shows the sex ratio of White and Black males per 100 females.

TABLE 4.13
SEX RATIOS FOR WHITES AND BLACKS
1860 – 2011

Year	White Sex Ratio	Black Sex Ratio
1860	105.3	99.6
1870	102.8	96.2
1880	104.0	97.8
1890	105.4	99.5
1900	104.9	98.6
1910	106.6	98.9
1920	104.4	99.2
1930	102.9	97.0
1940	101.2	95.0
1950	99.0	93.7
1960	97.4	93.3
1970	95.3	90.8
1980	94.8	89.6
1990	95.9	89.8
2000	96.4	90.5
2003	97.8	91.0
2005	98.1	91.2
2010	98.3	87.4
2011	98.6	87.7

Source: 1860-2005, U.S. Bureau of the Census.
http://www.infoplease.com/ipa/A0110384.html
2010 U.S. Census, http://www.census.gov/population/age/data/2010comp.html
2011 U.S. Census, http://www.census.gov/population/age/data/2011comp.html.

Demographers generally suggest that a relatively equal proportion of males and females is optimal for social stability. Over time, among Whites, there has been a large shift from a relative surplus of males to a slight underrepresentation of males, but the sex ratio is still reasonably close to parity. However, among African Americans, there has been a consistent excess of females to males. Note that the Black sex ratio fell to 95 in 1950 and has oscillated within the 90–91 range since 1970, an indicator of potential instability in social relationships.

The concept of *institutional decimation* was used earlier to characterize the social processes that contribute to a distorted sex ratio among Blacks by limiting the survivability of Black males. Consistent with this perspective, Steven Messner and Robert Sampson argue that declines in the sex ratio are associated with increased family instability and increased criminal violence, which, in turn, lead to more incarceration of males and a further worsening of the sex ratio.[66] Following the guidance of Du Bois, it is important to examine how these sex ratio shifts are affecting marriage formation patterns.

The percentage of Black men (age 15 and older) who have ever been married fell sharply from 64 percent in 1950 to 41 percent in 1998, whereas White men experienced a much smaller decline, from 70 percent to 60 percent. Conversely, during the same period, the percentage of never-married Black women doubled from 21 percent to 41 percent, reflecting, to some extent, the effects of decisions to delay marriage and childbirth to attend college and establish careers. By 2000, Black men at all ages were more likely to be married than Black women. The median age at marriage for Black men decreased between 1990 and 2000, and is now lower than the median age at marriage for Black women, a highly unusual phenomenon. Even more startling is that the increases in marriage for Black men did not occur among employed Black males but was confined to those who were not employed! Marriage rates continued to decline between 1990 and 2000 for young Black men who worked. In fact, in 2000, the percentage of ever-married men in institutions increased dramatically, and the percentage of ever-married men among the noninstitutional population was virtually unchanged. Thus, a significant proportion of the formation of family involving Black males at the end of the decade involved incarcerated Black males. This phenomenon poses serious challenges for the socialization of off-spring and for overall community stability.

Specific studies examining marital factors affecting conflict within the Black family are relatively few and the findings are speculative and inconclusive. A common fault of most literature on the subject is that Black family life is usually compared with the normative cultural values and behaviors of Whites, which is based on Eurocentric ideals. However, family conflict and derivative emotional responses develop out of culturally specific behavioral patterns. White or European social theorists do not apply a Black or Afrocentric frame of reference to interpret, analyze, or understand internal conflict within White families. Although many social and behavioral experiences are shared between Black and White Americans, the effects of racism, discrimination, and political and economic dominance are not felt or reacted to similarly. Undeniably, racism and oppression have affected, and continue to affect, the quality of Black family life. Therefore, more race specific studies relative to African American intra-family relations or conflict should precede comparative and cross-cultural investigations. White and non-White "objective" differentiations may obscure, rather than clarify, factors contributing to Black family conflict.

Separations or divorces are the results of failed marital relationships and, to an extent, reflect deficiencies in the values and moral codes of the society. Over time, increasing fidelity to Eurocentric and capitalistic philosophies of individual rights and moral freedom, as opposed to collective welfare and responsibility, has caused many African Americans to abandon traditional African-oriented family values. Some White social theorists devote an inordinate amount of effort to studying and reporting Black family "deviance" and dysfunction, while ignoring the moral decline, racism, legitimized aberrant family structures, liberal divorce laws, sexual crimes and pathologies, and drug and alcohol abuse characteristic of an increasing number of White families. Social problems and dysfunctions in the Black family are presented as if they are characteristic of Black culture and not influenced in part by White cultural dominance, racism, and economic disparity.

African American family conflicts or marital dissolutions, like those in any other human unions, can occur for intimate and personal reasons devoid of any external factor or stimulus. However, external socioeconomic forces do intervene and affect relationships between marital partners. The social effects of racism and of economic discrimination are among the direct and indirect causes of an infinite number of Black family conflicts that often culminate in separation and divorce. It is important to note, however, that between 1950 and 1998, trends in divorce were similar between Blacks and Whites, increasing from 3 percent to 12 percent among Blacks and from 2 percent to 11 percent among Whites.

Unfortunately, it is difficult to determine quantitatively the extent to which racism and economic discrimination, per se, affect the marital stability of Black families. Nevertheless, White sociologist Reynolds Farley found that Black men and women of higher socioeconomic status (SES) are more likely to maintain their marriages than lower SES Blacks. The study uncovered minor differences in the prevalence of divorce, and socioeconomic factors were strongly associated with widowhood and desertion. Widowhood and desertion were both inversely related to socioeconomic status. African Americans with low status jobs were more likely to be widowers than men with prestigious occupations. The socioeconomic variables considered were education, occupation, and income; and income was the most strongly linked to marital stability. Lower incomes were associated with a greater likelihood of marital separation.[67]

Robert B. Hill contends, in a more recent work, that institutionalized racism and structural discrimination significantly affect the functioning of both low-income and middle-income Black families. Hill further asserts that discriminatory socioeconomic policies, whether intended or unintended, have in effect undermined Black family stability. He contends "that institutional racism has contributed significantly to the erosion of the social and economic well-being of black families ..." and "... that the sharp increases in unemployment, poverty and one-parent families among blacks were due, in large part, to the structurally discriminatory effects of major economic forces and policies."[68]

Various studies demonstrate that there is a relationship between spousal abuse and income level among Blacks. In effect, the higher the level of family income, the lower the level of abuse reported. Black families encounter institutional economic racism and discrimination in the form of unemployment,

4

underemployment, and underpayment in the labor force. The social trauma and stigma of being unemployed can cause mental health problems. It has been observed that increased mental hospital admissions and higher suicide rates have coincided with increased and extended periods of state or national unemployment. The persistent disproportionate unemployment experienced by members of African American families, documented previously, along with underemployment and inadequate income, unquestionably contribute to psychological and interpersonal stress and distort the emotional climate of Black families.[69]

This discussion has attempted to cast the African American family in an Afrocentric analysis and ideology mold. In contrast with the views of Daniel P. Moynihan and others of his persuasion who attribute the social ills and instabilities of the Black family to factors internal to Black households and communities, African American Studies analysts focus on the external forces of social, political and economic racism and oppression. It would be intellectually naive to deny that dysfunctions and inadequacies do not exist in Black family life. Still, it is even more illogical that the Black family should assume total responsibility for its debilitated condition (blame the victim) and, thereby, absolve White America of four hundred years of subjugation and oppression of African Americans.

There is no need to debate the validity of the Weak-Family theory or the Strong-Family theory. What is needed is a reconciliation and synthesis of both schools of thought. The African American family is both weak and strong. It is weak because Black people as a whole lack sufficient political and economic power to confront effectively the ill-intentions of powerful segments of White society. The strength of the Black family is evident in its survival after centuries of slavery. Significant proportions of each generation of African American families are stronger, attain more success, and are more able to influence social dynamics than the preceding ones. There is also evidence of the resurgence of the extended family tradition among Blacks. Black family reunions have become increasingly popular, particularly after the release of Alex Haley's book *Roots*, and its movie in the mid-1970s, led to a burgeoning interest in family genealogy. What started as small extended-family gatherings have now expanded into regional and even national affairs, some even sponsored by major corporations and foundations.

The data in the table document that the ratio of Black males to Black females is almost at an all-time low, while it has been relatively stable in recent decades for Whites. This divergent pattern places significant negative pressure on traditional processes of family formation and maintenance. Traditional family formation involving Black males has also been altered by increases in interracial marriages.

Young Black men are out-marrying at very high rates (much higher than among women), although the overwhelming majority of U.S. marriages remain racially endogamous, i.e. they consist of two persons belonging to the same racial group. About 97 percent of marriages involving Blacks and Whites involve partners of the same race (2007 data). At the same time, the incidence of interracial marriage between Blacks and Whites has been growing substantially in recent years. Nevertheless, the general patterns can be observed below in Table 4.14.

TABLE 4.14
MARRIED COUPLES OF SAME OR MIXED RACES
Selected Years, 1960–2010 (000s)

Year	Total Married Couples	Total Black/White Interracial Couples	Black Husband, White Wife	White Husband, Black Wife	White/ Other Race*	Black/ Other Race*
1960	40,491	51	25	26	90	7
1970	44,598	65	41	24	233	12
1980	49,714	167	122	45	450	34
1985	51,114	164	117	47	599	29
1990	53,256	211	150	61	720	33
1995	54,937	328	206	122	988	76
2000	56,497	363	268	95	1,051	50
2002	57,919	395	279	116	1,222	57
2007	60,676	464	338	126	1,688	129
2010	60,384	558	390	168	1,723	132

Source: U. S. Census Bureau, Current Population Reports, Series, "Household and Family Characteristics: March 2003," and earlier reports. Data for 2007 extracted from Infoplease http://www.infoplease.com/ipa/A0884200.html. Data for 2010 comes from U.S. Census Bureau, Statistical Abstract of the United States: 2012, Table. 60, Interracial Married Couple by Race and Hispanic Origin of Spouses: 1980 to 2010. http://www.census.gov/compendia/statab/2012/tables/12s0060.pdf

As the data indicate, there is a large gap between the numbers of interracial marriages involving Black men and White women compared with those involving White men and Black women. The gap increased significantly beginning in the 1970s and expanded again during 1995–2000. Overall, the instability in the pattern of interracial marriages involving Blacks, compared with the steady increase in the number of interracial marriages involving other groups, suggests that the legacy of institutional racism is alive and well as it relates to contemporary trends in mate choices.

Interracial dating and marriages are sources of social and emotional controversy between African American males and females. Few recent studies relate the sociopolitical, psychological, and economic factors that give rise to Black/White interracial relationships. Delores Aldridge's essay "Interracial Marriages: Empirical and Theoretical Considerations" is an exception and provides an impressive review of literature on the subject.[70]

Traditionally, Black/White interracial marriages involved middle and upper-income Black males marrying lower-class White women and, conversely, high-income Black females were choosing lower status White men. In other words, higher status Blacks tend to marry Whites who are down the social and income ladder, whereas Whites marry Blacks who are their social and income superiors. However, in recent years, such unions are becoming more socioeconomically equal.[71] At the same time, tensions surrounding interracial marriages tend to focus on discussions about the status of middle-class African Americans. However, the marriage sex-ratio imbalance among middle-class African Americans reflects not only numerical imbalances in specific age cohorts but also a lack of mutual or reciprocal acceptability between Black males and females based on educational and occupational statuses. The rate of Black females completing four or more years of college significantly exceeds that of Black males. Thus, the shortage is reflected structurally when Black women may not choose to marry men who have less education or occupational status.[72]

One can logically assume that both unity and conflict patterns exist universally between men and women. The nature of the issues and social circumstances binding or dividing males and females within and across groups are determined by societal codes that are either egalitarian or inequitable in regards to sex, race, and culture. Maulana Karenga asserts that Black male/female relationships are affected more by societal rather than personal factors. Karenga posits that the causative factors are inherent in the three major American value systems: capitalism, racism, and sexism.[73]

Since the 1960s, scholars and politicians have developed a monadic or gender specific approach to studying or analyzing the African American community. This approach has led to the separate categorization of socioeconomic problems affecting Black males and females. Consequently, there is an abundance of literature publicizing the distinct and sometimes competing socioeconomic conditions of the Black male and female. This practice alone has promoted a kind of intra-community political division between Black men and women. Moreover, it has aided those interests that benefit by dividing and controlling specific groups. Criticism of this approach is not to deny that racism and its attendant properties have often differentially affected the Black male and female. It must, however, be emphasized that many of the negative statistical analyses and implications can be, and have been, manipulated and distorted by some politicians and the media to the detriment of all African Americans.

The proliferation of news and/or information focusing on the Black male's proclivity toward crime and juvenile delinquency; homicidal or "fratricidal" rate; unemployment; school drop-out rate or ineducability; drug proneness; violence; family irresponsibility; and a host of other social dysfunctions is a paradigmatic example. These social problems of Black males do exist, but they apply to much less than one-half of the total African American male population in the United States. Sociologist Jewelle Taylor Gibbs states one case in point in exploding the Black male drug myth:

> This stereotype grossly misrepresents the actual incidence of drug use by black youth, and it illustrates the hypocrisy of a society that views substance abuse by blacks and whites differently. Film and television generally depict the drug problem as having a black face, but according to figures from the National Institute of Drug Abuse, whites account for 80 percent and blacks for 20 percent of overall illicit drug use. While "crack" has been widely publicized as an inner-city problem, cocaine was popularized in the 1970s as a white middle-class recreational drug, glamorized by Hollywood celebrities and purchased by Wall Street stockbrokers and suburban yuppies.[74]

The negative statistical profile and conditions of the African American male gained such enormous attention that in 1991 a group of Black and White political leaders and scholars joined to establish the 21st Century Commission on African American Males, for the purpose of assisting Congress in developing a national policy for addressing the crisis facing Black men. Clearly, this was a noble undertaking by well-intentioned leaders. However, it is illogical to assume that the social dysfunctions and plight of the Black male occur within a vacuum without also adversely affecting Black females and children. Concentrating on and imputing the problem only to the Black male tends to veil the inequitable and subordinate status of all Black Americans.

In contrast to approaches that foreground conflicts between Black males and females, African American Studies specialists are interested in promoting strategies that ensure the wholesome development of children in all types of households. There is increased interest in parallel parenting and co-parenting initiatives as strategies to reduce the extent to which conflict between parents adversely affects children's well-being. Legally, parallel parenting is a form of custody and guardianship order in which such authority transfers from parent to parent, as the children are exchanged. This type of arrangement is often necessary when two estranged parents cannot co-parent successfully. In this type of arrangement, the two parents communicate as infrequently as possible and each handles issues as they arise during the time that they have custody of the child.[75] African American Studies advocates are more interested in promoting healthy co-parenting relationships. Co-parenting comprises all the activities related to communicating, negotiating and making decisions regarding children between both parents when they are estranged. The website WeParent.com is one of the most useful resources to facilitate successful co-parenting. The website declares that WeParent is "on a mission to support and facilitate a co-parenting 'revolution' among African American parents" who are willing "to face the challenges of co-parenting in order to enjoy the fulfillment of raising healthy, whole children."[76]

African American Religion and the Black Church

Religion of some nature, form, or practice is virtually a universal phenomenon. However, the definition of the term religion is less generic because it is culturally determined, and, like numerous terms or words of European origin, religion loses some of its conventional meaning in translation from a Eurocentric to an African or Afrocentric frame of reference. This becomes apparent when one studies John S. Mbiti's *African Religions and Philosophy*. For Africans, the whole of existence is a religious phenomenon, and all natural organic and inorganic creations have religious meanings. Religion is manifest in the material and the spiritual, in song and music, and libation and festivity. The spiritual conception of God is instinctive.[77] African Americans are reputed to be immensely religious because of their African culture and background.

E. Franklin Frazier rejected the notion that Black Americans have retained their African religion and religious practices and contended that the African religious traditions were destroyed with slavery and oppression in America. He asserted that the enslaved Africans and subsequent freedmen became totally influenced by the White Christian religion.[78] However, the majority of historians and religious scholars do not endorse Frazier's theory or assumptions. Contemporary scholars, especially Black theologians, concede that there were some discontinuities because of slavery and the influence of White Christian practices but insist that the continuities far outweigh the elements of African religious culture that were lost.

Few, if any, Africans were converted to Christianity before their arrival in the New World. Enslavement prevented open worship of divinities, speaking indigenous languages, or practicing traditional rituals, except clandestinely. Many enslaved Africans brought to the Americas from the West Coast of Africa were Muslims. Enslaved Africans were either persuaded or forced to accept Christianity. Through Christianity, Africans were counseled to be passive, obedient, and patient and were told that their reward for succeeding in demonstrating these virtues would be eternal life or Heaven. Religion, as imposed by Europeans and Americans, was intended not so much to save the "heathen" but more to instill docility in the minds of the enslaved Africans and thereby discourage rebellion. The purpose for which Christianity may have been intended was only partially effective because Africans could never reconcile the religious teachings of love, compassion, and righteousness with their plight of suffering and oppression.

Therefore, African American religion was born out of the contradictions of slavery, and it developed as a spiritual means to protest racism and to achieve independence from White authority. An account of the origin and development of Black separate or

130

independent religion and church has been given in the preceding chapter on African American history. A summary will suffice here for the purposes of reflection and continuity. As discussed previously in Chapter 3, in many White churches, Blacks in the North initially worshiped on a segregated basis.

The first recorded movement by Blacks to form their own independent church began in 1787, when Richard Allen, Absalom Jones, and other Black worshippers walked out of St. George's Methodist Church in Philadelphia when they were ordered from their knees to move to the balcony. This incident eventually led to the founding of the African Methodist Episcopal Church (AME), one of the major Black religious denominations existing today. The establishment of the AME Church was followed by the organization of the African Methodist Episcopal Zion Church denomination in 1796, and several independent Black Baptist churches were founded in major northern cities after 1809. About the same time, quasi-free Blacks had begun to organize separate churches in the South. These Black churches or groups were subjected to strict surveillance by the slavemasters for obvious reasons.

African American religion and churches were founded on the principles of protest and liberation. Early Black ministers were at the forefront of abolitionist movements and contributed to the oratorical denouncement of slavery. Black ministers and church leaders conceived and led the major slave revolts. Gabriel Prosser, who planned the Virginia uprising of 1800, was a devout Methodist, and Denmark Vesey, author of the most elaborate slave revolt in South Carolina in 1822, was also a Methodist leader. Nat Turner, a Baptist minister from Virginia, organized the largest slave revolt in American history. It is also important to note, as documented by Richard Turner, that Islamic beliefs played a significant role in inspiring resistance to the institution of slavery.[79] Thus, the tradition of Black ministers and religious leaders functioning as activists in liberation struggles in the United States began in the seventeenth century and continues into the twenty-first century.

Many of the prominent leaders of the Civil Rights Movement of the 1960s were ministers, including Martin Luther King Jr., Malcolm X, and Jesse Jackson. These, and other ministers, were supported by thousands of their church members and followers. Black religious denominations will hardly deny that they are not only religious but also political and economic institutions serving the interests of African Americans. Black religion has adapted to conform to the needs of its constituents. The most pressing needs of African Americans are freedom, equality of opportunity, and social justice.

The early Black churches were involved in a variety of activities that created social capital. Many operated Sunday schools and/or day schools. Curry insists some church buildings "were deliberately constructed so as to include facilities for a school."[80] Some Black churches raised and contributed funds to purchase enslaved Blacks and thereby enabled less constrained family formation and maintenance.[81]

The crusade against slavery, in fact, provided a focal point for many of the non-ritualistic activities of the early Black Church Movement. Gayraud Wilmore maintains that in the 1830s the Black Church provided the ideological and organizational foundations for subsequent antislavery initiatives. He suggests that the spirit of uplift and self-reliance cultivated in the independent churches originally infused the Convention Movement and that, in a sense, the Civil Rights Movement was the secular adjunct of the Black Church. He argues further that the growing radicalization of abolitionism in the 1840s and 1850s cannot be separated from the influence of Black religion.[82]

With the end of the Civil War, however, the Black Church faced the major challenge of uniting the institutional church developed by free Blacks with the "invisible church" that had served enslaved Blacks. This challenge precipitated both the formation of state conventions and national bodies, associated with some denominations, and a split between "progressive" and "conservative" church leaders. In the context of our discussion, the disagreement can be interpreted as differences in views about whether church-based social capital creation activities should be reoriented in the wake of the end of the era of enslavement. Nelsen and Nelsen suggest:

> The progressives ... realized that religion without education could not successfully uplift the race. The conservatives viewed the new group as a threat to the church, for they continued to believe that the individual existed for the glory of the church rather than the church for the benefit of the individual.[83]

Adherents to the conservative ideology were ill-equipped to meet the new challenges that arose in

4

urban areas associated with the Great Migration. The Pentecostal churches emerged, in part, as "deliberate, conscious, organized efforts of migrants to create a more satisfying mode of existing by refurbishing rural religious behavior to an urban environment."[84] The "storefront," which served as the place of worship for many churches in the early years, served as a stabilizing force within the chaotic milieu of residential and commercial succession in which Blacks were displacing previous migrants to the urban core.

The rapid urbanization of Blacks also prompted a renewed interest in Islam as a means to social emancipation. Noble Timothy Drew Ali founded the Moorish Science Temple Movement in New Jersey in 1913. The Great Depression of the 1930s would provide the seedbed for the emergence of the movement that later came to be known as the Nation of Islam in the ghettos of Detroit, under the leadership of Wallace Fard Muhammad.[85]

The terms *Black religion* and *Black Church* imply more than race/color differentiation from White religion and church. The authentic Black Church has traditionally been significantly different from White religion in role, objectives, form and manner of worship, and in practice. Although the Black churches that seceded from the White Methodist and Baptist denominations borrowed much of the evangelical and ecclesiastical practices from White churches, African Americans soon developed their own styles and orders of service.[86] Theologians Gayraud S. Wilmore and James H. Cone refer to the term *Black Church* as that institution or group of Christian denominations owned and operated, at least at the local level, by people of African descent. Wilmore and Cone offer another definition of the Black Church that is more or less ideological in nature. It relates to the "cultural and attitudinal factors and values descriptive of those who claim membership in such a church."[87]

In any event, Black or African American religion and church are more than a fusion of European and African religious cultures and values. The explicit political orientation and objectives of many Black churches make them different from White religious institutions. But, beyond their historical political tradition, the authentic Black Church differs from the conventional White church in emotional expression, devotional activity, and in musical or choral style and performance. Contemporarily, as during slavery, the more removed from White institutional influence, the more distinctive are African American religious

and church characteristics. The musical and worship styles of Black Americans are closely linked to African ritualistic and festive traditions.[88] Fused with Christian practices of European origin, a distinctive style of Black religious service emerged. However, some scholars suggest that enslaved preachers first established the contemporary style of African American ministers. Ethnomusicologist Portia K. Maultsby characterizes the dramatic and intense style of early Black preachers as

1. the use of vocal inflections, which produced a type of musical tone or chant, and facilitated the dramatic and climatic style of preaching;
2. the use of repetition for highlighting phrases of text;
3. the use of rhythmic devices for stress and pacing; and
4. the use of call-responses structures to stimulate "spontaneous" congregational responses.[89]

Based on current research, authentic sound recordings, and live performances, Maultsby relates Black spirituals and the modern free-style collective musical and individual lyrical improvisations of African American gospel music to West African influences.[90]

New interpretations of the Black religious tradition were inspired by the struggles of the Civil Rights, Black Power, and Black Studies Movements of the late 1960s. The concept of a *Black Theology* was forged by a group of "radical" Black clergy who met to formulate a statement supporting the use of, and ideology reflected by, the term *Black Power*. The impetus for this meeting was the rejection of the Black Power ideology by moderate Black leaders associated with the National Committee of Negro Churchmen (NCNC), later changed to the National Conference of Black Christians (NCBC). The meeting produced a statement entitled, "'Black Power': Statement by National Committee of Negro Churchmen," published in the *New York Times* on July 31, 1966. Prominent signatories to the document included the Revs. Benjamin Payton, Gayraud Wilmore, and Nathan Wright.

The ideological and institutional basis of Black Theology "was to build an alternative to the liberal and neo-orthodox theologies of the American religious establishment."[91] Thus as James H. Cone states, "Black preachers and civil rights activists of the 1960s initiated the development of a black theology that rejected racism and affirmed the black struggle for liberation as consistent with the gospel of Jesus."[92]

Black Theology was created as a distinct religious movement, essentially, for the purpose of relating to the oppressed masses of Blacks and for comforting them in their struggles against racism and discrimination. Excerpts from a statement by the National Committee of Black Churchmen, issued June 13, 1969, reads: "Black theology is a theology of liberation... It is the affirmation of black humanity that emancipates black people from white racism, thus providing authentic freedom for both white and black people."[93] Although Black Theology is not enthusiastically endorsed by some Black liberals and integrationists, it is a movement and a respected approach to racial and ethnic theology that is consistent with the ideology and mission of African American Studies.

In a similar vein, during the 1970s, a group of African American women theologians initiated a systematic challenge to the traditional sexism in Black churches. Leading figures in this effort included Jacquelyn Grant, Katie Cannon, and Delores Williams. The backbone and majority membership of the Black Church has always been women, but their roles have always been heavily circumscribed. This is especially true *vis à vis* the role of minister and higher leadership positions within the various denominations. Jacquelyn Grant declared in 1979, "[I]f the liberation of women is not proclaimed, the church's proclamation cannot be about divine liberation. If the church does not share in the liberation struggle of Black women, its liberation struggle is not authentic."[94] The sentiments expressed by Grant have been refined and systematized into what is described as "Womanist theology." Like its Black Theology counterpart, however, its impact on the practices of Black churches has been limited, although the ordination of women ministers and church leaders has expanded significantly in some denominations.[95]

The most comprehensive documentation of the role of Black women as principal agents has been undertaken by Bettye Collier Thomas.[96] Collier-Thomas successfully demonstrates how "black women have woven their faith into their daily experiences" as well as their "centrality to the development of African American religion, politics, and public culture."[97] This positioning has been accomplished through the creation of "an organizational network that has been indispensable to the fight against racism, sexism, and poverty.[98]

The Black community's tenuous relationship with Black Theology was highlighted in March 2008, when then Presidential candidate Barack Obama publicly severed his ties with his long-time minister, Jeremiah Wright of the Trinity United Church of Christ in Chicago. Wright had made several comments that infuriated some potential voters, such as asserting that the September 11, 2001 attacks were an outcome of U.S. actions abroad. In the wake of the controversy, Wright was removed from Obama's African American Religious Leadership Committee.[99] In addition, Obama found it necessary to repudiate his past affiliation with Wright in a statement entitled, "On My Faith and My Church." In the statement, Obama noted that Wright preached the social gospel and that the church membership practices social justice through various ministries including housing the homeless and supporting HIV/AIDS victims.[100] Many African Americans felt that Wright had been badly treated by Obama, but few proponents of Black Theology, and/or social capital, rallied to his defense, leaving widespread misconceptions about this religious tradition.

Concepts and ideologies may change, but the basic structures of social institutions often remain intact. The purposes and functions of the Black Church have been virtually unchanged since the Revolutionary War and on into the twenty-first century. Historically, it has been an institution that has provided mental and emotional escape from oppression for African Americans. The Black Church's social, cultural, and political functions have been summarized, but more needs to be stated relative to its economic contributions toward the betterment of the Black community.

Since the Reconstruction era, many African American religious denominations and churches have organized mutual aid or insurance societies to cope with the crises of sickness, death, and burial of its members. In large urban areas, beginning mostly with the Great Migration of the early twentieth century, Black religious organizations and denominational units have established childcare centers, low-income housing, credit unions, and various other socioeconomic auxiliaries. The Church's founding of several Black educational institutions was mentioned in the previous chapter.

Either independently, or in association with White religious denominations, private enterprise, or the federal government, African American churches have engaged in numerous economic development projects in the Black community. With the strength and

4

support of the Black Church, national organizations for the improvement of the economic condition of Blacks were founded during the 1960s and 1970s. Notably, the Rev. Martin Luther King, Jr. initiated Operation Breadbasket in Atlanta as a selective buying organization aimed at getting Blacks hired by White businesses. Rev. Jesse Jackson is recognized for having started People United to Save Humanity (PUSH). The PUSH organization negotiated multimillion dollar contracts for construction and/or employment of Blacks with major corporations. Opportunities Industrialization Centers (OIC) was founded by Rev. Leon Sullivan, of Zion Baptist Church of Philadelphia, to train young unemployed Blacks for jobs that were advertised in the daily newspapers. All of these organizations were developed with the backing of African American churches. Black Church members were often called on to support picketing or boycotting initiatives designed to pressure discriminatory firms and businesses to employ Blacks.[101]

African American religious denominations and churches are the sustaining force of Black communities throughout the United States. The foresightedness of the early Black Church in establishing schools and colleges has provided for the education and training of thousands of Black teachers, doctors, lawyers, scientists, engineers, and other professionals. Collectively, African American religious denominations and churches are probably the wealthiest of all Black-owned social institutions, even if one only considers their massive holdings in real estate. The Black minister has been compared with the traditional African tribal chief or clan leader. W. E. B. Du Bois wrote in his classic work, *The Souls of Black Folk*, "The Negro Church of to-day is the social centre of Negro life in the United States, and the most characteristic expression of African character."[102]

Today, there are eight major historically Black Christian denominations: African Methodist Episcopal; African Methodist Episcopal Zion; Christian Methodist Episcopal; Church of God in Christ; National Baptist Convention of America; National Baptist Convention, USA; National Missionary Baptist Convention; and the Progressive National Baptist Convention. These eight major Black denominations alone encompass some 65,000 churches and about 20 million members. In addition, there are many independent or quasi-independent Black churches or church networks.[103]

C. Eric Lincoln and Larry Mamiya report, in *The Black Church in the African American Experience*, that almost three-quarters of Black churches surveyed were engaged in community outreach programs that include day care, job search, substance abuse prevention, and food and clothing distribution. At the time of their study in the late 1980s, few churches received government funding to support these social service initiatives, and most clergy expressed concerns about receiving government money. Only about 8 percent of churches surveyed received any federal government funds.[104] However, at the dawn of the twenty-first century, George W. Bush's "Faith-Based Initiatives" program changed the landscape and prompted a major drive among many Black churches to seek federal funds to support outreach efforts. Although legitimate arguments can be advanced in support of such efforts, this initiative blurs the traditional distinction between church and state. It complicates social capital creation by introducing competition between churches and traditional social service institutions rather than fostering greater cooperation and complementarity.

The Bush administration's motives for supporting Black Church outreach initiatives, as suggested in the previous chapter, go well beyond any concerns about improving conditions in Black communities. Rather, there is a political objective to reduce the influence of traditional civil rights organizations by wooing Black preachers into the Republican camp. These Republican ministers, in turn, are expected to convince a significant portion of their congregations to follow their pastors' lead. The Bush initiative has been facilitated by the decline in denominationalism, along with the rise of Black megachurches and the growing prominence of a "prosperity gospel" that places greater emphasis on material well-being in lieu of the traditional concern with Black spirituality and redemptive salvation.[105]

There is already an observable shift in the political activities of Black ministers. In fact, the question has been raised whether the rise of mega-churches is consistent with the civil rights and social agendas needed to serve the contemporary interests of the large number of economically disadvantaged African Americans. Although the Black Church has been increasingly visible in elections, it has not used its influence to affect public policy on critical issues. A 2002 survey found that most clergy had worked in voter registration drives during the last decade and/or provided transportation to the polls for voters. However, fewer than 25 percent said they were involved in issues, such as, civil rights, affirmative action and welfare reform, and most had no direct involvement with public policy issues other than public education.[106] Viewed from this perspective, the sudden interest in political issues demonstrated by some Black ministers during the 2004 presidential election is curious, especially since they remained silent on the issues indicated above, but, instead, mobilized their congregations to oppose gay rights and abortion rights.

It is also important to recognize that the nature of Islamic social capital creation in Black communities has changed. During the 1960s and 1970s, the Nation of Islam, under the leadership of Elijah Muhammad, dominated Islamic life among African Americans. However, a split within the Nation led to the establishment of an orthodox Islamic movement, in 1978, led by Wallace Dean Muhammad, which left Louis Farrakhan as leader of Elijah Muhammad's movement. Many of the African American mosques unassociated with the Nation of Islam have become major contributors to social capital creation in inner city communities by openly opposing drug dealing and promoting socially conservative attitudes toward dress, family life, sexual conduct, and religious worship. Between one and two million African Americans now claim Islam as their religion.[107]

The growing interest in African-based religions is especially significant. African-based religious movements began to appear in the United States during the 1950s, as a result of migration from Africa and the Caribbean, and African Americans soon became converts. The religions in question include Haitian Voodoo, Santeria, Lucumi, and the traditional African religions of Akan and Orisa/Ifa.[108] The Oyotunji African Village in Sheldon, South Carolina, is one of the most institutionalized expressions of the resurgence of interest in traditional African spirituality and lifestyles. This self-sufficient village was founded in 1970 by Oserjeman Adefunmmi I and, at its apex, included approximately two hundred residents. The growing interest in modern Africa-based religions led to the founding of the National African Religion Congress, in 1999, to ensure the survival of African-based religions and the certification of priests and priestesses worldwide.[109] The accessibility of written materials describing traditional African religions has improved significantly in recent years, as exemplified by Maulana Karenga's translations of ancient Egyptian and Yoruba spiritual texts.[110]

Social capital creation in Black communities remains integrally connected with religious worship and religious institutions. One of the challenges facing African American Studies is to engage leaders, representing various religious traditions in order to identify ways of strengthening social capital creation efforts further, while simultaneously maintaining an appropriate balance between the spiritual and the secular dimensions of African American culture.

African Americans and Educational Institutions

Elementary and Secondary Education

Formal and informal educational institutions transmit the culture, values, and standard of living of a society. As noted previously, Du Bois conceptualized education as a critical means for strengthening community ties and for standardizing intergenerational transmission of values, beliefs, and commitments. The era of slavery denied African Americans the opportunity to develop and implement self-determined educational goals, policies, and practices. Although there was a brief wave of optimism during the Reconstruction period, when significant efforts were undertaken to provide education to freedmen, these efforts were largely abandoned by 1870. In the wake of this policy shift, southern states moved rapidly to lay the foundations for a system of educational apartheid. Their efforts were strengthened by the U.S. Supreme Court's 1883 invalidation of the Civil Rights Act of 1875 and codified as official government policy in the *Plessy v. Ferguson* (separate but equal) decision of 1896. The *Plessy v. Ferguson* decision was broadly interpreted to include all public facilities and institutions, including schools.

Many of the racial problems, tensions, and even racial violence that have characterized American society might have been averted if educational facilities and institutions for Blacks and Whites had, indeed, been made equal. Instead, disparities in the quality of public schools and facilities between Blacks and Whites increased markedly. If courageous cohorts of Black teachers and administrators had not dedicated their lives to provide the best possible education to students under severe externally-imposed constraints, the only possible outcome would have been generations of educationally ill-prepared and academically handicapped African Americans. However, within the abyss of racism and social separation that prevailed, a significant sociopsychological benefit did accrue to Black children under the system. Under separation, the school was truly an institution located in the African American community, operated by Black professional educator role models,

4

and under the influence of other Black cultural and social institutions.

The segregated Black school, although comparatively inadequate and unequal, was a product of the African American community, and it responded to the needs of the community as much as the racist society would allow. In many instances, the segregated school provided a nurturing environment in which students could develop a positive self-concept and a strong collective cultural ethos could be fostered. There are various historical case studies, such as Vanessa Siddle Walker's important study of the Caswell Country Training School during the 1940s and 1950s, which highlights the agency of Black parents, teachers, and principals in maintaining an exemplary Black school despite poor funding from the local and state governments.[111] Walker's work suggests that even when Black schools have been underfunded, strong Black leadership may help provide Black students with a better education than integrated schools.

Du Bois had, in fact, authored a defense of segregated schools in 1935, predicting that desegregation would lead to a decline in the number of Black teachers, a problematic learning environment for students, and limited instruction focusing on the history and culture of people of African descent. He argued that dedicated and competent Black teachers were better suited to understand and teach Black children than racist White teachers in integrated schools. Adequately funded and equipped, Black schools were a more pressing and immediate necessity for Blacks than Black children studying with White children.[112]

These concerns provide a useful frame of reference for assessing the outcomes of the decision by the U.S. Supreme Court in 1954 in *Brown v. Topeka Board of Education*, which reversed the fifty-eight-year-old *Plessy* decision. The Court essentially concluded "that in the field of public education the doctrine of separate but equal has no place. Separate educational facilities are inherently unequal." The ruling meant that segregation in all state schools was unconstitutional. The Court further decreed that desegregation was to proceed with "all deliberate speed." Subsequently, school authorities were ordered to submit plans for desegregation, and the federal courts would decide if the plans were in compliance with the decision of 1954.

Although the 1954 school desegregation decision ostensibly offered a potential antidote to the previous oppressive external imposition of unequal educational opportunities, the policy shift raised many complex legal and political questions and was resisted vigorously and

violently in the South. The original decision was supplemented in 1955 by a second case, known informally as *Brown II*. In *Brown II*, the Court set forth guidelines that placed the primary responsibility for setting the pace of desegregation on local school officials. Although federal district courts were to continue their jurisdiction and oversight of school desegregation cases, they could allow school districts to proceed carefully and gradually to complete school desegregation. The use of the language "with all deliberate speed" in the 1955 implementation order was a compromise designed to maintain unanimity among the justices. In addition, the Court decided that it would not treat desegregation cases as class actions and offer class-wide relief. This meant that only the named plaintiffs were entitled to a remedy and that each individual school district would have to be sued separately. The Court left many crucial questions unresolved and allowed lower courts to muddle through these issues until 1968. Even after the Court clarified several points in the *Green v. New Kent County School Board* case in 1968, the issues were framed almost entirely in terms of what forms of remedy were available to the courts. The Court did not approach desegregation implementation in terms of the rights of Black school children. Thus, the 1955 order set in motion a confusing and inconsistent pattern of enforcement that persists to this day.[113]

Pertinent questions raised by the decision, some of which are still unanswered, include: Is desegregation the same as integration? What are the different legal implications of *de facto* versus *de jure* segregation?[114] If intentional segregation was proven, which race should be bussed or transported? Did the quality of the school matter? Was it to be automatically assumed that—given equally trained faculty and similar facilities—Blacks would have higher educational achievement just by simply being among White students and teachers? What would be the positive and/or negative benefits of desegregation to White students or to Black students? The preceding questions are only a few among many that were generated by the Court's desegregation ruling.

In response to the first question, social theorists like to differentiate between the terms *desegregation* and *integration*. *Desegregation* implies the mere physical mixing of persons without regard to race, color, or socioeconomic status. It can be a rather mechanical process in the execution of one's civil rights. *Integration* is a subjective, psychological, and attitudinal social process. True integration is achieved only when two or more races or groups develop mutual respect for each other. A degree of cultural assimilation, interaction, and interpersonal relationships must exist, including intermixing and mutual acceptance as valued participants in each race's or group's social and family institutions.[115] In other words, desegregation is a preliminary stage toward the societal goal of equitable integration. In relation to education, neither optimum desegregation nor integration has been achieved for Blacks on a national scale in American society.

De facto and quasi *de jure* segregation are facts of life within the American educational system. Even though the practices are not as blatant or easily observable as they were during the 1950s and 1960s, tacit racial "segregation" in education, of one form or the other, continues. Segregation has been transformed into institutional racism, and, thus, produces the same result.

The record of desegregation efforts in the public schools over the last five decades can be described at best as tepid. Although desegregation actually increased somewhat in the 1980s, during the 1990s the Supreme Court began a continuing process of relaxing supervision over school districts. In 1991, in an Oklahoma City case, the Supreme Court held that lower courts could end desegregation orders in school districts that had attempted in good faith to comply, even if this would result in immediate resegregation. In 1992, in *Freeman v. Pitts*, the Supreme Court held that courts could end some aspects of school desegregation orders even if schools had never complied with other aspects. In addition, in the 1995 case *Missouri v. Jenkins*, the Supreme Court overturned a plan for magnet schools in Kansas City that was designed to attract White students back into the inner city. The Court said that the plan was unjustified and unnecessary to achieve desegregation. It also rejected the argument that increased spending on education could be justified in order to remedy reduced achievement by students in inner city schools. Since 1995, forty-five school districts across the country have been declared "unitary"—that is, sufficiently desegregated—and have had their federal desegregation orders rescinded by the courts. In essence, then, the policy at the dawn of the twenty-first century is very different from the vision in *Brown*. Today, schools may be segregated by race as long as it is not due to direct government fiat. The contemporary demographic reality is that Black students in central cities are educated in schools with virtually no White schoolmates, with demonstrably inferior facilities and educational opportunities.[116] The likelihood of even greater racial segregation increased significantly with the June 2007 Supreme Court decision in two cases involving voluntary school desegregation plans in Louisville, Kentucky (*Meredith v. Jefferson County Board of Education, No. 05-915*) and Seattle, Oregon (*Parents Involved in Community Schools v. Seattle School District No. 1, No. 05-908*). The Court's decision is another step backward, following three earlier decisions limiting mandatory desegregation in the 1990s. In a 5–4 decision, the Court rejected the methods many school districts use to retain some level of racial desegregation in a rapidly resegregating society. The invalidated methods attempted to maintain diversity within each school by limiting transfers on the basis of race, or by using race as a "tiebreaker" for admission to particular schools. Both programs had been upheld by lower federal courts and were similar to operating plans in hundreds of school districts around the country. The available research suggests that policies available to school districts in the wake of the decision are likely to be much less effective in constraining resegregation. Strategies that are still permitted include school site selection, minor boundary adjustments, and active, targeted recruitment for schools of choice. The Court narrowly upheld (5–4) the principle established in the 1978 *Bakke* case that the goal of integrated education is a "compelling interest." The designation of education as a "compelling interest" means that narrowly tailored programs that are designed to increase integration may still have the potential to survive future constitutional challenges. However, the decision serves to continue the overall trajectory of marginalizing African American students.[117]

The data in Table 4.15 below indicate the extent to which public elementary and secondary school students attended schools populated primarily by non-White students in 2007-08. Almost 50 percent of Black students attended schools with Black populations of 50 percent or more. In contrast, almost 90 percent of White students attended schools where Black students comprised less than 25 percent of the student body.

TABLE 4.15

PERCENTAGE DISTRIBUTION OF PUBLIC ELEMENTARY AND SECONDARY BLACK, WHITE, AND HISPANIC SCHOOL STUDENTS BY PERCENT BLACK ENROLLMENT IN SCHOOL: 2007-2008

Percentage Distribution

Race/Ethnicity	Less than 25 percent	25–49 percent	50–74 percent	75 percent or more
Black	27.8	23.8	17.1	31.2
White	89.7	7.9	1.9	.4
Hispanic	84.4	11.5	3.0	1.0

SOURCE: U.S. Department of Education, National Center for Education Statistics, Table 7.4, Percentage Distribution of Public Elementary and Secondary School Students of each Racial/Ethnic Group, by Percentage Enrollment in School of selected Racial/Ethnic Group: 2007-08 http://nces.gov

4

In the 2000-2001 school year White students attended schools that are 80 percent White, while the average student body of a Black student was 28 percent White, and for Hispanics the figure was 31 percent. In 1987, the average student body of a Black student's school was 37 percent White, about 6 percentage points higher than it was in 2000. The White percentage in the average Hispanic student's school fell by about the same percentage during the same period.[118]

Trends in dropout rates provide a useful indication of the extent to which current educational policies hamper efforts to build social capital in Black communities. Table 4.16 below contains information about the proportion of persons between 16 and 24 years old who are high school dropouts for various years between 1980 and 2010. The data indicate that the proportion of dropouts has dropped significantly among all groups.

TABLE 4.16
STATUS DROPOUT RATES PERSONS 16 – 24 YEARS OLD
BY RACE AND ETHNICITY
Selected Years, 1980 – 2010

Year	Black	White	Hispanic
1980	19.1	11.4	35.2
1985	15.2	10.4	27.6
1990	13.2	9.0	32.4
1995	12.1	8.6	30.0
2000	13.1	6.9	27.8
2005	10.4	6.0	22.4
2008	9.9	4.8	18.3
2010	8.0	5.1	15.1

Source: U.S. Department of Education, National Center for Education Statistics, STATUS DROPOUT RATES OF 16 – THROUGH 24 YEAR-OLDS IN THE CIVIL-IAN, NONINSTITUIONALIZED POPULATION, BY RACE/ETHNICITY: October Current Population Survey (CPS) 1980-2008 Data for 2009 is from the National Center for Education Statistics, http://nces.gov.

The overrepresentation of Black students in Special Education is also claimed by some to be a direct outgrowth of the manner in which school desegregation has been implemented. Five of the seven states today with the highest overrepresentation of African Americans labeled *mentally retarded* are located in the South, where Jim Crow education practices were most entrenched— Mississippi, Alabama, North Carolina, South Carolina, and Florida. However, over time, the tracking of Black students into Special Education has become a national problem. Daniel Losen and Gary Orfield found that, nationally, Blacks are nearly three times more likely to be identified as mentally retarded than White students, nearly twice as likely to be labeled *emotionally disturbed*, and 30 percent more likely to be categorized as having a specific learning disability.[119]

Given the discouraging educational trends discussed in the preceding paragraphs, it is not unreasonable to ask if the benefits derived from limited efforts to provide desegregated educational opportunities for Black children have warranted the costs that have been imposed on Black communities. African Americans have borne most of the burdens and hardships of desegregation. It is they who have witnessed the closure of schools in their community, suffered the unpleasantness of having their children bussed into often hostile White neighborhood schools, and experienced the loss or demotion of Black principals, teachers, and staff. On the other hand, there is a continuing dispute about the educational advantages accruing to Black students from desegregation. One of the most common complaints or grievances registered by Black students matriculated at predominantly White schools is that they experience a sense of loss of their racial identity and a feeling of cultural alienation. Along with other critical interventions, if educational institutions do not institute curriculum changes that promote appreciation and understanding of cultural diversity, predominantly White academic environments can intensify Black students' struggle for scholastic achievement and psychological survival. Their plight is further exacerbated in many cases by the lack of Black teachers and professional role models.

There is a critical need to scrutinize carefully whether teachers are actually prepared to assist students in developing the orientation and skills necessary to contribute to the creation of social capital within Black communities. The manner in which teacher competency is measured does not address this issue and focuses exclusively on general knowledge. Teacher competency tests with questionable validity constitute one of the major threats to the diversity of the teacher population. By 1990, about thirty-eight thousand Black, Latino, and other minority teachers had been removed from elementary and secondary classrooms as a result of failure to pass competency tests.[120] Such tests do not measure teacher commitment to students or their neighborhoods and disqualify many potential teachers who might not only be very successful in educating students, if given an opportunity, but who also could potentially foster social capital formation outside the classroom setting. It is in this context that some researchers claim school desegregation policies have ignored the voices of Black teachers and have not adequately considered the impact of desegregation on Black communities.

There is also a serious problem in retaining qualified Black teachers. In a 1994-95 study, 6.6 percent of African American teachers who were teaching in 1993-94 actually left the profession. This attrition is a disproportionate problem in inner cities because the teacher turnover rate is higher in schools with higher proportions of African American and Latino students.[121] Table 4.17 provides more recent information that suggests a mixed picture regarding trends in the representation of Black teachers. The percentage of Black elementary teachers in public schools is declining, while representation in private elementary schools is increasing. The percentage of Black teachers in public and private secondary schools is increasing, albeit the percentage in private institutions is extremely small.

TABLE 4.17
PERCENT OF ELEMENTARY AND SECONDARY
AFRICAN AMERICAN TEACHERS
PUBLIC AND PRIVATE SCHOOLS
1999–2000 AND 2007-2008

Level/Type	1999–2000	2007–2008
Public Elementary	8.4	7.4
Public Secondary	6.7	7.0
Private Elementary	4.7	5.2
Private Secondary	1.8	1.9

SOURCE: U.S. Department of Education, National Center for Education Statistics, Contexts of Elementary and Secondary Education, Teachers and Staff, Table A-31-1. Number and percentage distribution of full-time teachers, by school level, sector, and selected teacher characteristics: School years 1999-2000 and 2007-08. http://nces.ed.gov/programs/coe/tables/table-tsp-1.asp

The patterns described above are fueling growing ambivalence about the viability of current approaches to the integration of public education as a means of enhancing social capital creation. In fact, some critics have questioned the credibility of the original Social Science evidence that played such a pivotal role in the *Brown* case, that is, the famous doll studies conducted by noted psychologists Kenneth and Mamie Clark. The Clarks asked groups of Black children to choose between Black and White dolls in terms of which was nicer, which one they would like to play with, and which had the nicer color. The Black children generally selected the White dolls and typically chose Black dolls when asked which dolls looked bad. The Clarks concluded that Black children had negative attitudes about themselves and about their cultural background. Several researchers have criticized the studies and have conducted similar investigations with very different results.

Other commentators note that there is a tendency to overlook the beneficial attributes of good all-Black schools and to underestimate the magnitude of the burden that desegregation places on Black children and families when students are bussed away from their community schools to schools in White suburbs.[122] Sociologist James S. Coleman, whose 1960 seminal study was used to support school desegregation, later reversed his conclusion that African American students absolutely learn better in integrated classrooms. Coleman confessed that desegregation had proven to be much more complicated than many had realized. Furthermore, he rejected the belief that an all-Black school is inherently inferior and stated that "there have been and there are all-black schools that are excellent schools by any standard."[123]

Concurrent with the retreat by the courts from the aggressive pursuit of educational equality, the Bush administration introduced a new thrust, euphemistically described as "No Child Left Behind" (NCLB). The much touted and criticized NCLB initiative set forth in the Elementary and Secondary Education Act (ESEA) focuses almost exclusively on standards and testing, with no attention to addressing the environmental and ecological barriers that militate against successful academic achievement. NCLB requires every state to establish a formula for determining "adequate yearly progress" (AYP) toward the goal of all students attaining the "proficient" level on state assessments of reading and math by 2014 and to implement sanctions for failure to meet progress. Schools where the proportion of passing students is below the minimum standard are characterized as "In Need of Improvement" (INOI). Although there is no question that mastery of fundamental skills is a prerequisite for future academic success, critics charge that NCLB narrows the concept of educational progress to the attainment of acceptable reading and math scores on tests of dubious reliability.[124]

The factors contributing to disappointing achievement test performances by Black students and to their diminished educational goals and aspirations cannot be addressed by fiat. There are economic implications associated with substandard school facilities, as well as social and environmental factors, which plague low-income school districts and neighborhoods that worsen school outcomes. In addition, Black and other minority group social scientists have long contended that achievement or standardized tests are, in part, based on White middle-class norms, values, and experiences, and, thus, are culturally biased.

Data collection and maintenance requirements associated with NCLB could amount to as much as $35 billion annually, at the same time that most states are wrestling with massive deficits that require some states actually to reduce funding for education.[125] The National Education Association (NEA), the largest national teachers' organization, is challenging the requirements in court. The NEA's concerns include the fact that NCLB does not provide the funding for schools to provide the mandated supplemental services.[126] Pervasive segregation and resource disparities place inner-city schools at the greatest risk of being classified as INOI. One estimate suggests that as many as 70 percent of all schools are at risk of being labeled INOI.[127] Classification as INOI can lead to various consequences. As an example, when a Title I school fails to meet adequate yearly progress (AYP) goals for two or more consecutive years, parents of children in that school have the choice to transfer their children to another school.

The most fundamental policy question that must be addressed to reduce educational outcome disparities is how to make the availability of educational resources more equal. This was, in fact, a key dimension of the legal strategy that produced the *Brown* decision, namely, the demonstration that disparities in funding and facilities created a situation in which separate facilities were clearly unequal. Prominent scholar Derrick Bell of the NYU Law School has argued that if the *Plessy v. Ferguson* decision had not been overturned, it might have been possible to mount more effective challenges requiring school districts to equalize funding for schools serving Black and White students.

In the current operating environment of public schools, resource disparities severely restrict the provision of quality education, and the problem is magnified in inner cities. In central cities, schools are taxed with the expectation, not faced in most suburbs, to take on social transformation roles formerly performed by other agencies or organizations. Public schools are being unfairly expected "to supply our antidote to drugs and gang violence ... with a mélange of in-school social programs, anticrime initiatives, and after-school services

that once were the domain of families, churches, and neighbors."[128]

From the perspective reflected in the preceding discussion, it is clear that the lower educational achievement of African Americans is not caused by their lack of social mixing with Whites but by the unequal and inadequate funding and staffing of predominantly Black schools, coupled with general patterns of oppression that challenge effective family functioning. Many policy makers continue to ignore this fact, and focus, instead, on the perceived general dysfunction of public education systems as the source of persistent educational outcome disparities. These critics clamor for a greater role for private educational providers, and charter schools have emerged as their policy alternative of choice.

Charter schools are self-governing, nonsectarian, public schools, often run by private companies that operate largely outside the authority of local school boards. They have greater flexibility than traditional public schools in areas of policy, hiring, and teaching techniques. The "charter" establishing each such school is a performance contract describing the school's mission, program, goals, students served, methods of assessment, and ways to measure success. The length of time for which charters are granted varies, but most are granted for three to five years. At the end of this period, the entity granting the charter may renew the school's contract. Charter schools are accountable to their sponsor—usually a state or local school board—to produce positive academic results and adhere to the charter contract.

The basic concept of charter schools is that they exercise increased autonomy in return for accountability. They are presumably accountable for both academic results and fiscal practices to several groups: the sponsor that grants them, the parents who choose them, and the public that funds them. Of the nation's 88,000 public schools, 3,000 are charters that educate more than 600,000 students. Their ranks are expected to grow as No Child Left Behind identifies thousands of schools for possible closing because of poor test scores. To put this movement into a broader context, it is useful to note that in 1999 Blacks comprised 17 percent of all public school students and 9 percent of all private school students. In that same year, Black students comprised slightly over 27 percent of all public charter school students, and they were even more disproportionately represented in newly-created public charter schools and in previous private schools converted to public charter schools. Forty percent of Black students attending public charter schools were attending schools in which the proportion of Black students was 30 percent or greater.[129]

The first national comparison of test scores among children in charter schools and regular public schools surprisingly revealed that charter school students were generally performing worse than comparable students in regular public schools. Fourth graders attending charter schools tested about half a year behind students in other public schools in both reading and math. Beyond the general comparisons, the researchers also compared urban charters to traditional schools in cities by examining low-income children in both settings. They found that in virtually all instances, the charter students did worse than their counterparts in regular public schools.[130]

These findings cast serious doubt on the credibility of the trumped up claims by advocates that charter schools offer parents an escape from moribund public schools. However, some researchers insist that it is too soon to judge charter schools and claim students will derive positive benefits over a longer term after the interventions have neutralized previous negative educational experiences. The record to date, however, is not promising. More than eighty charter schools have been forced to close around the country, largely because of questionable financial dealings and poor performance. Nevertheless, a significant number of Black religious and secular organizations were convinced by the early marketing efforts and have established charter schools. Some of these schools offer an African-centered curriculum based on African Studies scholarship. Such a curriculum may well have empowering effects for those Black students fortunate enough to gain admission. In addition, consistent with the emphasis in Africana Studies on learning from the past, administrators and faculty operating such schools are likely to be more successful if they study the successful educational practices used to foster success in schools serving African American students during the Jim Crow era.

For all their positive virtues, however, charter schools, even those organized by self-conscious African American educators, will not solve the long-standing structural inequities consigning the vast majority of Black students to poorly funded traditional public schools. The activist tradition of Africana Studies mandates that efforts be directed toward empowering parents and supporters to demand accountability from administrators, teachers, and politicians, as was the case

in the heyday of the community empowerment movement that crystallized in the 1960s. Only informed, committed, and organized political action by parents, supporters, educators, administrators, and students can achieve educational reforms promoting healthy social capital formation.

Many African Americans are championing single-gender academies as a strategy to address the educational crisis in many Black communities, which is disproportionately disadvantaging African American males. In September 1991, then President George Bush, Sr., was roundly criticized for his praise of the city of Detroit's efforts to create all-male, African-centered elementary schools for at-risk Black males. Earlier that year, Detroit's Malcolm X Academy had become one of the nation's first single-gender public schools in the United States to address the alarming drop-out rate of African American males.[131]

Nearly two decades after the establishment of the Malcolm X Academy in Detroit, "Urban Prep Academy for Young Men" in Chicago, the nation's first all-male, all-African American high school, received major national media attention for achieving a 100% college enrollment rate. Located in the Englewood section of southwest Chicago, this charter school placed 107 seniors into 72 different colleges across the country.[132] Urban Prep's phenomenal success is now stirring a wave of support and interest among scholars and educators regarding the merits of single-sex education, and it comes at a time when the high school drop-out rate for African American males is nearly 50 percent in some cities.

The National Urban League's *State of Black America* report in 2008 recommended that all-male schools with a strong emphasis on mentoring could help keep Black boys "focused on their education and away from distractions that could lead them down the wrong paths".[133] The Urban League's position reflects commitment to culturally responsive (CRT) approaches to addressing the persistent disparities experienced by African American males, a grass-roots movement that is gaining momentum. Further, a recent survey of African American K-12 and higher education experts and practitioners overwhelmingly affirmed the Urban League's advocacy and direction on this issue.[134]

In light of Urban Prep's remarkable accomplishment, discussed previously, calls for similar experimental initiatives are likely to emerge in many urban school districts. Such innovations strike a resonant historical

4

chord among many African American households which desire a greater degree of educational self-determination for African Americans in the United States. African American advocates of single-gender education observe that complex schooling, social, and cultural factors contribute significantly to African American male under-achievement. Concerned that the current state is a "crisis" created by crowded schools, inexperienced teachers, fatherless homes, and negative pop cultural influences, they assert that more public school programs that avail single-sex schooling and culturally responsive interventions, such as mentoring and African American men as role models, are needed to provide pragmatic interventions and solutions.

There are some initiatives underway that strike a medium between full-fledged single-sex academies and more traditional reform efforts. The Benjamin E. Mays Institute (BEMI) is an example of such a blended approach. Located in Hartford, Connecticut, BEMI is reporting significantly improved academic success and has introduced an Afrocentric, school-based approach to educational reform that has demonstrated significant improvements in academic outcomes between those African American males who participate in BEMI's mentoring program and those who do not.[135] BEMI, although not a single-sex school, provides single-sex classroom education using culturally responsive strategies that aim to impact the development of students' racial identity, while reinforcing the community's support and commitment to them.[136] Randolph Potts labels this type of curriculum and community-centered approach or praxis "emancipatory education."[137] Thus, although not as far-reaching as the single-sex academy model, this initiative is clearly consistent with the CRT ideological position, with its strong emphasis on racial identity development and mentoring.

Marlon James asserts a "power-centered" instead of "problem-centered" approach is needed in single-gender schools to transcend the myriad complex social and academic challenges associated with educating urban African American males. Therefore, in addition to transforming the school's structural, philosophical and cultural environment, teacher effectiveness, principal leadership, and counseling support must also be appropriately realigned in single-gender schools and classrooms. More research is needed in this area, particularly in relation to assessing the impact of culturally responsive pedagogy and mentoring programs.[138]

In addition to the identity-enhancing potential of all-male academies, as noted previously, the BEMI also incorporates innovative mentoring interventions. This focus is laudable because various research has found that mentored males have significantly better academic achievement than non-mentored males.[139] BEMI's results, though small-scale and limited in participant selection and research design, are encouraging, in lieu of findings from three large-scale random studies of school-based mentoring programs for youth that found no program effects on academic achievement.[140] These studies, which examined the Big Brothers Big Sisters of America, Communities in Schools of San Antonio, and the U.S. Department of Education's Student Mentoring Program, did reveal important differences across a variety of areas, including agency inclusion criteria, program models, and implementation effectiveness and support.[141] CRT scholars and advocates maintain that extensive mentoring efforts must be a critical dimension of all-male African American academies, if they are to be successful in fundamentally addressing the continuing structured racial inequities faced by African Americans in U.S. society and educational systems.

Higher Education

Since the era of enslavement, African American leaders have championed higher educational attainment as the key to sustained development among African Americans and to the creation of social capital. For example, Du Bois insisted "the foundations of knowledge in this race, as in others, must be sunk deep in the college and university if we would build a solid, permanent structure."[142] Du Bois used evidence of the growing number of Blacks with college degrees and their success to argue for broadening opportunities for college attendance and against efforts to restrict educational opportunities to vocational curricula. Using Du Bois's broad measure as a benchmark, degree completion trends over the last forty years suggest that there is a sufficient number of college-educated Blacks to support stable and thriving communities.

The percentage of African American men with a bachelor's degree or more in 2002 was over 3.5 times the percentage (4.5%) in 1964, and the 2002 percentage for African American women was more than 5 times higher than in 1964 (3.4%). These substantial gains helped African American adults to reduce differences between their college completion rates and those of Whites. In 1964, White men were 2.7 times more likely than African American men to hold a bachelor's degree. By 2002, they were only twice as likely to do so. Similarly, in 1964, the percentage of White women with college degrees was twice that for Black women. This ratio had fallen to 1.5 times more likely by 2002.

As can be seen from Table 4.18, increases in the proportion of Black men and women enrolled in college have generally kept pace with gains for Whites, leaving the differential fairly constant. The enrollment of Black women between 2005 and 2008 is a noteworthy exception. The proportion of Black women enrolled in college fell more than 3 percentage points between these two years.

Given the historical debate about the relative merits of vocational and liberal arts instruction, it is useful to compare growth rates in baccalaureate and associate degree completion. Associate degrees tend to be more vocationally focused than baccalaureate degrees and have experienced an increase in popularity because many students from all backgrounds perceive that they provide easier transitions to employment. Table 4.19 below presents baccalaureate and associate degree completion data for selected years covering the last decade. The proportion of associate degrees has remained relatively stable over this period, although it has been trending up slightly.

Many educators have sounded alarms about the disproportionate gains in college completion and degree attainment achieved by Black women compared to Black men. This trend was discussed previously in relation to Black families and Black male-female relationships. As illustrated in Tables 4.19 and 4.20, differentials in degree attainment between Black men and women have been growing at all levels since the mid-1970s.

The disparities in higher education enrollment between Black men and women place a disproportionate burden on Black women to contribute high-level educational and economic inputs into the creation of social capital. The challenge is magnified by the persistence of gender–specific enrollment and occupational specialization patterns. If the current trends continue, Black women will have to move more aggressively into nontraditional fields to provide the types of knowledge and expertise traditionally acquired by males to sustain adequate social capital creation in Black communities.

The data in Table 4.21 below show the numbers of degrees conferred in 2002-2003 by field of study for Black men. There has been a large shift toward business, while enrollment in other areas has remained relatively stable. Comparable information for Black women is presented in Table 4.22. Enrollments in business have increased, but the proportion of business majors has

not increased due to significant increases in enrollment in health professions. This latter trend is encouraging, given the disproportionate health care needs of African Americans.

The enrollment and degree attainment gains described previously have occurred at the same time that there has been a decline in the role of Historically Black Colleges and Universities (HBCUs) as degree producers. The eminent African American educator and philosopher Carter G. Woodson once admonished that "the education of any people should begin with the people themselves."[143] Historically, HBCUs have been the major source of Black college graduates. Lincoln University in Pennsylvania, founded in 1854, and Wilberforce University in Ohio, founded in 1856, are cited as the first Black colleges in the United States. However, other less successful institutions were initiated prior to Lincoln and Wilberforce universities in 1839, 1842, 1849, and 1851.[144] The majority of these colleges and universities are located in the South. In spite of their threatened existence because of the politics of integration, over one hundred of these colleges still exist. Until 1965, 90 percent of African Americans in college attended historically black colleges.

The data in Table 4.23 below allow an assessment of the contemporary importance of HBCUs to the production of highly educated Blacks who can potentially contribute to the creation of social capital in Black communities. The data compare total Black enrollments in HBCUs and total Black enrollment in all colleges and universities. As indicated, only 9 percent of African American college students were enrolled in HBCUs in 2009.

In the context of the monumental historical role of HBCUs in generating social capital in Black communities, shifting enrollments could be problematic for Black community social capital formation in the twenty-first century. A century ago, at the dawn of the twentieth century, Du Bois averred, "the function of the Negro college ... is clear: it must maintain the standards of popular education, it must seek the social regeneration of the Negro, and it must help in the solution of problems of race contact and cooperation."[145] In fact, despite monumental challenges, HBCUs still account for a large share of Blacks receiving Bachelor's degrees in the biological, physical, and technical sciences, and in engineering and mathematics. And, despite the increasing number of African Americans enrolling at predominantly White colleges and universities, the number of graduates of HBCUs has been increasing, as documented below in Table 4.23.

TABLE 4.18

PERCENTAGE OF BLACK AND WHITE MALE AND FEMALE 18- TO 24 YEAR-OLDS ENROLLED IN COLLEGES AND UNIVERSITIES
Selected Years, 1980 - 2008

Year	Black Males	Black Females	White Males	White Females
1980	17.7	21.3	28.9	26.7
1985	20.3	19.3	30.8	29.3
1990	25.8	24.7	35.6	34.7
1995	26.0	28.7	37.0	38.8
2000	25.1	35.2	36.2	41.3
2005	28.2	37.6	39.4	46.1
2008	29.7	34.2	41.7	46.9

Source: U.S. Department of Commerce, Census Bureau, Current Population Survey (CPS), selected years, October 1980-2008.

TABLE 4.19

ASSOCIATE AND BACCALAUREATE DEGREES AWARDED TO BLACKS 1998-99, 2003-04 AND 2008-09 (000) AND PERCENTAGES OF DEGREES CONFERRED ON FEMALES

Year	Total Degrees	Bacc. Degrees	Assoc. Degrees	Percent Assoc.	Percent Female Bacc.	Percent Female Assoc.
1998-1999	159.6	102.2	57.4	35.9	65.9	66.2
2003-2004	212.4	131.2	81.2	38.2	66.6	68.0
2008-2009	258.1	156.6	101.5	39.3	65.9	68.5

Source: U.S. Department of Education, National Center for Education Statistics, 1998-99, 2003-04, and 2008-09 Integrated Postsecondary Education Data System (IPEDS), "Completions" Survey (IPEDS-C-99) and Fall 2004 and 2009.

TABLE 4.20

MASTER'S, FIRST-PROFESSIONAL, AND DOCTORAL DEGREES AWARDED TO BLACKS 1998-99, 2003-04, AND 2008-09 (000) AND PERCENT OF DEGREES AWARDED TO FEMALES

Year	Total Master's	Total First-professional	Total Doctoral	Percent Female Master's	Percent Female First-professional	Female Doctoral
1998-1999	32.5	5.3	2.1	69.1	58.8	59.1
2003-2004	50.7	5.9	2.9	71.1	62.1	65.0
2008-2009	70.0	6.6	4.4	71.8	62.0	66.5

Source: U.S. Department of Education, National Center for Education Statistics, 1998-99, 2003-04, and 2008-09 Integrated Postsecondary Education Data System (IPEDS), "Completions" Survey (IPEDS-C-99) and Fall 2004 and 2009.

TABLE 4.21

BACHELOR'S DEGREES CONFERRED TO BLACK MEN
By Selected Major Fields of Study: 2002-03 and 2008-09

Field	2002–03		2008–09	
	Total Degrees	Percent of Total Degrees	Total Degrees	Percent of Total Degrees
Business	10,804	42.6	15,035	47.3
Computer Science	3,491	13.8	2,813	8.8
Education	1,748	6.9	1,601	5.0
Engineering	2,137	8.4	2,362	7.4
Health Professions	1,035	4.1	1,987	6.3
Liberal Arts/ Social Sciences	6,137	24.2	7,994	25.1
Total	25,352		31,792	

Source: U.S. Department of Education, National Center for Education Statistics, Integrated Postsecondary Education Data System (IPEDS), "Completions," (November 2002) and Fall 2009.

TABLE 4.22

BACHELOR'S DEGREES CONFERRED TO BLACK WOMEN
By Selected Major Fields of Study: 2002-03 and 2008-09

Field	2002–03		2008–09	
	Total Degrees	Percent of Total Degrees	Total Degrees	Percent of Total Degrees
Business	19,942	42.1	24,497	42.4
Computer Science	3,049	6.4	1,509	2.6
Education	5,175	10.9	5,044	8.7
Engineering	1,139	2.4	897	1.6
Health Professions	6,959	14.7	11,840	20.5
Liberal Arts/ Social Sciences	11,132	23.5	13,890	24.1
Total	47,396		57,677	

Source: U.S. Department of Education, National Center for Education Statistics, Integrated Postsecondary Education Data System (IPEDS), "Completions," (November 2002) and Fall 2009.

The contemporary contributions of HBCUs to the creation of social capital in Black communities are documented in the report, "The Historically Black Colleges and Universities: A Future in the Balance."[146] The report makes a persuasive case for the continuing social efficacy of HBCUs. It highlights the critical and disproportionate role of HBCUs in producing the current generation of Black leaders in a variety of fields. Nearly 80 percent of Black officers in the U.S. military are HBCU graduates. So are 80 percent of Black federal judges, 60 percent of Black attorneys, and 50 percent of Black teachers in public schools.

TABLE 4.23
TOTAL BLACK ENROLLMENT AT HBCUS AND TOTAL BLACK UNDER-GRADUATE ENROLLMENTS AT ALL COLLEGES AND UNIVERSITIES
Selected Years, 1980 - 2008

Year	HBCU Black Enrollment	Total Black Undergraduates	HBCUs' Black Enrollment as % of all Black Undergraduates
1980	191.0	1106.8	17.3
1990	208.7	1247.0	16.7
2003	253.3	2068.4	12.2
2009	264.1	2919.8	9.0

Source: U.S. Department of Education, National Center for Education Statistics, "Fall Enrollments in Institutions of Higher Education," (2004 and 2009).

Moreover, the case is made that educational outcomes generated by HBCUs are distinguishable from those associated with traditionally White institutions. The report emphasizes that HBCUs serve a disproportionately disadvantaged clientele while maintaining low tuition. Various factors are identified as contributing to the success of HBCUs in educating students from lower-socioeconomic strata. These include (a) expertise in providing remedial preparation for students who start out with weak high-school backgrounds; (b) provision of a supportive social, cultural, and racial environment; (c) greater involvement of students in campus activities and (d) a high level of interaction with faculty, and particularly Black role models.[147]

The report also argues that HBCUs constitute economic and political resources to all members of their respective communities. A number of HBCUs have, for example, formed partnerships with urban elementary and secondary schools. In addition, approximately 50 HBCUs are taking part in international projects. It is clear, then, that the emphasis in desegregation policy on eradicating "racially identifiable" institutions has the potential to erode educational diversity in ways that reduce the capabilities of public systems to respond to new challenges, such as the major demographic changes anticipated in the next few decades.

With predominately White higher education institutions aggressively recruiting Black students, the question arises whether HBCUs will remain an important part of U.S. higher education in the twenty-first century. Several HBCUs have been forced to close or are in

jeopardy of losing accreditation. Morris Brown College in Atlanta and Mary Holmes College in West Point, Mississippi, for example, have lost accreditation. As of this writing Grambling State University in Grambling, Louisiana, is on probation following revelations of accounting discrepancies.

While HBCUs have made, and continue to make, important contributions to social capital creation in Black communities, it is not clear that they have sought to develop educational philosophies and courses of study that differ in any fundamental way from those found at predominantly White institutions. If both types of institutions are emphasizing education primarily as a means of enhancing individual upward mobility, then White colleges will be perceived by many as preferred alternatives.

At the turn of the twentieth century W. E. B. Du Bois envisioned HBCUs as producers of group leaders who would comprise his "Talented Tenth." However, in 1930 he criticized HBCUs for not "establishing that great and guiding ideal of group development and scholarship."[148] Scolding students for their gullibility, he noted, "The average Negro undergraduate has swallowed hook, line, and sinker, the dead bait of the White undergraduate who, born in an industrial machine, does not have to think and does not think."[149] Carter G. Woodson offered a similar critique and inveighed, "No systematic effort toward change has been possible, for, taught the same economics, history, philosophy, literature, and religion which have established the present code of morals, the Negro's mind has been brought under the control of his oppressor."[150]

Du Bois revised his conception of leadership in 1948 when he asserted:

My Talented Tenth must be more than talented, and work not simply as individuals. Its passport to leadership was not alone learning, but expert knowledge of modern economics as it affected American Negroes, and in addition to this and fundamental, would be its willingness to sacrifice and plan for such economic revolution in industry and just distribution of wealth, as would make the rise of our group possible.[151]

Du Bois also outlined a vision for the potential of HBCUs as change agents that would produce leaders and citizens who could change the destiny of the world:

The university must become not simply a center of knowledge but a center of applied knowledge and guide of action ... starting with present conditions and using the facts and the knowledge of the present situation of American Negroes, the Negro university expands toward the possession and the conquest of all knowledge. It seeks from a beginning of the history of the Negro in America and in Africa to interpret all history; from a beginning of social development among enslaved Africans and freedmen in America and Negro tribes and kingdoms in Africa, to interpret and understand the social development of all mankind in all ages. It seeks to reach modern science of matter and life from the surroundings and habits and attitudes of American Negroes and thus lead up to understanding of life and matter in the universe.[152]

Given Du Bois's challenge, it is ironic that African American Studies has become more firmly established at predominantly White institutions than at HBCUs. Many African American Studies specialists have taken up Du Bois's challenge and attempted to develop new analytical tools and models of social change. In recent years, many HBCUs have begun to embrace African American Studies more fully, and increased efforts in this direction will undoubtedly lead to enhanced social capital creation in Black communities.

In general, HBCUs' future viability depends, like all higher education institutions, on quality leadership that devotes constant and dedicated attention to people, programs, and plant. The best possible administrators, faculty, and students must function within flexible programs of study conducted in the best possible facilities and must be adept at using the latest available research and instructional technologies.

African American Studies specialists are particularly interested in enrollments in Black/Africana Studies majors. As of the year 2000, it was reported that there were approximately 50 degree-granting departments and over 200 programs housed in units with various titles, including Black Studies, African American Studies, African Studies, Africana Studies, or African Diaspora Studies, in colleges and universities across the United States.[153] In 2000, "colleges granted 604 undergraduate degrees, 70 master's degrees, and 7 doctoral degrees" in African American Studies.[154] More recent data indicate that in 2007 there were 311 institutions offering certification in Black/Africana Studies.[155]

Unfortunately, the expansion of opportunities for graduate study in Black/Africana Studies is not the only trend associated with Black/Africana Studies. While units at some institutions are experiencing enhancements, retrenchments are occurring at others. The Africana Studies Research Center at Cornell University is a case in point. In December 2010, without consultation with the faculty, the Provost declared his intention to eliminate the Center's autonomy and transfer the unit to the College of Arts and Sciences. In response, over 1,000 supporters circulated a petition seeking rescission of this decision. In addition, the Association for the Study of African American Life and History and the National Council for Black Studies both authored letters strongly criticizing the move and calling for a reversal of the decision. So far, all of these efforts have proven unsuccessful.[156]

African Americans and Sports Institutions

Sports play an important role in Western society. Americans have always exhibited a passion for sports as spectators and participants. Sports influence a wide range of other social institutions, occupy a significant fraction of total media output (whether television, radio, or print media), play an increasing role in the maintenance of public health, and control extensive economic resources. While popular mythology in American life often suggests that the sports arena represents the American dream of social mobility and equality, this has certainly not been the case for Black Americans.

In contrast, self-organized recreational activities in Black communities have historically contributed to the development of a sense of unity in the Black community. The greatest strength of sport and recreation may have been their potential to transcend social and class barriers for Blacks. In addition, sport fostered self-organization, creativity and expression within the Black community, and served a vital role in developing a sense of unity among Blacks. Circumstances in which Blacks competed successfully against Whites provided evidence for both the Black community and outsiders that challenged myths of Black inferiority. Successful competitors who also demonstrated a political commitment to overturning oppression were celebrated as cultural warriors. Despite these important contributions of sports to the stock of social capital in Black communities, scholars, including Du Bois and Frazier, criticized what they perceived as an overemphasis on sports and sports figures in Black communities as detrimental to what were perceived as "higher" cultural pursuits.

Self-organized athletic activities were sometimes at odds with the organized play movement introduced into mainstream White society in the early 1900s and subsequently extended to Black communities. This movement, with its supervised playgrounds and recreation centers, operated in conscious opposition to Black street culture and to the character of sport fostered by street culture. However, the organized play movement was beneficial in bringing about tangible results, such as community pools, gymnasiums, and playing fields. In spite of this, the new facilities, as well as the existing settlement houses, community centers, and YMCAs, often failed to meet Black communities' needs. Moreover, from the late 1920s through the 1940s, Black social clubs, sports entrepreneurs, and athletes themselves enabled community-based sports to thrive. Self-organized national competitions encompassed a variety of sports that included not only tennis and golf but also Indianapolis-style auto racing. These various community-based recreational activities have provided the foundation for the subsequent large-scale involvement of Blacks in sports at the professional, collegiate, and interscholastic levels.[157]

The desegregation of sports as a product of the Civil Rights Movement has led to disproportionate representation and success by Blacks in selected sports at both the professional and collegiate levels. This pattern has induced various "race-oriented" explanations to account for the phenomenon. A number of sportscasters and scholars have put forth the theory that Blacks are natural athletes because of their physiological and physical characteristics. Such a theory implies that Blacks are genetically superior to Whites, at least, in athletics. Others have fostered the claim that Blacks are more proficient at "reactive activities" and that Whites excel in those sports requiring "self-paced activity." In recent years, the number of so-called scientific explanations for Blacks' alleged superiority in athletics has proliferated. However, an examination of much of the literature reveals no convincing evidence of anthropometric, physiological, or anatomical differences between Blacks and Whites that inherently or permanently would cause either to be superior or inferior in athletic performance beyond long practice and dedicated training.[158]

However, the fostering of popular racial conceptions relative to sports without fully exploring the most logical nonracial explanations has had negative social, educational, and political effects on African Americans. Indeed, most sports sociologists concur that the reasons for the success and disproportionate participation of Blacks in sports are social, economic, and cultural, and not biological as some racialists claim. More important is that African Americans have gained prominence and success in only five major sports activities—basketball, football, baseball, boxing, and track and field. Until recently, Blacks have been conspicuously absent or barely represented in golf, tennis, hockey, soccer, skiing, and a host of other competitive sports in America. Gary A. Sailes and other sports sociologists have noted that, generally, Black communities lack the facilities, equipment, peer-models, instruction, or programs to participate in these sports, and, consequently, they gravitate toward those athletic activities that require minimal facilities and funds.[159]

In his essay, "On the Issue of Race in Contemporary American Sports," Harry Edwards implies that racism is the reason why some White Americans are willing and eager to concede that African Americans are superior athletically, while at the same time such a genetically claimed attribute is not accorded people of African descent in any other sphere of human activity. The implication may be, regardless how subtle, that Blacks are superbly talented for certain athletic achievement but lack the intellect to excel in various other sports activities or even in such positions as quarterback in football or as a pitcher in baseball. Indeed, in addition to economic constraints, institutional racism in high revenue sports, such as golf, hockey, and tennis, serves to inhibit and discourage many African Americans from participation.[160]

Participation in intercollegiate athletics has become the primary entry path to professional athletics in some sports, such as football and men's and women's basketball. In addition, intercollegiate athletics can provide an important enhancement to the life and spirit of an academic community. Participation in committed athletic training and competition can be deeply rewarding for students and can foster character through discipline and team membership. However, the rapid growth of commercial influences in high profile intercollegiate sports and the increased tendency toward professional performance standards has the potential to distort the development of student athletes. In efforts to increase

4

competitiveness and accommodate the interests of the entertainment industry, institutions of higher education have reduced the priority and the importance of wholesome personal and academic development in college athletes. The drawing power and winning capabilities of Black athletes have greatly increased their economic value to colleges and universities in three major sports: basketball, football, and track. Particularly in football and basketball, the fan attraction and star playing ability of Black athletes are essential to the financial maintenance of major White college and university athletic budgets, alumni support, and general student recruitment. Competition and rivalry in the recruitment of star Black athletes during and after the 1960s have led to the use of questionable academic practices to attract and retain them at almost any cost. Collegiate Black athletes make little direct contribution to social capital creation in Black communities, except at HBCUs. Unlike professional athletes, collegiate student-athletes do not have financial resources to make direct investments in social capital creation, and socialization influences at predominately White institutions tend to shift their orientation away from identification with communities of origin. As a consequence, success in professional athletics includes no guarantee that the previous support provided to athletes during their formative years will be reciprocated by direct investments in future generations. In the contemporary world, the primary effects of collegiate athletes on Black community social capital are indirect and include role-modeling *vis-à-vis* former teammates, schoolmates, and community members, along with a sense of pride for those who identify with their individual or team accomplishments.

Participation in K-12 sports programs remains virtually the only access point for intercollegiate athletics. Participation in school sports programs also contributes to social capital creation in several ways. For the individual, participation in interscholastic athletics increases popularity and social connections. Non-athletes also benefit from school sports programs because sport events are important parts of the social calendar and increase social networking opportunities.

In the context of African American Studies, the examination of sports raises many of the same issues as the preceding scrutiny of educational institutions. In fact, one of the issues highlighted in this section is the interaction between sports and educational institutions. The central issue that motivates the following examination is the extent to which the role of sports in building social capital in Black communities has been diminished in the eras of desegregation and commoditization of athletics. Another central issue is the extent to which the participation of Blacks in mainstream sports mirrors patterns of stratification found in the other U.S. institutions. There are also important corollary issues, including the changing significance of athletic role models and the effects of images they project, as well as the extent to which there is persistent imbalance in the focus on athletics versus other life activities, as suggested by Du Bois and Frazier. The intellectual approach of African American Studies mandates that these issues be examined in historical perspective.

Boxing

Boxing has had a unique influence on social capital creation in Black communities and on race relations. This distinct impact stems from the high priority assigned to "manliness" in Western culture. For White America, "manliness" was the racially coded male virtue, a combination of masculinity and restraint that, in theory, only Whites possess, as they are the bearers of the burden of empire and civilization. As a consequence, challengers to this image who were forged in the cauldron of Black racial oppression became important standard bearers for the race. The first known Black boxer, Tom Molineaux, dates back to 1810. However, Arthur John "Jack" Johnson (1878–1946) emerged as the major counterforce to the myth of White physical supremacy by becoming the first Black to win the heavyweight boxing championship of the world in 1910.[161] Prior to that time racial mores as a symbolic declaration of White physical superiority precluded Whites fighting Blacks for the heavyweight championship. However, former champion Jim Jeffries was forced to violate this standing policy because Jack Johnson knocked out then-champion Tommy Burns, in Australia in 1908, to become the "unofficial" world champion. Johnson was not officially given the title until 1910 when he finally fought and beat Jeffries in Las Vegas, after Jeffries had come out of retirement to become the first of many so-called "great White hopes." After the Johnson-Jeffries fight, race riots erupted. The Texas Legislature banned films of his victories over Whites for fear of more riots. In 1913, Johnson was forced to flee the United States because of trumped up charges of violating stipulations in the Mann Act against transporting White women across state lines for prostitution. He married three White women over the course of his life. Johnson lost his championship to Jess Willard in Cuba in 1915, during his exile, and was arrested on his return to the United States in 1920. He served a brief time in prison in Leavenworth, Kansas, and attempted unsuccessfully to regain his previous acclaim after his release.

Joe Louis (Joe Louis Barrow), the legendary "Brown Bomber," held the world's heavyweight title from June 22, 1937, until June 25, 1948, and made twenty-five successful title defenses, a division record. He was the first African American to achieve national hero worship, previously reserved only for Whites, as a result of his defeat of Germany's then-champion Max Schmeling, who was widely regarded as a Nazi symbol. Louis exhibited an extraordinary level of patriotism during World War II, which further cemented his image as a symbol of national unity and purpose in a racially divided country. He donated his purses twice to military relief funds and endeared himself even more to the American public by declaring that the U.S. would win the war "because we're on God's side." Although some Blacks considered him an "Uncle Tom," Joe Louis retained credibility among many Blacks by refusing to be photographed with a slice of watermelon in a proposed advertisement.[162]

The continuing saga of Muhammad Ali, formerly Cassius Clay, reflects elements of the stories of both Johnson and Louis. Ali became the first man to win the heavyweight title three times and revolutionized the sport by introducing a style diametrically opposed to orthodox teachings. As Cassius Clay, he won a light heavyweight gold medal at the 1960 Olympics and began his ascent to the heavyweight crown. In 1964, he shocked the world by defeating the seemingly invincible Sonny Liston for the heavyweight title. After the fight, Clay announced that he had accepted the teachings of Islam and changed his name to Muhammad Ali. In 1967, Ali, citing his religious beliefs, refused induction into the U.S. Army. He was arrested, his boxing license was suspended, and he was stripped of the heavyweight title. Ali was sentenced to five years in prison but was released on appeal, and his conviction was overturned three years later, which enabled him to return to boxing. Despite three years of inactivity, on his return to the ring Ali posted wins over Jerry Quarry and Oscar Bonavena, which set up a showdown between then-champion, Joe Frazier and him. In the bout with Frazier, Ali lost by a unanimous decision but regained the heavyweight crown in 1974 by beating George Foreman in Kinsasha, Zaire. Ali successfully defended the title until 1978, when Olympic gold medalist Leon Spinks won an upset

victory. However, Ali made history when he defeated Spinks six months later in a rematch to capture the crown a third time.[163]

Ali has become increasingly involved in domestic politics and international human rights initiatives over the course of his life. Despite his previous high profile counter-cultural activities, Ali has become increasingly popular with mainstream Americans, partially in sympathetic response to his courageous battle against Parkinson's disease. Ali actively supported Jimmy Carter's presidential candidacy in 1980 and worked the floor of the Democratic National Convention in New York City. He moved into the realm of international diplomacy in 1985 when he attempted, unsuccessfully, to secure the release of four kidnapped Americans in Lebanon. Ali has met with many important dignitaries, including former President Clinton, Queen Elizabeth II, Nelson Mandela, and Pope John Paul II. Despite the progress of Parkinson's syndrome, Ali remains active in raising money for the Muhammad Ali Foundation and still appears at sports tributes and fund-raisers.

Tennis

Ali's evolution parallels, in some respects, the precedent established by tennis star, Arthur Ashe. Ashe first gained national attention in 1963 when he became the first African American selected to play for the United States Davis Cup team. In 1969, Ashe was instrumental in forming what later became the Association of Tennis Professionals (ATP) that laid the foundation for tennis professionals to earn large purses. More significantly, in that same year, he was denied a visa to play in the South African Open because of the South African government's apartheid policies. He called for South Africa's expulsion from both the tennis tour and Davis Cup competition and began a long campaign for human rights for Black South Africans and other oppressed people. Ashe and actor Harry Belafonte organized Artists and Athletes Against Apartheid in 1975 to advocate for economic sanctions that ultimately contributed significantly to the end of apartheid. Even as his activism expanded, in 1975, at the age of 31, Arthur Ashe enjoyed one of his finest seasons ever and one of the shining moments of his career by winning Wimbledon and attaining the ranking of number one in the world.

Arthur Ashe passed away on February 6, 1993, after a heroic battle with AIDS, which he acquired through a blood transfusion. He used his celebrity status to raise awareness about AIDS, and, just prior to his death, he

4

established the Arthur Ashe Institute for Urban Health (AAIUH) to promote improved health care and education for urban residents. His athletic accomplishments included three Grand Slam singles titles and over eight hundred career victories. He paved the way for future stars that include Venus and Serena Williams by co-founding the National Junior Tennis League, which now has more than a thousand chapters. Recognizing the potential synergies between athletics and social capital creation, Ashe was instrumental in raising large amounts of money for the United Negro College Fund. Arthur Ashe will be remembered most for using his status as an elite tennis player as a worldwide platform to speak out about and demonstrate how to ameliorate inequities, both in the tennis world and in society as a whole.[164]

Contemporary Athletes

In many respects, the international acceptance of Ashe and Ali has paved the way for contemporary Black athletes participating in individual professional sports to achieve similar levels of celebrity. The ascendance of Tiger Woods and the Williams sisters as celebrated athletes with diverse fan support bases in sports where Blacks have traditionally had limited visibility provides useful insights regarding variations in how athletics is linked to social capital formation in contemporary Black America. Woods's father, whose military background emphasized discipline and adherence to conventional protocols, carefully mentored Tiger in this mold. Woods honed his skills at Stanford University prior to turning pro and has manifested an ambiguous racial presentation, which is reinforced by his multiracial parentage and his selection of a mate. At the same time, he has committed significant personal resources to expand opportunities for inner-city youth to learn the game of golf.

In a similar vein, Richard Williams deliberately prevented the mainstream tennis establishment from interfering with the early socialization of Serena and Venus Williams. Of course, Richard Williams was portrayed as an eccentric iconoclast until the Williams sisters began to dominate their classically trained White competitors. The Williams sisters stand on the shoulders of Althea Gibson, who preceded Arthur Ashe as a trailblazer in breaking down the barriers of segregation in tennis. Gibson became the first African American to win championships at Grand Slam tournaments that include Wimbledon, the French Open, and the United States Open in the late 1950s. In 1957, she was the first Black voted Female Athlete of the Year by the Associated Press, and she won the honor again in 1958. Gibson also went on to contribute to the desegregation of professional golf, although she failed to match her achievements in tennis.[165] In some sense, then, the early development of both Tiger Woods and the Williams sisters is a throwback to the days when the relationship between athletics and social capital creation in Black communities was internally controlled. The Williams sisters, unlike Woods, have failed to embrace the sports establishment fully. The sisters, and especially Venus, project an overt image of Black pride forged in inner-city Compton, California, but at the same time, they project sufficient "mainstream" linguistic and stylistic behaviors to attract White fans. They, like Woods, have been heavily involved in increasing participation of inner city youth in their sport. The contemporary visibility and success of Tiger Woods in golf and Serena and Venus Williams in tennis have increased interest in these sports, but participation opportunities are limited, and the sports are not as amenable to the free-flowing style that is manifested, for example, in inner-city basketball.

As a transition to the discussion of professional team sports, it is useful to note that the public personas of Louis, Ashe, Gibson, the Williams sisters, and Woods differ markedly from the intimidating "bad boy" image that has become pervasive among many Black male professional football and basketball players. The preferred contemporary representation in these sports appears to mimic some of the elements of the personas of Johnson and Ali.

Professional Team Sports

Unlike boxing, which fosters a spirit of individualism, team sports emphasize collective work toward a common goal. However, the nature of that goal and the manner in which its collectivism is manifested was altered drastically by desegregation and the commoditization of professional team sports.

In the case of baseball, while Blacks and Whites often played openly against each other in the North in the late nineteenth century, by the late 1880s, the game became mostly segregated by color. The first all-Black professional team, the Argyle Athletics founded in 1885, was based in Babylon, New York. The team played many exhibition games against both Black and White teams and was later renamed the Cuban Giants in an effort to make the Black squad more acceptable to White spectators.[166]

The initial effort to establish Black professional baseball leagues took root in 1920 with the formation of the Negro National League (1920–31, 1933–48). Other Black leagues included the Eastern Colored League (1923–28), and the Negro American League (1937–60). The leagues were based initially in cities such as Chicago, New York City, Detroit, St. Louis, and Kansas City, which had large and growing Black populations as a result of the twentieth century northward Black migration. Pittsburgh, however, was the home of two of the most successful teams. The leagues struggled for survival during the Great Depression, and, even though prosperity returned in the 1940s, desegregation of the major leagues would spell the demise of the Negro Leagues. However, the Negro American League (NAL) actually continued with league and all-star games through 1961.[167]

During their heyday, Negro League baseball teams were a major attraction in Black communities, and some teams played in specifically designated stadiums. The 7,500-seat Hinchliffe Stadium, in Paterson, New Jersey, was built in 1932 as a Depression-era public works project at a cost of $240,000. It was home to the New York Black Yankees of the Negro National League in the 1930s and 1940s. The only other remaining Negro League stadium is the Rickwood Stadium, built in 1910 in Birmingham, Alabama, which was home to the Birmingham Black Barons. The overall history and legacy of the Negro Leagues are being carefully preserved by the Negro Leagues Baseball Museum in Kansas City, Missouri.[168]

The signing of the Kansas City Monarch's rookie shortstop, Jackie Robinson, in 1945, by the Brooklyn Dodgers signaled the beginning of the decline of the Negro Leagues. Few Negro League veterans got opportunities to play in the majors. Those who did play were younger men, such as pitcher Don Newcombe and outfielder Larry Doby (Newark Eagles), catcher Roy Campanella (Baltimore Elite Giants), and outfielders Minnie Minoso (New York Cubans), Willie Mays (Birmingham Black Barons), and Hank Aaron (Indianapolis Clowns). Although most of these players spent most of their careers as major league stars, the major league teams were slow in adding Black players. Boston was the last to integrate its roster in 1959. While the major and minor leagues had opened up to African Americans, many major league quality players were never promoted from the minors because of their color, and most of the major league teams were resistant to having more than just a few Blacks on the roster. This pattern contributed to efforts by owners of the Negro Baseball League teams to continue operation, as a means of providing development and playing opportunities for Black players.[169]

Unlike baseball, basketball had no organized Black leagues; thus barnstorming became the modus operandi. The New York Rennaissance, Harlem Globetrotters, and the Philadelphia Tribunes were three of the well-known teams of the 1930s. Named after the Harlem Renaissance Ballroom, which served as the team's home court, the Rens were organized in 1923, played for twenty-seven seasons, and compiled a 2,588–539 record. They played each day of the week and twice on Sundays. The Rens introduced a new style of play predicated on speed, short crisp passes, and relentless defense, a style that was completely opposite to the traditional and methodical play of White players. Although the Rens was undoubtedly the best team in basketball from 1932 to 1936, when they compiled a 473–49 record, the team was not truly recognized as the best team in basketball until 1939, when it defeated the National Basketball League champion Oshkosh All-Stars to win the first ever World Professional Basketball Tournament.[170] The Harlem Globetrotters, founded as the Savoy Big Five, was initially the Midwest counterpart to the Rens. After team promoter Abe Saperstein purchased the team and it won the World Professional Basketball Tournament in 1940 by defeating the Chicago Bruins, the team was renamed the Harlem Globetrotters.[171] There were also two notable teams comprising Black women during the 1930s, the Chicago Romas and the Philadelphia Tribunes. The Tribunes traveled throughout the South introducing Black girls to basketball and was generally regarded as the top Black women's team of its day before it disbanded in 1940.[172]

The integration of professional basketball resulted from a shortage of White players created by World War II. Black players had already gained the attention of White leagues and organizers through interracial competition in connection with the barnstorming tours of Black teams. The National Basketball League, a forerunner of the National Basketball Association, became the first major professional basketball league of the modern era to allow Black basketball players to play in 1942, with two teams integrating their rosters that season. Integrated rosters expanded until the league's final season in 1948-49.

The success of Black players in the National Basketball League smoothed the integration of the National Basketball Association, created in 1949–50 through the merger of the Basketball Association of America and the National Basketball League. The new league integrated its teams the next year, with Black players joining four teams. Earl Lloyd became the first Black player to play in an NBA game on October 31, 1950.[173]

Professional football, born in the 1890s, came to maturity under the leadership of George Halas, principal founder of the National Football League. In contrast with the situation in baseball, efforts to develop the equivalent of the Negro Leagues were unsuccessful. However, college teams did not totally exclude Blacks; so, in theory at least, this was a potential route of entry into the professional game. Fritz Pollard was one of the early pioneers, becoming one of only two Black players in the American Professional Football Association in 1920, which later became the National Football League. Unfortunately, many African Americans who achieved stardom in college football were never given a chance to play in the NFL. Blacks organized their own professional teams and leagues. The most successful team was the New York Brown Bombers. Black teams existed in many cities, but talented players were overlooked or shunned by NFL owners until 1946. The NFL remained segregated until 1946, when Kenny Washington and Woody Strode played for the Los Angeles Rams. At the same time, Bill Willis and Marion Motley played for the Cleveland Browns of the then All America Football Conference (AAFC), one of the two leagues created in 1944 to compete with the NFL.[174]

The Black press considered the desegregation of professional football one of the top stories of 1946; only the debut of Jackie Robinson with the Montreal Royals was regarded as more important in the sports field. The success of the Cleveland Browns, on the field and at the gate, led to the desegregation of other AAFC teams. However, with the exception of the Detroit Lions who signed two Blacks in 1948, NFL owners did not actively pursue Black players until the early 1950s. With the collapse of the AAFC in 1950, the NFL added new teams, including the Browns. Cleveland's success in the NFL led many NFL owners gradually to add Black players.[175]

Even though desegregation of professional sports has produced visible and significant opportunities for Black athletes, it is also important to understand how the desegregation process disrupted social capital creation in Black communities. The current demographic representation profile of Black athletes is very different than existed during either the Jim Crow segregation era or the early years of desegregation. At the professional level, as is evident from the data in Table 4.24, Blacks dominate the NBA, NFL, and WNBA rosters. The representation rate in both sports was relatively stable throughout the 1990s. In contrast, the proportion of Black players has been declining in major league baseball, while Latinos account for over 25 percent of all players.

TABLE 4.24
RACIAL COMPOSITION OF SELECTED PROFESSIONAL SPORTS TEAMS PERCENTAGES
Selected Years

Season	NBA	NFL	MLB	WNBA
2009–10				
White	18	30	62	20
Black	77	67	9	67
Latino	3	1	27	0
2005–06				
White	22	32	60	34
Black	73	66	8	63
Latino	3	<1	29	1
1999–2000				
White	22	32	60	32
Black	78	67	13	64
Latino	<1	<1	26	2
1995–1996				
White	20	31	62	
Black	80	67	17	
Latino	0	0	20	
1989–1990				
White	25	40	70	
Black	75	60	17	
Latino	0	0	13	

Source: Racial and Gender Report Card, Various years.
http://www.tidesport.org/racialgenderreportcard.html

Stacking, or positional segregation, has been a traditional concern in examining racial representation patterns in football and baseball. In the past, it has been argued that positions presumably requiring greater intelligence have an overrepresentation of Whites, while

Blacks disproportionately fill positions where speed and reactive ability are highly valued. In football, the primary "thinking" position is the quarterback, while "skill" positions—that is, running back, wide receiver, cornerback, and safety—have been overpopulated by Blacks. Pitchers and catchers are the primary "thinking" positions in baseball, while speed and reactive ability are crucial for outfielders.

Many observers agree that stacking has declined as a concern in the NFL as the number of Black quarterbacks has increased, although Blacks still dominate the skill positions. However, stacking is still a concern in major league baseball, as Blacks accounted for only 3 percent of pitchers and 1 percent of catchers in 2002. The percentage of African American pitchers in 2002 was less than one-half of what it was in 1983.

While, in general, concern about Black representation in the playing ranks of professional teams has been declining, the same cannot be said about coaching positions. The absence of minority coaches is such an important issue to the NFL that they have designed a program to ensure the availability of quality coaches of color. The Minority Coaching Fellowship Program was established in 1987 to prepare minority coaches for potential employment as full-time NFL assistant coaches. All NFL teams participated in the program in 2000, and, since its creation, more than five hundred coaches have gone through the training camps.

Although the position of head coach is the most visible symbolic management position, it is necessary to examine employment patterns more broadly. The most comprehensive information available is contained in the annual "Racial & Gender Report Card" issued by the Institute for Diversity and Ethics in Sport and the DeVos Sport Business Management Program at the University of Central Florida. This is a comprehensive research document that analyzes the practice of hiring women and people of color in the NBA, NFL, Major League Baseball, Major League Soccer, the WNBA, the NCAA and its member institutions. A weighted letter grade is generated separately for race and gender inclusion, as well as for a combined score. Table 4.25 presents the grades for race inclusion for 2010 for the various sports organizations. The grades indicate ongoing improvement in all sports organizations. However, while progress is occurring, it is not yet sufficient to transform itself into the social-equalizing and apolitical institution it is purported to be.

TABLE 4.25

ASSESSMENT OF PROGRESS IN ACHIEVING RACIAL EQUITY
Selected Professional Sports

Sport	Grade
WNBA	A
NBA	A
NCAA	B
MLB	A
MLS	A
NFL	A

Source: Racial & Gender Report Card, 2010
http://www.tidesport.org/racialgenderreportcard.html

The penultimate issue associated with the examination of racial equity in professional sports is the ownership of franchises, which remained, until the recent purchase of the NBA's new Charlotte franchise in 2003 by Black Entertainment Television founder and CEO Robert Johnson, an all-White exclusive club. Even as more progress will undoubtedly be witnessed in all the problem areas discussed above, it is important to keep in mind that sports management participation and ownership are not panaceas that can engender collective upward social mobility of African Americans. Underneath the media-hype, cheering, and gladiatorial atmosphere of sports events lie the social maladies of racism, discrimination, and inequality that afflict the broader society. It is in this context that a detailed examination of sports at the intercollegiate and interscholastic levels is necessary.

Intercollegiate and Interscholastic Athletics

The dominant historical role of HBCUs in educating Black collegians was naturally replicated in intercollegiate athletics. In the face of racial segregation and discrimination, African Americans established their own athletic organizations and programs. In 1893, Tuskegee Institute (now Tuskegee University) in Alabama held the first major Black track and field meet in the country. The Central Intercollegiate Athletic Association (CIAA), founded in 1912 and now comprising twelve historically Black colleges and universities, was the only major collegiate conference to hold regular track and field meets for athletes at predominantly Black colleges and universities for nearly 20 years.[176]

The CIAA initiated a basketball tournament in 1946. Then North Carolina College coach John

McClendon was a major figure who invented the half-court press, the Four Corners offense, and the fast break.[177] The first Black college football game took place in North Carolina in 1892, when Biddle College defeated Livingston College. Although, intercollegiate football was racially integrated in the 1890s (in the North), in general, African American football players were not welcome on White campuses until the late 1950s, and not until the late 1960s in the Deep South. Jim Crow segregation forced the development of separate teams and leagues for Black players. Thereafter, Black college football became a major social event on campus that brought students and alumni together.[178]

The self-controlled and high-quality social capital formation processes associated with these self-organized ventures would be greatly disrupted by the desegregation of intercollegiate athletics. In the case of basketball, as far back as the early twentieth century, African Americans had played on basketball teams at some predominantly White colleges, including Harvard, Amherst, Oberlin, and Ohio Wesleyan. However, these early Black athletes often came from middle-class families in the North. Team captain George Gregory Jr., led Columbia University to the league title in 1930–31 and became the first African American named to an All-America team. Notable players at White colleges during the next two decades included Jackie Robinson and Don Barksdale of UCLA, Bill Russell at the University of San Francisco, and Wilt Chamberlain at the University of Kansas.[179]

In 1950, City College of New York became the first NCAA Champion with three African Americans in the starting lineup. Oscar Robertson achieved national stardom between 1958 and 1960 at the University of Cincinnati by becoming the first African American to be a three-time Player of the Year. For the first time, during the 1966 NCAA Championship game, an all-Black starting five defeated an all-White starting five when Texas Western defeated Kentucky. This event began to convince predominately White schools that recruiting more Black players in the future was essential.[180]

Although coaches and college administrators at many White institutions were initially reluctant to recruit more Black athletes, particularly those from working and lower-class backgrounds, the dexterity and skill of African American basketball players led to gradual acceptance of Black athletes on White school teams and aggressive recruitment efforts. Blacks who competed successfully on White teams had to be, demonstrably and unequivocally, better or superior in athletic ability and performance than their White teammates.

The same reality confronted Black football players at predominantly White colleges during the era of segregation. Black athletes played at various predominantly White schools in the early twentieth century, but Blacks had to have extraordinary ability and a serene temperament to play for desegregated college teams. Although there were a few exceptions, southern colleges usually refused to play against desegregated teams. Consequently, Blacks were often benched, or games were cancelled in the 1930s.[181]

By 1960, some of the most racist southern universities found themselves on the losing sides of battles with integrated teams. Such schools included the all-White University of Alabama, whose head coach swore he would never let a Black man play on his team. However, by 1971, even the University of Alabama had capitulated. By 1970, there was already a disproportionate number of Blacks playing on racially integrated football teams in the South.[182]

The integration of college and professional sports in the U.S. went hand in hand with the Black assertiveness that began during World War II. The influence of the Black Power Movement on some Black athletes was dramatically demonstrated at the 1968 Olympics in Mexico City, where John Carlos and Tommy Smith raised their Black-gloved fists and bowed their heads solemnly while the U.S. National Anthem was played during the medal ceremonies. Most Americans reacted extremely negatively to this adamant, though brief, gesture, and the two men and others presumed to have conspired with them suffered discrimination after the 1968 Olympics and had disproportionate difficulty finding good jobs.

This protest was, in fact, a well-planned initiative of the Olympic Project for Human Rights (OPHR), organized by sociologist Harry Edwards. The project focused on the linkages between athletes and the community circumstances in which they were socialized. It was an effort to link up with the broader Civil Rights Movement and challenge the myth that sports was a venue dominated by brotherhood and harmony. The media only focused on the raised fists, but the whole pose—including bowed heads and shoelessness—was intended as a statement about the poor conditions of Black people in the United States. Participants Tommie Smith and John Carlos had, in fact, been involved in organizing the Black Student Union and the Black Studies program at San Jose State long before the Olympic Project for Human Rights.[183]

Although Black males are disproportionately represented on collegiate football and basketball teams, their limited presence in other sports dramatically reduces the overall degree of sports overrepresentation. The information in Table 4.26 provides a snapshot of participation rates for Black and White males and females in 2000, 2005, and 2009. Statistical profiles are provided for all athletes participating in inter-collegiate sports at Division I, II, and III institutions—Division III schools do not offer athletic scholarships.

The data confirm Black male and female overrepresentation on athletic teams at Division I and II institutions, although overrepresentation of Black men is significantly higher. The overrepresentation of Black males declines significantly at Division III schools and Black women are not over-represented at these institutions.

TABLE 4.26
PERCENTAGE REPRESENTATION OF BLACKS AND WHITES AMONG INTER-COLLEGIATE ATHLETES DIVISION I,II, AND III
2000, 2005, and 2009

Race/ Gender	Division I			Division II			Division III		
	2000	2005	2009	2000	2005	2009	2000	2005	2009
Black Men	22.9	24.8	24.8	19.3	22.3	24.5	7.6	8.9	9.1
White Men	64.4	62.2	63.8	70.0	66.6	64.7	80.1	82.5	82.1
Black Women	13.8	15.4	16.0	10.6	12.1	13.9	4.2	5.1	5.1
White Women	72.6	70.5	71.3	79.9	76.7	75.1	83.1	85.9	86.2

Source: Student-Athlete NCAA Student-Athlete Ethnicity Report 1999-2000 – 2008-09 http://www.ncaapublications.com/productdownloads/SAEREP10.pdf

As suggested previously, critics charge that as the economic value of athletics has increased, concerns about the academic performance and long-term well-being of Black, and sometimes White, student athletes are often relegated to secondary importance. Allegations directed at universities include disregard for traditional academic requirements and standards in recruiting high-risk Black student athletes, special arrangements for class attendance and course selection to keep marginal students eligible, and tracking into "Mickey Mouse" and nondegree courses to facilitate practice schedules and absenteeism due to travel requirements. In addition, even in recent years, several major college

athletic programs have been fined, or otherwise sanctioned, for paying "out-of-pocket" money or providing gifts to satisfy the needs of some Black athletes. Black athletes often unwittingly participate in these unethical exploitative practices because of the lure and prospect of becoming a famous and wealthy professional sports figure.

Both critics and institutions use graduation rates as a means to adjudicate the charges and denials of the exploitation of Black athletes. Tables 4.27 and 4.28 below provide time series graduation rate data for Black and White males and Black and White females respectively at Division I schools. The data allow a comparison of the graduation rates for student cohorts six years after first entering college for athletes and for all students (non-athletes and athletes). Graduation rates for Black male, Black female, and White female athletes are higher than for their non-athlete peers. This is not the case for White male athletes. Black male athletes have experienced significant relative improvement in graduation rates relative to all Black male students, and White male athletes and White male non-athletes. A similar pattern has been manifested for Black female athletes. Notably, the graduation rates for both Black female athletes and non-athletes are substantially higher than for their Black male counterparts.

TABLE 4.27
SIX-YEAR GRADUATION RATES FOR BLACK AND WHITE MALE ATHLETES AND ALL BLACK AND WHITE MALE STUDENTS COHORTS ENTERING COLLEGE
Selected Years, 1985-2005 (Percent Graduating)

Year Entering	Black Male Athletes	Black Male Students	White Male Athletes	White Male Students
2005	49	39	69	66
2002	49	38	62	62
1995	43	34	59	59
1990	43	33	57	57
1985	34	30	55	55

Source 2003 Graduation Rates Report for NCAA Division I Schools and "NCAA Research Related to Graduation Rates of Division I Student-Athletes," 1984-2002, November 2009; NCAA Research Staff, "Trends in Graduation-Success Rates and Federal Graduation Rates at NCAA Division I Institutions NCAA," (October 2012). http://www.ncaa.org/wps/wcm/connect/public/ncaa/pdfs/2012/D1GsrFgrTrendsPdf

Differences in the graduation rates of Black and White male and female athletes have declined sharply and much faster than for non-athletes.

Even though the data presented may assuage some of the traditional concerns about the disproportionate exploitation of Black athletes, they certainly underscore the concerns raised earlier in the chapter about the overall status of Blacks in higher education. Although the basis for traditional concerns about the treatment of Black athletes has eroded somewhat and there is no question that participation in intercollegiate sports has provided thousands of underprivileged Blacks an opportunity to attend college, the differential graduation "success" of athletes may inappropriately reinforce beliefs that athletics is a relatively easy route to college completion. Moreover, there is little general understanding among would-be superstars about the astronomical odds against success in the professional ranks or in moving into coaching positions.

TABLE 4.28
SIX-YEAR GRADUATION RATES FOR BLACK AND WHITE FEMALE ATHLETES AND ALL BLACK AND WHITE FEMALE STUDENTS COHORTS ENTERING COLLEGE
Selected Years, 1985-2005 (Percent Graduating)

Year Entering	Black Male Athletes	Black Male Students	White Male Athletes	White Male Students
2005	64	48	75	67
2002	63	49	74	67
1995	60	45	72	64
1990	59	42	70	61
1985	44	36	65	58

Source 2003 Graduation-Rates Report for NCAA Division I Schools and "NCAA Research Related to Graduation Rates of Division I Student-Athletes," 1984-2002, November 2009; NCAA Research Staff, "Trends in Graduation-Success Rates and Federal Graduation Rates at NCAA Division I Institutions NCAA," (October 2012). http://www.ncaa.org/wps/wcm/connect/public/ncaa/pdfs/2012/D1GsrFgrTrendsPdf

Black athletes face enormous obstacles in obtaining positions in the coaching, managing, and executive ranks at colleges and universities as well as in professional sports. As noted by Harry Edwards, Black athletes who graduate with marginal skills, who do not graduate at all, or even who play successfully professionally, have limited likelihood of moving into coaching positions.

Few social theorists recommend that African American youth be discouraged from sports participation. Many of those who have successfully managed athletic and academic careers have made significant and enduring contributions toward the development and uplift of the Black community. Certainly, African American youth should have the option or opportunity to pursue a career in sports, in addition to having access to the scientific, medical, legal, academic, technical or vocational professions; however, contributions to social capital should be a primary concern that informs the guidance provided to young, impressionable Black males and females.

There is no question that the celebrity status of some high-profile athletes is inducing mimicry and adulation among younger fans, as evidenced, for example, by the popularity of urban attire sponsored by athletes. Cultural behaviors originating in inner-city neighborhoods are transforming the ethos of professional sports. From the vantage point of owners, there are often negative consequences, such as the negative publicity associated with various encounters between players and law enforcement agencies.

For a variety of reasons, professional football has been more successful than professional basketball in slowing this transformation process. As noted previously, Blacks do not dominate the football rosters as overwhelmingly as is the case in basketball. Of course, there is no question that Black players have set the bar in conceiving the exuberant end zone exhibitions of gleeful triumph that have replaced the reserved modesty once thought appropriate for gridiron heroes. However, football uniforms and the nature of the game limit exhibitionist opportunities, and fines have proved to be an effective deterrent because, in many cases—except for star athletes—there is a pool of players available to replace offenders.

In contrast, the influence of coaches on basketball players is declining as more players move directly from high school into the professional ranks and miss even the limited exposure to discipline required in the college game. The negative outcomes accompanying the deepening impact of Black athletes on professional football and basketball are tolerated, not only because of the players' centrality to competitive success, but also because they generate tremendous revenues by marketing sports attire and athletic footwear.[184]

It is not at all clear that the growing influence of Black urban culture in professional basketball and football has positive feedback effects on social capital creation in Black communities. As noted by Harry Edwards, "Today's black athlete is very different. Their identity is different—they live in a rich, largely White world, a world where black individuality is tolerated so long as it is without reference to the black community. If you asked them about the history of the black athlete, many couldn't tell you much. They don't find that history relevant to their world. Some even get angry when you ask them about it ... And the worse part about it is not that they are ignorant of this history, but they are militantly ignorant. The sad part about it is that when people forget how things came about, they are almost certainly doomed to see them go. And I think that is where this generation of black athletes may be headed in sports."[185] The pattern Edwards describes is a serious concern to Africana Studies scholar/activists.

Pro- and Anti-Social Youth and Young Adult Collectives

As noted previously, Du Bois believed that inter-generational transmission of knowledge, values, and beliefs is essential for a group to develop over time and enable it to adapt effectively to changing circumstances. In African American communities, this process has always involved the challenge of balancing various internal and external socializing influences. In the preceding sections of this chapter, we have discussed the historical and contemporary role of selected institutions within communities that serve this purpose, specifically, families and religious institutions. We have also examined the socializing influences that were at one time primarily community-controlled but are now largely externally controlled, such as, formal education and sports. In all cases, such institutions are typically organized and managed by representatives of older generations. There are legitimate questions about whether traditional designs are adequate for addressing the contemporary challenges facing younger African Americans. More generally, African Americans Studies specialists are very concerned that the connections among older and younger cohorts of African Americans that facilitate the transfer of knowledge, values, and social commitment are weakening and are being supplanted by external influences, such as, mass media and peer socialization practices that disrupt communities. The negative effects of weakened intergenerational ties span the socioeconomic spectrum. These issues are explored by examining youth collectives that involve both upwardly mobile and marginalized Black youth and young adults.

Black Greek-Letter Organizations (BGLOs)

For over a century, Black Greek-Letter Organizations (BGLOs), Black fraternities and sororities based in colleges and universities, have played a vital role in cultivating the leadership that has enabled African Americans to continue the struggle for freedom and justice. As Gloria Harper Dickinson observes, the founders of the first eight Black Greek- Letter Organizations were scholar-activists slightly more than one generation removed from slavery.[186] Dickinson suggests that the two factors which influenced the decision to establish these organizations were the tradition of organizing for the "good of the race" and "a naming pattern that overtly affirmed the connection between black North American institutions, organizations, and people and their African ancestry."[187] The strong initial commitment to social uplift championed by BGLOs contrasts strongly with the primarily social focus of White fraternities and sororities. The uplift value has been perpetuated through graduate chapters that continue affiliation beyond the undergraduate period by engaging in various service projects that contribute to community well-being.

The differences in orientation between Black and White fraternities and sororities reflect, in part, the perpetuation of a long tradition that dates back to traditional African societies and the early communal organizations established by free Blacks in the U.S. Asa Hilliard suggests that the pledge rituals associated with BGLOs bear strong similarities to the "Mystery Schools" of ancient Egypt and the initiation systems of West Africa.[188] The first rituals adopted by BGLOs were influenced by African-inspired Masonic rituals and practices. Dickinson also informs us that "the counter-clockwise circular movement, percussion, calls, chants, call-response, ritualistic garb, and performance styles that later became synonymous with BGLOs all had African precedents."[189] In addition, the branding practiced by some BGLOs reflects scarification and tattooing practices found among many African groups.

There are five fraternities and four sororities distinguished as the "Divine Nine" comprising the National Pan Hellenic Council. Alpha Phi Alpha, established at Cornell University in 1906, was the first national collegiate fraternity BGLO. Kappa Alpha Psi, established at Indiana University in 1911, was the second Black fraternity. Two Black fraternities were subsequently established at Howard University: Omega Psi Phi (1911) and Phi Beta Sigma (1914). Iota Phi Theta was formed at Morgan State University in 1963. Three of the four Black collegiate sororities belonging to the NPHC were founded at Howard University: Alpha Kappa Alpha (1908); Delta Sigma Theta (1913); and Zeta Phi Beta

(1920). The fourth, Sigma Gamma Rho, was established at Butler University in 1922.[190] Efforts to establish collegiate BGLOs preceded the formation of national bodies, including Alpha Kappa Nu at Indiana University in 1903 and Gamma Phi at Wilberforce University in 1905.[191]

There are also "sweetheart" programs associated with fraternities that are not considered Greek but have names that reflect affiliation with specific fraternities, for example, Alpha Angels, Kappa Sweethearts, Que Pearls, Sigma Doves, and Iota Sweethearts. These organizations typically perform activities traditionally associated with women and are comparable to the roles performed by women's auxiliary groups in churches and other organizations, such as, hosting parties and fundraising. Critics of such entities regard them as exploitative and patriarchal. However, these auxiliaries were very popular in the 1960s and 1970s, but the national leadership of Black fraternities has discouraged continuation of sweetheart organizations since the 1990s.[192]

The impressive list of prominent leaders who belong to BGLOs speaks to the significance of fraternities and sororities as critical socializing agents. Focusing on the original eight BGLOs, Alpha Phi Alpha's alumni include W. E. B. Du Bois, Martin Luther King, Jr., Thurgood Marshall, Jesse Owens, Adam Clayton Powell, Jr., and Paul Robeson. Alpha Kappa Alpha's famous alumnae include Marian Anderson, Ella Fitzgerald, Coretta Scott King, and Rosa Parks. Ralph Abernathy, Horace Mann Bond, Daniel "Chappie" James, Jr., Arthur Schomburg, and Leon Sullivan are among the prestigious alumni of Kappa Alpha Psi. Omega Psi Phi has contributed, among other outstanding leaders, Benjamin Hooks, Jesse Jackson, Vernon Jordan, Ernest Just, and Roy Wilkins. The alumnae of Delta Sigma Theta include Elizabeth Catlett, Shirley Chisholm, Ruby Dee Davis, Dorothy Height, and Mary Church Terrell. The noteworthy group of Phi Beta Sigma alumni includes George Washington Carver, James Weldon Johnson, Alain Locke, Huey P. Newton, Kwame Nkrumah, A. Philip Randolph, and Harold Washington. Hattie McDaniel, Rev. Willie T. Barrow, and Cathy Hughes are a few of the many prominent alumnae of Sigma Gamma Rho. Zeta Phi Beta's prominent members include Gwendolyn Brooks, Zora Neale Hurston, Madame C.J. Walker, and Sarah Vaughn.[193]

Although BGLOs have obviously provided strong leadership for Black communities as well as important venues for networking and social activities on college campuses, they have been subjected to several criticisms. Tamara Brown, et al., observe that "for all the good they have accomplished, BGLOs have not escaped the structural racism in this country unscathed. Like other African American individuals and institutions, they have struggled with the problems of elitism, colorism, and violence; with how to develop an identity that affirms their African heritage despite messages and images of a savage and uncivilized African continent; and with many other problems endemic to having been formed in a racist U.S. society."[194]

Traditionally, many BGLO social activities were designed to cultivate White middle-class values and, particularly, in the case of sororities, some women were excluded from membership based on physical appearance, including skin pigmentation, hair texture, and socioeconomic background. In the context of African American Studies, one of the more interesting research findings is that sorority membership appears to contribute positively to Black identity development, while the same is not the case for fraternity membership. This issue is related to another raised by Tamara Brown, et al., namely, whether BGLOs have lost their momentum and focus vis-à-vis racial uplift over time, "particularly in light of the new membership intake process, racial integration, and the changing educational, economic, social, and political participation of African Americans in U.S. Society." [195]

There are also concerns about the extent to which membership in BGLOs has negative effects on academic performance. Some studies have found positive impacts of BGLO membership on college adjustment, cognitive skill development, and extramural participation. However, despite these positive outcomes, BGLOs typically perform very poorly academically compared with White fraternities and sororities at the same institution.[196]

The most damning criticism leveled at BGLOs, particularly fraternities, focuses on the violence practiced in pledging, hazing, and initiation that has led to several high profile deaths. According to Ricky Jones, these practices reflect a deeper problem: "For the black man, violence and struggle have become reified as tools for acquiring social rewards. They have become achievements in and of themselves because everything else seems to have failed."[197] Although pledging and initiation processes have been revised, the traditional practices persist underground. This is the context in which Jones uses the term educated gangs to characterize violent behavior within Black fraternities and maintains that "very little difference is found in the gang practice of new members being 'beaten in' and the physical hazing that BGFs [Black Greek Fraternities] employ."[198]

This perspective is shared by Deborah Prothrow-Stith who suggests that "from a developmental perspective ... anti-social groups such as youth gangs and pro-social groups such as fraternities have a great deal in common. Both kinds of associations exist to provide members with an interim emotional base, one that gives substance to the ambiguity the adolescent feels when he is between the dependency of childhood and the independence of adulthood."[199]

The recognition that important parallels exist between BGLOs and gangs informs African American Studies perspectives on socializing and empowering youth. These parallels compel us to pursue comprehensive approaches to youth socialization that require as nuanced an understanding of gangs as we have of BGLOs.

Black Gangs

It may seem strange to treat Black gangs as a social institution. However, these collectives permeate many Black communities, affect the quality of life of all residents, and significantly influence the socialization of a large proportion of young Blacks. Various studies provide a wealth of evidence about the negative effects of gangs via drugs, dysfunctional sexual relations, and other criminal activity on the social and economic stability of Black communities. However, it is imperative to identify strategies to mobilize the potential for such collectives to contribute to the accumulation and use of social capital to support community liberation and uplift efforts and to reduce dysfunctional behaviors. In addition, these collectives function in part as alternative sources of identification to schools and athletic activities, as discussed previously, and the interests of African American Studies require that the forces that make gangs a preferred option relative to more traditional adolescent activities be examined in some detail.

Although the majority of young people do not belong to gangs, gang members often have a strongly felt presence in schools and neighborhoods because of the aura of actual and potential violent actions. Across all area types (urban, suburban, rural), most gang members are African American and/or Latino. While males dominate gangs, in 2007 6.6 percent of gang members were female. Table 4.29 details the demographic composition of gangs for selected years. The most recent data indicate that the proportion of gang members comprised of

African Americans is declining, while the representation of other groups is increasing.

TABLE 4.29
RACE/ETHNICITY OF GANG MEMBERS
Selected Years, 1996 – 2008

Race/Ethnicity of Gang Members	1996	1999	2002	2004	2006	2008
Black or African American	35.6	30.9	35.7	37.8	35.2	31.8
Hispanic or Latino	45.2	47.3	47.0	48.7	49.5	50.2
White	11.6	13.4	10.4	7.9	8.5	10.5
All Other	7.5	8.4	6.9	5.7	6.8	7.6

Source: National Youth Gang Center, National Youth Gang Survey Analysis. http://www.nationalgangcenter.gov/Survey-Analysis/Demographics.

Gangs often evolve from informal groups whose members have a common experience of being marginalized from more conventional adolescent experiences. Members of gangs tend to be low academic achievers who perceive that they have few "legitimate" opportunities. Gangs fulfill a variety of psychological/emotional functions that include serving as an interim emotional base during the transition from childhood dependency to adult independence; satisfying the need to belong to a group separate from families; and providing goals, a worldview, and a place to feel valued. Like BGLOs, gangs incorporate rituals that help define the group and the individual's place in the group, and both demonstrate membership by wearing identifiable colors, symbols, or clothing.[200]

When young males come together as a gang, the group enables them to commit acts of violence and other antisocial behavior that the individual members might not commit on their own.[201] In fact, the threat of violence from outside groups is often the catalyst that leads to the transformation of a relatively innocuous neighborhood group into a gang. Many gangs need outside threats to define themselves. Scott Decker argues that territorial gangs, in particular, cohere around the presence of (or potential presence of) rival gang members on their "turf." Threats from another gang or other groups (like the police) build cohesiveness and attract new members.[202]

Much gang violence takes the form of retaliation. Both the threat of retaliation from other gangs and the obligation to make good on their own threats to react violently if attacked increases the likelihood of violence. Decker argues that to stave off the threat from a rival gang, gang members try to arm themselves with more dangerous and more sophisticated weapons, and thereby create the neighborhood equivalent of an "arms race." When gang members engage in violent behavior, they create a protective aura shielding them from other gangs and nongang groups and individuals. The common knowledge that gang members are willing and able to respond with deadly violence increases their social isolation from community residents who fear potential victimization. The increased separation further increases the likelihood of antisocial behavior.[203]

Even though the problem of gang violence in Black communities is one of the major sources of social instability, Prothrow-Stith argues that the media presents a distorted view of youth gangs, and that gangs are not all territorial, drug-selling groups of youth who are intensely violent at some points and quiet at other times. Available data indicate that only about one in seven gang members are involved in the drug trade.[204]

There are actually three different types of gangs, each with distinctive characteristics. Scavenger gangs, prone to erratic behavior and to engage in violence on a random, unplanned basis, are the least organized and least "successful" gangs. Territorial gangs, as described by Decker, are also known as fighting gangs. They are turf-loyal and highly organized, with elaborate initiation rituals and other traditions and practices that set them off from nonmembers. They often wear clothing that identifies them as gang members—their "colors." Fighting is a major activity of territorial gangs and gives gang members a chance to prove themselves and increase their stature within the gang. The primary purpose of territorial gangs is social, not economic; and, although some sell drugs, many do not. In contrast, corporate gangs, also known as crews, are highly organized criminal conspiracies set up to sell drugs at maximum profit. Turf, colors, and other symbols that are important for other kinds of gangs are not relevant for corporate gangs. Instead, discipline, secrecy, and a strict code of behavior are expected of every member, and punishment for mistakes can be extreme. Even though members of corporate gangs may not be well educated, they are often highly intelligent, and leaders must be capable of strategic planning, personnel management, and money management.[205] The belief that gangs evolve over time into more highly organized and dangerous entities has been challenged by Prothrow-Stith. She argues, in particular, that the common stereotype of territorial gangs often "upgrading" to corporate gangs is invalid.[206]

Most research conducted on gangs has focused on gangs in poor neighborhoods. However, Mary Pattillo's study of a gang operating in a middle-class Chicago neighborhood provides useful insights into how such collectives might be mobilized and reoriented to enhance rather than deplete social capital.[207] As noted previously, Black middle-class neighborhoods have higher internal poverty rates and are closer to high-poverty and high-crime areas than White middle-class neighborhoods. This fact presents particular challenges to residents' efforts to keep the neighborhood safe and stable. Mary Pattillo describes how gang members in a middle-class Black community cooperate with law-abiding residents to keep crime down. She found that gang members were long-time residents who had strong ties in the community. Most gang members were the sons, grandsons, or friends of other neighborhood residents. The gang controlled specific community resources, such as local parks, and managed them in ways that fostered stability. Community members perceived that gang members generally behaved civilly, discouraged fighting, and avoided excessive use of profanity. Although engaged in criminal activity themselves, gang members provided oversight to ensure that crime did not spiral out of control in their neighborhood.[208]

Pattillo also found that gang members seemed to share many of the basic values of the law-abiding residents of the neighborhood. Gang members approached their drug involvement in a manner very similar to the way in which law-abiding neighbors related to their "middle-class" jobs. Gang members were not petty pushers but occupied a middle rung in the trade by obtaining drugs from higher-ups and selling them to street dealers. Like law-abiding residents, gang members wanted to get ahead in their industry and be able to provide for their families. Pattillo reports members were taught to be successful and passed on those "middle-class orientations" to their children.[209]

The problem for many law-abiding middle-class Blacks, then, is how to relate to gangs that share many of the same ultimate goals for protecting the neighborhood as they do. Since even the gang members contribute, in their own way, to the shared community goals of security and stability, it is very difficult to reject their efforts. At the same time, gang involvement fuels the astronomical incarceration rates discussed previously, forestalls educational attainment and occupational mobility, and has adverse consequences for family formation and functioning. Whereas gang-related violence had been declining in the second half of the 1990s, in many cities, gang-related violence, fueled by a weak economy and the release of large numbers of gang members from prison, has escalated to the highest levels since the early 1990s.

Ironically, although some BGLOs have strayed from their founding ideologies, an evolving "Thug Life" ideology has been adopted by some gangs, as well as non-gang affiliated youth, in response to their marginalization from traditional avenues of empowerment. The late Tupac Shakur originated the concept of Thug Life with an acronym for the phrase, "The Hate You Gave Little Infants Fucks Everybody."[210]

The codes of Thug Life were designed to give order to the rise of gang violence and drug dealing and were signed by the heads of the Bloods and Cripps at a peace treaty picnic called the Truce Picnic in California in 1992. Paradoxically, the code defined certain illegal acts as unacceptable, but endorsed others. For example, the code prohibits neighborhood carjacking, drug sales in schools, and using children to sell drugs. It also prohibits snitching to authorities. The code also promotes various pro-social values and behaviors, including prohibition against rape and protection of the elderly. Although this code is regularly violated in Black communities, it might serve as a starting point for reshaping the socialization of gangs.

In approaching these issues, it may be possible to adapt some of the strategies used by various organizations to attract Black youth that continue to subscribe to nation-building ideologies. The Five Percent Nation, also known as the Nation of Gods and Earths, founded by Clarence Jowars Smith or Clarence 13X around 1964 is one example. The original meaning of the five percent is derived from one of the teachings of the Nation of Islam—that five percent of the population, called poor righteous teachers, will be called on to save the rest of humanity. The Five-Percenter doctrine holds that the Original Blackman is God, the Original Blackwoman is the planet Earth, and through the inner powers of the Gods and Earths, youth can be transformed and defeat oppressive powers. Every man, regardless of race, is defined as a God, and, as a consequence, there is no leader, per se. Five-Percenters congregate at meetings, called parliaments, which usually occur in public venues. Several prominent artists, including Rakim, Wu-Tang Clan, Brand Nubian, Busta Rhymes, Jus Allah, and Poor Righteous Teachers have played prominent roles in spreading the Five-Percenter doctrine through their music. Coded language is used to convey core principles designed to create a common language and ethos for urban youth.[211]

The New Black Panthers or New Black Panther Party (NBPP) is another collective that has ties to the Nation of Islam and has attracted a significant following among Black youth. Formally known as the New Black Panther Party for Self-Defense, the organization was founded in Dallas, Texas, in 1989. It has no ties to the original Black Panther Party, and, in fact, has been repudiated by former leaders of the original party. The NBPP was headed by former Nation of Islam Minister Khalid Abdul Muhammad, from the late 1990s until 2001. The membership of the NBPP expanded significantly as many disaffected members of the Nation of Islam shifted their allegiance. The NBPP was the primary sponsor of three Million Youth Marches held in 1998, 1999, and 2000. The NBPP subscribes to the Nguzo Saba (Seven Principles), developed by Maulana Karenga, and its platform includes self-determination for Black people, full employment, reparations, decent housing, quality health, African-centered educational institutions, a halt to police harassment and brutality, and an end to the death penalty.[212]

Unlike the Five-Percenters and the NBPP, the New Afrikan People's Organization (NAPO) does not have strong historical ties to the Nation of Islam. The chairman and cofounder of NAPO is prominent human rights attorney Chokwe Lumumba, who is based in Mississippi. He has served as NAPO's chairperson since its inception in 1984 and was re-elected to the position in 2004. In January 2007, he was successful in gaining reinstatement to the American Bar after being suspended for his battle against racist practices in the state, which included police harassment of Blacks in Jackson, Mississippi. NAPO continues the legacy of the Republic of New Afrika, which sought to establish an independent Black nation in five southern states, a platform similar to the Nation of Islam's. Lumumba was a member of the Black Legion of the Republic of New Afrika, having joined that organization in 1969. NAPO currently sponsors a variety of community-based youth programs, anticrime patrols, political education forums, legal service clinics, and various other community service activities.[213]

Multiple strategies are required to deal with the gang problem. Initiatives must be undertaken to reduce the structural pressures that lead to gang formation. Interventions in the socialization of adolescents must be developed that alter patterns of collective identity development and create stronger ties to the community. Collaborative efforts across community institutions must also be strengthened to enhance the social capital available to foster community stability.

4

Socioeconomic Strata of African Americans

Blacks and the Dialectics of Class

In the examination of Black social institutions in the preceding sections, there has been evidence of variations in the social and economic circumstances of different segments of the population. Some of these differences are related to differences in family structure; some are due to differences in educational attainment; some reflect differences in values and socialization; while others, such as, participation in gangs, are heavily influenced by age. Most of these variations are the expected product of complex community structures, but African American Studies is especially interested in the impact of class differentiation on the creation of social capital. The importance of class schisms can be seen, for example, by the growing suburbanization of the Black middle class and the impacts of this exodus on the quality of life of Blacks who continue to reside in central cities. Class is difficult to define in cogent and precise terms in relation to human rankings or hierarchical stratifications. The classical debate between Karl Marx and Max Weber over the economic, social, or political determinants of class may not be wholly useful in analyzing the few strata that exist within the Black community. Class, like so many social terms of European origin, loses some of its generic intent when viewed from an African or Afrocentric frame of reference. Thus, culture and cultural experiences influence concepts and perspectives of class. The constant and conditional factors of race, racism, and color in the United States that affect African Americans complicate and obscure conventional concepts of class.

Black capitalists and millionaires are not fully exempt from the derogatory status White racism imposes on them. On the other hand, there are certain persons and professional or occupational groups that may be rated median or high, as similarly classified within White society. From an Afrocentric point of view, Black social organization must not always be studied or analyzed on a comparative basis *vis-à-vis* White society. Since equitable Black/White integration in American society is remote, and assimilation is largely a fantasy, African American Studies focuses on establishing culture-specific gradations of status and standards of reference. Class, status, and progress for African Americans cannot be measured or evaluated solely on the bases of White standards. Economic, educational, professional, or occupational achievements may be given different culture-related weights and values by Blacks in contrast with Whites. Moreover, in a racist society, more than income, education, and occupation affect class.

Oliver C. Cox, an African American sociologist, undertook a very comprehensive examination of class in *Caste, Class & Race*. Cox supports the thesis that the capitalist virtue of individualism is the basis of social class. The legacy of individual and family accumulated success and material wealth is the ideal that provides the ideological foundations for social class distinctions. African Americans are, inevitably, influenced by capitalist goals and ideology. However, Cox's differentiation of social class and political class suggests that Blacks, in opposition to racism, collectively form a political class structure regardless of social class divisions. This perspective conflicts with the theory that political class and social class are distinct phenomena.[214] In other words, class consolidation exists in the Black political struggle against White racism and oppression, but ordinarily solidarity may not be characteristic of Black social classes.

African American Studies focuses on two distinctive forces that influence the dynamics of class among African Americans—segregation and color consciousness. Inquiries in Africana Studies have been shaped by Du Bois's view that class divisions among African Americans prior to World War II were a relatively minor problem because of a racial caste system whereby "the Negro leaders are bound to their own group."[215] He saw the potential for a widening class division among African Americans after WW II, such that "when the whole caste structure finally does fall, Negroes will be divided into classes even more sharply than now, and the main mass will become a part of the working class of the nation and the world."[216]

The Black "Middle Class"

Bart Landry's *The New Black Middle Class* delineates and differentiates the old and new Black middle and upper class from that of White society.[217] The segment of the African American population that Landry describes as the "new" Black middle class started to develop after the U.S. Supreme Court's *Brown v. Board of Education* school desegregation decision in 1954 and mushroomed during the 1960s. Generally, they are a first generation middle class, the sons and daughters of factory, farm, and domestic workers of the segregation and separate-but-equal eras.

Sociologist William Julius Wilson theorizes that there is increasing potential for conflict between African American social classes because of economic differentials. Wilson posits that the Equal Employment Opportunity acts and Affirmative Action programs resulting from the Civil Rights Movement of the 1960s created an economic gulf between those Blacks who were educated and prepared to avail themselves of the new opportunities and those who could not because they were unprepared and unskilled. Following the 1960s, there was an unprecedented rise in the numbers of African Americans holding previously unattainable White-collar jobs and positions. Many Blacks moved into positions as mid-level corporate and government managers, academic and technical professionals, supervisors, clerks, and salespersons with incomes ranging well above the middle-income range at that time of $20,000. This change in the occupational distribution of Black workers created a new Black economic class less affected by traditional racism. This is the view underlying Wilson's analysis, as reflected in his book's title, *The Declining Significance of Race*.[218]

The problem in accepting Wilson's theory as wholly valid is that the economic status or advancement of African Americans has never exempted them from the insidious and socially regressive affects of racism. Racism is responsible for the creation of their opportunity for economic elevation. Furthermore, the "economic class" of Blacks that Wilson claims is immune from racism is still restricted in economic ascent by new forms of so-called subtle racism. Thus, the disadvantage of race or of being Black has been neither diminished nor eliminated, but middle-income and low-income Blacks are affected by racism in different ways. The Black common laborer may have to endure derogatory treatment and racial epithets from a White foreman. Conversely, the Black corporate mid-manager or clerical assistant may be racially or culturally ostracized and denied advancement opportunities. The Black underclass youth may have difficulty in getting a college education, but the Black college graduate may well be underemployed relative to her or his true potential. Nevertheless, various scholars, including Martin Kilson and Lois Benjamin, have described how the new Black middle class has more freedom than the old Black middle class in pursuing individual goals outside Black communities.[219] Although they themselves are still subject to "residual racism," they have been able to create psychic and physical distance from Blacks of lower socioeconomic status in ways that were not feasible in the era of Jim Crow segregation.

Not only drugs, but most of the nation's other social maladies derive from the capitalist, materialist, moral-relativist, and racist values of the broader society. The Black male problem is a product of such values. The focus on the Black male is characteristic of a preponderance of sociological studies that scrutinize lower-income or more disadvantaged strata of populations. It is not that the problems and conditions of the Black underclass should be ignored, but academic and political integrity demand a more balanced perspective. Thus, it is important to develop a familiarity with socioeconomic class variation among African Americans.

Consistent with the methodological tenets of African American Studies, it is useful to review the available data to explore the extent of divergence in the fortunes of the Black lower and middle classes. For present purposes, the discussion focuses exclusively on income, although in later chapters other factors such as occupation and wealth will be examined.

The Gini ratio (or index of income concentration) is a measure of income equality ranging from 0 to 1. A value of 1 indicates perfect inequality; that is, one person has all the income. A zero value indicates perfect equality, that is, all people have equal income shares. Thus, lower values indicate more equal distributions. Table 4.26 contains the Gini ratios for Black and White family income for selected years between 1966 and 2001.

Table 4.30 contains the Gini ratios for Black and White family income for selected years between 1970 and 2009 and document a continuing increase in income inequality for both Black and White families. Moreover, Black family income continues to be distributed more unevenly than White family income.

TABLE 4.30

GINI RATIOS FOR BLACK AND WHITE FAMILIES
Selected years, 1970-2009

YEAR	Black	White
2009	.469	.422
2005	.470	.420
2000	.442	.425
1995	.457	.409
1990	.445	.384
1985	.430	.378
1980	.410	.353
1975	.386	.349
1970	.388	.345

Source: U.S. Census Bureau, Historical Income Tables – Families http://www.census.gov/hhes/www/income/data/historical/families/f04.xls

A more detailed picture emerges when the share of income received by each fifth of the population is examined. The total number of families can be divided into five equal segments and the portion of total income received by each segment or quintile can be calculated. The results of such an analysis are presented in Table 4.31. The data show that the share of income received by the highest fifth, and especially the top five percent of Black families, has been increasing steadily at the expense of both the most disadvantaged and the Black middle class.

Who are these individuals and families that have made such extraordinary progress compared to other African Americans? Many are chief executive officers and other high-ranking corporate officers. In recent years, African Americans have been appointed to the top positions in several major corporations, including Merrill Lynch, American Express, Symantec, and AOL Time Warner. African Americans have also been appointed to high positions in Citigroup, Verizon, and General Electric, among others. There are also a number of media magnates, such as, Oprah Winfrey and Robert Johnson. Professional athletes and entertainers constitute a much larger group of individuals with exceptionally high earnings. Eugene Robinson argues that several of these figures have become a "transcendent elite," i.e., "a small but growing cohort with the kind of power, wealth, and influence that previous generations of African Americans could never have imagined."[220]

For affluent Blacks who do not qualify for Robinson's "transcendent" designation, however, the income advantage has not necessarily translated into a quality of life comparable to Whites with similar economic resources. The residential status of middle-class Black families is such that they have a much higher probability of neighborhood contact with persons in poverty, or near poverty, than Whites with comparable incomes. Douglas Massey and Nancy Denton argue that for Blacks, "high incomes do not buy entree to residential circumstances that can serve as springboards for future socioeconomic mobility."[221]

Richard Alba, John Logan, and Paul Bellair conclude, "even the most affluent blacks are not able to escape from crime, for they reside in communities as crime-prone as those housing the poorest whites."[222] From an analysis of 2010 data, John Logan reports that although affluent Blacks are less isolated than poor Blacks, affluent Blacks live in poorer neighborhoods than Whites with working class incomes in forty-eight of the fifty largest metropolitan areas.[223]

Home ownership has long been seen as a principal indicator of middle-class status. As can be seen from Table 4.32, the most recent housing boom resulted in a major increase in Black homeownership rates from 42.6 percent in 1994 to 49.4 percent in 2003. This increase reflects, in part, income gains experienced by many Blacks in the 1990s, along with housing policies designed to make home ownership more accessible for lower-income individuals. During this same period White homeownership rates increased from 70.2 percent to 75.5 percent. The impact of the ongoing housing crisis can be seen in the decline in the Black homeownership rate to 44.2 percent in 2010, while the White homeownership rate only fell to 74.2 percent.

The persisting disproportionate employment-related problems facing African Americans have contributed to disproportionate homeownership vulnerability in the wake of the ongoing housing crisis. Raul Ojeda of the UCLA North American Integration and Development Center found that, at the peak of the recent housing expansion, Black and Latino homeowners held high-cost mortgages between two and nine times the frequency of non-Hispanic Whites in high foreclosure regions. As a consequence, Black and Latino homeowners are at proportionately greater risk of defaulting on loans or vacating homes.[224] According to NeighborWorks America, African Americans currently account for a large percentage of homeowners suffering from the problem of foreclosure home auctions for sale in the U.S. In addition, African Americans have disproportionately sought counseling for foreclosure mitigation under the National Foreclosure Mitigation Counseling (NFMC) program. The NFMC has reported that among their clients holding mortgage loans with interest rates of eight percent or over, more than 35% are African Americans, even though only 20% of the country's subprime mortgages are held by African Americans.[225]

The problem of rising foreclosures among African Americans received heightened visibility when it was reported that the wealthiest predominantly Black county in the U.S., Prince George's County, Maryland, was experiencing a foreclosure crisis in 2011. In 2011, over half of the county's housing sales were properties in foreclosure.[226]

TABLE 4.31
SHARE OF AGGREGATE INCOME RECEIVED BY EACH FIFTH AND TOP 5 PERCENT OF BLACK FAMILIES:
Selected Years 1970 - 2009

Year	Lowest Fifth	Second Fifth	Third Fifth	Fourth Fifth	Highest Fifth	Top 5 Percent
2009	3.1	8.7	14.6	23.6	50.0	21.3
2005	3.0	8.6	14.6	23.7	50.0	20.7
2000	3.6	9.3	15.4	23.9	47.8	19.2
1995	3.3	8.7	15.2	24.1	48.7	20.0
1990	3.3	8.6	15.6	25.3	47.3	17.3
1985	3.7	9.1	15.7	25.2	46.3	16.8
1980	4.3	9.6	16.1	25.5	44.5	15.2
1975	4.9	10.2	16.8	25.3	42.8	14.7
1970	4.6	10.6	16.8	24.9	43.1	15.2

Source: U.S. Census Bureau, Historical Income Tables – Families. http://www.census.gov/hhes/www/income/data/historical/families/f02B.xls

TABLE 4.32
HOMEOWNERSHIP RATES OF BLACKS AND WHITES
Selected years (4th quarter) 1994 - 2010

YEAR	Black Homeownership Rate	White Homeownership Rate
1994	42.6	8.7
1997	45.1	71.9
2000	47.8	73.9
2003	49.4	75.5
2006	48.2	76.0
2008	46.8	74.8
2010	44.2	74.2

Source: Bureau of the Census, Current Population Survey/Housing Vacancy Survey, Series H-111, http://www.census.gov/hhes/www/housing/hvs/historic/files/histtab16.xls.

The paradoxes of Black middle-class status are heightened by the phenomenon of color-consciousness, which represents a potential barrier to the exercise of collective political and economic power. There is conflicting evidence regarding the extent to which this phenomenon continues to differentiate the life chances of lighter-skinned and darker-skinned Blacks. Several studies using data from the 1970 to 1982 period have found that lighter complexioned Blacks had advantages over darker-complexioned counterparts in terms of education, occupational prestige, and income. One study found that the family income of very light African Americans was more than 50 percent greater than that of very dark Blacks. Very light individuals were more likely to be employed as professionals and technical workers.[227] However, a recent study by Aaron Gullickson re-analyzes the previous data and takes into account the fact that skin tone may have a different effect on younger cohorts of African Americans than on older ones. This issue was not addressed adequately in previous studies. Gullickson concludes that, for persons born after 1940, there has been a significant decline in advantages associated with skin tone in educational and occupational attainment. He claims that "the decline was so dramatic that skin tone does not appear to have been relevant at all for cohorts born in the early 1960s."[228] He also finds that there was a further decline in the significance of color from the early 1980s until the early 1990s *vis-à-vis* occupational attainment. However, he cautions that "there has been no change in the importance of skin tone in the marriage market, where lighter skin still plays an important role in providing access to high quality spouses."[229] This phenomenon has permeated popular culture, both mainstream and Black-controlled, with lighter skinned-women disproportionately represented. This phenomenon, of course, parallels the growth in interracial marriages and relationships discussed previously. Another study assessing the role of skin-color differences in the Black community revealed that "while color stratification and differences persist in the Afro-American community, they make little difference in terms of the attitudinal configuration of Afro-American society and politics."[230]

Race may not be significant in an individual, case-by-case Black-White situation. Based on their personal experience, some Blacks and Whites choose not to see race as an issue or rely on racial identity to develop coping strategies in everyday interactions. Individually, many African Americans have made miraculous gains in income and position in American society, but from a collective perspective, even an unlearned observer can see that the basic economic-political power imbalance between Whites and Blacks has not changed materially since Reconstruction. If institutional racism is not a major contributing factor to the imbalance, then social theorists have yet to offer another logical explanation.

The Black middle class is a dynamic socially mobile group striving to lift itself out of the depths of historical oppression and poverty. Beyond economic aspirations and achievements, the Black middle-class is differentiated from the lower class by a pattern of behavior expressed in stable family and social organizational

4

relationships. This segment of the Black community is concerned with "front" and "respectability," and has a drive for "getting ahead."[231] The contemporary Black middle class is marked more by their social and civic responsibility, especially, in relation to the advancement of the race. Since the late 1960s, a growing number of the Black middle-class have been drawn to African history and culture and thus provide a connection to those Blacks in lower-income groups who subscribe to aspects of Black cultural nationalist ideology. The commonality of experiences that cut across class lines is embodied in a collective survival ethos that activates during periods of crisis.

The Black Poor and "Underclass"

It is the custom to refer to those people who are economically disadvantaged and impoverished as the lower class. The term *lower class* connotes more than economic destitution. It also implies social deviance or moral corruption. Therefore, it must be emphasized that ,in spite of popular conception, Blacks who are at the bottom of the economic ladder are not necessarily moral degenerates or criminals. Consistent with the prevailing racist ethos of the country, low character, low morals, low intelligence, proneness to crime, drugs, shiftlessness, laziness, and lack of ambition are traits that are generally ascribed to the Black poor. Low income does not automatically make one a criminal or a social deviant. If it is concluded that poor and low-income persons are inevitably prone to vice and criminality, then sociologists may find it difficult to explain the large number of White-collar crimes, drug enterprising activities, and moral corruption increasingly associated with wealthy people, high-income corporate officials, and the socially prominent.

In recent years, attempts have been made to further stratify the Black poor. The term *underclass* is used increasingly by some contemporary social theorists to describe a substratum of the lower class. Although Gunnar Myrdal is credited with having alluded to the term in the 1960s, it increased in popular usage with the publication of Douglas G. Glasgow's *The Black Underclass*. Glasgow describes the underclass as the hundreds of thousands of destitute Black men and women mired in economic poverty and social decay who are unskilled, jobless, and detached from the mainstream of society primarily because of institutional racism. In Glasgow's opinion, the underclass is distinguished from the lower class basically by its lack of social mobility.[232]

William Julius Wilson also asserts that the Black lower class is a heterogeneous grouping and that the underclass is a more impoverished segment of the lower class. Underclass Black families are likely to be headed by females, and the community is characterized by large numbers of "adult males with no fixed address—who live mainly on the streets, roaming from one place of shelter to another."[233]

Some social theorists apply the concept of underclass to all American poor or disadvantaged ethnic groups. However, Garry L. Rolison argues that underclass means more than just being poor, and, furthermore, in America, it is based more on racial rather than ethnic identification. White or near-White ethnic groups possess the potential for assimilation into the dominant society. The physical visibility of many Blacks prohibits their attainment of dominant-group membership. Consequently, Rolison defines the underclass as:

... that subgroup of the propertyless engaged in capitalist social relations who are denied the exchange of their labor power as an interactive function of their subordinate class position and racial membership. As a result, members of the underclass are simultaneously underemployed and tend to belong to an unprivileged racial group.[234]

Whether one agrees with Rolison's contention or not, there are sharp differences in the social effects and outcomes of ethnic versus race discrimination. Ethnic groups have entered the society and have become a part of the mainstream with comparative minimal difficulty, whereas African Americans, as a whole, remain economically differentiated and socially unassimilated.

The Black underclass is found mostly in impoverished and physically deteriorating urban areas. It includes a highly disproportionate number of the nation's school dropouts, welfare recipients, drug abusers, juvenile delinquents, and adult criminals. These are not inherent behavioral characteristics; but, because of their social and economic environment and circumstance, these individuals are forced to endure a life of hopelessness, despair, and moral decay. The plight of the Black urban underclass is worsened or compounded because of the flight of White city-dwellers and entrepreneurs to the suburbs, thus, taking with them the tax base needed to maintain the metropolis. Wilson is correct when he points out that it is not only the flight of Whites but also the attendant exodus of middle-class and working low-income Blacks from the cities that negatively affects the plight of the underclass. The underclass is left without role models and with weakened social institutions, such as, churches, schools, and other social organizations, when middle-class and working Blacks leave the community pursuing Whites for jobs in the suburbs.[235] Increasingly, members of the underclass also face negative conditions resulting from gentrification, i.e. inner city re-development initiatives designed to attract young white middle-class dwellers, which further weakens traditional community institutions as Black residents are forced to move from their traditional neighborhoods.

The major distinguishing characteristic between lower-class Blacks and the underclass is that of limited social mobility. For lower-class Blacks, poverty may be a transitory condition; but members of the underclass are locked into a situation where they lack adequate schooling, skills, and training to obtain meaningful and long-term employment. Unemployed and socially isolated, Black youth develop and adopt illegitimate economic means of subsistence and survival. They may rely on drugs as a livelihood or as an escape from harsh reality. Underlying the images of improvements in housing quality and reductions in crime rates, contemporary cities are plagued by large areas where poverty and unemployment are pervasive, vacant lots and abandoned dwellings abound, and the underground economy is the most vibrant economic sector. An update of the classic 1968 *Kerner Commission Report* assessing conditions thirty years later used the metaphor "locked in the poorhouse" to describe the conditions currently facing many inner-city residents.[236]

Robert Blauner and other social theorists have described communities of lower-class and underclass Blacks as analogous to colonies under a colonial system of oppression and exploitation. Ghetto residents have little or no power to improve their economic lot. They exist as a cheap source of labor, and nearly all of the economic institutions in their communities are owned and controlled by Whites outside the ghetto. Blacks are kept in a state of dependency and subject to deliberate suppression by the White power structure, including its law enforcement and judicial agencies. Although *colonialism* is defined as one country having economic and political dominance over another foreign nation, the term *internal* or *domestic colonialism* has been used to describe the African American experience in the United States. The ghetto is simply a domestic colony rendered powerless

under capitalist exploitation and racist ideology and controlled by powers external to it.[237]

As noted previously, some members of the lower class can and do experience some degree of social mobility. Such prospects were heightened in the 1990s by public policies designed to relocate poor families to the suburbs. The dominant approach to reducing poverty concentrations has been rental vouchers that allow the poor to move into more affluent neighborhoods.[238] However, many questions have been raised regarding how much dispersal programs can solve the problem of concentrated poverty. In fact, some researchers have claimed that residents dispersed outside central cities had been carefully selected to minimize resistance from suburban residents. The screening process includes selecting smaller families, families more likely to be employed, and families who had kept up with housekeeping and rental payments. The movement of poor people to the suburbs has been limited by the ability of suburban municipalities to grant waiting list preferences to their own residents. As a result, voucher holders typically concentrate in areas of low-socioeconomic status, where there is affordable housing, and generally follow existing patterns of integration.[239]

Vouchers have resulted in significantly less poverty concentrations than other forms of subsidized housing. Voucher users are less concentrated than public housing residents, and they reside in neighborhoods with less poverty, less racial segregation, and greater levels of home ownership.[240] Studies of scattered-site housing show that residents live in neighborhoods with higher median incomes, median housing values, median rents, and higher ownership rates.[241] Although some relocated households experience improved school quality, safer neighborhoods, and improved economic opportunities, others do not reap any of these positive benefits.[242]

There was, in fact, a dramatic decline in concentrated poverty in the 1990s, enabled by a strong economic expansion, as discussed previously. At the same time, there has been a substantial growth of poverty in suburban areas. Paul Jargowsky finds that in 2000 there were more concentrated poverty neighborhoods in suburban areas than in rural ones. Poverty rates increased along the outer edges of central cities and in the inner-ring suburbs of many metropolitan areas, including metropolitan areas that experienced large declines in poverty concentration.[243] One of the downsides of dispersal strategies is that it is more difficult to provide services to needy families. Unfortunately, subsequent to

4

2000, as the economic expansion petered out, poverty levels have again risen, as discussed previously. Between 2000 and 2001, the number of children of all races living in poverty increased by 700,000 and the number of Black children under the age of 18 living in extreme poverty reached the highest level since the government began collecting such data in 1980.

Elderly Black women constitute one of the most disadvantaged and vulnerable sub-populations. The difficulties of all elderly women, but particularly Black women, are exacerbated because of their longer life expectancy compared to men. More than three-fifths of all income received by elderly women comes from Social Security, and two-thirds of elderly women rely upon Social Security for a majority of their income. Moreover, one-third rely on Social Security for at least 90 percent of their income. For one elderly woman in five, Social Security is the sole source of income.[244]

The situation is even worse for elderly Black women. Average Social Security benefits are smaller for African Americans than for Whites due to lower average earnings during working years. Before receiving Social Security, 65.9 percent of African American women age 65 and older were poor in 1993-1997, compared to 52.4 percent of White women. Social Security benefits substantially reduce poverty for both groups, but the proportion of elderly women in poverty was nearly three times greater for African Americans (34.8 percent) than for Whites (12.7 percent). Because lifetime benefits are so closely related to the length of life and African Americans have shorter life spans, they are at a disadvantage, receiving a far poorer return on payroll taxes than do comparable Whites—approximately one percentage point less.[245] The problem is compounded because Social Security benefits cannot be transferred between generations.

Current trends suggest that the problems will worsen in the future. The proportion of African American women who will be unmarried at age 62, according to Social Security's projections, also will rise over time and will be substantially higher than the proportion of White elderly women. Never married African American women will increase from 5.1 for those born during the depression era to 18.6 percent for Baby Boomers. The proportion of elderly divorced women will grow from 14.8 percent for depression era African Americans to 24 percent for African American Baby Boomers. The proportion of never married 62-year-old African American Baby Boomers is more than two times that of Whites.

Thus, elderly, unmarried African American women face a triple threat—their race, gender, and marital status increase the possibility of living in poverty.[246]

In analyzing the various trends in class stratification and differentiation discussed in this section, African American Studies analysts are especially focused on how developments in the 1990s have reinforced the shared interests of Blacks across class lines. Although some Blacks have experienced significant upward economic mobility, as noted previously, many have not been able to distance themselves either physically or emotionally from the conditions affecting lower-class Blacks. The critical challenge is to identify strategies by which Black-controlled social institutions that serve Black populations can be mobilized and/or reorganized to confront the diverse forces and the challenges that limit opportunities for Blacks in all socioeconomic categories in the first decades of the twenty-first century.

Conclusion

The various issues examined from a sociological perspective in this chapter also have psychological, economic, and political dimensions. As a consequence, many of these same topics will be reexamined in subsequent chapters from other disciplinary perspectives. This process is illustrative of the distinctive African American Studies methodological approach that focuses on synthesizing multiple disciplinary perspectives to develop holistic perspectives that generate insights and strategies to enhance both individual agency and collective social functioning among African Americans.

As emphasized repeatedly, a key dimension of African American Studies methodology is to translate analyses into concrete interventions that can improve the quality of life for African American individuals, families, and communities. African American studies does not seek to reinvent the wheel, rather to the extent that existing projects can be identified that embody the multi-disciplinary African American studies approach to problem solving, such projects are championed and endorsed. As an example, the Harlem Children's Zone (HCZ), founded by Geoffrey Canada, addresses many of the issues highlighted in this chapter. This is a unique, holistic approach to rebuilding 100 blocks of Central Harlem, with the goal of creating a sustaining environment for children from birth through college. The support network includes in-school, after-school, social-service, health and community-building programs. Parents and families are targeted as well as the children.[247]

As described by Patricia Reid-Merritt, since its founding in 1968, the National Association of Black Social Workers (NABSW), has actively sought to realize the Social Work profession's values that include: the inherent rights and dignity of all people; the right to self-determination; societal responsibility to provide resources; and commitment to social change and social justice.[248] According to Reid-Merritt, the NABSW has mounted "an attack on societal racism while working simultaneously to strengthen the social fiber of the Black community."[249] The initiatives of the NABSW have been significantly influenced by the work of Black psychologists and Black sociologists. From the vantage point of African American Studies, the important role of Kawaida theory and Afrocentricity in informing the program of the NABSW is especially noteworthy.[250] The organization has taken progressive positions on a variety of important topics that significantly impact Black communities. Key areas where the NABSW has announced policy positions include Equal Opportunity and Affirmative Action, public assistance, employment, housing, political empowerment, preservation of the Black family, the Black aged, Black youth, teenage pregnancy, health issues, domestic violence, and cross-cultural counseling.[251] The position of the NABSW on transracial adoption has received the most attention. The organization has maintained staunch opposition to transracial adoption. This position was enunciated in the context of growing concerns about the mistreatment of Black children in the Child Welfare System. The statement was linked to a series of recommendations to address identified shortcomings. Reid-Merritt relates how the NABSW established an initiative, labeled "A Fist Full of Families," that spurred an increase in adoption by Black families.[252] In the current era of public discourse regarding "biracialism and non-racialism," the efforts of the NASBW face continuing external challenges.

Community-based efforts to strengthen Black families could be effectively organized around Black family reunions. There are several organizations that sponsor and/or research Black family reunions, including the annual National Council of Negro Women's Black Family Reunion celebrations, the Tom Joyner Family Reunion, and the Black Family Reunion Institute at Temple University.[253] In addition, to the development of cooperative empowerment strategies, Black family reunions can also serve as venues for cultivating greater knowledge of Black history in the context of the exploration of family history. In fact, family history seminars are an increasingly popular component of many Black family reunions. These activities have yet unrealized potential to create and sustain collective identity as globalization proceeds, which can, in turn, foster broader creative inter-familial empowerment initiatives.

Questions & Exercises

1. Define and discuss the concept of Black Sociology. What are some of the traditional sociological paradigms that many Black social theorists find problematic when applied to the African American experience?

2. Write a brief essay analyzing the terms race, color, and culture in the context of American society.

3. Debate the issue of African American intraclass conflict theorized by William Julius Wilson in his provocative book *The Declining Significance of Race*.

4. James Stewart and Joseph Scott introduced the concept of "institutional decimation" to characterize social control mechanisms targeted at Black males. Explain and discuss their theory in relation to the crisis of the African American family.

5. Examine Daniel P. Moynihan's study, *The Negro Family: The Case for National Action*, in relation to the counter-arguments it provoked among Black social theorists.

6. Which socioeconomic factors account most for the marriage sex ratio imbalance among middle-class African Americans?

7. Milton Gordon outlined seven stages that occur before a minority race or ethnic group is assimilated into a dominant society. Analyze each stage and discuss the progress of Blacks towards assimilation in American society.

8. The African American church is the sustaining force of most Black communities throughout the United States. How may George W. Bush's "Faith Based Initiatives" of the twenty-first century potentially affect the traditional role and operation of the Black church?

9. In 1954, Chief Justice Earl Warren and the U.S. Supreme Court overturned the "separate but equal" clause of the 1896 *Plessy v. Ferguson* decision. Debate whether this reversal was based on moral, economic, or political considerations.

10. In an attempt to improve the declining quality of American public education, President George W. Bush introduced a "No Child Left Behind" national education program. Examine the tenets of this initiative and explain why it failed to gain widespread support.

11. Examine Black and White racial integration patterns in athletics/sports institutions in America. What effects have racial and social integration of sports had on other aspects of American society?

12. Substantial residential racial "segregation" still exists in the United States. What are the underlying factors contributing to its persistence and growth?

Social Responsibility Projects

1. Identify neighborhoods in your community that are experiencing high levels of social distress and the organizations working to stem further deterioration. Volunteer to work with one or more of these organizations.

2. Identify community-based organizations that are working to provide support for families in need. Volunteer to work with one or more of these organizations.

3. Identify organizations that are serving the interests of military veterans. Volunteer to work with one or more of these organizations.

4. Identify churches that are actively involved in efforts to improve the neighborhoods in which they are located. Volunteer to work with one or more of these church-based projects.

5. Identify after-school programs in your community that provide tutoring and other support for students. Volunteer to work with one or more of these projects.

6. Identify community-based organizations working to reduce gang-related violence in your community. Volunteer to work with one or more of these organizations.

7. Organize a family-history seminar for your family reunion that connects your family history to the broad outlines of African American history.

8. Identify student organizations that support the Black/Africana Studies unit at your institution. Become an active member of one or more of these groups. If none exist organize a group in consultation with the unit head and faculty.

4

NOTES AND REFERENCES

1. P. Berger and B. Berger, *Sociology* (New York: Basic Books, Inc., 1972), 21-22.

2. See R. Wallace and A. Wolf, *Contemporary Sociological Theory* (Englewood Cliffs NJ: Prentice Hall, 1991), 18-25, 140 and M. Weber, *Basic Concepts in Sociology*. Translated by H.P. Secher (Westport CT: Greenwood Press, 1976).

3. B. Jones, "The Tradition of Sociology Teaching in Black Colleges," in *Black Sociologists*, ed. by J. Blackwell and M. Janowitz (eds.), (Chicago: The University of Chicago Press, 1974): 122-123.

4. See R. Jones, "Black Sociology: 1890-1917," *Black Academy Review* Vol. 2, nos. 1-4 (Winter 1971): 43-67.

5. R. Coulburn and W. E. B. Du Bois, "Mr. Sorokin's Systems," *Journal of Modern History 14* (1942): 511-512.

6. E. Frazier, "The Negro Family in Chicago," in G. Edwards (ed.) *E. Franklin Frazier on Race Relations* (Chicago: University of Chicago Press, 1968), 27–28).

7. Coulburn and Du Bois, "Mr. Sorokin's Systems," 511–512.

8. W. E. B. Du Bois, "The Atlanta Conferences," *Voice of the Negro 1* (March 1904): 85.

9. Ibid.

10. R. Staples, "What is Black Sociology? Toward a Sociology of Black Liberation," in J. Ladner (ed.) *The Death of White Sociology* (New York: Vintage Books, 1973), 161-172.

11. D. Richards, "The Ideology of European Dominance," *The Western Journal of Black Studies* Vols. 3/4 (Winter 1979): 244.

12. W. E. B. Du Bois, "The Development of a People," *International Journal of Ethics XIV* (April 1904): 293.

13. O. Klineberg, *Race Differences* (New York: Harper & Brothers Publishers, 1935), 18.

14. See R. Benedict, *Race: Science and Politics* (New York: The Viking Press, 1945), 22-38.

15. R. Hill, "Economic Forces, Structural Discrimination and Black Family Instability," in H. Cheatham and J. Stewart (eds.), *Black Families: Interdisciplinary Perspectives* (New Brunswick: Transaction Publishers, 1990), 89.

16. Benedict, *Race: Science and Politics*, 26.

17. See St. Clair Drake, *Black Folk Here and There* Volume 2 (Los Angeles: Center for Afro American Studies, University of California, 1990), 1-76.

18. F. Welsing, "The Cress Theory of Color-Confrontation," *The Black Scholar* (May 1974): 38.

19. For further study of the history and problems of mulatto Africans see "White by Day... Negro by Night," *Ebony* (November 1975), 80-83 and A. Poussaint, "The Problems of Light-Skinned Blacks," *Ebony* (February 1975), 85-91.

20. J. Rose, *Introduction to Sociology* (Chicago: Rand McNally College Publishing Co., 1980), 74-75.

21. *Religious Tolerance* (www.religioustolerance.org/chr_trend.htm).

22. S. Cohn, *Race, Gender, and Discrimination at Work* (Boulder, Colorado: Westview, 2000), 26.

23. A. Chimezie, "Theories of Black Culture," *The Western Journal of Black Studies* Vol. 7 (4) (Winter 1983): 218-219.

24. C. Torrance, "Blacks and the American Ethos: A Reevaluation of Existing Theories," *Journal of Black Studies Vol. 21 (1)* (September 1990): 82-83.

25. A. Abdel-Daim, "The Dialectics of Culture: Arab and American Relations," *The Western Journal of Black Studies* Vol. 3 (1) (Spring 1979): 3.

26. M. Gordon, *Assimilation in American Life* (New York: Oxford University Press, 1964), 71.

27. R. Walters, "Toward a Definition of Black Social Science," in J. Ladner (ed.) *The Death of White Sociology* (New York: Vintage Books, 1973), 197.

28. Robert Staples' perspectives on Black sociology were obtained through an exchange of letters and telephone conversations. Also see R. Staples, *Introduction to Black Sociology* (New York: McGraw Hill, 1976).

29. See T. Kershaw, "The Emerging Paradigm in Black Studies," *The Western Journal of Black Studies* Vol. 13 (1) (Spring 1989), 45-51.

30. D. Forsythe, "Radical Sociology and Blacks," in J. Ladner (ed.) *The Death of White Sociology* (New York: Vintage Books, 1973), 233.

31. W. E. B. Du Bois, Carter G. Woodson, Melville Herskovits, and John W. Blassingame are among those who write about the African continuities evident in African American family life. These authors are referenced in various sections in this book.

32. For an in depth study of the African family see, N. Sudarkasa, "African and Afro-American Family Structure: A Comparison," *The Black Scholar* (November/December 1980), 37-60; and C. A. Diop, *The Cultural Unity of Black Africa* (Chicago: Third World Press, 1978).

33. See J. Blassingame, *The Slave Community* (New York: Oxford University Press, 1979), 149-191; and H. Gutman, *The Black Family in Slavery and Freedom 1750-1925* (Vintage Books, 1977), 3-44.

34. E. Frazier, *The Negro Family in the United States*. Revised and abridged edition. (Chicago: University of Chicago Press, 1966). Originally published in 1939, 362.

35. See D. Moynihan, *The Negro Family: The Case for National Action* (Washington, D.C.: U.S. Department of Labor, 1965).

36.   R. Dennis, "Theories of the Black Family: The Weak-Family and Strong-Family Schools as Competing Ideologies," *The Journal of Afro-American Issues* (Summer/Fall 1976), 315-328.

37.   See A. Billingsley, *Black Families in White America* (Englewood Cliffs NJ: Prentice-Hall, 1968); R. Hill, *The Strength of Black Families* (New York: Emerson Hall Publishers, 1972); and R. Staples, *Introduction to Black Sociology* (New York: McGraw-Hill, 1976).

38.   See N. Hare, "What Black Intellectuals Misunderstood About the Black Family," *Black World XXV* (March 1976), 5-14.

39.   Daphne Lofquist and Renee Ellis, "Comparison of Estimates of same-Sex Couples from the American Community Survey and Current Population Survey." http://paa2011.princeton.edu/download.aspx?submissionId=110986.

40.   Defense Equal Opportunity Management Institute, "FY Summary Representation of Race/Ethnicity Groups and Women in the Active Armed Forces, 1997-2007."

41.   Michelle Alexander, *The New Jim Crow, Mass Incarceration in the Age of Colorblindness*, (New York: The New Press, 2010).

42.   Defense Equal Opportunity Management Institute, "FY Summary Representation of Race/Ethnicity Groups and Women in the Active Armed Forces, 1997-2007."

43.   Blassingame, *The Slave Community*, 149-191 and K. Stampp, *The Peculiar Institution* (New York: Vintage Books, 1956).

44.   Ibid.

45.   B. Omolade, *The Rising Song of African American Women* (New York: Routledge, 1994), 15.

46.   See, for example, Eleanor Seaton, Cleopatra Caldwell, Robert Sellers, & James S. Jackson, "The Prevalence of Perceived Discrimination among African American and Caribbean Black Youth," *Developmental Psychology* 44 (5), September, 2008, 1288–1297 and Ming-Te Wang & James Huguley, "Parental Racial Socialization as a Moderator of the Effects of Racial Discrimination on Educational Success Among African American Adolescents," *Child Development* 83 (5), (September/October 2012), 1716–1731.

47.   C. Franklin, "White Racism as the Cause of Black Male-Female Conflict: A Critique," *The Western Journal of Black Studies* Vol. 4 (1) (Spring 1980), 42-49.

48.   See C. Franklin, "Black Male-White Male Perceptual Conflict," *The Western Journal of Black Studies* Vol. 6 (1) (Spring 1982), 2-9.

49.   K. Jewell, "Black Male/Female Conflict: Internalization of Negative Definitions Transmitted through Imagery," *The Western Journal of Black Studies* Vol. 7 (1) (Spring 1983), 43-55.

50.   See M. Wallace, *Black Macho and the Myth of the Superwoman* (New York: The Dial Press, 1978), 3-33.

51.   J. Stewart and J. Scott, "The Pimp-Whore Complex in Everyday Life," *Black Male/Female Relationships* 1 (2), (1979), 11-15.

52.   D. Pilgrim, "Jezebel Stereotype," Jim Crow Museum of Racist Memorabilia, Ferris State University. http://www.ferris.edu/news/jimcrow/jezebel/.

53.   Jewell, "Black Male/Female Conflict."

54.   C. Rennison and S. Welchans, "Intimate Partner Violence," *U.S. Department of Justice, Office of Justice Programs, Bureau of Justice Statistics*, NCJ 178247 (May 2000). http://www.opj.usdoj.gov/bjs/abstract/ipv.htm.

55.   Ibid.

56.   Rennison and Welchan, "Intimate Partner Violence."

57.   L. Dugan, D. Nagin, and R. Rosenfeld, "Do Domestic Violence Services Save Lives?" *NIJ Journal* (250).

58.   C. Diop, *The Cultural Unity of Black Africa*, 45.

59.   S. Hatchett and A. Quick, "Correlates of Sex Role Attitudes Among Black Men and Women: Data from a National Survey of Black Americans," *Urban Research Review, Howard University Institute for Urban Affairs and Research,* Vol. 9 (2), (1983).

60.   A. White, "Talking Feminist, Talking Black: Micromobilization Processes in a Collective Protest Against Rape," *Gender and Society* 13 (1), Special Issue: Gender and Social Movements, Part 2, (February 1999): 77.

61.   White, "Talking Feminist," 95.

62.   A. White, "African American Feminist Fathers' Narratives of Parenting," *Journal of Black Psychology* 32 (1) (2006): 66.

63.   N. Hare and J. Hare, *The Endangered Black Family* (San Francisco: Black Think Tank, 1984), 25.

64.   See D. Aldridge, (ed.) "Black Women in the American Economy," *Special Issue of the Journal of Black Studies* 20 (2) (1989); D. Aldridge, *Focusing, Black Male-Female Relationships* (Chicago: Third World Press, 1991); D. Aldridge, "Womanist Issues in Black Studies: Towards Integrating Africana Women into Africana Studies," *The Afrocentric Scholar* 1 (1), (1992): 167-182; V. Gordon, *Black Women, Feminism, Black Liberation: Which Way?* Revised edition. (Chicago: Third World Press, 1987); C. Hudson-Weems, "Cultural and Agenda Conflicts in Academia: Critical Issues for Africana Womens' Studies," *Western Journal of Black Studies* 13 (4),(1989): 181-189; C. Hudson-Weems, *Africana Womanism: Reclaiming Ourselves* (Troy, MI: Bedford Publishers, 1993); C. Hudson-Weems, "Africana Womanism and the Critical Need for Africana Theory and Thought", *The Western Journal of Black Studies* (Summer 1997): 70-84.

65.   Du Bois (1908), 36.

66.   S. Messner and R. Sampson, "The Sex Ratio, Family Disruption, and Rates of Violent Crime," *Social Forces* 69 (3), (March 1991): 693-713.

67. R. Farley, "Trends in Marital Status Among Negroes," in C. Willie (ed.), *The Family Life of Black People* (Columbus OH: Merrill Publishing Co., 1970), 72-183.

68. Hill, "Economic Forces, Structural Discrimination and Black Family Instability," 87-105.

69. See O. Uzzell and W. Peebles-Wilkins, "Black Spouse Abuse: A Focus on Relational Factors and Intervention Strategies," *The Western Journal of Black Studies* Vol. 13 (1) (Spring 1989) and G. Johnson, "Underemployment, Underpayment, and Psychosocial Stress Among Working Black Men," *The Western Journal of Black Studies,* Vol. 13 (2) (Summer 1989).

70. See D. Aldridge, "Interracial Marriages: Theoretical Considerations," *Journal of Black Studies,* Vol. 8 (3), (March 1978).

71. For an empirical investigation of Black/White dating and sexual contacts see R. Staples, *The World of Black Singles* (Westport CT: Greenwood Press, 1981), 137-163.

72. See J. Gibbs, "Developing Intervention Models for Black Families: Linking Theory and Research," in Cheatham and Stewart, *Black Families*, 330-331.

73. M. Karenga, *Introduction to Black Studies* (Inglewood CA: Kawaida Publications, 1982), 218.

74. J. Gibbs, "Called Anything But a Child of God," *Focus, Joint Center for Political and Economic Studies* Vol. 19 (12) (December 1991).

75. See, for example, Family Mediation Center, Child Custody Parenting Plans. http://www.coparenting.com/bookandcd.html.

76. WeParent.com. http://www.weparent.com/about/weparent/.

77. J. Gibbs, "Called Anything But a Child of God," *Focus, Joint Center for Political and Economic Studies* Vol. 19 (12), (December, 1991).

78. E. F. Frazier, *The Negro Church in America* (New York: Schocken Books, 1966; 1964), 1-19.

79. R. Turner, *Islam in the African-American Experience* (Bloomington, IN: Indiana University Press, 1997).

80. L. Curry, *The Free Black in Urban America, 1800-1850* (Chicago: The University of Chicago Press, 1981), 193.

81. Ibid.

82. G. Wilmore, *Black Religion and Black Radicalism: An Interpretation of the Religious History of Afro-American People* (Maryknoll, NY: Orbis Books, 1983).

83. H. Nelsen and A. Nelsen, *The Black Church in the Sixties* (Lexington: The University Press of Kentucky, 1975).

84. I. Harrison, "The Storefront Church as a Revitalization Movement," in. H. Nelsen, et al. (eds.), *The Black Church in America* (Lexington: The University Press of Kentucky, 1971), 244.

85. See Turner, *Islam in the African-American Experience.*

86. G. Wilmore, "The Case for a New Church Style," in C. Eric Lincoln (ed.), *The Black Experience in Religion* (New York: Anchor Books, 1974), 34-44.

87. G. Wilmore and J. Cone, *Black Theology* (Maryknoll, NY: Orbis Books, 1979), 241.

88. See M. Herskovits, *The Myth of the Negro Past* (Boston: Beacon Press, 1958), 207-260.

89. P. Maultsby, "The Use and Performance of Hymnody, Spirituals, and Gospels in the Black Church," *The Western Journal of Black Studies* Vol. 7 (3), (Fall 1983): 164.

90. See P. Maultsby, "Influences and Retentions of West African Musical Concepts in U.S. Black Music," *The Western Journal of Black Studies* Vol. 3 (3), (Fall 1979): 197-212.

91. Wilmore and Cone, *Black Theology*, 18.

92. J. Cone, *For My People* (Maryknoll, NY: Orbis Books, 1991) 18.

93. Ibid., 53.

94. J. Grant, "Black Theology and the Black Women," in J. Cone and G. Wilmore (eds.), *Black Theology: A Documentary History, Volume I: 1966-1979* (Maryknoll, NY: Orbis Books, 1979), 328.

95. See A. Pinn, *The Black Church in the Post-Civil Rights Era* (Maryknoll, NY: Orbis Books, 2002).

96. Bettye Collier-Thomas, *Jesus, Jobs, and Justice, African American Women and Religion* (New York: Alfred A. Knopf, 2010).

97. Collier-Thomas, *Jesus, Jobs, and Justice*, xvi.

98. Collier-Thomas, *Jesus, Jobs, and Justice*, xvi.

99. "Controversial Minister off Obama's Campaign," (March 14, 2008). http://articles.cnn.com/2008-03-14/politics/obama.minister_1_obama-campaign-reverend-wright-sermons?_s=PM:POLITICS.

100. Barack Obama, "On My Faith and My Church," (March 14, 2008). http://www.huffingtonpost.com/barack-obama/on-my-faith-and-my-church_b_91623.html.

101. See G. Lloyd, "The Black Church and Economic Development," *The Western Journal of Black Studies* Vol. 1 (4), (December 1977): 273.

102. W. E. B. Du Bois, *The Souls of Black Folk* (New York: The New American Library, 1969; 1903), 213.

103. Pinn, *The Black Church in the Post-Civil Rights Era.*

104. C. Eric Lincoln and L. Mamiya, *The Black Church in the African American Experience* (Durham, NC: Duke University Press, 1990).

105. Pinn, *The Black Church in the Post-Civil Rights Era*, 138-139.

106. R. Smith, "The Public Influences of African-American Churches: Contexts and Capacities" Report submitted to the Pew Charitable Trust by The Public Influences of African-American Churches Project, The Leadership Center at Morehouse College (2002).

107. Turner, *Islam in the African-American Experience.*

108. See A. Pinn, *Varieties of African-American Religious Experience* (Minneapolis, MN: Fortress Press, 1998).

109. For information about the Oyotunji Village see the official website http://www.oyotunjivillage.net/oyo2_001.htm. For information about the National African Religion Conference go to the official website, http://www.narcworld.com/purpose.htm.

110. M. Karenga, *Selections from the Husia, Sacred Wisdom of Ancient Egypt* (Los Angeles: Kawaida Publications, 1984); M. Karenga, *Maat, The Moral Ideal in Ancient Egypt: A Study in Classical African Ethics* (New York: Routledge, 2004); M. Karenga, *Odu Ifa: The Ethical Teachings* (Los Angeles: University of Sankore Press, 1999).

111. S. Walker, *Their Highest Potential: An African American School Community in the Segregated South* (Chapel Hill, NC: University of North Carolina Press, 1996).

112. W. E. B. Du Bois, "Does the Negro Need Separate Schools?" *Journal of Negro Education,* 4 (2) (1935): 328-335; W. E. B. Du Bois, "A Negro Nation Within A Nation," *Current History, 42* (1935); 265-270; W. E. B. Du Bois, "The Hampton Idea," in H. Aptheker (ed.) *The Education of Black People: Ten Critiques, 1906–1960* (Amherst: University of Massachusetts Press, 1973).

113. See J. Balkin, "Brown as Icon," in J. Balkin, (ed.) *What "Brown v. Board of Education" Should Have Said* (New York: New York University Press, 2001), 3-28.

114. *De facto,* a Latin phrase meaning "in fact but not in law," refers to unintentional or non-government influenced segregation resulting from the conventional policy of building schools to serve specific neighborhoods regardless of race. *De jure,* on the other hand, is a Latin phrase meaning "by right" or "legally." *De jure* segregation occurs where public officials deliberately conspire or manipulate to maintain or assure the existence of segregation. For example, school districts could deliberately "gerrymander" school districts or attendance border lines.

115. See K. Clark, "Desegregation: The Role of the Social Sciences," *Teachers College Record* (October, 1960), 16-17.

116. Balkin, "Brown as Icon."

117. See, "Response to U.S. Supreme Court Decision about Voluntary School Integration," The Civil Rights Project, http://www.civilrightsproject.ucla.edu/policy/court/voltint.php.

118. Gary Orfield and Chungmei Lee, "Brown at 50: King's Dream or *Plessy's* Nightmare?" The Civil Rights Project, Harvard University, January 2004. http://www.civilrightsproject.harvard.edu/research/reseg04/brown50.pdf.

119. D. Losen and G. Orfield (eds.), *Racial Inequity in Special Education* (Cambridge, MA, Harvard Education Publishing Group, 2002).

120. "Tests Keep Thousands of Minorities Out of Teaching" *Fair Test Examiner* (Winter 1989). http://fairtest.org/examarts/winter89/smitahtt.htm.

121. S. Whitener and K. Gruber, *Characteristics of Stayers, Movers, and Leavers: Results from the Teacher Followup Survey: 1994-95* (NCES 97-450) (Washington, DC: U.S. Department of Education. National Center for Education Statistics, 1997).

122. J. Morris, "A Pillar of Strength: An African American School's Communal Bonds with Families and Community since Brown," *Urban Education,* 33 (5) (1999): 584-605.

123. Cited from, *The Adams Report: A Desegregation Update, Institute for Services to Education, Inc.,* (Washington, D.C. September, 1978), 3.

124. Inadequate Funding Makes NCLB Worse, *FairTest Examiner* (Winter-Spring) (2003). Available at http://fairtest.org/examarts/Wint-Spring%2003%20double/Funding.html (page no longer available).

125. Ibid.

126. G. Toppo, "Teachers union plans lawsuit over federal funds," *USATODAY* online (February 2003), http://www.usatoday.com/news/education/2003-07-02-nea-usat_x.htm.

127. "Seventy Percent of Schools to "Fail,'" *FairTest Examiner* (Winter-Spring), http://fairtest.org/examarts/Wint-Spring%2003%20double/Funding.html.

128. P. Grogan and T. Proscio, *Comeback Cities, A Blueprint for Urban Neighborhood Revival* (Boulder, CO: Westview Press, 2000), 223.

129. U.S. Department of Education, National Center for Education Statistics, Schools and Staffing Survey, 199-2000 "Public Charter School Survey," http://nces.ed.gov/surveys/sass/tables/table_10.asp.

130. F. Nelson, B. Rosenberg, and N. Meter, *Charter School Achievement on the 2003 National Assessment of Educational Progress* (American Federation of Teachers, August 2004).

131. "Bush's Backing of All-Male Schools Is Criticized," *New York Times* online (September 9, 1991), http://www.nytimes.com/1991/09/11/education/bush-s-backing-of-all-male-schools-is-criticized.html.

132. "Every Urban Prep senior is college-bound," *Chicago Tribune* online (March 5, 2010), http://articles.chicagotribune.com/2010-03-05/news/ct-met-urban-prep-college-20100305_1_metal-detectors-college-school-leaders.

4

133. National Urban League, *The State of Black America® Recommends A Blueprint for Economic Equality to Close Gaps Between Blacks and Whites* (Silver Spring, MD: Beckham Publications Group, 2008).

134. Anthony Mitchell & James Stewart, "The Westinghouse experiment: African-American educators think all-male-schools might improve prospects for Black males", *The Pittsburgh Post-Gazette* (2010, September 30), B 7.

135. D. M. Gordon, Iwamoto, N. Ward, , R. Potts; R. & E. Boyd, "Mentoring urban Black Middle School Male Students: Implications for Academic Achievement," *The Journal of Negro Education,* 78 (3), (Summer, 2009): 277-289, 362-364.

136. Ibid.

137. R. G. Potts, "Emancipatory education versus school-based prevention in African American communities," *American Journal of Community Psychology*, 31 (1/2) (2003, March): 173-183.

138. Marlon James, "Never quit: the complexities of promoting social and academic excellence at a single-gender school for urban African American males," *Journal of African American Males in Education,* 1 (3), (2010): 167-195.

139. D. M. Gordon, Iwamoto, N. Ward, , R. Potts; R. & E. Boyd, "Mentoring Urban Black Middle School Male Students: Implications for Academic Achievement," *The Journal of Negro Education,* 78 (3), (Summer, 2009): 277-289, 362-364.

140. M. Wheeler, T. Keeler, & D. DuBois, "Review of three recent randomized trials of school-based mentoring: Making sense of mixed findings," *Society for Research in Child Development Social Policy Report,* 24 (3), (2010): 1-27.

141. Ibid.

142. Du Bois, *Souls of Black Folk*, 108.

143. Carter G. Woodson, *The Mis-Education of the Negro* (Washington, D.C.: The Associated Publishers, Inc. 1933), 32.

144. For a historical account of predominantly Black colleges see, Alton Hornsby, Jr., "Historical Overview of Black Colleges," *The Western Journal of Black Studies* (Fall 1978) v. 2(3): 162-166.

145. Du Bois, *Souls of Black Folk*, 108-9.

146. Committee L on the Historically Black Institutions and the Status of Minorities in the Profession, "The Historically Black Colleges and Universities: A Future in the Balance," *Academe* (January/February, 1995).

147. Ibid.

148. W. E. B. Du Bois, "Education and Work," *Journal of Negro Education 1* (1931). Reprinted in H. Aptheker, (ed.) *The Education of Black People: Ten Critiques 1906-1960* (Amherst: The University of Massachusetts Press, 1973), 68.

149. Ibid.

150. Woodson, *Mis-Education*, iii.

151. W. E. B. Du Bois, "The Talented Tenth Memorial Address," *The Boule Journal 15* (October, 1948): 8.

152. W. E. B. Du Bois, "The Field and Function of the Negro College," Alumni Reunion Address, Fisk University, 1933. Reprinted in H. Aptheker (ed.) *The Education of Black People: Ten Critiques 1906-1960, 95-96.*

153. National Center for Education Statistics, "Digest of Education Statistics, 2000," http://nces.ed.gov/pubs2001/digest/.

154. Marjorie Coeyman, "Black Studies on The Move," *Christian Science Monitor* (February 12, 2002): L11, 14.

155. Abdul Alkalimat, *Africana Studies in the US* (March 2007), www.eblackstudies.org.

156. Max Schindler, "National Organizations Oppose Africana Studies and Research Center Overhaul," *Cornell Sun* online (January 24, 2011), http://www.cornellsun.com/.

157. "History of the NRA Organization." http://www.nrpa.org/content/default.aspx?documentId=721. "The Community basis of sports in Pittsburgh." http://northbysouth.kenyon.edu/2000/Intro/Community%20basis%20in%20Pitt.htm.

158. See E. Smith, "The Genetically Superior Athlete: Myth or Reality," in T. Anderson, *Black Studies: Theory, Method and Cultural Perspectives* (Pullman, WA: Washington State University Press, 1990), 120-131.

159. G. Sailes, "A Socioeconomic Explanation of Black Sports Participation Patterns," *The Western Journal of Black Studies* Vol. 11 (4), (Winter 1987): 164-167.

160. H. Edwards, "On the Issue of Race in Contemporary American Sports," *The Western Journal of Black Studies* (Fall 1982): 141.

161. H. Ploski and J. Williams (eds.), *The Negro Almanac* (New York: John Wiley & Sons, 1983), 905-922; See also G. Ward. *Unforgivable Blackness: The Rise and Fall of Jack Johnson* (New York: A.A. Knopf, 2004).

162. See R. Bak, *Joe Louis: The Great Black Hope* (Dallas, TX: Taylor Publishing, 1996).

163. See D. Remnick, *King of the World: Muhammad Ali and the Rise of an American Hero* (New York: Random House, 1998).

164. See A. Ashe and A. Rampersad, *Days of Grace: A Memoir* (New York: Ballantine Books, 1994).

165. See A. Gibson, *I Always Wanted to be Somebody*, Edited by Ed Fitzgerald, (New York: Harper & Row, 1958).

166. See M. Morrison, "Negro League Baseball, History and Key Players in Baseball's Gone—But not Forgotten—League," http://www.info-please.com/spot/negroleague1.html, and A. O'Toole, *The Best Man Plays: Major League Baseball and the Black Athlete, 1901-2002* (Jefferson City, NC: McFarland & Co., 2003).

167. See P. McKissack and F. McKissack, *Black Diamond: The Story of the Negro Baseball Leagues* (New York: Scholastic, 1994).

168. For information about Hinchcliffe Stadium visit the Ball Park Watch website, http://www.ballparkwatch.com/news/sept20_26.htm. For information about the Rickwood Stadium visit http://www.baseballpilgrimages.com/rickwood.html.

169. See A. Rampersad, *Jackie Robinson: A Biography* (New York: A.A. Knopf, 1997). See also McKissack and McKissack, *Black Diamond*; Morrison, "Negro League Baseball;" and O'Toole, *The Best Man Plays*.

170. See B. Kuska, *Hot Potato: How Washington and New York Gave Birth to Black Basketball and Changed America's Game Forever* (Charlottesville, VA: University of Virginia Press, 2004). Also see http://www.hoophall.com/halloffamers/NY%20Renaissance.htm and http://www.nba.com/history/encyclopedia_rens_001214.html.

171. See B. Green, *Spinning the Globe: The Rise, Fall, and Return to Greatness of the Harlem Globetrotters* (Harper-Collins, 2005).

172. See http://www.jimcrowhistory.org/scripts/jimcrow/sports.cgi?state=Pennsylvania and "Freedom to Play, The Life & Times of Basketball's African American Pioneers," http://www.hoophall.com/exhibits/freedom_barnstorming.htm.

173. See "Freedom to Play, The Life & Times of Basketball's African American Pioneers," http://www.hoophall.com/exhibits/freedom_nba.htm.

174. See M. Maltby, *The Origins and Development of Professional Football, 1890-1920. Garland Studies in American Popular History and Culture.* (Garland Publishing, 1997) and A. Levy, Tackling Jim Crow: Racial Segregation in Professional Football (Jefferson, NC: McFarland, 2003).

175. Ibid.

176. The official website of the CIAA is http://www.theciaa.com/.

177. See G. Rich, "What will the CIAA Add Next?," *Independent Weekly*, February 27, 2002, http:/indyweek.com/durham/20002-02-27/tri-angles.html.

178. See M. Hurd, *Black College Football, 1892-1992: One Hundred Years of History, Education, & Pride* (Donning Publishers, 2000).

179. See "White College, Blacks Join In," *Freedom to Play, The Life and Times of Basketball's African American Pioneers.* http://www.hoophall.com/exhibits/freedom_white_colleges.htm.

180. Ibid.

181. See J. Watterson, *College Football: History, Spectacle, Controversy* (Baltimore, MD: Johns Hopkins University Press, 2000).

182. Ibid.

183. D. Leonard, "What Happened to the Revolt of the Black Athlete? A Look Back Thirty Years Later," An Interview with Harry Edwards, *Color Lines* 1 (1) (Summer 1998), http://www.arc.org/C_Lines/CLArchive/story1_1_01.html.

184. See K. McNutt, *Hooked on Hoops: Understanding Black Youths' Blind Devotion to Basketball* (African American Images, 2002) and T. Boyd, *Young Black Rich and Famous: The Rise of the NBA, the Hip Hop Invasion and the Transformation of American Culture* (New York: Doubleday, 2003).

185. Leonard, "What Happened to the Revolt of the Black Athlete?," 6.

186. G. Dickinson, "Pledged to Remember: Africa in the Life and Lore of Black Greek-Letter Organizations," in *African American Fraternities and Sororities: The Legacy and the Vision*, T. Brown, G. Parks, and C. Phillips (eds.) (Lexington, KY: The University Press of Kentucky, 2005), 11.

187. Dickinson, "Pledged to Remember," 12-13.

188. A. Hilliard, "Pedagogy in Ancient Kemet," in *Kemet and the African Worldview: Research, Rescue and Restoration*, ed. M. Karenga and J. Carruthers (Los Angeles: University of Sankore Press, 1986) 138-39.

189. Dickinson, "Pledged to Remember," 19.

190. See C. Torbenson, "The Origin and Evolution of College Fraternities and Sororities," in *African American Fraternities and Sororities*, ed. Brown et al., 60-61.

191. M. Washington & C. Nunez, "Education, Racial Uplift, and the Rise of the Greek-Letter Tradition: The African American Quest for Status in the Early Twentieth Century," in *African American Fraternities and Sororities*, ed. Brown et al., 137.

192. M. Stombler & I. Padavic, "Sister Acts: Resistance in Sweetheart and Little Sister Programs," in *African American Fraternities and Sororities*, ed. Brown et al., 233-68.

193. This information was obtained from official websites of BGLOs and unofficial websites identifying prominent BGLO members.

194. T. Brown, C. Phillips, and G. Parks, "Future Directions," *African American Fraternities and Sororities*, ed. Brown et al., 465.

195. Brown, et al., eds., "Future Directions," 468.

196. S. Harper, L. Byars, and T. Jelke, "How Black Greek-Letter Organization Membership Affects College Adjustment and Undergraduate Outcomes," *African American Fraternities and Sororities*, ed. Brown et al., 393-416.

197. R. Jones, *Black Haze, Violence, Sacrifice, and Manhood in Black Greek-Letter Fraternities* (Albany, NY: SUNY Press, 2004), 108.

198. Jones, *Black Haze*, 81.

199. D. Prothrow-Smith, *Deadly Consequences* (New York: HarperCollins, 1991), 97.

200. See D. Prothrow-Stith, *Deadly Consequences* (New York: HarperCollins, 1991).

201. Ibid.

202. S. Decker, "Collective and Normative Features of Gang Violence," *Justice Quarterly 13*, (1996): 251-261.

203. Ibid.

204. Prothrow-Stith, *Deadly Consequences.*

205. Prothrow-Stith, *Deadly Consequences.*

206. Prothrow-Stith, *Deadly Consequences.*

207. M. Pattillo, "Sweet Mothers and Gangbangers: Managing Crime in a Black Middle-class Neighborhood," *Social Forces* 76 (1998), 765-770.

208. Ibid.

209. Ibid.

210. "Thug Life," *Urban Dictionary*, http://www.urbandictionary.com/define.php?term=thug%20life.

211. Information about the Five-Percent nation was obtained from several websites.

212. Information about the New Black Panthers was obtained from several websites.

213. Information about the New Afrikan Peoples Organization was obtained from several websites.

214. See O. Cox, *Caste, Class & Race* (New York: Doubleday & Co., 1948. Reprint, Modern Reader, 1970), 148-150, 154-162.

215. W. E. B. Du Bois, "Negroes and the Crisis of Capitalism," *Monthly Review* 4 (April 1953): 483.

216. Ibid.

217. B. Landry, *The New Black Middle Class* (Berkeley: The University of California Press, 1987).

218. W. Wilson, *The Declining Significance of Race*, 2nd ed. (Chicago: The University of Chicago Press, 1978; 1980), 19-23, 120-121.

219. M. Kilson, "The Black Bourgeoisie Revisited: From E. Franklin Frazier to the Present," *Dissent* 30 (1), (Winter, 1983); L. Benjamin, *Three Black Generations at the Crossroads, Community, Culture and Consciousness* (Chicago: Burnham, 2000).

220. Eugene Robinson, *Disintegration, The Splintering of Black America* (New York: Doubleday, 2010), 140.

221. Douglas Massey & Nancy Denton, *American Apartheid: Segregation and the Making of the Underclass* (Cambridge: Harvard University Press, 1993), 153.

222. Richard Alba, John Logan, and Paul Bellair, "Living with Crime: The Implications of Racial/Ethnic Differences in Suburban Location," *Social Forces* 73 (1994), 395-434.

223. John R. Logan, "Separate and Unequal: The Neighborhood Gap for Blacks, Hispanics and Asians in Metropolitan America," US2010 Project (Brown University July 2011). http://www.s4.brown.edu/us2010/Data/Report/report0727.pdf.

224. R. Ojeda, "The Continuing Home Foreclosure Tsunami, Disproportionate Impacts on Black and Latino Communities." A William C. Velasquez White Paper (October, 2009).

225. "How Many Home Auctions For Sale Belong to African American Homeowners?", *Foreclosure News.* (June 10, 2011), http://www.eforeclosuremagazine.com/foreclosure-auctions/how-many-home-auctions-for-sale-belong-to-african-american-homeowners#ixzz1RQWX0SCG.

226. "Will Foreclosures Ruin America's Richest Black County?" (June 16, 2011), http://atlantapost.com/2011/06/16/will-foreclosures-ruin-americas-richest-black-county/.

227. V. Keith and C. Herring, "Skin Tone and Stratification in the Black Community," *American Journal of Sociology* 97 (3), (1991): 760-778.

228. A. Gullickson, "The Significance of Color Declines: A Re-analysis of Skin Tone Differentials in Post-Civil Rights America," (mimeograph), March 2004, p. 21.

229. Ibid.

230. R. Seltzer and R. Smith, "Color Differences in the Afro-American Community and the Differences They Make," *Journal of Black Studies* Vol. 21 (3), (March 1991): 284-285.

231. Although some of the characteristics have been transformed since the 1960s, for an excellent study of the Black middle-class, see, St. Clair Drake and H. Cayton, *Black Metropolis, Vol. II* (New York: Harper Torchbooks, 1962), 658-715.

232. D. Glasgow, *The Black Underclass* (San Francisco: Jossey-Bass, Inc. Publishers, 1980). Reprint, (Vintage Books, 1981), vii-ix, 7-11.

233. Wilson, *The Declining Significance of Race*, 158-157.

234. G. Rolison, "An Exploration of the Term Underclass as it Relates to African-Americans," *Journal of Black Studies* Vol. 21 (3), (March 1991): 296-297.

235. See W. Wilson, "The Ghetto Underclass and the Social Transformation of the Inner City," *The Black Scholar Vol. 19* (3), (May/June 1988): 13. See also, "The American Underclass," *Time*, (August 29, 1977), 14-27.

236. F. Harris and L. Curtis, (eds.) *Locked in the Poorhouse, Cities, Race, and Poverty in the United States* (Lanham, MD: Rowman & Littlefield, 1998).

237. See R. Blauner, "Internal Colonialism and Ghetto Revolt," *Social Problems,* Vol. 16 (Spring 1969): 393-408.

238. A. Schwartz and K. Tajbakhsh, "Mixed Income Housing: Unanswered Questions," *Cityscape* 3 (2) (1997): 71-92.

239. Ibid.

Chapter 5

Black Psychology and Psychological Well-Being

American and African American Psychology

A Synopsis of Psychology and Race

There is an inevitable link between psychology and race in any situation where peoples of distinct cultures and races relate, interact, or interpret each other's behaviors. Indeed, *psychology* is the study or process of assessing human behavior and mental acts. Race, culture, and class often serve as correlative variants. Like sociology, American psychology developed from classical European thought and philosophy of the eighteenth and nineteenth centuries. Some of the early philosophical contributors to modern psychology include Wilhelm Wundt, Hermann Ebbinhaus, Carl Stumpf, Sigmund Freud William McDougall, Francis Galton; and Edward B. Titchener. The field was heavily influenced by Germans, however, the philosophies and racial suppositions of Charles Darwin, Francis Galton, and Herbert Spencer (British), are particularly significant to Black or African peoples. Thus, White American psychology is European race-specific, in terms of its philosophical origin and behavioral foundation, and it may not be wholly relevant or applicable in the analysis or treatment of Blacks or African Americans.

A review of much of the introductory literature will reveal that psychology is defined in many ways depending, largely, on the method of approach or the orientation of its many branches of study. Because psychology deals with the boundlessness of the human mind and behavior, it is characterized by much divisiveness and theoretical fragmentation.[1]

Modern psychology is divided into several subdisciplines that include developmental psychology, child psychology, clinical psychology, social psychology, personality psychology, cognitive psychology, and community psychology. *Developmental* psychology focuses on changes that occur over a person's life cycle. In a similar vein, *child* psychology focuses on children's cognitive, emotional, and social development. *Cognitive* psychology explores how humans acquire thoughts and ideas and how they use and organize knowledge. *Clinical* psychology is a subfield that examines means of assessing, preventing, reducing, and rehabilitating psychological distress, disabilities, and dysfunctional behaviors and of enhancing psychological well-being. *Social* psychology examines how a person's thoughts, feelings, and behaviors are influenced by the presence of other people. And, finally, *community* psychology examines how individuals interact with other individuals, social groups, clubs, churches, schools, families, neighborhoods, and the larger culture and environment.[2] All of these subareas clearly have potential relevance for the exploration of the psychological well-being of African Americans. However, this potentiality has been blunted by the intrusion of racist ideology into the ways in which mainstream psychologists have approached the study of African Americans.

Euro-American psychology has a close historical relationship with the field of anthropology, which is one of the reasons that much of the early study was focused on the physical and cultural characteristics of the non-White or so-called non-literate races of mankind. Physical or anatomical differences in the cranial capacity of the skull were once used to determine the extent of civilization or intelligence of a people. During the early twentieth century, American psychologists took particular interest in conducting tests designed to differentiate between Whites and the intelligence of "primitive" people: Blacks, certain Asian groups, Native Americans, and Pygmies.[3] Building on the "survival of the fittest" philosophy of Charles Darwin, the social Darwinist concepts of Herbert Spencer, and the race-difference implications and eugenics concepts of Francis Galton, American functionalist psychologist James M. Cattell developed and nurtured the idea of mental testing and measurements. However, American psychology seems to have been influenced more by philosophers and psychologists in the vein of Darwin and Galton.[4]

Historically, a significant number of White American psychologists or behavioral scientists have taken an interest in race research related to Black people. Even during the mid-twentieth century, it was implicitly and explicitly argued in some studies that Blacks were mentally and intellectually inferior. The studies were based on flawed, culturally-biased methodology and White supremacist models, and it served to fuel racial antagonism after the 1954 school desegregation decision by the U.S. Supreme Court.

The genetic theory and the heredity theory of Black intellectual inferiority was revived by Arthur R. Jensen in an article in the *Harvard Educational Review* in 1969 entitled, "How Much Can We Boost IQ and Scholastic Achievement?" Jensen claimed that genetic inferiority limits Blacks' ability to improve scores on standard intelligence tests. However, in contrast to this thesis, a psychiatric study of Blacks by A. Kardiner and L. Ovesey had previously suggested that historical racism, environmental influences, and dysfunctional compensatory behavior—rather than heredity—accounted for gaps in test scores.[5] The perceived mental deficiency of African Americans was disquieting, but not as much as the fact that the findings were made by White behavioral theorists and were racially biased. Invariably, such studies were based on White middle-class cultural norms. Blacks or Africans have been constantly scrutinized and studied by European people who have historically debased and "scientifically" adjudged them intellectually inferior. Frances Cress Welsing has mounted a global and provocative challenge to the traditional psychological

establishment. As suggested by the following statement, she maintains that White supremacy and race-awareness are significant psychological factors in the genetic survival of the White race regardless whether they are consciously or subconsciously manifested:

> All major and minor behavior-energy crystallization or behavior-units in the global white collective — no matter how simple or complex, old or new, short-or long-lived must conform, in the final analysis, to the basic behavior-energy equation of white over non-white (or white power over nonwhite powerlessness).[6]

Welsing insists that this orientation derives from psychological paranoia associated with the global numerical minority status of Whites in comparison to Black, brown, red, and yellow peoples. *The Cress Theory of Color Confrontation* holds that the numerical and "color inadequacy of whiteness necessitates a social structure based on white superiority."[7]

Although "scientific" efforts to prove that people of African descent are genetically predisposed to intellectual inferiority to Europeans are subsumed under the subdiscipline of cognitive psychology, they have heavily influenced the research interpretations of traditional psychologists in other subdisciplines. It was claimed, for example, that African Americans retained child-like psychological developmental characteristics throughout their lifetimes and that the intellectual development of Black children was uniformly slower than that of Whites.[8] Social and community psychological studies typically found the behaviors of African Americans to be dysfunctional or inadequate for coping with the demands of daily life.

The colonial and anthropological approaches of traditional psychology toward the study of African Americans have resulted in a form of scientific racism that has been challenged by contemporary Black psychologists. These pioneers have produced a distinct body of work that rejects the claims of universality advanced by traditional psychologists based on the assumption that many psychological processes may be race-culture specific. Research conducted and results obtained by progressive Black psychologists have already proven to be quite different from those of traditionalists.[9] Many of the assumptions and approaches employed by progressive Black psychologists overlap significantly with those employed by African American Studies specialists. As an example, the examination of the psychological dimensions of racial identity is an important component of the work of many Black psychologists. Race is ingrained in the social fabric of American society and affects the subconscious and unconscious thoughts of Blacks and Whites whenever and wherever the two races interact or relate.

Some Black psychologists emphasize the historical foundations of contemporary problems and graphically illuminate the myriad negative psychological consequences experienced by African Americans that emanate from the historical and continuing system of oppression that conditions Black existence. For too many African Americans, racism has either consciously or subconsciously induced self-alienation, a sense of powerlessness, social isolation, cultural obfuscation, and hopelessness. At the same time, progressive Black psychologists emphasize that White racism is also indicative of individual and collective psychopathic personality or mental disorders among Whites.

Consistent with the orientation of African American Studies on the agency of African Americans, some progressive Black psychologists focus primary attention on the development of strategies to neutralize the negative factors that hamper effective individual and collective psychological functioning. One such strategy is a call for the reintroduction of traditional African values and behaviors to counteract Eurocentric impositions.[10]

Definition and Development of Black Psychology

The preceding discussion emphasized the race/culture specific nature of the term and concept of *psychology*. African Americans may not wholly defer to European definitions and conceptions relative to the study of human behavior and mental activity. In contrast to a psychology founded solely on European or Asian ideas, the psychology of African Americans is more directly related to African ways of understanding the human existence.[11] John S. Mbiti makes the point that the behavior of Africans is based primarily upon religious, spiritual (spirits), ancestral, and mystical beliefs germane to the history and culture of Africa. In other words, Africans have their own ontology or concept of universal reality. Consequently, African people behave and are motivated by what they believe, and what they believe is based on what they experience.[12]

Slavery, racism, and some degree of acculturation have not obliterated certain African ontological beliefs and foundations. Consequently, Afrocentric psychologists argue that the African American experience is sufficiently different from that of White Americans to warrant its own branch of study. Furthermore, racism, discrimination, oppression, and cultural obfuscation have created, more than ever, the need for different psychological approaches toward the analysis of Black behavior and mentality. While many White psychologists have concentrated on measuring the mental or intellectual disparities between certain races or ethnic groups, contemporary Black psychologists seem more concerned with differentiating between the race-ethnic social realities or worldviews of races or ethnic groups.

The origin of the concept of psychology in this discussion is important only in relation to the race or culture to which it is intended to apply. In the European tradition, the concept is said to have originated as early as the fourth and fifth centuries B.C., with the thoughts and philosophies of Plato, Aristotle, and other Greek scholars. Wilhelm Wundt is credited with having started the first psychological laboratory in Leipzig, Germany in 1879.[13] Proponents of an African (Black) psychological foundation trace its beginnings back to the ancient Kemet (African-Egyptian) civilization around 3200 B.C.[14]

The contemporary organized concept of Black psychology began during the late 1960s, almost concomitantly with the call for a Black sociology and during the nationwide quest and demand for Black/African American Studies departments and programs. The Civil Rights, Black Power, and Black Studies Movements of the 1960s generated the optimum social, political, and educational environments for the creation of racially and culturally unique fields of academic inquiry. It was natural that the struggle for social justice and political and economic freedom would also include the long suppressed desire of Black Americans for intellectual liberation.

The modern field of Black or African psychology developed out of the formation of the Association of Black Psychologists (ABP) in 1968. During this era, a number of other African American professional organizations were formed apart from the traditional White academic associations. In particular, the ABP group of psychologists began to discover that the application of Eurocentric normative behavioral values and patterns to Black experience norms often yielded less than reliable findings and implications because Black (African) behavioral norms and ethos might differ significantly from White (European) behavior patterns, mental motivations, and cultural values on which traditional psychology is founded. Blacks have not been well-served by the field of psychology in the problem areas of education, self-concept and personality development, intra-group conflict, child and family relations, mental health therapy, and counseling with the use of unadjusted conventional European models.[15]

In *The Psychology of Blacks*, Joseph L. White and Thomas A. Parham discuss the objectives of their work: "Black psychology and the psychology of Blackness reflect an attempt to build a conceptual model that organizes, explains, and leads to understanding the psycho-social behavior of African-Americans based on the primary dimensions of an African-American world view."[16] In defining and enumerating the objectives of Black psychology, most of its proponents tend to broaden its perspective while not totally dismissing the utility and value of traditional psychology. Adelbert H. Jenkins asserts, "[T]here are existing viewpoints in contemporary Western psychology that can also be used to make a fuller and fairer assessment of the Afro-American."[17] Norman Cook and Sumiko Kono allude to Black psychology as existing as "the third great psychological-philosophical tradition" leading the way towards a more equalitarian or "universal psychology" that embraces "a theory of the human psyche which is broad enough to include the characteristic elements of mind in all cultures ... not merely Black culture."[18] Some African American psychologists see Black psychology as a reactive response to White psychology, whereas others assert that Black (African) psychology is reactive, proactive, and inventive.

It is obvious from the various positions or views taken by Black psychologists that there exist somewhat distinct schools of psychological thought on the study of African Americans. Maulana Karenga has characterized the African American schools of thought as traditional, reformist, and radical. The traditional school seems to support and apply conventional Eurocentric paradigms and norms toward the analysis of Black behavior. Roger Wilcox's edited volume, *The Psychological Consequences of Being a Black American*, is an example of the traditionalist orientation. The volume uses traditional disciplinary sub-classifications and research designs. The editor suggests the

book represents "somewhat of an artificial dichotomy in that the overall research of Black psychologists does not essentially differ from the research of other American psychologists."[19]

In contrast, the reformists do not take traditional approaches at face value and attempt to make adaptive changes in conventional psychological thought to conform to the Black American experience. However, their approach focuses exclusively on the experience of African Americans in the West and exhibits little regard for African foundations.

Radical or revolutionary theorists argue that the African ethos is the primary normative basis for the analysis of African American personality and behavior. Independent of European psychological theory, radical theorists employ and include African religion, philosophy, spiritualism, ritualism, concept of time, and worldview as the foundation of Black psychology.[20] Daudi Azibo's edited volume, *African Centered Psychology*, and Kobi K. K. Kambon's *African/Black Psychology in the American Context: An African-Centered Approach* are representative works in this tradition.[21]

The Afrocentric psychologist contends that oppositional racial-cultural psychological proclivities exist between Blacks/Africans and Whites/Europeans. Joseph A. Baldwin postulates that African Americans and White Americans function psychologically under distinct "cosmologies." These cosmological systems, "therefore, represent fundamentally different ontological systems and cultural definitions, which reflect their distinct approaches to conceptualizing, organizing and experiencing reality."[22] The racial-cultural ethos of the European American is characterized by its quest for control and mastery over nature, "survival of the fittest" ethics, future orientation, individualism, materialism, artificiality, intervention and aggression, White supremacy, and racism.[23] In an oppositional sense, the African American cosmology is said to be oriented towards achieving harmony and unity with nature, collectivism, egalitarianism, spiritualism, and ritualism.[24]

In their influential work, *Roots of Soul: the Psychology of Black Expressiveness-An Unprecedented and Intensive Examination of Black Folk Expression in the Enrichment of Life*, psychologists Alfred B. Pasteur and Ivory L. Toldson also affirm the theory that Black/African and White/European minds perceive and interpret universal phenomena somewhat differently, and, thus, their expressive behavior and value systems are in sharp contrast. The expressive differences of Blacks are explained as the result of the hemispheric specialization of the right side of the brain. The right hemisphere is postulated to be the seat of creative and artistic capacities, which accounts for the cultural pre-dilection of Blacks for a form of rhythm, motion, and language or rhetoric that is distinct from the ordered, structured, and control-oriented expressive behavior of Whites. Pasteur and Toldson observe further that the impact of Black expressiveness upon the White world has been an altering one—bringing it closer in feeling and sensibility, in rhythm and motion to that of Africa.[25] Molefi K. Asante extensively discusses the implications of cultural expressiveness in Blacks in *The Afrocentric Idea*. Asante expounds on the psychological aspects of rhythm and styling in the language delivery or rhetoric of Black Americans.[26]

African ethos and philosophies cannot be excluded from the development of Black psychological theory. In discussing the foundation of Black psychology, Wade W. Nobles states:

> Black Psychology must concern itself with the question of "rhythm." It must discuss at some great length, "the oral tradition." It must unfold the mysteries of the spiritual energy now known as "soul." It must explain the notion of "extended self" and the "natural" orientation of African peoples to insure the "survival of the tribe." Briefly, it must examine the elements and dimensions of the experiential communalities of African peoples.[27]

Indeed, fields of study are the products of the culture or cultures from which they are derived. Differences in historical experience affect virtually all paradigms or approaches to the study of a particular ethnic group or race of people.

The traditional Euro-American disciplines of today have taken many decades and perhaps centuries to develop into their present stage of intellectual respectability and academic practicality. Black psychology as well as other emerging subfields in African American Studies, must develop new or modified methodological and scientific theoretical guidelines to achieve academic credibility. Conflicting ideologies and competing paradigms will occur and are "healthy" for the refinement of a developing discipline. Considering the morass of repressive social and political conditions from which African American studies evolved during the 1960s, the progress and development of

Black psychology, sociology, history, and the various other fields of study constituting African American studies have been phenomenal.

Psychohistorical Approaches to Understanding African Americans

Psychohistory and African Americans

The relatively new field of psychohistory may provide important theoretical insights into the yet unfulfilled objectives of freedom and equality for Blacks in the United States. Social, political, and economic inequality, inequity, and injustice continue for Blacks, as a race of people, more than one hundred forty years after the Emancipation of 1863 and even after passage of the Civil Rights laws of the 1960s. After almost five hundred years of Black oppression (of varying degrees), nontraditional paradigms must be examined to offer theoretical explanations or reasons for this social reality. Germane to any psychoanalytic explanation of the African American condition is the question: How much of the oppression endured by African Americans is involuntary, and how much is voluntary? Although the effects of racism and racial oppression are real, the experiential dimension might be psychogenetic.

Peter Loewenberg submits that psychohistory is a synthesis between the disciplines of history and psychoanalysis. Furthermore, psychohistory "seeks the function of the unconscious in human behavior as evidenced by life styles, adaptations, creativity and sublimations, character ... Psychohistory is oriented to dynamic psychology in which the present reality interacts at all times with and is related to the personal and social past of the person in the unconsciousness."[28]

Psychohistory may offer not only reasons, but also potential solutions, for advancing the cause of Black social, political, and economic liberation in America. Psychohistory is an approach to the study of history using the techniques of psychoanalysis to explain actions or even motivations. It is a powerful interpretive field that can be used to explain the historically remote sociocultural, political, and economic attitudes or behaviors of an individual or a race of people that are manifested unconsciously in the present. This discussion is concerned with the transference and countertransference of feelings, attitudes, behaviors, personalities, and loves and hates that may be rooted in the historical experiences of African Americans during and after slavery.

Lloyd Demause states in his work, *Foundations of Psychohistory*, that psychohistory is the science of historical motivation.[29] The Black psychohistorian seeks to research the unconscious motivations that shaped African Americans' experiences during slavery and Jim Crow to explain present social, political, and economic attitudes and behaviors that are counterproductive to the implementation of contemporary liberation strategies.

Full or "real" racial integration between Blacks and Whites has proved elusive for more than four hundred years. Racial oppression, injustice, and inequality—overtly and covertly—continue to exist. The observable behavior of Whites demonstrates a lack of commitment to full integration of African Americans into the social mainstream. Yet, each succeeding generation of African Americans continues to advocate and seek more integration rather than strategic independence from oppressive forces. From the vantage point of psychohistory, a question arises about whether or not this predilection somehow originated with an historical fear of running away from the slaveholder. To the extent that such a fear was inculcated among enslaved Blacks, it may have contributed to a contemporary reluctance to engage in behaviors that reflect an orientation emphasizing self-sufficiency and self-determination. In other words, is it reasonable to pose the question, "Are African Americans currently afflicted with a psychohistorical dilemma that reinforces dependency on Whites?"

Many wealthy Black athletes, entertainers, and other professionals or celebrities donate millions of dollars to White-owned or controlled organizations and institutions, while ignoring the needs of Black independent educational institutions and community organizations. Are such actions a reflection of historical memory of the times when Blacks were forced to transfer some or most of their earnings or crops to the slave master or plantation owner?

Many African American politicians and speakers appear reluctant to mention or quote confrontational freedom fighters and civil rights activists, such as David Walker, Henry Highland Garnet, Marcus Garvey, Kwame Ture (Stokely Carmichael), Malcolm X, or Louis Farrakhan, before predominantly White audiences. However, these same public figures will readily invoke the memory of other figures, like Frederick Douglass or Martin Luther King, Jr. Does this selectivity reflect psychohistorical dimensions, the fear of provoking the wrath of White listeners?

Psychohistory is not only germane to the study of the African American condition; it is also useful for interpreting the general dysfunctional state of race relations in American society. America is bedeviled by a history of unjust and disharmonious relations between the White "majority" population and the "minority" Black, Native American, Latino, Asian, and other non-White populations. Interdisciplinary inquiries using the tools of psychoanalysis and history may well yield new insights into the psychogenic and phylogenic origins of White supremacy attitudes, racism, dominance/subordination syndromes, and xenophobic proclivities.

Psychological Dimensions of Oppression

Behavioral Effects of Slavery and Racism

Much has been written and observed concerning the social and behavioral patterns of African Americans that are attributed to the experiences of historical slavery and contemporary racism. It would be virtually impossible for a people to endure more than three hundred years of enslavement and not be psychologically affected or for the effects not to be culturally transmitted to some extent across generations. Moreover, it should not be difficult to understand that the mentality, emotions, personality, social behaviors, and values of Blacks may still be consciously, subconsciously, or unconsciously affected by slavery. Legalized segregation, the core of racist ideology and racism, ceased in America less than forty years ago with the U.S. Supreme Court's desegregation decision of 1954. With the continuation of individual and institutional racism in the society, African Americans are still burdened with various forms of psychological oppression.

Slavery must be understood as a form of physical and psychological torture to grasp its horrendous and indelible effects. Slavery was, in fact, an unending torture of the minds, bodies, and souls of Africans. Peter Suedfeld's study, *Psychology and Torture,* offers a chilling perspective about the slavery experience. Blacks were tortured basically for the same five reasons Suedfeld lists as rationales for torturing prisoners of war—information, incrimination, indoctrination, intimidation, and isolation.[30] Enslaved Africans were tortured to reveal information on revolts and to incriminate and betray fellow slaves. Torture was used to indoctrinate the slave with the values and wishes of the slaveholders and to force the abandonment of his African beliefs and practices. Torture and beatings were standard methods of intimidation employed to deter rebellion and to instill docility. Isolation was a form of torture in itself. Unapproved and unwarranted congregations were met with punishment.

Describing how psychological manipulation was practiced during slavery can provide useful insights into the probable contemporary psychological effects on African Americans. Enslaved African Americans were brainwashed (which engendered self-rejection and alienation); were made to fear their captors (Whites); and were forced to develop a dependency on slave masters (White society). Some of these attitudes and dispositions have been passed on and are reflected in the behavior of many African Americans. It is possible to compare these psychological responses to those exhibited by prisoners of war. Parallels with the treatment of prisoners of war are drawn here to highlight the concern that military psychiatrists, and the American public in general, have for war veterans who have been subjected to oppression and torture. In contrast, there has been little concern expressed about the long-term psychological consequences of enslavement. The Korean and Vietnam Wars show prime examples. Presenting veterans' experiences as prisoners of war as similar to that of former slaves is not an extreme analogy. Extreme cruelty and inhumane acts of oppression inflicted by one group on another psychologically affects both the victims and the victimizers.

Psychologists and sociologists differ on the extent and significance of the effects of slavery on contemporary African Americans. However, clinical psychologists Na'im Akbar and Bobby E. Wright are prominent among Black behavioral scientists who subscribe to the theory that slavery has had a continuing influence on the psychology of African Americans. Akbar argues that certain African American individual behaviors are influenced by collective factors that are historically remote.[31] Although we must acknowledge that slavery developed some strengths as well as weaknesses in the African character, a developmental focus necessarily emphasizes negative effects that require amelioration. From a psychohistorical perspective, Akbar describes destructive attitudes of many contemporary African Americans that may have derived from slavery. The dispositions and attitudes are related to property, work, leadership, "clowning," personal inferiority, community division, family instability, and color consciousness.[32] Attitudes toward work of some African Americans might be attributed to the slavery experience. Slaves worked with no compensation for their labor. Consequently, work was viewed as punishment, and some enslaved Blacks developed a hatred for work.

According to Akbar, the master's fine house, exquisite clothes, and luxurious material possessions created mixed attitudes in the minds of enslaved Blacks. On one hand, it caused them to resent property and property ownership. They also developed an unconscious delight in destroying or vandalizing property. The opposite effect was that property and material goods caused the enslaved African to be unnaturally attracted to expensive, flashy clothes or goods. This resulted in a tendency toward conspicuous consumption. This theory is similar to Franz Fanon's indication of the psychological dynamics that existed between the colonizer and the colonized in *The Wretched of the Earth.*[33] Indeed, the psychological effects of slavery are analogous to Fanon's behavioral concepts of colonialism in the Third World.

The leadership crisis and lack of unity in the Black community may also have its attitudinal origins in slavery. Emerging leaders of the slave community were eliminated or co-opted to serve the interests of slave masters. Therefore, out of fear, a hesitancy to exercise strong leadership developed, coupled with a collective suspicion targeting anyone attempting to assume leadership roles. Politically detrimental divisions within Black communities may have roots in the stratification introduced by slave masters between field and house slaves.

The illusory, superior social status afforded to quasi-free Blacks and mulattos during slavery was designed for the purpose of dividing and subordinating African-descended people regardless of status. Intraracial color consciousness was learned from

Whites and emulated by African Africans during and after slavery, and, unfortunately, is reemerging as a divisive factor in Black communities. Many White slave masters would elevate and educate their Black offspring conceived through rape or miscegenation. The psychological effects of color prejudice have had attitudinal and personality influences on African Americans.[34]

The psychological effects of slavery on the Black family's stability have been discussed in previous chapters. Behavioral or personality traits, such as self-rejection, personal inferiority, and acquiescence to White domination are slave-acquired characteristics according to Akbar in *Chains and Images of Psychological Slavery*. Perhaps the most controversial slavery-acquired trait that Akbar mentions is "clowning." He implies that overrepresentation of African Americans in the entertainment and sports fields developed from the opportunity allowed slaves to serve as jesters, clowns, or fools for the masters' entertainment. Akbar also refers to the majority of comedy based film and media roles Blacks have been allowed to play.

Na'im Akbar, a clinical psychologist, and Franz Fanon, a psychiatrist, contend in their works that both slavery and colonialism caused their victims to internalize destructive behavioral characteristics that contributed to their continuing oppression long after liberation or decolonization has been achieved. All psychologists may not concur that the historical effects of slavery still influence African American behavior and status. However, it is imperative that Black psychology consider in its academic and therapeutic purposes and objectives the historical variables that have impacted the life experiences of Black or African people.

Even if the idea that some Black behaviors derive from the effects of slavery is minimized or discounted, the thesis that African Americans suffer psychologically from post-slavery racist oppression is generally affirmed by many Black psychologists. The psychological effects of racist oppression have caused social dysfunction, aberrant behavior, and cultural alienation. Racism still impacts the mental health of African Americans.[35] Racism is the abstract component of physical racial slavery. Although the physical bondage of slavery has ended, racism keeps Blacks in a state of psychological oppression and bondage.

Psychotherapy, Mental Health, and African Americans

In 1968, the National Advisory Commission on Civil Disorders reported that the United States was headed towards the permanent establishment of two societies, one predominantly White and the other largely Black.[36] More than twenty years later, in 1989, a study approved by the National Research Council revealed that racial separation in American life had remained relatively the same.[37] Thus, it is obvious that African Americans have maintained, basically, a distinct social and cultural ethos apart from European Americans since the landing of the first twenty Africans at Jamestown in 1619. Consequently, a major contention of Black psychotherapists is that orthodox Western psychology and clinical approaches are not usually adapted to accommodate the distinct behavioral styles, personalities, and mental functioning of African people.

In spite of significant differences in cultural origins, ethos, behavior, and personal values between Blacks and Whites, psychologist K. Alan Wesson argues that the White psychotherapist uses the Anglo-American standards as tools for comparison, judgment, and measurement of the Black man and his society. However, given the existence of significant cultural differences, it is totally inappropriate for a White person to judge and evaluate a Black person using White standards, assuming inaccurately that Blacks' behavior is no different from Whites'. Many White analysts have, unfortunately, taken the view that Blacks are merely White men with Black skins.[38]

Black self-diagnosis and psychotherapy are essential elements to be considered in the treatment of the mental health problems of African Americans. Recognition that European paradigms may not be totally applicable in defining and diagnosing African or Black American mental disorders has led to the development of Black mental health models. Among prominent Afrocentrist mental health theorists are: Daudi Ajani ya Azibo, Joseph A. Baldwin, and Wade W. Nobles.[39]

Azibo, Baldwin, and Nobles think that effective therapy for African Americans must begin with knowledge of African (Black) psychology, philosophy, culture, and personality theory. African mental health models must involve dimensions of spirituality in concurrence with mental and emotional factors in psychotherapy. Thus, the European psychologist's knowledge, methodologies, and behavioral perceptions may be inadequate for dealing with the African psyche. The overriding assumption is that diagnosis and therapy are more accurately and effectively provided when the clinician and client have the same racial identity, and their culture, history, and values are more in common.

However, an African definitional system or standard is established in order to measure and determine the subject's degree of disorientation or deviance from the African, as opposed to the European, norm. Black personality research proposes to learn how and why a high level of African/Black consciousness enhances the psychological functioning of African Americans. It is known that a positive concept of one's self is a first step towards good mental health. Research studies do not accurately or reliably measure the effect that racism and discrimination have had on the mental health of African Americans. Individuals differ in their ability to cope or to tolerate racial bigotry, denigration, and persecution. Even though it may be difficult to quantify in biological terms the impact that racism has upon an individual or group, it is undeniable that racial oppression negatively affects the psychological or mental health of Blacks. Beyond the negative behavioral and personality effects discussed in the previous topic, racism and racial antagonism cause African Americans to suffer undue *depression, stress, anger,* and *hypertension.* Unsuccessful adaptation and coping strategies for these maladies can lead to serious social and biological dysfunctions.[40]

Depression is generally perceived as manifested by a dejected emotional attitude or mood resulting from feelings of inadequacy, helplessness, hopelessness, loss, or loneliness. Stress may be described as a physiological/emotional response to an act or threat to one's physical well-being. According to literature on the subject, depression might be caused by numerous psychological, biological, or even genetic factors. Thus, the intention here is not to give the impression that racism is the only or primary cause of depression and stress in African Americans. One may logically assume, however, that injurious treatment or unpleasant experiences resulting from exposure to racism or racist conditions and acts may contribute to the symptoms of depression or stress.

No racially identifiable African American person can consciously or subconsciously escape the effects of racism and racial subjugation in the United States. Encountering the effects of racism or race-consciousness is a daily, indeed hourly, experience for Black people, whether in the workplace, the school, the market, the bank, or on the street. A Black person sees himself or herself functioning at a negative, disparate level in almost every social, political, and economic sphere of American society. Black Americans are confronted and subjected almost totally to White authority figures in employment, education, commercial and financial institutions, social and government institutions, law enforcement and judicial systems, and in the media.

Race and color, more than other factors, determine the collective quality of life, achievement potential, health, and life-chances of African Americans. From this social reality of Black life, some symptoms of depression and stress inevitably develop. Black/African psychology further suggests that there are forms of depression and stress disorders peculiar to African Americans as a consequence of their distinct social reality.

Some psychotherapists report that many Black clients allude to feelings of worthlessness when asked to describe themselves. They seem to struggle to maintain a sense of positive self-regard in the face of oppressive circumstances. However, some manage to develop successful coping mechanisms that enable them to respond defensively to feelings of anxiety, fear, and anger generated by a hostile or overbearing environment. African Americans may also push themselves harder to overcome the stereotypes of being Black and to succeed. The tremendous effort that is required to do this is awesome and may, in itself, be a contributor to or cause of the high incidence of depression, stress, anger and/or hypertension in Black people.[41]

Black psychiatrists William H. Grier and Price M. Cobbs wrote *Black Rage* during the height of the Civil Rights Movement in 1968.[42] In a chapter discussing mental illness and the treatment of Black Americans, the writers describe the psychological "Black Norm." In essence, they speak of the natural tendency of Blacks to be wary and internally rebellious against a social system that is set against them. Blacks develop a profound distrust of their White fellow citizens and exercise eternal and unrelenting vigilance to protect themselves from humiliation, mistreatment, or physical hurt. Consequently, Grier and Cobbs state, they develop "a sadness and intimacy with misery which has become a characteristic of black Americans. It is a *cultural depression* and a *cultural masochism.*"[43]

Black anger often stems from the perception of having been treated unfairly or discriminated against, which can cause frustration and generate aggression. The Black Norm attitude Grier and Cobbs describe can be attributed to the African American experience

5

of having been reduced or relegated to insignificant and "minority" roles in the school, workplace, community, or society as a whole. Commenting on such marginalized roles, psychotherapist Betty Davis observes:

> As a consequence of racial roles in society, it is normal for Blacks to express anger as a healthy response to oppression and racism, better known as sublimation. Psychotherapists must begin to recognize and accept this anger as a healthy cultural response and assist Black clients to find constructive outlets for these feelings, instead of labeling them pathological. The clients' responses to stressors and/or behaviors through self-actualization may be a valuable means of support in working through the reactions to feelings of anger or aggression.[44]

Professional opinions and writings of Black psychologists and psychotherapists confirm that psychological reactions to race problems and racism are an integral part of the Black psyche. Thus, such factors should not be excluded as relevant psychological variables in the diagnosis and treatment of depression, stress, anger, or hypertension in African Americans.

Hypertension, which can be caused by physical, physiological, and/or psychosocial factors, is a major health problem of Blacks in the United States. However, research relating to the etiology of hypertension from psychosocial conditions is inconclusive. It is believed that the enhanced risk of hypertension among Blacks is attributable to a combination of psychological, biological, socioeconomic, sociocultural, and ecological factors. Whereas depression, subjective and chronic stress, anger and anxiety are known to be contributors to hypertension, socioeconomic factors (inadequate and inappropriate diet, poverty), and chemical dependency (alcohol, tobacco, drugs) are equally suspected.[45] The psychosocial experiences and socioeconomic conditions of Blacks are different from those of Whites because of racism and various psychological forms of oppression. This differential factor may be responsible for the higher incidence of hypertension among the African American population.

Racial oppression has been shown to have both direct and indirect effects in causing symptoms of depression and stress in both middle- and lower-income African Americans. The economic and political barriers to social mobility are prime contributors to Black stress and depression. Discrimination and prejudice based on race impede the employment and job advancement of African Americans, both of which can contribute to various symptoms related to mental disorders.[46] Even on the job, African Americans may experience feelings of social isolation, race-related anxiety, and cultural alienation. Often Blacks must adopt White "normative" or protective coping behaviors in order not to jeopardize their employment, especially in major American corporations.[47] Similar psychologically-related experiences are reported by Blacks in academic and government employment.

Working conditions or exploitative working situations can have the effect of lowering self-esteem and may create psychological tensions that contribute to symptoms of stress, anxiety, and depression.[48] Because of such negative race-related psychosocial experiences, Blacks are at a disproportionate risk for mental health disorders. Various researchers have documented that the harassment and discrimination experienced by African American employees in the workplace induce defensive responses, stress, and stress-related medical problems. F. M. Baker concludes that physical ailments can be induced by stress associated with confronting racism, frustration, and hostile working conditions.[49] Lawrence Houston states, "The denial of illness to avoid absences from work results in hypertension, coronary artery disease, and increased morbidity."[50] These problems are exacerbated when managerial personnel fail to respond appropriately to eliminate the sources of harassment and discrimination. To illustrate, Houston observes that the level of frustration experienced by African Americans increases "when it is recognized that those who have been placed, democratically, into the highest positions of power and leadership are unsympathetic, insensitive, and often callous regarding the plight of minorities."[51]

Psychology of Black Identity, Personality, and Self-concept

The perspective of Africana Studies specialists regarding minimal requirements for coherent study of the experiences of people of African descent in their psychological dimensions has been cogently summarized by Diane Pinderhughes:

[T]o understand individual behavior or emotion one must consider the relationships among the individual, the family, and the social system, the value orientations of the individual, family, subgroup, and social system, the geographical setting, and the interpenetration of all these systems and processes that operate in a reverberating and reciprocal manner. All of these factors influence and are influenced by each other, and they must all be taken into account in any understanding of culture.[52]

Racial and Ideological Identity

One of the most destructive psychological consequences of slavery was the loss or obfuscation of the African's distinct human identity. Adelbert Jenkins avers that "one of the major contributions that a stable African background gave to the enslaved Africans and their descendants was a basis for a sense of competence as human beings."[53] During slavery, every effort was made by the oppressor to obliterate, diminish, or disregard the African's individual self-concept and collective identity as a people. This was an essential step in dehumanizing the enslaved. During and since slavery, Black people have continually struggled to reassert and enhance their racial collectivity and to reestablish their cultural identity.

The identity reconstruction process has been fraught with various psychological difficulties and ideological conflicts among the former African slaves. Black people have had to wrestle with differences in self-identification engendered by the slavery experience, on the one hand, and with identifications attributed to them by Whites, on the other. In this context, Hussein Bulhan observes:

When the oppressor's harsh prohibitions and threats are enacted in family and interpersonal relations, problems of oppression and hence of violence become infused with a confounding ambivalence and guilt. This intensity of oppression, when even loved ones have adopted the oppressor's values and norms, is most difficult to change... What is more, the institutionalization of oppression in daily living also entails an internalization of the oppressor's values, norms, and prohibitions. Internalized oppression is most resistant to change, since this would require a battle on

two fronts: the oppressor within and the oppressor without.[54]

Bulhan even questions whether traditional socializing institutions can insulate individuals from massive assaults on the psyche:

Even if the family remains relatively intact or little tarnished by this violent social order, the attack on the self is merely postponed until one moves away from the intimate circle of the family to the ubiquitous violence of the wider social world. Thus black children who grow up in a healthy family environment sooner or later come up against massive social forces that undermine and sometimes overwhelm their development.[55]

These assaults on collective identity have been characterized by Bulhan as a "cognitive and affective 'Middle Passage' in the cultural deracination of blacks."[56] He argues that "like the historic Middle Passage involving the movement of bodies across the Atlantic Ocean ... so too the uprooting of psyches from their culture to their insertion into another, in which the basic values were pro-White and anti-Black, elicited a victimization difficult to quantify, but very massive."[57]

Identification is defined by some behavioral theorists as a psychological phenomenon that serves to increase feelings of worth and importance by identifying with, or taking on the characteristics, values, or cultural attributes of some person or group that is well-received by others.[58] Identification is psychologically essential for ego development and maintenance of the individual or group. A person normally has a related individual and collective identity. However, sometimes individual and collective identities are in conflict. A person may choose or prefer an identification that is consistent with his or her social reality, or one that allows escape from reality.

The identification dilemma for Blacks in America has been and continues to be caused by psychological and ideological conflicts of perceptual racial identification and acceptance. In other words, Blacks have always deliberated over whether to seek the acceptance of and identification with Whites or to adopt and declare a Black or African identity distinct from that of European Americans. Race-related assimilationist, integrationist, cultural nationalist, and separatist ideologies have been divisive elements affecting the thought and philosophy of Black Americans.

5

In response to ideological differences, the collective identification or race label of Blacks in America has changed, or a popular identity has existed concurrently with others at various times during the course of American history. The changes referred to are Black self-identifications and not attributed identifications.

The racial identification changes have been influenced by corresponding changes in the political, economic, social, and cultural outlook and condition of Black people, which in turn have altered their psychological inclinations and ideological perspectives.[59] From slavery to the present, the various names Blacks have adopted for racial identification include: African, Ethiopian, Colored, Negro, Afro-American, African American, and Black.

Beverly H. Wright posits that, historically, changes in the collective identification of Blacks have been directly related to their external or internal locus of control of events and circumstances affecting their condition. Blacks are externally oriented when they feel that they are powerless to influence social and political events affecting their condition. When Blacks feel that they can effect or change social and political events, they become more internally oriented. For example, during the "Colored Era" Blacks felt powerless to affect White hostility and oppression. The "Negro Era" was one in which Blacks began to exert moral suasion, court appeals, and peaceful protest. It was an era that produced hope and a weakening of the external forces that stifled their courage and initiative. Thus, they became more internally motivated. The "Black Era," commencing in the 1960s, represented a period of open defiance, rebellion, retaliatory violence, and a demand for Black Power.[60] This period was an era of self-definition, irrespective of attributed racial identifications. During the Black Era, Blacks have had more internal influence over their condition than at any other era in American history.

Sterling Stuckey found that the term *Negro* was once strongly associated with *slave*, especially, in the South. Negro was often pronounced demeaningly as *nigra* or *nigger* by southern Whites. Stuckey also informs us that the terms *colored* and *brown* were preferred by many of the light-skinned Africans of mixed-race ancestry who formed much of the free Black population.[61] Historically, as well as today, the term *African* reflects a pride in being a member of the Black race. The term *African* was used in the titles of many Black organizations that originated during and shortly after the slavery era. Yet, there were Black assimilationists and integrationists who adamantly opposed any Black organization having a title that would indicate its racial origin or constituency.[62]

Much of the variability of Black racial identification has been related to the collective political consciousness of Blacks during different stages of American social and economic development. However, underlying any ideological rationale is the psychological factor of Black self-concept. The terms *African American* and *Black* gained popular usage only after millions of Black Americans had begun to develop attitudes of "self-love" and a strong Black or African consciousness.

Prior to the Civil Rights and Black Power Movements of the 1960s, it could be said that most Blacks possessed weak African-centered psychological orientations. Consistent with the Frederick Douglass assimilation philosophy and aspirations, a significant segment of the Black population tended to view with disdain any identity symbol that would jeopardize their acceptance by Whites or would be contrary to Eurocentric values and standards. This mental attitude has been described or alluded to by Leachim T. Semaj, Na'im Akbar and other Afrocentric psychologists as an anti-self disorder or alien race preference disorientation.[63] It should be noted, however, that part of the reason why many Black Americans avoided identification with Africa was because of the negative depiction of continental Africans in the media as cannibals, savages, and primitive barbarians by Europeans and Americans.

Josephine Moraa Moikobu attempted to reveal the nature, character, and extent of Black American and African identification in a study of students. Moikobu revealed that Black Americans and Africans relate on a common basis according to specific *internal* and *external dimensions* of identity. *Internal dimensions* of identity apply to inherent attributes that come about through genetic constitution, over which the individual has no control, such as color and ancestry. *External dimensions* of identity are those based on political, social, and economic forces, including certain cultural phenomena. For example, Black Americans expressed their internal dimensions of identity with Africans in terms of their mutual color (Blackness), common race, and ancestry. In terms of their external dimensions of identity, they saw Whites as a common oppressor, similar suffering from racism, and a unified stance against the notion of White supremacy. Black Africans saw as internal dimensions of identity the commonality of Blackness and similar exposures to White prejudices and racism. They listed as external dimensions of identity with Black Americans their mutual struggle for political and economic power, common views toward colonization and international affairs, and African behaviors. Since Black Americans are "citizens" of the United States and, differentially, Africans are members of African "independent" states, the two peoples have less commonality in external dimensions of identity.[64]

At the beginning of the 1990s, national polls indicated that Black Americans prefer the racial identification of *Black* by a significant margin. A study conducted among Black students at a California university and an Arizona university supported previous surveys that *Black* is the more contemporary and socially acceptable race label as compared with *Black American*, *Afro-American*, and *Black Afro-American*, and others. Those preferring Black American wished to express ethnic pride as well as a degree of patriotism because "my people built this country." Those selecting *Afro-American* wished to emphasize their African ancestry and argued that "our roots are not in America."[65] This student survey may have limited use because it was not stated whether the terms *African* and *African American* were listed on the questionnaire. A more recent poll indicates interesting variations in preferences based on age and location of residence. In a study published in 2005, Lee Sigelman and his co-authors examined preferences for labels by using the National Survey of Black workers regarding the terms *Black* and *African American*. Sigelman, et al., found that, overall, preferences were evenly split between the two terms. There were no differences between males and females, but older Blacks were less likely to prefer *African American*. Residents of large cities were more likely to prefer *African American*. Respondents who scored higher on the racial identification scale the researchers used tended to prefer the term *African American*. One of the more interesting findings of the study is that individuals who had attended schools where Blacks or Whites were in the distinct majority were less likely to prefer *African American* than those who had attended schools with balanced student populations.[66]

Since the 1960s, Blacks have been more inclined to accept or acknowledge an African identification. After more than three hundred years of rejection and denial of equal opportunity, the reclamation of African heritage and values may be therapeutic for the psychological functioning of Blacks in America. Until Blacks are accorded equal rights, justice, and opportunity, they may increasingly repudiate Eurocentric values and ideology and embrace an African ethos and identification. The African American has always had to endure the mental travail of "double-consciousness," feeling one's "twoness—an American, a [Black]; two souls, two thoughts, two unreconciled strivings; two warring ideals in one dark body, whose dogged strength alone keeps it from being torn asunder," as was so eloquently described by W. E. B. Du Bois.[67]

Ever since the late 1930s, the matter of African American/Black self-concept or self-esteem has been an academic concern. For various reasons, it is assumed that slavery and the subjugated post-slavery experience of Blacks have afflicted them with attitudes and dispositions of self-derogation. The Black Power and Black Pride movements of the 1960s ushered in an era of psychological reversal of many of the previously held perceptions African Americans may have held of themselves. Yet, some behavioral and social theorists argue that vestiges of negative Black self-concepts still afflict the psyche of many African Americans.

Black *self-concept* is a term specifically used to define or refer to an African American's perception of his or her own worthiness. In general, self-concept is how one characterizes or perceives one's self in relation to others at any specific time and under certain societal or global conditions. Black self-concept is related to all of the psychological elements of Black identity and personality previously discussed. Therefore, Black self-concept may also be described as a conscious, preconscious, subconscious, or unconscious psychological phenomenon. From an analysis of various studies, it is evident that various concepts and definitions of Black self-concept exist.

Research on the Black self-concept has received much criticism. First, many of the studies are perceived as one-dimensional because color-awareness has been used as the primary determinant of Black positive or negative self-concept. Self-evaluation might be based on several factors, including color. Secondly, White people are always used as the model race of comparison. Indeed, much of the research on the Black self-concept has been initiated by White investigators.[68] Thirdly, the preponderance of subjects have been pre-school, primary, and high school children or adolescents.

During the period 1939 to 1973 alone, over one hundred studies and re-studies related to the measurement or determination of the Black self-concept have been conducted. Many more empirical studies have been executed up to the present date. The findings have been as varied and inconclusive as the myriad methodologies and techniques employed in research testing. Although a few of these studies tend to refute the negative Black self-concept theory, most reveal that for various reasons the color white (and implicitly White people) are held in higher esteem by Black children than their own color and race.[69]

Interest in Black self-concept research and theory became a popular academic pursuit after 1939, when Black psychologists Kenneth B. Clark and Mamie P. Clark developed the Black and White "dolls test" to determine children's racial awareness and preferences.[70] In successive studies by the Clarks and by others, it was inferred that Black children's choice of White dolls was indicative of their individual and group self-hatred. Criticism of the Clarks' methodology led to numerous variations. Other tests have included not only dolls but assorted methodologies using photographs, movies, crayons, colored pictures, etc. No attempt will be made here to discuss the voluminous studies of the Black self-concept. However, some recent studies seem to infer that many Black children, even thirty years after the Civil Rights and Black Power Movements, have color preferences for White people rather than for people of their own race. It is important to note that Sharon and Gopaul McNicol stated in their study that Black "parents may be implicitly guiding their children's experience" when they "buy only white dolls for their children."[71]

Logically, one may assume that the inclination for some Black children to prefer and admire White dolls or people more than Black dolls and their own race is a behavioral trait that is, in part, acquired from their African American parents. The cultural and social values of children are initially and profoundly influenced through parental relationships and the home environment. Consequently, Black self-concept studies have been grossly misguided. It would be far more progressive for African American adults to be subjected to Black/African consciousness tests and studies than Black children. Children who originate from strong African/Black centered households are bound to reflect some of the same characteristics in the choices they make in their daily lives.

One must realize that attitudes and beliefs in White supremacy are basically learned by White children from their parents and adult role models. Because of their religious and spiritual nature, Black parents tend to teach their children egalitarian values and to love everybody. Certainly, there is a religious variable that may influence children's social values and racial behaviors. Then, too, the insidious institutional racism that prevails in the public school system and schools cannot be ruled out as a major negative socialization factor affecting the self-concept of Black children. Educational subject matter, perspectives, and pictures in textbooks are White and European oriented. For the most part, American authority figures, folklore symbols, and media models are White.

Thus, a tremendous amount of research is not necessary to determine if, and why, Black children may be prone to prefer and to identity with Whites. The causes of such behavior are well-known. White cultural hegemony and institutional racism are powerful forces that can have a debilitating effect on the self-concept of children and adult African Americans. Consequently, doll tests and similar color-choice experiments are of little value in treating the root causes of Black low self-esteem. The motive and implications of these White/Black dolls color awareness tests seem to reinforce the ethnocentrism of Whites and focus unwarranted attention on the myth of White superiority.

The process of racial identity development is interwoven with mechanisms by which individuals develop the general capacity to function in the broader social milieu. Many reformist Black psychologists conceptualize the development of a stable Black identity as requiring "transformation" of a preexisting identity structure. This transformation is seen largely as a reaction to externally generated oppression.

During the 1960s and 1970s several "transformation" models were proposed. The most prominent is the model of Nigrescence developed by William Cross.[72] Cross's analysis is grounded in a conception of self-concept with two components: personal identity and reference group orientation. He introduces the possibility that an individual can be mentally healthy in terms of personal identity while, at the same time, not have a strong orientation toward a concept of African Americans as a distinct cultural collective. Reference group orientation, according to Cross, encompasses a variety of constructs that include racial identity, group identity, race awareness, racial ideology, race evaluation, race esteem, race image, and racial self-identification.[73]

More recent research focusing on the Cross model has provided support for the basic framework. Frank Worrell, et al., have examined the extent to which the stage definitions are consistent across students attending predominately Black (HBCUs) and predominantly White colleges and universities (PWIs). The researchers found four of the profiles—pre-encounter assimilation, pre-encounter mis-education, pre-encounter self-hatred, and immersion-emersion anti-White among students at both types of institutions, although there are some distinctive features that distinguish profiles among students attending HBCUs from those attending PWIs. Multicultural internalization profiles were found only among PWI students. Interestingly, there was limited evidence of the presence of internalized Afrocentric profiles at either type of institution.[74]

Nigrescence, for Cross, "is a *resocializing* experience that seeks to transform preexisting identity (a non-Afrocentric identity) into one that is Afrocentric by overcoming barriers to wholesome identity development created by social forces that induce an identity that reflects deracination and/or deculturation."[75] The model posits that individuals go through several stages in developing an awareness of individual and collective racial identity, that is, pre-encounter, encounter, immersion-emersion, and internalization/transformation. In the *pre-encounter stage*, persons "hold attitudes toward race that run from low salience to race-neutral, to anti-Black." The *encounter* stage entails two steps: experiencing an encounter and personalizing it. The third stage, *immersion-emersion*, first involves total submersion into "the world of Blackness," pursued in a highly emotional manner ideally, followed by a "leveling-out" period during which an individual uses a more intellectually driven approach to the pursuit of Black interests. According to Cross, this leveling-out process "results in the discovery that one's first impressions of Blackness were romantic and symbolic, not substantive textured and complex ... [and leads] toward association with groups or persons who are demonstrating a 'more serious' understanding of, and commitment to, Black issues," although the intensity of this phase can presumably lead some individuals to regress to earlier stages.[76]

The fourth stage involves the *internalization* of the new identity. Cross maintains, "For the 'settled' convert, the new identity gives high salience to Blackness, with the degree of salience determined by ideological considerations. At one extreme are nationalists, whose concern for race leaves little room for other considerations, for others Blackness becomes one of several (biculturalism) or many saliences (multiculturalism)."[77] He also insists, however, that "new challenges (e.g., a new Encounter) may bring about the need to recycle through some of the stages[, but] the successful resolution of one's racial identity conflicts makes it possible to shift attention to other identity concerns, such as religion, gender and sexual preferences, career development, social class and poverty, and multiculturalism."[78] Beverly Vandiver, who has collaborated with Cross in developing instruments to measure the expanded model, along with Cross and other researchers, have found that a multicultural inclusiveness orientation is more important than acceptance of members of other racial groups in the internalization stage.[79]

Research focusing on this model has been limited largely to testing the accuracy of stage definitions through the development of batteries of questions and the administration of instruments containing these questions to carefully selected samples of African Americans. Janet Helms notes that one of the limitations associated with this research is that the scales designed to measure model stages of Black identity have been used primarily "with college and university samples exclusively and thus one must ask whether it has heuristic value for other types of populations."[80]

Since most African Americans are not enrolled in institutions of higher education, results of studies of identity development of college students cannot be generalized to the larger population of young African Americans or to other segments of the African American population. There is a need to pay particular attention to the re-socialization of those caught up in the criminal justice system and in those activities that increase the likelihood of engagement with that system. A. Wade Boykin and Constance Ellison assert:

African American youth come to accept, reject, combine, blend, or otherwise negotiate the socialization dictates and messages emanating from the mainstream, minority and Afrocultural experiences. These outcomes, which translate into a given constellation of behaviors, values, beliefs, and roles, will serve expressive, instrumental, and terminal functions in the course of one's life. The

5

acceptance, rejection, and negotiation through the three realms principally transpire in the contexts of certain socialization agencies, in particular the family, school, media, and peer group. What constellation of outcomes actually obtains can be linked to the varying quality of the processes of socialization which prevailed in one's life and to the relative draw or repulsion of the various socialization ecologies.[81]

The negative socialization experiences of young African Americans increase the possibility that many will recycle through earlier stages on a periodic basis or "drop out." Cross describes "dropping out" as choosing to reject Blackness, sometimes "with considerable enthusiasm, becoming almost *reactionary* in disappointment with and opposition to the 'Blackness' thing."[82]

There are also severe limitations on the existing knowledge about the dynamics of racial identity among adults. A 1988 study by Clifford Broman, et al. reports that racial group identification was strongest among older Blacks and the least educated Blacks living in urban areas. Generally, higher education was associated with lower degrees of racial group identification for urban dwellers. College-educated Blacks living in the North and South were, however, more likely to have a higher level of racial group identification than college-educated Blacks living in the West.[83] A study by Vetta Thompson, approximately a decade later, found that early socialization that led to the inculcation of positive attitudes toward Black culture and continuing engagement with other African Americans increased the importance of racial identity for African American adults. Racial identity was heightened by perceptions of injustice and intergroup inequity. Moreover, she found that the salience of racial identity was largely unaffected by the intensity of an individual's integration experiences.[84]

There is also some limited evidence of variations in identity dynamics across socioeconomic classes. Upward socioeconomic class mobility poses significant challenges to sustaining and maintaining a collective sense of racial identity. Lois Benjamin, based on an analysis of the values and beliefs of one hundred Black elites employed in a broad cross-section of White-collar occupations, reports:

The color line and the acceptance of the value orientation of democracy, freedom, equality, individualism, progress and achievement result in a dual value system ...This dual value orientation is a source of conflict which manifests itself in their personal and collective identity. The way the Black elite experience the conflict of the color line is on an individual level, though it has a collective component—it is a shared experience.[85]

Lois Benjamin suggests that the potential exists for this group to develop a heightened racial collective consciousness "if ... the Black elite can externalize their response [to racism] and create messages from their subjective experiences that will lead to proactivity."[86] In a similar vein, Adelbert H. Jenkins asserts:

Biculturality is not simply a (relatively static) trait ... It is more properly thought of as an ongoing *process* or style of activity that characterizes the way Blacks have tended to deal with the realities of America. ... [Using] the capacity to imagine and use alternatives in conceptualizing a particular situation... [I]n their everyday efforts to enhance their competence many African Americans are intent on affirming their own cultural identity and are also open to making use of other cultural ways of adapting, depending on cultures, at least, individualism and collectivism need not be mutually exclusive.[87]

Jenkins insists that, although many Blacks suffer the "double jeopardy" of oppressive race and social class pressures, they do not seem to show greater mental disturbance than do Whites of similar socioeconomic status. This suggests that African Americans from all socioeconomic levels can develop a sufficient repertoire of cross-cultural interaction skills to forestall psychic collapse in the face of contemporary patterns of racial oppression.[88]

The processes described by Jenkins can be understood as a type of "identity negotiation," in which persons engage in a conscious and mindful process of shifting behaviors to achieve optimal outcomes during encounters with others, as James Stewart and Ronald Jackson observe:

Identity negotiation is about coordinating one's identity to match, complement or not resist the presence of other cultural identities. As with any relationship, if others do not coordinate relationships with us in a fair, equitable manner, relational possibilities may dissolve. However, if one feels coerced and his/her life possibilities, financial means of survival or some other major factor is at stake, certain cultural contacts may be more appealing despite coercion.[89]

Despite the preceding optimistic research findings that suggest the persistence of effective psychological resistance to deracination and efforts to distort racial identification, it is important to recognize the limitations of individualized efforts. Ronald Walters offers the cogent reminder that "in the Diaspora, the contradiction of possessing more than one identity has never been resolved and will not be as long as the basic identity of Africa continues to be the footstool of the world and African people ... are everywhere subordinated."[90]

African/Black Ordered and Disordered Personality

The emphasis on reconstructing the African personality structure as a fundamental basis for addressing the psychological challenges facing African Americans is the starting point for the radical school of Black psychology. The researchers question whether the process of psychological metamorphosis by which a deracinated African/African American is transformed into an African embracing *psychological Blackness*, as posited by Cross and other adherents to the reformist school, can be sustained. *Psychological Blackness* refers to a developmental system of psychogenic (spiritual, emotional, biochemical) and behavioral traits that are fundamental to African people. Radical theorists argue that any transformational theory that does not emphasize and promote the continuity of African-centered culture and thought, individually and/or collectively, within the African American psyche is misoriented.

As Daudi Azibo and Jeanene Robinson insist, "a psychological state in which the African person's orientation is the prioritization of the defense, development, and maintenance of African life and culture represents normalcy in African psychological functioning by most Afrocentric accounts."[91] Azibo and Robinson assert that the end stage for Cross, *internalization*, is actually a sophisticated regression to his beginning stage of pre-encounter. Such retrogression would not allow psychological Africanity to attain its logical conclusion. Thus, functional and therapeutic Black identity and personality theories must prioritize the defense, development, and maintenance of African life and culture.[92]

It is important to note that the radical school uses *personality* rather than identity as its core construct. Like so many abstract psychological words and concepts, there is no consensus on a specific definition of personality. Personality has various meanings and implications, depending on the objectives of the clinician or the impressions one gains from observing the behavioral characteristics of another person. Behavioral scientists lean toward the belief that the essence of an individual's personality emanates from the depths of the inner-self and transcends mere observable traits. Personality may be differentially defined based on Eurocentric or Afrocentric worldviews and perspectives.

However, Gordon Allport's definition that "personality is the dynamic organization within the individual of those psychophysical systems that determine his characteristic behavior and thought"[93] serves as a partial bridge between Afrocentric and Eurocentric concepts. Although Eurocentric behavioral scientists concur that culture and personality are closely related, Afrocentric psychologists stress the interrelatedness of race and culture relative to the African or Black personality. From the framework of Black personality theory, one's psychological experience is inextricably related to race. Joseph A. Baldwin asserts that biological and psychological phenomena are interrelated and interdependent, as defined by the natural order, such that psychological experience derives from a biological basis. Thus, each biogenetic (racial) type has its own distinct set of psychological and behavioral traits or dispositions.[94]

Their unique environment, institutions, values, socioeconomic and political experiences, and African ethos influence Black Americans to behave within a prescribed set of functional psychological norms. Race and culture are powerful forces that contribute to Black personality development and normal psychological functioning. However, racism and White cultural hegemony can have dysfunctional effects on African self-consciousness and cause the development of a disordered Black personality. Therefore, basic to the principles and practice of Black psychology are the definition and delineation of behavioral traits and attitudinal characteristics that constitute a normal African/Black personality.

5

Irene Atwell and Daudi Azibo propound that Africans/Blacks have "normal" or "correct" personalities when they have beliefs, values, attitudes, and behaviors that are African oriented; recognize themselves as African and Black; prioritize the interests, survival, and proactive development of Africans/Blacks; and support a standard of conduct that neutralizes people and things that are anti-African.[95] The objective of a Black normalcy concept is not to be ethnocentric or anti-others, but to recognize the potential of psychological dysfunction, which often results from an anti-self personality. Pro-self or pro-own group does not necessarily translate into being anti-others.

Because mental health may be determined by correct or normal psychological and behavioral functioning, Azibo has constructed a nosology of African personality disorder, referred to hereafter as the Azibo Nosology. The Azibo Nosology is a diagnostic system or guide for an Africentric representation of personality. It makes three prefatory points for consideration of mental order or mental disorder in Blacks. First, it explicates the nature of the relationship between personality order and personality disorder. Secondly, it advances the criticality of the self in personality or mental order and disorder. Thirdly, in spite of the risk of being criticized for its moral emphasis, the nosology promotes values and contends that they are fundamentally inherent in the diagnostic process.[96] The nosology lists and diagrams eighteen disorders peculiar to the African/Black personality. The Azibo Nosology represents a compilation of personality disorder theories from a host of Black behavioral theorists including those of Azibo.

While it is not possible to discuss all eighteen disorders in this survey, attention is given to a few that are perhaps more notable and lucid. Psychological misorientation, mentacide, alien-self disorder, anti-self disorder, psychological brainwashing, oppression violence, and self-destructive disorders, for example, have been alluded to in previous discussions. Most of these disorders are almost self-explanatory.

Psychological misorientation means that the individual functions without an African-centered belief system, whereby alien values and concepts exist at the expense of psychological Blackness. *Mentacide* has the effect of rendering the Black/African psyche void, and the vacuum is filled with unnatural and unwarranted acceptance, admiration, and allegiance to European, Arab, or any other alien groups, regardless of the denigrating opinions these groups may have toward

Africans or the injustice and inhumanity Blacks suffer at their hands. Mentacide has been figuratively described as the rape or murder of a person's mind.[97]

Alien-self-disordered Black persons tend to view themselves and world phenomena totally from a Eurocentric or alien perspective. They prefer intimate social and personal relationships with an alien group rather than with their own. An individual with an *anti-self disorder* is willing and is often chosen by an alien group to work against the survival of his own people. Racism and the psychology of oppression are instrumental in the development of alien-self and anti-self personality disorders. *Psychological brainwashing* results in the development of a mental disorder that impels the individual to inform or collaborate with the alien group. The individual may even extol the merits of being oppressed and indulge in self-blame. *Oppression violence* is a reaction to an oppressive milieu or environment. The individual may engage in unpremeditated violent acts, directed at in-group or out-group members. These various forms of behavior are analogous to the mental disorders Franz Fanon observed during a Third World liberation movement from colonialism. *Self-destructive personality* disorders are manifested in deviant behaviors, such as drug and alcohol abuse, suicide, fratricide, or Black on Black crime. It includes all those behaviors that are destructive not only to the individual but to the collective Black society.[98]

The Azibo Nosology does not contend that European-centered psychology is totally inapplicable in the diagnosis of Blacks. However, the African-centered Azibo Nosology is applicable to many of the personality disorders peculiar to Africans/Blacks. Throughout the emerging field of Black/African psychology, new or alternate Afrocentric psychotherapy models are being developed. Some will subsume existing methodologies, and others may counterpoise Eurocentric psychological paradigms. Subsequently, Azibo has identified forty "pscho-cultural perpetrations" imposed on African Americans that have resulted in what he describes as "psycho-cultural decimation," and he argues that this historical and continuing mentacide constitutes a basis for payment of reparations to the descendants of survivors of enslavement.[99] The issue of reparations is discussed in detail in Chapter 7.

Radical Black psychologists are developing instruments for empirical research to test the efficacy of their theories. Their work parallels the efforts of reformist school psychologists to refine racial identity research.

Joseph A. Baldwin and Yvonne R. Bell, for example, developed an instrument in 1985 descriptively titled "The African Self-Consciousness Scale: An Africentric Personality Questionnaire."[100] More recently, Azibo developed a "Black Personality Questionnaire" based on Robert Williams' 1981 formational concept of psychological Blackness, and Robinson and Azibo have developed the "African Self-Conscious Scale."[101]

Gender and Black Psychological Research

The astute reader will note that the discussion to this point has not addressed the issue of whether there are differences in the psychological functioning of, and challenges confronted by, African American males and females. It is absolutely critical to explore these issues for, as Barbara Omolade declares:

> The historical oppression of black women and men should have created social equality between them, but even after the end of slavery when the white patriarch receded, maleness and femaleness continued to be defined by patriarchal structures, with black men declaring wardship over black women. In the black community, the norm of manhood was patriarchal power, the norm of womanhood was adherence to it, though both men and women selected which aspects of these norms they would emphasize.[102]

Patricia Hill Collins suggests that women of African descent have developed unique psychological coping strategies as a consequence of the distinctive aspects of their oppression:

> On certain dimensions Black Women may more closely resemble Black men, on others, White women, and on still others Black women may stand apart from both groups. Black women's both/and conceptual orientation, the act of being simultaneously a member of a group and yet standing apart from it, forms an integral part of Black women's consciousness.[103]

The reformist school of Black psychology is largely silent on whether gender differences in socialization create variations in the process of developing self-efficacy and/or in cultivating racial identity. To illustrate, Adelbert Jenkins admits, "except at certain explicit points I do not distinguish between psychological issues affecting Black women as distinct from those affecting

Black men."[104] In a similar vein, William Cross acknowledges the possibility that there are gender-specific differences in the Nigrescence process but fails to address this issue systematically.[105]

The radical school of Black psychology has also been criticized for its treatment of gender. In this case, critics allege that the African societies that provide the basis for the models of psychological functioning that are used to define the norms are the same African societies that promote hierarchical male-female relationships of the type now being challenged by progressive African feminists.

It is critical that specialists work closely with progressive members of the various schools of thought in Black Psychology to confront biases that constrain the understanding of gender dimensions in identity development. To accomplish this objective, some reformulation of research techniques used to explore psychological issues may be required. The radical school is correct in emphasizing the need to use African society as a reference group, but the research must engage both historical and contemporary gender-specific psychological dynamics and not be delimited by traditional psychological research techniques. As Kim Vaz opines: "Unless we create a climate in psychology that is more amenable to alternative methods of carrying out research that are not heavily dependent on technology, our information about women in developing countries becomes the study of women's behavior in the developed world, not a true psychology of women."[106]

Research on how gender-specific psychological processes affect individual, family, and community dynamics using the type of interdisciplinary research methods advocated by African American Studies specialists is likely to yield important new insights. As Du Bois suggested in 1901, there are many delicate differences in race [and gender] psychology that are beyond the capacity of "crude social instruments" to uncover, understandable only through nonempirical methods."[107]

Psychopolitical Implications of the American Media

African Americans and the Media

From the perspective of African American Studies. a serious challenge facing specialists in the field

5

and the various schools of Black Psychology is overcoming the pervasive negative effects of the mass media on the psychological health of people of African descent. It would be hard to counter the assertion that the mass media constitute powerful agencies influencing the mind, thought, and behavior of American people. The media in the context of this discussion means all audio or visual materials or devices that influence the mind. Whether experienced via billboard, print, film, or broadcast media, the messages conveyed are designed to persuade, socialize, and control the minds of people who observe, listen, or view the content. The mass media have minimal, if any, restraints in the United States and serve basically as self-arbiters of psychological, cultural, social, and political messages. Historically, the mass media have been influential agencies in the field of race relations and have served as formidable antagonists to the social progress of African Americans.

Of the various media, Blacks have been adversely affected most by the television and film industries. When television began to emerge as the most popular medium of the American public during the late 1940s, African Americans, regardless of their socioeconomic strata, made whatever sacrifices that were necessary to acquire this intriguing electronic box and to view the fun and paradisiacal fantasies of the White world. Blacks did not initially appear on television except as menial and subservient characters, such as buffoons, butlers, doorman, porters, valets, and waiters. There were sporadic and short-term appearances by Blacks in a few programs in the North, but in the South, Blacks were not shown except as deviants and criminals on news casts. The brief duration of the Nat King Cole Show (1956) and talented Black performers on the Ed Sullivan Show (1948–71) were among the few exceptions.[108]

During the early 1960s, African Americans were still restricted to roles characterized as "Black parts," although a few made occasional appearances in regular network series. The quantity of Black characters did not increase until the 1970s when they began to star in a number of comedy shows. Whites have always tolerated and appreciated Blacks in the roles of comedians, athletes, and entertainers (singer and dancers). On the whole, the general stereotypical images and roles of Blacks on television have continued since the 1970s, although a few became hosts and co-hosts of various programs during the 1980s. Blacks were seldom cast in strong character roles, and their lives and experiences were usually unidimensional. A relative decline in the presence of Blacks in television and film was observed in the early 1980s.

Perhaps, one of the most positive contributions that television has made to the progress of African Americans was its explicit and extensive coverage during the 1960s of the Civil Rights Movement, including the Montgomery Bus Boycott. The major networks showed to the world, and in vivid detail, the brutality that was being inflicted on Blacks by Whites as they struggled for freedom and justice. Since the 1960s, the media have reverted to politico-psychological devastation of the Black psyche by portraying and reinforcing negative aspects of African American life.

The White-dominated media have the power to create images and assign definitions to certain non-White groups within the society. Positive images are assigned to Whites and negative images are ascribed to Blacks. Images are the vehicles for creating definitions. Thus, Blacks may define themselves based on the media or television images they have internalized. If negative images are transmitted and internalized, self-destructive or alien-self behavior patterns may develop. John Henrik Clarke discusses the power of such images:

> Because what we see about ourselves often influences what we do about ourselves, the role of image and the control of the mind is more important now in a media-saturated society than ever before in history. ...The image before the African child of today, both in Africa, the United States and throughout the world, is a clear indication of what they will be as adults and what they will think as adults.[109]

People in the American society rely extensively on visual media images for forming their social, political, and economic opinions. The negative images of Blacks that Whites internalize can perpetuate the myth of Black inferiority and White supremacy.

Not only are the media's distortions and stereotypes of Black social reality disturbing, but the conspicuous absence or nonportrayal of African Americans is equally appalling. The subliminal message conveyed by the absence of African American models and actors from the media is that Blacks are a nonentity in American society. Nearly all U.S. households own at least one television set. More than 98 percent of the characters or models in television are White. Yet, Blacks watch television an average of twenty-four hours per week whereas

Whites watch television an average of seventeen hours per week. This could mean that African/Black people are internalizing European/American culture and values at a faster rate than White people. The potential negative psychological effects on Black identity, personality, and self-concept are quite obvious. There is almost an inseparable relationship between the media and culture.

If one is non-White, the media are effective in alienating one from one's own race. Blacks who downplay their racial identity and lack own-race commitment are lauded, consulted, and frequently featured. Conversely, Blacks who demonstrate a pro-Black bias and a strong commitment to struggle are ignored or discredited. This is a politico-psychological aspect of the mass media.[110]

Although Black women appear in so-called "mainstream" commercials and advertisements of the print or broadcast media, their images are carefully managed to reinforce prevailing notions of beauty and cultural dominance. More often than not, in group scenes of commercials and advertisements, one symbolic Black female fleetingly appears, but there is hardly ever more than one. One wonders if the media have adopted a quota system. Tony Brown, an eminent Black journalist, explains why this is so:

> What you're looking at is more of the unconscious racism which assumes that blacks should never be in the majority. So as long as advertisers can create a world in which blacks are always in the minority, it seems to keep white people safe, or give them a false sense of security. ...And since two-thirds of the world is not white, they're only fooling themselves.[111]

Often when more than one Black is portrayed, it is in a stigma-oriented commercial. It appears that a disproportionate number of Black models promote personal care products.[112] For example, African Americans are frequently used in commercials advertising medication to ameliorate constipation, a pattern that reinforces stereotypes about the dietary practices of Blacks and their health implications.

Social and Psychological Media Influences

Social psychology offers a valid framework for the study of media influence and the socialization of power. As noted previously, this subfield is concerned with the study of individual behavior in a social setting or with the influence of other people or individuals. The American media primarily represents and promotes the culture, values, and experiences of White Americans. In other words, the media is predominantly Eurocentric in ethos, philosophy, and worldview. Racism, oppression, and the dehumanization of African/Black people are germane to the Eurocentric ethos. Consequently, the messages, imagery, and models transmitted by the media reflect, explicitly or implicitly, the attitudes, beliefs, and interests of the dominant society. A social psychological approach may determine the degree or extent African American individual or group behavior is affected by American print and electronic media, including movies and television.

Every society provides for and requires socialization of its population. However, in a racist society certain elements of socialization function as a system of control over diverse racial-ethnic groups.[113] Parents, siblings, teachers, adults, and peers are the major socializing agents in the life of children, but the media—the internet, books, magazines, newspapers, movies, and television—are agents of socialization for children and adults alike. The social process of the media is one of stimulus and response. The politico-psychological racial messages, imagery, and models communicated by the media may provide the stimuli that result in negative psychological and social responses and consequences for Black Americans.

The media also function as an auxiliary to educational institutions. They define and enforce the social norms of the dominant society on the individual and/or racial-ethnic groups. Through racial messages, imagery, and models, the media define and construct the social role, position, and pattern of behavior expected of a minority racial-ethnic individual or group. With few exceptions, the media reflect the social norms, values, and experiences of White America and European culture. Through media programming, Blacks are inundated with the arts and literature, and the social and scientific achievements of people of European descent. The paucity or absence of positive African/Black messages, images, and models of achievement affirms the supremacy of White culture and social values. The predominance of White aesthetic expressions creates respect for the established order, and an attitude of political and psychological submission to the ideological myth of White cultural supremacy within the psyche of many Blacks.

5

Obfuscation and Bifurcation of Black Identity and Personality

We have discussed the powerful influence of the media, particularly television and movies, in shaping Black identity and attitudes concerning social reality. The deluge of social experiences, speech patterns, and physical traits peculiar to the White race can have obfuscating or bifurcating effects on Black self and group identity, self-esteem, and social reality.[114] An *obfuscated identity* is evident when one is confused or unclear as to one's individual or collective racial identity. Identity bifurcation is related to Du Bois's concept of "double-consciousness," discussed previously.

On a cognitive individual basis, racial and group identification is essential to normal psychological functioning. However, race biases and negative political representations in the media may contribute to dysfunctional Black identity. The dangers of an oppressed minority assuming the identification of the oppressor are clear. White political and psychological control and oppression are assured when African Americans or Blacks, consciously or subconsciously, renounce Africa/Black identity totally in favor of an "alien" European/White identification.

Even today, there are few Black heroes or extraordinary persons featured in film or a television series. Only sports and entertainment personalities are acclaimed and showered with adoration. Rarely are Black scientists, economists, politicians, or other professional authority figures portrayed or consulted in the media, unless the topic of discussion is race or race relations. The African American's image in the media and on television is restricted to Whites' conception of Black life and culture. African Americans are represented and have achieved prominence in most professional and occupational fields, but the media, for racial and psycho-political reasons, have historically failed to project a balanced perspective of the Black experience.

In the context of the earlier discussion of gender issues, there is no question that the portrayal of misogyny in contemporary African American popular culture in the popular media also constitutes a major threat to the cultivation of a viable collective identity. Although unsophisticated media consumers may applaud the prevalence of scantily clad Black men and women parading their sexual prowess in music videos and films, African American Studies specialists insist on asking why such images are welcomed by media magnates. The simple answer is that they intensify the misorientation process, as described by radical psychologists, by promoting disharmonious Black male-female relationships and thereby hamper political mobilization to address structural oppression.

Through processes described above, the media are heavily implicated in what Aaron Gresson characterizes as a shift in the locus of meaning production from the group to the individual. Gresson describes one particular manifestation of this phenomenon among African Americans as the "Black apocalypse"—"the clash between Black privatization and Black collusion."[115] This conflict is heightened by the short-circuiting of collective memory, which generates a condition of "Black Amnesia." For Gresson, Black Amnesia is "a collective forgetting of the one-ness of personal and political life and their relation to racial domination" and can include "Black self-hatred as both an individual and collective phenomenon."[116]

The insidious destruction of collective racial memory requires a complex and systematic "recovery" project. The recovery would entail not only intervention to restore an individual's capacity to function effectively as a member of a conscious collective, but also the restoration of traditional social institutions to enhance the capacity to support personal identity development and mental health and the creation of new institutions to meet new challenges beyond the capacity of existing institutions. Gresson suggests that "this response is a recovery response, an attempt to gain back something of the balance—whether good, bad or different—that we once knew."[117]

Biracial/Multiracial Identity Discourses

The recovery process is complicated by the contemporary "biracialism" narrative that has been pushed into the forefront by the election of President Barack Obama. Indeed, Obama's victory was heralded by many as concrete evidence of America's transition to a "post-racial" society. Obtaining the support of a substantial proportion of the White electorate involved heavy emphasis on the candidate's multiracial lineage and international background, both of which were viewed by many Whites as distinguishing him from the modal African American. Even though Obama classified himself as Black when he completed his 2010 Census form,[118] this narrative revolved around the following features:

- his father was Kenyan;
- his mother was a White woman from Kansas;
- he was born in Hawaii;
- he spent a substantial portion of his early childhood in Indonesia; and
- he was reared subsequently by his White grandparents in the American Midwest.

In some respects, the discourse regarding biracial/ multiracial identities can be seen as an alternative to the recovery narrative. Developing a new identity that embraces multiple heritages could be seen by some as an alternative to the difficult task of recovering a "Black" identity. Among psychologists, there has been controversy about the applicability of the type of identity development models discussed previously for biracial or multiracial individuals. As noted by Raushanah Hud-Aleem and Jacqueline Countryman, in the 1980s, biracial individuals were assumed to identify with the same race as their parent of color, thus conforming to the historic "one drop rule," which assigned any individual with documentable African ancestry as Black.[119] They observe that challenges from multiracial individuals to this convention led to new concepts of biracial identity development as well as the inclusion of a biracial option on the U.S. Census beginning in 2000.[120] Some researchers have developed stage models of biracial/multiracial identity development with similarities to those discussed previously. As an example, the Poston Biracial Identity Development Model consists of five stages: personal identity, choice of group categorization; enmeshment/denial, appreciation, and integration. The individual is presumed to begin from an initial personal identity that entails no awareness of his/her mixed heritage into a stage where an initial choice of group identity is formed as a result of external influences. Subsequently the individual may experience guilt regarding the denial of the salience of other elements of his/her heritage and begin exploration of this other heritage. In the fifth stage, the individual may still identify with one group but appreciate "the integration of their multiple racial identities."[121]

In contrast, the Continuum of Biracial Identity (COBI) model allows biracial individuals to locate an identity any place along a "blended continuum." This continuum is bounded by singular racial identities, i.e. Black or White. Location along the continuum is subject to change in response to various influences. In this model, all choices, including singular identities, can result in a wholesome psychological state.[122] Consistent with the COBI model, Hud-Aleem and Countryman maintain that biracial children do not necessarily experience emotional or relational problems if they are raised by appropriately conscious parents. However, they allow that biracial children experience unique issues including "glares, strange looks, and comments about their family structure."[123]

The radical school of Black Psychology, of course, disagrees with the assessment that biracial identity can result in mental health comparable to that achieved by individuals who are grounded in their Black identity. Moreover, Africana Studies specialists would expect that systematic racism will produce episodes that generate cognitive dissonance that pushes individuals along the continuum toward a singular Black identity. As a consequence, even individuals who attempt to avoid Black identity recovery dynamics by prioritizing an alternative heritage will invariably be forced to undertake some variation of the recovery process.

Toward Individual and Collective Psychological Recovery

Gresson's recovery perspective is similar to Hussein Bulhan's idea of a psychology of liberation that gives "primacy to the empowerment of the oppressed through organized and socialized activity with the aim of restoring individual biographies and a collective history derailed, stunted, and/or made appendage to those of others."[124]

The critical issue for African American Studies specialists is how to expedite this recovery process. Consistent with the emphasis on psychohistorical approaches at the beginning of this chapter, Linda Myers reminds us that any viable recovery approach should focus on the "history of the spirit/mind analysis of individuals through autobiography and biography, and racial groups, the sexes, cultural groups, nations, and so on through ethnography, folklore, and ethno-methodology."[125]

Rites of Passage Programs

African Studies is strongly committed to programs that assist African Americans of all ages in developing and maintaining a positive sense of themselves as a collective group actively engaged in shaping their own destinies and contributing to the advancement of humankind. Rites of Passage programs constitute an especially important vehicle for promoting this psychological orientation. Mafori Moore, et al., describe a rite of passage as "a permission or right or chance to move to a higher level of human social and educational development."[126] Mafori, et al. emphasize that "the permission is granted by the community/society and signifies the successful completion of a developmental process and the earning of the respect of the community in doing so."[127] The Black Power Movement spurred widespread interest in the creation and/or resurrection of Rites of Passage programs, and a large number of community-based organizations have been involved in offering such programs for decades. These programs exhibit a diversity of designs, but most involve the immersion of participants in selected recreations of selected traditional African cultural rituals. Some are based on the Nguzo Saba originated by Maulana Karenga. Rites of Passage programs have been developed for both males and females.

There is an impressive body of literature describing various Rites of Passage programs. Early examples include Frank Fair's, *The Orita for Black Youth: An Initiation into Christian Adulthood* and Nathan and Julia Hare's, *Bringing the Black Boy to Manhood: The Passage*.[128] Mafori Moore, et al., published one of the first Rites of Passage programs for females: *Transformation, A Rites of Passage Manual for African American Girls*.[129] Mary Lewis also developed a Rites of Passage program for females during this same period: *Herstory, Black Female Rites of Passage*.[130]

Marilyn and Warren Maye have adapted the Orita construct using Maulana Karenga's Kwanzaa principles in *Orita, Rites of Passage for Youth of African Descent in America*.[131] Paul Hill is one of the foremost advocates of Rites of Passage programs. Hill emphasizes that these programs constitute "a strategy for life cycle development and not a panacea for resurrection of the masses."[132] However, he also maintains that there is significant potential for collective enhancement; "Aside from life cycle development, Rites-Of-Passage can focus on substance abuse rehabilitation, teen pregnancy and self development or therapeutic milieu."[133]

In a similar vein, Lathardus Goggins has argued that "Families, churches, and community organizations that provide African centered rites of passage as an essential healthy part of the development of a person, just as proper nutrition and exercise are important, [and] provide a proactive and positive encounter."[134] Referring to the previous discussion of stage models of identity development, Coggins proposes that Rites of Passage programs can develop a post-immersion stage of "African self-consciousness, which is necessary for true integration."[135]

Paul Hill is the founder of the National Rites of Passage Institute, which, "in collaboration with communities, other organizations, practitioners and scholars" seeks to elevate "the understanding and value of culturally-based rites of passage to the point that it is an integrative part of child, youth and community development at all levels of system."[136] This formalized network of Rites of Passage advocates is strongly supported by many African American studies specialists.

Differences in designs, objectives, curricula, and sources of support have introduced substantial diversity in the population of Rites of Passage programs serving African American males. Warfield-Coppock has developed one of the most useful classification schemes to illustrate this diversity.[137] She presents a typology of six types of programs: (1) Community-based; (2) Agency or organizationally-based; (3) School-based; (4) Church-based; (5) Therapeutic; and (6) Family-based. This diversity creates difficulty in efforts to assess the overall efficacy of programs because there may be differences in objectives, design, access to resources, and other factors. The existing psychological research examining the dynamics of identity development and transformation and of racial socialization strongly supports the validity of Rites of Passage programs as a potential vehicle for cultivating positive identity among African American males and for cultivating attitudes and behaviors that diverge from anti-social tendencies. However, the research is less clear regarding likely long-term impacts of participation.[138]

Expanding Identity Contours

The "re-ethnification" of the African-descended population in the U.S. offers new opportunities to address historical and contemporary psychological dilemmas. Increased immigration from various African, Caribbean, and South American countries is producing

204

distinctive collectives of persons of African descent with linguistic, religious, and political orientations markedly different from those of domestic African Americans. There is a need for a systematic strategy to interweave the identity construction processes of domestic and immigrant African-descended collectives to produce a collective transformation stage of shared identity. Such a strategy should attempt to initiate shared immersion-emersion experiences that can subsequently produce a composite African-based identity of the type envisioned by radical Black psychologists. Achieving this outcome will require much more extensive interaction between domestic African Americans and their immigrant counterparts

than currently exists. One of the benefits to domestic African Americans would be an opportunity to explore the contours of contemporary African identity and develop an understanding of how Africa's own encounter with the West has altered the configuration of African identity. Conversely, peoples of African descent socialized outside the U.S. would come to appreciate more fully how the particular characteristics of the system of oppression faced here precipitated existing identity configurations among domestic African Americans. Through a joint exploration of the process of parallel identity adaptation, the foundations

National Rites of Passage Institute founder Paul Hill with program participants

Questions & Exercises

for pursuing a viable proactive approach to composite African identity development could emerge and lead to new forms of empowerment and political mobilization.

1. Define Black psychology and discuss its academic validity and implications.

2. Differentiate among traditional, reformist, and radical African American psychological schools of thought as characterized by Maulana Karenga.

3. Explain how traditionalist psychology may have influenced public policy to the social, economic, and political detriment of African Americans.

4. Psychohistory is proposed as a paradigm for analyzing the historical consciousness of African Americans. It may also be useful in interpreting the racial attitudes and supremacy behaviors of White Europeans and Americans. Discuss.

5. How have racism and discrimination based on color and race affected the mental health of African Americans?

6. Components of racial identity, personality, and self-concept theories are more complex for African Americans than for any other race or ethnic group in America. Debate.

7. Discuss the meanings of African/Black ordered and disordered personalities.

8. Write an analytical essay explaining how various media, including television and film, billboard, and print, may contribute to negative socialization, stereotyping, and personality disorders among African Americans. Discuss the politico-psychological implications of this pattern.

9. Compare perceived differences in the early socialization of Black males and females with those of White males and females.

Social Responsibility Projects

1. Survey the resources in your college or university library that examine the psychology of African Americans. If these resources are absent or not up to date, request that the library update the holdings in this area.

2. Identify one or more Rites of Passage programs in your community and volunteer to provide assistance in operating the program.

3. Identify what, if any, support programs are on your campus that offer mental health care services for African American students. Make an assessment of the extent to which the interventions that are used are consistent with the approaches discussed in this chapter. If not, make the providers aware of the literature in this chapter.

4. Encourage family members and friends who are experiencing mental health problems to seek help from providers who use interventions consistent with the frameworks discussed in this chapter.

5. If friends and/or family are reluctant to seek support from credentialed mental health providers, organize a support group as a short-term measure to provide assistance.

5

Notes and References

1. See D. Schultz and S. Schultz, *A History of Modern Psychology*, 4th ed. (San Diego: Harcourt Brace Jovanovich, 1987), 4.
2. See "Areas of Psychology – Subfields of Psychology," http://psychology.about.com/library/weekly/aa021503a.htm.
3. R. Guthrie, *Even the Rat was White* (New York: Harper and Row, 1976), 29-46.
4. Schultz and Schultz, *A History of Modern Psychology*, 50-51.
5. A. Kardiner and L. Ovesey, *The Mark of Oppression* (New York: Norton, 1951).
6. F. Cress Welsing, *The Isis Papers* (Chicago: Third World Press, 1991), 44.
7. Ibid., 9.
8. See, for example, George Ferguson, *The Psychology of the Negro* (Wesport, CT: Negro Universities Press, 1916).
9. For a review of many essays by Black psychologists and behavioral scientists on the psychology of African Americans, see R. Jones, ed., *Black Psychology* (New York: Harper & Row, 1972).
10. See, for example, M. Karenga, *Introduction to Black Studies* (Inglewood CA: Kawaida Publications, 1982), 326-51.
11. See N. Cook and S. Kono, "Black Psychology: The Third Great Tradition," *Journal of Black Psychology* 3 (February 1977): 18-28.
12. J. Mbiti, *African Religions and Philosophy* (Garden City, NY: Anchor Books, 1970), 5, 20-21.
13. Schultz and Schultz, *A History of Modern Psychology*, 1-2.
14. K. Kambon, *African/Black Psychology in the American Context: An African-Centered Approach* (Tallahassee, FL: Nubian Nation Publications, 1998).
15. See G. Jackson, "The Origin and Development of Black Psychology: Implications for Black Studies and Human Behavior," *Studia Africana* 1 (fall 1979), 270-86.
16. J. White and T. Parham, *The Psychology of Blacks* (Englewood Cliffs, NJ: Prentice Hall, 1990), 23.
17. A. Jenkins, *The Psychology of the Afro-American* (New York: Pergamon Press, 1982), xvi.
18. See N. Cook and S. Kono, "Black Psychology: The Third Great Tradition," *Journal of Black Psychology* 3 (February 1977): 18-28.
19. R. Wilcox, ed., *The Psychological Consequences of Being a Black American* (New York: John Wiley & Sons, 1971), vii.
20. M. Karenga, *Introduction to Black Studies* (Inglewood CA: Kawaida Publications, 1982), 326-51.
21. See D. Azibo, ed., *African Centered Psychology: Culture-Focusing for Multicultural Competence* (Durham, NC: Carolina Academic Press, 2003) and K. Kambon, *African/Black Psychology in the American Context: An African-Centered Approach* (Tallahassee, FL: Nubian Nation Publications, 1998).
22. J. Baldwin, "Psychological Aspects of European Cosmology in American Society," *Western Journal of Black Studies* 9 (winter 1985): 216.
23. Ibid., 217-72.
24. See D. Richards, "The Implications of African-American Spirituality," in *African Culture*, ed. M. Asante and K. Asante (Westport CT: Greenwood Press, 1985).
25. A. Pasteur and I. Toldson, *Roots of Soul* (Garden City, NY: Anchor Press/Doubleday, 1982), 4-26.
26. See M. Asante, *The Afrocentric Idea* (Philadelphia: Temple University Press, 1987).
27. W. Nobles, "African Philosophy: Foundations for Black Psychology," in *Black Psychology*, ed. R. Jones (New York: Harper & Row, 1972): 31.
28. P. Loewenberg, *Decoding the Past* (Berkeley, Los Angeles, London: University of California Press, 1985), 3-15.
29. L. Demause, *Foundations of PsychoHistory* (New York: Creative Roots, 1982), i-ii.
30. P. Suedfeld, *Psychology and Torture* (New York: Hemisphere Publishing Co., 1990), 2-3.
31. N. Akbar, *Chains and Images of Psychological Slavery* (Jersey City: New Mind Productions, 1984). Akbar has described certain continuing effects of slavery in the first of two essays comprising the book.
32. Ibid., 9-40.
33. See F. Fanon, *The Wretched of the Earth* (New York: Grove Press, 1963).
34. For a study of color prejudice among Blacks, see O. Edwards, "Skin Color as a Variable in Racial Attitudes of Black Urbanites," *Journal of Black Studies* 3 (June 1972): 473-83.
35. J. Landrum-Brown, "Black Mental Health and Racial Oppression," in *Handbook of Mental Health and Mental Disorders Among Black Americans*, ed. D. Ruiz (New York: Greenwood Press, 1990), 113.
36. *Report of the National Advisory Commission on Civil Disorders* (Washington, D.C.: U.S. Government Printing Office, 1968).
37. G. Jaynes and R. Williams, eds., *A Common Destiny* (Washington, D.C.: National Academy Press, 1989), 103.
38. K. Wesson, "The Black Man's Burden: The White Clinician," *Black Scholar* (July-August 1975): 13-14.
39. See D. Azibo, "Treatment and Training Implications of the Advances in African Personality Theory," *Western Journal of Black Studies* (spring 1990): 53-62; J. Baldwin, "African Self-Consciousness and the Mental Health of African Americans," *Journal of Black Studies* 15 (2): 177-94; and W. Nobles, "Black People in White Insanity: An Issue for Black Community Health," *Journal of Afro American Issues* 4 (1976): 21-27.

40.   See D. Azibo, "Treatment and Training Implications of the Advances in African Personality Theory," *Western Journal of Black Studies* (spring 1990): 53-62; J. Baldwin, "African Self-Consciousness and the Mental Health of African Americans," *Journal of Black Studies* 15 (2): 177-94; and W. Nobles, "Black People in White Insanity: An Issue for Black Community Health," *Journal of Afro American Issues* 4 (1976): 21-27.

41.   For a comprehensive study of Black mental and physical health issues, see R. Jones, ed., *Black Adult Development and Aging* (Berkeley: Cobb & Henry Publishers, 1989).

42.   W. Grier and P. Cobbs, *Black Rage* (New York: Basic Books, 1968; Bantam edition, 1969).

43.   Grier and Cobbs, *Black Rage*, 149.

44.   B. Davis, "Anger as a Factor and an Invisible Barrier in the Treatment of Black Clients," *Western Journal of Black Studies* 4 (spring 1980): 29, 30.

45.   H. Myers, N. Anderson, and T. Strickland, "A Biobehavioral Perspective on Stress and Hypertension in Black Adults," in *Black Adult Development and Aging*, ed. R. Jones (Berkeley: Cobb & Henry Publishers, 1989), 311-36.

46.   H. Neighbors and S. Lumpkin, "The Epidemiology of Mental Disorder in the Black Population," in *Handbook of Mental Disorder Among Black Americans*, ed. D. Ruiz (New York: Greenwood Press, 1990), 55-68.

47.   T. Anderson and W. Harris, "A Socio-Historical and Contemporary Study of African Americans in U.S. Corporations," *Western Journal of Black Studies* 14 (fall 1990): 174-81.

48.   See G. Kaluger and C. Unkovic, *Psychology and Sociology* (Saint Louis: C.V. Mosby, 1969), 179-210.

49.   F. Baker, "The Afro-American Life Cycle: Success, Failure, and Mental Health," *Journal of the National Medical Association* 79 (1987): 630. See also K. James, C. Lovato, and G. Khoo, "Social Identity Correlates of Minority Workers' Health," *Academy of Management Journal* 37, no. 2 (1994): 383-96.

50.   L. Houston, *Psychological Principles and the Black Experience* (Lanham, MD: University Press of America, 1990), 107-8.

51.   Houston, *Psychological Principles*, 108.

52.   D. Pinderhughes, *Understanding Race, Ethnicity and Power* (New York: The Free Press, 1989), 6.

53.   A. Jenkins, *Psychology and African Americans: A Humanistic Approach*, 2nd ed. (Needham Heights, MA: Allyn & Bacon, 1995), 20.

54.   H. Bulhan, *Frantz Fanon and the Psychology of Oppression* (New York: Plenum Press, 1985), 123.

55.   Ibid.

56.   Bulhan, *Frantz Fanon*, 189.

57.   Ibid.

58.   Kaluger and Unkovic, *Psychology and Sociology*, 199.

59.   See R. Staples, *Introduction to Black Sociology* (New York: McGraw-Hill, 1976), 286-94.

60.   B. Wright, "Ideological Changes and Black Identity during Civil Rights Movements," *Western Journal of Black Studies* 5 (fall 1981): 186-97.

61.   S. Stuckey, *Slave Culture* (New York: Oxford University Press, 1987), 198-99.

62.   Ibid., 202-09.

63.   See L. Semaj, "The Black Self, Identity, and Models for a Psychology of Black Liberation," *Western Journal of Black Studies* 5 (fall 1981).

64.   J. Moikobu, *Blood and Flesh: Black American and African Identification* (Westport Ct: Greenwood Press, 1981), 91-96.

65.   F. Piven and R. Cloward, *Regulating the Poor: Functions of Public Welfare*, 2nd ed. (New York: Vintage Books, 1993).

66.   L. Sigelman, S. Tuch, and J. Martin, "What's In a Name: Preference for 'Black' Versus 'African American' Among Americans of African Descent," *Public Opinion Quarterly* 69 (Fall 2005): 429-38.

67.   W. E. B. Du Bois, *Souls of Black Folk* (New York: New American Library, 1969), 45.

68.   V. Gordon, *The Self-Concept of Black Americans* (Washington D.C.: University Press of America, 1977), 72-73.

69.   Gordon, *The Self-Concept of Black Americans*, 26-55. Gordon outlines and summarizes the results of more than a hundred studies from 1939 to 1973.

70.   K. Clark and M. Clark, "The Development of Consciousness of Self and the Emergence of Racial Identification in Negro Preschool Children," *Journal of Social Psychology* 10 (1939), 591-99.

71.   S. McNicol and G. McNicol, "Racial Identification and Racial Preference of Black Preschool Children in New York and Trinidad," *Journal of Black Psychology* 14 (February 1988): 67.

72.   W. Cross, "The Negro-to-Black Conversion Experience," *Black World* (July 1971): 13-27; "Black Families and Black Identity: A Literature Review," *Western Journal of Black Studies* 2 (1978), 111-24; "The Thomas and Cross Models on Psychological Nigrescence: A Literature Review," *Journal of Black Psychology* 4 (1978): 13-31.

73.   W. Cross, *Shades of Black: Diversity in African American Identity* (Philadelphia: Temple University Press, 1991).

74.   F. Worrell, B. Vandiver, B. Schaefer, W. Cross, Jr., and P. Fhagen-Smith, "Generalizing Nigrescence Profiles: Cluster Analyses of Cross Racial Identity Scale (CRIS) Scores in Three Independent Samples," *Counseling Psychologist* 34 (July 2006): 519-47.

75.   Cross, *Shades of Black*, 148-49, 190.

5

76. Ibid., 207.

77. Ibid.

78. Ibid., 210.

79. B. Vandiver, P. Fhagen-Smith, K. Cokley, W. Cross, & F. Worrell, "Cross's Nigresence Model: From Theory to Scale to Theory," *Journal of Multicultural Counseling and Development* 29 (2001): 174-200.

80. J. Helms, "The Measurement of Black Racial Attitudes" in *Black and White Racial Identity: Theory, Research and Practice*, ed. J. Helms (Westport, CT: Greenwood Press, 1990), 33-47.

81. A. Boykin and C. Ellison, "The Multiple Ecologies of Black Youth Socialization: An Afrographic Analysis" in *African-American Youth, Their Social and Economic Status in the United States*, ed. R. Taylor (Westport, CT: Praeger, 1995), 123.

82. Cross, *Shades of Black*.

83. C. Broman et al., "Racial Group Identification Among Black Adults," *Social Forces* 67, no. 1 (1988): 146-58.

84. V. Sanders Thompson, "Variables Affecting Racial-Identity Salience Among African Americans," *Journal of Social Psychology* 139, no. 6 (1999): 748-61.

85. L. Benjamin, *The Black Elite, Facing the Color Line in the Twilight of the Twentieth Century* (Chicago: Nelson-Hall, 1991), 43.

86. Ibid., 94.

87. Jenkins, *Psychology and African Americans*, 273.

88. Jenkins, *Psychology and African Americans*, 272.

89. R. Jackson and J. Stewart, "Negotiation of African American Identities in Rural America: A Cultural Contracts Approach," *Journal of Rural Community Psychology* E4, 1 (2001), http://www.marshall.edu/jrcp/JacksonStewart.htm, 6.

90. R. Walters, *Pan-Africanism in the African Diaspora: An Analysis of Modern Afrocentric Political Movements* (Detroit, MI: Wayne State University Press, 1993), 387.

91. D. Azibo and J. Robinson, "An Empirically Supported Reconceptualization of African-U.S. Racial Identity Development as an Abnormal Process," *Review of General Psychology* 8, (4) (2004): 252.

92. Ibid., 249-64.

93. G. Allport, *Pattern and Growth in Personality* (Ft. Worth: Holt, Rinehart and Winston, 1961), 28.

94. J. Baldwin, "Notes on an Africentric Theory of Black Personality."

95. I. Atwell and D. Azibo, "Diagnosing Personality Disorder in Africans," *Western Journal of Black Studies* 5 (fall 1981): 173-74; "Blacks Using the Azibo Nosology: Two Case Studies," *Journal of Black Psychology* 17 (spring 1991): 3.

96. Ibid., 3-4.

97. See D. Azibo, "African-centered Theses on Mental Health and a Nosology of Black/African Personality Disorder," *Journal of Black Psychology* 15 (spring 1989): 173-214.

98. Ibid.

99. Daudi Azibo, "The Psycho-cultural Case for Reparations for Descendants of Enslaved Africans in the United States," *Race, Gender, & Class 18* (1-2), 2011, 7-36.

100. J. Baldwin and Y. Bell, "The African Self-Consciousness Scale: An Africentric Personality Questionnaire," *Western Journal of Black Studies* 9 (summer 1985): 61-68.

101. D. Azibo, "Black Personality Questionnaire: A Review and Critique," in *Handbook of Tests and Measurements for Black Populations*, vol. 2, ed. R. Jones (Hampton, VA: Cobb & Henry, 1996), 241-49.

102. B. Omolade, *The Rising Song of African American Women* (New York: Routledge, 1994), 15.

103. P. Hill Collins, *Black Feminist Thought: Knowledge, Consciousness and the Politics of Empowerment* (New York: Routledge, 1991), 207.

104. Jenkins, *Psychology and African Americans*, xi.

105. Cross, *Shades of Black*.

106. K. Vaz, "Making Room for Emancipatory Research in Psychology: A Multicultural Feminist Perspective," in *Spirit, Space & Survival, African American Women in (White) Academe*, ed. J. James and R. Farmer (New York: Routledge, 1993), 96.

107. W. E. B. Du Bois, "The Relation of the Negroes to the Whites in the South," *Annals of the American Academy of Political and Social Science* 18 (July 1901): 121-22.

108. G. Hill and S. Hill, *Blacks on Television* (Metuchen, NJ: The Scarecrow Press, 1985), 1-7.

109. J. H. Clarke, *African World Revolution* (Trenton, NJ: Africa World Press, Inc., 1991), 329-30.

110. S. Peterson-Lewis and A. Adams, "Televisions' Model of the Quest for African Consciousness: A Comparison with Cross's Empirical Model of Psychological Nigrescence," *The Journal of Black Psychology* 16 (spring 1990): 55-72.

111. T. Brown, "Racism on TV," *Detroit Free Press*, December 27, 1979, 1.

112. See R. Davis, "Television Commercials and the Management of Spoiled Identity," *Western Journal of Black Studies* Vol. 11 (2) (summer 1987): 59-63.

113. Some of the social psychology theories presented here have been adapted from F. Sanford, *Psychology* (Belmont, CA: Wadsworth Publishing, Co., 1965), and R. Bootzin et al., *Psychology Today* (New York: Random House, 1983).

114. See R. and S. Hatchett, "The Media and Social Reality Effects: Self and System Orientation of Blacks," *Communications Research* 13 (January 1986): 97-123.

115. A. Gresson, *The Recovery of Race in America* (Minneapolis, MN: University of Minnesota Press, 1995), 16.

116. A. Gresson, *Black Amnesia* (Baltimore: Transformation Books, 1990), 6, 11.

117. Gresson, *The Recovery of Race*, xi.

118. Sam Roberts and Peter Baker, "Asked to Declare His Race, Obama Checks 'Black,'" *New York Times*, April 2, 2010, http://www.nytimes.com/2010/04/03/us/politics/03census.html.

119. Raushanah Hud-Aleem and Jacqueline Countryman, "Biracial Identity Development and Recommendations in Therapy," Psychiatry 5 (11) (November 2008), 37–44, http://www.innovationscns.com/biracial-identity-development-and-recommendations-in-therapy/.

120. Ibid.

121. WSC Poston, "The Biracial Identity Development Model: A Needed Addition," *Journal of Counseling Development* 69 (1990): 152–155.

122. K. Rockquemore and T.A. Laszloffy, "Moving Beyond Tragedy: A Multidimensional Model of Mixed-Race Identity" in *Raising Biracial Children*, (Lanham, MD: AltaMira Press, 2005), 1–17.

123. Hud-Aleem and Countryman, "Biracial Identity Development and Recommendations in Therapy."

124. Bulhan, *Frantz Fanon*, 277.

125. L. Myers, "Transpersonal Psychology: The Role of the Afrocentric Paradigm," in *African American Psychology, Theory, Research and Practice*, ed. A. Burlew et al. (Newbury Park, CA: Sage Publications, 1992), 15.

126. Mafori Moore, Gwen Akua Gilyard, Karen King, and Nsenga Warfield-Coppock, *Transformation, A Rites of Passage for African American Girls* (New York: Stars Press, 1987), 11.

127. Ibid.

128. Frank Fair, *The Orita for Black Youth: An Initiation into Christian Adulthood* (Valley Forge, PA: Judson Press, 1977); Nathan Hare and Julia Hare, *Bringing the Black Boy to Manhood: The Passage* (San Francisco: The Black Think Tank, 1985).

129. Moore, et al. *Transformation, A Rites of Passage for African American Girls*.

130. Mary Lewis, *Herstory, Black Female Rites of Passage* (Chicago: African American Images, 1988).

131. Marilyn Maye and Warren Maye, Orita, *Rites of Passage for Youth of African Descent in America* (New York: Faithworks, 2000).

132. Paul Hill, Jr., *Coming of Age, African American Male Rites-of-Passage* (Chicago: African American Images, 1992), 104.

133. Ibid.

134. Lathardus Goggins, *African Centered Rites of Passage and Education* (Chicago: African American Images, 1996), 64.

135. Ibid.

136. National Rites of Passage Institute, http://www.ritesofpassage.org/.

137. N. Warfield-Coppock, "The Rites of Passage Movement: A Resurgence of African-Centered Practices for Socializing African American Youth," *Journal of Negro Education*, 61 (4), 1992: 471-482.

138. See, for example, J. DeGruy, et al., "Racial Respect and Racial Socialization as Protective Factors for African American Male Youth," *Journal of Black Psychology*, 2011: 1-26; G. Nicolas, et al., "A Conceptual Framework for Understanding the Strengths of Black Youths," *Journal of Black Psychology* 34, 2008: 261-280; K. Resnicow, et al. Development of a Racial and Ethnic Identity Scale for African American Adolescents: The Survey of Black Life," *Journal of Black Psychology* 25, 1999: 171-188; and H. Stevenson Jr., "Relationship of Adolescent Perceptions of Racial Socialization to Racial Identity," *Journal of Black Psychology* 21, 1995: 49-70.

5

Noted Firsts in Politics and Public Policy

Hiram Rhodes Revels, the first African American to serve in Congress (1870)

Shirley Chisholm, the first African American woman elected to Congress

Carol Mosely-Braun, the first African American woman senator

Thurgood Marshall, first African American Supreme Court Justice

Louis Stokes, founding member of the Congressional Black Caucus

Eric Holder, first African American Attorney General

Condoleeza Rice, the first Black woman secretary of state

Dr. Minnie Jocelyn Elders, the first African American Surgeon General

Colin Powell, the first African American Secretary of State

Chapter 6

Politics and Public Policy

An Overview of Black Political Initiatives

Political Science and the Nature of Black Politics

Modern political science, like other areas of human study in the industrialized West, is a culture-specific examination of the allocation, application, and transfer of power in collective decision-making. From a Eurocentric worldview, the study of politics is traced to the ancient Greeks (500 to 300 B.C.). Some scholars maintain that "Plato may be called the father of political theory and Aristotle the parent of political science, at least in the West."[1] From this perspective, *political science* is broadly defined as a study of the principles and organization of the government of states. Thus, politics is the practical and functional exercise of policy making and rule of the state or government.

The limited scope of this approach to the study of political behavior is clearly inadequate for addressing the concerns of African American Studies. Attribution of the historical origins of the study of politics to the ancient Greeks ignores the record of the Egyptian and Ethiopian civilizations that thrived in North Africa as early as 6000 to 4000 B.C., which we discussed in the chapter on Black history. Emphasis on the evolution of political systems in the West also denies the relevance of examining the sophisticated West African states of Ghana, Mali, and Songhay that thrived and declined from A.D. 700 to 1600. Surely, these African civilizations and states were developed under sound culture-specific political principles, methods, and governmental structures.

Dismissal of the relevance of African societies for a comparative study of the evolution of political systems also extends to the study of the political experiences of African Americans. As noted by African American political scientist Mack Jones, researchers who examine the Black political experience in America have tended to look "not to the black political experience for guidance in developing ... a conceptual scheme, but rather to the political experience of other people."[2] Jones states that "a frame of reference for black politics should not begin with superficial comparisons of blacks and other ethnic minorities in this country or elsewhere, because such an approach inevitably degenerates into normative reformist speculation around the question of what can be done to elevate blacks to the position occupied by the group with which they are being compared."[3]

In the context of political science and its general concern with the allocation of power, for African American Studies the most useful approach to the study of African American political experiences would entail an examination of the "power struggle between blacks and whites, with the latter trying to maintain their superordinate position" in part through articulating and institutionalizing a belief in their inherent superiority.[4] Historically, slavery, segregation, and overt oppression excluded Blacks from *conventional* participation in the political affairs of the state. Even presently, it is questionable whether African Americans, with their comparative lack of power and representation, can affect government policy through conventional politics. The politics of Black Americans have been devoted to the objective of eliminating their disfranchisement and inequity based on race. Black politics is predicated on the abolition of racism and White oppression. The meaning and exercise of Black politics are often different from those of Whites, even though both races participate in the same political process.

Political scientist Hanes Walton, Jr., argues that "theorists of the black political experience in the virtual nonparticipation era of *slavery*, in the limited-participation era of *segregation*, and in the current evolving-participation era of *desegregation* have hypothesized in a holistic way that the very nature of black politics is centered on instrumentalism."[5] Walton emphasizes that in each of these eras, Black politics served as "an *instrument* of psychological, social, and political salvation" and "developed and became an integral feature of the black community."[6] The implication of his understanding of Black politics is that "those who moved to participate and involve themselves as elected officials, political leaders, or political activists were expected to use politics and the political arena as a device, procedure, or technique to help the race and its community. For those who did not operate with this 'sense of community,' the community retaliated by imposing various sanctions against them."[7]

The organic connection that historically existed between leaders and their constituencies in Black communities developed from a system Hanes Walton, Jr., describes as "invisible politics," a system that has operated historically in Black communities.[8] The concept of *invisible politics* is especially important for understanding the significant political role played by African American women in various historical eras. Gayle Tate has documented their participation in *Unknown Tongues, Black Women's Activism in the Antebellum Era, 1830–1860.*[9]

Most contemporary studies of Black politics fail to focus adequate attention on the important role of "invisible politics" in establishing the foundation for the subsequent success of both "movement politics" and "electoral politics." Movement politics, undergirded by invisible politics, was the dominant form of Black political activity prior to the passage of the Voting Rights Act of 1965. Some of the most effective Black political activities have included strikes, boycotts, demonstrations, civil disobedience, and marches.[10] Historically, Blacks have used these various strategies and techniques to influence the enactment of public policy to alleviate racial segregation, oppression, and discrimination.

Cedric Robinson has developed the most comprehensive "movement approach" to the study of Black politics. In *Black Movements in America*, Robinson discusses the relatively unknown history of Black mass political movements in the US from the colonial era to the modern Civil Rights Movement. He argues that the very different experiences of enslaved and freed Blacks produced two distinct political tendencies: a culture of resistance, and a culture of accommodation.[11] In a complementary study, *Black Protest, 350 Years of Documents and Analyses*, Joanne Grant provides a rich resource that documents the history of Black political movements.[12]

The dramatic rise of Black elected officials in the wake of the passage of the Voting Rights Act of 1965, along with several subsequent extensions and modifications, has given rise to the belief that African Americans have advanced from protest politics to accommodative electoral politics. This perception has been driven by the dramatic increase in the number of Black elected officials (BEOs). The number of BEOs has increased from 1,469 in 1970 to over 10,500 in 2011. The elected offices held by Blacks range from board/council members to state and municipal judiciary posts, mayors, state treasurers, and at the national level, President of the United States. In recent years, the rate of Black females being elected to public office in America has surpassed that of Black males by a 5-1 margin. There is also a generational shift in Black political leadership underway, with younger Black elected officials in their 30s and 40s being elected increasingly as older officials are retiring. This trend is likely to accelerate, and a growing proportion of new elected officials is likely to be female because of their disproportionate success in educational and occupational advancement compared to Black men.

The election of Barack Obama to the US presidency in 2008 was seen by many as a penultimate achievement in the arena of electoral politics. However, African American Studies specialists have retained a healthy skepticism regarding over-reliance on electoral politics as a means to catalyze ongoing efforts to achieve social and economic equity. Insights regarding this issue can be distilled by assessing whether public policies introduced by the Obama administration have significantly improved the quality of life for African Americans relative to policies instituted during previous administrations. Another critical issue is whether or not the BEOs are positioned in ways that can produce improvements in the quality of life of African Americans and other historically oppressed groups. Answering these and other related questions first requires exploration of the extent to which a collective consensus exists among Blacks regarding political and related objectives. In other words, in the twenty-first century, is there a shared Black political agenda?

Black Political Ideologies

Some commentators have argued that beyond rhetoric and symbolism a viable Black political ideology has not been developed, or at least sustained, since slavery. The implication is that Blacks have conformed to or adopted the political ideologies of White or European people.[13] Those who dismiss the significance of Black ideology are prone to view it only from a functional or practical basis. However, *ideology*, for the purpose of this discussion, is meant to include the various classifications of ideas, beliefs, theories, thoughts, or philosophies Blacks have expressed over the years in the liberation of their race. Just because African Americans have not possessed the power, means, and resources to effectuate or realize certain ideologies does not imply an absence of Black political ideology. Black political ideologies have been forged from the consciousness of Black people in individual and collective responses to their circumstances.

The political ideologies of White Americans are based on their beliefs in and practice of individualism, materialism, capitalism, and White supremacy.[14] Even though the influence and effect of dominant White American ideologies are significant, Black political ideologies are shaped more by efforts to construct a collective identity and the state of race relations in the United States at a particular time. At least three distinct racial or race relations ideologies have historically influenced and guided political ideology and activity in the Black community. Each of these political strands has been a divisive as well as an organizing element within the Black community. Although the underlying values and characteristics of these ideologies overlap, they can be broadly differentiated into three categories: assimilationism, separatism, and Black nationalism.

Frederick Douglass was the foremost architect and promoter of racial integration and assimilationism as a political ideology during slavery and after Emancipation. The moral and theoretical bases for desegregation, school integration, voting equality, social equality, and social-mixing can be found throughout his voluminous works and writings.[15] The spirit and racial philosophy of Frederick Douglass influenced the organization and political ideology of the NAACP, the premier Black political organization and catalyst for Black politics in the twentieth century. The integrationist ideology of the NAACP and the Urban League is reflected in their membership. Both organizations are interracial in character and depend, to some extent, on White liberals' support.

Booker T. Washington was the most visible public figure identified historically with the political philosophy of separatism. His famous "Atlanta Compromise" address in 1895 pronounced separatism as a viable alternative to Black/White social and economic integration. When Washington enunciated his separatist ideology, it created one of the greatest political divisions among Blacks in the African American experience. The ideology of Black separatism was diametrically opposed to the integrationist ideals of Frederick Douglass and W. E. B. Du Bois, as discussed earlier in Chapter 3.

The classical version of Black separatism advocated by Booker T. Washington in 1895, however, is not entirely comparable to modern separatist ideology. Washington's accommodationist advice during that time was for Blacks not to agitate for social, intellectual, and professional equality with Whites. Contemporary separatists exhort Blacks not only to equal Whites but to surpass them as a tribute to and redemption of their African heritage. Modern Black separatism is difficult to define because of its similarity to Black nationalism. In his book *Black Separatism in the United States*, Raymond L. Hall states that Black separatism is a subcategory of Black nationalism.[16] Hall has produced an excellent work on Black separatism, but his differentiation between Black separatism and nationalism lacks clarity. The reason may be that the two ideologies borrow from and subsume each other. Another reason is the ambiguity of the territorial division factor.

Neither integrationism, separatism, nor Black nationalism is absolute in its definition and distinguishing values. Each ideology shares similarities with the other. Integrationists, for example, are zealous in their fight to desegregate public facilities and institutions. Yet, they have lobbied and mounted vigorous

6

political campaigns to maintain the predominantly Black historical colleges and universities. Integrationists are not likely to seek significant desegregation of the Black Church or Black religious denominations. Although Black nationalists may believe in all-Black enterprises, they do not reject White markets and patronage.

Realizing the futility and improbability of territorial division or land separation, modern separatist ideology envisions a form of equitable racial coexistence with Blacks controlling the major social and economic institutions in the Black community. Self-determination and self-sufficiency are essential to the values of separatist ideology. Separatists are determined to have pride in Blackness and to maintain their separate Black identity. Black separatism and nationalism are fueled by skepticism that the White-dominated political establishment will ever truly commit itself to a regime characterized by racial justice and equality.

Some variants of Black nationalism incorporate an African-centered orientation. These constructions of contemporary Black nationalism foster identification with African states and the belief that the redemption of Africa is imperative for the liberation of African people in both America and Africa. Marcus Garvey was the foremost exponent of this form of Black nationalism in America during the 1920s. In addition to his return-to-Africa theme, Garvey instilled into the consciousness of the masses of Blacks a sense of self-worth and economic independence from Whites. Yet, Garvey was an avid believer and practitioner of capitalism. Evidence of the nexus between Black separatism and nationalism was Garvey's admiration of Booker T. Washington.[17]

Black integrationist, separatist, and nationalist political ideologies crystallized as formal and distinct approaches to Black liberation near the end of the nineteenth and early twentieth centuries. Although the major exponents are long since deceased, their racial uplift ideologies still have a profound and active effect on contemporary African American politics. Martin Luther King, Jr., reinvigorated efforts to implement the integrationist-assimilationist ideology of Frederick Douglass during the Civil Rights Movement of the 1960s. During this same period, Malcolm X was the flamboyant standard-bearer of the proponents of Black separatist-nationalist ideology. Integrationist and separatist ideologies have always been in conflict and have caused much political disunity in the Black community. Martin Luther King, Jr., and Malcolm X were ideological and political adversaries during the 1960s era, just as Jesse Jackson and Louis Farrakhan (the present Black nationalist Muslim leader) are today. In the political climate of the early twenty-first century, integration-oriented Black organizations and leadership, such as the NAACP and Urban League, are the most influential and receive the preferred attention of the White liberal establishment. At the same time, a new conservative religious leadership is emerging that embraces many elements of the classic Booker T. Washington position, although they do not endorse his willingness to eschew political rights. Prominent conservative Black religious leaders include Bishop T. D. Jakes (Dallas), the Rev. Herb Lusk (Philadelphia), Bishop Eddie Long (Atlanta), and the Rev. Harry Joe Walters (Republican National Committee).

While "liberalism" and "conservatism" may aptly describe White political orientations in the United States, Black political ideologies do not conform in all aspects to these concepts. Too little attention has been given to the notion that Blacks view liberal and conservative ideologies from different sociopolitical perspectives. Historically, African Americans have identified with and supported a liberal social agenda. This would seem natural because liberalism subscribes to egalitarian human principles. At the same time, White and Black liberals have never shared an ideological consensus. The differences between Black and White perceptions of liberal and conservative are not easily discernible, but they derive from different connotations of the terms *liberal* and *conservative*.

Political theorists now prefer to distinguish between classical and modern liberal philosophy. Classical liberalism strongly advocates the use of government intervention and funding to bring about solutions to many social and economic problems affecting society. Furthermore, the government is perceived as the guarantor of egalitarian principles and programs. This form of liberalism became popular as a result of Franklin D. Roosevelt's initiatives, or "New Deal," to overcome the social devastation created by the Great Depression. The New Deal was comprised of government sponsored economic and social programs.[18] Although the New Deal programs were not intended or designed to address racial inequality, Blacks benefited (under segregated programs) along with the general population. Therefore, Blacks began to associate racial uplift with liberal democratic politics.

Blacks perceive a liberal political philosophy as conducive to fighting and reducing the social ills of racism or racial inequality. On the other hand, Whites become disdainful of liberalism when it focuses on altering the racial status quo. White political theorists seldom, if ever, inject the term *racism* in liberal or conservative ideology. The word *racism* and its implications permeate the works or literature of Black political scientists. Nevertheless, through conventional and unconventional means, Blacks forced the issues of racism and civil rights into liberal democratic politics. Democratic Party administrations from Franklin D. Roosevelt to Lyndon Johnson were coerced into creating a policy linkage between conceptions of liberalism and civil rights. As a result, government intervention focused not just on promoting general economic growth and social well-being but also on reducing racial inequality and social injustice. Classical White liberals never intended for the race issue to be a major tenet of liberalism.

The broadening of the scope or umbrella of liberalism to include not only Blacks but also gays, feminists, and the organized interests of labor and environmental groups led to wide-scale abandonment of the Democratic Party by some Whites, especially in the South. In the 1980 presidential election, the crossover to the Republican Party was especially pronounced. It was clear to the Democrats after the 1984 election that a new liberal ideology had to be developed in order to "save" the Party. Thus, a modern or neoliberal political philosophy has emerged. Modern liberalism or neoliberalism reflects greater value-orientation and advocates a strong role of government in promoting economic growth by developing and subsidizing high technology. Neoliberal philosophy represents a marked shift from social to economic liberalism.[19]

Modern liberalism, in its broadest sense, differs from classical liberalism in the role and function of government. According to William S. Maddox and Stuart A. Lilie,

> modern liberals, while still valuing private property and the market, are willing to support government intervention to promote individual welfare and to regulate the economy. At the same time, liberals argue fairly consistently that in terms of one's personal activity outside the economic realm, the individual should remain free of governmental restriction.[20]

One difference between Black and White interpretations and expectations of liberalism is implicit in Maddox and Lilie's emphasis on "individual welfare." Modern Democratic and Republican liberalism now stresses individual rather than group rights. Liberalism to Blacks may mean a philosophy committed to the struggle of group or racial rights and equality.

Following the loss of momentum by the Civil Rights Movement during the mid-1970s, a small number of African American academic professionals began to articulate a "conservative" ideology that contrasted sharply with traditional Black liberal philosophy. Considering the history and role that White conservatism has played in the repression of Black justice and freedom, one may find it difficult to rationalize the existence of a Black conservative ideology. However, as in the case of liberalism, Blacks and Whites may concur on certain conservative principles but for different reasons. Before such an anomaly can be understood, one must have a general idea of the meaning of American conservatism.

Conservatism is an attitude or a philosophy that opposes change. It seeks to maintain tradition or the status quo. Conservatives oppose what they see as liberals' disregard of an objective moral order, or their support of moral relativism. Conservatism places private property and economic freedom above all other freedoms. Conservatives believe in minimal interference of government in the lives of people and business, except to establish law and order and to protect property rights.[21] Maddox and Lilie suggest that "conservatism has been associated with support for all basic American values, attachment to big business, [fundamentalist] religious approaches to politics, and general closed-mindedness."[22] One of the more popular conceptions of conservatism is the belief in self-reliance, or rugged individualism. This latter characteristic has a significant appeal to Black conservatives.

Black conservatives posit that the maximum benefit from government intervention on behalf of civil rights has already been obtained. Therefore, they believe that the traditional mono-dimensional Black liberal philosophy of civil rights agitation is outmoded and that new self-help economic policies should be developed. For the most part, Black liberals do not agree entirely with such an assumption. Political scientist W. Avon Drake contends that the foundation of Black conservative philosophy was laid by Booker T. Washington during the last half of the nineteenth and early twentieth centuries. Modern proponents of Black conservative ideology include Thomas Sowell

6

and Shelby Steele, both of the Hoover Institution, and Walter Williams of George Mason University. Drake has perceptively summarized four key points that synthesize the theoretical underpinnings of Black conservatism:

1. the premise that racism cannot fully explain Black economic subordination;
2. the premise that political power will not ensure economic success for Blacks;
3. the argument that a free market offers the best opportunity for Black progress;
4. the assertion that Blacks hold the key to their socioeconomic salvation in America.[23]

Some Black conservatives purport that most social problems besetting Blacks are of their own making, and that local, state, and government programs will do little to solve them. These conservatives depreciate the value of affirmative action programs. Black conservatives tend to soft-pedal racism, blame the victim, and let the White establishment off the hook.[24]

Gayle Tate and Lewis Randolph examine Black conservative thought in detail in their anthology *Dimensions of Black Conservatism in the United States*.[25] One critic, Frank Wilson, observes that the scope of the writings of Black conservatives is generally limited to "cultural concerns bearing on race and ethnicity, including critiques of affirmative action and multiculturalism."[26] In fact, Wilson reports that early tensions between Black and White conservatives were such that Supreme Court Justice "Clarence Thomas has mentioned that early on black conservatives were not generally received in public-policy discussions aside from caricatures and sideshows."[27]

As we consider both the history of political engagement by African Americans and the contemporary political landscape, it is important to keep in mind that there is significant ideological diversity. As noted below in Table 6.1, even two and a half decades ago, there was a significant proportion of Blacks self-identifying as "conservative."

More recent information from a Pew Research Center report reaffirms the diversity of political ideology among African Americans (see Table 6.2). The report uses a larger range of ideological positions than was used in the study summarized in Table 6.1, but if all of the categories other than Liberals and Democrats are combined and considered under the broad banner of "Conservative," the proportion of conservatives is very similar to that reported in Table 6.1 (26 percent versus 24 percent and 22 percent).

Contemporary Black conservatives are not novel in their advocacy of self-reliance and self-determination. Marcus Garvey, Elijah Muhammad, and Malcolm X were forerunners of the Black self-help philosophy. One of the critical differences, however, between historical approaches and contemporary strategies is the almost total absence of efforts by modern conservatives to become actively engaged in concrete efforts to address persisting inequalities. This is perhaps one reason why their appeal has been limited. As will be discussed later in the chapter, the growing appeal of conservative political ideology in Black communities derives largely from the emergence of a new generation of Black conservative religious leaders.

TABLE 6.1

SELF-IDENTIFIED IDEOLOGICAL POSITIONS IN THE BLACK COMMUNITY

Percentages by Sex, 1972–1982

Ideological Position	Black Men	Black Women
Liberals	44	39
Moderates	32	39
Conservatives	24	22
Totals	100	100

Source: Hanes Walton, Jr. Invisible Politics (Albany, NY: State University of New York Press, 1985), 33.

TABLE 6.2

REPRESENTATION OF BLACKS ACROSS THE PEW RESEARCH CENTER'S POLITICAL TYPOLOGIES

Typology	Black Representation
Solid Liberals	9
Hard-Pressed Democrats	35
New Coalition Democrats	30
Post-Moderns	6
Disaffecteds	8
Libertarians	1
Main Street Republicans	2
Staunch Conservatives	0
Bystanders	9

Source: Pew Research Center, "Beyond Red vs. Blue: The Political Typology," Released May 4, 2011.

http://people-press.org/2011/05/04/beyond-red-vs-blue-the-political-typology/

African American Studies wholeheartedly endorses self-help uplift efforts, but its insistence on eradicating institutional racism and discrimination and the overwhelming consensus among its practitioners that both social cancers persist make the field largely incompatible with most other tenets of contemporary Black conservatism. As a consequence, these conservative views have been the subject of many critical analyses in African American Studies professional literature.

Black Political Mobilization: Eighteenth Century to 1955

As early as the late eighteenth century, free Blacks succeeded in establishing independent institutions that addressed not only daily living concerns but also the need to challenge the foundations of the slavery regime. The creation of institutions was facilitated by a rapid growth in the size of the free Black population from several sources that included manumissions following military service during the Revolutionary War and natural increases. The free Black population increased from negligible numbers at the start of the American Revolution to 60,000 in 1790 and to nearly 234,000 in 1820, with most of this growth concentrated in the rural upper South.[28] The growth of the southern free Black population also sparked increased efforts by many enslaved Blacks to gain their freedom. Joseph Scott suggests that there were an unusually large number of revolts and attempted revolts between 1790 and 1802, as well as a pronounced increase in the number of enslaved Blacks who took flight from bondage.[29] Several major rebellions occurred; some were led by free Blacks. In addition, sabotage of equipment and property occurred frequently. These developments prompted southern states to introduce restrictions on the practice of manumission and to establish a variety of restrictions on the movement and rights of free Blacks. Suffrage did exist for a few "free" Blacks in the South, and, to some extent, among those in some northern states. A limited number of free Blacks voted in Tennessee in 1834 and in North Carolina in 1835. Although their vote was not large, Blacks were given equal suffrage and voted in Massachusetts, Maine, New Hampshire, and Vermont in 1840. New York and Rhode Island imposed property qualifications.[30]

In the face of restrictions on participation in electoral politics, free Blacks employed "invisible politics" strategies through community institutions, developing the means to fight for full citizenship rights and the end of slavery. Urban residential segregation enabled free Blacks to develop independent institutions and to develop collective strategies to uplift and to challenge the institution of slavery and institutional discrimination. Gayle Tate argues that "antebellum organizations, associations, and societies were the outgrowth of black women's developing political consciousness and community activism" and that "free black female activists, continuing or paralleling the role of slave women with the slave community, became nexus women, recruiting targeted members as well as other community members to organizations and community participation."[31] Tate makes the critical points that: (a) the political activities of free Blacks emerged from a focus on resistance to slavery; and (b) that Black women constituted the organizing force for invisible politics.

Patricia Hill Collins has argued that enslaved Black women forged and sustained a culture of resistance in enslaved communities.[32] Nancy Naples suggests that this resistance was embedded in enslaved women's labor activity in ways that blurred mothering, political action, and labor activity.[33] Elaborating on this interpretation, Gayle Tate argues, "Within the plantation system, slave women created autonomous spaces where they could activate their labor will as a protest mechanism in stimulating broad-based community resistance. They played the role of 'nexus women,' weaving the disparate elements of communities into a cohesive unit so that both resources and resistance could be maximized over a protracted period of time."[34]

The worldview that enabled enslaved African women to undertake such a monumental role in the Black liberation struggle had its origins in the pre-slavery ethos of African societies. Tate observes,

> Slave women understood their collective oppression in the context of their female work collectives, African traditions that kept freedom a living memory, and their own longing for freedom ... Their labor will activated a climate of collective and intergenerational resistance; the politicization of the slave community on the issue of existing inequalities and the continuous exploitation of labor; and gender as a mode of social organization on the plantation, where female work collectives created the space for discourse and resistance to emerge.[35]

6

As White repression to Black liberation efforts intensified, free Blacks transformed invisible political activities into visible movements. The Negro Convention Movement, for example, initiated in the 1830s, represented, in part, a national effort among free Blacks to exercise a collective impact on political policies affecting the fate of all peoples of African descent. This strategy marked a qualitative shift from the early forms of collective organization that were largely geared toward creating localized community-level infrastructures to address daily living concerns. Tate observes that the establishment of mutual benefit societies facilitated "the community's thrust for self-reliance, as well as black women's desire for community leadership and economic survival."[36] Moreover, "mutual benefit societies countered Northern racial attitudes, emphasized black pride, and were intertwined with the abolitionist movement that was gaining currency in northern cities."[37]

Consistent with the earlier discussion of the tensions between integrationist and nationalist ideologies, the struggle against slavery created a dilemma. The Abolition Movement was clearly interracial, but achieving interracial solidarity proved problematic. A repeated criticism advanced by Black abolitionists against their White comrades was that Blacks were seen as "exhibits" rather than as advocates for their own liberation, and there were clear limits on what most White abolitionists were willing to do to defend Black rights.[38]

As a consequence, greater cooperation emerged between free Black men and women to develop more self-determined liberation initiatives. By the late 1830s, many Black women were being recruited actively by Black men to become antislavery speakers, and many Black male leaders "worked on political committees with black women, particularly vigilance committees and antislavery societies, where women were active participants and recognized leaders."[39]

In addition to fostering greater cooperation between free Black men and women, the ambiguous relationship between Black and White antislavery advocates was also a catalyst for stronger ties between free and enslaved Blacks. Various private practices and public policies also facilitated stronger relationships. In many southern urban areas, Blacks were sometimes allowed to "live out" and "hire their own time." These "rights" not only blurred the distinction between free Blacks and enslaved Blacks in urban areas, they also enabled the development of collaborative antislavery activities. During the 1850s, federal policies reinforced the link between the lives of enslaved and free Blacks. As noted by Joe Trotter, the Fugitive Slave Law of 1850 "not only undercut the fugitive network but also weakened the free Black community by increasing penalties for persons aiding and abetting runaways."[40] In a similar vein, in the *Dred Scott* case of 1857, "the U.S. Supreme Court undermined the liberty of free Blacks as well as the enslaved."[41]

The progressive retrenchment of the rights of "free" Blacks led to an intensification of nationalist sentiments among many. The 1854 Negro Convention of free Blacks called for the creation of a self-contained economic network composed of Black workers and entrepreneurs. In effect, prior to the Civil War, law and public policy had created what Cheryl Harris describes as a de facto "property right" in Whiteness, protected by limiting the type of relief available to oppressed groups.[42] Protection of the property interest in Whiteness was and is achieved, in part, by treating race as "immutable and biological" and by "treating whiteness as the basis for a valid claim to special constitutional protection."[43]

The institutionalization of a property right in Whiteness meant that even after the formal end of slavery, full citizenship for African Americans would remain an unfulfilled dream, despite passage of the Thirteenth, Fourteenth, and Fifteenth Amendments to the Constitution. Early developments during the Reconstruction period appeared to offer the possibility that Blacks might be incorporated as full partners in post-Civil War politics. In fact, after the passage of the Fifteenth Amendment in 1870, Black Republicans gained significant political influence in the South.

Congress removed home rule from the southern states and divided the area into five military districts following the Civil War. New southern reconstruction governments were established that operated under the protection of the Army, and Blacks played a significant political role in establishing and operating these governments. Besides voting in large numbers, Black males were elected to local, state, and federal offices. In addition, Blacks comprised a majority of the delegates to the state constitutional conventions in South Carolina and Louisiana as well as 40 percent in Florida. Although not as well represented in other states, Black delegates still played an important role in crafting the new Constitutions. The reconstruction governments instituted an impressive range of progressive policies, including establishing systems of public education and building many new hospitals and other social service facilities.

At the national level between 1869 and 1901, two Blacks served in the US Senate and twenty served as members of the House of Representatives. Senators Hiram Rhodes Revels and Blanche Kelso Bruce were elected from Mississippi and served. P. B. S. Pinchback was also elected to the Senate from Louisiana but was not permitted to take his seat. He did serve as Lieutenant Governor of Louisiana, and, for three days, as Acting Governor. Northern Blacks were also active in electoral politics during this period, mobilizing in support of Republicans through various entities, including Black Republican Clubs. Although still disenfranchised, Black women helped mobilize the Black male electorate and insured that their voices would be heard through participation in meetings, rallies, and other political events. In some cases, Black women voted on political stances and participated in the selection of delegates.

The brief foray of Blacks into southern electoral politics was short-circuited by chaos created during the presidential election of 1876, when no victor emerged. In order to placate the South, Republican presidential candidate Rutherford B. Hayes agreed to withdraw federal Reconstruction enforcement officials in exchange for southern electoral votes. This became known as the Compromise of 1877. Hayes' compromise led directly to the complete dismantling of the initial political gains achieved by Blacks from passage of the Thirteenth, Fourteenth, and Fifteenth Amendments. In 1883, the Civil Rights Act of 1875 was declared unconstitutional, which allowed again the virtual disfranchisement of Blacks in the South. The public was primed to accept the exclusion of Blacks from electoral politics, in part, by slander campaigns caricaturing Black legislators as corrupt and inept. By 1890, eight southern states had disfranchised all Black voters through the revision of their constitutions. The South became a one-party region under the domain of White supremacy and Democratic Party politics. The Democratic Party prevailed exclusively in the South until 1964.[44]

Faced with their progressive removal from the arena of electoral politics, Blacks returned to movement politics in efforts to prevent wholesale re-subjugation. In a manner similar to efforts undertaken in connection with the Abolitionist movement, Blacks attempted to forge alliances with Whites. In the 1880s and 1890s, agrarian discontent was the spark igniting the creation of the Greenback Party and the Populist Movement. For a time it appeared as if the Populist Movement would provide a vehicle for interracial cooperation to counteract the adverse distributional consequences of economic transformation, but the movement split along racial lines.

The basis for cooperation around agricultural issues was the shared oppression being exacted by commercial agricultural interests on Black and White farmers and farm workers. Farmers initiated widespread organizational efforts to levy political influence and promote policies to improve the lot of farmers and farm workers. Farmers denounced grain elevators and speculators, agricultural futures markets, and mechanization of harvesting and processing. Blacks were especially concerned about the institutionalization of the infamous system of debt peonage that effectively shackled rural Blacks to the land. Vagrancy laws and related legislation were also used to coerce Black workers to rebuild southern infrastructure.

As was the case with the Abolitionist Movement, Black-White co-operation proved elusive in confronting challenges in the agricultural South. Targeted coercion of rural Blacks who left Whites relatively unaffected limited the extent and effectiveness of efforts to build interracial alliances. The predominantly White National Grange and the Farmers' Alliance Movement became major focal points for resistance efforts against oppressive forces. However, Black farmers felt compelled to organize their own counterpart in 1888—the Colored Farmers' National Alliance and Cooperative Union. At its peak, the Alliance claimed a membership of 1.2 million members in twelve states. It collapsed after a failed attempt to mount a strike of cotton pickers, which was opposed by the White Farm Alliance.[45]

Faced with systemic oppression in southern agriculture, some Blacks were able to "vote with their feet" and migrate to the West and North. Collective organization of migration sometimes occurred, as in the case of the two hundred thousand "exodusters" who migrated to the Midwest, especially to Kansas and Oklahoma, in the late 1870s. There was, in fact, a movement to make Oklahoma and Texas all-Black states. The Exoduster Movement had strong religious underpinnings, as suggested by the term *exodusters*,

6

which refers to the biblical exodus of the Israelites from bondage in Egypt.

Kenneth Hamilton has identified sixty-four all-Black towns that were established between 1877 and 1915. The phenomenon of Black town creation spanned thirteen states, although Oklahoma alone accounted for at least half, with Texas hosting the second largest number.[46] Various researchers have emphasized how these initiatives enabled Blacks to exercise self-government, escape discrimination and abuse, have a greater likelihood of being able to depend on neighbors for financial assistance, and have open markets for their crops. Entrepreneurs in these communities started every imaginable kind of business, including newspapers, and they advertised throughout the South for settlers. Hamilton argues, however, that the primary motivation of the persons who established these towns was economic and not political, although they used visions of a racial utopia to attract followers. Hamilton concludes that "developers of the predominantly Black town sites seemed to differ from promoters of White towns only in that they attempted to capitalize on race to secure inhabitants."[47] The contemporary parallel in electoral politics is the use of political office by some Black elected officials for personal aggrandizement rather than public service, and by their using calls for racial unity to maintain their elected positions.

In addition to the issue of less than altruistic motives behind the organizers of all-Black towns, Whites were largely unsympathetic to the efforts of Blacks to establish independent political jurisdictions. White citizens in Oklahoma, for example, undertook efforts to discourage additional Black migration once statehood was obtained, and, in addition, to segregate Blacks into areas that were not economically viable. One of the most notorious examples of White hostility to successful Black self-determination occurred in Tulsa, Oklahoma, where a major race riot occurred on June 1-2, 1921, when Blacks attempted to prevent incarcerated comrades from being lynched. During the course of the riot, both cars and airplanes were used in an all-out assault against Black citizens. Bombs dropped from planes caused extensive property damage and loss of life. Forty-four blocks of property were destroyed in the conflagration. In all, nearly seventy Blacks and twenty Whites lost their lives at Tulsa.

Even prior to this still largely unrecognized and unresolved tragedy, similar oppressive experiences in several states had forced some exodusters to migrate again to other locations, including Canada, Mexico, and Africa. Because the economies of most all-Black towns centered on agriculture, the onset of the "Great Depression" spelled doom for most, as they were unable to survive the fallout of declining demand, railroad failures, and population loss.

The specter of racial violence, and especially lynching, became one of the principal foci of Black political efforts in the late nineteenth and early twentieth centuries. Between 1892 and 1902, there were over 580 lynchings in Mississippi, over 530 in Georgia, over 490 in Texas, as well as large numbers in other states.[48] It was estimated by 1918, that over 2,500 Blacks had been lynched. Public acceptance of widespread violence against Blacks was fueled, in part, by the *Plessy v. Ferguson* decision of the United States Supreme Court in 1896, that established the doctrine of "separate but equal" as official government policy in race relations. In the *Plessy* case, as in the 1883 decision, the Court held that laws requiring segregation did not necessarily imply inferiority of one race with respect to another. By the beginning of the twentieth century, all sections of the Fourteenth Amendment had been nullified by Court decisions with the exception of citizenship provisions.

Consistent with the earlier discussion of diversity in Black political ideology, there were various attempts to use visible and invisible movement politics to confront racial domination. Black leaders favoring direct action had to contend with the accommodationist approach of Booker T. Washington, as discussed in Chapter 3. His Atlanta Compromise speech in 1895 served as a call to arms for many progressive Blacks.

W. E. B. Du Bois and twenty-nine other prominent Black men established the Niagara Movement in 1905 (named for the location of the group's second meeting at Niagara Falls in July 1905). Although formal membership was restricted to men, as in the case of other organizational initiatives, several Black women played prominent, but largely invisible, roles in facilitating the organizing efforts. In February 1905, for example, Mary B. Talbert hosted a planning session to prepare for the first formal Niagara Movement meeting. As of 1906, women were able to participate in the Niagara Movement as full-fledged members. Verina Morton Harris Jones, the first woman of any race to practice medicine in the state of Mississippi, was one of the women who participated in both the 1905 and 1906 Niagara meetings.[49] The Niagara Movement renounced Booker T. Washington's accommodationist policies and successfully organized approximately thirty chapters in various states. It was never, however, able to attract mass support and disbanded in 1910. The group's activities were largely restricted to distributing pamphlets and lobbying against Jim Crow segregation. It was especially active in waging protests against the treatment of Black soldiers assigned to an army regiment at Fort Brown, Texas, in 1906. Responding to repeated incidents of physical assaults on Black soldiers by Brownsville, Texas, residents, a group of approximately twenty Black soldiers fired weapons into several buildings and killed two people. Although the perpetrators were never identified, then-President Theodore Roosevelt dishonorably discharged 167 Black soldiers, an action that was favorably described by one staunch segregationist as an "executive lynching." This miscarriage of justice was not reversed until the 1970s.

That incident, along with the Springfield, Illinois, Race Riot of 1908, signaled the need for more assertive and effective organizational initiatives to stem the tide of racial violence and suppression of rights. A previous riot in 1904 resulted in the lynching of a Black man and the torching of several houses occupied by Blacks. The 1908 riot was precipitated by false accusations of rape by a White woman against a Black man. Despite the accuser's retraction of the charges, local Whites were intent on lynching the accused and were outraged when authorities secretly sprinted him from the town. In retaliation, two innocent Black men were lynched, and several Black-occupied homes were burned. Five thousand state militiamen had to be mobilized to quell the violence.[50]

These horrific events contributed to the attempt to make the Niagara Movement interracial. W. E. B. Du Bois invited Mary White Ovington, a settlement worker and socialist, to become the Movement's first White member. Other White liberals subsequently joined, which led to the demise of the Niagara Movement in 1908 and the formation of the NAACP in 1909.

The two prominent Black women involved in the formation and subsequent activities of the NAACP, Ida B. Wells-Barnett and Mary Church Terrell, played a critical role in prodding the NAACP to become active in the anti-lynching movement. Their initiatives flowed directly from the self-organizing efforts by Black women who built on the tradition of invisible politics practiced during the slavery and post-slavery eras. As discussed in a previous chapter, Ida B. Wells-Barnett is especially noteworthy for spearheading the anti-lynching crusade. When her exposé of the atrocities and twisted logic of lynching were largely ignored outside the Black press in the US, she took the case to England. There she was able to mobilize the British press to initiate fact-finding trips to the US and encourage British reformers to organize anti-lynching societies. When she returned to the US, her anti-lynching efforts were channeled successfully through the existing network of Black Women's clubs. This strategy was made possible because of the 1895 merger of the two most powerful federations of urban Black female societies, the Colored Women's League and the National Federation of Afro-American Women, to form the National Association of Colored Women (NACW), with Terrell serving as the organization's first president. During the late nineteenth century, the motto "Lifting As We Climb" emerged to describe a concept of shared social responsibility in which upper- and middle-class women worked to share their success by giving back to the community and helping the less fortunate.

Wells-Barnett worked with colleagues in New York and Chicago clubs to promote the anti-lynching campaign through the journal *The Women's Era*. As noted by Cedric Robinson, the NAACP was not comfortable with Wells-Barnett's militant tactics, but, responding to her international reputation, the organization vigorously took up the anti-lynching crusade "to become the staunchest organized opposition to lynching." The NAACP pursued its efforts largely through advocacy of the passage of a federal anti-lynching bill, an initiative that still has not been successful. The NAACP's emphasis on redress through legislative enactments and the judicial system carried over into its efforts to confront Jim Crow segregation in other venues, including 1917 legal challenges to voter exclusion in Oklahoma and residential segregation ordinances in Baltimore, New Orleans, and other cities in Louisiana.

The unprecedented level of violence exercised against Blacks in Tulsa prompted a more militant response among some Blacks. The official organ of the African Blood Brotherhood (ABB), the *Crusader*, asserted that the underlying motive of Whites in the Tulsa carnage was to grab African American

6

oil lands. This Marxist, anti-capitalist interpretation evolved from an earlier Black nationalist orientation. The ABB was founded by Cyril Briggs, who migrated from the Caribbean Island of Nevis to Harlem in 1905 and began writing for the *Amsterdam News* in 1912. He formed the ABB in 1917, which was built on the model of a secret fraternity and organized in "posts" with a centralized national organization based in New York City. He established *The Crusader* in 1918 to focus on the struggle for self-determination and Black pride. *The Crusader* exposed southern lynchings and northern job discrimination. In an early editorial, Briggs called for the establishment of a separate Black state in the United States. This would later become one of the positions of the American Communist Party, with which the ABB had some ties.

The 1920 ABB Convention defined resistance to the KKK, support for a united front of Black organizations, and promotion of higher wages and better working conditions for Black workers as paramount. While calling for "racial self-respect," it also argued that cooperation with "class-conscious white workers" was necessary. *The Crusader* declared that while the oppression of Blacks was more severe, Blacks and Jews shared a historic experience of persecution. This constitutes one example of the early exploration of possible Black-Jewish alliances that would become important in the modern Civil Rights Movement.

Opposing Garvey's economic nationalist movement, the ABB members did not consider "Africa for the Africans" with unbridled capitalist development very attractive. Briggs contended that socialism and communism were operative in Africa long before these modes of social organization were proposed by Europeans and that they should form the basis for African independent states. This, and other positions advanced by the ABB, highlighted a weakness in traditional integrationist and Black nationalist political discourse. Specifically, both tend to ignore constraints imposed by national and global political economies. Structural analyses that might be considered Socialist- or Communist-inspired are usually dismissed or ignored out of fear of repercussions from powerful elites. Precluding the exploration of structural barriers to Black liberation is dysfunctional, particularly as globalization has increasingly worsened the plight of African Americans and Africans.

The general tendency of integrationist values to trump all other ideological positions was particularly pronounced in the struggle between Garvey and more conventional Black leaders in the 1920s, as discussed earlier. Ironically, Du Bois, a staunch opponent of Garvey, would himself be subsequently banished from his position in the NAACP in the early 1930s for daring to challenge integrationist orthodoxy in essays, such as "A Negro Nation Within the Nation." With indirect censorship of political ideas in mainstream political discourse, Communists preserved militant resistance in the strategic repertoire of political responses. This militant option would be reactivated during the 1960s Black Power Movement. Following World War II, as the Cold War intensified, mainstream leaders would again scurry to avoid charges that the growing grassroots clamor for equal citizenship rights was a Communist ploy rather than a self-determined response to continuing racial oppression.

Fear within the White establishment that social critiques, articulated by Garveyites and more radical Black political groups, would gain a strong foothold in Black communities enabled Black women to carve out political space to rejuvenate the practice of "invisible politics" to create social capital. This social capital would prove crucial in the success of the modern Civil Rights Movement. In addition, Black women were also able to move into the vanguard in efforts to influence national politics directly. This latter role was obviously enabled by the passage of the Nineteenth Amendment to the Constitution in 1920 that extended the franchise to women.

The ability of Black women's organizations to influence public officials was also enhanced by northern Blacks' growing electoral strength which was fueled by the first wave of the Great Migration from the South. The Great Migration created the first large, urban Black communities in the North. During 1910–1930, the Black population in northern cities increased by about 20 percent. Chicago, Detroit, New York, and Cleveland experienced some of the largest increases. Blacks won many local elections throughout the North after World War I. In 1928, Chicagoan Oscar De Priest became the first Black to serve in the US Congress since 1901 and the first ever from the North. Northern Blacks also began to display electoral clout by influencing election outcomes in races where all contenders were White. Blacks helped elect and defeat Whites who supported or opposed civil rights advances in Ohio, Kansas, and California. At the same time, gains from Black electoral participation were restricted both by the relative size of the electorate and deliberate discriminatory arrangements.

During the 1800s, and even after the Rutherford B. Hayes betrayal in the Compromise of 1877, Blacks generally supported the Republican Party. They had good reasons to be loyal and dedicated to Republican politics because the Constitutional Amendments passed on behalf of their enfranchisement, the Emancipation, and the first Civil Rights Act were promoted and passed under traditional or radical Republicanism. A noticeable shift of the majority of African Americans from the Republican to the Democratic Party occurred in 1936 after the first term of the Roosevelt New Deal era. Blacks did not change their loyalty to the Democratic Party instantaneously. Instead, there was a gradual transition, beginning initially at the local level. Indeed, there always were some northern Blacks who supported selective Democratic candidates, and so did a number of southern Blacks who retained suffrage.[51] It is evident that Blacks generally avoided association with the Democratic Party prior to 1936 because of the overt racial meanness, and, particularly, the anti-Black attitudes of most White Democrats. Yet, it was the anti-Black and ultra-conservative sentiment that Republicans developed after 1877 that drove Blacks away from the Republican Party, their initial political benefactors. The first Black Democratic Congressman, Arthur Mitchell, was elected in 1934 by defeating Republican Oscar De Priest.

With the escalating shift in the political affiliation of northern Blacks, the important role of Mary McLeod Bethune in energizing the political potential of Black women cannot be overstated. Joyce Hanson affirms her contribution, noting that while president of the National Association of Colored Women, Mary McLeod Bethune transformed the organization into a cohesive body that served as the official voice of African American women on public issues.[52] One of her principal strategies involved preparing African American women to assume decision-making positions in government. Through the National Council of Negro Women, formed by Bethune in 1935, she "cultivated a female culture of resistance and fostered female autonomy."[53] In addition to the goal of appointments of African American women to boards and committees, the council also sought "to eliminate discriminatory legislation in housing, health, employment, public accommodations, and political representation."[54]

Bethune served in the administration of President Franklin Roosevelt as Director of the Office of Minority Affairs. In this role, she was able to wrest a significant degree of control from White administrators of the National Youth Administration programs in various states. As suggested previously, this was accomplished by having qualified African Americans appointed to key decision-making positions within the state administrative structure.

Bethune's most visible and influential role at the national level was associated with her organization of President Roosevelt's "Black Cabinet," an informal group of Black advisors. She was the only female member of this Cabinet but was clearly its most influential member. Bethune "used her position to arrange public conferences between civil rights activists and key government officials that focused government attention on economic, political, and social inequality."[55]

Charles Hamilton Houston, Dean of the Howard University Law School, was one of the approximately twenty luminaries comprising the "Black Cabinet." At the time, Houston was already playing a critical role in reshaping the legal contours of the battle for equal rights. As Jack Greenberg notes, "not until Howard University in the '30s began graduating numbers of Negro lawyers trained in civil rights did the race relations picture begin to change."[56] The impact of Houston's efforts can be seen from the success rate of the NAACP in civil rights litigation. Hanes Walton reports that the NAACP won twenty-six out of twenty-eight cases brought before the United States Supreme Court prior to 1958.[57]

World War II set in motion a complex set of events that would lay the foundations for the modern Civil Rights and Black Power Movements. Blacks continued to use a mix of electoral, movement, and invisible politics to continue the battle for equal rights. The March on Washington Movement, launched in 1941 by A. Philip Randolph of the Brotherhood of Sleeping Car Porters, was the most militant initiative. The Movement challenged segregation in the armed forces and discrimination in employment in defense industries and threatened to undertake a mass march on Washington, D.C. The march was called off after President Roosevelt met with Randolph and Walter White of the NAACP and issued Executive Order 8802, banning racial discrimination in government employment, defense industries, and training programs. The order also created the Fair Employment Practices Committee to implement its provisions.

6

On the electoral front, Black voters were regularly electing officials in a number of Northern states, as well as in Kentucky and West Virginia at the eve of World War II. These newly elected officials actively fought against segregation and racism. The activities of the Political Action Committee of the Committee for Industrial Organization in defeating prominent anti-Black Congressmen helped mobilize the support of Black labor for Franklin D. Roosevelt in 1944. Widespread Black support for Roosevelt was also stimulated by his desegregation of federal departments and the elimination of selected discriminatory arrangements in the armed forces.

In the immediate post-War period, Blacks were successful in building on the political momentum created during World War II. Many Black veterans returned from overseas assignments with new perspectives on American race relations and became involved in efforts to effect political change. Their allies included many members of the Black middle and working classes who had benefited from employment in war industries. For many Black workers, involvement with industrial unions had heightened their political awareness and commitment to social change.

The potential for southern Black electoral gains was enabled by the Supreme Court's decision in *Smith v. Allwright* (1944) that removed barriers to voting by Blacks in primary elections. The number of Black registered voters doubled between 1946 and 1947. This sparked massive Black voter registration in the South during the 1950s.[58] The *Smith v. Allwright* decision declared the White primary system unconstitutional. The White primary was a system initiated in the southern states to bar Black political participation. Blacks used their growing electoral clout to support Harry Truman's candidacy in 1948. Blacks contributed significantly to his margin of victory in California, Illinois, and Ohio. Widespread Black electoral support was given to Harry S. Truman partly in response to his desegregation of the armed forces.

White resistance in the South to the multipronged assault by Black activists on Jim Crow segregation intensified. The reaction of national leaders was partially conditioned by the need to project a positive image of human rights commitment in international circles. The global realignment that followed World War II forced the national government to confront the threat that Jim Crow segregation posed to international relations. Many colonies in Asia and Africa gained their independence from European domination after the War, and the Cold War struggle with the Soviet bloc nations forced the United States to court the good will of these emerging nations. The persistence of Jim Crow segregation provided ample fodder for the Soviet bloc's propaganda initiatives, and, recognizing this threat, American diplomats urged officials to end domestic segregation to facilitate the struggle against Communism abroad.

Black leaders recognized the importance of international public opinion as well. In 1947, under the auspices of the NAACP, Du Bois authored the document "An Appeal to the World: A Statement on the Denial of Human Rights to Minorities in the Case of Citizens of Negro Descent in the United States of America and an Appeal to the United Nations for Redress."

The continuing record of lynchings was the most visible evidence of the disjunction between articulated values and the realities of the condition of Blacks in the United States. Thus, the lynching of 14-year-old Emmett Till in Mississippi in 1955 was especially momentous in fueling the modern Civil Rights and Black Power Movements. As Clenora Hudson-Weems observes, Till was the "sacrificial lamb of the Civil Rights Movement."[59] He was killed for allegedly wolf-whistling at a White woman. He was kidnapped and murdered by the woman's husband and three accomplices. Till's murder occurred after two consecutive years in which no lynchings had occurred or were reported. The hiatus in lynching had led the Tuskegee Institute to declare that "lynching as traditionally defined and as a barometer for measuring the status of race relations in the South, seems no longer a valid index of such relationships."[60]

The lynching of Emmett Till galvanized national and international attention, in part, because the activism of Black community leaders and the Black press created a common purpose between Blacks in the South and the North. As Weems observes, labor unions, the NAACP, Black churches, and other organizations sponsored numerous speaking engagements for Till's mother, Mamie Bradley, and Rayfield Mooty, a labor activist and second cousin to the victim. Till's casket was open at his funeral in Chicago and pictures of his mutilated face were featured prominently in Black newspapers. The Black press covered the trial of the perpetrators extensively, and public outrage escalated when an all White, all male jury proclaimed the accused assailants innocent after one hour of deliberation.

Louis Burnham, the editor of *Freedom*, said shortly after Till's death, "The fight to avenge the murder of Emmett Louis Till has become a symbol of the Negro people's bitter struggle for first-class citizenship." Burnham's assessment was prescient, for the Till case established a firm foundation for continuing collaboration between northern and southern Blacks to end the Jim Crow regime.

The era of Black protest that developed from the violent school desegregation rebellions, racial atrocities, and the Montgomery Bus Boycott of the mid-1950s did more to arouse the national civic consciousness of African Americans than any other events in American history. Partly as a result of the urgency of this period, Congress passed Civil Rights Acts in 1957 and in 1960 to protect Black voting rights. It also established a Commission on Civil Rights as an investigative agency. Other non-electoral political tactics and activities, such as, the student sit-ins and freedom rides of the 1960s, also galvanized Black politics in the North and South.

Grassroots Activism and the Civil Rights Movement

Much of the literature that has examined the modern Civil Rights and Black Power Movements has focused on the role of national figures, like Martin Luther King, Jr., as the principal agents driving the movement. The traditional focus on national leaders and highly visible events creates the impression that the movements were geographically undifferentiated and were independent of local issues. Recent scholarship challenges this interpretation and highlights the distinctive character of each local effort. Jeanne Theoharis and Komozi Woodward argue cogently, in *Groundwork: Local Black Freedom Movements in America*, the need to foreground "the interconnections between churches, unions, black self-help organizations, and earlier civil rights actions."[61] This view is consistent with the emphasis on "invisible politics" discussed previously. The focus on local liberation struggles does not negate the existence of a broader collective struggle. The various contributors to *Groundwork* show how liberation struggles were waged in a variety of urban and rural settings. In many respects, the linkages between local and national interests were mediated through local affiliates of national and regional organizations, such as the NAACP and the Southern Christian Leadership Conference.

In the same way, several essays document that the Black Power Movement, like the Civil Rights Movement, had local origins. As noted by Theoharis and Woodard, many of the articles in the volume "document the native character and indigenous dimensions of Black Power organizations and the role of the NAACP, particularly the organization's Youth Councils, as incubators for militant activism in many cities. The synergy between the Black Power approach and more integrationist approaches worked to generate greater responsiveness to Black concerns from the American political system. The vision and strategies used to pursue Black Power politics provide, in many ways, a benchmark to assess the contemporary emphasis on traditional electoral politics. Thus, the politics of the Black Power Movement is examined prior to the record of traditional electoral politics.

The Politics of Black Power

When Kwame Ture (Stokely Carmichael) enunciated the shrill cry, "Black Power!"—from the back of a flatbed truck at the rally of the Voter Registration March Against Fear, in Greenwood, Mississippi, in June of 1966—the effect was both electrifying and disturbing to the minds of Blacks and Whites. It was a psychologically liberating experience for millions of African Americans. For over three hundred years, successive generations of Black people had been socialized and conditioned into believing that it was prohibitive and impossible to associate power with Blackness or Africanity. Conversely, Whites had been psychologically influenced for centuries to believe that power was an exclusive right of European people.

Initially and ironically, the most vocal critics and denunciators of the slogan Black Power were several traditional integrationist leaders, who seemed willing to surrender all claims to power as long as they could be socially merged and accepted into White society.[63] On the other hand, Whites were not about to share political or economic power with formerly enslaved Blacks whom they deemed humanly and intellectually inferior. Because of the controversy and the intense emotion that the slogan "Black Power" generated, progressive and mostly youthful proponents had to divert and devote much of their effort to defining and explaining the concept of Black Power and to easing

6

the fears of "Uncle Tom" Blacks and liberal Whites. Conservative Whites fully understood the meaning of power, regardless of the shade or color in which it came. Kwame Ture (Stokely Carmichael), the leading spokesman and advocate of Black Power, attributed to the term a clear and logical political meaning. In essence, Carmichael explained that the political system of America is structured and designed to render Black people socially and economically powerless. The majority of Blacks lacked adequate education and were economically deprived and without property. Therefore, it was imperative for Black people to have power to make, or to participate in making, the decisions that govern their lives and to effect social change in American society.[63]

The aspect of Black Power ideology that evoked the most concern and dissent was the advocacy of Black self-determination. Self-determination, economic self-sufficiency, and Black pride were not new concepts proposed for the political empowerment of African Americans. Marcus Garvey and other early Black philosophers had already authored and articulated the principles of self-determination. However, integrationists perceived any ideas or actions promoting Black independence as regressive and supportive of the degrading social system of segregation. They fearfully and inaccurately contended that Black Power was synonymous with segregation. The psycho-political implications of Blacks realizing any measure of independence from Whites are clear. As has already been referred to in the works of Franz Fanon, colonization or slavery politically socializes many of its subjects into accepting dependency on the oppressor as a normative state. An ostensibly "free" person may unconsciously resist the idea of "breaking away" or functioning without the scrutiny, approval, or supervision of the "enslaver."

The politics of Black Power conflict in many ways with integration as it is currently implemented in American society. Symbolic or token representation of Blacks in the political system in the name of integration does not translate, in effect, into actual power-sharing. Simple desegregation cannot achieve Black power. Token desegregation does not alter White control over matters affecting the quality of life and destiny of the Black community. Black Power means an assertion of Black identity and the recognition and operation of a Black political agenda. Since America is still divided, basically, into Black and White

communities, Black Power advocates support political control or ownership of the social and economic institutions within the Black community.

Integration has been extolled as a panacea for racial equality by many. However, Black Power advocates charge that integration has too often served as a political ploy for the socioeconomic elevation of a relatively few system-accommodating individuals, rather than for the uplift of African Americans as a whole. Manning Marable, for example, remarked that "racial integration has produced the symbols of progress and the rhetoric of racial harmony without the substance of empowerment for the oppressed."[64] Thus, significant divergence exists between Black Power and integration politics. An overriding question is: Can African Americans achieve some measure of political parity or power under the existing two-party system?

The political history of African Americans reveals that they have often attempted or succeeded in establishing independent political parties or organizations to project and to protect their political interests. Organizing and maintaining separate or independent political organizations are consistent with Black Power ideology. One of the most important goals and accomplishments of Black Power advocates during the Civil Rights Movement was their assistance in the establishment of the Mississippi Freedom Democratic Party (MFDP) in 1964. The purpose of the MFDP was to challenge and to end discriminatory exclusion of Blacks from the regular White-controlled Democratic Party. The MFDP challenged the seating of the regular Democratic delegates at the national convention in Atlantic City, but their claim was rejected. The seating of five White Congressmen from Mississippi was challenged by the MFDP in 1965 on the grounds that Blacks had been excluded in the primary and general elections. The House of Representatives voted to dismiss the challenge. Subsequently, the MFDP did achieve some successes. In 1968, a group of former MFDP delegates, calling themselves the Loyal Democrats of Mississippi succeeded in being seated as the sole Mississippi delegation to the Democratic National Convention.

In 1966, SNCC organized a Black independent political party in Lowndes County, Alabama (80 percent Black population) for the purpose of nominating candidates for the offices of sheriff, tax assessor, and members of the school board. The party was called the Lowndes County Freedom Organization (LCFO). It used the Black panther as its ballot symbol. The LCFO slate lost the election by a narrow margin because of violence on election day. Carmichael later used the Lowndes County experience to define and rationalize the political slogan of Black Power. With Blacks in a position to elect sheriffs, they could put an end to police brutality. Black tax assessors could collect and channel funds for the building of better Black schools and roads to serve the Black community.[65]

At the national level, active exploration of establishing an independent Black political party reflected the viewpoint articulated by Ronald Walters, "There needs to be some political organization capable of providing the option of running a candidate in the general election, or of throwing the organization's support to either one party or the other in accord with the outcome of the bargaining."[66] In some respects, this approach involves the fusion of movement and electoral politics.

The genesis of an organized Black revolt against the traditional Democratic and Republican two-party political system occurred when African Americans held the National Black Political Convention in Gary, Indiana, on March 10-12, 1972. More than 10,000 Black participants and 3,000 Black registered delegates from forty-six states came to Gary to adopt a National Black Agenda based on the common interests and political objectives of the masses of Black people in the United States. As one political analyst wrote, "Gary leaped past the limits and concepts of its conceivers, the Black elected officials and the Congressional Black Caucus."[67] The Black media reported much factionalism as might be expected at any political convention. Irreconcilable differences between Black Power/Nationalists and Black elected officials precluded, at that time, formation of a Black independent party. However, a holistic and unified African spirituality prevailed at the convention. The National Black Political Assembly was organized as the continuum of the Gary convention and has met annually in various other cities.

A Black independent political party, the National Black Independent Political Party was actually formed in 1980, but a truly viable Black political party remains an unrealized objective. Continuing efforts to establish such an entity, to be described later in this chapter, are driven in part by the increasingly indistinguishable policies of the Democratic and Republican Parties with respect to racial equity. If this trend continues,

it will serve to fuel the independent party initiative smoldering in the arena of Black politics.

The success of a Black independent political party depends on mobilization of significant support from registered and voting African Americans residing in many political jurisdictions. Creative use of invisible politics will be required to achieve such an outcome. The purpose of such a political party may not be to have its own slate of winning candidates but to negotiate or bargain for benefits between the two traditional parties. The goals of Black Power politics are to sustain a posture of independence, develop as a pivotal-force in the electorate, and to exercise leverage in the two-party American political system. Black Power political activists ultimately seek to change the social and economic order to one that is free of racial inequality and injustice.

Efforts to revive the idea of an independent Black political party and develop a group-specific agenda were also put forward at the National Black Agenda Convention, held in Boston, in March 2004. This conference drew state lawmakers, activists, and political stalwarts, such as Richard Hatcher, the former Mayor of Gary, Indiana, who was a key figure at the 1972 convention. It remains an open question whether Black Power politics, traditional Black electoral politics, invisible politics, or a combination thereof can achieve this outcome.

6

Political Education and the Media

The effectiveness of invisible and electoral politics depends critically on the existence and operation of communication vehicles to educate and mobilize constituents. These are part and parcel of the set of internal channels of communication developed by all societies to facilitate the exchange of information vital for maintaining community well-being. Such communication channels range from the "grapevine" that operates informally, for example, through discourse in beauty and barber shops, to more formal entities, such as, newspapers, magazines, and radio. African American Studies specialists are particularly interested in how such communication networks have been used to promote liberation and uplift and in the factors affecting success in promoting these objectives.

Black Newspapers

Black newspapers have been the primary printed source of information relevant to the struggle against racism since the early 1800s. Various commentators have concluded that Black newspapers have consistently demanded democracy, protested injustice, challenged White statements on race, presented positive images of Black people, and sought to perfect American democracy. Black newspapers have also acted as both a "mirror" of Black life in America and a facilitator of efforts to define a collective identity.

John B. Russwurm and Samuel E. Cornish established the first African American newspaper, *Freedom's Journal*, in 1827, with a mission to defend free Blacks. However, Russwurm and Cornish disagreed on editorial policy, and the newspaper only lasted until 1829. Other short-lived Black newspapers appeared in New York City, Albany, Philadelphia, Pittsburgh, and Columbus, Ohio. Frederick Douglass' newspaper, the *North Star*, established in 1847, survived until 1860. The educated free Black target audience was too small in most locales to support a weekly newspaper financially, and most publishers lacked adequate funds to subsidize losses over an extended period of time. Nevertheless, over forty Black newspapers were founded before the start of the Civil War, and by 1855, the Black press had spread westward to Kansas and even to San Francisco.[68]

The South's first Black newspaper, *L'Union*, appeared in New Orleans during the Civil War. By the end of 1865, Black newspapers had been established in Louisiana, Alabama, Tennessee, South Carolina, and Georgia, and Black newspapers were published in most of the former slave states within a few years. During the Reconstruction Era Black newspapers consistently protested the Black Codes—the laws passed by southern states to limit the freedom of the formerly enslaved Blacks—and outbreaks of racial violence. Between 1861 and 1877, an estimated 115 Black newspapers appeared across the nation, but most lasted less than two years. However, the growth of literacy among formerly enslaved Blacks laid the foundation for the emergence of more long-lived newspapers during the 1880s and 1890s.[69]

Between 1880 and 1890, more than five hundred new Black newspapers began publication. By 1910, over 275 Black newspapers were being published in cities throughout the United States, reaching a cumulative circulation of half a million readers. During the period 1895–1915, over twelve hundred Black newspapers nationwide were providing critical information to African Americans, although, as had been the case during earlier periods, many ceased publication after a few years. In the face of growing violence against African Americans, the Black Press tended to adopt a less militant stance after Reconstruction. However, those editors who spoke too freely risked losing life and property, and angry White mobs destroyed the offices of several Black newspapers—notably, the *Memphis Free Speech* in 1892 and the *Record* in Wilmington, North Carolina, in 1899. The *California Eagle*, founded in 1879, reached out to African Americans in the rest of the nation and called for them to seize opportunities available in the growing cities of the West, especially Los Angeles. The newspaper even challenged the nascent film industry and led a boycott that spread nationwide against D.W. Griffith's *Birth of a Nation*.[70]

During the early twentieth century, Black newspapers took a leadership role in investigative reporting on lynching by countering biased reports in White newspapers. Black newspapers also covered race riots, poor living conditions and poor education for Blacks, political and economic inequality between the races, and rising street crime. Robert Abbott's founding of the *Chicago Defender* in 1905 ushered in a new era in Black journalism. The *Defender's* sensational reporting gained wide popularity, and circulation grew to almost 300,000 by 1920. More than two-thirds of the circulation came from outside Chicago, and the *Defender* also enjoyed great popularity in the South. "The Great Northern Drive," started during World War I (WW I), was the newspaper's most famous crusade. The *Defender* urged southern Blacks to move North to take advantage of war jobs in the northern cities and escape southern brutality.[71]

During World War II, the *Pittsburgh Courier* instituted a comparable political mobilization effort by initiating the "Double V" campaign that called for victory overseas against Germany and Japan as well as victory at home against Jim Crow. Many other Black newspapers supported this initiative, and the *Courier's* circulation grew to approximately 270,000. FBI Director J. Edgar Hoover and President Franklin D. Roosevelt sought to use sedition charges to suppress Black newspapers during World War II, however, this effort was successfully thwarted by then-Attorney General, Francis Biddle.[72] After World War II, Black newspapers played an important role in the Civil Rights

Movement by reporting and providing commentary on the milestones of the period: the lynching of Emmett Till, the desegregation of the armed services, *Brown v. Topeka Board of Education*, the Montgomery Bus Boycott, the Freedom Riders, and the March on Washington.[73]

Since the 1960s, the role of the Black press has not been as significant, in part because integration induced the mainstream press to increase coverage of Black issues and to diversify its reporting and editorial ranks. About 210 Black newspapers are operating in the United States, most of which are weeklies, but many of which operate with marginal profits and skeletal staffs, often relying on wire services to provide their news content. However, a recent study of readers of over 100 Black newspapers in 55 cities found that these readers are better educated and wealthier than the general Black population and that most are not regular readers of mainstream daily papers. The National Newspaper Publishers Association, a federation of more than 200 Black community newspapers that have operated since the 1940s, claims that Black newspapers have a combined circulation of over 15 million. Thus, Black newspapers remain an important source of information for a large number of Black readers. Because most of these papers are weeklies, they provide less continuous information to readers than is available through mainstream dailies.

As more Black journalists have been employed by mainstream newspapers, there have been organized efforts to address continuing problems experienced by Black journalists. The National Association of Black Journalists was created in 1975, in part, to foster "an exemplary group of professionals that honors excellent and outstanding achievements by Black journalists, and outstanding achievement in the media industry as a whole, particularly when it comes to providing balanced coverage to the Black community and society at large."[74] Despite significant growth in the number of Black journalists, it is not clear that there is sufficient critical mass to change the core culture of mainstream newspapers. To illustrate, in some prominent Black columnists expressed concerns about their limited impact in the book *Thinking Black: Some of the Nation's Best Columnists Speak Their Mind*.[75]

The local nature of Black newspapers limits their potential impact and reduces the likelihood of replicating the type of successful national mobilization efforts undertaken by the *Chicago Defender* and the *Pittsburgh Courier*. The first national Black newspaper, the *National Leader*, began publication in 1987 in Philadelphia as a weekly. However, it was soon forced to switch to monthly publication and ceased publication in 1989 because of insufficient readership.[76]

African American Studies specialists are also concerned about the limited range of political ideas presented in Black and mainstream newspapers. With a few exceptions, there is remarkably little incisive criticism of policies that worsen the plight of African Americans and a wholesale absence of discussion on unorthodox solutions. The only widely read counterforce to narrowly framed political discussion is *The Final Call*, the successor to *Muhammad Speaks*, first published in 1961, which, at one time, had a weekly circulation of over 900,000. *The Final Call* began publication in 1979 as part of Louis Farrakhan's efforts to rebuild the former Nation of Islam.[77]

Black Magazines

Like newspapers, magazines have a long history of serving as an important source of information for African Americans on politics and current events. *Freedom's Journal*, which began publication in New York City in 1827, is sometimes described as the first Black magazine rather than the first newspaper, as it was represented in the previous section. Other periodicals described as magazines that were published during this period include the *National Reformer* (1833), *The Colored American Magazine* (1837-1841), the *Mirror of Liberty* (1837), and Frederick Douglass's *Monthly* (1858-1861). Like Black newspapers of the era, these magazines focused much of their content on the battle against the slavery regime.[78]

Emerge was a contemporary magazine that preserved and refined the tradition of the early Black magazines of the 1800s. Launched in 1989 by Wilmer C. Ames, *Emerge* operated as a national, issues-oriented newsmagazine for upscale, educated African Americans until its demise in June 2000. The magazine offered incisive political commentary and featured a Who's Who of famous writers and public figures. The tag line of *Emerge*, "Our Voice in Today's World," positioned the organ as an alternative to superficial discussions. George Curry succeeded Ames as editor and refined *Emerge*'s 'no holds barred' approach to in-depth coverage of newsworthy domestic events and global issues. Among Curry's most provocative acts was the use of covers on two issues that

6

featured caricatures of Justice Clarence Thomas, one as a lawn jockey. Vanguarde Media Group Inc., the publisher of *Emerge* (which was at that time owned by B.E.T. Holdings Inc., the parent company of Black Entertainment Television cable network), made the decision to halt publication in June 2000, presumably because the magazine had a relatively small and stagnant circulation of 160,000 and was losing money. At the time of the decision, Vanguarde claimed that a re-launch was planned, with focus on a broader, lifestyle publication—code words indicating that the successor to *Emerge* would manifest a decidedly reduced political content. However, the replacement publication never materialized. Fortunately, *Emerge*'s legacy is not entirely lost, as some of the best material has been compiled in an edited volume, the *Best of Emerge Magazine*.[79]

The major magazines or journals that were established at the beginning of the twentieth century include a new version of the *Colored American Magazine*, *The Horizon*, and *Voice of the Negro*. As Abby Johnson and Ronald Johnson observe, "These were 'race periodicals,' involved first in political and social occurrences and then in Black literature."[80] The publication of Black magazines entered a new stage of development when the NAACP initiated publication of *The Crisis* in 1910. Two other important magazines were also started during this period by organizations attempting to represent the interests of, and provide services to, African Americans. A. Philip Randolph and Chandler Owen began publishing the socialist-oriented *Messenger* in 1917, and this journal became the outlet for the Brotherhood of Sleeping Car Porters until it ceased publication in 1928. The Urban League's journal, *Opportunity*, was published from 1923 until 1949.[81]

Black popular magazines, with a primary purpose of amusing and entertaining rather than conveying political information and informing public opinion, also appeared in the early twentieth century. Examples include: *McGirt's Magazine* (1903–1907), *Alexander's Magazine* (1905–1909), and *Competitor* (1920–1921). Chicago became an especially important site for the publication of such magazines, including *Half Century* (1916–1925), *American Life Magazine* (1926–1928), *Bronzeman* (1929–1933), and *Abbott's Monthly* (1930–1933). The typical content of these journals included light fiction, confessional stories, success stories, gossip columns, discussion of fashion, home-making, and sports.[82]

In many respects, these journals were the forerunners of more modern variants of Black popular magazines, such as, *Ebony*, *Jet*, and *Essence*. John H. Johnson (deceased 2005), the founder of Johnson Publications, began publishing *Ebony* in 1945. Headquartered in Chicago, it is the largest Black-owned magazine in the world. *Ebony* was created, in part, to counter stereotypical portrayals of Blacks in White-owned newspapers, magazines, and broadcast media. *Ebony* also played a crucial role in keeping readers informed of the struggle for civil rights in the 1950s and 1960s. A number of Black journalists began their careers at *Ebony* in covering the Civil Rights Movement and mass campaigns for social justice. *Ebony*'s content emphasizes positive aspects of Black life and features articles on education, history, politics, literature, art, business, personalities, civil rights, sports, entertainment, music, and social events.

Jet, Johnson Publications' other major magazine, first appeared in 1951. Its most well-known feature is "Beauty of the Week," a centerfold picture of a smiling 20-something-year-old in a bathing suit. *Jet*'s content includes news and features sports, fashion, education, Black history, entertainment, business, society, religion, and African affairs, but entertainment is its primary focus. Each issue includes a listing of Black performers appearing on network TV during that week. However, *Jet* has also served a functional political role on occasion, for instance, when a graphic photo of Emmett Till's bruised face was published following his lynching in 1955. That picture helped to amplify outrage over the lynching and to galvanize national support for the struggle against Jim Crow segregation and racial violence.

Essence began publishing in May 1970 as a magazine addressing the concerns of contemporary African American women from ages 18 to 35, but subsequently expanded its focus to more mature women as well. *Essence* covers career and educational opportunities, fashion and beauty, health and fitness, parenting, food, and travel. Unlike Johnson Publications, which has retained its independence, Essence Communications was acquired by Time, Inc., in March 2005,

Many of the most recent additions to the ranks of Black magazines target the Hip Hop generation. Quincy Jones launched *VIBE* in 1993 in partnership with Time Warner, and it soon became the fastest-growing music magazine in history. *VIBE* chronicles urban music—rap, house, reggae, hip hop, techno and pop rhythm and blues. It also covers fashion and politics. Time Warner sold its stake in *VIBE* in 1996, and the magazine has been able to pursue its own vision.

Although the various popular magazines offer some relevant political information embedded in lighter fare, the content and coverage are inadequate to meet the pressing needs of African Americans. One of the major communication network deficits currently facing African Americans is the absence of a focused political magazine of the type that debuted in the 1800s.

Black Book Publishers

Donald Joyce reminds us that Black-owned book publishing houses have been in existence since the second decade of the 1800s. The earliest publishers were associated with religious denominations and produced works supporting religious instruction and interpretation for laymen and clergy. Joyce reports that the oldest Black book publisher is the AME Book Concern, established in 1817. Cultural and civil rights organizations—the American Negro Academy, the Association for the Study of Afro-American Life and History, the NAACP, and the Urban League—have also been active as book publishers. Book publishing has also existed at several HBCUs, such as, Atlanta University, Fisk University, Hampton University, Howard University, and Tuskegee University. Hampton has the longest book publishing history, which dates back to 1879.[83]

Commercial book publishers constitute the largest body of Black book publishers and include magazines and newspapers that also publish books, as well as firms whose activities are restricted to book publishing. The number of commercial Black-owned book publishers has expanded significantly since the 1960s. As Joyce observes, several new publishers focused attention on meeting "the demand for new books about blacks that resulted from the black revolution."[84] These publishers have been major outlets for the scholarship produced by African American Studies specialists. Scholarly publications are generally not highly profitable, and those publishers that have survived have demonstrated impressive dedication and commitment to the values and objectives of African American Studies. Representative publishers that continue to serve an important role for African American

Studies scholars and students include: Africa World Press (Trenton), Black Classic Press (Baltimore), Kawaida Publications (Los Angeles), and Third World Press (Chicago). The materials published by these houses play a particularly important role in compensating for the dearth of political commentary and educational content in other media.

Black Radio, Television, and Internet-based Media

In contrast with the many opportunities to use independent Black newspapers and magazines as vehicles to foster liberation struggles, lack of control created many obstacles to the successful use of radio to pursue similar aims. As noted by Brian Ward, radio stations devoted entirely to Black-oriented programming did not appear until 1948 (WDIA-Memphis and WOOK-Washington), and the first Black-owned station did not materialize until 1949 (WERD-Atlanta).[85] By the mid-1950s, according to Ward, there were twenty-two southern stations wholly devoted to Black audiences, along with another twenty-four airing over thirty hours of Black-oriented programming a week.[86] A Black-oriented programming service, the National Negro Network, began operation in 1954.

Prior to this period, there had been a protracted struggle regarding the representation of Blacks in radio programming. Black organizations, including the Urban League and the NAACP, sought active involvement in programming to counter the stereotyping that characterized the typical portrayal of Blacks, which mirrored caricatures in films, as discussed previously. The NAACP and other organizations vigorously protested the playing of songs containing the words "nigger," "darky," and "coon" on the network program *Wings Over Jordan,* which had originated as *Negro Hour* in Cleveland during the late 1930s.[87]

The NAACP's early efforts to influence the representation of Blacks in radio programming involved consultation with prominent members, including W. E. B. Du Bois, Walter White, and Roy Wilkins, for the "Black" episode in the twenty-six-week series *Americans All, Immigrants All,* produced for CBS by the federal government's Office of Education in 1938 and 1939. There were intense disagreements among consultants regarding whether to emphasize the politics of inclusion by highlighting Black allegiance to America or to emphasize a more nationalist representation. In the end, the politics of inclusion prevailed.[88]

6

Freedom's People, broadcast in 1941 and 1942, was another government-sponsored series that made use of Black consultants in script development. As Barbara Savage relates, "African Americans who helped mold the series used the show to spotlight the irreconcilable conflict between America's ideological myths and its continued unjust treatment of Blacks."[89] Elaborating, she concludes, "the political arguments contained in *Freedom's Struggle* clearly reflected the influence of Black intellectuals ... and Black activists ... and [was] consistent with the views being advanced by Black organizations, although it was necessarily a truncated and less explicit version."[90]

The Urban League's *The Negro and National Defense* program, directed by Ann Tanneyhill, was broadcast on CBS in 1941. The show used a star-studded variety show that included brief messages about the organization's vocational campaign to generate wartime employment opportunities for Blacks. Tanneyhill also scripted "Heroines in Bronze," an episode for CBS's *Spirit of '43* series that dramatized the historical and contemporary importance of Black women in American life.[91]

During the post-World War II period, local radio stations were able to take a more aggressive approach to programming than networks had been willing to support.[92] *New World A'Coming* and *Destination Freedom* have received the most attention from researchers. *New World A'Coming* was first broadcast by WMCA in New York in 1944. It used the war as a springboard to call for concrete action rather than platitudes to eliminate inequality and discrimination. *Destination Freedom* originally aired weekly on WMAQ radio in Chicago in the late 1940s and early 1950s. The broadcasts focused on African American heroes and sheroes, including Louis Armstrong, Jackie Robinson, Harriet Tubman, and Ida B. Wells.[93]

Black radio played an important role in advancing the objectives of the Civil Rights Movement, although Brian Ward cautions that the NAACP had to wait until the early 1960s to get any significant positive southern radio exposure, and, "only a few, mostly Black-oriented, southern stations actually became flag-waving champions of desegregation and Black voting rights."[94] During the 1950s and 1960s, Black disc jockeys were among the first messengers of the Civil Rights Movement by announcing meetings, conducting interviews with civil rights leaders, and keeping listeners informed about developments in the struggle for equality and justice.[95] They were also inclined to give significant airplay to R&B songs with political thrusts.

As the Black Power Movement crystallized, many activists were disappointed at the limited levels of "communal advocacy and the quality of public affairs broadcasting and news reporting on Black-oriented radio, even at the growing number of stations that were under Black ownership or management."[96] This situation worsened as the liberation struggle waned and industry consolidation increasingly limited the flexibility of local stations. In-depth news reporting has been one of the major casualties of conglomeration. The decline of Black radio news has, according to *Black Commentator*, conditioned listeners to expect mundane news broadcasts. *Black Commentator* argues, in fact, that "the near death of Black radio news has been a major factor in the erosion of Black political organization, nationwide" and that "chains like Radio One gradually eliminated news from the mix, passing off syndicated or local talk, instead, and pretending that morning news jockeys could double as news people."[97]

Industry consolidation also affects the type of political commentary likely to be prevalent on AM talk radio programs targeting Blacks. In 2004, New York station WLIB announced that it would become part of Progress Media's "Air America Radio," a predominately White, liberal talk network. The station's Afrocentric programming, and most notably the *Global Black Experience* show, hosted by Imhotep Gary Byrd, was, unfortunately, a casualty of this merger. Black talk radio has been growing steadily around the country.[98] The best available research indicates that Black ownership is critical for drawing and sustaining an audience.[99] In this regard it is significant that the Black-owned Radio One group supports daily talk shows hosted, respectively, by Michael Eric Dyson and the Rev. Al Sharpton. Prior to this initiative, the only national talk show targeting Black listeners was *The Bev Smith Show*, based in Pittsburgh and hosted by Bev Smith.

The *Tom Joyner Morning Show* is, however, the most widely heard and influential radio show currently on the air with 8 million listeners on 115 stations.[100] As Melicia Victoria Harris-Lacewell reports, "On a daily basis, Tom Joyner acts as kind of cultural groundskeeper for African Americans."[101] The show revolves around its "old school" musical offerings but incorporates extensive comedy and commentaries reminiscent of those offered by Black disc jockeys during the Civil Rights Movement. Conversely, *Tony Brown's Journal* which aired 1968-2008, was the only long-running television show offering information and politically relevant programming targeting African Americans. *Black Journal*, created in 1968 by New York's public station WNET-TV shortly after the release of the Kerner Commission Report, was the predecessor of *Tony Brown's Journal*. The program features guest discussion, commentaries, and documentaries and has an audience of 5 million viewers on more than 240 public television stations.

Public television as a venue constrains political dialogue to a greater extent than is desirable for African American Studies specialists. However, there is even greater concern about the co-optation of the *America's Black Forum* television show by right-wing conservatives. The show bills itself as "the only credible weekend news source for African American perspectives on national issues."[102] This initiative points to the need for alternative news sources on television and underscores the problematic nature of the decision by BET executives in 2005 to eliminate serious news coverage. Recent research indicates that African American consumers are 21 percent more likely than all viewers to watch late local news—about one-third of all Blacks typically watch the late local news.[103]

New Urban Entertainment TV, a planned African American-focused cable network that intended to offer a nightly 30-minute broadcast similar to ABC's *World News Tonight*, was forced to cease operations in 2002. Even though Tom Joyner launched a short-lived one-hour syndicated television show in fall 2005, there was no effort to incorporate news content. TV One, which has succeeded in creating an alternative to BET that targets viewers between ages 24 and 54, announced in July 2013 that it intends to present a live one-hour, weekday morning news program slated to premiere September 2013.[104]

To some extent, the dearth of news and political commentary in traditional Black media is being addressed by new Internet alternatives. The most popular is *BlackPlanet.com*, which in 2007 reported approximately 16 million members. In contrast, Tom Joyner's Web site, *BlackAmericaWeb.com*, had about 800,000 registered users in 2007. There are other African American websites that also offer both news and political commentary, including "Black Voices, "The Root," "News One," and "Black News."[105] However, for

these Internet initiatives to succeed in becoming principal vehicles for informing and educating Black citizens, it will be necessary to overcome the "digital divide."

The increasing use of the Internet by traditional Black newspapers and magazines provides a potential opportunity to reduce lack of access to, or comfort levels with, traditional news sources. The critical issue is how to ensure access to the Internet and education about how to use it. One strategy advocated by Abdul Alkalimat, formerly head of Black Studies at the University of Toledo, involves placing personal computers with Internet access into barber and beauty shops. As Harris-Lacewell states, "Ordinary African Americans, in the context of their everyday talk with one another, reproduce complex patterns of political belief."[106] She further emphasizes that "the barbershops, and beauty parlors, more than the churches, the schools, or the radio, exist as spaces where Black people engage each other as peers, where nothing is out of bounds for conversation, and where the serious work of 'figuring it out' goes on."[107] Consistent with this theme, the "Healthy Black Families Project" of the University of Pittsburgh's Center for Minority Health received a grant in 2004 that would, among other initiatives, teach residents in a predominantly Black area of Pittsburgh to improve nutrition, increase exercise, and promote disease prevention by training barbers, beauticians, church leaders, and community center administrators to convey information to customers and clients and encourage them to participate in educational programs offered through the project.[108] This is the type of initiative that African American Studies specialists enthusiastically support.

The potential of social media to serve as a power tool of movement politics was demonstrated in the case of the fatal shooting of black teenager Trayvon Martin in Sanford, Florida, on February 26, 2012, by a self-appointed urban watch vigilante named George Zimmerman. Zimmerman stalked Martin, who was wearing a "hoodie" and returning to his father's residence after purchasing a package of Skittles candy from a local convenience store. While some of the facts remain unclear, it is clear that Zimmerman continued to pursue Martin after being explicitly told to cease and desist by 911 operators. If it were not for the power of social media, this would have likely become another quasi-lynching case that received little attention, as the police initially declined to charge

6

Zimmerman. However, as a result of the strategic use of social media, this case became a global story that put the issues of racial justice, inequality, and gun laws in the public and political dialogue. The critical dynamic leading to the release of the 911 tapes that document Zimmerman's actions and the levying of charges of second-degree murder against him were set in motion, first, by a March 8, 2012, press conference held by Trayvon's father, Tracy Martin, calling for Zimmerman's arrest, and, second, by an on-line petition started by Howard University Law School alumnus, Kevin Cunningham, on the website *www.Change.org*, demanding that Sanford Police charge Zimmerman with a crime.[109]

This on-line initiative was quickly supported by a widespread exhibition of traditional protest politics across the country that made extensive use of hoodies and packages of Skittles as props to emphasize the gross injustice surrounding Martin's killing. The broad base of support was exemplified by the tweet that LeBron James posted of a picture of the Miami Heat wearing hoodies, with their heads bowed in support of Trayvon Martin.[110] Opening arguments in the trial of George Zimmerman took place in June 2013.

Hopefully one of the extrapolations that African American Studies specialists can develop from this case study is a strategy to use social media to generate sustained political engagement, in addition to mobilization to respond to egregious cases of racial and other oppression.

Blacks and Electoral Politics

African American Voter Patterns and Characteristics

Before the passage of the Voting Rights Act of 1965, it was generally understood that in the South the lack of Black political participation was often the result of fear of Whites and various forms of intimidation. The political machines and Black civic and political organizations of the urban North generated a significant Black electorate. However, the traditional parties and their political bosses were the recipients of the benefit from the Black electorate, while African Americans received comparatively few rewards for their political participation.

Since 1965 and the phenomenal increase in Black voter registrants, political scientists have sought to analyze Black voter behavior and the characteristics of the Black electorate. In the South, particularly after the fear of violence, intimidation, and voter discrimination has subsided, too little political participation and apparent apathy still exist among African Americans. Compared with the number of eligible Black voters and those who actually vote, the lack of political participation is not merely regional but national in scope and concern. The perception has been that voting among African Americans has been exercised more by the better educated, lower-middle and upper-income groups than among the larger lower-income classes, although the available research is not conclusive regarding education, income and occupation. In fact, there remains uncertainty regarding the primary determinants of Black voting or non-voting behavior.

In one study, it was found that extensive non-voting among Blacks could not be attributed to fear. Moreover, Black voting could not be specifically related to higher levels of education, income, and occupation. Of these three factors, income appeared to have the greater association, although it was not shown to be the case in all elections. The efforts of Black political and civic organizations have the greatest effect in motivating the Black electorate.[111] In general, it might be concluded that social pressures within the Black community concomitant with regional political, social, and economic histories significantly affect Black electoral participation and voter turn-out.

In addition to demographic or socioeconomic factors, political scientists also advance political efficacy theory to explain the degrees of interest and participation of citizens in the electorate. *Political efficacy* has been defined as the sense or feeling that a person can influence political outcomes through his or her participation in the electoral process.[112] Related to political efficacy is one's belief and confidence in the integrity of the government or system. This has been described as political trust. Thus, political efficacy and trust may combine to have a tremendous impact on Black political participation.[113] If it is presumed that Blacks are cynical or suspect of the political efficacy of the government in relationship to the benefits they receive, how does their attitude differ from that of Whites? A study by Philip E. Secret and James B. Johnson found that Blacks have a significantly lower sense of political efficacy than Whites. However, the presumption that

Blacks have a significantly lower trust in government than do Whites was not supported.[114]

It is logical to assume that demographic and socioeconomic factors do affect perceptions of political efficacy and trust. Psychologically, Blacks who may experience increased income and higher occupational status may develop a greater sense of civic responsibility. In contemporary Black politics, age may be a factor and affects older Black voters differently from younger ones. For one thing, older voters may have a personal frame of reference regarding the Black Power, Black Pride, and Civil Rights Movements of the 1960s and the sacrifices in suffering and lives that made full political participation for African Americans possible. Therefore, the extent to which Black heritage and cultural consciousness have been transmitted to younger generations must be considered as a factor in Black political participation. Future research may be able to ascertain the relationships among Black consciousness, socioeconomic and political efficacy, and trust factors as influences on Black electoral participation.

There has been some indication in recent years of a convergence of views between Blacks and Whites on major social and economic issues. However, the order of priority and significance each group places on these issues is different. In a survey conducted in 1984, African Americans cited unemployment first, government poverty programs second, and civil rights third as principal issues of concern. Whites shared the belief that unemployment was the primary issue, but named the federal deficit and inflation as the most important secondary issues. By 1986, both Blacks and Whites listed unemployment, high cost of living, and drug abuse as the most important issues. However, they differed in the ranking of these issues. In the order of priority, Blacks cited unemployment, the high cost of living, and drug abuse. Almost conversely, Whites' order of ranking was drug abuse, unemployment, and the high cost of living. African Americans advocated government intervention and affirmative action programs as ways of solving these problems, whereas Whites continued to oppose government social programs.[115] In spite of some similarities with other population groups, African American political participation, political concerns, and problems remain quite distinct. More recent survey information from the mid-1990s confirms these earlier conclusions. Blacks are more interested than other groups in preserving religion and respect for elders, as well as ethnic traditions and symbols.[116]

Although detailed assessments of the determinants of Black voting behavior await further research, the examination of trends in voter registration and voting in national elections during presidential election years is very instructive. This information is presented on the following page in Table 6.3. Although the percentage of voting-age Blacks who are registered voters is not significantly lower than that of voting-age Whites, the proportion of Blacks who actually vote is substantially less than for Whites. The lower proportions for Hispanics reflect the fact that many are not US citizens. In the context of the discussion of the impact of Black voters on presidential politics in the next section, the figures for 1992, 1996, 2000, and 2004 are especially useful for projecting future developments. There was a larger upsurge in Black voting in 2000 followed by a larger upsurge among Whites in 2004.

The data in Table 6.3 reveal a dramatic upsurge in registration and voting percentages associated with the 2008 election that produced the first Black President, Barack Obama. Although the percentage of registered White votes increased more than was the case for African Americans, the voting percentage increase was greater for African Americans. However, the most dramatic increases for registration and voting occurred among Hispanics, who voted overwhelmingly for Barack Obama, as did African Americans.

The dramatic gains in Black voter participation in 2008 occurred despite systematic efforts to diminish Black voting power initiated during the 2000 election. In the 2000 presidential election, over 4 percent of the ballots were invalidated due to outdated punch-card machine technology. Over a decade prior to the election, the National Bureau of Standards had recommended that punch card systems be replaced. Data indicate that ballots cast by Blacks were rejected at a rate of 14.4 percent, whereas those cast by non-Blacks were invalidated at a much lower rate of 1.6 percent. This discrepancy was partly because older punch card machines were disproportionately placed in inner-city locations. Prior to the 2000 election, there were no national standards on decisions regarding technologies, and standards were left to local and state election officials. The "Help America Vote Act" was passed in the wake of the Florida electoral controversy and included provisions to provide economic resources

6

to states and localities for purchasing modern voting machines. Other electoral reforms have generally focused on improving election day logistics, including better training for poll workers, better management of voter lists, and voters' ability to check their voting status.

In the wake of the 2000 Presidential election debacle, Congresswoman Eddie Bernice Johnson led an effort in the US House of Representatives requesting the United Nations (UN) to deploy election observers across the United States to monitor the 2004 Presidential election, citing the pattern of disenfranchisement of black voters during the 2000 Presidential election as one rationale. The proposed UN monitoring did not occur, and the 2004 election was not devoid of efforts to disenfranchise Black voters. In Milwaukee, Wisconsin, for example, fliers from a nonexistent Milwaukee Black Voters League were distributed in Black neighborhoods, warning residents that they could not vote if they had any type of legal violation, including traffic tickets. The flier claimed that anyone who voted and had a violation on the record would be subject to a prison term of ten years and the loss of custody of children.[117]

In fact, in the wake of the 2008 election voter suppression efforts have intensified across the country, targeting racial/ethnic groups and disadvantaged subgroups. These efforts have gained momentum as a result of a decision by the Supreme Court earlier in 2008, just prior to the primary election, which upheld Indiana's 2005 voter-identification law. In a 6-3 decision, the Court held that a requirement to produce photo identification is not unconstitutional and that the state has a "valid interest" in improving election procedures as well as deterring fraud. Opponents of the law had argued that the law imposed unjustified burdens on people who are old, poor or members of minority groups and less likely to have driver's licenses or other acceptable forms of identification. There are similar laws in over 20 states, and in the wake of the 2010 Republican victories in several states, additional suppression efforts have been initiated.[118] Research conducted by Gabriel R. Sanchez, Stephen A. Nuño, and Matt A. Barreto provides evidence of the disproportionate impact of photo identification requirements on people of color. They found that Whites clearly had the highest rates of valid identification and that Latinos, African Americans, and Asian Americans are less likely to have a state issued ID that meets the criterion established by the Supreme Court.[119] For specialists in African American Studies, these voter-suppression efforts conjure up memories of the poll taxes and grandfather clauses that were used to

disenfranchise Blacks in the South following the Civil War which were not overturned until passage of the Voting Rights Act of 1965. Ironically, conservative politicians continue to pursue efforts to weaken the federal oversight mandated by this law, an outcome that would undoubtedly further disenfranchise Black and Latino voters.

As illustrated in Table 6.3, despite efforts to restrict Black voter turnout, in 2012, Blacks actually voted at a higher rate (66.2 percent) than non-Hispanic Whites (64.1 percent) for the first time, spurring the re-election of Barack Obama. African American Studies specialists are encouraged by this demonstration of agency and resistance. At the same time, however, while concerns about Black voter disenfranchisement tend to emerge in connection with Presidential elections, there are structural issues that are of special concern to African American Studies specialists. A case in point is at-large voting, as opposed to district-based voting, which dilutes Black representation by preventing Black voters to benefit from the residential segregation imposed on them. The permanent loss of the franchise by convicted felons in many states is another pernicious source of Black voter disenfranchisement.

In the 2000 election, approximately 7 percent of otherwise eligible Blacks were barred from voting in the United States because of felony convictions. Interestingly, Florida is among the most flagrant of the disfranchising states which excludes Blacks for this reason, with 13.8 percent barred for felony convictions.[120] Thus, restoration of the voting rights of convicted felons must be a major public policy initiative.

More generally, Africana Studies specialists insist that community organizations must be mobilized to ensure that provisions of the Voting Rights Act are strictly enforced. Protection of the voting rights of Blacks were undermined by Supreme Court decisions in redistricting cases in Louisiana and Georgia in 2000 and 2003 and in Texas in 2006.

In all likelihood, efforts to disenfranchise Black (and Latino) voters will gain momentum in the wake of the June 2013 Supreme Court decision in *Shelby County v. Holder*. In this case, Shelby County, Alabama, challenged the constitutionality of Section 5 of the Voting rights Act of 1965. This provision requires that certain states, i.e., Alabama, Georgia, Louisiana, Mississippi, South Carolina, Texas, Virginia, Arizona, and Alaska, as well as certain cities in other states, to obtain federal permission before enacting changes in voting practices. The Voting Rights Act was passed, in part, to outlaw explicitly discriminatory voting practices that existed in the 1960s, including poll taxes and literacy tests. Section 5 was declared unconstitutional in a 5-4 vote reflecting the split on the Court between conservative and liberal justices. The majority opinion argued that the formula used to determine which jurisdictions were subject to the preclearance provision was anachronistic and that current voting patterns, described previously, document that barriers to voting confronting African Americans have largely been eradicated. The dissenters cited numerous examples of ongoing disenfranchisement efforts. The Court substituted its own judgment for that of the US Congress, which had repeatedly reauthorized the law in 1970, 1975, 1982, and 2006. The majority opinion suggested that Congress could update the coverage formula and resurrect the preclearance requirement. However, this was obviously an unrealistic recommendation in the face of the extreme political polarization among federal legislators. In effect, the decision has neutered the most successful Civil Rights era legislative enactments. In the future, victims of racially motivated voting rights violations will only be able to seek remedies after violations have occurred under another section of the Act.[121]

TABLE 6.3
PERCENTAGE OF THE VOTING AGE POPULATION VOTING AND REGISTERED PRESIDENTIAL ELECTION YEARS 1972 - 2012 WHITES, BLACKS, AND HISPANICS

	PCT Voting			PCT Registered		
Year	White	Black	Hispanic	White	Black	Hispanic
1972	69.1	52.1	37.5	68.3	65.5	41.4
1976	64.5	48.7	31.8	64.9	58.5	37.9
1980	60.9	50.5	29.9	68.4	60.0	36.3
1984	61.9	55.8	32.6	69.6	66.3	40.1
1988	59.1	51.5	28.8	67.9	64.5	35.5
1992	63.6	54.0	28.9	70.1	63.9	35.0
1996	56.0	50.6	26.7	67.7	63.5	35.7
2000	56.4	53.5	27.5	65.7	63.6	34.9
2004	60.3	56.2	28.0	67.9	64.3	34.3
2008	66.1	64.7	49.9	73.5	69.7	59.4
2012	64.1	66.2	48.0			

Source: 1972 – 2008 - US Census Bureau, "Voting and Registration in the Election of (various years)," *Current Population Reports* (Washington, D.C.: US Department of Commerce, various years); 2012 - Thom File "The Diversifying Electorate—Voting Rates by Race and Hispanic Origin in 2012 (and Other Recent Elections)," *Current Population Survey* (May 2013).

Moreover, there were charges of attempts to manipulate voting behavior and invalidate ballots cast by Black voters in a variety of jurisdictions in the 2000, 2004, and 2006 elections.

In addition to initiating steps to maximize the impact of votes cast by Blacks, there is an equally pressing need to develop a sophisticated voter education campaign that operates continuously and incorporates assessments of the performance of elected officials. Such an initiative is necessary to ensure that voters make informed decisions when casting ballots and are not unduly influenced by candidates' advertising around election time. Such an educational campaign can help to counter the increasingly sophisticated use of political marketing to influence voters. Political marketing involves the use of marketing and business practices by candidates, politicians, political parties, lobbyists, political action committees, and interest groups. The use of propaganda by these interest groups to influence voters is increasing both through traditional radio and media advertising as well as via telephone and Internet communications.

Presidential Politics

The increased electoral power and political influence of African Americans by 1960 contributed to the crucial margin of votes necessary for the successful election of President John F. Kennedy. Significant, too, in the development of the "new" Black politics was the extensive voter registration and voter education projects conducted from 1962 to 1964 by all the major civil rights organizations, which included the NAACP, SNCC, and CORE.

There is conventional wisdom that the Black vote can be the decisive factor in presidential elections. This assessment hinges on the idea of a Black voting bloc that overwhelmingly supports a particular candidate. Given such a bloc, under certain political circumstances, the African American electorate can be the decisive factor in determining the outcome of a presidential election. Following the passage of the 1965 Voting Rights Act, the Black vote was expected to be of increasing strategic significance in presidential primaries and in the general election. However, this has not always proven to be the case, and the most recent elections raise the question of the stability of a Black voting bloc.

In his landslide victory in 1964, Lyndon B. Johnson received 90 percent of the Black vote. However,

6

his ultraconservative Republican opponent, Barry Goldwater, won the electoral votes of Mississippi, Alabama, Georgia, Louisiana, and South Carolina, despite large Black registered voter populations in these states.[122] Thus, it would appear that the Black vote was not critical in the Johnson election.

In the presidential election of 1968, Democratic presidential candidate and civil rights advocate Hubert H. Humphrey lost to conservative Republican Richard M. Nixon in spite of Black support for the liberal Democratic ticket. Political scientist Ronald W. Walters attributes the ineffectiveness of the Black vote in this election to low Black voter turnout. Walters further speculates that "the low turnout implied a boycott of the Democratic candidate by blacks, a negative sanction in the eyes of party leaders and strategists—black and white."[123] In 1972, the Republican candidate, Richard Nixon, won handily again in his re-election bid against Democratic candidate George S. McGovern. McGovern received 90 percent of the Black vote.

The year 1972 was particularly significant in the history of Black politics. Andrew Young of Atlanta became the first Black elected to Congress from the Deep South since Reconstruction.[124] Shirley Chisholm, a Democratic Member of the House of Representatives from New York, became the first Black woman to declare and run for the presidency of the United States. However, the Democratic Convention held at Miami Beach nominated Senator George McGovern. Chisholm received 151.95 of the 2,000-plus ballots on the first roll call. Overall, however, there is no evidence that the Black vote had any meaningful impact on the election outcome.

In contrast, the Black vote was crucial in the victory of Jimmy Carter in 1976, and political theorists generally acknowledge that the African American vote provided his margin of victory. It was essential for Carter, a southerner, to carry the South. He could not have done this without the large Black voter registration in the southern states.

Conservative Republican Ronald Reagan defeated Jimmy Carter in his re-election bid of 1980. Carter's ineffective domestic economic policy and failed foreign policy and actions taken during the Iran hostage crisis contributed to his general unpopularity. In addition, a failing economy and accrued White backlash from affirmative action and equal opportunity programs that were responsible for Black progress during the 1970s kindled the fires of racial antagonism and racism. Ronald Reagan appealed to the base instincts and racist attitudes of southern Whites and ultraconservatives who overwhelmingly supported his election and reelection bids for the presidency in 1980 and 1984. As a consequence, the Black vote was unable to turn the tide in favor of the Democrats.

A historic event of the 1984 campaign and election year was Rev. Jesse Jackson's serious bid for the presidency. A Black "disciple" of the 1960s Civil Rights Movement, Jackson's political strategy was to develop a "Rainbow Coalition" of Blacks, Hispanics, women, and other oppressed members of American society. Jackson made extensive use of the political influence and power of the Black Church in mobilizing for the nomination. However, at the San Francisco National Convention, the Democratic Party selected Walter F. Mondale as the presidential nominee to oppose Ronald Reagan in 1984. Nevertheless, Jackson had an unprecedented impact on the campaign. More Blacks than ever participated in the Democratic Convention. There were 697 Black delegates representing 17.7 percent of the total. Even though Jackson's candidacy for the nomination was marred with intra-racial and intra-party controversy and disputes, Black politics were propelled to new heights in the American political arena.[125]

Jackson's second bid for the Democratic presidential nomination in 1988 was even more successful. Jesse Jackson received three times more White votes than he did in the 1984 primaries. Jackson doubled his overall primary vote to 6.6 million ballots compared with 3.15 million in comparable primaries in 1984. He won 2.1 million White votes in 1988 (12.5 percent) compared with 650,000 (5 percent) in 1984. Nevertheless, Jackson's candidacy remained almost wholly dependent on Black voters. He received 92 percent of all ballots cast by Blacks, or approximately 4.3 million votes.[126]

The Republicans won their third consecutive presidential election in 1988 with George H. Bush, defeating Michael Dukakis. Although nine out of every ten Blacks voted for Dukakis, this support was insufficient to affect Bush's presidential victory. Blacks were caught up in the age-long dilemma of being virtually written off by the Republicans and taken for granted by the Democrats. Linda F. Williams, in comparing the 1984 and 1988 elections, states, "The Democratic party has attempted to hold on to black voters, its most loyal constituency, while downplaying black influence in the party in hopes of stemming the flight of white voters."[127]

This same pattern has been evident in more recent elections although, beginning with the 1992 campaign, the Republicans initiated more aggressive attempts to cultivate Black voters. Bill Clinton, former Governor of Arkansas, positioned himself as a "New Democrat" in the 1992 election. Although he rejected many of the traditional liberal positions of the Democratic Party, Black voters nevertheless gave him overwhelming support, and analysts suggest that the support of Black women was especially critical. At the same time, it is important to recognize that in 1992, the Black vote was only 8 percent of the total electorate. In the 1992 election, exit polls showed that the proportion of White women who voted for Clinton was larger than for White men (44 to 34 percent) but significantly less than for Black women (86 percent).

Clinton's support among Blacks in general, and Black women in particular, was even more robust in the 1996 election, whereas support among White women and men eroded. In 1996, the Black vote accounted for 10 percent of the total compared with 8 percent in 1992. The proportion of White women and men supporting Clinton in 1996 fell to 42 and 31 percent, respectively. However, among Black women, Clinton received 89 percent of the vote. This figure is especially remarkable given the fact that Ross Perot received 7 percent of the Black vote in 1996.

Black women's staunch support for the Democratic Party harks back to the tradition established during the administration of Franklin Roosevelt by Mary McLeod Bethune and the NCNW. Building on her legacy, Black women have served at the helm of the Congressional Black Caucus, the National Black Caucus of State Legislators, and the National Black Caucus of Local Elected Officials. Consistent with the tradition of "invisible politics" discussed previously, in both the 1992 and 1996 campaigns, Black women worked behind the scenes in churches, parent groups, and civic organizations.

As noted in Chapter 3, the election in 2000 of George W. Bush, son of former President George H. W. Bush, was the most controversial election since the 1870s. Amid allegations of disfranchisement of Black and other voters, primarily in Florida, it eventually required certification by the Supreme Court. Despite Republican efforts to recruit Black voters through cultivation of conservative religious leaders, Black support for Al Gore was solid. Bush's share of the Black vote (9%) was actually less than his father had received in 1992 or that garnered by Bob Dole in 1996. Bush's 2000

Black vote was the lowest total received by any Republican presidential candidate since 1964, when Barry Goldwater received only 6 percent. In the 2000 presidential race, 94 percent of Black women voted for Al Gore, which continued the previous pattern of Black female bloc voting.

Overall, the potential of Black males to impact presidential elections has been eroding as a result of the high incarceration rates discussed in Chapter 4. As noted by the Washington, D.C.-based Sentencing Project, and Human Rights Watch, over 4.2 million Americans were prohibited from voting in the 2000 presidential election because they were in prison or had in the past been convicted of a felony. Of that number, more than one-third, or 1.8 million disfranchised potential voters, are African American males. This represents 13 percent of all Black males of voting age in the US.

In the 2004 election, George Bush not only successfully mobilized broad-based support from his core White conservative constituency but also built on the wedge established in the 2000 election between liberal and conservative Blacks. Overall voter turnout was 11 percent higher than in 2000. Fifty-eight percent of Whites voted Republican, whereas 41 percent voted Democratic. Eighty-eight percent of Blacks voted Democratic, and 11 percent voted Republican. Among Hispanics, 43 percent voted Republican, and 56 percent voted Democratic. Bush's Black support represented a slight gain over his 2000 support from 9 to 11 percent. This result is consistent with the GOP strategy of creating an impression that fundamental splits exist within Black ranks, thereby subverting the credibility of mainstream leaders who hold to the historical Black political consensus. There was no intention to recruit large numbers of Blacks to the GOP because this would dilute the party's appeal to Whites.

This strategy was implemented, in part, by supporting groups like "Blacks for Bush" that rallied around his faith-based initiatives and by exploiting highly visible controversies surrounding abortion rights and gay marriage rights. Many conservative Black religious leaders subordinated traditional political and economic concerns and urged constituents to support the Republican ticket solely on the basis of shared views on these two issues.

Black Republicans played an especially critical role in producing a Bush victory in Ohio, where Bush garnered about 16 percent of the Black vote. In Florida, Bush's support among African Americans rose 6

6

percentage points to 13 percent. Although the 2004 election was decided in Ohio, the extent of alleged disfranchisement of Black voters that occurred was of insufficient magnitude to alter the outcome. If the converse had been true, this would have constituted an ironic twist to the Black voting bloc theory, discussed previously, whereby a combination of unusual bloc voting coupled with selective disfranchisement would have enabled the Black vote to be the decisive factor in the election outcome.

A significant development during the 2004 election was targeted efforts to register disaffected young Blacks and Latinos, along with progressive young adults of other groups, and to get them to the polls through activities sponsored by the Hip-Hop Summit Action Network, which hip-hop mogul Russell Simmons backed. The Network used popular performers to draw young potential voters to voter registration and issue forums. The stated goal of the Network was to create an independent agenda that would address the particular concern of young people at extreme risk of experiencing dislocation as globalization proceeds. The Hip-Hop Summit Action Network succeeded in registering thousands of young voters, but its overall impact is not clear. Forty-five percent of Whites voted Democratic, compared with 37 percent of 33- to 44-year-olds. Among Blacks, 86 percent of 18- to 29-year-old Blacks voted Democratic, compared with 89 percent of 33- to 44-year-olds. One longer-term outcome of the Network may have been to lay the foundation for reinforcing shared intergenerational interests among Blacks.

Barack Obama's Path to the Presidency

As noted elsewhere in this text, the election of President Barack Obama in 2008 marked a hallmark in the nexus between African Americans and Presidential politics. Obama's trajectory to the Presidency is remarkable in many ways. Between 1985 and 1988, he worked as a community organizer in Chicago, prior to enrolling in Harvard Law School. After graduation, he returned to Chicago, continued activities as a community organizer, and married Michelle Robinson in 1992. Obama's first elected position was as an Illinois State Senator, a position that he held from 1997 until 2004. In 2000, he was unsuccessful in seeking the Democratic nomination to run for a seat in the US House of Representatives. Obama was propelled into the national arena via the keynote speech that he delivered at the Democratic Party's national convention in Boston on July 27, 2004.

In January 2005, Barack Obama became the third African American US Senator since Reconstruction, and the fifth in history. During his tenure, he served on both the Foreign Relations and Veteran's Affairs Committees. In January 2007, Senator Obama formed an exploratory committee as a first step towards a presidential bid. He announced his candidacy in February 2007.

Obama's candidacy benefited significantly in the early stages from Oprah Winfrey's endorsement in December 2007. He was subsequently victorious over Hillary Clinton in the Iowa primary in January 2008. A see-saw race ensued that included a loss in New Hampshire and a victory in South Carolina. The Super Tuesday primaries on February 5, 2008, were not decisive, but Obama subsequently mounted a string of ten victories. The contest continued, however, and Clinton won the Texas primary on March 4th. Clinton subsequently suspended her campaign in early June, and, on August 28th, Obama was officially installed as the Democratic nominee, paving the road to his electoral victory in November.

The strategy that produced Obama's primary and general election victories involved efforts to build a quasi-social movement, as opposed to relying on traditional party apparatuses and voter mobilization techniques. Sean Willenz describes the driving vision as "electing a 'post-partisan president' as the leader, not of a nation or even of a political party, but of a personalized social movement." This vision drew upon the successes of some previous social movements, including the Civil Rights and Farm Workers Movements. The strategy emphasized grassroots organizing, with a heavy emphasis on the use of modern social media. According to Willenz, numerous "Camp Obamas" were created to train thousands of campaign volunteers. In soliciting, these volunteers were trained to focus on general campaign themes, i.e., "hope" and "change," as opposed to specific policy positions.

This grassroots campaign dovetailed neatly with the grassroots Black politics tradition discussed previously. Thus it was no accident that Obama received broad support through the Hip-Hop Research and Education Fund and PowerPAC. In fact, the Hip-Hop Summit Action Network initiated a national campaign to mobilize the Hip-Hop generation of youth in Philadelphia in March 2008.[128]

The coalition mobilized in support of candidate Obama was indeed impressive. In addition to garnering overwhelming support from Blacks and Hispanics,

Obama won 43 percent of White voters including 54 percent of young White voters.[129] As a consequence, for some optimistic observers, the solid electoral victory by President Obama marked a sea change in American race relations. However, obtaining the support of a substantial proportion of the White electorate involved emphasizing Obama's multi-racial lineage and international background that were seen as distinguishing him from the modal African American. From this vantage point, Obama's victory was heralded by many as concrete evidence of the transition to a "post racial" society.

The Re-election of Barack Obama

In many respects, the re-election of Barack Obama as US President in November 2012 was even more remarkable than his election in 2008. As documented in Chapters 4 and 7, the pace of recovery from the Bush-era recession during the President's first term was lackluster at best. Historically, an unemployment rate in the 8 percent range would preclude the re-election of a sitting president. However, Obama was able to overcome this handicap, to the surprise of his Republican adversaries, who used every conceivable tactic to defeat him, including spending massive amounts of money on attack ads. Obama's opponents focused much of their attack on the Affordable Health Care Act, dubbed "Obama Care," which had surprisingly survived a US Supreme Court challenge as the result of an unexpected affirmative vote from Supreme Court Chief Justice Roberts. Many of the attacks on Obama Care, as well as those directed at other policies, were unabashedly racist, such as the image created with Obama's face superimposed on the body of a "witch doctor" and the words Obama Care spelled with the communist sickle and hammer replacing the "C" in Care.

More generally, the racist reaction to the Obama candidacy that erupted in the 2008 election campaign resurfaced with a vengeance in 2012. Even the official Republican campaign slogan, "Take Back America," subtlety implied that the government had been taken over by some presumably "un-American" forces.

The successful 2012 re-election of Barack Obama hinged on several factors, including an extensive voter mobilization effort initiated through Black churches, successful challenges to voter suppression policies in several states, strong support from Latinos and Asians that complemented overwhelming Black support, and the active support of former President Bill Clinton. As noted previously, for the first time in history, a higher proportion of Blacks voted than Whites. As reported by Paul Taylor, Obama won 80% of the non-White vote (including 93% of Blacks, 73% of Asian Americans and 71% of Hispanics) and just 39% of the White vote. That constellation of votes by race gave Obama a popular vote victory margin of 4.7 million and an Electoral College victory of 332-206.[130]

The Obama Presidency and the Limits of Racial Tolerance

The initial election of Barack Obama catalyzed a firestorm of hysteria from that segment of the US electorate that could not envision the possibility of an African American President. Even years after his election, the so-called "Birther" movement continues to claim that Barack Hussein Obama is not an American citizen, and many persist in the belief that he is a closet Muslim, despite the flack that arose during the presidential campaign over his membership in a church formerly pastored by Rev. Jeremiah Wright. President Obama has been subjected to a number of unprecedented insults and threats, including various depictions of him as the Joker character from Batman comic books and films.

Obama was called "a liar" during a speech to the US House of Representatives and Senate on September 9, 2009, by Representative Joe Wilson of South Carolina. Although the House of Representatives subsequently passed a resolution of disapproval (a mild rebuke), eleven Democrats actually voted against the resolution and only seven Republicans voted in favor.[131]

An even more racist example of the anti-Obama hysteria emerged in May 2010, when, Marilyn Davenport, an Orange County, California, Republican official sent an email depicting President Barack Obama as a chimpanzee. She was subsequently officially censured by the local party's executive committee.[132]

The most ominous manifestation of the anti-Obama hysteria, however, has been the increase in death threats following his election. A 2009 report indicated that since Obama took office, the rate of threats against the president increased 400 per cent from the 3,000 a year under President George W. Bush.[133]

The anti-Obama commotion has morphed into a quasi-political movement euphemistically labeled the "Tea Party," with "Tea" constituting an acronym for "taxed enough already." While presumably protesting big government personified in their minds by President Obama and his presumed socialist ideology, racial

6

enmity directed at the President has been both overtly and covertly evident at various functions. The racist sentiment seething just below the surface of the feigned non-racist anti-government posture is evident from the results of an April 2010 *New York Times* survey. The survey found that the 18 percent of Americans identifying themselves as Tea Party supporters tend to be Republican, White, male, married, and older than 45. Their animosity toward the president is fueled, in part, by perceptions that the policies of the Obama administration are disproportionately directed at helping the poor. The survey found that 92 percent of Tea Party supporters believe President Obama is moving the country toward socialism, and an overwhelming majority held the view that he does not share the values by which most Americans live. Instructively, 25 percent thought that the administration favors Blacks over Whites — compared with 11 percent of the general public. Tea Party supporters are also more likely than the general public, and even Republicans, to say that too much has been made of the problems facing Black people.[134]

The findings of this survey, as well as the various incidents and threats mentioned previously, cast serious doubts about the credibility of assertions that the election of President Obama marks the beginning of a transition to a post-racial America. Instead, it may well be the case that the US is entering into a period in which racial hostility actually intensifies, as the conservative backlash to the presence of an African American in the most powerful position in the world continues to escalate along with xenophobia regarding undocumented immigrants. This outcome would be anticipated as more likely by many African American Studies scholar/activists, who maintain that racism remains embedded, perhaps indelibly, deep inside the US psyche.

The Obama Presidency and African Americans

The findings of a November 2009 Pew Research Organization report indicated that "Blacks' assessments about the state of black progress in America have improved more dramatically during the past two years than at any time in the past quarter century."[135] In 2009, 39 percent of respondents said that the situation for Blacks was better than five years ago, compared to 20 percent in 2007. Fifty-three percent of respondents in 2009 said that life in the future would be better for Blacks, compared to 10% who said it would be worse. The comparable figures for the 2007 survey were 44% and 21%, respectively. The report attributes this rapid shift in opinion directly

to optimism regarding the election of President Barack Obama.[136]

Although most African Americans have remained supportive of President Obama, even this base has eroded somewhat in the face of limited improvements in the life circumstances in most Black communities. The prominent role of public figures Tavis Smiley and Cornell West in voicing these concerns is highlighted in Chapter 7. The saliency of their criticisms has been magnified by the administration's reluctance to put forth policy proposals that might be perceived by opponents on the Right as exclusively benefiting Black people. The one exception to this pattern was the announcement of a White House Initiative on Historically Black Colleges and Universities. Otherwise, the Obama administration has attempted to promote the position that African Americans can be less concerned about group-specific policies because they will benefit significantly from broadly focused initiatives. This message has been disseminated through special communications highlighting how the administration's policies would benefit Blacks in February 2010, February 2011 (Black History Month), and April 2011. To illustrate, the 2010 statement, entitled "Expanding Opportunities for African-American Families," discusses how African American families would benefit from several administration initiatives, e.g., tax cuts, health care reform, pension reform, college financial aid reform, housing finance reform, and reinvigorated civil rights enforcement.[137] This "semi-covert" approach to promoting Black interests can be contrasted to the more visible efforts waged by the administration in support of other groups, such as undocumented workers (most of whom are Hispanic), and lesbian and gay military servicepersons.

One strategy used by the Obama administration to blunt criticism regarding the failure to address the needs of Black communities directly has been to appoint Blacks and members of other underrepresented groups to important positions in the administration. Several Black women have been appointed to prominent positions, including Valerie Jarrett as White House senior adviser, Susan Rice as United States Ambassador to the United Nations, Margaret Hamburg as FDA commissioner, MD, and Regina Benjamin as Surgeon General.[138] Obama has, in fact, has set records for the number of women and minorities nominated to important positions. In all, 25% of administration appointees during the first term were African Americans, 10% have been Hispanics, and 11% have been Asian Americans.[139]

However, as Obama's second term proceeds, calls for him to address Black concerns more directly have escalated. As an example, shortly after the inauguration in January 2012, NAACP President and CEO, Benjamin Jealous went on nationwide television to condemn the administration's job creation record. He charged that the Black unemployment rate was one percent higher than when Obama assumed office. Congressional Black Caucus (CBC) members have become increasingly disaffected with the administration's failure to address the unemployment crisis in Black communities.[140] The CBC's frustration has been heightened by the failure of Obama to meet formally with CBC members since May 2011.[141] The CBC's increasingly public rebukes of the Obama administration have not focused exclusively on economic matters. Democratic Rep. Marcia L. Fudge of Ohio, the chairperson of the Congressional Black Caucus, penned a letter to President Obama challenging the lack of racial/ethnic diversity in administrative appointments in his second term.

In assessing the record to date of the Obama administration in furthering the advancement of Blacks, African American Studies specialists would first interrogate the history of efforts to promote freedom and equality through coordinated use of movement and electoral politics. This history reveals that improvements in the condition of Blacks in the US resulting from Presidential action, legislative enactments, and judicial decisions have been achieved only grudgingly after sustained non-electoral political action, i.e., "movement politics." This "outsider" strategy has reflected the continuing reality that desired changes require convincing non-supporters to change positions under threat of social unrest.

Although Barack Obama's election and re-election channeled movement politics messaging, this rhetoric and the networks that facilitated his election were largely abandoned after he took office. As a consequence, there was no outside force in play that could countervail the extreme right wing backlash that Obama encountered. The vision of "hope and change" has evaporated as the administration's policies in many areas, such as regulation of financial institutions and prosecution of war in Iraq and Afghanistan, failed to exhibit much of a difference from those of his predecessor. The double whammy of an abandoned movement and non-progressive policies (even in the case of the Health Care Reform Act) disappointed many supporters.

Through the lens of African American Studies, the record of the Obama administration highlights the limits of electoral politics without a symbiotic relationship to movement politics. This perspective is reinforced when the structural barriers to promoting Black interests in legislative venues is examined.

Black Congressional and Senatorial Representation

Similar to the influence of Black voters in presidential elections, the extent of Black representation in the US House of Representatives and the US Senate is conditioned by the geographic distribution of the Black population. The first Blacks elected to Congress in the twentieth century came from northern urban areas experiencing burgeoning population growth from the Great Migration. Increases in the number of Black Congressmen in these areas were stymied by the gerrymandering practices—used by White-controlled state legislatures in both the North and the South—to distribute Blacks across districts so that they did not constitute a numerical majority of potential voters. As a consequence of population patterns and discriminatory state action, between 1900 and 1971, fifteen Blacks served in the US House of Representatives, and only one of them, Shirley Chisholm of New York, was a woman. To put this figure in perspective, it is useful to note that twenty Blacks served in the House of Representatives between 1870 and 1900.

In many cases, legal challenges under the Voting Rights Act were required to create the potential for more Black congressional representatives to be elected. The prevailing practice is generally to draw districts so that Blacks, Hispanics, and Whites each have their own representatives. The policy is sometimes described as the creation of majority-minority districts. This practice is controversial but has contributed to increases in the number of Black congressional representatives.

As can be seen from Table 6.3 below, in 1965 there were only six Black House Members. The number did not reach twenty until 1985. The next sizeable increase occurred in 1993, an outcome of Clinton's successful presidential campaign.

Consistent with the previous discussions of the critical role of Black women in advancing Black political interests, in the 109th Congress, fourteen of the Black lawmakers were female (33.3 percent), compared with 15.7 percent for the House of Representatives as a whole. Moreover, two-thirds of these legislators were either widowed, separated, or divorced, which reflect

6

general Black population demographics. Their marital status and social circumstances differ markedly from those of congressional representatives as a whole, 86 percent of whom were married.

As can be seen from Table 6.4, the total number of Blacks serving in the 112th Congress increased slightly from the two preceding elections to 44. Thirteen of these representatives are women. Thus, although the overall number of Black female elected officials continues to increase, there appears to be a glass ceiling in national politics. While Black Congressmen were able to impact policy development when the Democrats held a majority of the seats in the House, this power evaporated when the Republicans took control of the House in 2010.

TABLE 6.4
NUMBER OF BLACKS IN THE US CONGRESS
1965-2011

Congress (Year)	Blacks in Congress	Congress (Year)	Blacks in Congress
89th (1965)	6	101st (1989)	24
90th (1967)	7	102nd (1991)	26
91st (1969)	10	103rd (1993)	40
92nd (1971)	14	104th (1995)	40
93rd (1973)	17	105th (1997)	39
94th (1975)	18	106th (1999)	38
95th (1977)	17	107th (2001)	38
96th (1979)	16	108th (2003)	39
97th (1981)	18	109th (2005)	42
98th (1983)	21	110th (2007)	41
99th (1985)	21	111th (2009)	41
100th (1987)	23	112th (2011)	44

Source: Catherine Tate, *Black Faces in the Mirror*, Table 2.3; "Membership of the 108th Congress: A Profile," CRS Report for Congress, October 25, 2004; "Membership of the 109th Congress: A Profile," CRS Report for Congress, March 23, 2005; "Membership of the 110th Congress: A Profile," CRS Report for Congress, September 3, 2008; "Membership of the 111th Congress: A Profile," CRS Report for Congress, December 27, 2010; "Membership of the 110th Congress: A Profile," CRS Report for Congress, September 3, 2008; "Membership of the 112th Congress: A Profile," CRS Report for Congress, March 1, 2011.

Because of their limited numbers, Black congressional representatives have long recognized the need to band together in efforts to promote Black interests. The institutionalization of this effort is the Congressional Black Caucus, formed in 1971, by thirteen Black Members of the US House of Representatives. Initially, the CBC depicted itself as a unified bloc of legislators representing the national Black community. The function of the CBC has broadened to address a wide range of national concerns through legislative processes. Nevertheless, it has remained devoted to improving the condition of Blacks and minorities and to fighting racism.[142]

Several commentators, including Lani Guinier, have argued that minority numerical representation would be enhanced if the method of selecting congressional representatives was changed from a single-member plurality system to one where seats are allocated in proportion to votes received by each party. However, there is no incentive for elites to change the current system that protects White privilege. When Guinier was being considered for a position in the Clinton administration, she was dubbed the "quota queen" for having the temerity to suggest changes in voting protocols to increase Black and Hispanic representation, and her nomination was withdrawn. Thus, it appears that the current level of Black representation in the House of Representatives is unlikely to increase and more probably will decrease over time.[143]

Caucus Members are generally unified on economic and racial issues but have had only a limited impact on public policy formation because of their limited numbers. This impact is even less when the Republican Party is in the majority and/or a Republican president is in office. One assessment of the Caucus concludes that it is institutionally weak, has become less confrontational over time, and has achieved only a "modest" record in delivering policy substance to the Black community.[144] This assessment gains some credence when votes on recent pieces of legislation are examined. Surprisingly, approximately a quarter of the CBC Members supported the Bush administration's proposals to tighten bankruptcy restrictions and provide additional subsidies for oil exploration. Twenty percent also supported the Bush administration's proposed reductions in estate taxes. These votes may suggest that corporate interests are having a greater influence on Black congressperson's votes on non-civil rights issues than in the past and are influencing support of positions that may not serve the interests of the majority of Blacks.[145]

Prospects for impacting the work of the US Senate are even more dismal. Prior to the election of Barack Obama in 2004, the last Blacks to sit in the Senate were Edward Brooke, a moderate Republican who was elected in Massachusetts in 1967 and who was the first Black Senator since 1881, and Carol Mosely Braun, Obama's immediate predecessor. A Black presence in the Senate was maintained temporarily when Roland Burris was appointed to fill out Obama's term. However, the Senate was left without a Black member when Republicans gained the seat in 2010. Ironically, Black representation in the Senate was re-established in December 2012, when Republican Governor Nikki Haley of South Carolina appointed Republican Congressman Tim Scott to fill out the term of Senator Jim DeMint, who resigned to assume leadership of the Heritage Foundation, a conservative think tank.[146]

The limited representation of Blacks in both the House and Senate has contributed to the inability of the Obama administration to move its agenda forward. It is unlikely that the mid-term 2014 election will improve the prospects of legislative enactments that will improve the quality of life for African Americans.

Black Mayors

The year 1967 was a turning point for Blacks in electoral politics. It marked the election of Black mayors in two of America's largest cities—Carl Stokes of Cleveland, Ohio, and Richard Hatcher of Gary, Indiana. The Cleveland and Gary mayoral elections were especially significant because, as William E. Nelson and Philip J. Meranto explain, these victories were achieved on the strength of the mass mobilization of the Black vote for independent political action. In these elections, Black voters appeared to turn their backs on White-controlled political organizations to vote for politically independent Black candidates dedicated to expanding Black control over broad sectors of local government.[147]

During the 1970s, Black mayors were also elected in Washington, D.C., Atlanta, Georgia, New Orleans, Louisiana, Los Angeles, California, and other US cities. The 1980s saw the election of Black mayors in Chicago, Philadelphia, New York City, and other cities throughout the country. Harold Washington was elected as the first Black mayor in Chicago's history in 1983. Washington ran on a platform that emphasized reform and the rejection of traditional machine politics. Washington had previously served as a Democratic member of the Illinois House of Representatives from 1965–77. There his legislative initiatives had included welfare rights, fair employment practices, human rights, fair housing practices, and recognition of the birthday of Rev. Martin Luther King as a state holiday. Washington was able to win the mayoral election in 1983 and a reelection bid in 1987 by mobilizing a coalition of Black, White, and Latino voters and by overcoming the vicious race-baiting tactics used by his adversaries. Washington's reforms achieved some successes, but his untimely death in 1987 brought an unhappy end to the promise of a new political dispensation for Black Chicagoans.[148]

African Americans have also presided as mayors of hundreds of small predominantly Black cities, such as, Oakland, Spokane, and Hartford. By 1990, the year that the first Black was elected Governor—Democrat L. Douglas Wilder of Virginia—the total number of Black mayors was 318.

Statistics show that as a result of Black high return migration, more than half the nation's Blacks live in the South and in cities and towns with an unprecedented number of Black mayors. According to the National Conference of Black Mayors, in 2005 there were approximately 539 Black mayors in the country, and the states with the most cities led by Blacks are southern: 71 in Mississippi, 52 in North Carolina, 49 in Texas, 47 in Louisiana, 45 in Alabama, and 41 in Georgia.[149]

As of 2008 there were 46 Black mayors of cities with populations of 50,000 or greater, with 27 heading cities with 100,000 or more residents. Nine of these mayors were women. In 2010, the ranks of Black women mayors increased with the election of Stephanie Rawlings-Blake as Mayor of Baltimore. She became the only Black female mayor leading a city with a population greater than 100,000.

The office of mayor, titular and pompous, is more ceremonial than powerful. No mayors have full control of the cities over which they preside. A Black mayor often serves with predominantly White city council members who may be insensitive to his or her initiatives to improve the condition of the Black community. Whites control the economic and corporate structures of the city, county, and state. Therefore, Black mayors and other Black elected officials may often have to compromise African American interests and appease more powerful Whites in order to direct even minimal benefits to the Black community. To overcome this factor, Black mayors have been most effective in securing federal revenues for development of social and economic projects that benefit the Black underclass.[150]

Considering the monumental odds against their success, the benefits Black elected officials have been able to direct to Black communities are noteworthy. As Nelson and Meranto observed in the early Cleveland and Gary experiences, Black mayors made a positive difference in the lives of Black citizens in these cities. The mayors of Cleveland and Gary oversaw the construction

6

of public housing units, establishment of day-care centers and health clinics, and attacked problems of employment and drug abuse. They assisted Black entrepreneurship and encouraged high-levels of minority hiring in administrative and managerial municipal positions, which permanently lifted thousands of African Americans into the middle-income class.[151]

Although Black mayors may have received most of their support from Blacks, they cannot ignore White concerns. The proliferation of Black mayors, especially in cities with minority Black populations, has led political analysts to develop various theories of White/Black cross-over voting. In the majority of cities, Whites own and control most of the businesses or economic enterprises. Thus, the Black mayor must look beyond his own community to the White corporate power structure, the state, and the federal government for funding and assistance. In other words, regardless of how impressive the titles of the few Black elected officials, White people still maintain overall economic and political power. Yet, in cities or districts where Blacks represent a near or complete majority, White political candidates must also be attentive to the Black electorate. There is, however, one difference. White candidates do not have to employ deracialized rhetoric to appeal to Black voters, which Black candidates must apparently exhibit, or prefer to articulate, in order to obtain White cross-over votes.

Efforts by Black mayors, as well as other mayors, to improve the quality of life for residents have been frustrated by contemporary patterns of globalization. Efforts by cities to strengthen international economic linkages by attracting multinational corporations have not benefited low-income residents as much as the higher income, highly educated urban residents. Although large investments in community-driven neighborhood revitalization projects have led to improvements in housing and neighborhood quality for many families in high-poverty areas, these gains have also been accompanied by significant negative outcomes. The adverse aspects of revitalization efforts include inadequate attention to improvements in public education and employment, and high rates of incarceration. New, higher income, residents often choose private educational options over public education. This leads to declined enrollments in public schools and reduced state support that is based on enrollment. Businesses that begin to cater to a more affluent base of consumers tend to offer only low-paying service jobs to original residents. In addition, many original resident owners find themselves unable to pay the higher property taxes and are forced to sell their residences and move to a cheaper community and seek new employment and schooling options. Some remaining residents, faced with declining legal options, turn to illegal activity in order to survive.

Adverse consequences resulting from the failure to address these issues are becoming more visible as the positive outcomes generated by the economic expansion of the late 1990s have dissipated.

African Americans who relocate to suburban jurisdictions to escape some of the negative characteristics of central cities often experience significant loss of political power. This can occur even in areas where Blacks are relatively affluent and constitute a large proportion of the population, as Valerie Johnson's study of Black political incorporation in Prince George's County, Maryland, documents.[152]

The economic crisis that began in 2007 has had disastrous effects on the ability of cities to meet the needs of their citizens. In 2009, nine in ten city finance officers reported problems in meeting fiscal needs. These problems have been sparked by lower consumption, which reduces sales tax revenues; increased property foreclosures and declines in property values, which lower property tax revenues; job losses, which lower income tax receipts; or record state budget shortfalls. In many cities, the local response to deteriorating conditions has consisted of service cutbacks, layoffs, and delayed or canceled infrastructure projects, or general service cuts. In addition, drastic cuts in state aid to cities have significantly exacerbated fiscal problems.[153]

Statewide Elected Offices

The subordinate position of cities relative to state governments limits the extent to which mayors, including Black mayors, can implement programs that improve the well-being of their constituents. Budget cuts implemented by state governments in recent years have affected all residents, not only city dwellers. Between 2007 and 2012, states implemented $290 billion in cuts to public services and $100 billion in tax and fee increases. These actions lengthened the recession and delayed the recovery by destroying hundreds of thousands of jobs and debilitating education, health care, and other social infrastructure initiatives.[154]

The fiscal circumstances of states have been worsened by the expiration of emergency federal aid at the end of 2011. Moreover, the federal government has been advancing spending cuts that are expected to further reduce federal funding for state and local governments.[155]

Historically, urban areas have not fared well in state-level policy decision-making compared to rural areas. Since African Americans are disproportionately located in urban areas they are unduly victimized by the power imbalance between urban and rural areas. The negative implications of the urban-rural schism for African Americans are heightened by the dramatic under-representation of Black legislators at the state level.

In 2009, there were 628 Black state legislators in office out of 7382 (9 percent). The representation rates were comparable for Houses of Representatives and Senates.[156] Black women accounted for approximately one-third of Black state legislators in 2012.

TABLE 6.5
STATE WITH THE LARGEST OVER- AND UNDER-REPRESENTATION OF BLACK STATE LEGISLATORS
2009

State	% African Americans in State	% African Americans in the Legislature	Over Representation in the Legislature
Ohio	12.0%	14.4%	2.4%
Illinois	15.0%	17.5%	2.5%
Nevada	8.0%	11.1%	3.2%
California	6.7%	10.8%	4.1%
State	% African Americans in State	% African Americans in the Legislature	Under Representation in the Legislature
Louisiana	31.9%	18.1%	-13.8%
Delaware	20.9%	8.1%	-12.8%
Virginia	19.9%	10.0%	-9.9%
Mississippi	37.2%	28.7%	-8.5%
Georgia	30.0%	22.5%	-7.6%
South Carolina	28.7%	21.8%	-7.0%

Source: Factoid: Black State Legislators in 2009
Posted by lunchcountersitin on April 16, 2009. http://allotherpersons.wordpress.com/2009/04/ 16factoid-black-state-legislators-in-2009/ (site no longer available.)

Electoral Politics and the Judiciary

Although judges are not elected at the federal level, election politics significantly influence appointments.

Federal judges are recommended to the Senate by the President and appointment requires a super majority (60 votes). While there have been examples where federal judges have surprised supporters who expected decisions to reflect a particular ideological orientation, in general judicial decisions do reflect the ideology of the nominating President. Because judicial appointments have no term limitations, depending on the level of appointment (District, Court of Appeals, Supreme Court), a President can influence the boundaries of public policy long after his or her term of office has ended. This phenomenon is and has been a central dynamic in shaping the trajectory of the struggle for freedom and equity waged by African Americans.

As noted in Chapter 3, the Supreme Court has been progressively retrenching legislative civil rights protections for Blacks. However, the retrenchment process actually begins in Federal, District, and Appeals Courts, where cases are first litigated. As of May 2012, Blacks comprised approximately 14% of sitting Federal District judges (85/616) and 11% (18/165) of sitting Federal Appeals Court judges. These figures, which are roughly proportional to population representation, are the result of appointments made by the Bush, Clinton, and Obama administrations. Despite the plaudits given to Lyndon Johnson for appointing Thurgood Marshall to the Supreme Court, only about 4% of his District Court appointees were Black, slightly better than the 3.4% figure for Richard Nixon. Jimmy Carter was the first President to appoint a significant number of non-Anglos to District judgeships—over 21 percent, two-thirds of whom were Black. Only 2 percent of Reagan's district court appointments were Black.

During the administration of President Bill Clinton (1993-2001), a dramatic change took place. Over 17 percent of the judges appointed to the District Court judgeships by Clinton were Black. The Clinton initiative to make the bench more accurately reflect US gender and racial demographics was evident in the ranks of the appellate judges as well. A third of his appointees were women, and more African-Americans, Hispanics, and Asians were appointed to the Appellate Court bench by Clinton than by any other president. Somewhat surprising is the fact that President George W. Bush also increased the courts' diversity. Almost one-third of his District Court appointments were women and racial/ethnic minorities, although obviously these judges reflect a very different judicial philosophy than those appointed by Clinton.[157]

6

As of May 2012, President Obama had made 188 nominations for federal judgeships, of which 133 had been confirmed. His most significant achievements have been the successful nominations of Supreme Court Justices Sonia Sotomayor and Elena Kagan. Fourteen of Obama's nominees for the lower courts are African American women. Obama has had more difficulty in getting nominees confirmed for Federal District judgeships than Presidents Clinton and Bush.

The numbers of African Americans appointed by Presidents Clinton, Bush, and Obama currently sitting on the District and Appeals benches as of May 2012 are shown below in Table 6.6.

TABLE 6.6
NUMBER OF SITTING AFRICAN AMERICAN FEDERAL DISTRICT AND APPEALS JUDGES APPOINTED BY PRESIDENTS CLINTON, BUSH AND OBAMA
May 2012

President	District Court	Appeals Court
Clinton	35	7
Bush	18	4
Obama	18	6

Source: "Diversity on the Bench," History of the Federal Judiciary. Federal Judiciary Center. http://www.fjc.gov/servlet/nDsearch?race=African+American.

It is important to recognize that the figures for Clinton and Bush reflect eight years of office, compared to less than four for Obama. Ten of Clinton-appointed sitting judges are African American females, eight of Bush-appointed sitting appointees, and eleven of Obama appointees. It is reasonable to expect that there is a nontrivial degree of ideological diversity across the three sets of appointees reflecting the orientations of the nominating President. Thus, it is doubtful that a consensus regarding judicial philosophy exists with respect to civil rights issues.

The most critical pattern shaping the future of civil rights is the overall composition of the Supreme Court. Despite the appointment of Justices Sotomayor and Kagan, mentioned previously, there is currently a solid conservative majority in place resulting from appointments during the Bush administration (2005). Decisions rendered under the leadership of Chief Justice Roberts clearly signal that further retrenchment of hard-fought civil rights gains is virtually guaranteed. For African American Studies specialists, this means that expanded efforts are needed to mobilize engagement in both electoral and protest politics.

Assessing Black Political Leaders and Organizations

Critical Perspectives on Black Political Leadership

As Katherine Tate observes, it is not enough that a few minorities take part in deliberation, "their members must constitute a 'critical mass' so that they become willing enough to enunciate minority positions ... and be interspersed across the wide array of committees and subcommittees and other levels of government."[158] The preceding discussion has highlighted the skewed distribution of Blacks in elected office in positions that have limited power to influence the quality of life and opportunities for Blacks. Any useful assessment of the effectiveness of Black elected officials and political organizations must begin from the indisputable fact that Whites possess the power and control over the major political and economic institutions of American life.

As noted previously, throughout the history of the Black experience in America, the primary need and principal role for Black leaders have been to champion the freedom of African people and to deliver them from the inhumane circumstance of White racism and oppression. The philosophy, approach, and method of each true leader may have varied, but his or her objective remained constant. Those persons who have historically stood, or who presently stand, ready to risk their personal well-being to press for the liberty and uplift of Black people are the ones who measure up to the criteria of true Black political leadership. The profile of Black leadership has been a popular area of study, especially during and subsequent to the 1960s. Social scientists have analyzed the racial ideology of Black leaders, revealed how they acquire leadership status, studied their various styles and unique appeals, and attempted to quantify the level of support and confidence that they have earned among Blacks. The quality of Black leadership has been measured in terms of the degree of commitment the leader has exhibited in promoting the best interests of the Black community. Politically, a Black leader is despised or esteemed on the basis of the rights and resources he or she can demand or negotiate from the White-dominated system for the uplift and benefit of the Black community. The difficult problem that confronts Black leaders is whether or not they can be politically cooperative with Whites and still be competitive enough to forge social and economic benefits for their Black constituency. All eminent Black spokespersons are not truly Black leaders.

Historically and presently, many African Americans who have been designated, or who have been promoted, as Black leaders might be described more appropriately as racial diplomats, as charismatic spokesmen, or as ceremonial agents of non-Black interests. Many so-called Black leaders are not stewards of the Black community but are creations of the news media. These persons are often selected and promoted by White politicians, or serve as representatives of political organizations, whose purposes and commitments are inconsistent with the welfare and best interests of African Americans.

Chuck Stone, former assistant to dynamic African American Congressman Adam Clayton Powell, characterized Negro politicians who exploit Blacks with their favored status among Whites as "Uncle Toms" and "ceremonial Negro leaders."[159] Stone's characterization of two such types of leaders reveals that neither poses a threat to the White power structure and neither is willing to disturb the power structure or to "rock the boat." Both types hold their positions of leadership at the whim and on the terms of Whites, and neither is prepared to utilize their influence to energize or to organize the masses of Blacks for an assault on racism. The difference between them is that the ceremonial Negro leader tries "to keep his or her political tracks covered in the [Black] community" and often gives the impression or puts up the facade of challenging "the periphery of the white power structure," while the Uncle Tom has little involvement with the Black community and functions basically out of "naked fear" of White people.[160]

Some contemporary Black political leaders conform to the above descriptions, but recent indications are that Black leadership that is solely anointed and legitimated by Whites cannot so easily deliver the votes and "souls" of the Black community to the White power structure. Although the ballot has increased the number of Black public officials, low-income Blacks and the Black underclass have experienced relatively little change in their condition. Despite the great surge in the number of Black elected officials, Black leadership still lacks real power to effect social change.

Black political leaders who have little identity or familiarity with Black issues and concerns become alienated from the African American community. Fair minded, or at least politically wise, White candidates may often have an equal opportunity of appealing to the Black electorate. For Black candidates to attain more and higher elective offices, they must attract more non-Black votes. The trend toward Black candidates attracting more White voters was evident in the 1988 elections. The question is, as Black candidates improve in their ability to gain White voters, will it affect their political efficacy to the African American community?

Redistributive benefits traditionally anticipated by African American communities as a result of the election or appointment of Black governing or supervising officials include:

1. More federal and private (philanthropic) funding.
2. An increase in numbers of Blacks employed in various municipal and governmental work forces.
3. Appointment of more Blacks to commissions and review boards.
4. More expenditure for municipal education and social welfare.
5. An environment created by Black political power in city hall in which Black business thrives.
6. Less police brutality (fewer Whites killing Blacks), although the crime rate remains constant.[161]

A discussion and analysis of Black leadership is not complete without including the role of the church in producing the majority of Black leaders. In the African American experience, religion has never been separated from politics. This is the primary reason why most of the struggles for freedom, justice, and civil rights, from the eighteenth century to the present, have taken place in the Black Church and have been led by Black ministers.[162] The numbers of Black ministers who have played a role in liberation and civil rights struggles are too numerous to treat here. However, it is important to mention some of the most important ones, such as, Henry Highland Garnet (1815–1882), a contemporary of Frederick Douglass in the early antislavery crusades. Garnet was a pastor as well as a political activist. Many of the slave insurrections were planned and executed by ministers, of whom Denmark Vesey (1767-1822) was one of the most renowned. Vesey, a Methodist minister, used the church as a base for planning one of the most famous revolts. A few of the most prominent ministers or religious leaders who were political activists during

6

the 1960s include Congressman Adam Clayton Powell, Martin Luther King Jr., Malcolm X, and Jesse Jackson. Thus, it is not surprising that after the passage of the Voting Rights Act, a large number of Black elected officials are ministers.

It would be erroneous to assume that all Black ministers have been active advocates and supporters of the freedom and uplift of the Black masses. Many ministers have been suppressors of African American resistance movements and have also been used as pawns to promote the political interests of the White establishment. The Black preacher unquestionably wields much influence over millions of Blacks. However, one study found that the role and behavior of Black ministers were geared toward the congregation's expectations, which affected the kind of apathetic, active, or very active political leadership a particular minister might exhibit. A conservative minister might emphasize spiritual leadership within the church devoid of any political activism. A moderate minister might not initiate political activism but would respond to the congregation's willingness to act on specific social and political issues. The liberal minister was found to initiate political activism.[163] Regardless of these variations, African American ministers have been primary motivators of Black political activism and the mainstay of Black leadership. The preceding comments provide a context for evaluating the political behavior of the new breed of conservative Black ministers who are entering the political arena.

Adolph Reed has argued that a new type of Black leader emerged after the Civil Rights Movement. Whereas Black leaders, including elected leaders, had traditionally come from the Black Church, as increasing numbers of Blacks were elected, Black ministers were displaced as the source of Black leadership.[164] Reed's assessment is controversial because, as suggested previously, one of the key dynamics during the 2004 presidential election was the return of the Black minister as a major political force. Ironically, the new breed of Black-minister-turned-political-advocate is pursuing a political agenda that reduces the historically established priority of the Black freedom struggle. This new conservative mantra may be transferred to constituents who begin to seek elected and appointed positions in a manner that could further weaken the battle for racial justice.

This development raises the question, given the apparent declining linkage between Black "leaders" and traditional Black interests, of whether race should be the only—or even the principal—criterion the Black electorate should consider in its voter decision-making. A Black face alone does not guarantee that an official will prioritize the best interests of the Black community or those of African American people in general. In many cases, a White candidate may best serve the interests of the Black community. For example, as noted in Chapter 3, Clarence Thomas's nomination caused much controversy and divided support among African Americans, and he was also opposed by several White feminist groups. For most Blacks, Thomas's consistent votes in opposition to the articulated interests of the majority of Black people would seem to disqualify him unquestionably from the status of Black leader. There is some indication that some Black organizations are now willing to violate the historical taboo against publicly criticizing Blacks appointed to high positions whose record clearly indicates limited linkage to the Black community. Jane Mansbride and Katherine Tate assert that "the appointment of Clarence Thomas to the Supreme Court of the United States may have served as a milestone ... in the Black community, as some African American organizations ... opposed Thomas's nomination despite [the fact that he is Black]."[165]

If the Thomas nomination is indeed an important turning point, perhaps Black organizations will begin to address the criticism Robert Smith raises in *We Have No Black Leaders*. Smith argues that Black organizations and their leaders have been ineffective in representing and promoting Black interests over the last three decades. These failures, according to Smith, stem from a combination of limited resources, incompetent leaders, and misguided strategies.[166] There are, of course, other perspectives. Ollie Johnson and Karin Stanford counterpose Smith by arguing that "despite occasional scandals and internal struggles, Black political organizations have been the Black community's strongest advocates and defenders, and following the passage of the 1960s civil rights legislation, these groups mobilized their resources to guarantee implementation of the new federal and local laws."[167]

The Leadership Conference on Civil Rights (LCCR), founded in 1950 by A. Philip Randolph, Roy Wilkins, and Arnold Aronson (a leader of the National Jewish Community Relations Advisory Council), is the paradigmatic example of resource mobilization to support implementation of civil rights legislation. The LCCR has coordinated the national legislative campaign on behalf of every major civil rights law since 1957. It comprises more than 180 national organizations, representing persons of color, women, children, labor unions, individuals with disabilities, older Americans, major religious groups, gays and lesbians, and civil liberties and human rights groups.[168]

From the vantage point of Africana Studies, the critical question is: Given the declining federal commitment to the enforcement of civil rights and the limited success of electoral politics in enhancing the lives of people of African descent, to what extent is it feasible to revive Black organizations and movement politics to counterbalance the shortcomings of electoral politics? In addition, the heavy reliance of Black organizations on external support is seen by many as a major stumbling block to political efficacy. Adolph Reed, for example, argues that one weakness facing many Black organizations is an unhealthy linkage between African American leaders and powerful external benefactors. On the other hand, Charles Jones insists that "outside elites provide African American leaders with critical resources needed to enhance and fortify their respective leadership positions."[169]

In the face of these competing perspectives, we should examine how individual organizations that played a critical role during the Civil Rights Movement are adapting to the current period in which electoral politics is paramount and is dominated by conservative interests.

Assessing Black Political Organizations

The NAACP has been long regarded as the premier civil rights organization. Its major asset continues to be a membership of approximately half a million, with a network of local branches and state-level organizations. Robert Smith argues that the NAACP's traditional emphasis on anti-defamation, litigation, and lobbying have been undermined by four factors: (1) declining support from Whites, (2) the changing nature of racism, (3) Republican control of the federal government, and (4) resource constraints. Of these, the changing nature of racism from overt to covert and the Supreme Court's continuing movement away from race-conscious discrimination remedies have made it difficult for the NAACP to redefine its agenda in a way that connects to the concerns of younger Blacks and that garners visibility as a continuing force in the contemporary liberation struggle.[170]

In contrast with the active civil rights advocacy of the NAACP, the National Urban League was built around a social work model that emphasized the provision of direct services to the Black community. Although it has attempted to reinvent itself and take a more activist posture in recent years, Jennifer Wade and Brian Williams report that it faces major challenges in the areas of funding, staffing, and leadership. The Urban League is heavily dependent on corporate support and external funding to support projects. The Southern Christian Leadership Conference (SCLC) played an especially critical role in mobilizing grassroots support during the Civil Rights Movement. The challenges it faced were not compatible with the development of long-term plans or projects. In recent years, the SCLC has attempted to take a more strategic approach to addressing the concerns of its constituents. However, F. Carl Walton concludes that these efforts have not been very successful and that the organization has lost the support of many ministers. Some of the erosion of engagement with the SCLC reflects efforts by individual ministers to undertake economic development initiatives by using their own congregations' resources concomitant with a reduction in commitment to addressing persisting civil rights inequities.[171]

The concern with economic empowerment is not new and, in fact, was a central component of the agenda of Operation People United to Save Humanity (Operation PUSH), founded by Rev. Jesse Jackson in 1971. Evolving out of Operation Breadbasket, which advocated economic boycotts against discriminatory businesses, Operation PUSH developed an agenda that focused simultaneously on economic opportunity and political empowerment. The political empowerment initiatives consisted primarily of voter registration and voter education drives that were continued following the merger of Operation PUSH with the Rainbow Coalition in 1995. However, the Rainbow/PUSH Coalition has made African American business development and economic mobility the centerpiece of its agenda through the Wall Street Project, which seeks to exert influence and/or gain some control over mainstream financial institutions and expanding opportunities for Black-owned businesses.[172]

Turning attention to movements and organizations outside the orbit of mainstream politics, African American Studies sees the lack of sustained activity following the Million Man March in 1995 as one of the greatest disappointments in recent years. Claude Clegg argues that Louis Farrakhan missed a unique opportunity to take on a greater leadership role in the liberation

6

struggle. Clegg contends that in the early years of the twenty-first century, "Farrakhan has constructed no grand philosophy or practical program beyond small-scale entrepreneurial capitalism."[173]

In contrast, the agenda of the Black Radical Congress (BRC), established in 1998, attempts "to address a myriad of issues and organize socialists, revolutionary nationalists, and feminists to oppose actively all forms of oppression, 'including class exploitation, racism, patriarchy, homophobia, anti-immigration prejudice and imperialism.'" The BRC builds on the tradition of the National Black Political Assembly Convention held in 1972. As Valerie Johnson observes, "Although the BRC maintains that its agenda is not an intention to replace or displace existing organizations, parties, or campaigns, it was a clear rejection of business as usual and the strategies and tactics of mainstream Black political organizations."[174] Johnson suggests, however, that the BRC has not offered substantive strategies.

Viable Domestic Political Strategies for the Twenty-first Century

The preceding assessment of the efficacy of Black political leadership and Black political organizations leaves little room for optimism. Confronting constraints on successful independent political initiatives by Blacks, some commentators insist that a reversal in Black political fortunes can only be accomplished by a greater emphasis on coalition building. Coalitions must be pursued carefully and strategically, and, further, be informed by historical experience. John Henrik Clarke, the eminent African historian, once stated, in essence, that Blacks are one of the most naive of peoples in instances where Black/White political alliances or coalitions have been formed.[175] In the context of this inference, Clarke was recounting the historical experiences of Africans (Egypt, Ethiopia) with the Greeks and Romans more than 1600 to 2000 years ago. Other historians relate the tragic experience of the Black freedmen in their attempts to ally or coalesce with White Populists near the end of the nineteenth century.[176] The most controversial and precarious coalition attempts and experiences of Blacks with other races or ethnic groups, and, indeed, intra-racially, occurred in the twentieth century.

Dialectics of Black Alliances and Coalitions

Maulana Karenga has suggested that the reason Blacks have failed to achieve more profitable and substantial political relationships with other groups is because they have not observed the basic distinction between a coalition and an alliance. Karenga argues that an "alliance is a long-term ongoing unity based on common interests and common basic principles whereas a coalition is a short-term working association based on specific short-term goals."[177] The basis or rationale for any political relationship between persons or groups is self-interest. Historically, it appears that African Americans have sustained extended coalitions and/or alliances with other groups, while their own immediate self-interests have been poorly or unequally served.

Coalition is a political strategy resorted to when one faction of individuals cannot singly achieve its goals and objectives without the support and aid of another external faction that has similar objectives or who stands to reap specific benefits as a result of mutual cooperation. Individuals or groups coalesce to achieve certain goals or benefits. The motive is self-interest. However, often, in political coalitions, there exist different self-interests that can lead to unequal results or benefits for one of the factions. Coalition-building was a functional factor of Black politics during slavery, during the abolitionist and Reconstruction periods, and has been, even more so, in the twentieth century. The common patterns or attempts by Blacks to form coalitions that cross racial lines include:

1. Blacks and White liberals
2. Blacks and Jews
3. Blacks and Organized Labor
4. Blacks and other racial-ethnic groups

Although the above list is not comprehensive, it presents both those coalitions of the most historical significance, as well as those most likely to be useful for addressing contemporary issues.

Blacks and White Liberals

The most common, debatable, and frequently assessed coalition has been the one that, variously, has existed between Black and White liberals. Whether relating to Black/White liberal coalitions or to Blacks coalescing with other groups, the classical discussion of the "Myths of Coalition" in Stokely Carmichael and Charles

V. Hamilton's book, *Black Power: The Politics of Liberation in America*, incisively analyzes the misconceptions of coalition. Carmichael and Hamilton posit that it is mythical and a fallacy to assume that: (1) Black interests are identical with the interests of White liberals and other reform groups; (2) powerless and insecure people can develop effective and trusting relationships with politically and economically powerful groups; and (3) coalitions can be developed and sustained on a purely moral, collegial, or sentimental basis.[178]

Black liberals might be characterized as those who seek integration with Whites, but who also demand redress from Whites and the government for their unequal economic and political plight. White liberalism is egalitarian in nature, but it remains to be seen how far Whites have ever been prepared to go towards relinquishing or sharing power with Blacks. Real or significant integration between the races has not occurred. The NAACP and the Urban League are the most prominent and effective civil rights organizations that have been established to improve race relations and to redress the wrongs of racism. These organizations were initially biracially focused and administered. They were, and still are, to some extent, partly dependent on a few economically and politically powerful Whites for funding and support.

The NAACP and the Urban League have been responsible for forging major social, political, and economic gains for Blacks. However, for more than eighty years of Black/White coalition within these organizations, Blacks have participated and functioned more from a position of weakness than from strength. No one can say for sure how much the prohibitive pressures and attitudes of eminent White benefactors have restricted or restrained some of the more aggressive and expeditious civil rights actions of these organizations. However, one may observe and logically assume that, in order to preserve Black/White liberal coalitions, cautious and non-intimidating approaches towards civil rights litigation and action have been and still must be pursued. A successful and effective coalition can result only if the constituent factions are of equal strength or at least can demand equal respect. Black Power advocates disdain Black/White coalitions because of the tendency of Whites to control the organizations.

Some political analysts argue that the primary political objectives of Blacks are no longer race-specific. This view is shared by many Black conservatives who believe that many social and economic policies transcend race or are not racially related. Under such a premise, race issues are impertinent in Black/White political coalitions. In electoral politics the Black candidate, especially, must succumb regarding policy initiatives and must acquiesce to a deracialized rhetoric to vie successfully for office.[179]

Deracialized politics implies that the high disproportionate rates of Black poverty, unemployment, homelessness, disease, crime, and incarceration are related solely to economic variables and social dysfunctions independent of racial injustice and discrimination. Deracialized political philosophy functions on the assumption that all institutional barriers to social, political, and economic equality based on race, color, and culture have been eliminated. Thus, power cannot be discerned as being inordinately possessed by any single race or ethnic group. Racism and discrimination must become obsolete, and, indeed, so must White and Black politics and coalitions. Such a utopian state of race relations is yet to be consummated in American society.

Blacks and Jews

Historically, Blacks and Jews have been perceived as having maintained, from time to time, a type of political or moral coalition in the area of civil rights. However, in business and economic dealings, Blacks have been known to possess anti-Semitic attitudes toward White liberal Jews. Jewish people have supported and have been highly active in Black civil rights organizations, but many African Americans feel that they have been economically exploited by Jews.[180] Prior to the 1960s, Jewish researchers virtually dominated or controlled the scholarship on African Americans. The factors that incline Blacks and Jews to coalesce politically are their similar histories of suffering and persecution. Blacks point to the long suffering of slavery, and Jews point to the experience of the Holocaust. Beyond this vestige of moral sentiment, Blacks and Jews have little in common.

C. Eric Lincoln perceptively notes that Jews are persecuted primarily because of their religion and Blacks because of their race and color. Jews can be Jewish or otherwise, but Blacks cannot change their race or color. Lincoln writes that "being white, individual Jews have behaved more or less like other whites, and that they have been neither better nor worse than other whites with whom they are associated."[181]

A new era of strained Black-Jewish relations began during the late 1970s when Jewish leaders demanded the resignation of Black Ambassador Andrew Young, when

6

he supposedly made contact with members of the Palestine Liberation Organization. During the same period, the Jewish community opposed affirmative action for African Americans. Jewish intellectuals gave credence to White claims concerning the impropriety of "reverse discrimination" and "quotas" to remedy historical discrimination against Black Americans. Blacks were also concerned about the trade and military alliance Israel had maintained with the oppressive and racist regimes of South Africa. The following statement sums up the political implications of Black-Jewish coalitions:[182]

> There is no question that individual Jews and Jewish organizations and their leaders have worked as part of a liberal coalition with Blacks and organized labor to form a powerful political force for social and economic reform in the United States. It is also clear that Jewish organizations and leadership have done so when it is in their perceived interest to do so as do we. It is reasonable to believe that they will continue to work with Blacks when they believe that it is in their interest to be allied with Blacks and their aspirations.

Seemingly irreparable breaches developed in Black-Jewish relations during the 1984 and 1988 presidential elections involving Rev. Jesse Jackson and Muslim leader Minister Louis Farrakhan. Jackson lost some support when he failed to disassociate himself from Mr. Farrakhan's criticism of Jews during the 1984 campaign when Mr. Farrakhan's Nation of Islam endorsed Mr. Jackson. Although Farrakhan distanced himself from presidential politics in the 1988 campaign, ghosts of 1984 haunted the Jackson campaign limiting support from Jewish interests. Although in the early decades of the 21st century there are fewer instances of highly visible conflicts between Blacks and Jews there are also few examples of concrete collaboration. Thus, it appears that for the foreseeable future, it appears that each group will independently use whatever power and influence it has to pursue its own political objectives.

Blacks and Organized Labor

Organized labor has had a longstanding interest and active involvement in efforts to promote the civil rights of groups facing discrimination. Despite this fact, the degree of cooperation between organized labor and civil rights advocacy groups has been largely episodic. Over time, the two constituencies have developed different approaches to addressing civil rights issues, and it is often difficult to resolve seemingly competing foci, despite what would appear to be clearly overlapping interests. There was, of course, extensive collaboration between organized labor and civil rights groups during the Civil Rights Movement. However, prior to that time, and, subsequently, less cooperation was and is the norm. The increasing economic vulnerability experienced by racial/ethnic minorities and workers has forced organizations representing both groups to expand their traditional agendas. For example, civil rights organizations are focusing increasingly on issues of economic empowerment—with concerns about the deteriorating employment prospects of Blacks at the top of the new agenda—and large numbers of unorganized Black workers in the South constitute a potential vital constituency for organized labor. If organized labor and traditional civil rights groups are to be in the vanguard of forces generating a new movement for economic justice, then it is important to examine and better understand the historical and contemporary sources of friction on employment-related issues as a necessary precursor to forging an effective coalition to confront current political and economic challenges associated with globalization.

Nelson Lichtenstein has argued that the creation of structures that provided avenues for individual workers to seek redress outside the collective bargaining framework is a major culprit that has contributed both to weakening the labor movement and to the dilution of synergies between the Civil Rights Movement and organized labor. Specifically, he suggests:

> The 1963 March on Washington signals the moment when work rights underwent a fundamental shift in their meaning and method. Indeed, the summer of 1963 may well be taken as the moment when the discourse of American liberalism shifted decisively out of the New Deal/laborite orbit and into a world in which the racial divide colored all politics. From the early 1960s onward the most efficacious and legitimate defense of American job rights would be found not as a collective initiative, as codified in the Wagner Act and advanced by the trade unions, but as an individual claim to a worker's civil rights based on one's distinctive race, gender or other attribute. From a legislative point of view the decisive moment in this transformation came when, during the great political opening that followed the Birmingham demonstrations of May

1963, legislation governing fair employment practices was rolled into the 1964 civil rights laws as Title VII.[183]

This critique is both misleading and shortsighted. Specifically, it ignores the history of discrimination experienced by Blacks at the hands of unions and the racism exhibited by White workers before and subsequent to the Civil Rights Movement. The negative experiences of Blacks with organized labor date back to the nineteenth century, and produced, as in the case of other venues, a tradition of self-organization as epitomized by A. Philip Randolph's organization of the Brotherhood of Sleeping Car Porters. James Stewart has documented how Black steelworkers had to wage an insurgent campaign to force the union to implement aggressive nondiscriminatory policies.[184]

There are signs that some important changes are occurring within organized labor. In the 1990s, the AFL-CIO established alliances with Black ministers and created a new Economic Education Project. Developing alliances between organized labor and Black church leaders reflects the type of holistic approach to the pursuit of racial equity that Black workers were seeking during the 1960s. The Economic Education Project outline asserts that "the labor movement must stand for inclusion and social justice. ...Workers must have access to jobs and training, and must receive equitable pay, regardless of their race, gender or sexual orientation. The results of past and current discrimination must be remedied by methods which include affirmative action." The outline also declares, "Unions play a crucial role in uniting workers of all races and both genders around their common interests as workers. When unions have been at their best, reducing wage and job quality differences between workers of different races and genders has been an important goal of our policies, and we must redouble our efforts in these areas."[185] As the twenty-first century unfolds, further development of such educational approaches and coalition-building initiatives have the potential to serve the interests of both Blacks and workers. However, this type of initiative is likely to suffer as a result of the fragmentation of the AFL-CIO that occurred in 2005.

Blacks and Other Racial/Ethnic Groups

America is populated with various racial-ethnic groups who are negatively affected socially, politically, and economically because of their minority status. Efforts to form national political coalitions and alliances in the past have proved largely ineffective because each group experiences discrimination, exploitation, racism, or alienation in different ways. Differences in the cultural, social, and economic objectives of Blacks, Hispanic, Asian, and Native Americans have often been divisive. Yet, there have been times when these differences have been bridged briefly enough to achieve mutual political gains. Black coalitions with other racial-ethnic minority groups have also been problematic because of intraclass dynamics within each of these groups. Although Jesse Jackson based his political campaigns of 1984 and 1988 on a Rainbow Coalition, there has been little or no evidence to show how solidly he attracted other minority racial and ethnic voters.

The concepts of race and ethnicity can be confusing if one is attempting to stratify the diverse population groups in the United States. Obviously, racially defined minorities are not perceived the same as ethnically defined minorities. In this book, African American and Black are meant to refer to descendants and all immigrants from Africa and the Caribbean of Black stock. Hispanic/Latino may refer to those persons who trace their heritage to Spanish-speaking countries that may have White, Black, or Brown phenotypes. The Asian classification includes Japanese, Chinese, Korean, Filipinos, non-native Indians, Vietnamese, and other Asian and Pacific Islanders. When White or White American is mentioned, it has meant those persons of European descent who consider themselves non-Hispanic.[186]

For political purposes, the term *minority* generally applies only to groups physically distinct from the European-American majority in the United States. A minority status in America usually implies a group with a history of discrimination and social stratification, whereas *ethnicity* refers to a national identity and distinct culture and language.[187] Defining and stratifying such groups are important to Black politics and the prospect of coalition initiatives. If current Hispanic and Asian immigration and birth rates continue to increase at the present rate, in a half-century or more (2050 or 2080), non-Hispanic Whites will comprise less than half of the total US population. Each racial minority or ethnic group has its own legitimate self-interests that may not be conducive to coalition but can result in intense inter-group conflict. Blacks can no longer assume "automatic" coalitions with other racial-ethnic groups without carefully assessing mutual interests and common goals.

6

257

Irrespective of the extent of inter-group competition, the vulnerability of Blacks and Latinos to the vagaries of globalization mandates serious exploration of the development of strategic coalitions. Continuing attacks on affirmative action clearly provide a rallying point for the development of the type of coalition proposed. Blacks and Hispanics/Latinos are the principal targets of efforts to curtail affirmative action programs in higher education. Moreover, both Black and Hispanic/Latino children are disproportionately attending schools with substantial resource deficits as a result of de facto segregation.

There are, of course, difficult barriers to overcome in forming a Black-Latino coalition. Joel Kotkin opines, "Many older, more established communities—both African American and Anglo—will feel themselves overwhelmed and in some sense, displaced by the energetic newcomers, both in the marketplace and, over time, in the political arena."[188] In a similar vein, Alvin Toffler argues that "in addition to traditional conflict between majority and minorities, democratic governments must now cope with open warfare *between* rival minority groups, as happened in Miami, for example, between Cuban and Haitian immigrants, and elsewhere in the United States between African Americans and Hispanics."[189]

In many respects, Los Angeles is the principal testing ground for the likelihood of developing viable Black-Latino coalitions. Peter Skerry finds that Mexican Americans in Los Angeles have been willing to endure double and summer sessions to alleviate crowding in neighborhood schools rather than participate in busing schemes designed to promote desegregation. He also suggests that Latino concerns with bilingual education have been pursued in a manner that creates potential conflicts with the agendas pursued by Blacks.[190]

The electoral results in the 2005 Los Angeles Democratic mayoral primary election suggest that the potential for coalition is increasing although serious problems remain. Antonio Villaraigosa defeated incumbent James Hahn, in part by making significant inroads into Hahn's previous solid support among Black voters. In the 2001 contest between these same two candidates, Hahn won 80 percent of the Black vote. During the 2005 campaign, Villaraigosa undertook extensive outreach efforts designed to overcome the history of Black–Brown rivalries over jobs, housing, and political power, including several visits to Black churches. He was endorsed by a prominent group of Black supporters that included

"Magic" Johnson and US Rep. Maxine Waters. This collaboration may be the prototype for a new kind of multiracial coalition, with Latinos in the lead and with African Americans playing a key role along with White liberals and Jews.

At the national level, as of this writing, the most recent flash point affecting Black–Latino relations were comments made about Blacks by Mexican president Vicente Fox in May 2005. In defending the positive impact of Mexican immigrants on the US, he asserted that Mexican immigrants were taking jobs that even Blacks would not do. This assessment was received with outrage by many traditional Black leaders, and Fox was forced to backtrack, although he refused to apologize formally even after separate meetings with Revs. Jesse Jackson and Al Sharpton. If this controversy could produce a commitment for ongoing discussion and exploration of strategies to pursue mutual interests, the likelihood of developing stronger Black–Latino coalitions in specific urban areas could be enhanced.

Despite the intransigence of these and other barriers to Black–Latino collaboration, a focused effort to overcome them must be undertaken if the foundation for a viable future for both populations is to be constructed. Blacks and Hispanics/Latinos need to develop strategies to maximize access to the social services necessary to support stable communities in the next century. Such a strategy must have at least three components: (a) organizing and funding self-provision of social services, (b) lobbying local government agencies to provide services equitably, and (c) undertaking political action and community education to increase the priority assigned to social services. The incident with President Fox emphasizes that efforts to build Black–Latino coalitions must conceptualize the project in global rather than simply national or local terms.

Recognition of the need for systematic evaluation of potential Black–Latino coalitions harks back at least to the mid-1990s. A conference involving Black, Mexican American, and Puerto Rican American academics and activists on "Urban Challenges for Blacks and Latinos in the 1990s: Strategies of Contention and Collaboration" was held at the University of Illinois at Chicago's Center for Urban Economic Development in September 1995. This meeting produced the volume *The Collaborative City: Opportunities and Struggles for Blacks and Latinos in U.S. Cities, in 2000*, and offers a variety of well-researched analyses of the potential and difficulties associated with developing viable Black–Latino coalitions.[191] Additional initiatives of this type will be required to provide the foundation for successful Black–Latino coalitions.

New Approaches to Electoral and Movement Politics

The viability of Black political initiatives in the twenty-first century may not be as critically dependent on coalescing with external groups as on developing strategies to address the increasing diversity of political interests among Blacks. Not only is there a need to mediate the traditional ideological schism between Black liberals and Black power/nationalists, it is also crucial to engage the issues advanced by Black conservatives and Black radical groups. Moreover, as suggested previously, there are the unresolved issues of the gender divide in political engagement and the generational divide between Civil Rights generation cohorts and the Hip-Hop generation. Unless these political fault lines receive attention, they are likely to widen and significantly erode the potential for collective action.

The potential for deeper splits is evidenced by the plans of Black conservative ministers to expand their political engagement beyond that undertaken during the 2004 election. There is a continuing effort to promote a so-called Black Contract With America on Moral Values. This is an effort to promote biblical-based action by government and churches to promote conservative priorities including banning same-sex marriages and abortions and expanding school vouchers. The Black Contract is loosely patterned on then-House Speaker Newt Gingrich's "Contract With America" of the mid-1990s. The "Mayflower Compact for Black America" Movement has similar objectives and plans to organize in key states ahead of the future elections.

Black conservative religion-based activism is being challenged by Black ministers who subscribe to the traditional consensus regarding the requirements for full citizenship. The presidents of four Black Baptist denominations with 15 million members have agreed to move towards a common agenda and a set of positions that include a higher minimum wage, cancellation of recent tax cuts, investment in public education, reauthorization of the Voting Rights Act of 1965, a moratorium on the privatization of prisons, reinvestment in children's health insurance, and increased global relief for Black nations, such as Sudan and Haiti.

In May 2005, Minister Louis Farrakhan and Revs. Jesse Jackson and Al Sharpton announced joint plans to hold another mass march on Washington. The "Millions More March" held on October 10, 2005 was designed, in part, to commemorate the tenth anniversary of the Million Man March of 1995. Unlike its predecessor, the Millions More March included both men and women, in response to one of the critiques of the earlier effort. The planners also assured potential supporters that there would be systematic follow-up activities, a major criticism levied against the 1995 venture. The timing of this initiative, coming in the aftermath of the Katrina debacle, signals to the US body politic that there is an ongoing liberation struggle being waged by politically-conscious segments of Black communities. However, the fact that the principal organizers are members of the traditional male Civil Rights era shows that the effort is not responsive to the disproportionate role of Black women in Black politics and the need to engage younger Blacks in the freedom struggle.

In the electoral arena, controversial votes by some Black Members of the US House of Representatives signal a need to make Black politicians more accountable between elections to their constituencies. One strategy, similar to that used by various watchdog groups, would involve the regular publication and interpretation in the Black popular media of the votes on key issues affecting Black communities, coupled with demands by activists that legislators provide a justification for votes that appear not to represent the interests of their constituents. More generally, there are important lessons to be learned from the tactics used by conservative and progressive political action committees (PACs) during the 2004 elections. The progressive organization Move-On was virtually the only visible force challenging conservative domination of the political advertising landscape. Move-On was able to raise funds to mount a very effective campaign, largely through electronic solicitations. There is an urgent need to form a progressive Black PAC that can develop and broadcast political education advertisements on a regular basis to maintain Black engagement with the electoral process between political campaigns.

Local Black elected officials, especially mayors, need to become better versed on how globalization processes—such as dispersal of Blacks through gentrification of inner city neighborhoods and the suburban isolation of poor Blacks—are hampering efforts to improve the lives of their constituents. Community self-reliance

6

should be emphasized rather than an unthinking pursuit of multinational firms with no community loyalties. Self-reliance, according to Michael Shuman, should be a legitimate objective of local government regulation, as much as local health, safety, and environmental protection should be. Black elected officials should also embrace the aims of the environmental racism and environmental justice movements that advocate redevelopment policies that are in balance with nature, honor the cultural integrity of communities, and provide fair access for all to the full range of resources. For example, existing transportation policies (highways, light rail networks, and other suburban-friendly public transportation modes) disadvantage inner city residents, not only in terms of services provided, but also through the disproportionate health hazards associated with pollution from transport modes such as buses that burn diesel fuel.

Black elected officials must also support living wages in their communities that will require employers to raise the pay of low-wage workers sufficiently to enable them to escape poverty. More generally, Black elected officials at all levels should join coalitions that attempt to ensure that global trade agreements are not structured in ways that lead to the destruction of local corporations that are friendly to communities. Michael Shuman insists that "the most insidious feature of the WTO [World Trade Organization] is that it systematically strips communities of powers they could otherwise use to protect themselves against the adverse effect of the global economy, and to promote community corporations," yet few community leaders are aware of its power and reach.[192]

International Politics

Historical Perspectives

Alvin Tillery has argued that the engagement of African Americans in the US with foreign policy is "fundamentally bound up with their activities in the domestic environment."[193] At the same time, Ronald Walters has argued convincingly that this engagement has also been directed toward promoting "foreign policy justice."[194] Understandably, Africa has always been the primary geographical area of concern, with the issues of enslavement, colonization, and neo-colonialism dominating the agenda at various periods in history. The enduring focus of African Americans in the US on Africa and the Diaspora has been fueled by perceptions of a shared ancestral heritage. However, as Tillery clearly documents, the manner in which this legacy has been interpreted has shifted over time and has varied among individuals and across socio-economic classes, organizations, and ideological orientation.[195]

At various points in time, individual African Americans have operated in the international arena outside the framework of formal government and non-governmental organizations. This has been especially true during periods when official government policies actively, or passively, supported the oppression of people of African descent. One example, the successful repatriation of formerly enslaved Blacks to Africa by Black shipbuilder Paul Cuffee, was mentioned in Chapter 3. When Cuffee returned to the US to recruit additional emigrants, he encountered resistance from many "free" Blacks, because a White organization, the American Colonization Society (ACS), had co-opted the repatriation initiative while he was abroad.[196] The ACS initiative drew suspicion from free Blacks who perceived it as a means to maintain slavery and remove a quasi-free population that complicated the political discourse.

The founding of Liberia, mentioned in Chapter 3, was initiated by the ACS and President James Madison arranged public funding for the group despite large-scale protests by free Blacks.[197] When Liberia declared independence in 1847 Britain was the first nation to extend formal recognition. Notably, the United States delayed recognition until 1862 because of fears of the impact this might have on the issue of slavery domestically and the objections some might have to the presence of Black diplomats in Washington.[198]

During the Civil War era, and subsequently, African Americans attempted to regain the initiative in exploring opportunities to relocate to Africa. Martin Delany attempted to establish a state for African Americans in Africa via negotiations with indigenous leaders and by self-organizing among Blacks. He led an exploration party to the Niger Delta in 1859 to identify a feasible location for a settlement and signed an agreement with local leaders who permitted settlers to live on "unused land" in return for using their skills for the community's good. Unfortunately, the treaty was later dissolved due to warfare in the region, opposition by White missionaries, and the advent of the US Civil War.[199]

After Delany became a customs inspector in Charleston, South Carolina, in 1873, he became an active supporter of the Liberian Exodus Joint Stock Steamship Company, established in 1877 as an organization which arranged transport of emigrants to Liberia. Delany served as chairman of the finance committee, and in 1878, the company purchased a ship—the *Azor*—for the voyage. Delany served as president of the board as planning proceeded for the voyage, and two hundred six emigrants departed on the voyage, with the majority establishing permanent residence in Liberia. Unfortunately, due to financial hardships, the company was forced to sell the *Azor* after it returned to Charleston.[200]

Bishop Henry McNeal Turner also promoted emigration during this period. However, unlike Delany, Turner channeled much of his advocacy through the White-controlled ACS. Turner was roundly attacked in the Black press when he supported an unsuccessful 1890 bill that would have provided federal aid to US Blacks migrating to Liberia (Delany had also supported this bill). Understandably, many Blacks suffering under post-Reconstruction oppression in the South wanted to explore emigration options, but Black elites staunchly opposed this approach to confronting institutional racism.

The tug-of-war over Liberian emigration was complicated by the appointment of US Blacks as liaisons to the Liberian government. President Grant appointed James Milton Turner as Minister to Liberia in 1871. Turner incurred the anger of Liberia's leaders (emigrants from the US) because of his opposition to emigration. Turner accused the Liberian government of colluding with the ACS to suppress information about the poor conditions experienced by emigrants. Turner left the post and returned to the US in 1878. President Garfield continued the pattern of appointing US Blacks as Ministers of Liberia when Henry Highland Garnet was chosen in 1881. Although Garnet subsequently moved to Liberia, he died two months after arrival.[201]

In a broader context, as Ronald Walters observed, "when African Americans became government officials in the foreign policy establishment, they exercised opposition to what they considered regressive American policies, but their position meant that they also had to become midwives of policies their government demanded should be carried out."[202] Walters notes that this dilemma "often created a conflict between the progressive intentions of such officials and their official roles."[203] Walters informs us that the first African American representative in foreign affairs appointed by a president was Ebenezer Bassett. Bassett was appointed Ambassador to Haiti in 1869 by President Grant.[204]

Tillery argues that the ascendancy of Booker T. Washington as anointed spokesperson for Black interests in 1895 effectively shelved the emigration issue until the emergence of Marcus Garvey.[205] Instead of emigration from the US, the partitioning of Africa by European colonial powers initiated by the Berlin Conference of 1884-1885 shaped the trajectory of the engagement of US Blacks with African issues for the first 60 years of the 20th century.

Bishop Henry McNeal Turner played a pivotal role in mobilizing early opposition to European colonialism by organizing a major conference in 1893. He, along with other prominent African Americans, participated in another major conference in 1895. These meetings were precursors to the Pan-African meeting held in London in 1900, organized by West Indian lawyer Henry Sylvester Williams. Although W. E. B. Du Bois was not initially involved in planning this meeting, he played a prominent role, serving as chair of the committee that drafted the address titled, "To the Nations of the World." This manifesto demanded that the colonial European powers institute reforms in their treatment of Africans. Although the address was largely ignored by the colonizers, the meeting set in motion an ongoing Pan-African Movement focused on the liberation of colonized Africans, in which Blacks in the US would be actively involved.[206]

The end of World War I spurred Du Bois to organize the first Pan-African Congress held in Paris in 1919 partly as an effort to influence deliberations at the Versailles Peace Conference. He had received support from the NAACP in pursuing this initiative. Funding for the meeting was supplied by various US Black civil rights and fraternal organizations, including the NAACP, the Elks, and the Masons. In addition to Du Bois, several prominent African Americans from the US attended, including John Hope, President of Morehouse College, and noted historian, Rayford Logan. Several Black American organizations also attempted to impact the outcomes of the Versailles Conference, including the UNIA, the Hamitic League, and the International League of Darker Peoples.[207]

Brenda Plummer asserts that "the interwar epoch witnessed the contemporary world taking shape in the increased industrialization and urbanization of the black population."[208] She maintains that "the black college, the black church, the black press, and black organizations

6

proved to be not only tools of civil rights insurgency, but also building blocks to construct an emancipatory view of race in the global setting."[209]

The Pan-African Congress reconvened in London in August 1921 and in Brussels in September of the same year. Participants denounced both imperialism in Africa and racism in the United States and demanded local self-government for colonial subjects. Subsequent 1923 meetings in London and Lisbon addressed the conditions of the African Diaspora, as well as the global exploitation of Black workers. Two hundred eight delegates from twenty-two American states and ten foreign countries reconvened for another Pan-African Congress in New York in 1927.[210]

Ethiopia moved to center stage in the minds of internationally-focused African Americans in the wake of the Italian invasion in 1935. Italy had previously attempted unsuccessfully to colonize Ethiopia in the late 1880s. The Black press was instrumental in mobilizing awareness of Italy's second attempt at colonization. Efforts were initiated under the auspices of the African Legion and the International Black League to recruit volunteers to fight on behalf of Ethiopia. Although thousands attended rallies in support of Ethiopia, Tillery concludes that "very few blacks were willing to give up their US citizenship or risk imprisonment by violating the neutrality laws."[211] A group of African Americans, organized under the auspices of the Lincoln Brigade, went to Spain in 1936 to fight Fascism. Many Brigade members had wanted to go to Ethiopia to fight Mussolini's army.[212]

The Council on African Affairs (CAA), formerly the International Committee on African Affairs, was established in 1937 as a lobbying group opposing colonialism. Black YMCA field secretary, Max Yergan, formed the inter-racial organization, and the founding members included Paul Robeson, Ralph Bunche, and President Mordecai Johnson of Howard University.[213]

Penny Von Eschen suggests that the "global dynamics unleashed by World War II generated expanded discourse among U.S. African Americans regarding linkages to people of African descent around the world."[214] At the same time, the financial crisis induced by the Great Depression and the military exigency generated by World War II necessitated the suspension of the Pan-African Congress for a period of eighteen years.

The Pan-African Movement was revived in Manchester, England, in 1945, and Du Bois was named as president of the conference. Congress participants unequivocally demanded an end to colonialism in Africa and encouraged the use of strikes and boycotts to end exploitation by colonial powers. The final declaration urged colonial and subject peoples of the world to unite and assert their rights to reject those seeking to control their destinies. This politically assertive stance was supported by a new generation of African American activists, including the actor and singer Paul Robeson, the minister and politician Adam Clayton Powell, and the educator and political activist William Hunton, Jr.[215]

In June of the next year, the CAA organized a mass gathering attended by 15,000 people "to demonstrate to the Truman administration and fledgling United Nations the depth of support within U.S. civil society for policies that would hasten decolonization in Africa."[216] The U.N. was also viewed as a potential agent for addressing the condition of American Blacks. In October 1947 the NAACP filed a petition in the United Nations entitled "An Appeal to the World," that protested the treatment of Blacks in the United States. W.E.B. Du Bois was the principal author of this petition, which was rejected by the UN Commission on Human Rights in December 1947. This petition was endorsed by some 36 domestic organizations, including several Black fraternities and sororities, the National Council of Negro Women, and the National Baptist Convention. Fifteen African and non-American Diasporan organizations also endorsed the petition.[217]

The CAA went into rapid decline after being targeted by the Truman administration's anti-Communist crusade. The CAA had a long record of cooperation with the Communist Party-USA and Paul Robeson, who served as chair of the CAA executive committee, was an avowed Marxist. Even after Du Bois joined the organization and assumed a leadership role in 1948 following his expulsion from the NAACP, the organization was unable to maintain its viability and went out of existence in 1955.[218]

The advocacy undertaken by the CAA was taken up by other organizations. The American Committee on Africa was formed in 1953 to support African liberation struggles against colonialism. Its activities included lobbying the United Nations and US government officials, publishing pamphlets and a magazine, and reporting on liberation struggles for both the public and policy-making audiences. Bayard Rustin, Martin Luther King, Jr. and Eleanor Roosevelt all played important roles in the organization's campaigns.[219]

Efforts to bring attention to the plight of US Blacks also continued in international forums. In 1951, William Patterson, Chairman of the Civil Rights Congress (CRC), delivered a petition to the United Nations Committee on Human Rights in Geneva, Switzerland, claiming that the US government was complicit in genocide against African Americans. The petition, titled "We Charge Genocide," included documentation of 153 killings and other human rights abuses that occurred between 1945-1951.[220]

Penny Von Eschen asserts that a "severing of international and domestic politics in the early Cold War and the silencing of anti-imperialist and anticapitalist politics" muted African American engagement in the anti-colonial struggle in the 1950s.[221] Moreover, Plummer reports that at the end of the 1950s only about "two dozen Afro-Americans in the Foreign Service Staff Corp" and they "remained relegated to the Canary Islands, Africa, or other hardship posts."[222]

Ronald Williams insists that "because Ghana's independence (and that of the numerous nation-states that won their freedom struggles shortly thereafter) coincided with the civil rights movement under way in the United States, many African Americans began to reconceptualize the African continent and their relationship to it."[223] The 1961 assassination of Prime Minister Patrice Lumumba of the Congo sparked a demonstration in a UN Security Council meeting by 85 persons that included several public figures, such as Max Roach, Abby Lincoln, and Maya Angelou.[224] Ironically, Ralphe Bunche, who was then serving as UN Undersecretary for Special Political Affairs, felt compelled to deliver a speech the next day apologizing for the demonstration.[225] Bunche's route to this position included a stint as adviser to the US Department of State and to the military on Africa and colonial areas of strategic military importance during World War II, analyst in the Office of Strategic Services, and Acting Chief of the Division of Dependent Area Affairs in the US State Department. Bunche had been awarded the Nobel Peace Prize in 1950 for his role as a mediator between Israel and the Arab States.[226]

Martin Luther King, Jr., A. Phillip Randolph, Whitney Young, James Farmer, and Dorothy Height formed the American Negro Leadership Conference on Africa (ANLC) in 1962.[227] According to Plummer, the group's platform included "a 'Marshall Plan for Africa,' more black foreign service appointments, sanctions against South Africa, and firm support for new governments and liberation movements."[228] When these demands were issued, "there were no black American desk officers in USAID, the State Department (including the Bureau of African affairs), or any other agency related to foreign policy."[229] Plummer reports that the ANLC successfully linked segregation and apartheid in South Africa and forced "the U.S. Navy to cancel calls at South African ports."[230]

Ronald Williams describes the Organization for African American Unity (OAAU) as the "first effort in the 1960s to mobilize African Americans around a Pan-Africanist nationalist program."[231] He observes that "the OAAU's preeminence as a 1960s Pan-African nationalist organization is particularly notable in light of the dominant integrationist dogma of the civil rights movement."[232] Ronald Williams also discusses the international activities of Robert Williams' Revolutionary Action Movement and Amiri Baraka's Congress of African People.

US Black groups were able to unite across the political ideological spectrum in fighting for the eradication of South African apartheid. Williams argues that "the crystallization of the integrationist, nationalist, and Pan-Africanist camps... enabled anti-apartheid to evolve into a worldwide movement, started initially by African Americans, but evolving into a cause around which people of all races and nationalities rallied."[233]

Ronald Williams avers that the Congressional Black Caucus (CBC), founded in 1971, played a pivotal role in fueling the Anti-apartheid Movement in the 1970s and 1980s. He concludes that the CBC and its Members "served as the foundation for the formal involvement of African Americans in U.S. foreign policy" and "gave birth to TransAfrica, the institutionalized African American foreign policy lobby that would advocate issues related to Africa and the Caribbean."[234]

TransAfrica, founded by Randall Robinson, was especially instrumental in organizing opposition to US policy via daily protests outside the South African Embassy, undertaken under the auspices of the Free South Africa Movement (FSAM). Between 1984 and the enactment of sanctions legislation in October 1986, approximately six thousand people were arrested while picketing the South African embassy and consulates. Demonstrators included eighteen members of the US House of Representatives and one US Senator. Because of his involvement in one of the protests, former Sen. Lowell Weicker of Connecticut became the

6

first senator in US history to be arrested for an act of civil disobedience.[235]

Then-President Reagan had been following a policy of "Constructive Engagement" that emphasized evolutionary change pursued through non-confrontational mechanisms and that recognized common strategic interests of the United States and South Africa. These interests were promoted as a justification for unilateral action, as opposed to multilateral approaches through organs like the United Nations.[236] Following the lead of some of his predecessors, Reagan attempted to use Black representation as a means to neutralize opposition. He tapped Black career foreign services officer William Perkins as Ambassador to South Africa in 1986, and Perkins served in this role from 1987 to 1990. Perkins had joined the Foreign Service in 1972 and had previously served in various posts in African countries.[237]

With the support of the FSAM, Tillery recounts that "in 1986, the CBC engineered the passage of the Comprehensive Anti-Apartheid Act over Ronald Reagan's veto."[238] He claims that "this was the first time in U.S. history that a racial or ethnic minority successfully challenged the authority of a sitting president on a foreign policy issue and won."[239]

The activities of the Rev. Leon Sullivan to combat apartheid, undertaken under the auspices of the International Council for Equality of Opportunity Principles (ICEOP), are less well-known. He formulated the Sullivan Principles (The Principles), a corporate code of conduct formally announced in 1977, as an effort to influence the behavior of multinational corporations operating in South Africa. Sullivan's effort drew heavily on the traditions of domestic Black political activism and on his experience in creating and operating Opportunities Industrialization Centers of America (OIC), a major community-based organization providing employment preparation services.[240]

Sullivan was eventually forced to withdraw his support for The Principles as the South African government remained intransigent and The Principles became linked, in the public view, to Reagan's constructive engagement policies. In June 1987, he called for withdrawal of all United States companies from the Republic of South Africa, and for a total United States embargo against South Africa, until statutory apartheid was ended, and Blacks have a clear commitment for equal political rights.[241]

South Africa was not the only African country that received the attention of American Black elites during the 1970s and 1980s. President Jimmy Carter appointed Andrew Young to serve as the United States Ambassador to the United Nations. Young became the first African-American to serve in the position and was instrumental in achieving a settlement in Rhodesia between antagonists Robert Mugabe and Joshua Nkomo. The settlement enabled Mugabe to take power as Prime Minister of Zimbabwe. Young was forced from this position in August 1979 after meeting with representatives of the Palestine Liberation Organization.[242]

The grassroots strategies implemented by Randall Robinson and Leon Sullivan have survived and continue to serve as a linkage between American Blacks and Blacks in Africa and non-American Diasporan communities. Ronald Williams concludes that "TransAfrica remains a force in organizing prominent African Americans around issues related to Africa and African Diaspora."[243] Continuing, he relates that "the group continues to coordinate African American foreign policy efforts toward Africa, the Caribbean, and Latin America, through protest activities, policy briefs, and position papers."

Subsequent to his withdrawal of support of The Principles, Sullivan focused his efforts on expanding the work of the International Foundation for Education and Self-Help (IFESH), which he founded in 1981. The mission of IFESH is to support African nations in their efforts to eradicate poverty, disease, and inequity through self-help partnership programs, and, as of 2009, there were IFESH programs operating in 12 sub-Saharan African countries.[244] In effect, IFESH represents the extension of the domestic OIC development model to the international arena.

Sullivan organized the first of what is now termed the Leon H. Sullivan Summits in 1991. The biennial Summit serves as a means to foster cooperation among leaders throughout the Diaspora. Each Summit is hosted by a different African country. Continuing the vision that guided the original vision of the Sullivan Principles, the key strategic objective of the Summit is to foster corporate investments on the African continent.[245] However, just as important is the fact that the Summit has provided an unparalleled opportunity for African American activists and political figures to establish direct linkages, laying the foundation for international activism.

The circle that began with the enunciation of the original Sullivan Principles was completed when Rev. Sullivan and then UN Secretary-General Kofi Annan formally introduced the Global Sullivan Principles of Social Responsibility (GSP) at a special session at the United Nations headquarters in 1999. Like the original Sullivan Principles, the GSP constitute a voluntary code of conduct, and over 120 companies, including most signatories to the original Principles, are endorsers.[246] In essence, the GSP restates the original objectives of the Sullivan Principles while broadening their applicability beyond South Africa and modifying them to reflect the contemporary challenges of globalization. The website of the Leon H. Sullivan Foundations indicates: "The objectives of the Global Sullivan Principles are to support economic, social and political justice by companies where they do business; to support human rights and to encourage equal opportunity at all levels of employment, including racial and gender diversity on decision making committees and boards; to train and advance disadvantaged workers for technical, supervisory and management opportunities; and to assist with greater tolerance and understanding among peoples; thereby, helping to improve the quality of life for communities, workers and children with dignity and equality."[247]

Sullivan was not alone in recognizing the importance of focusing attention on building strong economic linkages in response to global economic developments. Prior to his appointment as Secretary of Commerce during President Clinton's first administration (the first African American to hold this position), Ronald (Ron) Brown brought attention to this issue after a visit to sub-Saharan Africa in 1990. He emphasized the importance of trade and investment and led several trade missions to Africa, including one to South Africa, a few days after sanctions were lifted by the United States.[248] He also opened a US commercial center in South Africa, now named after him; opened and expanded commercial offices in regional hubs throughout Africa; and supported the passage of the African Growth and Opportunity Act (AGOA). Unfortunately, Brown perished, along with 34 other passengers, in a 1996 plane crash in Croatia. Brown's legacy continues through various initiatives including an annual African Affairs Lecture Series and the Bay Area Africa Initiative, whose main goals are to create a better business climate in African countries, improve the perception of Africa in the Bay Area, and increase Bay Area business engagement in Africa.[249]

William Jones reports that "between 1996 and 1998, the Africa Growth and Opportunity Act began to take form as one of the most significant African policy initiatives in the post-civil rights, post-Southern African liberation, and post-Cold War era."[250] The Act, which guides economic and trade policy toward Africa, was signed into law by then President Clinton in 2000 and has subsequently has been expanded and extended through 2015.[251] Jones relates that the CBC supported the legislation, "although without the level of unanimity historically accompanying issues related to Africa and domestic racial issues."[252]

Jones observes that "the impact and success of the AGOA remain a matter of contention," noting that the "U.S. foreign policy establishment and the supporters of the AGOA maintain that the act had led to marked progress in the economic development of participant African states."[253] In contrast, Jones relates that "TransAfrica assesses the impact of the AGOA as negative because of its view that sweatshops and associated environmental problems have proliferated."[254] Another watchdog organization, Africa Action, "believes that the negative impact of other financial institutions such as the International Monetary Fund and the World Bank far outweighs the benefits of the AGOA."[255]

Ronald Williams aptly suggests that "the appointments of [Colin] Powell and [Condoleeza] Rice as secretary of state by Republican administrations... complicate notions of solidarity among African Americans in debates about U.S. foreign policy toward Africa."[256] Charles Henry is much more direct, asserting that "Although both have linked their racial experiences to their work, neither... raised the status of Africa (excluding Egypt) as a foreign policy priority or moved aggressively to solve any of the continent's many problems."[257] From this perspective, it is instructive to compare their inaction with the proactive posture of Ron Brown as Secretary of Commerce during the first Clinton administration. Moreover, Henry decries the fact that Powell and Rice were "the most visible spokespersons for a foreign policy that many Africans and many African Americans reject."[258] Henry is particularly critical of Rice, lamenting that she even "backed away from Powell's declaration of genocide in Rwanda," opposed "any resolutions dealing with environment and human rights concerns in Nigeria," and "undercut Haiti's Aristide by threatening Jamaica and other Caribbean governments that offered to harbor him."[259]

The Obama Era

Then-Secretary of State, Hillary Clinton outlined the Africa policy of the Obama administration in a January 2009 presentation to the Senate Foreign Relations

6

Committee. Clinton indicated that the Obama administration's foreign policy objectives for Africa focus on security and include "combating al-Qaida's efforts to seek safe havens in failed states in the Horn of Africa; helping African nations to conserve their natural resources and reap fair benefits from them; stopping war in Congo; [and] ending autocracy in Zimbabwe and human devastation in Darfur."[260] Susan Rice, who was confirmed as the US Permanent Representative to the U.N. in January 2009 and named National Security Advisor in 2013, has played an important role in shaping this policy. Rice served as US Assistant Secretary of State for African Affairs from 1997-2001 in the Clinton administration. Johnnie Carson serves as US Assistant Secretary of State for African Affairs in the Obama Administration.

In June 2012, President Obama released a major policy directive entitled, "U.S. Strategy Toward Sub-Saharan Africa."[261] This document essentially reaffirms the policies set forth in the 2009 declaration. Among other accomplishments, it touts investments in development partnerships to foster sustained economic growth, promote food security, increase resilience to climate change, and improve the capacity of countries and communities to address HIV/AIDS, malaria, and other health threats. The report also notes that Africa is the focus of three key presidential development initiatives: the Global Health Initiative, Feed the Future, and the Global Climate Change Initiative. Unfortunately, there has been relatively limited-action engagement with African countries in most of these areas in comparison to other countries, especially China. Ironically, Obama has been less engaged with Africa than either of his two immediate predecessors, former Presidents Clinton and Bush. President Obama did not undertake a major visit to African countries until June 2013, when he and his family visited Senegal, South Africa, and Tanzania.

African American Studies specialists should take special note of the discussion of peace and security issues in the Obama administration's documents. The report declares that the US played a major role "in the birth of South Sudan, supporting the African Union Mission in Somalia, and working with regional partners to counter the predatory Lord's Resistance Army." Although not discussed directly, it is important to recognize that the United States Africa Command, AFRICOM, is one of the key ingredients in the implementation of the administration's Africa policy. AFRICOM is one of six Defense Department regional military headquarters and was declared a fully unified command on

October 1, 2008. The stated mission of AFRICOM is to collaborate with other US government agencies and international partners to conduct "sustained security engagement through military-to-military programs, military-sponsored activities, and other military operations as directed to promote a stable and secure African environment in support of U.S. foreign policy." AFRICOM is based in Germany because no African country has been willing to serve as a host for this operation.[262]

A number of organizations have raised alarms regarding the formation of AFRICOM and the implications for the militarization of Africa in connection with the "War Against Terror" and competition for African resources. As an example, ResistAFRICOM is one of the more visible campaigns comprised of concerned U.S- and Africa-based organizations and individuals opposed to AFRICOM. According to ResistAFRICOM, the Pentagon is attempting to increase access to Africa's oil and to wage a new front in the Global War on Terror without regard for the needs or desires of African people. ResistAFRICOM maintains that AFRICOM is in league with major oil companies and private military contractors and serves as the latest frontier in military expansionism, violating the human rights and civil liberties of Africans.[263]

Some critics of AFRICOM also charge that it will become a major tool in attempting to neutralize the growing influence of China in Africa. Africa registered 5.8 percent economic growth in 2007, its highest level ever, in part because of Chinese investment. Experts say the roads, bridges, and dams built by Chinese firms are low cost, of good quality, and were completed in a fraction of the time such projects usually take in Africa. China has cancelled $10 billion in bilateral debt from African countries, sends doctors to treat Africans across the continent, and hosts thousands of African workers and students in Chinese universities and training centers. In return for these development projects, China has been able to obtain long-term contractual access to major oil supplies needed to fuel its continuously expanding economy. Several concerns about China's role in Africa have been voiced by a range of people—from human rights groups to international observers to Africans themselves. These concerns include charges that Chinese companies underbid local firms and do not hire and train African workers. It is reported that Chinese infrastructure deals often stipulate that up to 70 percent of the labor must be Chinese.[264]

African American Studies specialists resonate with the critiques of AFRICOM and are especially wary of the potential "recolonization" of Africa as an element of a new superpower conflict. Externally supported military interventions in Cote d'Ivoire and Libya in 2011 heighten these concerns, although both were undertaken by multi-national forces rather than unilaterally by the US. In contrast to the robust opposition to colonialism and apartheid in South Africa in previous eras, voices of dissent by American Blacks against African militarization policy has been relatively muted. Ironically, one precedent that may have contributed to this lack of dissent is "Operation Restore Democracy," the September 1994 invasion of Haiti by US troops that returned to power Jean-Bertrand Aristide, the elected president who had been overthrown three years earlier in a bloody military coup. Charles Henry concludes that pressure from TransAfrica and the Congressional Black Caucus probably had a significant effect on the decision to intervene militarily.[265]

Africa is also experiencing another form of colonialism—hydro-colonialism. There is currently a major land rights grab occurring in many African countries by multinational corporations based in several countries. These land deals involve large-scale, industrial agriculture operations that will consume massive amounts of water. Nearly all are located in major river basins with access to irrigation. They occupy fertile and fragile wetlands, or are located in more arid areas that can draw water from major rivers. In some cases, the farms directly access ground water by pumping it up. These water resources are lifelines for local farmers, pastoralists and other rural communities. Many already lack sufficient access to water for their livelihoods. Citigroup insists that in the not-so-distant future, water will become "the single most important physical-commodity based asset class, dwarfing oil, copper, agricultural commodities and precious metals."[266]

Notably, several of the major targets of these land acquisition moves are countries where recent political unrest has been prevalent. Approximately 5 million hectares have been leased to foreign interests in Egypt, Sudan and South Sudan since 2006. Other countries targeted in this hydro-colonialism scheme include Cameroon, Kenya, Mali, Mozambique, Senegal, and Tanzania.

Combatting the New Colonialism and Promoting 21st Century Pan-Africanism

Recent developments strongly indicate that even under the Obama administration, the US government cannot be viewed as a strong opponent of contemporary neo-colonialism in Africa. Moreover, existing efforts by non-governmental organizations appear insufficient to influence current policy. And engagement by US Blacks in international affairs, including African affairs, has declined markedly from previous eras.

From the vantage point of African American Studies, there is a need to catalyze the reconnection of domestic and international politics with respect to the circumstances of people of African descent. In the words of Charles Henry, what is needed is a new self-critical Pan-Africanism "that includes the 150 million South Americans of African descent."[267] Fortunately, the infrastructure to produce such a transnational consciousness and political movement is being created. Minion K.C. Morrison has summarized the deliberations of the first two meetings of the Legislative Caucus of Afro-Descendant Legislators in the Americas that occurred in 2003 and 2004. The goals established for the initial meeting included raising the visibility of socioeconomic conditions confronting Afro-descendants in the Western hemisphere, creating a network of Afro-descendant legislators and civil society organizations dedicated to Afro-descendant communities in the hemisphere, and elaborating a legislative plan of action to promote racial equality.[268]

Actions taken by the African Union (AU) have created space for members of the African Diaspora in the Western hemisphere to become more directly involved in shaping Africa's future. The AU defines the African continent as being divided into six geographical regions — North Africa, South Africa, West Africa, East Africa, Central Africa, and the African Diaspora (the sixth region).

As described by David Horne, Article 3(q) of the AU's amended Constitutive Act, "invite(s) and encourage(s) the full participation of the African Diaspora as an important part of our continent, in the building of the African Union."[269] Although currently, only the Economic, Social and Cultural Council have designated spaces for 20 members from the Diaspora, in the future "there will be places for the African Diaspora in many other advisory committees, subcommittees and working groups, including, ultimately, the Pan African Parliament, which will pass legislation for the entire continent by approximately 2015."[270]

Consistent with the social responsibility mandate of Africana Studies, specialists should actively support these contemporary Pan-African initiatives and work actively to highlight the linkages between domestic and international struggles against racial oppression.

6

As noted by Elliott Skinner, "knowledge of the attempts of African Americans to use both diplomatic and symbolic means to protect and advance the cause of black nationality, both on the continent of Africa and in the diaspora, is part of the continuing effort by African Americans to achieve full equality in the United States."[271]

Loretta Lynch, the first Black female Attorney General, is sworn in by Vice President Joe Biden using Frederick Douglass's bible (2015.)

US Department of Justice

Questions & Exercises

1. The terms *invisible politics*, *movement politics*, and *electoral politics* have been introduced to identify or typify African American systems of political participation. Describe and analyze each of these methods.

2. Historically and contemporarily, Blacks have benefited from the political cultures of resistance and accommodation. Support, refute, or explain this assertion.

3. What are the essential differences between segregation, separatism, and Black Nationalism in the context of the circumstances facing Blacks in the US?

4. How do Black liberal and conservative philosophies differ or compare with White liberal and conservative philosophies in American politics?

5. Some political theorists suggest that the principles and policies of the Democratic and Republican Parties are becoming indistinguishable relative to the interests of African Americans. Consequently, the idea of a Black independent party has been revived. Discuss the pros and cons of an African American independent political party.

6. Discuss the traditional role of Black newspapers and magazines as information sources. Describe the factors that have diminished this traditional role.

7. Defend or refute the following statement: "Radio and television stations owned or controlled by Blacks should not be overly concerned with providing news and political information because their principal role is to provide entertainment."

8. Research and discuss the invisible role Black women have played in American politics. To what extent is the invisibility of women's politics functioning today?

9. Historically and presently, what benefits have White Americans gained through political coalitions with African Americans? Have such coalitions been mutually and equally rewarding for both parties?

10. Discuss the reasons why alliances formed between organized labor and African Americans have been episodic rather than enduring.

11. How will geopolitics and global economic policies of the twenty-first century affect the social, economic, and political welfare of African Americans?

6

Social Responsibility Projects

1. Organize an on-line political forum to increase political awareness and knowledge of critical events affecting the well-being of African Americans.

2. Conduct a survey to determine the political orientation of your classmates and friends, disseminate the findings and organize a forum to discuss your findings.

3. Organize a letter-writing campaign asking the Governor of your state to increase support for the urban municipalities in your state.

4. Organize your classmates and friends to undertake a voter registration campaign.

5. Organize a letter-writing campaign asking legislators to reject or repeal voter photo identification laws.

6. Organize a letter-writing campaign urging the US Senate to conduct timely reviews of nominations for federal judgeships.

7. Organize or participate in a "get-out-the vote campaign" to provide transportation for voters to travel to the polls.

8. Organize a panel discussion of state legislators to explore strategies to increase support for urban communities in your state. Write letters-to-the-editor or opinion editorials in your college and/or local newspaper discussing political developments affecting African Americans.

9. Organize a panel discussion with representatives of the Embassies of several African and African Daisporan countries to promote greater understanding of common political interests.

NOTES AND REFERENCES

1. C. Rodee, T. Anderson and C. Christol, *Introduction to Political Science* (New York: McGraw-Hill, 1967), 6.
2. M. Jones, "A Frame of Reference for Black Politics," in *Black Political Life in the United States*, ed. L. Henderson (San Francisco: Chandler, 1972), 7.
3. Ibid., 7-8.
4. Jones, "A Frame of Reference for Black Politics," 9.
5. H. Walton, *Black Politics and Black Political Behavior* (Westport, CT: Greenwood, 1996), 5.
6. Ibid.
7. Walton, *Black Politics*, 5-6.
8. H. Walton, *Invisible Politics: The Politics of Black and Tans* (Metuchen, NJ: Scarecrow Press, 1975).
9. G. Tate. *Unknown Tongues: Black Women's Activism in the Antebellum Era, 1830-1860* (East Lansing, MI: Michigan State University Press, 2003).
10. See H. Walton, *Black Politics* (Philadelphia: J.B. Lippincott, 1972), 2, 10.
11. C. Robinson, *Black Movements in America* (New York: Routledge, 1997).
12. J. Grant, ed., *Black Protest: 350 Years of Documents and Analyses* (New York: Fawcett Columbine, 1968).
13. For a historical essay on the lack of Black ideological development, see R. Jones, "In the Absence of Ideology: Blacks in Colonial America and the Modern Black Experience," *Western Journal of Black Studies* 12 (spring 1988): 30-39.
14. See M. Thorne, *American Conservative Thought Since World War II* (New York: Greenwood Press, 1990).
15. See P. Foner, *The Life and Writings of Frederick Douglass*, vol. 4 (New York: International Publishers, 1955).
16. R. Hall, *Black Separation in the United States* (Hanover, NH: University Press of New England, 1978), 1.
17. See J. Turner, "Historical Dialectics of Black Nationalist Movements in America," *Western Journal of Black Studies* 1 (September 1977): 164-183.
18. See R. Rothenberg, *The Neoliberals* (New York: Simon and Schuster, 1984), 45-46.
19. Rothenberg, *The Neoliberals*, 107-08.
20. W. Maddox and S. Lilie, *Beyond Liberal and Conservative* (Washington, D.C.: Cato Institute, 1984), 13-14.
21. Thorne, *American Conservative Thought Since World War II*, 4, 44, 81-82, 89.
22. Maddox and Lilie, *Beyond Liberal and Conservative*, 16.
23. W. Drake, "Black Liberalism, Conservatism and Social Democracy: The Social Policy Debate," *Western Journal of Black Studies* 14 (summer 1990): 118-19.
24. H. Boyd, "Black Conservatives," *Lies of Our Times* 2 (January 1991), 10.
25. G. Tate and L. Randolph, ed., *Dimensions of Black Conservatism in the United States: Made in America* (New York: Palgrave Macmillan, 2002).
26. F. Wilson, "Neoconservatives, Black Conservatives, and the Retreat from Social Justice," in *Dimensions of Black Conservatism in the United States*, ed. Tate and Randolph, 193.
27. Ibid., 193.
28. J. Trotter, *The African American Experience* (Boston, MA: Houghton Mifflin, 2001), 128.
29. J. Scott, *The Black Revolts: Racial Stratification in the U.S.A.: The Politics of Estate, Caste, and Class in the American Society* (Cambridge, MA: Schenkman Publishing, 1976), 80.
30. B. Quarles, *The Negro in the Making of America* (New York: MacMillan, 1964), 88, 92.
31. Tate, *Unknown Tongues*, 17.
32. P. Collins, *Black Feminist Thought: Knowledge, Consciousness and the Politics of Empowerment* (New York: Routledge, 1991).
33. N. Naples, ed., *Community Activism and Feminist Politics: Organizing Across Race, Class, and Gender* (New York: Routledge, 1998).
34. Tate, *Unknown Tongues*, 11.
35. Tate, *Unknown Tongues*, 32.
36. Tate, *Unknown Tongues*, 68.
37. Tate, *Unknown Tongues*, 69.
38. Trotter, *The African American Experience*, 232.
39. Tate, *Unknown Tongues*, p. 85.
40. Trotter, *The African American Experience*, 219.
41. Trotter, *The African American Experience*, 219.
42. C. Harris, "Whiteness as Property," *Harvard Law Review*, 106 (June 1993): 1768.
43. Ibid., 1768, 1775.
44. Walton, *Black Politics*, 86-91.

6

45. See E. Ayres, *The Promise of the New South* (New York: Oxford University Press, 1992), 220.

46. K. Hamilton, *Black Towns and Profit, Promotion and Development in the Trans-Appalachia West, 1877-1915* (Urbana, IL; University of Illinois Press, 1991); see also N. Crockett, *The Black Towns* (Lawrence: University of Kansas Press, 1979).

47. Hamilton, *Black Towns and Profit*, 4.

48. C. Robinson, *Black Movements in America* (New York: Routledge, 1997), 105.

49. "The Niagara Movement Centennial at Harpers Ferry: Ten Questions (and Answers) That Help Explain Why This Meeting is Worth Remembering," National Parks Conservation Association, http://www.npca.org/niagara/q-a.html.

50. Trotter, *The African American Experience*, 337.

51. Ibid., 100.

52. J. Hanson, *Mary McLeod Bethune & Black Women's Political Activism* (Columbia, MO: University of Missouri Press, 2003).

53. Ibid., 9.

54. Hanson, *Mary McLeod Bethune*, 9.

55. Hanson, *Mary McLeod Bethune*, 9.

56. J. Greenberg, "The Capacity of Law to Affect Race Relations," in *Society and the Legal Order*, ed. R. Swartz and J. Skolnick (New York: Basic Books, 1970), 404.

57. Walton, *Black Politics*.

58. See L. Henderson, "Black Politics and American Presidential Elections," in *The New Black Politics*, ed. M. Preston, L. Henderson, and P. Puryear (New York: Longman, 1982), 7-8.

59. C. Hudson-Weems, *Emmett Till: The Sacrificial Lamb of the Civil Rights Movement*, 3rd ed. (Troy, MI: Bedford Publishing, 1994).

60. J. Stewart, foreword to *Emmett Till: The Sacrificial Lamb of the Civil Rights Movement*, xv.

61. Theoharis and Woodward, *Groundwork*, 6.

62. See C. Fager, *White Reflections on Black Power* (W.B. Eerdmans, 1967), 41-43.

63. S. Carmichael, *Stokely Speaks* (New York: Vintage Books, 1971), 18-19.

64. M. Marable, "The Rhetoric of Racial Harmony," *Sojourners* 19 (August/September 1990): 17.

65. Carmichael, *Stokely Speaks*, 19-21.

66. R. Walters, *Black Presidential Politics in America* (New York: State University of New York Press, 1988), 139.

67. See W. Strickland, "The Gary Convention and the Crisis of American Politics," *Black World*, October 1972, 18-23.

68. See T. Seybert, "The Historic Black Press—Overview Essay," The History of Jim Crow, http://www.jimcrowhistory.org/resources/lessonplans/hs_es_black_press.htm.

69. Ibid.

70. T. Seybert, "The Historic Black Press."

71. T. Seybert, "The Historic Black Press."

72. Patrick S. Washburn, *A Question of Sedition: The Federal Government's Investigation of the Black Press During World War II* (New York, Oxford University Press, 1986).

73. T. Seybert, "The Historic Black Press."

74. "NABJ: About NABJ," www.nabj.org/about/v-print/story/10p-8c.html.

75. D. Wickham, ed., *Thinking Black: Some of the Nation's Best Columnists Speak Their Mind* (New York: Three Rivers Press, 1997).

76. A. Bennett, "Making a Way Out of No Way: First, You Have to Find the Capital," *NABJ Journal* 15 (April 1970): 16.

77. A. Muhammad, "Muhammad Speaks: A Trailblazer in the Newspaper Industry," *Final Call*, www.finalcall.com/national/savioursday2k/m_speaks.htm; "The Final Call: Continuing a Tradition," *Final Call*, www.finalcall.com/national/savioursday2k/final_call.htm.

78. See A. Johnson and R. Johnson, *Propaganda and Aesthetics: The Literary Politics of African-American Magazines in the Twentieth Century* (Amherst, MA: University of Massachusetts Press, 1979, 1991).

79. G. Curry, ed., *The Best of Emerge Magazine* (New York: One World/Ballantine, 2003).

80. Ibid., 1.

81. Johnson and Johnson, *Propaganda and Aesthetics*.

82. Johnson and Johnson, *Propaganda and Aesthetics*.

83. D. Joyce, *Black Book Publishers in the United States: A Historical Dictionary of the Presses, 1817-1900* (New York: Greenwood Press, 1991).

84. Joyce, *Black Book Publishers in the United States*, xiv.

85. B. Ward, *Radio and the Struggle for Civil Rights in the South* (Gainesville, FL: University of Florida Press, 2004).

86. Ibid.

87. B. Savage, *Broadcasting Freedom: Radio, War, and the Politics of Race, 1938-1948* (Chapel Hill, NC: University of North Carolina Press, 1999).

88. Ibid.

89. Savage, *Broadcasting Freedom*, 63-64.

90. Savage, *Broadcasting Freedom*, 104.

91. Savage, *Broadcasting Freedom*.

92. See J. Dates and W. Barlow, *Split Image: African Americans in the Mass Media*, 2d ed. (Washington, DC: Howard University Press, 1993).

93. Savage, *Broadcasting Freedom*.

94. Ward, *Radio and the Struggle for Civil Rights in the South*, 179.

95. Ibid.

96. Ward, Radio and the Struggle for Civil Rights, 362.

97. "Many Ways to Pressure Black Radio," *Black Commentator*, E-Mailbox, 46. http://www.blackcommentator.com/46/46_email.html.

98. K. Carrillo, "Air America Will Displace Black Talk on WLIB," SacObserver.com, March 23, 2004, http://www.sacobserver.com/news/032304/wlib_air_america_radio.shtml.

99. C. Squires, "Black Talk Radio: Defining Community Needs and Identity."

100. D. Jones, "Marketing to the Masses Tends to Miss Many: Radio Host Has Pointers for Reaching Black Audience, *USA TODAY*, August 15, 2005, B.3.

101. M. Harris-Lacewell, *Barbershops, Bibles and BET: Everyday Talk and Black Political Thought* (Princeton, NJ: Princeton University Press, 2004), 244.

102. G. Ford and P. Gambel, "America's Black Rightwing Forum: The Grotesque Devolution of a Black News Program," *Black Commentator* 20 (December 2002). http://www.blackcommentator.com/20_commentary_1.html.

103. Scarborough Research, "Hispanics and African-Americans Make Headlines as Avid Viewers of Late Local News," *Scarborough Research* (2005).

104. See www.thefutoncritic.com/news/2013/07/09/tv-one-announces-plans-for-live-daily-morning-news-program-news-one-now-to-be-hosted-by-roland-s-martin-886105/20130709tvone01/ #bbuXDX22OMD2coAx.99.

105. The URL for BlackPlanet.com is http://www.blackplanet.com/. The URL for BlackAmericaWeb.com is www.blackamericaweb.com/. The URL for Black Voices.com is bv.channel.aol.com/.The URL for NewsOne.com is httpnewsone.com/. The URL for BlackNews.com is http://www.blacknews.com/.

106. Harris-Lacewell, *Barbershops, Bibles and BET*, 163.

107. Harris-Lacewell, *Barbershops, Bibles and BET*, 163.

108. A. Semuels, "$1.4 Million in Grants Boost Pitt's Healthy Black Family Project," *Pittsburgh Post Gazette*, August 24, 2005, sec. E, 1, 3.

109. See Kelly McBride, "Trayvon Martin Story Reveals New Tools of Media Power, Justice," Poynte.org, (March 23, 2012), http://www.poynter.org/latest-news/making-sense-of-news/167660/trayvon-martin-story-a-study-in-the-new-tools-of-media-power-justice/. The on-line petition can be found at the following website: http://www.change.org/petitions/prosecute-the-killer-of-our-son-17-year-old-trayvon-martin.

110. Gene Demby, "LeBron James Tweets Picture Of Miami Heat Wearing Hoodies In Solidarity With Family Of Trayvon Martin," *The Huffington Post* (March 23, 2012, http://www.huffingtonpost.com/2012/03/23/lebron-heat-trayvon-tweet_n_1375831.html.

111. See D. St. Angelo and P. Puryear, "Fear, Apathy, and Other Dimensions of Black Voting," in The New Black Politics, ed. Preston et al., 128.

112. J. Pierce and A. Carey, "Efficacy and Participation: A Study of Black Political Behavior," *Journal of Black Studies* (December 1971): 202.

113. See P. Secret and J. Johnson, "Political Efficacy, Political Trust, Race and Electoral Participation," *Western Journal of Black Studies* (summer 1985): 74-83.

114. Ibid., 78.

115. See L. Williams, "Significant Trends in Black Voter Attitudes," *The Black Scholar* 17 (November/December 1986): 24-25.

116. Market Segment Research & Consulting, *The MSR&C Ethnic Market Report: A Portrait of the New America* (Coral Gables, FL: Market Segment Research & Consulting, 1996).

117. Letter to the Honorable Kofi Annan, July 1, 2004. S Schultze, "Campaigns Condemn Political Flier, Paper Aimed at Black Voters Falsely States Voting Rules," JSOnline [Posted: 29 October 29, 2004], journalsentinel.com.

118. David Stout, "Supreme Court Upholds Voter Identification Law in Indiana," New York Times (April 29, 2008), http://www.nytimes.com/2008/04/29/washington/28cnd-scotus.html.

119. Gabriel R. Sanchez, Stephen A. Nuño, and Matt A. Barreto, "The Disproportionate Impact of Photo-ID Laws on the Minority Electorate," (May 24, 2011), http://www.latinodecisions.com/blog/2011/05/24/the-disproportionate-impact-of-stringent-voter-id-laws/.

120. "Felony Costs Voting Rights for a Lifetime in Nine States," *New York Times*, November 3, 2000.

6

121. Shelby County, Alabama v. Holder, Attorney General, et al. Certiorari to the United States Court of Appeals for the District of Columbia Circuit. No. 12–96. Argued February 27, 2013—Decided June 25, 2013, http://www.supremecourt.gov/opinions/12pdf/12-96_6k47.pdf

122. Walters, *Black Presidential Politics in America*, 10.

123. Walters, *Black Presidential Politics in America*, 32.

124. See L. Bennett, *Before the Mayflower* (Chicago: Johnson Publishing, 1962; reprinted by Penguin Books, 1984), 594-97.

125. See A. Reed, *The Jesse Jackson Phenomenon* (New Haven: Yale University Press, 1986).

126. E. Dionne, "Jackson Share of Votes by Whites Triples in '88," *New York Times*, June 13, 1988, A-13.

127. L. Williams, "The 1988 Election in Review," *Focus, Joint Center for Political and Economic Studies* 16, nos. 11&12 (November-December 1988): 3.

128. "National Hip-Hop Team Vote 2008 Campaign to Be Launched in Pennsylvania," (March 16, 2008), http://www.reuters.com/article/2008/03/16/idUS73167+16-Mar-2008+BW20080316.

129. Maria Krysan and Nakesha Faison, "Racial Attitudes in America: A Brief Summary of the Updated Data," http://igpa.uillinois.edu/programs/racial-attitudes/data/white/t33supp.

130. Paul Taylor, " The Growing Electoral Clout of Blacks Is Driven by Turnout, Not Demographics," (December 26, 2012), http://www.pewsocialtrends.org/files/2013/01/2012_Black_Voter_Project_revised_1-9.pdf.

131. "House chastises South Carolina representative who called Obama a liar," (September 15, 2009), http://www.guardian.co.uk/world/deadlineusa/2009/sep/15/usa-democrats.

132. "Offensive email sender censured by OC GOP," (May 4, 2011), http://seattletimes.nwsource.com/html/nationworld/2014964364_apusobamaoffensiveemail.html.

133. Ronald Kessler, *In the President's Secret Service: Behind the Scenes with Agents in the Line of Fire and the Presidents They Protect* (New York: Random House, 2009).

134. The New York Times CBS Poll, "National Survey of Tea Party Supporters, April 5-12, 2010," (2010), http://documents.nytimes.com/new-york-timescbs-news-poll-national-survey-of-tea-party-supporters.

135. "Blacks Upbeat about Black Progress, Prospects: A Year after Obama's Election," (2010) Pew Research Center Publications (January 12), http://pewresearch.org/pubs/1459/year-after-obama-election-black-public-opinion.

136. "Blacks Upbeat about Black Progress, Prospects: A Year after Obama's Election," op. cit.

137. "Expanding Opportunities For African-American Families," President Obama's Fiscal 2010 Budget Overview, *A New Era Of Responsibility: Renewing America's Promise*, http://www.nbcsl.org/PresidentBudget/01_AFAMfactsheet.pdf.

138. Gabriel Winant, "Obama White House Brings Black Women to Power, White House Advisers And Staff Form Strong Support Network," (Mar 18, 2009), http://www.newser.com/story/53645/obama-white-house-brings-black-women-to-power.html.

139. "Obama's push for court diversity hits snag," *USA Today*, June 15, 2010, http://www.usatoday.com/news/washington/judicial/2010-06-15-diversity-lower-courts_N.htm.

140. Donald Lambro, "Black Leaders Open Fire on Obama Over Unemployment," *Freerepublic.com*, March 29, 2013, http://www.freerepublic.com/focus/f-news/3002164/posts.

141. William Douglas, "Black Caucus, Marcia Fudge press White House on high-level appointments," *Washingtonpost.com*, March 24, 2013, http://articles.washingtonpost.com/2013-03-24/politics/37989948_1_immigration-laws-president-obama-obama-white-house.

142. See M. Barnett, "The Congressional Black Caucus and the Institutionalization of Black Politics," *Journal of Afro-American Issues* 5 (summer 1977): 201-27.

143. See L. Guinier, *The Tyranny of the Majority: Fundamental Fairness in Representative Democracy* (New York: The Free Press, 1994).

144. See R. Singh, *The Congressional Black Caucus: Racial Politics in the U.S. Congress* (Thousand Oaks, CA: Sage, 1998).

145. "Black Caucus Losing Cohesion," *The Black Commentator* Issue 135, April 21, 2005, http://www.blackcommentator.com/135/135_cover_black_ caucus.html.

146. "Haley names Tim Scott as DeMint's successor," *CNN.com*, December 17, 2012, http://politicalticker.blogs.cnn.com/2012/12/17/haley-to-announce-demints-replacement-at-noon/.

147. W. Nelson and P. Meranto, *Electing Black Mayors* (Columbus, OH: Ohio State University Press, 1977), 68.

148. See R. Browning, D. Marshall, and D. Tabb, *Racial Politics in American Cities* (New York: Longman, 1990).

149. "Columbus to Host National Conference of Black Mayors," April 25, 2005, http://www.experiencecolumbus.com/press_releases.cfm?pressrelease_ id=78. The website of the National Conference of Black Mayors is http://www.ncbm.org/.

150. See H. George, "Black Power in Office: The Limits of Electoral Reform," *Western Journal of Black Studies* 9 (summer 1985): 84-95.

151. Nelson and Meranto, *Electing Black Mayors*, 374-75.

152. V. Johnson, *Black Power in the Suburbs: The Myth of African American Suburban Political Incorporation* (Albany, NY: State University of New York Press, 2002).

153. Mark Muro, "Fiscal Challenges Facing Cities: Implications for Recovery," http://www.brookings.edu/papers/2009/1118_cities_fiscal_challenges_muro_hoene.aspx.

154. Center on Budget and Policy Priorities, "Out of Balance: Cuts in Services Have Been States' Primary Response to Budget Gaps, Harming the Nation's Economy." http://www.cbpp.org/cms/index.cfm?fa=view&id=3747.

155. Elizabeth McNichol, Phil Oliff & Nicholas Johnson, "States Continue to Feel Recession's Impact," March 21, 2012, http://www.cbpp.org/cms/index.cfm?fa=view&id=711.

156. "African American Legislators 2009," National Black Caucus of State Legislatures and the National Conference of State Legislatures, http://www.ncsl.org/LegislaturesElections/LegislatorsLegislativeStaffData/AfricanAmericanLegislators19922009/tabid/14781/Default.aspx.

157. See B. Perry, "Can the Judiciary be 'Representative'?" *Insights on Law & Society* 2(10), (Fall 2001).

158. K. Tate, *Black Faces in the Mirror: African Americans and Their Representatives in the U.S. Congress* (Princeton, NJ: Princeton University Press, 2003), 158.

159. C. Stone, *Black Political Power in America* (New York: Dell Publishing Co., 1970), 168-69.

160. Ibid.

161. For a comparison of studies on the results of Black elected officials, see H. Wilson, "Black Electoral Outcomes and Policy Impacts," *Western Journal of Black Studies* 11 (spring 1987): 24-28; and G. Lowenstein, "Black Mayors and the Urban Black Underclass," *Western Journal of Black Studies* 5 (winter 1981): 278-314.

162. See G. Wilmore and J. Cone, *Black Theology* (Maryknoll, NY: Orbis Books, 1979), 534.

163. W. Jones, H. Wingfield, and A. Nelson, "Black Ministers: Roles, Behavior, and Congregation Expectations," *Western Journal of Black Studies* 3 (summer 1979): 99-103.

164. Reed, *The Jesse Jackson Phenomenon*.

165. J. Mansbridge and K. Tate, "Race Trumps Gender: Black Opinion on the Thomas Nomination," *PS: Political Science and Politics* 25, no.3 (1992).

166. R. Smith, *We Have No Leaders: African Americans in the Post-Civil Rights Era* (Albany: State University of New York Press, 1996).

167. O. Johnson and K. Sanford, "Introduction: The Relevance of Black Political Organizations in the Post-Civil Rights Era," in *Black Political Organizations in the Post-Civil Rights Era* (New Brunswick, NJ: Rutgers University Press, 2002), 5.

168. Information about the LCCR can be found on the following website: http://www.civilrights.org/about/lccr/.

169. C. Jones, "From Protest to Black Conservatism, The Demise of the Congress of Racial Equality," in *Black Political Organizations*, ed. Johnson and Sanford, 82.

170. C. Jones, "From Protest to Black Conservatism, The Demise of the Congress of Racial Equality," in *Black Political Organizations*, ed. Johnson and Sanford, 82.

171. F. Walton, "The Southern Christian Leadership Conference: Beyond the Civil Rights Movement," in *Black Political Organizations*, ed. Johnson and Sanford, 132-49.

172. See K. Sanford, "Reverend Jesse Jackson and the Rainbow/PUSH Coalition: Institutionalizing Economic Opportunity," in *Black Political Organizations*, ed. Johnson and Sanford, 150-69.

173. C. Clegg, "'You're Not Ready for Farrakhan': The Nation of Islam and the Struggle for Black Political Leadership, 1984-2000," in *Black Political Organizations*, ed. Johnson and Sanford, 130.

174. V. Johnson, "Where Do We Go From Here? Facing the Challenges of the Post-Civil Rights Era," in *Black Political Organizations*, ed. Johnson and Sanford, 207.

175. See J. H. Clarke, "Black/White Alliances: A Historical Perspective," *Black Pages Series* (Chicago: Institute of Positive Education, 1970), 1- 22.

176. For a study of the near Black/White alliance in the South, see C. V. Woodward, *The Strange Career of Jim Crow* (New York: Oxford University Press, 1966), 60-82.

177. M. Karenga, *Introduction to Black Studies* (Inglewood CA: Kawaida Publications, 1982), 254.

178. S. Carmichael and C. Hamilton, *Black Power* (New York: Vintage Books, 1967), 60.

179. For a discussion on de-emphasis of race in coalition building, see M. Morris, *The Politics of Black America* (New York: Harper & Row Publishers, 1975), 196-302.

180. See J. Wilson, *Negro Politics* (New York: The Free Press, 1960), 155-61.

181. C. Eric Lincoln, *Race, Religion and the Continuing American Dilemma* (New York: Hill and Wang, 1984), 180.

182. Part of a statement read by Julian Bond and adopted unanimously by the Black American Leadership Meeting, Wednesday, August 22, 1979, NAACP National Office, New York, NY.

6

183. N. Lichtenstein, "Civil Rights Culture and the Eclipse of Job Rights in the American Workplace," Paper Presented at the Labor History Workshop, Penn State University, November 5, 1995, 5.

184. J. Stewart, "The Pursuit of Equality in the Steel Industry: The Committee on Civil Rights and Civil Rights Department of the United Steelworkers of America, 1948-1970, in *African Americans, Labor, and Society*, ed. P. Mason (Detroit: Wayne State University Press, 2001), 165-201.

185. AFL-CIO, "Economics Education, What is Our Message, What are Our Goals," mimeo, n. d.

186. These descriptions are based on K. Crews and P. Chancellier, *U.S. Population: Charting the Change*, Population Reference Bureau (Washington, D.C., 1988). They are confirmed by more recent projections.

187. See R. Staples, "The Emerging Majority: Non-White Families in the United States," *Family Relations*, 37 (1988).

188. J. Kotkin, *Tribes: How Race, Religion, and Identity Determine Success in the New Global Economy* (New York: Random House, 1993), 254.

189. A. Toffler, *Future Shock* (New York: Random House, 1970), 249.

190. See P. Skerry, *Mexican Americans: The Ambivalent Minority* (New York: The Free Press, 1993).

191. See J. Bentancur and D. Gills, eds., *The Collaborative City, Opportunities and Struggles for Blacks and Latinos in U.S. Cities* (New York: Garland Publishing, 2000).

192. M. Shuman, *Going Local, Creating Self-Reliant Communities in a Global Age* (New York: Routledge, 2000), 160.

193. Alvin Tillery, *Beyond Homeland and Motherland, Africa, U.S. Foreign Policy, and Black Leadership in America* (Ithaca, NY: Cornell University Press, 2011), 5.

194. Ronald Walters, "Racial Justice in Foreign Affairs," in Michael Clemons, ed. *African American in Global Affairs, Contemporary Perspectives* (Boston: Northeastern University Press, 2010), 1-30.

195. Tillery, op. cit.

196. Tillery, op. cit., 17.

197. Tillery, op. cit., 19.

198. US Department of State, "Founding of Liberia," http://future.state.gov/when/timeline/1830_timeline/founding_liberia.html.

199. Tillery, op. cit., 36.

200. Tillery, op. cit., 37.

201. Elliott Skinner, *African Americans and U.S. Policy Toward Africa 1850-1924, In defense of Black Nationality* (Washington: Howard University Press, 1992), 108.

202. Walters, op. cit. 7.

203. Walters, op. cit., p. 7.

204. Walters, op. cit., 7, 9.

205. Tillery, op. cit., 42.

206. Saheed Adejumobi, "The Pan-African Congress," in *Organizing Black America: An Encyclopedia of African American Associations*, Nina Mjagkij, ed. (New York: Garland Publishing, Inc., 2001).

207. Skinner, op. cit., 394-5.

208. Brenda Plummer, *Rising Wind, Black Americans and U.S. Foreign Affairs, 1935-1960* (Chapel Hill: University of North Carolina Press, 1996), 36.

209. Plummer, op. cit., 36.

210. Adejumobi, op. cit.

211. Tillery, op. cit., 69.

212. Plummer, op. cit., 61.

213. Plummer, op. cit., 79.

214. Penny Von Eschen, *Race Against Empire, Black Americans and Anticolonialism, 1937-1957* (Ithaca, NY: Cornell University Press), 7.

215. Adejumobi, op. cit.

216. Tillery, op. cit., 72.

217. Plummer, op. cit., 180-1.

218. Tillery, op. cit., 73-4.

219. Von Eschen, op. cit., 143.

220. Plummer, op. cit., 202.

221. Von Eschen, *Race Against Empire*, 186.

222. Plummer, op. cit., 271.

223. Ronald Williams, "From Anticolonialism to anti-Apartheid: African American Political Organizations and African Liberation, 1957-93," in Clemons, op. cit., 67.

224. Plummer, op. cit., 302.

225. Tillery, op. cit., 99.

226. Tillery, op. cit., 99.

227. Plummer, op. cit., 307.

228. Plummer, op. cit., 308.

229. Plummer, op. cit., 308.

230. Plummer, op. cit., 310-1.

231. Ronald Williams, "From Anticolonialism to anti-Apartheid: African American Political Organizations and African Liberation, 1957-93," in Clemons, op. cit., 72.

232. Ronald Williams, op. cit., 72.

233. Ronald Williams, op. cit., 78.

234. Ronald Williams, op. cit., 79.

235. Baker, *The United States and South Africa: The Reagan Years*, 29. See also Nesbitt, *Race for Sanctions* and Culverson, *Contesting Apartheid.*

236. James Stewart, "Amandla! The Sullivan Principles and the Battle to End Apartheid in South Africa, 1975-1987," *The Journal of African American History* 96 (1), (Winter 2011): 62 – 89.

237. Juan Williams, "A Black Ambassador to Apartheid South Africa," NPR, October 24, 2006, http://www.npr.org/templates/story/story.php?storyId=6369450.

238. Tillery, op. cit., p. 126.

239. Tillery, op. cit., p. 126.

240. Stewart, op. cit.

241. "Statement to Signatory Company Representatives to the Sullivan Principles on June 3, 1987 at 10:14 a.m.," *ICEOP Records*, Box 2, File 8.

242. See Michael Clemons, "Conceptualizing the Foreign Affairs Participation of African Americans: Strategies and Effects of the Congressional Black Caucus and TransAfrica," in Clemons, op. cit., 46.

243. Ronald Williams, op. cit., 81.

244. The stated goals of IFESH are to assist sub-Saharan African countries through literacy, basic education, and the creation of employment and income-generating opportunities for youths, increasing health awareness to vulnerable populations, and stabilizing populations through conflict mitigation and resolution, http://www.ifesh.org/index.php.

245. The Sullivan Foundation, http://www.thesullivanfoundation.org/summit/about/history/.

246. The Sullivan Foundation, http://www.thesullivanfoundation.org/gsp/endorsers/charter/default.asp.

247. The Sullivan Foundation, http://www.thesullivanfoundation.org/gsp/principles/gsp/default.asp.

248. White House Fact Sheet, http://clinton4.nara.gov/Africa/19980331-9503.html.

249. "The Annual Ronald H. Brown African Affairs Series, September 18th – 26th, 2009," http://www.cfanet.org/cms/wp-content/uploads/2009/12/Ronald-H.-Brown-African-Affairs-Series-2009-Final-Report.pdf; Bay Area Africa Initiative, http://export.gov/california/oakland/eg_us_ca_023415.asp.

250. William Jones, "Congress and Africa's Constituency: The Development of the Africa Growth and Opportunity Act and the Intersection of African American and Business Interests," in Clemons, op. cit., 94.

251. Jones, op. cit., 94.

252. Jones, op. cit., 112.

253. Jones, op. cit., 114.

254. Jones, op. cit., 115.

255. Jones, op. cit., 115.

256. Ronald Williams, op. cit., 81.

257. Charles Henry, "The Rise and Fall of Black Influence on U.S. Foreign Policy," in Clemons, op. cit., 192.

258. Henry, op. cit., 192.

259. Henry, op. cit., 216.

260. Charles Corey, "Hillary Clinton Outlines Obama's Africa Policy," January 24, 2009, http://allafrica.com/stories/200901240009.html.

261. *U.S. Strategy Toward Sub-Saharan Africa*, June 2012, http://www.whitehouse.gov/sites/default/files/docs/africa_strategy_2.pdf.

262. United States Africa Command, "About the Command," http://www.africom.mil/about-the-command; See also, John Vandiver, "GAO Questions Keeping AFRICOM in Germany," Stars and Stripes (September 10, 2013), http://www.stripes.com/news/europe/gao-questions-keeping-africom-in-germany-1.240176.

263. ResistAfricom. http://salsa.democracyinaction.org/o/1552/t/5717/signUp.jsp?key=3094.

6

264. Stephanie Hanson, "China, Africa, and Oil," (June 6, 2008), Council on Foreign Relations. URL: http://www.cfr.org/china/china-africa-oil/p9557.

265. Henry, op. cit., 216.

266. "Willem Buiter Thinks Water Will Be Bigger Than Oil," (July 21, 2011), http://ftalphaville.ft.com/blog/2011/07/21/629881/willem-buiter-thinks-water-will-be-bigger-than-oil/.

267. Henry, op. cit., 216.

268. Minion K.C. Morrison, "The Emergence of a Legislative Caucus of Afro-Descendant Legislators in the Americas: Context, Progress, and Agenda Setting," in Clemons, op. cit., 264-5.

269. David Horne, "The African Union and the African Diaspora: An Information Kit, (Jun 02, 2011), http://afrikanunityofharlem.wordpress.com/the-african-union-and-the-african-diaspora/.

270. Horne, op. cit.

271. Skinner, op. cit., 526.

President Barack Obama and First Lady Michelle Obama watch the 2009 Inaugural Parade from the viewing stand in front of the White House, Washington, D.C.

William Edward Burghardt DuBois, scholar, activist and leader of the Niagara Movement.

Sojourner Truth, women's activist and preacher.

Patrice Lumumba, independence leader and the first democratically elected Prime Minister of the Congo.

Trackwomen for the Baltimore and Ohio Railroad Company. 1943

Million Man March. October 16, 1995.

Jesse Jackson surrounded by marchers carrying signs advocating support for the Hawkins-Humphrey Bill for full employment.

President Theodore Roosevelt and Booker T. Washington.

Booker T. Washington's funeral casket.

Moorland-Spingarn Research Center

George Washington Carver, was a botanist and inventor best known for his work with peanuts, sweet potatoes and soybeans.

Moorland-Spingarn Research Center

Charles Drew, physician and heart surgeon known for his work with transfusions and blood storage.

Mae Jemison, first African American female astronaut, aboard the space shuttle *Endeavour*.

Moorland-Spingarn Research Center

Henry O. Flipper, the first African American graduate of West Point.

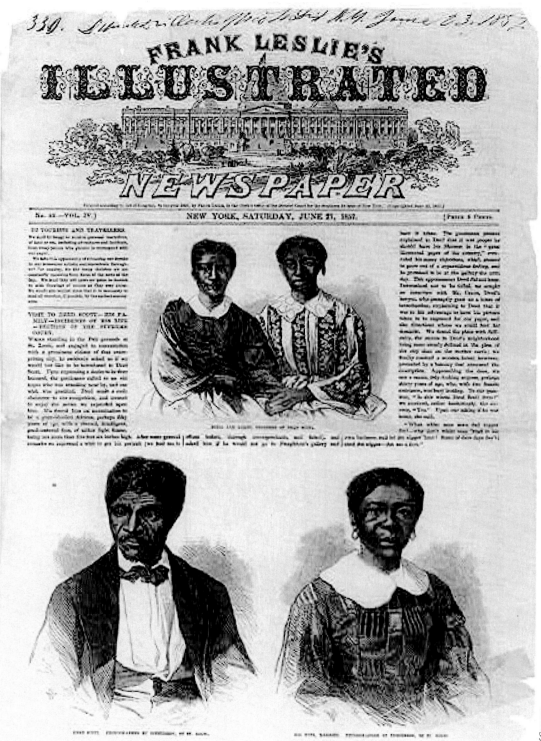

Illustrations of Eliza and Lizzie, the children of Dred Scott; and Dred Scott and his wife, Harriet on the front page of Frank Leslie's Illustrated Newspaper on June 27, 1857.

Madame C. J. Walker, one of the most succesful business women during the early twentieth century.

President Barack Obama awards the 2013 Presidential Medal of Freedom to Oprah Winfrey in the East Room of the White House, Nov. 20, 2013.

Mary McLeod Bethune, activist and educator who founded a private school for African Americans, later to become Bethune-Cookman University.

Maggie L. Walker, the fist woman bank president (of any race) of a charter bank in the US.

Malcolm X, (el-Hajj Malik el-Shabazz), inspirational leader and prominent activist in the struggle for human and civil rights

Randall Robinson, prominent leader and activist in the movement to end apartheid in South Africa.

Henry McNeal Turner, pioneering church organizer and missionary for the AME Church, Reconstruction Era politician, and early Black Nationalist

Kwame Ture, (Stokely Carmichael), Pan-African nationalist, former member of SNNC, The Black Panther Party and founder of All African Peoples Revolutionary Party

Anna Julia Cooper, activist, author, and major contributor to the formation of the Colored Women's YWCA.

Asa Hilliard, educator, psychologist and researcher of African history, culture and education.

Mary Church Terrell, educator and proponent of suffrage for Black women.

Octavia Butler, writer best known for her science fiction works.

Walter Mosley writes in multiple genres, and is one of the most versatile and admired writers of his generation.

Phillis Wheatley, one of the best-known poets in pre-nineteenth-century America, and first Black female published poet.

Melvin Van Peebles, actor, director, playwright and composer, just as famous for introducing a new era of African American focused films

Cab Calloway, singer and band leader who rose to fame as an entertainer during his years performing at Harlem's Cotton Club.

Oscar Micheaux movie advertisement. Micheaux is best known as early African American film producer and director.

Ella Fitzgerald with musicians at the Muray Garber Studio.

Zora Neale Hurston, writer, beating the Hountar, or Mama drum.

First African American Nobel Peace Prize winner Ralph Bunch with Marian Anderson, the first African American woman to perform with the New York Metropolitan Opera.

It should be remembered that the murder of Breonna Taylor on March 13, 2020, occurred some two months before that of George Floyd.

George Floyd's murder sparked demonstrations around the world.

George Floyd Facebook page

Black Lives Matter protest. Washington DC, 2020.

dreamstime.com

Whitehouse.gov

Black voters played a critical role in forging the 2020 election victory of President Joe Biden and Vice President Kamala Harris.

Stacey Abrams Twitter

Stacey Abrams, was unquestionably the most visible opponent of voter suppression and advocate for fair elections leading up to the 2020 elections.

Raphael Warnock Campaign Photo

Georgia's first and newly elected Black Senator, Raphael Warnock (D-GA).

Chapter 7

Individual and Collective Economic Empowerment

Economic Theories and the Black Experience

Traditional Economic Theories: A Critique

All societies must develop the capacity to produce the basic goods and services needed by their inhabitants. In addition, they must institute various rules for, and the means of, distributing benefits to members. Production of goods and services is generally accomplished through some combination of coercion and volunteerism. Most modern economic theories, and particularly what is called *neoclassical economics*, emphasize volunteerism and tout the efficacy of capitalist/competitive market economies in which individuals make decisions that are claimed to yield the greatest benefits. The competitive market is presented as an idealized allocation mechanism that deters or prevents powerful agents from taking advantage of those with fewer resources. Adam Smith, generally regarded as establishing the foundations of modern neoclassical economic thought, describes the market as "an invisible hand" that enables individuals to maximize their well-being and societies to allocate resources and produce goods efficiently.

Presumably, a competitive market discourages those agents who would otherwise engage in various forms of excessive profit-seeking from doing so. Smith assumes that consumers choose the lowest price and that entrepreneurs strive for the highest rate of profit. He insists that consumers' choices "direct" investment money to the most profitable industry. Modern

neoclassical economists make similar arguments in asserting that racial discrimination cannot persist in competitive markets because discriminators will incur economic losses.

In a competitive market economy, all agents are supposedly free to select jobs consistent with their own initiative and skills. Individuals are assumed to be sufficiently empowered to make fully informed decisions regarding schooling and training and to undertake "investments" that will increase their ability to compete for high status—high paying occupations. In modern parlance, the term *human capital* is used to describe the knowledge and skills possessed by individuals that earn returns in the form of wages/salaries.

The term *human capital*, however innocuously intended, shows the need to examine critically how economic theories have treated the experiences of people of African descent. The use of the term *capital*, in reference to human endowments, raises red flags for some because Africans are one of the few populations that have actually been treated specifically as *capital* on a large-scale by the institution of chattel slavery. Such considerations are of little concern to neoclassical economists, who typically think of social identities as characteristics associated with an individual that are not economically productive, although they may have economic consequences. As a result, the scrutiny of race is relegated to a secondary status relative to other forces deemed to be more important for economic decision making.[1]

The neoclassical approach to the examination of factors associated with economic disparities among groups has been formalized within the subfield of "economics of discrimination." Few economists would deny that African Americans and other groups historically have been the victims of economic discrimination. As a consequence, most research examining discrimination focuses on the period after the passage of major civil rights legislation. There is a continuing debate between the researchers who insist that discrimination continues to produce racial disparities and the conservatives who argue that discrimination has been virtually, if not completely, eliminated in influencing economic outcomes for Blacks. The latter group includes some Blacks, for example, Thomas Sowell and Walter Williams. This group asserts that economic disparities persist because Blacks have a "dysfunctional culture" that does not put a very high premium on self-reliance and deferred gratification. Such interpretations typically claim that the principal contemporary manifestation of discrimination is "statistical," rather than deriving from the individual tastes and preferences of employers, consumers, and other agents. This "sanitized" form of discrimination places major responsibility on victims, in their search for equitable treatment, to modify their behavior to alter others' perceptions. Blacks are depicted as having developed an over-reliance on government subsidies and on special treatment programs, such as, public welfare and affirmative action, respectively. Critics describe such argumentation as the "new racism."[2] Africana Studies, of course, rejects these neoconservative formulations. As stated in a previous chapter, Africana Studies specialists insist that historical patterns continue to influence contemporary social dynamics.

Fortunately, there are many African American economists whose research findings support the perspective of African American Studies. In *Persistent Disparity: Race and Economic Inequality in the United States Since 1945* (1998), William Darity and Samuel Myers focus on the policy implications of a simultaneous "widening gap in general inequality between the top and the bottom of the income distribution and the consequent squeeze on the middle" and a "widening gap in racial inequality between blacks and whites." They conclude that "policies, such as affirmative action, that address current market discrimination and disparities, may fail to win political support when there is a widening of general inequality. Yet, even those policies may be less than fully effective if some or most of the current labour market inequality rests on historic disparities transmitted from one generation to the next."[3]

In addition to the limitations of traditional economic theory in examining the microeconomic dimensions of the experiences of Blacks, it is not clear that conservative neoclassical economists have an adequate understanding of the destructive effects of economic domination as experienced by peoples of African descent. Adam Smith's celebratory treatise on capitalism, *The Wealth of Nations*, was published in 1776, during the height of the slave trade and only slightly prior to the invention of the cotton gin that would dramatically increase the demand for enslaved Africans in what is now the southern United States. The essential tenets of Adam Smith's capitalism are freedom, laissez-faire or non-interference by government in business, and individualism.[4] Freedom, ironically, is the fundamental right that Blacks have historically been denied. Moreover, Blacks have relied partly on government economic intervention for the limited economic progress that has been achieved. Efforts by individuals to improve their economic circumstances have been continually hampered by systemic discrimination.

The institution of slavery coerced Blacks into playing a major role in generating pre-Civil War economic growth in the US. Slavery enabled most of the product of Black labor to be appropriated by various non-Black interests. Not only were the products of Black labor and ingenuity appropriated by Whites, but conditions were imposed on Blacks who left a continuing legacy of racial inequality in economic and non-economic outcomes following emancipation. Faced with a variety of structural barriers and individual impediments at the end of the Civil War, Blacks struggled to increase incomes and improve their economic welfare. The difficulty of this struggle cannot be overstated for, as emphasized by Roger Ransom and Richard Sutch, "unlike the indentured servants of Colonial America, blacks received no freedom dues; land redistribution was aborted and blacks were forced to begin their lives as free men and women without money, without tools, without work animals, without assets of any kind [and] their economic, political, and social freedom was under constant attack by the dominant white society, determined to preserve racial inequalities."[5] Opportunities to acquire human capital and pursue economic ventures outside agriculture remained severely restricted. The absence of significant investment in the education of Black children perpetuated high illiteracy rates among adults, which "remained muted by expanding media efforts to promote Black business development. The most prominent example is the magazine *Black Enterprise*, which founder Earl Graves characterizes as "a vehicle to teach the black entrepreneur how to tap into the billions of dollars generated by Blacks." The magazine was launched in 1970 and was the first publication designed for African American entrepreneurs and corporate executives.

Systematic critiques of efforts to pursue Black empowerment by active commitment to capitalism and capitalist institutions have come largely from outside the cohort of professional Black economists. Sociologist Oliver Cox is best known for his treatise *Caste, Class, and Race* (1948), in which he argues that racial antagonisms are organically linked to the class struggle between capital and labor rather than simply a manifestation of a racial caste system. However, he systematically examines the origin and development of capitalism in three volumes: *Foundations of Capitalism* (1959); *Capitalism and American Leadership* (1962); and *Capitalism as a System* (1964). Cox foresees an eventual downfall of capitalism and emergence of socialism as the dominant economic system.[24] Du Bois also carefully scrutinized the expansion of global capitalism after World War II and advised Blacks not to fall into the trap of becoming ardent supporters of capitalism in the essay, "Negroes and the Crisis of Capitalism" (1953).[25] Following in their footsteps, James Boggs opines in 1971, "The creation of a middle class of Black capitalists would make the distribution of income inside the Black community less equal, not more equal. It would be the source of greater chaos and disorder inside the Black community, because the layer at the bottom of the Black community, far from seeing these Black capitalists as models and symbols to be admired and imitated, would be hostile to and strike out at them."[26]

Boggs's critique was part of an intense debate on strategies to promote Black economic advancement that began in the late 1960s and persists to this day. *Black Economic Development* (1969), edited by William Haddad and G. Douglas Pugh, is one of the first collections that highlight competing perspectives on how to address economic disparities. Various essays promote entrepreneurship, critique the potential of small businesses, advocate separatist approaches to development, and scrutinize the role and intentions of the federal government.[27] Many of these same issues are revisited some thirty years later in an edited

volume by Thomas Boston and Catherine Ross, *The Inner City: Urban Poverty and Economic Development in the Next Century* (1998).[28]

Robert Browne had a significant impact in shaping the research and activist agendas of contemporary Black economists. He founded the Black Economic Research Center (BERC) in 1969, as an "economic laboratory" where young Black economists conducted a variety of research projects. Concurrently, he founded the *Review of Black Political Economy*, as a journal focusing specifically on a broad spectrum of issues related to the economic status of African American and Third World peoples. Browne's writings in the *Review of Black Political Economy* explore a wide range of topics that include barriers to Black participation in the US economy, cash flows in the ghetto community, political and economic challenges, and prospects for Black economic development, education, and community development corporations. He believed that the history of Black oppression in the US necessitated both reparations and affirmative action.

Browne's interest in the plight of Black farmers and the loss of Black-owned farmland led him to create the Emergency Land Fund (ELF) in 1971, and, in 1973, to publish *Only Six Million Acres*, a monograph documenting the problem. In 1985, the ELF merged with the Federation of Southern Cooperatives as the Federation of Southern Cooperatives/Land Assistance Fund. The agency continues to assist in efforts to aid Black farmers and to retain Black-owned land. Browne expanded the focus on self-help and on preserving and enhancing community economic resources by creating the Twenty-First Century Foundation, which has provided approximately $2 million in funding for projects and organizations.[29]

Recent monographs by Black economists bear a direct or indirect imprint of Robert Browne's work. They include: *A Different Vision: African American Economic Thought* (1997), *Blacks in Rural America* (1995), *African Americans and Post-Industrial Labor Markets* (1997), *Leading Issues in Black Political Economy* (2002), and *African Americans in the U.S. Economy* (2005).[30]

African American Studies specialists are particularly interested in the strategies explored by Browne and other economists to promote Black community development. Various articles examining this topic were published in the *Review of Black Political Economy* during the 1970s. This body of work was

7

complemented by several books that include: Frank Davis', *The Economics of Black Community Development* (1972) and William Tabb's, *The Political Economy of the Black Ghetto* (1970).[31] These titles were supplemented by the edited volume of William Cash and Lucy Oliver, *Black Economic Development: Analysis and Implication* (1975).[32]

Strategies to promote Black community development explored in these collections focus both on traditional approaches, such as Black entrepreneurship, and on historical efforts to construct semi-autonomous economic networks with broad opportunities for participation and ownership. Such efforts can be traced back to the Convention Movement that thrived during the 1830s and 1850s and to the Reconstruction era initiative that the Colored National Labor Convention of 1869 established. This convention led to the formation of the Colored National Labor Union, which involved a wide range of constituencies: entrepreneurs, government clerks, ministers, and politicians.[33] W. E. B. Du Bois coined the expression "group economy movement' to describe the effort to establish economic networks, and, as late as 1935, Du Bois believed the continued growth of the "group economy" provided the potential for the creation of a "Negro Nation within the Nation."[34]

African American Studies specialists are especially interested in exploring cooperative principles as one component of a multifaceted strategy to strengthen the economic infrastructure of Black America as alternatives to existing capitalist enterprises. Stratification Economics directs African American Studies specialists to focus on the extent to which racial hierarchies are reproduced through the operation of labor markets and the social processes that foster wealth accumulation.

Stratification, Labor Market Outcomes and Wealth Disparities

Employment, Earnings, and Discrimination

In contrast to the traditional perspective that impersonal markets determine labor outcomes for Blacks, particularly after the passage and implementation of anti-discrimination laws, the perspective of African American Studies has been shaped by the emerging subfield of "stratification economics," as introduced by several progressive African American economists. *Stratification economics* examines how institutions are organized and operated to achieve acceptable levels of efficiency, while accommodating patterns of racial domination in institutions that are critical to the normal functioning of the US political economy. Racial disparities and racial discrimination are treated as endemic features of the US economy and social systems. Discrimination based on race permeates a myriad of institutional practices in ways that are virtually impossible to neutralize or eradicate totally.

Racial stratification in economic institutions leads to the disproportionate assignment of high status positions (those associated with control over allocation of resources, distribution of economic benefits, and high incomes) to members of the dominant group. The collective outcome of stratification processes across organizations is the institutionalization of a hierarchy of dominant and subordinate statuses among racial groups. Recognition of the dynamic character of racial stratification processes differentiates the *Black Political Economy* (BPE) paradigm from most other analytical approaches that explore structural forces in perpetuating racial economic inequality.

The primary focus and purpose of this section is to highlight the challenges associated with the shift in the core employment-generating sector from manufacturing to services and the challenges associated with expanding globalization that Black workers face. However, to understand these challenges, it is first necessary to examine how the employment opportunities of Blacks were circumscribed during the first half of the twentieth century when manufacturing was the core economic engine.

The outbreak of World War I severely restricted the influx of European immigrants, and the demand for industrial labor during World War I provided unprecedented employment opportunities for Blacks in the North. Between 1910 and 1920, the net outmigration of Blacks from the South was about 454,000, which was spurred, in part, by floods and boll weevil crop destruction that crippled southern agriculture.[35] As noted previously, Black economist George Edmund Haynes was given the responsibility of mobilizing many of these migrants to support the war effort.

Following World War I, rapid technological change pushed more Blacks out of the agricultural sector. By 1930, the percentage of Black males employed in the agricultural sector had fallen from 58 percent in 1910 to 45 percent. For Black females, the comparable figures were 52 percent and 27 percent, respectively. However, the opportunities for manufacturing employment for Blacks, during and immediately following World War I, largely occurred in non-unionized industries. This pattern served to institutionalize racial wage inequality because the average hourly wage in union industries was $1.01 in 1926, whereas the comparable figure for nonunion industries was 49 cents. Blacks were also being pushed out of relatively better-paying positions as artisans. Black artisans as a proportion of all artisans fell in the carpentry, bricklaying, plastering, and painting crafts in both the South and in the United States as a whole.[36]

Racism in the union movement limited the opportunities for Blacks to obtain union jobs. To minimize the potential adverse economic impact of unorganized workers, the American Federation of Labor (AFL) decided in 1890 to give direct charters to Blacks who were not accepted into White locals. In 1902, of the 40,000 Blacks who belonged to the AFL, over half belonged to one union—the United Mine Workers. Forty-three internationals had no Black membership, and twenty-seven had only a few Black members. The Brotherhood of Sleeping Car Porters, organized by A. Philip Randolph, was a direct response to the exclusionary practices of the Railroad Brotherhoods. Randolph's union became affiliated with the AFL in 1929, with a membership, at that time, of 35,000, which was about half of the total Black membership of the AFL.[37]

Between 1930 and 1940, Blacks were pushed out of the agricultural sector in increasing numbers by technological change and public policy. There were 192,000 fewer Black tenants and 150,000 fewer White tenants in 1940 than in 1930. Expanded industrial employment opportunities generated by World War II contributed to a net out-migration of 1.6 million Blacks from the South between 1940 and 1950. By 1950, the proportion of Black males employed in agriculture had fallen to 0.25. The comparable figure for Black females was 0.10.[38]

Initially, the movement for unionization in mass production industries displayed some potential for altering the subordinate economic status of Blacks. This movement was spearheaded by the Committee for Industrial Organization, which was staffed primarily by the United Mine Workers and existed independently of the AFL from 1937 to 1955. However, by the time of the AFL-CIO merger in 1955, the CIO had largely abandoned any vigorous commitment to an improvement in the position of Black workers through direct union action. Partly as a consequence of limited union advocacy for equal employment opportunity, Black workers continued to be channeled into low-paying occupations. Between 1910 and 1950, the proportion of Black males employed as operatives increased from 0.06 to 0.22, and the proportion employed as service workers increased from 0.06 to 0.14, virtually accounting for the entire shift out of agriculture. For Black women, the decline in the proportion employed in agriculture from 0.52 to 0.10 is almost totally explained by increases in the proportions employed as service workers (0.04 to 0.19), operatives (0.02 to 0.15), clerical and sales (0.00 to 0.05), and household workers (0.39 to 0.42).[39]

A marked improvement in Black economic progress occurred after World War II. There was a rise in Black per capita income from a pre-war $384 to $1,070 in 1956. Black participation in the defense and peacetime industries from 1940 to 1950 accounted for much of the increase. In addition, significant occupational advances were made by African Americans from 1940 to 1956. A shift from farm jobs to non-farm and urban occupations, accompanied by a resumption of migration from rural areas to the cities and from the South to the North, contributed to much of the economic improvement of the Black population. Even before the Civil Rights Movement began in 1956, one in every three urban Black families owned their own home.[40] However, Black economic progress was minimal in comparison to White advancement during this period. Nevertheless, following World War II Blacks experienced a new era of political and economic consciousness. One might conclude that a broader Black "middle-class" began to develop during the two decades following 1945.

As illustrated in Table 7.1, differences in income between Black and White full-time workers are larger for men than for women. The differential for men is essentially unchanged between 2000 and 2011, after falling to its 1990 level in 2010. The differential for women was also unchanged between 2000 and 2011, after experiencing a decline in 2010 to the lowest level since the 1970s. The earnings differential between Black men and women has continued to be less than that for their White counterparts, and in both cases the gains for women seem to have plateaued.

7

TABLE 7.1
MEDIAN EARNINGS OF YEAR-ROUND, FULL–TIME WORKERS 1970 – 2011
Constant 2011 Dollars

	1970	1980	1990	2000	2010	2011
Median earnings						
White male	47,674	49,784	48,179	50,462	51,769	50,070
White female	27,975	29,306	33,444	36,887	38,551	37,719
Black male	32,916	35,205	35,222	39,313	38,006	39,483
Black female	22,387	27,734	30,094	32,767	33,322	33,501
Female:male ratios						
White	.58	.59	.69	.73	.74	.75
Black	.68	.79	.85	.83	.88	.85
Black:white ratios						
Men	.69	.71	.73	.78	.73	.79
Women	.80	.95	.90	.89	.86	.89

Source: US Bureau of the Census, *Table P-38. Full-Time, Year-Round White Workers by Median Earnings and Sex:1967 to 2011*, http://www.census.gov/hhes/www/income/data/historical/people/P38W_2009.xl.

As noted previously, the US economy has undergone a massive transformation from an industrial to a service economy. Thus, the post 1960s period has been characterized by a precipitous decline in the industrial sector and the emergence of the services sector as the principal engine of economic growth. In the US as a whole, private service-producing industries accounted for nearly 90 percent of the job growth in the 1990s and increased their share of total non-farm employment by more than 4 percentage points. The expanded labor force participation of women accounts for much of the growth in employment in the service sector. The magnitude of these shifts can be seen in the shifts in the occupational distributions of Black and White workers indicated in Table 7.2.

TABLE 7.2
OCCUPATIONAL DISTRIBUTION OF BLACK AND WHITE WOMEN AND MEN 1960 – 2010

White Women	White Women	White Women	White Women	Black Women	Black Women	Black Women	Black Women
1960	1980	2000	2010	1960	1980	2000	2010
Professional/technical							
12.2	17.0	22.1	27.3	6.8	13.8	17.8	23.1
Managers							
5.5	7.4	14.8	14.2	2.0	3.4	10.7	10.7
Office/Admin. Support							
32.5	36.0	23.7	20.8	10.1	29.3	24.0	19.4
Sales							
9.8	7.3	13.2	11.7	1.5	2.8	10.9	11.4
Construction/Maintenance/Production/Operatives/Transportation							
16.0	13.1	8.5	5.5	15.1	17.3	11.2	7.0
Service							
20.3	17.9	15.8	20.1	60.1	32.8	23.5	28.3
Agriculture							
2.7	1.7	1.3	0.4	4.5	0.5	0.2	0.2
Total							
100.0	100.0	100.0	100.0	100.0	100.0	100.0	100.0

White Men	White Men	White Men	White Men	Black Men	Black Men	Black Men	Black Men
1960	1980	2000	2010	1960	1980	2000	2010
Professional/technical							
12.3	16.1	16.3	17.6	3.7	8.2	12.2	13.7
Managers							
15.2	15.3	15.8	17.2	4.0	5.6	8.9	9.8
Office/Admin. Support							
7.2	6.2	5.0	6.0	6.2	8.4	8.5	9.9
Sales							
7.0	6.4	11.9	10.7	1.9	2.5	7.6	8.4
Construction/Maintenance/Production/Operatives/Transportation							
43.8	44.1	37.9	33.8	55.7	56.0	43.2	36.5
Service							
5.7	7.9	6.5	13.6	16.0	16.5	12.6	21.2
Agriculture							
8.8	4.1	4.0	1.1	12.5	2.8	2.1	0.5
Total							
100.0	100.0	100.0	100.0	100.0	100.0	100.0	100.0

Source: US Bureau of Labor Statistics, *Employment and Earnings*, various years.

The economic transformation described previously can be seen most easily in the drastic decline in the proportion of Black and White men working in construction, maintenance, production, operative, and transportation occupations between 1960 and 2009. However, there are several other trends that should be noted. There has been a large increase in the proportion of all groups employed in the professional/technical, manager, and sales categories, but these gains have been especially pronounced among Black men and women. Among Black women, the drastic decline in the proportion of service sector jobs after 1960 is the result of the collapse of private household employment that provided an especially important source of income prior to the desegregation era. Finally, there is a continuing decline in employment in the agricultural sector.

At the time of the passage of the Social Security Act and the National Labor Relations Act in the mid-1930s, 95 percent of domestic workers were Black women in the South. A number of researchers, including Rebecca Sharpless, have examined their experiences.[41] However, Black women domestic workers were also prevalent in the North. To illustrate, Elizabeth Clark-Lewis carefully documents the migration of Black women to Washington D.C. and their travails as domestic workers.[42] In both regions of the country, Black domestic workers endured extensive discrimination, long hours, and physical and sexual abuse to support their families and to lay the foundations for future advancement. Sharpless argues, for example, that these work experiences served as a bridge from old labor arrangements to new ones in somewhat less oppressive manufacturing, clerical, and professional occupations.

Both domestic and farm workers were explicitly excluded from the Social Security Act and the National Labor Relations Act. There is an ongoing debate about whether these exclusions were racially motivated. These exclusions have been one catalyst for ongoing efforts by domestic workers to gain basic employment rights. A monumental victory was achieved on September 31, 2010, when Governor Patterson signed the Domestic Workers Rights Bill into law. Among other provisions, this law provides for:

- The right to overtime pay at time and a half after 40 hours of work in a week, or 44 hours for in-home workers;
- A day of rest every seven days, or overtime pay if it is waived;

- Three paid days of rest annually after one year of work;
- The removal of the domestic workers exemption from the Human Rights Law, and the creation of a special cause of action for domestic workers who suffer sexual or racial harassment;
- The extension of statutory disability benefits to domestic workers, to the same degree as other workers; and
- A study by the Commissioner of Labor on the practicality of extending collective bargaining rights to domestic workers.[43]

The decline of manufacturing jobs, a vast majority of which were unionized, has had a significant negative impact on the earnings of all workers, especially Blacks. Several studies indicate that while manufacturing employment accounted for only about 20 percent of total employment in the mid-1980s, about 50 percent of all workers displaced as a result of plant closings/relocations had been employed in manufacturing. Blacks have been significantly over-represented among displaced workers (see, for example, Jacobson, LaLonde, and Sullivan, 1993), and, as a result, have experienced disproportionate income losses.

The information presented in Table 7.3 documents the ongoing importance of unions as a mechanism to reduce earnings inequality for Black men in particular. As indicated in the table, Black men not represented by unions earn only 73 percent as much as those represented by unions. In contrast, White male non-union workers earn 83 percent as much as those represented by unions. Black female non-union workers fare better than White female non-union workers in relation to those represented by unions. There is a much smaller earnings gap between Black and White male union workers than is the case for non-union workers—the respective ratios are .84 and .66. This is not the case for Black female workers. The union and non-union earnings ratios are, respectively .83 and .88.

The earnings and employment stability of Blacks have also been adversely affected by cutbacks in government employment. As can be ascertained from Table 7.4, the proportion of Black women and women increased dramatically between 1950 and 1980, at a rate far larger than that for the overall work force. Declines in the proportion of workers employed in the public sector began in the 1980s and is continuing. These declines are accelerating in the wake of the latest recession. Since January 2009, more than 425,000 state and

7

local government workers have lost their jobs. As many as 800,000 additional public sector jobs could be eliminated through fiscal year 2012. The impact of such cutbacks on Black workers would be enormous. Black men and women are employed in higher-paying jobs in the public sector compared to their counterparts in the private sector and earn higher median earnings than in other sectors.

TABLE 7.3

UNION REPRESENTATION AND RELATIVE EARNINGS OF BLACK AND WHITE MALE AND FEMALE WORKERS 2010

	Black Men	White Men	Black Women	White Women
Percent of Workers Represented by Unions	16.2	13.7	13.8	12.2
Median Weekly Earnings of Full-time Workers Represented by Unions	$827	$985	$720	$872
Median Weekly Earnings of Full-time Workers Not Represented by Unions	$606	$817	$574	$651
Ratio: Non-Union Earnings/Union Earnings	.73	.83	.79	.75
Ratio: Black Union Earnings/White Union Earnings	.84		.83	
Ratio: Black Non-Union Earnings/White Non-Union Earnings	.66		.88	

Source: Bureau of Labor Statistics, Table 1, "Union Affiliation of Employed Wage and Salary Workers by Selected Characteristics," http://www.bls.gov/news.release/union2.t01.htm; Table 2, "Median weekly Earnings of Full-Time Wage and salary Workers by Union Affiliation and Selected Characteristics," http://www.bls.gov/news.release/union2.t02.htm.

TABLE 7.4

PROPORTION OF EMPLOYED AFRICAN AMERICANS AND ALL AMERICANS WORKING IN GOVERNMENT, 1950 – 2010

Year	Black Men	Black Women	All Men*	All Women*
1950	10.1	10.0	14.4	11.1
1960	14.5	14.3	16.4	13.1
1970	24.3	19.1	20.0	15.7
1980	31.2	22.9	21.2	16.1
1990	26.1	20.8	18.4	14.7
2005–2007	23.3	18.0	19.0	12.9
2008–2010	23.6	18.3	19.4	13.6

* Excludes Blacks for 2005-2007 and 2008-2010
Sources: 1950-1990 - Lynn Burbridge, "Government, For-Profits, and Third-Sector Employment Differences by Race and Sex, 1950-1990." Special Report, Wellesley College, Center for Research on Women, (1994). Reprinted in Mary King, "Globalization and African Americans: A Focus on Public Employment," in *African Americans and the US Economy*; 2005-2009 - Steven Pitts, "Black Workers and the Public Sector," Research Brief: UC Berkeley Labor Center, April 4, 2011, http://laborcenter.berkeley.edu/blackworkers/blacks_public_sector11.pdf.

The employment and earnings of Black workers are also adversely affected by what is termed the *spatial mismatch* between where jobs are located and where potential workers reside. Although this phenomenon was first identified as a barrier to Black employment in the 1960s, renewed interest emerged in the 1980s and persists. African Americans generally have the longest travel times to work in all regions of the country where public transit is available, and low-income minorities have longer travel times than low-income Whites.[44] Spatial mismatch patterns are more complex than the traditional concern with inner-city residents experiencing difficulty traveling to suburban job sites. Downward pressure on incomes and status of all workers from global competition has trickled down in ways that are intensifying conflicts over valuable commercial and residential space in urban areas. Intense political battles have been, and are being, waged for control of city government by globalization-friendly constituents. Globalization proponents want to make cities more attractive to global corporations. Low-income Black residents generally lack the skills to compete effectively for high-paying central city employment opportunities generated as a result of globalization. As a consequence there is now a second wave of erosion of accessible well-paying jobs in central cities that disadvantages Black inner-city residents. This second wave of job loss exacerbates the previous pattern of spatial mismatch that resulted from the earlier relocation of manufacturing and wholesaling firms from urban to suburban locations.

The especially important role of information processing in the current global economy has led to intense inter-city competition for college-educated workers who provide preferred staff for the local offices of multinational corporations. In many cities, urban planners are creating residential opportunities and social spaces in the heart of the city in close proximity to places of work for these workers. This allows them to improve their quality of life. As a consequence, in many cities, a new pattern of suburban-type residential segregation is emerging that disperses Blacks away from the most valuable commercial areas in inner cities. This development parallels the racial geographical patterns found in South Africa.

The impact of these various developments on the economic status of African Americans has been compounded by the growing presence of new sources of more easily controllable labor to fill low-paying, low-status jobs, especially in the services sector.

Foreign-born workers in the labor force have been growing faster than their population representation, and immigrants are disproportionately employed in business services, construction, durable and nondurable manufacturing, health care, and personal services.[45]

The increasing availability of low-wage workers has increased the vulnerability of traditional full-time workers. Not only have incomes stagnated, but many workers have also experienced large reductions in benefits, with low-income workers experiencing particular hardship. Less than one-fifth of low-income workers have access to employer-sponsored pension plans, and significant racial differentials exist in pension coverage. In 1991, 56.2 percent of White full-time workers participated in employer-sponsored pension plans. By 2000, this figure had increased to 59 percent. In contrast, for African American workers, 51.4 percent of full-time workers participated in employer-sponsored pension plans in 1991, but, by 2000, this figure had fallen to 49.7 percent.[46]

The preceding discussion does not address the issue of the growing labor market non-participation rate for Black males. The high rates of incarceration, discussed in the preceding chapter, reflect public policy decisions to manage Black males with low levels of human capital in ways that maximize social control. Many Black males are now being forced to provide cheap labor for prison industries that are, in some cases, competing with civilian suppliers. Meaningful analysis of this phenomenon requires a racial stratification framework rather than the type of inquiries generally undertaken in the subfield of the economics of discrimination.

Traditional studies in the subfield of economics of discrimination generally take a narrow focus in comparing labor market outcomes across groups. Such studies depend critically on the distinction between racial disparities and racial discrimination. The differences in labor market outcomes discussed to this point summarize well-known and largely undisputed interracial economic disparities. As Patrick Mason observes, "There is no disagreement that there are large and persistent racial differences in compensation, hours, and working conditions ... there is considerable disagreement among economists regarding how much—if any—of this inequality is due to racial discrimination within the labor market."[47]

The idea of unqualified, or under-qualified, Black workers seems to be very real in the minds of Whites.

Research by Major Coleman indicates that 75 percent of Whites believe that it is very likely, or somewhat likely, that less qualified Blacks get jobs or promotions before more qualified Whites do. However, few Blacks accept the idea that Blacks are unqualified. Seventy-five percent of Blacks say it is not likely that a less qualified Black person will get a job or promotion before a more qualified White. Nearly all of the available evidence indicates that Blacks are as qualified, or more qualified, for their jobs and positions, than are Whites.[48]

Disparities can conceivably result from factors other than discrimination, such as average difference in skills. Differences in skills translate into productivity differences that will generate differences in compensation. In fact, some conservatives argue that Black–White earnings differences simply reflect the greater productivity of White workers. Economists also make a distinction between racial discrimination in the labor market and in the non-labor market that contributes to racial inequality in labor market outcomes. Examples of non-market discrimination include differential access to high-quality schools, information and social capital, parental resources, and financial resources. Patrick Mason's research and his review of various studies lead him to conclude that "nearly all of the Black-White racial inequality in earnings can be attributed to discrimination, either within the labor market or in non-labor-market activities that affect skill accumulation and other vital aspects of income attainment."[49]

Blacks and Whites differ in their perceptions of the sources of interracial disparities. Blacks attribute interracial disparities in jobs, income, and housing mainly to discrimination, while the majority of Whites believe that discrimination against Blacks is no longer operative. Many believe that they are actually the victims of "reverse discrimination." The tendency to scapegoat Blacks to rationalize stagnation or declines in economic well-being enables the globalization processes discussed previously to intensify and further erode economic prospects.

Some conservative economists contend that contemporary labor market discrimination against Blacks has been eliminated. Much of the disagreement between economists, like Mason, and conservatives stems from the way in which economists typically attempt to measure discrimination. Much of the research in the subfield of the economics of discrimination uses statistical models that treat

7

discrimination as a "residual" that is left after all of the other factors that influence earnings have been accounted for, factors such as, age, experience, and geographical region. Depending on the assumptions used, it is possible to come to totally different conclusions when the same data are examined.

It is possible, however, to examine the extent of discrimination more directly by using audit studies. As Mason states, "Audit studies are labor market experiments where carefully matched pairs of individuals (Black–white or Hispanic–non-Hispanic white) who are otherwise equal, except for their racial identity, are sent into the labor market to obtain employment at the same set of businesses."[50] Typically, audit studies find rates of employment discrimination against African Americans and Latinos in excess of 25 percent.[51]

It is also important to understand the resurgence of discrimination based on skin color. This type of discrimination results in African Americans and Latinos with the darkest skin tones and most non-European phenotypes receiving lower incomes, having less stable employment, and obtaining less prestigious occupations than their counterparts who are lighter or have more European physical features. Skin-shade studies have, in fact, demonstrated that workers with dark complexions face sizable penalties in the labor market. Keith and Herring found that skin tone had a larger impact on educational attainment than sex, region, or urban location. Skin tone was found to be the major determinant of occupational status—other than an individual's education. Similarly, skin tone had a larger impact on personal income and family income than either parental education or urban location.[52]

In February 2010, the Obama administration announced intentions to strengthen civil rights enforcement efforts. This effort was welcome news to African American Studies specialists. Table 7.5 below presents information about the number of employment discrimination cases received and resolved by the Equal Employment Opportunity Commission. As is evident from the table, data for 2009 and 2010 show, indeed, an increase in both cases received and resolved compared to the last four years of the Bush administration. Civil Rights enforcement was dramatically weakened during the Bush administration in comparison to the Clinton administration. To illustrate, during 2000, the last year of the Clinton administration, there were 28,945 cases received and 33,188 resolved. The fact that more cases were resolved than received

reflects the carryover of cases received during previous years.

TABLE 7.5
RACE-BASED COMPLAINTS AND RESOLUTIONS
EQUAL EMPLOYMENT OPPORTUNITY COMMISSION
FY 2005 – FY 2010

	2005	2006	2007	2008	2009	2010
Receipts	26,740	27,238	30,510	33,937	33,579	35,890
Resolutions	27,411	25,892	25,882	28,321	31,129	37,559

Source: Equal Employment Opportunity Commission, "Race-Based Charges, FY 1997 – FY 2010," http://www.eeoc.gov/eeoc/statistics/enforcement/race.cfm

One of the most egregious and ominous indications of the persistence of racial discrimination in the workplace has been the continuing phenomenon of nooses used to intimidate Black workers. The display of nooses in the workplace has been recognized as an egregious form of workplace racial harassment by the US Equal Employment Opportunity Commission (EEOC). Such cases have received special attention since 2000, and the EEOC continues to intervene actively in such cases.[53]

As noted previously, there has been a dramatic decline in agricultural employment. This is symptomatic of the overall high level of marginalization experienced by Blacks living in rural communities. In contrast to the highly visible nature of the difficulties Black workers face in urban areas, the economic status of African Americans in rural areas has had relatively limited visibility in recent years. However, to ignore the plight of rural African Americans would be a tremendous disservice, both to the legacy of the ongoing struggle to achieve overall racial economic parity and to current efforts to ameliorate the particular disadvantages rural Blacks face.

In *Blacks in Rural America*, Donald Bellamy and Alfred Parks reported that counties with less-educated populations had the highest growth in per capita income, primarily from an influx of low-wage jobs.[54] On the other hand, Louis Swanson, Rosalind Harris, Jerry Skees, and Lionel Williamson found that large concentrations of Blacks in particular counties persist as pockets of underdevelopment as a result of a combined cultural and exploitative legacy.[55] Using the construct of "employment hardship" to compare the plight of Blacks in rural areas to their central city counterparts and to compare the circumstances of rural Blacks and Whites, Leif Jensen concluded that employment hardship is most prevalent among non-metropolitan African Americans, Hispanics, and Native Americans.[56] Theodore Davis has identified various sources of income inequities between Blacks and Whites in non-metropolitan southern counties. These sources include structural differences in labor market attachment, social characteristics, and human capital endowments. One of Davis' more interesting conclusions is that traditional political empowerment strategies are less effective in non-metropolitan communities, in part because of the absence of multiple political groups that are actively involved in public resource allocation decisions.[57]

African American Studies specialists are attempting to decipher how political and economic agents bent on re-establishing the previous racial order are developing new strategies that include masking their objectives in language touting "color blind" policies. New types of discriminatory behavior have emerged that involve symbolic racism, so called because its practitioners are not assumed to act out of self-interest. Instead, practitioners of symbolic racism are said to act from a feeling of resentment that Blacks willfully refuse to adhere to the traditional American values of hard work, self-reliance, and individualism. These perspectives undergird new practices, such as "rational" statistical discrimination and racial profiling, as well as screening ethnic-sounding names in making hiring decisions. At the same time, both overt and subtle racial harassment and the erection of barriers to upward mobility in the workplace have intensified.

The Obama Administration and the Black Employment Crisis

President Obama came to office in the midst of the worst economic crisis facing the United States since the Great Depression. Obama's principal response to this crisis was to announce what was termed the "American Recovery and Reinvestment Plan," or economic stimulus package, in January 2009. In announcing the plan, the then President-elect indicated that it "not only creates jobs in the short-term but

spurs economic growth and competitiveness in the long-term."[58]

The various components of the stimulus package were presumably designed to provide assistance to low- and middle-income Americans, strengthen the nation's infrastructure, and invest in states that were struggling with falling revenues. Most importantly, the President set the goal of creating or preserving at least 3 million jobs over the next two years.[59] The cost of the final stimulus bill that was implemented was about $787 billion dollars. A poll of 50 economists conducted by USA Today one year later resulted in a median estimate that 1.2 million jobs were saved by the package. In other words, without the package, the December 2009 unemployment rate would have been 10.8 percent compared to the actual rate of 10.0 percent.[60] Achieving the President's job creation goal has been a major challenge during an unprecedented tepid recovery.

The weak pattern of job recovery has had especially dire consequences for African Americans as documented previously. From the vantage point of African American Studies, it is important to question why policies implemented by the Obama administration have not improved the well-being of African Americans. Careful scrutiny of both the design of programs and the underlying philosophy can provide useful insights. In fact, the manner in which some of the Federal stimulus spending was disbursed could have been expected to exacerbate, rather than mitigate, economic inequality. To illustrate, a significant portion of the first wave of economic stimulus funding targeted highway and road construction. Unfortunately, this industry does not have a good track record in employing African Americans. In a study of 18 major urban areas, Todd Swanstrom of Saint Louis University found that Black employment in this industry would be larger by over 42,000 workers if Blacks were employed at the same proportion as in other industries.[61] And an analysis by the Kirwan Institute at Ohio State University reports that of $13 billion or so direct federal contracts awarded in 2009 to small businesses as part of the stimulus effort, only 2.5% of the receiving businesses were owned by Blacks.[62] These findings constitute a testimonial not only to the fact that stimulus funding was not likely to improve the economic well-being of Blacks, but also to the weakness of the Black business sector. Although the number of Black-owned businesses has increased sharply over the years,

7

the vast majority are sole proprietorships (over 92 percent). The proportion of all Black workers working for Black-owned enterprises in 2002 was only about 5 percent.[63]

Efforts to highlight how the administration's efforts have impacted African Americans couch these anticipated gains in terms of non-race focused initiatives. The White House has undertaken three such communication outreach efforts, launched respectively during Black History Month, in February 2010 and 2011 and in April 2011. Despite these extensive communication outreach initiatives there is growing concern among some African Americans that President Obama has not been aggressive enough in addressing the continuing employment plight of African Americans. A public confrontation between celebrated civil rights activist Rev. Al Sharpton and public intellectual Cornell West is perhaps the most visible example of a growing division among African Americans in the assessment of the efficacy of the Obama administration with respect to quality of life enhancement expectations. The two public personalities engaged in a heated discussion about President Obama in April 2011 on the MSNBC special, "The Black Agenda." During the debate, West argued that the President has failed to do enough to reduce Black unemployment and that Obama was no more than a "black mascot" for the rich. Sharpton offered a spirited defense of the President and challenged Ivory Tower academics to become directly involved in community-based self-help initiatives. The pair continued their discourse at the National Newspaper Publishers Association's annual conference in Chicago in June 2011.[64]

The theme of the 2011 National Urban League conference was "Jobs Rebuild America," and it underscored the growing concern about the disproportionate unemployment wreaking havoc in Black communities.[65] The organization released a report during the conference entitled, "At Risk: The State of the Black Middle Class," which asserted that the recession has begun to erode the Black middle class. In response, NUL President and CEO, Marc Morial launched the "War on Unemployment" open letter petition to President Barack Obama and Congress to take decisive action.[66]

Subsequently, Morial and NAACP President Ben Jealous met with President Obama to insist that the social safety net not become a casualty of agreements to reduce the national debt and to urge him to act on

the job-creating solutions contained in the National Urban League's 12-point *Jobs Rebuild America* plan.[67]

Tavis Smiley and Cornel West, who have been consistent critics of the Obama administration's failure to target the Black unemployment crisis, launched "The Poverty Tour: A Call to Conscience" on August 6, 2011, to dramatize the magnitude of poverty's impact on America by taking stock of various social programs that have been successful in preventing people from succumbing to poverty as well as to call attention to the numbers of people who have been less successful in coping with the effects of the recession. The tour began in Wisconsin, and town hall meetings were held in nine states before it ended in Memphis on August 12th. The tour sparked substantial controversy and backlash including disruption of the town hall meeting in Detroit with a pro-Obama protest.[68]

On August 8, 2011, the Congressional Black Caucus launched the "For the People" Jobs Initiative that included job fairs and town hall meetings in five cities: Cleveland, Detroit, Los Angeles, Atlanta and Miami.[69] Thousands of job seekers lined up for hours at a time to attend each of the events.

For African American Studies specialists, the continuing unemployment crisis overwhelming Black America and the grassroots responses to this crisis underscore several important points. First, African American Studies must continue to expand its focus on policy analyses to strengthen governmental and grassroots efforts to address the perpetual structural employment lacuna confronting Black America. Second, African American Studies scholar/activists must become more actively engaged with those community-based organizations struggling to prepare job seekers and to identify employment opportunities as part of the discipline's social responsibility mission. Finally, African American Studies must never shirk from its responsibility to "speak truth to power" in calling for accountability from all parties, including President Obama, with respect to their responsibility to ferret out the continuing discrimination and exploitation experienced by African Americans and other groups.

Wealth Disparities and Barriers to Wealth Accumulation

Disparities in Wealth Accumulation

Growing income inequality among Blacks serves to exacerbate existing wealth gaps between Blacks and Whites. In other words, racial wealth disparities have persisted, and even increased, even though many differences in income and education have declined. It is important to realize that two families with the same income, but widely different wealth levels, are not in the same financial position. As economist Edward Wolff observes, "The wealthier family is likely to be better able to provide for its children's educational and health needs, live in a neighborhood characterized by more amenities and lower levels of crime, have greater resources that can be called upon in times of economic hardship, and have more influence in political life."[70]

Generally, the term *wealth* is used to characterize what is known as net worth. *Net worth* is a measure of everything a household owns (assets) minus everything owed to creditors (liabilities). Financial assets are the cornerstone of asset-building and wealth creation because they can generate additional wealth. Many financial assets generate income in the form of interest or dividends. Other financial assets, such as stocks, also provide opportunities for capital gains. Capital gains result from increases (appreciation) in the market value of an asset (financial or non-financial) and are realized when assets are sold for a profit. It must be recognized, however, that significant risks exist because a capital asset can decline as well as increase in value. A prime example is the rapid decline in the price of technology stocks that occurred in 2001.

Non-financial assets, such as a homeowner's primary residence, vehicles, and net equity in businesses are also important components of wealth or net worth but are generally less liquid than financial assets. The majority of the wealth held by most households, in fact, consists of the equity in their principal residence (the value of the residence minus outstanding mortgages).

The historical experiences of African Americans have generated distinct differences in the goals associated with saving and investing compared with Whites. A 1998 survey of high-income investors conducted by Ariel Mutual Funds and Charles Schwab found that retirement was the most important goal for 58 percent of Whites, compared with 37 percent of African Americans. Conversely, for 26 percent of African Americans, sending a child to college was the most important goal, compared with 17 percent of Whites. There was also a difference in the proportion, indicating that obtaining a better life style was the most important goal—17 percent of African Americans versus 9 percent of Whites.[71]

The differences in expected life spans of African Americans and Whites, along with the continuing impacts of employment and other forms of discrimination, make it absolutely imperative that African Americans develop and follow a strategic plan to build assets and accumulate wealth. Ideally, such a plan should be developed and implemented early in life, but it is important that the asset-building and wealth accumulation process be well underway as middle age approaches.

The 1998 Employment Confidence Survey conducted by the Employee Benefit Research Institute (EBRI) indicated that only half of African Americans thought they would have enough money to live comfortably in retirement compared with 61 percent of all persons surveyed. Although 63 percent of the total population had started saving for retirement, the comparable figure was only 47 percent for African Americans; and among those who had begun saving for retirement, there was a marked disparity. Among African Americans, 28 percent had saved less than $10,000, compared with 16 percent of the total population.[72]

Differences in savings and investment goals between Blacks and Whites combine with persisting disparities in wealth and structural barriers in ways that hamper wealth accumulation for Blacks. There is no doubt that dramatic disparities in wealth persist between African Americans and Whites. Periodic surveys of sample populations are used to measure the magnitude of these disparities. The median net worth of African American and White families for selected years is shown below in Table 7.6. As can be seen from the table, the relative wage gap ballooned during the boom of the mid-2000s, and declined somewhat during the recession. The absolute magnitude of the wealth differential remains enormous and is a

7

stark reminder of the impact of centuries of economic exploitation.

TABLE 7.6
MEDIAN NET WORTH OF WHITE AND AFRICAN AMERICAN FAMILIES SELECTED YEARS (2011 $1000)
Median Value

Year	Whites	African Americans	Ratio: White/Black
2001	150.4	25.0	6.0
2004	162.2	25.9	6.3
2007	179.4	17.9	10.0
2010	130.6	15.5	8.4

Source: Federal Reserve Bulletin, June 2012, February 2009, February 2006.

Overall, the share of income devoted to savings by African Americans is less than for Whites, but, as Edward Wolff observes, "Much of this difference is attributable to the fact that (average) savings rates rise with income, and African Americans have lower incomes than Whites."[73] Equalizing savings rates would require equalization of income, as the income gap itself contributes significantly to the racial wealth gap. If this were possible, the result would be significant. Using 1994 data, Wolff predicts, "Raising African American incomes to the level of those of white families... would cause the racial wealth ratio to jump by as much as 10 percentage points."[74]

Portfolio differences exist even for comparable high-income African American and White households. In the 1998 survey conducted by Ariel and Schwab, high-income African American investors were found to favor investments that provided lower long-term returns than those selected by White counterparts. Specifically, high-income African American investors disproportionately consider real estate to be a better overall investment than stocks, as opposed to the pattern for high-income White investors.[75] Other important differences were found as well: Whites saved more for nonretirement goals, contributed greater amounts to retirement accounts, and were more likely to use brokerages or mutual fund companies to invest most of their money than their African American counterparts.[76]

African American Studies specialists promote collective approaches to wealth creation and accumulation. Savings clubs and investment clubs can concurrently serve individual goals while also generating sufficient capital to leverage opportunities outside the reach of individual small investors. The Black Bank

Initiative argues that "informal institutions of financial intermediation like investment clubs and rotating savings and credit associations are just as important as formal institutions like minority-owned commercial lending institutions as we pursue wealth creation, financial literacy, and community development."[77]

The persisting wealth gap between African Americans and Whites reflects the cumulative effects of both past and present racism and of persistent inequality in opportunities. Moreover, these wealth differences provide material incentives that encourage the continual reproduction of racism in American society. A wide gap exists between the wealth of young Black and White household heads, even before either has had time to accumulate savings from earnings. This gap results from the fact that many young White household heads often get a head start in wealth accumulation from gifts and inheritances from parents and grandparents. In fact, research indicates children of parents with very little wealth and children of parents with extensive wealth rarely end up with wealth that is very different from that of their parents.[78] One critical reason for this close correspondence between parents' and children's wealth is that wealthier parents are more able to make significant investments in their children's education or, in economic parlance, human capital. According to the US Department of Agriculture, depending on a family's income, the cost of raising a child from birth through age 17 can range from $120,000 to $250,000, and these figures do not include the cost of college attendance. To cover these costs requires a systematic approach to asset-building and wealth accumulation if children are expected to be competitive in an increasingly global society.

Asset-building and wealth accumulation are important not only to provide heirs with an advantage in meeting the challenges of the future, but also for collective economic empowerment. There is an urgent need to promote asset-building and wealth accumulation to prevent African Americans from being left behind as the process of inter-generational wealth and power transfer proceeds. Transferring wealth between generations provides a measure of financial security and can enhance upward mobility. Within the next decade, the largest intergenerational transfer of wealth ever seen in modern civilization will begin in the United States. The wealth accumulated in the US from the post-World War II period to the present day is enormous and will be passing to the next generation between now and the year 2050. Economists estimate that this intergenerational transfer may range from $40 trillion to $136 trillion dollars. The recipients of this wealth will become tomorrow's power brokers.

Intergenerational transfers among Blacks are constrained, in part, by the inability to accumulate sufficient sources of income prior to retirement to transfer wealth either during retirement years or at the time of death. As noted earlier in this chapter, African Americans are too disproportionately dependent on income from Social Security to provide for financial needs during retirement. Income from investments provides one-fifth of the income of the White elderly but less than 10 percent of the income of the African American elderly. The dependence on Social Security income is increasingly ominous because of the increased uncertainty of relying on employer-sponsored pension plans as a future source of retirement income. Less than one-fifth of low-income workers have access to employer-sponsored pension plans. In 1991, 56.2 percent of White full-time workers participated in employer-sponsored pension plans. By 2000, this figure had increased to 59 percent. The situation was very different for African American workers. In 1991, 51.4 percent of African American full-time workers participated in employer-sponsored pension plans, but by 2000, this figure had fallen to 49.7 percent.[79]

Building wealth can also ensure that surviving relatives are not burdened by costs resulting from the death of a primary breadwinner, nor are forced to alter their lifestyle significantly as a result of reduced income. Burial and related expenses are often covered by life insurance policies, but, unfortunately, the amount of coverage required to cover fully funerals and related expenses is often underestimated, and savings or other sources must be tapped to cover the balance. African Americans have faced unique challenges in using life insurance as a means to protect loved ones from economic hardships. Jim Crow segregation also limited the opportunities for African Americans to accumulate wealth through insurance policies.

It is important to explore the persistence of the racial gap in wealth accumulation. Edward Wolff suggests that "the wealth of Whites rises more steeply than that of African Americans with increases in such characteristics as income and education."[80] Between 1998 and 2001, the median income of White families increased by 10 percent, whereas that of African American families increased by 20.3 percent.[81] Yet, as noted previously, there was no relative improvement in the median net worth of African American families. In a similar vein, the ratio of the mean wealth of African Americans to that of Whites in 1994 was almost identical for all levels of educational attainment; thus, differences in educational attainment do not explain either the magnitude or the persistence of racial wealth disparities. The situation is extremely problematic for lower-income African Americans without college degrees. In 1998, the average African American family in this category, headed by a person 21 to 34 years old with a high school diploma, had wealth holdings of less than $2,000. Moreover, approximately 70 percent of the assets of such families consisted of vehicles.[82]

The failure to implement a systematic asset-building and wealth accumulation plan early in life can lead to what is described as "middle-age hardship." The condition of middle-age hardship includes, among other characteristics, family income below 150 percent of the poverty threshold and living in rental property.[83] Two-thirds of families who experience chronic middle-age hardship were also found to experience old-age hardship, and African Americans were among the groups most likely to experience both middle-age and old-age hardship.

More generally, lower-income individuals are likely to face the double challenge of low incomes and lack of assets. According to Robert Haveman and Edward Wolff, "A household is considered to be 'asset-poor' if the access... to wealth-type resources is insufficient to enable 'basic needs' [to be met] for some 'limited period of time.'"[84] African Americans are twice as likely to be asset-poor as Whites, although the differential declined between 1984 and 1999.[85]

Even African Americans who have college degrees and have positions paying high incomes have difficulty maintaining parity with their White counterparts with similar incomes. A study of changes in wealth holdings between 1995 and 1998 for a sample of African American and White families earning between $50,000 and $140,000 found that, in 1995, African American families in this category actually had wealth holdings 4 percent higher than their White counterparts. However, by 1998 the wealth holdings of African American families were 14 percent lower than that of the cohort of White families.

In 1993, the home ownership rate for African Americans was 42.0 percent. By 1999, this figure had increased to 46.7 percent.[86] This increase reflects, in part, income gains experienced by many Blacks in the 1990s along with housing policies designed to make home ownership more accessible for lower-income individuals. Home ownership among African Americans reached 48.1 percent, its highest point in history, in the fourth quarter of 2001. The pattern in 2002 was not quite as promising, although the homeownership rate for African Americans rose to 47.5 percent from 47.1 percent in the third quarter.

Despite these gains, institutional discrimination continues to limit home ownership opportunities for many Blacks. Melvin Oliver and Thomas Shapiro describe, for example, how higher mortgage rejection rates constrain the ability of young African American families to use home ownership as a platform to build wealth. Moreover, even when homeownership is attained, discrimination, in combination with other factors, reduces the returns on this investment for many African American homeowners. African Americans often receive higher average interest rates for home mortgages, comparable to those of Whites, and housing in communities with a high proportion of African American residents does not appreciate as much as housing in predominantly White communities. In addition, as the economic growth experienced during the 1990s has waned, bankruptcies and foreclosures among Black homeowners have increased significantly.

One of the processes, typically overlooked, by which wealth disparities have been perpetuated is through the expropriation of land owned by Black farmers. By 1982, the figure had been reduced by half to 3 million acres. Several reports have been produced documenting the plight of Black farmers, and a number of factors contributing to land loss have been identified, which include lack of access to credit, partition sales, tax sales, and foreclosures. Discrimination against Black farmers by officials of the US Department of Agriculture has been highlighted as a major culprit in worsening the circumstances of Black farmers.

Black farmers have fought back by using a variety of tactics. They have formed several organizations in an effort to stem further land loss and to challenge discriminatory practices. Among those organizations are the Black Farmers' Agricultural Association (BFAA), the National Black Farmers' Association (NBFA), and the Land Loss Prevention Project. A major legal challenge was initiated via the *Pigford v. Veneman*

(formerly known as *Pigford v. Glickman*) class action lawsuit filed by 401 African American farmers from Alabama, Arkansas, California, Florida, Georgia, Illinois, Kansas, Missouri, Mississippi, North Carolina, Oklahoma, South Carolina, Tennessee, Texas, and Virginia, alleging that the USDA discriminated against them on the basis of their race in its farm credit and non-credit benefit programs. The legal strategy was complemented by direct action tactics that included a protest in front of the White House in December 1996 and a march from the USDA headquarters to the Capitol building in March 1997. In that same month, the Congressional Black Caucus held hearings on the Black farmers' charges.

On April 14, 1999, a Consent Decree to resolve the case was approved over the objections of many farmers and support groups. The US Department of Agriculture finally acknowledged that it had stacked the deck against the farmers by denying loans that could have kept them in business. At a March 1998 hearing to assess the proposed terms of the consent decree, more than forty Black farmers and support groups—which included the BFAA, the Federation of Southern Cooperatives, Land Loss Prevention Project, and the NAACP—asked the judge to throw out the proposed Consent Decree. This request was denied, and two tracks known as *Track A* and *Track B* were created to provide compensation. *Track A* provided compensation in the amount of $50,000, whereas applicants could obtain larger compensation under *Track B* if they could prove that they had incurred larger losses. Black farmers supported by the Land Loss Prevention Project went to court to have the Consent Decree set aside but were unsuccessful.

The process of applying for compensation was cumbersome, and many eligible farmers missed the original filing deadline, which was subsequently extended. There have been continuing allegations of mismanagement of the settlement process. Congressional hearings in 2004 addressed concerns about the large number of claims from Black farmers that were summarily rejected, because they arrived after the filing deadline due to inadequate notification of the potential claimants. As of November 2002, of the approximately 21,000 eligible farmers, only about 13,000 (or 60 percent) had been approved for a cash settlement and debt relief. The approved disbursements amounted to about $780 million, much less than the original $2.5 billion estimate of the value of the settlement. The high rate of denial (9,000 or 40 percent) has spurred additional direct action, such as takeovers and attempted takeovers of Farm Service Agency offices in Tennessee, Arkansas, and Louisiana in 2002. In addition, a new lawsuit was filed in September 2004 but was dismissed in 2005. Thus, Congressional action was the last hope for the many Black farmers left out of the original settlement.[87]

In June 2008, then-President Bush signed a law providing claimants with a right to pursue their discrimination claims if they had petitioned to participate in *Pigford*, but did not have their petitions considered because they were filed late. The law did not "re-open" the *Pigford* case; rather it provided a new right to sue. The bill made $100 million available to settle claims.

After nearly two years of litigation, attorneys for tens of thousands of farmers and attorneys for USDA entered into a Settlement Agreement that would require Congress to fund an additional $1.15 billion for successful claimants (which would bring total funding for valid claims to $1.25 billion) on February 18, 2010. In May 2011, the presiding judge approved the preliminary Settlement, with a final approval hearing scheduled for September 1, 2011. Under the terms of the settlement, claimants can receive up to $50,000 plus a payment to be applied to debt owed (if any) to USDA, plus a tax payment worth 25 percent of that person's cash and loan awards under an expedited process. An alternative claims process will allow claimants to pursue actual damages up to $250,000.[88]

The ongoing saga of institutional assaults on Black farmers underscores the continuing validity of Joyce Allen-Smith's assessment in 1995: "As we approach the twenty-first century... prospects to alleviate poverty and improve the well-being of rural blacks in the near future remain dim."[89] The plight of Black farmers also highlights why African American Studies specialists are less concerned about distinctions between market and non-market discrimination than economists. The various forms of discrimination are so tightly intertwined that efforts to disentangle them statistically are largely empty intellectual exercises.

The preceding discussion indicates that racial wealth inequality is entrenched in the fabric of American society and that a variety of forces interact to produce and sustain wealth disparities. African American Studies specialists contend that only a multifaceted approach can alter the dynamics that reproduce unequal wealth distributions. The edited volume *Wealth Accumulation & Communities of Color in the United States* provides a useful compilation of the most recent relevant research in this area.[90]

Black Consumer Power: Myth or Reality?

Consumer Expenditures and Economic Well-Being

The exacerbation of the problem of wealth disparities has been largely overlooked, in part, because many commentators claim that African American purchasing constitutes a potential form of economic power. The argument typically incorporates two claims. The first is that the value of the consumer purchases made by African Americans is larger than the value of goods and services produced by the vast majority of countries. This argument, of course, ignores the critical distinction between purchasing and consuming a good or service and having the capacity to exercise sufficient control over economic resources to mobilize production processes and create markets. The second claim is that if Black consumers can mobilize selective patronage (either boycotts or coordinated efforts to support Black-owned businesses), it would enable Blacks to exercise leverage against non-Black owned businesses that engage in employment or consumer discrimination.

Both of these claims have a long history. In a 1935 government publication, Eugene Jones argues, "The annual purchasing power of approximately 890,000 Negroes in the South's 17 largest cities has been estimated as $308,000,000. This is most significant when compared with the nation's 1929 export trade of $224,619,486 with Mexico and all Central America; $208,969,847 with the West Indies and the Bermudas; and $374,851,619 with Argentina, Brazil and Chile."[91] The "Don't Buy Where You Can't Work" Movement was initiated in 1931 in Chicago and spread to Pittsburgh, Philadelphia, New York, Boston, Baltimore, Richmond, and Atlanta. The movement utilized pickets and boycotts to force discriminating businesses to hire sales clerks in stores located in predominantly Black neighborhoods. The strategy received legal endorsement in a 1935 case in Maryland, in which the court supported "the general purpose of colored persons to improve the condition of their race" by refusal

7

to buy where Blacks are not employed. This ruling was upheld by the US Supreme Court in 1938.[92]

There is no question that consumer purchases by Blacks have been rapidly increasing as illustrated below in Table 7.7. There is a conventional wisdom that the savings rate of African Americans is lower than that of Whites because, presumably, African Americans have a cultural preference for consumption over savings. This conventional wisdom is fueled by regular announcements touting the significant purchasing power of African Americans. However, it is not at all clear that this image stands up to serious scrutiny. The fallacy of the conventional wisdom is also evident from an examination of the growth rate in consumer expenditures shown in Table 7.7. The data demonstrate how Black consumer expenditures slowed considerably as a result of the recession. Moreover, Black consumer expenditures have not grown substantially faster than White consumer expenditures.

TABLE 7.7
AVERAGE EXPENDITURES OF BLACK AND WHITE CONSUMER UNITS AND PERCENTAGE GROWTH BETWEEN PERIODS
Selected Years 1990 – 2009 (Current Dollars)

Year	Blacks	Pct Growth	Whites	Pct Growth
1990	19,130		28,989	
1995	23,739	24.1	33,373	15.1
2000	28,152	18.6	39,406	18.1
2005	32,849	16.7	48,077	22.0
2009	35,311	7.5	50,723	5.5
Consumer units 2009	14,659,000			
Total Expenditures	$517 Billion			

Source: US Department of Labor, Bureau of Labor Statistics, Consumer Expenditure Survey, Expenditure Shares Tables, Various Years http://www.bls.gov/cex/csxshare.htm

It is also useful to compare the proportion of expenditures by Blacks and Whites for various categories of goods and services. Data for 2011 are presented below in Table 7.8. Focusing on large expenditure categories, the data indicate that African Americans under-spend disproportionately on health care, education, and pensions and insurance and overspend on housing relative to Whites. The impact of the differences in proportions spent on human capital investments is exacerbated by the significant difference in the absolute amount of expenditures between African American and White households.

One of the key implications of the preceding comparison is that it is critical to ensure that African Americans receive equivalent value per dollar expended. An even more critical implication is the need to eliminate, if not reverse, the discrepancies in expenditures on health care and education. As noted in previous sections, investments in human capital (which include health status) are absolutely essential for successful labor market outcomes and wealth accumulation. To address these discrepancies, however, requires some understanding of two important economic concepts.

TABLE 7.8
PERCENTAGE OF TOTAL EXPENDITURES IN 2011 WHITE AND AFRICAN AMERICAN HOUSEHOLDS AND TOTAL EXPENDITURES ($)
Percent of Total Expenditures

Expenditure Category	Whites	African Americans
Food	13.0	12.9
Alcohol	1.0	.5
Housing	33.3	38.2
Apparel	3.4	4.6
Transportation	16.7	16.2
Health Care	6.9	5.2
Entertainment	5.4	3.9
Personal Care	1.3	1.5
Tobacco	.7	.7
Education	2.1	1.3
Reading	.2	.1
Miscellaneous	1.6	1.4
Contributions	3.5	3.7
Life Ins/Pensions	10.9	9.8
Total Expenditures	$51,113	$36,644

Source: Bureau of Labor Statistics. *Consumer Expenditures in 2011.* http://www.bls.gov/cex/2009/share/race.pdf

Public Goods and Economic Well-Being

The consumer purchases discussed so far involve expenditures by individuals and households from their own income. This excludes consumption of what economists call public goods. Public goods are assets that multiple persons can enjoy simultaneously and that can provide benefits without creating scarcity because each person can gain from them without diminishing the consumption of others. Moreover, it is impossible to prevent people from gaining access to a public good. A public good is the opposite of a *private good*, which is an asset that can easily be divided into parts to sell on the market, (such as a loaf of bread) whose owner can exclude others from using it and, which cannot be used again once it has been consumed. Private businesses avoid the provision of public goods because public goods do not make profits and non-payers cannot be excluded from using them. As a consequence, public goods are typically provided by governments and financed through taxes or fees.

The preceding technical description of public goods is usually expressed in popular discourse as "goods provided by the government" or "goods the government ought to provide the public." Proponents of privatization often argue that too much of our resources are allocated to public goods. Advocates of privatization, more often than not, have sufficient incomes to purchase merchandise or services provided by public goods and are seeking to reduce taxes paid to subsidize public goods. However, when governments reduce public goods in favor of privatization, typically, those with limited incomes and those dependent on public goods are left with fewer goods and services and lower quality goods and services..

The two consumption categories in which Blacks spend disproportionately less relative to Whites— health care and education—are also the most vulnerable to cutbacks in public expenditure. In the case of health care, the Medicaid program was designed to provide support to dependent children and their mothers, the disabled, and the elderly, with additional groups added in the late 1980s. In 2000, Medicaid provided support to 21.6 million children and 9.6 million adults. Medicaid has reduced racial and ethnic disparities in access to insurance coverage. However, non-Whites sometimes receive different treatment from Whites, even when they have the same insurance coverage and see the same physicians. In addition, non-White residents are much more likely than White residents to live in an area where Medicaid prescribing rules will constrain their physician. Thus, efforts to reduce Medicaid budgets and introduce private provider schemes are likely to exacerbate both the quality and quantity of medical services consumed by poor African Americans.[93]

In the area of education, the implementation of voucher programs and the creation of charter schools constitute efforts to privatize what had previously been a public good. National opinion polls conducted by the Joint Center for Political and Economic Studies found that Blacks are more likely than Whites to support vouchers.[94] Critics of vouchers argue that they could further increase funding inequities and the stratification of students by income, race, and social background. Available information suggests that vouchers increase inequity by diverting money from students currently served by the public schools to students who already go to private schools.

Charter schools have spread rapidly across the country and have received funding from federal, state, and local budgets. Part of their allure is the combination of the independence and autonomy of private schools with the public support and free tuition of public schools. Unfortunately, the available evidence does not suggest that charter schools have overcome the most difficult problems presented to them by the adverse effects on human capital accumulation. For example, non-White students are disproportionately enrolled in charter schools without college preparatory curricula.[95]

The overall evidence suggests that privatization of education is not leading to higher quality educational achievement or to human capital investment for Blacks. At the same time, the diversion of resources from public education is further eroding the quality of public education consumed by most African Americans. All school choice programs, public school choice as well as voucher and charter school programs, are increasing student stratification by income and other family background characteristics without necessarily producing academic gains. In assessing efforts to privatize public education, it is also important to recognize that the timing of these efforts overlaps with legal decisions to pursue public school desegregation.

The preceding discussion of educational options illustrates the need for a comprehensive approach to optimize Black consumption behavior. We require an approach that recognizes a mix of both private and public goods is needed. Because African Americans with lower incomes depend heavily on public goods, direct political action in the form of protests, demonstrations, and lobbying will be increasingly necessary to slow the tide of privatization. This approach to Black consumption behavior suggests a more sophisticated use of consumer boycotts and selective patronage than has been attempted to date. There is, in fact, some evidence that the traditional use of consumer boycotts is evolving to meet the new challenges posed by increasing corporate power.

7

The Rainbow Push Coalition's Wall Street Project uses subliminal threats of boycotts to gain support for inclusion, opportunity, and economic growth for African Americans and other people of color through pacts with corporate America. In contrast with the initial use of boycotts in the 1930s to obtain sales jobs, the Wall Street Project focuses on global hiring and promotion practices, representation on corporate boards, awarding more business to minority companies, and increasing the amount of business minority firms conduct with each other.[96]

Karin Sanford raises the critical question of whether initiatives like the Wall Street Project, "with its primary focus on employment and support for African American businesses, somehow counteract capitalism's inherent unfairness and greed?"[97] In elaborating on the implications of this question, Sanford counterpoises the thrust of the Wall Street Project against an alternative thrust advocated by Manning Marable, that is: family-oriented strategies focusing on more equity in the distribution of income that would include living wage policies.[98] These conflicting perspectives provide the context for the expanded discussion of Black capitalism in the following section.

Black-owned Business and the Vision of Black Capitalism

Black Capitalism and Liberation: A Critique

As noted previously, Abram Harris was one of the first Black economists to express skepticism about relying on the growth of Black business ownership as the linchpin of a strategy to promote economic advancement. One of the great ironies is that the term *Black capitalism* actually originated during the Nixon administration. Then-President Nixon issued Executive Order 11458 in 1969, establishing the Office of Minority Business Enterprise (OMBE). This office had the responsibility of coordinating and working with the Small Business Administration (SBA), and other federal agencies, to provide advisory services and financial aid to minority enterprise. The OMBE was Nixon's response to the demands of African Americans for Black power. Consequently, Nixon reaped political benefits by giving the government

a role in reviving and fostering the concept of Black capitalism.[90]

The OMBE established field offices nationwide for the purpose of channeling technical assistance and aiding the loan-applications of minority businesses, working in conjunction with numerous local business development organizations. Within a few years after the establishment of OMBE, federal loans and guarantees and SBA assistance quadrupled. Federal procurement set-aside programs were initiated and privately capitalized Minority Enterprise Small Business Investment Companies (MESBIC) were initiated during this period. More than a dozen federal agencies, and twice as many private organizations, have functioned since the 1970s to promote, advise, and increase Black entrepreneurship. It is remarkable that, in spite of the difficulty of debt financing and widespread credit discrimination that Black entrepreneurs experience, they have continued to grow in spite of adverse economic cycles.

In 1971, Nixon signed Executive Order 11625 requiring all federal agencies to develop plans for Minority Business Enterprise contracting. Complementing these efforts was a 1969 amendment to the Small Business Administration Act establishing the SBA §8(a) program that specified a percentage of federal contracts would be awarded to minority businesses. In 1971, the §7(a) loan guarantee program for loans to minority-owned businesses was passed, as was the §504 Certified Development Company Loan Program for the purchase of fixed assets by minority-owned businesses. The cluster of mandates and programs embodied the idea of *Black capitalism* and implemented a new approach to asset-building in minority communities.[100]

Black business ownership is essential for the development of African American communities. This is imperative since the Black and White races still occupy, basically, segregated neighborhoods. When Whites own businesses located in the Black community, the profits from those enterprises are returned to White Americans for the development of their communities and social institutions. Seldom, if ever, do White businesses invest in or develop the Black community from which they derive their profits. Race of ownership and control of business determine which community reaps the majority reward from entrepreneurship. Therefore, in discussing Black economic development, a sharp distinction must be made between Black *proprietary* versus Black *participatory* entrepreneurship.

Proprietary Black entrepreneurship means Black majority ownership of the capital assets of an enterprise, with Blacks having decision-making power over the personnel, materials, resources, and all matters pertaining to its economic as well as social functions. *Participatory* Black entrepreneurship exists where Blacks share only marginally, or not at all, in the ownership of the business, even though they may participate at high management levels. Participatory entrepreneurial Blacks have no ultimate decision-making responsibility or power relative to the execution of a firm's activities or the allocation of its economic resources.[101] Following the 1960s Civil Rights Movement, many African Americans were placed symbolically on corporation boards and in vice corporate management positions. Ordinarily, these Blacks possess neither the power nor influence to alter corporate policy that will affect African American entrepreneurs or the Black community favorably. Social integration and participatory entrepreneurship are of little benefit without a commensurate measure of Black proprietary economic power and influence. Although profit is the life-blood and primary motive of business activity, Black-owned businesses often make policy on behalf of the economic, political, and social interests of the Black community. Proprietary and participatory Black entrepreneurship constitute a form of Black/White economic coexistence that will exist indefinitely in the United States.

Since Abram Harris expressed his doubts in the mid-1930s, there has been ongoing criticism of efforts to promote Black capitalism and the strategy to use Black-owned businesses for community development. E. Franklin Frazier described Black business as a social myth and argued that the accumulation of wealth by a few Blacks would not solve the race problem in America. He further stated that the myth "served to exaggerate the economic wellbeing of [Blacks] in the United States and to whet the appetites of the black bourgeoisie... "[102] Frazier's criticism of Black capitalism was followed during the early 1970s by two books: *The Myth of Black Capitalism* by Earl Ofari and *Black Awakening in Capitalist America* by Robert L. Allen.[103] Manning Marable's *How Capitalism Underdeveloped Black America*, which is highly critical of Black capitalism, appeared in 1983.[104] The debate concerning the merits of Black capitalism and Black-owned businesses

has not, however, retarded the continuing expansion in the number of Black-owned enterprises.

Growth and Impact of Black Business

The data in Table 7.9 document the rapid growth in the number of Black-owned businesses in the fifty years between 1863 and 1913. Many enterprising African Americans were able to utilize skills obtained during slavery to establish businesses, and urbanization provided opportunities to take advantage of population concentrations. W. E. B. Du Bois's study of Black businesses conducted in 1899 and 1900 indicated that some former house servants had been able to establish themselves as barbers, restaurant owners, and caterers. Former field workers had established themselves in a variety of occupations including gardeners, grocers, and florists. Some Blacks trained as skilled craftsmen on plantations had successfully made the transition to become builders, contractors, brick masons, painters, and blacksmiths.[105]

TABLE 7.9
NUMBER OF BLACK-OWNED BUSINESSES,
1863 – 1913

Year	Total Number of Businesses
1863	2,000
1873	4,000
1883	10,000
1893	17,000
1903	25,000
1913	40,000

Source: US Bureau of the Census, *The Social and Economic Status of the Black Population in the United States*, 78.

The National Business League founded by Booker T. Washington in 1900 provided important social and psychological stimuli for Black business development. The purpose of the National Business League was to give encouragement and inspiration to potential, and practicing, Black business persons. More than 600 state and local branches of the organization existed by the end of 1915.[106] In addition, Marcus Garvey's ideology of Black economic self-determination, Black pride rhetoric, and his mass following sustained the momentum of African American business progress through the 1920s. African American business growth and development continued in spite of the racial violence and racism that followed the end of World War I. Some historians note

7

that the race riots tended to drive Blacks closer together. Consequently, Blacks "thus aroused, then, became not only racially conscious, but economically conscious. From this realization [Blacks] began to enter business in a larger measure."[107]

Significant development of Black businesses thus continued between the years 1900 and 1929. Major African American publishers and newspapers were established during this period. The most extraordinary Black business woman of this time was Madame C.J. Walker. By 1917, she had established a million-dollar company in Indianapolis, Indiana, that manufactured hair and skin preparations and other cosmetic products.[108] The Depression (1929-1933) took its toll in the number of Black businesses that failed. However, many Black businesses survived this critical period. According to historian Lerone Bennett, Jr., by 1939, 57,195 Black-owned retail and service establishments existed with annual income far exceeding 100 million dollars. Their total income represented less than one percent of the National Income.[109]

Growth in the number of Black-owned businesses from the early part of the twentieth century through the 1960s can best be described as geometric, as can be seen by comparing the 163,000 figure for 1969 in Table 7.10 with the 40,000 figure in Table 7.9. Politico-psychological influences resulting from the 1954 school desegregation ruling, the Montgomery Bus Boycott, and the Black Power/Black Pride Movement contributed to the upsurge in African American business and economic development through the 1970s. During the dramatic unfolding of these three phenomena, Blacks revived their interest in building and patronizing their own businesses. White establishments that practiced segregated services, seating, or eating policies were boycotted by Blacks. Consequently, Black entrepreneurs began to build new businesses or improve existing facilities to accommodate members of their own race. A new capitalist spirit was generated among African Americans and many started business enterprises with less than one-thousand dollars as initial capital.

As is evident from Table 7.11, growth continued at a very rapid pace between 1969 and 2007. Moreover, women were establishing businesses much more frequently than men. In 2007, 47.4 percent of Black-owned businesses were owned by women, compared to 38 percent in 1997. While growth in the number of Black-owned businesses is impressive, it is important to note that there is a high degree of geographic concentration.

To illustrate, 30 percent of all Black-owned firms are found in three states: New York, Georgia, and Florida.

Given the dramatic increase in the number of Black-owned businesses, why does there continue to be such skepticism about the potential for Black-owned businesses to contribute significantly to Black community economic development? Several issues account for this skepticism, including industry concentrations, limited markets served, and the extent of employment generation. As shown in Table 7.11, in 2007, 38 percent of Black-owned businesses were operating in two sectors: (1) health care and social assistance; and, (2) repair, maintenance, personal and laundry services. The list in Table 7.12 indicates that retail trade still generates the most receipts, reflecting the continuing importance of targeting Black consumer markets, although the ability of Black-owned firms to monopolize this market has declined significantly over time.

The weakening linkage between the fortunes of Black-owned businesses and Black consumers underscores the cautions expressed in the previous section regarding the excessive trumpeting of Black consumer power as a measure of collective economic power. Although highly publicized threats of consumer boycotts have exacted some concessions from high-profile firms, like Denny's, their capitulation is likely more a result of the desire to avoid negative publicity than concerns about losses due to a decline in purchases by Blacks. Growing individualism among Black consumers is reducing the credibility of threats of consumer boycotts as a means to force businesses to guarantee economic equity.

Turning to the issue of employment generation by Black-owned businesses, there is no question that the number of Black-owned businesses with paid employees and the number of employees in these firms have increased sharply between 1977 and 2007, as documented in Table 7.13 below. Research indicates that Black-owned firms are much more likely to employ Black workers than non-Black firms.

At the same time, it is important to recognize that the magnitude of employment provided by Black-owned business is only a small proportion of the Black labor force. As shown in Table 7.13, the percentage of Black-owned firms with paid employees, as a percentage of all Black-owned firms continues to decline. Female-owned Black businesses account for 30 percent of all Black-owned businesses with paid employees, and female-owned businesses are less likely to have employees than male-owned businesses. The relatively small proportion of total Black employment accounted for by Black-owned businesses raises the question of the extent to which it is feasible to believe that this figure can grow further. This will require overcoming traditional problems that limit the survivability of Black-owned businesses and lead them to organize disproportionately as sole proprietorships, without paid employees, rather than other business models operating with paid employees. Black-owned businesses, in particular, are much more likely to be small, with earnings less than $25,000. Moreover, the survival rates of new businesses owned by Blacks are the lowest, compared with other business groups. Economist Timothy Bates argues that the principal barriers to strengthening the employment generating potential of Black-owned businesses are difficulty in obtaining sufficient capital, declining access to government contracts resulting from legal challenges to programs that set-aside a specified portion of contracts for minority-owned firms, and the tendency for Black-owned businesses to be located in economically depressed areas.[110] However, Robert Fairlie and Alicia Robb maintain that the lack of prior experience working in family businesses is a more important cause of the limited success of most Black-owned businesses.[111] From the vantage point of Africana Studies, one of the greatest threats to the future vitality of Black-owned businesses is the continuing assault on affirmative action programs. This constitutes one dimension of a larger movement toward restricting economic gains generated by the struggles of the 1960s.

The continuing problems limiting the development of successful Black-owned businesses that can contribute to community development are often overlooked due to the visibility of what are presumed to be high-profile success stories. As an example, much attention has been focused on the emergence of hip-hop media moguls as successful entrepreneurs. On closer inspection, however, many of these firms are not purely Black-owned and are heavily underwritten by external capital. As noted by Dipannita Basu, "Hip-hop labels such as Def Jam, Roc-a-Fella, and Bad Boy, are not really 'independent.' They act as intermediaries within the production of music... In essence they are no more than titular CEOs who are 'media moguls by name, millionaires by bank balance, but paid staff nevertheless.'"[112] Several of the Hip-Hop clothing lines have come under fire for allegedly using sweatshops in foreign countries to produce attire. Such circumstances are at the very least ironic, given the chronic unemployment problem faced by African Americans.

There are, of course, many contemporary examples of successful Black entrepreneurs and top-level corporate executives not associated with the Hip Hop Movement. Oprah Winfrey became a billionaire in the US by leveraging the stunningly successful "Oprah Winfrey Show." Buoyed by the success of that venture, she established an independent television network, OWN. Winfrey has donated generously to many institutions, including Morehouse College and the National Museum of African American History and Culture. In addition, she established the Oprah Winfrey Leadership Academy for Girls in South Africa. Cathy Hughes has also built a fortune by leveraging her involvement in popular media. Hughes served as Vice President and General Manager of Howard University's radio station (WHUR), where she pioneered the format (known as the "Quiet Storm") that revolutionized urban radio and aired on almost 500 stations across the country. Hughes later founded the media company Radio One, which was subsequently expanded into TV One, an independent network. In many respects, the success of these media moguls repeats the experience of the legendary late John H. Johnson, who built a fortune through media acquisitions that included *Ebony* and *Jet* magazines. At the time of his death in 2005 at the age of 87, Johnson had major holdings in book and magazine publishing, cosmetics, television and radio. In 1982, Johnson was cited as the first African-American on *Forbes* magazine's list of the 400 wealthiest Americans.

It is also important to acknowledge African Americans who have also risen to the top echelons of major corporations not directly involved in providing services to Black consumers or to African American interests. As an example, in 1987, Reginald Lewis bought Beatrice International Foods, a snack food, beverage, and grocery store conglomerate, for $985 million, and renamed it TLC Beatrice International Holdings, Incorporated. At the time, this was the largest African American-owned and -managed business in the U.S., reporting revenue of $1.8 billion in 1987. At its peak in 1996, TLC Beatrice International had sales of $2.2 billion and was number 512 on Fortune magazine's list of 1,000 largest companies. Lewis also established The Reginald F. Lewis Foundation in 1987, and the Foundation has supported many non-profit programs and organizations, including Howard University and the Reginald F. Lewis Museum of Maryland African American History & Culture. More contemporary Black CEOs include Rosalind Brewer (Sam's Club), Ursula M. Burns (Xerox), Kenneth I. Chenault (American Express), Steve Davis (Bob

7

Evans Farms), Roger W. Ferguson, Jr. (TIAA-CREF), Kenneth C. Frazier (Merck & Co.), Kim Saunders (M&F Bancorp), and Don Thompson (McDonald's).

There are a few examples of major initiatives by former athletes that demonstrate that conscious efforts to use businesses as a vehicle for community development can be successful. Former major league baseball player Hank Aaron has been successful in using franchise agreements to penetrate the market for fast food in predominantly Black communities. Aaron organized the 755 Restaurant Corporation in 1995. The company, based in Atlanta, operates thirteen Church's Chicken franchises and three Popeye's Chicken and Biscuits franchises in Atlanta, Georgia, and Charlotte, North Carolina. Aaron's 755 Doughnut Corporation operates a Krispy Kreme franchise in the predominantly Black west end of Atlanta.[113]

The initiatives undertaken by the Johnson Development Corporation, founded by former basketball star Earvin "Magic" Johnson, provide an even broader range of benefits to community residents. The corporation was formed in 1993 and has focused much of its energies on creating entertainment complexes, restaurants, and retail centers in underserved urban and suburban communities such as the one with Loews Cineplex Entertainment. Similar partnerships have been established with Starbucks Coffee and Carlson Restaurants (TGI Friday's). The corporation is also involved in urban development projects via the Canyon-Johnson Urban Fund. Johnson has also become involved in the development of financial intermediaries that are targeting lending and other activities in inner city communities. He and other investors, including entertainer Janet Jackson, hold controlling interests in the Los Angeles-based Founders Bank of Commerce. In 2001, Founder's Bank (now named OneUnited Bank) merged with the Boston Bank of Commerce to create the first bicoastal African American bank.[114]

The efforts of former New York Knicks point guard, Stephon Marbury, to eliminate the pressure felt by youngsters and parents to spend exorbitant amounts on the latest sneakers was another initiative that sparked the interest of many African American Studies specialists. Marbury's "Starbury" shoes retailed for $14.98, a far cry from the $200 price of some "Air Jordan" shoes and the over $100 commanded by some shoes marketed by Kobe Bryant and LeBron James. The Starbury line also included apparel like hoodies, jackets and jerseys, all priced at $9.98 or less. The items are sold exclusively at Steve and Barry's University Sportswear stores.

When the Starbury shoes first debuted, what had been envisioned as a month's supply sold out within days. *Business Week* named the line one of its best products of 2006, and the trade magazine, *Footwear News*, named Starbury the "2006 Footwear Launch of the Year."

Although some critics questioned the quality of Starburys, the high performance basketball shoes were made with similar construction and materials as the most expensive top brands. Marbury wore Starburys in every game, as did former Detroit Pistons center, Ben Wallace, who developed his own signature Starbury shoe. Consumers of all ages, community leaders, and media across the country embraced the Starbury initiative and many called it a "Movement" that was revolutionizing the footwear and apparel industries. From the vantage point of African American Studies, it would have been desirable if this movement had expanded. Unfortunately, the retailer, Steve & Barry's, filed for bankruptcy in July 2008, effectively ending this promising venture.[115]

The Starburys venture raised the visibility of the linkages between African Americans and the global economy. Like many other brands, Starburys were made in China, and some critics claimed that the low price was only possible through the exploitation of low-paid workers. Marbury's spokespeople claim, however, that Starburys are not produced in sweatshops and that the low price reflects a business model that eliminates middleman markups and uses word of mouth advertising to promote sales, as opposed to high-cost national advertising campaigns. While Marbury's efforts clearly enhanced the purchasing power of African Americans, a broader initiative will be necessary to transform the economically depressed communities in which many former Starbury customers reside without gainful employment. Marbury himself seemed to be aware of the magnitude of the problems he was trying to address. In the wake of Hurricane Katrina, he pledged about $500,000 of his own money to help victims of the catastrophe, a level of generosity matched by few, if any, other high profile Black athletes.[116]

TABLE 7.10
NUMBER OF BLACK-OWNED BUSINESSES
1969 – 2007

Year	Number
1969	163,073
1972	194,986
1977	231,203
1982	357,000
1997	823,499
2002	1,197,567
2007	1,921,881

Source: US Bureau of the Census, Survey of Black-Owned Businesses, various years

TABLE 7.11
INDUSTRIES WITH THE LARGEST NUMBER OF BLACK-OWNED FIRMS
2007

	Number	% of Total
Health care and social assistance	365,140	19
Repair and maintenance and personal and laundry services	358,332	19
Administrative and support and waste management and remediation services	216,742	11

Source: US Bureau of the Census, Survey of Black-Owned Businesses 2007.

TABLE 7.12
INDUSTRIES OF BLACK-OWNED FIRMS WITH THE LARGEST RECEIPTS
2007

1. Retail trade
2. Health care and social assistance
3. Wholesale trade
4. Construction
5. Professional, scientific, and technical services

Source: US Bureau of the Census, Survey of Black-Owned Businesses 2007.

TABLE 7.13
NUMBER OF BLACK-OWNED FIRMS WITH PAID
EMPLOYEES AND NUMBER OF EMPLOYEES
1977 – 2007

Year	Black firms with paid employees	Percent of all Black firms	Number of Employees
1977	39,968	17.3	164,177
1982	37,841	12.3	121,373
1987	70,815	16.7	220,467
2002	94,518	7.9	753,978
2007	106,824	5.6	921,032

Source: US Bureau of the Census, Survey of Black-Owned Businesses, various years.

Social Entrepreneurship

Consistent with its emphasis on fostering social change, African American Studies specialists prioritize the application of entrepreneurial and other business principles to solve social problems. The systematic application of entrepreneurial principles to promote collective empowerment is termed "Social Entrepreneurship." Private sector entrepreneurs generally measure success via performance in generating profits. In contrast, a social entrepreneur is also focused on producing positive outcomes for society or particular subgroups. Although social entrepreneurs are commonly associated with the voluntary and not-for-profit sectors, social entrepreneurship can also be associated with for-profit ventures.

In response to the recent recession, both African American men and African American women have become increasingly involved in social entrepreneurship ventures. Bret Johnson has profiled four African American males involved in impressive social entrepreneurship ventures.[117] In a similar vein, Toats has documented the important work of six African American female social entrepreneurs.[118]

African American Studies scholars/activists have a mandate to support efforts to develop additional Black social entrepreneurs. One strategy could involve partnerships with educational institutions providing such instruction. As an example, Andrea Johnson argues that HBCUs must take the lead in training Black social entrepreneurs. She describes the development and implementation of an Introduction to Social Entrepreneurship course for students at North Carolina Agricultural & Technical State University.[119]

Black-owned Banks

An examination of the liberating potential of Black-owned business would not be complete without an analysis of the status of Black-owned banks. Magic Johnson's initiatives in this area signify the unparalleled importance of financial intermediaries as a basis for stable local economies. A bank is an organization, usually a corporation, chartered by a state or federal government, which does most or all of the following: receives demand deposits and time deposits; honors instruments drawn on them, and pays interest on them; discounts notes, makes loans, and invests in securities; collects checks, drafts, and notes; certifies depositor's checks; and issues drafts and cashier's checks.

7

Although African Americans established a solid track record of saving during the slavery era through benevolent and beneficial societies, their first experience with large-scale banking proved to be disastrous. Congress incorporated the Freedmen's Savings and Trust Company in 1865 as a banking institution for the former enslaved Africans "to receive on deposit such sums of money as may be offered... and investing the same in the stocks, bonds, treasury notes or other securities of the United States." The bank was a massive failure, as corrupt bureaucrats swindled its depositors out of millions of dollars.[120] Although this devastating loss temporarily set back the process of wealth accumulation and saving, between 1888 and 1934, approximately 135 Black-owned banks were established. The first Black-owned and administered banks were organized in 1888. The Capital Savings Bank of Washington, D.C., opened October 1888, and the Grand Fountain United Order of True Reformers Bank opened in Richmond, Virginia.[121] By 1933, Black banks, savings and loan institutions, and insurance companies had accumulated approximately $4.2 billion in total assets. Seventy-five of the 135 established banks failed before 1936. As late as 1962, only ten commercial banks were minority controlled.[122]

As noted previously, Black-owned banks have been largely written off as insignificant by prominent economists, including Abram Harris and Andrew Brimmer. Traditionally, Black-owned banks were heavily dependent on government deposits and limited to making loans in risky markets. However, in recent years, Black-owned banks have experienced some resurgence and have, thus far, survived waves of both consolidation and innovation in the banking industry. Carver Federal Savings Bank (New York), One United Bank (Boston), Liberty Bank and Trust Company (New Orleans), Industrial Bank (Washington, D.C.), and Citizens Trust Bank (Atlanta) are currently among the largest Black-owned banks.[123] It must be kept in mind, however, that just as is the case for other types of Black-owned business, the economic clout of Black-owned banks is miniscule relative to the largest US financial institutions. At the same time, however, Black financiers are moving into some of the more prestigious and lucrative areas of the industry. Several Black-owned investment banks have been established, most of which are located in New York. Investment banks are financial institutions that deal primarily with raising capital, corporate mergers and acquisitions, and securities trades.

Insurance Companies

Black-owned insurance companies have the longest tradition of providing critical financial services to African Americans. The Black Church learned, taught, and practiced the art of pooling the resources of many in order to care for the needs or misfortunes of a few. From this statistical reality and capability, the idea of Black self-insurance was conceived and led to the establishment of several insurance companies.[124] From 1865 to 1915, concurrent with the development of church mutual aid societies, Black fraternal orders were formed. The Black Church, benevolent societies, and the fraternal orders amassed huge capital funds from assessments, dues, and fees. Often church mutual aid societies and the fraternal orders joined in ventures to form banks as well as insurance companies.

The two largest Black insurance companies existing today were founded by two formerly enslaved Blacks, both of whom, coincidentally, previously worked as barbers. John Merrick, a former agent of the Order of True Reformers, was the principal organizer of North Carolina Mutual of Durham in 1898. In 1905, Alonzo F. Herndon bought the assets of several church mutual aid associations and formed what is now the Atlanta Life Insurance Company.[125]

During the era of Jim Crow segregation, African Americans confronted systemic discrimination and could generally only buy life insurance from Black-owned companies. These companies generally offered only small, affordable "penny" policies, with modest burial benefits, and no cash value. In 1947, there were 211 Black-owned insurance companies. When large White-controlled companies began selling life insurance policies to African American customers, African Americans were charged higher premiums because of shorter life spans. This practice has been challenged in the courts, and large insurers, including American General and Metropolitan Life, have been forced to provide restitution to African American policyholders who were overcharged for burial policies in the 1950s. Nevertheless, Black-owned insurance companies have progressively lost ground in competing with White-controlled companies.

The challenges facing Black insurance companies have forced some of those companies to develop new strategies for economic viability. Currently, there are only nine remaining Black-owned insurance companies in the National Insurance Association, an umbrella organization for African American insurers. North

Carolina Mutual, the oldest and largest African American-managed life insurance company, is focusing more of its attention on providing accident, health, and life insurance to large employers. In a similar vein, in 2001, Atlanta Life transformed itself into the Atlanta Life Financial Group, which added Atlanta Life Investment Advisors to the traditional insurance business. Atlanta Life has stopped opening new individual accounts but has invested heavily in reinsurance, by forming partnerships with larger companies to offer group policies. It has also established a partnership with funeral homes to offer "preneed" insurance to cover funeral expenses.[126]

Continuing Challenges

Although Black businesses undoubtedly play a vital role in Black communities, African American Studies specialists share the skepticism expressed by various authors cited previously regarding the viability of Black business development as the core element of a comprehensive economic empowerment strategy for Blacks. This skepticism provides the foundation for an examination of alternative approaches to the pursuit of Black community economic development in the following section.

Community Political-Economic Development

Defining Black Community Development

The problem of defining Black political-economic development lies in differentiating it from both a global concept of economic development and the more limited concept of business formation. Conventional economic theory cites human resources, natural resources, capital formation, and technology as key processes and fundamental factors that define and measure economic development. The inherent objective of economic development in this sense is to produce goods and services to satisfy human needs and wants. Thus, economic development means the process of improving the production capability of a country or society to meet the consumption requirements of its people.

Black political-economic development differs from general economic development only in the sense that it is race-specific. It is race-specific because Blacks are a politically oppressed people and comprise a disparate segment of American society. Therefore, as an oppressed race, political liberation is equal with and fundamental to all of the other factors of economic development. Beyond these distinctions, the production and consumption analysis of economic development is also applicable to African Americans.

It is crucial to understand the distinctions between the individually-focused economic improvement strategies discussed in previous sections (participation in labor markets, wealth creation, consumption monitoring, and business ownership), and the explicit collective approaches to political-economic development of Black communities. In this discussion, the latter strategy involves a more inclusive approach that promotes concurrent efforts to improve individual outcomes and the systematic creation of social capital as defined in Chapter 4. Comprehensive approaches to political-economic development also prioritize broad-based ownership of economic assets as opposed to individual wealth creation that leads to greater inequality. Such broad-based ownership and participation is deemed necessary to foster a wholesome collective identity and a shared commitment to sustainable political-economic development.

Of the key factors and processes necessary to generate economic development, human resources (professional and occupational skills) and capital formation are seen as the most important and effective factors in developing the Black economy.[127] Black economic development and self-determination can occur only if African Americans acquire the professional, technical, and scientific training and skills to produce the goods and services necessary for the sustenance of the Black community. Moreover, they must be able to produce enough to promote economic exchanges and develop interdependent relationships with other groups. There has always been a correlation between the economic advancement of African Americans and the number of Black academic professionals, scientists, engineers, and technicians, etc., graduated from American colleges and universities.

William M. Harris, a prominent urban planner, has proposed a three-phase model for the development and empowerment of the Black community. The first phase involves building a sense of community through programs that raise Black consciousness. The second phase is devoted to the identification of problems, formation of the goals, and the development of strategies for eliminating barriers to economic development. During this phase, the participation of, or the contributions by, non-Blacks or outside groups is limited to technical

7

assistance for the achievement of goals and objectives. The third phase tests the operation of plans designed to promote self-development and greater self-sufficiency in the Black community.[128]

Historical Community Development Initiatives

The historical roots of political-economic development initiatives can be seen in the earliest efforts of free Blacks to achieve a modicum of economic security through self-help organizations. Two types of societies emerged in the last quarter of the eighteenth century: benevolent societies and beneficial societies. The former were essentially philanthropic organizations, whereas the latter entailed the collection of weekly dues to provide support for members in the event of calamities, including unemployment, illness, or death. One of the first beneficial societies organized in a major city, The Free African Society (1787), was the same organization that facilitated the establishment of the African Methodist Episcopal Church.[129] The greatest growth in the number of benevolent societies occurred between 1820 and 1850, with a substantial number directly or indirectly connected to Black religious congregations.[130]

The Chesapeake Marine Railway and Dry Dock Company was one of the first examples of a cooperative business venture. This enterprise was owned entirely by Blacks and was organized in response to the 1865 dismissal of Black mechanics and longshoremen from employment in the Baltimore shipyards following protests by White workers. The Black workers raised seed capital of $10,000 by selling $5 shares that enabled the purchase of a shipyard and railway.[131]

Du Bois's vision of a "group economy movement" was discussed in the introduction of this chapter. The growth of the group economy, as Du Bois observed in 1906, was such that "half of the Black population came within its orbit and that for 100,000 urban Blacks and 200,000 Black farmers it approached 'a complete system.' "[132] Du Bois's optimism in the possibility of creating a self-sustaining economic network among African Americans was fueled, in part, by his belief that elements of the Rochdale Cooperative Movement, which originated in Britain, could be adapted by Blacks. E. Franklin Frazier also expressed interest in exploring this possibility.

The Rochdale Cooperative Movement was established in 1844 by a small number of weavers who had been fired and blacklisted by former employers. The Rochdale Pioneers codified their operating policies into what are commonly known as the Rochdale Principles. Cooperatives are member-owned and controlled businesses in which all members have an equal say in the governance of the business: one member, one vote. This organizational structure differs significantly from traditional corporate ownership. Cooperatives establish limits on the return on investment and on share holdings and discourage profit-seeking investments; they encourage instead local control and investments by users. Cooperatives also engage in educational efforts, buy goods from other cooperatives, and provide development assistance to groups attempting to organize other co-ops and otherwise contribute to strengthening and sustaining local communities.[133]

As late as 1935, Du Bois believed that the continued growth of the "group economy" provided the potential for the creation of a "Negro Nation within the Nation."[134] Although Du Bois's use of the term *nation* was largely euphemistic, because he did not advocate the creation of a separate independent nation, this was indeed the position advocated by the American Communist Party in the early 1930s. The so-called Black Nation thesis in its classical form was enunciated by the American Communist Party in 1928, was later modified in a 1930 resolution, and was formally codified in Harry Haywood's *Negro Liberation* (1948). The thesis is based on Stalin's definition of a nation, set forth in "Marxism and the National Question" (1913), that defines a nation as "a historically constituted, stable community of people formed on the basis of a common language, territory, economic life and psychological makeup manifested in a common culture." The nation was to consist of the agglomeration of "Black belt" counties in which African Americans constitute a majority. This classical formulation was rendered obsolete, however, by the continuing northern migration of Blacks that resulted, over time, in many of the original counties changing from majority Black to majority White.[135]

The idea of a separate Black nation state in the South was resurrected by Elijah Muhammad of the Nation of Islam (NOI). Muhammad did not use population location as a criterion to justify his scheme. Rather, five southern states were to be turned over as a form of reparations for past injustices. Large numbers of Blacks seeking to escape the forms of oppression experienced in northern urban areas envisioned a return to the South. The five-state proposal was based on two criteria: (a) relative population size, and (b) the ability of the land to sustain necessary levels of agricultural production. Malcolm X explains the vision:

The Honorable Elijah Muhammad says that the size of the territory can be judged according to our population. If a seventh of the population of this country is black, then give us a seventh of the territory, a seventh part of the country. And that is not asking too much because we already worked for the man for four hundred years.[136]

Both Malcolm X and Elijah Muhammad understood that, even if the domestic proposal were implemented, there would be a long transition period during which African Americans would remain engaged principally in the American political economy. Muhammad noted that Blacks earned and contributed billions of dollars annually to the national economy (GNP) through unnecessary expenditures for fine automobiles, clothes, alcohol, tobacco, and drugs. The Muslim's economic plan was for their salary and wage earners to contribute from one to ten dollars a month to develop a national equity or capital fund to buy land and to invest in Black-owned businesses. However, the economic functioning of African Americans in the American political economy was to be undertaken as preparation for eventual disengagement, rather than as a strategy to achieve economic integration:

The Honorable Elijah Muhammad says... [b]etter jobs won't solve our problems. An integrated cup of coffee isn't sufficient pay for four hundred years of slave labor. He also says that a better job, a better job in the white man's factory, or a better job in the white man's business, or a better job in the white man's industry or economy is, at best, only a temporary solution. He says that the only lasting and permanent solution is complete separation on some land that we can call our own.[137]

Even though Malcolm's break with the Nation of Islam precipitated his rejection of the separate nation state model, both before and after the rift, he maintained an unswerving commitment to an urban community-based development model. Malcolm believed, for example, that it would be possible to channel the energies and resources devoted to hedonistic pursuits, both legal and illegal, into a comprehensive development program:

[T]he money that we used to throw away when we were Christians—nightclubbing and drinking and smoking and participating in these other acts of immorality—the money we save when we become Muslims—we channel it into these small business

enterprises and try to develop them where they can provide some job opportunities for the rest of our people.[138]

It is interesting to note that Malcolm's vision of development is organized around the same type of small business development model that has been the foundation of the Black capitalist business development strategy discussed in the previous section. Consequently, it is not clear whether it is consistent with the political-economic development concept presented in the introduction to this section. Most of the small businesses started by Elijah Muhammad's followers were not owned by the collective Nation of Islam but by individual Muslims. Neither Malcolm nor Elijah Muhammad was able to conceive of a more cooperative model of business organization to serve as a foundation for community-wide development, although his language seems to imply that such a model was needed, as illustrated in his speech "The Ballot or the Bullet."[139]

In this speech, Malcolm discusses the economic philosophy of Black Nationalism. For him, the economic implications of Black Nationalism "only means that we should own and operate and control the economy of our community."[140] The failure to follow such a strategy leads to a situation where Black communities become slums.[141] Malcolm maintained that the economic philosophy of Black Nationalism helps African Americans "become conscious of the importance of controlling the economy of our community."[142] The need for a re-education campaign to accomplish this objective was emphasized.[143] The principal outcome of this strategy would be a situation wherein, "If we own the stores, if we operate the businesses, if we try and establish some industry in the community, then we're developing to the position where we're creating employment for our own kind."[144] The use of "we" in Malcolm's formulation, unfortunately, seems to be a rhetorical tactic rather than a concrete suggestion for collective ownership strategies.

The economic philosophy of the NOI can be usefully contrasted with that adopted by the Republic of New Africa (RNA). Some of the delegates who attended a March 1968 Black Nationalist political convention held in Detroit formulated a "Declaration of Independence" designed, in part, to build an independent Black nation. The RNA is best known for a major confrontation with the police and FBI in Jackson, Mississippi, resulting from its efforts to launch its nation-building program. Following several nonviolent confrontations with the Jackson police and the FBI, on

7

August 18, 1971, a gun battle erupted at the headquarters of the RNA, resulting in the death of one police officer. Eleven RNA members were arrested and prosecuted. The RNA had declared sovereignty over the same five "Black Belt" southern states originally identified by Elijah Muhammad in his economic plan: Mississippi, Louisiana, Alabama, Georgia, and South Carolina. The RNA maintained that the land should be ceded by the US government as part of the reparations due Blacks for enslavement. The RNA also demanded a payment of $10,000 per person as compensation for the failure of the federal government to deliver on its promise of "40 acres and a mule" following the Civil War. The initial RNA officers were President Robert Williams, First Vice President Gaidi Obadele, Minister of Information Imari Abukari Obadele I, and Treasurer Obaboa Okono. In contrast with the implicit individualistic philosophy of the NOI, the RNA framed its economic vision by adapting the Tanzanian model of Ujamaa villages that emphasized cooperative economics and community self-sufficiency.[145]

In many respects, the economic development strategy pursued in Philadelphia by Rev. Leon Sullivan embodied the same principles. Sullivan originated what was called the *10-36 plan* in his Philadelphia church in 1962. Congregation members were asked to contribute $10 for 36 months to undertake a community economic development effort. Most of these monies were channeled into the purchase of shares in Zion Investment Associates, a for-profit holding company or community development corporation. This holding company generated Progress Enterprises, a subsidiary that undertook construction of Progress Plaza Shopping Center and an apartment building. Other ventures included a garment manufacturing plant and a chain of convenience stores. Although, as indicated previously, the majority of members' subscriptions constituted cooperative investments, 10 of the 36 payments were used to fund nonprofit social services through the Zion Non-Profit Charitable Trust. Thus, the emergent strategy incorporated provisions for growth enhancing activities alongside vehicles to accomplish redistribution. From one church, the number of churches participating in Sullivan's 10-36 program reached 400.[146]

Neither this economic development initiative, nor the complementary efforts to provide social services, were ever intended, in and of themselves, to be the sole solution to the economic plight of Black Americans. In 1964, Rev. Sullivan spearheaded the formation of Opportunities Industrialization Centers of America (OIC), a community based vocational training and job placement operation that, at its height, was operating in over 160 cities. One of the distinctive features of the OIC approach has been the development of a close working relationship with the private, corporate sector. This facilitated job placement activities and generated corporate contributions that enabled OICs to keep the training cost per participant relatively low. The expansion of the scope of OICs operations depended critically on local ministers in the various communities, a pattern consistent with its origins.[147]

The expansion of Sullivan's community-based development model was stymied by what might be described as the "hijacking" of his model by the federal government. It became the prototype for the Community Development Corporation (CDC) initiative that was first authorized in the special impact provisions of Title VII of the EEO Act of 1964. CDCs were given a broad mandate for a wholistic approach to community development by engaging in a wide variety of activities from housing rehabilitation to health care delivery.[148] CDCs were empowered to encourage business start-ups and to provide technical assistance, and sometimes they had access to concessionary finance for community-based businesses.

One of the distinguishing characteristics of the initial CDC concept was the explicit effort to foster formation through existing neighborhood institutions, as opposed to designing new organizations. This approach contrasts with that taken, for example, in the Model Cities Program (MCP), established in 1969. The implementation of MCP virtually ignored existing institutions and attempted to create entirely new, presumably representative structures. As a consequence, the underlying sense of community was upset, and, predictably, chaos erupted in many locales. The MCP was originally designed as a program that would permit a number of well-funded "model cities" to demonstrate different approaches to poverty reduction and urban renewal. When implemented, the idea of a few cities winning out in a competition for the available funds—so that best practices could be generated and later imitated—was replaced by an allocation process that doled out available federal monies to all cities that met eligibility criteria and filed applications for the money. The more subtle transformation, however, was a massive shift away from a focus on community development to one that emphasized poverty reduction.[149]

Community-based control of resources was significantly reduced when MCP was replaced by the Community Development Block Grant program (CDBG) in 1974. The emphasis on poverty reduction was also a casualty, such that, by 1974, asset-building directed to low-income people, whether for economic development or housing, was no longer a component of anti-poverty programs.[150] Instead, as noted by Gary Dymski, cities were given more tools to use federal funds for asset-building projects that would, at best, have only indirect benefits for lower-income people.[151]

Contemporary Public Policy Barriers

Beginning in the early 1980s, the Reagan administration began a process of retrenchment and funding reduction in federal anti-poverty and urban policy that is ongoing. Declining federal support for urban asset-building and poverty-reduction induced states and localities to create enterprise zones in the late 1970s and to offer tax incentives to firms that locate production sites and/or create jobs in designated areas. These initiatives would be modified by the Clinton administration in the 1990s and repackaged as empowerment zones and empowerment communities. Dymski concludes that such areas, unfortunately, do not lead to employment in low-income areas or neighborhoods where non-Whites reside.[152]

Faced with a changing political and economic climate, many Community Development Corporations (CDCs) became heavily involved in efforts to improve housing conditions in inner-city neighborhoods. CDCs were responsible for constructing approximately 125,000 low- or moderate-income housing units between CDC's inception in the 1960s and 1988. CDCs were also involved in a variety of business ventures leading to the development of over 16 million square feet of commercial or industrial space, loans to or investments in 2,200 community businesses, and direct ownership of over 400 businesses. These commercial activities either created or retained some 90,000 jobs.[153] Successful retail developments have been established by CDCs in several cities that include Boston, Charlotte, Chicago, Detroit, Houston, Los Angeles, Miami, New York, and Philadelphia. However, Grogan and Proscio observe that many initiatives involved an "oasis strategy," in which Community Development Corporations and others have carved out areas of revitalization and relative stability "while the forces that would undo their fragile improvements crouched just outside the door."[154]

The success of CDCs ironically contributed to a new move to locate White-owned businesses in central city locations to take advantage of Black consumers' purchasing power, an ironic development in the context of the earlier discussion of consumption. A 1995 article by business strategist Michael Porter, published in the *Harvard Business Review*, asserts that inner-city consumer markets offer a very attractive target for large-scale retailers and service providers but that land parcels were often too small in inner-city areas to permit efficient businesses to locate there. He also argued that government should provide tax incentives to facilitate the opening of inner-city markets to mainstream businesses.[155] Although the limitations of Porter's analysis were analyzed comprehensively in the volume *The Inner City, Urban Poverty and Economic Development in the Next Century*, he was able to mobilize business leaders to support his approach. Although there were some positive outcomes for Black business owners, the overall thrust of Porter's initiative was to open new markets for large firms.[156]

This strategy was institutionalized in the New Market Initiative Program implemented by the Clinton administration in 1999.[157] It has been complemented by accelerating "gentrification" efforts, that is, recruitment of high-earning Whites to establish residences in central city neighborhoods. Although it might appear at first glance that an influx of higher-income residents is a boon for development potential indices discussed in a previous chapter, it is important to keep in mind, as Smith observes, that "developments... emphasiz[ing] attracting high-income tenants are more likely to favor amenities and a traditional design over celebrating the cultural tradition of a community."[158] The effort to attract high-income residents can erode a critical cultural asset that could anchor bona fide revitalization efforts.

Any discussion of political-economic community development would be incomplete without a discussion of the increasing involvement of Black churches in community development projects. Case studies of individual churches that have established economic empowerment ministries reveal a range of activities somewhat similar to those undertaken by Leon Sullivan. Such initiatives include developing low-income and senior housing projects, operating credit unions and investment clubs, providing job training, offering entrepreneurship programs, and operating private schools.[159] A number of churches have organized community development

7

corporations to facilitate their efforts although the Sullivan model, emphasizing broad-based ownership, has not yet been replicated. In addition to individual church ministries, there are also coalitions of churches taking advantage of economies of scale. In some cities, these coalitions are becoming major leaders in urban revitalization planning and development. In Atlanta, for example, the Concerned Black Clergy, a consortium of 100 predominantly Black congregations, is forming a partnership with the Bank of America and the Fulton County Housing Authority to pursue a mixed-use development project in the East Point area. Two hundred-forty churches in Washington, D.C., have established a coalition to seek equitable lending policies by financial institutions. This initiative has resulted in approximately $250 million in loans from local banks. Similar coalitions are operating in Pittsburgh and St. Louis. At the national level, the Congress of National Black Churches operates a national homeownership program as well as a wholly owned for-profit development subsidiary.[160]

This church-based economic development movement comes at a critical juncture when traditional Black political power is on the decline. W. E. B. Du Bois, no doubt, would applaud the current movement as having the potential to be the hub of a new "group economy movement." At the same time, the caution he advanced remains relevant, that is, the Black Church should avoid evolving into "large social and business institutions catering to the desire for information and amusement of their members [while] warily avoiding unpleasant questions both within and without the Black world."[161] Thus, it is critical that Black church-based development leaders collaborate with secular organizations, such as the Urban League and the NAACP, and incorporate opportunities for broad-based ownership in their commercial ventures.

Community groups are increasingly waging successful campaigns to implement community benefits agreements to ensure that the current wave of urban revitalization and gentrification do not lay waste to Black communities, as was the case for the first wave of urban renewal. Such agreements typically involve contractual commitments regarding employment opportunities, purchases from community businesses, and infrastructure investments in connection with major redevelopment projects. The agreement between activists in the Hill District of Pittsburgh and the Pittsburgh Penguins hockey team is a prime example. Ironically,

this area was the first casualty of the first wave of urban renewal in the 1950s, however, this time, the residents learned the lessons of the past and came prepared to confront the Penguins management when plans were announced to build a new arena in the same area.[162]

Reparations: A Potential Boon to Community Development?

Formal initiatives to seek reparations for various types of damages incurred by African Americans during the slavery era provide a new context for discussions about future possibilities for community political-economic development. Reparations claims are different from other civil rights remedies that address post-slavery racial harms. Affirmative action, for example, was designed to combat existing racism against Blacks and did not attempt to compensate Black people for uncompensated labor during the slavery era.

Reparations claims incorporate ethical as well as economic justifications, but the present examination is limited to the economic justifications and potential use of reparations payments. Public discussion of proposals to pay reparations to African Americans for the oppression and exploitation experienced by their ancestors during the slavery era has intensified in recent years, as evidenced by reparations claims recently advanced at the World Conference Against Racism (WCAR) in September 2001 in Durban, South Africa. Unfortunately, serious consideration of the issue at the WCAR was thwarted by the United States and its allies. A growing grassroots movement has been largely responsible for advancing the goals of the reparations movement. Formal reparations demands were made to the White religious community by James Forman on May 4, 1969. Forman's famous Black Manifesto, in essence, demanded that Whites pay reparations to Black people for two centuries of forced slavery and another hundred years of Black servitude to the White power structure.[163] Proponents and opponents of the Manifesto and reparation demands continued spirited debates during the 1970s.

Currently, a variety of groups are active in educational and advocacy efforts. They include the Republic of New Africa, the National Coalition of Blacks for Reparations in America, and the African Reparations Movement. Contemporary efforts to pursue reparations claims are built upon earlier analytical examinations of possible political and legal strategies and direct attempts to seek reparations. Boris Bittker's classic volume, The

Case for Black Reparations, identifies many of the critical issues that frame the current debate.[164] Bittker uses the experiences of various groups to whom reparations or quasi-reparations payments have been made to generate a line of argument that would support reparations for Blacks. These include payments to Native Americans for treaty violations, reparations to Japanese Americans for internment during World War II, and payments to Jewish Holocaust victims. More recent legal strategies are also informed by successful litigation resulting in payments to survivors of the Rosewood massacre and payments to survivors of the Tuskegee experiment.

Bittker's analysis leads him to conclude that "Congress or some other public body... will have to decide in the end whether a program of reparations should consist of individual or group payments, specific monetary programs, or some combination of these, and will have to face all the subordinate difficulties that each of these alternatives would bring in its wake."[165] However, Bittker's assumption that Congress is a likely venue in which to advance reparations claims is not borne out by either historical or contemporary experience. The proposal developed by Walter Vaughn published in 1891 was one of the first formal efforts to seek reparations for Blacks. Vaughn's "Freedom Pension Bill" was described as "a rational proposition to grant pensions to persons of color emancipated from slavery." In describing the reaction to his proposal, Vaughn states that "rebuffs were expected and have been abundant. Discouragement has appeared in every possible form. White men have frowned and combated, while many influential and educated Negroes have been incredulous and doubtful."[166] Needless to say, Vaughn's bill was never enacted. Callie House, an African American woman who had been enslaved prior to the end of the Civil War, took up the call for reparations and in the early 1900s organized the first national Black grassroots movement in history, which culminated in the formation of the National Ex-Slave Mutual Relief and Pension Association. House identified approximately $68 million in taxes ($1.2 billion in 2005 dollars) on Confederate cotton seized by the Union forces as the source from which reparations payments should be made. The organization thrived until House was imprisoned by the Justice Department for allegedly engaging in mail fraud—a technique that would later be used to undermine Marcus Garvey.[167]

Representative John Conyers introduced a bill in 1989 calling for creation of a presidential commission to study the question of reparations for African Americans.

The Conyers bill (originally HR 40, now HR 891) was put forward after passage of the Civil Liberties Act of 1988, which granted reparations to Japanese Americans interned during World War II. Despite the fact that several cities, including Detroit, Cleveland, and the District of Columbia, passed resolutions endorsing this initiative, there has been no meaningful action, although it has been re-introduced annually since 1989. The Conyers bill calls for appropriating $8 million to establish a commission to study reparations proposals for African Americans.[168]

The economic basis of reparations claims advanced by both Vaughn and Bittker are the economic losses incurred by Blacks as a result of slavery. Although they are described in general terms, more recently several economists have attempted to measure the gains accruing to Whites and the losses experienced by Blacks that are attributable to the slavery regime. Attention to this issue has been guided by the efforts of Richard America, who includes several important studies in his book *The Wealth of Races*.[169] Richard Vedder, Lowell Gallaway, and David Klingaman estimate that approximately 25 percent of the total income in the southern states was attributable to slave exploitation. According to their calculations, by 1860, enslaved Blacks were only receiving sustenance amounting to about one-third of the value of the products they were producing. They calculate that the total wealth accumulated from slavery by the onset of the Civil War was about $3.2 million in 1859 dollars.[170] This is the same figure calculated by Roger Ransom and Richard Sutch.[171] James Marketti estimates the present value as of 1983 of losses incurred by Africans resulting from enslavement during the period 1790 to 1860 and finds, depending on what assumptions are used, that the value in 1983 dollars of losses ranged from $2.1 to $4.7 billion.[172] Larry Neal calculates a figure of $1.4 trillion using similar techniques.[173] The magnitude of potential claims and collective White unwillingness to take responsibility for historical injustices are important sources of ongoing resistance to serious consideration of reparations proposals, as well as the obvious difficulty in developing precise estimates of reparations due.

Several lawsuits have been filed in recent years seeking damages from companies that provided the financial underpinnings and infrastructure of the slavery regime. Specifically, suits were filed in 2002 seeking class-action status for descendants of enslaved Blacks in the US, in California, Illinois, Louisiana, New Jersey, New York, and Texas. Edward Fagan and Roger Wareham are the

7

two lead attorneys in five of these cases. The suits sought restitution, punitive damages, and the creation of a historical commission to study the companies' actions before the Civil War. Four of these cases were consolidated and transferred to Illinois for adjudication. The defendants in these cases are J.P. Morgan Chase & Co., R. J. Reynolds Tobacco Company, CSX Corporation, Aetna Incorporated., Brown Brothers Harriman and Company, New York Life Insurance Company, Norfolk Southern Corporation, Lehman Brothers Corporation, Lloyd's of London, Union Pacific Railroad, Brown & Williamson, Liggett Group Incorporated, Canadian National Railway, Southern Mutual Insurance Company, American International Group, Fleet Boston, and Loews Corporation.[174]

The consolidated suit was dismissed in July 2005, with the presiding judge declaring that the plaintiffs failed to show any injury done to them that can be traced to the companies. The case will obviously be appealed, but this decision is indicative of the difficulties plaintiffs face in advancing "derivative claims," or claims brought by someone other than the direct victim. Several legal strategies have been proposed to increase the likelihood of success in litigation. It might be useful to position current African Americans not simply as victims but as heirs and claimants of lost wages. Another strategy could focus on persuading the legal system to recognize group rights in addition to traditional individual rights. By using such a strategy, reparations claims could focus, in part, on the broader concept of "underdevelopment" resulting from the systematic enslavement and exploitation of the African American population. The system of slavery, thereby, ensured that money and other resources were channeled to Whites and denied to African Americans.[175] Reparations claims could then focus, in part, on remedying the broad-based harm that produced broad-based benefits to Whites via slavery and segregation.

The success of future litigation is uncertain, particularly if the position adopted in the Illinois case establishes a precedent that "the historical record clearly shows that the President and Congress have the constitutional authority to determine the nature and scope of the relief sought in this case, not the courts." At the same time, new municipal and state disclosure laws, designed to identify corporations that had financial involvement in supporting slavery, are likely to yield a large quantity of information that can strengthen future legal pleadings. A number of states and municipalities have passed legislation requiring corporations to divulge links with slavery, including California, Chicago, and Los Angeles. Such disclosures may cause sufficient embarrassment that corporations take proactive efforts to protect their public images, as opposed to being drawn into lengthy litigation. In 2005, Wachovia Bank, the nation's fourth largest, issued a formal apology acknowledging that two of the company's ancestral banks—the Bank of Charleston and the Georgia Railroad and Banking Company—owned enslaved Africans and accepted captives as collateral for loans. Such apologies could eventually lead to voluntary reparations payments.

Assuming that a pool of reparations payments from firms were to materialize, how should such funds be distributed and utilized to achieve the largest possible developmental impact? Assuming that payments would be designated for individuals, the first problem would be preventing "imposters" from gaining access to payments. William Darity and Dania Frank suggest two criteria for eligibility: (1) an individual must prove that they had at least one ancestor who was enslaved in the United States; and (2) demonstrate prior self-identification as Black on a legal document at least ten years before the beginning of the reparations program.[176]

Darity and Frank also discuss various forms by which payments might be made to individuals. The most simple would be lump-sum payments to eligible individuals. This approach would have the least long-term developmental impact for the various reasons discussed in previous sections. Alternatively, a trust fund could be established to which eligible Blacks could apply for grants for various asset-building projects, including homeownership, additional education, or start-up funds for self-employment. Obviously, this option would have greater developmental impact than the first option. In a similar vein, payments could be made in the form of vouchers, rather than cash, which could be used for asset-building purposes, including the purchase of financial assets. Another approach could provide reparations-in-kind, rather than cash or quasi-cash payments. Darity and Frank suggest, for example, guaranteed schooling beyond the high school level or guaranteed medical insurance.[177]

Another approach to reparations would be to create new institutions to promote collective well-being in the Black community. Such institutions could be designed to consider reparations for encouraging individual recipients to pool resources for the accumulation of social capital and collective wealth holding.

For example, a national CDC entity could be created with the expressed purpose of underwriting community development projects, such as entrepreneurial ventures, infrastructure projects, etc. Individuals would be guaranteed a minimum return on invested reparations payments and would receive a lump sum payment at retirement.

It would, of course, be possible to create combinations of the various designs. The development of payment plans should be guided by several principles, as proposed by Darity and Frank. Their research suggests that any form of payment that does not include disincentives for recipients to purchase goods and services from non-Blacks will exacerbate the forces that reduce the income of Blacks relative to Whites. Consequently, it might be useful to mandate partial payment of reparations in the form of vouchers redeemable only at goods and service providers affiliated with Black-owned businesses. Darity and Frank also note that "without significant productive capacity in place before reparations, a lump-sum payment could actually result in an absolute decline in Black income."[178] This finding implies that a first priority use of reparations payments should be to create institutions that increase what economists call the "absorptive capacity" to receive and utilize funds efficiently. Finally, Darity and Frank insist that African Americans should not bear the tax burden of financing their own reparations payments, therefore reparations income should be tax-free.[179]

Darity's and Frank's proposals are consistent with the perspective that emerges from an African American Studies-based analysis of the reparations issue. It is imperative that various reparations activist groups take the necessary steps to have concrete plans in place to guide reparations payment processes, if, and when, such payments are initiated by corporations.

Carlton Waterhouse argues that African Americans should pursue a reparations program of institutional development within Black communities – with or without government support. In the absence of government support Waterhouse argues that a reparations program can be implemented through the pooling of existing internal resources.[180] Andre Smith and he have examined whether the laws of tax exemption and charitable organizations and tax exempt status may be conferred upon organizations whose stated goals are to repair the community of a particular race.[181] Waterhouse also insists that it is imperative that the intended beneficiaries of reparations programs play an active role in their design and implementation.[182]

More generally, a systematic approach is needed to overcome the various problems identified in this chapter and to promote sustainable political-economic development. The problems include: (1) the absence of a collective economic liberation ideology; (2) systemic barriers limiting opportunities to obtain adequate advanced education and business training; (3) externally created difficulty in procuring capital and credit; (4) external and self-generated barriers to saving and wealth accumulation and the transfer of wealth; and, (5) psychological resistance caused by cultural alienation to organizing to attain cooperative goals.

Globalization: A New Challenge to Community Development?

The growing challenges associated with globalization necessitate action to address the organizational and psychological constraints summarized in the last section. Ironically, the proposals advanced by critics of globalization who seek to protect vulnerable US communities bear remarkable similarities to those of the Black political-economic development movement discussed previously. Michael Shuman argues for increasing community self-reliance and asserts, "The only way communities can ensure their economic well-being is to stop chasing multinational firms with no community loyalties, and to start investing in community corporations."[183] He advocates local investment in community corporations that provide employment and supply goods and services for local consumption. This approach is almost a direct restatement of Black political-economic development strategies advocated in the late 1960s and early 1970s! Shuman does, however, have additional strategic and policy dimensions that should be incorporated into future Black political-economic development advocacy. Specifically, he claims that community self-reliance should be a legitimate objective of local government regulation, similar to local health, safety, and environmental protection.[184]

The concerns of the Environmental Racism and Environmental Justice Movements should also be assigned high priority in Black political-economic development strategizing. These movements advocate redevelopment policies that are attuned to nature, honor the cultural integrity of communities, and provide fair access for all to the full range of resources. The movement especially challenges metropolitan sprawl because it is not environmental-friendly and is fostered by inequitable policies. As noted in the earlier

7

discussion of spatial mismatch, existing transportation policies (highways, light rail networks, and other suburban-friendly public transportation modes) disadvantage inner city residents in the services provided and in the negative impacts on health of the modes of transportation that are accessible.[185] The ideology and objectives of the Environmental Racism and Environmental Justice Movements should be sufficiently uncontroversial to allow cooperation across groups with very different ideologies.

The "Living Wage" Movement is another locally-oriented policy thrust that attacks the negative consequences of globalization. This movement seeks to force employers to raise the pay of low-wage workers sufficiently to enable them to escape poverty. Advocacy for local legislation mandating a minimum "living wage" has had some success, but it needs broader support from Blacks who are among the groups most vulnerable to becoming the "working poor." Advocacy for a "living wage" at the local level should be coordinated with state and national efforts to increase the statutory minimum wage. Black political-economic development planners cannot, however, take an isolated approach to addressing local and domestic US concerns. As William Julius Wilson observes, "The lesson for those committed to fighting inequality, especially those involved in multiracial coalition politics is to pay close scrutiny to fiscal, monetary, and trade policies that may have long-term consequences for the national and regional economies, as seen in future earnings, jobs and concentrated poverty."[186] To confront international developments effectively will require conscious efforts to organize the equivalent of what Joel Kotkin describes as "global tribes." Global tribes, which he argues includes the British, Jews, Japanese, Chinese, and Asian Indians, are said to have three critical characteristics: (1) a strong ethnic identity and sense of mutual dependence, that helps the group adjust to changes in the global economy and political order without losing its essential unity; (2) a global network based on mutual trust that allows the tribe to function collectively beyond the confines of national or regional borders; and (3) a passion for technical and other knowledge from all possible sources, combined with an essential open-mindedness that fosters rapid cultural and scientific development critical for success in the late-twentieth-century world economy.[187] According to Kotkin, "The power of global tribes derives from their successful coalescing of two principles that, in classic liberal thought, have been separated: an intrinsic 'tribal' sense of unique historical and ethnic identity and the ability to adapt to a cosmopolitan global economy."[188]

Conscious development of global tribal affinity among people of African descent would resurrect the historical efforts to promote Pan-Africanism with a special emphasis on global economics in addition to strengthening political power. The discussion of the need to cultivate a new pan-African identity in Chapter 5 would be a key component of such a strategy.

The events surrounding Hurricane Katrina point to the need for Black organizations and communities to develop independent, local self-help, community-based plans and procedures for various types of emergencies. The development of such plans should involve the widest possible collaboration with individuals and groups, including churches, resident boards of housing projects, neighborhood associations, parent-teacher organizations, and neighborhood school officials. The technology and information management capabilities necessary to maintain local plans in a national electronic clearinghouse that can be updated annually should be developed. In addition, the self-help fundraising efforts initiated to assist Katrina's victims should be continued indefinitely to create a national disaster relief fund that could be accessed by individuals and groups victimized by future disasters. Specific attention should be focused on ensuring that property owners are not further victimized by unscrupulous land grab efforts by speculators and opportunists.

Questions & Exercises

1. Class antagonism between owners of capital and labor is a concern of socialist and capitalist theorists. However, neither classical nor neoclassical economists adequately factor in the impacts of race and racism. In what ways do slighting the implications of race and racism in economic transactions affect the validity or efficacy of modern economic theory?

2. How does racial stratification as discussed in this chapter differ from overt racial discrimination in American society?

3. What socioeconomic factors contribute most to the overwhelming disparity in the wealth accumulation of Blacks compared with Whites?

4. Historically, large labor unions and federations, such as the AFL-CIO, have had a mixed record in fighting racial discrimination. Given this history, even though non-union employers like Walmart pay relatively low wages, how important is it for African Americans to consider alliances with the labor movement in efforts to improve economic well-being?

5. Federal programs designed to promote and facilitate minority business enterprise have had little effect or success in the development of large multimillion dollar Black-owned businesses. Support or refute this statement.

6. The "group economy" was promoted as a strategy to pursue community economic development. The group economy concept has, demonstrably, been more successful among Asian, Arab, Hispanic, and other racial-ethnic groups than among African Americans. Discuss some of the socioeconomic and political factors that might explain this phenomenon.

7. The purchasing power of African Americans is approaching $800 billion annually. Discuss some of the reasons why these massive consumer expenditures have not resulted in a much greater increase in the number and economic viability of Black-owned businesses.

8. The contemporary plight of African Americans results, to a significant extent, from the economic oppression and exploitation experienced by their ancestors during the slavery era. Reparations have been proposed to compensate Black people for uncompensated labor extracted during the slavery era. Write a critical analysis of the merits and weaknesses of the various reparations proposals discussed in this chapter.

9. Explain why and how the expanding globalization of economic activity may prove to be disadvantageous to African American salaried professionals and unskilled laborers in the United States.

Social Responsibility Projects

1. Identify a community-based organization that provides support for job seekers and/or the unemployed and volunteer your services.

2. Work with your family members to develop and implement a long-term wealth-building strategy.

3. Identify a community-based organization that promotes consumer literacy and provide assistance in outreach efforts.

4. Organize a savings or investment club to advance collective wealth generation.

5. Identify a local Community Development Corporation and become involved in one or more projects.

6. Determine if your place of worship is involved in economic development activities and, if so, begin working with the responsible person. If not, encourage your religious leader to initiate such initiatives.

54. D. Bellamy and A. Parks, "Economic Development in Southern Black Belt Counties: How Does it Measure Up?" in *Blacks in Rural America,* ed. Stewart and Allen, 79-102.

55. L. Swanson, R. Harris, J. Skees and L. Williamson, "African Americans in Southern Rural Regions: The Importance of Legacy," in *Blacks in Rural America*, ed. Stewart and Allen, 103-18.

56. L. Jensen, "Employment Hardship and Rural Minorities: Theory, Research, and Policy," in *Blacks in Rural America*, ed. Stewart and Allen, 119-38.

57. T. Davis, "Income Inequities between Black and White Populations in Southern Nonmetropolitan Counties," in *Blacks in Rural America*, ed. Stewart and Allen, 139-52.

58. "Obama's Stimulus Plan," The Progress Report, (January 5, 2009), http://www.huffingtonpost.com/the-progress-report/obamas-stimulus-package_b_155279.html.

59. "Obama's Stimulus Plan," The Progress Report, (January 5, 2009), http://www.huffingtonpost.com/the-progress-report/obamas-stimulus-package_b_155279.html.

60. Paul Wiseman and Barbara Hansen, "Exclusive: Obama stimulus reduced our pain, experts say," *USA Today*, January 25, 2010, http://www.usatoday.com/money/economy/2010-01-25-usa-today-economic-survey-obama-stimulus_N.htm.

61. T. Swanstrom, "The Road to Jobs: Patterns of Employment in the Construction Industry in Eighteen Metropolitan Areas," unpublished manuscript (August 30, 2007).

62. K. Thompson, "Advocates Struggle to Measure Stimulus Relief for Minority Businesses," Washingtonpost.com, January 18, 2010, http://www.washingtonpost.com/wp-dyn/content/article/2010/01/17/AR2010011702910.html.

63. U.S Bureau of the Census, Survey of Black Owned Businesses, Washington: GPO, 2006.

64. Jackie Jones, "Sharpton, West to Debate on Obama, Black Agenda," *BlackAmericaWeb*, June 21, 2011, http://www.blackameri-caweb.com/.

65. National Urban League, http://www.nul.org/2011conference/2011/welcome.

66. National Urban League, http://org2.democracyinaction.org/o/5666/p/dia/action/public/?action_KEY=7766.

67. National Urban League, "The State of Black America 2011: Jobs Rebuild America: Putting Urban America Back to Work," http://www.iamempowered.com/sites/default/files/12-point_jobs_rebuild_america_plan.pdf .

68. The Poverty Tour, http://www.povertytour.smileyandwest.com.

69. "Congressional Black Caucus' 5-city job fair tour kicks off in Cleveland with thousands turning out," Cleveland.com, August 08, 2011, http://www.cleveland.com/business/index.ssf/2011/08/congressional_black_caucus_fiv.html. See also Marcia Pledger, "CBC Launches "For The People" Jobs Tour," http://newsone.com/nation/thegrio1/cbc-jobs-fairs/.

70. E. Wolff, "Racial Wealth Disparities: Is the Gap Closing?" *Public Policy Brief No. 66A* (Annandale-on-Hudson, NY: The Levy Economics Institute of Bard College, 2001), 3.

71. H. McCall, "The Savings Gap: Savings and Investing by African Americans," (1998), accessed 5/10/2003, http://www.osc.state.ny.us/reports/other/savings.htm, (1998).

72. Ibid.

73. K. Charles and E. Hurst, "The Correlation of Wealth Across Generations," (December 2002), http://faculty.chicagobooth.edu/erik.hurst/research/final_resub_jpe_dec2002.pdf.

74. P. Purcell, "Pension Sponsorship and Participation: Summary of Recent Trends," *CRS Report for Congress* (Washington, D.C.: Congressional Research Service, 2001).

75. Wolff, "Racial Wealth Disparities," 2.

76. A. Aizcorbe, A. Kennickell, and K. Moore, "Recent Changes in U.S. Family Finances from the 1998 and 2001 Survey of Consumer Finances," *Federal Reserve Bulletin* (January 2003):1-32.

77. "Investment Club," Black Bank Initiative, http://www.blackownedbank.com/?page_id=4.

78. R. Haveman and E. Wolff, "Who are the Asset Poor? Levels, Trends, and Composition, 1983-1998," unpublished manuscript (2001).

79. A. Caner and E. Wolff, "Asset Poverty in the United States, 1984-1999: Evidence from the Panel Study of Income Dynamics," *Economics Working Paper Archive* at WUSTL (September 2002).

80. Straight, "Black-White Wealth."

81. Wolff, "Racial Wealth Disparities," 2.

82. Ibid, 3.

83. McCall, "The Savings Gap."

84. Ibid.

85. Wolff, "Racial Wealth Disparities."

86. Office of Policy Development and Research, "Homeownership: Progress and Work Remaining." Issue Brief No. III, US Department of Housing and Urban Development (December 2000).

7

87. The preceding information is derived from the websites of several organizations including the Land Loss Project,http://www. landloss.org/; Federation of Southern Cooperatives Land Assistance Fund, http://www.federationsoutherncoop.com/; and The Land Loss Fund, http://www.federationsoutherncoop.com/.

88. United States District Court for the District of Columbia (*In re* Black Farmers Discrimination Litigation), Misc. No. 08-mc-0511 (PLF), Settlement Agreement, February 18, 2010 (Revised and Executed as of May 13, 2011), https://www.blackfarmer-case.com//SettlementAgreement.aspx.

89. J. Allen-Smith, "Introduction," in *Blacks in Rural America*, ed. Stewart and Allen, 15-16.

90. J. Nembhard and N. Chiteji, eds., *Wealth Accumulation & Communities of Color in the United States* (Ann Arbor: The University of Michigan Press, 2006).

91. Cited in A. Harris, *The Negro as a Capitalis*t, 214.

92. See A. Harris, T*he Negro as a Capitalist*, especially 216-17.

93. See A. Headen and N. Masia, "Exploring the Potential Link Between Medicaid Access Restrictions, Physician Location, and Health Disparities," *American Journal of Managed Care* (January 2005): SP021-SP026.

94. See the website of the Joint Center for Political and Economic Studies http://jointcenter.org/databank/NOP/reports/1999_educ_report.htm.

95. See E. Frankenberg and C. Lee, "Charter Schools and Race: A Lost Opportunity for Integrated Education," *Education Policy Analysis Archives* 11 (September 2003). Retrieved from http://epaa.asu.edu/epaa/v11n32/.

96. See "Rainbow/PUSH-Wall Street Project," *Black Enterprise*, February 2005.

97. K. Sanford, "Jesse Jackson and the Rainbow/PUSH Coalition," in *Black Political Organizations in the Post-Civil Rights Era*, ed. O. Johnson and K. Sanford (New Brunswick, NJ: Rutgers University Press, 2002), 168.

98. Manning Marable, "Civil Rights or Silver Rights?" Znet Commentary, January 2, 2000.

99. See for example, T. Cross, *Black Capitalism: Strategy for Business in the Ghetto* (New York: Antheneum, 1974).

100. Ibid.

101. T. Anderson, "Black Entrepreneurship and Concepts toward Economic Coexistence," *Western Journal of Black Studies* (Summer 1982): 84.

102. E. Franklin Frazier, *Black Bourgeoisie* (New York: Collier Books, 1962), 144-45.

103. E. Ofari, *The Myth of Black Capitalism* (New York: Modern Reader, 1970); R. Allen, *Black Awakening in Capitalist America* (Garden City, NJ: Anchor Books, 1970).

104. M. Marable, *How Capitalism Underdeveloped Black America* (Boston: South End Press, 1983).

105. W. E. B. Du Bois, T*he Negro in Business: Report of a Social Study made under the direction of Atlanta University; together with the Proceedings of the Fourth Conference for the Study of the Negro Problems, held at Atlanta University, May 30-31, 1899.* (Atlanta: Atlanta University Press, 1899).

106. See Seder and Burrell, "Getting it Together," 11-12.

107. J. Harmon, A. Lindsay and C. Woodson, *The Negro as a Business Man* (College Park, MD: McGrath Publishing Co., 1929, Reprint 1969), 24.

108. See Seder and Burrell, "Getting it Together," 10-11.

109. L. Bennett, Jr., "Money, Merchants, Markets: The Quest for Economic Security," *Ebony*, Part 11 (1975), 77.

110. T. Bates, Banking on *Black Enterprise, The Potential of Emerging Firms for Revitalizing Urban Economies* (Washington, D.C.: Joint Center for Political and Economic Studies, 1993).

111. R. Fairlie and A. Robb, "Why Are Black-Owned Businesses Less Successful than White–Owned Businesses? The Role of Families, Inheritances, and Business Human Capital," unpublished manuscript. (May 2003).

112. D. Basu, "A Critical Examination of the Political Economy of the Hip-Hop Industry," in *African Americans in the U.S. Economy*, ed. Conrad et al., 267.

113. See J. Whitehead and J. Stewart, "African American Athletes," in *African Americans in the U.S. Economy*, ed. Conrad et al.

114. Ibid.

115. Andria Cheng, "Steve & Barry Bankruptcy Further Pressures Malls," *The Wall Street Journal*, July 9, 2008, http://www.market-watch.com/story/steve-barrys-bankruptcy-deals-another-blow-to-malls.

116. For information about the Starbury initiative see the Starbury website:www.starbury.com. (site discontinued).

117. Bret Johnson, "4 Change-Makers Poised for Success," *The Root*, November 5, 2012, http://www.theroot.com/views/4-changemakers-poised-success.

118. Toats, "6 African American Women Making Their way as Social Entrepreneurs," Madamenoire.com, January 10, 2012, http://madamenoire.com/96654/african-american-women-making-their-way-as-social-entrepreneurs/.

119. Andrea Johnson, "Teaching Social Entrepreneurship at Historically Black Colleges and Universities: Implications for the Future," Institute for Entrepreneurship Leadership & Innovation, Howard University, http://www.theeliinstitute.org/

faculty-repository/75-teaching-social-entrepreneurship-at-historically-black-colleges-and-universities-implications-for-the-future.

120. See Seder and Burrell, "Getting It Together."
121. See Seder and Burrell, "Getting It Together."
122. See Seder and Burrell, "Getting It Together."
123. See the annual *Black Enterprise* lists of the largest Black-owned firms for updated information.
124. For a brief chronology of Black economic and educational development from 1865 to 1915, see J. Franklin, *From Slavery to Freedom* (New York: Alfred A. Knopf 1967), 382-412.
125. See Seder and Burrell, "Getting It Together."
126. Information about these insurers can be obtained from the company websites.
127. See T. Anderson, "Black Affirmative Action: Strategies Towards Self-Help and Self-Determination," *Humboldt Journal of Social Relations* 14, nos. 1&2 (FW/S.S. 1986/87): 185-94.
128. W. Harris, *Black Community Development* (San Francisco: R&E Publishers, 1976).
129. See Seder and Burrell, "Getting It Together."
130. Ibid.
131. See Seder and Burrell, "Getting It Together."
132. W. E. B. Du Bois, "The Economic Future of the Negro," *Publications of the American Economic Association* 7 (1906): 219-42.
133. For additional information, see J. Birchall, *Co-op: The People's Business* (Manchester: Manchester University Press, 1994).
134. W. E. B. Du Bois, "A Negro Nation Within a Nation," *Current History* 42 (June 1935): 265-70.
135. For additional information, see E. Hutchinson, *Blacks and Reds: Race and Class in Conflict, 1919-1990* (Lansing, MI: Michigan State University Press, 1995).
136. Malcolm X, "The Black Revolution," *The End of White World Supremacy: Four Speeches by Malcolm X*, ed. B. Goodman (New York: Merlin House, 1971), 72. This speech was delivered in 1963.
137. Ibid, 73-74.
138. Malcolm X, "The Black Revolution," 84-85.
139. Malcolm X, "The Ballot or the Bullet," in *Malcolm X Speaks, Selected Speeches and Statements*, ed. G. Breitman (New York: Pathfinder Press, 1989), 23-44. Speech delivered in Cleveland, Ohio, April 3, 1964.
140. Ibid.
141. Malcolm X, "The Ballot or the Bullet," 39.
142. Malcolm X, "The Ballot or the Bullet," 39.
143. Malcolm X, "The Ballot or the Bullet," 39.
144. D. Cunnigan, "Bringing the Revolution Down Home: The Republic of New Africa in Mississippi," *Sociological Spectrum* 19, 1 (1999): 63-92.
145. Malcolm X, "The Ballot or the Bullet," 39.
146. See P. Patterson, "Community Development Corporations," in *Black Economic Development*, ed. Cash and Oliver, 276-281 and J. Stewart, "Building a Cooperative Economy: Lessons from the Black Experience," *Review of Social Economy* 42, no. 3 (1984): 360-68.
147. See Stewart, "Building a Cooperative Economy."
148. See Patterson, "Community Development Corporations."
149. See G. Dymski, "New Markets" or Old Constraints? Financing Community Development in the Post-'War on Poverty' Era," unpublished manuscript (2005).
150. Ibid.
151. Dymski, "New Markets."
152. Dymski, "New Markets."
153. D. Imbroscio, *Reconstructing City Politics* (Thousand Oaks, CA: Sage, 1997).
154. P. Grogan and T. Proscio, *Comeback Cities, A Blueprint for Urban Neighborhood Revival* (Boulder, CO: Westview Press, 2000), 54.
155. M. Porter, "The Competitive Advantage of the Inner City," *Harvard Business Review* (May-June 1995): 55-71.
156. See T. Boston & C. Ross, eds., *The Inner City, Urban Poverty and Economic Development in the Next Century* (New Brunswick, NJ: Transaction Publishers, 1997).
157. Dymski, "New Markets."
158. A. Smith, "Mixed-income Housing Developments: Promise and Reality," Joint Center for Housing Studies of Harvard University (2002).
159. W. Malone, *From Holy Power to Holy Profits: The Black Church and Community Economic Empowerment* (Chicago: African American Images, 1994).

7

160. See J. Stewart, "The Black Church as a Religio-Economic Institution," in *Flight in Search of Vision*, ed. J. Stewart (Trenton, NJ: Africa World Press, 2004), 261-76.

161. W. E. B. Du Bois "Of the Faith of the Fathers," *Souls of Black Folk* (1903). Reprinted in *The Black Church in America*, ed. H. Nelsen, R. Yokley, R. and A. Nelsen (New York: Basic Books, 1971), 38.

162. D. Jones, "Hill District Group, Firms Collaborate on Master Plan," Post-gazette.com, January 26, 2010, http://www.post-gazette.com/pg/10026/1031027-53.stm#ixzz0gYzjKTri.

163. R. Lecky and H. Wright, eds., "Reparations Now? An Introduction," in *Black Manifesto* (New York: Sheed and Ward, 1969), 1-4.

164. B. Bittker, *The Case for Black Reparations* (New York: Random House, 1973).

165. Ibid., 86.

166. W. Vaughn, *Vaughn's 'Freedmen's Pension Bill'* (Chicago, 1891). Reprinted by (Freeport, New York: Books for Libraries Press, 1971).

167. See M. Berry, *My Face is Black is True: Callie House and the Struggle for Ex-Slave Reparations* (New York: Albert A. Knopf, 2005).

168. See R. Allen, "Past Due: The African American Quest for Reparations," in *African Americans in the U.S. Economy*, ed. Conrad et al., 319-26.

169. R. America, ed., *The Wealth of Races: The Present Value of Benefits from Past Injustices* (Westport, CT: Greenwood Press, 1990). See also R. America, ed., *Paying the Social Debt* (Westport, CT: Praeger, 1993).

170. R. Vedder, L. Gallaway, and D. Klingaman, "Black Exploitation and White Benefits: The Civil War Income Revolution in America," The Wealth of Races, 125-37.

171. R. Ransom and R. Sutch, "Who Pays for Slavery in America," *The Wealth of Races*, 31-54.

172. J. Marketti, "Estimated Present Value of Income Diverted During Slavery in America," *The Wealth of Races*, 107-23.

173. L. Neal, "A Calculation and Comparison of the Current Benefits of Slavery and an Analysis of Who Benefits in America," *The Wealth of Races*, 91-105.

174. It should also be noted that in 1995 a reparations lawsuit demanding $100 million was filed against the federal government in the Ninth Circuit Court of Appeals, but the suit, *Cato v. United States*, was rejected.

175. The argument would follow the general outlines found in W. Rodney, *How Europe Underdeveloped Africa* (Washington, DC: Howard University Press, 1981).

176. W. Darity and D. Frank, "The Economics of Reparations," in *African Americans in the U.S. Economy*, ed. Conrad et al., 334-38.

177. Ibid.

178. Darity and Frank, "The Economics of Reparations," 336.

179. Darity and Frank, "The Economics of Reparations."

180. C. Waterhouse, "Avoiding Another Step in a Series of Unfortunate Legal Events: A Consideration of Black Life under American Law from 1619 to 1972 and a Challenge to Prevailing Notions of Legally Based Reparations," *Boston College Third World Law Journal*, 2006.

181. C. Waterhouse and A. Smith," No Reparation Without Taxation: Applying the Internal Revenue Code to the Concept of Reparations for Slavery and Segregation," *Florida International University Legal Studies Research Paper No. 08-2.*

182. C. Waterhouse, "The Good, the Bad, and the Ugly: Moral Agency and the Role of Victims in Reparations Programs," Show Abstract *University of Pennsylvania Journal of International Economic Law,* 31 (1), 2009.

183. Shuman, *Going Local*, 7.

184. Shuman, *Going Local.*

185. See R. Bullard, *Dumping in Dixie: Race, Class, and Environmental Quality* (Boulder, CO: Westview Press, 1990); and R. Bullard, G. Johnson, and A. Torres, eds., *Sprawl City: Race, Politics, and Planning in Atlanta* (Washington, DC: Island Press, 2000).

186. W. Wilson, "There Goes the Neighborhood," New York Times.com, June 16, 2003, http://www.nytimes.com/2003/06/16/opinion/there-goes-the-neighborhood.html.

187. J. Kotkin, *Tribes: How Race, Religion, and Identity Determine Success in the New Global Economy* (New York: Random House, 1993).

188. Ibid. 16.

Chapter 8

African American Arts and Humanities

The Role and Evaluation of Creative Production

There is an unfortunate but continuing tendency among many casual observers to treat various forms of creative expression as the principal source material for African American Studies. However, as has been demonstrated in the preceding chapters, the mission of the field to contribute directly to improving the quality of the lived experiences of people of African descent necessitates a heavy emphasis on social sciences for understanding reality. This does not mean, however, that creative expression is ignored or relegated to a secondary position in African American Studies. Rather, it means that specialists in African American Studies focus special attention on creative works that complement the ideological and political objectives of the field and on the interpretation of works that promote community development.

There is no question that, for many people, the day-to-day exposure to various popular media, such as music and film, is the principal source of ideas about how to cope with social reality. However, excessive attachment to unfiltered products of popular culture can be dangerous, because embedded messages can foster anti-social beliefs and behaviors—particularly when such media are largely controlled by external forces that practice institutional racism. Well-conceived "criticism" can play a critical role in enabling willing consumers to decipher the messages embedded in cultural products and limit the potentially negative effects on individual and social psyches. Criticism, in

this sense, simply means discourse about a particular area, such as literature. Literary criticism, for example, includes the description, analysis, interpretation, and evaluation of literary works. Similar definitions apply to other fields, including the visual arts, film, television, music, and theater. Criticism also includes discussions of the principles, theory, and aesthetics associated with particular fields, and scholars engaged in such studies are called *critics*.

Some approaches to criticism are more compatible with the mission and ideology of African American Studies than others. There is an ongoing disagreement among commentators regarding the extent to which creative artists should restrict the subject matter and content of their work to promote collective political objectives. Critics see such an expectation as infringing on individual artistic freedom, and, thereby, hampering the exploration of new and innovative subjects in ways that could potentially lead to inferior artistic products. In contrast, in his 1935 essay, "A Negro Nation Within a Nation," W. E. B. Du Bois argues, "There exists today a chance for the Negroes to organize a co-operative state within their own group. By letting Negro farmers feed Negro artisans, and Negro technicians guide Negro home industries, and Negro thinkers plan this integration of co-operation, while Negro artists dramatize and beautify the struggle, economic independence can be achieved."[1] Thus Du Bois charged creative artists with the responsibility of using their talents to further community development. Recognizing that Black creative artists differ widely in their political and artistic commitments, African American Studies simply chooses to focus its primary energies on studying the more overtly

325

politically conscious creative artists and their works. Consistent with the interdisciplinary nature of the field, African American Studies attempts to develop a composite approach to the study of Black creative arts that reflects insights from various schools of criticism within different fields. African American Studies specialists are especially interested in how the content of political messages embedded in artistic works changes over time. Another special interest is the degree of similarity in the type of messages found in different forms of artistic expression during a particular period. The overarching rubric that guides much of the literary and artistic criticism undertaken within African American Studies is the concept of a "Black Aesthetic."

The Black Aesthetic

According to the Oxford English Dictionary, the word *aesthetic* is of Greek origin and is associated with beauty or the appreciation of beauty. Aesthetic is also used to refer to a set of principles underlying the work of a particular artist or artistic movement. It connotes sensitivity to beauty, or an act or feat perceived as creative, artful, and in good taste. Aesthetics is the philosophy of the nature and function of beauty and its standard in art and culture. Aesthetics can relate to objects or materials within the physical realm, such as, paintings, sculpture, and crafts; and to those concrete and abstract human activities, behaviors, or motions that appeal to the senses as dance, music, and drama. However, an absolute universal aesthetic does not exist. Aesthetics or beauty can be an individual perception, but more often it is based on the values and ideals of a group or society. Thus, culture, race, and tradition may determine or influence the aesthetic nature and beauty of an object or phenomenon. In other words, beauty is relative, and a sense of aesthetic relativism must prevail if the art of peoples of different cultures is to be fairly evaluated and appreciated.

Aesthetic evaluation is not immune to ethnocentrism, egoism, and prejudice, or oppressive political racism. Such negative aspects of aesthetic appraisal are why African American and African cultural inventions have been relegated to an inferior status by European and Western critics of the arts and humanities. Even without the impact of racism on aesthetic systems and standards, beauty in the classical Western or White European sense cannot be applied uncritically to African or African American arts.

Art is the creative expression of human feelings, thoughts, and observations, rendered in a compelling style and structure that has been shaped by the experiences of the society from which it is produced. As a consequence, European aesthetic standards are not easily translatable into any of the various African cultures. When the European colonizers raided African villages and societies in the seventeenth and eighteenth centuries, under the guise of making scientific inquiry, they discovered an assortment of African "art objects," many of which were figurines, masks, carved ivory, and castings in bronze and brass. Europeans routinely classified such objects as *primitive African art*, in contrast to the art of White "civilized" societies.[2] Physical paraphernalia were not the only aspects of African culture that were classified as crude or primitive by the Europeans. African dance, music, and song were also described as primitive or savage in nature.

In the African tradition and frame of reference, objects, dance, music, and song were not perceived as art but as functional creations and symbols of life. The artifacts and activities were used and employed in birth, marriage, harvest, festive, and burial rituals and ceremonies. In contrast, the European conceptualization of the value of art is its historically inherent apolitical nature and function. From a European perspective, art is a thing of beauty to be seen, or from which to derive personal sensual pleasure or sensation. In African societies, "art" objects, music, dance, pantomime or drama "were a functioning, collective and integral part of society, not a cultural appendage."[3] More succinctly, Carlton and Barbara Molette describe the Black aesthetic as being "related to its usefulness, that is, art-for-peoples' use . . . in contrast to the Eurocentric elitist art-for-art's sake tradition."[4]

Kariamu Welsh-Asante has provided a useful framework for evaluating the quality of creative production. She argues that in traditional African societies, "if an artistic product is functional, meaning if it promotes positive, transformative beliefs and practices, then it is valuable and therefore beautiful and good."[5] Welsh-Asante has proposed the Nzuri model to further assess the value of an artistic product. The seven evaluative criteria in the Nzuri model are (1) meaning, (2) ethos, (3) motif, (4) mode, (5) function, (6) method/technique, and (7) form.[6]

Black or African American art and art forms are often treated and viewed as "less than," or unrefined, by White American art and literary critics. Stemming from the slavery and colonial periods, the nadir of the Black experience in American history, Black song, music, dance, and poetry were regarded as curious and primitive until the second decade of the twentieth century. However, by the 1940s, the unique, soul-stirring, and "beautiful" nature of Black arts became so appealing to Euro-Americans and Europeans that they began unabashedly to imitate, emulate, and co-opt African American music, dance and rhetoric. Still, Black cultural creativity is categorized as *fine art* only to the extent that it conforms to European classical culture and standards. White Western culture and arts are paraded universally as the model and experience to pursue for all other peoples and cultures. Most White scholars and their disciples have historically attempted to define, validate, or invalidate the aesthetic achievements of the non-White world.

The essence of the Black Aesthetic is that the arts and writings of African Americans be judged based on their own cultural, political, and economic history. Black arts and literary works are most authentic when they reconstruct the conditions, experiences, and core values of African Americans creatively in relation to the broader society and the world. To preserve the authenticity of a Black aesthetic, the concept of beauty, values and standards of White European culture cannot authoritatively displace the culture and worldviews of Black people.[7]

Beauty is not limited to how an object, an individual, or a group appears, but includes how it, he/she, or they contribute to the survival, function, and betterment of the race and of mankind. African Americans can least afford to perceive art and beauty solely in terms of looks or inutility, antiquity, and sensual appeal. Blacks or Africans, who have been regarded and portrayed as primitive, savage, and ugly people, have enlightened the world with creative material and spiritual expression. Their aesthetic creativity emanates from their struggles, as well as from their music, dance, drama, and literature. In that sense, beauty can be seen in the perseverance and triumphs of an oppressed people.

The existence of a Black Aesthetic has long been recognized by scholars. W. E. B. Du Bois argued in 1925 that there was undoubtedly a certain group expression of Negro art, which included: essays examining Black life, its aspirations, and the problems of the color line; autobiographies of formerly enslaved Blacks and notable Blacks; and poetry, novels, paintings, sculpture, music, and plays that have emerged from the collective experience.

The Black Aesthetic is a branch of the unique cultural system of African Americans. The culture of African Americans is the product and process of the cumulative historical, social, political and economic forces that have shaped or molded it over time. Authentic Black creativity evolved from the struggle of people of sub-Saharan ancestry to survive and thrive with dignity in diverse, often hostile, social and geographical arenas. Cultural creativity begins first with the need to survive. An out-group who appreciates the visual or performing arts of Blacks should also appreciate the historical and cultural context from which they are derived. Any criticism must take into consideration the culture and core values of African American and African peoples. Although cross-cultural comparison of Black arts is perhaps inevitable, critical analysis from others that is purely ethnocentrically motivated must be accepted with reservations or rendered invalid.

The foundations for the contemporary understanding of the Black Aesthetic derive, to a large extent, from the creative energies unleashed by African Americans during the New Negro Movement and the Harlem Renaissance. To understand how the Harlem Renaissance laid the foundations for later views about the need for an organic relationship between art and political struggle, it is useful to keep in mind W. E. B. Du Bois' thoughts in 1897 in his classic monograph *The Conservation of Races*:

> For the development of Negro genius, of Negro literature and art, of Negro spirit, only Negroes bound and welded together, Negroes inspired by one vast ideal, can work out in its fullness the great message we have for humanity ... For the accomplishment of these ends we need race organizations, a Negro school of literature and art, and an intellectual clearing house, for all these products of the Negro mind, which we may call a Negro Academy. Not only is all this necessary for positive advance, it is absolutely imperative for negative defense.[8]

Although Blacks had established their artistic and literary capabilities long before the Reconstruction era,

8

the New Negro Movement and the Harlem Renaissance are generally cited as the flowering period of Blacks in the arts and humanities. Although there is some overlap in the timing of the Harlem Renaissance and the New Negro Movement, the Harlem Renaissance was essentially dismantled by the Great Depression but the New Negro Movement persisted. African Americans made phenomenal advances in visual and performing arts (music, dance, theater, art), but the most significant gains were made in the literary field. Prior to the 1920s, much of Black arts and writings were compromising and imitative of Whites, except for the earlier protest or moralizing writings. The Harlem Renaissance was the period when Blacks departed from tradition and developed a revitalized sense of racial pride and self-expression.

The Harlem community of New York City may have been the hub of African American artistic and literary activity, but its effects and the participants-contributors were dispersed nationwide. The development and flourishing of Black cultural activity during the 1920s may be attributed to several complementary factors. Without regard to rank in weight or significance, they can be listed as: (1) the mass migration, urbanization and industrialization of Blacks following the war; (2) the considerable increase in the number of Black graduates from Black colleges in the South and North; (3) the influence of Marcus Garvey in the development of Black racial pride and awareness, and (4) the attraction of White tourists, patrons, scholar-writers, and publishers to the activities of Harlem.[9]

The most renowned Black writers and poets of the Harlem Renaissance period were Langston Hughes, James Weldon Johnson, Claude McKay, and Countee Cullen. African American artists, theater groups, and writers came together during the 1920s and produced imaginative Black theater and musical productions. Some of the most notable theater personalities, dancers, musicians and performers include Paul Robeson, Josephine Baker, Florence Mills, Eubie Blake, and Noble Sissle. Their expression was a welcomed departure from the Blackface and Minstrelsy shows that prevailed prior to the 1920s. The Harlem Renaissance period launched the vanguard of nationally renowned Black singers and musicians, as well as jazz—the music created by Blacks. Blues singer Bessie Smith and jazz bandleaders Jelly Roll Morton, King Oliver, Duke Ellington, and Louis Armstrong are only a few of the famous artists who began their careers during the

New Negro Movement. The African idiom in painting and sculpture also gained popularity during the 1920s when foundations and galleries were established for the development of Black artists and for the exhibition of their works.[10]

The outpouring of Black cultural expression during the Harlem Renaissance subsided somewhat during the Depression and race-riot torn years of the 1930s and 1940s. However, during World War II, between 1940 and 1945, the New Negro Movement and Black political activity increased concomitantly with cultural activities that continued from the Harlem Renaissance. During the early 1940s, Black political leaders A. Philip Randolph, Walter White, Adam Clayton Powell and their respective organizations petitioned the Roosevelt administration for civil rights and social justice. At the same time, noted Black musicians Dizzy Gillespie, Charlie Parker, and Thelonious Monk were making their debut. In art, Charles White, Elizabeth Catlett, and Romare Bearden were outstanding during the period. On stage, Katherine Dunham, Pearl Primus, and Eartha Kitt received rave reviews. Richard Wright and Langston Hughes produced major works during this period. Even during its decline, Harlem remained a major center of Black cultural and political activity.[11]

Political struggle and freedom stimulate cultural creativity in the arts and humanities. A review of African American history reveals that the artistic and literary production of Blacks increase during and following major political triumphs in civil rights struggles. Based on this theory, many writers compare the Civil Rights Movement and its aftermath of the 1960s and 1970s with the Harlem Renaissance period. Some humanist scholars refer to the decades of the 1960s and 1970s as the Black Arts Movement (BAM).

The Harlem Renaissance of the 1920s and the Black Arts Movement of the 1960s and 1970s differed significantly, with the exception that both eras resulted in a tremendous increase in Black creative and literary productivity. The motivating force of the Harlem Renaissance was one of Black self-discovery and race vindication. In short, it could be considered a vindicating movement. African Americans wanted to prove that they were equally as talented as Whites. Most Black creative artists sought to correct the traditionally negative racial stereotypes that Whites and some Blacks continued to perpetuate. With new-found racial pride, Blacks discovered that they possessed artistic talents and literary skills that even many Whites acknowledged and admired. The prevailing social philosophy and objective of many Black artists and writers were consistent with integration and assimilation. The Black idiom and political activism were implicitly, but not blatantly, stated in the works of most Harlem Renaissance artists and writers. With the exception of Marcus Garvey's adherents, the Harlem Renaissance largely involved the Black bourgeoisie. The masses of Blacks were engaged as consumers and observers, not participants.[12]

The 1960s marked a rebirth or renaissance of Black arts and literature that had begun during the 1920s. The Black community abounded with politically and socially creative music, song, African dance, theater, poetry and literature. White critics were quick to assess these works as political and propagandistic protest with little, if any, aesthetic or artistic merit. What Whites did not understand was that Black artists and their works were in harmony with the functional nature of Black aesthetics. Black arts and writings during the 1960s served as the driving force for the development of African American Studies nationwide, and they continue to fuel the political fires of Black liberation in the twenty-first century.

The Black Arts Movement developed out of the political struggle for social justice, economic equity, and educational opportunity. Black arts and literary works were inspired by the Movement and, for the most part, were the products of it. All social stratifications of the Black community, including students, were constructively engaged, in one way or another, in the liberation struggle. Although a variety of groups engaged in the struggle for power, the Movement was divided into two primary ideological camps. One side sought integration and cultural fusion. The other advocated separatism, or Black nationalism, and cultural distinctiveness as solutions to the country's race problem. The Black Arts Movement also revived interest in Africa, the mother country. The aim of the African American intellectual was to participate in the struggle for liberation and justice. The Black Power and Black Arts Movements were the foundations of Black Studies programs and departments and ushered in an era when African American intellectuals would assume authority for the interpretation of Black cultural and historical experience. In conjunction with the Civil Rights Movement, the cultural and educational plight of Blacks improved, and the entire social

and economic structure was affected. The masses, therefore, benefited significantly from the Black Power and Black Arts Movements.

The Black Arts Movement (BAM) roughly spanned the period 1964–76 and was linked closely to the ethos of the Black Power Movement. BAM engendered the creation of a large body of poems, plays, and essays, much of which employed distinctive modes of expression. Writers developed hyperbolic language in attacks against racism and celebrated the linguistic conventions of African American folk and urban lifestyles. Writers innovated new forms of discourse that included techniques borrowed from various musical genres, especially jazz. BAM creative artists generated "polyvocal" cultural products that were disseminated by a variety of "cultural transmitters," such as, scholars, writers, painters, editors, and popular culture media. African American poets, for example, performed readings for diverse audiences, including students on college campuses across the country, and produced recordings with musicians and choirs that were comparable to the outreach initiatives of Africana Studies.

BAM artists altered traditional language by coining new terms and extensively using words and phrases from various African languages. They also made special use of "Black English." Many of the works they produced embodied the African American Studies commitment to the primacy of history in examining social conditions. For example, tribute poems celebrate heroic historical figures. The emphasis of African American Studies on the agency of people of African descent was also reflected in works that celebrated how African Americans had struggled to overcome oppressive conditions.

The aesthetic qualities of Black protest arts and political tactics have been widely copied by groups around the world in search of redress from oppression. The Black Aesthetic includes the silent and dignified rebellion of Rosa Parks and the compelling oratory of Martin Luther King, Jr. and Jesse Jackson. Great literary achievements—works of art, drama, music, and song—were developed during and following the Civil Rights Movement of the 1960s. There has always been an aesthetic quality to committed struggles for right and justice.

However, such aesthetic and artistic qualities have not proven sufficient to alter the racism, social injustice, and economic inequality suffered by African Americans. White America has appropriated

8

much of African American music, dance, art forms, and rhetoric, while subordinating African people as a race. Manning Marable sums up race relationships in America when he states, "Whites' affinity and tolerance for blackness are largely cultural, not racial. Many Whites have learned to appreciate African-derived elements of music, dance, and religious rituals, but would not endorse the sharing of power or material privileges, which would undermine the stratification of race."[13]

Defining and refining a Black aesthetic was a major focus of academic critics, such as, Addison Gayle and Stephen Henderson; of cultural workers, such as, Larry Neal and Hoyt Fuller; and of poets, such as, Amiri Baraka and Carolyn Rodgers. Many of the artists who employed a "Black aesthetic" used approaches that displayed important similarities to the efforts by Africana Studies specialists to develop interdisciplinary modes of inquiry. Several BAM poets used jazz to frame their poetry, especially "free jazz." BAM artists prioritized the radical dimensions of jazz, reinterpreted the music, and disseminated their interpretations through poetry.

BAM has been criticized by some analysts for its constructions of "Blackness," manhood, and womanhood. One body of research focuses on excavating the distinctive literary and artistic traditions of Africana women.[14] There are also ongoing initiatives to establish the contours of a Black feminist school of artistic and literary criticism that would reflect the particular stance of Africana women.[15] Other contemporary critics, such as Trey Ellis, champion a "new Black Aesthetic." This new Black Aesthetic stresses mixed cultural heritage over Black cultural nationalism in its satirical and parodic construction of texts to explore dimensions of African American literature that go beyond "the race problem."[16] While the right of creative artists and critics to approach their subject matter from any vantage point is not subject to challenge, this artistic and critical approach obviously lies outside the boundaries of the traditional conception of African American Studies. As noted previously, artistic and literary criticism undertaken under the auspices of African American Studies is concerned especially with the products of cultural workers who self-consciously approach their craft as a vehicle to foster social change and whose cultural products embody themes, linguistic conventions, and images congruent with the vision of Africana Studies.

James Stewart suggests three general criteria for assessing the degree of alignment between specific creative/critical cultural products and Black/Africana Studies. The three criteria are: (1) the similarity between the values and images found in a work or approach and those of African American Studies; (2) the degree to which history and historical explanations of contemporary phenomena are reflected; and (3) the extent to which cultural workers self-consciously approach their craft as a vehicle to foster social change. These criteria are useful for assessing traditions and contemporary trends in various expressive modes.[17]

As mentioned in Chapter 6, Garveyism represented the separatist-nationalist and "back-to-Africa" sentiment during the Harlem Renaissance. Carter G. Woodson introduced Negro History Week in 1926. The artistic legacy and the books and writings of the Harlem Renaissance were the initial, and sometimes only, Black-authored reference sources for the development of African American Studies programs established in colleges and universities beginning in 1968. In assessing and comparing the Harlem Renaissance with the Black Arts Movement four decades later, one might conclude that the Movements reinforced and complemented each other. If the Harlem Renaissance had not occurred and proven culturally and artistically fruitful, the Black Arts Movement would have been without foundation or focus. Consequently, it would have inevitably faltered and failed to effect social and cultural change.

African American Music

Black Musical Traditions

Of the cultural arts, African American music is the most indigenous to American society. Black people have been the primary source of a folk and popular music that is "Native American," that is, not a direct extension of European forms and types of music. Black music is so rhythmically and harmonically distinctive that it has been difficult for others to comprehend, perform, and imitate it culturally.[18] The forms of music that Blacks have contributed to American musical culture are spirituals, gospel, blues, jazz, and, more recently, rap.

A close scrutiny of Black musical traditions is critical for understanding the dynamics of the Black liberation struggle. As Leroi Jones [now Amiri Baraka] states, "[I]f the music of the Negro in America, in all its permutations, is subjected to a socio-anthropological as well as musical scrutiny, something about the essential nature of the Negro's existence in this country ought to be revealed, as well as something about the essential nature of this country, i.e., society as a whole."[19] In a similar vein, Samuel Floyd asserts that "all black music making is driven by and permeated with the memory of things from the cultural past and that the viability of such memory should play a role in the perception of and criticism of works and performances of black music."[20] Alain Locke even proposed that changes in predominant African American musical genres were closely correlated with major transformations in the socio-political-economic milieu of African Americans.[21]

The rhythmic forms of Black music are basically African. Melville Herskovits' *The Myth of the Negro Past*, a major scholarly study, affirms African musical and cultural retentions by Black Americans in spite of slavery and the antebellum period.[22] Since this classic work was published in 1941, numerous scholars have substantiated that Black Americans have retained the cultural, tonal, rhythmic, and technical musical traditions of Africa. Africa has also influenced the music, song, and dance of Central America, South America, the Caribbean, and all other regions where Africans were transported during the Atlantic slave trade.

Melanie Bratcher argues that "African American singers are not always aware that their stylization of sound is decidedly African" and that "they may not be aware that those sound effects are connected to African cultural values."[23] She maintains that "many African American singers use specific sound motions and sound qualities, such as slurs, guttural tones, bends, drops, moans, shouts, raspiness, and call-and-response to express something deeper than the lyrics alone can convey."[24]

Initial studies of African retentions in Black American music were related to religious songs and music—the spirituals and gospel. However, technical analyses have revealed that African patterns of melody, harmony, and rhythm are also found in blues, jazz, and other forms of African American music. Lazarus Ekwueme points out, for example, that the roots of the "blue note" in Black American blues songs, spirituals, work chants, and folk songs lie in African music. The blue note is the presence of the flattened third and

seventh degrees in the major scale.[25] Rhythm patterns common in Africa are prevalent in the music of African Americans. Ekwueme states that it is not uncommon to find that Black American musical patterns use quarter notes in combination with dotted quarters, resulting in a proportional time value of two against three. The employment of two versus three, in combination and sometimes "in contradiction," is a basic character of African musical rhythm. The presence of mixed rhythmic units of double and triple time, and combinations of these in a counterpoint of rhythms, contribute to that lilting, propelling force described as syncopation in Black music.[26] Various writers have noted that the "call and response" and the "call and refrain" patterns in Black music have been derived exclusively from African musical traditions.

African American music, undoubtedly, contains some elements of European cultural, musical, and performance practices. However, Black American music has been able to maintain its own distinctiveness and identifiable African characteristics of melody, harmony, and rhythm. Moreover, in a popular and quantitative sense, Black music has influenced and modified Euro-American concepts of melody, rhythm, harmony, and instrumental deployment. In any of its forms, Black music can be emotional and intense, melancholy and blue, meditative and tender, or dynamic and explosive. It is an artful and abstract testimony of the slavery, suffering, oppression, resilience, and freedom experiences of African Americans. For African Americans and Africans, music is more than entertainment; it is functional and therapeutic to their religious, social, and political existence.

The Spiritual and Gospel Music

The African American spirituals may be categorized as folk music because they have been handed down and often revised from generation to generation. The original authors or composers are generally unknown or have been forgotten. Spirituals, in their purest form, evolved out of the enslavement experience of African Americans. Alain Locke wrote that the spirituals are Blacks' "great folk-gift, and rank among the classic folk expressions in the whole world because of their moving simplicity, their characteristic originality, and their universal appeal."[27] W. E. B. Du Bois was even more profound and poetic in his acclaim of the African American spiritual. Du Bois states, in essence, that the Black folk-song (spiritual) is the rhythmic cry of

8

enslaved Blacks; that it stands, not only as music indigenous to America, but as the most beautiful expression of human experience originated on this side of the seas; and that it remains the singular spiritual heritage of the nation and the greatest gift of Black people.[28] The acclaim for the spirituals is well deserved; they are appreciated by all races and have been performed in most nations of the world.

According to Eileen Southern, a renowned Black musicologist, when the spirituals began is unknown. It is known that spirituals were sung by Blacks many years before the first collection of songs by enslaved Blacks was formally published in 1867. Spirituals began their rise to national and international prominence in 1871, when a student concert troupe was formed at Fisk University under the leadership of George L. White. The idea for the student concert group arose from the dire need for funds for the operation of Fisk University, an institution that was organized primarily for Blacks after the Civil War. The concert troupe eventually became known as the Fisk Jubilee Singers. They were catapulted into national and international fame when they were invited by Henry Ward Beecher to perform in Brooklyn, and, subsequently, in Boston on the occasion of the World Peace Jubilee in 1872. Praise of the group's performance was so exuberant that the singers went on to perform before heads of state in Europe and Great Britain. In a few years, the group had raised over $150,000, which was used to erect a new building, called *Jubilee Hall*, on the Fisk University campus.[29] The success of the Fisk Jubilee Singers encouraged the formation of similar spiritual choirs at Black institutions in Hampton, Virginia; Tuskegee, Alabama; and Atlanta, Georgia. However, as music historians point out, the character of the genuine folk-spirituals had been transformed in the course of relocation from the plantation and Black Church to the concert stage. Although spirituals have undergone adaptation and change of original venue, they remain a valuable contribution to American culture.

Evidence suggests that the development of the spiritual took place in the independent Black churches of the North during the 1770s and 1780s, although, indeed, spirituals of some nature were also sung in the South. During this period, Richard Allen and fellow-worshippers walked out of the White Methodist church in Philadelphia and eventually organized the African Methodist Episcopal Church. Allen compiled

a hymnal for the use of his congregations. The hymnal contained hymns already in circulation, folk songs, and many original and unorthodox songs, and the distinction that was made between hymns and spirituals at that time may have been the earliest record of a formal collection of spirituals. The verses of these spirituals in the hymnal had been improvised and were transferred, undoubtedly, by ministers and church members as they visited from one congregation to the other throughout the country.[30]

The notion that Black spirituals are sorrowful songs is a one-dimensional perspective, as an analysis of the verses and words will reveal the psychological and therapeutic value of these songs to an enslaved and oppressed people. Religious in nature, they generally express hope for divine deliverance from bondage, burdensome toil, and suffering. Most of the songs reflect the yearnings of Blacks to escape to a refuge called *heaven*. A commonly sung spiritual follows:

STEAL AWAY TO JESUS

Steal away, steal away,
Steal away to Jesus;
Steal away, steal away home,
I ain't got long to stay here.

This song has dual connotations. It expresses a desire for spiritual relief from suffering. On the other hand, it is recorded that the song served as a coded message to signify an actual escape plan, secret meeting or uprising. Another song with similar implications is:.

DEEP RIVER

Deep river, my home is over Jordan
Deep river, Lord,
I want to cross over into campground,
Lord, I want to cross over into campground
Lord, I want to cross over into campground.[31]

Various interpretations have been given to these early Negro spirituals. Whether spirituals were sung for their opiate effect, or whether they were to be taken literally cannot be determined. From a contemporary Black perspective, spirituals have essentially the same meaning and significance as they did during the antebellum period whether they are presented in concert arrangements or in folk performances.

African American gospel song and music, in contradistinction to any other gospel forms, evolved out of the Black Church. The development of gospel music did not begin in the traditional or conventional denominations of the church, such as the Baptist, Methodist, Presbyterian, and Catholic, but in the more fundamentalist Pentecostal or "sanctified" churches. The foot stomping, handclapping, and rhythmic body movements associated with the performance of gospel music were deemed somewhat sacrilegious in traditional worship services. However, Black gospel music is essentially a derivative of and transition from spiritual songs. The primary difference between spiritual and gospel performance is the obligatory accompaniment of the piano and electric organ. Tambourines, drums, guitar, and brass musical instruments are also commonly used as accompaniments to gospel songs. The performance of spirituals is mostly *a cappella*, solemn and intense, but also moving and emotional. Gospel music has a tempo similar to that of Black secular music, with its riffs, ostinatos, call and response, obbligatos, voice exclamations, and rocking in time.[32]

Black gospel music gained in general popularity from 1945 to 1955. Its growing popularity led to the formation of gospel choirs that toured and performed, mainly for Black church-goers, in rented halls and auditoriums throughout the country. Gospel music was no longer limited to the small sanctified or storefront church and began to gain national appeal. Gospel music created much controversy and division initially because some perceived its beat and style to be inappropriate or sacrilegious in religious worship service and because earlier gospel stars (and some present gospel artists and groups) performed at night clubs and in various other secular settings. Sister Rosetta Tharpe, an early national gospel singer, started in the church and then moved to the night club circuit. In 1957, another gospel artist and group, Clara Ward and the Ward Singers, performed at the Newport Jazz Festival. However, other noted gospel artists, such as James Cleveland, Andrae Crouch, and Shirley Caesar, at one time, refused to perform outside the church or a religious milieu. By the late 1960s and early 1970s, gospel music became widely accepted and was performed in the Baptist, Methodist, and other traditional congregations. Through recordings, radio, and television programs, it was received into the homes of listeners and viewers nationally and internationally. Noted gospel singer Mahalia Jackson performed at one of the inaugural parties for President John F. Kennedy. Eventually, gospel was performed at Carnegie Hall.[33] Because Black gospel music is appreciated at the Newport Jazz Festival and at Carnegie Hall, its characterization as sacred or secular music remains an open question.[34] Nevertheless, as of the 1990s, gospel music continues as a stable and growing tradition in the Black Church. The Gospel Music Association, founded in 1964, serves as an umbrella trade organization to promote gospel music.

Gospel singing has been adopted and is appreciated among most African American church groups because it is more culturally related to the African custom of performer-audience participation. During gospel performances, the congregation responds by singing along, clapping their hands, and tapping their feet in harmony and rhythm with the singer or choir. Thomas A. Dorsey, gospel writer and the Father of Gospel Music, felt that traditional hymns and church music failed to enliven or to instill the spirit of rejoicing among church members. In commenting on the pre-gospel era, Dorsey states: "The people were singing so dead, so disinterested in the church. The church needed something to fire them up."[35] African traits of harmony, rhythm, beat, and style of performance are unmistakably evident in the music of African Americans. Thus, spirituals, gospel, blues, jazz, and rap music are Afrocentric culturally and ethnically. In recent years, an increasing number of artists have incorporated contemporary hip-hop music into the gospel tradition in an effort to attract younger audiences. Leading artists in this movement include Kirk Franklin, Mary Mary, Trinitee 5:7, Yolanda Adams, Fred Hammond, and Hezekiah Walker.

The Blues and African Americans

Music historians are uncertain regarding the specific origin of blues music and songs in America. It is known and acknowledged that the blues evolved and developed out of the oppressed and tragically ironic experience and condition of southern Blacks during and after the Civil War. The antecedents of the blues were the rhythmically melancholic and functional work chants and field hollers of enslaved Blacks, prisoners, rail hands, and sharecroppers. The rhythm, beat, and melody structures of the blues are clearly consistent with the musical cultures of West Africa, with evident residual strains from Central, Southern, and Eastern Africa.[36] In the US South during the early

8

1900s, it was commonplace to find, in most towns, a Black blues player picking a guitar on a street corner or to see itinerant blues troubadours performing their sorrowful songs at honky-tonks and parties in the Black community. Prior to the 1920s, the blues might be categorized as the *down-home country blues*.

W.C. Handy is generally regarded as Father of the Blues because, according to some music scholars, he was the first person to write or orchestrate the blues. Two of his most popular blues compositions are "Memphis Blues" (1912) and "St. Louis Blues" (1914). Some scholars suggest that big band-orchestrated blues may be the musical bridge to jazz. However, Ferdinand "Jelly Roll" Morton is generally recognized as the first great composer and jazz piano player. As a teenager, Jelly Roll worked as a piano player in the whorehouses of Storyville, Tennessee, and traveled the Deep South until about 1917. He was variously a gambler, pool shark, pimp, vaudeville comedian, and a pianist. Jelly Roll was an important transitional figure between ragtime and jazz piano styles. He played on the West Coast from 1917 to 1922, and then moved to Chicago where he had a major hit with his 1923 version of "Wolverine Blues." He formed the Red Hot Peppers band, which played a hot New Orleans style jazz, and made a series of classic records on the Victor label.[37]

The highly orchestrated style of blues should be distinguished, partly, in style and adherents, from the folk blues songs and music that developed among Blacks earlier in the South. W.C. Handy and Gertrude "Ma" Rainey (the earliest known professional blues singer) are credited with popularizing the blues through commercial records. This style of blues, performed in European orchestral form, appealed to urban Blacks and to some Whites alike.

The tonal quality and structure of the blues are related to the spiritual and to gospel music. However, the blues is generally secular or worldly in content and motive. Early blues artists and enthusiasts were leery and dubious of a religion or a God who would relegate Black people to such an oppressed social and economic position. Blues music and song are based on the immediate and material reality of Black life. They reflect the hurt and pain of lost jobs, lost loves, sexual desires, infidelity, hardship, White racism, despair and anguish. Yet, some blues have a degree of spiritual flavor because of the performer's exclamatory interjection of phrases like, "O Lordy" or "God have mercy."

The blues is basically a folk music with verses and stanzas that have been passed along and sometimes modified from one blues singer to another. The songs have rhyming lines and closely parallel poetic form. The traditional or more frequently performed blues is a twelve-bar, three-line stanza song. The first line is repeated twice and the third is a response to the previous two lines. The singer "calls and responds" to him/herself in a falsetto, slurring, shouting, whining, moaning style. Variations in blues form may include a reduction to eight measures or an expansion to sixteen measures. The verses may vary from two to six lines with complex repetitions of lines or phrases.[38]

As mentioned earlier, down-home country blues prevailed in the South prior to the 1920s. Early classic "down-home" blues artists included Huddie (Leadbelly) Ledbetter, Blind Lemon Jefferson, Son House and Robert Johnson. Blind Lemon Jefferson's songs were almost always autobiographical. The following are typical three-line stanza songs of Blind Lemon Jefferson:

(Example of hardship)

I stood on the corner and almost bust my head
I stood on the corner and almost bust my head
I couldn't earn enough to buy me a loaf of bread.

(Example of sexual imagery)

Mmmmm-mm, black snake crawling in my room.
Mmmmm-mm, black snake crawling in my room
And some pretty mama better get this black snake soon.[39]

A popular blues stanza rendered by contemporary blues artists Bobby "Blue" Bland is similar to this:

(Example of loneliness or forlornness)

I'm driftin' and driftin' like a ship out on the sea.
I'm driftin' and driftin' like a ship out on the sea.
And I ain't got nobody, in this whole world to care for me.

The uniqueness of the blues melody is its altered harmonic scale or "blue notes" that reflect the Africanisms mentioned in the discussion of gospel music. Musicologist Eddie S. Meadows provides a technical explanation:

In the Blues scale the concept of the neutral third is the result of the Black American's attempt to retain his African musical identity. The diatonic scale contains major and minor thirds and major and minor sevenths. Both are virtually unknown in most African cultures. Since these tones were not present in most African scales, Blacks of the antebellum period had to choose between the major and minor thirds and sevenths of the diatonic scale when making music. The compromise was to use neither the major nor minor third, but, rather, to use thirds and sevenths that wavered between the two and were therefore "neutral." Each of the tones lies at a midpoint between the major and minor intervals. Although this scale is known as the Blues scale, it permeates all Black American music: Blues, Gospels, Jazz, Spirituals, and Soul music. It can be achieved through vocal inflection, through instrumental inflections, and by striking the flatted and natural thirds and sevenths simultaneously. Blues guitarists used the bottleneck technique to achieve this same effect.[40]

In spite of cultural dilution and commercialization of the blues, the African influence still remains.

The Delta country of the South produced the earliest and greatest growth and development of classic down-home blues. In the 1940s and 1950s, the blues "migrated" to big cities where distinctive styles promoted by various artists developed. From the Delta basic blues form, a Memphis style emerged, whose major proponents included B.B. King, Bobby Bland, Albert King, Junior Parker, and Little Milton. The blues that was played on the traditional acoustic guitar was replaced with the innovative "one-string" electric guitar techniques of B.B. King, T-Bone Walker, Albert King, and Freddie King. The blues and many of the Memphis artists moved to Chicago where a Delta-based Chicago style evolved. Famous Chicago bluesmen include Muddy Waters, Elmore James, and Howlin' Wolf. Memphis Minnie, a Chicago-based Blueswoman, was a pioneer in using the electric guitar and became one the most influential recorded blues performers.[41] Many of these artists, such as, Sonny Boy Williamson, Willie Nix, Walter Horton, and John Lee Hooker recorded with White recording companies in Jackson, Mississippi, and in Memphis, Tennessee, before moving North. Blues singer-guitarists Muddy Waters, Howlin' Wolf, John Lee Hooker, and Lightnin'

Hopkins are among those categorized as "low-down dirty" blues artists.[42] Robert Cray, Albert Collins, and Johnny Copeland (deceased) are among the relatively few younger Black artists carrying on the Memphis/ Chicago blues traditions.

Melanie Bratcher has examined the blues song performances of three major female performers: Bessie Smith, Billie Holiday, and Nina Simone. She argues that "their songs function in the capacity of preserving African heritage for Black people and encouraging alternative models of behavior and attitude toward Black women.[43]" Continuing, Bratcher observes that "the most prevalent themes and messages in their lyrics address social ills, particularly imprisonment (incarceration), race relations, and love-induced depression."[44]

Only a fractional number of renowned Black blues artists are mentioned in this discussion. A complete history of the blues in America requires a full-length book. It is unfortunate that, at one time, the interest of African Americans in their blues heritage waned. However, British and other European nationalities have always loved and treasured Black blues music. When European and White American rock artists began to imitate Black blues singers and to use blues music to propel them into world-wide stardom, African American interest in the blues was revived.

It is important to recognize that there is a largely unappreciated social realism and critical tradition in the blues. It is, of course, unrealistic to expect that traditional blues could exhibit the type of aggressive, challenging political commentaries that were fueled, for example, by the Black Power Movement. Instead, blues artists used their finely honed descriptive skills to highlight the effects of oppression in ways designed to raise the awareness of sympathetic external audiences and/or to promote solidarity among African Americans by documenting common experiences and enhancing the resolve to survive in the face of daily oppression. The precedents for political expression established by blues artists, in fact, laid the foundation for the broader patterns of political expression reflected in succeeding musical genres.

Several blues writers and performers used their artistic talents to challenge the systemic oppression Blacks experienced during the post-World War I and Depression eras. Bessie Smith's rendition of "Poor Man's Blues," which was recorded in 1928, is a good example.[45] The social and political conditions of the

8

1920s and 1930s had a major influence on the political commentaries of blues artists. The Great Depression, WPA policies, prison farms, and lynching were among the specific topics explored in the blues. The onset of the Great Depression in 1929 prompted several blues artists to record songs, directed at both internal and external audiences, which documented the disproportionate suffering Blacks experienced. Alfred Fields's "'29 Blues," and Blind Lemon Jefferson's "Tin Cup Blues," both of which are essentially documentaries, are examples.[46] Some blues artists directed sharp criticism at the failure of government programs, in particular, the WPA, such as, Big Bill Broonzy in his "Unemployment Stomp" (1938).[47] Blues artists effectively chronicled how "southern justice" intensified exploitation and consolidated external social control, as in Vera Hall's "Another Man Done Gone" and Bukka White's "Parchman Farm Blues" (1940).[48] One of the best indictments of the US government's discriminatory racial practices—while calling on Blacks to contribute to the World War II effort—is provided by Waring Cuney's "Uncle Sam Says" (1941), performed by Josh White.[49] In the post-World War II era, new musical genres emerged and subsequently assumed the role of the blues as a major artistic outlet for Black political commentary. At the same time, however, blues artists responded to the changing times as illustrated by Homer Harris's "Atomic Bomb Blues" (1946).[50]

The Civil Rights and Black Power Movements, along with the Vietnam War, would later infuse a greater assertiveness into some blues lyrics, such as "Backlash Blues" (1967), performed by Nina Simone.[51] Other blues artists also commented on the Vietnam War, including Junior Wells in "Viet Cong Blues."[52]

Jazz: The Musical Creation of African Americans

More has been written about jazz than perhaps any other African American art form. However, the treatment of jazz here will be limited to a brief discussion of its origin, nature, and development, as well as some of its early and contemporary contributors. The most phenomenal aspect of jazz music is that it evolved from the social culture of African Americans, descendants of enslaved Blacks of the American South. Because early jazz grew rapidly in popularity and was appreciated and imitated by White American

and European musicians from its inception, some critics are reluctant to classify it as Black music. Nonetheless, most scholars and music historians acknowledge the African roots and origins of jazz. Other ethnic groups have contributed to jazz development, but the basic "rhythmic language" of the music is derived from the musical culture of African Americans. Jazz is an instrumental extension of the spiritual, gospel, and blues.

The rhythmic complexity, the execution, the polyrhythmic performance, the inflections, and the syncopation of jazz are indisputably African in nature. There is no precedent of these musical characteristics in European music.[53] Many of the African characteristics of jazz are reported to be derived from the Congo and Angola or the Central and South West regions of Africa. New Orleans, the birthplace of jazz, had significant populations of Blacks from these African regions through the Atlantic slave trade.[54] On holidays and allowed recreational occasions, enslaved Blacks would assemble in New Orleans at a place known as *Congo Square*. In Congo Square, they would perform indigenous African festive music and dances. The participants dressed in their finest, and the women, men and children danced and shouted to the rhythms of the bamboula and tom-tom drums. They used anklet bells and other crude, but ingeniously devised, castanet and marimba-type instruments.[55] By the late nineteenth and early twentieth centuries, a distinct Black music began to develop in Storyville, a renowned red-light district of New Orleans. The music eventually became known as *jazz*, although the exact origin of the term *jazz* is unknown. African American bands performed in the cabarets of the Storyville section of the French Quarter, in street parades, and in funeral processions. Daphne Harrison describes the evolution of jazz as a music that "rose from the brothels, the party houses, the river saloons, and whisky joints, from the funeral processions, the blue hollers and the street cries of Southern Blacks, and merged imperceptibly with the European quadrilles, waltzes, folk tunes, and hymns of Whites."[56] White orchestras, under the influence of Black musicians, developed a type of Dixieland jazz that became popular beyond the New Orleans area. This "jazz" was perceptively different from the authentic timbre of African American jazz.

The closing of Storyville in 1917 and the migration of Blacks to northern cities led to a dispersal of Black musicians from New Orleans and the spread of jazz music to the urban areas of the North and Midwest. Black combos in the big cities continued to play the blues–rag–jazz type of music they had been accustomed to playing. Joe "King" Oliver and Louis Armstrong were the initial and principal purveyors of Black New Orleans jazz to the cities of Chicago, New York, and Los Angeles.

It must be pointed out that preceding and contributing to the development of jazz was a distinctively Black-created music tempo called ragtime. As the restrictive and inhibiting forces of slavery diminished, Blacks began to develop music and entertainment suited to their own tastes and pleasure. They were fascinated with the piano, and in the process of mastering this instrument, Black musicians created a kind of piano-rag music adapted to the dance of Black folk. The unique syncopated music was a natural and perfect accompaniment to the Black folk dance called the cakewalk.[57] White America became aware of ragtime music when it was played in Black minstrel shows and musical comedies during the late 1890s. They adopted and contributed to its style. This genre reigned in popularity in America and Europe until about 1917.

Essentially, ragtime became a synthesis of African American and European musical traditions. Ragtime players performed for meager wages in saloons and in honky-tonk cafes along the Mississippi River and the eastern seaboard, where a piano player could substitute for an orchestra because the pianist could maintain a steady bass beat with the left hand while the right hand played the syncopated melody and rhythms. Scott Joplin (1868–1917), a Black musician and composer, is generally acknowledged as a major figure in the development and popularization of ragtime. He was famous for having published several masterpieces; one of the most notable was "Maple Leaf Rag." Few will deny that ragtime was a prime musical forerunner of jazz. The improvisation of popular songs allowed upcoming jazz artists and bands to break away from rhythmic and emotional constraints. Later, the jazz artists of the 1920s and 1930s, such as "Jelly Roll" Morton, Louis Armstrong, and Earl Hines, would blend ragtime with the blues, folk, and popular tunes, and inject jazz rhythms. Thus, to a great extent, jazz was derived or evolved from ragtime.[58] However, ragtime's "limited rhythmic language, and narrow emotional range" would later contribute to its demise.

Jazz followed almost the same route northward as its precursor the blues—from New Orleans to Memphis, Kansas City, and St. Louis to Chicago. However, jazz took on a new flavor in New York and spread with alacrity to Paris and London. By 1926, the music had acquired profound critics and devotees. Despite the racial origin of jazz and the racist and oppressive era in which it developed, White orchestra leaders were attracted to African American music and its musicians. Jazz sparked unprecedented interracial collaboration. It is generally known among jazz enthusiasts that famous White musicians, such as, Glenn Miller, Tommy Dorsey, Harry James, Bennie Goodman, and Jack Teagarden, would avail themselves of every opportunity to visit night clubs in Chicago and New York's Harlem to learn from, and to consort with, Black jazz artists. Eventually, White musicians would capitalize on jazz and receive greater economic rewards and more social accolades than the Black originators of the music. Yet, White musicians played a major role in establishing jazz as a universal musical art form.

In the mid- and late-1930s, philosopher and writer Alain Locke perceived the formation of three different schools or styles of jazz. The jumping, jamming, and swing style that emanated from Chicago was called *hot jazz*. The jazz that became popular in New York, and subsequently in Paris and London, stressed melody and flowing harmony. It was classified as *sweet jazz*, and the more sophisticated or refined hybrid style was described as *classic jazz*.[59] Although most Black jazzmen could be experimentally competent in all styles, Louis Armstrong, Earl Hines, and Coleman Hawkins were included, at that time, as the principal purveyors of hot jazz. Fletcher Henderson, Duke Ellington, Lester Young, Art Tatum, Erroll Garner, Count Basie, Lionel Hampton, and a host of other Black and White bandleaders and jazz artists ushered in the era of sweet, sophisticated, swing, and classic jazz.

By the mid-1940s, the enthusiasm for big band swing, classic, and classical jazz had climaxed. New and younger Black jazz musicians who had been mentored by the earlier jazz greats came on the scene. During World War II and the early 1950s, there was an emergent rebellion against political conservatism and a movement to reject conservatism and classicism in the arts and humanities. A cultural rebellion occurred in Europe and in America and ushered in an avant garde era. In music, bebop was the avant garde counterpart to jazz conservatism. Charlie Parker (alto

8

sax), Dizzy Gillespie (trumpet), Thelonious Monk (piano), Kenny Clarke (drums), Max Roach (drums), and Bud Powell (piano) were the founders of bebop, or the modern jazz movement. The new jazz was initially repudiated by many conventional jazz enthusiasts. However, bebop, in a way, was a rebellion by Black jazz artists against the White-dominated music industry and racism. Bebop was a declaration of Black musical independence.

Following the brief span of the bebop era, proponents of a *cool* modern jazz emerged. Many music writers labeled this music *West Coast jazz, hard bop,* or the *second stage of traditional bebop.* Black artists and groups in this category include the Miles Davis Quintet, Clifford Brown–Max Roach Quintet, the Modern Jazz Quartet, John Coltrane, Horace Silver, Charlie Mingus, Sonny Rollins, Ornette Coleman, Sonny Stitt, Eric Dolphy, Hubert Laws, and John Lewis.[60] This style of jazz was antithetical to the European classical art and musical tradition, with improvisation as its essence. Technical and innovative creativity in the execution of a piece, song, or ballad was expected of each individual performer, and any attempt to match or duplicate the feelings of a previous artist was deemed unimaginative. Because jazz is a living and functional art reflective of the artist's depth of emotion and feeling at a given moment or time of performance, an authentic Black jazz artist never played the same piece of music the same way twice. Jazz does not require the player to adhere strictly to a fossilized rhythm, pitch, timbre or the feelings and emotions of dead composers or artists as in European classical music, and the freedom inherent in the expressiveness of African spirituality is perhaps why White Americans and Europeans find African American music appealing.

Black music, including jazz, is still denied recognition as a fine art form. It is often assumed that early jazz musicians had not studied music and that Blacks excel technically only in rhythm. The truth is that most or all of the early Black musicians studied music through an apprentice system, although most did not receive music degrees. Furthermore, Black musicians have also been the most innovative harmonic and melodic players in jazz.[61] The unfortunate aspect of jazz history is that African Americans have never reaped significant economic rewards from their musical creativity. White musicians, critics, and researchers have capitalized on jazz and other Black music both economically and artistically. The leading night clubs and music halls seldom seek African American jazz artists to perform because White musicians now successfully imitate Black jazz culture. Although jazz is taught at major colleges and universities, there are few if any Blacks employed as faculty in the music departments. The sad truth is that while many elements of Black music and culture are accepted by White Americans, in general, Black artists and Black people are not.

Commercialization and the commercial specifications that have influenced Black jazz artists since the 1960s have diluted the originality and authenticity of jazz. In order to make a living, many contemporary Black jazz artists have found it necessary to crossover, or to fuse their jazz orientation and talent with rock music culture. Unless African Americans make a special effort to encourage young Blacks to appreciate their jazz heritage and to choose jazz careers, jazz as a Black musical art form will cease to exist.

Both the scholarly study of jazz and its representation in various media reflect systematic efforts to sever its connection to its cultural origins. Recent historical explorations of jazz de-emphasize its African and African American roots and highlight contributions of European Americans. In a similar vein, so-called smooth jazz FM stations prioritize the pop jazz recordings of European American musicians. Jazz studies programs have also contributed to the growing disconnection of jazz from its cultural moorings. These programs emphasize transforming the music into a notated format similar to traditional European genres. This involves a form of musicological reductionism designed to allow strict replication in performance. This process makes jazz compatible with traditional European performance, but it distorts the essence of traditional jazz performance in its cultural context.

It is necessary to challenge efforts to sever jazz from Black culture, especially now when cultural expression among Blacks appears limited to hip-hop and associated genres. It is especially important to highlight aspects of the jazz tradition that are most compatible with African American Studies. Some jazz composers and performers have directly contributed their unique artistic perspectives to the modern Black liberation movement. Max Roach's "Garvey's Ghost" (1961) invokes historical efforts to promote self-determination, and his "Man from South Africa" (1961) invites comparisons between the oppression of American Blacks under Jim Crow laws and of South African

Blacks under apartheid.[62] Herbie Hancock's "I Have a Dream" (1969) captures the spirit of Martin Luther King, Jr.'s nonviolent approach to the struggle for racial justice, and Archie Shepp's "Malcolm, Malcolm, Semper Malcolm" (1965) pays tribute to uncompromising warrior Malcolm X.[63] In each case, the composition's stylistic characteristics were designed creatively to convey the intended political sentiments in the language of jazz.

Rhythm and Blues—Soul Music

Each category of African American music reflects the social, political, and economic conditions of Black people during various periods of American history. Even though the categorization of African American music is useful for analytical or academic purposes, the music itself is a continuum of the cultural and spiritual forces from which it derived. The rhythmic, harmonic, and melodic nature of authentic Black music is African. Its emotional dynamism and spiritual excitement are founded on the religious beliefs and practices of Black people in America.

The Black music that became known as *rhythm and blues* in the 1950s developed from the sound, feelings, and religious aura of the Black Church. Literally and figuratively, the Black Church spawned the talent that created rhythm and blues in the same manner that it had done for spirituals, gospel, blues, and jazz. Many rhythm and blues artists sang previously in church choirs and choral groups. In addition, rhythm and blues music was shaped and influenced by the same social, political, and economic factors of Black discontent that gave rise to the Civil Rights Movement of the 1950s and 1960s and the Black Church was the spiritual force and political garrison that sustained the Movement. Thus, the music, lyrics, and timbre of rhythm and blues reflect, substantially, the religious influence, and the social, political, and economic experiences of African Americans from the 1950s through the 1970s.

It is not surprising that rhythm and blues, like the spirituals, gospel, and blues, had its primary development in the South with a preponderance of its artists southern born and bred; in spite of northern migration, the South still contained the largest Black population. Following World War II, the prospects for racial advancement appeared promising and millions of Black youth, at that time, yearned for a musical medium that would be spiritually uplifting—one to which they could relate and which they could use to describe their love relationships in a hopeful and inspiring manner. The traditional country and urban blues did not suffice because it was basically melancholy and appealed mostly to the older generations, and jazz was limited in its ability to provide the lyrical expressions and dance rhythms that appealed to teenagers and young adults. A lively more, upbeat, and rhythmic type of music developed among young Blacks in major cities of the South and in the ghettos of the North.

White record companies found it profitable to market Black music in the Black community. Prior to 1949, the term *race record* was used by recording companies to identify records made by Black artists. The popular trade paper *Billboard* substituted *rhythm and blues* (R & B) for the word *race* to designate the new Black music that had begun to develop by the 1950s.[64]

White youth were overwhelmingly attracted to the rhythm and blues music that was being played on spot radio programs targeted at the Black community. Initially, rhythm and blues records were not made available in stores accessible to Whites or in White neighborhoods. Thus, White retailers faced a growing demand from White youth to stock rhythm and blues records. Radio stations in major cities, North and South, filled the airwaves with rhythm and blues music with the primary intent of appealing to the African American market. Soon rhythm and blues became the dominant music of most pop radio stations.[65] It is necessary to recall that prior to the mid–1950s, especially in the South, Whites did not generally allow their children to listen to Black music or to emulate Black dance. Many Whites referred to African American popular music as *nigger music*, and it was forbidden because of its "immoral" nature. Nevertheless, because of its popularity and profitability, White artists recorded their versions of rhythm and blues music to cash in on and capture the broadening market. These White recordings were called *covers*. The word *cover* was also used to describe the practice of placing a Black artist's photograph on the album cover of a White artist's recording of a rhythm and blues hit song.

The Black sound, with its sexual connotations and physical gyrations characteristic of rhythm and blues music performance, prompted various White artists to enter the field in imitation of Blacks. White segregated concert audiences in the South would not think

8

of watching Black artists perform rhythm and blues music, but they enthusiastically accepted White imitations. Elvis Presley, who has been dubbed the *King of Rock and Roll*, was heavily influenced by Black rhythm and blues artists. The term *rock and roll*, it should be noted, was coined for performances of rhythm and blues music by White artists. Even though some White writers fuse and attribute rock and roll to African Americans, the term did not originate in the Black community, nor was it ever intended to refer to Black music. The hit song "Hound Dog," which propelled Elvis Presley to fame, had been recorded three years earlier by Black female blues singer, Big Mama Thornton.[66]

During the height of the Civil Rights Movement, Blacks began to refer to rhythm and blues music as soul music. At least two styles and two tempos of the music existed. In one style the lead singer was harmonically backed up by a group, and they invoked the African call-and-response pattern clearly derived from the Black gospel choir format. The other style involved group harmony, where an American popular song or an original lyric was treated as a sentimental ballad. Each artist or group was capable of rendering an upbeat rhythmic-dance piece or the sentimental ballad. The rhythm and blues groups were distinguished by their unique naturalistic names, such as, the Flamingoes, the Orioles, the Ravens, the Midnighters, the Drifters, and the Clovers. However, individual male and female artists dominated the rhythm and blues or soul field. Some of the early upbeat rhythm and blues artists included Chuck Berry, Little Richard, James Brown, and Bo Diddley. The lyrics and rhythms of these rhythm and blues stars influenced Elvis Presley and, also, such European rock groups as the Beatles and the Rolling Stones. Since rhythm and blues was an extension or modernization of the blues, bluesmen like B.B. King, Bobby Bland, Muddy Waters, Charles Brown, and Amos Milburn were influential during the rise of R&B. Others in the rhythm and blues style and tradition include individual male singers Sam Cooke, Lloyd Price, Solomon Burke, Jackie Wilson, Johnny Ace, and Chuck Willis. Ruth Brown, Dinah Washington, LaVern Baker, and Little Esther Phillips were among the early dynamic female rhythm and blues artists.[67]

Groups and individual singers of the 1960s and 1970s include Ike and Tina Turner, the Impressions, the Isley Brothers, the Fifth Dimension, Aretha Franklin, Otis Redding, Wilson Pickett, and numerous others. One of the greatest boosts to rhythm and blues music occurred when Motown, the Black-owned record company of Detroit, began to discover and produce a seemingly unlimited number of rhythm and blues stars. Under the leadership of founder Berry Gordy, Motown produced nationally famous rhythm and blues groups and singers, including Diana Ross and the Supremes, the Temptations, Smokey Robinson and the Miracles, the Marvelettes, the Jackson Five, the Four Tops, Gladys Knight and the Pips, Marvin Gaye, Martha Reeves and the Vandellas, and many others.

The astounding development, growth and popularity of rhythm and blues, or soul music, through the decades of the 1950s, 1960s, and 1970s were, undoubtedly, the result of rising social, economic, and political expectations from the Supreme Court's desegregation decision of 1954 and the subsequent Civil Rights Movement. The impact of these two developments also affected family life and social relationships between Black males and females. James Stewart insists that the positive expressions of Black social consciousness in Black rhythm and blues music of the 1960s performed a unique social function in the Black community. However, that aspect of Black male–female relationships was lost in the rhythm and blues music of the 1970s. Stewart argues that the rhythm and blues music of the 1960s projected a highly romantic and Platonic view of male–female relationships. In contrast, much of the music of the 1970s was materialist and earthy in character. The 1970s music and song indicated a somewhat flippant resignation to romantic and marital breakup and a proclivity to sexual exploitation. The integrationist ideology that prevailed at the time led to an implicit acceptance by Blacks of general societal values.[68] The character, pattern, and style of any music change over a period of time, as artists seek to modify or expand their musical talent, and as other cultural group influences dilute or distort original forms. Commercialization, profit seeking, and the artificiality of electronic music have obscured the traditional rhythm and blues sound and style. In addition, the social, economic, and political milieu that prevails today has changed from that of a few decades ago.

As is true of other genres discussed previously, it is critical to highlight the linkage between art and politics in rhythm and blues. William van Deburg writes, "As an indigenous expression of the collective African American experience (soul music) served as a repository of racial consciousness [that transcended] the medium of entertainment [and] provided a ritual in song with which African Americans could identify and through which they could convey important in-group symbols."[69] In a similar vein, disc jockey Reggie Lavong declares, "Like blues, soul music reflects, defines, and directs the strategies, expectations, and aspirations of black Americans."[70] During the Civil Rights and Black Power eras, racial segregation established distinct spaces in which African Americans listened to and experienced music. These places included family gatherings, informal interactions among friends, parties, organization meetings, and movie houses. Segregated community theaters facilitated the generation of group specific interpretations of political messages. The political significance of rhythm and blues songs was further enhanced by some African American disc jockeys' use of their shows as platforms for political education. Van Deburg contends that "more overtly political music often made little impact on national record charts, [but] the message of these songs was spread underground via a modern-day 'grapevine telegraph.' "[71]

The basic type of political commentary in rhythm and blues is the "documentary," which "provide[s] a running commentary on the state of Black culture."[72] In general, documentaries highlight the negative conditions prevalent in Black communities, whereas, what James Stewart describes as "All God's Children Declarations," tout the common interests and shared experiences of African Americans and other groups to argue for equal treatment, removal of barriers to equality, and a reduction of inter-group conflict. Stewart identifies other types of commentaries that include "Defiant Challenges," which demand, rather than entreat, external forces to cease and desist from exploitative behavior; "Awareness Raising Self-Criticism," which are designed to educate listeners about the seriousness of a particular set of circumstances and to document the need for corrective action; "Collective Self-Help Solutions," which attempt to sharpen political consciousness but have the further objective of providing guidance for solving community problems; and "Revolutionary Manifestos," which frame problems in Black communities within broader patterns of global oppression.[73]

Rap Music and Hip-Hop Culture

The new Black musical idiom of the mid-1980s and 1990s that is reflective of the contemporary African American experience is rap music or hip-hop, and commentaries found in the more political songs can be classified by employing the same categories used for rhythm and blues. Rap music originated or evolved out of the street culture of African American and Puerto Rican youths during the mid-1970s within the New York vicinities of the South Bronx, Brooklyn, and Queens. Three radio disc jockeys (DJs), Kool Herc, Grandmaster Flash, and Afrika Bambaataa, are credited with having popularized rap music. The first rap record, "Rapper's Delight," was released in 1979; it was a stunning commercial success and was marketed internationally. It listed among the Top Ten on the popular charts in the United States, and more than two million copies were sold.[74] Prior to this breakthrough, rap had been considered by the entertainment media to be too Black and rhetorically explicit for the masses.

Although rap has some Hispanic and White rock influences, it is overwhelmingly an African American art form. Rap was initiated by urban youth who sought positive diversion from violence and drug abuse. Rap music is an art form of rhythm, rhetoric, and rhymes consistent with the African musical and oral tradition. Blacks have always found that music, verbal dexterity, and dance are psychologically therapeutic in their struggle for survival against racism and oppression,[75] and it provided a means of relief from economic deprivation, unemployment, and social despair. A vivid description of Black verbal and musical dexterity, as evidenced in rap, is provided by Alfred B. Pasteur's and Ivory L. Toldson's explication of the Black vernacular:

> Black vernacular is both poetic and prosaic... Whether written or oral, black vernacular has long been of interest to those captivated by beauty that arises from the artistic sequencing of words. Be it in the form of sermon, rap, dozens, signifying, folk tale, song (shouts, spirituals, gospels, field hollers, rhythm & blues, reggae, jazz), it emotionally stirs and seizes upon transmission. Black vernacular is explosive with emotional power.[76]

An entire culture has been created around rap music based on the Black vernacular. The culture is commonly known as hip-hop.

Hip-hop music embodies a myriad of disconnected issues and phenomena from African symbolism, anarchy, capitalism, communalism, Islamic fundamentalism, social protest, sexual imagery, break dancing, mural and graffiti art, Black history, pedagogy, violence, materialism, drug abstinence, egoism, to obscenity.[77] Hip-hop emerged, in part, as a rebellion against the more conventional music of the 1970s and 1980s, in the same manner that bebop challenged conventional jazz in the 1950s. Rap music was initially rejected and spurned by MTV and the music media. But today, its purveyors and fans include people of all socioeconomic classes, races, and ethnic groups.

Some of the early rap groups included The Sugar Hill Gang, Grandmaster Flash and the Furious Five, Kurtis Blow, Public Enemy, Erik B. and Rakim, L.L. Cool J., 2 Live Crew, Heavy D and the Boyz, and Dr. Jekyll and Mr. Hyde. Early prominent female rappers included Roxanne Shante, JJ Fad, M.C. Lyte, and Queen Latifah. Popular contemporary rappers include the late Tupac Shakur, Ice Cube, Snoop Dog, Outkast, Missy Elliot, Lil' Kim, T.I., Eve, Trina, Ludacris, Kanye West, Lil Wayne, Common, and Lil John, to name a few.

The presence of popular female rap artists does not, however, absolve artists from addressing continuing charges of misogyny in the lyrical content of many songs. In discussing the misogynistic dimensions of rap, Harold Kruse appropriately asserts "no popular music in recent years has been as explicitly coded as male in popular discourse as rap."[78] Gender dynamics in rap music has been critiqued by a large number of commentators. From an historical context, Charise Cheney maintains that "Although extremely sensational, the sexual politics of rap nationalists was an extension of a centuries-old tradition of black male politicking that has never been apologetic for or restrained in its desire for male power."[79] In a similar vein, Ronald Jackson and Sakile Camara argue that even the female thug image in hip hop "is merely emblematic of a master narrative—old guard, male representation of women as feisty, overactive, sexualized mistresses."[80] However, Layli Phillips, Kerri Reddick-Morgan, and Dionne Stephens identify another tendency. They argue that some female rappers have used hip hop as a platform "to critique the sexism of men of their same race," while concurrently "express[ing] solidarity with men of their same race or ethnicity in their critique of and struggle against mainstream society's racism, classism, and race sexism (which affects both men and women of color)."[81]

The most intriguing and appealing aspect of rap music is the execution of its rhythm, rhetoric, and rhyme. In addition to body dexterity and imagery, Houston A. Baker Jr., describes rap music as "hybridity":

> Black sounds (African drums, bebop melodies, James Brown shouts, jazz improvs, Ellington riffs, blues innuendoes, doo-wop croons, reggae words, calypso rhythms). ...But the most acrobatic of the techniques is the verb and reverb of the human voice pushed straight out, or emulated by synthesizers, or emulating drums and falsettos—the rhyming, chiming sound that is a mnemonic for black urbanity.[82]

Some commentators have criticized rap for its lack of traditional Eurocentric musical characteristics. These criticisms fail to appreciate African-influenced musical characteristics, including the musicality of the spoken and performed word. Brackett explains that "the sounds of rap recordings challenge preconceptions on their own: in rap, voices do not sing or produce melody in any conventional sense, but they do not merely speak words either. Instead they produce 'rhythmicized speech' ... in which variations of tone and relative pitch create a melody in much the same way that a non-pitched percussion instrument might."[83] According to Brackett, rappers' musicality "is expressed in phrasing, articulation, rhythm, and tone rather than in the manipulation of discrete pitches."[84] Patricia Washington and Lynda Shaver suggest that "Rap music videos continue the themes and traditions of the Blues."[85] Elaborating on this observation, the authors declare, "Like the blues, rap reveals the effects of community conditions and the development of rappers as organic intellectuals."[86]

The priority of the spoken word in rap music extends the contributions of artists such as Gil Scott Heron, who described himself as a "Bluesician," attempting to resurrect the tradition of political commentary in the blues. Tracing his lineage directly to Langston Hughes, Heron enunciated the intent to "adapt certain theories [used by] ... Robeson, Hughes, and Others [and] ... working these theories in our own context around South Africa, life concerns, and daily living."[87] The Last Poets, a group of Black nationalist spoken word artists who emerged during the late 1960s, are also considered progenitors of rap. In 2005, The Last Poets teamed up with rapper Common to record "The Corner," a song about Black life in the inner cities. Contemporary "spoken word" artists have adapted this tradition to introduce a new genre of stand-up poetry, much of which expresses overt political commentary. In fact, many of the criticisms that ostensibly focus on the musical characteristics of rap are often actually disguised opposition to the political ideologies and social values projected in the medium. Musical criticisms of rap, as well as of earlier genres, including jazz, "frequently mingle with a sense of threat to the social order, for these genres have often brought together new social and cultural alliances, or have focused attention on the dispossessed and marginalized."[88]

The broad impact of rap music can be seen in the fact that most purchasers of rap CDs are White, and "white listeners, who were generally more affluent, [have] exercised a disproportionate influence over what the industry perceived as market-place trends."[89] The record companies pay particular attention to White consumers of rap because "as in nearly all forms of cultural production, making a profit in popular music production is a difficult and complicated project."[90] The profit motive, as suggested in Chapter 7, imposes serious challenges to sustaining the authenticity and political potential of rap music. One of the more instructive historical examples of the potential loss to community development that occurs when financial control over cultural production is lost is provided by the sad saga of the Corporation, founded in 1921, which released several records under the Black Swan label. Although the label initially recorded world-class musicians, such as Fletcher Henderson and Ethel Waters, it ceased operations in 1924 as a result of competition and price-cutting by White-owned labels, such as Okeh, Paramount, and Columbia.

In engaging hip hop, Africana specialists should become familiar with the burgeoning body of literature that is examining the genre. Examples include Jeffrey Ogbar's *Hip-Hop Revolution: The Culture and Politics of Rap* and the volume edited by Derrick Alridge, James Stewart and V.P. Franklin entitled, *Message in the Music: Hip Hop History and Pedagogy*.[91] In promoting the social responsibility agenda of African American Studies, scholar/activists would do well to follow the suggestion of Pero Dagbovie to help restore what he describes as hip hop's "historical revivalism." Dagbovie proposes that "If mainstream Hip Hop artists in conjunction with black historians produced CD with a

dozen tracks, which recounted black history from the shores of Africa to the present, millions of black youth would be able to recite black history, feel the black past, and internalize aspects of the enduring black struggle for liberation."[92]

Classical Music (European)

African American Studies specialists are careful to use the adjective "European" to modify the term "classical music." This convention is necessary, in part, because the term "classical" implies a certain prestige and status over and above other musical forms. When it is used solely to refer to European music, the music of other cultures is implicitly relegated to a second class status. In contrast, the best examples of African, African American, and other African Diasporan musical compositions and performances are classified as "classics" within the context of African American Studies. This perspective influences the manner in which the involvement of African Americans, in refining and performing European classical music, is treated and discussed below.

Most African American Studies specialists view the engagement of Blacks with European classical music as playing an important role in refuting racist assertions that Blacks were unable to appreciate or master the compositional and performance skills required to contribute to European "high culture." The important achievements of African Americans in all of the various roles associated with this musical genre, i.e., composers, symphony conductors, instrumentalists, and concert and opera singers, provide irrefutable counter evidence invalidating racist claims. John Gray's bibliographical guide to literature, examining Blacks in European classical music, provides a comprehensive roadmap to relevant writing on this subject.[93] The principal interest of most African American Studies specialists with the engagement of Blacks with classical European music is the efforts of some to move beyond the mastery of European styles, *per se*, and expand the boundaries of the genre in ways consistent with the values and interests of African American Studies. The following discussion focuses on selected examples of such transformative activities.

In the area of classical composition, the contributions of Robert Nathaniel Dett are especially noteworthy. Dett was born in Ontario, Canada, and graduated from the Oberlin Conservatory of Music in 1908, with the distinction of being the first person of African

8

descent to receive a Bachelor of Music degree in composition. While at Oberlin, Dett developed a deep appreciation of the musical sophistication of "Negro Spirituals" that became the focus of his career. Dett also studied at the American Conservatory of Music, Columbia University, Northwestern University, the University of Pennsylvania, and Harvard University. He received the Bowdoin Literary Prize in 1920 at Harvard for his thesis, "Negro Music." Dett taught for 20 years at Hampton University, where he composed works for piano and for mixed choir, many of which were arrangements of spirituals. In 1930, he took the Hampton Institute Choir on a 40-city tour of Europe and the United States. During his career, Dett composed approximately 100 works for piano, orchestra, chorus, and solo voice, and he won a variety of compositional and literary awards.[94] Dett saw his work in preserving the spiritual as valuable for both Blacks and Whites, insisting that:

> It occurred to the writer that if a form of song were evolved which contained all the acceptable characteristics of Negro folk music and yet would compare favorably in poetic sentiment and musical expression with the best class of church music, it would ... save to the Negro and his music all the peculiar and precious idioms, and as work of art would be as great to white people as to the colored people, while at the same time such composition would constitute the development of a natural resource."[95]

In a similar vein, William Grant Still made important strides in infusing material based on African American culture into operatic and orchestral performance genres. Still composed eight operas including, "Troubled Island" (1941), the first opera by a Black person staged by a major opera company—the New York City Opera Company (1949). Still was also the first Black to conduct a major symphony orchestra (Los Angeles Philharmonic, 1936).[96] Still attempted to establish a national Negro symphony orchestra, whose members would have "jazz training, which would increase their virtuosity and thus enable them to execute passages that were generally difficult for musicians trained only in the European school of performance."[97] Over the course of his career, Still produced approximately one hundred compositions, including "symphonies, operas, ballets, orchestral works for chorus or solo voice, works for band, choir, piano, voice, and chamber pieces for winds or strings."[98]

It is also important to recognize the unique influence of female composers. Margaret Bonds, for example, was born in 1913 and studied piano at the Coleridge-Taylor Music School and Northwestern University. Entering Northwestern in 1929, she was not allowed to live on campus or to use the University's facilities. However, despite these barriers, Bonds received her Masters degree in music in 1934 and became the first African American to perform with the Chicago Symphony Orchestra that same year. In the 1950s, Bonds composed a number of works using the writings of Langston Hughes, including "Songs of the Season" and "Three Dream Portraits." She also wrote the music for Hughes' play, "Shakespeare in Harlem" and composed Leontyne Price's famous rendition of "He's Got the Whole World in His Hands" (1963).[99]

In the contemporary era, Anthony Davis', "X: The Life and Times of Malcolm X," is an innovative attempt to infuse content reflecting the 1960s struggle for liberation into an operatic format. This opera debuted in 1986 in New York, performed by the New York City Opera. It is a biographical treatment of the life of Malcolm X, with special attention focused on his conflict with Elijah Muhammad. In contrast to the traditional operatic focus on vocalism, "X" is an example of message theater that incorporated extensive, atonality, repetitive chants, and modern jazz elements.[100]

Among the many classical African American singers, the life and activities of contralto Marian Anderson and baritone Paul Robeson are of special interest to African American Studies specialists. Anderson, who was born in Philadelphia, is noted for several performances that broke barriers, including a solo recital at Carnegie Hall on December 30, 1928. Her most famous concert was the result of the refusal of the Daughters of the American Revolution (DAR) to allow Anderson to perform at Washington, D.C.'s Constitutional Hall in 1939. This blatant discrimination precipitated widespread protest, and First Lady Eleanor Roosevelt and Walter White of the NAACP, along with others, were successful in persuading Secretary of the Interior, Harold Ickes, to arrange a free open-air concert on the steps of the Lincoln Memorial for Easter Sunday, April 9th. On this date, Marian Anderson sang before 75,000 people and was also heard by millions of radio listeners. She is also recognized as the first Black singer who was a regular member of the New York Metropolitan Opera. Anderson was awarded the American Medal of Freedom in 1963 by President Lyndon Johnson. Aside from these accomplishments, African American Studies specialists celebrate her for her early opposition to segregation that included the insistence on "vertical" seating in segregated cities so that Black audience members could sit in all parts of performance venues, including the orchestra section. By 1950, Anderson was refusing to sing anywhere where the audience was segregated.[101]

Paul Robeson is highly celebrated by African American Studies specialists for both his artistic accomplishments and his political activism. Robeson refined his performance skills while still in law school. His first professional performance occurred in 1922, as the lead in a 1922 Broadway theatrical production, "Taboo," and he was also a replacement cast member in Eubie Blake's and Noble Sissle's pioneering all-black musical, "Shuffle Along." Robeson appeared in a 1924 revival of Eugene O'Neill's, "The Emperor Jones" and premiered in O'Neill's, "All God's Chillun Got Wings." Robeson performed as Othello in a 1930 London production and in a 1932 Broadway revival of Oscar Hammerstein's and Jerome Kern's musical, "Showboat." This production featured Robeson's highly acclaimed rendition of "Ol' Man River."[102] Robeson was criticized by some members of the "New Negro Movement" because of his role as a chicken thief in "Emperor Jones." Between 1934 and 1937, Robeson performed in several films that presented Blacks in other than stereotypical ways, including "Sanders of the River" (1935), "King Solomon's Mines" (1937) and "Song of Freedom" (1937), and, by 1939, he had begun to refuse roles that portrayed Blacks negatively and to insist on changes in movie scripts.[103]

Robeson, and his longtime pianist and arranger Lawrence Brown, played a pivotal role in bringing spirituals into the classical music repertory. His 1925 recital at the Greenwich Village Theater was the first in which a Black soloist sang an entire program of spirituals, and he subsequently established an international reputation as a concert singer. Robeson sang a wide range of material, including sentimental popular tunes, work songs, political ballads, and international folk music, but continued to emphasize interpretations of the spirituals as the hallmark of his performances.[104]

Robeson's political activism began to blossom in the early 1930s when he became an honorary member of the West African Students' Union, through which he became acquainted with African students Kwame Nkrumah and Jomo Kenyatta, future presidents of Ghana and Kenya, respectively. He subsequently co-founded the Council on African Affairs to aid in African liberation.[105]

During a trip to the Soviet Union in 1934 to discuss the making of the film "Black Majesty," Robeson began to study Marxism and socialist systems in the Soviet Union. Robeson's activism and interests in the Soviet Union made him a primary target of anti-communist political interests, and he was called before the California Legislative Committee on Un-American activities in October 1946. Although Robeson declared that he was not a member of the Communist Party, he praised the Party's fight for equality and democracy. In 1949, Robeson embarked on a European tour during which he spoke out against the discrimination and injustices faced by Blacks in the US. Robeson's activities received significant attention in the US media, leading to violent assaults upon his return from abroad. In 1950, the federal government refused to allow Robeson to travel outside the US unless he agreed not to make any speeches. During this domestic exile Robeson continued to speak out in public forums and through his own monthly newspaper, "Freedom," which became his primary oratory and advocacy platform from 1950 to 1955. His autobiography, *Here I Stand*, was published in 1958 through a London publishing house.[106]

Robeson's battle to regain his passport was successful in 1958, a victory he announced at a May 10, 1958, concert at New York's Carnegie Hall. Subsequently, Robeson traveled to England, the Soviet Union, Austria, and New Zealand from 1958 to 1963, returning to the US after experiencing recurring health problems. Robeson's contributions to the liberation struggles of people of African descent and other oppressed peoples resulted in many awards and recognitions, including a 1965 salute chaired by actors Ossie Davis and Ruby Dee, writer James Baldwin, and many other supporters.[107]

8

African American Visual and Performing Arts

Black Art and the Evolution of the Black Artist

In a general sense, art is the creation of things or imagery by humans that display or manifest form, beauty, or perceptions that interest or attract. Usually, art is considered the product of, by, and for a particular culture or society, although it may be assessed—appreciated or depreciated—by other cultures. A society or culture determines the merits and functions of its own art. The universal appeal of an art object or concept may not be deliberate but simply incidental. The discussion here is related to African American creations in specific visual arts—painting and sculpture. Each race, culture, or ethnic group has distinctive approaches to painting, drawing, and sculpting.

Black art, in this context, may be defined as African American creative influences and contributions in the fields of painting and sculpture in America. Black art is demonstrably racial in context and reflects the symbolism of Africa and the social experiences of Black people in the United States and the world. Black art as an aesthetic ideology began to develop in the twentieth century when African American artists gradually refused to succumb totally to European and White American concepts of art forms, beauty, and social reality. Like Black music, Black art first developed to serve the interests of the Black public or community. Subsequently, its quality and appeal broadened and won the acclaim of other peoples. From an Afrocentric perspective, the works of African American painters or sculptors that do not reflect the Black art concept and idiom to some degree fall into the category of general art.

Black art portrays social, political, and economic realities from a Black perspective. It offers an alternative to the stereotypes of African Americans created by Europeans and White Americans. Black art treats those aspects and paradigms of the Black past and present that have enabled African Americans to survive and to prevail against slavery, oppression, and racism. Black art reflects the condition, hopes, despair, aspirations, triumphs, losses, imagination, joys, and sorrows of Black people. The Black artist seeks to define and redefine universal phenomena from an African worldview. The elements of protest and politics can be manifested in Black art without neutralizing or nullifying its aesthetic quality and appeal.[108] Although the Black artist has been unavoidably influenced by European and other cultures, threads of Afrocentrism differentiate Black art from general art.

The Black painter and sculptor have been confronted historically with the task of withstanding the belittlement and disregard of White American art critics. Even within the inclusive rationale of cultural relativism, the works of African American artists are rarely accorded the status of fine art. Consequently, proponents of the Black Arts Movement refused to appease White historians and critics who systematically ignored and omitted the works and accomplishments of African American artists. As a result, a proliferation of African American art organizations, museums, and galleries were established, especially, during and after the 1960s.

The inherent talent and skill of African American artists are attributable to their African heritage. As in the field of Black music, enslaved Africans brought to the New World a variety of skills that might be classified as arts and crafts. West Coast and Equatorial Africa from which most African Americans descended, were noted for the art of wood and metal sculpture, metal forging, wood carving, ivory and bone carving, weaving, and pottery. In America, testimonials to the artistic skills and abilities of the enslaved African can be seen in the intricate ironwork designs of colonial mansions, and, especially, in the forged balconies and grill work of many public and domestic buildings of New Orleans. Architecture and building were the outlets that provided much of the opportunity for enslaved Blacks to ply or demonstrate their craft and artistic abilities.[109] When Blacks were introduced to the European tradition of easel painting on canvas and to sculpture mediums in the nineteenth century, their works were highly imitative of European art in subject matter, style, and technique. Of the few Black artists who can be documented, Edward M. Bannister (1828–1901) was the first to achieve distinction as a painter. Edmonia Lewis (1845–1890), a woman, was the first Black sculptor of note. Painter Henry O. Tanner (1859–1937) and sculptor Meta Warrick Fuller (1877–1968) departed from the European orientation and produced works that directly engaged their Black heritage and existence. The works depicting Black subjects by Tanner and Fuller may have been the first to inspire the concept of "Black art."

Black art did not begin to receive recognition until about 1928, when philanthropist William E. Harmon established a foundation to aid and develop African American artists. The Harmon Foundation, through its financial awards and exhibitions, influenced the development of art education programs at many African American colleges and universities. Initially, most African Americans strived for recognition as *mainstream* artists rather than as Negro artists. However, by

1931, there was an attitudinal change. At the Harmon Foundation-sponsored exhibition that year, Black subjects and backgrounds predominated, and, according to Alain Locke, the quality, profundity, and vitality of the work improved as the artists grappled with familiar and well-understood subject matter.[110] A psychology of oppression and racism had misled earlier Black artists to avoid producing works relevant to their own race and experience. More than a half-century ago, Alain Locke, a formally trained philosopher, wrote that for the Black artist, "a real and vital racialism in art is a sign of artistic objectivity and independence and gives evidence of a double emancipation from apologetic timidity and academic imitativeness."[111] The adoption of a Black aesthetic ideology should not prevent an African American artist from expanding beyond this realm.

The New Deal programs instituted by President Franklin D. Roosevelt during the Depression years were a windfall for the growth and development of Black and White actors, writers, and artists. As a measure to decrease massive unemployment in large cities, like New York and Chicago, the federal government became the patron of thousands of artists by paying them through the Works Progress Administration (WPA) to produce murals, easel paintings, etchings, sculpture, and other art that eventually were placed in public buildings and museums. The purpose of the program was to put unemployed artists to work, to develop a trend and a body of art that depicted the American ethos, and to democratize art—to bring it into the daily life of the average citizen. Many Black artists who had begun to develop during the Harlem Renaissance period were helped immensely by the WPA program.

The Black experience was the major theme of African American art during this period. The works of Aaron Douglas and James Lesesne Wells were within this culturally conscious realm. Other artists who actively produced work depicting the experiences of Blacks from the Depression through World War II include painter Archibald Motley (1891–1981); sculptress Augusta Savage (1900–1962); sculptress Selma Burke (1900–1995); painter Hale Woodruff (1900–1980); painter William H. Johnson (1901–1970); sculptor Richmond Barthé (1901–1981); painter Lois Mailou Jones (1905–1998); painter-sculptor-muralist Charles Alston (1907–1972); painter-muralist William Carter (1909–1996); painter Ernest Crichlow (1914–);

painter-illustrator Charles Sebree (1914–1985); painter-collagist Romare Bearden (1914–1988); sculptress and painter Elizabeth Catlett (1915–); painter Eldzier Cortor (1916–); painter Charles White (1918–1979); and painter Jacob Lawrence (1917–2000).[112] The 1950s and 1960s spawned a large cadre of politically-conscious Black artists. The works of these artists reflect a strong sense of Black pride, Black culture, civil rights awareness, militancy, and Pan-Africanism. During this period, a major school of Black artists rejected the Eurocentric notion of "art-for-arts-sake" and substituted "art-for-peoples'-sake." Under the aura and momentum of the Black Power, Black Pride, and Civil Rights Movements, the number of Black museums, galleries, and community art centers dramatically increased all over the country. The Studio Museum of Harlem was organized in 1969 as a facility where artists could display their work, hold meetings, and conduct other art-related activities. It is now a major African American cultural center in New York. Among the prominent art exhibited there are the works of the famous Harlem Renaissance photographer James Van Der Zee.

During the 1960s, the African Community of Bad Relevant Artists (AfriCobra), a coalition of Black artists, was founded. The purpose of AfriCobra was to establish a Black aesthetic school of thought derived from traditional African art and African American culture. While the artists agreed to retain their artistic individuality, AfriCobra set forth certain collective principles characteristic of the Black aesthetic as follows: Free Symmetry, "meaning rhythmic syncopation in design, music, and movement"; Shine, "meaning luminosity through dynamic contrasts of color, form, and spatial relationships"; Jam-packed and Jellytight Compositions, "meaning form-filled and fullfield surface design"; Awesome Imagery; and Koolaid Color.[113] All African American artists do not subscribe to the Black aesthetic concept. Some reject the notion that there should be an identifiable Black art aesthetic. African American art, like Black music, is influenced by the social and economic conditions of Blacks and by changes in their political ideology. The Black Arts period of the 1960s fostered many positive socio-psychological changes in the Black community. In many African American lower and middle-income homes, Black- or African-oriented paintings and sculpture are now a part of the decor which previously included only European and Victorian art.

8

Many African American churches replaced the symbolic blond, blue-eyed portrait of Christ with a Black one in harmony with their own race and image. The popular social theory of the past two decades has been cultural pluralism. However, cultural pluralism and diversity translate into cultural specificity and identity.

As a result of the cultural and Civil Rights Movements of the 1960s, there now exist in various areas of the arts hundreds, or perhaps thousands, of Black artists. However, since the late 1970s, there has been a retrenchment in civil rights and in progressive race relations in the United States. Consequently, many Black artists and African Americans in general have increased their interest in Black art and African culture. There is, in fact, a large group of contemporary African American artists who are carrying on the tradition of positive representation of the experiences of Black Americans established by Depression-era Black artists. These include Charles Bibbs, Raymond Cody, Verna Hart, Marian Howard, Annie Lee, Faith Ringgold, Dane Tilghman, and Gilbert Young.

Black visual artists have provided the most consistent body of work with positive representations. There appears to be fewer negative influences on such work because of less commercial pressure. In many respects, the trajectory of the visual arts and the commitment of conscious artists serve as a standard by which other genres can be compared.

Nell Painter has examined the contributions of Black visual artists to the presentation of the history of African Americans. She maintains that "the work of black artists contradicts demeaning conventional images of black people and puts black people's conception of themselves at the core of African American history. Whereas U.S. culture has depicted black people as ugly and worthless, black artists dwell on the beauty and value of black people."[114] Painter insists, further, that the content of the representations can clearly be distinguished from broader representational tendencies: "Throughout the twentieth century... black visual artists depicted two kinds of images repeatedly that were seldom featured in American fine art: ordinary, working people and violence inflicted upon people of African descent."[115]

Black Theater and Dance

Creativity in the entertainment arts has always been an acclaimed and popular tradition of African Americans. However, African Americans have never reaped just and equitable rewards for the amusement and artistic enrichment they have contributed to American society through their creative talents and skills. During the voyage from Africa, enslaved Blacks were forced to act, dance, and entertain their captor crews on the decks of the slave ships. In the New World, the ritualistic acts, symbols, music, song, and dance of Africans provided amusement and entertainment for Whites on plantations, city squares, and riverboats throughout the South. When free Blacks of the North formed their own playhouses and shows, they were often greeted with laughter and derision from White spectators. In theater, more than in any other area of entertainment, Black actors and actresses were forced to perform in stereotypical, comic, and buffoonish roles to satisfy the prejudicial humor of White Americans. Even in the twentieth century, Blacks were generally cast by Whites in stereotypical roles in theater, film, and television. The racism and discrimination that were so pervasive in American and European stagecraft provoked and inspired the development of Black theater, an approach to theatrical productions that incorporates the type of Black aesthetic previously described.

Theater

It is generally believed that African participation in drama in America started in minstrel shows that originated among enslaved Blacks. Captive African Americans would entertain themselves by mimicking the mannerisms, walking, and talking styles of their enslavers. Whites found performances by enslaved Blacks to be amusing and began to adopt a style of performance in which they would apply black makeup to their faces (blackface) and engage in stereotypical imitations of Blacks. This performance style came to be known as *minstrelsy*. Whites in blackface started a theatrical trend of projecting Blacks as lazy, shiftless, simple, dialect-speaking people with kinky hair and large lips. Blacks themselves did not participate in minstrel shows until after the Civil War. When Blacks began to form their own minstrel shows, they also blackened their faces and painted their lips to amuse White audiences. Black minstrelsy had the advantage of incorporating original Black routines, materials, and dances.[116]

Minstrelsy was a popular form of entertainment for almost a century, and, unfortunately, its negative impact on the image and psyche of Black and White Americans has endured.

The African Americans' attempt to provide an alternative to the caricature of minstrelsy began in New York with the formation of a Black theater company that eventually led to the organization of the African Grove Theatre in 1821. Understandably, serious African American theater at that juncture in history had a European frame of reference. The repertory of the African Grove Company included such productions as *Tom and Jerry*, Shakespeare's *Othello*, *Hamlet*, and *Richard the Third*. Two of the foremost Black actors of the time were James Hewlitt and Ira Aldridge. Henry Brown, producer and director of the African Grove Company, also wrote and directed the first drama by a Black man, *The Drama of King Shotaway*, which was performed at the African Grove Theatre.[117]

Some music historians believe that other Black dramatic companies also performed at the African Grove Company and that other companies existed between the time of the decline of the African Grove Theatre and the Civil War. There is reference to the Creole Dramatic Company of New Orleans that performed from 1859–70. A few Black musical companies, which included the Hyers Sisters Combination of Sacramento, California, and the Original Colored Opera Company of Washington, D.C., were active during the late nineteenth century. It is important to note that, after 1876, Black actors, singers, and dancers were often used in the performances of the classic *Uncle Tom's Cabin*.[118] As minstrel shows declined in popularity around 1890, they were replaced with burlesque and vaudeville musical comedies. These shows often used Black females as principal performers and in chorus lines. Even though the musical comedies were still like minstrels in format, they did provide an opportunity for African Americans to engage in playwriting and musical composition. The first show produced and stage-managed by Blacks was *A Trip to Coontown*. The show had both structure and continuity and combined music with the plotline. It was written by Bob Cole in 1898. In the same year, Will Marion Cook composed the music, and Paul Laurence Dunbar wrote the lyrics, to *Clorindy, the Origin of the Cakewalk*. The skit played in a major Broadway theater.

On the negative side, some African American actors and show persons, such as, Ernest Hogan, Bert Williams, and George Walker contributed to the development of stereotypical images of the Black race by performing as dimwits and buffoons on stage. They acquired substantial personal wealth for playing these roles, but, undoubtedly, were affected psychologically. Certainly, the dignity of African people was tarnished. From a positive perspective, these show persons paved the way for hundreds of African Americans to receive training and to practice more serious stagecraft in the decades that followed.

During the Harlem Renaissance, Black theater flourished along with Black musical, visual, and literary arts. W. E. B. Du Bois and a group of Black intellectuals established the ideological foundations for Black theater during the Harlem Renaissance. Du Bois believed that African American theater should have plots that accurately depict Black life and should be written by Black playwrights. He also insisted that the theater must cater primarily to Black audiences and be supported and sustained by their entertainment and approval. To facilitate this support, Du Bois believed that theaters should be physically located in Black neighborhoods near the mass of ordinary Black people. Du Bois organized the Krigwa Players to implement his ideas about Black theater, and for a brief period, the company did produce and perform works embodying his perspectives. The company's plays addressed topics such as lynching and the Underground Railroad. The most ambitious effort was the epic, *The Star of Ethiopia*, written by Du Bois as part of the NAACP's celebration of the fiftieth anniversary of the Emancipation Proclamation. The play depicts five epochs in African and African American history, beginning with the discovery of iron and extending to Black progress since the Emancipation Proclamation.[119]

Several Black theaters and theater companies were active in Harlem during the 1920s. The Lincoln, Lafayette, and the Crescent were the most notable theaters. By the end of the decade, these theaters had produced such famous actors as Paul Robeson and Charles Gilpin. As noted previously, Robeson gained fame for his role in *All God's Chillun Got Wings*, and Gilpin played the leading role in *The Emperor Jones*. The Federal Theatre Project, under the sponsorship of the WPA during the Depression of the 1930s, enabled Black actors to receive serious professional training.

8

Subsequently, in the 1940s, African Americans were cast in roles of greater depth and humanity. In 1943, Paul Robeson was the first Black to play the title role of Othello on Broadway.[120] The 1950s were marked by the organization of various small production companies, the most successful of which included the two companies of the Negro Art Players. Blacks began to write and produce numerous plays, of which the most significant of the period was Lorraine Hansberry's award winning *A Raisin in the Sun*.

The concept of Black Theater—art-for-people's-sake—came to the fore at the height of the 1960s Civil Rights Movement. Both small and large Black community theaters mushroomed in several major cities and on college and university campuses throughout the country. Integrationist ideals competed with Black Pride and Black Separatist ideologies, and the theater productions reflected these contentions. Many of the plays focused on American racism and dwelled on themes relevant to the Black political and economic plight, as well as on the social experiences of Black communities. Melvin Van Peebles had the unique distinction of having two plays on Broadway during the same year (1972), the musicals *Ain't Supposed To Die a Natural Death* and *Don't Play Us Cheap*. *Ain't Supposed to Die a Natural Death* was nominated for seven Tony Awards. *Don't Play Us Cheap*, adapted from his novel *The Party in Harlem*, was nominated for two Tony Awards and was released as a film in 1973.[121] In addition to these two plays, two other successful Black-oriented productions played on Broadway during the mid-1970s: *The Wiz* and *For Colored Girls Who Have Considered Suicide When the Rainbow Is Enuf*.

The institutionalization of Black Theater is reflected in the ongoing work of the National Black Theatre Festival (NBTF), an international outreach program of the North Carolina Black Repertory Company. The NBTF was founded in 1989 by Larry Leon Hamlin. This initiative is designed to unite Black theater companies across the United States. The 1989 NBT Festival offered thirty performances by seventeen professional Black theater companies and attracted national and international media coverage. The NBT Festival is held biennially and attracts a national and international audience of more than 55,000 people over a six-day period.[122]

Funding of the arts, public and private, is affected directly by the state of the economy and the preferences of political administrations. A major factor contributing to the upsurge of Black community theater in the 1960s and 1970s was the funding support received from the National Endowment of the Arts, from federal and municipal programs, and from corporate foundations. Adverse economic conditions and the conservative posture of the Reagan and Bush administrations of the 1980s and 1990s led to decreases in the availability of funds and resources in support of Black theater. Nevertheless, Black theater is active and thriving in major American cities such as Chicago, New York, Atlanta, Los Angeles, Pittsburgh, and Seattle.

Consistent with the definition of the Black aesthetic and the discussion of the Black Arts Movement, Black theater as a distinct African American art form is a dramatic reflection of the culture, values, and experiences of African Americans. Its performance portrays their hopes, despair, joys, sorrows, triumphs, failures, fortunes, and tragedies. Black theater is functional beyond its propensity to entertain because its objective is to inform, to communicate, and to relate the social, political, and economic experiences of Black people with other peoples of the world. Black theater reflects the reality of racism, colonialism, and oppression, yet it retains its artistic commitment. In so doing, it is an aesthetic vehicle for promoting social change. Black theater defines and evaluates itself based on the cultural values, standards, and experiences of African Americans. Therefore, Black theater is distinct from both general theater and the theater of other cultures.

The type of dramatic, historical epic represented by Du Bois' *The Star of Ethiopia* is, of course, the type of production championed by African American Studies specialists because of its emphasis on the primacy of history in generating relevant social knowledge. Unfortunately, there have been few efforts to build on this tradition. The most notable exception is August Wilson who completed a ten-play cycle in 2005, shortly before his death, that chronicles the African American experience in the twentieth century. All ten of these plays are situated in the Hill district of Pittsburgh and two—*The Piano Lesson* (1986), which examines the 1930s, and *Fences* (1985), which focuses on the 1950s—won Pulitzer Prizes. The play that examines the earliest decade, the 1900s, is *Gem of the Ocean* (2003), whereas *Radio Golf* (2005) explores the 1990s.[123]

Dance

The study of dance in African American Studies begins with an understanding of the differences in the relationship between music and dance in African societies and in Western societies. Olly Wilson argues that in the West there is "conceptual assumption of a division between consciously organized sound (music) and movement associated with that sound."[124] Wilson insists that in African and African American cultures, there is no such separation and the association "of motion and music, provides us with a framework within which to analyze the historical development of music and its 'foreground characteristics.'"[125] Kariamu Welsh Asante has identified seven core dimensions of African and African American dance that are useful for conceptualizing and describing dance: polyrhythm, polycentrism, holism, curvilinearity, dimensionality, repetition, and epic memory.[126] The synthesis of these components constitutes a "'mode of intellectual energy' that communicates various values."[127]

African American Studies specialists focus on the multiple roles of public dance—purification, affirmation, and celebration.[128] In the absence of external influences, the constantly changing forms of African American public dances would, to borrow the words of Ralph Ellison, reflect a "dynamic process in which the most refined styles from the past are continually merged with the play-it-by-eye-and-by-ear improvisations" invented for the purposes of interacting wholesomely with the environment and entertainment.[129] In addition, Black public dance plays a critical role in creating a sense of shared culture and identity through a common experience across regional, class, and age differences.[130]

The first public dances of enslaved Africans in the United States were direct reflections of music and dance forms in African societies. In traditional African societies, there is no formal separation between music and dance, as is the case in Western societies. As noted by Jacqui Malone, "Although some African cultures do feature music purely for listening pleasure, music that accompanies dance, or dance-beat-oriented music is much more prevalent."[131] Malone asserts that "African American vernacular dance is characterized by propulsive rhythm [and] black Americans demand a steady beat in their dance music. Although the beat can be embellished, the basic rhythm provides the dancer with dramatic exits and entrances."[132]

During the time of enslavement African Americans drew upon various African traditions in performing public dances during Saturday night socials, church services, funerals, and holidays. Lynne Emery indicates that the dances were typically accompanied by "the banjo, fiddle, quills, tambourine, bones, or, infrequently, a drum or pots and pans beaten like drums—or just the human voice with clapping and stamping."[133] The influence of African music and dance on Black public dance was not limited to the South. During the early 1700s, Blacks regularly performed African dances in northern cities. The persistence of African traditions in Black public dance is most evident in New Orleans, especially prior to the Hurricane Katrina disaster. Dancing at Congo Square in New Orleans began in the early 1800s and, according to Emery, "The African drum, transported to the West Indies but prohibited in most parts of the United States, seems to have re-emerged in Congo [S]quare."[134] Variants of these dances have been an integral feature of annual New Orleans Mardi Gras celebrations.

African American Studies specialists are especially interested in the Black concert dance tradition that celebrates African and African American cultures. Asadata Dafora [Horton] is a principal pioneer of this genre. His 1934 performance of Kykunkor, which is considered a classic, includes a breath-stopping dance by a witch doctor accompanied by frenzied drum rhythms. According to Emery, "Kykunkor proved that black dancers working with material from their own heritage could be successful on the American concert stage."[135]

Pearl Primus and Katherine Dunham further elevated the culturally-representative Black concert dance tradition in the 1940s. Pearl Primus was born in Trinidad and studied anthropology, along with various dances of Africa, to develop her repertory, which included "protest dances" designed to draw attention to racial inequality. Among such compositions were "Strange Fruit," which dealt with the reaction of a woman to a lynching and "The Negro Speaks of Rivers," which debuted on Broadway in 1944. In 1959, Primus was named director of Liberia's Performing Arts Center, which was founded with the goal of "discovering, restoring, reviving, and expanding African dance and allied cultures."[136]

Katherine Dunham majored in anthropology at the University of Chicago and did field research in the West Indies, where she gathered material for future stage productions. In 1939, she was named dance director of the New York Labor Stage. Dunham established the Dunham School of Dance in New York in 1945, which continued to operate until 1955. Among African American Studies specialists, Dunham is best known for her work with disadvantaged Black youth in East St. Louis, Illinois, which she began in the late 1960s. In collaboration with Southern Illinois

8

University, Dunham developed a cultural arts program, including dance, drama, martial arts, music, and the humanities, which was taught at the Performing Arts Training Center where she served as director. The Katherine Dunham Museum, which celebrates Dunham's accomplishments, was opened in 1977.[137]

The best known contemporary concert dance company is the Alvin Ailey American Dance Theatre formed in 1958. This company has served as a platform for the works of several Black choreographers. Ailey's approach to modern dance emphasizes both abstract styles of performance and material drawn directly from African and African American cultures.[138]

Black colleges and universities have been important contributors to the concert dance tradition. The Hampton Dance Group's performance in New York in 1937 emphasized themes taken directly from African and African American experiences. The most successful integration of dance into African American Studies has been achieved by the African American Dance Company, a unit within the Department of African American and African Diaspora Studies at Indiana University.[139]

Contemporary African American Studies specialists do not limit their interest to concert dance. Rather, it is recognized that "along with spaces allocated for sacred purposes, the street is one of the oldest and most significant performance outlets in history... [and] has served as a creative learning and performing environment in its own right and as a springboard to theatrical performance outlets."[140] This recognition spurs interest in the examination of how various contemporary vernacular dance forms, such as, break dancing and line dances, like the Cha-Cha Slide, continue the tradition of innovation and expression. African American Studies specialists are also interested in deepening the understanding of the role that Black fraternity and sorority step shows, as well as Black college marching bands, have played in preserving and extending the public Black dance tradition. The competitive interaction associated with the step show and band competition plays a critical role in spurring innovation and leads to new routines and dances.[141]

In a broader sense, African American Studies specialists should explore how the interconnections between popular dance and music contributed to the creation of a national Black popular culture. From this vantage point, the role of the television show *Soul Train* in popularizing selected musical genres and dance styles deserves special scrutiny. Created by Don Cornelius,

who passed away in 2012, the show aired weekly on national television from 1971 to 2006. In the early years, the main fare consisted of rhythm and blues and soul performances, although funk, jazz, disco, and gospel artists have also appeared. In later years, consistent with changes in musical tastes, the show increasingly featured hip hop artists. It is important to recognize that the Soul Train dancers, known originally as the Soul Train Gang, were critical for generating the show's world-wide popularity.[142]

The most popular theatrical productions examining the experiences of Black Americans have tended to be musicals, rather than dramas. To some extent this preference is natural. African American music, song, and dance are integral to the performance of Black theater. From the days of minstrelsy to the present, African-derived music and dance have generally accompanied the performance of Black theater. African derived and oriented dances include the juba, calinda, and bamboula. African American-influenced dances are the hambone, Charleston, shuffle, cakewalk (ragtime), slow drag, bebop, and Lindy Hop (jitterbug). In addition, a myriad of African American originated dances developed along with rhythm and blues music of the 1950s, 1960s, and 1970s.[143]

Beginning in the 1960s, native African dance and dancers were often presented or fused with Black theater. A significant number of Black theater and dance companies were formed during the Black Arts era of the 1960s, and many still exist. Some are specifically identified as *Black* or *African* Dance Theater.[144]

Considering the important role of music and dance in Black Theater, one wonders if the heavy emphasis on musicals and comedy has been detrimental to the sophisticated, dramatic exploration of important issues by Black theater. This concern arises from what could be described as a resurgence of the minstrelsy tradition in various entertainment genres, including stand-up comedy and most television programs focusing on Blacks. The emphasis on comedic depiction has been integrated into the most popular type of contemporary Black theatrical performance, so-called Gospel Plays. These plays have been popularized by Tyler Perry, who plays the character of a gun-toting grandma named Madea Simmons. Perry has had eight plays on tour, all of which were cheaply produced, vaudeville-style church services that are reminiscent of Greek morality plays and choruses. There are several other producers of this type of play, and the titles clearly signal the moral message, including *Real Men Pray* and *I'm Doing the Right Thing... With the Wrong Man.* The plots tend to be similar and relatively simple, typically including a wronged woman (or, occasionally, man), the no-good man (or, occasionally, woman), an easily accessible lover (milkman, janitor, or mechanic), the evils of drugs or alcohol, a comically over-the-top gay man (usually a hairdresser), and a cathartic "come-to-Jesus" moment.[145] From the perspective of African American Studies, such plays perform a constructive role in providing an alternative to the degradation of traditional values that are propagated through many other popular cultural genres. The plays are especially popular among Black women over 25 years old. At the same time, the simple solutions to life's problems proposed in these presentations are viewed by African American Studies specialists as inadequate in addressing the complex problems facing Black communities. Consequently, African American Studies specialists are committed to assisting Black Theater specialists in strengthening efforts to build and sustain Black theatrical productions that build on the legacy established by W. E. B. Du Bois and August Wilson. The Kuntu Repertory Theatre, housed in the Department of Africana Studies at the University of Pittsburgh, is a prime example of the integration of theater into the fabric of African American Studies. The mission of Kuntu, which has operated since 1974, is to "examine Africana life from a sociopolitical, historical perspective and to combine the salient features of theater that educate, entertain, and move both performers and audiences to social action."[146]

Blacks in Film and Television

In many respects the history of Blacks in movies and on television parallels that of Blacks in theater. Conscientious Black filmmakers, television writers, and actors and actresses have had to grapple with the problem of stereotypes. In taking up the challenge, Blacks involved in the film and television industries have had to decide whether to promote a Black aesthetic through independent venues or to attempt to nudge mainstream interests toward more authentic and realistic portrayals of Black experience. D.W. Griffith's infamous *Birth of a Nation* (1915) depicted Blacks as incompetent darkies intent on raping White women and the members of the Ku Klux Klan as heroes. The film was roundly criticized by the NAACP and others, and a group of independent Black filmmakers released director Emmett J. Scott's *The Birth of a Race* in 1919 as a response. Although this film was largely ignored, Black filmmaker Oscar Micheaux's

first feature-length film, *The Homesteader* (1919), and *Within Our Gates* (1920) were more effective in countering the explicit and implicit racist messages in *Birth of a Nation*.[147]

In pursuing filmmaking, Blacks have been hampered by the costs of the enterprise. Even though Michaeux had some success during the era of silent movies, he went bankrupt before eventually returning to produce sound films in the 1930s. His important films during the 1920s addressed subject matter that mainstream Hollywood producers refused to explore, including lynching, Black success myths, and color-based caste. Representative titles are *Body and Soul* (1924), starring Black athlete, singer, and activist Paul Robeson; *Within Our Gates* (1920); and *The Symbol of the Unconquered* (1921).[148] Black filmmakers were hit hard by the Great Depression. The direct financial impacts were exacerbated by the emergence of sound films that allowed Hollywood to exploit Black musical traditions. Black filmmakers lacked the resources to invest in sound filmmaking or to rewire theaters in Black communities.[149] Although there were some limited successes in subsequent decades, a new Black independent film movement would not emerge until the 1970s. This new movement embraced a variant of the "Black aesthetic" and insisted that Black expression be appreciated on its own terms.

Black critic James Snead has argued that a Black cinema must "coin unconventional associations for black skin within the reigning film language" to replace well-known stereotypical images. Melvin Van Peebles' movie, *Sweet Sweetback's Baadasssss Song* (1971), marks an important milestone in this effort. The film opens with the statement, "Dedicated to all the Brothers and Sisters who had enough of the Man," which is followed by the credit, "Starring: The Black Community." Ironically, *Sweet Sweetback* is often identified as the first movie to usher in the blaxploitation film genre because of its extensive use of traditional stereotypes and its celebration of anti-social behavior. However, critics who make this claim fail to realize that Van Peebles, unlike the Hollywood interests that usurped these themes, was concerned with Black empowerment and economic control. Van Peebles's film was designed to foster interest in, and commitment to, Black cultural products independently produced by, and for, a primarily Black audience. Van Peebles's continuing commitment to these values is evidenced by his creation of the MVP Foundation in 2003. The mission of the MVP Foundation is

8

to provide educational assistance for economically disadvantaged youths. The Foundation gives yearly scholarships and grants in any field of study but especially in those fields that promote excellence in the hard sciences and in business.[150]

Other participants in the movement to create a culturally authentic Black film genre have taken different routes. Some filmmakers, for example, are linked to quasi-independent channels, as opposed to Hollywood, as production and distribution venues. These producers utilize niche distributors, such as, the Black Filmmakers Foundation, California Newsreel, and Women Make Movies, Inc., rather than rely solely on mass markets. Women filmmakers have been prominent in this movement. Kathleen Collin's *The Cruz Brothers and Miss Malloy,* Ayoka Chinzira's satiric *Hair Piece: A Film for Nappy Headed People* (1985), and Julie Dash's *Daughters of the Dust* (1991) are examples of this effort.[151]

Spike Lee is most well-known of the new Black filmmakers. In the spirit of Oscar Micheaux, Lee has explored themes that Hollywood has been unwilling to explore. In *She's Gotta Have It* (1986), he satirizes the double standard imposed on women in multiple relationships compared with men. *School Daze* (1988) explores the conflict between light-skinned and dark-skinned Blacks on a Black college campus. The highly acclaimed 1989 film *Do The Right Thing* portrays the simmering racial tensions between Italians and African Americans in Brooklyn's Bedford-Stuyvesant section that erupt when a White police officer kills a Black man. In *Jungle Fever* (1991), Lee addresses the issue of interracial sex, as confounded by color, class, and family ties.[152] Spike Lee's 1992 film, *Malcolm X,* played a major role in elevating the Black leader to mythic status and spurred a resurgence of interest in Malcolm among young Blacks of that era. Lee again addresses contemporary political issues in *Get on the Bus* (1996), which tracks the journey of twelve men from Los Angeles to Washington, D.C., to take part in the Million Man March. The highly diverse assemblage manifests the wide range of interests, personalities, and perspectives that constitute challenges for African American Studies activists attempting to mobilize and empower Blacks.[153]

As the influence of Black filmmakers increased, new opportunities were created for Black actors and actresses, as major studios made efforts to attract Black audiences. According to Donald Bogle, the traditional film roles available to Blacks were highly circumscribed and can be classified into five archetypes: Toms, Coons, Mulattoes, Mammies, and Bucks.[154] A cursory examination of contemporary cinema suggests that many Black characters still conform to the old stereotypes. Bogle contends that, historically, the best Black actors who had to play such roles actually subverted and transcended the stereotyping and gave pleasure to Black and White audiences.[155] The extent to which contemporary Black actors exhibit this same facility is a subject of much debate.

However, it is important to recognize the stellar achievements of Denzel Washington and Halle Berry in 2002 when, for the first time in the seventy-four-year history of the Academy Awards ceremonies, a pair of African Americans captured the Best Actor and Best Actress awards in the March 24 ceremonies in Los Angeles. Halle Berry won for her performance playing the bereaved widow of a death-row inmate who falls in love with a racist prison guard in *Monster's Ball*. Denzel Washington, who previously had won Best Supporting Actor in 1989 for his role in the movie *Glory,* won Best Actor for his role as a rogue cop in the movie *Training Day*.[156]

While acknowledging the significance of these accomplishments, there are legitimate questions about why their performances in roles that portray negative representations of Black life were deemed meritorious, whereas earlier solid performances by both Berry and Washington in roles that portrayed Blacks in a positive manner were overlooked. In some respects the lionization of these particular roles reflects the potential emergence of new stereotypes added to the traditional ones that are still alive and well.

The tendency to gravitate toward traditional stereotypes is exemplified by the resurgence of films resembling "Blaxploitation" films or, alternatively, "gangsploitation" films beginning in the 1990s. The original Blaxploitation films were the brainchild of Hollywood magnates and were released primarily between 1971 and 1975. They included such well-known offerings as *Superfly*. It is estimated that there were approximately two hundred such films based on a formulaic structure that involved violence, drugs, sex, street talk, fancy clothes and cars, and "getting over on the man." Ultimately, Black audiences realized they were being exploited and abandoned the theaters.[157] James Stewart argues that the wide dissemination of Blaxploitation films directly diluted the potential of important Black Power Movement (BPM) cultural symbols to facilitate political mobilization and collective action. This was accomplished by the systematic imposition of invisibility on the BPM and/or the misrepresentation of the BPM as dysfunctional, disorganized, opportunistic, and impotent. Stewart further insists that the propagation of this negative imagery complemented the direct physical assaults and disinformation campaigns that were waged by governmental officials against BPM organizations and their leaders. According to Stewart, this "Neutering" of the Black Power Movement set in motion a persistent pattern of compromised cultural production that continues to constrain contemporary efforts to develop and implement mass-based resistance to racial oppression.[158]

The new genre of Blaxploitation films has been fueled by the Hip-Hop/Rap Music Movement and made possible by the success of independent Black filmmakers. The exact origins are in dispute, but the release of *I'm Gonna Get You Sucka* in 1988 is one important benchmark. Other significant films include John Singleton's *Boyz 'N' The Hood* (1991), Mario van Peebles's *New Jack City* (1991), Ernest Dickerson's *Juice* (1992), and Albert and Allen Hughes' *Menace II Society* (1993). Other representative titles include *Dead Presidents*, *Set It Off*, and *Poetic Justice*. Like their 1970s predecessors, these films typically highlight music and violence, with a story line that pretends to say something genuine about the Black experience. This trend in Black cinematic production is problematic, especially if it fosters destructive behavior in Black communities and propagates distorted representations of Black life and culture.[159] The representation of Blacks on television is no less guilty of perpetuating stereotypes. Donald Bogle provides a comprehensive history of Blacks on network television in *Primetime Blues: African Americans on Network Television*. His examination of trends in each decade leads to the conclusion that the full range of Black humanity has not been reflected in television offerings during any period and in any genre, ranging from sitcoms, to lawyer and cop programs, to Westerns, to sci-fi, or dramas.[160]

Until the emergence of Black Entertainment Television (BET), the presence of Blacks on television was largely restricted to sitcoms, which are generally segregated. As Gloria Gutierrez explains, television sitcoms were created at the end of WWII. The first sitcom with an all-Black cast, *Amos 'n' Andy*, was created in the early 1950s. The show was canceled after seventy-eight episodes in response to protests by the NAACP, which complained about the blatant stereotypes propagated by the show.[161] The foundation for the next sitcom featuring a Black cast was laid by the success of *All in the Family* (1971) produced by Norman Lear. The main character's (Archie Bunker) resistance to social change, including race relations and his comedic interactions with his upwardly mobile Black neighbors, the Jeffersons, led to the spin-off of the second African American sitcom, *The Jeffersons*, in 1975. *The Jeffersons* successfully broke into mainstream television. It aired over 250 shows over a ten-year run and compiled Nielsen ratings among the top 25 for eight years.[162]

Black situation comedy received another boost in 1984 with the debut of *The Cosby Show*. The show explored the world of the upper-middle-class Huxtable family, headed by Dr. Cliff Huxtable (Cosby), an OB-GYN doctor, and his wife, Clair, an attorney. The show dealt primarily with parenting issues and avoided controversial topics such as race. Although some critics argued that the Huxtable family's troubles were far from typical, the show was highly popular. It rated as TV's most widely viewed show from 1985 to 1988 and remained in the top 20 shows for eight years.

More recent African American sitcoms have proliferated on several networks and have regressed more toward the *Amos 'n' Andy* formula. United Paramount Network (UPN) aired six Black sitcoms (four of them new) back-to-back in 1996. This format is not unusual because, as has been the case for other sitcoms with a common target audience, TV networks have often scheduled Black sitcoms in blocks on a given night of the week. Even though this has helped to foster an audience for many of these shows, it has been criticized as creating a "ghetto" for them. They are less likely to be watched by non-Black viewers, who might tune in early for a "White" show they are already interested in or stay tuned in after another show has finished. Building on this precedent, UPN had emerged as the most prolific broadcaster of Black sitcoms, scheduling one or two nights of programming each week featuring such shows. In spite of the increase in Black sitcoms, the shows have remained confined to comedic situations where the cast is of the same racial background. Miriam Miranda concludes from her research on African American sitcoms that the Black community prefers Black sitcoms because they are able to identify with the life issues that are depicted. "[W]hat black viewers appreciate the most about black sitcoms is watching 'ordinary events' in black communities portrayed in comical ways on television."[163] The segregation of racial groups in sitcoms has been so successful that television networks have noticed

8

that profits are higher; therefore, they feel encouraged to continue the same racial and social structure in their shows.

From the vantage point of African American Studies, the history of Blacks in television leads us to agree with Bogle that Blacks involved as performers or writers have not been sufficiently aggressive to compel networks to air more politically conscious shows. Cosby, who had a top-rated show on television, actually had the leeway necessary to incorporate political themes but chose not to do so. Moreover, the experience with BET under Black-ownership suggests that even Black ownership and control are insufficient to employ the media for collective empowerment.

BET's hip-hop music video-dominated programming has come under sharp attack from many sources, including some hip-hop performers. Several of the station's programming decisions provide justification for such criticism. Such decisions include cutbacks of BET's public affairs department, the firing of *BET Tonight* talk show host and social commentator Tavis Smiley in March 2001; and the canceling of *BET Tonight*, as well as, the youth panel program *Teen Summit* and the morning news broadcast *Lead Story*. The airing of Nelly's music video *Tip Drill*, highlighting virtually naked women engaged in playful antics in a hot tub on BET's *Uncut* show in December 2003, sparked a continuing protest against the station's programming on several college campuses, including Spelman College. African American Studies specialists applaud the activism displayed by students fighting for more responsible programming. The issue of BET's stereotypical representations of African American culture has been exacerbated by the sale of the network to Viacom, which was first announced in November 2000. A cursory review of BET programming since that time provides no reason to be optimistic that the behaviors of Viacom's executives will differ significantly from those of Hollywood producers who championed the Blaxploitation film genre of the 1970s.

The visibility of African Americans on television has been significantly enhanced by the emergence of two Black-owned TV networks—Oprah Winfrey's OWN and Cathy Hughes' TV One. Although the programming on OWN generally does not target an African American audience, treatments of Black life and culture that are offered typically resist sensationalized images and content. In contrast, TV One targets African American adults with a broad range of programming,

including original lifestyle discussions, documentaries, movies, concert performances, and classic series from the 1970s–2000s.

Unfortunately the positive impacts of the programming of OWN and TV One are partially neutralized by reality shows on other networks that reinforce prevailing negative stereotypes, particularly of Black women, such as the *Real Housewives of Atlanta* and *Basketball Wives*.

The Literature of African Americans

Defining Black Literature

The concept of *Black literature* is used in the same context as Black music, Black art, and Black theater. Black literature is the creative written and oral expression of people of African descent and is particularly related to the cultural and sociopolitical experiences of African Americans. Black literature, as used in this text, is consistent with the own-race or self-defining, self-evaluating, and self-legitimating stance that a group of African American literary critics adopted during the 1960s. Black literature projects the reality and mythology of Black life and experience. The representation of Blacks or Africans—their history, life, or culture—in Black literature is considerably different from such depictions in White American literature. Much of the literature of African Americans reflects over 250 years of struggle and protest that American history and literature generally omit.

The concept of *Black literature* is not shared by all African American writers. There are those who seek to avoid having their work racially classified and to avoid being identified as Black writers. Consequently, a distinction might be made between Black literature and literature by Black writers. Some Black writers may seek to underplay the significance of their race, with the notion that they may gain broader acceptance of their work. Writers identified as African Americans may face the risk, or problem, of being underread and underrepresented in the White-dominated literary world. Thus, the ethnological, racial, or political character of the literature may be sublimated to gain White appeal. On the other hand, the growing swell of race pride and racial consciousness that began during the Harlem Renaissance and intensified during the 1960s has caused

African Americans to prefer and to seek literature created from a Black perspective. After centuries of seeing themselves through the eyes of others, the appeal of books by Black authors and of periodicals focusing on the African American experience has increased dramatically in academic and popular circles. Still, in the majority of schools and in many fields, even the most highly visible Black writers are unknown. With the burgeoning of Black literature during the twentieth century, there is no reason why Black literature or the literary works of African Americans should not be given equitable recognition and treatment. Black literature, like Black history, is an integral part of American literature.

Because of their success in achieving cultural hegemony, White writers are not usually confronted with the need to conceal their racial identity or obscure their Eurocentric experience and orientation to gain universal recognition. Consequently, White literary works are read, celebrated, and emulated by many other cultures.

In the absence of literary capitulation, a race or culture must create or produce its own literature, and critique and support its own writers. Universal interest or appeal of a race's or culture's literature may occur, but it is often incidental. Black literature incorporates a historic, political, folkloric, parabolic, metaphoric, and sometimes mythological style characteristic of that expressed in Molefi Asante's *The Afrocentric Idea*.[164] Whether one reads the addresses or writings of David Walker, Frederick Douglass, Booker T. Washington, W. E. B. Du Bois, Langston Hughes, Martin Luther King Jr., Margaret Walker, Malcolm X, or Jesse Jackson, the uniqueness of Black literary expression is evident. It is a style that attracts the attention of other groups without compromising its integrity. Yet, there have been times in the history of African American literature, when life and liberty were at stake and some forms of accommodation were prudent or strategic.

The unique cultural ethos of African Americans is manifested across various literary genres. The extent to which distinctive cultural features are evident depends both on the intent and orientation of individual authors and the degree of flexibility associated with the conventional format of specific genres. Different cultures may have particular preferences for certain types of expressive modes. In addition, political, economic, and social conditions may influence the choice of modes of expression available to a given group. The oral tradition in most African societies is more institutionalized than the use of the written word. Although ancient writing traditions do exist on the African continent, in most African societies, art forms are oral rather than literary. In contrast to written literature, African orature is orally composed and transmitted and is often created to be communally performed as an integral part of dance and music. The oral tradition incorporates five key elements: myth, legend, song, tale, and oratory.

Although slavery took Africans from their homeland, they were able to retain much of the oral traditions of each country and region and to integrate such traditions into Western written literary formats. Two of the earliest genres used by enslaved Africans that involved adaptations of the African oral tradition were poetry and the slave narrative.

Black Literature of the Eighteenth and Nineteenth Centuries

The first documented example of formal poetry by an enslaved Black in what is now the US is Lucy Terry's ballad "Bars Fight." Terry, a semi-literate enslaved Black, recreates a Native American massacre that occurred in Deerfield, Massachusetts, in this work. Assisted by his owner, Jupiter Hammon published the poem "An Evening Thought, Salvation by Christ, with Penitential Cries" in 1761. In 1786, Hammon wrote "An Address to the Negroes of the State of New York" and delivered it before the African Society of New York City. The address was published the following year.

Phillis Wheatley is the most recognized Black poet of this period. She was born in Senegal, was enslaved, and was brought to America. She was educated in her owner's household. With the help of her owners, she published numerous poems, letters, and memoirs of her life. Wheatley's poems reflect the traditional European genre of the time.[165]

The enslaved poets of the eighteenth century are not regarded as having made a significant contribution to African American life and history beyond vindication, or having proven that Blacks possessed the ability to master European literary style and thought. Hammon and Wheatley have been dismissed by Black cultural nationalists as irrelevant because of the accommodationist and servile themes of their prose and poetry. Hammon, for example, published the poem "The Kind Master And The Dutiful Servant" in 1783. The poem seems obviously supportive of the slave system, as one verse reads:

8

Dear Master, that's my whole delight,
Thy pleasure for to do;
As for grace and truth's insight,
Thus far I'll surely go.[166]

Phyllis Wheatley's poem, "On Being Brought From Africa To America," expresses gratitude for her having been kidnapped from Africa and enslaved:

Twas mercy brought me from my Pagan land,
Taught my benighted soul to understand
That there's a God, that there's a Saviour too:
Once I redemption neither sought nor knew,
Some view our sable race with scornful eye,
"Their color is a diabolic die,"
Remember, Christians, Negroes, black as Cain,
May be refin'd and join th' angelic train.[167]

A few literary scholars look beyond the groveling nature of these poems by enslaved Blacks to find some esoteric innuendos of religious sarcasm and subversion. However, these enslaved poets of the eighteenth century were forced to consider and choose among the same three options for responding to oppression as African American writers of the twentieth century: accommodation, protest, or escape.[168] Their adaptation of the European literary format clearly constrained their expressive possibilities and can be considered as largely experimental, given the general inaccessibility of this genre to the mass of enslaved Blacks.

For the large cohort of enslaved Blacks, storytelling, an important dimension of African oral tradition, played a critical role in enabling their survival. Storytelling is an essential part of cultural survival because stories serve as a form of social cement. The "words" of the Black narrative tradition have often originated in speech, not on paper. Robert Hemenway reminds us that "this tradition eventually became a reservoir of stylized expression that helped black people survive and affirm themselves as a culturally unique group [and w]hen black people began to publish in fairly significant numbers during the last half of the nineteenth century, the tradition crossed over into written literature."[169]

The stories collected by Joel Chandler Harris from Blacks, as told through the fictional character Uncle Remus, were typical of those created by Blacks during the slavery era. In these tales, the lowly Brer Rabbit, the hero, is successful in consistently outsmarting more powerful predators—the fox, bear, and wolf. As Robert Hemenway observes, "Like the Aesop fables, which were brought to Greece by black slaves, these tales had their origin in Africa's complex pantheon of animal deities."[170] Hemenway comments that most Whites, and even Harris, the collector of the tales, were initially unaware that these tales were disguised protests against slavery. The stories only gained stature as "literature" after they were put into children's books.

The slave narratives produced during the eighteenth and nineteenth centuries are especially important because many focus directly on proactive efforts to overcome oppression. Approximately six thousand formerly enslaved Africans from North America and the Caribbean provided written accounts of their lives during the eighteenth and nineteenth centuries. About 150 of the narratives were published as separate books or pamphlets. From the 1770s to the 1820s, these narratives first appeared in England. The authors frequently identify themselves as Africans rather than slaves. Interestingly, many of these narratives often focus on their conversion to Christianity. Examples of such narratives include: *A Narrative of the Most Remarkable Particulars in the Life of James Albert Ukawsaw Gronniosaw, an African Prince*, published in Bath, in 1772, and *The Interesting Narrative and the Life of Olaudah Equiano or Gustavus Vassa, the African*, published in London, in 1789.

Responding to the oppression experienced under chattel slavery, many slave narratives written after 1820 focus on the evils of the institution— slave auctions, family disruption, and descriptions of escapes. These narratives, approximately eighty of which were published between 1835 and 1865, provide important documentary evidence of the abolitionist movement. The format and style of these narratives reflect more of the characteristics typically associated with literature than earlier narratives. The most well-known of these narratives include: *The History of Mary Prince, a West Indian Slave* (London 1831); *A Narrative of the Life of Frederick Douglass, an American Slave* (Boston 1845); *Narratives of the Sufferings of Lewis and Milton Clarke, Sons of a Soldier of the revolution, during a Captivity of more than Twenty years among the Slaveholders of Kentucky* (Boston 1846); *Narrative of William Wells Brown, a Fugitive Slave* (Boston 1847); and *Incidents in the Life of a Slave Girl, by Harriet Jacobs* (Boston 1861).

Consistent with the antislavery focus of many slave narratives, other forms of prose produced by African Americans prior to the Civil War was also directed at overturning the slavery regime. The seeds for the future development of Black consciousness, cultural nationalism, revolutionary nationalism, and Pan-Africanism were sown by writers and orators, such as, David Walker, Henry Highland Garnet, Frederick Douglass, and James Forten. Antislavery and related political ideas increasingly permeated Black writings.

David Walker's Appeal, published in a pamphlet in 1829, was a drastic change from the servile themes of the enslaved writers of the 1700s. Walker's writings were precursory to the Black pride proponents of the twentieth century. An excerpt from the *Appeal* reads:

> They think because they hold us in their infernal chains of slavery, that we wish to be white, or of their color—but they are dreadfully deceived—we wish to be just as it pleased our Creator to have made us. ...Now, I ask you, had you not rather be killed than be a slave to a tyrant, who takes the life of your mother, wife, and dear little children?[171]

Building upon the resistance literature of David Walker, Henry Highland Garnet espoused a more strident militancy. His paper, "An Address to the Slaves of the United States," urges enslaved Blacks in the South to rise up in arms. The writings and addresses of Frederick Douglass are masterpieces of literary eloquence and dynamism. Although Douglass' writings were devoid of the strident themes that characterized the works of Walker and Garnet, he was equally effective in the art of moral persuasion.

The literary excellence of early African American writers is reflected even in their letters and petitions to government authorities. James Forten's series of letters to the Pennsylvania legislature protesting a bill that would halt the migration of free Blacks to Philadelphia are often included in anthologies of African American literature. Expressions of protest and anguish also appeared in the works of renowned Black poets, such as Frances Ellen Harper, during the mid-1800s.

The adaptation of the novel genre as a mode of affirmation did not occur until the 1850s. Notably, the first two novels, [William Wells] Brown's *Clotel or The President's Daughter: A Narrative of Slave Life in the United States* (1853) and Frank Webb's *The Garies and Their Friends* (1857), were first published in London, not in the United States."[172] Martin R. Delany's *Blake; or The Huts of America: A Tale of the Mississippi Valley, the Southern United States and Cuba* (1859), and Harriet E. Wilson's *Our Nig: or Sketches from the Life*

of a Free Black, In a Two-Story White House, North. Showing That Slavery's Shadows Fall Even There (1859), which are written in the tradition of the slave narrative are the first novels published by Black Americans in the United States.[173]

By the end of the Civil War, African American novelists were preoccupied with the Black liberation struggle, but no new African American novel was published until James Howard's *Bond and Free* (1886). However, some Black writers, like Frances Ellen Watkins Harper, continued to serialize novels for predominantly Black audiences in Black periodicals and magazines. During this period, Black novelists were compelled to have their works printed privately, or to make compromises to appeal to predominantly White readers, and most chose to compromise by moderating their militancy "while persevering in the artistic attempt to counter the white literary distortions of reality and the experiences of black people."[174]

During this same period, Paul Laurence Dunbar (1872–1906) emerged as a profound African American poet who wrote about Black life with realistic and functional simplicity. Dunbar was the first to gain national recognition as a Black poet. He dignified the language of the vernacular or the dialect of common Black people by using it formally with emotion and compassion in his poetry. Dunbar's poetry and short stories reflect the psychological oppression of Black people. This is clearly evident in one of his most often quoted poems "We Wear the Mask" (1895):

> We wear the mask that grins and lies,
> It hides our cheeks and shades our eyes—
> This debt we pay to human guile;
> With torn and bleeding hearts we smile,
> And mouth with myriad subtleties.
> Why should the world be overwise
> In counting all our tears and sighs?
> Nay, let them only see us while we wear the mask.
> We smile, but, O great Christ, our cries
> To Thee from tortured souls arise.
> We sing, but oh the clay is vile
> Beneath our feet, and long the mile;
> But let the world dream otherwise
> We wear the mask.

8

Black Writers and Literature of the Twentieth Century

The literary achievements of Black writers and poets of the eighteenth and nineteenth centuries laid the foundation for the proliferation of African American literature in the twentieth century. Race riots and oppression at the beginning of the century raised racial consciousness among Blacks and empowered Black writers and intellectuals. Although the aura of the 1920s revived and stimulated African American creativity in music, art, and theater, the Harlem Renaissance was basically a literary movement. The Renaissance, or the "New Negro Movement," brought to the fore writers and poets of future fame, such as, Claude McKay, Langston Hughes, Countee Cullen, and Jean Toomer. Scholar-writers and civil rights activists W. E. B. Du Bois and James Weldon Johnson became dominant figures in the fight for freedom and justice during this period. During and following the Renaissance period, many Black novelists and fiction writers emerged. Such writers include Nella Larsen, Jessie Redmon Fauset, Wallace Thurman, and Rudolph Fisher.[175]

The Black rebellious spirit and sentiment of the period were militantly set forth by Claude McKay in his poem "If We Must Die." The plight, despair, and aspirations of African Americans were poetically expressed in Langston Hughes' "The Negro Speaks of Rivers." Perhaps, Hughes was the most accomplished and acclaimed poet of the period. Although W. E. B. Du Bois' sociological classic, *Souls of Black Folk*, and his novel, *The Quest of the Silver Fleece*, were written earlier, they influenced the spirit of the Renaissance Movement. Black intellectual James Weldon Johnson established his literary reputation in 1927, with a collection of folk sermons in verse—*God's Trombones*. Today, he is mostly remembered as the author of the poem "Lift Every Voice and Sing," which was set to music and now serves as the Black National Anthem. Bell observes that "by and large, the New Negro turned to Africa and African American folklore for the authenticity and authority of a usable ethnic past," and they transformed the nineteenth century image of Africa "as a primitive land [and] a site of shame and self-hatred for many Black Americans."[176]

With the crash of the stock market in 1929 and the beginning of the Great Depression, the momentum behind the Harlem Renaissance dissipated. One response to the vacuum was the effort of some novelists to explore the Black folk tradition as a source of cultural renewal. The primary example is Zora Neale Hurston, who used her training in anthropology as a guide to an analytical inquiry into Black folk culture. However, in Hurston's efforts to integrate Black folk culture into her novels, Trudier Harris argues that the "historical folklore themes" overwhelm the literary creation as "the excessively metaphorical language becomes an added character, plugging up the cracks between them and plot, not a smoothly woven, integral part of the whole."[177]

The publication of Richard Wright's *Native Son* in 1940 ushered in a new naturalistic treatment in the Black novel that stressed "the violence and pathological personalities that result from racial oppression and economic exploitation."[178] Bernard Bell argues that between 1952 and 1962, Black novelists moved away from naturalism and retreated as well from experimentation with the nonracial themes that some had undertaken in the 1940s and early 1950s. The dominant movement that emerged emphasized "the rediscovery and revitalization of myth, legend, and ritual as appropriate sign systems for expressing the double consciousness, socialized ambivalence, and double vision of the post–World War II experiences of black Americans."[179] This shift in emphasis set the stage for developments in the 1960s and 1970s.

A new orientation, or a redefinition, of African American literature and poetry developed with the advent of the 1960s and the Civil Rights Movement. Amiri Baraka [Leroi Jones] was the leading change agent and promoter of the new "relevant" Black literature. Baraka deplored a Black literature that capitulated totally to the Eurocentric tradition, that was devoid of a Black identity, ethos or cultural frame of reference. Several other young Black writers and poets believed that Black literature should reflect the reality of the Black experience and conform to the needs of Black people.[180] The Black Arts Movement of the sixties differed from the Renaissance of the 1920s in that it fostered a conscious form of Black cultural nationalism.

The 1960s was a period of racial violence, social unrest, and reformation. Consequently, a school of "revolutionary" Black writers and poets emerged. These writers wrote in the angry vein of David Walker and Henry Highland Garnet and simulated the tone of Claude McKay's poem "If We Must Die." Often the style and format violated traditional prose and poetic standards. Self-satire, Black love, revolutionary rhetoric, social criticism, ghetto strife, and Africanity characterized some of the writings of the revolutionary poets. The poetry was delivered in a manner to elicit intermittent response from the audience.

There are far too many Black writers, novelists, and poets whose work appeared from the 1930s through the 1970s to comment on each individually. However, it may serve study and research purposes to list *some* of the major contributors to African American literature who followed in the spirit of the Harlem Renaissance:

Richard Wright, novelist
Sterling Brown, poet, critic
James Baldwin, novelist, essayist
Frank Yerby, novelist
Ralph Ellison, novelist, essayist
Chester Himes, novelist
Robert Hayden, poet
Zora Neale Hurston, novelist
John O. Killens, novelist
Margaret Walker, poet, novelist
Arna Bontemps, poet, novelist
Ann Petry, novelist, critic
Melvin B. Tolson, poet
J. Saunders Reddings, author, critic
Gwendolyn Brooks, poet
Leroi Jones (Amiri Baraka) poet, playwright, essayist
Don L. Lee (Haki A. Madhubuti) poet, writer
Julius Lester, writer, essayist, critic
Paule Marshall, novelist, writer
Addison Gayle, essayist, critic
Maya Angelou, writer, poet
Sonia Sanchez, poet, playwright
Nikki Giovanni, poet
Toni Cade Bambara, writer, poet
Mari Evans, poet
Alice Childress, playwright, novelist
Ishmael Reed, novelist, poet
Ernest J. Gaines, novelist
Clarence Major, poet, novelist
Ed Bullins, dramatist, essayist
Toni Morrison, novelist

Black Poets

Several poets, including Gwendolyn Brooks, Sonia Sanchez, Dudley Randall, Eugene Redmond, and Haki Madhubuti, have garnered extensive attention from African American Studies specialists. Gwendolyn Brooks is celebrated for her dramatic representations of the life experiences of urban African Americans. Her first collection of poems, *A Street in Bronzeville* (1945), brought her instant critical acclaim. Her ability to resonate with the struggles of residents of Bronzeville stemmed, in part, from her work as

secretary of the Chicago NAACP in the 1930s. Her second book of poetry, *Annie Allen* (1949), won a Pulitzer Prize for poetry, the first awarded to an African American, and her collection *In the Mecca* (1968) is also highly regarded. Brooks also wrote children's poetry: *Bronzeville Boys and Girls* (1956) and *We Real Cool* (1960), which remains her most popular. Brooks was appointed Poet Laureate of Illinois in 1968 and was named Consultant in Poetry by the Library of Congress in 1985.[181]

Sonia Sanchez is an enduring figure who emerged during the Black Arts Movement. Her poems offer incisive analyses of racial struggle and gender oppression. She combines an innovative use of language, especially Ebonics, with a panoramic view of history to create verbal images that are unmatched by any other poet. She has authored more than fifteen books of poetry. *Homecoming* (1968) was her first book. Other volumes include *We a Baddddd People* (1970), *It's a New Day: Poems for Young Brothas and Sistuhs* (1971), *Homegirls & Handgrenades* (1985), winner of an American Book Award, *Like the Singing Coming Off of Drums* (1999), and *Bum Rush the Page: A Def Poetry Jam* (2001). Sanchez received the Robert Frost medal in poetry in 2001.[182]

Eugene Redmond is recognized for his work as a poet, playwright, critic, editor, and educator. His first volume of poetry, *A Tale of Two Toms, or Tom-Tom (Uncle Toms of East St. Louis and St. Louis)* was published in 1968. Subsequent volumes include *A Tale of Time & Toilet Tissue* (1969), *Songs from an Afro/Phone* (1972), and *Eye on the Ceiling* (1991). Like Sanchez, he makes extensive use of basic rhythms and music in his poetry. Many of his poems have a rap-like beat and contain direct references to jazz, blues, spirituals, soul music, and Black musicians. Redmond is the author of *Drumvoices: The Mission of Afro-American Poetry, A Critical History* (1976), a survey of Black poetry from 1746 to 1976 that took eight years to research. *Drumvoices* explores the "complex web of beliefs, customs, traditions, and significant practices that tie diasporan black cultures to their African origins." He is also editor of *Drumvoices Revue*. Redmond served as a senior consultant to Katherine Dunham at Southern Illinois University's Performing Arts Training Center from 1967 to 1969.[183]

Dudley Randall is well known both as a poet and publisher as well as a leading figure in the Black Arts Movement in Detroit. The publication of his poem, "Ballad of Birmingham," written in the wake of the 1963

8

church bombing in which four Black girls were killed, set in motion the establishment of Broadside Press in 1965. Broadside poems were published on a single piece of paper, were sold for $1 or $2, and were extremely popular. Subsequent publications included an anthology, numerous chapbooks, and a series of critical essays. Broadside Press became the most important Black press in America by cementing the reputations of several renowned African American poets, including Margaret Walker, Sonia Sanchez, Audre Lorde, Sterling Plumpp, Melba Boyd, Clarence Major, and Haki Madhubuti.[184]

Haki R. Madhubuti is a widely celebrated poet, publisher, editor, and educator. He is not only a pivotal figure in the development and sustenance of a strong Black literary tradition that reflects the ethos of the Black Arts Movement, but is also involved in institution building as advocated by African American Studies specialists. Madhubuti is founder, publisher, and chair of the board of Third World Press (1967), co-founder of the Institute of Positive Education/New Concept School (1969), and co-founder of the Betty Shabazz International Charter School (1998) in Chicago, Illinois. Third World Press is publisher of Tavis Smiley's popular volume, *Covenant With Black America*. Madhubuti has published over twenty books of poems and essays. His book *Black Men: Obsolete, Single, Dangerous: The African American Family in Transition* (1990) has sold over a million copies, and his literary work has been anthologized in over thirty publications.[185]

Some contemporary Black female poets, such as, Marilyn Nelson and Rita Dove, utilize traditional forms and employ them to explore universal themes. Others, including Harryette Mullen, Jessica Care Moore, Honoree Fanonne Jeffers, Elizabeth Alexander, and Chezia Thompson Cager are experimenting with path breaking approaches to explore the deep contours of identity and contemporary Black life.[186]

The tradition of progressive Black poetry forged during the Black Arts Movement has been partially revived by contemporary spoken word artists who have adopted the genre of slam poetry. Slam poetry, a form of performance poetry, is associated with a competitive poetry event—a "slam." The popularity of this genre grew immensely with the creation of the HBO series, *Def Poetry Jam*, produced by Russell Simmons. Poetry slams originated in Chicago around 1984 and subsequently spread to Ann Arbor, San Francisco, and New York City. The first national slam poetry competition was held in 1990. Slam poetry encompasses a very broad range of voices, styles, cultural traditions, and approaches to writing and performance. Some performances are heavily layered with Black cultural symbolism, including the use of African drums for accompaniment and the rhythmic and stylistic elements of West Indian dub poetry.[187]

Black Novelists

The most creative, prolific, and critically acclaimed novelists of the 1970s and 1980s have been Black women. Even though there are numerous women writers, Toni Morrison, Alice Walker, and Terry MacMillan are foremost in the eyes of critics. According to one positive critic, Morrison is a powerful fiction writer whose works abound in mystical occurrences—conjurations, superstitious manifestations, and spiritual visitations. She artistically interweaves the physical and spiritual worlds in an African continuum that is characteristic of true African Americaness.[188]

Morrison's novels include *The Bluest Eye* (1970); *Song of Solomon* (1977); *Tar Baby* (1981); and *Beloved* (1987). *Beloved* is the first volume of a trilogy that includes *Jazz* (1992) and *Paradise* (1997). *Jazz* is of special interest to African American specialists because of its creative integration of blues and jazz thematics and aesthetics. As Tracey Sherard observes, Morrison's "pervasive signification on blues, jazz, and Harlem imagery, as well as her allegorical use of the narrator as technological composite of the phonograph and record to 'play' cultural narratives which its characters both respond to and resist creates an African American female 'crossroads' from which readers can and should re-audit the music and history of 1920's Harlem."[189]

Alice Walker is a novelist, essayist, and poet. She is the author of a number of collections of short stories and poems. Her novels include *Meridian* and *The Color Purple*. Walker focuses on sensitive and controversial subjects relating to Black male/female relationships and the pains and burdens of Black life. Her works border on the feminist idiom to the extent that they may be perceived as portraying negative images of Black men. The film made from her novel, *The Color Purple*, received mixed reviews among African Americans.

Terry MacMillan is another important contemporary African American novelist. Her first novel, *Mama*, was published in 1987 and received a National Book Award. MacMillan's second novel, *Disappearing Acts*, was published in (1989). Her third novel, *Waiting to Exhale* (1992), led to significant public acclaim, although it was attacked by some critics for excessive male bashing. The movie based on the novel was big news as a Black movie event in 1995. MacMillan's more recent books include *How Stella Got Her Groove Back* (1996), also a successful movie, *The Interruption of Everything* (2005), and *Who Asked You?* (2013). Other contemporary Black female novelists also continue the momentum of the 1970s and 1980s. This group of authors include Olympia Vernon and Tayari Jones.[190]

The theme and focus of the literary works of Black writers are not static but change as they are affected by social, political, and economic factors that impact African American life and experience. The Black consciousness movements of the 1920s and 1960s have generated voluminous books—novels, essays, and other writings—by and about African Americans. In the post-Civil Rights era, new motifs and sub-genres have emerged that reflect the erosion of collective consciousness. Some novelists are pursuing distinctively nonracial themes, whereas others are producing "Black chick lit," a sub-genre that typically centers on single women balancing the demands of their personal and professional lives. Still others are writing increasingly popular Black romance novels. Confronted with this continually changing landscape, African American Studies specialists need a solid understanding of the strengths and weaknesses of various popular approaches to literary criticism. Such an understanding is useful for identifying sub-genres and individual works most closely aligned to the missions of African American Studies.

Literary Criticism and African American Studies

Consistent with the general view of African American Studies specialists regarding authenticity of analysis, Bernard Bell notes that "the consensus of contemporary specialists in the fields of African American literary history and criticism is that the African American literary tradition is best understood and appreciated by interpreting its merits within the context of its own indigenous nature and function."[191]

There are various approaches to literary criticism that have some attraction for African American Studies specialists. Bell's approach emphasizes the strengths of Afro-American folk art and its potential for a tradition of Black American high art. Key elements of his interpretations have been presented in the previous section.

Henry Louis Gates has produced another influential approach to Black literary criticism. Influenced by post-structuralist theories that emphasize the primacy and fluidity of language, Gates' analysis in *Signifying Monkey* prioritizes linguistic innovation. He treats literature as a system of cultural signs that has only limited connection to social reality. This position is clearly inconsistent with the holistic framework advocated by African American Studies specialists in which, to paraphrase the words of Du Bois, the cause and explanation of current events lies in the past. Gates proposes that the rhetorical strategy of "signifying," which makes extensive use of stylized and sometimes indirect insults, is the key metaphor in Black literature. To Gates' credit, he looks to traditional Africa to ground his analysis, by using the divine trickster figure of the Yoruba people, Esu-Elegbara, as his archetype. Normally, African American Studies specialists would view the effort to construct a theory from specific African origins to be a constructive strategy, but Gates' effort is problematic because it anoints a particular African cultural tradition as the exemplar of all African cultures. In addition, his regard for traditional Africa is not matched by an appreciation of the efforts of African American literati to define a "Black aesthetic." As Houston Baker observes, Gates maintains that advocates of a Black aesthetic "postulated a tautological, literary-critical circle assuming that the thought of an Afro-American literary text was 'black thought' and, hence, could be 're-thought' only by a black critic."[192]

Baker, who offers a third approach to Black literary criticism, rejects Gates narrow interpretation of the Black aesthetic. In *Blues, Ideology, and Afro-American Literature*,[193] Baker champions the blues as key to a meaningful interpretation of Black literature. His methodology is grounded in what is characterized as the "anthropology of art," which is based on the guiding assumption "that works of Afro-American literature and verbal art cannot be adequately understood unless they are contextualized with the interdependent systems of Afro-American culture."[194] In addition, consistent with the tenets of African American Studies, Baker declares "the contextualization of a work of literary or verbal art … is an 'interdisciplinary' enterprise in the most contemporary sense of that word."[195] He insists that "rather than ignoring (or denigrating) the research and insights of scholars in the nature (sic), social, and behavioral sciences, the anthropology of art views such efforts as positive, rational attempts to comprehend the full dimensions of human behavior."

Baker's proposal to develop a synthesis of social science and literary analysis methodologies is very similar to ideas advanced by Garry Potter, who insists that science and art have the same objects of knowledge and

8

that literary criticism functions in a manner that parallels social science.[196] According to Potter, it is simply the focus on the literary text as a medium, as a means to produce knowledge, that gives literary criticism its disciplinary distinctiveness.[197] African American Studies specialists are especially supportive of efforts to integrate analyses from the sciences and humanities; this is the essence of African American Studies. In a similar vein, within the field of literary criticism, there is value in combining the approaches of Bernard Bell, Henry Louis Gates, and Houston Baker. However, consistent with a recurring theme in this text, there is also a need to pay special attention to the treatment of gender in literary criticism. Clenora Hudson-Weems is the principal force in the development of Africana Womanist Literary Theory that parts company with feminist literary criticism that prioritizes sexism over racism as oppressive forces stifling African American women[198]:

> Many feel that Africana women fiction writers have a critical mission to "tell it like it is." And since literature in general should reflect life, it is important that the literature of Africanist Womanist writers speak the truth—the whole truth. When the Africana womanist writes about male-female relationships, for example, she must present them in all dimensions. She must explore the dynamics of the relationships, which go far beyond the mere surface interaction between the man and the woman. She must realistically and objectively examine the dominant forces at play, forces that dictate the very nature of the conflicts and the ways they are handled. These forces, in many instances, are deeply rooted in economics, particularly the economic failure of the Africana man.[199]

Literary criticism within African American Studies has been less influenced by the work of Black feminist literary critics. This is because, as observed by Madhu Dubey, "the contemporary black feminist discourse on identity is motivated by an impulse to displace the prescriptive model of black identity, unified around the sign of race, that was promoted to Black Aesthetic critics."[200] At the same time, Dubey argues that "contemporary black feminist literary theory extends the Black Aesthetic gesture of challenging the dichotomy between art and ideology."[201]

There are several contemporary African-centered approaches to literary criticism developed by female scholars that are especially well-suited for African

American Studies. Georgene Bess Montgomery has originated the Ifa Paradigm as a vehicle for text interrogation. Ifa is a classical Yoruban spiritual system whose central message focuses on the Goodness of and in the world; the chosen status of humans in the world; the criteria of a good world; and the requirements for a good world. Bess Montgomery's Ifa paradigm "examines ways in which the Orisa, the ancestors, colors, numbers, conjurers, conjuring, divination, initiation, ritual, magic are manifested in Caribbean and African American literary texts and demonstrates how to identify and decode signs and symbols central to Ifa located in the texts."[202] Within this context, application of the Ifa paradigm involves addressing two questions: (1) Does the story's use of symbolic language suggest the influence of African cultural traditions in the Diaspora?; and, (2) What cultural traditions are specifically represented in the work and how are these traditions manifested in the community that nurtured the creation of the work?[203] Bess Montgomery's analysis of four works applying the Ifa Paradigm leads her to conclude that "this paradigm, then, much like the Black Aesthetic, is a system by which one can evaluate the artistic endeavors of African Diasporic people, a system that reflects a profound understanding of their cultural specificities."[204]

Chezia Thompson Cager has developed an alternative approach to literary criticism that reconceptualizes how plots are structured. She suggests that traditional criticism treats plots as progressing linearly through several stages from an introduction, to the onset of a conflict, to a climax, and finally to a resolution. In contrast, Thompson Cager suggests that greater insights can be gained by conceptualizing a plot via what she characterizes as "The Vertical Technique." The Vertical Technique is described as "an analytical device that uses elements of the African and African-American historic situation to present the worldview of Africana people."[205] It treats a crisis as initiating descent into an increasingly negative state of affairs. Eventually a process of regeneration is initiated that can be thought of as re-establishing an upward trajectory. Thompson Cager proposes that the Vertical Technique be used in combination with the "Blues Motif" to "expand traditional notions of literary classification and broaden the boundaries of criticism and literary history to include works with roots deep in the oral and musical patterns of African-American life."[206] The Blues Motif foregrounds the African-American vernacular tradition, with blues music at its core, as an essential component of American culture and art, which is especially evident in creative production of African Americans, including literature. Thompson Cager argues that "The Blues motif, as a literary tool, augments the Vertical Technique's macrostructural view at the microstructural level by focusing on specific, individual images containing the dialectical symbolism."[207]

What then are the potential benefits of integrating these various perspectives on literary theory into the examination of Black literature in African American Studies? Such an approach would be useful for interpreting novels that interweave the past, present, and future. Trudier Harris notes that a significant number of Black novelists "have drawn upon African-American history (American in the broadest connotations) in developing their novels, poetry, and short fiction."[208] Toni Morrison, for example, in *Song of Solomon*, presents a modernized version of the myth of flying Africans. This myth is linked to a rebellion by a group of enslaved Igbo who overcame slavers off the coast of St. Simons, Georgia, and, according to folklore, magically transformed themselves into birds and flew back to Africa.[209] In Octavia Butler's *Kindred*, the heroine is an African American woman of mixed ancestry who becomes telekinetically and psychokinetically linked to her White great-grandfather, who is part of an enslaver family. She is forced to revisit the past and protect him on several occasions when he is in mortal danger.[210]

Octavia Butler has also provided fictional perspectives that are valuable for engaging the concern of African American Studies with the future of people of African descent. In *Parable of the Sower* and *Parable of the Talents*, she envisions a future in which the type of rightwing political and religious ideology currently in ascendance has destroyed the social fabric. The heroine is a Black Baptist preacher's empathic visionary daughter who feels the pain of others. She establishes a religious community in northern California which becomes the social force that restores social harmony.[211]

W. E. B. Du Bois's novels are all historical treatises presented in the format of the novel. Du Bois consciously employed this technique to allow more flexibility in examining his subject matter. In the postscript to his last novel of the trilogy *The Black Flame*, Du Bois states:

The basis of this book is documented and verifiable fact, but the book is not history. On the contrary, I have used fiction to interpret those historical facts which otherwise would not be clear. Beyond this I have in some cases resorted to pure imagination in order to make unknown and unknowable history relate an ordered tale to the reader. ...If I had time and money, I would have continued this pure historical research. But this opportunity failed and time is running out. Yet I would rescue from my long experience something of what I have learned and conjectured and thus I am trying by the method of historical fiction to complete the cycle of history which has for half a century engaged my thought, research and action.[212]

Du Bois argued that on occasion this methodology was preferable to traditional historical discourse, "provided that the methodology was explicitly acknowledged beforehand."[213] In other words, linkages among fictional, artistic, and analytical discourse can be used in African American Studies as a new approach to generate knowledge.

The potential gains from combining literary and social science methods are further illustrated by James Stewart's analysis of characters in Du Bois' novels. The characters provided Du Bois with a means for developing a correspondence between the type of observations conducted by scientists and those made by writers of fiction. Stewart uses the characters to assess the expositional power of three contemporary approaches to understanding the development of racial identity as discussed in Chapter 5.[214] Potentially useful integration of social science and humanistic modes of inquiry are not restricted solely to literature. James Stewart offers an example of a synthesis involving a qualitative social science study by sociologist Joseph Scott and songs performed by rhythm and blues singer Millie Jackson. The subject matter was male-sharing relationships (romantic triangles). Stewart concludes that the treatment of the two interpretations as parallel types of information provides a richer understanding of the phenomenon than either approach achieves singly.[215]

The approach recommended by Stewart can be employed with other nontraditional methods of examining Black novels, including the use of elements of psychoanalysis as Claudia Tate proposes. Tate believes that "psychoanalysis... can help us not only analyze black textuality but also effectively explain important aspects of the deep psychological foundations of the destructive attitudes and behaviors of racism."[216] Success in this endeavor would undoubtedly dramatically advance the interests of African American Studies specialists.

8

Conclusion

The preceding discussion highlights how the various artistic and humanistic genres are intertwined. These interconnections underscore the need for the type of transdisciplinary approach to inquiry emphasized in this text. In addition, it is clear that all genres offer opportunities to advance the liberatory and social responsibility objectives of African American Studies. Finally, it is clear from the exposition that African American culture is continuously evolving and in all of its manifestations it continues to be a major force shaping the contours, not only of cultural trends in the US, but also global cultural patterns.

Questions & Exercises

1. Explain how creative arts can go beyond perceptions of beauty, form, motion, and sound to influence the social, political, and economic condition of a race or group of people.

2. Discuss and compare the Harlem Renaissance of the 1920s with the Black Arts Movement of the 1960s.

3. Was there an identifiable Black creative arts movement emergent during the 1980s and 1990s? If so, characterize and describe it.

4. Black music and song have generally reflected the social, political, and economic realities of African American communities. Refer to Chapter 5, and relate the implications of psychohistory to the lyrics and modes of Black music and to the nature and subjects of Black art.

5. Write a paper examining the beginnings, development, and popularization of rap music in America.

6. Defend or refute the following statement: "Rap music should not be supported by African American Studies specialists because too many songs degrade women and celebrate violence and other behaviors that have a negative impact on Black communities."

7. Discuss the differences between Eurocentric "art-for-art's-sake" and Afrocentric "art-for-peoples'-sake."

8. Why is the politicization of Black music and arts vital to the civil/human rights struggle and the progress of African Americans?

9. Discuss the differences in how African Americans are generally represented in visual arts versus film and television. Specify some of the factors that contribute to these differences in representation.

10. What are some of the distinctive expressive modes or nuances in American literature that distinguish the work of an African American writer from a writer of other racial or ethnic groups?

8

Social Responsibility Projects

1. Organize a book club that reads and discusses works that address themes of relevance to African American Studies.

2. Organize a discussion forum that explores the impact of hip hop on African American culture.

3. Organize a discussion forum that explores the representation of African Americans in television programming.

4. Work with appropriate departments and/or organizations to organize a film series that examines both historical and contemporary movies that address some of the concerns of African American Studies.

5. Work with appropriate organizations to organize a series of poetry slams to celebrate creativity and highlight important contemporary issues confronting African Americans.

6. Contact appropriate departments and/or organizations to organize an art exhibit featuring works by historical and contemporary artists that present powerful images of African American life and culture.

7. Organize a group to conduct an assessment of course offerings examining African American creative production. Present your findings to appropriate departments along with recommendations for new courses based on discussions in this text.

NOTES AND REFERENCES

1. W. E. B. Du Bois, "A Negro Nation Within a Nation," *Current History* 42 (June 1935): 270.

2. See C. Blair, "Perspective on African Art Criticism," 24 *Black World* (July 1975), 23-24, 71-78.

3. P. Klotman, ed., *Humanities Through the Black Experience* (Dubuque: Kendall/Hunt Publishing., 1977), 1.

4. C. Molette and B. Molette, *Black Theatre* (Bristol, IN: Wyndham Hall Press, 1986), 38.

5. Kariamu Welsh Asante, "The Aesthetic Conceptualization of Nzuri," in Kariamu Welsh Asante (ed.), *The African Aesthetic: Keeper of the Traditions*. (Westport, CT: Praeger, 1994), 9.

6. Melanie Bratcher, *Words and Songs of Bessie Smith, Billie Holiday, and Nina Simone: Sound Motion, Blues Spirit, and African Memory* (New York: Taylor & Francis, 2007), 16.

7. W. E. B. Du Bois, "The Social Origins of Negro Art," *Modern Quarterly* 3, no. 1 (1925): 53-56.

8. W. E. B. Du Bois, "Strivings of the Negro People," *Atlantic Monthly* 80 (August 1897), 194-98.

9. See N. Huggins, *Harlem Renaissance* (New York: Oxford University Press, 1971); see also, J. Emanuel, "Renaissance Sonneteers," *Black World* (September 1975): 34.

10. For a chronology and biographies of Black artists and literary figures of this period, refer to H. Ploski and J. Williams, eds., *The Negro Almanac* 4th ed. (New York: John Wiley & Sons, 1983).

11. The political-cultural nexus of the 1940s is treated more fully in A. Lynch, "Reflections on Black Culture in the Early Forties," *Black Books Bulletin* 6 (Spring 1978).

12. See also R. Hayden, "preface" to *The New Negro*, ed. A. Locke (New York: Atheneum, 1969), ix.

13. M. Marable, "The Rhetoric of Racial Harmony," *Sojourners* (August/September 1990): 17.

14. See for example, M. Busby, *Daughters of Africa: An International Anthology of Words and Writings by Women of African Descent: From the Ancient Egyptian to the Present* (New York: Pantheon Books, 1992) and F. Foster, *Written by Herself: Literary Production by African American Women, 1746-1892* (Bloomington: Indiana University Press, 1993).

15. See B. Christian, *Black Women Novelists: The Development of a Tradition, 1892-1976* (Westport, CT: Greenwood Press, 1980); B. Christian, *Black Feminist Criticism: Perspectives on Black Women Writers* (Paris: Elsevier Science, 1997); C. Wall, *Changing Our Own Words: Essays on Criticism, Theory, and Writing by Black Women* (New Brunswick: Rutgers University Press, 1989).

16. T. Ellis, "The New Black Aesthetic," *Callaloo* 38 (winter 1989): 233-43.

17. J. Stewart, "Reaching for Higher Ground: Toward an Understanding of Black/African Studies," *The Afrocentric Scholar* 1, no. 1 (1992): 1-63.

18. A. Locke, *The Negro and His Music* (Washington, DC: The Associates in Negro Folk Education, 1936), 1-7.

19. Cited in F. Kofsky, *Black Nationalism and the Revolution in Music* (New York: Pathfinder Press, 1970), 102.

20. S. Floyd, *The Power of Black Music* (New York: Oxford University Press, 1995), 10.

21. Locke, *The Negro and His Music*.

22. M. Herskovits, *The Myth of the Negro Past* (Boston: Beacon Press, 1958; Harper & Brothers, 1941).

23. Bratcher, *Words and Songs*, 90.

24. Bratcher, *Words and Songs*, 90.

25. L. Ekwueme, "African-Music Retentions in the New World," *The Black Perspective in Music* 2 (fall 1974), 134-35.

26. Ibid., 135.

27. Locke, *The Negro and His Music*, 18.

28. Du Bois also describes spirituals as "Sorrow Songs." See Chapter 14 in W. E. B. Du Bois, *The Souls of Black Folk* (New York: The New American Library, 1969; originally published in 1903).

29. E. Southern, *The Music of Black Americans* (New York: W.W. Norton & Co., 1971), 249-51.

30. See E. Southern, "An Origin for the Negro Spiritual," *Black Scholar* (Summer 1972): 8-13.

31. Several Black spirituals and speculative interpretations are presented in C. Dixon, *Negro Spirituals* (Philadelphia: Fortress Press, 1976).

32. See P. Maultsby, "The Use and Performance of Hymnody, Spirituals and Gospels in the Black Church," *Western Journal of Black Studies* 7 (Fall 1983): 161-71; see also M. Davis, "The Black Sacred Song," *Western Journal of Black Studies* 2 (Summer 1978): 140-41.

33. H. Boyer, "Contemporary Gospel Music: Sacred or Secular?" *Black Perspective in Music* 7 (Spring 1979): 5-6.

34. Ibid., 7-11.

35. "An interview with Thomas A. Dorsey," *Black Books Bulletin* 5 (Spring 1977): 22.

36. See J. Nketia, "The Study of African and Afro-American Music," *Black Perspective in Music* 1 (Spring 1973): 7-15; S. Charters, *The Bluesman* (New York: Oak Publications, 1967), 15-22.

37. See P. Pastras, *Dead Man Blues: Jelly Roll Morton Way Out West* (Berkeley, CA: Univ. of California Press, 2001).

8

38. Southern, *The Music of Black Americans*, 333-35.

39. The stanzas presented here and below are from the personal record collection of Talmadge Anderson. For an excellent pictorial, biographical, and autobiographical history of the Blues, see P. Oliver, *The Story of the Blues* (Philadelphia: Chilton Book Co., 1969).

40. E. Meadows, "African Retentions in Blues and Jazz," *Western Journal of Black Studies* 3 (Fall 1979): 183.

41. Maria Johnson, "Black Women Electric Guitarists and Authenticity in the Blues," in Eileen Hayes and Linda Williams, eds., *Black Women and Music, More than the Blues* (Urbana, IL University of Illinois Press, 2007), 51.

42. See M. Haralambos, *Right On: From Blues to Soul in Black America* (New York: Da Capo Press, 1979), 20-27.

43. Bratcher, *Words and Songs*, 1.

44. Bratcher, *Words and Songs*, 1.

45. B. Smith, "Poor Man's Blues," recorded August 24, 1928 in New York City, (W-146895-1, Columbia 14399).

46. A. Fields, "'29 Blues," recorded July 7, 1939 in Chicago, (WC 2646-A Okeh 06020). *News & The Blues, Telling It Like It Is* (Columbia Records, CBS Records, 1990); Blind Lemon Jefferson, "Tin Cup Blues," in *The Blues Line: A Collection of Blues Lyrics from Leadbelly to Muddy Waters*, comp. E. Sackheim and J. Shahn (Hopewell, NJ, 1969), 79.

47. Big Bill Broonzy, "Unemployment Stomp," recorded March 30, 1938 in Chicago, (C-2159-1 Vocalion 04205). *News & The Blues, Telling It Like It Is*.

48. V. Hall, "Another Man Done Gone" in J. Lomax and A. Lomax, *Folk Song U.S.A.*, p. 376. Lyrics reprinted in J. Cone, "The Blues, A Secular Spiritual," in *The Spirituals and the Blues: An Interpretation* (New York: Seabury, 1972); B. White, "Parchman Farm Blues." recorded March 7, 1940 in Chicago. (WC 2981-A Okeh 05683). *News & The Blues, Telling It Like It Is*.

49. W. Cuney, "Uncle Sam Says," Vocals by Josh White (Mercury Records, 1941) Defiance Blues. (House of Blues, 1998) (51416 1340 2).

50. H. Harris, "Atomic Bomb Blues," recorded September 27, 1946 in Chicago (CCO 4650) (Columbia (unissued)). *News & The Blues, Telling It Like It Is*.

51. L. Hughes and N. Simone, "Backlash Blues," recorded January 5, 1967 (EMI Waterford Music).

52. Junior Wells, "Viet Cong Blues," *Defiance Blues* (Songs of Polygram International, Inc. BMI.)

53. G. Sales, *Jazz: America's Classical Music* (Englewood Cliffs, NJ: Prentice-Hall, 1984), 26-28.

54. R. Thompson, "Kongo Influences on African American Artistic Culture," in *Africanisms in American Culture*, ed. J. Holloway (Bloomington, IN: Indiana University Press, 1990), 148-50.

55. F. Ramsey and C. Smith, eds., *Jazzmen* (New York: Limelight edition, 1985), 7-9.

56. D. Harrison, "Jazz: The Serious Music of Black Americans," *Western Journal of Black Studies* 2 (Fall 1978):198.

57. Southern, *The Music of Black Americans*, 311-314.

58. Sales, *Jazz: America's Classical Music*, 50-56.

59. Locke, *The Negro and His Music*, 84-87.

60. The categorization of jazz schools and artists are as varied as there are music writers and historians. Most of the writer-analysts of jazz have been White. Their concepts may be at variance with Black jazz enthusiasts and historians. For an interesting work by a White writer, see I. Gitler, *Swing to Bop* (New York: Oxford University Press, 1985).

61. L. Porter, "Some Problems in Jazz Research," *Black Music Research Journal* 8 (Fall 1988): 200.

62. M. Roach, "Garvey's Ghost," *Max Roach Percussion Bitter Sweet* recorded in 1961 in New York (MCA Records, 1962).

63. H. Hancock, "I Have a Dream," *The Prisoner* (Blue Note, April 18 – 23, 1969); A. Shepp, "Malcolm, Malcolm, Semper Malcolm," *Fire Music* (MCA Records, 1965, MCAD-39121).

64. A. Shaw, "Researching Rhythm & Blues," *Black Music Research*, Institute for Research in Black American Music (Fisk University, 1980), 871.

65. For a chronology of R&B music development see, R. Larkin, *Soul Music* (New York: Lancer Books, 1970).

66. Shaw, "Researching Rhythm and Blues," 72.

67. For a more comprehensive study of R&B or Soul music the book by P. Guralnick, *Sweet Soul Music* (New York: Harper & Row, 1986) is recommended.

68. J. Stewart, "Relationships Between Black Males and Females in Rhythm and Blues Music of the 1960s and 1970s," *The Western Journal of Black Studies* 3(3), (Fall 1979):186-195.

69. W. Van Deburg, *New Day in Babylon, The Black Power Movement and American Culture, 1965-1975* (Chicago: University of Chicago Press, 1992), 205.

70. Quoted in *Soul Music: The Birth of Sound in Black America*, by M. Haralambos (New York: Da Capo Press, 1974), 118.

71. Van Deburg, *New Day in Babylon*, 215.

72. Van Deburg, *New Day in Babylon*, 215.

73. J. Stewart, "Message in the Music: Political Commentary in Black Popular Music from Rhythm and Blues to Early Hip Hop," *Journal of African American History* (Fall 2005).

74. N. George, "Rapping Their Way to Gold," *Black Enterprise* (June 1982), 223.

75. See for instance, Lawrence W. Levin, *Black Culture and Black Consciousness: Afro-American Folk Thought from Slavery to Freedom* (Oxford: Oxford University Press, 1977); Sterling Stuckey, *Slave Culture: Nationalist Theory and the Foundations of Black America* (Oxford: Oxford University Press, 1988).

76. A. Pasteur and I. Toldson, *Roots of Soul* (Garden City, NY: Anchor Press, 1982) 28.

77. See R. Stephens, "What the Rap is About: Some Historical Notes on the Development of Rap Music and the Hip-Hop Movement," *Word* 1 (Spring 1991); and E. Wheeler, "Most of My Heroes Don't Appear on No Stamps: The Dialogics of Rap Music," *Black Music Research Journal* 11 (Fall 1991).

78. H. Kruse, "Gender," in *Key Terms in Popular Music and Culture*, ed. B. Horner and T. Swiss (Oxford, UK: Blackwell, 1999), 86.

79. Charise Cheney, "In Search of the 'Revolutionary Generation': (En)Gendering the Golden Age of Rap Nationalism," in Derrick Alridge, James Stewart, and V.P. Franklin, *Message in the Music, Hip Hop History & Pedagogy* (Washington, D.C.: The ASALH Press, 2010), 86.

80. Ronald Jackson and Sakile Camara, "Scripting and Consuming Black Bodies in Hip Hop Music and Pimp Movies," in Derrick Alridge, James Stewart, and V.P. Franklin, *Message in the Music, Hip Hop History & Pedagogy* (Washington, D.C.: The ASALH Press, 2010), 189.

81. Layli Phillips, Kerri Reddick-Morgan, and Dionne Stephens, "Oppositional Consciousness within an Oppositional Realm: The Case of Feminism and Womanism in Rap and Hip Hop, 1976-2004," in Derrick Alridge, James Stewart, and V.P. Franklin, *Message in the Music, Hip Hop History & Pedagogy* (Washington, D.C.: The ASALH Press, 2010), 91.

82. H. Baker, "Hybridity, the Rap Race and Pedagogy for the 1990s," *Black Music Research Journal* 11 (Fall 1991): 220-221.

83. D. Brackett, "Music," in *Key Terms in Popular Music and Culture*, ed. B. Horner & T. Swiss, 137.

84. Ibid.

85. Patricia Washington and Lynda Shaver, "The Language Culture of Rap Music Videos," in Joseph Adjaye and Adrianne Andrews, eds., *Language, Rhythm, and Sound* (Pittsburgh: University of Pittsburgh Press, 1997), 174.

86. Washington and Shaver, "The Language Culture of Rap Music Videos," 174.

87. "BBB Interviews Gil Scott-Heron," *Black Books Bulletin* 6, no. 3 (1979): 36.

88. Brackett, "Music," 128.

89. R. Potter, "Race," in *Key Terms in Popular Music and Culture*, ed. B. Horner and T. Swiss, 82.

90. M. Fenster and T. Swiss, "Business," in *Key Terms in Popular Music and Culture*, ed. Horner and Swiss, 227.

91. Jeffrey Ogbar, *Hip-Hop Revolution: The Culture and Politics of Rap* (Lawrence, KS: The University of Kansas Press, 2007) and Derrick Alridge, James Stewart, and V.P. Franklin, *Message in the Music, Hip Hop History & Pedagogy* (Washington, D.C.: The ASALH Press, 2010).

92. Pero Dagbovie, "'Of All Our Studies, History is Best Qualified to Reward Our Research': Black History's Relevance to the Hip Hop Generation," in Derrick Alridge, James Stewart, and V.P. Franklin, *Message in the Music, Hip Hop History & Pedagogy* (Washington, D.C.: The ASALH Press, 2010), 339.

93. J. Gray, compiler, *Blacks in Classical Music, A Bibliographical Guide to Composers, Performers, and Ensembles* (Westport, CT: Greenwood Press, 1988).

94. R. Jones, "R. Daniel Dett," Afrocentric Voices in "Classical" Music, http://www.afrovoices.com/dett.html.

95. R. Dett, "The Development of Negro Religious Music," Negro Music. Bowdoin Literary Prize Thesis, Harvard, 1920. In *The R. Nathaniel Dett Reader: Essays in Black Sacred Music: A Special Issue of Black Sacred Music: A Journal of Theomusicology* 5 (Fall 1991): 36.

96. J. Spencer, *The New Negroes and Their Music, The Success of the Harlem Renaissance* (Knoxville, TN: The University of Tennessee Press, 1997), 76.

97. Spencer, *The New Negroes and Their Music*, 77.

98. Spencer, *The New Negroes and Their Music*, 80.

99. R. Jones, "Margaret Bonds," Afrocentric Voices in "Classical" Music, http://www.afrovoices.com/dett.html.

100. D. Henahan, "Opera: Anthony Davis's X (The Life and Times of Malcolm X)," *New York Times* (September 29, 1986).

101. R. Jones, "Marian Anderson," Afrocentric Voices in "Classical" Music, http://www.afrovoices.com/dett.html.

102. http://www.africanamericans.com/PaulRobeson.htm.

103. Spencer, *The New Negroes and Their Music*, p. 18.

104. http://www.africanamericans.com/PaulRobeson.htm (site discontinued)

105. "Paul Robeson" AfricaWithin.com, http://www.africawithin.com/bios/paul_robeson.htm (site discontinued).

106. "Paul Robeson" AfricaWithin.com, http://www.africawithin.com/bios/paul_robeson.htm (site discontinued).

8

107. "Paul Robeson" AfricaWithin.com, http://www.africawithin.com/bios/paul_robeson.htm (site discontinued).

108. See A. Gayle, "Blueprint for Black Criticism," *First World* (Jan/Feb 1977): 41-45; see also R. Williams, "The Black Artist as Activist," *Black Creation* 3 (winter 1972): 42-45.

109. J. A. Porter, *Modern Negro Art* (New York: Dryden Press, 1943; reprinted Washington DC: Howard University Press, 1992), 27; and A. Locke, *Negro Art: Past and Present* (Washington, DC: Associates in Negro Folk Education, 1936), 15.

110. Locke, *Negro Art: Past and Present*, 61.

111. Locke, *Negro Art: Past and Present*, 61.

112. G. McElroy, R. Powell, and S Patton, eds., *African-American Artists 1880–1987* (Washington, DC: Smithsonian Institution, 1989).

113. Ibid., 103-04.

114. Nell Painter, *Creating Black Americans, African-American History and Its Meanings*, 1619 to the Present (New York: Oxford University Press, 2007), xvi.

115. Painter, *Creating Black Americans*, xviii.

116. See L. Thompson, "The Black Image in Early American Drama," *Black World* (April 1975):54-69; and S. Brown, "Negro in American Theatre," in *The Oxford Companion to the Theatre*, ed. P. Hartnoll (London: Oxford University Press, 1967), 672.

117. E. Southern, "The Origin and Development of the Black Musical Theatre," *Black Music Research Journal* (1981–1982): 2-5.

118. Ibid., 7-9.

119. W. E. B. Du Bois, "Krigwa Players Little Negro Theatre," *Crisis* 32 (July 1926):134-36.

120. See A. Morrison, "One Hundred Years of Negro Entertainment," in *International Library of Afro-American Life and History* ed. L. Patterson (Washington, DC: ASALH, 1976), 3-7.

121. G. Chaffin-Quiray, "Melvin Van Peebles," Senses of Cinema, http://www.sensesofcinema.com/contents/directors/03/van_peebles.html (site discontinued).

122. The website for the National Black Theater Festival is http://www.nbtf.org.

123. For a brief summary of Wilson's career and accomplishments with links to additional information, see "August Wilson," http://en.wikipedia.org/wiki/August_Wilson.

124. Olly Wilson, "The Association of Movement and Music as a Manifestation of a Black Conceptual Approach to Music-Making," in Irene Jackson, (ed.), *More than Dancing, Essays on Afro-American Music and Musicians* (Westport, CT: Greenwood Press, 1985), 10.

125. Wilson, "The Association of Movement and Music," 20.

126. Kariamu Welsh Asante, "Commonalities in African Dance: An Aesthetic Foundation", in Molefi Asante and Kariamu Welsh Asante, eds., *African Culture: Rhythms of Unity* (Trenton, NJ: Africa World Press, 1985), 3-12.

127. Bratcher, *Words and Songs*, 2.

128. J. Malone, *Steppin' On The Blues: The Visible Rhythms of African American Dance* (Urbana, IL: University of Illinois Press, 1996), 1.

129. R. Ellison, *Going to the Territory* (New York: Random House, 1986), 139.

130. Malone, *Steppin' On The Blues*, 4.

131. Malone, *Steppin' On The Blues*, 13.

132. Malone, *Steppin' On The Blues*, 33.

133. L. Emery, *Black Dance: From 1619 to Today* second, rev. ed. (Highstown, NJ: Princeton Book Company, 1988), 86–87.

134. Emery, *Black Dance*, 157–58.

135. Emery, *Black Dance*, 250.

136. Emery, *Black Dance*, 260.

137. Emery, *Black Dance*, 257.

138. Emery, *Black Dance*, 276.

139. Emery, *Black Dance*, 244.

140. Emery, *Black Dance*, 341.

141. Malone, *Steppin' On The Blues*, 213.

142. For additional information see the official Soul Train website, http://soultrain.com.

143. For a study of Black dance and music see, S. Floyd, "Afro-American Music and Dance," *Western Journal of Black Studies* 13 (Fall 1989).

144. For a directory of contemporary African dance companies, visit Open Directory – Arts: Performing Arts: Dance: Folk: African, http://dmoz.org/Arts/Performing_Arts/Dance/Folk/African/.

145. T. Brown, "'Mad Black Woman' Draws from Gospel 'Chitlin Circuit'," *The San Diego Union Tribune*, March 24, 2005, http://www.signon-sandiego.com/uniontrib/20050324/news_1c24black.html.

146. University of Pittsburgh, Pittsburgh Arts, http://www.pitt.edu/~pittarts/pitt/theatre/kuntu.html.

147. For a good history of the efforts by Blacks to produce independent films see M. Reid, *Redefining Black Film* (Berkeley, CA: University of California Press, 1993).

148. Ibid.

149. Reid, *Redefining Black Film*.

150. For additional information about the MVP Foundation, visit http://melvinvanpeebles.org/melvinvanpeebles_index. php.

151. For additional information about Black female filmmakers, see J. Bobo, *Black Women Film and Video Artists* (New York: Routledge, 1998).

152. For a concise history of Spike Lee's career and accomplishments, visit, http://www.imdb.com/name/nm0000490/.

153. Ibid.

154. D. Bogle, *Toms, Coons, Mulattoes, Mammies, and Bucks: An Interpretive History of Blacks in American Films* (New York: Viking Press, 1973).

155. Ibid.

156. See "Feature Presentation: African American Oscar Winners," Black Film Center/Archive, Indiana University, *http://www.indiana.edu/~bfca/features/oscars.html*.

157. For celebratory information about this genre see http://www.blaxploitation.com/.

158. James Stewart "Art, Politics, Cultural Studies, and Post-Structural Philosophy in Black/Africana Studies: Deciphering Complex Relationships." Unpublished manuscript.

159. See C. Waring, "Hot Chicks, Cool Dudes and Bad Muthas: Crime Time's Definitive Guide to Blaxploitation," CrimeTime.com, http://www.crimetime.co.uk/features/blaxploitation.php.

160. D. Bogle, *Primetime Blues: African Americans on Network Television* (New York: Farrar, Straus & Giroux, 2001).

161. P. Deane, "Amos 'n Andy Show: U.S. Domestic Comedy," Museum Broadcast Communications, http://www.museum.tv/archives/etv/A/htmlA/amosnandy/amosnandy.htm.

162. G. Gutierrez, "American Sitcoms: A Diversity of Flavors in Society," Contribution to English Media Culture (University of California, Santa Barbara) http://www.uweb.ucsb.edu/~monicamd/gloriapaper.html (site discontinued).

163. M. Miranda, "Black Sitcoms: A Black Perspective," Cercles (Orangeburg, SC: Claflin University, 2003), http://www.cercles.com/n8/chitiga.pdf.

164. Read M. Asante, *The Afrocentric Idea* (Philadelphia: Temple University Press, 1987).

165. Ploski and Williams, *The Negro Almanac*, 984, 998, 1001.

166. S. Ransome, ed., *J. Hammon, America's First Negro Poet* (Port Washington NY: Kennikat Press, 1970), 59.

167. P. Wheatley, *Poems On Various Subjects, Religious and Moral* (Philadelphia: 1786; facsimile reprinted New York: AMS Press, 1976), 13.

168. See A. Davis and S. Redding, eds., *Cavalcade* (Boston: Houghton Mifflin, 1971), 3.

169. R. Hemenway, "The Sacred Canon and Brazzle's Mule," *ADE Bulletin* 73 (winter 1982).

170. Ibid.

171. B. Chambers, ed., *Chronicles of Black Protest* (New York: Mentor Books, 1968), 58.

172. B. Bell, *The Contemporary African American Novel: Its Folk Roots and Modern Literary Branches* (Amherst, MA: University of Massachusetts Press, 2004), 95.

173. Ibid.

174. Bell, *The Contemporary African American Novel*, 97.

175. H. Baker, *Black Literature in America* (New York: McGraw-Hill, 1971), 140-43.

176. Bell, The *Contemporary African American Novel*, 106.

177. T. Harris, *Fiction and Folklore: The Novels of Toni Morrison* (Knoxville, TN: The University of Tennessee Press, 1991), 6.

178. Bell, *The Contemporary African American Novel*, 121.

179. Bell, *The Contemporary African American Novel*, 125.

180. See also, C. Everett, "'Tradition' in Afro-American Literature," *Black World* (December 1975): 20-35; and B. Bell, "Contemporary Afro-American Poetry as Folk Art," *Black World* (March 1973): 16-26.

181. "Gwendolyn Brooks," Poets.org, http://www.poets.org/poet.php/prmPID/165.

182. "Sonia Sanchez," *African American Literature Book Club*, http://authors.aalbc.com/sonia.htm.

183. J. Burton, "Eugene Redmond," Answers.com, http://www.answers.com/topic/eugene-redmond?cat=entertainment.

184. "A Foundation of Poetry, Dudley Randall," *The African American Registry*, http://www.aaregistry.org/historic_events/view/foundation-poetry-dudley-randall.

185. "Haki Madhubuti," *African American Literature Book Club*, http://aalbc.com/authors/haki.htm.

186. See K. Leonard, "African American Women Poets and the Power of the Word," in A. Mitchell and D. Taylor, eds., *The Cambridge Companion to African American Women's Literature.* (New York: Cambridge University Press, 2009), 168-186.

8

187.   See G. Glazner, (ed.), *Poetry Slam: The Competitive Art of Performance* (San Francisco: Manic D Press, 2000).

188.   C. Hudson-Weems, "Toni Morrison's World of Topsy-Turvydom: A Methodological Explication of New Black Literary Criticism," *Western Journal of Black Studies* 10 (Fall 1986): 134.

189.   T. Sherard, "Women's Classic Blues in Toni Morrison's Jazz: Cultural Artifact as Narrator," *Genders* 31 (2000), http://www.genders.org/g31/g31_sherard.html.

190.   See D. Williams, "Contemporary African American Women Writers," in A. Mitchell and D. Taylor, eds., *The Cambridge Companion to African American Women's Literature* (New York: Cambridge University Press, 2009), 71-86 and M. Dubey, "'Even Some Fiction Might be Useful': African American Women Novelists," in A. Mitchell and D. Taylor, eds., *The Cambridge Companion to African American Women's Literature* (New York: Cambridge University Press, 2009), 150-167.

191.   Bell, *The Contemporary African American Novel*, 388.

192.   H. Baker, "Generational Shifts and the Recent Criticism of Afro-American Literature, in *Paradigms in Black Studies: Intellectual History, Cultural Meaning, and Political Ideology*, ed. A. Alkalimat (Chicago: Twenty-First Century Books and Publications, 1990), 71-117.

193.   H. Baker, *Blues, Ideology and African-American Literature* (Chicago: University of Chicago Press, 1984).

194.   Baker, *Generational Shifts*, 115.

195.   Baker, *Generational Shifts*, 115.

196.   G. Potter, "Truth in Fiction, Science and Criticism," in *After Postmodernism, An Introduction to Critical Realism*, ed. J. Lopez & G. Potter (London: The Athlone Press, 2001), 183-95.

197.   Ibid.

198.   C. Hudson-Weems, *Africana Womanist Literary Theory* (Trenton, NJ: Africa World Press, 2004).

199.   C. Hudson-Weems, *Africana Womanism: Reclaiming Ourselves* (Bedford, 1993), 77.

200.   M. Dubey, "Introduction" to *Black Women Novelists and the Nationalist Aesthetic* (Bloomington, IN: Indiana University Press, 1994).

201.   Dubey, "Introduction."

202.   Georgene Bess Montgomery, *The Spirit and the Word, A Theory of Spirituality in Africana Literary Criticism* (Trenton, NJ: Africa World Press, 2008), 4.

203.   Montgomery, *The Spirit and the Word*, xiv.

204.   Montgomery, *The Spirit and the Word*, 197.

205.   Chezia Thompson Cager, *Teaching Jean Toomer's 1923 Cane (Studies in African-American Culture)* Volume 9 (New York: Peter Lang, 2006), 48.

206.   Thompson Cager, *Teaching*, 55.

207.   Thompson Cager, *Teaching*, 56.

208.   Harris, *Fiction and Folklore*, 191.

209.   T. Morrison, *Song of Solomon* (New York: Alfred A. Knopf, 1977).

210.   O. Butler, *Kindred* (Doubleday, 1979).

211.   O. Butler, *Parable of the Sower* (Four Walls Eight Windows, 1993); O. Butler, *Parable of the Talents* (Warner Books, 1998).

212.   W. E. B. Du Bois, postscript, *The Ordeal of Mansart* (Millwood, NY: Kraus Thomson Ltd., 1976). (Reprinted from Mainstream Publishers, 1957), 315.

213.   Ibid.

214.   J. Stewart, "Perspectives on Reformist, Radical, and Recovery Models of Black Identity Dynamics from the Novels of W. E. B. Du Bois," in *Flight in Search of Vision*, ed. J. Stewart (Trenton, NJ: Africa World Press, 2004), 107-27.

215.   J. Stewart, "Perspectives on Black Families from Contemporary Soul Music: The Case of Millie Jackson," *Phylon* (March 1980): 57-71.

216.   C. Tate, *Psychoanalysis and Black Novels: Desire and the Protocols of Race* (New York: Oxford University Press, 1998).

Chapter 9

Science, Technology, and the Future of African Americans

Introduction

As discussed in Chapter 1, African American Studies eschew distorted interpretations of the African American experience. Even though discussions of subject matter content in the preceding chapters have been organized to correspond with standard social science and humanistic disciplinary demarcations, wholesale distortions are often generated by relying exclusively on narrowly conceived models and canons associated with a single social science or humanistic approach. As the complexity of the human experience and the dynamic interaction between humans and their environments have become more apparent, there is growing awareness of the need to develop interdisciplinary research methods.

Ironically, the synthesis of methods of obtaining knowledge long pursued in African American Studies is now actually at the cutting edge of efforts to develop new approaches to generating socially useful knowledge. The growing impact of science and technology on the human experience is a major impetus for the shift toward more integrative research strategies. Conversely, the rapid pace of scientific discoveries, many of which challenge long-held facts of science, is leading many skeptics to challenge the privileged status of science as the principal source of knowledge for improving the human condition. The erosion of scientific influence is signaled by several developments. For many lay people, popular culture is increasingly supplanting science as the major purveyor of cultural imagery, values, and interpretations of social and physical phenomena. Even within the scientific establishment itself, soul-searching has increased among practitioners in various disciplines regarding the value of the current incremental approach to generating knowledge.

In the face of growing uncertainty regarding the optimal means to generate knowledge for guiding social change, a major challenge for specialists in African American Studies is to provide guidance to people of African descent for controlling the impact of scientific and technological research on their lives. The approach advocated in this chapter is to integrate perspectives into African American Studies from Science, Technology, and Society (STS) and from Future Studies (FS), two important emergent fields that address scientific and technological issues,

Science, Technology, and Society (STS) is an interdisciplinary field of study that seeks to explore and understand the many ways in which science and technology shape culture, values, and institutions, as well as how such factors shape science and technology. Future Studies (FS) is a systematic interdisciplinary analysis of present technological, economic, or social trends undertaken to predict the medium to long-term future. The core concept of Future Studies is the idea of alternative futures, which contends that individuals, groups, and cultures are not set on a deterministic path to a single unitary future. Rather, by using their powers of foresight and decision making, individuals and collectives can select from a wide range of future trajectories and outcomes and promote the most desirable. Thinking, debating, and shaping the future are especially essential today because of the complexity of scientific, technological, and societal interrelationships, the limits of financial resources, and the increasing rate of scientific and technological change. All of these phenomena reinforce the need for all parties affected by science and technology to develop a working understanding of these enterprises.[1]

Integrating Science and Technology Studies Into African American Studies

Although there is little disagreement that African Americans have been and still remain vulnerable to extraordinary victimization as a result of research, development, and the deployment of scientific and technological innovations, only a few scholars have advanced critiques that focus on group-specific concerns.[2] S.E. Anderson argues that one of the reasons for this silence is that "Blackfolk have to struggle against a double psych-barrier: Science as divine and mysterious, *and* science as non-black in the socio-historical sense."[3] He argues that "technological oppression and dependence blocks us from developing: (a) revolutionary black scientists, (b) scientific and technological alternatives, and (c) scientific education among the masses of blackfolk."[4] Although somewhat less radical, Lenneal Henderson's perspective points in the same general direction, with the assertion that "black participation in public technology must be multidimensional and diverse, vertical and horizontal."[5] Henderson insists, "Black input must include policy decisions, scientific and professional employment, White collar and blue-collar employment and, where necessary, legal and community action," and that this "participation and impact inventory can best be accomplished by more black involvement in the emerging discipline of 'technology assessment,' the attempt to analyze and make informed decisions about the implications of technological developments."[6]

From the vantage point of African American Studies, there is a pressing need to take up the challenges posed by Anderson and Henderson. The growing role of science and technology in shaping the lives of African Americans has long been recognized, for example, when W.E.B. Du Bois' pleads in 1933 that HBCUs focus their attention on "reach[ing] modern science of matter and life" through the experiences of peoples of African descent.[7] As Abdul Alkalimat observes, "The relationship between technological change and the economic, social, cultural, and political struggle of African American people is the missing link in the 'history of African American history.'"[8]

The continuing catastrophe experienced disproportionately by African Americans in 2005 in the wake of Hurricane Katrina has brought into sharp relief the need for systematic scrutiny of the impacts of modern science and technology on people of African descent. However, this travesty represents only the tip of the iceberg in assessing how science and technology can potentially worsen the long-term prospects for the survival of people of African descent. Similar attention is required in many areas where modern science and technology are heavily implicated in the conditions that affect the life chances of Blacks. A comprehensive understanding of the characteristics of modern science and technology and how they shape social options is required for Black organizations and individuals to be successful in addressing the challenges posed by the increasing impact of science and technology and the attendant risks. Armed with such knowledge, African Americans will be better equipped to harness science and technology and to use them to promote liberation rather than unwittingly supporting applications that intensify subjugation.

Understanding Science and Technology

A distinctive African American Studies analysis of the role of science and technology in the historical, contemporary, and prospective experiences of people of African descent can use key concepts developed by specialists in the field of STS as a point of departure. One of the key conclusions emerging from this field is an understanding that a salient feature of the modern world is the fusion of science and technology as a single enterprise, in contrast with their historical separation. RajkoTomovic observes that "the most powerful factors shaping our technology—union of science, research, and technology as well as extensive technological education—were almost nonexistent until the middle of the nineteenth century."[9] Fundamentally, as Robert McGinn concludes, "Technology as an activity existed long before the dawn of the era of modern technology in the mid-eighteenth century."[10]

Understanding the significance of technology in human societies is often obscured because the term technology has multiple meanings. McGinn identifies four distinct meanings: (1) technology as material products fabricated by humans; (2) technology as the "complex of knowledge, methods, materials, and if applicable, constituent parts (themselves technics) used in making a certain kind of technic"; (3) technology as a distinctive form or kind of human cultural activity, just as art, law, medicine, sport, and religion are often used to refer to distinctive forms of human practice; and (4) technology as the complex of knowledge, people, skills organizations, facilities, technics, physical resources, methods, and technologies that, taken together and in relationship to one another, are devoted to their search, development, production, and operation of technics.[11] For present purposes, it is important to keep in mind, as Harvey Brooks states, that "Technology does not consist of artifacts but of public knowledge that underlies the artifacts and the way they can be used in society."[12] From this vantage point, the term technology can be applied to a wide range of human endeavors. Brooks argues, in fact, that the activity of management can be characterized as a technology, "insofar as it can be described by fully specifiable rules ... and indeed a very large bureaucratic organization can be considered an embodiment of technology just as much as a piece of machinery."[13] In a similar vein, Bernard Gendron states, "A technology is any systematized practical knowledge, based on experimentation and/or scientific theory, which enhances the capacity of society to produce goods and services, and which is embodied in productive skills, organization or machinery."[14] Thus, as William Lowrance observes, technology should be seen as "disembodied knowledge and technical art, not just as hardware."[15] Social mechanisms are designed to foster technological development and application. Langdon Winner declares, "Consciously or not, deliberately or inadvertently, societies choose structures for technologies that influence how people are going to work, communicate, travel, consume, and so forth over a long period of time."[16] One key distinction between science and technology is that the outputs of technology are technics and technic-related intellectual constructs, while the output of science is theory-related knowledge of nature, including humans and their individual and social activities and behaviors.

It is especially critical to recognize that the modern linkage of science and technology occurred contemporaneously with the initial large-scale exploitation of African peoples. This is, of course, no mere coincidence for, as Tomovic reminds us, "The social structure of the world in the mid-eighteenth century shaped the basic features of modern technology, i.e., a high level of concentration of global decision power."[17] This origin fuels a contemporary dynamic whereby different people are differentially situated and possess unequal degrees of power as well as unequal levels of awareness. The dominant role of large corporations leads to circumstances in which "choices tend to become strongly fixed in material equipment, economic investment, and social habit, [such that] the original flexibility vanishes for all practical purposes

once the initial commitments are made."[18] In the modern era, then, the social goals that shaped technological development have included mass production, profit optimization, abuse of natural resources, and the development of management technologies. McGinn observes that "the dominant role played by technology in contemporary society is that of helping corporations survive and increase their profits, something assumed to translate into substantial benefits for society at large."[19]

Consistent with the emphasis within African American Studies on the agency of people of African descent rather than their oppression, African American Studies approaches to the study of science and technology are centered on several principles that Adam Banks proposes. First, African American Studies specialists emphasize that African Americans have demanded "full access to and participation in American society *and* its technologies on their own terms and [have worked] to transform both the society and its technologies, to ensure that not only Black people but all Americans can participate as full partners."[20] Second, to examine fully how African Americans have transformed technologies to meet their own needs, it is necessary to ask, "What cultural retentions do African Americans and other people of color bring to the technologies that they use?"[21] Third, consistent with the focus on using knowledge to improve the quality of life and empowering people to control their own destinies in African American Studies, the ideal approach would involve lay people in the effort to redesign the textual, physical, and virtual spaces they occupy rather than their relying on the presumed expertise of technological elites.[22]

The Significance of Future Studies

Two of the critical questions raised by the increasing control of technological innovations by corporations are: (1) What alternatives could generate more egalitarian outcomes? and (2) Why are people of African descent especially vulnerable to exploitation by corporate-controlled technological innovations? Such questions are most effectively addressed using the investigative tools of Future Studies. Wendell Bell notes, "The purposes of Future Studies are to discover or invent, examine and evaluate, and propose possible, probable, and preferable futures."[23]

Timothy Jenkins and Khafra Om-Ra Seti present a culture-specific Future Studies analysis in *Black*

9

Futurists in the Information Age. Affirming the assessment of McGinn, these authors identify multinational corporations as key actors shaping scientific and technological possibilities. They observe, "The loss of employment opportunities for unskilled, or even skilled labor as it has been known traditionally, promises a worldwide shift in unemployment and employability likely to be catastrophic to certain segments of the black workforce, and threatens Depression-like conditions."[24] Their study is described as "a wake-up call to technicians and non-technicians alike, to become vitally concerned with the sweeping technological undercurrents radically and silently changing the demographics of the future."[25] The technological innovations they predict will come into widespread usage during the twenty-first century include holographic imagery (three dimensional photographic images), virtual reality (computer simulated environments and models), advances in superconductivity that will enable highspeed levitated trains and ships, and hypersonic air travel.

Jenkins and Om-Ra Seti declare, "Black people need to understand that this is clearly the time to make dramatic changes in response to the enormous implications of these expected future developments [and] ... to develop strategic plans, hold conferences, and strongly consider reengineering many of our current organizations in order to fully participate in what we consider to be a period of incredible change."[26] Africana Studies specialists agree with this assessment and assert that in order to engage the future it is first necessary to understand how science and technology have been used historically, and currently, to suppress people of African descent and secondly to examine alternative liberating technological applications that Blacks have attempted to develop and implement.

Science, Technology, and the Oppression of African Americans

The typical assessment of the impact of Western science and technology on people of African descent begins with an examination of how Europeans used advances in military and transportation technologies in the seventeenth and eighteenth centuries to institutionalize the Atlantic slave trade. In the late eighteenth century, the cotton gin emerged as a major technological innovation in the US and served as a "powerful impetus to the expansion and consolidation of the Southern slave-based plantation system."[27]

An authentic historical perspective informed by African American Studies on scientific and technological impacts would link the exploitation of Africans arising from the invention of the cotton gin directly to subsequent patterns of exploitation. The plantation system relied heavily on enslaved craftsmen to construct buildings and other structures. Blacks were involved in designing many of the plantations throughout the Confederacy.

The post-Civil War experiences of African Americans were shaped jointly by the institution of sharecropping and a major technological revolution in agriculture during the 1880s. The invention of reapers, combines, and tractors made the operation of small farms uneconomical and led to the expulsion of huge numbers of Black sharecroppers from farmlands. At the same time, the sharecropping system ensured that African Americans would be unable to accumulate sufficient human and financial capital to participate equitably in the emerging industrial order. Increasing industrialization, the organization of trade unions in the North that excluded Blacks, and the economic depression that doomed Reconstruction largely eliminated the independent Black artisan. The demise of Black landowners in the aftermath of Reconstruction restricted opportunities for Black craftsmen and contributed to the demise of African Americans in the work of designing spaces.[28]

Various firearm and military technologies were used to reduce the likelihood that Blacks would attempt violent forms of resistance. Prohibitions against the sale of cheap handguns first appeared in the South following the Civil War. In several Deep South states, specific bans on the possession of arms by Blacks that originated in the slavery era were still enforced after the Civil War.

The forced exodus of Blacks from southern agriculture precipitated large-scale migration to northern urban areas undergoing industrial transformation. As noted in Chapter 7, Black migrants were relegated to the lowest status and most dangerous industrial jobs. This pattern of linkage to the industrial order established the terms on which African Americans would be connected to the ongoing post-industrial transformation. The transformation, as suggested previously, is currently generating disproportionate blue-collar job losses for African Americans.

In southern coastal cities where Blacks provided cheap labor, they were forced to live in areas most prone to storm damage and subject to the least well-designed technological applications to pre-vent flooding and related catastrophes. David Brooks relates, for example, how the hurricane that killed six thousand people in Galveston, Texas, in 1900 exposed racial animosities very similar to those that erupted in the wake of Hurricane Katrina. Following the Galveston storm, Blacks were falsely accused by the press of cutting off the fingers of corpses to steal wedding rings, a gross misrepresentation comparable to the depictions of looting by Blacks that dominated mainstream media reports in the wake of Hurricane Katrina.[29] Brooks also describes how the great Mississippi flood of 1927 led to the intense subjugation of Blacks. Reminiscent of the circumstances at the Super-dome in New Orleans in 2005, Blacks were rounded up into work camps, held by armed guards, and pre-vented from leaving as the waters rose. Brooks writes, "A steamer, the Capitol, played 'Bye Bye Blackbird' as it sailed away, [and t]he racist violence that followed the floods helped persuade many Blacks to move north."[30] In the aftermath of the 1927 flood, Brooks reports, "civic leaders intentionally flooded poor and middle-class areas to ease the water's pressure on the city, and then reneged on promises to compensate those whose homes were destroyed."[31]

Segregation and Social Control

The preceding discussion of the historical backdrop of the Hurricane Katrina catastrophe highlights the long-standing tradition of using technology and public pol-icy to control residential options available to African Americans.

As urban segregation intensified in the twenti-eth century, new policies were necessary to ensure technological superiority in firearms to quash rebel-lions. On June 1–2, 1921, Whites attacked the Black community of Tulsa, Oklahoma, with widespread mob violence. During the course of the conflagra-tion, both cars and airplanes were used in an all-out assault against Black citizens. Bombs dropped from planes caused extensive property damage and loss of life. Forty-four blocks of property were destroyed in the conflagration. In all, nearly seventy Blacks and twenty Whites lost their lives.[32] Military-style assaults on Black communities is not simply a past historical problem, as evidenced by the MOVE confrontation with Philadelphia police during the administration of Wilson Goode (a Black Mayor). John Africa founded what was to become MOVE in 1972 as the "Christian

Movement for Life." MOVE's ideology centered on ecological harmony including a return to a hunter-gatherer society. The group also rejected modern sci-ence, medicine, and technology. Members changed their surnames to Africa to demonstrate reverence for their continent of origin.[33] On May 13, 1985, the Phila-delphia Police Department, aided by military advisors, staged an early-morning assault on the headquarters of the MOVE organization. The raid was precipitated by complaints from neighbors regarding loud broad-casts of political messages and health hazards associ-ated with MOVE members' composting activities. In addition, several MOVE members were under indict-ment for various alleged offenses. Approximately ten thousand rounds of ammunition were fired at the house and a helicopter dropped a bomb on the roof. In the wake of the assault, eleven people, including five children, were killed, and only one adult MOVE mem-ber and one child in the structure survived.[34]

This vulnerability was made real by the fail-ure of Congress in 2005 to renew the ban on pur-chases of semi-automatic rifles. Assault weapons have become the weapon of choice by right-wing paramili-tary extremists. Racist paramilitary organizations that have acquired large caches of assault weapons include the Posse Comitatus, Aryan Nations, and The Order. Besides this external threat, Black communities also face increased risk of violence associated with gang turf wars connected to the drug trade. Assault weap-ons have become increasingly popular among gangs and individuals involved in dealing (slinging) drugs.[35] The threat posed by the presence of assault weapons within Black communities expands the vulnerability to violence from widespread cheap handguns. Hand-guns are used not only by criminal elements, but also by partners in domestic disputes and by neighbors engaged in arguments. Self-destructive patterns are reinforced by a judicial system that issues light sen-tences in cases involving Black-on-Black crime. With such grim realities, Black communities confront a quandary in trying to control the many forces that threaten to tear them apart from within (with exter-nal encouragement) and in developing self-protection mechanisms against external physical violence, while still creating conditions for long-term social stability and economic development.

The continuing vulnerability of Black communi-ties to violent assaults is partly a consequence of the segregation of poor Blacks into clearly identifiable

9

areas and the traditional design of public housing complexes that facilitate social control. As Leslie Weisman observes, "Public buildings that spatially segregate or exclude certain groups, or relegate them to spaces in which they are invisible or visibly subordinate, are the direct result of a comprehensive system of social oppression, not the consequences of failed architecture or prejudiced architects ... [Many] buildings are designed and used to support ... the maintenance of social inequality."[36] Black designers have had limited success in counteracting such design practices because they have largely been excluded from involvement in the design of public housing. Although opportunities to participate in urban design projects increased in the wake of the Civil Rights Movement, the withdrawal of federal support for low- and moderate-income housing under the Reagan and Bush presidencies reduced African American architectural practice in contemporary urban design. This pattern of exclusion is problematic for African American Studies specialists because there is a massive unmet housing need and persisting underdevelopment in many inner-city areas. Approximately 12 million households pay more than half of their monthly income for rent.[37] Besides the vulnerability of poor Blacks to external control, the broader pattern of racial segregation in cities creates an environment in which most Blacks have a high probability of experiencing policy discrimination and differential access to the benefits of technology.

Even though gentrification (movement of middle-class Whites into central city areas) is occurring in many cities, the experience of Black suburbanites suggests that the desegregated resettlement pattern is likely to be temporary and will lead, over time, to wholesale Black displacement, until formerly Black residential areas become resegregated as White residential areas. Even prior to the economic expansion of the 1990s, gentrification was occurring, and, continues to occur, in the same metropolitan areas with significant concentrations of poverty.

One of the most interesting patterns emerging from analyses of trends in poverty concentration is the substantial growth of poverty in suburban areas. Paul Jargowsky finds that in 2000 there were more poverty neighborhoods concentrated in suburban areas than in rural ones. Poverty rates increased along the outer edges of central cities and in the inner-ring suburbs of many metropolitan areas, including metropolitan

areas that experienced large declines in poverty concentration.[38] Housing vouchers and scattered-site public housing have contributed significantly to this dispersal of poverty. Under the voucher program, eligible families with a certificate or voucher find and lease a unit in the private sector and pay a portion of the rent (based on income, generally around 30 percent). The local housing authority pays the owner the remaining rent, subject to a cap referred to as "Fair Market Rent." Tenants can rent anywhere they choose and are not limited to specific complexes. Whites appear to have been more successful than nonwhites in using Section 8 vouchers away from poor and minority neighborhoods, and voucher holders in the suburbs tend to cluster in racially and economically defined neighborhoods.[39] Studies of scattered-site housing show that residents of such complexes do live in neighborhoods with higher median incomes, median housing values, median rents, and higher ownership rates.[40] However, whereas some relocated households experience improved school quality, safer neighborhoods, and improved economic opportunities, others did not reap any of these positive benefits.[41]

Racial Segregation and Surveillance

Segregation enables public officials to enhance the surveillance of both individuals and groups. Ongoing technological advances render this surveillance increasingly intrusive and a potential threat to the privacy rights of both individuals and groups. This weakening of individual rights has, unfortunately, gained a measure of social acceptance due to concerns about future terrorist attacks in the wake of the 911 tragedy. Cameras mounted on street corners constitute one of the technologies increasingly used for social surveillance. Although there may be some benefit to law enforcement, most of the time these cameras monitor people engaged in innocent and lawful activities. Such innocent activities, however, may be confidential and personally damaging if the tapes fall into the wrong hands. There is evidence that adequate controls are not in place. For example, officials in New Jersey are concerned because in several cases highway surveillance videos of freeway accidents have been posted on the YouTube website.[42]

African American Studies specialists are concerned that activists protesting racist policies are disproportionately targeted for surveillance. The New York City Police Department, for example, taped large segments of the Million Youth March in Harlem on Labor Day Weekend, 1998. Such surveillance is similar to that experienced by progressive Black activist organizations in the 1960s and 1970s under the FBI's COINTELPRO policy. Black organizations that protest against the war in Iraq and racist domestic policies are at special risk of becoming surveillance targets. In November 2003, the *New York Times* disclosed a classified FBI memo instructing state and local police officials in methods for targeting and monitoring the activities of antiwar protestors.[43]

Young African Americans who identify with hip-hop are also likely to become surveillance targets. In 2004, it was disclosed that New York City has developed a massive surveillance effort targeting hip-hop artists. The surveillance is focused presumably on uncovering criminal behavior, including drug-dealing and violence fueled by the rivalries between rappers. Using categories formulated by Adam Banks, it is important to note that the surveillance targets both the physical space claimed by hip-hoppers and the cultural space they have defined and created. Although initiated in New York, the surveillance of hip-hop artists has taken on a national character. New York City officials hosted a three-day "hip-hop training session" in May 2004 that was attended by officials from Miami, Atlanta, and Los Angeles. Reportedly, a six-inch-thick binder was distributed containing details about rappers with arrest records. The surveillance of hip-hop is becoming institutionalized, as evidenced by a special Hip-Hop Intelligence Unit in New York that (1) stakes out hotels, video shoots, and concerts; (2) scrutinizes the lyrics of songs to identify potential flash points for violent confrontations; and (3) monitors hip-hop on radio and TV stations.[44]

The New York Civil Liberties Union reported in 2006 that 3,100 surveillance cameras were operative in New York City, with many focused on people of color residing in housing projects.[45] Similar concerns were raised in Chicago by the ACLU of Illinois.[46]

The issue of the surveillance of citizens via cameras is not disconnected from the increased use of house arrest electronic monitoring by criminal justice systems. Use of such systems began in the early 1980s. After the federal crime bill calling for more alternatives to incarceration passed in 1994, use of electronic monitoring expanded significantly, with some 1,500 programs and 95,000 electronic monitoring units in existence at the beginning of 1998.[47] Such units are

typically used in cases involving individuals on pretrial status, home detention, probation, and parole, as well as in juvenile detention. GPS technology has greatly enhanced the capacity of this incarceration technology. It allows accurate, 24-hour monitoring of an individual's presence in the home. Authorities can trace activities for an entire day and pinpoint an offender's location at any given time. The tracking device can be programmed to specify "inclusion zones," where the person should be at a certain time (such as, home or work), and "exclusion zones" or "hot zones," where the person is not allowed to be (such as, near the home of a person the offender abused in a domestic violence incident).[48] By 2007, it was estimated that approximately 130,000 electronic monitoring units were deployed daily in the United States.

Racial Medical Experimentation

The relatively impersonal surveillance protocols discussed above have an equally ominous counterpart, namely medical experimentation on Black bodies. Harriet Washington has carefully documented examples of "experimental abuse and exploitation of African Americans from the first encounters in the New World through the post-Civil War era."[49] Washington argues that "Enslavement could not have existed and certainly could not have persisted without medical science."[50] She further maintains that "physicians were also dependent upon slavery, both for economic security and for the enslaved 'clinical material' that fed the American medical research and medical training that bolstered physicians' professional advancement."[51] Such experiments have had a long-lasting impact on how African Americans relate to institutionalized health care. Washington observes, "As African Americans came to learn of the experiments ... these experiments fed an aversion to the health system. They also harmed the community of African Americans by strengthening a perception of them as appropriate human fodder for research."[52]

Ironically, rather than recognizing the racism inherent in the involuntary use of Black bodies for medical experimentation, some researchers contend that Blacks were responsible for their own illnesses. This logic supported the view that experimental remedies were necessary to correct diseases caused by Blacks' inherent physical flaws, so "if an experimental procedure was painful or dangerous, the logic went, blacks had only themselves to blame, not the

9

surgeon."[53] This line of argument constituted an early form of the "blame the victim" rationale for racist policies that persists to this day. The view that Black bodies were expendable and did not warrant protection by public authorities was not restricted to the medical profession. As described by William Darity, several researchers actively involved in the American Economic Association during its formative years subscribed to the view that African Americans would eventually face extinction as a consequence of genetic deficiencies and social maladjustments. Proponents of this view refused to discard the underlying assumptions of Black genetic inferiority, even after demographic trends contradicted the predictions associated with this "Black Disappearance Hypothesis."[54]

The most infamous historical example of the use of African Americans as involuntary subjects in medical research is the so-called Tuskegee Experiment. In essence, the experiment involved the deliberate denial of treatment for syphilis to approximately four hundred African American men and their families in the Tuskegee, Alabama, area from 1930 to 1970. The experiment was conducted under the auspices of the Public Health Service. As noted by James Jones, "The Tuskegee Study had nothing to do with treatment. No new drugs were tested, neither was any effort made to establish the efficacy of old forms of treatment. It was a non-therapeutic experiment, aimed at compiling data on the spontaneous evolution of syphilis on black males."[55]

Institutionalized racism shaped the conceptualization of this experiment. The study's goal was to prove that presumed genetic differences in brain complexity between European Americans and African Americans would produce different physiological effects from advanced syphilitic infections. Specifically, it was hypothesized that, in the advanced stages, syphilis would attack the brains of European Americans. However, because the brains of African Americans were presumed to be genetically inferior, it was expected that the manifestations of advanced syphilis infections in Blacks would be observed in the muscular system. Even after it was clear that the hypotheses were inaccurate, the experiment was continued.

The Tuskegee Experiment has been one of many negative experiences with medical, scientific, and technological research that has contributed to tremendous apprehension among African Americans about their use as guinea pigs and the possibility of their being targets of genocidal policies. This fear has been projected in African American popular culture in a variety of ways. The creation legend propagated by Elijah Muhammad, of the Nation of Islam, attributed the emergence of the so-called Caucasian race to mutations resulting from biological experiments conducted by Yakub, "the big-head scientist." In *Message to the Blackman*, Elijah Muhammad asserts that Yakub "learned his future from playing with steel. It is steel and more steel that this made race (the white race), are still playing with."[56]

Frances Cress Welsing and other commentators have suggested that the fear of biological annihilation through genetic exchange is the foundation for much of the biological experimentation and general efforts to segregate African Americans.[57] The claim has also been advanced that the AIDS virus is a laboratory creation designed to annihilate people of African descent. Such speculations regarding conspiracies to use African Americans for biological experiments were reignited in the early 1990s by a controversy over a proposed "violence initiative" that was to be sponsored through the National Institutes of Health. The study was to be designed to identify young Black children between ages five and nine with genetic markers that presumably create a disposition for violence. One component of this project was a conference on "Genetic Factors in Crime: Findings, Uses and Implications" that was to be held at the University of Maryland in October 1993. Other agencies involved in the proposed research included the National Institute of Mental Health and the Centers for Disease Control.[58] The research focused on the role of the chemical serotonin in inducing violent behavior. Presumably, serotonin is associated with "prefrontal" changes in the brain that correlate with later tendencies toward violent behavior. One of the philosophical tenets underlying the study was that the focus of policies and programs designed to curb violence should be on defective individuals rather than on the underlying social causes. These defective individuals, according to this view, must be seen as suffering from genetic disorders that require special treatment. Planning for this project was shelved by the public outcry that arose once the initiative was exposed to the media by the Center for the Study of Psychiatry.

Although public scrutiny provides some protection from the victimization of civilians by medical researchers, the same is not true for prison inmates. Incarcerated Blacks are at distinct risk of becoming unwitting subjects in medical experiments. Prison authorities have access to a variety of medications to immobilize inmates. These vary from psychotropic drugs, such as anti-depressants, sedatives, and tranquillizers, to powerful hypnotics. Drugs employed as the chemical equivalents of strait jackets have become increasingly controversial as prison populations rise and larger numbers of inmates are "treated."

The most egregious recent example of racial experimentation with continuing implications for African Americans is the case of Henrietta Lacks, a Black tobacco farmer from southern Virginia, who was diagnosed with cervical cancer when she was 30. A doctor at Johns Hopkins Hospital extracted a sample of her tumor without her consent, and these cells proved to be the first human cells that did not die when grown in a laboratory. The HeLa cell line (named for Henrietta) was essential to developing the polio vaccine and subsequently in a variety of important research accomplishments, including cloning, gene mapping and in vitro fertilization. The scientists engaged in research using these cells undertook deliberate actions to obscure the origin of these cells and Lacks' identity did not become public until the 1970s. Lacks died in Baltimore in 1951, having received no compensation for the unsanctioned use of her body product. Moreover, her family has not benefited economically or socially from the cell line; when the story received national attention, it was reported that the family did not have adequate healthcare.[59]

Historical Liberating Uses of Science and Technology

As noted in the first chapter, one of the distinguishing characteristics of African American Studies is the systematic examination of how people of African descent have attempted to combat oppression. In the context of science and technology, this requires an exploration of how people of African descent have adapted modern science and technology creatively to further liberation objectives.

Traditional African Technologies

The conventional wisdom on both ancient Africa and modern Africa projects images of the continent with pre-industrial, underdeveloped African villages using low technologies to produce the means of subsistence. Contemporary problems in Africa are defined from this vantage point, as underdevelopment resulting from a lack of technological development. As a corollary, African Americans are implicitly treated as a population that was involuntarily forced to function in a technologically advanced culture. This traditional view of African peoples has, however, been challenged increasingly by a body of research that has sought to uncover a record of the development of "high" technologies that both preceded and paralleled "low" technologies. Ancient Egypt was the predominant example of a highly-technological African society that produced advances in navigation and exploration, astronomy, aeronautics, medicine, and mathematics. Technological advancement in areas, such as, steel-making and astronomy—purported to equal or exceed the technology produced much later in Europe and in the United States—have also been identified in other parts of ancient Africa.[60]

The hypothesis of African high technology "loss" is that it was the direct result of early European invasions, and the later invasions associated with the era of slavery and the slave trade. The demand for large numbers of Africans for enslavement presumably led to an intensity of efforts to capture Africans near large population centers, where high technology was also concentrated. Disruption of these centers would, then, not only abort the diffusion of high technology to the hinterlands, but also destroy indigenous capacity for technological development. Effective resistance to the European invasion was not possible because of the relative underdevelopment of weapons technologies in Africa.[61] Although the indigenous capacity for technological development in African societies was decimated by the European invasion, enslaved Africans brought critical agricultural, communication, and other technologies to the West that were integrated into the general technological repertoire. For example, the development of large-scale rice production in South Carolina resulted directly from the transfer of technology from West Africa by enslaved Africans.

9

Commemorating Victims of Enslavement

The traditions, customs, procedures, mourning practices, burial rites, and cemetery configurations of African Americans reflect both traditional African beliefs and practices as well as adaptations resulting from experiences in the Western hemisphere. The 1991 discovery in lower Manhattan of what has come to be known as the African Burial Ground has provided a unique window on how people of African descent both endured the holocaust of enslavement and commemorated its victims. The skeletal remains of 419 Africans have been recovered, examined, and re-interred in the memorial. As described in the US Park Services' Management Report, "The African Burial Ground demonstrates how individuals, singly and collectively, can create lives that transcend the inhumanity of forced immigration and enslavement, the burdens of the harshest labor, and the repression of cherished cultural and societal practices."[62] The Burial Ground was used for at least 100 years and the report notes that "The site held spiritual, social, and cultural meaning for this predominantly enslaved population."[63] Analysis of remains has revealed that "Individuals between the ages of nine and sixteen showed high stress that perhaps can be linked directly to the slave trade, as this was the prime age range for individuals subjected to enslavement and the trans-Atlantic passage."[64]

There is also evidence that infant and childhood health were worse for individuals born in New York than those born in Africa who died as adults in New York. This finding documents the oppressive conditions experienced during enslavement. Mothers were discovered who were buried with newborn or stillborn babies, documenting the importance of family and inter-generational cultural transmission. The report discusses how funerals offered a chance to express cultural identity in a relatively unsupervised context: "Even though laws prohibited customary night funerals and gatherings of large numbers of Africans, the evidence from the burial ground indicates that it continued as a focus of community identity for nearly a hundred years."[65]

African American funerary practices have clearly evolved in many ways over the years. Harking back to the era of enslavement, death was, and still is, often seen as an escape from misery, particularly for followers of Christianity. In some locales, such as New Orleans, parades with elaborate costumes and fun-filled jazz music became part of funerary tradition. Ironically, African American funerary traditions are being challenged increasingly, as small Black-owned funeral homes that have been managed by single families for generations are being bought by large conglomerates. This has resulted in the diminution of unique African American cultural funerary practices.[66]

Ironically, efforts are currently underway to create a memorial just outside of New Orleans for formerly enslaved African Americans. The two cemeteries in question contain the remains of more than 300 persons and are located on land that once constituted sugar plantations. Other long-forgotten burial sites used by Blacks have been located in Dallas, Texas, and Charleston, South Carolina.[67]

The Struggle for Freedom

A significant, but controversial, historical example of the use of technology to promote liberation is the employment of codes in quilts to provide guidance for enslaved Blacks attempting to escape to the North. As Adam Banks reminds us, "African American quilts helped slaves on the underground railroad by acting as maps of lands surrounding plantations, charting routes and distances to safe houses, including the distances between them, and advice on how to navigate those routes."[68] Although basic information about this practice has existed for some time, Jacqueline Tobin and Raymond Dobard have provided previously unknown details about Underground Railroad quilt patterns.[69] According to Ozella McDaniel Williams, in information provided to Tobin and Dobard, ten quilts were used to direct escaping slaves to take particular actions. Each quilt contained a particular pattern and was placed one at a time on a fence. As described by Williams, part of the code contained the following instructions: "There are five square knots on the quilt every two inches apart. They escaped on the fifth knot on the tenth pattern and went to Ontario, Canada. The monkey wrench turns the wagon wheel toward Canada on a bear's paw to the crossroads."[70]

It is important to acknowledge that there is still controversy among historians and scholars regarding whether or not escaping slaves actually used codes concealed within quilt patterns to follow the escape routes of the Underground Railroad. The case for the use of the codes is based on stories passed down through generations. Patricia Cummings is the leading skeptic in the forefront of challenging the quilt code theory.[71]

Whether or not the quilt code theory is accurate, it is significant that these quilts have now become collector's items of high value. This transformation reflects the process by which Blacks, and particularly Black women, have modified an indigenous technology—that previously provided a particular type of collective benefit—to another use that generates value within the context of contemporary social and commercial practices.

Navigating Industrialization and Urbanization

The pattern of oppression Africans in America experienced included mechanisms to appropriate technological innovations by African Americans. However, when the creative energies of African Americans were unleashed following the end of slavery, mastery of technological knowledge was evident. As both the westward expansion and industrial transformation proceeded, the perception of new opportunities to benefit from developing technological innovations spurred creative activity among African Americans. Unfortunately, the subordinate political status of Blacks and limited access to capital prevented innovators from transforming ideas into enterprises that could have a major impact on the collective development of Black communities. At least one inventor, Granville Woods, attempted to resist this pattern of absorption by major corporations. He refused Edison's attempts to hire him and instead formed the independent Woods Electric Company. In the end, however, Woods was forced to sell important patents to American Bell Telephone, Westinghouse, and General Electric between 1885 and 1900.[72] Woods' experience was typical of the pattern of discrimination and exclusion that has characterized the efforts of African Americans to participate in shaping the contours of modern science and technology, rather than simply becoming victims or passive consumers.

Blacks encountered similar resistance in efforts to capitalize on emergent automobile transportation technologies during the early twentieth century. As Charles Johnson states, in the early days of the automobile, Blacks "were expected to operate automobiles for Whites, but not to own them."[73] Yet, historically, a small group of Black inventors and entrepreneurs not only owned cars in the 1910s and the 1920s, but

took advantage of their automotive skill to run driving schools for chauffeurs and even start their own automotive companies. One of the main reasons that African Americans were attracted to the automobile was that it provided an opportunity to avoid Jim Crow segregation on trains and street cars.[74] In addition, automobiles offered a springboard into the middle class for some African Americans as chauffeuring, and, later, jitney services became a way for Black mechanics and drivers to own their own businesses and to achieve status comparable to that of Pullman porters. During the early era of the automobile, Blacks were able to own and control a large percentage of the taxicab business throughout the country, as well as a large proportion of garage and repair shop business.[75] However, Black automotive experts of the 1920s and the 1930s were largely ignored by the White automotive press and mainstream motor travel authorities, and the exclusion of Blacks from the migration to the suburbs limited long-term gains from these early successes.

Over time, the liberatory relationship between African Americans and the automobile increasingly shifted to one in which the automobile became both an indicator of, and a contributing factor to, unequal access to employment, goods, and services. Overall, approximately 19 percent of African Americans lack access to automobiles. The comparable figures for Latinos and Whites are 13.7 and 4.6 percent, respectively.[76] The problem is even more pronounced among poor African Americans. John Pucher and John Renne report that 33 percent of low-income African Americans lack access to an automobile. This is not simply a problem in inner-cities.[77] As noted by Alexandra Cawthorne, "the lack of a personal vehicle and limited access to efficient public transportation is a significant barrier to employment for poor people in many suburban communities."[78] According to Cawthorne, in such communities, lack of access to an automobile is especially problematic because "low-income families also need transportation to access supportive services, which are typically dispersed throughout a wide area."[79] The problems created by lack of access to an automobile are exacerbated by limited public transportation options. The Leadership Conference Education Fund insists that the lack of public transportation options hampers efforts to reduce poverty because "three out of five jobs that are suitable for welfare-to-work participants are not accessible by public transportation."[80]

9

The dire implications of lack of automobile access were grimly apparent in the wake of Hurricane Katrina. Alan Berube, Elizabeth Deakin, and Steven Raphael relate that "The evacuation failure in New Orleans was compounded by the racial segregation of the New Orleans metropolitan area. Given that most black households resided in predominantly black areas, black households without cars were physically surrounded by neighbors without cars, rendering an evacuation strategy based on private transportation particularly ineffective."[81] The circumstances that amplified the Katrina catastrophe are not unique. Research conducted by Meizhu Lui, Emma Dixon, and Betsy Leondar-Wright reveals that people of color in all eleven major cities that have experienced five or more hurricanes in the last 100 years disproportionately lack access to cars.[82] Moreover, survey data collected in the wake of Hurricane Katrina revealed that 27 percent of African Americans would be unable to obey an immediate evacuation order during a disaster due to lack of transportation. Thirty-three percent of Latinos and 23 percent of Whites indicated the same vulnerability.[83]

In some ways, the manner in which African Americans are disadvantaged by the lack of access to automobiles and reliable public transportation has been masked by the visibility of examples of conspicuous displays of ownership of expensive cars. The celebration of practices such as "ride Pimping" (the garish customization of vehicles, including spinner rims and lavish sound systems), reinforces the traditional stereotypes, often used by racist politicians to attack anti-poverty efforts, that project Blacks as owners of expensive cars that they cannot afford.

Clothing and Style

Clothing traditions among African Americans also reflect efforts to balance concerns of appearance and functionality. There is an ongoing fascination with "bling" and exotic clothing, including the urban attire associated with hip hop lifestyles. This emphasis on highly distinctive visual representations as a statement of strength in the face of oppressive conditions is a long-standing tradition. As described by Monica Miller, "Black people are known for 'stylin' out,' dressing to the nines, showing their sartorial stuff, especially when the occasion calls for it and, more tellingly, often when it does not."[84] One of the most ironic historical examples of this tradition is the use of some

enslaved boys as displays of wealth in part by dressing them in highly adorned costumes.[85]

It is important, however, to understand that these instances were far from typical. Slave traders regularly deprived West Africans of their clothes during the Middle Passage, and survivors were forced to find new ways to meet clothing needs and create distinctive styles.[86] In the words of Shane White and Graham White, African Americans successfully fashioned clothing out of adversity in ways that "made the lives of African Americans during the time of their enslavement bearable."[87] African American studies specialists should incorporate discussions of Black clothing traditions to help cultivate informed consumers who can successfully navigate the contemporary commercialization of fashion and attire that saps scarce community resources.

Food Production and Security

Slavery unquestionably created almost insurmountable food security problems for African Americans. Robert Fogel insists "excess death rates of children under 5 ... accounted for nearly all the difference between the overall death rates of U.S. slaves and U.S. whites during the late antebellum era."[88] Fogel also contends that the available evidence indicates that surviving infants were disproportionately undersized and the fact that small babies failed "to exhibit much catch up growth between birth and age 3 suggest chronic undernourishment during these ages."[89] Infants' postnatal problems originated with the malnourishment of pregnant women, who were subjected to "the intense routine of the gang system down to the eve of childbirth"[90] Pregnant women were not provided with nutritional supplementation that might have compensated for such high levels of physical activity. As a consequence, they generally failed to achieve sufficient weight gains "that would [normally] yield average birth weights and forestall infant death rates."[91] Although Fogel does not make the logical connection, surviving Black infants suffered short-term and long-term complications as a result of pre-natal and post-natal nutritional deficiencies. These conditions included impaired learning skills and chronic health problems.

Faced with these horrific conditions, African Americans exhibited remarkable creativity in adapting the historical food production technologies employed in traditional African societies. Many ingredients used in traditional African American cooking are indigenous to African culture, including okra, meat jerky, greens, yams (sweet potatoes in America), peanuts, rice, onions, sesame seeds, coffee, black-eyed peas, shea butter, watermelon, hot peppers, bananas, coconut, and cornmeal. African food preparation methods adapted in the US include: making stews that require long simmering periods and the use of large iron pots; communal cooking; combining fruit and meat in main dishes; and deep-frying meat and vegetables. The holocaust of enslavement necessitated the development of innovations to make use of all portions of animals' feet, brains, snout, and intestines (chitterlings); eating foods that are high in calories in order to acquire enough energy to work all day in the fields; and eating the wildlife of the region and using vegetables and fruit from gardens.[92]

Having been built on the tradition of rural agriculture, the career of George Washington Carver suggests the outlines of a model for specialists who seek to harness the potential of science and technology to foster holistic development for people of African descent. Ironically, Carver achieved national prominence for his work at Tuskegee Institute, located in the same environs as the infamous Tuskegee experiment discussed previously. Carver's research program was developed as an organic extension of the lived experiences of Black farmers in rural Alabama. He encouraged farmers to grow peanuts, sweet potatoes, and soybeans in an effort to reduce overdependence on cotton cultivation. Carver used his chemurgical skills to develop approximately three hundred consumer products from the peanut, one hundred from sweet potatoes, and seventy-five from the pecan in an effort to generate markets for these alternative crops. These products included adhesives, ink, shampoo, shaving cream, wood stain, food additives, and dehydrated foods. The sweet potato flour that he developed was used as military rations during World War II. One of the most impressive dimensions of Carver's achievements was that he refused to exploit his products for personal gain, insisting that he was simply executing his social responsibility to humanity.[93] African American Studies seeks to recultivate this type of selfless commitment to community and human progress among future members of the African American technological elite.

To some extent the contemporary efforts of the National Organization of Professional Black Natural Resources Conservation Service Employees builds on Carver's legacy of extending the efforts of Black farmers by providing access to modern technology. This group is attempting to address the problem of African American farmers and ranchers with limited resources who have made very little progress in reducing soil erosion and loss of wetlands. The organization, in partnership with the National Resource Conservation Service, conservation districts, Black land-grant institutions, and state and local conservation agencies, is attempting to stabilize Black farmers' land loss, increase agricultural productivity, keep agriculture profitable, and improve the environment, in part, by encouraging the use of low-cost initial conservation measures as a means of improving natural resource and environmental assets.[94]

In many respects, Carver's efforts were a forerunner to the Appropriate Technology Movement that originated in England in the early 1960s as an alternative strategy for international economic development. Proponents advocate technologies that are small in scale, democratically controllable, low in capital commitment, environmentally sustainable, and adaptable to local cultural conditions. Efforts to transplant the ideas into the American context have focused on the development of democratic and sustainable technologies that avoid excessive machinery and financial outlays.[95]

Architecture and Design

Black architects and designers also used their knowledge of design and technology to enhance the quality of life in African American communities. The establishment of HBCUs following the Civil War provided some unique design opportunities for Black architects. Black architects were also regularly called on to produce designs for Black churches. In 1941, the War Department awarded a $4.2 million contract to the Black firm McKissack & McKissack for construction of the Tuskegee Airbase.[96]

Greater contemporary involvement of African Americans as developers and disseminators of technologies appropriate for African American communities is desired, not because it will enhance societal integration, but because they can serve as protectors of their communities of origin. African American Studies specialists are generally opposed to technologies of acculturation and seek to develop and enhance technologies of cultural preservation, empowerment, and adaptation. At the same time, there is a simultaneous

9

need both to monitor and to engage "high technologies" in critical areas where rapid innovations in science and technology have the potential for unprecedented impacts on the lives of people of African descent.

Information Technology and the "Digital Divide"

Timothy Jenkins and Khafra Om-Ra Seti cogently observe that the "new information and communications revolution could easily bypass the minority communities of America, very much like the infamous interstate highways of old, providing few or no meaningful access ramps, unless they are carefully designed into the plans taking place now."[97] Extending this metaphor, they proclaim, "Indeed it has been graphically suggested that left to their own devices, minorities are most likely to be the major road kill of the Information Superhighway, with jobs flowing abroad, while those remaining in the country have unreachable high-tech entry requirements or offer a new form of house-bound bondage without hard-won worker fringe benefits or job security."[98] To document their case, the authors reviewed recent developments in computer technology, semiconductor technology, microchip design, laser beam technology and fiber optics, and optical disc technologies.

The existence and implications of a "digital divide" has captured the attention of technology analysts and important Black political leaders. In 2000, Rep. Maxine Waters (D-CA), declared: "Until we eradicate the divide that is growing between those who have access to the Net and those who do not have access, we must press on. We cannot afford to leave behind any of our children in this Information Age. Failure to bridge the gap will relegate our sons and daughters to sit in the backseat of the technology train on the Information Superhighway."[99]

The basic circumstances described in Waters' declaration are not in dispute, although the gap is declining. Whereas Black students were 16 percent less likely than White students to use a computer in school in 1984, the disparity had fallen to 6 percent by 1997. However, during the same period, Black and Hispanic students still lagged behind in using the latest technology in school, and their teachers were less prepared to use the latest technology.[100] Poor schools with predominantly minority students have twice as many students per computer, on average, as middle-class White schools. In addition, among students without a computer in the home, White students are much more likely than African American students to have used the World Wide Web, and also more likely to have accessed the Web at locations other than home, work, or school—at libraries, friends' houses, and community access points.[101] At the collegiate level, one study using late-1990s data found that 90 percent of private college freshman were using the Internet to conduct research and 80 percent regularly used e-mail. In contrast, the comparable usage rates for freshman at public HBCUs were 78 and 41 percent.[102] To bridge the gap, the Congressional Black Caucus has proposed that the federal government buy computers and provide computer access for disadvantaged Americans and offer cash grants to fund the training necessary to use computers effectively.[103]

Although the proposed initiatives could have a major impact on bridging the digital divide in urban areas, it is important to realize that the digital divide increasingly is not just between those who have computers and those who do not; even more, it is a divide between those who have low-cost high-speed Internet access and associated educational and entertainment options, and those who do not. Bridging the digital divide is especially challenging in rural areas, in part because rural schools tend to have the least funding and at present are less likely to have broadband access than other schools. Because satellite TV systems have limited bandwidth, satellite TV companies can only offer a certain number of TV channels to customers.[104]

Caution regarding differential access and outcomes in rural areas can be usefully extended to urban areas. African American Studies specialists and their allies must work to prevent the dumping of cheap Internet technologies on low-income and/or inner-city populations in a manner that leads to the "dumbing down" of the technology. African American Studies specialists can use the criteria suggested by Adam Banks to evaluate the types of access that are available. Banks reminds us that "for material access to have any effect on people's lives or on their participation in society, they must also have the knowledge and skills necessary to use those tools effectively," that is, they must have functional access.[105] However, even functional access is not sufficient: "Beyond the tools themselves and the knowledge and skills necessary for their effective use, people must actually use them; they must have experiential access, or an access that makes the tools a relevant part of their lives."[106]

The Community Technology Center program established during the Clinton administration is the major publicly-funded initiative to address the digital divide. The purpose of this program is to create and expand community technology centers that will provide disadvantaged residents of economically distressed urban and rural communities with access to information technology and related training. The program's focus is the use of technology-related instruction to improve the academic achievement of students in secondary schools. It is supported by the Community Technology Centers Network (CTCNet), a network of more than a thousand organizations committed to improving the educational, economic, cultural, and political life of their communities through technology. CTCNet provides resources and advocacy to improve the quality and sustainability of community technology centers and programs at the local, national, and international level and works together with its member organizations to provide networking, capacity building, program development, and partnership opportunities.

Black leaders throughout the US are beginning to regard CTCs as an essential part of African American communities, especially in inner cities and poverty zones. A survey of CTC users at forty-four community sites revealed that two-thirds of the users identified themselves as "non-White"—37 percent as African American. About 65 percent of the survey respondents reported taking classes at their CTC to improve their job skills, and, of 446 job seekers, 43 percent had either found a job or were closer to obtaining one.[107] Although CTCs have significant potential to address the digital divide, most CTCs are too heavily dependent on one-year government appropriations and foundation grants to develop long-term programming. Consequently, it is critical to mobilize increased public support for more permanent funding for CTCs and for multiyear grants. It is also critical to keep in mind that short-term initiatives of this type will not substitute for a comprehensive approach to the use of information technology to enhance educational outcomes. Such an approach must avoid stereotypes that hamper existing practices.

In many low-income schools, concerns about equipment damage leads to restrictions on usage. In addition, computers are more likely to be used for routine drills with limited cognitive challenge. The increased focus on high stakes testing under the No Child Left Behind (NCLB) regime further limits the educational potential of information technology by restricting the subject matter that it encompasses. Finally, teachers in schools in low-income communities generally have less training.

As noted previously, there is credible evidence that the digital divide is slowly being spanned. Whereas, in the late 1990s, White families were roughly twice as likely to own a home computer as Black families, middle-class Blacks in the US are now one of the fastest-growing segments of first-time buyers of home computers. According to a Pew Trust study, more than three and a half million African American adults went online for the first time in 2000, nearly doubling the size of the Black online population in 1999. The report indicates that 36 percent of all African American adults had Internet access in 2000, versus 23 percent in 1998. It is interesting to note that women have driven the growth of the Black Internet population. Black women are more likely to seek health, job, and religious information online, whereas men are more likely to seek sports and financial information.[108] Despite these gains, it is critical to recognize that the digital divide remains. The Pew study found that, overall, 50 percent of Whites had Internet access in 2000 compared with 36 percent of Blacks. In addition, 36 percent of Blacks with Internet access go online on a typical day, compared with 56 percent of Whites; and, 27 percent of Blacks with Internet access send or receive e-mail on a typical day compared with 49 percent of Whites.[109] Although Whites are more likely to own computers than African Americans, after taking income into account, younger, highly-educated African Americans are more likely than Whites to be working in computer-related occupations and have computer access at work.[110]

It is also important to recognize that African Americans make different use of the Internet from Whites. BlackAmericaweb.com and BlackPlanet.com are two of the most popular websites that cater specifically to African Americans. Adam Banks has conducted a detailed examination of the content and discourse on BlackPlanet and emphasizes how users of the website "keep Black discursive traditions alive."[111]

Linda Jackson and her colleagues report that African American females use the Internet more intensely and in more diverse ways than any other group. In contrast, African American males use the Internet less intensely and in fewer ways. They also found that African Americans were more likely to search for religious/spiritual information and information

9

about jobs than Whites. Moreover, even though fewer African Americans are online, they spend comparable amounts per capita on Internet shopping.[112] The authors conclude that a new digital divide has emerged that is characterized by African American females embracing information technology. African American females often surpass White males in use of the Internet, while African American males lag behind other groups with the exception of participation in playing video games.[113]

Another aspect of the new digital divide was illustrated in the shift in popularity from MySpace to Facebook described by Danah Boyd as "white flight." Boyd argues "to the degree that some viewed MySpace as a digital ghetto or as being home to the cultural practices that are labeled as ghetto, the same fear and racism that underpinned much of white flight in urban settings is also present in the perception of MySpace."[114] Cameron Marlow examined the use of Facebook by different racial/ethnic groups in 2009. He found that African Americans constituted about 6 percent of Facebook users in January 2006 compared to about 9½ percent of Internet users. By 2009, the two percentages had reached parity at slightly more than 10 percent.[115] Thus, the temporary MySpace/Facebook digital divide seems to have been bridged. It is notable that African American organizations, such as the Association for the Study of African American Life and History, have begun to use both Facebook and Twitter as communication vehicles.

African American interests are also increasingly present in the blogosphere. The Black Blogger Network currently serves as an online resource guide for Black Bloggers. Writers and journalists can post articles on the Network's website covering various topics, including increasing web presence, networking with other Black bloggers, blog-building techniques, and blog promotion.[116] The Black Weblog Awards was founded in 2005 to give recognition to Black bloggers (and those of the African Diaspora) that were largely overlooked by other Internet award events online. Black Weblog Awards annually selects the best Black bloggers in various categories including Faith Based, Fashion or Beauty, Gaming or Comics, Science or Technology, Political or News, Sports, Green Nature or Outdoor Living, Parenting, Travel, Food, Business, International, Health or Wellness, Hip Hop Blog, and Sex or Relationship.[117]

In addition to supporting bloggers focused on science and technology, political issues, international issues, and other topics of special concern to African American Studies, specialists should also explore opportunities to make more use of Facebook, Twitter, blogs, and podcasts to advance the mission of African American Studies. By increasing the use of this communication vehicle, Africana Studies organizations could become eligible for the Black Weblog Awards that recognize the best group blogs and podcasts as part of its mission.[118]

A variety of programs have been implemented in several communities that are worthy of note and support. One program focuses on providing affordable hardware and software for low-income residents coupled with instruction in how to use computers effectively. Other programs provide job training in areas that require computer literacy. Urban Ed., located in Washington, D.C., has developed a "Pathways to Prosperity" initiative that provides intensive advanced training in computer programming to low- to no-income youth and young adults.[119]

These initiatives have significant potential to connect computer use more directly to problem-solving, an apparent objective of many African American computer users. The Pew study found that online African Americans are proportionally more likely than online Whites to have searched for information about major life issues—new jobs, places to live, religious or spiritual information. At the same time, Blacks are also more likely to have sought entertainment online through music, video and audio clips, and instant messaging. Blacks under 30 years old disproportionately use the Internet for leisure activities, such as chat rooms, gaming, and use of multimedia resources.[120] A study by the Kaiser Family Foundation revealed that Black youths between 8 and 18 years old played video and computer games roughly 90 minutes a day—almost 30 minutes more than White youths. The disproportionate engagement of young Blacks with gaming, music, and video consumption is a critical public policy issue that warrants attention.

In the case of gaming, Jason Della Rocca, executive director of the International Game Developers Association observes, "Games are an expressive medium. They are an art form, just like movies, theater and literature and we're seeing, to a large extent, that the games that are being designed unconsciously include the biases, opinions, and reflections of their creators."[121] Black characters are strongly represented in sports games; however, outside of sports games, the representation of African Americans drops precipitously. African American characters are featured as gangsters and street people in games such as *Grand Theft Auto* and *50 Cent Bulletproof*.[122] The disproportionately high rate of video game play by Black boys, coupled with the manner in which African Americans are portrayed in violent video games is a matter of concern to African American Studies scholar/activists. The most current available evidence strongly suggests that exposure to violent video games, is a causal risk factor for increased aggressive behavior, aggressive cognition, and aggressive affect. In addition, such exposure is associated with decreased empathy and increased antisocial behavior.[123] In contrast to games, much of the dysfunctional imagery in music and videos is produced and perpetuated by Blacks themselves.

The Obama Administration and the Digital Divide

President Obama's Broadband Initiative constitutes an attempt to address the persisting digital divide between Blacks and Whites. According to a report issued by the Leadership Conference on Civil Rights Education Fund, teenagers who have access to home computers are 6 to 8 percentage points more likely to graduate from high school than are teenagers who do not have home computers.[124] The American Recovery and Reinvestment Act (ARRA) of 2009 appropriated $7.2 billion to the Department of Agriculture's Rural Utilities Service and the Department of Commerce's National Telecommunications Information Administration (NTIA) to invest in broadband infrastructure and access. This initiative has resulted in the creation of two programs, the most significant of which is the NTIA Broadband Technology Opportunities Program, designed to provide grants to fund broadband infrastructure, public computer centers, and sustainable broadband adoption projects.[125]

Broadband adoption by African Americans currently stands at 56 percent, up from 46 percent in 2009. This 22-percent year-over-year growth rate is well above the national average and by far the highest growth rate of any major demographic group. Over the last year, the broadband-adoption gap between Blacks and Whites has been cut nearly in half. In 2009, 65 percent of White Americans and 46 percent of Black Americans were broadband users (a 19-percentage-point gap). By contrast, in 2010, 67 percent of Whites and 56 percent of African Americans were broadband users (an 11-percentage-point gap).[126]

In the case of gaming, efforts are currently underway to increase the involvement of young African Americans in the design of video and computer games to counteract the tendency for Blacks to be portrayed as criminals. Roughly 80 percent of video game programmers are White, according to preliminary results from an International Game Developers Association survey. About 4 percent of designers are Hispanic and less than 3 percent are Black.[127] Mario Armstrong is part of a group that has started the Urban Video Game Academy, a virtual programming boot camp for "minorities."[128] African American Studies specialists with interests in this area could seek to establish a cultural education initiative in support of this effort.

It is important to recognize that increased use of information technologies also invites increased surveillance, an extension of the concerns about technological surveillance discussed previously. Spyware software, for example, can be used to collect information about a computer's hardware and software, web surfing, buying habits, passwords, e-mail addresses, and personal identification information. Surveillance spyware includes key loggers, trojans, and screen capture spyware. Such surveillance spyware is used by large companies and law enforcement agencies. The potential threats posed by this type of surveillance should serve as a reminder that, as noted by Adam Banks, "Equal access across the digital divide will always be illusory, as long as the power and poverty differential that undergirds it exists."[129]

Technology and Racial Health Disparities

Racial Health Disparities

African Studies specialists have a responsibility to examine the extent to which emergent high technologies constitute promising avenues to reduce racial health disparities, or, alternatively, new modes of social control and surveillance in the sense discussed in the previous section. Black-White health disparities have remained virtually unchanged since 1960, despite reduced gaps in housing, education, and income.

Life expectancy can be thought of as a type of composite indicator of how persons are able to navigate challenges to health over the life cycle. In 1970, life expectancy at birth for African American men was 60.0 years, and for Black females it was 68.3 years.

9

For White American males, life expectancy was 67.1 years, versus 74.7 years for females. In 2008, life expectancy for African American males had increased to 70.9 years, while life expectancy for African American females had improved to 77.4 years. The rates for White males and females also improved to 75.5 years and 80.5 years, respectively.[130] Thus, disparities in life expectancy have been reduced significantly over the last forty years. At the same time, some glaring disparities remain in causes of death and prevalence of diseases that are implicated in the persisting disparities in life expectancy. Differences in access to health care and quality of living circumstances contribute significantly to health disparities and differences in life expectancy.

Data for mortality (death) and morbidity (the incidence of a disease) are often presented in the form of rates measured as the number of occurrences per 1000 persons. This measure accounts for differences in population sizes. In examining Black-White standardized mortality ratios (SMRs), David Satcher, et al., found that SMR had changed very little between 1960 and 2000; it had actually worsened for infants and for African American men 35 years and older. Consistent with some of the trends reported in other chapters, SMR did improve for African American women. Using 2002 data, the authors estimated that the Black-White mortality gap could be eliminated and that 83,570 unnecessary deaths could be prevented each year.[131]

The infant mortality rate for African Americans was 13.59 in 2000, compared to 5.70 for European Americans. The rates for both groups had changed very little by 2006, i.e., 13.35 and 5.58, respectively. At the other end of the life cycle, age-adjusted death rates for coronary heart disease and stroke in 2006 for African Americans were 161.6 and 61.6, compared to 134.2 and 41.7 for White Americans. Homicide is a cause of death where disparities are especially large. In 2007, homicide death rates for African American males and females were, respectively, 41.4 and 6.4. The rates for White American males and females were 3.7 and 1.8, respectively. AIDS has exacted a disastrous toll on Black communities. As of 2006, the cumulative number of African Americans who have died of AIDS was 218,000. In 2006, approximately twice as many African Americans died from AIDS as White Americans (7,426 versus 3,860).[132]

Morbidity statistics provide another important perspective on health disparities. As an example, data for 2005-2008 indicate that the age-adjusted percentage of African American adults suffering from hypertension was 42.0 percent compared to 28.8 percent for White Americans. In 2004, the age-adjusted percentages of African American and White adults diagnosed with diabetes were, respectively, 10.3 and 6.7. Comparable figures for 2008 were 10.4 and 7.3 percent.

Obesity is a major risk factor associated with these and other diseases. Table 9.1 presents information regarding the prevalence of obesity for African Americans and White Americans. The data clearly indicate that obesity constitutes a major barrier to reducing health disparities among African Americans, and especially for African American females.

TABLE 9.1
PREVALENCE OF OBESITY
AFRICAN AMERICANS AND WHITE AMERICANS
2005-2008
(Percent)

Sex	Age Range	African Americans	White Americans
Female	2 – 19	24	14
	20 – 39	47	29
	40 – 59	52	37
	60 or older	55	32
Male	2 – 19	18	15
	20 – 39	37	26
	40 – 59	37	36
	60 or older	37	35

Source: National Health and Nutritional Examination Survey, United States 2005-2008.

Returning to the issue of HIV/AIDS, major disparities exist for HIV infections. In 2005, the infection rates for African American and White males were, respectively, 118.0 and 16.4. Rates for 2008 were 131.9 and 16.6, respectively. For African American and White females, the respective rates in 2005 were 56.9 and 2.8. Rates for 2008 were 56.0 and 2.9. African American females accounted for 65 percent of all new HIV/AIDS diagnoses among women in 2006 and were 23 times more likely to be diagnosed with AIDS than White women. In 2004, African Americans accounted for 70 percent of new HIV diagnoses among teenagers. African Americans represent a disproportionate share of HIV infections from injection drug use and, as a result, are more frequently co-infected with hepatitis C.

The Obama Administration and Racial Health Disparities

The preceding discussion of racial mortality and morbidity disparities provides a context for examining the response of the Obama administration. The signature legislation impacting the health status of African Americans is the Patient Protection and Affordable Care Act (PPACA), signed into law on March 23, 2010.[133] Some of the important provisions in this wide-ranging legislation include:

- prohibiting the denial of coverage for children based on pre-existing conditions;
- prohibiting insurance companies from rescinding coverage;
- establishing consumer assistance programs in the states;
- providing free preventive care;
- providing access to insurance for uninsured Americans with pre-existing conditions;
- extending coverage for young adults; and
- expanding coverage for early retirees.[134]

The potential value of these provisions for African Americans is easy to document. In 2008, for example, 19.1 percent of African Americans had no health care coverage compared to 10.8 percent of non-Hispanic White Americans.[135] This differential clearly indicates that Blacks have proportionately more to gain from expanding coverage to the uninsured and other provisions of the PPACA.

Conservatives have mounted several challenges to this law that introduce significant uncertainty into whether its potential benefits will ever be realized. More ominously, even some of the existing health programs that have been shown to benefit African Americans in large numbers, such as Medicaid, are in jeopardy of significant cuts as negotiations aimed at reducing the national debt proceed. A recent study examining the Oregon Health Care Experiment found that Medicaid recipients are far more likely to receive health care than the uninsured. Citizens with Medicaid coverage were also found to be 30 percent more likely to experience a hospital stay, 35 percent more likely to have an outpatient visit to a doctor, and 15 percent more likely to take prescription drugs, compared to similar low-income citizens not enrolled in the program. Those who enrolled in Medicaid also experienced subsequent improvements in their finances: they were 35 percent less likely to experience out-of-pocket medical expenses and had a 25 percent decline in unpaid medical bills sent to collection agencies.[136]

Additionally, as a complement to the White House's efforts to improve health outcomes nationwide, First Lady Michelle Obama is spearheading a major effort to reduce childhood obesity. Her program, called Let's Move, is focused on ending childhood obesity in a single generation.[137] It is a response to the report of the White House Task Force on Childhood Obesity, issued in May 2010, which found that the obesity rate of non-Hispanic Black American boys aged 12 to 19 years was 19.8 percent compared to 16.6 percent for their non-Hispanic White American male counterparts. For African American and White American girls of the same ages, the rates were significantly more disparate: 29.2 percent compared to 14.5 percent. These data highlight the potential for the First Lady's initiative to have a disproportionate impact on African American females in particular.[138]

The Obama administration's efforts to combat the HIV/AIDS epidemic also have the potential to benefit African American women and men disproportionately. For the years 2003 to 2007, African American males and females together accounted for about 50 percent of all HIV/AIDS cases in each year. Although most cases involving African Americans are males, as noted previously there is a disproportionate burden borne by African American women. The relative prevalence of HIV/AIDS among African American women is four times that for their White and Hispanic American counterparts.[139] In response to these findings, the Obama administration unveiled a campaign to reenergize the nation's HIV/AIDS efforts in April 2009. Under the auspices of the Centers for Disease Control and Prevention, $45 million was designated for expenditure over five years for radio ads, transit signs, airport dioramas, online banner ads, and online videos in English and Spanish.[140] In July 2010, the administration announced plans to step up enforcement of antidiscrimination laws affecting HIV/AIDS patients, redirect resources to alleviate health disparities of those infected with HIV/AIDS, and increase the accessibility and quality of health care for those with HIV/AIDS.[141]

While these efforts are laudable, there remain structural impediments to reducing racial health disparities related to the earlier discussion of persisting racial segregation. To illustrate, in 2009, 26.1 percent

9

of African American men and 29.8 percent of African American women lived in unhealthy housing, compared to 22.2 percent of White men and 23.3 percent of White women. In the 2006 – 2008 period, 15.2 percent of African Americans resided in counties that did not meet National Ambient Air Quality Standards for particulate matter compared to 9.7 percent of White Americans. In the 2007-2009 period, 40.0 percent of African Americans resided in counties that did not meet National Ambient Air Quality Standards for ozone versus 32 percent of White Americans.

One adverse consequence of the disproportionately unhealthy living environments of African Americans is disproportionately higher rates of incidence of asthma, especially among children, irrespective of socioeconomic status as illustrated below in Table 9.2. Asthma rates are higher for male children than female children and lower for adult males than females for both African Americans and White Americans.

TABLE 9.2
PREVALENCE OF ASTHMA AMONG AFRICAN AMERICAN AND
WHITE CHILDREN AND ADULTS BY POVERTY LEVEL
2006-2008
(Percent)

Socioeconomic Group	Children	Adults
Poor African Americans	15.8	10.9
Poor White Americans	10.1	13.3
Near-poor African Americans	14.3	8.1
Near-poor White Americans	9.5	9.1
Non-poor African Americans	13.6	6.5
Non-poor White Americans	7.6	6.8

Source: United States, National Health Interview Survey, 2006-2008

Another health hazard disproportionately experienced by African Americans is exposure to dangerous levels of lead. Exposure to lead in housing poses a significant health risk to young children. Lead is highly toxic when absorbed into the body, and it is most harmful to children under age six because it is easily absorbed. Pregnant women and women of child-bearing age are also at increased risk, because lead ingested by the mother can cross the placenta and affect the unborn fetus. According to the Centers for Disease Control, approximately 310,000 American children, the equivalent of 1.6 percent of children aged 1-5, had too much lead in their blood based on 2002 data. The CDC found that 3.1 percent of African-American children aged 1-5 are still lead-poisoned, significantly higher than for the whole population of children in that age group.[142]

Clearly, technological innovations will be required to address the health barriers associated with unhealthy living environments. African American Studies specialists must establish partnerships with environmental scientists to seek ways of mitigating the adverse impacts of pollution, environmental stressors, and other factors that adversely impact health status. The need for African American Studies specialists to become more engaged with specialists in the biological, natural, and physical sciences and the medical professions is especially critical as it relates to reproductive technologies and emergent efforts to develop customized medical interventions for specific populations.

Areas where such collaboration can be fruitful include confidentiality protection for health conditions such as AIDS, and community education to inform victims of treatment options. Many African Americans still believe that the high rates of AIDS infections among Blacks is the result of a genocidal conspiracy, a belief fueled by the historical experiences with medical research discussed previously. Education campaigns are needed regarding safe sexual practices and the dangers of sharing intravenous needles, and advocates for programs that will improve the overall health status of vulnerable individuals. High infection rates are partly conditioned by nutritional deficiencies, related to subordinate socioeconomic status, that weaken the immune system. Infection and malnutrition are synergistic, as increased susceptibility to infection results from both protein and energy malnutrition and deficiencies of specific micronutrients, such as iron, zinc, and vitamins.[143]

Reproductive Technologies

The reproductive technologies of concern to African American studies specialists include both those associated with the prevention and termination of pregnancies and new technologies that offer opportunities for non-traditional procreation, such as in-vitro fertilization.

Building on the preceding discussion of mortality and morbidity, disparities in preterm births is one important indicator of disparity. In 2007, the total preterm birth rate for African Americans was 11.5 compared to 18.3 for White Americans.[144] The Centers for Disease Control (CDC) observes that the gap between non-Hispanic Whites and non-Hispanic Blacks in preterm birth risk has narrowed somewhat during the past two decades. However, the CDC notes that this reduction has resulted from increases in preterm births among non-Hispanic Whites, as opposed to reductions in preterm births among African Americans. The causes of these disparities identified by the CDC include differences in socioeconomic status, prenatal care, maternal risk behaviors, infection, nutrition, stress, and genetics.[145]

As Dorothy Roberts notes, the introduction of birth control pills was viewed with skepticism by many in Black communities.[146] Although birth control pills gave Black women greater control over reproduction than ever before, the historical use that White-dominated birth control programs had played in furthering racial injustice raised legitimate suspicions regarding the underlying motives. Roberts recounts that "as black Americans agitated for their civil rights, the white backlash included reproductive regulation [and] the pill was introduced at a time when scientists such as Arthur Jensen and William Shockley were promoting genetic explanations of racial differences in intelligence-test scores."[147]

The introduction of birth control pills occurred concurrently with the coercive sterilization of thousands of poor Black women under federally funded programs during the 1960s and 1970s. Roberts describes how women were threatened with termination of welfare benefits or denial of medical care for failure to "consent" to the procedure, a practice so widespread in the South that it was called a "Mississippi appendectomy."[148] Moreover, such practices were not limited to the South, as "teaching hospitals in the North also performed unnecessary hysterectomies on poor Black women as practice for their medical residents."[149]

Contraceptive sterilization became increasingly popular as a method of birth control beginning in the mid-1960s. However, as noted by Rebecca Kluchin, "before it became a popular method of birth control, sterilization was a tool of eugenics, the science of racial betterment that developed around the turn of the twentieth century."[150] What Kluchin characterizes as "neo-eugenics" continued the eugenics legacy in the post-baby boom years. However, neo-eugenics reflected "contemporary social anxieties, including blacks' demands for racial equality, Mexican immigration, antipoverty programs, the expansion of welfare, and fears of overpopulation."[151] Back in the 1950s, Black women in the South became targets of forced sterilization via hysterectomy, commonly referred to as 'Mississippi appendectomies.' Women "entered

hospitals to have abdominal surgery and left, unknowingly, without their uteruses."[152] In the post-baby boom period, forced sterilization practices changed and spread in the late 1960s and early 1970s through newly established federal family planning programs, and during this period, "Increasingly, poor women of color entered hospitals for labor and delivery, where the neo-eugenic physicians who treated them forced them to undergo tubal ligation."[153]

According to Kluchin, civil rights leader Fannie Lou Hamer was the first activist to speak out against sterilization abuse in 1964, having been the victim of such a process herself in 1961.[154] In 2011, renewed attention was focused on the practice of forced sterilization as a result of developments in North Carolina. Sterilizations began in North Carolina in 1929 and continued at least through 1973, with over 7,600 individuals, 85 percent of whom were women, subjected to this procedure.[155] North Carolina ranked third in the United States for the total number of people sterilized. More than 30 states enacted laws allowing surgical sterilization for certain people, although not all of them carried out such procedures.[156]

African Americans represent 39 percent of those sterilized in North Carolina over the entire period; but by the latter 1960s, they constituted 60 percent of those sterilized, while comprising only a quarter of the population.[157] In 2011, Democratic Gov. Beverly Perdue created a five-person task force to decide how to compensate victims of forced sterilization. The task force recommended that $50,000 be distributed to as many as 2,000 people.[158] In July 2013 the North Carolina General Assembly approved compensation for the remaining victims of the sterilization program. Governor Pat McCrory subsequently signed the law authorizing a $10 million compensation package that will be distributed among living victims by 2015.[159] This is the first time a state has moved to compensate victims of eugenics programs.

Dorothy Roberts uses this history to explain the divergence of interests between Black women and the White-dominated Women's Movement that focuses myopically on abortion rights at the expense of other aspects of reproductive freedom, including the right to bear children. The Women's Movement also misunderstands criticism of coercive birth control policies. Approximately one and a third million abortions occur annually in the US. Although about 63 percent of abortion patients are White, Black women are more than three times as likely to have an abortion as White

9

women, and Hispanic women are two and a half times as likely.

Past concerns about the potential systematic use of abortions to practice genocide against Blacks were resurrected in 2005 based on comments by former Secretary of Education William Bennett while discussing how the crime rate in the US could be reduced if all Black babies in the US were aborted. Although Bennett bore the brunt of the attacks for expressing in a public forum what many others privately believe, his comments were largely a summary of research findings by some economists involved in examining the relationship between abortion and crime.[160] Thus, there is a body of "legitimate" social science research that can support targeted medical research and technological applications that threaten long-term Black survival.

Given the historical genocidal applications of reproductive control technologies experienced by Blacks and the contemporary suggestions of possible use of such technologies in the future, historical concerns about birth control pills are completely understandable. Many perceived the pill as "just another tool in the White man's efforts to curtail the black population."[161] More recently, efforts to encourage poor Black women to use long-lasting contraceptives, such as, hormonal implants and injectable contraceptives, have resurrected the debate about race and birth control.

Similar types of concerns have been voiced regarding new reproductive technologies that expand procreation options. Viewed from an economic perspective, some critics have argued that the female body's generative capacity is now a new area of investment for profit-seeking scientists, medical engineers, and entrepreneurs. According to this line of argument, reproductive technologies have been developed not because women need them but because capital and science need women for the continuation of their model of growth and progress. In addition, these technologies further increase the capability of paternalistic interests to control women's reproductive capacity.[162]

These new technologies include in vitro fertilization, surrogacy, and embryo transfer. In vitro fertilization (IVF) is a method of infertility treatment in which an egg and sperm are joined in a laboratory container (in vitro means "in glass"). This is in contrast with normal in vivo conception, in which fertilization occurs in the fallopian tube of a woman's reproductive tract. The first human IVF baby, Louise Brown, was born in England in 1978, and the first IVF baby in the United States was born in 1981. Although assisted reproductive technologies (ART) are used by only 1 percent of all women of reproductive age and by only 7 percent of all women who seek services for infertility, over 35,000 babies are born annually in the US by using these technologies.[163]

These technologies are attractive to many Whites because they help infertile couples have a child of their own, help women avoid bearing handicapped children, and help reduce the risks associated with pregnancy and child-bearing. However, some Black commentators have expressed concern because such technologies involve a "deconstruction of motherhood" as a unified biological process, and this has chilling parallels to the way in which chattel slavery forced enslaved Black women to bear children for whom they had no legal claim as mothers.[164] Dorothy Roberts applies the concept of Reprogenetics to discuss the special hazards associated with these new reproductive technologies that confront Black women.

According to Roberts, "Reprogenetics intensifies a dual system of reproduction in which primarily Whites benefit from technologies enabling them to bear the children they want while minority and immigrant women are the primary subjects of welfare reform and other measures aimed at limiting their childbearing."[165] Roberts observes that "poor and minority women have little access to reprogenetic technologies[,] and the images promoting these technologies are almost always of white people."[166] In addition, the available research indicates that use of assisted reproductive technologies (ART) is 20 percent less likely to result in a live birth for African American women than for Whites. Miscarriage rates were also higher among Black, non-Hispanic patients, especially among younger patients.[167]

As Dorothy Roberts observes, the racial dimensions of IVF are not well understood, and may relate, in part, to the stereotype that excess fertility, not infertility, is a more important Black reproductive issue. Although Black women in the United States have infertility rates one and a half times higher than White women, White women use ART techniques at rates twice as high as those of Blacks. IVF is also closely intertwined with class status because the costs of IVF are in the $10,000 per month range, it is not always covered by private insurance, and it is even less likely covered by public medical insurance.

Many African American Studies specialists concur with Dorothy Roberts that there is nothing contradictory about advocating women's access to contraceptive and reproductive technological options while opposing abusive population control practices. In the spirit of African American Studies, Roberts insists that social justice requires equal access to safe, user-controlled contraceptives, an end to the use of birth control as a means of population control, and advances in reproductive rights that overtly incorporate mechanisms to promote racial equality.[168]

Racial Medicine and Genetic Sequencing

Research that has identified possible race-specific responses to IVF technologies is only a minor example of new approaches to the study of "racial medicine." Recent advances in medical research have created a potentially revolutionary approach to the treatment of diseases that disproportionately affect particular population groups. A heart failure medication was approved in 2005 by the Food and Drug Administration (FDA) specifically for African Americans. This is the first time that a drug has been approved that targets a single racial group, although there are approximately thirty "race-specific" drugs under development. The potential benefits of the medicine are beyond dispute. In clinical trials, co-sponsored by the Association of Black Cardiologists, there were 43 percent fewer deaths than among those who did not receive the drug.[169]

The case for targeted medications is straightforward because ethnic and racial minorities are subject to greater risks if they are prescribed a so-called equivalent medicine when substantial evidence indicates that, in some cases, dosage adjustment may be necessary or that the drug has toxic side effects because they cannot tolerate the standard dosage levels.[170] Although different groups are susceptible to different diseases and respond differently to some drugs and other treatments, women and minorities have not been included in health research studies in adequate numbers.[171]

Whether intentional or not, there is solid evidence that researchers have excluded Blacks and other non-Whites from clinical trials. This pattern elevates the issue of broad-based inclusion of non-Whites in clinical trials as a Civil Rights as well as a sociopolitical issue.[172] Congress enacted the National Institutes of Health Revitalization Act of 1993, requiring researchers to include women and non-Whites as subjects in clinical research trials. The law also mandates that NIH conduct outreach efforts to recruit both groups.

The Centers for Disease Control (CDC) established a similar policy in 1995.[173]

Despite these legal mandates, the desired outcomes have been difficult to achieve because of resistance from both researchers and potential participants. Some researchers have objected because inclusion of specific demographically defined subgroups in clinical trials requires different methodologies. Opponents have argued that the required protocols increase the difficulty of completing studies. Many Blacks are reluctant to participate in health research studies from fear of being used as a guinea pig in Tuskegee-type studies. In addition, many Blacks have personally experienced abuse in hospitals and clinics, which fuels a fear of participating in research studies.[174]

Substantial caution should be exercised in the exploration of future race-specific medications. The history of racial science in the Western world, not to mention the Tuskegee experiment discussed earlier in this chapter, provides sufficient reasons to advocate a cautious approach. The essential premise of racial science has been that fundamental differences between people reflect the existence of identifiable racial or ethnic groups. Europeans have been trumpeted as the "superior" race, whereas people of African descent have been assigned to the lowest rung on the evolutionary ladder. Although most contemporary researchers discount traditional notions of clearly defined racial groups and racial hierarchies, racist extremists could still attempt to use the search for racial medicines as a justification for promoting traditionally racist scientific perspectives.

Caution is also warranted because no fixed racial identifiers can predict how an individual responds to a disease or a drug treatment because of the considerable genetic variability within any racial group. As a consequence, it is likely that the new pill may fail some patients identified as "Black," whereas some "White" potential beneficiaries will not have access because of their non-Black racial profile. In essence, medical scientists are using race as a crude surrogate for what they assume are unidentified genetic differences. Eventually researchers hope to develop medical treatments based on an individual's genes and life experiences, not on membership in some loosely defined racial or ethnic category. Thus, race-based prescribing makes sense only as a temporary measure.

There is also a linkage between the development of racial medicines and the state of genetic research

9

related to the Human Genome Project. Although the prevailing interpretation of the findings of such research is that there is greater genetic variation within members of populations presumed to be associated with a racial group than between supposedly different groups, the identification of "racial drugs" has reopened debates about whether distinctive genetic characteristics that underlie racial classifications will be identified in future research. The National Institutes of Health has, in fact, funded a project, "A Paradox of Genetic Research: Race, Ethnicity, and Disease," with the goal of stimulating communication between genetic researchers and community organizations regarding research on genetic disease. The project aims to: (1) understand how and why investigators link genetic disease to named populations; (2) understand how community organizations respond to genetic research and disease linkages; (3) stimulate a dialogue between genetic researchers and community organizations on social risk, the processes of community consultation, and informed consent; (4) develop materials that begin to inform researchers about the implications of using racial and ethnic variables in genetic research and about social and ethical issues of importance to community organizations; and (5) develop materials that begin to inform community organizations about the methods, goals, risks, and benefits of genetic research, and the processes of community consultation and informed consent.[175] Such medical and genetic research must be carefully monitored to minimize the potential for misuse.

The development of monitoring mechanisms can be informed by the perspectives advanced by "Black Social Science" advocates in the early 1970s. These scholars argued that the production of research of value to Black communities requires engaged analysts with organic ties to the community under study. Harris and McCullough suggest, "Black communities must be studied by black people for our own self-interest [because] we cannot afford to be misled by the interpretations and conclusions of statistical studies done by Whites who are interested in preserving the status quo. We must gather the data, analyze and interpret them for our own needs and purposes."[176] Some twenty years later Black social scientists, like Stanfield, were still expressing similar concerns:

Research in the social sciences is one of the last areas in U.S. society in which social inequality is taken as a given. It is assumed that researchers have expertise that is beyond the comprehension of those they study. ...Unless we find adequate ways of liberating the research process in the social sciences, there will be mounting questioning of the relevance of scientific inquiry, especially from the empowering institutions and communities of people of color in the United States and abroad. No longer can social scientists hide behind the ivy-covered walls of academia and their research laboratories, assuming they can study whomever they want to, whenever they please."[177]

Careful monitoring is especially needed to ensure that expanded DNA testing does not become another tool to practice invidious forms of discrimination. Although personal medical information is protected by law, an individual's medical records can be easily accessed by someone working in a medical clinic, a hospital, or a nursing home. Many employers are very interested in taking advantage of increasingly precise, available, and affordable genetic testing to reduce the costs associated with insuring the health of employees whose genetic profiles indicate a high probability that they will experience future health problems. While engaging in such surveillance exposes the employer to a vast array of potential litigation and liability related to the Americans with Disabilities Act, the Fourth Amendment, Title VII of the Civil Rights Act, and state legislation designed to protect genetic privacy, there are strong incentives to take such risks. Given the history of African Americans, it takes no stretch of the imagination to understand that Blacks are likely to be disproportionately victimized by such practices. As a consequence, an important policy objective is to mobilize support for strict confidentiality of medical records coupled with strong sanctions for violations.

Returning to the issue of genetic research, African American Studies specialists should also pay especially close attention to new tests created in recent years that have turned DNA into a popular tool for determining ancestry. Quantitative techniques are being used to estimate an individual's bio-geographical ancestry. Such an analysis can produce evidence of historical genetic exchanges. For example, one person may be classified as 90 percent African and 10 percent European. Conversely, another individual might be identified as having a 100 percent East Asian profile. The company African Ancestry uses these techniques to focus specifically on people of African descent and is able to determine if an individual has a genetic profile similar to individuals living in specific countries or regions.[178]

This technology has critical implications for several public policy areas. Widespread findings of extensive genetic exchanges could undercut the foundations of traditional "racial science" that has undergirded public policy for centuries, as discussed previously. If such findings were not contradicted by future research that supports traditional racial classifications, interests desiring to eliminate the use of traditional racial classifications and outlaw the collection of data by race would gain influence. African American Studies specialists would, of course, oppose such a policy change because it could make it more difficult to track continuing inequalities arising from social rather than the genetic construction of race.

In the longer term, it is possible to envision efforts to develop genetic "therapies" that would allow individuals to alter their genetic make-up to approximate that of some desired population group. In some respects such an application of new DNA identification technologies would constitute the modern equivalent of previous technologies with similar objectives. Rebecca Herzig describes how x-ray technology was adapted to encourage epilation (removal of excess hair) among southern European immigrants in the early twentieth century as a means to achieve a "normal" White skin.[179] Although African Americans had limited access to this particular technology, both southern Europeans and African Americans have made extensive use of skin-bleaching products. Nadinola skin bleaching cream, the first such product in the US market since 1889, initially contained 10 percent ammoniated mercury, a highly toxic agent with serious health implications. More modern skin-lightening creams include the active ingredient hydroquinone, now banned in many countries.[180] Paradoxically, in studies of contemporary excessive use of skin lightening creams in African countries, this chemical has been found to cause hyper-pigmentation (darkening) of the skin.[181] Hair-straightening technologies, the most well-known of which were pioneered by Madam C. J. Walker, are also examples of the attempts to alter physical characteristics, motivated, in part, to closer approximate White standards of beauty and physical characteristics.

Widespread DNA ancestry testing could also have negative ramifications for the process of determining eligibility for reparations payments, assuming that

these eventually materialize. This is why the eligibility criteria proposed in Chapter 7 are essential for developing guidelines regarding reparations payments, in particular the requirement of proof that someone claiming to be of African descent had an ancestor who was actually enslaved.

The preceding discussion emphasizes the potentially negative outcomes that could result from widespread DNA ancestry testing, but there are also possible benefits that should be explored. The capability to trace ancestry to particular regions can reinforce global African identity constructs and create the potential for functional Pan-Africanist political and economic initiatives. Such testing could enable the systematic creation of the type of "Global Tribes" described in Chapter 7. African American Studies specialists can play a key role in facilitating the realization of this potential. Specifically, outreach efforts could be undertaken to recruit African American and African community members to participate in ancestry investigation workshops that include not only testing, but also a series of discussions about the implications of the results and how connections to communities of origin can promote development both in regions of origin and in the Diaspora. Such dialogues can help forge the new type of African identity described in Chapter 5.

Grassroots Strategies to Combat Racial Health Disparities

African American Studies specialists must simultaneously become involved in efforts to combat the exploitation of the genetic resources on the African continent via the Human Genome Diversity Project (HGDP). This project seeks to collect the DNA from indigenous populations that are "disappearing" (as well as others). Native American and some Asian communities were in the forefront of raising objections to this project, raising legitimate questions about why the investigators were not helping them survive instead of worrying about generating hypotheses and constructing narratives based on their DNA. They were also concerned about the interpretation and misuse of these data and their commercialization. Rapid developments in biotechnology over the last two decades have enabled corporations and scientists to alter nature's handiwork for commercial profit. The patent, a tool originally created to insure that inventors could share in the financial returns and

9

benefits derived from the use of their inventions, has become the primary mechanism through which the private sector advances its claims to ownership over genes, proteins, and entire organisms. Unfortunately, there has not been a statement from the Organization of African Unity (OAU), or its successor the African Union (AU), about the taking of biological materials from African peoples (from Cairo to the Cape). Nor have any of the major African American community or rights organizations made official statements about the harvesting of the DNA of people of African descent. Any future African human genomics and diversity project must, as with its Asian counterpart, be under the auspices of Africans who are the primary investigators and African American Studies specialists should be partners in any such efforts.[182]

African American Studies favors a comprehensive "cradle to grave" (and beyond) approach to reducing racial health disparity and maximizing the health status of African Americans that makes use not only of institutional resources, but also recognizes and utilizes grassroots collaborative resources. Such an approach includes initiatives, such as, quality pre-natal care for expectant mothers, parenting seminars for parents, reduction of environmental health hazards, access to adequate nutrition, access to high-quality health care services, and support for caregivers.

There is also a need for a crisis intervention strategy to respond to economic and other catastrophes that heighten food insecurity and create acute health hazards. As an example, the National Black Church Initiative (NBCI), a coalition of 34,000 churches across the United States, is pledging to feed an additional 100,000 families in 2012 in response to a surge in hunger that has been caused by the economic downturn.[183]

More generally, a strategy is needed to improve nutritional practices and combat institutional barriers to healthy eating, such as "food deserts." Marc Weigensberg and colleagues studied whether dietary fat intake above current Acceptable Macronutrient Distribution Range (AMDR) guidelines was associated with greater insulin resistance in Black and White children. They found that Black children with dietary fat intake above current AMDR guidelines had lower insulin sensitivity and higher acute insulin response to glucose than those who met AMDR guidelines. This was not the case for White children.[184] Marcia Schmidt and her collaborators compared fast-food intake and diet quality for Black and White girls. They found that Black girls consumed fast foods more frequently than

White girls for all ages. This means that Black girls are consuming more calories, total fat, saturated fat, and sodium than White girls. Higher fat intake is associated with higher risk for cardiovascular disease, obesity, and elevated cholesterol. In addition, White girls tended, more than Black girls, to decrease the consumption of saturated fats as a percentage of calories consumed as they aged, while the frequency of fast-food consumption increases with age for both Black and White girls.[185]

The disproportionate consumption of fast foods is partially related to the presence of "food deserts" in many African American neighborhoods. Food deserts are areas with poor access to healthy and affordable food. Jason Block and colleagues found in a study of several communities that predominantly Black neighborhoods had 2.4 fast-food restaurants per square mile compared to 1.5 restaurants in predominantly White neighborhoods.[186] Kimberly Morland and fellow researchers found that if communities do not have access to supermarkets that offer a wide variety of foods at reasonable prices, poor and minority communities also may not have equal access to the variety of healthy food choices available to nonminority and wealthy communities.[187]

African American Studies specialists should become involved in community-based efforts to address the problem of food deserts. One such initiative has been undertaken by the Community Health Councils (CHC), a nonprofit community-based organization in South Los Angeles. CHC worked with the African Americans Building a Legacy of Health Coalition and research partners to combat health disparities with a focus on cardiovascular disease (CVD) and diabetes which concentrated on the issue of food deserts.[188]

There are also several initiatives that target the problem of food deserts by increasing access to healthy foods by encouraging community-based food production. The Detroit Black Community Food Security Network, formed in 2006, is an important example. The Network operates a two-acre model urban farm located in Rouge Park in Northwestern Detroit. The enterprise includes organic vegetable plots, two bee hives, a hoop house for year round food production, and a composting operation. Produce is grown using sustainable, chemical-free practices, and sold at D-Town Farm, Eastern Market, and urban growers markets throughout Detroit. An annual Harvest Festival is held that showcases the farming operations. There is also an Ujamaa Cooperative Food Buying Club that provides community residents with affordable food. Finally, there is also a Food Warriors Youth Development Program that involves a partnership with three African- centered schools to introduce elementary school students to agriculture.[189] Many Black farmers are also embracing organic and other sustainable farming methods. Urban farming projects that use vacant lots are springing up in many Black neighborhoods. There are also a growing number of books and other resources promoting more healthy dietary choices and food preparation practices among African Americans.[190]

Turning to community-based initiatives targeting racial health disparities more broadly, at the national level since 2002, *The Tom Joyner Morning Show's* "Take A Loved One to The Doctor" has raised health and wellness awareness in the Black community via this national, health awareness campaign. The Black Barbershop Health Outreach Program focuses on screening, educating, and referring men to local health care resources. According to the organization's website, over 30,000 men in over 500 barbershops in 38 cities have been screened since the program's inception in 2007.[191] Beauty shops are also serving as an important venue for addressing racial health disparities. As an example, The Women's Collaborative, a prevention program of the AIDS Foundation of Chicago, increases HIV awareness and primary care services for African-American and Latina women through beauty and nail salons, barbershops and beauty supply stores.[192] These types of initiatives constitute ideal potential partners for African American Studies outreach efforts.

The collaboration between faculty members at the University of Illinois at Urbana-Champaign and the local organization Sister Net is an innovative use of information technology to promote health equity. The Afya (Swahili for "health") project uses a participatory action research approach to provide Sister Net members with improved health information and services while enhancing their computer and Internet literacy. Sister Net is a local network of African American women committed to improving health outcomes through monitoring and altering lifestyles, behaviors, and support systems. The project's objective is "to develop a practical vision for library engagement in community health and the digital divide that promotes social justice through community-wide alliances that model more democratic and participative

relationships. Afya is concerned, fundamentally, with developing new social technologies (ways that people communicate and collaborate) as well as new digital tools and resources."[193]

More generally, the widespread distrust of the medical establishment is not likely to abate until more Blacks are involved in biomedical research and health care delivery. Only 0.37 percent of biomedical research funds are awarded to Black scientists, which reflects the paucity of Blacks pursuing medical scientific and research careers.[194] It is hoped that the training of such professionals will include exposure to African American Studies courses and possible pursuit of double majors or minors.

Environmental Racism and Justice

The topics examined thus far in this chapter can be readily understood in accordance with conventional notions of "science" and "technology." However, as previously mentioned, perspectives from STS studies have fostered discussion on technologies and their social functions. Exploration of the constructs of environmental racism and environmental justice/injustice provides an illustration of Langdon Winner's reminder, cited previously, of how societies choose structures for technologies that influence how people are going to work, communicate, travel, and consume over extended periods of time.[195]

Environmental Racism

Among other manifestations, environmental racism involves targeting African American communities as sites for noxious facilities, locally unwanted land uses, and environmental hazards. Air pollution and lead exposure among urban African Americans have been documented and exposed. Robert Bullard argues that environmental discrimination results, in part, from the inability of Black communities to mobilize sufficient political power to oppose location of toxic facilities successfully. An egregious example of such cases is that the sister plant to the Union Carbide plant in Bhopal, India, the site of one of the most tragic environmental disasters, is located in the predominantly Black area of Institute, West Virginia. Because the plant in West Virginia was unincorporated, the

9

community received no direct tax benefits from the plant and lacked the capacity for self-protection that might result from incorporation.[196] This type of environmental racism has been aided and abetted by the inaction of the federal government. The Environmental Protection Agency (EPA) had not specifically examined the social impact of its policies on minority and poor working-class communities until the early 1990s, when former President Clinton issued the Executive Order "Federal Actions to Address Environmental Justice in Minority Populations and Low-Income Populations" on February 11, 1994.

Environmental Justice

Even such advances as the federal environmental justice initiative do not address the fundamental problems. Environmental racism is not limited to disproportionate environmental risks to people of African descent. More common manifestations are the dilapidated infrastructures in Black communities that are more likely to experience catastrophic failure in the public service delivery of technologies of inferior quality. Several scholars have examined how some cities were specifically designed to institutionalize racial segregation and quality of life disparities. Amy Bix observes, "The process of designing and constructing municipal services and systems carried important implications for race, class, and community life."[197] This view is buttressed by studies of the history of the development of public utilities in Denver and Kansas City, the design of the Long Island parkways in New York, as well as a variety of studies of "urban renewal" and urban highway construction initiatives of the 1960s and 1970s.

The processes by which suburbs developed were closely linked to the mass production technologies of automobiles and highway construction. These processes were coupled with federal housing policies that enabled Whites to relocate from cities to suburbs. As noted previously, some African Americans benefited from the rapid ascendance of the automobile as a personal transportation technology. However, until the late 1960s, discrimination limited their ability to use the mobility associated with the automobile to expand their housing options beyond the inner city. Moreover, public transportation policies (highways, light rail networks, and other suburban-friendly public transportation modes) were deliberately designed to deprive inner city residents of quality services and to disadvantage the

negative health consequences of the pollution produced by the accessible public transit technologies.

The above policy bias persists. As researchers Ravindra Krovi and Claude Barnes report, African Americans generally have the longest travel times to work in all regions of the country where public transit is available, and low-income minorities have longer travel times than low-income Whites.[198] Overall, the authors conclude, "it appears that minority groups have to travel longer to seek high-income or even part-time low-skilled opportunities relative to Whites. There is also some evidence that transit systems are not as well integrated in minority neighborhoods [increasing] commute time ... because of longer distances to transit points."[199] The Turner Foundation and Ford Foundation are funding a major transportation equity project in Atlanta and several other cities to explore these issues in more detail.[200]

Even as Blacks have moved into the suburbs, new surveillance technologies have been installed to reduce potential social disruption. Recurring charges of excessive police surveillance have led to the expression "driving while Black" to describe the inordinate stopping of Blacks by law enforcement agents for no apparent reason. The new surveillance technologies are essentially refined versions of those used to discourage Black motorists from driving on open roads in the early twentieth century.[201] The preceding discussion illustrates the complexities of monitoring and assessing the many and multifaceted ways science and technology can be used to reinforce existing inequalities. In the spirit of the earlier discussion of the goals of future studies, a useful starting point for community-based systems for assessing scientific and technological impacts is the development of a common vision for a desired social environment. Such an initiative has been undertaken by the Environmental Justice Movement, which advocates the design and implementation of technologies in balance with nature, honors the cultural integrity of communities, and provides fair access for all to the full range of resources.

Delegates to the First National People of Color Environmental Leadership Summit held in October 1991, in Washington D.C., drafted and adopted seventeen principles of Environmental Justice. Since then, The Principles have served as a defining document for the growing grassroots movement for environmental justice. Eight of these principles especially relevant to the core concerns of African American Studies are presented below:

2) Environmental Justice demands that public policy be based on mutual respect and justice for all peoples, free from any form of discrimination or bias.

1. Environmental Justice affirms the fundamental right to political, economic, cultural, and environmental self-determination of all peoples.

6) Environmental Justice demands the cessation of the production of all toxins, hazardous wastes, and radioactive materials, and that all past and current producers be held strictly accountable to the people for detoxification and the containment at the point of production.

7) Environmental Justice demands the right to participate as equal partners at every level of decision-making, including needs assessment, planning, implementation, enforcement, and evaluation.

8) Environmental Justice affirms the right of all workers to a safe and healthy work environment without being forced to choose between an unsafe livelihood and unemployment. It also affirms the right of those who work at home to be free from environmental hazards.

9) Environmental Justice protects the right of victims of environmental injustice to receive full compensation and reparations for damages as well as quality health care.

12) Environmental Justice affirms the need for urban and rural ecological policies to clean up and rebuild our cities and rural areas in balance with nature, honoring the cultural integrity of all our communities, and providing fair access for all to the full range of resources.

13) Environmental Justice calls for the strict enforcement of principles of informed consent, and a halt to the testing of experimental reproductive and medical procedures and vaccinations on people of color.[202]

African American Studies specialists endorse these principles and support the work of groups associated with the Environmental Justice Movement.

A variety of "green initiatives" that are being undertaken by African American community-based organizations in various cities. One example is the Urban Green Growth Collaborative in the East End of the City of Pittsburgh. The focus of this program is intertwining existing services and moving this experience towards a

Green pre-workforce opportunity and/or livable wage opportunities. The coordination of these services and the role of the Urban Green Growth Collaborative provide multiple opportunities for consumers in the green economy, construction, janitorial, hospitality, and retail; and in emerging businesses within the East End of the City of Pittsburgh.[203]

On a larger scale, the National Black Church Initiative (NBCI), a faith-based coalition of 34, 000 churches comprised of 15 denominations and 15.7 million African Americans dedicated to the eradication of racial disparities around the world, is in the forefront in implementing environmental policy in the faith community and in offering its perspective on environmental policy both domestically and globally. The mission of this initiative is the utilization by NBCI of its enormous moral authority and influence to support policies and programs to educate its congregants on the importance of the environment as it relates to their faith and to preserve the environment for all future generations.[204] NBCI will be working with ten environmental organizations to achieve its objectives. The NBCI website asserts: "We also are committed to combating the scourge of environmental racism and creating green, sustainable environments throughout our faith-based communities across the country."[205] The example of Florida Avenue Baptist Church in Washington, D.C., is cited as an example of success. This church made a $600,000 investment in solar panels that reduced its $3,000 monthly electricity bill by $450 (15%), and it is anticipated that solar power will generate 25% of the electricity consumed. Federal subsidies and local incentives helped it to raise 30% ($18,000) of the required funding, and a US Department of Labor grant enabled the local solar firm to train and hire 80 workers to do the construction and retrofitting.[206]

The NAACP Climate Justice Initiative constitutes another important effort to address the disproportionate vulnerability of African Americans to the consequences of environmental degradation. The initiative has several goals, including: (1) increasing awareness and understanding of the connection between climate change and the quality of life in Black communities; and (2) cultivating a "Black-Green Pipeline" by "working with institutions to increase paid internship opportunities for students of color as well as working with unions and others to advance economic opportunities afforded by the emerging green economy." The Initiative is also advancing an advocacy agenda focusing on clean energy,

9

transportation equity, food justice, equity in urban/rural development, economic empowerment/green economy, health justice, education justice, disaster planning, and housing justice.[207]

These types of initiatives constitute exciting opportunities for African American Studies scholar/activists to become both partners and path breakers in promoting an environmental ethic that can foster sustainable improvements in the quality of life for people of African descent, in both the domestic and global contexts. The imperative that African American Studies focus attention on the environmental justice issue is heightened by the research reported by J. Andrew Hoerner and Nia Robinson that finds that "people of color, indigenous peoples, and low-income communities bear disproportionate burdens from climate change itself, from ill-designed policies to prevent it, and from the side effects of energy systems that cause it."[208] According to the authors, although African Americans emit nearly 20 percent less greenhouse gases than non-Hispanic Whites on a per capita basis, they are significantly more vulnerable to its effects than non-Hispanic Whites. Some examples include greater vulnerability to higher energy bills and economic downturns caused by global energy price shocks. In addition, Hoerner and Robinson note that "the six states with the highest African American population are all in the Atlantic hurricane zone and are expected to experience more intense storms resembling Katrina and Rita in the future."[209]

Africana Studies and Space Exploration

Future Africana Studies specialists will be challenged to extend humanistic African values and the principles of the Environmental Justice Movement to the realm of space exploration and colonization. The principal mandate will be to ensure that the horrific history created by European colonization is not repeated, as humans seek to establish bases beyond planet Earth. As a prelude, African Americans have had important roles as humanizing agents in several futuristic science fiction series, including Nichelle Nichols as Lt. Uhura in the original Star Trek series (1966 – 1969) and Avery Brooks as Captain Sisko in the series Star Trek: Deep Space Nine. More recently Zoe Saldana reprised the role of Uhura in the 2009 film Star Trek and in the 2013 film Star Trek into Darkness. In addition to these cinematic representations, imagined images of African Americans engaged in space travel have also appeared in other genres. One example is the 1975 album, Mothership Connection, by

Parliament. The title song, "Mothership Connection (Star Child)," includes the lyrics,

"Well all right, Starchild
Citizens of the Universe, recording angels
We have returned to claim the pyramids
Partying on the mothership
I am the mothership connection...."

Discussing the imagery embedded in this album, band leader George Clinton related, "We had put black people in situations nobody ever thought they would be in, like the White House. I figured another place you wouldn't think black people would be was in outer space. I was a big fan of Star Trek, so we did a thing with a pimp sitting in a spaceship shaped like a Cadillac, and we did all these James Brown-type grooves, but with street talk and ghetto slang."[210]

The representations of Blacks in the space travel-science fiction cinematic genre are undergirded by a strong tradition of extensive involvement by African Americans in bona fide aerospace ventures. Robert Henry Lawrence, Jr., was named the first African American astronaut in 1967, but Guion Bluford has the honor of being the first African American to travel into space. Bluford's first mission was aboard the space shuttle Challenger in 1983. Bluford's career is additionally noteworthy because he had the opportunity to travel into space more than once, serving on three additional shuttle missions prior to his retirement. However, Bluford was not the first person of African descent to undertake an extraterrestrial voyage. This designation belongs to a Cuban astronaut, Arnaldo Tamayo-Mendez, who was part of the Soviet mission Salyut 6 in 1980. The first African American to make a spacewalk was Bernard Harris, Jr., who served as Payload Commander on the first flight of the joint Russian-American Space Program (February 2-11, 1995). Mae Jemison is widely known as the first African-American woman to become a US astronaut. She was the science mission specialist on the Spacelab-J shuttle mission (September 12-20, 1992), a cooperative mission between the United States and Japan.[211]

African Americans have also been represented among those whose lives have been lost in fatal accidents associated with space exploration. Robert Lawrence died in December 1967 when his jet crashed at Edwards Air Force Base, California, during a training mission. Ronald E. McNair died on January 28, 1986, when the space shuttle Challenger exploded after launch from the Kennedy Space Center, Florida. And, Michael Anderson died on February 1, 2003, over the southern United States when space shuttle *Columbia* and her crew perished during re-entry, 16 minutes prior to the scheduled landing.[212]

Several African Americans have contributed to the US space program in other important roles. For example, physicist Arthur Walker was appointed in 1986, by then-President Ronald Reagan, to serve on the commission that investigated the explosion of the space shuttle *Challenger*. In her role at the National Space Science Data Center, Astrophysicist Beth A. Brown is involved in the Multiwavelength Milky Way project, an outreach initiative intended to make information about the galaxy accessible to educators, students, and the general public. This type of educational outreach is one objective of the TV series, *Cosmos: A Spacetime Odyssey*, hosted by Neil deGrasse Tyson, Frederick P. Rose Director of the Hayden Planetarium at the American Museum of Natural History.[213]

The 2009 appointment of Charles Frank Bolden, Jr., a Marine Corps Major General and astronaut to be senior administrator of NASA is one of the most notable milestones during the Obama presidency. NASA has set a goal of transporting humans to the planet Mars by 2050. In a video released in April 2010, titled "NASA's New Era of Innovation and Discovery," Bolden said, "We're gonna turn science fiction into science fact." Bolden also told interviewers that one of the primary goals he was given by President Obama was to "help re-inspire children to want to get into science and math."[214]

Some Black space pioneers continue to be actively involved in educational and other public service efforts that bring African American sensibilities to space exploration efforts. Nichelle Nichols has served on the Board of Governors of the National Space Society, a nonprofit, educational space advocacy organization. Mae Jemison founded the Jemison Group, Inc., to research, develop and implement advanced technologies suited to the social, political, cultural and economic context of the individual, especially for the developing world. She is currently working on humanity's first starship. Her goal is "to help change the world by leading the effort to send and sustain humans in interstellar space travel within the next 100 years."[215]

In looking toward the future, Africana Studies specialists must position themselves to infuse humanity's quest to explore outer space with values and behaviors inspired by African sensibilities and moderated by the calamitous experiences of people of African descent under various global regimes. Students can be inspired to pursue careers in science and technology in general, and space exploration specifically, by demonstrating the linkages between historical achievements, such as, those of the Dogon and of Benjamin Banneker, and the efforts of contemporary space pioneers. Through such interventions, Africana Studies can conceivably expand its future reach beyond the confines of this planet to the far reaches of the universe.

Technology and the Future of African American Studies

The preceding discussion of technology in the context of African American life and experience suggests that African American Studies must expand its existing orientation to include the study of design and technology in the curriculum as well as embrace information technology more aggressively. Efforts to integrate design studies and architectural studies into the Africana Studies curriculum and research agenda can assist Black architects to generate viable answers to a salient and lingering question Melvin Mitchell raises, namely, "What does Black Architecture look like?"[216] Mitchell provides one obvious answer to this question: "Any architecture undertaken for the purpose of the individual and/or group empowerment of African-Americans (ownership and control are litmus tests)."[217] However, he also laments that Black architects have not developed a Black design aesthetic that compares with the Black aesthetic in literature and the arts, as discussed in Chapter 8. In addition, Mitchell suggests that Black architects must redefine the traditional ways in which non-Black architects relate to stakeholders to become integral to Black communities. He observes: "Black community support is plausible only when ... architects step completely outside of the box of academically promoted orthodoxy of how an architect is supposed to relate to the marketplace. The cues and clues abound in the actions of other black entrepreneurs in the world of music, entertainment, and other vital culture sensitive business enterprises."[218] Moreover, he argues that "the crucial responsibility of a black architect to Black America is to envision and conceptualize productive new environments, create value, and deliberately reflect African-American culture where none of those things currently exists."[219]

9

In Mitchell's view, Black architects must draw on a variety of Black musical traditions, a perspective consistent with the interdisciplinary approach championed by African American Studies specialists. Specifically, he suggests that the foundations of a Black design aesthetic can be found in: "a) the obvious architectonic music and style composed or played by Bolden, Joplin, Armstrong, Ellington, Miles, and Coltrane; b) the visual style of all of the movies made by Spike Lee and John Singleton, et al.; and c) many of the street-based videos made by the two African-American socio-economic class extremes of Howard University—business major Sean 'P Diddy' Combs and New Orleans public housing project spawned Master P (Percy Miller)."[220]

Adam Banks also provides important insights regarding approaches to integrating design and architectural studies into the fabric of African American Studies. Among other values, he espouses "an approach to design that encodes freedom directly into spaces and artifacts, in a sense, an approach that embeds the technical communication, the instructions, the documentation, into the artifacts and spaces themselves."[221] Another salient value proposed by Banks is "a willingness to use every means available in design, even dated and discarded technologies, and spaces and artifacts of the everyday."[222]

Melvin Mitchell offers a vision that integrates the realm of design, control of space, and liberating uses of information technology to guide collaboration between architects, information technology experts, and African American Studies specialists:

> The common denominator meeting point of much of the telecommunications driven revolution is where African-Americans live and sleep each night. They sleep in some form of building structure, also known as their house, and rarely thought of as 'architecture.' How the next generation of black architects is to be socialized in their chosen academic environments to relate to the question of how other blacks will be housed in the twenty-first century is a major issue for both groups in their struggle to exist as viable cultural entities.[223]

African American Studies specialists can play a major role in addressing that question and in implementing the transformation model proposed by Mitchell:

> The key to a twenty-first century black architectural practice renaissance requires that young black architects position themselves in the middle of an inevitable integration of all of the cultural art forms of Black America. The home or place of residence is the physical centerpiece and lynchpin of a true music–art–architecture triptych that must be fashioned around the integrated economic and cultural needs of large sectors of Black America that will continue to live together.[224]

In addition to examining the role of information technology to enhance design studies, there is also a need to explore how information technology can be used to enhance the entire range of instruction in African American Studies.

In the article "Will the Revolution be Digitized? Using Digitized Resources in Undergraduate Africana Studies Courses," James Stewart presents suggestions on the use of Internet-based documents as supplemental resources in undergraduate African American Studies courses.[225] Most existing courses rely heavily on traditional print scholarship supplemented by various audio and visual materials in analog formats. Although traditional print resources will continue to constitute the bedrock of African American Studies instruction, there are several potential benefits that can be derived from expanding sources of instructional materials and pedagogical approaches.

The learning styles of traditional-age college students today are generally more tactile and visually oriented than earlier generations. At the same time, African American Studies courses disproportionately attract students from digitally-under-served populations. As a consequence, using digitized resources in African American Studies classes can enhance students' capacities with information technologies and contribute to bridging the "digital divide," as discussed previously. In addition, given the proliferation of digitized misinformation spread through e-mail and various websites exemplified by the myriad of "urban myths," use of digitized resources can help students develop critical electronic literacy skills for making informed judgments about the accuracy of digitized information. Developing such skills serves both individual and collective long-term social survival and the empowerment objectives of African American Studies.

Consistent with the general empowerment objectives of African American Studies, use of digitized resources in instruction should encourage students to think of themselves as potential knowledge producers rather than passive information consumers. Moreover, instructors must ensure that neither the technology itself, nor digitized content, induce undesired shifts in overall philosophical orientation or instructional goals. The most functional efforts to introduce digitized resources into African American Studies courses will be closely aligned with the historical mission and trajectory of the field and with the orientation of existing printed resources that have demonstrated instructional value. Many of the websites Stewart discusses in his study include multimedia digitized resources with links to other websites, searchable full-text databases, bibliographies, digitized images of visual and narrative materials, interactive GIS-based maps and databases, non-GIS searchable databases, video and audio clips, and specially prepared introductory and other narrative material that help guide users.

"E Black Studies" (http://www.eblackstudies.org/), spearheaded by Abdul Alkalimat at the University of Toledo, is one of the few examples of the dedicated use of the Internet to serve the interests, concerns, and needs of African American Studies. The project's mission is identified as allowing "one stop shopping for everyone in the field of Africana Studies" with respect to providing "information ... in all academic fields that focus primarily on Africa and the African Diaspora." The site also supports upper-division instruction via extensive links provided to African American Studies journals too often overlooked as potential supplemental resources for upper-division instruction.[226] The long-term vision guiding this effort is the creation of an online research archive that can support both instruction and additional research. The creation of such an archive would realize the vision set forth a decade ago by W.E.B. Du Bois in which he proposed a 100-year-long research program that would provide a systematic database that could be tapped to examine the major questions for African American Studies specialists to seek answers.

It is important to keep in mind that computer-based software packages also constitute a means to integrate digitized information into classroom instruction. The most well-known is Microsoft Encarta Africana.[227] This two-CD ROM resource contains a virtual storehouse of information. The available information is, in fact, not restricted to what is stored on the CD ROM. Some inquiries activate links to various websites. A downside of computer-based software packages compared with Internet resources is the cost associated with acquiring the software. Whereas the web-based resources discussed in the Stewart study are free, this is not the case for Microsoft Encarta Africana, although the cost is relatively reasonable. As in the case of web-based resources

and textbooks, issues related to ideology and to orientation are relevant in making decisions about the use of software packages. As instructors' comfort levels and expertise with information technologies increase, students could be assigned to work on projects involving the development of digitized materials as part of a capstone seminar in African American Studies. Finally, as Africana Studies instructors and researchers continue to explore new opportunities to use information technologies, we may produce a new generation of scholar/activists for whom the revolution will be digitized!

However, as technology continues to advance, the importance of a trans-disciplinary approach to African American Studies will become increasingly apparent. While taking full advantage of the new possibilities for inquiry and engagement that have become available, it is important to keep the core principles of African American Studies in the foreground. There are five characteristics that can be useful in differentiating Africana Studies analyses from inquiries more appropriately identified with other intellectual traditions: (a) rejection of "victimology" orientations in favor of approaches focusing on efforts by African Americans to shape their own destiny (Africana agency); (b) interpretation of contemporary developments through a framework of analysis that explores the effects of historical forces in shaping current conditions (continuing historical influences); (c) use of multiple analytical methods and modes of presentation to understand and articulate the complexities of the experiences of peoples of African descent (wholism/multidimensionality); (d) exploration of policy implications (simultaneous pursuit of academic excellence and social responsibility); and (e) exploration of historical and continuing cultural and political linkages between Africans in Africa and Africans in the Diaspora (pan-Africanism). While no individual investigation is likely to incorporate all of these elements, the absence of characteristics (a) and (b) generally suggests that a particular research study is more appropriately identified with a field of inquiry other than Africana Studies, per se. Conversely, studies incorporating a larger number of these characteristics are more representative of the type[228] of Africana Studies scholarship envisioned by founders than those exhibiting fewer of these elements.

9

Questions & Exercises

1. Scientific and technological advances have had both positive and negative effects on the well-being of African Americans. Discuss whether the net effect of these advances has improved or worsened the overall situation of African Americans.

2. Implicit in this chapter's discussion is the concern that Blacks may have as much to fear from covert domestic scientific and technological experimentation as from forces external to the United States. Refute or support this assumption.

3. The diversity of race and culture may affect the purpose and usage of information technology. What distinct cultural attributes should designers and manufacturers of computers adhere to in addressing the needs and desires of African Americans?

4. Support or refute the following assertion: Because reducing the number of Black babies is an unstated objective, Black women should universally resist reproductive technologies that enable abortions.

5. Targeted racial-ethnic medical prescriptions may produce negative or positive benefits. Analyze the pros and cons of race-specific medications and treatments. Discuss the extent to which sufficient scientific genetic research has been conducted to validate this practice.

6. Identify and evaluate the risks associated with two forms of environmental racism experienced in many predominantly Black communities.

7. Select two of the principles of Environmental Justice presented in this chapter and discuss how policies consistent with these principles could improve the quality of life in predominantly Black communities.

8. Describe some ways in which information technology is being used to enrich instruction in African American Studies. What types of new applications might further enhance the learning experience of students?

Social Responsibility Projects

1. Organize a group and conduct research to determine the extent to which surveillance cameras are being used in your community. Share the findings of your research with local residents.

2. Organize a "Healthy Eating Club" that focuses on consumption of nutritious foods and physical fitness.

3. Encourage your family members to modify their eating habits to consume less fast and high-fat content foods.

4. Identify organizations in your community that are working to combat food deserts and work with one or more as a volunteer.

5. Identify groups in your community that are monitoring air and water quality and work with them as a volunteer.

6. Identify video games that portray African Americans stereotypically, refuse to purchase or play such games and encourage others to do the same.

7. Determine if there is a program in your community that encourages residents to take a loved one to the doctor. If so, work with the program as a volunteer. If not, organize such a program.

8. Query your local barber or beauty shop operator to find out if he or she currently participates in the Black Barbershop Health Outreach Program or a program similar to the Chicago Women's Collaborative. If so, work with the program. If not, work with your provider to organize such a program.

9. Find out if your church currently participates in the National Black Church Initiative. If so, volunteer to work on green growth initiatives. If not, encourage the church leadership to join the initiative and promote environmental awareness and a sustainable environment.

10. Organize a Facebook group to share information relevant to the goals and concerns of African American Studies.

9

NOTES AND REFERENCES

1. For a detailed analysis of the contours of Future Studies, see W. Bell, *Foundations of Future Studies*, vols. 1 and 2 (New Brunswick, NJ: Transaction Publishers, 1997).

2. See for example, S. Anderson, "Science, Technology and Black Liberation," *The Black Scholar* 5, no. 3 (1974): 2-8; L. Henderson, "Public Technology and the Metropolitan Culture," *The Black Scholar* 5 (March 1974): 9-18; M. Hendrix, J. Bracy, J. Davis, and W. Herron, "Computers and Black Studies: Toward the Cognitive Revolution," *Journal of Negro Education* 53 (1984): 341-50; R. Johnson, "Science, Technology, and Black Community Development," *Western Journal of Black Studies* 4, no. 3 (1980): 212-16; and W. King, "Enhancing Scientific and Technical Literacy in Afroamerican Communities," mimeo (1992).

3. Anderson "Science, Technology and Black Liberation," 3.

4. Anderson "Science, Technology and Black Liberation," 5.

5. Henderson "Public Technology and the Metropolitan Culture," 14.

6. Ibid.

7. W.E.B. Du Bois, "The Field and Function of the Negro College," alumni reunion address, Fisk University, 1933. Reprinted in *W.E.B. Du Bois, The Education of Black People, Ten Critiques 1900-1960*, ed. H. Aptheker (Amherst, MA: University of Massachusetts Press, 1973), 83-102.

8. A. Alkalimat, "*Technological Revolution and Prospects for Black Liberation in the 21st Century*," CyRev online, (Posted 2001), http://www.net4dem.org/cyrev/archive/issue4/articles/liberation/Liberation1.htm.

9. R. Tomovic, "Technology and Society," in *Science and Technology in the Transformation of the World*. Proceedings of the First International Seminar on the Transformation of the World, Belgrade, Yugoslavia, ed. A. Abdel-Malek, et al. (October 1979), 53.

10. R. McGinn, *Science, Technology and Society* (Englewood Cliffs, NJ, Prentice-Hall, 1991), 20.

11. McGinn, *Science, Technology and Society*, 14–15.

12. H. Brooks, "Technology, Evolution and Purpose," *Daedalus* 109, no. 1 (1980): 66.

13. Ibid.

14. B. Gendron, *Technology and the Human Condition* (New York: St. Martin's Press, 1977), 23.

15. W. Lowrance, *Modern Science and Human Values* (New York: Oxford University Press, 1985), 34.

16. L. Winner, "Do Artifacts Have Politics?" *Daedalus* 109, no. 1 (1980): 27.

17. Tomovic, "*Technology and Society*," 54.

18. Ibid., 56.

19. McGinn, *Science, Technology and Society*, 7.

20. A. Banks, *Race, Rhetoric, and Technology, Searching for Higher Ground* (Mahwah, NJ: Lawrence Erlbaum, 2006), 2.

21. A. Banks, *Race, Rhetoric, and Technology*, 44.

22. A. Banks, *Race, Rhetoric, and Technology*, 44.

23. W. Bell, *Foundations of Futures Studies, History, Purposes, and Knowledge, Human Science for a New Era, Vol. 1* (New Brunswick, NJ: Transaction Publishers, 2003), 111.

24. T. Jenkins and K. Om-Ra Seti, *Black Futurists in the Information Age* (San Francisco: KMT, 1997), 22.

25. Ibid., viii-ix.

26. Jenkins and Om-Ra Seti, *Black Futurists in the Information Age*, 77-78.

27. McGinn, *Science, Technology and Society*, 118–19.

28. V. Kaplan, *Structural Inequality: Black Architects in the United States* (Lanham, MD: Rowman & Littlefield, 2006), 21.

29. D. Brooks, "The Storm After the Storm," *New York Times*, September 1, 2005.

30. Ibid.

31. Brooks, "The Storm After the Storm."

32. See for example, J. Patrick, "The Tulsa, Oklahoma Race Riot of 1921," *Exodus* online, http://www.exodusnews.com/HISTORY/History007.htm.

33. John Anderson and Hilary Hevenor, *Burning Down the House: MOVE and the Tragedy of Philadelphia* (New York: W.W. Norton & Co., 1987).

34. See, for example, W. Stevens, "Police Drop Bomb on Radicals' Home in Philadelphia," *New York Times*, May 14, 1985.

35. "Drug Traffickers, Paramilitary Groups..." Violence Policy Center, http://www.vpc.org/studies/awadrug.htm.

36. L. Weisman, *Discrimination by Design: A Feminist Critique of the Man-Made Environment* (Urbana, IL: University of Illinois Press, 1992), 35.

37. A. Smith, *Mixed-income Housing Developments: Promise and Reality* (Boston, MA: Joint Center for Housing Studies of Harvard University, 2002).

38.   P. Jargowsky, *Stunning Progress, Hidden Problems: The Dramatic Decline in Concentrated Poverty in the 1990s. Living Census Series* (Washington, D.C.: Brookings Institution, May 2003).

39.   J. Hartung and J. Henig, "Housing Vouchers and Certificates as a Vehicle for Deconcentrating the Poor: Evidence from the Washington, D.C. Metropolitan Area," *Urban Affairs Review 32*, 3 (1997): 403–19.

40.   G. Goetz, "The Effects of Subsidized Housing on Communities," *Just in Time Research: Resilient Communities.* (Minneapolis: University of Minnesota Press, 2000).

41.   Smith, *Mixed-income Housing Developments.*

42.   "YouTube Rubbernecking has NJ Officials Seeing Red," ZDNet Government, May 23, 2007, http://government.zdnet.com/?p=3173.

43.   "Hip Hop Journalist Davey D on Police Surveillance of Rappers, the National Hip Hop Convention and the 2004 Election," Democracynow.org, Monday April 19, 2004, http://www.democracynow.org/print.pl?sid=04/04/19/156250.

44.   G. Younge, "U.S. Police Put Hip-Hop Under Surveillance," *Guardian*, March 11, 2004, http://www.theguardian.com/world/2004/mar/11/arts.usa.

45.   *Who's Watching? Video Camera Surveillance in New York City and the Need for Public Oversight*, A Special Report of the New York Civil Liberties Union, Fall 2006, http://www.nyclu.org/pdfs/surveillance_cams_report_121306.pdf.

46.   *Chicago's Video Surveillance Cameras: A Pervasive and Unregulated Threat to our Privacy*, A Report from the ACLU of Illinois, February 2011, http://il.aclu.org/site/DocServer/Surveillance_Camera_Report1.pdf?docID=3261.

47.   National Institute of Justice, "Keeping Track of Electronic Monitoring," *National Law Enforcement and Corrections Technology Center Bulletin* (October 1999), http://www.justnet.org/Lists/JUSTNET%20Resources/Attachments/859/Elec-Monit.pdf.

48.   National Institute of Justice, "Keeping Track of Electronic Monitoring."

49.   H. Washington, *Medical Apartheid: The Dark History of Medical Experimentation on Black Americans from Colonial Times to the Present* (New York: Doubleday, 2006), 19.

50.   Washington, *Medical Apartheid*, 26.

51.   Washington, *Medical Apartheid*, 26.

52.   Washington, *Medical Apartheid*, 73.

53.   Washington, *Medical Apartheid*, 73.

54.   W. Darity, "Many Roads to Extinction, Early AEA Economists and the Black Disappearance Hypothesis," *History of Economics Review* 21 (1994): 47-64.

55.   J. Jones, *Bad Blood: The Tuskegee Syphilis Experiment* (New York: Free Press, 1981), 2.

56.   E. Muhammad, *Message to the Blackman in America* (Chicago: Muhammad Mosque of Islam, No. 2, 1965), 112.

57.   See F. Welsing, *The Cress Theory of Color-Confrontation and Racism (White Supremacy)* (Washington, D.C.: Frances L. Cress-Welsing, 1972).

58.   P. Breggin, "The Violence Initiative: A Racist Biomedical Program for Social Control," *The Rights Tenet* (summer 1992): 3-8.

59.   Rebecca Skloot, *The Immortal Life of Henrietta Lacks* (New York: Random House, 2010).

60.   I. Van Sertima, ed., *Blacks in Science: Ancient and Modern* (New Brunswick, NJ: Transaction Books, 1983).

61.   I. Van Sertima, ed., *Blacks in Science: Ancient and Modern* (New Brunswick, NJ: Transaction Books, 1983).

62.   National Park Service, *Draft Management Recommendations for the African Burial Ground*, http://www.africanburialground.gov/ABG_FinalReports.htm, p. v.

63.   National Park Service, *Draft Management Recommendations for the African Burial Ground*, p. 9.

64.   National Park Service, *Draft Management Recommendations for the African Burial Ground*, p. 11.

65.   National Park Service, *Draft Management Recommendations for the African Burial Ground*, pp. 11-12.

66.   "African American Funerals and Cemeteries," http://www.memorials.com/Headstones-African-American-Funerals-and-Cemeteries-information.php

67.   Rick Jervis, "Initiative Aims to Find Lost Grave Sites of Slaves," USAToday.com, February 2, 2012, http://www.usatoday.com/news/nation/story/2012-02-02/slave-burial-sites/53083254/1..

68.   A. Banks, *Race, Rhetoric, and Technology*, 125.

69.   J. Tobin and R. Dobard, *Hidden in Plain View: A Secret Story of Quilts and the Underground Railroad* (New York: Anchor, 2000).

70.   Tobin and Dobard, *Hidden in Plain View*, 22.

71.   Patricia Cummings, "An American Quilt Myth: The Secret Quilt Code of the Underground Railroad," http://www.quiltersmuse.com/an-american-quilt-myth.htm.

72.   See L. Haber, *Black Pioneers of Science and Invention* (New York: Harcourt, Bracey and World, 1990) and V. Sammons, *Blacks in Science and Medicine* (New York: Hemisphere Publishing Corporation, 1991).

73.   C. Johnson, *Patterns of Negro Segregation* (New York: Harper, 1940), 124.

74.   W. Pickens, "Jim Crow in Texas," *The Nation*, August 15, 1923, 156.

9

75. K. Frantz, "'The Open Road': Automobility and Racial Uplift in the Interwar Years," in *Technology and the African-American Experience, Needs and Opportunities for Study*, ed. B. Sinclair (Boston: MIT Press, 2004), 131-53.

76. Steven Raphael and Alan Berube, "Socioeconomic Differences in Household Automobile Ownership Rates: Implications for Evacuation Policy," paper prepared for the Berkeley Symposium on "Real Estate, Catastrophic Risk, and Public Policy," March 23, 2006, http://urbanpolicy.berkeley.edu/pdf/raphael.pdf.

77. John Pucher and John Renne, "Socioeconomics of Urban Travel: Evidence from the 2001 NHTS," *Transport Quarterly* 57 (2003): 49–77 http://policy.rutgers.edu/faculty/pucher/TQPuchRenne.pdf.

78. Alexandra Cawthorne, "Trouble in the Suburbs: Poverty Rises in Areas Outside Cities," Center for American Progress, October 27, 2010, http://www.americanprogress.org/issues/2010/trouble_in_the_suburbs.html.

79. Cawthorne, "Trouble in the Suburbs."

80. The Leadership Conference Education Fund, "Where We Need to Go: A Civil Rights Roadmap for Transportation Equity," (March 2011), 3, http://www.aapd.com/what-we-do/transportation/where-we-need-to-go.pdf.

81. Alan Berube, Elizabeth Deakin, and Steven Raphael, "Socioeconomic Differences in Household Automobile Ownership Rates: Implications for Evacuation Policy," (June 2006), http://socrates.berkeley.edu/~raphael/BerubeDeakenRaphael.pdf.

82. Meizhu Lui, Emma Dixon, and Betsy Leondar-Wright, "Stalling the Dream: Cars, Race and Hurricane Evacuation." United for a Fair Economy's Third Annual Report, *State of the Dream 2006*, January 10, 2006, http://www.faireconomy.org/files/pdf/stalling_the_dream_2006.pdf.

83. Irwin Redlener, et al. *Follow-Up 2005: Where the American Public Stands on Terrorism and Preparedness after Hurricane Katrina & Rita: A Follow-Up to the 2005 Annual Survey of the American Public by the National Center for Disease Preparedness*. Columbia University Mailman School of Public Health, (2005).

84. Monica Miller, *Slaves to Fashion, Black Dandyism and the Styling of Black Diasporic Identity* (Durham, NC: Duke University Press, 2009), 1.

85. Ibid., 3.

86. Helen Foster, *'New Raiments of Self': African American Clothing in the Antebellum South*. Oxford, UK: Berg, 1997, 24.

87. Shane White and Graham White, *Stylin': African American Expressive Culture from Its Beginnings to the Zoot Suit* (Ithaca, NY: Cornell University Press, 1998), 36.

88. Robert Fogel, *Without Consent or Contract, The Rise and Fall of American Slavery* (New York: W.W. Norton, 1989), 144.

89. Ibid., 143.

90. Fogel, *Without Consent or Contract*, 145.

91. Fogel, *Without Consent or Contract*, 145.

92. This information is taken from Kenyon.edu, http://northbysouth.kenyon.edu/2002/Food/NBSFOOD/Food%20History.htm.

93. K. Manning, *Black Apollo of Science* (New York: Oxford University Press, 1983).

94. The website of the National Organization of Professional Black Natural Resources Conservation Service Employees can be found at http://nopbnrcse.memberlodge.org/

95. See the definition of appropriate technology online at http://en.wikipedia.org/wiki/Appropriate_technology.

96. V. Kaplan, *Structural Inequality: Black Architects in the United States*, 21.

97. A. Jenkins and Om-Ra Seti, *Black Futurists in the Information Age*, 10-11.

98. Ibid., 11.

99. Representative Maxine Waters, "Rep. Waters Joins President Clinton in Launch of Digital Divide New Markets Initiative Tour," Press Release, April 4, 2000.

100. A. Krueger, "The Digital Divide in Educating African-American Students and Workers" (March 2000), Princeton University IRS Working Paper No. 434, http://ssrn.com/abstract=223749.

101. D. Hoffman and T. Novak, "Bridging the Racial Divide on the Internet," *Science* 280 (April 1998): 390-91.

102. L. Sax, A. Astin, W. Korn, and K. Mahoney, "The American Freshman: National Norms for Fall 1998," Higher education Research Institute, UCLA Graduate School of Education & Information Studies http://www/acenet.edu/news/press_release/1999/01January/freshman_sur-vey.html.

103. Noted on the Congressional Black Caucus' website technology section on April 16, 2002 at http://www.house.gov/ebjohnson/cbctechnolo-gymain.htm.

104. J. Meredith, "Closing the New Digital Divide: African-Americans Call Upon the FCC to Allow Improved High-Speed Internet Access."

105. Banks, *Race, Rhetoric, and Technology*, 41.

106. Banks, *Race, Rhetoric, and Technology*, 42.

107. For information about Community Technology Center initiatives see the CTC-Net website, at http://www.ctcnet.org.

108. T. Spooner and L. Rainie, "African-Americans and the Internet," Pew Internet & American Life Project (2000), http://www.pewinternet.org.

109. Ibid.

110. T. Novak and D. Hoffman, "Bridging the Digital Divide: The Impact of Race on Computer Access and Internet Use," Vanderbilt eLab Manuscripts, February 2, 1998, http://www.ehcweb.ehc.edu/faculty/ljcumbo/PDFS/hoffman_novak.pdf.

111. A. Banks, *Race, Rhetoric, and Technology*, 8.

112. A. Marks, "Digital Divide Narrows: Minorities Closing High-tech Gap," *Christian Science Monitor*, January 25, 2000.

113. Linda Jackson, et al., "Race, Gender, and Information Technology Use: The New Digital Divide," *Cyberpsychology & Behavior* 11(4), (2008), http://academics.hamilton.edu/ebs/pdf/NDD.pdf.

114. Danah Boyd, "White Flight in Networked Publics? How Race How Race and Class Shaped American Teen Engagement With MySpace and Facebook," in *Race After the Internet*, eds. L. Nakamura and P. Chow-White, *Digital Race Anthology* (New York: Routledge, 2011), 203-222, http://www.danah.org/papers/2009/WhiteFlightDraft3.pdf.

115. Cameron Marlow, "How Diverse is Facebook?," Facebook.com, December 16, 2009, http://www.facebook.com/note.php?note_id=205925658858&id=8394258414&ref=mf.

116. The Black Bloggers Network, http://www.blackbloggernetwork.com/about/.

117. "Black Weblog Awards A Celebration of Black Social Media," http://www.blackweblogawards.com/home/

118. Ibid.

119. See the Urban Ed, Inc. website for additional information, http://www.urbaned.org/6_about_urbaned.html.

120. Spooner and Rainie, "African-Americans and the Internet."

121. "Video game industry seeking minorities," NBCNews.com, http://www.msnbc.msn.com/id/8837488/ August 5, 2005.

122. Dmitri Williams, Nicole Martins, Mia Consalvo and James D. Ivory, "The Virtual Census: Representations of Gender, Race and Age in Video Games," *New Media Society* 11 (2009): 815-834.

123. Craig Anderson, et al., "Violent Video Game Effects on Aggression, Empathy, and Prosocial Behavior in Eastern and Western Countries: A Meta-analytic Review," *Psychological Bulletin* 136 (2), (March 2010): 151-173.

124. Leadership Conference on Civil Rights Education Fund, "Are We Really a Nation Online? Ethnic and Racial Disparities in Access to Technology and Their Consequences," CivilRights.org, September 20, 2005, http://www.civilrights.org/publications/nation-online/.

125. Marcus-Alexander Neil, "President Obama's Broadband Initiative Will Attempt to Bridge the Nation's Growing Digital Divide," CivilRights.org, September 4, 2009, http://www.civilrights.org/archives/2009/09/673-broadband.html.

126. Aaron Smith, "Home Broadband 2010," A Pew Internet and American Life Project Report, Pew Internet, August 11, 2010, http://pewinternet.org/Reports/2010/Home-Broadband-2010/Summary-of-Findings.aspx.

127. Ibid.

128. "Video game industry seeking minorities."

129. A. Banks, *Race, Rhetoric, and Technology*, 123.

130. U.S. National Center for Health Statistics, "Death: Preliminary Data for 2008," *59*(2), (December 2010), http://www.census.gov/compendia/statab/2012/tables/12s0105.pdf.

131. D. Satcher, G. Fryer, Jr., J. McCann, A. Troutman, S. Woolf and G. Rust, "What If We Were Equal? A Comparison of The Black-White Mortality Gap In 1960 And 2000," *Health Affairs* 24 (2), 459.

132. Centers for Disease Control, "2006 HIV/AIDS Surveillance Report," (2008).

133. Public Law 111-148, 124 Stat. 119, to be codified as amended at scattered sections of the Internal Revenue Code and in 42 U.S.C.

134. "Provisions of the Affordable Care Act, by Year." (Washington, DC: U.S. Department of Health and Human Services, retrieved July 12, 2011), http://www.healthcare.gov/law/about/order/byyear.html.

135. Carmen DeNavas-Walt, Bernadette Proctor, and Jessica Smith, "Income, Poverty, and Health Insurance Coverage in the United States: 2008." *Current Population Reports* (September 2009), 60-236 (RV).

136. Amy Finkelstein, Sarah Taubman, Bill Wright, Mira Bernstein, Jonathan Gruber, Joseph P. Newhouse, Heidi Allen, Katherine Baicker, and the Oregon Health Study Group, "The Oregon Health Insurance Experiment: Evidence from the First Year" (NBER Working Paper No. 17190). Cambridge, MA: National Bureau of Economic Research, (July 2011).

137. "Michelle Obama: 'Let's Move' Initiative Battles Childhood Obesity," ABCNews.com, February 9, 2010, http://abcnews.go.com/GMA/Health/michelle-obama-childhood-obesity-initiative/story?id=9781473.

138. *Solving the Problem of Childhood Obesity Within a Generation. Report to the President*, (Washington, DC: White House Task Force on Childhood Obesity, May 2010).

9

139.   Centers for Disease Control and Prevention, "Cases of HIV Infection and AIDS in the United States and Dependent Areas, by Race/Ethnicity, 2003–2007," HIV/AIDS Surveillance Supplemental Report, 14 (2009), http://www.cdc.gov/hiv/surveillance/resources/reports/2009supp_vol14no2/pdf/table1.pdf.

140.   "Obama Administration Putting AIDS Back on Nation's Radar," USAToday.com, April 7, 2009, http://www.usatoday.com/news/health/2009-04-07-AIDS-CDC-HIV_N.htm.

141.   "Obama Administration Releases AIDS Strategy with Important Anti-Discrimination Policies," ACLU.org, July 13, 2010, http://www.aclu.org/hiv-aids/obama-administration-releases-aids-strategy-important-anti-discrimination-policies.

142.   "Understanding New National Data on Lead Poisoning," Community Environmental Resource Center, http://cehrc.org/chil_ar/chil_ar_lead_poisoning_bll_data_factsheet/.

143.   Nevin Scrimshaw and John Paul SanGiovanni, "Synergism of Nutrition, Infection, and Immunity: An Overview," *American Journal of Clinical Nutrition* 66(4), (1997): 64S-77S.

144.   CDC, *CDC Health Disparities and Inequalities Report – United States, 2011. Morbidity and Mortality Weekly Report, Supplement. 60* (January 14, 2011).

145.   Ibid.

146.   D. Roberts, "Black Women and the Pill," *Family Planning Perspectives* 32 (March/April 2000). See also D. Roberts, *Killing the Black Body: Race, Reproduction, and the Meaning of Liberty* (New York: Vintage, 1997).

147.   Ibid.

148.   Roberts, "Black Women and the Pill."

149.   Ibid.

150.   Rebecca Kluchin, *Fit to be Tied, Sterilization and Reproductive Rights in America, 1950-1980* (New Brunswick: NJ: Rutgers University Press, 2009), 1

151.   Kluchin, *Fit to be Tied*, 19.

152.   Kluchin, *Fit to be Tied*, 6.

153.   Kluchin, *Fit to be Tied*, 7.

154.   Kluchin, *Fit to be Tied*, 177.

155.   State Library of North Carolina, "Eugenics in North Carolina," http://statelibrary.dcr.state.nc.us/dimp/digital/eugenics/index.html.

156.   Martha Waggoner, "Payouts Urged in N.C. Sterilization Case," PostandCourier.com, January 11, 2012, http://www.postandcourier.com/news/2012/jan/11/payouts-urged-nc-sterilization-case/.

157.   Rebecca Sinderbrand, "A Shameful Little Secret," *Newsweek* 33, March 28, 2005, 1.

158.   Waggoner, "Payouts Urged."

159.   "North Carolina agrees to compensate sterilization victims for 45-year eugenics program," RT.com, http://rt.com/usa/north-carolina-eugenics-program-932/.

160.   See J. Donohue and S. Levitt, "Further Evidence that Legalized Abortion Lowered Crime: A Reply to Joyce," NBER Working Paper No. 9532 (March 2003). This view is also presented in S. Levitt and S. Dubner, *Freakonomics: A Rogue Economist Explores the Hidden Side of Everything* (New York: Harper-Collins, 2005).

161.   Roberts, "Black Women and the Pill."

162.   M. Mies, "New Reproductive Technologies: Sexist and Racist Implications," *Quilt* (1994): 41–42.

163.   This information is taken from the families.com website: http://encyclopedias.families.com/in-vitro-fertilization-494-495-ecc.

164.   Ibid.

165.   D. Roberts, "Race and the Biotech Agenda," Presentation at the Symposium, "The Next Four Years, the Biotech Agenda, the Human Future: What Direction for Liberals and Progressives?" (1994).

166.   Ibid.

167.   A. Bowser, "Positive Outcomes for Assisted Reproduction Less Likely in Black, Asian Women," *Medscape*, October 18, 2004, http://www.medscape.com/viewarticle/491497.

168.   Roberts, "Black Women and the Pill."

169.   See the website of the African American Heart Failure Trial (A-HeFT), http://www.aheft.org/about.asp.

170.   V. Randall, "Gender, Race and Ethnicity: Experiences with Three Health Care Related Issues," vol. 1, The Role of Governmental and Private Health Care Programs and Initiatives, The Health Care Challenge: Acknowledging Disparity, Confronting Discrimination, and Ensuring Equality, a Report of the United States Commission on Civil Rights (September 1999), http://academic.udayton.edu/health/08civilrights/01-03-05Research.htm (site no longer available).

171.   J. LaRosa, B. Seto, C. Caban, and E. Hayunga, "Including Women and Minorities in Clinical Research," *Applied Clinical Trials* 4 (May 1995): 31; J. Bennett, "Inclusion of Women in Clinical Trials—Policies for Population Subgroups," *New England Journal of Medicine* 329 (July 22, 1993): 288-92.

172. O. Brawley and H. Tejeda, "Minority Inclusion in Clinical Trials Issues and Potential Strategies," *Journal of the National Cancer Institute Monographs*, no. 17 (1995): 56.

173. Pub. L. No. 103-43, 107 Stat. 122 (codified in scattered sections of 8, and 42 U.S.C. [1994 & Sup. II. 1996]).

174. Brawley and Tejeda, "Minority Inclusion in Clinical Trials," 56.

175. "A Paradox of Genetic Research: Race, Ethnicity, and Disease," Center for the Study of Society & Medicine, http://www.societyandmedicine.columbia.edu/genetics_red.shtml.

176. J. Harris and W. McCoullough, "Quantitative Methods and Black Community Studies," in *The Death of White Sociology*, ed. J. Ladner (New York: Random House, 1973), 336.

177. J. Stanfield, "Methodological Reflections, An Introduction." In *Race and Ethnicity in Research Methods*, ed. J. Stanfield & R. Dennis (Newbury Park, CA: Sage Publications, 1993), 32-33.

178. The website of the African Ancestry website can be found at http://www.africanancestry.com/index.html.

179. Rebecca Herzig, "The Matter of Race in Histories of American Technology," in *Technology and the African-American Experience*, ed. B. Sinclair (Cambridge, MA: MIT Press, 2004), 155-70.

180. See A. Mire, "Pigmentation and Empire, The Emerging Skin-Whitening Industry," A CounterPunch Special Report, Counterpunch.com, July 28, 2005, http://www.counterpunch.org/2005/07/28/the-emerging-skin-whitening-industry.

181. M. Bongiorno and M. Aricò, "Report: Exogenous Ochronosis and Striae Atrophicae Following the Use of Bleaching Creams," *International Journal of Dermatology* 44 (February 2005): 112.

182. Shomarka Keita and James Stewart, "Ethics, Identity, Genetics, Patrimony and Power in the Harvesting of DNA from Africa," Council for Responsible Genetics, http://www.councilforresponsiblegenetics.org/GeneWatch/GeneWatchPage.aspx?pageId=273&archive=yes.

183. National Black Church Initiative, http://www.naltblackchurch.com/about/current-programs.html.

184. Marc Weigensberg, "Dietary Fat Intake and Insulin Resistance in Black and White Children, *Obesity Research*. 13(9), (September 2005), 1630-7.

185. Maria Schmidt, et al., "Fast-Food Intake and Diet Quality in Black and White Girls." The National Heart, Lung, and Blood Institute Growth and Health Study. *Archives of Pediatrics and Adolescent Medicine* 159 (July 2005), 626-631.

186. Jason Block, et al. "Fast Food, Race/Ethnicity, and Income: A Geographic Analysis," *American Journal of Preventive Medicine* 27(3), (October 2004): 211-7.

187. Kimberly Morland, et al. "Neighborhood Characteristics Associated with the Location of Food Stores and Food Service Places," *American Journal of Preventive Medicine* 22(1), (January, 2002): 23-9.

188. LaVonna Lewis, et al., "Transforming the Urban Food Desert From the Grassroots Up: A Model for Community Change," *Family & Community Health Issues* 34 (Supplement S1, January/March 2011): S92–S101.

189. Detroit Black Community Food Security Network, accessed 2/25/2010, http://detroitblackfoodsecurity.org/.

190. See, for example, Tracye Lynn McQuirter, *By Any Greens Necessary: A Revolutionary Guide for Black Women Who Want to Eat Great, Get Healthy, Lose Weight, and Look Phat* (Chicago: Lawrence Hill Books, 2010); Angela Medearis, *The Kitchen Diva! The New African-American Kitchen* (New York: Lake Isle Press, 2008); and Bryant Terry, *Vegan Soul Kitchen: Fresh, Healthy, and Creative African-American Cuisine* (Cambridge, MA: Da Capo Press, 2009); and Afroculinaria.com, a website that explores the culinary traditions of Africa, African America and the African Diaspora, http://afroculinaria.com/.

191. "The Black Barbershop Health Outreach Program," http://blackbarbershop.org/.

192. K. Aleisha Fetters and Sheila Dichoso, "HIV Prevention Enters Salons, Barbershops," Medill Reports, March 12, 2009 http://news.medill.northwestern.edu/chicago/news.aspx?id=123525.

193. See A. Bishop, I. Bazzell, B. Mehra, and C. Smith, "Afya: Social and Digital Technologies that Reach across the Digital Divide," *First Monday* 6 (April 2001), http://www.firstmonday.org/issues/issue6_4/bishop/.

194. L. Fortson, "Biomedical Research Warfare," *Black Issues in Higher Education*, (March 1999): 25.

195. L. Winner, "Do Artifacts Have Politics?" *Daedalus* 109, no. 1 (1980): 27.

196. R. Bullard, *Dumping in Dixie: Race, Class and Environmental Quality* (Boulder, CO: Westview Press, 1990).

197. A. Bix, "A Bibliography of Technology and the African American Experience," in *Technology and the African-American Experience*, ed. B. Sinclair, 207.

198. R. Krovi and C. Barnes, "Work-Related Travel Patterns of People of Color," in *Travel Patterns of People of Color*, ed. Battelle (Columbus, OH: Battelle, 2000).

199. Ibid., 62.

200. Environmental Justice Resource Center (n. d.) Atlanta Transportation Equity Project Summary, http://www.ejrc.cau.edu/atepannouncement.htm.

201. See K. Frantz, "'The Open Road': Automobility and Racial Uplift in the Interwar Years."

9

202. The Proceedings to the First National People of Color Environmental Leadership Summit are available from the United Church of Christ Commission for Racial Justice, 475 Riverside Drive, Suite 1950, New York, NY 10115.

203. See the website of Action Housing, http://www.actionhousinggreen.org/partnerships.php.

204. The National Black Church Initiative, http://www.naltblackchurch.com/environment/index.html.

205. Ibid.

206. The National Black Church Initiative.

207. NAACP Climate Change Initiative, http://www.naacp.org/pages/climate-justice-initiative-about.

208. J. Andrew Hoerner and Nia Robinson, "Just Climate Policy —Just Racial Policy," *Race Poverty & the Environment: A Journal for Social and Environmental Justice*, Urban Habitat, http://urbanhabitat.org/cj/hoerner-robinson.

209. Hoerner and Robinson, "Just Climate Policy."

210. Jeff Niesel, (2013-06-26). "Cleveland - Music - Turn This Mutha Out". Clevescene.com. (June 26, 2013).

211. This information is extracted from, "Space/Astronomy," About.com. URL: http://space.about.com/od/astronomyspacehistory/tp/Black_History_Month.htm.

212. Ibid.

213. "Space/Astronomy, op. cit."

214. "Space/Astronomy, op. cit."

215. "Space/Astronomy, op. cit."

216. M. Mitchell, *The Crisis of the African-American Architect: Conflicting Cultures of Architecture and (Black) Power, 2d rev. ed* (Lincoln, NE: iUniverse, 2003), x.

217. Mitchell, *The Crisis of the African-American Architect*, xiii.

218. Mitchell, *The Crisis of the African-American Architect*, 276.

219. Mitchell, *The Crisis of the African-American Architect*, 276.

220. Mitchell, *The Crisis of the African-American Architect*, xii-xiii.

221. A. Banks, *Race, Rhetoric, and Technology*, 129.

222. A. Banks, *Race, Rhetoric, and Technology*, 129.

223. Mitchell, *The Crisis of the African-American Architect*, 296.

224. Mitchell, *The Crisis of the African-American Architect*, 296-97.

225. J. Stewart, "Will the Revolution be Digitized? Using Digitized Resources in Undergraduate Africana Studies Courses," *Western Journal of Black Studies* 27 (fall 2003): 194-204.

226. The website for the eBlack Studies can be found at http://www.eblackstudies.org.

227. K. Appiah, & H. Gates, *Microsoft Encarta Africana* (Microsoft 2000).

228. James Stewart, "Riddles, Rhythms, and Rhymes: Toward an Understanding of Methodological Issues and Possibilities in Black/Africana Studies," in Timothy Wong, ed. *Ethnic Studies Research, Approaches and Perspectives* (Lanham, MD: AltaMira Press, 2008), 179-217.

Select Bibliography

"A Foundation of Poetry, Dudley Randall." African American Registry. (n.d.). http://www.aaregistry. org/historic_events/view/foundation-poetry-dudley-randall

Abdel-Daim, A. "The Dialectics of Culture: Arab and American Relations." *The Western Journal of Black Studies* 3 (Spring 1979): 2–7.

Adarand Constructors, Inc. v. Pena, 515 U.S. 200 (1995).

Adejumobi, S. "The Pan-African Congress." In *Organizing Black America: An Encyclopedia of African American Associations*, edited by N. Mjagkij. New York: Garland Publishing, 2001.

Administration on Aging, U.S. Department of Health and Human Services. "A Statistical Profile of Black Older Americans Aged 65+." *Snapshot*, February 2006. http://www.aoa.gov/aoaroot/ press_room/products_materials/pdf/stat_profile_black_aged_65.pdf.

AFL-CIO. "Economics Education, What Is Our Message, What Are Our Goals." Unpublished manuscript, n.d.

"African American Funerals and Cemeteries." Accessed August 16, 2014. http://www.memorials. com/Headstones-African-American-Funerals-and-Cemeteries-information.php.

"African American Heart Failure Trial." (n.d.). A-HeFT. http://www.medscape.org/ viewarticle/494186.

African Ancestry. http://www.africanancestry.com/home/.

Aizcorbe, A., A. Kennickell, and K. Moore. "Recent Changes in U.S. Family Finances from the 1998 and 2001 Survey of Consumer Finances." *Federal Reserve Bulletin* (January 2003). http://www. federalreserve.gov/pubs/bulletin/2003/0103lead.pdf.

Akbar, N. *Chains and Images of Psychological Slavery*. Jersey City: New Mind Productions, 1984.

Alba, R. A., J. R. Logan, and P. E. Bellair. "Living with Crime: The Implications of Racial/Ethnic Differences in Suburban Location." *Social Forces* 73 (1994): 395–434.

Aldridge, D. "Interracial Marriages: Theoretical Considerations." *Journal of Black Studies* 8 (March 1978): 355–68.

————. ed. "Black Women in the American Economy." Special issue, *Journal of Black Studies* 20, no. 2 (1989).

————. *Focusing: Black Male–Female Relationships*. Chicago: Third World Press, 1991.

————. "Womanist Issues in Black Studies: Towards Integrating Africana Women into Africana Studies." *Afrocentric Scholar* 1, no. 1 (1992): 167–82.

Aldridge, D., and C. Young. *Out of the Revolution: The Development of Africana Studies*. Lanham: Lexington Books, 2000.

Alexander, M. *The New Jim Crow: Mass Incarceration in the Age of Colorblindness*. New York: The New Press, 2010.

Alkalimat, A. "Africana Studies in the US." March 2007. Accessed August 16, 2014. eblackstudies. org.

————. "Technological Revolution and Prospects for Black Liberation in the 21st Century." *CyRev* (2001). http://www.net4dem.org/cyrev/archive/issue4/articles/liberation/liberation.pdf.

Alkalimat, A., and Associates. *Introduction to Afro-American Studies: A Peoples College Primer*. Chicago: 21st Century Publications, 1986.

Allen, R. *Black Awakening in Capitalist America*. Garden City, NY: Anchor Books, 1970.

————. "Past Due: The African American Quest for Reparations." In *African Americans in the U.S. Economy*, edited by C. A. Conrad, J. Whitehead, P. L. Mason, and J. Stewart. Lanham: Rowman & Littlefield, 2005.

Allen-Smith, J. "Introduction." In *Blacks in Rural America*, edited by J. B. Stewart and J. E. Allen-Smith. New Brunswick: Transaction Publishers, 1995.

Alliance for Healthy Homes. "Understanding New National Data on Lead Poisoning." http://www. nchh.org/Portals/0/Contents/hps_lead_BLL_data_factsheet.pdf. Accessed September 29, 2014.

Allport, G. *Pattern and Growth in Personality*. Ft. Worth: Holt, Rinehart and Winston, 1961.

Alpers, E., and A. Roberts. "What Is African Studies? Some Reflections." *African Issues* 30, no. 2 (2002): 11–18.

Alridge D., J. Stewart, and V. P. Franklin, eds. *Message in the Music, Hip Hop History and Pedagogy*. Washington, DC: The ASALH Press, 2010.

America, R., ed. *Paying the Social Debt*. Westport: Praeger, 1993.

————. *The Wealth of Races: The Present Value of Benefits from Past Injustices*. Westport: Greenwood Press, 1990.

American Civil Liberties Union. "Obama Administration Releases AIDS Strategy with Important Anti-discrimination Policies." July 13, 2010. https://www.aclu.org/hiv-aids/obama-administration-releases-aids-strategy-important-anti-discrimination-policies.

"An Interview with Thomas A. Dorsey." *Black Books Bulletin* 5 (Spring 1977).

Anderson, C., A. Shibuya, N. Ihori, E. Swing, B. Bushman, A. Sakamoto, H. Rothstein, and M. Saleem. "Violent Video Game Effects on Aggression, Empathy, and Prosocial Behavior in Eastern and Western Countries: A Meta-analytic Review." *Psychological Bulletin* 136, no. 2 (March 2010): 151–73.

Anderson, S. E. "Science, Technology and Black Liberation." *The Black Scholar* 5, no. 6 (1974): 2–8.

Anderson, T. "Black Affirmative Action: Strategies towards Self-Help and Self-Determination." *Humboldt Journal of Social Relations* 14, no. 1/2 (1987): 185–94.

———. "Black Entrepreneurship and Concepts toward Economic Coexistence." *The Western Journal of Black Studies* 6 (Summer 1982): 80–88.

Anderson, T., and W. Harris. "A Socio-historical and Contemporary Study of African Americans in U.S. Corporations." *The Western Journal of Black Studies* 14 (Fall 1990): 174–81.

Appiah, K. *In My Father's House: Africa in the Philosophy of Culture*. New York: Oxford University Press, 1992.

Appiah, K., and H. Gates. *Microsoft Encarta Africana*. Redmond, WA: Microsoft, 2000.

Aptheker, H. *Abolitionism*. Boston, MA: Twayne Publishers, 1989.

———. *American Negro Slave Revolts*. New York: Columbia University Press, 1943.

"Areas of Psychology—Subfields of Psychology." Accessed August 16, 2014. http://psychology. about.com/library/weekly/aa021503a.htm.

Asante, M. *Afrocentricity: The Theory of Social Change*. New York: Amulefi, 1980.

———. *The Afrocentric Idea*. Philadelphia: Temple University Press, 1987.

Ashe, A., and A. Rampersad. *Days of Grace: A Memoir*. New York: Ballantine Books, 1994.

Association for the Study of Afro-American Life and History. *The International Library of Afro-American Life and History*. Washington, DC: Association for the Study of Afro-American Life and History, 1976.

Atwell, I., and D. Azibo. "Diagnosing Personality Disorder in Africans (Blacks) Using the Azibo Nosology: Two Case Studies." *The Journal of Black Psychology* 17 (Spring 1991): 1–22.

Aubrey, L. "African Americans in the United States and African Studies." *African Issues* 30, no. 2 (2002): 19–23.

Ayres, E. *The Promise of the New South*. New York: Oxford University Press, 1992.

Azibo, D., ed. *African Centered Psychology, Culture-Focusing for Multicultural Competence*. Durham: Carolina Academic Press, 2003.

———. "African-Centered Theses on Mental Health and a Nosology of Black/African Personality Disorder." *The Journal of Black Psychology* 15 (Spring 1989): 173–214.

———. "Black Personality Questionnaire: A Review and Critique." In *Handbook of Tests and*

Measurements for Black Populations, edited by R. L. Jones, vol. 2. Hampton, VA: Cobb and Henry, 1996.

―――. "The Psycho-cultural Case for Reparations for Descendants of Enslaved Africans in the United States." *Race, Gender & Class* 18, no. 1–2 (2011): 7.

―――. "Treatment and Training Implications of the Advances in African Personality Theory." *The Western Journal of Black Studies* 14 (Spring 1990): 53–65.

Azibo, D., and J. Robinson. "An Empirically Supported Reconceptualization of African–U.S. Racial Identity Development as an Abnormal Process." *Review of General Psychology* 8, no. 4 (2004): 249–64.

Bak, R. *Joe Louis: The Great Black Hope*. Dallas: Taylor Publishing, 1996.

Baker, F. "The Afro-American Life Cycle: Success, Failure, and Mental Health." *Journal of the National Medical Association* 79, no. 6(1987): 625–33.

Baker, H. *Black Literature in America*. New York: McGraw-Hill, 1971.

―――. *Blues, Ideology and African-American Literature*. Chicago: The University of Chicago Press, 1984.

―――. "Generational Shifts and the Recent Criticism of Afro-American Literature." In *Paradigms in Black Studies: Intellectual History, Cultural Meaning, and Political Ideology*, edited by A. Alkalimat. Chicago: Twenty-First Century Books and Publications, 1990.

―――. "Hybridity, the Rap Race and Pedagogy for the 1990s." *Black Music Research Journal* 11, no. 2 (Fall 1991): 217–28.

Baldwin, J. "African Self-Consciousness and the Mental Health of African Americans." *Journal of Black Studies* 15, no. 2 (1984): 177–94.

―――. "Notes on an Africentric Theory of Black Personality." *The Western Journal of Black Studies* 5, no. 2 (Fall 1981): 53–71.

―――. "Psychological Aspects of European Cosmology in American Society." *The Western Journal of Black Studies* 9 (Winter 1985): 216–23.

Baldwin, J., and Y. Bell. "The African Self-Consciousness Scale: An Africentric Personality Questionnaire." *The Western Journal of Black Studies* 9 (Summer 1985): 61–68.

Balkin, J. "Brown as Icon." In *What "Brown v. Board of Education" Should Have Said*, edited by J. Balkin, 3-28. New York: New York University Press, 2001.

Bander, E., ed. *Turmoil on the Campus*. New York: H.W. Wilson, 1970.

Banks, A. *Race, Rhetoric, and Technology: Searching for Higher Ground*. Mahwah: Lawrence Erlbaum, 2006.

Barnett, M. "The Congressional Black Caucus and the Institutionalization of Black Politics." *Journal of Afro-American Issues* 5 (Summer 1977): 201–27.

Basu, D. "A Critical Examination of the Political Economy of the Hip-Hop Industry." In *African Americans in the U.S. Economy*, edited by C. A. Conrad, J. Whitehead, P. L. Mason, and J. Stewart, 258-70. Lanham: Rowman & Littlefield, 2005.

Bates, T. *Banking on Black Enterprise: The Potential of Emerging Firms for Revitalizing Urban Economies*. Washington, DC: Joint Center for Political and Economic Studies, 1993.

"BBB Interviews Gil Scott-Heron." *Black Books Bulletin* 6, no. 3 (1979): 36–41.

Beck, A. "Prison and Jail Inmates at Midyear 1999." Bureau of Justice Statistics Bulletin, U.S. Department of Justice, Office of Justice Programs, April 2000.

Bell, B. "Contemporary Afro-American Poetry as Folk Art." *Black World* (March 1973):16-35

———. *The Contemporary African American Novel: Its Folk Roots and Modern Literary Branches*. Amherst: University of Massachusetts Press, 2004.

Bell, W. *Foundations of Future Studies*. Vols 1 and 2. New Brunswick: Transaction Publishers, 1997.

Bellamy, D., and A. Parks. "Economic Development in Southern Black Belt Counties: How Does It Measure Up?" In *Blacks in Rural America*, edited by J. B. Stewart and J. E. Allen-Smith. New Brunswick: Transaction Publishers, 1995.

Benedict, R. *Race: Science and Politics*. New York: Viking Press, 1945.

Benjamin, L., J. Stewart, and J. Allen-Smith, eds. *The Black Elite: Facing the Color Line in the Twilight of the Twentieth Century*. Chicago: Nelson Hall, 1991.

Benjamin, L. *Three Black Generations at the Crossroads: Community, Culture and Consciousness*. Chicago: Burnham, 2000.

Bennett, A. "Making a Way Out of No Way: First, You Have to Find the Capital." *NABJ Journal* 15 (April 1970).

Bennett, J. "Inclusion of Women in Clinical Trials: Policies for Population Subgroups." *The New England Journal of Medicine* 329 (July 1993): 288–92.

Bennett, L. *Before the Mayflower*. Chicago: Johnson Publishing, 1982; reprinted by Penguin Books, 1984.

———. *Forced into Glory: Abraham Lincoln's White Dream*. Chicago: Johnson Publishing, 1999.

———. "Money, Merchants, Markets: The Quest for Economic Security." *Ebony*, Part II, November 1975

Bentancur, J., and D. Gills, eds. *The Collaborative City, Opportunities and Struggles for Blacks and Latinos in U.S. Cities*. New York: Garland Publishing, 2000.

Berger, P., and B. Berger. *Sociology*. New York: Basic Books, 1972.

Berlin, I. *Slaves Without Masters*. New York: Vintage Books, 1976.

Berry, M. *Black Resistance, White Law*. New York: Appleton-Century-Crofts, 1971.

select bibliography

————. *My Face Is Black Is True: Callie House and the Struggle for Ex-Slave Reparations*. New York: Albert A. Knopf, 2005.

Berube, A., E. Deakin, and S. Raphael. "Socioeconomic Differences in Household Automobile Ownership Rates: Implications for Evacuation Policy" (June 2006). http://socrates.berkeley.edu/~raphael/BerubeDeakenRaphael.pdf . Accessed September 29, 2014.

Billingsley, A. *Black Families in White America*. Englewood Cliffs: Prentice Hall, 1968.

Birchall, J. *Co-op: The People's Business*. Manchester: Manchester University Press, 1994.

Bishop, A., I. Bazzell, B. Mehra, and C. Smith. "Afya: Social and Digital Technologies That Reach across the Digital Divide." *First Monday* 6 (April 2001). http://www.firstmonday.org/issues/issue6_4/bishop/.

Biskupic, J. "Obama's Push for Court Diversity Hits Snag." *USA Today*, June 15, 2010. http://www.usatoday.com/news/washington/judicial/2010-06-15-diversity-lower-courts_N.htm.

Bittker, B. *The Case for Black Reparations*. New York: Random House, 1973.

Bix, A. "A Bibliography of Technology and the African American Experience." In *Technology and the African-American Experience*, edited by B. Sinclair, 197-234. Cambridge, MA: The MIT Press, 2004.

Black America Web. Accessed September 2, 2014. http://www.blackamericaweb.com/.

"Black Caucus Losing Cohesion." *The Black Commentator* 135 (April 21, 2005). http://www.blackcommentator.com/135/135_cover_black_caucus.html.

Black Voices. Accessed September 1, 2014. http://bv.channel.aol.com/.

Black Weblog Awards. Accessed September 2, 2014. http://www.blackweblogawards.com/home/.

BlackPlanet. http://www.blackplanet.com/.

"Blacks Upbeat about Black Progress, Prospects: A Year after Obama's Election." Pew Research Center Publications (January 12, 2010). http://www.pewsocialtrends.org/2010/01/12/blacks-upbeat-about-black-progress-prospects/. Accessed September 29, 2014.

Blair, C. "Perspective on African Art Criticism." *Black World*, July 24, 1975.

Blassingame, J. *The Slave Community*. New York: Oxford University Press, 1979.

Blauner, R. "Internal Colonialism and Ghetto Revolt." *Social Problems* 16, no. 4 (1969): 393–408.

Block, J., R. Scribner, and K. DeSalvo. "Fast Food, Race/Ethnicity, and Income: A Geographic Analysis." *American Journal of Preventive Medicine* 27, no. 3 (October 2004): 211–17.

Blum, J. M., W. S. McFeely, E. S. Morgan, A. M. Schlesinger Jr., and K. M. Stampp. *The National Experience*. 2nd ed. New York: Harcourt, Brace & World, 1968.

Bobo, J. *Black Women Film and Video Artists*. New York: Routledge, 1998.

Boggs, J. "The Myth and Irrationality of Black Capitalism." In *Black Business Enterprise: Historical and Contemporary Perspectives*, edited by R. W. Bailey. New York: Basic Books, 1971.

Bogle, D. *Primetime Blues: African Americans on Network Television*. New York: Farrar, Straus and Giroux, 2001.

———. *Toms, Coons, Mulattoes, Mammies, and Bucks: An Interpretive History of Blacks in American Films*. New York: Viking Press, 1973.

Bohmer, P. "Marxist Theory of Racism and Racial Inequality." In *African Americans in the U.S. Economy*, edited by C. A. Conrad, J. Whitehead, P. L. Mason, and J. Stewart, 94-100. Lanham: Rowman & Littlefield, 2005.

Bongiorno, M., and M. Aricò. "Exogenous Ochronosis and Striae Atrophicae Following the Use of Bleaching Creams." *International Journal of Dermatology* 44 (February 2005): 112–15.

Bootzin, R. R., E. F. Loftus, and R. B. Zajonc. *Psychology Today*. New York: Random House, 1983.

Bositis, D. *Black Elected Officials: A Statistical Summary 2001*. Washington, DC: Joint Center for Political and Economic Studies, 2003.

Boston, T., ed. *A Different Vision: African American Economic Thought*. Vol. I. New York: Routledge, 1997.

———. *Leading Issues in Black Political Economy*. New Brunswick: Transaction Publishers, 2002.

Boston, T., and C. Ross. *The Inner City: Urban Poverty and Economic Development in the Next Century*. New Brunswick: Transaction Publishers, 1998.

Bowser, A. "Positive Outcomes for Assisted Reproduction Less Likely in Black, Asian Women." *Medscape* (October 18, 2004). http://www.medscape.com/viewarticle/491497.

Boyd, D. "White Flight in Networked Publics? How Race and Class Shaped American Teen Engagement with MySpace and Facebook." In *Race after the Internet*, edited by L. Nakumura and P. Chow-White. New York: Routledge, 2011. http://www.danah.org/papers/2009/WhiteFlightDraft3.pdf.

Boyd, H. "Black Conservatives." *Lies of Our Times* 2 (January 1991).

Boyd, T. *Young Black Rich and Famous: The Rise of the NBA, the Hip Hop Invasion and the Transformation of American Culture*. New York: Doubleday, 2003.

Boyd, V. *Wrapped in Rainbows: The Life of Zora Neale Hurston*. New York: Scribner, 2003.

Boyer, H. "Contemporary Gospel Music: Sacred or Secular?" *The Black Perspective in Music* 7 (Spring 1979):5-58.

Boykin, A., and C. Ellison. "The Multiple Ecologies of Black Youth Socialization: An Afrographic Analysis." In *African-American Youth: Their Social and Economic Status in the United States*, edited by R. L. Taylor, 93-128. Westport: Praeger, 1995.

Brackett, D. "Music." In *Key Terms in Popular Music and Culture*, edited by B. Horner and T. Swiss, 124-40. Oxford, UK: Blackwell, 1999.

Bratcher, M. *Words and Songs of Bessie Smith, Billie Holiday, and Nina Simone: Sound Motion, Blues Spirit, and African Memory*. New York: Taylor & Francis, 2007.

Brawley, O., and H. Tejeda. "Minority Inclusion in Clinical Trials: Issues and Potential Strategies." *Journal of the National Cancer Institute Monographs* 17 (1995): 55–57.

Breggin, P. "The Violence Initiative: A Racist Biomedical Program for Social Control." *The Rights Tenet* (Summer 1992).

Breitman, G., ed. *Malcolm X Speaks: Selected Speeches and Statements*. New York: Pathfinder Press, 1989; Grove Press, First Evergreen Black Cat edition, 1966.

Brimmer, A. "The Black Banks: An Assessment of Performance and Prospects." *Journal of Finance* 26 (May 1971): 379–405.

Broman, C., H. Neighbors, and J. Jackson. "Racial Group Identification among Black Adults." *Social Forces* 67, no. 1 (1988): 146–58.

Brooks, D. "The Storm After the Storm." *The New York Times*, September 1, 2005 http://www.nytimes.com/2005/09/01/opinion/01brooks.html?_r=0 . Accessed September 29, 2014.

Brooks, H. "Technology, Evolution and Purpose." *Daedalus* 109, no. 1 (1980): 65–81.

Broonzy, B. "Unemployment Stomp." Recorded March 30, 1938, in Chicago. (C-2159-1 Vocalion 04205). In *News & the Blues, Telling It Like It Is*. Columbia Records, CBS Records, 2001.

Brown, S. "Negro in American Theater." In *The Oxford Companion to the Theater*, edited by P. Hartnoll. London: Oxford University Press, 1967.

Brown, T. " 'Mad Black Woman' Draws from Gospel 'Chitlin Circuit'." *San Diego Union Tribune*, March 24, 2005, 24. http://www.signonsandiego.com/uniontrib/20050324/news_1c24black.html.

———. "Racism on TV." *Detroit Free Press* 149 (December 27, 1979): 237.

Brown, T., C. Phillips, and G. Parks. "Future Directions." In *African American Fraternities and Sororities: The Legacy and the Vision*, edited by T. L. Brown, G. S. Parks, and C. M. Phillips, 465-70. Lexington: University Press of Kentucky, 2005.

Browning, R., D. Marshall, and D. Tabb. *Racial Politics in American Cities*. New York: Longman, 1990.

Bulhan, H. *Frantz Fanon and the Psychology of Oppression*. New York: Plenum Press, 1985.

Bullard, R. *Dumping in Dixie: Race, Class, and Environmental Quality*. Boulder: Westview Press, 1990.

Bullard, R., and A. Torres, eds. *Sprawl City: Race, Politics, and Planning in Atlanta*. Washington, DC: Island Press, 2000.

Bunch, L. "A Vision for the National Museum of African American History and Culture." http://nmaahc.si.edu/About/Mission.

Bunzel, J. "Black Studies at San Francisco State." *Public Interest* (August 1968). http://www.nationalaffairs.com/public_interest/detail/black-studies-at-san-francisco-state. Accessed September 30, 2014.

Burton, J. "Eugene Redmond." *Answers* (n.d.). http://www.answers.com/topic/eugene-redmond?cat=enter tainment.

Busby, M., ed. *Daughters of Africa: An International Anthology of Words and Writings by Women of African Descent: From the Ancient Egyptian to the Present.* New York: Pantheon Books, 1992.

Butler, O. *Kindred.* New York: Doubleday, 1979.

———. *Parable of the Sower.* New York: Warner Books, 1993.

———. *Parable of the Talents.* New York: Warner Books, 1998.

Caner, A., and E. Wolff. "Asset Poverty in the United States, 1984–1999: Evidence from the Panel Study of Income Dynamics." Economics Working Paper Archive at Washington University in St. Louis, St. Louis, MO, September 2002.

Carmichael, S. *Stokely Speaks.* New York: Vintage Books, 1971.

Carmichael, S., and C. Hamilton. *Black Power: The Politics of Liberation in Americas Politics.* New York: Vintage Books, 1967.

Carrillo, K. "Air America Will Displace Black Talk on WLIB." *The Sacramento Observer* (March 23, 2004). http://www.sacobserver.com/news/032304/wlib_air_america_radio.shtml. Page no longer available.

Cash, W., and L. Oliver, eds. *Black Economic Development: Analysis and Implications.* Ann Arbor, MI: Graduate School of Business Administration, University of Michigan, 1975.

Cawthorne, A. "Trouble in the Suburbs: Poverty Rises in Areas outside Cities." Center for American Progress (October 27, 2010). http://www.americanprogress.org/issues/poverty/news/2010/10/27/8457/trouble-in-the-suburbs/. Accessed September 30, 2014.

Center on Budget and Policy Priorities. "Out of Balance: Cuts in Services Have Been States' Primary Response to Budget Gaps, Harming the Nation's Economy" (April 18, 2012). http://www.cbpp.org/cms/index.cfm?fa=view&id=3747.

Centers for Disease Control. "HIV/AIDS among African Americans" (February 2005).

Centers for Disease Control and Prevention. "Cases of HIV Infection and AIDS in the United States and Dependent Areas, by Race/Ethnicity, 2003–2007." *HIV/AIDS Surveillance Supplemental Report* 14 (2009). http://www.cdc.gov/hiv/surveillance/resources/reports/2009supp_vol14no2/pdf/table1.pdf.

Centers for Disease Control and Prevention. "CDC Health Disparities and Inequalities Report – United States, 2011." *Morbidity and Mortality Weekly Report, Supplement* 60 (January 14, 2011).

Chaffin-Quiray, G. "Melvin Van Peebles." *Senses of Cinema* (n.d.). http://sensesofcinema.com/2003/great-directors/van_peebles/.

Chamarik, S. "Technological Self-Reliance and Cultural Freedom." In *Human Rights and Scientific and Technological Development*, edited by C. G. Weeramantry. New York: United Nations Press, 1990.

Chambers, B., ed. *Chronicles of Black Protest*. New York: Mentor Books, 1968.

Champagne, D. "Toward a Multidimensional Historical Comparative Methodology: Context, Process, and Causality." In *Race and Ethnicity in Research Methods*, edited by J. H. Stanfield and R. M. Dennis, 233-53. Newbury Park, CA: Sage Publications, 1993.

Charles, K., and E. Hurst. "The Correlation of Wealth Across Generations." Unpublished manuscript, December 2002.

Charters, S. *The Bluesman*. New York: Oak Publications, 1967.

Cheney, C. "In Search of the 'Revolutionary Generation': (En)Gendering the Golden Age of Rap Nationalism." In *Message in the Music: Hip Hop, History, & Pedagogy*, edited by D. P. Alridge, J. B. Stewart, and V. P. Franklin, 70-89. Washington, DC: The ASALH Press, 2010.

"Chicago's Video Surveillance Cameras: A Pervasive and Unregulated Threat to our Privacy." A Report from the ACLU of Illinois, February 2011. https://www.aclu.org/blog/free-speech-national-security/surveillance-cameras-chicago-extensive-pervasive-and-unregulated. Accessed September 30, 2014.

Chimezie, A. "Theories of Black Culture." *The Western Journal of Black Studies* 7 (Winter 1983): 216–28.

Christian, B. *Black Feminist Criticism: Perspectives on Black Women Writers*. Paris: Elsevier Science, 1997.

———. *Black Women Novelists: The Development of a Tradition, 1892–1976*. Westport: Greenwood Press, 1980.

Clark, K. "Desegregation: The Role of the Social Sciences." *Teachers College Record* 62, no. 1 (October 1960): 1–17.

Clark, K., and M. Clark. "The Development of Consciousness of Self and the Emergence of Racial Identification in Negro Preschool Children." *Journal of Social Psychology* 10 (1939): 591–99.

Clark Hine, D., and S. Small. *Black Europe and the African Diaspora*. Urbana: University of Illinois Press, 2009.

Clark-Lewis, E. *Living In, Living Out: African American Domestics in Washington, D.C., 1910–1940*. Washington, DC: Smithsonian Institution Scholarly Press, 1994.

Clarke, J. *African World Revolution*. Trenton, NJ: Africa World Press, 1991.

———. *Black/White Alliances: A Historical Perspective* (Black Pages Series). Chicago: Institute of Positive Education, 1970.

———, ed. *Marcus Garvey and the Vision of Africa*. New York: Vintage Books, 1974.

———. "The University of Sankore at Timbuctoo: A Neglected Achievement in Black Intellectual History." *The Western Journal of Black Studies* 1 (June 1977): 142–46.

Clear, T. "Backfire: When Incarceration Increases Crime" (1996). http://www.doc.state.ok.us/DOCS/OCJRC/Ocjrc96/Ocjrc7.htm (page no longer available).

Clegg, C. " 'You're Not Ready for Farrakhan': The Nation of Islam and the Struggle for Black Political Leadership, 1984–2000." In *Black Political Organizations in the Post-Civil Rights Era*, edited by O. Johnson and K. Stanford, 90-131. New Brunswick: Rutgers University Press, 2002.

Clemons, M. "Conceptualizing the Foreign Affairs Participation of African Americans: Strategies and Effects of the Congressional Black Caucus and TransAfrica." In *African American in Global Affairs, Contemporary Perspectives*, edited by M. L. Clemons, 33-64. Boston, MA: Northeastern University Press, 2010.

Coeyman, M. "Black Studies on the Move." *Christian Science Monitor* (February 12, 2002http://www.csmonitor.com/2002/0212/p11s02-lehl.html. Accessed September 30, 2014.

Cohn, S. *Race, Gender, and Discrimination at Work*. Boulder: Westview Press, 2000.

Coleman, M. "African American Popular Wisdom Versus the Qualification Question: Is Affirmative Action Merit-Based?" *The Western Journal of Black Studies* 27 (Spring 2003): 35–44.

College of Letters & Science. *Opt for Undergraduate Studies in Afro-American Studies*. Milwaukee, WI: University of Wisconsin-Milwaukee, 1991.

Collier-Thomas, B. *Jesus, Jobs, and Justice, African American Women and Religion*. New York: Alfred A. Knopf, 2010.

Collins, P. *Black Feminist Thought: Knowledge, Consciousness and the Politics of Empowerment*. New York: Routledge, 1991.

Committee L on the Historically Black Institutions and the Status of Minorities in the Profession. "The Historically Black Colleges and Universities: A Future in the Balance." *Academe* 81, no. 1 (January/February 1995): 49–57.

Cone, J. *For My People*. Maryknoll, NY: Orbis Books, 1991.

Conrad, C., and G. Sherer. "From the New Deal to the Great Society: The Economic Activism of Robert C. Weaver." In *A Different Vision: African American Economic Thought*, edited by T. D. Boston, 290-301., vol. 1. New York: Routledge, 1997.

select bibliography

Conrad, C., J. Whitehead, P. Mason, and J. Stewart, eds. *African Americans in the U.S. Economy*. Lanham: Rowman & Littlefield, 2005.

Cook, N., and S. Kono. "Black Psychology: The Third Great Tradition." *The Journal of Black Psychology* 3 (February 1977): 18–28.

Cooper, A. J. "The Negro as Presented in American Literature (1892)." In *The Voice of Anna Julia Cooper: Including a Voice from the South and Other Important Essays, Papers and Lectures*, edited by C. Lemert and E. Bhan, 134-60. Lanham: Rowman & Littlefield, 1998.

Corey, C. "Hillary Clinton Outlines Obama's Africa Policy," allAfrica.com (January 24, 2009). http://allafrica.com/stories/200901240009.html.

Coulburn, R., and W. E. B. Du Bois. "Mr. Sorokin's Systems." *Journal of Modern History* 14 (1942): 500–21.

Cox, L. *Lincoln and Black Freedom*. Columbia, SC: University of South Carolina Press, 1981.

Cox, O. *Caste, Class and Race*. New York: Doubleday, 1970; originally published in 1948.

Crews, K., and P. Chancellier. *U.S. Population: Charting the Change*. Washington, DC: Population Reference Bureau, 1988.

Crockett, N. *The Black Towns*. Lawrence: University Press of Kansas, 1979.

Cross, T. *Black Capitalism: Strategy for Business in the Ghetto*. New York: Anthenum, 1974.

Cross, W. "Black Family and Black Identity: A Literature Review." *The Western Journal of Black Studies* 2 (1978): 111–24.

———. *Shades of Black: Diversity in African American Identity*. Philadelphia: Temple University Press, 1991.

———. "The Negro-to-Black Conversion Experience." *Black World* (July 1971): 13-31.

———. "The Thomas and Cross Models on Psychological Nigrescence: A Literature Review." *The Journal of Black Psychology* 5, no. 1 (1978): 13–31.

Cruse, H. *Plural but Equal*. New York: William Morrow, 1987.

———. *The Crisis of the Negro Intellectual*. New York: William Morrow, 1967.

Cummings, P. "An American Quilt Myth: The Secret Quilt Code of the Underground Railroad." http://www.quiltersmuse.com/an-american-quilt-myth.htm (page no longer exists)

Cuney, W. "Uncle Sam Says." Vocals by Josh White (Mercury Records, 1941). In *Defiance Blues* (House of Blues, 1998).

Cunnigan, D. "Bringing the Revolution down Home: The Republic of New Africa in Mississippi." *Sociological Spectrum* 19, no. 1 (1999): 63–92.

Curry, G., ed. *The Best of Emerge Magazine*. New York: One World/Ballantine, 2003.

Curry, L. *The Free Black in Urban America, 1800–1850*. Chicago: The University of Chicago Press, 1981.

Dagbovie, P. " 'Of All Our Studies, History Is Best Qualified to Reward Our Research': Black History's Relevance to the Hip Hop Generation." In *Message in the Music, Hip Hop History & Pedagogy*, edited by D. P. Alridge, J. B. Stewart, and V. P. Franklin, 321-44. Washington, DC: The ASALH Press, 2010.

Dalfiume, R. *Desegregation of the U.S. Armed Forces*. Kansas City: University of Missouri Press, 1969.

Daniels, W. *Black Journals of the United States*. Westport: Greenwood Press, 1982.

Darity, W. "Many Roads to Extinction: Early AEA Economists and the Black Disappearance Hypothesis." *History of Economics Review* 21 (1994): 47–64.

Darity, W., and D. Frank. "The Economics of Reparations." In *African Americans in the U.S. Economy*, edited by C. A. Conrad, J. Whitehead, P. L. Mason, and J. Stewart, 334-39. Lanham: Rowman & Littlefield, 2005.

Darity, W., and S. Myers. *Race and Economic Inequality in the United States Since 1945*. Cheltenham: Edward Elgar, 1998.

Dates, J., and W. Barlow. *Split Image: African Americans in the Mass Media*. 2nd ed. Washington, DC: Howard University Press, 1983.

Davis, A., and S. Redding, eds. *Cavalcade*. Boston, MA: Houghton Mifflin, 1971.

Davis, B. "Anger as a Factor and an Invisible Barrier in the Treatment of Black Clients." *The Western Journal of Black Studies* 4 (Spring 1980): 29–32.

Davis, F. *The Economics of Black Community Development*. Chicago: Markham Publishing, 1972.

Davis, M. "The Black Sacred Song." *The Western Journal of Black Studies* 2 (Summer 1978): 138–41.

Davis, R. "Television Commercials and the Management of Spoiled Identity." *The Western Journal of Black Studies* 11 (Summer 1987): 59–63.

Davis, T. "Income Inequities between Black and White Populations in Southern Non-Metropolitan Counties." In *Blacks in Rural America*, edited by J. B. Stewart and J. E. Allen-Smith, 139-52. New Brunswick: Transaction Publishers, 1995.

Deane, P. "Amos 'n Andy Show: U.S. Domestic Comedy." *Museum of Broadcast Communications* (n.d.). http://www.museum.tv/archives/etv/A/htmlA/amosnandy/amosnandy.htm.

Decker, S. "Collective and Normative Features of Gang Violence." *Justice Quarterly* 13, no. 2 (1996): 243–64.

"Dedication." In *African Americans in the U.S. Economy*, edited by C. A. Conrad, J. Whitehead, P. L. Mason, and J. Stewart, xii. Lanham: Rowman & Littlefield, 2005.

Defense Equal Opportunity Management Institute. "FY Summary Representation of Race/Ethnicity Groups and Women in the Active Armed Forces, 1997–2007."

DeGruy, J., J. Kjelldtran, H. Briggs, and E. Brennan. "Racial Respect and Racial Socialization as Protective Factors for African American Male Youth." *The Journal of Black Psychology* 38, no. 4 (2012): 395–420.

Demause, L. *Foundations of Psychohistory*. New York: Creative Roots, 1982.

Demby, G. "LeBron James Tweets Picture of Miami Heat Wearing Hoodies in Solidarity with Family of Trayvon Martin." *The Huffington Post* (March 23, 2012). http://www.huffingtonpost.com/2012/03/23/lebron-heat-trayvon-tweet_n_1375831.html.

DeNavas-Walt, C., B. Proctor, and J. Smith. "Income, Poverty, and Health Insurance Coverage in the United States: 2008." *Current Population Reports* (September 2009) http://www.census.gov/prod/2009pubs/p60-236.pdf. Accessed September 30, 2014.

Dennis, R. "Theories of the Black Family: The Weak-Family and Strong-Family Schools as Competing Ideologies." *Journal of Afro-American Issues* (Summer/Fall 1976): 315-28.

Detroit Black Community Food Security Network. Accessed August 26, 2014. http://detroitblackfoodsecurity.org/.

Dett, R. "The Development of Negro Religious Music." Negro Music. Bowdoin Literary Prize Thesis, Harvard, 1920. In *The R. Nathaniel Dett Reader: Essays in Black Sacred Music: A Special Issue of Black Sacred Music: A Journal of Theomusicology* 5 (Fall 1991.

Dickinson, G. "Pledged to Remember: Africa in the Life and Lore of Black Greek-Letter Organizations." In *African American Fraternities and Sororities: The Legacy and the Vision*, edited by T. L. Brown, G. S. Parks, and C. M. Phillips, 11-36. Lexington: The University Press of Kentucky, 2005.

Dionne, E. "Jackson Share of Votes by Whites Triples in '88." *The New York Times*, June 13, 1988.

Diop, A. "Cultural Well-Being." *First World* 2, no. 3 (1979).

Diop, C. *The Cultural Unity of Black Africa*. Chicago: Third World Press, 1978.

Diouf, S. *Dreams of Africa in Alabama: The Slave Ship Clotilda and the Story of the Last Africans Brought to America*. New York: Oxford University Press, 2007.

———. *Servants of Allah: African Muslims Enslaved in the Americas*. New York: New York University Press, 1998.

Dixon, C. *Negro Spirituals*. Philadelphia: Fortress Press, 1976.

Donohue, J., and S. Levitt. "Further Evidence That Legalized Abortion Lowered Crime: A Reply to Joyce" (NBER Working Paper No. 9532, March 2003). Cambridge, MA: National Bureau of Economic Research.

Dormon, J., and R. Jones. *The Afro-American Experience*. New York: John Wiley & Sons, 1974.

Drake, S. *Black Folk Here and There*. Vol. 1. Los Angeles: UCLA Center for Afro-American Studies, 1987.

———. *Black Folk Here and There*. Vol. 2. Los Angeles: UCLA Center for Afro-American Studies, 1990.

Drake, S., and H. Cayton. *Black Metropolis*. Vol. 2. New York: Harper Torchbooks, 1962.

Drake, W. "Black Liberalism, Conservatism and Social Democracy: The Social Policy Debate." *The Western Journal of Black Studies* 14 (Summer 1990): 115–22.

"Drug Traffickers, Paramilitary Groups . . ." *Violence Policy Center* (n.d.). http://www.vpc.org/studies/awadrug.htm. Accessed September 30, 2014.

Dubey, M., " 'Even Some Fiction Might Be Useful': African American Women Novelists." In *The Cambridge Companion to African American Women's Literature*, edited by A. Mitchell and D. K. Taylor, 150-67. New York: Cambridge University Press, 2009.

Du Bois, W. E. B. "A Negro Nation Within a Nation." *Current History* 42 (1935): 265–70.

———. "Apologia." In *The Suppression of the African Slave Trade to the United States of America, 1638-1870*, 327-29. New York: Schocken Books, 1969.

———. *Black Reconstruction in America 1860-1880*. New York: Atheneum Publishers, 1971; originally published in 1935.

———. "Does the Negro Need Separate Schools?" *The Journal of Negro Education* 4, no. 2 (1935): 328–35.

———. "Education and Work." *The Journal of Negro Education* 1 (1931): 60–74; reprinted in *The Education of Black People: Ten Critiques 1906–1960*, edited by H. Aptheker. Amherst, MA: University of Massachusetts Press, 1973.

———. "Krigwa Players Little Negro Theatre." *Crisis* 32 (July 1926): 134–36.

———. "Negroes and the Crisis of Capitalism." *Monthly Review* 4 (April 1953).

———. "Of the Faith of the Fathers." In *Souls of Black Folk*, 1903. Reprinted in *The Black Church in America*, edited by H. M. Nelsen, R. L. Yokley, and A. K. Nelsen. New York: Basic Books, 1971.

———. "Postscript." In *The Ordeal of Mansart*. Millwood, NY: Kraus Thomson, 1976.

———. "Race Relations in the United States 1917–1947." *Phylon* 9, no. 3 (1948): 234–47.

———. "Strivings of the Negro People." *Atlantic Monthly* 80 (August 1897).

———. "The Atlanta Conferences." *Voice of the Negro* 1 (March 1940): 85–89.

———. *The Autobiography of W. E. B. Du Bois*. New York: International Publishers, 1968.

———. "The Beginning of Slavery." *Voice of the Negro* 2 (February 1905): 104–6.

———. "The Conservation of Races" (American Negro Academy Occasional Paper No. 2, 1897). Reprinted in *W.E.B. Du Bois Speaks: Speeches and Addresses 1890–1919*, edited by P. S. Foner. New York: Pathfinder Press, 1970.

————. "The Development of a People." *International Journal of Ethics* 14 (April 1904): 292–311.

————. "The Economic Future of the Negro." *Publications of the American Economic Association* 7 (1906): 219–42.

————. "The Field and Function of the Negro College." Alumni Reunion Address, Fisk University, 1933. Reprinted in *The Education of Black People: Ten Critiques 1900–1960*, edited by H. Aptheker. Amherst, MA: University of Massachusetts Press, 1973.

————. "The Hampton Idea." In *The Education of Black People: Ten Critiques, 1906–1960*, edited by H. Aptheker. Amherst, MA: University of Massachusetts Press, 1973.

————. *The Negro American Family: Report of a Social Study Made Principally by the College Class of 1909 and 1910 of Atlanta University, under the Patronage of the Trustees of the John F. Slater Fund; Together with the Proceedings of the 13th Annual Conference for the Study of the Negro Problems, Held at Atlanta University on May 27, 1902.* Atlanta: Atlanta University Press, 1908.

————, ed. *The Negro Artisan: Report of a Social Study Made under the Direction of Atlanta University; Together with the Proceedings of the Seventh Conference for the Study of Negro Problems, Held at Atlanta University, on May 27, 1902.* Atlanta: Atlanta University Press, 1902.

————. *The Negro in Business: Report of a Social Study Made under the Direction of Atlanta University; Together with the Proceedings of the Fourth Conference for the Study of the Negro Problems, Held at Atlanta University, May 30–31, 1899.* Atlanta: Atlanta University Press, 1899.

————. "The Relation of the Negroes to the Whites in the South." *The Annals of the American Academy of Political and Social Science* 18 (July 1901): 121–40.

————. "The Social Origins of Negro Art." *The Modern Quarterly* 3, no. 1 (1925).

————. *The Souls of Black Folk.* New York: The New American Library, 1969; originally published in 1903.

————. "The Talented Tenth Memorial Address." *Boulé Journal* 15 (October 1948): 3–13.

————. "The Upbuilding of Black Durham." *World's Work* 13 (January 1912): 334–38.

Dugan, L., D. Nagin, and R. Rosenfeld. "Do Domestic Violence Services Save Lives?" *NIJ Journal* 250 (2003): 20–25.

Dymski, G. " 'New Markets' or Old Constraints? Financing Community Development in the Post-'War on Poverty' Era." Unpublished manuscript, 2005.

eBlack Studies. Accessed August 26, 2014. http://www.eblackstudies.org.

Edwards, G. "E. Franklin Frazier." In *Black Sociologists: Historical and Contemporary Perspectives*, edited by J. E. Blackwell and M. Janowitz. Chicago: The University of Chicago Press, 1974.

Edwards, H. *Black Students.* London: The Free Press, 1970.

———. "On the Issue of Race in Contemporary American Sports." *The Western Journal of Black Studies* 6 (Fall 1982): 138–44.

Edwards, O. "Skin Color as a Variable in Racial Attitudes of Black Urbanites." *Journal of Black Studies* 3 (June 1972): 473–83.

Ekwueme, L. "African-Music Retentions in the New World." *The Black Perspective in Music* 2 (Fall 1974): 128–44.

Elkins, S. *Slavery*. Chicago: The University of Chicago Press, 1959.

Ellis, T. "The New Black Aesthetic." *Callaloo* 38 (Winter 1989): 233–43.

Ellison, J. *Ten Black Economists of Note 1850–1950* (A Report Prepared for the Board of Governors, Federal Reserve System). Gaithersburg, MD: Mid-Atlantic Economic Research Corporation, 1990.

Ellison, R. *Going to the Territory*. New York: Random House, 1986.

Emanuel, J. "Renaissance Sonneteers." *Black World*, September 1975.

Emery, L. *Black Dance, from 1619 to Today*. 2nd ed. Hightstown, NJ: Princeton Book Company, 1988.

Environmental Justice Resource Center. "Atlanta Transportation Equity Project Summary" (n.d.). http://www.ejrc.cau.edu/atepannouncement.htm.

Ernst, S. "Nooses Emerge as Symbols of Hatred in the Workplace." *DiversityInc*, July 18, 2000.

Everett, C. " 'Tradition' in Afro-American Literature." *Black World*, December 1975.

"Expanding Opportunities for African-American Families." President Obama's Fiscal 2010 Budget Overview. A New Era of Responsibility: Renewing America's Promise (2010). http://www. nbcsl.org/PresidentBudget/01_AFAMfactsheet.pdf (page no longer available).

Experience Columbus. "Columbus to Host National Conference of Black Mayors" (April 25, 2005). http://www.experiencecolumbus.com/press_releases.cfm?pressrelease_id=78.

Fager, C. *White Reflections on Black Power*. Grand Rapids, MI: W. B. Eerdmans Publishing, 1967.

Fair, F. *The Orita for Black Youth: An Initiation into Christian Adulthood*. Valley Forge, PA: Judson Press, 1977.

Fairlie, R., and Robb, A. "Why Are Black-Owned Businesses Less Successful than White-Owned Businesses? The Role of Families, Inheritances, and Business Human Capital." Unpublished manuscript, May 2003.

Family Mediation Center. "Child Custody: Parenting Plans." Accessed August 27, 2014. http://coparenting.com/bookandcd.html.

Fanon, F. *The Wretched of the Earth*. New York: Grove Press, 1963.

select bibliography

Farley, E. "The Fugitive Slave Law of 1850 Revisited." *The Western Journal of Black Studies* 3 (Summer 1979): 110–15.

Farley, R. "Trends in Marital Status Among Negroes." In *The Family Life of Black People*, edited by C. V. Willie. Columbus: Merrill Publishers, 1970.

"Feature Presentation: African American Oscar Winners." Black Film Center/Archive, Indiana University. http://www.indiana.edu/~bfca/features/oscars.html (page no longer available.)

Federation of Southern Cooperatives Land Assistance Fund. Accessed August 27, 2014. http://www.federationsoutherncoop.com/.

"Felony Costs Voting Rights for a Lifetime in Nine States." *The New York Times*, November 3, 2000. http://www.nytimes.com/2000/11/03/us/felony-costs-voting-rights-for-a-lifetime-in-9-states.html. Accessed September 30, 2014.

Fenderson, J., J. Stewart, and K. Baumgartner, eds. *Expanding the History of the Black Studies Movement* (A Special Issue of the Journal of African American Studies). 2012.

Fenster, M., and T. Swiss. "Business." In *Key Terms in Popular Music and Culture*, edited by B. Horner and T. Swiss, 225-38. Oxford, UK: Blackwell, 1999.

Ferran, L. "Michelle Obama: 'Let's Move' Initiative Battles Childhood Obesity" (February 9, 2010). http://abcnews.go.com/GMA/Health/michelle-obama-childhood-obesity-initiative/story?id=9781473.

Fetters, K., and S. Dichoso. "HIV Prevention Enters Salons, Barbershops" (March 12, 2009). http://news.medill.northwestern.edu/chicago/news.aspx?id=123525.

Fields, A. "29 Blues." Recorded July 7, 1939, in Chicago (WC 2646-A Okeh 06020). In *News & the Blues, Telling It Like It Is*. Columbia Records, CBS Records, 1990.

Finkelstein, A., S. Taubman, B. Wright, M. Bernstein, J. Gruber, J. P. Newhouse, H. Allen, and K. Baicker. "The Oregon Health Insurance Experiment: Evidence from the First Year" (NBER Working Paper No. 17190, July 2011). Cambridge, MA: National Bureau of Economic Research.

Floyd, S. "Afro-American Music and Dance." *The Western Journal of Black Studies* 13 (Fall 1989): 130–38.

———. *The Power of Black Music*. New York: Oxford University Press, 1995.

Fogel, R. *Without Consent or Contract: The Rise and Fall of American Slavery*. New York: W. W. Norton, 1989.

Foner, P. *History of Black Americans*. Westport: Greenwood Press, 1983.

———, ed. *The Life and Writings of Frederick Douglass*. 4 Vols. New York: International Publishers, 1975.

Ford, G., and P. Gambel. "America's Black Rightwing Forum: The Grotesque Devolution of a Black News Program." *Black Commentator* 20 (December 12, 2002). http://www.blackcommentator. com/20_commentary_1.html.

Forsythe, D. "Radical Sociology and Blacks." In *The Death of White Sociology*, edited by J. Ladner, 213-33. New York: Vintage Books, 1973.

Fortson, L. "Biomedical Research Warfare." *Black Issues in Higher Education*, March 1999.

Foster, F. *Written by Herself: Literary Production by African American Women, 1746–1892*. Bloomington: Indiana University Press, 1993.

Foster, H. *'New Raiments of Self': African American Clothing in the Antebellum South*. Oxford, UK: Berg, 1997.

Frankenberg, E., and C. Lee. "Charter Schools and Race: A Lost Opportunity for Integrated Education." *Education Policy Analysis Archives* 11 (September 2003). http://epaa.asu.edu/ojs/ article/view/260/386. Accessed September 30, 2014.

Franklin, C. "Black Male–White Male Perceptual Conflict." *The Western Journal of Black Studies* 6 (Spring 1982): 2–9.

———. "White Racism as the Cause of Black Male–Female Conflict: A Critique." *The Western Journal of Black Studies* 4 (Spring 1980): 42–49.

Franklin, J. *From Slavery to Freedom*. New York: Alfred A. Knopf, 1967.

Frantz, K. " 'The Open Road': Automobility and Racial Uplift in the Interwar Years." In *Technology and the African-American Experience, Needs and Opportunities for Study*, edited by B. Sinclair, 131-54. Boston, MA: The MIT Press, 2004.

Frazier, E. *Black Bourgeoisie*. New York: Collier Books, 1962.

———. *The Negro Church in America*. New York: Schocken Books, 1966.

———. "The Negro Family in Chicago." In *E. Franklin Frazier on Race Relations*, edited by G. F. Edwards. Chicago: The University of Chicago Press, 1968.

———. *The Negro Family in the United States*. Rev. ed. Chicago: The University of Chicago Press, 1966; originally published in 1939.

"Freedom to Play, The Life & Times of Basketball's African American Pioneers." http://www. hoophall.com/exhibits/freedom_barnstorming.htm (page no longer available.)

Gayle, A. "Blueprint for Black Criticism." *First World*, January/February 1977).

Gendron, B. *Technology and the Human Condition*. New York: St. Martin's Press, 1977.

George, H. "Black Power in Office: The Limits of Electoral Reform." *The Western Journal of Black Studies* 9 (Summer 1985): 84–95.

George, N. "Rapping Their Way to Gold." *Black Enterprise*, June 1982.

Gibbs, J. "Called Anything But a Child of God." *Focus: Magazine of the Joint Center for Political and Economic Studies* 19 (December 1991).

———. "Developing Intervention Models for Black Families: Linking Theory and Research." In *Black Families: Interdisciplinary Perspectives*, edited by H. E. Cheatham and J. B. Stewart. New Brunswick: Transaction Publishers, 1990.

Gibson, A. *I Always Wanted to Be Somebody*, edited by E. Fitzgerald. New York: Harper & Row, 1958.

Gilroy, P. *The Black Atlantic: Modernity and Double-Consciousness*. Cambridge, MA: Harvard University Press, 1993.

Gitler, I. *Swing to Bop*. New York: Oxford University Press, 1985.

Glasgow, D. *The Black Underclass*. San Francisco: Jossey-Bass, 1981.

Glatthaar, J. *Forged in Battle*. New York: Meridian, 1991.

Glazner, G., ed. *Poetry Slam: The Competitive Art of Performance*. San Francisco: Manic D Press, 2000.

Goetz, G. *The Effects of Subsidized Housing on Communities: Just in Time Research Resilient Communities*. Minneapolis: University of Minnesota, 2000.

Goggins, L. *African Centered Rites of Passage and Education*. Chicago: African American Images, 1996.

Gordon, D., D. Iwamoto, N. Ward, R. Potts, and E. Boyd. "Mentoring Urban Black Middle School Male Students: Implications for Academic Achievement." *The Journal of Negro Education* 78, no. 3 (Summer, 2009): 277–89.

Gordon, M. *Assimilation in American Life*. New York: Oxford University Press, 1964.

Gordon, V. *Black Women, Feminism, Black Liberation: Which Way?* Rev. ed. Chicago: Third World Press.

———. "The Coming of Age of Black Studies." *The Western Journal of Black Studies* 5 (Fall 1981): 231–36.

———. *The Self-Concept of Black Americans*. Washington, DC: University Press of America, 1977.

Grant, J., ed. *Black Protest: 350 Years of Documents and Analyses*. New York: Fawcett Columbine, 1968.

———. "Black Theology and the Black Women." In *Black Theology: A Documentary History, Volume I: 1966–1979*, edited by J. H. Cone and G. S. Wilmore. Maryknoll, NY: Orbis Books, 1979.

"Granville Woods." The Black Inventor Online Museum. http://blackinventor.com/granville-woods/. Accessed September 30, 2014.

Gray, J., ed. *Blacks in Classical Music: A Bibliographical Guide to Composers, Performers, and Ensembles*. Westport: Greenwood Press, 1988.

Green, B. *Spinning the Globe: The Rise, Fall, and Return to Greatness of the Harlem Globetrotters*. New York: Harper-Collins, 2005.

Greenberg, J. "The Capacity of Law to Affect Race Relations." In *Society and the Legal Order*, edited by R. Swartz and J. Skolnick. New York: Basic Books, 1970.

Greene, L., and C. Woodson. *The Negro Wage Earner*. Washington, DC: Associated Publishers, 1930.

Gresson, A. *Black Amnesia*. Baltimore: Transformation Books, 1990.

———. *The Recovery of Race in America*. Minneapolis: University of Minnesota Press, 1995.

Grier, W., and P. Cobbs. *Black Rage*. New York: Basic Books, 1986.

Grogan, P., and T. Proscio. *Comeback Cities: A Blueprint for Urban Neighborhood Revival*. Boulder: Westview Press, 2000.

Groys, B. *Art Power*. Cambridge, MA: The MIT Press, 2008.

Guinier, L. *The Tyranny of the Majority, Fundamental Fairness in Representative Democracy*. New York: The Free Press, 1994.

Gullickson, A. "The Significance of Color Declines: A Re-analysis of Skin Tone Differentials in Post-Civil Rights America." Unpublished manuscript, March 2004.

Guralnick, P. *Sweet Soul Music*. New York: Harper & Row, 1986.

Guthrie, R. *Even the Rat Was White*. New York: Harper & Row, 1976.

Gutierrez, G. "American Sitcoms: A Diversity of Flavors in Society." Contribution to English Media Culture, University of California, Santa Barbara, n.d. http://www.uweb.ucsb.edu/~monicamd/gloriapaper.html (page no longer available).

Gutman, H. *The Black Family in Slavery and Freedom 1750–1925*. New York: Vintage Books, 1977.

"Gwendolyn Brooks." *Poets.org* (n.d.). http://www.poets.org/poet.php/prmPID/165.

Haber, L. *Black Pioneers of Science and Invention*. New York: Harcourt, Bracey & World, 1990.

Haddad, W., and G. Pugh. *Black Economic Development*. Englewood Cliffs: Prentice Hall, 1969.

"Haki Madhubuti." African American Literature Book Club. Accessed September 2, 2014. http://aalbc.com/authors/haki.htm.

Hall, R. *Black Separation in the United States*. Hanover, NH: University Press of New England, 1978.

Hall, V. "Another Man Done Gone." Folk Song U.S.A. Reprinted in J. Cone. "The Blues: A Secular Spiritual." In *The Spirituals and the Blues: An Interpretation*, 120. New York: Seabury, 1972.

Hamilton, K. *Black Towns and Profit: Promotion and Development in the Trans-Appalachia West, 1877–1915*. Urbana: University of Illinois Press, 1991.

Hancock, H. "I Have a Dream." Recorded April 18–23, 1969. In *The Prisoner* (Blue Note Label).

Hanson, J. *Mary McLeod Bethune and Black Women's Political Activism*. Columbia, MO: University of Missouri Press, 2003.

Hanson, S. "China, Africa, and Oil" (June 9, 2008). Council on Foreign Relations. http://www.cfr. org/china/china-africa-oil/p9557.

Haralambos, M. *Right on: From Blues to Soul in Black America*. New York: Da Capo Press, 1979.

———. *Soul Music: The Birth of Sound in Black America*. New York: Da Capo Press, 1974.

Hardy, C., L. Malone, V. Wilson, M. Obama, and M. Morial. *The State of Black America 2011: Jobs Rebuild America: Putting Urban America Back to Work*. New York: National Urban League Publications Unit, 2011.

Hare, N. "The Challenge of a Black Scholar." *The Black Scholar* (December 1969).

———. *The Hare Plan*. San Francisco: The Black Think Tank, 1991.

———. "The Meaning of Black Studies." *Graduate Journal* (University of Texas at Austin) 8, no. 2 (1971).

———. "What Black Intellectuals Misunderstood about the Black Family." *Black World*, March 25, 1976.

Hare, N., and J. Hare. *Bringing the Black Boy to Manhood: The Passage*. San Francisco: The Black Think Tank, 1985.

———. *The Endangered Black Family*. San Francisco: The Black Think Tank, 1984.

Harmon, J., A. Lindsay, and C. Woodson. *The Negro as a Business Man*. College Park, MD: McGrath Publishing, 1929. Reprint 1969.

Harper, S., L. Byars, and T. Jelke. "How Black Greek-Letter Organization Membership Affects College Adjustment and Undergraduate Outcomes." In *African American Fraternities and Sororities: The Legacy and the Vision*, edited by T. L. Brown, G. S. Parks, and C. M. Phillips, 393-416. Lexington: The University Press of Kentucky, 2005.

Harris, A. *The Negro as Capitalist: A Study of Banking and Business among American Negroes*. New York: American Academy of Political and Social Science, 1936.

Harris, C. "Whiteness as Property." *Harvard Law Review* 106 (June 1993): 1707–91.

Harris, F., and L. Curtis, eds. *Locked in the Poorhouse: Cities, Race, and Poverty in the United States*. Lanham: Rowman & Littlefield, 1998.

Harris, H. "Atomic Bomb Blues." Recorded September 27, 1946, in Chicago (CCO 4650; Columbia, unissued). In *News & the Blues, Telling It Like It Is*. Columbia Records, CBS Records, 1990.

Harris, J., and W. McCoullough. *Africans and Their History*. New York: New American Library, 1972.

———. "Quantitative Methods and Black Community Studies." In *The Death of White Sociology*, edited by J. A. Ladner, 331-43. New York: Random House, 1973.

Harris, L. *Philosophy Born of Struggle*. Dubuque, IA: Kendall/Hunt Publishing Company, 1983.

Harris, R. "Coming of Age: The Transformation of Afro-American Historiography." In *Paradigms in Black Studies*, edited by A. Alkalimat, 107-21. Chicago: Twenty-First Century Books and Publications, 1990.

Harris, W. *Black Community Development*. San Francisco: R&E Publishers, 1976.

Harris-Lacewell, M. *Barbershops, Bibles and BET: Everyday Talk and Black Political Thought*. Princeton: Princeton University Press, 2004.

Harrison, D. "Jazz: The Serious Music of Black Americans." *The Western Journal of Black Studies* 2 (Fall 1978): 196–201.

Harrison, I. "The Storefront Church as a Revitalization Movement." In *The Black Church in America*, edited by H. M. Nelsen, R. L. Yokley, and A. K. Nelsen. Lexington: The University Press of Kentucky, 1971.

Harrison, P., and J. Karberg. *Prison and Jail Inmates at Midyear 2003*. Washington, DC: Office of Justice Programs, U.S. Department of Justice, May 2004.

Hartung, J., and J. Henig. "Housing Vouchers and Certificates as a Vehicle for Deconcentrating the Poor: Evidence from the Washington, D.C. Metropolitan Area." *Urban Affairs Review* 32, no. 3 (1997): 403–19.

Hatchett, R., and S. Hatchett. "The Media and Social Reality Effects: Self and System Orientation of Blacks." *Communications Research* 13 (January 1986).

Hatchett, S., and A. Quick. "Correlates of Sex Role Attitudes among Black Men and Women: Data from a National Survey of Black Americans." *Urban Research Review* 9, no. 2 (1983): 1–11.

Haveman, R., and E. Wolff. "Who Are the Asset Poor? Levels, Trends, and Composition, 1983–1998." Unpublished manuscript, 2001.

Hayden, R. "Preface." In *The New Negro*, edited by A. L. Locke. New York: Atheneum, 1969.

Haynes, G. *The Negro at Work during the World War and during Reconstruction*. Washington, DC: Government Printing Office,1921.

Headen, A., and N. Masia. "Exploring the Potential Link Between Medicaid Access Restrictions, Physician Location, and Health Disparities." *The American Journal of Managed Care* (January 2005). http://www.ajmc.com/publications/issue/2005/2005-01-vol11-n1SP/Jan05-1980pSP021-SP02/.

select
bibliography

Hecht, M., and S. Ribeau. "Sociocultural Roots of Ethnic Identity." *Journal of Black Studies* 21 (June 1991): 501–13.

Helms, J. "The Measurement of Black Racial Attitudes." In *Black and White Racial Identity: Theory, Research and Practice*, edited by J. E. Helms. Westport: Greenwood Press, 1990.

Hemenway, R. "The Sacred Canon and Brazzle's Mule." *ADE Bulletin* 73 (Winter 1982): 26–32.

Henahan, D. "Opera: Anthony Davis's X [The Life and Times of Malcolm X]." *The New York Times*, September 29, 1986. http://www.nytimes.com/1986/09/29/arts/opera-anthony-davis-s-x-the-life-and-times-of-malcolm-x.html.

Henderson, L. "Black Politics and American Presidential Elections." In *The New Black Politics*, edited by M. B. Preston, L. J. Henderson, and P. L. Puryear. New York: Longman, 1982.

———. "Public Technology and the Metropolitan Culture." *The Black Scholar* 5 (March 1974).

Hendrix, M., J. Bracy, J. Davis, and W. Herron. "Computers and Black Studies: Toward the Cognitive Revolution." *The Journal of Negro Education* 53 (1984): 341–50.

Henri, F. *Black Migration*. Garden City, NY: Anchor Books, 1976.

Henry, C. "The Rise and Fall of Black Influence on U.S. Foreign Policy." In *African American in Global Affairs, Contemporary Perspectives*, edited by M. L. Clemons, 192-222. Boston, MA: Northeastern University Press, 2010.

Herskovits, M. *The Myth of the Negro Past*. Boston, MA: Harper & Brothers, 1941.

Herzig, R. "The Matter of Race in Histories of American Technology." In *Technology and the African-American Experience*, edited by B. Sinclair, 155-70. Cambridge, MA: The MIT Press, 2004.

Higginbotham, A. *In the Matter of Color, Race and the American Legal Process: The Colonial Period*. New York: Oxford University Press, 1978.

Hill, I. *The Deacons for Defense, Armed Resistance and the Civil Rights Movement*. Chapel Hill: The University of North Carolina Press, 2004.

Hill, P. *Coming of Age, African American Male Rites-of-Passage*. Chicago: African American Images, 1992.

Hill, R. "A Positive Look at Black Families." *Manpower* 4, no. 1 (January 1972): 24–27.

———. "Economic Forces, Structural Discrimination and Black Family Instability." In *Black Families: Interdisciplinary Perspectives*. New Brunswick: Transaction Publishers, 1990.

———. *The Strength of Black Families*. New York: Emerson Hall Publishers, 1972.

Hill, G., and S. Hill. *Blacks on Television*. Metuchen, NJ: The Scarecrow Press, 1985.

Hilliard, A. "Pedagogy in Ancient Kemet." In *Kemet and the African Worldview: Research, Rescue and Restoration*, edited by M. Karenga and J. H. Carruthers. Los Angeles: University of Sankore Press, 1986.

Hine, D. *Black Women in White: Racial Conflict and Cooperation in the Nursing Profession, 1890–1950*. Bloomington: Indiana University Press, 1989.

———, ed. *Black Women's History: Theory and Practice*. Brooklyn: Carlson Publishers, 1990.

Hine, D., E. Brown, and R. Terborg-Penn, eds. *Black Women in America: An Historical Encyclopedia*. Brooklyn: Carlson Publishers, 1993.

Hine, D., and K. Thompson. *A Shining Thread of Hope: The History of Black Women in America*. New York: Broadway Books, 1998.

"Hip Hop Journalist Davey D on Police Surveillance of Rappers, the National Hip Hop Convention and the 2004 Election." *Democracy Now!* (April 19, 2004). http://www.democracynow. org/2004/4/19/hip_hop_journalist_davey_d_on. Accessed October 1, 2014.

"History of the NRA Organization." http://www.nrpa.org/content/default.aspx?documentId=721 (page no longer available.)

Hodges, N. *Black History*. New York: Monarch Press, 1971.

Hoene, C., and M. Muro. "Fiscal Challenges Facing Cities: Implications for Recovery." http://www. brookings.edu/papers/2009/1118_cities_fiscal_challenges_muro_hoene.aspx.

Hoerner, J., and Robinson, N. "Just Climate Policy—Just Racial Policy." *Race, Poverty & the Environment*. http://urbanhabitat.org/cj/hoerner-robinson.

Hoffman, C., T. Snyder, and B. Sonnenberg. *Historically Black Colleges and Universities, 1976–1994* (NCES 96-902). Washington, DC: National Center for Education Statistics, U.S. Department of Education, 1996.

Hoffman, D., and T. Novak. "Bridging the Racial Divide on the Internet." *Science* 280 (April 1998): 390–91.

Holahan, J., and A. Ghosh. "The Economic Downturn and Changes in Health Insurance Coverage, 2000–2003." *Kaiser Commission on Medicaid and the Uninsured* (September 2004). http:// kaiserfamilyfoundation.files.wordpress.com/2013/01/the-economic-downturn-and-changes-in-health-insurance-coverage-2000-2003-report.pdf. Accessed October 1, 2014

Horne, D. "The African Union and the African Diaspora: An Information Kit" (June 2, 2011). http:// www.ourweekly.com/features/african-union-and-african-diaspora-information-kit (page no longer available).

Hornsby, A. "Historical Overview of Black Colleges." *The Western Journal of Black Studies* 2 (Fall 1978).

———. *The Black Almanac*. Woodbury, NY: Barron's Educational Series, 1973.

"House Chastises South Carolina Representative Who Called Obama a Liar." *The Guardian* (September 15, 2009). http://www.guardian.co.uk/world/deadlineusa/2009/sep/15/usa-democrats.

Houston, L. *Psychological Principles and the Black Experience*. Lanham: University Press of America, 1990.

Hud-Aleem, R., and J. Countryman. "Biracial Identity Development and Recommendations in Therapy." *Psychiatry* 5, no. 11 (November 2008): 37–44. http://www.ncbi.nlm.nih.gov/pmc/articles/PMC2695719/.

Hudson-Weems, C. "Africana Womanism and the Critical Need for Africana Theory and Thought." *The Western Journal of Black Studies* 21 (Summer 1997): 70–84.

———. *Africana Womanism: Reclaiming Ourselves*. Troy, MI: Bedford Publishers, 1993.

———. *Africana Womanist Literary Theory*. Trenton, NJ: Africa World Press, 2004.

———. "Cultural and Agenda Conflicts in Academia: Critical Issues for Africana Womens' Studies." *The Western Journal of Black Studies* 13, no. 4 (1989): 185–89.

———. *Emmett Till: The Sacrificial Lamb of the Civil Rights Movement*. Troy, MI: Bedford Publishers, 1994.

———. "Toni Morrison's World of Topsy-Turvydom: A Methodological Explication of New Black Literary Criticism." *The Western Journal of Black Studies* 10 (Fall 1986): 132–36.

Huggins, N. *Harlem Renaissance*. New York: Oxford University Press, 1971.

Hughes, E. "The Negro's New Economic Life." *Fortune*, September 1956.

Hughes, L., and N. Simone. "Backlash Blues." Recorded January 5, 1967. In *Defiance Blues*. (House of Blues, 1998). EMI Waterford Music.

Hungerford, T. "The Persistence of Hardship over the Life Course" (Working Paper No. 367, December 2002). Annandale-on-Hudson, NY: The Levy Economics Institute of Bard College.

Hunter, H. "The Political Economic Thought of Oliver C. Cox." In *A Different Vision, African American Economic Thought*, edited by T. D. Boston, vol. 1, 270-89. New York: Routledge, 1997.

Hurd, M. *Black College Football, 1892–1992: One Hundred Years of History, Education, and Pride*. Virginia Beach: The Donning Company Publishers, 2000.

Hutchinson, E. *Blacks and Reds: Race and Class in Conflict, 1919–1990*. Lansing: Michigan State University Press, 1995.

"Inadequate Funding Makes NCLB Worse." *FairTest Examiner* (Winter–Spring 2003). http://fairtest.org/examarts/Wint-Spring%2003%20double/Funding.html.

Institute for Services to Education. *The Adams Report: A Desegregation Update*. Washington, DC: Institute for Services to Education, September 1978.

"Introduction to Afro-American Studies." *eBlack Studies*. Accessed August 27, 2014. http://eblackstudies.org/intro/.

"Investment Clubs." *The Black Bank Initiative*. http://www.blackownedbank.com/?page_id=4.

Jackson, G. "The Origin and Development of Black Psychology: Implications for Black Studies and Human Behavior." *Studia Africana* 1 (Fall 1979).

Jackson, J. *Introduction to African Studies*. New York: Carol Publishing Group, 1990; originally published in 1970.

Jackson, L., Y. Zhao, A. Kolenic III, H. Fitzgerald, R. Harold, and A. Von Eye. "Race, Gender, and Information Technology Use: The New Digital Divide." *CyberPsychology & Behavior* 11, no. 4 (2008). http://academics.hamilton.edu/ebs/pdf/NDD.pdf.

Jackson, R., and S. Camara. "Scripting and Consuming Black Bodies in Hip Hop Music and Pimp Movies." In *Message in the Music, Hip Hop History & Pedagogy*, edited by D. P. Alridge, J. B. Stewart, and V. P. Franklin, 178-203. Washington, DC: The ASALH Press, 2010.

Jackson, R., and J. Stewart. "Negotiation of African American Identities in Rural America: A Cultural Contracts Approach." *Journal of Rural Community Psychology* E4, no. 1 (2001). http://www.marshall.edu/jrcp/JacksonStewart.htm.

James, K., C. Lovato, and G. Khoo. "Social Identity Correlates of Minority Workers' Health." *Academy of Management Journal* 37, no. 2 (1994): 383–96.

James, M. "Never Quit: The Complexities of Promoting Social and Academic Excellence at a Single-Gender School for Urban African American Males." *Journal of African American Males in Education* 1, no. 3 (2010): 167-195.

James, P. *The Real McCoy*. Washington, DC: Smithsonian Institution Scholarly Press, 1989.

Jargowsky, P. *Stunning Progress, Hidden Problems: The Dramatic Decline in Concentrated Poverty in the 1990s* (The Living Census Series). Washington, DC: The Brookings Institution, May 2003.

Jaynes, G., and R. Williams, eds. *A Common Destiny*. Washington, DC: National Academy Press, 1989.

Jefferson, B. "Tin Cup Blues." In *The Blues Line: A Collection of Blues Lyrics from Leadbelly to Muddy Waters*, edited by E. Sackheim. Hopewell, NJ: Ecco Press, 1969.

Jenkins, A. *Psychology and African Americans: A Humanistic Approach*. 2nd ed. Needham Heights: Allyn & Bacon, 1995.

———. *The Psychology of the Afro-American*. New York: Pergamon Press, 1982.

Jenkins, T., and K. Om-Ra Seti. *Black Futurists in the Information Age*. San Francisco: KMT, 1997.

Jensen, L. "Employment Hardship and Rural Minorities: Theory, Research, and Policy." In *Blacks in Rural America*, edited by J. B. Stewart and J. E. Allen-Smith. New Brunswick: Transaction Publishers, 1995.

Jervis, R. "Initiative Aims to Find Lost Grave Sites of Slaves." *USA Today*, February 2, 2012. http://www.usatoday.com/news/nation/story/2012-02-02/slave-burial-sites/53083254/1.

Jewell, K. "Black Male/Female Conflict: Internalization of Negative Definitions Transmitted through Imagery." *The Western Journal of Black Studies* 7 (Spring 1983): 43–48.

Johnson, A., and R. Johnson. *Propaganda and Aesthetics: The Literary Politics of African-American Magazines in the Twentieth Century*. Amherst, MA: University of Massachusetts Press, 1979.

Johnson, C. *Patterns of Negro Segregation*. New York: Harper & Row, 1940.

Johnson, G. "Underemployment, Underpayment, and Psychosocial Stress Among Working Black Men." *The Western Journal of Black Studies* 13 (Summer 1989): 57–65.

Johnson, J. A., D. Musial, G. E. Hall, D. M. Gollnick, V. L. Dupuis. *Introduction to the Foundations of American Education*. Boston, MA: Allyn & Bacon, 1969.

Johnson, K. *Uplifting the Women and the Race: The Lives, Educational Philosophies, and Social Activism of Anna Julia Cooper and Nannie Helen Burroughs*. New York: Garland Publishing, 2000.

Johnson, M. "Black Women Electric Guitarists and Authenticity in the Blues." In *Black Women and Music, More than the Blues*, edited by E. M. Hayes and L. F. Williams. Urbana: University of Illinois Press, 2007.

Johnson, O., and K. Sanford, eds. *Black Political Organizations in the Post-Civil Rights Era*. New Brunswick: Rutgers University Press, 2002.

———. "Introduction: The Relevance of Black Political Organizations in the Post-Civil Rights Era." In *Black Political Organizations in the Post-Civil Rights Era*, edited by O. Johnson and K. Sanford, 1-13. New Brunswick: Rutgers University Press, 2002.

Johnson, R. "Science, Technology, and Black Community Development." *The Western Journal of Black Studies* 4, no. 3 (1980): 212–16.

Johnson, V. *Black Power in the Suburbs: The Myth of African American Suburban Political Incorporation*. Albany: SUNY Press, 2002.

———. "Where Do We Go from Here? Facing the Challenges of the Post-Civil Rights Era." In *Black Political Organizations in the Post-Civil Rights Era*, edited by O. Johnson and K. Sanford, 202-16. New Brunswick: Rutgers University Press, 2002.

Joint Center for Political and Economic Studies. http://jointcenter.org.Accessed October 1, 2014.

——*Focus: Magazine of the Joint Center for Political and Economic Studies* (December 1980).

———. *Political Trendletter* (March 1988).

Jones, B. *Quest for Equality: The Life and Writings of Mary Eliza Church Terrell, 1863–1954*. Brooklyn: Carlson Publishers, 1990.

————. "The Tradition of Sociology Teaching in Black Colleges." In *Black Sociologists*, edited by J. E. Blackwell and M. Janowitz. Chicago: The University of Chicago Press, 1974.

Jones, C. "From Protest to Black Conservatism: The Demise of the Congress of Racial Equality." In *Black Political Organizations in the Post-Civil Rights Era*, edited by O. Johnson and K. Sanford, 80-98. New Brunswick: Rutgers University Press, 2002.

Jones, D. "Marketing to the Masses Tends to Miss Many: Radio Host Has Pointers for Reaching Black Audience." *USA Today*, August 15, 2005. http://usatoday30.usatoday.com/educate/college/careers/Advice/adv8-15-05.htm. Accessed October 1, 2014.

Jones, J. *Bad Blood: The Tuskegee Syphilis Experiment*. New York: The Free Press, 1981.

————. *Labor of Love, Labor of Sorrow: Black Women, Work, and Family from Slavery to Freedom*. New York: Basic Books, 1985.

Jones, M. "A Frame of Reference for Black Politics." In *Black Political Life in the United States*, edited by L. J. Henderson. San Francisco: Chandler, 1972.

Jones, R. "Margaret Bonds." In *Afrocentric Voices in "Classical" Music* (n.d.). http://www.afrovoices.com/dett.html.

————. "Marian Anderson." In *Afrocentric Voices in "Classical" Music* (n.d.). http://www.afrovoices.com/dett.html.

————. "R. Daniel Dett." In *Afrocentric Voices in "Classical" Music* (n.d.). http://www.afrovoices.com/dett.html.

Jones, R. L., ed. *Black Adult Development and Aging*. Berkeley: Cobb & Henry Publishers, 1989.

————. *Black Haze, Violence, Sacrifice, and Manhood in Black Greek-Letter Fraternities*. Albany: SUNY Press, 2004.

————, ed. *Black Psychology*. New York: Harper & Row, 1972.

————. "Black Sociology: 1890–1917." *Black Academy Review* 2 (Winter 1971): 43–67.

————. "In Absence of Ideology: Blacks in Colonial America and the Modern Black Experience." *The Western Journal of Black Studies* 12 (Spring 1988): 30–39.

Jones, W. "Congress and Africa's Constituency: The Development of the Africa Growth and Opportunity Act and the Intersection of African American and Business Interests." In *African American in Global Affairs, Contemporary Perspectives*, edited by M. L. Clemons, 93-117. Boston, MA: Northeastern University Press, 2010.

Jones, W., H. Wingfield, and A. Nelson. "Black Ministers: Roles, Behavior, and Congregation Expectations." *The Western Journal of Black Studies* 3 (Summer 1979): 99–103.

Joyce, D. *Black Book Publishers in the United States: A Historical Dictionary of the Presses, 1817–1900*. New York: Greenwood Press, 1991.

July, R. *A History of African People*. New York: Charles Scribner's Sons, 1970.

Kain, J. "Housing, Segregation, Negro Employment, and Metropolitan Decentralization." *The Quarterly Journal of Economics* 82 (1968): 175–97.

———. "The Spatial Mismatch Hypothesis: Three Decades Later." *Housing Policy Debate* 3 (1992): 371–460.

Kaluger, G., and C. Unkovic. *Psychology and Sociology*. St. Louis, MO: C. V. Mosby Co., 1969.

Kambon, K. *African/Black Psychology in the American Context: An African-Centered Approach*. Tallahassee: Nubian Nation Publications, 1998.

Kaplan, V. *Structural Inequality: Black Architects in the United States*. Lanham: Rowman & Littlefield, 2006.

Kardiner, A., and L. Ovesey. *The Mark of Oppression*. New York: W.W. Norton, 1998.

Karenga, M. *Introduction to Black Studies*. Los Angeles: Kawaida Publications, 1982.

———. *Kawaida Theory: An Introductory Outline*. Inglewood, CA: Kawaida Publications, 1980.

———. *Maat, the Moral Ideal in Ancient Egypt: A Study in Classical African Ethics*. New York: Routledge, 2004.

———. *Odu Ifa: The Ethical Teachings*. Los Angeles: University of Sankore Press, 1999.

———. *Selections from the Husia: Sacred Wisdom of Ancient Egypt*. Los Angeles: Kawaida Publications, 1984.

Keita, S., and J. Stewart. "Ethics, Identity, Genetics, Patrimony and Power in the Harvesting of DNA from Africa." *GeneWatch* 23 (May–June 2010). http://www.councilforresponsiblegenetics.org/GeneWatch/GeneWatchPage.aspx?pageId=273. Accessed October 1, 2014.

Keith, V., and C. Herring. "Skin Tone and Stratification in the Black Community." *American Journal of Sociology* 97, no. 3 (1991): 760–78.

Kershaw, T. "The Emerging Paradigm in Black Studies." In *Black Studies: Theory, Method, and Cultural Perspectives*, edited by T. Anderson. Pullman, WA: Washington State University Press, 1990.

———. "The Emerging Paradigm in Black Studies." *The Western Journal of Black Studies* 13 (Spring 1989): 45–51.

Kessler, R. *In the President's Secret Service: Behind the Scenes with Agents in the Line of Fire and the Presidents They Protect*. New York: Random House, 2009.

Kilson, M. "The Black Bourgeoisie Revisited: From E. Franklin Frazier to the Present." *Dissent* 30 (Winter 1983): 85–96.

King, W. "Enhancing Scientific and Technical Literacy in Afroamerican Communities." Unpublished manuscript, 1992.

Klineberg, O. *Race Differences*. New York: Harper & Brothers, 1935.

Klotzman, P., ed. *Humanities through the Black Experience*. Dubuque, IA: Kendall/Hunt Publishing Company, 1977.

Kluchin, R. *Fit to Be Tied, Sterilization and Reproductive Rights in America, 1950–1980*. New Brunswick: Rutgers University Press, 2009.

Kofsky, F. *Black Nationalism and the Revolution in Music*. New York: Pathfinder Press, 1970.

Kotkin, J. *Tribes: How Race, Religion, and Identity Determine Success in the New Global Economy*. New York: Random House, 1993.

Kovel, J. *White Racism: A Psychohistory*. New York: Vintage Books, 1970.

Krovi, R., and C. Barnes. "Work-Related Travel Patterns of People of Color." In *Travel Patterns of People of Color*, edited by Battelle. Washington, DC: Federal Highway Administration, 2000. http://www.fhwa.dot.gov/ohim/trvpatns.pdf. Accessed October 1, 2014.

Krueger, A. "The Digital Divide in Educating African-American Students and Workers" (Princeton University IRS Working Paper No. 434, March 2000). http://ssrn.com/abstract=223749.

Kruse, H. "Gender." In *Key Terms in Popular Music and Culture*, edited by B. Horner and T. Swiss, 85-100. Oxford, UK: Blackwell, 1999.

Krysan, M., and N. Faison. "Racial Attitudes in America: A Brief Summary of the Updated Data" (2008). http://igpa.uillinois.edu/programs/racial-attitudes/data/white/t33supp.

Kusimo, P. "Rural African Americans and Education: The Legacy of the Brown Decision." *Eric Digest* (EDO-RC-98-4, January 1999). http://www.ericdigests.org/1999-3/brown.htm . Accessed October 1, 2014.

Kuska, B. *Hot Potato: How Washington and New York Gave Birth to Black Basketball and Changed America's Game Forever*. Charlottesville, VA: University of Virginia Press, 2004.

Ladner, J., ed. *The Death of White Sociology*. Baltimore: Black Classic Press, 1973.

Land Loss Project. Accessed August 27, 2014. http://www.landloss.org/.

Landrum-Brown, J. "Black Mental Health and Racial Oppression." In *Handbook of Mental Health and Mental Disorders among Black Americans*, edited by D. Ruiz, 113-32. New York: Greenwood Press, 1990.

Landry, B. *The New Black Middle Class*. Berkeley: University of California Press, 1987.

———. "The New Middle Class, Part I." *Focus: Magazine of the Joint Center for Political and Economic Studies* (September 1987).

Larkin, R. *Soul Music*. New York: Lancer Books, 1970.

LaRosa, J., B. Seto, C. Caban, and E. Hayunga. "Including Women and Minorities in Clinical Research." *Applied Clinical Trials* 4 (May 1995).

Leadership Conference on Civil Rights Education Fund. "Are We Really a Nation Online? Ethnic and Racial Disparities in Access to Technology and Their Consequences" (September 20, 2005). http://www.civilrights.org/publications/nation-online/.

Lecky, R., and H. Wright, eds. "Reparations Now? An Introduction." In *Black Manifesto*. New York: Sheed & Ward, 1969.

Leonard, D. "What Happened to the Revolt Black Athlete? A Look Back Thirty Years Later: An Interview with Harry Edwards." *Color Lines* 1 (Summer 1998). http://www.arc.org/C_Lines/CLArchive/story1_1_01.html.

Leonard, K. "African American Women Poets and the Power of the Word." In *The Cambridge Companion to African American Women's Literature*, edited by A. Mitchell and D. K. Taylor, 168-86. New York: Cambridge University Press, 2009.

Levitt, S., and S. Dubner. *Freakonomics: A Rogue Economist Explores the Hidden Side of Everything*. New York: HarperCollins, 2005.

Levy, A. *Tackling Jim Crow: Racial Segregation in Professional Football*. Jefferson, NC: McFarland, 2003.

Lewis, L., L. Galloway-Gilliam, G. Flynn, J. Nomachi, L. C. Kenner, and D. C. Sloane. "Transforming the Urban Food Desert from the Grassroots up: A Model for Community Change." Supplement, *Family & Community Health Issues* 34, no. S1 (January/March 2011): S92–101.

Lewis, M. *Herstory: Black Female Rites of Passage*. Chicago: African American Images, 1988.

Lincoln, C. *Race, Religion and the Continuing American Dilemma*. New York: Hill & Wang, 1984.

Lincoln, C., and L. Mamiya. *The Black Church in the African American Experience*. Durham: Duke University Press, 1990.

Lloyd, G. "The Black Church and Economic Development." *The Western Journal of Black Studies* 1 (December 1977): 270–75.

Locke, A. *Negro Art: Past and Present*. Washington, DC: Associates in Negro Folk Education, 1936.

———. *The Negro and His Music*. Washington, DC: Associates in Negro Folk Education, 1936.

Loewenberg, P. *Decoding the Past*. Berkeley: University of California Press, 1985.

Lofquist, D., and R. Ellis. "Comparison of Estimates of Same-Sex Couples from the American Community Survey and Current Population Survey." http://paa2011.princeton.edu/download.aspx?submissionId=110986.

Logan, J. *Separate and Unequal: The Neighborhood Gap for Blacks, Hispanics and Asians in Metropolitan America* (US2010 Project). Providence, RI: Brown University, July 2011. http://www.s4.brown.edu/us2010/Data/Report/report0727.pdf.

Losen, D., and G. Orfield. *Racial Inequity in Special Education: Civil Rights Project, Harvard University*. Cambridge, MA: Harvard University Press, 2002.

Lowenstein, G. "Black Mayors and the Urban Black Underclass." *The Western Journal of Black Studies* 5 (Winter 1981): 278–84.

Lowrance, W. *Modern Science and Human Values*. New York: Oxford University Press, 1985.

Ludlow, L. "Assorted Reactions to Calling Blacks African Americans." *San Francisco Examiner*, December 22, 1988.

Lui, M., E. Dixon, and B. Leondar-Wright. "Stalling the Dream: Cars, Race and Hurricane Evacuation." United for a Fair Economy's Third Annual Report. State of the Dream, January 10, 2006. http://www.faireconomy.org/files/pdf/stalling_the_dream_2006.pdf.

Lynch, A. "Reflections on Black Culture in the Early Forties." In *Black Books Bulletin*, vol. 6, edited by H. R. Madhubuti. Chicago: Institute of Positive Education, Spring 1978.

Maddox, W., and S. Lilie. *Beyond Liberal and Conservative*. Washington, DC: Cato Institute, 1984.

Madhubuti, H., and M. Karenga. *Million Man March/Day of Absence: A Commemorative Anthology: Speeches, Commentary, Photography, Poetry, Illustrations, Documents*. Chicago: Third World Press, 1996.

Malone, J. *Steppin' on the Blues: The Visible Rhythms of African American Dance*. Urbana: University of Illinois Press, 1996.

Malone, W. *From Holy Power to Holy Profits: The Black Church and Community Economic Empowerment*. Chicago: African American Images, 1994.

Maltby, M. *The Origins and Development of Professional Football, 1890–1920* (Garland Studies in American Popular History and Culture). New York: Garland Publishing, 1997.

Malveaux, J. "Missed Opportunity: Sadie Tanner Mossell Alexander and the Economics Profession." In *A Different Vision: African American Economic Thought*, edited by T. D. Boston, vol. 1, 123-28. New York: Routledge, 1997.

———. "Tilting Against the Wind: Reflections on the Life and Work of Dr. Phyllis Ann Wallace." In *A Different Vision: African American Economic Thought*, edited by T. D. Boston, vol. 1, 129-35. New York: Routledge, 1997.

Manning, K. *Black Apollo of Science*. New York: Oxford University Press, 1983.

Mansbridge, J., and K. Tate. "Race Trumps Gender: Black Opinion on the Thomas Nomination." *PS: Political Science and Politics* 25, no. 3 (1992): 488–92.

"Many Ways to Pressure Black Radio." *Black Commentator*, E-Mailbox, Issue 46. http://www.blackcommentator.com/46/46_email.html.

Marable, M. "Civil Rights or Silver Rights?" *Znet Commentary* (January 2, 2000). http://www.hartford-hwp.com/archives/45a/239.html. Accessed October 1, 2014.

———. *How Capitalism Underdeveloped Black America*. Boston, MA: South End Press, 1983.

———. "The Modern Miseducation of the Negro: Critiques of Black History Curricula." Black Studies Curriculum Development Course Evaluations, Conference I, Institute of the Black World, Atlanta, 1981.

———. "The Rhetoric of Racial Harmony." *Sojourners* 19 (August/September 1990).

———. *W. E. B. Du Bois: Black Radical Democrat*. Boston, MA: Twayne Publishers, 1986.

Market Segment Research & Consulting. *The MSR&C Ethnic Market Report: A Portrait of the New America*. Coral Gables, FL: Market Segment Research & Consulting, 1990.

Marketti, J. "Estimated Present Value of Income Diverted during Slavery." In *The Wealth of Races: The Present Value of Benefits from Past Injustices*, edited by R. F. America. Westport: Greenwood Press, 1990.

Marks, A. "Digital Divide Narrows: Minorities Closing High-tech Gap." *ABC News*, January 25, 2000. http://www.abcnews.go.com/sections/tech/DailyNews/csm_divide000126.html.

Marlow, C. "How Diverse Is Facebook?" (December 16, 2009). http://www.facebook.com/note.php?note_id=205925658858&id=8394258414&ref=mf.

Mason, P. "Persistent Racial Discrimination in the Labor Market." In *African Americans in the U.S. Economy*, edited by C. A. Conrad, J. Whitehead, P. L. Mason, and J. Stewart, 141-50. Lanham: Rowman & Littlefield, 2005.

Massey, D., and N. Denton. *American Apartheid: Segregation and the Making of the Underclass*. Cambridge, MA: Harvard University Press, 1993.

Maultsby, P. "Influences and Retentions of West African Musical Concepts in U.S. Black Music." *The Western Journal of Black Studies* 3 (Fall 1979): 197–215.

———. "The Use and Performance of Hymnody, Spirituals, and Gospels in the Black Church." *The Western Journal of Black Studies* 7 (Fall 1983): 161–71.

Maye, M., and W. Maye. *Orita, Rites of Passage for Youth of African Descent in America*. New York: Faithworks Publishing, 2000.

Mbiti, J. *African Religions and Philosophy*. Garden City, NY: Anchor Books, 1970.

McBride, K. "Trayvon Martin Story Reveals New Tools of Media Power, Justice." *Poynte* (March 23, 2012). http://www.poynter.org/latest-news/making-sense-of-news/167660/trayvon-martin-story-a-study-in-the-new-tools-of-media-power-justice/.

McCabe, K. "African Immigrants in the United States." US in Focus, Migration Policy Institute (July 2011). http://www.migrationinformation.org/article/african-immigrants-united-states.

———. "Caribbean Immigrants in the United States." US in Focus, Migration Policy Institute (April 2011). http://www.migrationinformation.org/USfocus/display.cfm?id=834.

McCall, H. "The Savings Gap, Savings and Investing by African Americans" (1998). http://www.osc.

state.ny.us/reports/other/savings.htm.

McElroy, G., R. Powell, and S. Patton, eds. *African-American Artists 1880–1987*. Washington, DC: Smithsonian Institution Scholarly Press, 1989.

McEvoy, J., and A. Miller, eds. *Black Power and Student Rebellion*. Belmont: Wadsworth Publishing, 1969.

McGinn, R. *Science, Technology and Society*. Englewood Cliffs: Prentice Hall, 1991.

McKinnon, J. *The Black Population in the United States: March 2002* (Current Population Reports, April 2003). Washington, DC: U.S. Census Bureau.

McKissack, P., and F. McKissack. *Black Diamond: The Story of the Negro Baseball Leagues*. New York: Scholastic, 1994.

McNichol, E., P. Oliff, and N. Johnson. "States Continue to Feel Recession's Impact" (March 2, 2012). http://www.cbpp.org/cms/index.cfm?fa=view&id=711.

McNicol, S., and G. McNicol. "Racial Identification and Racial Preference of Black Preschool Children in New York and Trinidad." *The Journal of Black Psychology* 14 (February 1988): 65–68.

McNutt, K. *Hooked on Hoops: Understanding Black Youths' Blind Devotion to Basketball*. Chicago: African American Images, 2002.

McQuirter, T. *By Any Greens Necessary: A Revolutionary Guide for Black Women Who Want to Eat Great, Get Healthy, Lose Weight, and Look Phat*. Chicago: Lawrence Hill Books, 2010.

Meadows, E. "African Retentions in Blues and Jazz." *The Western Journal of Black Studies* 3 (Fall 1979): 180–85.

Medearis, A. *The Kitchen Diva! The New African-American Kitchen*. New York: Lake Isle Press, 2008.

Membership of the 109th Congress: A Profile (CRS Report for Congress, March 23, 2005). http://www.senate.gov/reference/resources/pdf/RS22007.pdf. Accessed October 1, 2014.

Meredith, J. "Closing the New Digital Divide: African-Americans Call upon the FCC to Allow Improved High-Speed Internet Access." *National Center for Policy Analysis*, No. 411 (May 2002). http://www.nationalcenter.org/NPA411.html.

Messner, S., and R. Sampson. "The Sex Ratio, Family Disruption, and Rates of Violent Crime." *Social Forces* 69 (March 1991): 693–713.

Mies, M. "New Reproductive Technologies: Sexist and Racist Implications." *Quilt*, January 1, 1994.

Miller, M. *Slaves to Fashion, Black Dandyism and the Styling of Black Diasporic Identity*. Durham: Duke University Press, 2009.

Miranda, M. "Black Sitcoms: A Black Perspective." *Cercles* 8 (2003): 46–58. http://www.cercles.com/n8/chitiga.pdf.

Mire, A. *Pigmentation and Empire: The Emerging Skin-Whitening Industry* (A CounterPunch Special Report, 2005). http://www.counterpunch.org/mire07282005.html.

Mitchell, M. *The Crisis of the African-American Architect: Conflicting Cultures of Architecture and (Black) Power*. 2nd rev. ed. Lincoln, NE: iUniverse, 2003.

Moikobu, J. *Blood and Flesh: Black American and African Identification*. Westport: Greenwood Press, 1981.

Molette, C., and B. Molette. *Black Theater*. Bristol, IN: Wyndham Hall Press, 1986.

Moody, S. "Anna Julia Cooper, Charles Chesnutt, and the Hampton Folklore Society—Constructing a Black Folk Aesthetic through Folklore and Memory." In *New Essays on the African American Novel: From Hurston and Ellison to Morrison and Whitehead*, edited by L. King and L. Selzer. New York: Palgrave, 2008.

Moody-Turner, S., and J. Stewart. "Gendering Africana Studies: Insights from Anna Julia Cooper." *African American Review* 43, no. 1 (Spring 2009): 35–44.

Moore, M., G. Gilyard, K. King, N. Warfield-Coppock, and G. Hassan. *Transformation: A Rites of Passage Manual for African American Girls*. New York: The Star Press, 1987.

Morland, K., S. Wing, A. Roux, and C. Poole. "Neighborhood Characteristics Associated with the Location of Food Stores and Food Service Places." *American Journal of Preventive Medicine* 22, no. 1 (January, 2002): 23–29.

Morris, J. "A Pillar of Strength: An African American School's Communal Bonds with Families and Community Since Brown." *Urban Education* 33, no. 5 (1999): 584–605.

Morris, M. *The Politics of Black America*. New York: Harper & Row, 1975.

Morrison, A. "One Hundred Years of Negro Entertainment." In *International Library of Afro-American Life and History*, edited by L. Patterson. Washington, DC: The ASALH Press, 1976.

Morrison, M. "Negro League Baseball, History and Key Players in Baseball's Gone—But Not Forgotten—League" (n.d.). http://www.infoplease.com/spot/negroleague1.html.

———. "The Emergence of a Legislative Caucus of Afro-Descendant Legislators in the Americas: Context, Progress, and Agenda Setting." In *African American in Global Affairs, Contemporary Perspectives*, edited by M. L. Clemons, 249-82. Boston, MA: Northeastern University Press, 2010.

Morrison, T. *Song of Solomon*. New York: Alfred A. Knopf, 1977.

Moynihan, D. *The Negro Family: The Case for National Action*. Washington, DC: U.S. Department of Labor, 1965.

Muhammad, A. "Muhammad Speaks: A Trailblazer in the Newspaper Industry." *The Final Call* (n.d.). http://www.finalcall.com/national/savioursday2k/m_speaks.htm.

Muhammad, E. *Message to the Blackman in America*. Chicago: Muhammad Mosque of Islam, No. 2, 1965.

Myers, H., N. Anderson, and T. Strickland. "A Biobehavioral Perspective on Stress and Hypertension in Black Adults." In *Black Adult Development and Aging*, edited by R. L. Jones. Berkeley: Cobb & Henry Publishers, 1989.

Myers, L. "Transpersonal Psychology: The Role of the Afrocentric Paradigm." In *African American Psychology, Theory, Research and Practice*, edited by A. K. Burlew, W. C. Banks, H. P. McAdoo, and D. Ajani Ya Azibo, 5-17. Newbury Park, CA: Sage Publications, 1992.

Naples, N., ed. *Community Activism and Feminist Politics: Organizing across Race, Class, and Gender*. New York: Routledge, 1998.

Nash, G. *Race and Revolution*. Madison: Madison House, 1990.

National Advisory Commission on Civil Disorders. *Report of the National Advisory Commission on Civil Disorders*. Washington, DC: U.S. Government Printing Office, 1968.

National Association of Black Journalists. Accessed August 28, 2014. http://www.nabj.org/.

"National Black Caucus of State Legislatures and the National Conference of State Legislatures. Number of African American Legislators" (2009). http://www.ncsl.org/research/about-state-legislatures/african-american-legislators-2009.aspx.

National Black Church Initiative. Accessed August 28, 2014. http://www.naltblackchurch.com/about/current-programs.html.

National Center for Education Statistics, U.S. Department of Education. *National Assessment of Educational Progress (NAEP)* (2003 Reading Assessment, January 2004). http://nces.ed.gov/nationsreportcard/pubs/main2003/2005453.asp. Accessed October 1, 2014.

National Center for Education Statistics, U.S. Department of Education. "Schools and Staffing Survey, 1999–2000" (Public Charter School Survey, May 2002). http://nces.ed.gov/pubs2002/2002313.pdf. Accessed October 1, 2014.

National Center for Education Statistics, U.S. Department of Education. "State Nonfiscal Survey of Public Elementary/Secondary Education, 1991–1992 and 2001–2002." The NCES Common Core of Data (CCD) (n.d.). http://nces.ed.gov/ccd/stnfis.asp. Accessed October 1, 2014.

"National Hip-Hop Team Vote 2008 Campaign to Be Launched in Pennsylvania" (March 16, 2008). http://www.reuters.com/article/2008/03/16/idUS73167+16-Mar-2008+BW20080316.

National Institute of Justice. "Keeping Track of Electronic Monitoring." *National Law Enforcement and Corrections Technology Center Bulletin* (October 1999). http://www.docstoc.com/docs/42325828/Keeping-Track-of-Electronic-Monitoring.

National Park Service. "Draft Management Recommendations for the African Burial Ground." http://www.africanburialground.gov/ABG_FinalReports.htm (site discontinued).

Neal, L. "A Calculation and Comparison of the Current Benefits of Slavery and an Analysis of Who Benefits." In *The Wealth of Races: The Present Value of Benefits from Past Injustices*, edited by R. F. America. Westport: Greenwood Press, 1990.

Neighbors, H., and S. Lumpkin. "The Epidemiology of Mental Disorder in the Black Population." In *Handbook of Mental Health and Mental Disorders among Black Americans*, edited by D. Ruiz, 55-70. New York: Greenwood Press, 1990.

Neil, M. "President Obama's Broadband Initiative Will Attempt to Bridge the Nation's Growing Digital Divide." The Leadership Conference, September 4, 2009. http://www.civilrights.org/archives/2009/09/673-broadband.html.

Nelson, F., B. Rosenberg, and N. Meter. *Charter School Achievement on the 2003 National Assessment of Educational Progress*. Washington, DC: American Federation of Teachers, 2004.

Nelsen, H., and A. Nelsen. *The Black Church in the Sixties*. Lexington: The University Press of Kentucky, 1975.

Nelson, W., and P. Meranto. *Electing Black Mayors*. Columbus: The Ohio State University Press, 1977.

Nembhard, J., and N. Chiteji, eds. *Wealth Accumulation and Communities of Color in the United States*. Ann Arbor: University of Michigan Press, 2006.

Netter, S. "President Obama Takes Responsibility for Democrats' Loss, Saying, 'I've Got to Do a Better Job'." *ABC News*, November 3, 2010. http://abcnews.go.com/Politics/vote-2010-elections-president-obama-takes-responsibility-democrats/story?id=12046360.

New York Civil Liberties Union. "Who's Watching? Video Camera Surveillance in New York City and the Need for Public Oversight" (A Special Report, Fall 2006). http://www.nyclu.org/pdfs/surveillance_cams_report_121306.pdf.

News One. "Obama and Congressional Black Caucus Finally Getting along" (December 13, 2011). http://newsone.com/2000206/obama-congressional-black-caucus-unite/.

Nicolas, G., J. Helms, M. Jernigan, T. Sass, A. Skrzypek, and A. DeSilva. "A Conceptual Framework for Understanding the Strengths of Black Youths." *The Journal of Black Psychology* 34 (2008): 261–80.

Nketia, J. "The Study of African and Afro-American Music." *The Black Perspective in Music* 1 (Spring 1973): 7–15.

Nobles, W. "African Philosophy: Foundations for Black Psychology." In *Black Psychology*, edited by R. Jones. New York: Harper & Row, 1972.

———. "Black People in White Insanity: An Issue for Black Community Health." *Journal of Afro-American Issues* 4, no. 1 (1976): 21–27.

Novak, T., and D. Hoffman. "Bridging the Digital Divide: The Impact of Race on Computer Access and Internet Use." *eLab Manuscripts* (1998). http://elab.vanderbilt.edu/research/papers/html/manuscripts/ race/science.html.

Obama, B. "On My Faith and My Church" (March 14, 2008). http://www.huffingtonpost.com/barack-obama/on-my-faith-and-my-church_b_91623.html. http://www.huffingtonpost.com/barack-obama/on-my-faith-and-my-church_b_91623.html. Accessed October 1, 2014.

"Obama's Stimulus Package." *The Progress Report* (January 5, 2009). http://www.huffingtonpost.com/the-progress-report/obamas-stimulus-package_b_155279.html. http://www.huffingtonpost.com/the-progress-report/obamas-stimulus-package_b_155279.html. Accessed October 1, 2014.

Ofari, E. *The Myth of Black Capitalism*. New York: Modern Reader, 1970.

Office of Juvenile Justice and Delinquency Prevention. *Summary* (1998 Youth Gang Survey, November 2000). . https://www.ncjrs.gov/pdffiles1/ojjdp/183109.pdf. Accessed October 1, 2014.

Office of Policy Development and Research. *Homeownership: Progress and Work Remaining* (Issue Brief No. III). Washington, DC: U.S. Department of Housing and Urban Development, December 2000.

Ogbar, J. *Hip-Hop Revolution: The Culture and Politics of Rap*. Lawrence: University Press of Kansas, 2007.

Ogbu, J. "Racial Stratification and Education." In *U.S. Race Relations in the 1980s and 1990s*, edited by G. E. Thomas. New York: Hemisphere Publishing Corporation, 1990.

Ojeda, R. "The Continuing Home Foreclosure Tsunami, Disproportionate Impacts on Black and Latino Communities" (A William C. Velasquez Institute White Paper, October, 2009). http://community-wealth.org/content/continuing-home-foreclosure-tsunami-disproportionate-impacts-black-and-latino-communities. Accessed October 2, 2014.

Oliver, M., and T. Shapiro. *Black Wealth/White Wealth: A New Perspective on Racial Inequality*. New York: Routledge, 1995.

Oliver, P. *The Story of the Blues*. Philadelphia: Chilton Book Company, 1969.

Omolade, B. *The Rising Song of African American Women*. New York: Routledge, 1994.

Onwubu, C. "The Intellectual Foundation of Racism." In *Black Studies: Theory, Methods and Cultural Perspectives*, edited by T. Anderson. Pullman, WA: Washington State University Press, 1990.

Orfield, G., and C. Lee. "Brown at 50: King's Dream or Plessy's Nightmare?" *The Civil Rights Project, Harvard University* (January 2004). http://civilrightsproject.ucla.edu/research/k-12-education/integration-and-diversity/brown-at-50-king2019s-dream-or-plessy2019s-nightmare/orfield-brown-50-2004.pdf. Accessed October 1, 2014.

O'Toole, A. *The Best Man Plays: Major League Baseball and the Black Athlete, 1901–2002*. Jefferson, NC: McFarland and Company, 2003.

Painter, N. *Creating Black Americans, African-American History and Its Meanings, 1619 to the Present*. New York: Oxford University Press, 2007.

————. *Sojourner Truth: A Life, a Symbol*. New York: W.W. Norton, 1996.

Panis, C., and L. Lillard. "Socioeconomic Differentials in the Return to Social Security" (RAND Corporation Working Paper No. 96-05, February 1996). http://www.rand.org/content/dam/rand/pubs/drafts/2008/DRU1327.pdf. Accessed October 1, 2014.

Pasteur, A., and I. Toldson. *Roots of Soul*. Garden City, NY: Anchor Press/Doubleday, 1982.

Pastras, P. *Dead Man Blues: Jelly Roll Morton Way out West*. Berkeley: University of California Press, 2001.

Patrick, J. "The Tulsa, Oklahoma Race Riot of 1921." *Exodus Online* (n.d.). http://www.exodusnews.com/HISTORY/History007.htm (page no longer available.).

Patterson, P. "Community Development Corporations." In *Black Economic Development: Analysis and Implications*, edited by W. L. Cash and M. L. Oliver. Ann Arbor: Graduate School of Business Administration, University of Michigan, 1975.

Pattillo, M. "Sweet Mothers and Gangbangers: Managing Crime in a Black Middle-Class Neighborhood." *Social Forces* 76 (1998): 747–74.

"Paul Robeson." *Africa within*. http://www.africawithin.com/bios/paul_robeson.htm (site no longer available.)

Perry, B. "Can the Judiciary Be 'Representative'?" *Insights on Law & Society* 2 (Fall 2001).

Peterson, W., M. Novak, and P. Gleason. *Concepts of Ethnicity*. Cambridge, MA: Belknap Press of Harvard University Press, 1982.

Peterson-Lewis, S., and A. Adams. "Television's Model of the Quest for African Consciousness: A Comparison with Cross' Empirical Model of Psychological Nigrescence." *The Journal of Black Psychology* 16 (Spring 1990): 55–72.

Phillips, L., K. Reddick-Morgan, and D. Stephens. "Oppositional Consciousness within an Oppositional Realm: The Case of Feminism and Womanism in Rap and Hip Hop, 1976–2004." In *Message in the Music, Hip Hop History & Pedagogy*, edited by D. P. Alridge, J. B. Stewart, and V. P. Franklin, 90-112. Washington, DC: The ASALH Press, 2010.

Pickens, W. "Jim Crow in Texas." *The Nation*, August 15, 1923.

Pierce, J., and A. Carey. "Efficacy and Participation: A Study of Black Political Behavior." *Journal of Black Studies* 2, no. 2 (December 1971): 201–23.

Pilgrim, D. "Jezebel Stereotype." Jim Crow Museum of Racist Memorabilia, Ferris State University. Accessed August 28, 2014. http://www.ferris.edu/news/jimcrow/jezebel/.

Pinderhughes, D. *Understanding Race, Ethnicity and Power*. New York: The Free Press, 1989.

Pinn, A. *The Black Church in the Post-Civil Rights Era*. Maryknoll, NY: Orbis Books, 2002.

————. *Varieties of African-American Religious Experience*. Minneapolis: Fortress Press, 1998.

Piven, F., and R. Cloward. *Regulating the Poor: The Functions of Public Welfare*. Rev. ed. New York: Vintage Books, 1993.

Ploski, H., and J. Williams, eds. *The Negro Almanac*. New York: John Wiley & Sons, 1983.

Plummer, B. *Rising Wind, Black Americans and U.S. Foreign Affairs, 1935–1960*. Chapel Hill: The University of North Carolina Press, 1996.

Porter, J. *Modern Negro Art*. New York: Dryden Press, 1943.

Porter, K., K. Larin, and W. Primus. *Social Security and Poverty among the Elderly: A National and State Perspective*. Washington, DC: Center on Budget and Policy Priorities, 1999.

Porter, L. "Some Problems in Jazz Research." *Black Music Research Journal* 8 (Fall 1988): 195–206.

Porter, M. "The Competitive Advantage of the Inner City." *Harvard Business Review*, May–June 1995, 55–71.

Poston, W. "The Biracial Identity Development Model: A Needed Addition." *Journal of Counseling Development* 69 (1990): 152–55.

Potter, G. "Truth in Fiction, Science and Criticism." In *After Postmodernism: An Introduction to Critical Realism*, edited by J. Lopez and G. Potter. London: Athlone Press, 2001.

Potter, R. "Race." In *Key Terms in Popular Music and Culture*, edited by B. Horner and T. Swiss, 71-84. Oxford, UK: Blackwell, 1999.

Potts, R. "Emancipatory Education versus School-Based Prevention in African American Communities." *American Journal of Community Psychology* 31, no. 1–2 (March, 2003): 173–83.

Poussaint, A. "The Problems of Light-Skinned Blacks." *Ebony*, February 1975.

President's Initiative on Race. *One America in the 21st Century, Forging a New Future: The President's Initiative on Race* (The Advisory Board's Report to the President). Washington, DC: U.S. Government Printing Office, 1998.

President's National Advisory Commission on Civil Disorders. *Report of the National Advisory Commission on Civil Disorders*. Washington, DC: U.S. Government Printing Office, 1968.

Prothrow-Stith, D. *Deadly Consequences*. New York: HarperCollins, 1991.

"Provisions of the Affordable Care Act, by Year." Washington, DC: U.S. Department of Health and Human Services. http://www.healthcare.gov/law/about/order/byyear.html (page no longer available.).

Pucher, J., and J. Renne. "Socioeconomics of Urban Travel: Evidence from the 2001 NHTS." *Transport Quarterly* 57 (2003). http://policy.rutgers.edu/faculty/pucher/TQPuchRenne.pdf.

Purcell, P. *Pension Sponsorship and Participation: Summary of Recent Trends* (CRS Report for Congress). Washington, DC: Congressional Research Service, 2001.

Quarles, B. *The Negro in the Making of America*. New York: Macmillan, 1964.

"Rainbow/PUSH-Wall Street Project." *Black Enterprise*, February 2005.

Rampersad, A. *Jackie Robinson: A Biography*. New York: Alfred A. Knopf, 1997.

Ramsey, F., and C. Smith, eds. *Jazzmen*. New York: Limelight, 1985.

Ranciere, J. *The Politics of Aesthetics*. Translated by Gabriel Rockhill. New York: Continuum, 2004.

Randall, J., and D. Donald. *The Civil War and Reconstruction*. Boston, MA: D. C. Heath and Company, 1961.

Randall, V. "Gender, Race and Ethnicity: Experiences with Three Health Care Related Issues." In *The Role of Governmental and Private Health Care Programs and Initiatives, the Health Care Challenge: Acknowledging Disparity, Confronting Discrimination, and Ensuring Equality* (A Report of the United States Commission on Civil Rights), vol. I. Washington, DC: U.S. Government Printing Office, 1999. http://academic.udayton.edu/health/08civilrights/01-03-05Research.htm (page no longer available.)

Ransby, B. *Ella Baker and the Black Freedom Movement*. Chapel Hill: The University of North Carolina Press, 2003.

Ransford, O. *The Slave Trade*. London: John Murray Publishers, 1971.

Ransom, R., and R. Sutch. *One Kind of Freedom: The Economic Consequences of Emancipation*. New York: Cambridge University Press, 1977.

———. "Who Pays for Slavery?" In *The Wealth of Races: The Present Value of Benefits from Past Injustice*, edited by R. F. America. Westport: Greenwood Press, 1990.

Ransome, S., ed. *J. Hammon, America's First Negro Poet*. Port Washington, NY: Kennikat Press, 1970.

Raphael, S., and A. Berube. "Socioeconomic Differences in Household Automobile Ownership Rates: Implications for Evacuation Policy." Paper prepared for the Berkeley Symposium on "Real Estate, Catastrophic Risk, and Public Policy," Berkeley, CA, March 23, 2006. http://urbanpolicy.berkeley.edu/pdf/raphael.pdf.

Reddick, L. "The Negro Policy of the United States Army, 1775–1945." *The Journal of Negro History* 34, no. 1 (1949): 9–29.

Redding, S. *They Came in Chains*. Philadelphia: J. B. Lippincott & Company, 1950.

Redlener, I., and D. Berman. "Follow-Up 2005: Where the American Public Stands on Terrorism and Preparedness after Hurricane Katrina & Rita: A Follow-Up to the 2005 Annual Survey of the American Public by the National Center for Disease Preparedness." *Journal of International Affairs* 59, no. 2 (Spring/Summer 2006): 87-103.

Reed, A. *The Jesse Jackson Phenomenon*. New Haven: Yale University Press, 1986.

Reid, M. *Redefining Black Film*. Berkeley: University of California Press, 1993.

Reid-Merritt, P. *Righteous Self Determination: The Black Social Work Movement in America.* Baltimore: Inprint Editions, 2010.

Religious Tolerance. http://www.religioustolerance.org/. Accessed October 1, 2014.

Remnick, D. *King of the World: Muhammad Ali and the Rise of an American Hero.* New York: Random House, 1998.

Rennison, C., and S. Welchans. *Intimate Partner Violence* (NCJ 178247, 2000). Bureau of Justice Statistics, Office of Justice Programs, U.S. Department of Justice. http://www.bjs.gov/index.cfm?ty=pbdetail&iid=1002 . Accessed October 1, 2014.

Resnicow, K., R. Soler, R. Braithwaite, M. Selassie, and M. Smith. "Development of a Racial and Ethnic Identity Scale for African American Adolescents: The Survey of Black Life." *The Journal of Black Psychology* 25 (1999): 171–88.

"Responses to U.S. Supreme Court Decision About Voluntary School Integration." The Civil Rights Project, UCLA. http://www.civilrightsproject.ucla.edu/policy/court/voltint.php.

Rhodes, J. *Mary Ann Shadd Cary: The Black Press and Protest in the Nineteenth Century.* Bloomington: Indiana University Press, 1998.

Riach, P., and J. Rich. "Field Experiments of Discrimination in the Market Place." *The Economic Journal* 112 (November 2002): F480–518.

Rich, G. "What Will the CIAA Add Next?" *Independent Weekly*, February 27, 2002. http:/indyweek.com/durham/2002-02-27/triangles.html.

Richards, D. "Implications of African-American Spirituality." In *African Culture: The Rhythms of Unity*, edited by M. Kete Asante and K. Welsh Asante, 207-32. Westport: Greenwood Press, 1985.

———. "The Ideology of European Dominance." *The Western Journal of Black Studies* 3, no. 4 (Winter 1979): 244–50.

Richardson, M., ed. *Maria W. Stewart, America's First Black Woman Political Writer: Essays and Speeches.* Bloomington: Indiana University Press, 1987.

Richardson, P. *Empire and Slavery.* London: Longmans, Green & Company, 1968.

Roach, M. "Garvey's Ghost." Recorded in New York (Impulse!, 1961). In *Max Roach Percussion Bitter Sweet*

Robbins, R. "Charles S. Johnson: Scholarship, Advocacy, and Role Balance." In *Black Sociologists: Historical and Contemporary Perspectives*, edited by J. Blackwell and M. Janowitz. Chicago: The University of Chicago Press, 1974.

Roberts, D. "Black Women and the Pill." *Family Planning Perspectives* 32 (March/April 2000): 92–93.

————. *Killing the Black Body: Race, Reproduction, and the Meaning of Liberty*. New York: Vintage Books, 1997.

————. "Race and the Biotech Agenda." Presentation at the Symposium on "The Next Four Years: The Biotech Agenda, the Human Future: What Direction for Liberals and Progressives?" New York City, 1994.

Roberts, S., and P. Baker. "Asked to Declare His Race, Obama Checks 'Black'." *The New York Times*, April 2, 2010. http://www.nytimes.com/2010/04/03/us/politics/03census.html.

Robinson, C. *Black Movements in America*. New York: Routledge, 1997.

Robinson, E. *Disintegration: The Splintering of Black America*. New York: Doubleday, 2010.

Rockquemore, K., and T. Laszloffy. "Moving beyond Tragedy: A Multidimensional Model of Mixed-Race Identity." In *Raising Biracial Children*, edited by K. A. Rockquemore and T. A. Laszloffy, 1-17. Lanham: AltaMira Press, 2005.

Rodee, C., T. Anderson, and C. Christol. *Introduction to Political Science*. New York: McGraw-Hill, 1967.

Rodney, W. *How Europe Underdeveloped Africa*. London: Bogle L'Ouverture, 1972.

Rogers, I. "The Black Campus Movement and the Institutionalization of Black Studies, 1965–1970." In *Expanding the History of the Black Studies Movement* (A Special Issue of the Journal of African American Studies), edited by J. Fenderson, J. Stewart, and K. Baumgartner. *Journal of African American Studies* vol. 16, no. 1 (March 2012): 21-40.

Rolison, G. "An Exploration of the Term Underclass as It Relates to African-Americans." *Journal of Black Studies* 21 (March 1991): 287–301.

Rose, J. *Introduction to Sociology*. Chicago: Rand McNally College Publishing Company, 1980.

Rothenberg, R. *The Neoliberals*. New York: Simon & Schuster, 1984.

Rusche, G., and O. Kirchheimer. *Punishment and Social Structure*. New York: Columbia University Press, 1939.

Sailes, G. "A Socioeconomic Explanation of Black Sports Participation Patterns." *The Western Journal of Black Studies* 11 (Winter 1987): 164–67.

Sales, G. *Jazz: America's Classical Music*. Englewood Cliffs: Prentice Hall, 1984.

Sammons, V. *Blacks in Science and Medicine*. New York: Hemisphere Publishing Corporation, 1991.

Samuelson, P., and W. Nordhaus. *Economics*. New York: McGraw-Hill, 1989.

Sanchez, G., S. Nuño, and M. Barreto. "The Disproportionate Impact of Photo-ID Laws on the Minority Electorate" (May 24, 2011). http://www.latinodecisions.com/blog/2011/05/24/the-disproportionate-impact-of-stringent-voter-id-laws/.

Sanford, F. *Psychology*. Belmont: Wadsworth Publishing, 1965.

Sanford, K. "Reverend Jesse Jackson and the Rainbow/PUSH Coalition: Institutionalizing Economic Opportunity." In *Black Political Organizations in the Post-Civil Rights Era*, edited by O. Johnson and K. Sanford, 150-69. New Brunswick: Rutgers University Press, 2002.

Satcher, D., G. E. Fryer, Jr., J. McCann, A. Troutman, S. H. Woolf, and G. Rust. "What If We Were Equal? A Comparison of the Black–White Mortality Gap in 1960 and 2000." *Health Affairs* 24, no. 2 (2005): 459–64.

Savage, B. *Broadcasting Freedom, Radio, War, and the Politics of Race, 1938–1948*. Chapel Hill: The University of North Carolina Press, 1999.

Sax, L., A. Astin, W. Korn, and K. Mahoney. "The American Freshman: National Norms for Fall 1998." Higher Education Research Institute, UCLA Graduate School of Education & Information Studies (1999). http://www.heri.ucla.edu/PDFs/pubs/TFS/Norms/Monographs/TheAmericanFreshman1998.pdf. Accessed October 1, 2014.

Scarborough Research. "Hispanics and African-Americans Make Headlines as Avid Viewers of Late Local News" (2005).

Schechter, P. *Ida B. Wells-Barnett and American Reform, 1880–1930*. Chapel Hill: The University of North Carolina Press, 2001.

Schindler, M. "National Organizations Oppose Africana Studies and Research Center Overhaul." *The Cornell Daily Sun*, January 24, 2011. http://cornellsun.com/blog/2011/01/24/national-organizations-oppose-africana-studies-and-research-center-overhaul/.

Schmidt, M., S. Affenito, R. Striegel-Moore, P. Khoury, B. Barton, P. Crawford, S. Kronsberg, G. Schreiber, E. Obarzanek, and S. Daniels. "Fast-Food Intake and Diet Quality in Black and White Girls: The National Heart, Lung, and Blood Institute Growth and Health Study." *Archives of Pediatrics and Adolescent Medicine* 159 (July 2005): 626–31.

Schultz, D., and S. Schultz. *A History of Modern Psychology*. 4th ed. San Diego: Harcourt Brace Jovanovich, 1987.

Schultze, S. "Campaigns Condemn Political Flier, Paper Aimed at Black Voters Falsely States Voting Rules." *JSOnline*, October 29, 2004. http://journalsentinel.com.

Schwartz, A., and K. Tajbakhsh. "Mixed Income Housing: Unanswered Questions." *Cityscape* 3, no. 2 (1997): 71–92.

Scott, J. *The Black Revolts, Racial Stratification in the U.S.A.: The Politics of Estate, Caste, and Class in the American Society*. Cambridge, MA: Schenkman Publishing, 1976.

Scrimshaw, N., and J. SanGiovanni. "Synergism of Nutrition, Infection, and Immunity: An Overview." *American Journal of Clinical Nutrition* 66, no. 4 (1997): 464S–77S.

Secret, P., and J. Johnson. "Political Efficacy, Political Trust, Race and Electoral Participation." *The Western Journal of Black Studies* (Summer 1985): 74–83.

select bibliography

Seder, J., and B. Burrell. "Getting It Together." In *Black Economic Development: Analysis and Implications*, edited by W. L. Cash and M. L. Oliver. Ann Arbor, MI: Graduate School of Business Administration, University of Michigan, 1975.

Seltzer, R., and R. Smith. "Color Differences in the Afro-American Community and the Differences They Make." *Journal of Black Studies* 21 (March 1991): 279–86.

Semaj, L. "The Black Self, Identity, and Models for a Psychology of Black Liberation." *The Western Journal of Black Studies* 5 (Fall 1981): 158–71.

Semuels, A. "$1.4 Million in Grants Boost Pitt's Healthy Black Family Project." *Pittsburgh Post-Gazette*, August 24, 2005. http://www.post-gazette.com/news/health/2005/08/24/1-4-million-in-grants-boost-Pitt-s-Health-Black-Family-Project/stories/200508240222. Accessed October 1, 2014.

"Seventy Percent of Schools to 'Fail'." *FairTest Examiner* (Winter–Spring 2003). http://fairtest.org/seventy-percent-schools-fail.

Seybert, T. "The Historic Black Press – Overview Essay." *The History of Jim Crow* (n.d.). http://www.jimcrowhistory.org/resources/lessonplans/hs_es_black_press.htm (page no longer available).

Sharpless, R. *Cooking in Other Women's Kitchens: Domestic Workers in the South, 1860–1960* (The John Hope Franklin Series in African American History and Culture). Chapel Hill: The University of North Carolina Press, 2010.

Shaw, A. "Researching Rhythm & Blues." *Black Music Research Journal* University of Illinois Press(1980): 71–79.

Shepp, A. "Malcolm, Malcolm, Semper Malcolm." *Fire Music*. MCA Records, MCAD-39121, 1965.

Sherard, T. "Women's Classic Blues in Toni Morrison's Jazz: Cultural Artifact as Narrator." *Genders* 31 (2000). http://www.genders.org/g31/g31_sherard.html. Accessed October 1, 2014.

Shin, P., K. Jones, and S. Rosenbaum. *Reducing Racial and Ethnic Health Disparities: Estimating the Impact of High Health Center Penetration in Low-Income Communities*. Washington, DC: Center for Health Services Research and Policy, George Washington University Medical Center, September 2003.

Shuman, M. *Going Local: Creating Self-Reliant Communities in a Global Age*. New York: Routledge, 2000.

Sigelman, L., S. Tuch, and J. Martin. "What's in a Name: Preference for 'Black' versus 'African American' among Americans of African Descent." *Public Opinion Quarterly* 69 (Fall 2005): 429–38.

Simms, M., and J. Malveaux, eds. *Slipping through the Cracks: The Status of Black Women*. New Brunswick: Transaction Publishers, 1986.

Singh, R. *The Congressional Black Caucus: Racial Politics in the U.S. Congress*. Thousand Oaks, CA: Sage Publications, 1998.

Skerry, P. *Mexican Americans: The Ambivalent Minority*. New York: The Free Press, 1993.

Skinner, E. *African Americans and U.S. Policy toward Africa 1850–1924: In Defense of Black Nationality*. Washington, DC: Howard University Press, 1992.

Skloot, R. *The Immortal Life of Henrietta Lacks*. New York: Random House, 2010.

Smith, A. *Home Broadband 2010* (A Pew Internet and American Life Project Report, August 11, 2010). http://pewresearch.org/pubs/1694/broadband-adoption-slows-dramatically-except-african-americans-little-interest-among-non-users.

———. *Mixed-Income Housing Developments: Promise and Reality*. Joint Center for Housing Studies, Harvard University, 2002.

Smith, B. "Poor Man's Blues." Recorded August 24, 1928, in New York City (W-146895-1, Columbia 14399).

Smith, C. "The Civil Rights Legacy of Ronald Reagan." *The Western Journal of Black Studies* 14 (Summer 1990): 102–14.

Smith, E. "The Genetically Superior Athlete: Myth or Reality." In *Black Studies: Theory, Method and Cultural Perspectives*, edited by T. Anderson. Pullman, WA: Washington State University Press, 1990.

Smith, M. *Debating Slavery, Economy and Society in the Antebellum American South*. Cambridge, UK: Cambridge University Press, 1998.

Smith, R. *The Public Influences of African-American Churches: Contexts and Capacities* (A Report Submitted to the Pew Charitable Trust by The Public Influences of African-American Churches Project, The Leadership Center at Morehouse College). Atlanta: Morehouse College, 2002.

———. *We Have No Leaders: African Americans in the Post-Civil Rights Era*. Albany: SUNY Press, 1996.

Solomon, M. *The Cry Was Unity: Communists and African Americans, 1917–1936*. Oxford, MS: University of Mississippi Press, 1998.

Solving the Problem of Childhood Obesity within a Generation (Report to the President). Washington, DC: White House Task Force on Childhood Obesity, May 2010.

"Sonia Sanchez." African American Literature Book Club (n.d.). http://authors.aalbc.com/sonia.htm.

Southern, E. "An Origin for the Negro Spiritual." *The Black Scholar* vol. 3, no. 10 (Summer 1972):8-13.

———. *The Music of Black Americans*. New York: W.W. Norton, 1971.

———. "The Origin and Development of the Black Musical Theater." *Black Music Research Journal* 2 (1981/1982): 1–14.

Spencer, J. *The New Negroes and Their Music: The Success of the Harlem Renaissance*. Knoxville, TN: The University of Tennessee Press, 1997.

Spero, S., and A. Harris. *The Black Worker*. New York: Columbia University Press, 1931.

Spooner, T., and L. Rainie. *African-Americans and the Internet* (Pew Internet & American Life Project, 2000). http://www.pewinternet.org/.

Stampp, K. *The Peculiar Institution*. New York: Vintage Books, 1956.

Stanfield, J. "Methodological Reflections: An Introduction." In *Race and Ethnicity in Research Methods*, edited by J. H. Stanfield and R. M. Dennis, 3-15. Newbury Park, CA: Sage Publications, 1993.

St. Angelo, D., and P. Puryear. "Fear, Apathy, and Other Dimensions of Black Voting." In *The New Black Politics*, edited by M. B. Preston, L. J. Henderson, and P. Puryear. New York: Longman, 1982.

Staples, R. *Introduction to Black Sociology*. New York: McGraw Hill, 1976.

———. "The Emerging Majority: Resources for Non-White Families in the United States." *Family Relations* 37 (1988): 348–54.

———. *The World of Black Singles*. Westport: Greenwood Press, 1981.

———. "What Is Black Sociology? Toward a Sociology of Black Liberation." In *The Death of White Sociology*, edited by J. Ladner, 161-72. Baltimore: Black Classic Press, 1998.

Starobin, R. *Industrial Slavery in the Old South*. New York: Oxford University Press, 1970.

Stephens, R. "What the Rap Is about: Some Historical Notes on the Development of Rap Music and the Hip-Hop Movement." *Word: A Black Culture Journal* 1 (Spring 1991): 53–83.

Stern, S. "The Call of the Black Panthers." In *Black Protest in the Sixties*, edited by A. Meier and E. M. Rudwick. Chicago: Quadrangle Books, 1970.

Sternberg, S. "Obama Administration Putting AIDS Back on Nation's Radar." *USA Today*, April 7, 2009. http://www.usatoday.com/news/health/2009-04-07-AIDS-CDC-HIV_N.htm.

Stevens, W. "Police Drop Bomb on Radicals' Home in Philadelphia." *The New York Times*, May 14, 1985.

Stevenson, H., Jr. "Relationship of Adolescent Perceptions of Racial Socialization to Racial Identity." *The Journal of Black Psychology* 21 (1995): 49–70.

Stewart, J., ed. *African Americans and Post-Industrial Labor Markets*. New Brunswick: Transaction Publishers, 1997.

———. "Art, Politics, Cultural Studies, and Post-Structural Philosophy in Black/Africana Studies:

Deciphering Complex Relationships." Unpublished manuscript, last modified February 2014. Microsoft Word file.

———. "Building a Cooperative Economy: Lessons from the Black Experience." *Review of Social Economy* 42, no. 3 (1984): 360–68.

———. "Foreword." In, 3rd ed., edited by C. Hudson-Weems, xix-xxiv. Troy, MI: Bedford Publishers, 2000.

———. "George Edmund Haynes and the Office of Negro Economics." In *A Different Vision, African American Economic Thought*, edited by T. D. Boston, vol. 1, 213-29. New York: Routledge, 1997.

———. "Globalization, Cities, and Racial Inequality at the Dawn of the 21st Century." *The Review of Black Political Economy* 31 (Winter 2004): 11–32.

———. "Historical Patterns of Black–White Political Economic Inequality in the United States and the Republic of South Africa." *The Review of Black Political Economy* 7, no. 3 (1977): 266–95.

———. "Message in the Music: Political Commentary in Black Popular Music from Rhythm and Blues to Early Hip Hop." *Journal of African American History* 90 (Fall 2005): 196–225.

———. "Perspectives on Black Families from Contemporary Soul Music: The Case of Millie Jackson." *Phylon* 41 (March 1980): 57–71.

———. "Perspectives on Reformist, Radical, and Recovery Models of Black Identity Dynamics from the Novels of W. E. B. Du Bois." In *Flight in Search of Vision*, edited by J. B. Stewart. Trenton, NJ: Africa World Press, 2004.

———. "Reaching for Higher Ground: Toward an Understanding of Black/African Studies." *The Afrocentric Scholar* 1, no. 1 (1992): 1–63.

———. "Relationships between Black Males and Females in Rhythm and Blues Music of the 1960s and 1970s." *The Western Journal of Black Studies* 3 (Fall 1979): 186–96.

———. "The Black Church as a Religio-Economic Institution." In *Flight in Search of Vision*, edited by J. B. Stewart. Trenton, NJ: Africa World Press, 2004.

———. "The Legacy of W. E. B. Du Bois for Contemporary Black Studies." *The Journal of Negro Education* 53, no. 3 (1984): 296–311.

———. "The Pursuit of Equality in the Steel Industry: The Committee on Civil Rights and Civil Rights Department of the United Steelworkers of America, 1948–1970." In *African Americans, Labor, and Society*, edited by P. L. Mason. Detroit: Wayne State University Press, 2001.

———. "Will the Revolution Be Digitized? Using Digitized Resources in Undergraduate Africana Studies Courses." *The Western Journal of Black Studies* 27 (Fall 2003): 194–204.

Stewart, J., and M. Coleman. "The Black Political Economy Paradigm and the Dynamics of Racial Economic Inequality." In *African Americans in the U.S. Economy*, edited by C. A. Conrad, J. Whitehead, P. L. Mason, and J. Stewart, 118-31. Lanham: Rowman & Littlefield, 2005.

select bibliography

Stewart, J., and J. Scott. "The Institutional Decimation of Black American Males." *The Western Journal of Black Studies* 2 (1978): 82–92.

―――. "The Pimp–Whore Complex in Everyday Life." *Black Male/Female Relationships* 1, no. 2 (1979): 11–15.

Stewart, J. B., and J. E. Allen-Smith. "Amandla! The Sullivan Principles and the Battle to End Apartheid in South Africa, 1975–1987." *The Journal of African American History* 96, no. 1 (Winter 2011): 62–89.

―――, eds. *Blacks in Rural America*. New Brunswick: Transaction Publishers, 1995.

―――. "Riddles, Rhythms, and Rhymes: Toward an Understanding of Methodological Issues and Possibilities in Black/Africana Studies." In *Ethnic Studies Research: Approaches and Perspectives*, edited by T. P. Fong, 179-218. Lanham: AltaMira Press, 2008.

Stombler, M., and I. Padavic. "Sister Acts: Resistance in Sweetheart and Little Sister Programs." In *African American Fraternities and Sororities: The Legacy and the Vision*, edited by T. L. Brown, G. S. Parks, and C. M. Phillips, 233-68. Lexington: The University Press of Kentucky, 2005.

Stone, C. *Black Political Power in America*. New York: Dell Publishing, 1970.

Stout, D. "Supreme Court Upholds Voter Identification Law in Indiana." *The New York Times*, April 29, 2008. http://www.nytimes.com/2008/04/29/washington/28cnd-scotus.html.

Straight, R. "Black–White Wealth: Asset Accumulation Differences by Race—SCF Data." Unpublished manuscript, 2002.

Strickland, W. "The Gary Convention and the Crisis of American Politics." *Black World*, (October 1972): 18-26.

Stuckey, S. *Slave Culture: Nationalist Theory and Foundations of Black America*. New York: Oxford University Press, 1987.

Sudarkasa, N. "African and Afro-American Family Structure: A Comparison." *The Black Scholar* vol. 11, no. 8 (November/December 1980): 37-60.

Suedfeld, P. *Psychology and Torture*. New York: Hemisphere Publishing Corporation, 1990.

Swanson, L., R. Harris, J. Skees, and L. Williamson. "African Americans in Southern Rural Regions: The Importance of Legacy." In *Blacks in Rural America*, edited by J. B. Stewart and J. E. Allen-Smith. New Brunswick: Transaction Publishers, 1995.

Swanstrom, T. "The Road to Jobs: Patterns of Employment in the Construction Industry in Eighteen Metropolitan Areas." Unpublished manuscript, August 30, 2007.

Tabb, W. *The Political Economy of the Black Ghetto*. New York: W.W. Norton, 1970.

Tanner, M. "Disparate Impact, Social Security and African Americans" (CATO Institute Briefing Paper No. 61, 2001). http://www.cato.org/sites/cato.org/files/pubs/pdf/bp61.pdf . Accessed October 1, 2014.

Tate, C. *Psychoanalysis and Black Novels: Desire and the Protocols of Race*. New York: Oxford University Press, 1998.

Tate, G. *Unknown Tongues, Black Women's Activism in the Antebellum Era, 1830–1860*. East Lansing: Michigan State University Press, 2003.

Tate, G., and L. Randolph. *Dimensions of Black Conservatism in the United States: Made in America*. New York: Palgrave Macmillan, 2002.

Tate, K. *Black Faces in the Mirror: African Americans and Their Representatives in the U.S. Congress*. Princeton, NJ: Princeton University Press, 2003.

Taylor, R. "The Study of Black People: A Survey of Empirical and Theoretical Models." In *Black Studies: Theory, Method, and Cultural Perspectives*, edited by T. Anderson. Pullman, WA: Washington State University Press, 1990.

Terry, B. *Vegan Soul Kitchen: Fresh, Healthy, and Creative African-American Cuisine*. Cambridge, MA: Da Capo Press, 2009.

"Tests Keep Thousands of Minorities Out of Teaching." *Fair Test Examiner* (Winter 1989). http://fairtest.org/examarts/winter89/smitahtt.htm (page no longer available).

"The American Underclass." *Time*, August 29, 1977.

The Associated Press. "Offensive Email Sender Censured by OC GOP" (May 4, 2011). http://seattletimes.nwsource.com/html/nationworld/2014964364_apusobamaoffensiveemail.html.

The Black Barbershop Health Outreach Program. https://www.facebook.com/BlackBarbershopHealthOutreachProgram.

The Black Bloggers Network. Accessed August 30, 2014. http://www.blackbloggernetwork.com/about/.

"The Community Basis of Sports in Pittsburgh" (2000). http://northbysouth.kenyon.edu/2000/Intro/Community%20basis%20in%20Pitt.htm.

"The Final Call: Continuing a Tradition." *The Final Call* (n.d.). http://www.finalcall.com/national/saviours-day2k/final_call.htm (page no longer available.).

The Land Loss Fund. Accessed August 30, 2014. http://www.federationsoutherncoop.com/.

The Leadership Conference Education Fund. "Where We Need to Go: A Civil Rights Roadmap for the National Black Church Initiative." Accessed August 30, 2014. http://naltblackchurch.com/.

The New York Times CBS Poll. "National Survey of Tea Party Supporters," April 5–12, 2010. http://documents.nytimes.com/new-york-timescbs-news-poll-national-survey-of-tea-party-supporters. Accessed October 1, 2014.

The White House. "U.S. Strategy toward Sub-Saharan Africa" (June 2012). http://www.whitehouse.gov/sites/default/files/docs/africa_strategy_2.pdf.

select bibliography

Thompson, K. "Advocates Struggle to Measure Stimulus Relief for Minority Businesses." *The Washington Post*, January 18, 2010. http://www.washingtonpost.com/wp-dyn/content/article/2010/01/17/AR2010011702910.html.

Thompson, L. "The Black Image in Early American Drama." *Black World*, vol. 26, no. 6 (April 1975): 54-69.

Thompson, R. "Kongo Influences on African American Artistic Culture." In *Africanisms in American Culture*, edited by J. E. Holloway. Bloomington: Indiana University Press, 1990.

Thompson, V. "Variables Affecting Racial-Identity Salience among African Americans." *The Journal of Social Psychology* 139, no. 6 (1999): 748–61.

Thompson Gager, C. *Teaching Jean Toomer's 1923 Cane* (Studies in African-American Culture). Vol. 9. New York: Peter Lang, 2006.

Thorne, M. *American Conservative Thought since World War II*. New York: Greenwood Press, 1990.

Tillery, A. *Beyond Homeland and Motherland, Africa, U.S. Foreign Policy, and Black Leadership in America*. Ithaca: Cornell University Press, 2011.

Tobin, J., and R. Dobard. *Hidden in Plain View: A Secret Story of Quilts and the Underground Railroad*. New York: Anchor, 2000.

Toffler, A. *Future Shock*. New York: Random House, 1970.

Tomovic, R. "Technology and Society." In *Science and Technology in the Transformation of the World* (Proceedings of the First International Seminar on the Transformation of the World, Belgrade, Yugoslavia, October 1979), edited by A. Abdel-Malek, G. Blue, and M. Pecujlic. Tokyo: The United Nations University. http://archive.unu.edu/unupress/unupbooks/uu01se/uu01se06.htm#technology and society. Accessed October 1, 2014.

Toppo, G. "Teachers Union Plans Lawsuit over Federal Funds." *USA Today*, February 7, 2003. http://www.usatoday.com/news/education/2003-07-02-nea-usat_x.htm.

Torbenson, C. "The Origin and Evolution of College Fraternities and Sororities." In *African American Fraternities and Sororities: The Legacy and the Vision*, edited by T. L. Brown, G. S. Parks, and C. M. Phillips, 37-66. Lexington: The University Press of Kentucky, 2005.

Torrance, C. "Blacks and the American Ethos: A Re-evaluation of Existing Theories." *Journal of Black Studies* 21 (September 1990): 72–86.

"Transportation Equity" (March 2011). http://www.protectcivilrights.org/pdf/docs/transportation/52846576-Where-We-Need-to-Go-A-Civil-Rights-Roadmap-for-Transportation-Equity.pdf.

Trotter, J. *The African American Experience*. Boston, MA: Houghton Mifflin, 2001.

Turner, J. "Historical Dialectics of Black Nationalist Movements in America." *The Western Journal of Black Studies* 1 (September 1977): 164–83.

Turner, R. *Islam in the African-American Experience*. Bloomington: Indiana University Press, 1997.

U.S. Bureau of the Census. *Survey of Black Owned Businesses*. Washington, DC: U.S. Government Printing Office, 2006.

U.S. Commission on Civil Rights. "Accessibility Issues." Chap. 6 in *Voting Irregularities in Florida during the 2000 Presidential Election*. Washington, DC: U.S. Government Printing Office, 2001.

U.S. Committee on Civil Rights. *Freedom to Be Free* (A Report to the President by the U.S. Committee on Civil Rights). Washington, DC: U.S. Government Printing Office, 1963

U.S. Department of Health, Education, and Welfare. *Black Studies: Issues in Their Institutional Survival*. Washington, DC: U.S. Government Printing Office, 1976.

U.S. Department of State. "Founding of Liberia" (n.d.). http://future.state.gov/when/timeline/1830_timeline/founding_liberia.html.

U.S. National Center for Health Statistics. *Death: Preliminary Data for 2008*. Vol. 59, No. 2 (December 2010). http://www.census.gov/compendia/statab/2012/tables/12s0105.pdf.

Uzzell, O., and W. Peebles-Wilkins. "Black Spouse Abuse: A Focus on Relational Factors and Intervention Strategies." *The Western Journal of Black Studies* 13 (Spring 1989): 10–16.

Van Deburg, W. *New Day in Babylon: The Black Power Movement and American Culture, 1965–1975*. Chicago: The University of Chicago Press, 1992.

Van Sertima, I., ed. *Blacks in Science: Ancient and Modern*. New Brunswick: Transaction Books, 1983.

———. *They Came before Columbus: The African Presence in Ancient America*. New York: Random House, 1976.

Vandiver, B., P. Fhagen-Smith, K. Cokley, W. Cross, and F. Worrell. "Cross's Nigresence Model: From Theory to Scale to Theory." *Journal of Multicultural Counseling and Development* 29 (2001): 174–200.

Vaughn, W. *Vaughn's "Freedmen's Pension Bill."* Freeport, NY: Books for Libraries Press, 1971; originally published in Chicago, 1891.

Vaz, K. "Making Room for Emancipatory Research in Psychology: A Multicultural Feminist Perspective." In *Spirit, Space and Survival: African American Women in (White) Academe*, edited by J. James and R. Farmer, 83-98. New York: Routledge, 1993.

Vedder, R., L. Gallaway, and D. Klingaman. "Black Exploitation and White Benefits: The Civil War Income Revolution." In *The Wealth of Races: The Present Value of Benefits from Past Injustices*, edited by R. F. America. Westport: Greenwood Press, 1990.

"Video Game Industry Seeking Minorities." *MSNBC*. Accessed August 5, 2005. http://www.msnbc.msn.com/id/8837488/.

Von Eschen, P. *Race against Empire, Black Americans and Anticolonialism, 1937–1957*. Ithaca: Cornell University Press, 1997.

Wade, J., and B. Williams. "The National Urban League: Reinventing Service for the Twenty-First Century." In *Black Political Organizations in the Post-Civil Rights Era*, edited by O. Johnson and K. Sanford, 40-53. New Brunswick: Rutgers University Press, 2002.

Wade, R. *Slavery in the Cities: The South, 1820–1860*. New York: Oxford University Press, 1964.

Waggoner, M. "Payouts Urged in N.C. Sterilization Case." *The Post and Courier*, January 11, 2012. http://www.postandcourier.com/news/2012/jan/11/payouts-urged-nc-sterilization-case/.

Walker, S. *Their Highest Potential: An African American School Community in the Segregated South*. Chapel Hill: The University of North Carolina Press, 1996.

Wall, C. *Changing Our Own Words: Essays on Criticism, Theory, and Writing by Black Women*. New Brunswick: Rutgers University Press, 1989.

Wallace, M. *Black Macho and the Myth of the Superwoman*. New York: The Dial Press, 1978.

Wallace, R., and A. Wolf. *Contemporary Sociological Theory*. Englewood Cliffs: Prentice Hall, 1991.

Walters, R. *Black Presidential Politics in America*. New York: SUNY Press, 1988.

———. *Pan-Africanism in the African Diaspora: An Analysis of Modern Afrocentric Political Movements*. Detroit: Wayne State University Press, 1993.

———. "Racial Justice in Foreign Affairs." In *African American in Global Affairs: Contemporary Perspectives*, edited by M. L. Clemons, 1-30. Boston, MA: Northeastern University Press, 2011.

———. "Toward a Definition of Black Social Science." In *The Death of White Sociology*, edited by J. Ladner, 190-212. New York: Vintage Books, 1973.

Walton, F. "The Southern Christian Leadership Conference: Beyond the Civil Rights Movement." In *Black Political Organizations in the Post-Civil Rights Era*, edited by O. Johnson and K. Sanford, 132-49. New Brunswick: Rutgers University Press, 2002.

Walton, H. *Black Politics and Black Political Behavior*. Westport: Greenwood Press, 1996.

———. *Black Politics*. Philadelphia: J. B. Lippincott & Company, 1972.

———. *Invisible Politics: The Politics of Black and Tans*. Metuchen, NJ: The Scarecrow Press, 1975.

Ward, B. *Radio and the Struggle for Civil Rights in the South*. Gainesville: University Press of Florida, 2004.

Ward, G. *Unforgivable Blackness: The Rise and Fall of Jack Johnson*. New York: Alfred A. Knopf, 2004.

Warfield-Coppock, N. "The Rites of Passage Movement: A Resurgence of African-Centered Practices for Socializing African American Youth." *The Journal of Negro Education* 61, no. 4 (1992): 471–82.

Waring, C. "Hot Chicks, Cool Dudes and Bad Muthas: Crime Time's Definitive Guide to Blaxploitation." *Crimetime* (n.d.). http://www.crimetime.co.uk/features/blaxploitation.php.

Washington, H. *Medical Apartheid: The Dark History of Medical Experimentation on Black Americans from Colonial Times to the Present*. New York: Doubleday, 2006.

Washington, J. *Alain Locke and Philosophy: A Quest for Cultural Pluralism*. New York: Greenwood Press, 1986.

Washington, M., and C. Nunez. "Education, Racial Uplift, and the Rise of the Greek-Letter Tradition: The African American Quest for Status in the Early Twentieth Century." In *African American Fraternities and Sororities: The Legacy and the Vision*, edited by T. L. Brown, G. S. Parks, and C. M. Phillips, 137-80. Lexington: The University Press of Kentucky, 2005.

Washington, P., and L. Shaver. "The Language Culture of Rap Music Videos." In *Language, Rhythm, and Sound*, edited by J. K. Adjaye and A. R. Andrews. Pittsburgh: University of Pittsburgh Press, 1997.

Waterhouse, C. "Avoiding Another Step in a Series of Unfortunate Legal Events: A Consideration of Black Life Under American Law from 1619 to 1972 and a Challenge to Prevailing Notions of Legally Based Reparations." *Boston College Third World Law Journal* 26, no. 2 (2006): 207–65.

Waterhouse, C. "The Good, the Bad, and the Ugly: Moral Agency and the Role of Victims in Reparations Programs." *University of Pennsylvania Journal of International Economic Law* 31, no. 1 (2009): 257–94.

Waterhouse, C., and A. Smith. "No Reparation without Taxation: Applying the Internal Revenue Code to the Concept of Reparations for Slavery and Segregation" (Florida International University Legal Studies Research Paper No. 08-28, February 3, 2010). http://papers.ssrn.com/sol3/papers.cfm?abstract_id=1547326. Accessed October 1, 2014.

Waters, M. "Rep. Waters Joins President Clinton in Launch of Digital Divide New Markets Initiative Tour." Press Release, April 4, 2000.

Watterson, J. *College Football: History, Spectacle, Controversy*. Baltimore: The Johns Hopkins University Press, 2000.

Weber, M. *Basic Concepts in Sociology*. Translated by H.P. Secher. Westport: Greenwood Press, 1976.

Weigensberg, M., G. Ball, G. Shaibi, M. Cruz, B. Gower, and M. Goran. "Dietary Fat Intake and Insulin Resistance in Black and White Children." *Obesity Research* 13, no. 9 (September 2005): 1630–37.

Weisberger, B. *Booker T. Washington*. New York: New American Library, 1972.

Weisman, L. *Discrimination by Design: A Feminist Critique of the Man-Made Environment*. Urbana: University of Illinois Press, 1992.

Wells, J. "Viet Cong Blues." In *Defiance Blues*. (House of Blues, 1998). Songs of Polygram International, Inc., BMI.

Welsh Asante, K. "Commonalities in African Dance: An Aesthetic Foundation" In *African Culture: The Rhythms of Unity*, edited by M. Kete Asante and K. Welsh Asante, 71-82. Westport: Greenwood Press, 1985.

Welsh Asante, K. "The Aesthetic Conceptualization of Nzuri." In *The African Aesthetic: Keeper of the Traditions*, edited by K. Welsh Asante. Westport: Praeger, 1994.

Welsing, F. *The Cress Theory of Color-Confrontation and Racism (White Supremacy)*. Washington, DC: Frances L. Cress-Welsing, 1972.

———. "The Cress Theory of Color-Confrontation." *The Black Scholar* (May 1974).

———. *The Isis Papers*. Chicago: Third World Press, 1991.

WeParent. Accessed August 30, 2014. http://www.weparent.com/about/.

Wesley, C. *In Freedom's Footsteps*. Cornwells Heights, PA: International Library of Afro-American Life and History, 1967.

Wesson, K. "The Black Man's Burden: The White Clinician." *The Black Scholar* (July–August 1975).

Wheatley, P. *Poems on Various Subjects, Religious and Moral*. Philadelphia: Facsimile, 1786; reprinted in New York: AMS Press, 1976.

Wheeler, E. "Most of My Heroes Don't Appear on No Stamps: The Dialogics of Rap Music." *Black Music Research Journal* 11 (Fall 1991): 193–216.

Wheeler, M., T. Keller, and D. DuBois. *Review of Three Recent Randomized Trials of School-Based Mentoring: Making Sense of Mixed Findings* (Society for Research in Child Development Social Policy Report, vol. 24, no. 3, 2010). http://www.mentoring.org/downloads/mentoring_1273.pdf. Accessed October 1, 2014.

White, B. "Parchman Farm Blues." Recorded March 7, 1940, in Chicago (WC 2981-A Okeh 05683). In *News & the Blues, Telling It Like It Is*. Columbia Records, CBS Records, 1990.

"White by Day. . . Negro by Night." *Ebony*, November 1975.

"White College, Blacks Join in." *Freedom to Play, The Life & Times of Basketball's African American Pioneers*. http://www.hoophall.com/exhibits/freedom_white_colleges.htm (page no longer available.)

White, D. "An Independent Approach to Black Studies: The Institute of the Black World (IBW) and Its Evaluation and Support of Black Studies." In *Expanding the History of the Black Studies Movement* (A Special Issue of the Journal of African American Studies), edited by J. Fenderson, J. Stewart, and K. Baumgartner. Journal of African American Studies vol. 16, no. 1 (March 2012): 70-88.

White, J., and T. Parham. *The Psychology of Blacks*. Englewood Cliffs: Prentice Hall, 1975.

White, S., and G. White. *Stylin': African American Expressive Culture from Its Beginnings to the Zoot Suit*. Ithaca, NY: Cornell University Press, 1998.

Whitehead, J., and J. Stewart. "African American Athletes." In *African Americans in the U.S. Economy*, edited by C. A. Conrad, J. Whitehead, P. L. Mason, and J. Stewart, 378-92. Lanham: Rowman & Littlefield, 2005.

Whitener, S., and K. Gruber. *Characteristics of Stayers, Movers, and Leavers: Results from the Teacher Follow-Up Survey: 1994–95* (NCES 97-450). Washington, DC: National Center for Education Statistics, U.S. Department of Education, 1997.

Wickham, D., ed. *Thinking Black: Some of the Nation's Best Columnists Speak Their Mind*. New York: Three Rivers Press, 1997.

Wilcox, P. "Integration or Separatism in Education: K-12." In *Integrated Education: Race and Schools*, vol. (January–February 1970); reprinted by Integrated Education Associates, Chicago. 23-33

Wilcox, R., ed. *The Psychological Consequences of Being a Black American*. New York: John Wiley & Sons, 1971.

Wilkerson, M., and J. Gresham. "The Racialization of Poverty." *The Nation*, July 24–31, 1989, 126-130.

Williams, C. *The Destruction of Black Civilization*. Chicago: Third World Press, 1974.

Williams, D. "Contemporary African American Women Writers." In *The Cambridge Companion to African American Women's Literature*, edited by A. Mitchell and D. K. Taylor, 71-86. New York: Cambridge University Press, 2009.

Williams, D., N. Martins, M. Consalvo, and J. D. Ivory. "The Virtual Census: Representations of Gender, Race and Age in Video Games." *New Media & Society* 11 (2009): 815–34.

Williams, J. "A Black Ambassador to Apartheid South Africa." *NPR*, October 24, 2006. http://www.npr.org/templates/story/story.php?storyId=6369450.

Williams, L. "Significant Trends in Black Voter Attitudes." *The Black Scholar* vol. 17 no.6 (November/December 1986): 24-27.

———. "The 1988 Election in Review." *Focus: Magazine of the Joint Center for Political and Economic Studies* 16 (November–December 1988): 3.

Williams, R. "From Anticolonialism to Anti-apartheid: African American Political Organizations and African Liberation, 1957–93." In *African American in Global Affairs: Contemporary Perspectives*, edited by M. L. Clemons, 65-90. Boston, MA: Northeastern University Press, 2010.

Williams, R. "The Black Artist as Activist." *Black Creation* 3 (Winter 1972).

Wilmore, G. *Black Religion and Black Radicalism: An Interpretation of the Religious History of Afro-American People*. Maryknoll, NY: Orbis Books, 1983.

————. "The Case for a New Church Style." In *The Black Experience in Religion*, edited by C. E. Lincoln. New York: Anchor Books, 1974.

Wilmore, G., and J. Cone. *Black Theology*. Maryknoll, NY: Orbis Books, 1979.

Wilson, F. "Neoconservatives, Black Conservatives, and the Retreat from Social Justice." In *Dimensions of Black Conservatism in the United States: Made in America*, edited by G. T. Tate and L. A. Randolph, 179-196. New York: Palgrave Macmillan, 2002.

Wilson, H. "Black Electoral Outcomes and Policy Impacts: A Review of the Literature." *The Western Journal of Black Studies* 11 (Spring 1987): 24–28.

Wilson, J. *Negro Politics*. New York: The Free Press, 1960.

Wilson, O. "The Association of Movement and Music as a Manifestation of a Black Conceptual Approach to Music-Making." In *More than Dancing: Essays on Afro-American Music and Musicians*, edited by I. V. Jackson, 9-24. Westport: Greenwood Press, 1985.

Wilson, W. *The Declining Significance of Race*. Chicago: The University of Chicago Press, 1978.

————. "The Ghetto Underclass and the Social Transformation of the Inner City." *The Black Scholar* vol. 19, no. 3 (May/June 1988): 10-17.

————. "There Goes the Neighborhood." *The New York Times*, June 16, 2003. http://www.nytimes.com/2003/06/16/opinion/there-goes-the-neighborhood.html?module=Search&mabReward=relbi as%3Ar. Accessed October 1, 2014.

Winant, G. "Obama White House Brings Black Women to Power, White House Advisers and Staff Form Strong Support Network" (March 18, 2009). http://www.newser.com/story/53645/obama-white-house-brings-black-women-to-power.html.

Winner, L. "Do Artifacts Have Politics?" *Daedalus* 109, no. 1 (1980): 121–36.

Wish, H. "American Slave Insurrections Before 1861." *The Journal of Negro History* 22 (July 1937): 299–320.

Wolff, E. "Racial Wealth Disparities: Is the Gap Closing?" (Public Policy Brief No. 66A, 2001). Annandale-on-Hudson, NY: Levy Economics Institute of Bard College.

"Women and Minorities in the 110th Congress." *Congressional Quarterly Weekly*, February 26, 2007. http://library.cqpress.com/cqalmanac/document.php?id=cqal07-1006-44894-2047197. Accessed October 1, 2014.

Woodard, C. *The Strange Career of Jim Crow*. New York: Oxford University Press, 1966.

Woodson, C. *Mis-education of the Negro*. Washington, DC: Associated Publishers, 1933.

Worrell, F., B. Vandiver, B. Schaefer, W. Cross, and P. Fhagen-Smith. "Generalizing Nigrescence Profiles: Cluster Analyses of Cross Racial Identity Scale (CRIS) Scores in Three Independent Samples." *The Counseling Psychologist* 34 (July 2006): 519–47.

Wright, B. "Ideological Change and Black Identity during Civil Rights Movements." *The Western Journal of Black Studies* 5 (Fall 1981): 186–98.

X, M. "Speech delivered at the Founding Rally of the OAAU, June 28, 1964.." In *Malcolm X Speaks: Selected Speeches and Statements*, edited by G. Breitman, 57-96. New York: Pathfinder Press, 1992 (originally published in 1970).

————. "The Ballot or the Bullet." Speech delivered in Cleveland, Ohio, April 3, 1964; reprinted in *Malcolm X Speaks: Selected Speeches and Statements*, edited by G. Breitman, 23-44. New York: Pathfinder Press, 1989.

————. "The Black Revolution." Speech delivered in 1963; reprinted in *The End of White World Supremacy: Four Speeches by Malcolm X*, edited by B. Goodman. New York: Merlin House, 1971.

Young, W. *Minorities and the Military*. Westport, CT: Greenwood Press, 1982.

Younge, G. "US Police Put Hip-Hop under Surveillance." *Guardian Unlimited*, March 11, 2004. http://arts.guardian.co.uk/news/story/0.11711.1166792,00.html. http://www.theguardian.com/world/2004/mar/11/arts.usa. Accessed October 1, 2014.

"YouTube Rubbernecking Has NJ Officials Seeing Red." *ZDNet Government*, May 23, 2007. http://government.zdnet.com/?p=3173.

Zinn, H. *SNCC—The New Abolitionists*. Boston, MA: Beacon Press, 1965.

Index

C

index

index

150921-180-22-50W